Child Case Management Practice

Second Edition

Child Case Management Practice

Second Edition

Editor-in-Chief
The Hon Mr Justice Ryder

General Editor
Iain Goldrein QC

Contributors
Edward Devereux
Barrister, Harcourt Chambers

District Judge Claire Gilham

Michael Gration
Barrister, 4 Paper Buildings

Teertha Gupta QC

Anne-Marie Hutchinson OBE
Partner, Dawson Cornwell

Malcolm Sharpe
Barrister, Atlantic Chambers

June Venters QC
Managing Partner, Venters Solicitors

His Honour Judge Bernard Wallwork

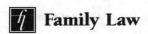

Published by Family Law
a publishing imprint of
Jordan Publishing Limited
21 St Thomas Street
Bristol BS1 6JS

British Library Cataloguing-in-Publication Data

A catalogue record for this book is available from the British Library.

ISBN 978 1 84661 264 0

Typeset by Letterpart Ltd, Reigate, Surrey
Printed and bound in Great Britain by CPI Antony Rowe, Chippenham and Eastbourne

This book is dedicated to Demi-Lou, the 'adopted' daughter of June Venters QC and her husband, who is a shining example of how the system can work with effective social services practice; decisive legal expertise; devoted and loving adoptive parents and, above all, with the child's welfare being and remaining of the utmost paramount concern.

FOREWORD

In 2009 I described *Child Case Management Practice* as being a new idea. Three years on and in a professional world so much more acutely attuned to delay than ever before, the concept behind this handbook is particularly relevant and necessary. It remains our guiding purpose to provide core skeleton arguments for the busy children practitioner for both the common and less common children applications to encourage careful adherence to best practice in the preparation and presentation of children cases. By using the materials in this handbook, the practitioner will find it easier to ensure that there is compliance with Practice Directions, in particular the Public Law Outline and the Revised Private Law Programme. The methodology remains consistent with best practice case management, ie the identification of the essential legal questions that are involved in a case so that they can be applied to an analysis of the facts and lead to the identification for the court of the key issue(s) upon which a decision is needed.

Iain Goldrein has brought an impressive and personal attention to detail in editing this work and has put together a specialist team of practitioners who have contributed some of their best arguments. The next three years will see many changes in family justice but the speed and accuracy of analysis of practitioners will be a requirement in every case. The second edition of this handbook will help to provide practitioners with that resource and will help pave the way for the reforms in which we will all be involved.

Sir Ernest Ryder
Royal Courts of Justice
September 2012

FOREWORD TO THE FIRST EDITION

Child Case Management Practice is based upon a new idea. It is not a competitor or substitute for your favourite textbook or procedural guide. It is a new handbook for the busy practitioner and judge, designed to provide core skeleton arguments for the most common and some less common children applications. Each free standing argument is drafted by a specialist contributor and describes the legal principles which underpin the proceedings and the authorities and materials which contain the principles involved. The arguments are supported by detailed cross references to both source materials and case digests from which additional authorities can be easily accessed to develop, fashion and apply the arguments provided. The overall approach is informed by a very careful adherence to best practice in the preparation and presentation of children cases. This is explained in the chapters which describe case management principles and practice by reference to Rules, Practice Directions and guidance. Not only is this a valuable resource to refresh the memory or inform the reader but the arguments are designed to identify the essential legal questions which are involved in a case so that they can be applied to an analysis of the facts and lead to the identification for the court of the key issue(s) upon which a decision is needed.

Iain Goldrein has combined his extensive experience as an author and commentator with the practitioner's eye for detail and practical application in his determination to find arguments which will help the practitioner and the judge. He has undertaken an immense task with dedication and great skill but the project is deliberately unfinished. It is our fervent hope that developments in the law will be reflected in regular new editions and the reader is strongly encouraged to become a contributor by submitting a skeleton argument which adds to, improves or changes that which has been written and collected so far. This is a book which is designed to service both your needs and the court's requirements. I hope you will find it an invaluable and helpful resource.

Sir Ernest Ryder
Royal Courts of Justice
January 2009

CONTENTS

Part IV
International Issues

Chapter 17
Forced Marriage and the Forced Marriage (Civil Protection)
Act 2007   **841**

TABLE OF CASES

References are to paragraph numbers.

TABLE OF STATUTES

References are to paragraph numbers.

TABLE OF STATUTORY INSTRUMENTS

References are to paragraph numbers.

TABLE OF PRACTICE DIRECTIONS

References are to paragraph numbers.

PART I

PRACTICE, EVIDENCE AND PROCEDURE

CHAPTER 1

LEGAL AID (PUBLIC FUNDING) AND REPRESENTATION

1.1 INTRODUCTION

The concept of legal aid arose following the Second World War in 1945, when the importance of social and legal justice was first recognised by the Rushcliffe Committee. Since that time legal aid has continued to develop and evolve. Most recently, following the report of Lord Carter of Coles ('A market-based approach to reform' published 13 July 2006), the legal aid system as a whole has gone through a period of significant change. Specifically with regard to the area of family law, the majority of these changes came into force on 1 October 2007, and further changes are to be implemented in April 2013 (see Legal Aid, Sentencing and Punishment of Offenders Act 2012) with regard to the withdrawal of public funding from private law children cases.

1.2 BACKGROUND

The government provides funding for legal aid to help people:

- protect their basic rights and get a fair hearing;

- access the court process to sort out disputes; and

- solve problems that contribute to social exclusion.[1]

The Access to Justice Act 1999 created the Legal Services Commission (LSC). The LSC has the following responsibilities:

- awards contracts for legal aid work to be undertaken by individual solicitors firms;

- administers the Legal Aid Scheme; and

- grants certificates of representation.

---

[1] Quoted from the LSC website: 'What is Legal Aid?'

The Community Legal Service, established by the LSC,[2] is the organisation which manages the Civil Legal Aid Fund on a day-to-day basis.

1.3   CIVIL LEGAL AID

Civil legal aid can fund:

- initial advice and assistance with any civil law problem (*Legal Help*);

- a solicitor who can speak on someone's behalf at court hearings, without formally representing them (*Help at Court*) (although Help at Court is not available in relation to family disputes);[3]

- help and advice on family disputes, including assistance with family mediation (*Family Help* (Lower) or *Family Help* (Higher));

- Family Mediation; and

- legal representation in court proceedings (*Legal Representation*).[4]

1.4   WHO QUALIFIES FOR LEGAL AID?

One factor that remains fundamental to the award of public funding to a client is that they must be both financially eligible (the 'means test') and satisfy the 'merits test' (save for Special Children Act proceedings where the party is the child, parent or has parental responsibility).

1.4.1   Financial eligibility: the means test

To qualify for Legal Help, the client must have a gross income of less than £2,350 per month, and a disposable income of less than £672 per month. In terms of capital assets, the client must have less than £8,000 in disposable capital. The Legal Help form (Controlled Work 1) contains the prescribed calculations to be carried out in order to assess financial eligibility. These limitations are altered from time to time and the LSC publishes a 'Keycard' periodically containing the current figures. The LSC also has an 'eligibility calculator' on its website.

If a client is in receipt of income support, income-based jobseeker's allowance or guarantee state pension credit, they are 'passported' and automatically qualify for public funding. Clients in receipt of any other state benefit must still satisfy the financial eligibility criteria.

---

2   Access to Justice Act 1999, s 4(1).
3   *Funding Code Criteria*, Section 11 Family, para 3A–055; 11.2.
4   Full definitions of each level of service can be found in the *Funding Code Criteria*, Section 2, para 3A–004.

When determining a client's financial eligibility for legal aid, copies of the client's pay slips must be retained or letters from their benefit provider confirming receipt of the relevant benefit in order to satisfy LSC audit requirements.

The client must be advised in writing that, should their financial circumstances change, the LSC will need to be advised of this and the client's eligibility will need to be reassessed.

The calculation as to whether the client will qualify for the Legal Help level of funding is a helpful guide to determine whether the client would further qualify for full Legal Representation if necessary. It may be the case that a client will be financially eligible for Legal Help, but may thereafter be required to pay a contribution to their legal costs should they go on to receive Legal Representation.

1.5 THE LEVELS AND SCOPE OF LEGAL AID: PRIVATE LAW CHILDREN CASES

Note: Further changes are to be implemented in April 2013 with regard to the withdrawal of public funding from private law children cases (these are *not* set out in the text below). See the Legal Aid, Sentencing and Punishment of Offenders Act 2012 for detail.

1.5.1 Controlled Work – Legal Help

1.5.1.1 Level 1 Initial advice – £94 (excluding VAT)

Level 1 covers the initial meeting with a client regarding a private family law issue and any work immediately following that meeting. The relevant application form is the Controlled Work 1.[5]

1.5.1.2 Level 2 Children & Finance

Level 2 (Family Help (Lower)) is payable where further work is carried out on a case beyond Level 1 where there is a significant family dispute relating to children and/or finance matters.[6] There is a separate fee for children and finance issues. This fee covers all work up to, but not including the issue of proceedings. If the client's matter involves both children and finance issues, both fees can be claimed.

An additional settlement fee is payable where the issue is fully settled at this Level. However, if the settlement breaks down within 6 months, the

---

[5] *Funding Code Decision Making Guidance – Family*, para 3C–175: 20.10(5).
[6] *Funding Code Criteria*, Section 11 Family, para 3A–055; 11.3.1 and see also, *Funding Code Decision Making Guidance – Family*, para 3C–175: 20.11(2).

settlement fee will be reclaimable by the LSC. A new matter can be started after 3 months to assist the client if there has been a material change in circumstances.[7]

There is no form to be used to progress a matter from Level 1 to Level 2, work simply continues to the next stage and both fees should be claimed accordingly. Occasionally in a private law case, it will be necessary to issue proceedings straight away and in those circumstances, Level 2 is 'leapfrogged' and an application for Full Representation is made as described below.

1.5.1.3   Level 2 Children (excluding VAT)

	Fee	Settlement Fee
London	£256	£153
Non-London	£221	£132

1.5.1.4   Level 2 Finance (excluding VAT)

	Fee	Settlement Fee
London	£268	£161
Non-London	£231	£139

1.5.1.5   Exceptional Case hourly rates

A case is considered 'exceptional' if the work done on the file equates to three times the amount of the fixed fee available. In those circumstances, the matter falls outside the fixed fee regime and reverts to payment according to hourly rates. The applicable rates are set out in the table below.

Activity	London rate	Non-London rate
Preparation, attendance and advocacy	£53.10 per hour	£50.05 per hour
Travel & waiting	£28.05 per hour	£28.05 per hour
Routine letters out and telephone calls	£4.10 per item	£3.95 per item

---

[7]   *Funding Code Decision Making Guidance – Family*, para 3C–175: 20.11(5)–(6).

1.5.2   Certificated (Licensed) Work: 'Level 3'

1.5.2.1   Family Help (Higher)

Where proceedings are issued, an application for a certificate of Family Help (Higher) should be made. This certificate covers all work up to, but not including preparation for a final hearing. This work continues to be paid at hourly rates, *however the introduction of fixed fees is expected in the future.* The application form is the CLS APP 3 and this should be submitted to the LSC for consideration along with the relevant means form to establish financial eligibility.

The most commonly used forms are as follows:

- CLS MEANS 1: for those clients in employment. The client's employer is also required to complete an L17 form.

- CLS MEANS 1a: for self employed clients.

- CLS MEANS 2: for those clients in receipt of income support or income-based jobseeker's allowance.

On receipt of a client's application forms, the LSC will firstly carry out various checks and assessments of the client's financial circumstances in order to establish eligibility. For example, the LSC will liaise with the Benefits Agency to ensure the client is in receipt of the benefits they claim to be. If financial eligibility is established, the LSC will then go on to consider the 'merit' in granting public funding to the client.

1.5.2.2   The merits test

Private law cases are merits tested. It is important to set out the reasons why the client's case has 'merit' with reference to the 'sufficient benefit test' set out in the Funding Code at para 3A–025. The CLS APP 3 form contains sections for the merit in the case to be explained.

1.5.2.3   Limitations

A Family Help (Higher) Certificate will be issued with a costs limitation, the standard limitation being £1,500. Extensions to the limitation will only be granted if extra work and the costs envisaged are justified. If an increase is required and there is little chance of the case being resolved without a final hearing, it may be more appropriate to apply for Legal Representation.

1.5.2.4   Mediation

It is a requirement of the LSC that a client in a private law case be referred to mediation as a way of resolving the dispute without going to court.[8] This referral should be made, except in certain specified circumstances that are set out in the *Funding Code Decision Making Guidance – Family*, para 3C–182, 20.16(4) (and on the CLS APP 7 form), for example, where the applicant has made allegations of domestic violence within the preceding 12 months, which have resulted in either police investigations or the issue of civil proceedings for the protection of the applicant. There is another similar exemption with regard to domestic violence situations, where the mediator does carry out an assessment and is then satisfied that the client has a reasonable fear of domestic abuse and the mediator certifies that the matter is not suitable for mediation. If there has been domestic violence in the past, but the client is still willing to mediate, then the mediation should proceed, although the *mediator* retains the right to refuse to conduct the mediation if there are significant safety concerns. A CLS APP 7 should be sent along with a CLS APP 3 application form where Legal Representation is required, when mediation has failed or is not appropriate.

1.5.2.5   Family Mediation

'Family Mediation' is a separate level of funding which allows for an assessment of whether mediation is a suitable means of solving the dispute, with consideration of the parties involved and in all the circumstances. Family Mediation will also fund the mediation process itself if the case is considered appropriate for mediation. If the assessment process decides that mediation is not suitable, the mediator will complete the CLS APP 7 form setting out reasons why mediation would not be appropriate. Similarly, if the mediation process begins and then subsequently breaks down, the mediator should complete the CLS APP 7 explaining the reason for the breakdown. The CLS APP 7 form can then be submitted to the LSC along with the substantive application form (CLS APP 3) when applying for Legal Representation.

1.5.2.6   Legal Representation

This covers preparation for and representation at a final hearing and any subsequent work. If a client is already receiving Legal Help (Higher), an application to amend the certificate to cover Legal Representation should be made; a new certificate will not be issued. Legal Representation continues to be paid at hourly rates, but again, the introduction of fixed fees is expected. Currently, certificates are issued with costs limitations. As

---

8   *Funding Code Decision Making Guidance – Family*, para 3C–182: 20.16.

and when a case nears its limitation, a CLS APP 8 form should be completed to increase the costs limitation and submitted to the LSC for consideration.

1.5.2.7 *Prior authority for disbursements*

In private law children cases, any anticipated expenditure on disbursements over £100 requires prior authority from the LSC. Typically, this will apply to instructing experts or obtaining tests, such as DNA testing. The relevant form to be completed is a CLS APP8.

1.6 THE LEVELS AND SCOPE OF LEGAL AID: PUBLIC LAW CHILDREN CASES

In Special Children Act proceedings, there is no means testing. Any parent or person with parental responsibility for a child will automatically be eligible for public funding, regardless of financial means, given the nature and seriousness of such cases.[9] If the party is not the child, parents or a person with parental responsibility they are required to make an application to court to be joined in the proceedings and, in these circumstances, public funding is means and merits tested as above.[10]

One of the significant changes introduced to legal aid for Special Children Act cases, as of 1 October 2007, coincided with the pilot of a new system by which child care cases are now managed by local authorities. The Public Law Outline was brought into force countrywide from April 2008 and requires local authorities to carry out much more work before issuing proceedings – see Chapter 3 for more detail. As a result, it has been considered important for parents (and those with parental responsibility) to have greater access to legal advice at an earlier stage in an attempt to avoid cases going to court. There are now two levels of fixed fee available for pre-proceedings work.

1.6.1 Controlled Work – Legal Help

1.6.1.1 *Level 1 – £144 (excluding VAT)*

Level 1 covers all public law children cases and initial advice. Where a provider attends a child protection case conference at this level, it is included in the fee. The relevant form is the Controlled Work 1 form and continues to be means tested. Legal Help also covers the completion of any necessary application for Legal Representation.[11]

---

9   *Funding Code Decision Making Guidance – Family*, para 3C–191: 20.26(2).
10   *Funding Code Decision Making Guidance – Family*, para 3C–191: 20.26(3).
11   *Funding Code Decision Making Guidance – Family*, para 3C–175: 20.10(3).

As with private law children cases, a matter will be considered 'exceptional' if the work carried out on the file equates to three times the available fixed fee. In these circumstances the matter will move to hourly rates from the fixed fee regime and revert to being paid according to hourly rates, as shown in the following table.

1.6.1.2   Hourly rates for Exceptional Cases

Activity	London Rate	Non-London Rate
Preparation, attendance and advocacy	£53.10 per hour	£50.05 per hour
Travel & waiting time	£28.05 per hour	£28.05 per hour
Routine letters out and telephone calls	£4.10 per item	£3.95 per item

1.6.1.3   Level 2 – Family Help (Lower) – £347 (excluding VAT)

Level 2 is only available to parents or those with parental responsibility and covers care and supervision proceedings under Children Act 1989, s 31 and is non-means and non-merits tested. This level becomes available when the relevant local authority issues a written notice of intention to issue proceedings[12] (see Chapter 3 on the Public Law Outline for more detail). Essentially, this level is designed to enable parents to access advice and support when liaising and negotiating with the local authority to resolve matters without the need to issue care proceedings. To move on to Level 2, a Controlled Work 1PL form should be completed.

If a client already has a written notice from the local authority when they first seek advice, the solicitor should use Level 2 (Family Help (Lower)) immediately and 'leapfrog' Level 1.

1.6.1.4   Hourly rates for Exceptional Cases (ie 3 times the fixed fee)

As above, a case can move to hourly rates from the fixed fee scheme if it is 'exceptional' and work thereafter will be paid according to the hourly rates shown in the following table.

---

12   *Funding Code Decision Making Guidance – Family*, para 3C–175: 20.11(3).

Activity	London Rate	Non-London Rate
Preparation, attendance and advocacy	£61.20 per hour	£57.25 per hour
Travel & waiting time	£30.30 per hour	£29.45 per hour
Routine letters out and telephone calls	£4.40 per item	£4.10 per item

1.6.1.5 Level 3 – Full Representation (excluding VAT) (Licensed Work)

Level 3 covers care and supervision proceedings under Children Act 1989, s 31 and related proceedings, and the fixed fee covers all work from the issue of proceedings onwards. Advocacy can be claimed separately at hourly rates and therefore is not included in the fixed fee.

Where advocacy is provided by counsel, they will claim for such work under the 'Graduated Fees Order'[13] where the application for funding was made before 9 May 2011. Where an application for funding is made on or after 9 May 2011, they will claim for such work under the 'Family Advocacy Scheme'.[14] Where advocacy is provided by a solicitor, including at any interim hearings, such work is claimed under hourly rates. A solicitor can also claim any associated travel and waiting time, and attendance at advocates' meetings, at the appropriate hourly rate. Preparation for attendance at hearings is claimed as part of the standard fixed fee. 'Advocacy' does not include attendance at court with counsel, since only one person may claim for advocacy services at any hearing.[15]

The relevant application form to apply for Legal Representation in this type of case is the CLS APP 5. When such an application becomes necessary, it is often the case that immediate work and attendance at a court hearing is required. It is therefore not practical to await the outcome of a decision by the LSC to grant funding, and given that these cases are non-means and non-merits tested in any event, the solicitor with conduct should devolve powers and submit the CLS APP 5 within 5 days of receipt of instructions.[16]

---

[13] Community Legal Service (Funding) (Counsel in Family Proceedings) Order 2001, SI 2001/1077.

[14] Community Legal Service (Funding) (Amendment) Order 2011, SI 2011/1027 and *Unified Civil Contract – Civil Specification: Section 10: Family* .

[15] *Unified Civil Contract – Civil Specification: Section 10: Family, paras 10.39–10.42.*

[16] Paragraph 10.32 Family Specification – suppliers have a specific devolved power to grant funding in Special Children Act cases. See also *Funding Code Decision Making Guidance – Family*, para 3C–191: 20.26; 13–15.

The CLS APP 5 has been further amended as of 1 October 2007 to include a question as to whether separate representation is appropriate, whereby it must be explained why there is a need for parents, for example, to be represented by separate solicitors. The aim of this provision is to benefit the legal aid fund and to enable cases to be dealt with more quickly. Separate representation is likely to be unnecessary where parents (or others with delegated parental responsibility) appear to have the same interests in the proceedings, and in the case of a couple, they are not living separate and apart. If separate representation is to be justified on the basis of a conflict of interests, details should be given.[17]

The fixed fee available varies depending on the party represented, the region and level of court, as shown in the table below.

Party	Court	No. of clients	Midlands	North	South	Wales
Child	Other	1	£2,405	£1,972	£2,761	£2,695
Child	Other	2+	£3,608	£2,958	£4,142	£4,043
Child	High	1	£3,199	£2,623	£3,672	£3,584
Child	High	2+	£4,799	£3,935	£5,508	£5,376
Joined Party	Other		£1,276	£986	£1,482	£1,606
Joined Party	High		£1,697	£1,311	£1,971	£2,136
Parent	Other	1	£3,156	£2,621	£3,589	£3,250
Parent	Other	2	£3,945	£3,276	£4,486	£4,063
Parent	High	1	£4,197	£3,486	£4,773	£4,323
Parent	High	2	£5,246	£4,358	£5,966	£5,404

A certificate can be revoked if the client has not engaged for a period of time and fails to provide instructions, since the solicitor cannot prepare a case up to and including final hearing without ongoing instructions from

---

[17] See *Funding Code Decision Making Guidance – Family*, para 3C–191; 20.26(15).

the client.[18] No time frame is given in the Guidance, it simply says 'where the client has failed to engage over a period of time or has disappeared'.

1.6.1.6 Hourly rates for Exceptional Cases

Again, a case will be considered 'exceptional' if the work done on the file will amount to *two times*[19] the available fixed fee and in those circumstances the case can 'escape' the fixed fee scheme and be paid according to the hourly rates shown in the table below.

Activity	Higher Courts	County Court and Magistrates Court
Writing routine letters	£4.70 per item	£4.10 per item
Receiving routine letters	£2.35 per item	£2.05 per item
Routine telephone calls	£4.70 per item	£4.10 per item
Preparation and attendance	£77.85 per hour (London rate) £73.15 per hour (Non-London rate)	£68.20 per hour (London rate) £64.90 per hour (Non-London rate)
Attending at court or conference with counsel	£41.25 per hour	£36.30 per hour
Advocacy	£77.85 per hour (London rate) £73.15 per hour (Non-London rate)	£71.50 per hour
Travelling and waiting time	£35.75 per hour	£32.45 per hour

Any certificates issued before 1 October 2007 will continue to operate according to the previous rules, whereby hourly rates continue to be applicable and the certificate will have a limitation. The initial limitation in a child care case is usually £5,000. In such cases, when the work in

---

[18] *Funding Code Decision Making Guidance – Family*, para 3C–191: 20.26(18) Revocation or discharge of certificates (September 2007).

[19] *Legal Aid Reform Provider Training Pack* (September 2007), p C6.

progress and disbursements are nearing the limitation, an application must be made to the LSC using a CLS APP8 to increase the costs limitation.

1.6.1.7 Very Expensive Cases

If a case goes on to reach the level of £25,000 it becomes a 'high cost case' and a High Cost Case Plan must be completed and submitted to the LSC Special Cases Unit to explain the work done to date, costs to date and anticipated work required before the case can be brought to a conclusion.[20]

See **1.9** for an example of a Case Plan which has to be submitted to the LSC for each stage of work to be undertaken in very expensive cases.

1.6.2 Emergency protection orders

Work carried out in respect of an application for an emergency protection order will continue to be paid according to hourly rates with a CLS APP 5 application form being submitted. If (and when) a case then progresses to an application for a care or supervision order under Children Act 1989, s 31, a second application for funding under the fixed fee scheme will be required.

1.6.3 Secure accommodation orders and child assessment orders

Both of these orders are categorised as Special Children Act proceedings and, therefore, public funding for both is granted on a non-means and non-merits tested basis. As with applications for Legal Representation for care and supervision orders, such applications should be made using the CLS APP 5 form. The CLS APP 5 makes it clear that the fixed fee scheme applies only to care and supervision orders and, accordingly, funding for a case regarding a secure accommodation order or a child assessment order would, like emergency protection orders, continue to be paid according to hourly rates.

1.6.4 Related proceedings

Where a client is already in receipt of Legal Representation in Special Children Act proceedings, further Legal Representation may be granted in related proceedings. For example, Legal Representation will be granted on an application for a placement order where that is being dealt with

---

[20] *Funding Code (Part B) – Procedures: Section 6 Referral to Special Cases Unit*; see also *LSC Manual*, Vol 3, Part C, Chapter 15.

together with the Special Children Act proceedings. Related proceedings will be dealt with on a non-means, non-merits tested basis.[21]

Applications for cover for appeals within public law proceedings under the Children Act 1989 are merits tested in the same way that other applications for representation within Children Act proceedings are merits tested, ie by reference to prospects of success.[22]

1.6.5 Placement and adoption orders

Legal Representation is unlikely to be granted where the application is uncontested. Despite poor prospects of success, an application for representation by natural parents to oppose the making of an order is unlikely to be refused if there have not been a previous placement order or adoption proceedings. The reason for this is that once a placement or adoption order has been made, natural parents are unlikely to have any ongoing involvement in the child's life (save for ongoing contact, if any) and, therefore, there is great justification for parents to be represented in such cases.

An applicant for an order may be refused Legal Representation if there is an alternative source of funding. For example, an applicant supported by the relevant local authority could be expected to be funded by that local authority.[23]

1.6.6 Special guardianship orders

A special guardianship order is a private law order and as such the Guidance specifically takes into consideration the 'No order principle' in Children Act 1989, s 1 when considering the prospects of success. The relevant local authority will have prepared a report for the court when any applicant has notified them of an intention to apply for a special guardianship order.[24] This report will also be considered by the LSC when looking at prospects of success. If there is an alternative means of funding, such as a supportive local authority, Legal Representation is likely to be refused.

---

[21] *Funding Code Decision Making Guidance – Family*, para 3C–192: 20.27 (September 2007).

[22] *Funding Code Decision Making Guidance – Family*, para 3C–194: 20.29 (September 2007).

[23] *Funding Code Decision Making Guidance – Family*, para 3C–195: 20.30 (September 2007).

[24] Children Act 1989, s 14A.

As for a respondent opposing such an order, the ways in which they currently exercise their parental responsibility will be considered when considering whether to grant Legal Representation.[25]

1.6.7 Inherent jurisdiction (wardship)

The inherent jurisdiction is now unlikely to be utilised since an appropriate remedy will be found under the Children Act 1989. Consequently, an application for Legal Representation in wardship cases is likely to be refused. In those cases where the use of wardship continues to be appropriate, the prospects of success and sufficient benefit in the case must be considered. Solicitors are required to consider if there is an alternative means by which the issues can be resolved.[26]

1.6.8 Prior authority for disbursements in public law cases

Prior authority is only required in child care cases where the anticipated disbursement is of an unusual nature, or is of an unusually large amount, for example if expenditure is in excess of £5,000 per funded party.[27] The CLS APP 8 form is used to apply for prior authority.

It is important to alert any expert instructed to the fact that the LSC can, under clause 19.2 of the Standard Terms in the Civil Unified Contract, specify maximum rates for experts' fees, by reference to type of expert and type of activity. Consequently, where the LSC have applied such maximum rates, fees incurred must not exceed these limits without prior authority to do so.[28] Amounts claimed by experts are always subject to assessment either by the court or by the LSC and it is therefore important to ensure that any expert instructed is aware that there is a risk that not all fees claimed will be paid, and additionally, that the firm instructing would not be liable to pay any shortfall.

1.7 EXPERTS AND RESIDENTIAL ASSESSMENTS

Under the terms of the Unified Civil Contract published in February 2007,[29] experts instructed in family cases where fees are likely to exceed £250 must keep accurate records of the time they spend working on a case. The expert must also agree to allow the LSC to audit their records should they wish to do so. Letters of instruction to experts should explain this requirement.

---

[25] *Funding Code Decision Making Guidance – Family*, para 3C–200.1: 20.36 (September 2007).

[26] *Funding Code Decision Making Guidance – Family*, para 3C–196: 20.31 (September 2007).

[27] *LSC Manual*, Vol 1, Part D, paras 1D–062.1–5.8(9) (September 2007).

[28] *Unified Contract – Civil Specification* (1 October 2007), para 8.38.

[29] Unified Contract Standard Terms 2007, clause 19.6.

From 1 October 2007, the LSC no longer fund residential assessments and local authorities will be asked to fund such assessments in Special Children Act proceedings.[30]

1.8 STATUTORY CHARGE

The statutory charge, often applied to any monetary award in civil law proceedings, does not apply to Children Act proceedings.

---

[30] *Funding Code Criteria*, para 3A–003: 1.3.

1.9 PUBLIC LAW CHILDREN ACT CASE PLAN

CASE INFORMATION

A. Summary of Case

B. Objectives

C. Case Analysis
The legal issues are:
The favourable facts are:
The unfavourable facts are:

D. Funding Code Assessment

E. Case Theory

CASE ACTIVITIES AND COSTS INFORMATION

F. & G. (i) Costs To-Date		COSTS
WORK		

I confirm that a copy of this case plan has been sent to the client.

(ii) Future Overall & Staged Costs			
		TIME ESTIMATE IN HOURS	COSTS
		SOLICITOR	COUNSEL	
Stage One				
Stage Two				
Conclusion – Review of Case Plan				

(iii) Costs Summary

	Profit Costs	Counsel's Fees	Disbursements	Total
				24,000
				£34,042.00

H. Cost Sharing Agreement

Not applicable

CASE MANAGEMENT INFORMATION

I. Team Personnel (including Solicitors Employees, Experts and Counsel and/or Solicitor Advocate)

1.10 LAW SOCIETY'S CHILDREN PANEL MEMBERSHIP

1.10.1 Membership list

Full current membership lists for children representatives, adult party representatives and local authority representatives are regularly posted on the Law Society website within the Children Panel Section.[31]

1.10.2 Types of Membership

Membership of the Law Society Children's Panel is open to both solicitors and Fellows of the Institute of Legal Executives (FILEX) who are *employed* by a solicitor.

There are two categories of membership:

1.10.2.1 *Private practitioner membership*

- Must be employed in private practice; and

- must satisfy the eligibility, experience and training criteria.

There are two types of membership available within this category:

(a) Children representatives

- Representation of all children in all family proceedings where there is provision to represent children; and
- representation of adult parties in public law proceedings under the Children Act 1989.

(b) Adult party representatives

- Representation of adult parties in public law proceedings under the Children Act 1989.

(NB – When being considered for private practitioner membership it is possible to request consideration as adult party representatives only. Subsequently it is possible to convert from adult party representative to child representative upon application to the Law Society and following an interview by a solicitor assessor and a children's guardian assessor who *may* recommend transfer of membership.)

1.10.2.2 *Local authority membership*

- Must be employed by local authority; and

---

[31]   www.panels.lawsociety.org.uk.

- must satisfy the eligibility, experience and training criteria.

1.10.2.3 Duration of membership

Membership lasts for 5 years. Thereafter, there is a requirement to demonstrate continued suitability to remain on the panel by successfully completing the re-accreditation process.

1.10.2.4 Eligibility

- Practising solicitor for at least 3 years.

- Fellow of the Institute of Legal Executives (FILEX) for at least 3 years, held fellowship of the Institute throughout that period and hold the Rights of Audience Matrimonial Proceedings Certificate (or other appropriate advocacy qualification awarded by the Institute of Legal Executives (ILEX)).

In addition:

- Must be employed by a solicitor.

- If employed by the local authority authorisation pursuant to Local Government Act 1972, s 223, replaces the need to hold an ILEX advocacy qualification.

1.10.2.5 Standards required of a Children Panel member

- Basic knowledge requirement.[32]

- Demonstrate experience by the conduct of cases for parties in public and other family proceedings as defined in the Children Act 1989.

- Demonstrate competence in the skills specified in Annex C[33] and have a good working knowledge of procedures in the appropriate courts.

- Good advocacy skills.

- Demonstrate a thorough awareness of ethical issues as may arise in children cases.

In addition, it is necessary to demonstrate relevant experience depending on the nature of the membership sought.

---

[32] Annex B – www.panel.lawsociety.org.uk.
[33] www.panel.lawsociety.org.uk.

1.10.2.6   Other requirements

- Completion of a compulsory training course with an approved provider prior to application for membership. Thereafter, application for membership must be made within 6 months of completing the course.

- A list of current providers can be found on the Law Society website.[34]

- Completion of application which is the first stage of assessment.

- Providing first stage of assessment is passed, all applicants for private practice membership will be subject to interview. This will be conducted by a solicitor assessor and children's guardian assessor.

Applicants for local authority membership will only be interviewed if application is considered borderline at the first stage of assessment.

1.10.2.7   Private practitioner membership

- Requires two referees who are familiar with the applicant's work and able to comment on suitability for membership, one of whom must be a children's guardian. The referees must not be employed by a partner within the firm employing the applicant.

- Local authority membership requires one referee who must be either a member of the judiciary or a private practice member of the Children Panel.

- Enhanced disclosure from the Criminal Records Bureau is required.

- All applicants for private practice membership are required to read and sign the undertaking attached at Annex A[35] which normally provides for the Children Panel private practitioner member to conduct the case personally; to consider whether it is in the best interests of the client to instruct another advocate; if it is in their best interests or necessary to instruct another advocate, to advise the client or children's guardian (if applicable) as to whom should be instructed and that, save in exceptional circumstances, any advocate so instructed will be either a Children Panel member (approved as a children representative if the client is a child) or a member of the Bar included in the practitioner's firm's approved counsel list. There is an additional requirement in such circumstances to obtain from that advocate an undertaking to attend and conduct the matter personally, unless an unavoidable professional engagement arises,

---

34   www.panel.lawsociety.org.uk.
35   www.panel.lawsociety.org.uk.

and to take all reasonable steps to ensure that, so far as reasonably practicable, a conflicting professional engagement does not arise.

1.10.2.8 Appointment as Children Panel solicitor

(a) By the children's guardian

A children's guardian appointed in a public law case has a duty to advise the court what is in the child's best interests from their professional point of view and also to communicate the child's wishes to the court. The children's guardian will appoint a solicitor whose client is the child.[36]

(b) By the court

In some areas there is a shortage of CAFCASS children's guardians and therefore it can fall to the court to appoint a solicitor for the child before a guardian is appointed.

The appointment of the solicitor for the child in care and supervision applications is dealt with pursuant to CA 1989, s 41(3)–(5). The solicitor for the child should be appointed in time to represent the child at the first hearing.

See: *A Statement of Good Practice in the Appointment of Solicitors for Children where it falls to the Court to do so in Specified Proceedings.*

Paragraph 4:

> '... a solicitor who fulfils this role should normally be an experienced member of the Law Society Children Panel. A solicitor should be regarded as being an experienced member of the Panel for these purposes if he/she has been a member of the Panel accredited to represent children for three years or more.'

Paragraph 5:

> 'The Law Society will make available to the Justices' Chief Executive in each Magistrates' Courts Committee area the full list of Panel members accredited to represent children ... The JCE will prepare a list identifying those members of the Panel practising in each Care Centre area in which that MCC has Family Proceedings Courts and will specifically identify those who have been on the Panel for three years or more ("the local list"). The JCE will send a copy of the local list to their Family Proceedings Courts, the Care Centre(s) and to CAFCASS offices responsible for Care Centre area(s).'

---

[36] Part 4, para 4.1.2 of *Good Practice in Child Care Cases* issued by the Law Society.

See also: *Representation of Children in Public Law Proceedings – Law Society Good Practice Note on Acting in the Absence of a Children's Guardian* (December 2006), which supersedes Appendix 8 of *Good Practice in Child Care Cases*.

1.10.2.9 Law Society and CAFCASS Guidance on the working relationship between Children Panel Solicitors and Children's Guardians

The guidance is issued by the Law Society's Children Law Sub-Committee and CAFCASS and replaces but reflects and builds on the Protocol for the Working Relationship between Children Panel solicitors and guardians ad litem issued by the Law Society's Children Law Sub-Committee in conjunction with the National Association of Guardians ad Litem and Reporting Officers (NAGLRO) and the Association of Guardians ad Litem and Reporting Officers Panel Managers (AGOLROPM) in March 2000. In addition, it should be read in conjunction with Part 4 of Good Practice in Child Care Cases published by the Law Society.

1.11 GUIDANCE FOR CHILDREN PANEL SOLICITORS

1.11.1 Professional practice

The Children Panel Solicitor should remain sensitive to the importance of the working relationship with the children's guardian.

A Children Panel Solicitor should ensure that they discuss with the children's guardian at the outset of a case their roles and expectations, including the need for the children's guardian to access and read the relevant social services files; what evidence is relevant and should be obtained; and whether any interviews should be conducted jointly. They should also ensure the guardian receives copies of all documents filed in the proceedings and copy correspondence (where relevant). It is also essential that the children's solicitor confirms to the children's guardian the need to keep a written record of all communications with the relevant social services department and other persons involved in the case.

In addition, a Children Panel Solicitor should:

- respond promptly to the children's guardian's request to act, including declining to act;

- be professional and promote the independent role of the children's guardian;

- remind the children's guardian of the need to be and to be seen to be open minded and even handed;

- provide competent representation;

- keep under review the need to avoid delay;[37]

- comply with the Children Panel Solicitor's personal undertakings; discuss and agree with the children's guardian the substitution of advocates for hearings, including selection of counsel;

- ensure counsel, where instructed, is fully and properly briefed;

- recognise the limits of own experience and seek advice from mentors or advise change of solicitor.

1.11.2 Representation of child

- Bear in mind the child is the client;

- see the child personally unless, in consultation with the guardian, it is considered inappropriate; seek guidance from the children's guardian concerning age and understanding and discuss with the children's guardian the issue of disclosure;

- keep under constant review the child's capacity with regard to separate representation;

- consult with the children's guardian about attendance of the child at court hearings;

- consider consulting with the child about the choice of advocate (only if the child is of sufficient age and understanding);

- discuss with the children's guardian the best way of advising the child and of informing the child of the outcome of hearings and important meetings.

1.11.3 Legal advice to children's guardian

Advice provided to the guardian should be prompt and should include advice on law; evidence; experts; procedure and appeal.

---

[37] CA 1989, s 1(2).

1.11.4   Guidance on acting in the absence of a children's guardian

The Law Society has issued guidance in relation to this topic.[38]

It is necessary to bear in mind that, where a solicitor has decided to act, he/she should conduct the proceedings in accordance with the instructions taken from the child where the child is able to provide instructions, having regard to their age and understanding.

If the child is not able to provide instructions, the solicitor should represent the child 'in furtherance of the best interests of the child'.[39]

It is important to remember that the solicitor should not undertake the guardian's professional role. The solicitor is not in a position to advise the court as to what is in the child's best interests.

The solicitor should, in the absence of the appointment of a children's guardian:

- critically appraise the local authority's actions and evidence; require the filing of further evidence if appropriate; ensure the court has sufficient evidence on which to base its decision and to test all the evidence at any contested hearing;

- continue throughout to seek the appointment of a children's guardian by CAFCASS;

- represent the child in accordance with instructions received from the child.

---

[38]   Law Society Guidance (October 2003).
[39]   Section 4 of the CA 1989 and FPR 2010, Chapter 8, r 16.29(5).

CHAPTER 2

ALLOCATION AND TRANSFER OF PROCEEDINGS

2.1 INTRODUCTION

The law and procedure relating to the allocation and transfer of family law proceedings is governed by the Allocation and Transfer of Proceedings Order 2008 ('the 2008 Order'), which came into force on 25 November 2008. The Children (Allocation of Proceedings) Order 1991 and all subsequent amendments to that Order have been revoked in full. A Practice Direction from the President of the Family Division also came into effect on 25 November 2008 and provides guidance in line with the 2008 Order. The stated objective of the Practice Direction is to 'ensure that the criteria for the transfer of proceedings are applied in such a way that proceedings are heard at the appropriate level of court; that the capacity of the magistrates' courts is properly utilised and that proceedings are only dealt with in the High Court if the relevant criteria are met'.[1]

2.2 STARTING PROCEEDINGS

Part 2, Section 1 of the 2008 Order provides an exhaustive list of the appropriate courts within which to start particular types of family law proceedings. Generally, most family matters must be commenced in the magistrates' court (family proceedings court). The 2008 Order also makes specific provision for certain proceedings that either must be started in a county court, or may be started in the High Court.

2.2.1 Starting proceedings in a magistrates' court

Article 5(1) of the 2008 Order sets out those proceedings that must always be started in the magistrates' court:

(a) Protection of children in an emergency under Children Act 1989, s 79K;

(b) Contribution orders under Children Act 1989, Sch 2, para 23;

---

[1] Practice Direction – Allocation and Transfer of Proceedings, November 2008, para 1.2.

(c)   Certain appeals under Children Act 1989, Sch 8, para 8;

(d)   Varying a placement order under Adoption and Children Act 2002, s 23;

(e)   Adoption orders (where there is no local authority involvement and no intercountry aspect involved[2]) under Adoption and Children Act 2002, s 50 or 51;

(f)   Appeals under Child Support Act 1991, s 20 (where proceedings are to be dealt with under the Child Support Appeals (Jurisdiction of Courts) Order 2002);

(g)   Parental orders under Human Fertilisation and Embryology Act 1990, s 30.

Article 5(2) of the 2008 Order sets out those proceedings that must be started in the magistrates' court, subject to two possible exceptions:

(a)   Acquisition of parental responsibility by a father under Children Act 1989, s 4;

(b)   Acquisition of parental responsibility by a step-parent under Children Act 1989, s 4A;

(c)   Secure accommodation under Children Act 1989, s 25;

(d)   Care and supervision orders under Children Act 1989, s 31;

(e)   Leave to change the surname of or remove from the UK, a child in care under Children Act 1989, s 33(7);

(f)   Parental contact with a child in care under Children Act 1989, s 34;

(g)   Education supervision orders under Children Act 1989, s 36;

(h)   Child assessment orders under Children Act 1989, s 43;

(i)   Emergency protection orders under Children Act 1989, s 44;

(j)   Extension, variation or discharge of emergency protection orders under Children Act 1989, s 45;

(k)   Emergency protection order by police officer under Children Act 1989, s 46(7);

---

[2]   See arts 5(1)(e) and para 6(c) and (d) of the 2008 Order.

(l)   Powers to assist in the discovery of children under Children Act 1989, s 48;

(m)   Recovery orders under Children Act 1989, s 50;

(n)   Warrant authorising a constable to assist in the exercise of certain powers to search for children under Children Act 1989, s 102;

(o)   Approval of arrangements to assist a child to live abroad under Children Act 1989, Sch 2, para 19.

The two potential exceptions to these matters being started in the magistrates' court are detailed in art 5(3) and (4) of the 2008 Order.

Article 5(3) provides that if proceedings for any of the above orders are to be commenced and there are already existing proceedings relating to the child before a county court or the High Court, and the application arises out of the same circumstances as the existing proceedings, the new proceedings can be started in the court in which the current proceedings are already pending.

Article 5(4) relates to applications under ss 4 and 4A of the Children Act 1989 (parental responsibility) which are started at the same time as proceedings in a county court or the High Court for a section 8 order (for residence or contact, for example). Applications under s 4 or 4A in relation to the same child, that are to start at the same time as an application for a section 8 order, must be commenced in the same court.

2.2.2   Starting proceedings in a county court

Article 6 of the 2008 Order provides for a small number of matters that must be started in a county court:

(a)   proceedings brought by an applicant under the age of 18:

(i)   under Children Act 1989, ss 10(2)(b), 11J(6) or 11O(7) (leave of the court to make an application); or
(ii)   under Family Law Act 1996, Pt IV (domestic violence provisions);

(b)   children under the age of 16 seeking leave of the court to make an application (Family Law Act 1996, s 43);

(c)   proceedings for a Convention adoption order;

(d)   proceedings for an adoption order under the Adoption and Children Act 2002 where s 83 of that Act (restriction on bringing children in) applies.

2.2.3 Starting proceedings in the High Court

Article 7 of the 2008 Order sets out the criteria for proceedings that can properly be started in the High Court, subject to the provisions of art 5(3) and (4) (as described above) and art 8 of the Order. Proceedings may be started in the High Court if:

(a)   the proceedings are exceptionally complex;

(b)   the outcome of the proceedings is important to the public in general; or

(c)   there is another substantial reason for the proceedings to be started in the High Court.

2.2.4 Starting other proceedings in the court where adoption proceedings are pending

Article 8 details those proceedings that must be started in the court where proceedings (concerning the same child) under the Adoption and Children Act 2002 are pending.

Where proceedings under s 50 or 51 of the Adoption and Children Act 2002 for an adoption order are pending, proceedings concerning the same child must be started in the same court for the following applications:

(a)   leave to apply for a residence order (Adoption and Children Act 2002, s 29(4)(b));

(b)   leave to apply for a special guardianship order (Adoption and Children Act 2002, s 29(5)(b));

(c)   applications for a section 8 order, where leave has been obtained under Adoption and Children Act 2002, s 28(1)(a) or 29(4)(b);

(d)   applications for a special guardianship order under Children Act 1989, s 14A, where leave has been obtained under Adoption and Children Act 2002, s 28(1)(b) or 29(5)(b);

(e)   leave to remove the child under Adoption and Children Act 2002, s 37;

(f)   leave to oppose the making of an order under Adoption and Children Act 2002, s 47(3) or (5).

Where proceedings under section 22 of the Adoption and Children Act 2002 for a placement order are pending, proceedings under that Act for leave to remove the child from local authority accommodation must be started in the same court in which proceedings are pending.[3]

Where proceedings under s 42(6) of the Adoption and Children Act 2002 for leave to apply for an adoption order are pending, proceedings under s 38(3)(a) or 40(2)(a) of that Act for leave to remove a child must be started in the same court in which proceedings are pending.[4]

2.2.5 Classes of county courts

The 2008 Order, Part 2 sets out the specific 'classes' of county court in which proceedings must be started. To hear certain types of family proceedings, a county court must be a Family Hearing Centre, a Care Centre, an Adoption Centre, an Intercountry Adoption Centre or a Forced Marriage County Court. Each county court within England and Wales is listed in Schedule 1 to the 2008 Order alongside which is noted the class of that court, indicating the types of proceedings that particular court is capable of hearing.[5] The Principal Registry of the Family Division of the High Court is treated as if it were all of the specified centres, and can therefore hear any family case.[6]

Article 9 of the 2008 Order provides that proceedings under the Children Act 1989 Parts 1 and 2 and Sch 1 which are to start in a county court must, subject to the provisions of art 8(1)(c) and (d) (as detailed above), commence in a designated Family Hearing Centre. Proceedings under Parts 3, 4 or 5 of the Children Act 1989 which are to be started in a county court must be commenced in a Care Centre. Article 10 deals with those proceedings under Part 4A of the Family Law Act 1996 and provides that such matters that are to be started in a county court must be commenced in a Forced Marriage County Court. Article 11 provides that proceedings under the Adoption and Children Act 2002 that are to be started in a county court must be commenced in either an Adoption Centre or an Intercountry Adoption Centre, depending on the nature of the adoption involved.

These provisions as to the class of individual county courts are also relevant to circumstances where proceedings are to be transferred between courts as detailed below. Only those courts that have the correct class status can accept transfers of proceedings of certain types.[7]

---

3   Allocation and Transfer of Proceedings Order 2008, art 8(2).
4   Allocation and Transfer of Proceedings Order 2008, art 8(3).
5   Allocation and Transfer of Proceedings Order 2008, art 2.
6   Allocation and Transfer of Proceedings Order 2008, art 3.
7   Allocation and Transfer of Proceedings Order 2008, Part 3, arts 20–22.

2.3 TRANSFER OF PROCEEDINGS

Whilst family law proceedings are required to be started in a particular court, the matter may not necessarily remain in that same court for the duration of the proceedings. The 2008 Order, Part 3 sets out the specific circumstances in which cases can be transferred between the different levels and classes of courts, and between particular individual courts. Proceedings can be transferred up, from the magistrates' court to the county court, or from the county court to the High Court. They can be transferred down from the High Court to the county court, or the county court to the magistrates' court, and proceedings can be transferred sideways to a court of the same level.

The paramount consideration for a court deciding on the appropriate forum to hear proceedings is the 'no delay' principle. Article 13 of the 2008 Order makes it clear that the court must have regard to the need to avoid delay in the proceedings. In circumstances where a higher court is considering a transfer down to a lower level of court, this should not be done if the transfer would cause the determination of proceedings to be delayed.

Paragraph 3.1 of the *President's Practice Direction – Allocation and Transfer of Proceedings* provides clear guidance regarding the transfer of proceedings and states that the issue of the most appropriate court to hear proceedings 'must be addressed by the court speedily as soon as there is sufficient information to determine whether the case meets the criteria for hearing in that court'. The paragraph also clearly states that such considerations must remain under review throughout the proceedings. Paragraph 4 of the Practice Direction provides additional guidance as to 'timeliness' and suggests, for example, that listing availability of courts should be ascertained before deciding where the proceedings should be heard.

2.3.1   Transfer from one magistrates' court to another

Article 14 of the 2008 Order details the circumstances in which it will be appropriate for a transfer between magistrates' courts. The 'transferring court' can only transfer to the 'receiving court' if it considers that:

(a) the transfer will significantly accelerate the determination of the proceedings;

(b) it is more convenient for the parties or for the child who is the subject of the proceedings for the proceedings to be dealt with by the receiving court; or

(c) there is another good reason for the proceedings to be transferred.

The President's Practice Direction – Allocation and Transfer of Proceedings, at para 7 details those factors that may make a sideways transfer to another magistrates' court appropriate:

(1)   the fact that a party is ill or suffers a disability which could make it inconvenient to attend at a particular court;

(2)   the fact that the child lives in the area of the other court;

(3)   the need to avoid delay.

These factors are equally applicable when a county court considers a sideways transfer to another county court (see **2.3.4**).

2.3.2   Transfer from a magistrates' court to a county court

Article 15 of the 2008 Order provides criteria for when proceedings can properly be transferred up from a magistrates' court to a county court. A magistrates' court may transfer the whole or any part of proceedings to a county court if it considers that:

(a)   the transfer will significantly accelerate the determination of the proceedings;

(b)   there is a real possibility of difficulty resolving conflicts in the evidence of witnesses;

(c)   there is a real possibility of a conflict in the evidence of two or more experts;

(d)   there is a novel or difficult point of law;

(e)   there are proceedings concerning the child in another jurisdiction or there are international law issues;

(f)   there is a real possibility that enforcement proceedings may be necessary and the method of enforcement of the likely penalty is beyond the powers of the magistrates' court;

(g)   there is a real possibility that a guardian ad litem will be appointed under rule 16 of the Family Procedure Rules 2010;

(h)   there is a real possibility that a party to the proceedings is a person lacking capacity within the meaning of the Mental Capacity Act 2005 to conduct the proceedings; or

(i)   there is another good reason for the proceedings to be transferred.

There are certain exceptions to these rules, detailed in art 15(2) and (3) of the 2008 Order, whereby some types of proceedings cannot be transferred from the magistrates' court. Generally, those matters that cannot be transferred relate to applications for emergency protection of children (see art 5(1)(a)-(c) and art 5(2)(i)-(l) for those proceedings that cannot be transferred from the magistrates' court).

The President's Practice Direction states in para 8.1 that a magistrates' court, when considering the issues outlined in art 15(1) (except those in art 15(1)(g) and (h)), is required to first consider whether another magistrates' court would have the suitable experience to deal with the issues which have given rise to a consideration of art 15, such that a sideways transfer might be more suitable than a transfer to a county court. Paragraph 8.2 of the Practice Direction provides further guidance to magistrates' courts in respect of considering a transfer under art 15(1)(a), namely that a transfer would significantly accelerate the determination of the proceedings. Information regarding the available hearing dates in other magistrates' courts and the relevant county court must be obtained and the fact that an earlier date is available in the county court will not of itself justify a transfer to the county court.

It is possible to appeal against the decision of a magistrates' court to refuse to transfer Children Act 1989 proceedings to a county court. An application may be made to a circuit judge for an order to transfer the proceedings to a county court, under art 25(1) of the 2008 Order. In such situations, the relevant procedure to lodge an appeal is contained within rr 12.9–12.11 of the Family Procedure Rules 2010. Under s 94(2) of the Children Act 1989, there is no right of appeal against the decision of a magistrates' court to decline jurisdiction and transfer proceedings to a county court if it considers that the case can be more conveniently dealt with by another court.

2.3.3 Transfer from a county court to a magistrates' court

Under art 16(1) of the 2008 Order, if on receiving a case from the magistrates' court, the county court considers that none of the criteria in art 15(1) of the 2008 Order apply to the proceedings, it must transfer the matter back to the magistrates' court. Similarly, under art 16(2) of the 2008 Order, a county court must transfer to a magistrates' court any proceedings which were started in the county court (except for those matters that must, under arts 5(3) and (4) and 8, be started in the county court) if it considers that the criteria in art 15(1) do not apply. This is with the exception of the criteria in art 15(1)(a), namely if a determination of the proceedings will be significantly accelerated by remaining at the county court, they should not be transferred to the magistrates' court.

The President's Practice Direction, para 9.2 lists those straightforward matters that should ordinarily be transferred to a magistrates' court if they have been started in the county court and the county court considers that none of the criteria in art 15(1)(b)-(i) apply. Those straightforward matters are:

(1) a residence order;

(2) a contact order;

(3) a prohibited steps order;

(4) a specific issue order;

(5) a special guardianship order;

(6) an order under Part IV of the Family Law Act 1996.

Where a county court orders the transfer of proceedings to a magistrates' court, this decision can be appealed under art 26 of the 2008 Order. Where the decision was made by a district judge or deputy district judge of the county court, the appeal lies to a circuit judge. Where the decision was made by a district judge or a deputy district judge of the Principal Registry of the Family Division, the appeal lies to a judge of the Family Division of the High Court.

2.3.4 Transfer of proceedings from one county court to another

Article 17 of the 2008 Order sets out when a county court may transfer proceedings to another county court. As with sideways transfers between magistrates' courts, the transferring county court must consider that:

'(a) the transfer will significantly accelerate the determination of the proceedings;
(b) it is more convenient for the parties or for the child who is the subject of the proceedings for the proceedings to be dealt with by the receiving court;
(c) ...[8]; or
(d) there is another good reason for the proceedings to be transferred.'

2.3.5 Transfer from a county court to the High Court

Under art 18 of the 2008 Order, a county court may transfer proceedings to the High Court if it considers that:

(a) the proceedings are exceptionally complex;

---

[8] Also contained in this Article (art 17(c)), is a provision that a county court may transfer proceedings to another county court where there is an occupation rights matter to be dealt with under s 59(1) of the Family Law Act 1996, if the property in question is situated in the district of the receiving court.

(b)   the outcome of the proceedings is important to the public in general; or

(c)   there is another substantial reason for the proceedings to be transferred.

Paragraph 5 of the *President's Practice Direction* provides extensive additional guidance as to the factors to be taken into consideration when dealing with the transfer of proceedings from or to the High Court. The court is required to take into account the following factors when deciding if the requisite criteria for a case to be heard in the High Court apply, namely whether:

'(1)   there is alleged to be a risk that a child concerned in the proceedings will suffer serious physical or emotional harm in the light of -
     (a)   the death of another child in the family, a parent or any other material person; or
     (b)   the fact that a parent or other material person may have committed a grave crime, for example, murder, manslaughter or rape,
     in particular where the essential factual framework is in dispute or there are issues over the causation of injuries or a material conflict of expert evidence;

(2)   the application concerns medical treatment for a child which involves a risk to the child's physical or emotional health which goes beyond the normal risks of routine medical treatment;

(3)   an adoption order is sought in relation to a child who has been adopted abroad in a country whose adoption orders are not recognised in England and Wales;

(4)   an adoption order is sought in relation to a child who has been brought into the United Kingdom in circumstances where section 83 of the Adoption and Children Act 2002 applies (restriction on bringing children in) and
     (a)   the person bringing in the child, or causing the child to be brought –
          (i)   has not complied with any requirement imposed by regulations made under section 83(4); or
          (ii)   has not met any condition required to be met by regulations made under section 83(5) within the required time; or
     (b)   there are complicating features in relation to the application;

(5)   it is likely that the proceedings will set a significant new precedent or alter existing principles of common law;

(6)   ...'

The Practice Direction then proceeds, in para 5.2, to list specific proceedings which are likely to fall within the criteria for hearing in the High Court. These proceedings are not listed here in full since they are of

---

9   A further consideration is outlined in relation to periodical payments, lump sums and property transfers in para 5.1(6), which is not detailed here since it is not relevant to child care practice.

an unusual nature, generally related to complex matters involving foreign jurisdictions. The most relevant type of proceedings to child care practice noted in the paragraph are those proceedings in which there is an application to remove a child permanently or temporarily from the jurisdiction to a non-Hague Convention country.

Paragraph 5.3 of the Practice Direction notes those factors which may be present in a case, but which will not normally mean that the High Court is automatically the appropriate venue for the proceedings to be heard:

(1)   intractable problems with regard to contact;

(2)   sexual abuse;

(3)   injury to a child which is neither life-threatening nor permanently disabling;

(4)   routine neglect, even if it spans many years and there is copious documentation;

(5)   temporary or permanent removal to a Hague Convention country;

(6)   standard human rights issues;

(7)   uncertainty as to immigration status;

(8)   the celebrity of the parties;

(9)   the anticipated length of the hearing;

(10) the quantity of evidence;

(11) the number of experts;

(12) the possible availability of a speedier hearing.

2.3.6   Transfer from the High Court

Article 19 of the 2008 Order provides that the High Court must transfer to a county court or a magistrates' court any proceedings which were started in, or transferred to the High Court if the High Court considers that none of the criteria in art 18 apply.

The President's Practice Direction, para 5.4 provides that proceedings which have needlessly been brought in the High Court under the 'there is another substantial reason for starting proceedings in the High Court' provision, will be transferred to a county or magistrates' court and the High Court may consider making appropriate costs orders.

2.3.7　The Public Law Outline: Guide to Case Management in Public Law Proceedings

See Chapter 3 for detailed discussion.

2.4　ALLOCATION TO JUDICIARY

If proceedings are either started in the county court or transferred to the county court (or the Principal Registry of the Family Division (PRFD)), the case is then allocated to a particular judge to maintain judicial continuity throughout the proceedings. The Family Proceedings (Allocation to Judiciary) Directions contain detailed schedules showing the categories of proceedings that different levels of judge can suitably hear. Cases will therefore be allocated to judges depending on the status of the individual judge and the nature of the proceedings themselves in order to ensure that the most serious matters are heard by appropriately qualified and experienced judges. Judges of the Family Division of the High Court can hear any family law proceedings.

2.5　TRANSFER TO THE PRINCIPAL REGISTRY OF THE FAMILY DIVISION

For the purposes of the commencement and allocation of family law proceedings, the PRFD is treated as a county court. Procedures have been in place since 30 October 2006 to deal with the transfer in of proceedings from FPCs. Such procedures are available elsewhere in England and Wales, which are published in local Practice Notes or Family Courts Plans by the individual Care Centres. The procedures were implemented following the Child Care Proceedings Review in May 2006 and the aim is to ensure that cases are fit to proceed and to achieve judicial continuity. The Gatekeeping and Allocation procedure for the PRFD is as set out below.

2.5.1　Procedure in the FPC to effect transfer

- Where the FPC decides to transfer, the parties are to be informed that the court file will be referred to the gatekeeper judge at the PRFD for allocation and initial directions. The judge will consider the case papers and give standard directions without the attendance of the parties or their legal representatives.

- At the conclusion of the hearing at which transfer is decided, the local authority and other parties must complete and file a 'judicial gatekeeping scrutiny form' containing information about the case relevant to allocation and initial directions. The form will accompany the file when it is transferred to the PRFD.

- Any request for a specific non-standard direction, or a request for a preliminary hearing prior to directions being given, must be stated in the gatekeeping form. The party must state what direction/order is sought, whether it is agreed or opposed and the reason for any preliminary hearing, with a time estimate. The legal representatives should draw to the attention of the gatekeeping judge any unusual or particularly complex circumstances within the form.

- Where it is clear there are exceptional circumstances and that an urgent hearing is needed, the FPC should contact the PRFD and fix a provisional date for hearing, not more than 5 days after the decision to transfer.

- The court file must be transferred as soon as practicable and in any event, not more than one working day after the hearing in the FPC.

- Where a decision to transfer is made and a substantive hearing is already fixed in the FPC, this should not be vacated until the gatekeeper judge confirms it is not required. The FPC legal advisor may contact the gatekeeper judge if there is a doubt about the appropriateness of transfer.

2.5.2 Procedure following transfer to the PRFD

Once the court file has been transferred, the gatekeeper judge will consider allocation within two working days of receipt. The judge will consider the case papers without a hearing and will:

- Consider whether the case should proceed in the Principal Registry (High Court or county court) or whether it may be appropriate to transfer the case back to the FPC or another court.

- Subject to the above, allocate the case to the appropriate level of court (High or county).

- Where the case is to proceed at county court level, allocate a case management judge.

- Give standard directions.

- Consider any other directions that may be required.

- If appropriate, fix a hearing to consider any additional directions or orders which may be required.

If the judge considers the case should be transferred back to the FPC or another court, a hearing will be fixed for that purpose and the court will give notice to the parties. The hearing is to be held within 14 days.

The gatekeeper judge will liaise with the list office/Clerk of the Rules as appropriate to fix the CMC or any preliminary hearing, before the allocated judge. The court will serve a copy of the order on all parties.

A2.1 APPENDIX 1:
ALLOCATION AND TRANSFER OF PROCEEDINGS ORDER 2008

PART 1
PRELIMINARY

1 Citation, commencement, interpretation and application

(1) This Order may be cited as the Allocation and Transfer of Proceedings Order 2008 and, subject to paragraph (2), shall come into force on 25th November 2008.

(2) Articles 6(a)(i), 9(1) and 20(1), in so far as they apply to section 11J(6) or 11O(7) of, and paragraphs 4 to 7 and 9 of Schedule A1 to, the 1989 Act, shall come into force on the same day as sections 4 and 5 of the Children and Adoption Act 2006 come into force.

(3) In this Order–

"the 1989 Act" means the Children Act 1989;
"the 1996 Act" means the Family Law Act 1996;
"the 2002 Act" means the Adoption and Children Act 2002;
"Convention adoption order" means an adoption order under the 2002 Act which, by virtue of regulations under section 1 of the Adoption (Intercountry Aspects) Act 1999 (regulations giving effect to the Convention), is made as a Convention adoption order;
"proceedings" means, unless the context otherwise requires, proceedings under–
    (a)   section 55A of the Family Law Act 1986 (declarations of parentage);
    (b)   the 1989 Act;
    (c)   section 20 of the Child Support Act 1991 (appeals);
    (d)   section 30 of the Human Fertilisation and Embryology Act 1990 (parental orders);
    (e)   Part 4 of the 1996 Act; and
    (f)   the 2002 Act.

(4) The provisions in this Order apply unless any enactment or rule provides otherwise.

2 Classes of county court

For the purposes of this Order there are the following classes of county court–

    (a)   family hearing centres, being those courts against which the word yes appears in column 2 of the table in Schedule 1;
    (b)   care centres, being those courts against which the word yes appears in column 3 of that table;

(c) adoption centres, being those courts against which the word yes appears in column 4 of that table;

(d) intercountry adoption centres, being those courts against which the word yes appears in column 5 of that table; and

(e) forced marriage county courts, being those courts against which the word yes appears in column 6 of that table.

3 Principal Registry of the Family Division

The principal registry of the Family Division of the High Court is treated, for the purposes of this Order, as if it were–

(a) a family hearing centre;

(b) a care centre;

(c) an adoption centre;

(d) an intercountry adoption centre; and

(e) a forced marriage county court.

4 Contravention of a provision of this Order

Where proceedings are started or transferred in contravention of a provision of this Order, the contravention does not have the effect of making the proceedings invalid.

PART 2
STARTING PROCEEDINGS

Section 1
Starting Proceedings in Specified Level of Court

5 Proceedings which must be started in a magistrates' court

(1) Proceedings under the following provisions must be started in a magistrates' court–

(a) section 79K of the 1989 Act (protection of children in an emergency);

(b) paragraph 23 of Schedule 2 to the 1989 Act (contribution order);

(c) paragraph 8 of Schedule 8 to the 1989 Act (certain appeals);

(d) section 23 of the 2002 Act (varying placement order);

(e) section 50 or 51 of the 2002 Act (adoption order), unless any local authority will be a party to the proceedings or article 6(c) or (d) applies;

(f) section 20 of the Child Support Act 1991 (appeals) where the proceedings are to be dealt with in accordance with the Child Support Appeals (Jurisdiction of Courts) Order 2002; and

(g) section 30 of the Human Fertilisation and Embryology Act 1990 (parental orders).

(2) Subject to paragraphs (3) and (4), proceedings under the following provisions must be started in a magistrates' court–

(a)   section 4 of the 1989 Act (acquisition of parental responsibility by father);

(b)   section 4A of the 1989 Act (acquisition of parental responsibility by step-parent);

(c)   section 25 of the 1989 Act (use of accommodation for restricting liberty);

(d)   section 31 of the 1989 Act (care and supervision orders);

(e)   section 33(7) of the 1989 Act (leave to change surname of, or remove from United Kingdom, child in care);

(f)   section 34 of the 1989 Act (parental contact etc. with children in care);

(g)   section 36 of the 1989 Act (education supervision orders);

(h)   section 43 of the 1989 Act (child assessment orders);

(i)   section 44 of the 1989 Act (emergency protection orders);

(j)   section 45 of the 1989 Act (extension, variation or discharge of emergency protection order);

(k)   section 46(7) of the 1989 Act (emergency protection order by police officer);

(l)   section 48 of the 1989 Act (powers to assist in discovery of children etc.);

(m)   section 50 of the 1989 Act (recovery orders);

(n)   section 102 of the 1989 Act (warrant authorising a constable to assist in exercise of certain powers to search for children etc.); and

(o)   paragraph 19 of Schedule 2 to the 1989 Act (approval of arrangements to assist child to live abroad).

(3)   Proceedings to which paragraph (2) applies which–

(a)   concern a child who is the subject of proceedings which are pending in a county court or the High Court; and

(b)   arise out of the same circumstances as gave rise to those proceedings

may be started in the court in which those proceedings are pending.

(4)   Proceedings under section 4 or 4A of the 1989 Act which are started at the same time as proceedings in a county court or the High Court for an order under section 8 of the 1989 Act (residence, contact and other applications in relation to children) in relation to the same child must be started in the court in which proceedings under section 8 are started.

6   Proceedings which must be started in a county court

Subject to article 7, proceedings–

(a)   brought by an applicant who is under the age of eighteen under–
   (i)   section 10(2)(b), 11J(6) or 11O(7) of, or paragraph 9(6) of Schedule A1 to, the 1989 Act (leave of the court to make an application); or
   (ii)   Part 4 of the 1996 Act;

(b)   under section 43 of the 1996 Act (leave of the court for applications by children under sixteen);

(c)   for a Convention adoption order; or

(d)   for an adoption order under the 2002 Act where section 83 of that Act (restriction on bringing children in) applies,

must be started in a county court.

7   Proceedings which may be started in the High Court

Subject to articles 5(3) and (4) and 8, proceedings may be started in the High Court only if–

(a)   the proceedings are exceptionally complex;

(b)   the outcome of the proceedings is important to the public in general; or

(c)   there is another substantial reason for the proceedings to be started in the High Court.

8   Proceedings which must be started in the court where proceedings under the 2002 Act are pending

(1)   Where proceedings under section 50 or 51 of the 2002 Act (adoption order) are pending, proceedings concerning the same child under–

(a)   section 29(4)(b) of the 2002 Act (leave to apply for a residence order);

(b)   section 29(5)(b) of the 2002 Act (leave to apply for a special guardianship order);

(c)   section 8 of the 1989 Act where section 28(1)(a) or 29(4)(b) of the 2002 Act applies (leave obtained to make application for a residence order);

(d)   section 14A of the 1989 Act where section 28(1)(b) or 29(5)(b) of the 2002 Act applies (leave obtained to make application for a special guardianship order);

(e)   section 37(a) of the 2002 Act (leave to remove the child); or

(f)   section 47(3) or (5) of the 2002 Act (leave to oppose the making of an adoption order),

must be started in the court in which the proceedings under section 50 or 51 are pending.

(2)   Where proceedings under section 22 of the 2002 Act (placement order) are pending, proceedings under section 30(2)(b) of that Act (leave to remove a child from accommodation provided by the local authority) must be started in the court in which the proceedings under section 22 are pending.

(3)   Where proceedings under section 42(6) of the 2002 Act (leave to apply for an adoption order) are pending, proceedings under

section 38(3)(a) or 40(2)(a) of that Act (leave to remove a child) must be started in the court in which the proceedings under section 42(6) are pending.

Section 2
Starting Proceedings in Specified Class of County Court

9   Starting proceedings under the 1989 Act

(1)   Subject to article 8(1)(c) and (d), proceedings under Part 1 or 2 of, or Schedule 1 or paragraphs 4 to 7 or 9 of Schedule A1 to, the 1989 Act which are to be started in a county court must be started in a family hearing centre.

(2)   Proceedings under Part 3, 4 or 5 of the 1989 Act which are to be started in a county court must be started in a care centre.

10   Starting proceedings under Part 4A of the 1996 Act

(1)   Proceedings under Part 4A of the 1996 Act which are to be started in a county court must be started in a forced marriage county court.

(2)   Article 7 applies to proceedings under Part 4A of the 1996 Act as it applies to other proceedings.

11   Starting proceedings under the 2002 Act

(1)   Subject to paragraph (2), proceedings under the 2002 Act which are to be started in a county court must be started in an adoption centre.

(2)   Proceedings for–

  (a)   a Convention adoption order; or
  (b)   an adoption order under the 2002 Act where section 83 of that Act applies

which are to be started in a county court must be started in an intercountry adoption centre.

PART 3
TRANSFER OF PROCEEDINGS

Section 1
General

12   Disapplication of enactments about transfer

The proceedings to which this Order applies are excluded from the operation of sections 38 and 39 of the Matrimonial and Family Proceedings Act 1984 (transfer of family proceedings).

13   General rules about transfer of proceedings

(1)   When making any decision about the transfer of proceedings under articles 14, 15, 17 and 18 the court must have regard to the need to avoid delay in the proceedings.

(2)   Articles 16 and 19 do not apply if the transfer of proceedings would cause the determination of the proceedings to be delayed.

(3)   The transfer of proceedings under this Part may be made at any stage of the proceedings and whether or not the proceedings have already been transferred.

Section 2
Transfer of Proceedings to Specified Level of Court

14   Transfer of proceedings from one magistrates' court to another

A magistrates' court (the "transferring court") may transfer proceedings to another magistrates' court (the "receiving court") only if the transferring court considers that–

(a)   the transfer will significantly accelerate the determination of the proceedings;

(b)   it is more convenient for the parties or for the child who is the subject of the proceedings for the proceedings to be dealt with by the receiving court; or

(c)   there is another good reason for the proceedings to be transferred.

15   Transfer of proceedings from magistrates' court to county court

(1)   Subject to paragraphs (2) and (3), a magistrates' court may transfer the whole or any part of proceedings to a county court only if the magistrates' court considers that–

(a)   the transfer will significantly accelerate the determination of the proceedings;

(b)   there is a real possibility of difficulty in resolving conflicts in the evidence of witnesses;

(c)   there is a real possibility of a conflict in the evidence of two or more experts;

(d)   there is a novel or difficult point of law;

(e)   there are proceedings concerning the child in another jurisdiction or there are international law issues;

(f)   there is a real possibility that enforcement proceedings may be necessary and the method of enforcement or the likely penalty is beyond the powers of a magistrates' court;

(g)   there is a real possibility that a guardian ad litem will be appointed under rule 16.3 or 16.4 of the Family Proceedings Rules 2010;

(h)   there is a real possibility that a party to proceedings is a person lacking capacity within the meaning of the Mental Capacity Act 2005 to conduct the proceedings; or

(i)   there is another good reason for the proceedings to be transferred.

(2)   Proceedings under any of the provisions mentioned in articles 5(1)(a) to (c) or 5(2)(i) to (l) may not be transferred from a magistrates' court.

(3)   Proceedings under section 25 of the 1989 Act (use of accommodation for restricting liberty) may not be transferred from a magistrates' court which is not a family proceedings court within the meaning of section 67 of the Magistrates' Courts Act 1980.

16   Transfer of proceedings from county court to magistrates' court

(1)   A county court must transfer to a magistrates' court proceedings which were transferred under article 15(1) if the county court considers that none of the criteria in article 15(1) applies.

(2)   Subject to articles 5(3) and (4), 6 and 8, a county court must transfer to a magistrates' court proceedings which were started in the county court if the county court considers that none of the criteria in article 15(1)(b) to (i) applies.

17   Transfer of proceedings from one county court to another

Subject to articles 16, 20, 21 and 22 a county court (the "transferring court") may transfer proceedings to another county court (the "receiving court") only if the transferring court considers that–

(a)   the transfer will significantly accelerate the determination of the proceedings;

(b)   it is more convenient for the parties or for the child who is the subject of the proceedings for the proceedings to be dealt with by the receiving court;

(c)   the proceedings involve the determination of a question of a kind mentioned in section 59(1) of the 1996 Act and the property in question is situated in the district of the receiving court; or

(d)   there is another good reason for the proceedings to be transferred.

18   Transfer of proceedings from county court to High Court

A county court may transfer proceedings to the High Court only if the county court considers that–

(a)   the proceedings are exceptionally complex;

(b)   the outcome of the proceedings is important to the public in general; or

(c)   there is another substantial reason for the proceedings to be transferred.

19   Transfer of proceedings from High Court

The High Court must transfer to a county court or a magistrates' court proceedings which were started in, or transferred to, the High Court if the High Court considers that none of the criteria in article 18 applies.

Section 3
Transfer of Proceedings to a Specified Class of County Court

20   Transfer of proceedings under the 1989 Act

(1)   Where proceedings under Part 1 or 2 of, or Schedule 1 or paragraphs 4 to 7 or 9 of Schedule A1 to, the 1989 Act are to be transferred to a county court, they must be transferred to a family hearing centre.

(2)   Where proceedings under Part 3, 4 or 5 of the 1989 Act are to be transferred to a county court, they must be transferred to a care centre.

21   Transfer of proceedings under the 2002 Act

(1)   Subject to paragraph (2), where proceedings under the 2002 Act are to be transferred to a county court, they must be transferred to an adoption centre.

(2)   Where proceedings for–

   (a)   a Convention Adoption Order; or
   (b)   an adoption order under the 2002 Act where section 83 of that Act applies,

are to be transferred to a county court, they must be transferred to an intercountry adoption centre.

22   Transfer of proceedings under Part 4A of the 1996 Act

(1)   Where proceedings under Part 4A of the 1996 Act are to be transferred to a county court, they must be transferred to a forced marriage county court.

(2)   Articles 17 to 19 apply to the transfer of proceedings under Part 4A of the 1996 Act as they apply to the transfer of other proceedings but as if the modification in paragraph (3) were made.

(3)   Article 19 is to be read as if "or a magistrates' court" were omitted.

Section 4
Transfer of Proceedings to Particular Court

23 Transfer of proceedings when arrested for breach of order under Part 4 of the 1996 Act

Where a person is brought before–

(a) the relevant judicial authority in accordance with section 47(7)(a) of the 1996 Act (arrest for breach of order); or

(b) a court by virtue of a warrant issued under section 47(9) of the 1996 Act,

and the matter is not then disposed of immediately, the relevant judicial authority or the court may transfer the matter to the relevant judicial authority or court which attached the power of arrest under section 47(2) or (3) of the 1996 Act or which issued the warrant.

24 Transfer of proceedings when arrested for breach of order under Part 4A of the 1996 Act

Where a person is brought before–

(a) the relevant judge in accordance with section 63I(3) of the 1996 Act (arrest for breach of order); or

(b) a court by virtue of a warrant issued under section 63J(3) of the 1996 Act,

and the matter is not then disposed of immediately, the relevant judge or the court may transfer the matter to the relevant judge or court which attached the power of arrest under section 63H(2) or (4) of the 1996 Act or which issued the warrant.

PART 4
APPLICATION FOLLOWING REFUSAL TO TRANSFER FROM MAGISTRATES' COURT TO COUNTY COURT AND APPEAL AGAINST TRANSFER TO MAGISTRATES' COURT BY COUNTY COURT

25 Application following refusal to order transfer of proceedings from magistrates' court to county court

(1) Where a magistrates' court refuses to order the transfer of proceedings to a county court under article 15(1), an application may be made for an order transferring proceedings to a county court.

(2) An application under paragraph (1) must be made–

(a) in relation to proceedings under the 2002 Act, to an adoption centre;

(b) in relation to proceedings under Parts 3, 4 and 5, to a care centre; and

(c) in any other case, to a family hearing centre.

(3)   In this article, "proceedings" means the proceedings under the 1989 Act or the 2002 Act and proceedings under section 55A of the Family Law Act 1986 (declarations of parentage).

26   Appeal against transfer of proceedings to magistrates' court by county court

Where a county court orders the transfer of proceedings to a magistrates' court under article 16, an appeal may be made against that decision–

> (a)   where the decision was made by a district judge or deputy district judge of a county court, to a circuit judge; or
>
> (b)   where the decision was made by a district judge or deputy district judge of the principal registry of the Family Division, to a judge of the Family Division of the High Court.

PART 5
REVOCATIONS, CONSEQUENTIAL AMENDMENTS AND TRANSITIONAL PROVISIONS

27   Revocations

Subject to article 29(2) and (3), the instruments listed in column 1 of the table in Schedule 2 (which have the references listed in column 2) are revoked to the extent indicated in column 3.

*28   Consequential amendments

(1)   Subject to article 29(4), the Family Proceedings Rules 1991* are amended as follows–

this section of ATPO 2008 remains in force despite the new FPR 2010 now being in force. No new SI amendment provisions have been given effect.

> (a)   in rule 2.39(1) for "where no such application as is referred to in rule 2.40(1) is pending the", substitute "The";
>
> (b)   omit rule 2.40;
>
> (c)   in rule 3.8(2) omit "but shall be treated, in the first instance, as an application to the High Court for leave";
>
> (d)   for rule 4.22(2A) substitute–

"(2A)   In relation to an appeal to the High Court under section 94, the documents required to be filed by paragraph (2) shall be filed in the district registry, being in the same place as a care centre within the meaning of article 2(b) of the Allocation and Transfer of Proceedings Order 2008, which is nearest to the court below."; and

> (e)   in rule 4.26 after paragraph (5) add–

"(6)   Where a local authority makes an application to a magistrates' court for a care or supervision order with respect to the child in relation to whom the direction was given, the local authority must inform the court that gave the direction of the application in writing.".

(2)   Subject to article 29(4), for rule 3A(8) of the Family Proceedings Courts (Matrimonial Proceedings etc.) Rules 1991 substitute–

> "(8)   Subject to any enactment, where an application for an occupation order or a non-molestation order is pending, the court may transfer the proceedings to another court of its own motion or on the application of either party; and any order for transfer shall be made in Form FL417.".

29   Transitional provisions

(1)   This Order applies, so far as practicable, to proceedings started before but not concluded by 25th November 2008.

(2)   Where, by reason of paragraph (1), this Order does not apply to particular proceedings which have been started but not concluded before the 25th November 2008, the Children (Allocation of Proceedings) Order 1991 or the Family Law Act 1996 (Part IV) (Allocation of Proceedings) Order 1997, as the case may be, continue to apply to those proceedings.

(3)   The Children (Allocation of Proceedings) (Appeals) Order 1991 continues to apply to–

(a)   an appeal started before 25th November 2008; and
(b)   an appeal in proceedings to which the Children (Allocation of Proceedings) Order 1991 still applies by virtue of paragraph (2).

(4)   The amendments in article 28 do not apply in relation to proceedings to which the Children (Allocation of Proceedings) Order 1991 or the Family Law Act 1996 (Part IV) (Allocation of Proceedings) Order 1997 still apply by virtue of paragraph (2).

(5)   In relation to an appeal in respect of a type of case before the commencement of section 10 of the Child Support, Pensions and Social Security Act 2000 for the purposes of that type of case, the reference to the Child Support Appeals (Jurisdiction of Courts) Order 2002 in article 5(1)(f) is to be read as a reference to the Child Support Appeals (Jurisdiction of Courts) Order 1993.

Schedule 1
Classes of county court

Column 1	Column 2	Column 3	Column 4	Column 5	Column 6
County court	Family Hearing Centre	Care Centre	Adoption Centre	Inter-country Adoption Centre	Forced Marriage county court
Aberystwyth County Court	Yes		Yes		
Accrington County Court	Yes				

Column 1	Column 2	Column 3	Column 4	Column 5	Column 6
County court	Family Hearing Centre	Care Centre	Adoption Centre	Inter-country Adoption Centre	Forced Marriage county court
Aldershot County Court	Yes				
Altrincham County Court	Yes				
Barnet County Court	Yes				
Barnsley County Court	Yes				
Barnstaple County Court	Yes				
Barrow in Furness County Court	Yes				
Basingstoke County Court	Yes				
Bath County Court	Yes				
Bedford County Court	Yes				
Birkenhead County Court	Yes				
Birmingham County Court	Yes	Yes	Yes	Yes	Yes
Bishop Auckland County Court*					
Blackburn County Court	Yes	Yes	Yes		Yes
Blackpool County Court	Yes				
Blackwood County Court	Yes				
Bodmin County Court	Yes				
Bolton County Court	Yes		Yes		
Boston County Court	Yes				
Bournemouth County Court	Yes	Yes	Yes	Yes	
Bow County Court	Yes		Yes		
Bradford County Court	Yes		Yes		Yes
Brecon County Court	Yes				
Brentford County Court	Yes				
Bridgend County Court	Yes				
Brighton County Court	Yes	Yes	Yes		
Bristol County Court	Yes	Yes	Yes	Yes	Yes
Bromley County Court	Yes		Yes		
Burnley County Court	Yes				
Burton-on-Trent County Court	Yes				
Bury County Court	Yes				
Bury St. Edmunds County Court	Yes				
Caernarfon County Court	Yes	Yes			
Cambridge County Court	Yes	Yes	Yes		
Canterbury County Court	Yes	Yes	Yes		

Column 1 County court	Column 2 Family Hearing Centre	Column 3 Care Centre	Column 4 Adoption Centre	Column 5 Intercountry Adoption Centre	Column 6 Forced Marriage county court
Cardiff County Court	Yes	Yes	Yes	Yes	Yes
Carlisle County Court	Yes	Yes	Yes		
Carmarthen County Court	Yes				
Chelmsford County Court	Yes	Yes	Yes		
Chester County Court	Yes	Yes	Yes	Yes	
Chesterfield County Court	Yes				
Chichester County Court	Yes				
Chorley County Court	Yes				
Clerkenwell & Shoreditch County Court	Yes				
Colchester and Clacton County Court	Yes				
Consett County Court*					
Coventry County Court	Yes	Yes	Yes		
Crewe County Court	Yes				
Croydon County Court	Yes		Yes		
Darlington County Court	Yes				
Dartford County Court	Yes				
Derby County Court	Yes	Yes	Yes		Yes
Dewsbury County Court	Yes				
Doncaster County Court	Yes				
Dudley County Court	Yes				
Durham County Court	Yes				
Eastbourne County Court	Yes				
Edmonton County Court	Yes				
Epsom County Court*					
Exeter County Court	Yes	Yes	Yes	Yes	
Gateshead County Court	Yes				
Gloucester County Court	Yes				
Grimsby County Court	Yes				
Guildford County Court	Yes	Yes	Yes		
Halifax County Court	Yes				
Harlow County Court*					
Harrogate County Court	Yes				
Hartlepool County Court	Yes				

Column 1	Column 2	Column 3	Column 4	Column 5	Column 6
County court	Family Hearing Centre	Care Centre	Adoption Centre	Inter-country Adoption Centre	Forced Marriage county court
Hastings County Court	Yes				
Haverfordwest County Court	Yes				
Hereford County Court	Yes				
Hertford County Court	Yes				
Hitchin County Court*					
Horsham County Court	Yes				
Huddersfield County Court	Yes				
Ilford County Court	Yes				
Ipswich County Court	Yes	Yes	Yes		
Keighley County Court	Yes				
Kendal County Court	Yes				
King's Lynn County Court	Yes				
Kingston-upon-Hull County Court	Yes	Yes	Yes		
Kingston-upon-Thames County Court	Yes				
Lambeth County Court	Yes				
Lancaster County Court	Yes	Yes	Yes		
Leeds County Court	Yes	Yes	Yes	Yes	Yes
Leicester County Court	Yes	Yes	Yes		Yes
Leigh County Court*					
Lincoln County Court	Yes	Yes	Yes		
Liverpool County Court	Yes	Yes	Yes	Yes	
Llanelli County Court	Yes				
Llangefni County Court	Yes		Yes		
Lowestoft County Court*					
Luton County Court	Yes	Yes	Yes		Yes
Macclesfield County Court	Yes		Yes		
Maidstone County Court	Yes				
Manchester County Court	Yes	Yes	Yes	Yes	Yes
Mansfield County Court	Yes				
Medway County Court	Yes	Yes	Yes		
Merthyr Tydfil County Court	Yes				
Middlesbrough County Court at Teesside Combined Court	Yes	Yes	Yes		Yes

Column 1	Column 2	Column 3	Column 4	Column 5	Column 6
County court	Family Hearing Centre	Care Centre	Adoption Centre	Inter-country Adoption Centre	Forced Marriage county court
Milton Keynes County Court	Yes	Yes	Yes		
Morpeth County Court	Yes				
Neath County Court	Yes				
Nelson County Court**					
Newcastle-upon-Tyne County Court	Yes	Yes	Yes	Yes	Yes
Newport (Gwent) County Court	Yes	Yes	Yes		
Newport (Isle of Wight) County Court	Yes				
Northampton County Court	Yes	Yes	Yes		
North Shields County Court	Yes				
Norwich County Court	Yes	Yes	Yes		
Nottingham County Court	Yes	Yes	Yes	Yes	
Oldham County Court	Yes				
Oxford County Court	Yes	Yes	Yes		
Penrith County Court*					
Penzance County Court*					
Peterborough County Court	Yes	Yes	Yes		
Plymouth County Court	Yes	Yes	Yes		
Pontefract County Court	Yes				
Pontypridd County Court	Yes	Yes	Yes		
Portsmouth County Court	Yes	Yes	Yes	Yes	
Preston County Court	Yes				
Rawtenstall County Court	Yes				
Reading County Court	Yes	Yes	Yes		
Reigate County Court	Yes				
Rhyl County Court	Yes	Yes	Yes		
Romford County Court	Yes		Yes		Yes
Rotherham County Court	Yes				
Runcorn County Court*					
St. Helens County Court	Yes				
Salford County Court*					
Salisbury County Court	Yes				
Scarborough County Court	Yes				
Scunthorpe County Court	Yes				

Column 1	Column 2	Column 3	Column 4	Column 5	Column 6
County court	Family Hearing Centre	Care Centre	Adoption Centre	Intercountry Adoption Centre	Forced Marriage county court
Sheffield County Court	Yes	Yes	Yes		
Shrewsbury County Court	Yes				
Skipton County Court	Yes				
Slough County Court	Yes				
Southampton County Court	Yes		Yes		
Southend County Court	Yes				
Southport County Court*					
South Shields County Court	Yes				
Stafford County Court	Yes				
Staines County Court	Yes				
Stockport County Court	Yes		Yes		
Stoke-on-Trent County Court	Yes	Yes	Yes		
Sunderland County Court	Yes	Yes	Yes		
Swansea County Court	Yes	Yes	Yes		
Swindon County Court	Yes	Yes	Yes		
Tameside County Court	Yes				
Taunton County Court	Yes	Yes	Yes		
Telford County Court	Yes	Yes	Yes		
Thanet County Court	Yes				
Torquay County Court	Yes				
Trowbridge County Court	Yes				
Truro County Court	Yes	Yes	Yes		
Tunbridge Wells County Court	Yes				
Uxbridge County Court	Yes				
Wakefield County Court	Yes				
Walsall County Court	Yes				
Wandsworth County Court	Yes				
Warrington County Court	Yes	Yes	Yes		
Watford County Court	Yes	Yes	Yes		
Welshpool and Newtown County Court	Yes				
Weston Super Mare County Court	Yes				
Weymouth County Court	Yes				
Whitehaven County Court*					

Column 1	Column 2	Column 3	Column 4	Column 5	Column 6
County court	Family Hearing Centre	Care Centre	Adoption Centre	Intercountry Adoption Centre	Forced Marriage county court
Wigan County Court	Yes				
Willesden County Court	Yes				Yes
Winchester County Court	Yes				
Wolverhampton County Court	Yes	Yes	Yes		
Woolwich County Court	Yes				
Worcester County Court	Yes	Yes	Yes		
Worthing County Court	Yes				
Wrexham County Court	Yes	Yes	Yes	Yes	
Yeovil County Court	Yes				
York County Court	Yes	Yes	Yes		

* County courts which ceased to be a family hearing centre from 4 July 2011, Allocation and Transfer of Proceedings (Amendment) Order, SI 2011/1460.

** County courts which ceased to be a family hearing centre from 1 February 2010, Allocation and Transfer of Proceedings (Amendment) Order, SI 2009/3319

Schedule 2
Revocations

Column 1	Column 2	Column 3
Title	Reference	Extent of revocation
The Children (Allocation of Proceedings) Order 1991	S.I. 1991/1677	The whole order
The Children (Allocation of Proceedings) (Amendment) Order 1993	S.I. 1993/624	The whole order
The Children (Allocation of Proceedings) (Amendment) Order 1994	S.I. 1994/2164	The whole order
The Children (Allocation of Proceedings) (Amendment) (No. 2) Order 1994	S.I. 1994/3138	The whole order
The Children (Allocation of Proceedings) (Amendment) Order 1995	S.I. 1995/1649	The whole order
The Children (Allocation of Proceedings) (Amendment) Order 1997	S.I. 1997/1897	The whole order
The Children (Allocation of Proceedings) (Amendment) Order 1998	S.I. 1998/2166	The whole order
The Children (Allocation of Proceedings) (Amendment) Order 1999	S.I. 1999/524	The whole order
The Children (Allocation of Proceedings) (Amendment) Order 2000	S.I. 2000/2670	The whole order

The Children (Allocation of Proceedings) (Amendment) Order 2001	S.I. 2001/775	The whole order
The Children (Allocation of Proceedings) (Amendment No. 2) Order 2001	S.I. 2001/1656	The whole order
The Children (Allocation of Proceedings) (Amendment) Order 2003	S.I. 2003/331	The whole order
The Children (Allocation of Proceedings) (Amendment) Order 2005	S.I. 2005/520	The whole order
The Children (Allocation of Proceedings) (Amendment No. 2) Order 2005	S.I. 2005/2797	The whole order
The Children (Allocation of Proceedings) (Amendment) Order 2006	S.I. 2006/1541	The whole order
The Children (Allocation of Proceedings) (Amendment No. 2) Order 2007	S.I. 2007/1099	The whole order
The Children (Allocation of Proceedings) (Appeals) Order 1991	S.I. 1991/1801	The whole order
The Family Law Act 1996 (Part IV) (Allocation of Proceedings) Order 1997	S.I. 1997/1896	The whole order
The Family Law Act 1996 (Part IV) (Allocation of Proceedings) (Amendment) Order 2005	S.I. 2005/2924	The whole order
The Mental Capacity Act 2005 (Transitional and Consequential Provisions) Order 2007	S.I. 2007/1898	Paragraph 23 of Schedule 1

A2.2　APPENDIX 2: PRACTICE DIRECTION – ALLOCATION AND TRANSFER OF PROCEEDINGS

1.1　This Practice Direction is given by the President of the Family Division under the powers delegated to him by the Lord Chief Justice under paragraph 2(2) of part 1 of Schedule 2 to the Constitutional Reform Act 2005 and is agreed by the Lord Chancellor.

1.2　The objective of this Practice Direction is to ensure that the criteria for the transfer of proceedings are applied in such a way that proceedings are heard at the appropriate level of court, that the capacity of magistrates' courts is properly utilised and that proceedings are only dealt with in the High Court if the relevant criteria are met.

1.3　This Practice Direction will come into effect on 25 November 2008. Where practicable, it applies to proceedings started before but not concluded by 25 November. The Practice Directions of 5 June 1992 (distribution of business) and 22 February 1993 (applications under the Children Act 1989 by children) are revoked except that they will continue to apply to any proceedings to which it is not practicable to apply this Practice Direction.

1.4 A reference to an article is a reference to the article so numbered in the Allocation and Transfer of Proceedings Order 2008.

PART 1

2 This Part of this Practice Direction applies to all family proceedings (whether or not the Allocation and Transfer of Proceedings Order 2008 applies to such proceedings).

Timing and continuing review of decision on appropriate venue

3.1 The issue as to which court is the most appropriate hearing venue must be addressed by the court speedily as soon as there is sufficient information to determine whether the case meets the criteria for hearing in that court. This information may come to light before, during or after the first hearing. It must then be kept under effective review at all times; it should not be assumed that proceedings will necessarily remain in the court in which they were started or to which they have been transferred. For example proceedings that have been transferred to a county court because one or more of the criteria in article 15 applies should be transferred back to the magistrates' court if the reason for transfer falls away. Conversely, an unforeseen late complication may require a transfer from a magistrates' court to a county court.

3.2 Where a court is determining where the proceedings ought to be heard it will consider all relevant information including that given by the applicant either in the application form or otherwise, for example in any request for proceedings to be transferred to another magistrates' court or to a county court under rule 6 of the Family Proceedings Courts (Children Act 1989) Rules 1991.

Timeliness

4.1 Article 13 and paragraph 12.1 require the court to have regard to delay. Therefore the listing availability of the court in which the proceedings have been started and in neighbouring magistrates' courts and county courts must always be ascertained before deciding where proceedings should be heard.

4.2 If a magistrates' court is considering transferring proceedings to a county court or a county court is considering transferring proceedings to the High Court but that decision is finely balanced, the proceedings should not be transferred if the transfer would lead to delay. Conversely, if the High Court is considering transferring proceedings to a county court or a county court is considering transferring proceedings to a magistrates' court but that decision is finely balanced, the proceedings should be transferred if retaining them would lead to delay.

4.3 Transferring proceedings may mean that there will be a short delay in the proceedings being heard since the papers may need to be sent to the court to which they are being transferred. The court will determine whether the delay is significant, taking into account the circumstances of the case and with reference to the interests of the child.

4.4 While there is no express reference in the Allocation and Transfer of Proceedings Order 2008 or in Part 3 of this Practice Direction to the length of the hearing or to judicial continuity such issues may be relevant.

Transfer of proceedings to or from the High Court

5.1 A court will take into account the following factors (which are not exhaustive) when considering whether the criteria in articles 7 or 18 or paragraph 11.2 or 12.3 apply, such that the proceedings ought to be heard in the High Court—

(1)   there is alleged to be a risk that a child concerned in the proceedings will suffer serious physical or emotional harm in the light of—

    (a)   the death of another child in the family, a parent or any other material person; or

    (b)   the fact that a parent or other material person may have committed a grave crime, for example, murder, manslaughter or rape,

in particular where the essential factual framework is in dispute or there are issues over the causation of injuries or a material conflict of expert evidence;

(2)   the application concerns medical treatment for a child which involves a risk to the child's physical or emotional health which goes beyond the normal risks of routine medical treatment;

(3)   an adoption order is sought in relation to a child who has been adopted abroad in a country whose adoption orders are not recognised in England and Wales;

(4)   an adoption order is sought in relation to a child who has been brought into the United Kingdom in circumstances where section 83 of the Adoption and Children Act 2002 applies and

    (a)   the person bringing the child, or causing the child to be brought—

        (i)   has not complied with any requirement imposed by regulations made under section 83(4); or

(ii) has not met any condition required to be met by regulations made under section 83(5) within the required time; or

(b) there are complicating features in relation to the application;

(5) it is likely that the proceedings will set a significant new precedent or alter existing principles of common law;

(6) where periodical payments, a lump sum or transfer of property are an issue—

(a) the capital value of the assets involved and the extent to which they are available for, or susceptible to, distribution or adjustment;

(b) any substantial allegations of fraud or deception or non-disclosure;

(c) any substantial contested allegations of conduct.

5.2 The following proceedings are likely to fall within the criteria for hearing in the High Court unless the nature of the issues of fact or law raised in the proceedings may make them more suitable to be dealt with in a county court—

(1) proceedings involving a contested issue of domicile;

(2) applications to restrain a respondent from taking or continuing with foreign proceedings;

(3) suits in which the Queen's Proctor intervenes or shows cause and elects trial in the High Court;

(4) proceedings in which an application is opposed on the grounds of want of jurisdiction;

(5) proceedings in which there is a complex foreign element or where the court has invited submissions to be made under Article 11(7) of Council Regulation (EC) No 2201/2003 of 27 November 2003 concerning jurisdiction and the recognition and enforcement of judgments in matrimonial matters and the matters of parental responsibility;

(6) proceedings in which there is an application to remove a child permanently or temporarily from the jurisdiction to a non-Hague Convention country.

(7) interlocutory applications involving—

(a) search orders; or

(b) directions as to dealing with assets out of the jurisdiction.

5.3 Proceedings will not normally be suitable to be dealt with in the High Court merely because of any of the following—

(1) intractable problems with regard to contact;

(2) sexual abuse;

(3) injury to a child which is neither life-threatening nor permanently disabling;

(4) routine neglect, even if it spans many years and there is copious documentation;

(5) temporary or permanent removal to a Hague Convention country;

(6) standard human rights issues;

(7) uncertainty as to immigration status;

(8) the celebrity of the parties;

(9) the anticipated length of the hearing;

(10) the quantity of evidence;

(11) the number of experts;

(12) the possible availability of a speedier hearing.

5.4 A substantial reason for starting proceedings in the High Court will only exist where the nature of the proceedings or the issues raised are such that they ought to be heard in the High Court. Where proceedings have been started in the High Court under article 7(c) or paragraph 11.2(4) and the High Court considers that there is no substantial reason for them to have been started there, the High Court will transfer the proceedings to a county court or a magistrates' court and may make any orders about costs which it considers appropriate.

PART 2

6 This Part of this Practice Direction applies to family proceedings to which the Allocation and Transfer of Proceedings Order 2008 applies.

Transfer of proceedings from one magistrates' court to another or from one county court to another

7 Where a magistrates' court is considering transferring proceedings to another magistrates' court or a county court is considering transferring proceedings to another county court, the court will take into account the following factors (which are not exhaustive) when considering whether it would be more convenient for the parties for the proceedings to be dealt with by the other court—

(1) the fact that a party is ill or suffers a disability which could make it inconvenient to attend at a particular court;

(2) the fact that the child lives in the area of the other court;

(3) the need to avoid delay.

Transfer of proceedings from a magistrates' court to a county court

8.1 Where a magistrates' court is considering whether one or more of the criteria in article 15(1) (except article 15(1)(g) and (h)) apply such that the proceedings ought to be heard in the county court, the magistrates' court will first consider whether another magistrates' court would have suitable experience to deal with the issues which have given rise to consideration of article 15. If so, the magistrates' court will then consider whether the proceedings could be dealt with more quickly or within the same time if they were transferred to the other magistrates' court rather than a county court. If so, the magistrates' court will transfer the proceedings to the other magistrates' court rather than a county court.

8.2 A magistrates' court may only transfer proceedings to a county court under article 15(1)(a) if it considers that the transfer will significantly accelerate the determination of the proceedings. Before considering a transfer on this ground, the magistrates' court must obtain information about the hearing dates available in other magistrates' courts and in the relevant county court. The fact that a hearing could be arranged in a county court at an earlier date than in any appropriate magistrates' court does not by itself justify the transfer of proceedings under article 15(1)(a); the question of whether the determination of the proceedings would be significantly accelerated must be considered in the light of all the circumstances.

Transfer of proceedings from a county court to a magistrates' court

9.1 A county court must transfer to a magistrates' court under article 16(1) proceedings that have previously been transferred under article 15(1) where the county court considers that none of the criteria in article 15(1) apply. In particular, proceedings transferred to a county court by a magistrates' court for resolution of a single issue, for example, use of the inherent powers of the High Court in respect of medical testing of a child or disclosure of information by HM Revenue and Customs, should be transferred back to the magistrates' court once the issue has been resolved.

9.2 Subject to articles 5(3), 6, 8 and 13 and paragraphs 4 and 12.1, straightforward proceedings for—

(1) a residence order;

(2) a contact order;

(3) a prohibited steps order;

(4) a specific issue order;

(5) a special guardianship order; or

(6) an order under Part 4 of the Family Law Act 1996

which are started in a county court should be transferred to a magistrates' court if the county court considers that none of the criteria in article 15(1)(b) to (i) apply to those proceedings.

PART 3

10 This Part of this Practice Direction applies to any family proceedings to which the Allocation and Transfer of Proceedings Order 2008 does not apply.

Starting proceedings

11.1 Subject to paragraph 11.2, family proceedings must be started in a county court.

11.2 Family proceedings may be started in the High Court only if—

(1) the proceedings are exceptionally complex;

(2) the outcome of the proceedings is important to the public in general;

(3) an enactment or rule requires the proceedings to be started in the High Court; or

(4) there is another substantial reason for starting the proceedings in the High Court.

Transferring proceedings

12.1 When making any decision about the transfer of proceedings the court must have regard to the need to avoid delay in the proceedings.

12.2 A county court will take into account the following factors (which are not exhaustive) when considering whether to transfer proceedings to another county court—

(1) whether the transfer will significantly accelerate the determination of the proceedings;

(2) whether it is more convenient for the parties for the proceedings to be dealt with by another county court; and

(3) whether there is another good reason for the proceedings to be transferred.

12.3 A county court will take into account the following factors (which are not exhaustive) when considering whether to transfer proceedings to the High Court—

(1) whether the proceedings are exceptionally complex;

(2) whether the outcome of the proceedings is important to the public in general;

(3) whether an enactment or rule requires the proceedings to be dealt with in the High Court; and

(4) whether there is another substantial reason for the proceedings to be transferred.

12.4 The High Court will also take into account the factors in paragraph 12.3 when considering whether to transfer proceedings to a county court.

The Right Honourable
Sir Mark Potter
The President of the Family Division

The Right Honourable
Jack Straw MP
The Lord Chancellor

CHAPTER 3

CASE MANAGEMENT: HOW TO USE THE PUBLIC LAW OUTLINE

3.1 INTRODUCTION

The purpose of this Chapter is to demonstrate the practical effect of the PLO in the context of local authority child care proceedings. The procedural changes are driven by the new Practice Direction of 2010, which fine-tunes that of 2008.[1]

It is misconceived to judge the PLO by reference to earlier practice, for such practice was not underpinned by 'front-end loading' (entrenched as that is by the PLO) nor by the new Overriding Objective, active judicial case management and *issue* driven litigation.

The new 'Letter before Proceedings' and the very substantial shift in authority to the Case Management Judge dovetails with the newly drafted duty to 'co-operate', mandating as it does very real levels of co-operation between the parties and the court.

Central to the PLO is the identification of the key/dominant issue(s). So important is the concept of the *'issue'* that the word is printed in *italics* throughout this text.

The PLO demands efficient litigation practice, and accordingly, central points of principle and practice are highlighted in the context of the demands made by the PLO.

This Chapter is also to be read in the context of the Case Digest;[2] its purpose is to provide a ready access to those cases which establish points/principles which are essential to everyday practice, and which are usefully at one's fingertips in any court hearing.

---

[1]   See **A3.2**.
[2]   See Chapter 18.

The Standard Variable Directions[3] are to be seen in the context of the Case Management Order; on the basis that the provisions can be 'cut and pasted' into the draft order, thus to tailor it to the needs of the individual case.

This Chapter is not intended to constitute a comprehensive practice manual for all child care work. Rather it focuses on the key features of child care procedure in the context of the new PLO. This is to provide the practitioner with immediate access to those key points which will help to render his or her file management more efficient in the new procedural environment.

The Chapter is fulfilled by the Appendices which are not to be viewed as the 'also ran' in the field, but are essential reading to achieve an effective grip on practice under the PLO.

3.2   AN ANALYSIS OF THE PUBLIC LAW OUTLINE

3.2.1   An introduction to the new documentation

(1)   **The documents identified:**

    (a)   Family Procedure Rules 2010, Part 12, Chapter 3.
    (b)   The new Practice Direction of April 2010, which is Practice Direction 12A of the new Family Procedure Rules 2010.
    (c)   C110: Application under the Children Act 1989 for a care or supervision order.
    (d)   Standard Directions on Issue.
    (e)   Standard Directions at First Appointment.

3.2.2   Key concepts in care proceedings which must be critically analysed to give effect to the PLO

(1)   **Transparency:**
    Such transparency underpins all aspects of family law practice from the openness of local authority reports and assessments to the reasoning process contained in medical reports.

(2)   **Threshold criteria:**
    These will be set out by the applicant local authority on issue of proceedings and may be revised as the case progresses. They comprise the salient assertions with regard to proof of the *Threshold criteria*.
    Practice points:

---

3   See **A3.19**.

- Facts to be set out clearly, simply and succinctly; any party must be able readily to understand their meaning.
- They should be proportionate; no more than is reasonably necessary.
- There should be no digression to comment on matters of inference, or discussion.
- In the event of the court finding such facts proved, the respondent(s) must be able to appreciate how far short he/she has fallen and what steps have to be taken to remedy that position (if capable of being remedied).

(3) **Welfare checklist:**

- Proportionality is central to the inter-action of 'threshold' and 'welfare'.
- Given the '*Letter before Proceedings*' it may be expected that fewer cases will require adjudication on 'threshold' and the hearing before the judge will turn substantially on the issue of how best, in accordance with the welfare checklist, to manage the risk.
- By reference to s 1(5) the options for the court range from 'no order' to adoption,[4] through the 'family assistance order', supervision,[5] care,[6] and special guardianship.[7]

(4) **Avoiding delay:**
Delay arises through poor case preparation, late issue and poor case management.

- Delay is likely to be prejudicial to paramount interests including—

  (i) The child's welfare. If there is to be delay in the resolution of any *issue* as to the future care/residence of any child, then the potential damage to that child of such delay must be consistently addressed by all parties and the court must be advised.
  (ii) The interests of other children at risk, whose safety may depend on local authority involvement.

- Delay which results in a disproportionate use of a local authority's resources—

  (i) has the potential seriously to impact on other children whose safety is at risk.

---

[4]   See Chapter 15.
[5]   See Chapter 13.
[6]   See Chapter 13.
[7]   See Chapter 8.

(ii) absorbs resources unnecessarily, which should be appropriated elsewhere.

(5) **Purposive or constructive delay:**
A distinction has to be drawn between time needed for the identification and narrowing of issues and the gathering of evidence on the one hand; and time for the testing out of care/contact or therapeutic arrangements which it is said could affect the order which the court will be required to make. The latter constitutes a significant minority of cases and in substance is not 'delay' in the pejorative sense, at all.

(6) **The inter-action of procedural compliance and local authority resources:**
The allocation of a local authority's resources must be based on case management which is by reference to procedural rules and legal principle. A failure adequately to comply with such rules and principle has the effect of distorting a local authority's care budget and the courts' own timetables.

(7) **Cases where family may not be known to the local authority – considerations for time-tabling:**
Cases may come before the court, particularly where proceedings have been precipitated for instance by non-accidental injury; or for reasons of immigration status or family profile; where the family is not formerly well-known to agencies. These cases should be identified and a detailed timetable drawn up at the First Directions Appointment and thereafter reviewed to ensure that these factors cause as little delay as can be achieved.

(8) **Split trial/Finding of fact:**
Grounds for a split trial—

- *For:* When there is a discrete *issue* which could be determinative of threshold; eg was it the parent who was the perpetrator of NAI, or did the parent fail to protect or secure appropriate assistance or treatment?
- *Against:* Delay arising from two hearings rather than one; discrete findings of fact may prevent the court assimilating a fuller and relevant picture.

(9) **Primary issues on a split trial hearing:**

- Given the regular reminders from the Court of Appeal as to how the drafting of these orders in split-trial cases can so easily slip into error[8] it is essential to specify precisely the facts which

---

8   See Case Digest.

the court is to be invited to find at the hearing, see the *President's Guidance in Relation to Split Hearings* May 2010.

- As to checklists in relation to discrete areas which may be expected to attract the 'split trial' jurisdiction, see **3.2.7** below.
- For a model split trial order see **A3.19** (NB – Parts 1 and 2 must be before the same judge), save in exceptional circumstances; see *Re G & B (Fact-Finding Hearing)* [2009] EWCA Civ 10.

3.2.3 Key features of the PLO

(1) **Introduction:**

The PLO provides for pro-active, interventionist, judicial case management throughout the case. The agenda is to narrow issues rather than increase them, and to narrow them at a stage very much earlier than has happened hitherto (so often at the court door). This is intended also to have the effect of reducing written material. The purpose of the PLO is to achieve the following—

- Welfare based guidance on allocation, case management and use of experts where necessary.
- Identification of the *Timetable for the Child* (and see also FPR 2010, r 12.23).
- Identification of key *issue*(s) for agreement and, if necessary, determination.
- Identification of cases requiring early final hearing.
- An issue resolution 'window' where the emphasis is on early neutral evaluation, ie avoiding the distress and delay of contested final hearings.
- Coordinated case management of placement and adoption processes.
- The CAFCASS analysis at each stage of the proceedings is to help identify issues from a welfare perspective and provide a quality control check for the local authority.

(2) **The juridical framework of the PLO:**

There are four requirements of the new system—

- *First*: Procedural fairness by local authorities, ie early preparation and disclosure (front-end loading, letter before action, consultation).
- *Second*: A timetable for the child.
- *Third*: *Key issue* identification by the court.
- *Fourth*: *Key issue* resolution by the court.

(3) **The Letter before Proceedings:**[9]

Practice points—

---

[9] See **A3.1**.

- it avoids the problem that had hitherto so frequently blighted this field of litigation: the parent(s) not knowing what they had done wrong and/or having no insight into what had gone wrong and/or not having the opportunity to demonstrate capacity to change.
- In the 'slow burn' type of case where a problem brews over time, the '*Letter before Proceedings*' affords to a parent a clearly expressed (and understood) opportunity to address what is wrong and to put it right.
- Stage 1 of the PLO pre-trial (see Annex A to Practice Direction 1) provides for 'Letters' – in the plural. This anticipates a first letter 'before proceedings' as set out above; and a second follow-up letter recording in terms where the parent has fallen short, notwithstanding the first letter, and the local authority involvement thereafter.

(4) How the 'Letter before Proceedings' operates:

- It sets out in plain language a statement and explanation of expectation to avoid proceedings wherever appropriate.
- It forecloses the argument before it is raised: '*I do not know what I have done wrong*'.
- Combined with the availability of legal help for significant adults pre-proceedings, it will secure agreement in many more cases.
- 'Threshold' can be expected to be clear in the face of non-compliance with a '*Letter before Proceedings*'. This will be the norm in the 'slow burn' cases of neglect etc. Different considerations may be expected to apply in the emergency situations of non-accidental injury and sex abuse.
- Integral to the *Letter before Proceedings* is the *Family Meeting* (see below).

(5) The significance of the Family Meeting under the PLO

- This is where the local authority, prior to launching proceedings, discusses its concerns and proposals in detail with families.
- It is one of the key concepts derived from best practice that are now required of the local authority.
- The agenda and matters to be covered are set out together with other pre-proceedings preparation in Department for Children Schools and Families (DCSF) Guidance.
- The result of the Family Meeting is also expected to be notified to families in writing to form the basis for discussion with their legal adviser (see Appendix 1).

(6) Party status in the context of the PLO:

The practice is much tighter than before—

- The requirements on the local authority prior to the issue of proceedings (dovetailing as it does with the letter before proceedings) are intended to ensure that all kinship care options have been fully explored, core assessments carried out and that care plans have been prepared and shared with families.
- If any person wishes to apply to become a party and apply for an order of the court in relation to a child's welfare, then such person must apply at the earliest reasonable opportunity.
- If an application is made later than it should have been, then very strong grounds will have to be made out as to—

   (i)   why such an application should be considered, and
   (ii) if such application were sufficiently strong and genuinely to be considered, why it was not made earlier.
   Timetable for the Child is immediately relevant here, as is culpable delay.
- Applications for McKenzie friends should be made at the First Appointment and the relevant individual will require court approval.[10]

(7)   **The new requirement for front-end loading:**

- The minimum standards expected of all local authorities are encapsulated in s 7 of the LASSA 1970.
- The guidance issued by central government with the PLO is set out at **A3.1** below. This will require local authorities in all but the most urgent cases to provide a minimum service to families and to the courts, with evidence in writing.
- Such social work, investigation and input will be open to scrutiny by the court by reference to the materials produced at First Appointment as comprised in the checklist set out in the Practice Direction at **A3.2**.

(8)   **Front-end loading in practice – the pre-proceedings checklist:**
   The local authority, on issue, is to file the specific documents recited in paragraph 10 of the Practice Direction.
   See the Pre-Proceedings Checklist of the PLO at para 26(31) below.

(9)   **Front-end loading and the emergency case:**
   If a child's welfare is at risk, the local authority must make an immediate court application. The absence of certain steps or documents is irrelevant in these circumstances.

---

10   See PD at para 13.2 and the Case Digest.

(10) **The central importance of the 'Timetable for the Child' under the PLO:**

- The Timetable for the Child will start to be constructed and set out on the face of all of the case management orders from the First Appointment.
- Such timetable is to include all significant legal and social, health and education care steps that are agreed or decided upon by the court.

(11) **The 'Timetable for the Child' – definition:**[11]
'Timetable for the Child' is defined by the rules as the timetable set by the court in accordance with its duties under ss 1 and 32 of the 1989 Act and should take into account dates of significant steps in the life of the child who is the subject of the proceedings; and should be appropriate for that child.

(12) **Timetable for the Child in the context of case management:**
The new Practice Direction explains the interaction of the Timetable for the Child and case management, in paras 3.2–3.9. The provisions in the new Practice Direction are sufficiently important to warrant looking at now, before reading further; please see **A3.2**.

(13) **Timetable for the Child – practice points:**
The child as an individual may have educational, health or emotional development needs which will indicate key events around which the timetable for court decisions about future care should be constructed so as to safeguard or promote welfare—

- Any proposed procedural step must be balanced against the child's timetable.
- The court will address the timetable for the child at each stage and in particular the commissioning of further reports or assessments.
- The actual (or potential) involvement of an Adoption Panel is a factor for the court to consider in setting a timetable for the child in individual cases.
- If there is more than one child, the 'Timetable for the Child' may be different in each case. This will require careful consideration by the court into all the circumstances. It may be that if the timetable for one child is well in advance of another, then the resolution of the proceedings for the first child should be addressed without further delay to him/her.

(14) **The central importance of the CAFCASS analysis under the PLO:**
This is a further step which entrenches the importance of the local authority achieving accurate and objective assessment prior to the

---

[11]   See PD at para 3.2.

issue of proceedings; the effect of the CAFCASS analysis is a quality control check on the approach of the local authority.

(15) **The CAFCASS analysis – definition:**
The document is provided for in the new Practice Direction at paras 3.10, 12.4. 13.3 and 26, and provides that there be an analysis in relation to the following, by reference to the following checklist in para 26.10—

- any harm or risk of harm;
- the child's own views;
- the family context, including advice relating to ethnicity, language, religion and culture of the child and other significant persons;
- the local authority work and proposed care plan;
- advice about the court process, including the Timetable for the Child; and
- identification of work that remains to be done for the child in the short and longer term.

The CAFCASS analysis is an evolving document. It should also make recommendations for outcomes in order to safeguard and promote the best interests of the child in the proceedings.

(16) **The CAFCASS analysis – in practice:**
This will be produced in three stages, initial, interim and final for use at First App, CMC, IRH and FH. The initial analysis may be brief given that the Cafcass officer at this stage will only just have been introduced to the family and in many cases it will not be feasible to produce such an analysis. However the format and topics covered will be similar, comprising—

- the child's needs, wishes and feelings;
- child's development;
- family abilities and vulnerabilities;
- parental relationship;
- work of other agencies;
- referral and support services for lesser interventions; options available to the court to meet the identified desired outcomes;
- likely effect of change on the children.

The second CAFCASS analysis is to be available for the CMC and/or the IRH and may be expected to advise inter alia upon the identification of the *key issue(s)* and any evidence that may be required, together with the planning process for the child and the child's timetable.

(17) **The re-cast Advocates' Meeting under the PLO:**
The primary function of this meeting is to draft the Case Management documents including the draft order and Local

Authority Summary. The parties must meet to discuss their positions, the *issues* and the evidential requirements at an Advocates' Meeting that does *not* take place on the morning of the hearing. It should take place in sufficient time for the Case Management Record (see PD, 26(13)) to be produced to the court no later than at 11.00am on the day before the CMC/IRH. Its primary agenda is to draft the Case Management Order (see 26(12) and Annex C of the PD Form PLO3).

(18) **The Case Management Conference and Issue Resolution Hearing – identification of *Key Issues* by the court:**
The role of the pro-active interventionist judge sees full expression here, being thrown into stark relief in para 3.20 of the new Practice Direction. Please turn to it now to appreciate its full extent and impact, together with paragraph 4 of the PD (expectations).

(19) **The six stages of the 2003 Protocol reduced to four in the new PLO:**
The new '*4 Stages*' are set out in the *Practice Direction* at para 10.2 and are explained below at **3.2.5**. The crucial feature is this: *Do not* list for final hearing (unless absolutely necessary) prior to the Issue Resolution Hearing. Experience has shown overwhelmingly that prior to the Final Hearing, the *issue*(s) sufficiently crystallises to result in the ELH for final hearing being almost invariably too long.

(20) **The Case Management Order:**
This Order mirrors the Active Judicial Case Management ordained by paras 3.19 and 3.20 of the *Practice Direction*. Please refer below for an explanation of this document in the context of the Case Management Record as a whole (as to which para 3.12). The *Practice Direction* defines the Case Management Order at para 3.15. This ties in with paras 5.8–5.11 of the new PD at in particular 5.10:

> 'There should be ongoing consideration of the draft Case Management Orders throughout the proceedings. The Draft Case Management Orders should serve as an aide Memoire to everyone involved in the proceedings of—
> – The Timetable for the Child;
> – The case management decisions;
> – The identified issues.'

(21) **The purpose of the Case Management Order:**
It is a precise snapshot of the shape of the case—

- As part of the *Case Management Record*, it sets out on its face a complete case management record of the proceedings thus far.
- There has been negotiated with the HMCS E-delivery Group that the order will be available to judges and practitioners alike as a formatted inter-active document that can be shared,

amended and then cut and pasted into the *familyman* orders system until such time as the new *familyman* system is available.
* Please see **A3.19** for a set of Model Directions. The purpose is to facilitate these being cut and pasted into the Case Management Order at the time of the Advocates' Meeting.

(22) **The new Overriding Objective and the entrenched duty to co-operate:** This is of singular importance as a key feature of the PLO and warrants its own section, see below at **3.2.4**.

3.2.3A   Linked criminal and care directions – timetable for the child

(1) Where there are parallel care and criminal proceedings against a person connected with the child for a serious offence against that child, linked directions hearings should take place as the case progresses (*Re SL* [2006] EWCA Crim 1902 and *Re A & B (One Parent Killed by the Other)* [2011] 1 FLR 783).

(2) The timing of proceedings in a linked criminal case (particularly if the child is to be interviewed or to give evidence) should appear in the *timetable for the child*.

(3) Local protocols may develop the guidance in *Re SL* (above) to achieve the following:

* Timetable the care and criminal proceedings in order to decide which should be heard first and at which level of court.
* Arrange administrative links and ensure service of copy documents such as draft schedules of findings, transcripts etc in both sets of proceedings.
* Determine the procedural and evidential issues in one case which impinge upon the other and arrange for disclosure; deal with public interest immunity questions; determine any joint experts and also requests for leave to interview children.
* Consider linked directions hearings, with the allocated care judge either conducting both himself, or in liaison with the nominated criminal judge.
* Ensure the *timetable for the child* covers all relevant events in both sets of proceedings.

3.2.4   The new overriding objective and the entrenched duty to cooperate

(1)   **The terms of the new Overriding Objective:**

'2.1 This Practice Direction has the overriding objective of enabling the court to deal with cases justly, having regard to the welfare issues involved. Dealing with a case justly includes, so far as is practicable:
(1) ensuring that it is dealt with expeditiously and fairly;
(2) dealing with the case in ways which are proportionate to the nature, importance and complexity of the issues;
(3) saving expense; and
(4) allotting to it an appropriate share of the court's resources, while taking into account the need to allot resources to other cases.'

(2) **The entrenching of that duty:**
The PD directly and indirectly assumes the Overriding Objective as underpinning the entire operation of the PLO; for example (at para 2.2)—

'The court must seek to give effect to the overriding objective when it—
(1) exercises the case management powers referred to in this Practice Direction; or
(2) interprets any provision in this Practice Direction.'

(3) **The duty to co-operate:**
This is so focal to the new environment that **para 20.2** of the new PD warrants setting out here in full—

'At each court appearance the court will ask the parties and their legal representatives—
(1) what steps they have taken to achieve co-operation and the extent to which they have been successful;
(2) if appropriate the reason why co-operation could not be achieved;
(3) the steps needed to resolve any issues necessary to achieve co-operation.'

(4) **Duty not to raise expectations:**
This duty of co-operation mandates that it is **not** the role of an advocate unreasonably to raise a client's expectations. Rather it is to facilitate the new procedural environment and enable the case management judge to control the three aspects of the interlocutory hearing, namely—

• How and when the *issue*(s) is to be resolved, ie—

(i) the style of hearing;
(ii) the evidence that is proportionately necessary;
(iii) the manner in which the evidence is received; and
(iv) the timetable for the child within which the process needs to be completed.

• Identification and resolution of the *issue*(s) at the earliest opportunity by considering the merits of the evidence using *early neutral evaluation* to facilitate the resolution of the *key issue(s)* and reduce or eliminate disagreements between the parties. In simple terms, a *neutral* evaluation is a clear indication that is not so interventionist as to require recusing oneself.

(5) **Pro-active judicial intervention:**
Such intervention has the effect of monitoring the state's compliance with the statutory duties imposed on local authorities by Parliament and also of the court's orders and directions. This is intended to result in greater procedural fairness in the evidence-collecting and decision-making processes undertaken by local authorities.

(6) **Entrenching the duty to co-operate:**
Lest there be any misunderstanding, the PD labours the duty to co-operate extensively (the *italics* are that of the editors)—

- **Para 3.17** – 'In each case there will be a Case Management Conference to enable the case management judge or case manager, **with the co-operation** of the parties, actively to manage the case and, at the earliest practicable opportunity to—

  (1) identify the relevant and key issues; and
  (2) give full case management directions including confirming the Timetable for the Child.'

- '**Para 3.20(3)** – (Active case management includes) encouraging the parties to *co-operate* with each other in the conduct of proceedings.'

- '**Para 5.5** – The parties should *co-operate* with the court in case management including the fixing of timetables to avoid unacceptable delay and in the crystallisation and resolution of the *issue*(s) on which the case turns.'

(7) ***Issue* identification and resolution:**
The parties are expected to work *co-operatively* with each other and the court at every stage to identify and to resolve and record the resolution of *key issues*. Where issues are identified, parties are expected to consider and record whether evidence or submissions are appropriate to resolve those *issues*, what form that evidence might take and when the *issue* should be resolved.

(8) **The impact of the '*Duty to Co-operate*' on advocacy**
Whilst it is the duty of every advocate to represent independently and fearlessly his own client, that is without more, an inadequate guide to the role of the advocate in family proceedings. Advocacy must be subject also to the Overriding Objective and the Duty to Co-operate. In family proceedings more than any other, the duty of the advocate to exercise a careful judgment as to what is relevant,

necessary and proportionate and what is not, has very carefully to be weighed. The ultimate duty is owed to the child in relation to whose welfare the judge has a constitutionally entrenched role. Thus given the dual key-signatures of the Overriding Objective and the Duty to Co-operate, advocacy which is disproportionately and unreasonably assertive can have the effect of generating an impression of undue protestation, which carries with it the risk of rebounding on a party whose interests the advocate may be seeking to advance.

3.2.5 A practical approach to the four stages of the PLO

(1) **Introduction to the four stages** (with greater detail below from **3.2.6** et seq):
For the Stages set out, see PD in Appendix at **A3.1**.

- *Stage 1:* There are two components—

  (i)   Issue of proceedings (the Pre-proceedings Checklist being in Form C110);
  (ii) First Appointment.

- *Stage 2:* There are two components—

  (i)   Advocates' Meeting;
  (ii) CMC.

- *Stage 3:* There are two components—

  (i)   Advocates' Meeting;
  (ii) Issue Resolution Hearing.

- *Stage 4:* Final hearing (in the event that the case genuinely justifies this).

(2) **Issue of proceedings:**
On day 1 and by day 3 the local authority files application Form and Annex Documents where available. The checklist is set out in 'Stage 1' of the Public Law Outline, see 10.2 et seq in Appendix 2 below. Where one of the adult parties lacks mental capacity for these purposes the Official Solicitor should now be invited to act on the basis of previously obtained medical reports, and any other special requirements for supportive advocacy/translation etc must also be identified.

(3) **Purpose of the First Appointment:**

- The court reviews these actions, and critically identifies the parties and potential parties.

- The court allocates and identifies what hearings will be required for contested interim care; split hearings for findings of fact in relation to key allegations (which may be capable at this stage of being flagged up); or on the other hand fast-track Early Final Hearing cases.
- There will fall to be considered arrangements for contested interim hearings, identifying the issues and evidence required.

See the checklist at Stage 1 of the PLO at 10.2 below.

(4) **Agenda for the first appointment:**
The focus is the identification of immediate risk factors as they bear upon the *issues* of interim care and/or alternative placement. Thus—

- **Prescribed prompts:** Using the Case Management Order/ standard directions on First Appointment as an aide memoire the court will record the current position, direct CAFCASS analysis for stage 2 together with a Case Summary from the local authority, and order the parties' outline position statements and witness statement(s).
- *Timetable for the child*: This will be created recording critical life events for the child or developmental factors influencing the timing of future hearings.
- **Checklist:**

    (i) Should the case be transferred up?
    (ii) Which parties can join in instructing common counsel (which potential parties are in fact supporting other parties' cases)?
    (iii) Alternatively are there potential splits between parties depending on the development of certain key issues or decisions on contested facts? Identify in advance the need for separate instructions.
    (iv) Are all alternatives to care being explored; have alternative family carers been approached and identified to the local authority?
    (v) Have missing people been traced?
    (vi) Is expert evidence reasonable, necessary and proportionate? What expert evidence is required and is it available within the timescale for decisions?

(5) **Advocates' Meeting prior to CMC:**[12]

- This is held no later than 2 days before the CMC with the draft Case Management Order to be filed on the same day or by agreement with the court no later than one full working day prior to the hearing. The advocates will consider the position

---

[12] Dealt with in detail below at **3.2.6**.

statements and the analysis of the guardian, and prepare the Case Management Order with the Local Authority Summary.

- On the evidence now available which *issue(s)* identified is/are now agreed; how should these be recorded as concisely as possible yet comprehensively?
- What is the *key issue(s)* and upon what evidence does each party rely in relation to it; when can it be predicted that such *issue(s)* will be resolved and how?
- Do the appropriate persons have party status?

See checklist at Stage 2 of the PLO, below.

This topic is covered in more detail below.

(6) **The Case Management Conference** (no later than day 45):

- The court will scrutinise compliance and allocation and using the Case Management Order as an aide memoire, prepare the case for *Issue(s) Resolution*.
- The court will now consider who has party status in relation to the *issues* and make contingent orders such as for disclosure and special measures.
- Orders will provide for potential carers to be nominated and for assessments, and order expert reports when appropriate with particular regard to availability.
- Full allocation and case management directions will be given using checklists. The timetable for the child will be confirmed in relation to each child.
- Further hearings ie for interim care or split hearing, will be flagged up (and if possible at this stage, timetabled), as will the *Issues Resolution Hearing* after evaluating the degree to which *issues* are likely to be contested.
- *Checklist*:

  (i)   Have the *key issue*(s) been identified?
  (ii) Has the case been narrowed down to the key question(s) upon which the threshold is said to be satisfied and the welfare of the child will be decided?
  (iii) Has the evidence been identified that will be necessary to determine the *key issue*(s)?
  (iv) In order to facilitate co-operation and avoid delay, have unreasonable expectations been managed and dispelled (to avoid investigation of unnecessary peripheral issues and unnecessary evidence)?
  (v)   Is the order consistent with the *Timetable for the Child*?
  (vi) See checklist at Stage 2 of the PLO (below).

(7) **The Issue(s) Resolution Hearing ('IRH'):**
The IRH (generally between 16 and 25 weeks) is intended to resolve and narrow issues. It is listed within the *'Timetable for the Child'*

when a relevant experts' meeting has taken place or other similar evidential steps have been completed.

- The IRH is preceded by an Advocates' Meeting, the purpose of which is—

  (i) to consider all updated analyses and position statements; and
  (ii) using the Case Management Order and Local Authority Case Summary, to record the progress of the case, defining any remaining *issue(s)*.[13]
- Checklist for IRH:

  (i) directions for any final hearing tailored to that *issue(s)*;
  (ii) identification of specific evidence and reports as to such *issues*;
  (iii) review of The '*Timetable for the Child*' when setting the date for final hearing;
  (iv) see checklist at Stage 3 of the PLO.
- Practice points for the IRH:

  − The first objective of this hearing is to achieve children's dispute resolution. The judge, using the draft Case Management Order and Local Authority Case Summary produced by the advocates, aims to resolve and refine *issues*, recording those that are not in dispute.
  − This hearing will be listed for a time when key evidential *issues* are expected to have crystallised. An IRH should be timetabled to take place soon after the evidence is filed and/or any experts' meeting has been undertaken.
  − The purpose of the IRH is in co-operation with the parties to crystallise the *key issue* (or if necessary, *issues*) upon which a final decision depends, and if possible, resolve the same.
  − The case management judge will be expected to be pro-active and interventionist. Parties should expect in appropriate cases a process of early neutral evaluation to be undertaken by the judge as to the merits of their positions and the evidence filed.
  − The judge will also identify any key remaining *issue(s)* (of fact or concerning proposed orders and plans for the child), and their extent with the objective of reducing the number and length of Final Hearings to those that genuinely remain in dispute.

---

[13] See further **3.2.8** below.

    –   The judge may feel able on the facts of the case to call a parent, or social worker or other expert to help clarify an *issue* or maybe resolve such *issue*, or to avoid a fully contested hearing.

(8) Final hearing:

This may be either earlier or later than 40 weeks, but it is expected that its timing and length will be directly referable to the needs of the child on the one hand and the complexity or otherwise of the key *issue(s)* on the other. If the timescale exceeds 40 weeks, the reason for this should be recorded on the face of the order; see Stage 4 of the PLO for checklist.

3.2.6 More detailed considerations relevant to the First Advocates' Meeting and the CMC – Stage 2

(1) The primary purpose of the Advocates' Meeting:

The primary purpose of any Advocates' Meeting is to narrow the *issues* and compile the Draft Case Management Order. That is a legal function, not a social services function. Thus—

- There should be brought to bear the professional rigour of *issue*-driven litigation: parties/social workers, and the children's guardian may be available outside with whom to canvas proposals, but the ultimate responsibility for the compilation of the draft Case Management Order is an exclusively *legal* function.
- Input from the social services is primarily through the Local Authority's Case Summary and Position Statement. Input from CAFCASS comes through the CAFCASS analysis.
- Practice Direction, para 5.9 provides that the local authority advocate should take the lead in preparing the Draft Case Management Order.

(2) Who should attend the Advocates' Meeting:

This is to be attended by advocates, litigants in person; and appointed McKenzie friends only who have the permission of the court to attend. Full co-operation by the advocates in case management and refining *issues* are essential elements underpinning the PLO.

(3) Risk factors:

The following is a range of risk factors to children and is intended to assist in the drafting of the *Case Management Order* and the *Local Authority Summary*. Teasing out the extent to which any of these factors may apply in the instant case is relevant not just to the present risk of injury but also to insight and capacity to change and the ability to provide safe enough parenting—

- domestic violence (risk of physical and emotional impact on children);
- drugs;
- drink (including of a partner);
- financial difficulties;
- chaotic lifestyle;
- neglect;
- ill-treatment of children;
- lack of control of children;
- school attendances;
- lack of hygiene;
- emotional abuse;
- mother's lack of candour (co-operation with authorities);
- mother's ability to separate from partner;
- safety of parenting having regard to above issues.

(4) **Practice points for the Advocates' meeting:**

- *Agenda* – Advocates are expected to work through the position statements, analyses and schedules using the Case Management Order to update the previous CMO; refine *issues*; record what remains in dispute (and not), the precise evidence relevant to each matter in dispute and consider what further orders are needed.
- *Position statement* – The position of the other parties to the proceedings will be updated at each stage and will constitute the parents' etc response to the Proposed Schedule of Findings on each *Key Issue*.
- *Case Management Order and the Local Authority Case Summary* – This is to be prepared by the advocates at the Advocates' Meeting. The local authority legal representative will e-mail the draft to the judge for use at the CMC or IRH as appropriate no less than one day prior to the hearing, by 11.00am. There was discussion as to this being two days before rather than one. Allowing just 1 day affords to the litigators some latitude. The corresponding obligation on the litigators has to be strict compliance with such timetable, failing which an unfair burden is cast upon the court service and the judge.
- *What is in issue?* – *Issues* can never be more than law, fact, discretion and/or expert evidence. This is central to analysing the question '*what is in issue?*' As to what is not agreed, is that *issue* necessary/proportionate?
- *Party status* – Ascertainment and investigation of those who ought to have non-automatic party status should only be that which is necessary, proportionate and reasonable. *Checklist for party status—*

(i) *Tracing?* (Date of birth, last known address, statements from extended family, statement from mother as to relationship.)

(ii) *Paternity testing* (Family Law Reform Act 1969, s 20).

(iii) *Members of extended family:* does any member of the extended family need party status – or – local authority assessment (with documentary disclosure to the person affected) with liberty to apply within a specified time of the assessment if negative? Note: the CMC is the last opportunity for nomination.

(iv) *Capacity and representation* (need for OS/NF if lacks capacity to instruct).

(5) **Core local authority evidence for consideration at the Advocates' Meeting:**
The central documents are—

- The core assessment will have been filed pursuant to Form C110. It is defined in para 26(16) of the PD.
- The Initial Social Work Statement is defined in the Practice Direction at para 26(23) of the Glossary.
- The Local Authority Case Summary is defined in para 26(26): It means a summary for each case management hearing in the form set out at Annex B to the Practice Direction and must include the information prescribed.[14] NB – This is to be seen in contrast to *'Other Parties Case Summaries'* which are defined in the Glossary at para 25(30) and to which full reference should be made.
- Final evidence and care plan/placement application and Annex B report.
- Consideration of residential assessment? (see below).
- Updated chronology and position statement.
- Any amended threshold criteria.
- Timetabling of adoption/placement report—

(i) Annex B report/Statement of Fact;
(ii) Guardian's report;
(iii) Statement of parent;
(iv) NB – The Family Justice Council has issued guidance on concurrent planning in care cases.
- Updated Timetable for the Child.

(6) **Checklist as to other matters to be addressed at the Advocates' First Meeting prior to the Stage 2 CMC, led by the LA:**

---

[14]   See **A3.1**.

- **Split trial?**[15] The issue should be flagged up, and if the *issue* is sufficiently clear, then directions for—

  (i)   hearing when (timetabling)?
  (ii) define *issue(s)*;
  (iii) witnesses;
  (iv) ELH.

  NB. President's Guidance (May 2010).

- **Statements of evidence to be obtained by local authority**— Examples—

  (i)   from social worker as to initial disclosures/alcohol/drugs/ domestic violence?
  (ii) statement from foster carer about disclosures;
  (iii) assessments of relatives likely to play any role in providing a home for the children or in contact;
  (iv) statements from any medical personnel as witnesses as to fact.

- **Statements of evidence from parties**: Statements should be timetabled and specify where appropriate the *issue* to be addressed. Matters which should be covered (by way of example, and where appropriate) include—

  (i)   extent of agreement with threshold criteria and any areas of dispute therewith;
  (ii) proposals as to long-term care of and contact with children;
  (iii) relationship with other relevant party/person;
  (iv) provide for any statement in response, *only* if necessary.

- **Records:** Examples—

  (i)   Education welfare records.
  (ii) School records: (Behaviour of child, presentation, attendance, co-operation (or lack of it), any incidents of concern observed).
  (iii) Contact records (but not to be in court bundle).
  (iv) Medical records: (Identifying relevant persons/parties. Checklist: mother/father/child/other potential carer with consent/midwifery, ambulance). Local authority to obtain records and leave to serve order on relevant authority; not to form part of the court bundle.
  (v)   Health visitor records: As a general rule no report is required unless the evidence is critical or in dispute (the records speak for themselves).
  (vi) Housing officer records (as to condition of house/ complaints of neighbours and original logs).

---

[15]   See **A3.19** for model order.

  (vii) Case conference minutes/strategy discussion minutes
        including LAC review/social services record (taking into
        account what is reasonable, necessary and proportionate).
  (viii) Transcripts of previous proceedings.

- **Tests:**
  Liver function and hair strand testing (consider reports from
  alcohol/drug related services); as to hair strand, see *London
  Borough of Richmond v B, W, B and CB* [2010] EWHC
  2905 (Fam).

(7) **Guardian:**
To update analysis and position statement.[16]

(8) **Residential assessments:**
If this is to be sought, mother's solicitor should file a report from the
home stating—

- What precisely is to be provided as a residential assessment – is
  it *Re G* compliant? If what is to be provided is a continuing
  course of education, training or psychotherapy/therapy to the
  parent with a view to giving her the opportunity to change
  sufficiently so as to become a safe and acceptable carer for the
  child, who is to fund?
- Their willingness to have a mother/partner and baby.
- What is involved in the assessment.
- The timescale.
- What is expected of the parents.
- Cost apportionment: what is the cost of the proposed
  assessment and the impact (if relevant) on local authority
  resources?
- What is the appropriate apportionment on cost?
- Whether mother and father will sign the appropriate
  agreement.
- Are there to be interim reports and, if yes, when? With
  disclosure of records?

3.2.7 Discrete themes at the Advocates' Meeting prior to CMC – relevant checklists

(1) **Domestic violence:**

- Admitted/denied?
- Statements (including schedule of incidents and police DV
  records).

---

16 See PD para 26(10) for the contents of the CG's '*Case Analysis and Recommendations*'.

- Insight/capacity to change (Behavioural profile/evidence of capacity to change? Psychiatrist/psychologist or DV Intervention Scheme).
- Facilities for change (DV programmes and a report from such programme?).
- Victim Realisation Programme? (Report? Timescale?)
- Evidence checklist—

    (i) police records of any 'call-out' to any address connected with any relevant party;
    (ii) police records of any relevant incident;
    (iii) if relevant, statements from police officers involved (examples of situations to be covered: circumstances of a child's removal, the state of the property, those present, reactions of those present to the removal);
    (iv) previous convictions;
    (v) timetable for hearing;
    (vi) who is to serve order on the police.

(2) **Non-accidental injury:**

- What injuries were suffered?

    (i) Nature and extent of injury.
    (ii) Mechanism/causation?
    (iii) Timing/probable timescale.
    (iv) Accidental or non-accidental? (If non-accidental, who is in the range of likely perpetrators?)
    (v) Failure to protect: If only one parent is found to be responsible for perpetration, did the other fail to protect; was the injury concealed?
    (vi) What would the child's manifestation of pain have been?
    (vii) Would a reasonable parent have realised the need for medical treatment? If yes, on what grounds?
    (viii) Delay – in seeking treatment or failure to disclose?
- Evidence checklist—

    (i) Should other persons be invited to intervene (and if they decline, use witness summons)? Alternatively, consider making potential perpetrators parties so that they are bound by court orders/findings.
    (ii) Ensure that any direction for a split trial also covers background evidence so that the facts which are sought to be found can be assessed in context.
    (iii) Findings the court is invited to make must be included in the order or be scheduled to the order (such schedule having as many columns as parties, so that each party can

respond to each of the findings of fact which the local authority invites the court to make).

(3) **Sexual abuse:**
Examples of issues likely to arise—

- Is there evidence of abuse?
- Nature of abuse?
- What is the probable cause?
- Would child have manifested pain/change of behaviour?
- Who is within the range of likely perpetrators?
- Is there an issue of failure to protect?
- What records are there of any complaint?
- Can a perpetrator be identified?
- Chronology of complaints (look at timescale).
- Evidence checklist—
  Examples—

  (i) Transcripts of ABE interviews.
  (ii) Witness statements in any criminal investigation.
  (iii) Records of 'call-outs'.
  (iv) Previous convictions of those who are in the range of possible perpetrators.
  (v) Reports of FME/notes of examinations/photographs.

(4) **Emotional abuse/ill-treatment/neglect/developmental delay:**

- *Analysis of facts* – Consider the nature of the factual allegations and the alleged effect on the child. Is there a medical/social work chronology from all the records that demonstrates the events upon which cause and effect might be considered?
- *Analysis of harm* – Will it be necessary to have a report from a consultant paediatrician/child psychiatrist/psychologist to consider extent of harm and the effect on the child's development and needs both currently and in the future.

(5) **Mental health:**

- Is there a need for a psychiatric report?
- Is the Official Solicitor required?
- Disclosure of medical records.

3.2.8 Considerations relevant to Advocates' Meeting after CMC and prior to IRH – Stage 3

(1) **Considerations in preparation for the Advocates' Meeting prior to the IRH in relation to the order made at the CMC:**

- Has there been non-compliance in relation to any order? If yes, what is the reason for such failure and what steps are proposed to remedy the default?
- What is agreed and not agreed? *Issue* of law and/or fact and/or expert evidence? Provide a clear and concise statement of *issues* outstanding. Is it necessary, reasonable and proportionate for the court to be invited to resolve *all* of them? Can their number be reduced?
- In relation to such *issues*, what evidence is required for their determination? What documents can be put in evidence without calling the maker (either because agreed, or questions are not to be put, or proportionality?)
- Is disclosure complete? Are there any remaining applications for specific disclosure?
- Is the core assessment complete?
- If there is to be a split trial, directions as to—

  (i) timetabling (hearing where, and when, before whom);
  (ii) define *issue*(s);
  (iii) witnesses;
  (iv) ELH.

(2) **Is the case ready for hearing?**
The following are examples of an evidence checklist—

- Have all statements of evidence been filed?
- Has CG checked that all the evidence is properly compiled? Does the CG's report cover the statutory requirements?
- Further witness statements?
- Addendum experts reports?
- Additional testing for drink/drugs?
- Report from contact supervisor?
- Any other records to be obtained?
- Social worker addendum report?
- Review of Timetable for the Child to achieve the conclusion of proceedings.
- Amended care plan.
- Allocation to appropriate list.

(3) **Case management practice:**
Checklist—

- Time estimate (including submissions and judgment).
- Venue?
- Which witnesses? (Use of interpreters? Special measures? Facilities for person with disability?)
- What evidence is agreed to be recorded in the Case Management Order?

- Video/telephone? Transcript.[17] Have arrangements been made for viewing/listening?
- Witness summonses?
- Trial bundles, indexed and up to date?
- Recommended reading list?
- Witness availability/template – witnesses as to fact and expert witnesses. The template should list the witnesses, the time of their availability and timescales for examination/cross-examination and re-examination.
- Skeleton arguments with indexed and paginated authorities?
- Confirm same judge.

(4) **The discipline of '*Issues*' and the trial bundle:**
Advocates and professionals are reminded that any trial bundle must contain nothing more than those documents required to adjudicate upon the *issues*. In the event of medical *issues*, the core medical notes should be distilled out of the range of medical records (and paginated and indexed as a separate bundle), the latter being kept entirely separate from the trial bundles. Any bundle for any hearing must be clearly indexed and paginated (and each part separated by numbered card dividers) whereby the following becomes immediately accessible—

- The threshold criteria, cross-referencing with documents in the core medical bundle.
- The Case Management Record (as a compilation of the case management documentation).
- CAFCASS analysis.
- The statements in support of any application.
- The statements opposing any such application.
- The professionals (including experts) report for each party.
- Minutes of any advocates' and professionals' meeting.

3.2.9   The children's guardian, the PLO and *issues*

(1) **Guardian – appointment and role:**
The investigation of the guardian covers four main areas—

- Studying papers (reports and statements, including the local authority care plan and local authority files).
- Interviews with the child and all relevant family members.
- Interviews of professionals involved: Including health and education; discussion with the local authority social worker, team manager, family support worker and contact supervisor.
- Observations of the child with significant adults (eg parents and carers, including at school and during contact).

---

[17]   See Hale J in *Re S* [1998] 1 FLR 798.

(2) **As to when a guardian is to be appointed:**

- Section 41(6) as to situations mandating a guardian—

  (i) Applications for care or supervision (s 31).
  (ii) Direction where the court is considering making an interim care order (s 37(1)).
  (iii) Applications to discharge or vary a care and supervision order (s 39(4)).
  (iv) Application for a residence order where the child is in care (s 8).
  (v) Application for contact where a child is in care (s 34).
- Note also appointment pursuant to rr 12.27 and 16.3 of the FPR 2010—

  (i) Applications for secure accommodation orders (s 25).
  (ii) Applications to change the surname of a child in care (s 33(7)).
  (iii) Applications for a child in care to live abroad (Sch 2, para 19(1)).
  (iv) Applications to extend a supervision order (Sch 3, para 6(3)).
  (v) Appeals in respect of applications set out at (i)–(iv) immediately above.
- Guardians can also be ordered in the following cases—

  (i) The Adoption and Children Act 2002 (adoption and placement orders);
  (ii) Human Fertilisation and Embryology Act (1990) (s 30 – applications for parental orders or under s 54 of the 2008 Act);
  (iii) Crime and Disorder Act 1998 (s 11 – applications for a child safety order).

(3) **If guardian has been appointed (see FPR 2010, Part 16, Chapters 6 and 7):**

- Name, and when appointed?
- Allocated (if previous proceedings, allocated?)
- Solicitor appointed, if yes – name?
- Has CAFCASS been notified? If no – why not?

(4) **Role of guardian:**
The guardian's role is critically to examine and appraise, and to report to the court. See FPR 2010, PD16A as to the role of the guardian, given his/her autonomy as an officer of the court: the

children's guardian (CG) must notify any person whose joinder might safeguard the interests of the child and must inform the court of—

- any such notification given;
- anybody the CG tried but failed to contact for this purpose;
- anybody the CG believes may wish to be joined.

Thus check that CG has addressed all significant persons involved in the child's care including a father without parental responsibility and significant adults in extended family? To minimise disruption, can the child be placed with familiar family or friends rather than with stranger foster parents?

(5) **The guardian and scrutiny of care plan:**

The guardian must scrutinize the care plan to assess that it appropriately meets the child's needs, whether the local authority has attributed sufficient weight to the children's wishes and feelings and the views of others, and how probable it is that the plan will succeed. The CG should also assess the plan against other options taking into account the Human Rights Act and proportionality.

(6) **Guardian's report and the PLO:**

- Under the PLO the guardian has a duty to provide information to the court from the earliest stage, and will formally report at initial (if feasible) interim and final stages. Reports are produced within a template that aims to avoid repetition including in each report only information which is new and relevant.
- Depending on how much is known, the first report to the court at First Appointment may be verbal, if it is feasible to report. The initial written report will be given at the first Case Management Conference. The guardian's main task at this stage is to appraise the work undertaken pre-proceedings, to establish if it meets standards and correctly identifies *issues* and whether there are any evidential gaps.
- The following headings will be covered in reports, conveying information cumulatively without repetition between reports or of other material filed in the case. Each successive report will identify areas of change as the case progresses—

  - Local Authority details.
  - Sources of Information.
  - Diversity information.
  - Risk Issues and Safety planning.
  - Analysis of key issues.
  - Parties position on key issues.
  - The children's views.

- Informing the child of the outcome.
- Recommendations at initial/interim/final stage.

3.2.10 Duties of local authorities – assessments

(1) **Guidance to local authorities has been re-issued**

- Under the PLO at First Appointment the court will consider whether pre-proceedings preparation has been carried out appropriately; for example all kinship care options should (to the extent that is possible) have been explored, and core assessments carried out, as required in the Integrated Children's System introduced within the Every Child Matters Initiative (www.everychildmatters.gov.uk). In the event that potential kinship carers have not come forward to avoid conflict with the parents, this issue should be further explored once proceedings have been commenced.

- If certain work has not been carried out pre-proceedings (depending on the type of case) the court may direct and timetable such work to ensure that it is carried forward as the case progresses. Assessments of attachment, parenting, general risk of harm, general issues of child development, the effect on parenting of substance dependence problems or mental health problems should be able to be satisfactorily dealt with by the social worker or the children's guardian.

(2) **Initial assessment:**
If the child is *assessed* as being *in need* and the local authority is concerned that the child is *suffering*, or is at risk of suffering, *significant harm,* the authority is *under a duty* to make, as soon as practicable and, in any event, *within 48 hours* of the authority receiving the information, such *enquiries* as it considers necessary to enable it to decide whether it should take action to safeguard or promote the welfare of the child (s 47(1) of the Act) and what action may be appropriate in the circumstances.

(3) **Core assessment:**

- A core assessment is defined in the PD (para 26(16)) as—

    'the assessment undertaken by the Local Authority in accordance with The Framework for the Assessment of Children in Need and their Families (Department of Health et al, 2000).'

    It is an in-depth assessment which addresses the central or most important aspects of the needs of a child and the capacity of his or her parents or caregivers to respond appropriately to these needs within the wider family and community context.

- The core assessment (which builds on the initial assessment when indicated) is the means by which full s 47 enquiries are carried out. In all cases where an initial assessment concludes that there is cause to suspect that a child is suffering or is likely to suffer significant harm, a core assessment should be completed, informed by the information obtained through an initial assessment.

(4) **Specialist assessments:**
These may be commissioned by the local authority from other agencies or independent professionals also as part of the s 47 investigation e g where there may be either organic or care elements in relation to a child's failure to thrive.

(5) **Kinship assessments:**
The local authority will produce an assessment of the kinship carer's capacity to provide appropriate care for the child using a standard framework. It should ensure, when assessing the wider family and environmental factors within the core assessment, that it has considered the capacity and willingness of the wider family to provide care for the child on a short or a longer-term basis.

(6) **Family Group Meetings:**
These may be a method whereby in some cases, local authorities convene meetings with the family to discuss their concerns and the plan for the child and explore alternative options involving family members as alternative carers or to offer other support.

(7) **Child's Chronology:**
By LAC (2005)3 every local authority is obliged to maintain a chronology that will be automatically updated when key events are recorded in their system, for example, when a child becomes looked after. Historic information will be entered into the system as it is discovered through assessment and other case activity and subsequently output. Specialised chronologies should be outputted for different purposes; ie health, education, change of carer histories and for use in court proceedings.

(8) **Questions to ask concerning assessments:**

- Have appropriate treatment programmes been explored to address particular issues for the children or parents?
- Do the parents have special needs and have they been offered support and advocacy?
- Have the appropriate specialist assessments been carried out to identify what the reasons are for the problems the child is suffering?

- Have the parents been contacted and their views sought, and have they been involved in all relevant meetings and kept informed of all processes?
- Is the family appropriately housed?
- Have health and education agencies full complied with their duties to assist the local authority and assess the child and offer services?
- Have the local authority's concerns been shared with the family as they have emerged and the alternatives explored at each stage?
- Have the appropriate resources been offered to support the family in caring for the child themselves through the provision of services? Have these alternatives been costed as against the costs of removal of the child and long-term placement?
- Have special guardianship/residence orders been explained and explored as an alternative to care? Where requested, has this assessment been carried out?
- Where special guardianship or residence orders have been discussed, have sufficient services been offered to support these options?
- Has it been made clear before asking family members to offer alternative care, that this would only be considered were the court to decide that the parents could not offer care themselves, and have they therefore been assessed pre-proceedings?
- Have the proceedings been launched prematurely?
- Have the proceedings been launched late and the risk to the child increased and the outcome of proceedings affected?
- Section 38(6) provides power to order assessments. Such assessments must be assessments of the child and not a back-door for treatment of a parent.[18]

3.3   INTRODUCTION AND INDEX TO THE 'PLO' DOCUMENTATION

(1)   **Philosophy underpinning the documentation:**
Central to the PLO is the Case Management Order. It is not to be read in isolation but in conjunction with—

- The *Local Authority Case Summary.*
- The *Case Management Record.*
- In care and supervision proceedings, any Letter before Proceedings and any related subsequent correspondence confirming the local authority's position to parents and others with parental responsibility for the child.

---

[18]   *Re C (A Minor) (Interim Care Order: Residential Assessment)* [1997] AC 489; *Kent County Council v G* [2005] UKHL 68.

- The Case Management Documentation (the documents in para 3.10 of the PD).
- Standard Directions on issue and on First Appointment.
- The Draft Case Management orders approved by the court.

(Parties will be expected to retain their own record containing copies of the documents on the court's Case Management Record).

(2) **The central importance of the Case Management Record:**

The concept is that this Case Management Record (see PD3.12) provides a comprehensive freeze-frame of the case at a particular moment in time. This is immensely helpful to both Bench and advocate, because—

- the judge can assimilate the core data very much more quickly than has hitherto been the experience;
- to achieve that result, the pre-proceedings material has to have been compiled accurately and succinctly by the local authority pursuant to s 7 of the LASSA 1970 and its protocols (in the appropriate cases);
- and given the work invested by the local authority, the advocates are empowered to home in on the *key issue*(s) in the case and approach the hearings with robust forensic discipline;
- The result of the PLO is to achieve formally, what had been the empirical experience of courts up and down the land; namely, that most cases *do* resolve without a final hearing. The experience has been that the *issue(s)* hitherto has crystallized too late to avoid compendious listings for final hearings (which did not in fact materialise) with the result that courts were booked so long in advance unnecessarily with great delay to cases coming up behind, with the obvious impact on a child's timetable;
- The engine which drives this machinery is the PLO Practice Direction.

(3) **Running through the Appendices to this Chapter:**

Appendix 1: Revision of the Public Law Outline
Appendix 2: Practice Direction 12A: Public Law Proceedings Guide to Case Management
Appendix 3: Practice Guidance 12 July 2010: McKenzie Friends (Civil and Family Courts)
Appendix 4: President's Guidance in Relation to Split Hearings
Appendix 5: Practice Direction 12B: The Revised Private Law Programme
Appendix 6: Forced Marriage Guidelines
Appendix 7: Acting in the Absence of a Children's Guardian
Appendix 8: Preparing for Care and Supervision Proceedings

Appendix 9: Guidelines for Judges Meeting Children who are subject to Family Proceedings

Appendix 10: Basic Guidance to Good Practice in Care Proceedings across London

Appendix 11: Arrangements to Assist Cafcass Pending Implementation of the Family Justice Review

Appendix 12: Joint Message from Sir Nicholas Wall, President of the Family Division and Anthony Douglas CBE, the Chief Executive of Cafcass

Appendix 13: Communicating with the Home Office in Family Proceedings

Appendix 14: President's Guidance in Relation to Out of Hours Proceedings

Appendix 15: Case Management Decisions and Appeals Therefrom (Bulletin No 2)

Appendix 16: Guidance in Cases Involving Protected Parties in which the Official Solicitor is being Invited to Act as Guardian ad Litem or Litigation Friend

Appendix 17: Protocol for Handling Secure Accommodation Applications under s 25

Appendix 18: Practice Management: Domestic Violence

Appendix 19: Standard Variable Directions Dovetailing with the Case Management Order

Appendix 20: The Children Act 1989 Guidance and Regulations, Vol 1, Court Orders, A Framework for the Care and Upbringing of Children, Chapter 3

Appendix 21: President's Direction of 24 July 2000: Human Rights Act 1998

Appendix 22: Practice Direction 27A: Family Proceedings: Court Bundles (Universal Practice to be applied in All Courts other than the Family Proceedings Court)

Appendix 23: Model Judgment Template

Appendix 24: Working Party of the Family Justice Council Guidelines

Appendix 25: The New Care Monitoring System

(4) Analysis of **the PLO Practice Direction:**
This is a crucial document. It must be read in detail and in full. It is the engine which drives through the procedural changes. It covers—

- Scope: para 1.
- The overriding objective: para 2.
- Court case management: para 3.
- Expectations (in the Nelsonian sense): para 4.
- How the parties should help court case management: para 5.
- Findings of Fact Hearings: para 6.
- Ethnicity, language, religion and culture: para 7.
- Adults who may be protected parties: para 8.

- Child likely to lack capacity to conduct the proceedings when he reaches 18: para 9.
- Outline of the processes and how to use the case management tools: para 10 (this includes the schedules which we associate with the PLO).
- Starting proceedings: para 11.
- What the court will do at the issue of proceedings: para 12.
- First appointment: para 13.
- Advocates' discussion/meeting and the draft Case Management Order: para 14.
- Case Management Conference (including comprehensive objectives): para 15.
- The Issue Resolution Hearing: para 16.
- Attendance at the Case Management Conference and the Issues Resolution Hearing: para 17.
- Flexible powers of the Court Service: para 18.
- Alternative Dispute Resolution: para 19.
- Co-operation: para 20.
- Agreed directions: para 21.
- Variation of case management timetable: para 22.
- Who performs the functions of the court: para 23.
- Technology: para 24.
- Other Practice Directions (including 'Bundles'): para 25.
- Glossary: para 26.

(5) **Particular features of the Practice Direction as to case management:**

- The new Overriding Objective and the duty of the parties to further that objective. This dovetails with an entrenched duty to co-operate under para 5.5 which implicitly prevents the raising of unreasonable expectations.
- The main principles of court case management including a comprehensive check list of what is involved in court case-management, set out in para 3.20.
- The expectation that cases will be conducted in accordance with the Case Management Documentation prescribed, in accordance with a Timetable for the Child.
- The Schedules which are the core documents of the PLO embracing the Pre-Proceedings Checklist and Stages 1, 2, 3 and 4.

3.4 THE JUDGE AND THE CARE PLAN

3.4.1 The duty of the court to scrutinise the care plan

It is essential that the court rigorously scrutinises the care plan.[19]

---

[19] See Wall J in *Re J (Minors) (Care Plan)* [1994] 1 FLR 253 at 258.

3.4.2 Why does the judge have to scrutinise the care plan?

- To ensure that the best possible services are put in place to support the placement of the child whether at home, with relatives or outside the birth family.

- Once a care order has been made, the court cannot control the operation of the care order by the local authority.

- Any social worker assigned to work with the children after a care order has been made will read the care plan first in order to gain an understanding of how the local authority (LA) was planning to meet the needs of the children.

- It is the care plan and not the court order that contains important decisions or agreements such as that the children will not be placed separately or that the LA has agreed to fund a child's current expensive placement for the foreseeable future.

This essential duty of scrutinising the care plan is now given statutory force by s 31(3A) of the Children Act 1989. This stipulates that:

> 'No care order may be made with respect to a child until the court has considered a plan (a section 31A Plan) for the future care of the child prepared under section 31A. The LA must keep any care plan under review and if they are of the opinion some change is required, revise the plan or make a new plan accordingly.'

See also Family Procedure Rules 2010, Practice Direction 12A – Public Law Proceedings Guide to Case Management: April 2010.

- A judge should be proactive in prompting the LA at each hearing to meet the child's needs and devise the best possible outcome for that child.

- The duty of scrutiny by the court begins at the first directions hearing and continues through every subsequent hearing.

- As the case unfolds, the care plan may well change and the court should be updated periodically. The court should check the progress of the case when interim care orders are renewed.

- It is good practice for the LA itself to notify the judge of major changes to the care plan which occur outside directions hearings.

- Evidence in support of the plan should be made available to the court. In particular, where placement details are available they should be made available to the court.[20]

3.4.3 How to scrutinise the interim care plan

- For example, at an Allocation Hearing, a Case Management Conference or a Directions Hearing.

- Ask yourself and if necessary pursue the following questions with the local authority:

  - If the child is living at home or with a relative under an interim care order ensure that the LA and the parents or relative enter into a signed working agreement so that the family is aware of what is expected of them by the LA and the LA sets out what support they will provide to the family. Working agreements are particularly useful in the situation where a party is limited to contact supervised by the LA, eg in making it clear that the carer should not permit unsupervised contact.
  - Why is this child not with his/her parents?
  - Why is this child not with his/her siblings? When are they to be placed together?
  - Why is this child not with part of the wider family? Cause enquiries to be made of the extended family as to who may wish to put themselves forward as carers in the event of the parents being unable to care for the child. Order viability assessments of relatives offering to care.
  - If there is a paternity issue give directions for DNA testing.
  - If the child is not with parents or wider family, who are the significant people to this child and what contact is proposed between them?
  - Will the proposed contact between the child and his parents be at an appropriate level?
  - What inter-sibling contact is to take place? (often overlooked)
  - How will any special needs of the child, including those related to education, health, disability, race, culture, language and religion, be met within the placement? What services need to be provided to meet the child's needs.
  - What are the arrangements for education? Can the child be maintained at the same school?
  - Are the funds in place to maintain the placement until final hearing?
  - Have sufficient attempts been made to communicate and consult with the parents?

---

[20] See further *Re J (Minors) (Care Plan)* [1994] 1 FLR 253 at 261F–262B; *Re L (Sexual Abuse: Standard of Proof)* [1996] 1 FLR 116; *Re T (A Minor) (Care Order: Conditions)* [1994] 2 FLR 423.

- What are the views of the child(ren)? How were they obtained?
- If the child's views are known and not being followed, why not?
- If the foster placement is vulnerable, what support can be put in to maintain the placement? Eg a nursery placement, advice from a psychologist or respite care. What is the contingency plan in the case of placement breakdown?
- Is the local authority twin tracking the case in order to prevent delay, eg planning for a return of the child home at the same time as putting in place the necessary groundwork for adoption? Concurrent planning avoids delay.
- Is the plan to place the child in the area of another local authority? If so the care plan needs to be developed in conjunction with the other LA who should be invited to attend all court hearings so that the judge can be confident that the LA in whose area the child is to live can and will meet the child's needs once a care order is made.
- Is the plan before you going to achieve the best possible outcome for the child in the circumstances?

3.4.4 How to scrutinise the final care plan

Ask yourself and if appropriate the local authority the following questions in the event of:

3.4.4.1 Placement at home

(1) What is the nature of the parental difficulty? Eg domestic violence, drug or alcohol abuse?

(2) What support package has been devised by the LA in order to monitor and protect the child or children in placement? Eg finding a nursery for the child, visits by health visitor and social worker.

(3) How many children are to be placed at home together? What are the ages of the children?

(4) Does the support package meet the needs of each child? Eg for input from a child psychologist or psychiatrist or speech therapist.

(5) Has a contract or working agreement been drawn up between the LA and the parents so that the parents understand what is expected of them and that breaches may result in removal of the children.

(6) How are the child's needs for education to be met?

(7) What is the contingency plan in case of placement breakdown? Is there a member of the extended family available who ought to be named as a potential carer if the current placement breaks down?

3.4.4.2   Care by the extended family

(1)   Has every effort been made to search out potential carers within the parents' families?

(2)   Does the care plan indicate whether placement will be under a care order or under a residence order, a residence order with a supervision order to the LA or a special guardianship order?

(3)   What support package is necessary to maintain the placement and meet the children's needs? Are the arrangements in place?

(4)   What financial payments will be made by the LA to the relatives, eg residence allowance or relative carer allowance?

(5)   What contact arrangements to the birth parents have been approved by the court? Are the details of the approved contact set out in the care plan? Should a s 8 contact order be considered?

(6)   What inter-sibling contact is to take place? Or contact with other significant relatives? Eg grandparents.

(7)   Has a contract or working agreement been drawn up and signed by the relative and the LA so that there is no doubt that the relative understands that he or she cannot permit unsupervised contact between the parents and the child?

(8)   How will the child's special needs for education be met? Or his health, disability, language, religious, race or cultural needs be met in this placement?

(9)   What contingency plan is in place in the event of placement breakdown. Is there another member of the extended family available who ought to be named as a potential carer?

3.4.4.3   Long-term foster care

(1)   Does the child agree with the plan for him to live with foster parents?

(2)   What support package is proposed to meet the needs of the child in the foster placement? Are the arrangements in place?

(3)   Is/are the promised specific resource(s) available? On what date will they become available?

(4)   What are the age(s) of the child(ren)?

(5)   Are the plans for parental contact and inter-sibling contact approved by the court set out in the care plan? Are the foster parents content with the planned contact with the family?

(6)   Do the foster parents need specific support (eg psychologist or respite periods) in order to prevent placement breakdown?

(7)   How will the child's special educational needs be met? Or his health, disability, religious, language, racial or cultural needs be met in placement.

(8)   What contingency plan is in place in the event of placement breakdown? Eg Is there another relative carer available? If so, specify them by name so that they can be considered in the event of placement breakdown.

(9)   Order the disclosure of any judgment or experts reports to the carers so that they are aware of the views of the judge and the experts as to the needs of the child.

3.4.4.4   Residential care

(1)   Why is the care plan for this child not to experience family life at home with parents or relatives or with foster parents? Is the residential placement really necessary?

(2)   Is the child already settled in the residential placement prior to the making of a care order?

(3)   NB – Do not finalise the care order until the child is in placement. It is not uncommon to find that the placement proposed for the child is either not available or those running the placement will not accept the child.

(4)   Are the specific resources required to further the interests of the child truly available at the proposed placement? Eg therapy or education. Ensure that the guardian visits the proposed placement.

(5)   Has the LA agreed that they will fund the proposed residential placement for the foreseeable future?

(6)   What are the proposals for contact with parents and siblings? Do they meet the child's needs? Are the arrangements approved by the court set out in the care plan?

(7)   How far away is the placement from the homes of those exercising contact? Will the LA be assisting by paying for the cost of travel to

contact or will the LA be conveying the siblings to the place of contact? Are the arrangements approved by the court set out in the care plan?

3.4.4.5 *Adoption*

(1) What is the size of the sibling group?

(2) How likely is it that the group can be placed together?

(3) What are the ages of the children?

(4) Is there any developmental delay in the child/any child in the group?

(5) Does the care plan correctly reflect the decision of the court as to which children must be placed together and which may have to be separated?

(6) Does the care plan specify the decision of the court as to how long the LA should search for a placement for all the children together and the point when separation may be necessary? Eg after a search for 6 or 9 months.

(7) If the children will or might be separated what are the plans for inter-sibling contact approved by the court and are they accurately recorded in the care plan?

(8) What are the plans for parental contact and have they been accurately recorded in the care plan?

(9) Ensure that any relevant judgments or medical reports are released to the prospective adopters so that they are aware of the views of the judge and the experts as to the needs of the children.

(10) Set out in the care plan any health, religious, cultural or educational needs of the children.

3.4.4.6 *Contact – important considerations*

(1) The care plan needs to state who are the important people to the child.

(2) With siblings the plan needs to state whether it is the local authority intention to place them together and if the plan is to separate them, what plans there are for inter-sibling contact.

(3)   In adoption cases the plan should state what is in the child's interests. If the wish is not to bind prospective, as yet unknown, adopters, the plan can state what the ideal situation is in respect of contact subject to the agreement of the adopters.

(4)   The contact plan needs to state long-term aims as well as current arrangements. Too many are short-term in nature.

(5)   If the contingency plan involves a change of residence, it should also set out the contingency plan for contact so far as it can be ascertained when the plan is drawn up.

3.4.5   What can the judge do if she/he disagrees with the contents of the care plan or has doubts that it can be implemented?

The court may refuse to make a care order:

If there is a fundamental disagreement between the judge and the LA eg where the LA plans to place a child for adoption but the judge has been persuaded that the child ought to be placed with grandparents or an aunt under a care order, a stalemate can arise. The judge will not approve the care plan and the LA will not amend its care plan. This situation is best resolved by the judge giving clear reasons in his judgment why he/she cannot approve the care plan and setting out the ways in which the judge invites the LA to change the care plan. The judge should then adjourn the case for an appropriate period of time to allow the LA to consider that invitation. If the LA witnesses have vehemently opposed changing the care plan it is pointless allowing the same social work team to consider the judgment as their views are entrenched. In that situation it is often helpful to ask the relevant Assistant Director of Children Services to consider your invitation to change the care plan and direct that they attend at court at the adjourned hearing in the event that the LA is still refusing to amend the care plan so that the reasons for such refusal can be explained by the Assistant Director to the judge personally.

Re X; Barnet London Borough Council v Y and X [2006] 2 FLR 998

Munby J (sitting as a county court judge) refused to endorse the LA's care plan and found that the LA's decision-making process had been flawed in a number of significant ways, eg the LA had created a plan which in reality was a plan of higher management which seemed to have an uncertain grasp of the facts and had placed unduly excessive weight upon factors having more to do with policy or principle than with the child's needs. Having particularised many failures in the LA's decision-making process the judge refused to approve the care plan because it was not in the best interests of the child.

Three weeks later the LA agreed to amend its care plan in accordance with the judgment of the court.

See *Re S and W (Care Proceedings)*,[21] where the Court of Appeal approved the above approach and roundly condemned the behaviour of the relevant LA. It is not in the interests of the child to have a stand off between the LA and the court which will result in delay. The shared objective of the LA and the court should be to achieve a result in the best interests of the child.[22]

If the LA will not accept the judgment of the court it may be necessary to make a residence order coupled with a supervision order or a family assistance order.

If the court is not satisfied about material aspects of the care plan it may decline to make a final care order.[23]

The judge may at final hearing continue the interim care order in order to give the LA time to work upon the care plan and allow it to crystallise to the satisfaction of the guardian and the judge.

NB – An interim care order is only to be used for its intended purpose and not, by extension, to provide the court with a continuing control over the LA.[24]

3.4.6 When in practice should the court withdraw from a case and make a final care order and when should the court retain control?

For example:

Do NOT hold the case until long term foster parents or an adoptive placement has been identified by matching the child with identified carers (*Re R (Care: Plan for Adoption: Best Interest)* [2006] 1 FLR 483).

By means of interim care orders DO continue to hold the case:

- where the care plan is for adoption and the LA Adoption Panel has not met and decided that adoption is in the best interests of the child, until the Panel's decision that the child should be placed for adoption has been ratified internally by the LA;

---

21   [2007] 2 FLR 275.
22   Ibid at 284.
23   See *Re J (Minors) (Care Plan)* [1994] 1 FLR 253.
24   See *Re L (Sexual Abuse: Standard of Proof)* [1996] 1 FLR 116; *Re J (Minors) (Care Plan)* [1994] 1 FLR 253.

- until the right residential placement has been found for the child and the guardian supports the placement and the LA have agreed to fund the placement;

- until the proposed rehabilitation to the parents or members of the extended family has been successful.

In *Re H (Children)* [2011] EWCA Civ 1218 the trial judge had made full care orders but directed assessments as to post-adoption contact. The Court of Appeal held that the judge had not had the necessary material on which to decide whether the child should be adopted. The court must not finally dispose of the matter when the facts are not as clearly known as can reasonably be expected. Before approving the local authority's care plan for adoption there should have been some assessment of the prospects of adoption succeeding and the issue of contact with the birth family was inextricably tied up with that.

By contrast, in *Re D O'H (Children)* [2011] EWCA Civ 1343 the Court of Appeal upheld the judge's decision to make final care orders approving a plan for adoption for the younger child whilst the issue of attachment to, and contact with, an older sibling remained to be determined. The judge had been entitled to find that adoption was required and that the issue of contact was to be determined within that context.

Sometimes:

- the 'lesser of two evils' arguments arises where a court is faced with the dilemma of making a care order based upon a plan perceived by the court as being not wholly in the interests of the child and returning the child to live with unsuitable parents (*Re S & D (Children: Powers of Court)* [1995] 2 FLR 456).

See *Re S and W (Care Proceedings)* [2007] 2 FLR 275 for an occasion when the Court of Appeal said that the LA were unable to rely upon the lesser of two evils argument as they had failed to reconsider their position in the light of the judgment given by the judge and in accordance with the invitation of the court (see p 283, paras [31]–[38]).

Sometimes the approval of a care plan will involve taking a step into the unknown.[25]

- The court can seek to persuade the LA to rethink its plan and in practice many do. Sometimes there arises an impasse between the LA and the judge who may have to accede to the inevitable and make a care order.

---

[25] See *Re J (Minors) (Care Plan)* [1994] 1 FLR 253.

3.4.7 Challenging the care plan

- In pending care proceedings the venue for challenging the plan is in the care proceedings rather than by judicial review. Further there is no need for separate Human Rights Act proceedings as there is a remedy within the proceedings. See *Re C (Adoption: Religious Observance)* [2002] 1 FLR 1119.

- There is jurisdiction under Senior Courts Act 1981, s 37 or County Courts Act 1984, s 38 or under the Human Rights Act 1998, s 8(1) for a county court or the High Court to grant an injunction in prospective or pending proceedings in order to restrain a local authority from changing the placement of a child pending the hearing of an extant or proposed adoption application.[26] In *Re H (Care Plan: Human Rights)* [2012] 1 FLR 191 the judge disagreed with the local authority's care plan to separate mother and child and declined to amend it. The Court of Appeal confirmed that the judge could injunct the local authority under s 8 HRA 1998 and should have been asked to do so at the hearing of the interim care order application.

- Where after the making of the care order the LA departs from the care plan, the parents may return the case to court by applying for the discharge of the care order.

- Alternatively where after the making of the care order, the LA has departed from the care plan for a child in such a manner as to breach the human rights of a party, the extended powers given to the court by HRA 1998, ss 6 and 7 may be exercised to grant such relief as may be appropriate. A human rights challenge to a care plan or the placement of a child should be heard in the Family Division and if possible by a judge who has experience of sitting in the Administrative Court.[27]

3.4.8 The Independent Reviewing Officer

- Section 118(1) of the Adoption and Children Act 2002 introduced the Independent Reviewing Officer who is charged with participating in, and monitoring, the LA's decisions in respect of reviews of 'looked after children'. The section inserts a new s 26(2A) to the Children Act 1989 giving the IRO power to refer the case to CAFCASS, if he considers it appropriate to do so.

---

[26] *Re H (Care Plan: Human Rights)* [2012] 1 FLR 191 and *Coventry City Council v O (Adoption)* [2011] 2 FLR 936.

[27] See *C v Bury MBC* [2002] 2 FLR 868; *Re M (Care: Challenging Decisions by Local Authority)* [2001] 2 FLR 1300; and *Hershman & McFarlane* Vol 1, Section C, paras 1140 and 1141.

- If there are concerns that there may be problems in the future in relation to certain parts of the care plan, then these should be directed in the order and included in the care plan as follows:

  (1) that the IRO be given a copy of the amended care plan and the court order;
  (2) that after 6 months the IRO should check certain specified aspects of the care plan; and
  (3) refer the case to CAFCASS if appropriate.

3.4.9 The Family Justice Review

The authors of the Family Justice Review recommended that the courts should not need to scrutinse the full detail of the care plan. In the Government's response to the review it indicated it would legislate to make clear that, although courts will still need to consider the core elements of a care plan, in the majority of cases the detail could and should be left to the local authority. At the time of writing, the proposed legislation is not in existence and therefore the guidance above continues to apply.

A3.1   APPENDIX 1:
REVISION OF THE PUBLIC LAW OUTLINE –
GUIDANCE FROM THE MINISTRY OF JUSTICE

Issue

The President of the Family Division and the Ministry of Justice have been working together (and in conjunction with other family justice agencies) to revise the 'Practice Direction Guide to Case Management in Public Law Proceedings'. This Practice Direction is more commonly known as the Public Law Outline, (the PLO).

•   Our aim is for revisions to the PLO to come into force on 6 April 2010.

•   The purpose of this note is to brief you about these changes and their impact – and for you to share this information with relevant colleagues in your organisation.

Background

The Review of the Child Care Proceedings System in England and Wales was issued jointly by the Department for Constitutional Affairs (now Ministry of Justice), the Department for Education and Skills (now Department for Children Schools and Families) and the Welsh Assembly Government, in May 2006.

The Care Review made a number of recommendations to improve the system for children and families subject to care proceedings. It encouraged early intervention to find resolutions before cases reach court, and identified ways to improve the quality of local authority applications. It also recognised there were benefits in simplifying the court process and improving case management procedures. The PLO was a key reform arising from the Care Review.

The Public Law Outline – 1 April 2008

The PLO was issued jointly by the President of the Family Division and the Ministry of Justice, on 1 April 2008, and applies to all care and supervision proceedings. As far as practicable, it is to be applied to all other family public law proceedings.

The PLO introduced a simpler, more streamlined process designed to minimise unnecessary delay, with greater emphasis on case management and advocacy preparation. Importantly, the timetable in each case would be focused around the needs of the individual child involved. It shifted the balance from the emphasis on a specific target time for completion of cases, to a more flexible requirement for cases to proceed at a speed appropriate to meet the needs of the individual child, known as 'Timetable for the Child'.

Reasons for change

A commitment was made to revisit the PLO, a year after it had been in operation. This was intended not as a wholesale revision or dilution of the PLO principles, but rather a fine-tuning exercise to make necessary changes and improvements to address any specific areas of operational concern.

We commissioned some research to help our understanding of how the PLO was operating. The report, 'An early process evaluation of the Public Law Outline in family Courts' (Brophy et al, July 2009), showed that overall, when implemented appropriately to the needs of the case, the PLO provides a clear structure for care and supervision cases. However, it also found that there was inconsistency in compliance with the PLO requirements, and that the PLO paperwork was seen as unwieldy and in need of streamlining. The research was used to help inform the key areas to be addressed when revising the PLO.

Work to revise the PLO has been led by the judiciary, and the key areas of focus were agreed following input from an inter-agency group comprising: the Ministry of Justice, Association of Directors for Children's Services, Cafcass, CAFCASS CYMRU, and the Welsh Assembly Government. In addition, an inter-agency Care Proceedings Implementation Steering Group (ISG) was tasked with reviewing the current PLO documentary requirements and recommending improvements.

What is not changing

The overall framework of the original PLO has not been affected by the changes. There are still the same four stages. The same timescales also apply to the each stage as before.

PLO stages 1–4, timescales and hearings

1. **Issue (on day 1 and by day 3)** – to ensure compliance with the pre-proceedings checklist and give initial case management directions and **First Appointment (by day 6)** – to allocate the case to the appropriate tier of court and give initial case management directions.

2. **Advocates' Meeting (no later than 2 days before the Case Management Conference)** – to prepare the draft Case Management

Order and the **CMC (no later than day 45)** – to identify issues that need resolving, confirm timetable for the child and give full case management directions.

3.   **Advocates' Meeting (between 2 & 7 days before the Issues Resolution Hearing)** – to prepare or update the draft Case Management Order and the **IRH (between 16 & 25 weeks)** – to resolve and narrow issues that need resolving and identify any remaining issues.

4.   Hearing set in accordance with the Timetable for the Child – **to determine any remaining issues**.

Each of the hearings should still take place within the same timescales as above, and in accordance with the **Timetable for the Child** – on which there is now a greater emphasis.

Applications for Emergency Protection Orders

EPOs will continue to be outside the scope of the PLO. The Practice Direction explicitly states that consideration should be given to applying the PLO to all public law proceedings and it will therefore be a decision to be taken by the court about how and when it is appropriate for the PLO to apply when an application commences by way of an EPO.

Key changes and benefits

It was agreed, that revision of the PLO should be focused on three key areas:

- reducing the burden of documentary requirements at issue

- clarifying the 'Timetable for the Child' principle

- improving the PLO forms

The revised PLO will streamline the documentary requirements on issue. It also provides further guidance on the principle relating to the Timetable for the Child, and how this needs to work with the overall framework of the PLO and the timescales of the various stages within it. In addition, the overly cumbersome original PLO forms have also been streamlined and simplified.

Pre-proceedings checklist

Some important changes have been made to the Pre-proceedings stage of the PLO – this makes a distinction between the checklist documents required at Issue, and other documents to be disclosed by the First Appointment – or as directed by the court.

This change is in response to the feedback received that the original documentary requirements were considered to be overly burdensome and have been streamlined as a result. Such a large volume of documentation was also not considered to be essential for the courts to have at the issue stage.

New application form C110

To inform the development of the new application form for care and supervision orders, we carried out a targeted two week consultation on the draft version, during January 2010. There was a high level of interest in the C110 consultation, generating 51 responses. Overall, the comments were very positive and welcomed the introduction of a bespoke application form.

The new form C110 contains an 'Annex' with a list of the 6 documents that need to be filed with the application at the time of issue. This requirement is in accordance with the revised PLO:

- **Social Work Chronology**

- **Initial Social Work Statement**

- **Initial and Core Assessments**

- **Letters before Proceedings**

- **Schedule of Proposed Findings**

- **Care Plan**

By introducing the Form C110, there will no longer be a requirement to use the existing prescribed application forms C1 and C13 to apply for a care or supervision order. It will also not be necessary to use a series of forms recommended for use under the PLO Practice Direction – which results in an overall reduction in forms.

Note: The C1 form will continue to exist, but will no longer be used for care and supervision applications and therefore some minor changes have been made to the heading of the C1 form to make this clear. Some consequential rule amendments are being made to cater for these minor changes to the C1 form.

Streamlining documentation

A series of forms were introduced with the PLO. Currently, the forms PLO1, 2 and 3 are annexed to the PLO. The revised PLO will not annex any forms. The changes are:

- **PLO1 Pre-proceedings checklist** – this form will be obsolete as the relevant information has been incorporated into the new C110 application form.

- **PLO2 Local Authority Case Summary** – the current form will be made obsolete. A Local Authority Case Summary will still be required, although no longer on a particular form. The information needed will be specified in the revised PLO.

- **PLO3 Draft Case Management Order** – this form will become obsolete, and the content for this order is set out in the revised PLO.

- **PLO4 Allocation Record and Timetable for the Child(ren)** – this form will be obsolete as the relevant information at issue stage, is incorporated into the C110.

- **PLO5 Standard Directions Form on Issue** – this form will become obsolete, and the content for these directions is set out in the revised PLO.

- **PLO6 Standard Directions Forms at First Appointment** – this form will become obsolete, and the content for these directions is set out in the revised PLO.

The changes mean that the documentary requirements have been reduced substantially and that overall the new forms are more appropriately tailored for use with the requirements of the revised PLO and more flexible and user-friendly.

These are

- **Form C110** – a new application form for care and supervision orders

- No longer a need to use the prescribed forms **C1 and C13**

- Also no longer a need to use the original PLO forms **PLO1, PLO2, PLO3, PLO4, PLO5 and PLO6**.

- The revised PLO will set out the information that should be included in the:

  - Standard Directions on Issue
  - Standard Directions at First Appointment
  - Case Management Order

Accessing the new forms

Prior to April 2010 – the new form C110 and the amended form C1 will be available on the HMCS website at: http://www.hmcourts-service.gov. uk/cms/index.htm

Courts will need to direct court users to the HMCS forms website for the new forms.

Old forms

From the 6 April 2010 – the existing C1, C13, PLO1, PLO2 PLO3, PLO4, PLO5 and PLO6 – will become obsolete. Courts need to ensure that they no longer accept these forms.

Rules

When the PLO was issued in April 2008, it was as a free-standing Practice Direction and is not supported by court rules. Therefore, revision of the PLO would not ordinarily require any amendment to the rules. However, this opportunity to revise the PLO is also being used to introduce a new application form to align with the PLO requirements.

The rule amendments make provision for the use of a new application form for care and supervision orders, Form C110. In addition, the rules will provide that only those of the documents which are specified in the 'Annex' to the Form C110 as are available should be filed at issue. The aim is to ensure that proceedings aimed at protecting children are not delayed by reason of a missing document. The new application form supports the revision to the PLO – for example, by referring to the documents set out in the Annex to the form C110 – and when the court should give directions relating to any missing Annex documents.

In addition, there will be a new rule, which makes express reference to the court setting the timetable for the proceedings for a care or a supervision order in accordance with the Timetable for the Child defined in the rule. The revisions to the PLO support this rule by giving greater emphasis to the Timetable for the Child. The key feature of the Timetable for the Child, is that it is a timetable which takes into account dates of the significant steps in the life of the child who is the subject of the proceedings and is appropriate for that child

Transitional arrangements

The changes to the PLO will not apply retrospectively. The revisions to the PLO will apply to applications issued from 6 April 2010. However, the court may direct in any individual case that the revised PLO will apply in whole or in part.

Training

During March 2010 there will be a series of regional conferences across the country, which are about reducing delay in care proceedings. These events will cover the new system wide target for care cases, and also cover the changes to the PLO. These are inter-agency events, open to all those involved in the care proceedings system. The details appear on the Ministry of Justice website for those wishing to attend:

http://www.justice.gov.uk/latest-updates/announcement260210b.htm

Also during March, as the revision of the PLO is being finalised, we are sharing information and briefing about the changes – ahead of them coming into force.

Conclusion

Our aim is for the revised PLO Practice Direction, new prescribed application Form C110, revised application Form C1, and the necessary rule amendments, all to come into force on 6 April 2010.

Publication

Prior to coming into force, the revised PLO Practice Direction will be issued electronically, on the HMCS website at: http://www.hmcourts-service.gov.uk/cms/479.htm

The changes mean:

- This is NOT a wholesale revision of the PLO

- Overall, the framework of the PLO is not changing

- The principles of the PLO remain intact

- Processes have been streamlined and simplified

There is no change to:

- Our commitment to avoid unnecessary delay

- The four stages of the PLO

- The Hearing types of the PLO

- Emphasis on robust case management

- Enhanced advocacy preparation

- Use of case management tools

- Focus on individual needs of the Child – the 'Timetable for the Child'

Contacts

The relevant contacts for this work in Family Law and Justice Division, Ministry of Justice:

Sian Simpkins
Tel: Tel: 0203 330 4122
Sian.Simpkins@justice.gsi.gov.uk

Surinder Sawali
Tel: 0203 330 3142
Surinder.Sawali@justice.gsi.gov.uk

A3.2 APPENDIX 2:
PRACTICE DIRECTION 12A
PUBLIC LAW PROCEEDINGS GUIDE TO CASE
MANAGEMENT: APRIL 2010

This Practice Direction supplements FPR Part 12

Scope

1.1 This Practice Direction applies to care and supervision proceedings. In so far as practicable, it is to be applied to all other Public Law Proceedings.

1.2 This Practice Direction replaces Practice Direction Guide to Case Management in Public Law Proceedings dated April 2008.

1.3 This Practice Direction will come into effect on 6 April 2010. The new form of application for a care or supervision order (Form C110) only applies to proceedings commenced on or after 6 April 2010. Subject to this it is intended that this Practice Direction should apply in so far as practicable to applications made and not disposed of before 6 April 2010. In relation to these applications –

(1) the Practice Direction Guide to Case Management in Public Law Proceedings dated April 2008 applies where it is not practicable to apply this Practice Direction; and

(2) the court may give directions relating to the application of this Practice Direction or the April 2008 Practice Direction. This is subject to the overriding objective below and to the proviso that

such a direction will neither cause further delay nor involve repetition of steps already taken or decisions already made in the case.

1.4 This Practice Direction is to be read with the rules and is subject to them.

1.5 A Glossary of terms is at paragraph 26.

The overriding objective

2.1 This Practice Direction has the overriding objective of enabling the court to deal with cases justly, having regard to the welfare issues involved. Dealing with a case justly includes, so far as is practicable –

    (1) ensuring that it is dealt with expeditiously and fairly;

    (2) dealing with the case in ways which are proportionate to the nature, importance and complexity of the issues;

    (3) ensuring that the parties are on an equal footing;

    (4) saving expense; and

    (5) allotting to it an appropriate share of the court's resources, while taking into account the need to allot resources to other cases.

Application by the court of the overriding objective

2.2 The court must seek to give effect to the overriding objective when it –

    (1) exercises the case management powers referred to in this Practice Direction; or

    (2) interprets any provision of this Practice Direction.

Duty of the parties

2.3 The parties are required to help the court further the overriding objective.

Court case management

THE MAIN PRINCIPLES

3.1 The main principles underlying court case management and the means of the court furthering the overriding objective in Public Law Proceedings are –

(1) **Timetable for the Child**: each case will have a timetable for the proceedings set by the court in accordance with the Timetable for the Child;

(2) **judicial continuity**: each case will be allocated to one or not more than two case management judges (in the case of magistrates' courts, case managers), who will be responsible for every case management stage in the proceedings through to the Final Hearing and, in relation to the High Court or county court, one of whom may be – and where possible should be – the judge who will conduct the Final Hearing;

(3) **main case management tools**: each case will be managed by the court by using the appropriate main case management tools;

(4) **active case management**: each case will be actively case managed by the court with a view at all times to furthering the overriding objective;

(5) **consistency**: each case will, so far as compatible with the overriding objective, be managed in a consistent way and using the standardised steps provided for in this Direction.

THE MAIN CASE MANAGEMENT TOOLS

The Timetable for the Child

3.2 The "Timetable for the Child" is defined by the rules as the timetable set by the court in accordance with its duties under section 1 and 32 of the 1989 Act and shall –

(1) take into account dates of the significant steps in the life of the child who is the subject of the proceedings; and

(2) be appropriate for that child. The court will set the timetable for the proceedings in accordance with the Timetable for the Child and review this Timetable regularly. Where adjustments are made to the Timetable for the Child, the timetable for the proceedings will have to be reviewed. The Timetable for the Child is to be considered at every stage of the proceedings and whenever the court is asked to make directions whether at a hearing or otherwise.

3.3 The steps in the child's life which are to be taken into account by the court when setting the Timetable for the Child include not only legal steps but also social, care, health and education steps.

3.4 Examples of the dates the court will record and take into account when setting the Timetable for the Child are the dates of –

(1) any formal review by the Local Authority of the case of a looked after child (within the meaning of section 22(1) of the 1989 Act);

(2)   the child taking up a place at a new school;
(3)   any review by the Local Authority of any statement of the child's special educational needs;
(4)   any assessment by a paediatrician or other specialist;
(5)   the outcome of any review of Local Authority plans for the child, for example, any plans for permanence through adoption, Special Guardianship or placement with parents or relatives;
(6)   any change or proposed change of the child's placement.

3.5   Due regard should be paid to the Timetable for the Child to ensure that the court remains child-focused throughout the progress of Public Law Proceedings and that any procedural steps proposed under the Public Law Outline are considered in the context of significant events in the child's life.

3.6   The applicant is required to provide the information needed about the significant steps in the child's life in the Application Form and to update this information regularly taking into account information received from others involved in the child's life such as other parties, members of the child's family, the person who is caring for the child, the children's guardian and the child's key social worker.

3.7   Before setting the timetable for the proceedings the factors which the court will consider will include the need to give effect to the overriding objective and the timescales in the Public Law Outline by which the steps in the Outline are to be taken. Where possible, the timetable for the proceedings should be in line with those timescales. However, there will be cases where the significant steps in the child's life demand that the steps in the proceedings be taken at times which are outside the timescales set out in the Outline. In those cases the timetable for the proceedings may not adhere to one or more of the timescales set out in the Outline.

3.8   Where more than one child is the subject of the proceedings, the court should consider and may set a Timetable for the Child for each child. The children may not all have the same Timetable, and the court will consider the appropriate progress of the proceedings in relation to each child.

3.9   Where there are parallel care proceedings and criminal proceedings against a person connected with the child for a serious offence against the child, linked directions hearings should where practicable take place as the case progresses. The timing of the proceedings in a linked care and criminal case should appear in the Timetable for the Child.

Case Management Documentation

3.10 Case Management Documentation includes the –

> (1) Application Form and Annex Documents;
> (2) Case Analysis and Recommendations provided by Cafcass or CAFCASS CYMRU;
> (3) Local Authority Case Summary;
> (4) Other Parties' Case Summaries.

3.11 The court will encourage the use of the Case Management Documentation which is not prescribed by the rules.

The Case Management Record

3.12 The court's filing system for the case will be known as the Case Management Record and will include the following main documents –

> (1) the Case Management Documentation;
> (2) Standard Directions on Issue and on First Appointment;
> (3) Case Management Orders approved by the court.

3.13 Parties or their legal representatives will be expected to retain their own record containing copies of the documents on the court's Case Management Record.

The First Appointment

3.14 The purpose of the First Appointment is to confirm allocation of the case and give initial case management directions.

The Case Management Order

3.15 The Case Management Order is an order which will be made by the court at the conclusion of the Case Management Conference, the Issues Resolution Hearing and any other case management hearing. It is designed to achieve active case management as defined in paragraph 3.20 below. The parties are required to prepare and submit to the court a draft of this order in accordance with paragraphs 5.8 to 5.10 below. The order will include such of the provisions referred to in the Glossary at paragraph 26(12) as are appropriate to the proceedings.

Advocates' meeting/discussion

3.16 The court will consider directing advocates to have discussions before the Case Management Conference and the Issues Resolution Hearing. Advocates may well find that the best way to have these discussions is to meet. Such discussion is intended to facilitate agreement and to narrow the issues for the court to consider. Advocates and litigants in person may take part in the Advocates' Meeting or discussions.

The Case Management Conference

3.17 In each case there will be a Case Management Conference to enable the case management judge or case manager, with the co-operation of the parties, actively to manage the case and, at the earliest practicable opportunity to –

(1) identify the relevant and key issues; and
(2) give full case management directions including confirming the Timetable for the Child.

The Issues Resolution Hearing

3.18 In each case there will be an Issues Resolution Hearing before the Final Hearing to –

(1) identify any remaining key issues; and
(2) as far as possible, resolve or narrow those issues.

ACTIVE CASE MANAGEMENT

3.19 The court must further the overriding objective by actively managing cases.

3.20 Active case management includes –

(1) identifying the Timetable for the Child;
(2) identifying the appropriate court to conduct the proceedings and transferring the proceedings as early as possible to that court;
(3) encouraging the parties to co-operate with each other in the conduct of the proceedings;
(4) retaining the Case Management Record;
(5) identifying all facts and matters that are in issue at the earliest stage in the proceedings and at each hearing;
(6) deciding promptly which issues need full investigation and hearing and which do not and whether a fact finding hearing is required;
(7) deciding the order in which issues are to be resolved;
(8) identifying at an early stage who should be a party to the proceedings;
(9) considering whether the likely benefits of taking a particular step justify any delay which will result and the cost of taking it;

(10) directing discussion between advocates and litigants in person before the Case Management Conference and Issues Resolution Hearing;

(11) requiring the use of the Case Management Order and directing advocates and litigants in person to prepare or adjust the draft of this Order where appropriate;

(12) standardising, simplifying and regulating –

    (a) the use of Case Management Documentation and forms;
    (b) the court's orders and directions;

(13) controlling –

    (a) the use and cost of experts;
    (b) the nature and extent of the documents which are to be disclosed to the parties and presented to the court;
    (c) whether and, if so, in what manner the documents disclosed are to be presented to the court;
    (d) the progress of the case;

(14) where it is demonstrated to be in the interests of the child, encouraging the parties to use an alternative dispute resolution procedure if the court considers such a procedure to be appropriate and facilitating the use of such procedure;

(15) helping the parties to reach agreement in relation to the whole or part of the case;

(16) fixing the dates for all appointments and hearings;

(17) dealing with as many aspects of the case as it can on the same occasion;

(18) where possible dealing with additional issues which may arise from time to time in the case without requiring the parties to attend at court;

(19) making use of technology; and

(20) giving directions to ensure that the case proceeds quickly and efficiently.

The Expectations

4.1 The expectations are that proceedings should be –

(1) conducted using the Case Management Tools and Case Management Documentation referred to in this Practice Direction in accordance with the Public Law Outline;

(2) finally determined within the timetable fixed by the court in accordance with the Timetable for the Child – the timescales in the Public Law Outline being adhered to and being taken as the maximum permissible time for the taking of the step referred to in the Outline unless the Timetable for the Child demands otherwise.

4.2 However, there may be cases where the court considers that the child's welfare requires a different approach from the one contained in the Public Law Outline. In those cases, the court will –

(1) determine the appropriate case management directions and timetable; and

(2) record on the face of the order the reasons for departing from the approach in the Public Law Outline.

How the parties should help court case management

MAIN METHODS OF HELPING

Good case preparation

5.1 The applicant should prepare the case before proceedings are issued. In care and supervision proceedings the Local Authority should use the Pre-proceedings checklist.

The Timetable for the Child

5.2 The applicant must state in the Application Form all information concerning significant steps in the child's life that are likely to take place during the proceedings. The applicant is to be responsible for updating this information regularly and giving it to the court. The applicant will need to obtain information about these significant steps and any variations and additions to them from others involved in the child's life such as other parties, members of the child's family, the person who is caring for the child, the children's guardian and the child's key social worker. When the other persons involved in the child's life become aware of a significant step in the child's life or a variation of an existing one, that information should be given to the applicant as soon as possible.

5.3 The information about the significant steps in the child's life will enable the court to set the Timetable for the Child and to review that Timetable in the light of new information. The Timetable for the Child will be included or referred to in the draft of a Case Management Order, the Case Management Order, Standard Directions on Issue and on First Appointment and the directions given at the Case Management Conference and Issues Resolution Hearing.

Case Management Documentation

5.4 The parties must use the Case Management Documentation.

Co-operation

5.5 The parties and their representatives should co-operate with the court in case management, including the fixing of timetables to avoid unacceptable delay, and in the crystallisation and resolution of the issues on which the case turns.

Directions

5.6 The parties will –

(1) monitor compliance with the court's directions; and
(2) tell the court or court officer about any failure to comply with a direction of the court or any other delay in the proceedings.

The Case Management Record

5.7 The parties are expected to retain a record containing copies of the documents on the court's Case Management Record.

Drafting the Case Management Order

5.8 Parties should start to consider the content of the draft of the Case Management Order at the earliest opportunity either before or in the course of completing applications to the court or the response to the application. They should in any event consider the drafting of a Case Management Order after the First Appointment.

5.9 Only one draft of the Case Management Order should be filed with the court for each of the Case Management Conference and the Issues Resolution Hearing. It is the responsibility of the advocate for the applicant, which in care and supervision proceedings will ordinarily be the Local Authority, to prepare those drafts and be responsible for obtaining comments from the advocates and the parties.

5.10 There should be ongoing consideration of the Case Management Orders throughout the proceedings. The Case Management Orders should serve as an *aide memoire* to everyone involved in the proceedings of –

(1) the Timetable for the Child;
(2) the case management decisions;
(3) the identified issues.

5.11 In paragraphs 5.4, 5.6 to 5.9 "parties" includes parties' legal representatives.

Findings of fact hearings

6   In a case where the court decides that a fact finding hearing is necessary, the starting point is that the proceedings leading to that hearing are to be managed in accordance with the case management steps in this Practice Direction.

Ethnicity, language, religion and culture

7   At each case management stage of the proceedings, particularly at the First Appointment and Case Management Conference, the court will consider giving directions regarding the obtaining of evidence about the ethnicity, language, religion and culture of the child and other significant persons involved in the proceedings. The court will subsequently consider the implications of this evidence for the child in the context of the issues in the case.

Adults who may be protected parties

8.1   The applicant must give details in the Application Form of any referral to or assessment by the local authority's Adult Learning Disability team (or its equivalent). The Local Authority should tell the court about other referrals or assessments if known such as a referral to Community Mental Health.

8.2   The court will investigate as soon as possible any issue as to whether an adult party or intended party to the proceedings lacks capacity (within the meaning of the Mental Capacity Act 2005) to conduct the proceedings. A representative (a litigation friend, next friend or guardian ad litem) is needed to conduct the proceedings on behalf of an adult who lacks capacity to do so ("a protected party"). The expectation of the Official Solicitor is that the Official Solicitor will only be invited to act for a protected party as guardian ad litem or litigation friend if there is no other person suitable and willing to act.

8.3   Any issue as to the capacity of an adult to conduct the proceedings must be determined before the court gives any directions relevant to that adult's role within the proceedings.

8.4   Where the adult is a protected party, that party's representative should be involved in any instruction of an expert, including the instruction of an expert to assess whether the adult, although a protected party, is competent to give evidence. The instruction of an expert is a significant step in the proceedings. The representative will wish to consider (and ask the expert to consider), if the protected party is competent to give evidence, their best interests in this regard. The representative may wish to seek advice about 'special measures'.

The representative may put forward an argument on behalf of the protected party that the protected party should not give evidence.

8.5 If at any time during the proceedings, there is reason to believe that a party may lack capacity to conduct the proceedings, then the court must be notified and directions sought to ensure that this issue is investigated without delay.

Child likely to lack capacity to conduct the proceedings when aged 18

9 Where it appears that a child is –

(1) a party to the proceedings and not the subject of them;
(2) nearing age 18; and
(3) considered likely to lack capacity to conduct the proceedings when 18, the court will consider giving directions relating to the investigation of a child's capacity in this respect.

Outline of the process and how to use the Main Case Management Tools

10.1 The Public Law Outline set out in the Table below contains an outline of –

(1) the order of the different stages of the process;
(2) the purposes of the main case management hearings and matters to be considered at them;
(3) the latest timescales within which the main stages of the process should take place.

10.2 In the Public Law Outline –

(1) "CMC" means the Case Management Conference;
(2) "FA" means the First Appointment;
(3) "IRH" means the Issues Resolution Hearing;
(4) "LA" means the Local Authority which is applying for a care or supervision order;
(5) "OS" means the Official Solicitor.

Public Law Outline

PRE-PROCEEDINGS	
PRE-PROCEEDINGS CHECKLIST	
Annex Documents (the documents specified in the Annex to the Application Form to be attached to that form where available):	**Other Checklist Documents which already exist on LA's files which are to be disclosed in the event of proceedings normally before the day of the FA:**
– Social Work Chronology	– Previous court orders & judgments/reasons
– Initial Social Work Statement	– Any relevant assessment materials
– Initial and Core Assessments	– Section 7 & 37 reports
– Letters Before Proceedings – Schedule of Proposed Findings	– Relatives & friends materials (e.g., a genogram)
– Care Plan	– Other relevant reports & records
	– Single, joint or inter-agency materials (e.g., health & education/Home Office & Immigration documents)
	– Records of discussions with the family
	– Key LA minutes & records for the child (including Strategy Discussion Record)
	– Pre-existing care plans (e.g., child in need plan, looked after child plan & child protection plan)

STAGE 1 – ISSUE AND THE FIRST APPOINTMENT	
ISSUE	**FIRST APPOINTMENT**
On DAY 1 and by DAY 3	**By DAY 6**
Objectives: To ensure compliance with pre-proceedings checklist; to allocate proceedings; to obtain the information necessary for initial case management at the FA	**Objectives: To confirm allocation; to give initial case management directions**

On Day 1:
– The LA files the Application Form and Annex Documents where available
– Court officer issues application
 	
– Court nominates case manager(s)
– Court gives Standard Directions on Issue including:
 	
   – Pre-proceedings checklist compliance including preparation and service of any missing Annex Documents
   – Allocate and/or transfer
 	
   – Appoint children's guardian
 	
   – Appoint solicitor for the child
 	
   – Case Analysis for FA
 	
   – Appoint a guardian ad litem or litigation friend for a protected party or any non subject child who is a party, including the OS where appropriate
   – List FA by Day 6
	– LA normally serves Other Checklist Documents on the parties
	– Parties notify LA & court of need for a contested hearing
	– Court makes arrangements for a contested hearing
	– Initial case management by court including:
	
	   – Confirm Timetable for the Child
	   – Confirm allocation or transfer
	   – Identify additional parties & representation (including allocation of children's guardian)
	
	   – Identify "Early Final Hearing" cases
	
	   – Scrutinise Care Plan
	
	– Court gives Standard Directions on FA including:
	
	   – Case Analysis and Recommendations for Stages 2 & 3
	   – Preparation and service of any missing Annex Documents
	   – What Other Checklist Documents are to be filed

– Make arrangements for contested hearing (if necessary) **By Day 3** – Cafcass/CAFCASS CYMRU expected to allocate case to children's guardian – LA serves the Application Form and Annex Documents, on parties	– LA Case Summary – Other Parties' Case Summaries – Parties' initial witness statements – For the Advocates' Meeting – List CMC or (if appropriate) an Early Final Hearing – Upon transfer

STAGE 2 – CASE MANAGEMENT CONFERENCE	
ADVOCATES' MEETING	**CMC**
No later than 2 days before CMC	**No later than day 45**
Objectives: To prepare the Draft Case Management Order; to identify experts and draft questions for them	**Objectives: To identify issue(s); to give full case management directions**
– Consider information on the Application Form, all Other Parties' Case Summaries and Case Analysis and Recommendations – Identify proposed experts and draft questions in accordance with Experts Practice Direction – Draft Case Management Order – Notify court of need for a contested hearing – File draft of the Case Management Order with the case manager/case management judge by 11am one working day before the CMC	– Detailed case management by the court – Scrutinise compliance with directions – Review and confirm Timetable for the Child – Identify key issue(s) – Confirm allocation or transfer – Consider case management directions in the draft of the Case Management Order – Scrutinise Care Plan – Check compliance with Experts Practice Direction – Court issues Case Management Order

	– Court lists IRH and, where necessary, a warned period for Final Hearing

STAGE 3 – ISSUES RESOLUTION HEARING	
ADVOCATES' MEETING	**IRH**
Between 2 and 7 days before the IRH	**Between 16 & 25 weeks**
Objective: To prepare or update the draft Case Management Order	**Objectives: To resolve and narrow issue(s); to identify any remaining key issues**

– Consider all other parties' Case Summaries and Case Analysis and Recommendations
 	
– Draft Case Management Order
 	
– Notify court of need for a contested hearing/time for oral evidence to be given
 	
– File Draft Case Management Order with the case manager/case management judge by 11am one working day before the IRH
	– Identification by the court of the key issue(s) (if any) to be determined
	
	– Final case management by the court:
	
	    – Scrutinise compliance with directions
	
	    – Review and confirm the Timetable for the Child
	
	    – Consider case management directions in the draft of the Case Management Order
	
	    – Scrutinise Care Plan
	
	    – Give directions for Hearing documents:
	
	        – Threshold agreement or facts/issues remaining to be determined
	
	        – Final Evidence & Care Plan
	
	        – Case Analysis and Recommendations
	
	        – Witness templates
	
	        – Skeleton arguments

	– Judicial reading list/reading time/judgment writing time
	– Time estimate
	– Bundles Practice Direction compliance
	– List or confirm Hearing
	– Court issues Case Management Order

STAGE 4	
HEARING	
Hearing set in accordance with the Timetable for the Child	
Objective: To determine remaining issues	
– All file & serve updated Case Management Documentation & bundle – Draft final order(s) in approved form	– Judgment/Reasons – Disclose documents as required after hearing

Starting the proceedings

Pre-proceedings Checklist

11.1 The Pre-proceedings Checklist is to be used by the applicant to help prepare for the start of the proceedings.

11.2 The Pre-proceedings Checklist contains the documents which are specified in the Annex to the Application Form. The rules require those documents which are known as the "Annex Documents" to be filed with the Application Form where available. The Annex Documents are –

(1) Social Work Chronology;
(2) Initial Social Work Statement;
(3) Initial and Core Assessments;
(4) Letters before Proceedings;
(5) Schedule of Proposed Findings; and
(6) Care Plan.

11.3 In addition, the Pre-proceedings Checklist contains examples of documents other than the Annex Documents which will normally be on the Local Authority file at the start of proceedings so that they can be served on parties in accordance with the Public Law Outline. These documents are known as the "Other Checklist Documents" and are not to be filed with the court at the start of the proceedings but are to be disclosed to the parties normally before the day of the First Appointment or in accordance with the court's directions and to be filed with the court only as directed by the court.

Compliance with Pre-proceedings Checklist

11.4 It is recognised that in some cases the circumstances are such that the safety and welfare of the child may be jeopardised if the start of proceedings is delayed until all of the documents appropriate to the case and referred to in the Pre-proceedings Checklist are available. The safety and welfare of the child should never be put in jeopardy because of lack of documentation. (Nothing in this Practice Direction affects an application for an emergency protection order under section 44 of the 1989 Act).

11.5 The court recognises that the preparation may need to be varied to suit the circumstances of the case. In cases where any of the Annex Documents required to be attached to the Application Form are not available at the time of issue of the application, the court will consider making directions on issue about when any missing documentation is to be filed. The expectation is that there will be a good reason why one or more of the documents are not available. Further directions relating to any missing documentation are likely to be made at the First Appointment. The court also recognises that some documents on the Pre-proceedings Checklist may not exist and may never exist, for example, the Section 37 report, and that in urgent proceedings no Letter Before Proceedings may have been sent.

What the court will do at the issue of proceedings

Objectives

12.1 The objectives at this stage are for the court –

(1)   to identify the Timetable for the Child;
(2)   in care and supervision proceedings, to ensure compliance with the Pre-proceedings Checklist;
(3)   to allocate proceedings;
(4)   to obtain the information necessary to enable initial case management at the First Appointment.

12.2 The steps which the court will take once proceedings have been issued include those set out in paragraphs 12.3 to 12.5 below.

Allocation

12.3 By reference to the Allocation Order, the court will consider allocation of the case and transfer to the appropriate level of court those cases which are obviously suitable for immediate transfer.

Other steps to be taken by the court

Directions

12.4 The court will –

   (1)   consider giving directions –

       (a)   appropriate to the case including Standard Directions On Issue;

       (b)   in care and supervision proceedings, relating to the preparation, filing and service of any missing Annex Documents and what Other Checklist Documents are to be filed and by when;

       (c)   relating to the representation of any protected party or any child who is a party to, but is not the subject of, the proceedings by a guardian ad litem or litigation friend, including the Official Solicitor where appropriate;

   (2)   appoint a children's guardian in specified proceedings (in relation to care and supervision proceedings the court will expect that Cafcass or CAFCASS CYMRU will have received notice from the Local Authority that proceedings were going to be started);

   (3)   appoint a solicitor for the child under section 41(3) of the 1989 Act where appropriate;

   (4)   request the children's guardian or if appropriate another officer of the service or Welsh family proceedings officer to prepare a Case Analysis and Recommendations for the First Appointment;

   (5)   make arrangements for a contested hearing, if necessary.

(A suggested form for the drafting of Standard Directions on Issue is Form PLO 8 which is available from HMCS)

Setting a date for the First Appointment

12.5 The court will record the Timetable for the Child and set a date for the First Appointment normally no later than 6 days from the date of issue of the proceedings and in any event in line with the Timetable for the Child.

Case managers in the magistrates' courts

12.6 In the magistrates' courts, the justices' clerk may nominate one but not more than two case managers.

The First Appointment

Objectives

13.1 The First Appointment is the first hearing in the proceedings. The main objectives of the First Appointment are to –

   (1)   confirm allocation; and
   (2)   give initial case management directions having regard to the Public Law Outline.

13.2 The steps which the court will take at the First Appointment include those set out in paragraphs 13.3 to 13.6 below.

Steps to be taken by the court

13.3 The court will –

   (1)   confirm the Timetable for the Child;
   (2)   make arrangements for any contested interim hearing such as an application for an interim care order;
   (3)   confirm in writing the allocation of the case or, if appropriate, transfer the case;
   (4)   request the children's guardian or if appropriate another officer of the service or Welsh family proceedings officer to prepare a Case Analysis and Recommendations for the Case Management Conference or Issues Resolution Hearing;
   (5)   scrutinise the Care Plan;
   (6)   consider giving directions relating to –

      (a)   those matters in the Public Law Outline which remain to be considered including preparation, filing and service of any missing Annex Documents and what Other Checklist documents are to be filed and by when;
      (b)   the joining of a person who would not otherwise be a respondent under the rules as a party to the proceedings;
      (c)   where any person to be joined as a party may be a protected party, an investigation of that person's capacity to conduct the proceedings and the representation of that person by a guardian ad litem or litigation friend, including the Official Solicitor where appropriate;
      (d)   the identification of family and friends as proposed carers and any overseas, immigration, jurisdiction and paternity issues;
      (e)   any other documents to be filed with the court;

(f) evidence to be obtained as to whether a parent who is a protected party is competent to make a statement.

(A suggested form for the drafting of Standard Directions on First Appointment is Form PLO 9 which is available from HMCS)

Early Final Hearing

13.4 Cases which are suitable for an early Final Hearing are those cases where all the evidence necessary to determine issues of fact and welfare is immediately or shortly available to be filed. Those cases are likely to include cases where the child has no parents, guardians, relatives who want to care for the child, or other carers. The court will –

(1) identify at the First Appointment whether the case is one which is suitable for an early Final Hearing; and
(2) set a date for that Final Hearing.

Setting a date for the Case Management Conference.

13.5 The court will set a date for the Case Management Conference normally no later than 45 days from the date of issue of the proceedings and in any event in line with the Timetable for the Child.

Advocates' Meeting/discussion and the drafting of the Case Management Order

13.6 The court will consider directing a discussion between the parties' advocates and any litigant in person and the preparation of a draft of the Case Management Order as outlined below.

Experts

13.7 A party who wishes to instruct an expert should comply with the Experts Practice Direction. Where the parties are agreed on any matter relating to experts or expert evidence, the draft agreement must be submitted for the court's approval as early as possible in the proceedings.

Advocates' Meeting/discussion and the drafting of the Case Management Order

14.1 The main objective of the Advocates' Meeting or discussion is to prepare a draft of the Case Management Order for approval by the court.

14.2 Where there is a litigant in person the court will consider the most effective way in which that person can be involved in the advocates discussions and give directions as appropriate including directions relating to the part to be played by any McKenzie Friend.

14.3 Timing of the discussions is of the utmost importance. Discussions of matters "outside the court room door", which could have taken place at an earlier time, are to be avoided. Discussions are to take place no later than 2 days before the Case Management Conference or the Issues Resolution Hearing whichever is appropriate. The discussions may take place earlier than 2 days before those hearings, for example, up to 7 days before them.

14.4 Following discussion the advocates should prepare or adjust the draft of the Case Management Order. In practice the intention is that the advocate for the applicant, which in care and supervision proceedings will ordinarily be the Local Authority, should take the lead in preparing and adjusting the draft of the Case Management Order following discussion with the other advocates. The aim is for the advocates to agree a draft of the Case Management Order which is to be submitted for the approval of the court.

14.5 Where it is not possible for the advocates to agree the terms of the draft of the Case Management Order, the advocates should specify on the draft, or on a separate document if more practicable –

(1) those provisions on which they agree; and
(2) those provisions on which they disagree.

14.6 Unless the court directs otherwise, the draft of the Case Management Order must be filed with the court no later than 11am on the day before the Case Management Conference or the Issues Resolution Hearing whichever may be appropriate.

14.7 At the Advocates' Meeting or discussion before the Case Management Conference, the advocates should also try to agree the questions to be put to any proposed expert (whether jointly instructed or not) if not previously agreed. Under the Experts Practice Direction the questions on which the proposed expert is to give an opinion are a crucial component of the expert directions which the court is required to consider at the Case Management Conference.

Case Management Conference

Objectives

15.1 The Case Management Conference is the main hearing at which the court manages the case. The main objectives of the Conference are to –

(1) identify key issues; and
(2) give full case management directions.

15.2 The steps which the court will take at the Case Management Conference include those steps set out in paragraphs 15.3 to 15.5 below.

Steps to be taken by the court

15.3 The court will –

(1) review and confirm the Timetable for the Child;
(2) confirm the allocation or the transfer of the case;
(3) scrutinise the Care Plan;
(4) identify the key issues;
(5) identify the remaining case management issues;
(6) resolve remaining case management issues set out in the draft of the Case Management Order;
(7) identify any special measures such as the need for access for the disabled or provision for vulnerable witnesses;
(8) scrutinise the Case Management Record to check whether directions have been complied with and if not, consider making further directions as appropriate;
(9) where expert evidence is required, check whether the parties have complied with the Experts Practice Direction, in particular the section on preparation for the relevant hearing and consider giving directions as appropriate.

Case Management Order

15.4 The court will issue the approved Case Management Order. Parties or their legal representatives will be expected to submit in electronic form the final approved draft of the Case Management Order on the conclusion of, and the same day as, the Case Management Conference.

Setting a date for the Issues Resolution Hearing/Final Hearing

15.5 The court will set –

(1) a date for the Issues Resolution Hearing normally at any time between 16 and 25 weeks from the date of issue of the proceedings and in any event in line with the Timetable for the Child; and

(2) if necessary, specify a period within which the Final Hearing of the application is to take place unless a date has already been set.

The Issues Resolution Hearing objectives

16.1 The objectives of this hearing are to –

(1) resolve and narrow issues;
(2) identify key remaining issues requiring resolution.

16.2 The Issues Resolution Hearing is likely to be the hearing before the Final Hearing. Final case management directions and other preparations for the Final Hearing will be made at this hearing.

Steps to be taken by the court

16.3 The court will –

(1) identify the key issues (if any) to be determined;
(2) review and confirm the Timetable for the Child;
(3) consider giving case management directions relating to –

(a) any outstanding matter contained in the draft of the Case Management Order;
(b) the preparation and filing of final evidence including the filing of witness templates;
(c) skeleton arguments;
(d) preparation and filing of bundles in accordance with the Bundles Practice Direction;
(e) any agreement relating to the satisfaction of the threshold criteria under section 31 of the 1989 Act or facts and issues remaining to be determined in relation to it or to any welfare question which arises;
(f) time estimates;
(g) the judicial reading list and likely reading time and judgment writing time;

(4) issue the Case Management Order.

16.4 For the avoidance of doubt the purpose of an Issues Resolution Hearing is to –

(1) identify key issues which are not agreed;
(2) examine if those key issues can be agreed; and

(3) where those issues cannot be agreed, examine the most proportionate method of resolving those issues.

16.5 The expectation is that the method of resolving the key issues which cannot be agreed will be at a hearing (ordinarily the Final hearing) where there is an opportunity for the relevant oral evidence to be heard and challenged.

Attendance at the Case Management Conference and the Issues Resolution Hearing

17 An advocate who has conduct of the Final Hearing should ordinarily attend the Case Management Conference and the Issues Resolution Hearing. Where the attendance of this advocate is not possible, then an advocate who is familiar with the issues in the proceedings should attend.

Flexible powers of the court

18.1 Attention is drawn to the flexible powers of the court either following the issue of the application in that court, the transfer of the case to that court or at any other stage in the proceedings.

18.2 The court may give directions without a hearing including setting a date for the Final Hearing or a period within which the Final Hearing will take place. The steps, which the court will ordinarily take at the various stages of the proceedings provided for in the Public Law Outline, may be taken by the court at another stage in the proceedings if the circumstances of the case merit this approach.

18.3 The flexible powers of the court include the ability for the court to cancel or repeat a particular hearing. For example, if the issue on which the case turns can with reasonable practicability be crystallised and resolved by having an early Final Hearing, then in the fulfilment of the overriding objective, such a flexible approach must be taken to secure compliance with section 1(2) of the 1989 Act.

Alternative Dispute Resolution

19.1 The court will encourage the parties to use an alternative dispute resolution procedure and facilitate the use of such a procedure where it is –

(1) readily available;
(2) demonstrated to be in the interests of the child; and
(3) reasonably practicable and safe.

19.2 At any stage in the proceedings, the parties can ask the court for advice about alternative dispute resolution.

19.3 At any stage in the proceedings the court itself will consider whether alternative dispute resolution is appropriate. If so, the court may direct that a hearing or proceedings be adjourned for such specified period as it considers appropriate –

(1) to enable the parties to obtain information and advice about alternative dispute resolution; and

(2) where the parties agree, to enable alternative dispute resolution to take place.

Co-operation

20.1 Throughout the proceedings the parties and their representatives should cooperate wherever reasonably practicable to help towards securing the welfare of the child as the paramount consideration.

20.2 At each court appearance the court will ask the parties and their legal representatives –

(1) what steps they have taken to achieve co-operation and the extent to which they have been successful;

(2) if appropriate the reason why co-operation could not be achieved; and

(3) the steps needed to resolve any issues necessary to achieve co-operation.

Agreed directions

21.1 The parties, their advisers and the children's guardian, are encouraged to try to agree directions for the management of the proceedings.

21.2 To obtain the court's approval the agreed directions must –

(1) set out a Timetable for the Child by reference to calendar dates for the taking of steps for the preparation of the case;

(2) include a date when it is proposed that the next hearing will take place.

Variation of case management timetable

22 It is emphasised that a party or the children's guardian must apply to the court at the earliest opportunity if they wish to vary by extending the dates set by the court for –

(1)   a directions appointment;
(2)   a First Appointment;
(3)   a Case Management Conference;
(4)   an Issues Resolution Hearing;
(5)   the Final Hearing;
(6)   the period within which the Final Hearing of the application is to take place; or
(7)   any Meeting/discussion between advocates or for the filing of the draft of the Case Management Orders.

Who performs the functions of the court

23.1 Where this Practice Direction provides for the court to perform case management functions, then except where any rule, practice direction, any other enactment or the Family Proceedings (Allocation to Judiciary) Directions ([2009] 2 FLR 51) provides otherwise, the functions may be performed –

(1)   in relation to proceedings in the High Court or in a district registry, by any judge or district judge of that Court including a district judge of the principal registry;

(2)   in relation to proceedings in the county court, by any judge or district judge including a district judge of the principal registry when the principal registry is treated as if it were a county court; and

(3)   in relation to proceedings in a magistrates' court by –

   (a)   any family proceedings court constituted in accordance with sections 66 and 67 of the 1980 Act;
   (b)   a single justice; or
   (c)   a justices' clerk.

23.2 The case management functions to be exercised by a justices' clerk may be exercised by an assistant justices' clerk provided that person has been specifically authorised by a justices' clerk to exercise case management functions. Any reference in this Practice Direction to a justices' clerk is to be taken to include an assistant justices' clerk so authorised. The justices' clerk may in particular appoint one but not more than two assistant justices' clerks as case managers for each case.

23.3 In proceedings in a magistrates' court, where a party considers that there are likely to be issues arising at a hearing (including the First Appointment, Case Management Conference and Issues Resolution Hearing) which need to be decided by a family proceedings court, rather than a justices' clerk, then that party should give the court written notice of that need at least 2 days before the hearing.

23.4 Family proceedings courts may consider making arrangements to ensure a court constituted in accordance with s 66 of the 1980 Act is available at the same time as Issues Resolution Hearings are being heard by a justices' clerk. Any delay as a result of the justices' clerk considering for whatever reason that it is inappropriate for a justices' clerk to perform a case management function on a particular matter and the justices' clerk's referring of that matter to the court should then be minimal.

Technology

24 Where the facilities are available to the court and the parties, the court will consider making full use of technology including electronic information exchange and video or telephone conferencing.

Other Practice Directions

25.1 This Practice Direction must be read with the Bundles Practice Direction.

25.2 The Bundles Practice Direction is applied to Public Law Proceedings in the High Court and county court with the following adjustments –

(1) add "except the First Appointment; Case Management Conference, and Issues Resolution Hearing referred to in the Practice Direction Public Law Proceedings Guide to Case Management: April 2010 where there are no contested applications being heard at those hearings" to paragraph 2.2;

(2) the reference to –

    (a) the "Protocol for Judicial Case Management in Public law Children Act Cases [2003] 2 FLR 719" in paragraph 6.1;

    (b) the "Practice Direction: Care Cases: Judicial Continuity and Judicial Case Management" in paragraph 15; and

    (c) "the Public Law Protocol" in paragraph 15, shall be read as if it were a reference to this Practice Direction.

25.3 Paragraph 1.9 of the Practice Direction: Experts in Family Proceedings Relating to Children dated April 2008 should be read as if "Practice Direction: Guide to Case Management in Public law Proceedings, paragraphs 13.7, 14.3 and 25(29)" were a reference to "Practice Direction Public Law Proceedings Guide to Case Management: April 2010, paragraphs 14.7, 15.3 and 26(33)".

Glossary

26 In this Practice Direction –

(1) "the 1989 Act " means the Children Act 1989;
(2) "the 1980 Act" means the Magistrates' Courts Act 1980;
(3) "advocate" means a person exercising a right of audience as a representative of, or on behalf of, a party;
(4) "Allocation Order" means any order made by the Lord Chancellor under Part 1 of Schedule 11 to the 1989 Act;
(5) "alternative dispute resolution" means the methods of resolving a dispute other than through the normal court process;
(6) "Annex Documents" means the documents specified in the Annex to the Application Form;
(7) "Application Form" means Form C110 and Annex Documents;
(8) "assistant justices' clerk" has the meaning assigned to it by section 27(5) of the Courts Act 2003;
(9) "the Bundles Practice Direction" means the Practice Direction Family Proceedings: Court Bundles (Universal Practice to be Applied in all Courts other than Family Proceedings Court) of 27 July 2006;
(10) "Case Analysis and Recommendations" means a written or oral outline of the case from the child's perspective prepared by the children's guardian or other officer of the service or Welsh family proceedings officer at different stages of the proceedings requested by the court, to provide –

  (a) an analysis of the issues that need to be resolved in the case including-

    (i)   any harm or risk of harm;
    (ii) the child's own views;
    (iii) the family context including advice relating to ethnicity, language, religion and culture of the child and other significant persons;
    (iv) the Local Authority work and proposed care plan;
    (v)   advice about the court process including the Timetable for the Child; and
    (vi) identification of work that remains to be done for the child in the short and longer term; and

  (b) recommendations for outcomes, in order to safeguard and promote the best interests of the child in the proceedings;

(11) "Case Management Documentation" includes the documents referred to in paragraph 3.10;
(12) "Case Management Order" means an order made by the court which identifies the Timetable for the Child, any delay in the proceedings and the reason for such delay and the key issues in

the proceedings and includes such of the following provisions as are appropriate to the proceedings –

(a) preliminary information:

  (i) the names and dates of birth of the children who are the subject of the proceedings;

  (ii) the names and legal representatives of the parties, and whether they attended the hearing;

  (iii) any interim orders made in respect of the children and any provisions made for the renewal of those orders;

(b) any recitals that the court considers should be recorded in the order, including those relating to:

  (i) any findings made by the court or agreed between the parties;

  (ii) any other agreements or undertakings made by the parties;

(c) orders made at the hearing by way of case management relating to:

  (i) the joinder of parties;

  (ii) the determination of parentage of the children;

  (iii) the appointment of a guardian ad litem or litigation friend (including the Official Solicitor where appropriate);

  (iv) the transfer of the proceedings to a different court;

  (v) the allocation of the proceedings to a case management judge;

  (vi) the filing and service of threshold criteria documents;

  (vii) the preparation and filing of assessments, including Core Assessments and parenting assessments;

  (viii) in accordance with the Experts' Practice Direction, the preparation and filing of other expert evidence, and experts' meetings;

  (ix) care planning and directions in any application for placement for adoption;

  (x) the filing and service of evidence/further evidence on behalf of the local authority;

  (xi) the filing and service of evidence/further evidence on behalf of the other parties;

  (xii) the filing and service of the Case Analysis and Recommendations;

  (xiii) the disclosure of documents into the proceedings held by third parties, including medical records, police records and Home Office information;

(xiv) the disclosure of documents and information relating to the proceedings to non-parties;

(xv) the listing of further hearings, and case management documentation to be prepared for those hearings;

(xvi) advocates' Meetings;

(xvii) the filing of bundles and other preparatory material for future hearings;

(xviii) technology/special measures;

(xix) media attendance and reporting;

(xx) linked or other proceedings;

(xxi) non-compliance with any court orders;

(xxii) such further or other directions as may be necessary for the purposes of case management;

(xxiii) attendance at court (including child/children's guardian);

(13) "Case Management Record" means the court's filing system for the case which includes the documents referred to at paragraph 3.12;

(14) "Case manager" means the justices' clerk or assistant justices' clerk who manages the case in the magistrates' courts;

(15) "Care Plan" means a "section 31A plan" referred to in section 31A of the 1989 Act;

(16) "Core Assessment" means the assessment undertaken by the Local Authority in accordance with The Framework for the Assessment of Children in Need and their Families (Department of Health et al, 2000);

(17) "court" means the High Court, county court or the magistrates' court;

(18) "court officer" means –

(a) in the High Court or a county court, a member of court staff ; and

(b) in a magistrates' court, the designated officer;

(19) "Experts Practice Direction" means the Practice Direction regarding Experts in Family Proceedings relating to Children;

(20) "genogram" means a family tree, setting out in diagrammatic form the family's background;

(21) "hearing" includes a directions appointment;

(22) "Initial Assessment" means the assessment undertaken by the Local Authority in accordance with The Framework for the Assessment of Children in Need and their Families (Department of Health et al, 2000);

(23) "Initial Social Work Statement" means a statement prepared by the Local Authority strictly limited to the following evidence –

(a) the precipitating incident(s) and background circumstances relevant to the grounds and reasons for making the application including a brief description of any referral and assessment processes that have already occurred;

(b) any facts and matters that are within the social worker's personal knowledge limited to the findings sought by the Local Authority;

(c) any emergency steps and previous court orders that are relevant to the application;

(d) any decisions made by the Local Authority that are relevant to the application;

(e) information relevant to the ethnicity, language, religion, culture, gender and vulnerability of the child and other significant persons in the form of a 'family profile' together with a narrative description and details of the social care and other services that are relevant to the same;

(f) where the Local Authority is applying for an interim order: the Local Authority's initial proposals for the child (which are also to be set out in the Care Plan) including placement, contact with parents and other significant persons and the social care services that are proposed;

(g) the Local Authority's initial proposals for the further assessment of the parties during the proceedings including twin track /concurrent planning (where more than one permanence option for the child is being explored by the Local Authority);

(24) "legal representative" means a –

(a) barrister,

(b) solicitor,

(c) solicitor's employee,

(d) manager of a body recognised under section 9 of the Administration of Justice Act 1985, or

(e) person who, for the purposes of the Legal Services Act 2007, is an authorised person in relation to an activity which constitutes the conduct of litigation (within the meaning of that Act), who has been instructed to act for a party in relation to the proceedings;

(25) "Letter Before Proceedings" means any letter from the Local Authority containing written notification to the parents and others with parental responsibility for the child of the Local Authority's plan to apply to court for a care or supervision order and any related subsequent correspondence confirming the Local Authority's position;

(26) "Local Authority Case Summary" means a document prepared by the Local Authority advocate for all case management hearings including –

(a) a recommended reading list and suggested reading time;

(b)   the key issues in the case;

(c)   any additional information relevant to the Timetable for the Child or for the conduct of the hearing or the proceedings;

(d)   a summary of updating information;

(e)   the issues and directions which the court will need to consider at the hearing in question, including any interim orders sought;

(f)   any steps which have not been taken or directions not complied with, an explanation of the reasons for non–compliance and the effect, if any, on the Timetable for the Child;

(g)   any relevant information relating to ethnicity, cultural or gender issues;

(27)   "justices' clerk" has the meaning assigned to it by section 27(1) of the Courts Act 2003;

(28)   "McKenzie Friend" means any person permitted by the court to sit beside an unrepresented litigant in court to assist the litigant by prompting, taking notes and giving advice to the litigant;

(29)   "Other Checklist Documents" means the documents listed in the Pre-proceedings Checklist which will normally be on the local authority file prior to the start of proceedings but which are not –

(a)   to be filed with the court on issue; or

(b)   Annex Documents.

(30)   "Other Parties' Case Summaries" means summaries by parties other than the Local Authority containing –

(a)   the party's proposals for the long term future of the child (to include placement and contact);

(b)   the party's reply to the Local Authority's Schedule of Proposed Findings;

(c)   any proposal for assessment / expert evidence; and

(d)   the names, addresses and contact details of any family or friends who it is suggested be approached in relation to long term care / contact or respite;

(31)   "Pre-proceedings Checklist" means the Annex Documents and the Other Checklist Documents set out in the Public Law Outline;

(32)   "Public Law Outline" means the Table contained in paragraph 10;

(33)   "Public Law Proceedings" means proceedings for –

(a)   a residence order under section 8 of the 1989 Act with respect to a child who is subject of a care order;

(b) a special guardianship order relating to a child who is subject of a care order;

(c) a secure accommodation order under section 25 of the 1989 Act;

(d) a care order under section 31(1)(*a*) of the 1989 Act or the discharge of such an order under section 39(1) of the 1989 Act;

(e) an order giving permission to change a child's surname or remove a child from the United Kingdom under section 33(7) of the 1989 Act;

(f) a supervision order under section 31(1)(*b*) of the 1989 Act, the discharge or variation of such an order under section 39(2) of that Act, or the extension or further extension of such an order under paragraph 6(3) of Schedule 3 to that Act;

(g) an order making provision for contact under section 34(2) to (4) of the 1989 Act or an order varying or discharging such an order under section 34(9) of that Act;

(h) an education supervision order, the extension of an education supervision order under paragraph 15(2) of Schedule 3 to the 1989 Act, or the discharge of such an order under paragraph 17(1) of Schedule 3 to that Act;

(i) an order varying directions made with an interim care order or interim supervision order under section 38(8)(*b*) of the 1989 Act;

(j) an order under section 39(3) of the 1989 Act varying a supervision order in so far as it affects a person with whom the child is living but who is not entitled to apply for the order to be discharged;

(k) an order under section 39(3A) of the 1989 Act varying or discharging an interim care order in so far as it imposes an exclusion requirement on a person who is not entitled to apply for the order to be discharged;

(l) an order under section 39(3B) of the 1989 Act varying or discharging an interim care order in so far as it confers a power of arrest attached to an exclusion requirement;

(m) the substitution of a supervision order for a care order under section 39(4) of the 1989 Act;

(n) a child assessment order or the variation or discharge of such an order under section 43(12) of the 1989 Act;

(o) an order permitting the Local Authority to arrange for any child in its care to live outside England and Wales under paragraph 19(1) of Schedule 2 to the 1989 Act;

(p) a contribution order, or the variation or revocation of such an order under paragraph 23(8), of Schedule 2 to the 1989 Act;

(q) an appeal under paragraph 8(1) of Schedule 8 to the 1989 Act.

(34) "rules" means rules of court governing the practice and procedure to be followed in Public Law Proceedings;

(35) "Schedule of Proposed Findings" means the schedule of findings of fact prepared by the Local Authority sufficient to satisfy the threshold criteria under section 31(2) of the 1989 Act and to inform the Care Plan;

(36) "section 7 report" means any report under section 7 of the 1989 Act;

(37) "section 37 report" means any report by the Local Authority to the court as a result of a direction under section 37 of the 1989 Act;

(38) "Social Work Chronology" means a schedule containing –

    (a) a succinct summary of the significant dates and events in the child's life in chronological order- a running record to be updated during the proceedings;

    (b) information under the following headings –

        (i) serial number;

        (ii) date;

        (iii) event-detail;

        (iv) witness or document reference (where applicable);

(39) "specified proceedings" has the meaning assigned to it by section 41(6) of the 1989 Act;

(40) "Standard Directions on Issue" mean directions made by the court which will include such of the directions set out in the Public Law Outline, Stage 1, column 1 as are appropriate to the proceedings;

(41) "Standard Directions on First Appointment" means directions made by the court which will include such of the directions set out in the Public Law Outline, Stage 1, column 2 and directions relating to the following as are appropriate to the proceedings –

    (a) the Timetable for the Child;

    (b) the joining of a party to the proceedings;

    (c) the appointment of a guardian ad litem or litigation friend including the Official Solicitor where appropriate for a protected party or non subject child;

    (d) allocation of the case to a case manager or case management judge;

    (e) experts in accordance with the Experts Practice Direction;

    (f) the interim care plan setting out details as to proposed placement and contact;

    (g) any other evidence (such as evidence relating to vulnerability, ethnicity, culture, language, religion or gender) and disclosure of evidence between the parties;

    (h) filing and service of the draft of the Case Management Order before the Case Management Conference;

    (i)   listing the Issues Resolution Hearing and Final Hearing;

    (j)   media attendance and reporting;

(42) "Strategy Discussion Record" means a note of the strategy discussion within the meaning of "Working Together to Safeguard Children" (2006);

(43) "Timetable for the Child" has the meaning assigned to it by the rules (see paragraph 3.2 of this Practice Direction).

Annex A: Form C110

	Click here to reset form	Click here to print form

C110

Application under the Children Act 1989 for a care or supervision order

To be completed by the court	
Name of court	
Date issued	
Case number	
Child(ren)'s name(s)	Child(ren)'s number(s)

Summary of application

Name of applicant

Name of respondent(s)

Child 1 - Name of child	Date of birth	Order(s) applied for (including interim orders)
	D D / M M / Y Y Y Y	
Name of mother	Name of father	Parental Responsibility ☐ Yes ☐ No

Child 2 - Name of child	Date of birth	Order(s) applied for (including interim orders)
	D D / M M / Y Y Y Y	
Name of mother	Name of father	Parental Responsibility ☐ Yes ☐ No

Child 3 - Name of child	Date of birth	Order(s) applied for (including interim orders)
	D D / M M / Y Y Y Y	
Name of mother	Name of father	Parental Responsibility ☐ Yes ☐ No

Child 4 - Name of child	Date of birth	Order(s) applied for (including interim orders)
	D D / M M / Y Y Y Y	
Name of mother	Name of father	Parental Responsibility ☐ Yes ☐ No

C110 Application under the Children Act 1989 for a care or supervision order (04.10) © Crown copyright 2010

1. The applicant

Name of applicant
(local authority or authorised person)

Name of contact

Job title

Address

Postcode

Contact telephone number

Mobile telephone number

Fax number

Email

DX number

Solicitor's details

Solicitor's name

Address

Postcode

Telephone number

Mobile telephone number

Fax number

Email

DX number

Solicitor's Reference

2

2. The child(ren)

Please give details of the child(ren) and the order(s) you are applying for.
If there are more than 4 children please continue on a separate sheet.

Child 1

Child's first name	
Middle name(s)	
Surname	
Date of birth	D D / M M / Y Y Y Y Gender ☐ Male ☐ Female
Name of Social worker and telephone number	
Is the child subject of a child protection plan?	☐ Yes ☐ No
Are there any health or disability issues relating to the child?	☐ Yes ☐ No
If Yes, please give details	
Who does the child live with?	
At which address does the child live?	
	Postcode ☐☐ - ☐☐☐
Please give the full names of any other adults living at the same address and their relationship to the child.	
Are there any contact arrangements in place for this child?	☐ Yes ☐ No

If Yes, please give details

Name of person	Frequency of contact	Supervised contact
		☐ Yes ☐ No
		☐ Yes ☐ No
		☐ Yes ☐ No
		☐ Yes ☐ No

3

Child 2

Child's first name	
Middle name(s)	
Surname	
Date of birth	D D / M M / Y Y Y Y Gender Male Female
Name of Social worker and telephone number	
Is the child subject of a child protection plan?	☐ Yes ☐ No
Are there any health or disability issues relating to the child?	☐ Yes ☐ No
If Yes, please give details	
Who does the child live with?	
At which address does the child live?	

Postcode ☐☐☐☐ ☐☐☐☐

Please give the full names of any other adults living at the same address and their relationship to the child.

Are there any contact arrangements in place for this child?   ☐ Yes   ☐ No

If Yes, please give details

Name of person	Frequency of contact	Supervised contact
		☐ Yes ☐ No
		☐ Yes ☐ No
		☐ Yes ☐ No
		☐ Yes ☐ No

4

Child 3 _____

Child's first name	
Middle name(s)	
Surname	

Date of birth D D / M M / Y Y Y Y   Gender ☐ Male ☐ Female

Name of Social worker and telephone number

Is the child subject of a child protection plan? ☐ Yes ☐ No

Are there any health or disability issues relating to the child? ☐ Yes ☐ No

If Yes, please give details

Who does the child live with?

At which address does the child live?

Postcode ☐☐☐ ☐☐☐

Please give the full names of any other adults living at the same address and their relationship to the child.

Are there any contact arrangements in place for this child? ☐ Yes ☐ No

If Yes, please give details

Name of person	Frequency of contact	Supervised contact	
		☐ Yes	☐ No
		☐ Yes	☐ No
		☐ Yes	☐ No
		☐ Yes	☐ No

Child 4

Child's first name

Middle name(s)

Surname

Date of birth [D D] / [M M] / [Y Y Y Y]   Gender ☐ Male   ☐ Female

Name of Social worker and telephone number

Is the child subject of a child protection plan? ☐ Yes   ☐ No

Are there any health or disability issues relating to the child? ☐ Yes   ☐ No

If Yes, please give details

Who does the child live with?

At which address does the child live?

Postcode [ ][ ][ ][ ] [ ][ ][ ][ ]

Please give the full names of any other adults living at the same address and their relationship to the child.

Are there any contact arrangements in place for this child? ☐ Yes   ☐ No

If Yes, please give details

Name of person	Frequency of contact	Supervised contact	
		☐ Yes	☐ No
		☐ Yes	☐ No
		☐ Yes	☐ No
		☐ Yes	☐ No

6

3. The respondents

If there are more than 2 respondents please continue on a separate sheet.

Respondent 1

Respondent's first name

Middle name(s)

Surname

Date of birth `D D` / `M M` / `Y Y Y Y`   Gender ☐ Male ☐ Female

Place of birth
(town/county/country, if known)

Current address

Postcode ☐☐☐☐ ☐☐☐☐

Telephone number

Are you aware of any relevant family court proceedings involving the respondent? ☐ Yes ☐ No

If Yes, give details (include type of order, date, name of court and case no.)

Relationship to the child(ren)

Name of child(ren)	Relationship	Parental Responsibility	
		☐ Yes	☐ No
		☐ Yes	☐ No
		☐ Yes	☐ No
		☐ Yes	☐ No

7

Respondent 2 _____

Respondent's first name

Middle name(s)

Surname

Date of birth | D D / M M / Y Y Y Y   Gender ☐ Male ☐ Female

Place of birth
(town/county/country, if known)

Current address

Postcode ☐☐☐ ☐☐☐

Telephone number

Are you aware of any relevant
family court proceedings
involving the respondent?   ☐ Yes   ☐ No

If Yes, give details (include type of order, date, name of court and case no.)

Relationship to the child(ren)

Name of child(ren)	Relationship	Parental Responsibility
		☐ Yes ☐ No
		☐ Yes ☐ No
		☐ Yes ☐ No
		☐ Yes ☐ No

8

4. Grounds for the application

The grounds for the application are that the child(ren) is suffering or is likely to suffer, significant harm and the harm or likelihood of harm is because the child is:

- [ ] not receiving care that would be reasonably expected from a parent
- [ ] beyond parental control

5. Why are you making this application?

Please give a brief summary of why you are making this application. You should include:

- the background circumstances
- the precipitating circumstances

In this summary it is not sufficient just to refer to existing or future documents.

9

6. Factors affecting ability to participate in proceedings

Do you have any reason to believe that any respondent or other person to be given notice of the application may lack capacity to conduct proceedings?

☐ Yes   ☐ No

If Yes, please give details

Provide details of any referral to or assessment by the Adult Learning Disability team, together with the outcome

Are you aware of any other factors which may affect the ability of the person concerned to take part in the proceedings?

7. Plans for the child(ren)

Please give a brief summary of the plans for the child(ren).

- **for supervision orders only,** any requirements which you will invite the court to impose under Part 1 of Schedule 3 Children Act 1989

In this summary it is not sufficient just to refer to or repeat the Care Plan.

8. Timetable for the child(ren)

The timetable for the child will be set by the court to take account of dates of the significant steps in the child's life that are likely to take place during the proceedings. Those steps include not only legal steps but also social, care, health and education steps.

Please give any relevant dates/events in relation to the child(ren)
• it may be necessary to give different dates for each child.

Are you aware of any significant event in the timetable, before which the case should be concluded?

☐ Yes   ☐ No

If Yes, please give a date

D D / M M / Y Y Y Y

and give your reasons

9. Your allocation proposal

You need to provide the court with your proposal for allocation of this case.

Please select from the following:

☐ magistrates' court

☐ county court (Care Centre)

☐ High Court

and give your reasons

11

10. Other court cases which concern the child(ren)

Are you aware of any other court cases, including cases concerning the children, which are relevant to this application?

☐ Yes

☐ No   If No, **go to section 11**

If Yes, give details (include type of order, date, name of court and case no.) and in cases where the child was represented the name of any guardian and solicitor for the child.

12

11. Others who should be given notice

Person 1

Person's first name

Middle name(s)

Surname

Date of birth D D / M M / Y Y Y Y   Gender ☐ Male ☐ Female

Address

Postcode

Relationship to the child(ren)

Name of child	Relationship	Parental Responsibility	
		☐ Yes	☐ No
		☐ Yes	☐ No
		☐ Yes	☐ No
		☐ Yes	☐ No

Relationship to the respondents

Name of respondent	Relationship

13

Person 2

Person's first name	
Middle name(s)	
Surname	
Date of birth	D D / M M / Y Y Y Y Gender ☐ Male ☐ Female
Address	
	Postcode ☐☐☐☐ ☐☐☐

Relationship to the child(ren)

Name of child	Relationship	Parental Responsibility
		☐ Yes ☐ No
		☐ Yes ☐ No
		☐ Yes ☐ No
		☐ Yes ☐ No

Relationship to the respondents

Name of respondent	Relationship

14

12. Signature

Print full name

Your role/position held

Signed

Applicant

Date   D D / M M / Y Y Y Y

13. Attending the court

If an interpreter will be required, you must tell the court now so that one can be arranged.

Are you aware of whether an
interpreter will be required?

☐ Yes   ☐ No

If Yes, please specify the language and dialect:

If attending the court, do any of the
parties involved have a disability for
which special assistance or special
facilities would be required?

☐ Yes   ☐ No

If Yes, please specifiy what the needs are:

Please state whether the court
needs to make any special
arrangements for the parties
attending court (e.g. providing a
separate waiting room or other
security requirements).

Court staff may get in contact with you about the requirements

15

continued over the page ⇨

Annex

This annex must be completed by the applicant with any application for a care order or supervision order.
The documents specified in this annex must be filed with the application if available.
If any relevant document is not filed with the application, the reason and any expected date of filing must be stated.
All documents filed with the application must be clearly marked with their title and numbered consecutively.

1. Social Work Chronology
(A succinct summary)

☐ attached   ☐ to follow

If **to follow** please give reasons why not included and the date when the document will be sent to the court.

2. Initial Social Work Statement

☐ attached   ☐ to follow

If **to follow** please give reasons why not included and the date when the document will be sent to the court.

3. Initial and Core Assessments

☐ attached   ☐ to follow

If **to follow** please give reasons why not included and the date when the document will be sent to the court.

4. Letters Before Proceedings

☐ attached   ☐ to follow

If **to follow** please give reasons why not included and the date when the document will be sent to the court.

5. Schedule of Proposed Findings

☐ attached   ☐ to follow

If **to follow** please give reasons why not included and the date when the document will be sent to the court.

6. Care Plan

☐ attached   ☐ to follow

If **to follow** please give reasons why not included and the date when the document will be sent to the court.

What to do once you have completed this form

Ensure that you have:

☐ attached copies of any **relevant** documents.

☐ **signed** the form at Section 12.

☐ provided a **copy** of the application and attached documents for each of the respondents, and for Cafcass or CAFCASS CYMRU.

☐ given details of the additional children if there are more than 4 in Section 2.

☐ given details of the additional respondents if there are more than 2 in Section 3.

☐ the correct fee.

It is good practice to inform Cafcass or CAFCASS CYMRU that you are making this application. The court will expect the local authority to have informed Cafcass or CAFCASS CYMRU that proceedings are being issued.

Have you notified Cafcass - Children and Family Court Advisory and Support Service (for England)

or

CAFCASS CYMRU - Children and Family Court Advisory and Support Service Wales.

☐ Yes   ☐ No

If Yes, please give the date of notification

| D | D | / | M | M | / | Y | Y | Y | Y |

Now take or send your application with the correct fee and correct number of copies to the court.

17

Annex B: Form PLO8

PLO8 Form – April 2010

Case Name:	Case Number:
HHJ/ District Judge/Justices' Clerk/Assistant Justices' Clerk:	Date:

Standard Directions on Issue

Preamble

Upon the proceedings having been referred to the Judge/Justice's Clerk/Assistant Justices Clerk for allocation and directions upon issue / transfer [*delete as appropriate*] and the court having considered the papers in the absence of the parties or their legal representatives

Pre-proceedings checklist compliance

[   ] The LA shall file and serve the documents set out in the table below by 2 pm on the date recorded alongside

each [*delete any which have been filed or are not applicable*]

	Category	Document	Date for filing
A	Annex documents		
1	Social Work Chronology		
2	Initial Social Work Statement		
3	Initial and Core Assessments		
4	Letters Before Proceedings		
5	Schedule of Proposed Findings		
6	Care Plan		
B	Other checklist documents		
8	Previous proceedings	Orders	
		Judgment/reasons	
9	Any relevant assessment materials	Section 7 & 37 reports	
		Relatives and friends materials (e.g. a genogram)	
10	Other relevant reports and records	Single, joint or inter-agency materials	
		Records of discussions with the family	
		Key LA minutes and records for the child, (inc. Strategy Discussion Record)	
11	Pre-existing care plans (e.g. child in need plan, looked after child plan & child protection plan)		
12	Other relevant pre-proceedings documents (specify)		

[   ]   The LA shall serve the application form and Annex documents filed with the court

by 2.00 pm on [{date}   ] on [{specify party or proposed party}

172   *Child Case Management Practice*

PLO8 Form – April 2010

Allocate and/or transfer

[   ]   The application[s] [is] [are] transferred to the

         □ [{*name*}   ] County Court   □ [{*name*}   /Inner London] FPC   □   High Court
         □ [other]

         [to be heard with Case No.   / FD   C   ]

[   ]   The proceedings are allocated for case management to / the proceedings are to be allocated by:

         Mr(s) Justice

         His / Her Honour Judge ..../ DFJ for {*name of care centre*}

         District Judge

         2 Case Managers in the FPC namely [   ]and[   ]

[   ]   [{*other*}]

Appointment of Children's Guardian / Children's Solicitor

[   ]   A Children's Guardian [(*name*)   )] shall be appointed for the child[ren]

OR

[   ]   [{*Solicitor's name*}

         of {*firm*}   ] is appointed as solicitor for the child[ren]

[   ]   [The Child(ren)'s Solicitor shall file and serve by 2.00 pm on [{*date*}   ] a Case Analysis and Recommendations document prepared by the Child(ren)'s Guardian for use at the First Appointment] OR [The Child(ren)'s Guardian shall be in a position to present an oral Case Analysis and Recommendations at the First Appointment]

The Case Analysis and Recommendations shall set out:

(a)   an analysis of the issues that need to be resolved in the case including-

         (i)   any harm or risk of harm;

         (ii)   the child's own views;

         (iii)   the family context including advice relating to ethnicity, language, religion and culture of the child and other significant persons;

         (iv)   the Local Authority work and proposed care plan ;

         (v)   advice about the court process including the Timetable for the Child; and

         (vi)   identification of work that remains to be done for the child in the short and longer term; and

(b)   recommendations for outcomes, in order to safeguard and promote the best interests of the child in the proceedings;

PLO8 Form – April 2010

Guardian ad litem/litigation friend/Official Solicitor

[   ]   The Official Solicitor is invited to act in these proceedings as the guardian ad litem or litigation friend on behalf

of the [M] [F] [non-subject child] {*name*}

Listing of First Appointment

[   ]   The application[s] are listed for a First Appointment [FA] before

    ☐ DJ / PRFD   ☐ CJ / RCJ   ☐ HCJ / RCJ   ○ FPC / Inner London

    ☐ [the allocated judge]

    on   at   (time estimate   )

[✓]   No document other than a document specified in these directions or in accordance with the Rules or Practice
Directions shall be filed by any party without the court's permission.

[✓]   Any application to vary these directions or for any other order is to be made to the allocated Judge/Justices'
Clerk/Assistant Justices' Clerk on notice to all parties.

Interim Hearings

[   ] the application by the [local authority] [mother] [father] [*other*   ]

for an interim [care] [supervision] [contact] [*other*   ] order is listed for hearing before

    ○ DJ / PRFD   ○ CJ / RCJ   ○ HCJ / RCJ   ○ FPC / Inner London

    ○ [the allocated judge]

    on   at   (time estimate   )

Compliance with directions

[✓]   All parties must immediately inform the [Case Progression Officer][Case Manager] on
                (tel)/   (fax)/[{*e-mail*}   ] if any party fails to adhere to any date
specified for filing any document.

Dated:

Signed: **HHJ/ DJ/[Assistant] JC**

Child Case Management Practice

Annex C: Form PLO9

PLO9 Form - April 2010

Case Name:	**Case Number:**
HHJ/ District Judge/Justices' Clerk/Assistant Justices' Clerk	**Date:**

Standard Directions at First Appointment

Parties to the Proceedings/Joinder of Parties/Official Solicitor

[√]   The parties to the proceedings are:

The Applicant LA..

The 1st Respondent (identify relationship: M / F) ....

The [   ] Respondent (identify relationship:) ....

The [   ] Respondent (identify relationship:) ....

The [   ] Respondent (a child) ....

The [   ] Respondent (a child) ....

The [   ] Respondent (a child) ....

[   ]   The Official Solicitor is invited to act in these proceedings as the guardian ad litem or litigation friend on behalf

of the [M] [F] [non-subject child] {name}   ]

[   ]   {name}   ] is joined as the [{specify}   ] Respondent to the proceedings

[for the purpose of determining {specify where appropriate}

Timetable for the Child

[   ]   The key dates and events in the Timetable for the Child(ren) are:

(a)

(b)

(c)

(d)

PLO9 Form - April 2010

Transfer / Allocation to Case Manager / Case Management Judge

[   ]   The application[s] [is] [are] transferred to the

☐ [{name}   ] County Court   ☐ [{name}   /Inner London] FPC   ☐ High Court
☐ [other]

[to be heard with Case No.   / FD   C   ]

[   ]   The proceedings are allocated for case management to / the proceedings are to be allocated by:

Mr(s) Justice

His / Her Honour Judge ..../ DFJ for {name of care centre}

District Judge

2 Case Managers in the FPC namely [   ] and [   ]

[   ]   [{other}]

Case Analysis and Recommendations

[   ]   The child(ren)'s solicitor shall file and serve by 2.00 pm on [{date}   ]

a Case Analysis and Recommendations document prepared by the Children's Guardian for use at the

Case Management Conference setting out:

(a)   an analysis of the issues that need to be resolved in the case including-

(i)   any harm or risk of harm;

(ii)   the child's own views;

(iii) the family context including advice relating to ethnicity, language, religion and culture of the child and other significant persons;

(iv)   the Local Authority work and proposed care plan;

(v)   advice about the court process including the Timetable for the Child; and

(vi)   identification of work that remains to be done for the child in the short and longer term; and

(b)   recommendations for outcomes, in order to safeguard and promote the best interests of the child in the

proceedings.

Annex documents and other checklist documents

[ ] The LA shall file and serve the documents set out in the table below by 2 pm on the date recorded alongside each *[delete any which have been filed or are not applicable]*

	Category	Document	Date for filing
A	Annex documents		
1	Social Work Chronology		
2	Initial Social Work Statement		
3	Initial and Core Assessments		
4	Letters Before Proceedings		
5	Schedule of Proposed Findings		
6	Care Plan		
B	Other checklist documents		
8	Previous proceedings	Orders	
		Judgment/reasons	
9	Any relevant assessment materials	Section 7 & 37 reports	
		Relatives and friends materials (e.g. a genogram)	
10	Other relevant reports and records	Single, joint or inter-agency materials	
		Records of discussions with the family	
		Key LA minutes and records for the child, (inc. Strategy Discussion Record)	
11	Pre-existing care plans (e.g. child in need plan, looked after child plan & child protection plan)		
12	Other relevant pre-proceedings documents (specify)		

Evidence / Documents for CMC/interim hearing

[ ] The LA shall file and serve by 2.00pm on [*{date}*]

    (i)   a Local Authority Case Summary prepared in accordance with the Practice Direction

    (ii)   the interim care plan(s) setting out details of any proposed placement and contact

    (iii)   any further evidence upon which they intend to rely including any evidence relating to vulnerability, ethnicity, culture, language, religion or gender

    (iv)   [*{other}*]

[ ] The [M] [F] [ ] [Respondents]   shall each file and serve by 2.00pm on [*{date}*]

(i) a Case Summary setting out

    (a)   their proposals for the long term future of the child (to include placement and contact);

    (b)   their reply to the Local Authority's Schedule of Proposed Findings;

    (c)   any proposal for assessment / expert evidence; and

    (d)   the names, addresses and contact details of any family or friends who it is suggested be approached in relation to long term care / contact or respite;

3

(ii) Initial witness statements

(iii) *[Other – specify]*

[   ]   Any party proposing to ask the court for permission to instruct an expert or for any other assessment must comply with the Experts' Practice Direction and provide details to the other parties before the advocates' meeting of the nature of the assessment or report required, the issue to which it is directed, the identity, CV and availability of the proposed assessor, the timescale, likely cost and method of funding.

[   ]   Any outstanding disclosure of relevant documents between the parties shall take place not later than 3 working days before the CMC advocates meeting.

Advocates Meeting

[   ]   The parties' lawyers and any unrepresented party shall attend an Advocates Meeting / Discussion for the purpose of identifying the key issue(s) and drafting the directions to be sought at the CMC and to draft a case management order for the court

[to take place at   p.m. on *{date}*   at *{venue}*   ] [by video / telephone conference]

OR

[to be arranged by the solicitor for the child(ren) / *{other}*   ] not later than [   ] *(2 days before the CMC)* / at [*{venue, date and time}*   ]] [by video / telephone conference]

[The court grants permission for *{name}*   to attend the Advocates Meeting as a McKenzie Friend for *{name of litigant in person}*   . The McKenzie Friend may assist by prompting, taking notes and giving advice but is not an advocate for the party concerned]

Case Management Order

[   ]   The LA shall file and serve by 11 a.m. one working day before the CMC:

      (i)   a completed draft case management order in typed form;

      (ii)   [*{other}*   ]

Where the above documents are filed by fax or e-mail original copies must be handed to the court at the hearing.

4

PLO9 Form - April 2010

Listing of CMC

[ ]   The application[s] are listed for a Case Management Conference [CMC] before

      ○ DJ / PRFD   ○ CJ / RCJ   ○ HCJ / RCJ   ○ FPC / Inner London

      ○ [the allocated judge]

      on   at   (time estimate   )

Interim Hearings

[ ]   the application by the [local authority] [mother] [father] [*other*   ]

for an interim [care] [supervision] [contact] [*other*   ] order is listed for hearing before

      ○ DJ / PRFD   ○ CJ / RCJ   ○ HCJ / RCJ   ○ FPC / Inner London

      ○ [the allocated judge]

      on   at   (time estimate   )

Other Hearings

[   ]   The Issues Resolution Hearing will take place on / not later than   *{specify date}*

[   ]   The Final Hearing will take place not later than   *{specify date}*

[   ]   The court is of the opinion that the case is suitable for an Early Final Hearing because

{specify reasons}

and the Final Hearing shall take place at*{venue, date & time}*

Other Orders

[   ]

[   ]   *[see attached sheet]*

[✓]   No document other than a document specified in these directions or in accordance with the Rules or Practice
Directions shall be filed by any party without the court's permission.

5

PLO9 Form - April 2010

[✓] In proceedings in / before the FPC, where a party considers that there are likely to be issues arising at a hearing (including the Case Management Conference and Issues Resolution Hearing) which need to be decided by a full Bench or District Judge (Magistrates' Court), rather than a Justices' Clerk/Assistant Justices' Clerk, then that party shall give the court written notice of that need as soon as possible and at least 2 days before the hearing. The notice shall specify:

    a) the nature of the issue(s);
    b) whether it is anticipated that an application will be contested by any party;
    c) the estimated length of hearing (where this is in excess of any existing time estimate).

[✓] Any application to vary these directions or for any other order is to be made to the allocated judge/case manager on notice to all parties.

Compliance with directions

[✓] All parties must immediately inform the [Case Progression Officer][Case Manager] on
        (tel)/   (fax)/[{e-mail}   ] if any party fails to adhere to any
date specified for filing any document.

Dated:

Signed: **HHJ/ DJ/Assistant JC**

A3.3   APPENDIX 3:
PRACTICE GUIDANCE 12 JULY 2010
MCKENZIE FRIENDS (CIVIL AND FAMILY COURTS)

1 This Guidance applies to civil and family proceedings in the Court of Appeal (Civil Division), the High Court of Justice, the County Courts and the Family Proceedings Court in the Magistrates' Courts.[1] It is issued as guidance (**not** as a Practice Direction) by the Master of the Rolls, as Head of Civil Justice, and the President of the Family Division, as Head of Family Justice. It is intended to remind courts and litigants of the principles set out in the authorities and supersedes the guidance contained in *Practice Note (Family Courts: McKenzie Friends) (No 2)* [2008] 1 WLR 2757, which is now withdrawn.[2] It is issued in light of the increase in litigants-in-person (litigants) in all levels of the civil and family courts.

1   References to the judge or court should be read where proceedings are taking place under the FPC(MP etc)R 1991, as a reference to a justices' clerk or assistant justices' clerk who is specifically authorised by a justices' clerk to exercise the functions of the court at the relevant hearing. Where they are taking place under the FPC(CA 1989)R 1991 they should be read consistently with the provisions of those Rules, specifically rule 16A(5A).

2   *R v Leicester City Justices, ex parte Barrow* [1991] 260, *Chauhan v Chauhan* [1997] FCR 206, *R v Bow County Court, ex parte Pelling* [1999] 1 WLR 1807, *Attorney-General v Purvis* [2003] EWHC 3190 (Admin), *Clarkson v Gilbert* [2000] CP Rep 58, *United Building and Plumbing Contractors v Kajla* [2002] EWCA Civ 628, *Re O (Children) (Hearing in Private: Assistance)* [2005] 3 WLR 1191, *Westland Helicopters Ltd v Sheikh Salah Al-Hejailan (No 2)* [2004] 2 Lloyd's Rep 535. *Agassi v Robinson (Inspector of Taxes) (No 2)* [2006] 1 WLR 2126, *Re N (A Child) (McKenzie Friend: Rights of Audience) Practice Note* [2008] 1 WLR 2743.

The Right to Reasonable Assistance

2 Litigants have the right to have reasonable assistance from a layperson, sometimes called a McKenzie Friend (MF). Litigants assisted by MFs remain litigants-in-person. MFs have no independent right to provide assistance. They have no right to act as advocates or to carry out the conduct of litigation.

What McKenzie Friends may do

3 MFs may: i) provide moral support for litigants; ii) take notes; iii) help with case papers; iv) quietly give advice on any aspect of the conduct of the case.

What McKenzie Friends may not do

4 MFs may not: i) act as the litigants' agent in relation to the proceedings; ii) manage litigants' cases outside court, for example by signing court documents; or iii) address the court, make oral submissions or examine witnesses.

Exercising the Right to Reasonable Assistance

5 While litigants ordinarily have a right to receive reasonable assistance from MFs the court retains the power to refuse to permit such assistance. The court may do so where it is satisfied that, in that case, the interests of justice and fairness do not require the litigant to receive such assistance.

6 A litigant who wishes to exercise this right should inform the judge as soon as possible indicating who the MF will be. The proposed MF should produce a short curriculum vitae or other statement setting out relevant experience, confirming that he or she has no interest in the case and understands the MF's role and the duty of confidentiality.

7 If the court considers that there might be grounds for circumscribing the right to receive such assistance, or a party objects to the presence of, or assistance given by a MF, it is not for the litigant to justify the exercise of the right. It is for the court or the objecting party to provide sufficient reasons why the litigant should not receive such assistance.

8 When considering whether to circumscribe the right to assistance or refuse a MF permission to attend the right to a fair trial is engaged. The matter should be considered carefully. The litigant should be given a reasonable opportunity to argue the point. The proposed MF should not be excluded from that hearing and should normally be allowed to help the litigant.

9 Where proceedings are in *closed court*, i.e. the hearing is in chambers, is in private, or the proceedings relate to a child, the litigant is required to justify the MF's presence in court. The presumption in favour of permitting a MF to attend such hearings, and thereby enable litigants to exercise the right to assistance, is a strong one.

10 The court may refuse to allow a litigant to exercise the right to receive assistance at the start of a hearing. The court can also circumscribe the right during the course of a hearing. It may be refused at the start of a hearing or later circumscribed where the court forms the view that a MF may give, has given, or is giving, assistance which impedes the efficient administration of justice. However, the court should also consider whether a firm and unequivocal warning to the litigant and/or MF might suffice in the first instance.

11 A decision by the court not to curtail assistance from a MF should be regarded as final, save on the ground of subsequent misconduct by the MF or on the ground that the MF's continuing presence will impede the efficient administration of justice. In such event the court should give a short judgment setting out the reasons why it has curtailed the right to assistance. Litigants may appeal such decisions. MFs have no standing to do so.

12 The following factors should not be taken to justify the court refusing to permit a litigant receiving such assistance:

(i) The case or application is simple or straightforward, or is, for instance, a directions or case management hearing;

(ii) The litigant appears capable of conducting the case without assistance;

(iii) The litigant is unrepresented through choice;

(iv) The other party is not represented;

(v) The proposed MF belongs to an organisation that promotes a particular cause;

(vi) The proceedings are confidential and the court papers contain sensitive information relating to a family's affairs.

13 A litigant may be denied the assistance of a MF because its provision might undermine or has undermined the efficient administration of justice. Examples of circumstances where this might arise are: i) the assistance is being provided for an improper purpose; ii) the assistance is unreasonable in nature or degree; iii) the MF is subject to a civil proceedings order or a civil restraint order; iv) the MF is using the litigant as a puppet; v) the MF is directly or indirectly conducting the litigation; vi) the court is not satisfied that the MF fully understands the duty of confidentiality.

14 Where a litigant is receiving assistance from a MF in care proceedings, the court should consider the MF's attendance at any advocates' meetings directed by the court, and, with regard to cases commenced after 1.4.08, consider directions in accordance with paragraph 13.2 of the Practice Direction Guide to Case Management in Public Law Proceedings.

15 Litigants are permitted to communicate any information, including filed evidence, relating to the proceedings to MFs for the purpose of obtaining advice or assistance in relation to the proceedings.

16 Legal representatives should ensure that documents are served on litigants in good time to enable them to seek assistance regarding their content from MFs in advance of any hearing or advocates' meeting.

17 The High Court can, under its inherent jurisdiction, impose a civil restraint order on MFs who repeatedly act in ways that undermine the efficient administration of justice.

Rights of audience and rights to conduct litigation

18 MFs do **not** have a right of audience or a right to conduct litigation. It is a criminal offence to exercise rights of audience or to conduct litigation unless properly qualified and authorised to do so by an appropriate regulatory body or, in the case of an otherwise unqualified or unauthorised individual (i.e., a lay individual including a MF), the court grants such rights on a case-by-case basis.[3]

   3   Legal Services Act 2007 s 12–19 and Schedule 3.

19 Courts should be slow to grant any application from a litigant for a right of audience or a right to conduct litigation to any lay person, including a MF. This is because a person exercising such rights must ordinarily be properly trained, be under professional discipline (including an obligation to insure against liability for negligence) and be subject to an overriding duty to the court. These requirements are necessary for the protection of all parties to litigation and are essential to the proper administration of justice.

20 Any application for a right of audience or a right to conduct litigation to be granted to any lay person should therefore be considered very carefully. The court should only be prepared to grant such rights where there is good reason to do so taking into account all the circumstances of the case, which are likely to vary greatly. Such grants should not be extended to lay persons automatically or without due consideration. They should not be granted for mere convenience.

21 Examples of the type of special circumstances which have been held to justify the grant of a right of audience to a lay person, including a MF, are: i) that person is a close relative of the litigant; ii) health problems preclude the litigant from addressing the court, or conducting litigation, and the litigant cannot afford to pay for a qualified legal representative; iii) the litigant is relatively inarticulate and prompting by that person may unnecessarily prolong the proceedings.

22 It is for the litigant to persuade the court that the circumstances of the case are such that it is in the interests of justice for the court to grant a lay person a right of audience or a right to conduct litigation.

23 The grant of a right of audience or a right to conduct litigation to lay persons who hold themselves out as professional advocates or professional MFs or who seek to exercise such rights on a regular basis, whether for reward or not, will however only be granted in exceptional circumstances. To do otherwise would tend to subvert the will of Parliament.

24 If a litigant wants a lay person to be granted a right of audience, an application must be made at the start of the hearing. If a right to conduct

litigation is sought such an application must be made at the earliest possible time and must be made, in any event, before the lay person does anything which amounts to the conduct of litigation. It is for litigants to persuade the court, on a case-by-case basis, that the grant of such rights is justified.

25 Rights of audience and the right to conduct litigation are separate rights. The grant of one right to a lay person does not mean that a grant of the other right has been made. If both rights are sought their grant must be applied for individually and justified separately.

26 Having granted either a right of audience or a right to conduct litigation, the court has the power to remove either right. The grant of such rights in one set of proceedings cannot be relied on as a precedent supporting their grant in future proceedings.

Remuneration

27 Litigants can enter into lawful agreements to pay fees to MFs for the provision of reasonable assistance in court or out of court by, for instance, carrying out clerical or mechanical activities, such as photocopying documents, preparing bundles, delivering documents to opposing parties or the court, or the provision of legal advice in connection with court proceedings. Such fees cannot be lawfully recovered from the opposing party.

28 Fees said to be incurred by MFs for carrying out the conduct of litigation, where the court has not granted such a right, cannot lawfully be recovered from either the litigant for whom they carry out such work or the opposing party.

29 Fees said to be incurred by MFs for carrying out the conduct of litigation after the court has granted such a right are in principle recoverable from the litigant for whom the work is carried out. Such fees cannot be lawfully recovered from the opposing party.

30 Fees said to be incurred by MFs for exercising a right of audience following the grant of such a right by the court are in principle recoverable from the litigant on whose behalf the right is exercised. Such fees are also recoverable, in principle, from the opposing party as a recoverable disbursement: CPR 48.6(2) and 48(6)(3)(ii).

Personal Support Unit & Citizen's Advice Bureau

31 Litigants should also be aware of the services provided by local Personal Support Units and Citizens' Advice Bureaux. The PSU at the Royal Courts of Justice in London can be contacted on 020 7947 7701, by

email at cbps@bello.co.uk or at the enquiry desk. The CAB at the Royal Courts of Justice in London can be contacted on 020 7947 6564 or at the enquiry desk.

Lord Neuberger of Abbotsbury
Master of the Rolls

Sir Nicholas Wall
President of the Family Division

A3.4   APPENDIX 4:
PRESIDENT'S GUIDANCE IN RELATION TO SPLIT HEARINGS
MAY 2010

From time to time issues will arise with which magistrates and judges at every level will have to grapple and which will cause difficulties. Against this background I intend from time to time to issue what I propose to call "Guidance" designed to help colleagues make difficult decisions. Self-evidently such Guidance is not designed to tell courts <u>what</u> to decide: the objective is to assist them in the process of going about the decision making progress. Plainly, it will be appropriate not to follow the Guidance in some circumstances: what I hope is that in a sufficiently large number of instances the Guidance will be of use and will help magistrates and judges in the decision making process.

Split Hearings (Bulletin Number 1)

Introduction

1 Over recent months and years it has become apparent to me that split hearings are: (1) taking place when they need not do so; and (2) are taking up a disproportionate amount of the court's time and resources.

2 I have therefore decided to issue the following Guidance in an attempt to assist judges and magistrates who are invited to direct split hearings.

3 Like all Guidance, what follows is not binding on the judiciary at any level. It is an attempt to identify good practice. Moreover, it is designed to apply in both private and public law proceedings.

4 In this Guidance, I propose to use the following terminology –

A "split hearing" is a hearing divided into two parts, during the first of which the court makes findings of fact on issues either identified by the parties or the court, and during the second part of which the court, based on the findings which it has made, decides the case.

A "fact finding hearing" is the first limb of a split hearing.

Guidance

5 Judges and magistrates should always remember that the decision to direct a split hearing or to conduct a fact finding hearing is a *judicial* decision. It is not a decision for *Cafcass* or for the parties. It is a decision to be taken by the court. Thus the court should not direct a fact finding hearing simply because the parties agree that one is necessary or because *Cafcass* says that it cannot report without one. Such considerations are, of course, to be taken into account, but they are not conclusive. In any event, the focus of any report is a matter for the court.

6 Judges and magistrates should always remember that a fact finding hearing is a working tool designed to assist them to decide the case. Thus a fact finding hearing should only be ordered if the court takes the view that the case cannot properly be decided without such a hearing.

7 Even when the court comes to the conclusion that a fact finding hearing is necessary, it by no means follows that such a hearing needs to be separate from the substantive hearing. In nearly every case, the court's findings of fact inform its conclusions. In my judgment it will be a rare case in which a separate fact finding hearing is necessary.

8 Thus, for example, the fact that domestic abuse is put forward by the residential parent of a child as a reason for denying the non-residential parent contact with the child is not automatically as reason for a split hearing with a preliminary fact finding hearing. As the President's *Practice Direction: Residence and Contact order: Domestic Violence and Harm* of 14 January 2009 [2009] 2 FLR 1400 makes clear, the court must consider the nature of any allegations, and the extent to which those allegations, if admitted or proved *"would be relevant in deciding whether to make an order about residence or contact and, if so, in what terms"* – see para [3] (emphasis supplied). In para [11] the court is again instructed to *"consider the likely impact of that issue (domestic abuse) on the outcome of the proceedings"* (emphasis supplied) and whether or not the decision of the court is likely to be affected by findings of domestic abuse. Plainly, if the allegations are unlikely to have any impact on the court's order, there is no need for a separate fact finding hearing.

9 In addition, in cases in which the court concludes that a fact-finding hearing is necessary, the *Practice Direction* requires the court to give directions designed to ensure that *"the matters in issue are determined expeditiously and fairly"* (emphasis supplied).

10 None of the foregoing is designed to minimise or trivialise domestic abuse or its effects on children and upon its other victims, or to discourage victims from coming forward with abuse allegations. I repeat

that the aim of the Guidance is to enable magistrates and judges fully to address their minds to the need for a separate fact finding hearing.

11 The rationale for split hearings in care proceedings was enunciated by Bracewell J in *Re S (Care Proceedings: Split Hearing)* [1996] 2 FLR 773 when, voicing the views of the Children Act Advisory Committee, she stated that consideration could usefully be given to whether or not there were questions of fact within a case which needed to be determined at an early stage. The advantages of doing so, she said were that early resolution of such facts "would enable the substantive hearing to proceed more speedily" and would enable the court to "focus on the child's welfare with greater clarity". Cases suitable for split hearings, she commented "would be likely to be cases in which there is a clear and stark issue, such as sexual abuse or physical abuse". Once again, the object was "to prevent delay and the ill-focused use of scarce expert resources". These factors should be borne in mind by the court when deciding whether or not to order a split hearing.

12 Magistrates and judges are reminded of the decision of the Court of Appeal in *Re C* [2009] EWCA Civ 994. They might also care to look at paragraphs 27 to 35 of my recent judgment in the case of *W (Children)* [2009] EWCA Civ 644, now also reported at [2009] 3 FCR 1.

13 Courts are also reminded of the provisions of the *Practice Direction: The Revised Private Law Programme* which came into effect from 1 April 2010.

Nicholas Wall
May 2010

A3.5   APPENDIX 5:
PRACTICE DIRECTION 12B
THE REVISED PRIVATE LAW PROGRAMME

This Practice Direction supplements FPR Part 12

1 Introduction

1.1 The Private Law Programme has achieved marked success in enabling the resolution of the majority of cases by consent at the First Hearing Dispute Resolution Appointment ("FHDRA"). It has been revised to build on the successes of the initial programme and to take account of recent developments in the law and practice associated with private family law.

1.2 In particular, there have been several legislative changes affecting private family law. The Allocation and Transfer of Proceedings

Order 2008 (the "Allocation Order"), requires the transfer of cases from the County Court to the Family Proceedings Court (FPC). Sections 1 to 5 and Schedule 1 of the Children and Adoption Act 2006 which came into force on 8 December 2008, amends the Children Act 1989 by introducing Contact Activity Directions, Contact Activity Conditions, Contact Monitoring Requirements, Financial Compensation Orders and Enforcement Orders.

1.3 There has been growing recognition of the impact of domestic violence and abuse, drug and alcohol misuse and mental illness, on the proper consideration of the issues in private family law; this includes the acceptance that Court orders, even those made by consent, must be scrutinised to ensure that they are safe and take account of any risk factors. Coupled with this is the need to take account of the duty on Cafcass, pursuant to s 16A Children Act 1989, to undertake risk assessments where an officer of the Service ("Cafcass Officer") suspects that a child is at risk of harm. (References to Cafcass include CAFCASS CYMRU and references to the Cafcass Officer include the Welsh family proceedings officer in Wales).

1.4 There is awareness of the importance of involving children where appropriate in the decision making process.

1.5 The Revised Programme incorporates these developments. It also retains the essential feature of the FHDRA as the forum for the parties to be helped to reach agreement as to, and understanding of, the issues that divide them. It recognises that having reached agreement parties may need assistance in putting it into effect in a co-operative way.

1.6 The Revised Programme is designed to provide a framework for the consistent national approach to the resolution of the issues in private family law whilst enabling local practices and initiatives to be operated in addition and within the framework.

1.7 The Revised Programme is designed to assist parties to reach safe agreements where possible, to provide a forum in which to find the best way to resolve issues in each individual case and to promote outcomes that are sustainable, that are in the best interests of children and that take account of their perspectives.

2 Principles

2.1 Where an application is made to a court under Part II of the Children Act 1989, the child's welfare is the court's paramount concern. The court will apply the principle of the "Overriding Objective" to enable it to deal with a case justly, having regard to the welfare principles involved. So far as practicable the Court will –

(a)   Deal expeditiously and fairly with every case;

(b)   Deal with a case in ways which are proportionate to the nature, importance and complexity of the issues;

(c)   Ensure that the parties are on an equal footing;

(d)   Save unnecessary expense;

(e)   Allot to each case an appropriate share of the court's resources, while taking account of the need to allot resources to other cases.

2.2 The court will give effect to the overriding objective when applying this programme and when exercising its powers to manage cases.

The parties are required to help the court further the overriding objective and promote the welfare of the child by the application of the welfare principle, pursuant to s 1(1) of the Children Act 1989.

This Programme provides that consideration and discussion of all issues will not take place until the FHDRA when parties are on an equal footing and can hear what is said to and by each other. This excludes the safety checks and enquiries carried out by Cafcass before the first hearing that are required for that hearing and deal only with safety issues.

At the **FHDRA** the Court shall consider in particular –

(a)   Whether and the extent to which the parties can safely resolve some or all of the issues with the assistance of the Cafcass Officer and any available mediator.

(b)   Risk identification followed by active case management including risk assessment, and compliance with the Practice Direction 14 January 2009: "Residence and Contact Orders: Domestic Violence and Harm".

(c)   Further dispute resolution.

(d)   The avoidance of delay through the early identification of issues and timetabling, subject to the Allocation Order.

(e)   Judicial scrutiny of the appropriateness of consent orders.

(f)   Judicial consideration of the way to involve the child.

(g)   Judicial continuity.

3 Practical arrangements before the FHDRA

3.1 Applications shall be issued on the day of receipt in accordance with the appropriate Rules of Procedure. It is important that the form C100 is fully completed, especially on pages 1, 2, 3, 10 and 11 otherwise delay may be caused by requests for information.

3.2 If possible at the time of issue, and in any event by no later than 24 hours after issue, or in courts where applications are first considered on paper, by no later than 48 hours after issue, the court shall

(i)   send or hand to the Applicant

(ii)   send to Cafcass

the following:

(a)   a copy of the Application Form C100, (together with Supplemental Information Form C1A) (if provided) (references to form C1A are to be read as form C100A following the introduction of this replacement form),

(b)   the Notice of Hearing,

(c)   the Acknowledgment Form C7,

(d)   a blank Form C1A,

(e)   the Certificate of Service Form C9,

(f)   information leaflets for the parties.

3.3 Save in urgent cases that require an earlier listing, the fully effective operation of this Practice Direction requires the FHDRA to take place within **4** weeks of the application. Where practicable, the first hearing must be listed to be heard in this period and in any event no later than within **6** weeks of the application. Where, at the time of introduction of this Programme, the Designated Family Judge/Justices' Clerk determines that it is not practicable to list the first hearing within 4 weeks, they should, in consultation with HMCS and Cafcass, formulate a timetable for revisiting the position and managing to list the FHDRA within 4 weeks.

3.4 Copies of each Application Form C100 and Notice of Hearing shall be sent by the court to Cafcass in accordance with 3.2 above.

3.5 The Respondent shall have at least 14 days notice of the hearing where practicable, but the court may abridge this time.

3.6 The Respondent should file a response on the Forms C7/C1A no later than 14 days before the hearing.

3.7 A copy of Forms C7/C1A shall be sent by the court to Cafcass on the day of receipt.

3.8 **NOTE:** This provision relates to cases that are placed in the FHDRA list for hearing other than by direct application in accordance with the procedure referred to in paragraph 3.1. Such listing may follow an application under the Family Law Act 1996, or a direction by the Court in other proceedings. In all such cases, or where the Court adjourns proceedings to a 'dispute resolution hearing' (sometimes called 'conciliation'), this will be treated as an adjournment to a FHDRA, and the documents referred to in para 3.2 must be filed and copied to parties and Cafcass for safety checks and enquiries, in the same way.

3.9 Before the FHDRA Cafcass shall identify any safety issues by the steps outlined below. Such steps shall be confined to matters of safety. Neither Cafcass nor a Cafcass Officer shall discuss with either party before the FHDRA any matter other than relates to safety. The Parties will not be invited to talk about other issues, for example relating to the substance of applications or replies or about issues concerning matters of welfare or the prospects of resolution. If such issues are raised by either party they will be advised that such matters will be deferred to the FHDRA when there is equality between the parties and full discussion can take place which will also be a time when any safety issues that have been identified also can be taken into account.

(a)   In order to inform the court of possible risks of harm to the child in accordance with its safeguarding framework Cafcass will carry out safeguarding enquiries, including checks of local authorities and police, and telephone risk identification interviews with parties.

(b)   If risks of harm are identified, Cafcass may invite parties to meet separately with the Cafcass Officer before the FHDRA to clarify any safety issue.

(c)   Cafcass shall record and outline any safety issues for the court.

(d)   The Cafcass Officer will not initiate contact with the child prior to the FHDRA. If contacted by a child, discussions relating to the issues in the case will be postponed to the day of the hearing or after when the Cafcass officer will have more knowledge of the issues.

(e)   At least 3 days before the hearing the Cafcass Officer shall report the outcome of risk identification work to the court by completing the Form at Schedule 2.

4 The First Hearing Dispute Resolution Appointment.

4.1 The parties and Cafcass Officer shall attend this hearing. A mediator may attend where available.

4.2 At the hearing, which is not privileged, the court should have the following documents:

(a)   C100 application, and C1A if any

(b)   Notice of Hearing

(c)   C7 response and C1A if any

(d)   Schedule 2 safeguarding information

4.3 The detailed arrangements for the participation of mediators will be arranged locally. These will include:

(a)   Arrangements for the mediator to ask the parties in a particular case to consent to the mediator seeing the papers in the case where it seems appropriate to do so.

(b)   Arrangements for the mediator to ask the parties to waive privilege for the purpose of the first hearing where it seems to the mediator appropriate to do so in order to assist the work of the mediator and the outcome of the first hearing.

(c)   In all cases it is important that such arrangements are put in place in a way that avoids any pressure being brought to bear in this connection on the parties that is inconsistent with general good mediation practice.

4.4 At the FHDRA the Court, in collaboration with the Cafcass Officer, and with the assistance of any mediator present, will seek to assist the parties in conciliation and in resolution of all or any of the issues between them. Any remaining issues will be identified, the Cafcass Officer will advise the court of any recommended means of resolving such issues and directions will be given for the future resolution of such issues. At all times the decisions of the Court and the work of the Cafcass Officer will take account of any risk or safeguarding issues that have been identified.

4.5 The Cafcass Officer shall, where practicable, speak separately to each party at court and before the hearing.

4.6 In the County Court, the Court shall have available a telephone contact to the Family Proceedings Court listing manager, diary dates for the appropriate Family Proceedings Court, or other means by which the

County Court, at the time of the hearing, will be able to list subsequent hearings in the Family Proceedings Court.

5 Conduct of the Hearing. The following matters shall be considered

5.1 **Safeguarding**:

(a)   The court shall inform the parties of the content of any screening report or other information which has been provided by Cafcass, unless it considers that to do so would create a risk of harm to a party or the child. The court may need to consider whether and how any information contained in the checks should be disclosed to the parties if Cafcass have not disclosed it.

(b)   Whether a risk assessment is required and when.

(c)   Whether a fact finding hearing is needed to determine allegations whose resolution is likely to affect the decision of the court.

5.2 **Dispute Resolution**:

(a)   There will be at every FHDRA a period in which the Cafcass Officer, with the assistance of any Mediator and in collaboration with the Court, will seek to conciliate and explore with the parties the resolution of all or some of the issues between them. The procedure to be followed in this connection at the hearing will be determined by local arrangements between the Cafcass manager, or equivalent in Wales, and the Designated Family Judge or the Justices' Clerk where appropriate.

(b)   What is the result of any such meeting at Court?

(c)   What other options there are for resolution e.g. may the case be suitable for further intervention by Cafcass; mediation by an external provider; collaborative law or use of a parenting plan?

(d)   Would the parties be assisted by attendance at Parenting Information Programmes or other activities, whether by formal statutory provision under section 11 Children Act 1989 as amended by Children and Adoption Act 2006 or otherwise?

5.3 **Consent Orders**:

Where agreement is reached at any hearing or submitted in writing to the court, no order will be made without scrutiny by the court. Where safeguarding checks or risk assessment work remain outstanding, the making of a final order may be deferred for such work. In such circumstances the court shall adjourn the case for no longer than 28 days to a fixed date. A written notification of this work is to be provided by Cafcass in accordance with the timescale specified by the court. If satisfactory information is then available, the order may be made at the adjourned hearing in the agreed terms without the need for attendance by the parties. If satisfactory information is not available, the order will not be made, and the case will be adjourned for further consideration with an opportunity for the parties to make further representations.

5.4 **Reports**:

(a) Are there welfare issues or other specific considerations which should be addressed in a report by Cafcass or the Local Authority? Before a report is ordered, the court should consider alternative ways of working with the parties such as are referred to in paragraph 5.2 above. If a report is ordered in accordance with Section 7 of the Children Act 1989, it should be directed specifically towards and limited to those issues. General requests should be avoided and the Court should state in the Order the specific factual and other issues that are to be addressed in a focused report. In determining whether a request for a report should be directed to the relevant local authority or to Cafcass, the court should consider such information as Cafcass has provided about the extent and nature of the local authority's current or recent involvement with the subject of the application and the parties, and any relevant protocol between Cafcass and the Association of Directors of Children's Services.

(b) Is there a need for an investigation under S 37 Children Act 1989?

(c) A copy of the Order requesting the report and any relevant court documents are to be sent to Cafcass or, in the case of the Local Authority, to the Legal Adviser to the Director of the Local Authority Children's Services and, where known, to the allocated social worker by the court forthwith.

(d) Is any expert evidence required in compliance with the Experts' Practice Direction?

5.5 **Wishes and feelings of the child**:

(a) Is the child aware of the proceedings?
How are the wishes and feelings of the child to be ascertained (if at all)?

(b) How is the child to be involved in the proceedings, if at all, and whether at or after the FHDRA?

(c)   If consideration is given to the joining of the child as a party to the application, the court should consider the current Guidance from the President of the Family Division. Where the court is considering the appointment of a guardian ad litem, it should first seek to ensure that the appropriate Cafcass manager has been spoken to so as to consider any advice in connection with the prospective appointment and the timescale involved. In considering whether to make such an appointment the Court shall take account of the demands on the resources of Cafcass that such appointment would make.

(d)   Who will inform the child of the outcome of the case where appropriate?

5.6 Case Management:

(a)   What, if any, issues are agreed and what are the key issues to be determined?

(b)   Are there any interim orders which can usefully be made (e.g. indirect, supported or supervised contact) pending final hearing?

(c)   What directions are required to ensure the application is ready for final hearing – statements, reports etc?

(d)   List for final hearing, consider the need for judicial continuity (especially if there has been or is to be a fact finding hearing or a contested interim hearing).

5.7 Transfer to FPC:

The case should be transferred to the FPC, pursuant to the Allocation and Transfer of Proceedings Order 2008 unless one of the specified exceptions applies. The date should be fixed at court and entered on the order.

6 The Order

6.1 The Order shall set out in particular:

(a)   The issues about which the parties are agreed.

(b)   The issues that remain to be resolved.

(c)   The steps that are planned to resolve the issues.

(d)   Any interim arrangements pending such resolution, including arrangements for the involvement of children.

(e)   The timetable for such steps and, where this involves further hearings, the date of such hearings.

(f)   A statement as to any facts relating to risk or safety; in so far as they are resolved the result will be stated and, in so far as not resolved, the steps to be taken to resolve them will be stated.

(g)   If it be the case, the fact of the transfer of the case to the Family Proceedings Court with the date and purpose of the next hearing.

(h)   If it be the case, the fact that the case cannot be transferred to the Family Proceedings Court and the reason for the decision.

(i)   Whether in the event of an order, by consent or otherwise, or pending such an order, the parties are to be assisted by participation in mediation, Parenting Information Programmes, or other types of parenting intervention, and to detail any contact activity directions or conditions imposed by the court.

6.2 A suggested template order is available as set out in Schedule 1 below.

7 Commencement and Implementation

7.1 This Practice Direction will come into effect on 1 April 2010. So that procedural changes can be made by all agencies, the requirement for full implementation of the provisions is postponed, but in any event it should be effected by no later than 4 October 2010.

Schedule 1

The suggested form of Order which courts may wish to use is PLP10 which is available from Her Majesty's Court Service.

Schedule 2

Report Form on outcome of safeguarding enquiries. See version for Cafcass in England and for CAFCASS CYMRU in Wales.

A3.6   APPENDIX 6:
FORCED MARRIAGE GUIDELINES

10 November 2009

The Guidance for local authorities and partner agencies is intended to provide additional advice and support to frontline local authority employees when they are considering making an application as a Relevant Third Party under the Forced Marriage (Civil Protection) Act 2007.

The Guidance can be found at http://www.fco.gov.uk/resources/en/pdf/ 3849543/forced-marriage-guidelines09.pdf

A3.7 APPENDIX 7:
ACTING IN THE ABSENCE OF A CHILDREN'S GUARDIAN

Law Society Practice Note
25 August 2009

(© The Law Society 2009)

Acting in the Absence of a Children's Guardian

1 Introduction

1.1 Who should read this practice note?

Solicitors who represent children in public law proceedings.

1.2 What is the issue?

This practice note clarifies what you should do if a court appoints you to represent children in cases where a guardian is not immediately available, or where there are delays between the order appointing a guardian in specified proceedings and the allocation of a guardian.

This practice note does not apply to situations in which a guardian has been appointed but you have not received instructions from the allocated guardian or where the guardian's physical attendance at court may not be possible.

This practice note replaces Appendix 8 of *Good Practice in Child Care Cases* and should be read in conjunction with the Public Law Outline and the President's Interim Guidance for England.

This advice has been endorsed by Resolution, the national organisation of family lawyers. See 4.3.4 Resolution for more information.

1.2.1 TANDEM MODEL

The Law Society supports the need for a tandem model of legal representation – a solicitor and a children's guardian. The tandem model provides a balance of welfare and legal support for children that is vital to ensuring that the best interests of the child are clearly articulated in court proceedings.

2 *Appointments to represent children*

The appointment by the court of the solicitor for the child is governed by section 41(3) Children Act 1989. The Law Society's document "Appointing a solicitor for the child in specified proceedings: guidelines for courts" April 2007 provides guidance on the appointment of the solicitor for the child.

The President's Interim Guidance for England provides that Designated Family Judges may make arrangements for care centres and/or groups of courts to enter into a CAFCASS duty advice scheme for the provision of advice to the court at the first appointment through the solicitor appointed under section 41(3) Children Act 1989. The guidance is intended to cease to have effect on 31st March 2010.

Note—The guidance was intended to cease on 31 March 2010 but has now been extended to have effect until at least 30 September 2010.

2.1 *Accepting an appointment*

You may decide whether or not to accept an appointment from the court to act for a child.

In making the decision, you should consider whether you are able and competent to represent that child in accordance with the professional duty to the client.

You should identify the child's best interests and vulnerability issues, including:

- the urgency of the case
- the impact of delay upon the child
- the age and understanding of the child.

You should carefully consider whether you are able to act promptly and personally, and whether you have sufficient experience and the appropriate expertise to deal with the case in the absence of a children's guardian. You may also consider making appropriate professional mentoring arrangements.

You should not refuse to accept instructions to represent a child solely on the basis of the non-availability of a children's guardian. There is likely to be significant work which you can undertake in and outside of court pending the involvement of a children's guardian in order to facilitate the smooth running of the proceedings, to clarify issues and plans and to probe and test evidence.

2.2 *Law Society Children Panel undertaking*

Members of the Law Society Children Panel must comply with the panel undertaking in all cases, whether or not a children's guardian is appointed. Continuity and consistency of representation for the child will be particularly important where no child's guardian is involved in the case.

3 Acting in the absence of a children's guardian

Having accepted an appointment to represent a child in the absence of a guardian you should conduct the proceedings in accordance with the instructions from the child where the child is able to understand the situation and give such instructions.

In default of instructions you should represent the child "in furtherance of the best interests of the child" in view of Section 41 of the Children Act 1989 and Rule 4.12 of the Family Proceedings Rules 1991. What work is necessary will be a matter of your professional judgement in the individual case.

You should not however undertake the guardian's professional role. You must not make welfare decisions and recommendations based on personal feelings. While you should act in accordance with the particular child's best interests, you are not in a position to advise the court what those interests are but you may make the court aware of all the available options, without specific recommendations.

3.1 Preparation

You should carefully read all papers before the first hearing and consider the appropriate resources required to support the case.

3.1.1 REQUEST AND COLLATE DOCUMENTS

You should request and collate as soon as possible all relevant papers including:

- copies from the local authority social services' records of all case conference minutes, and
- medical or other reports relating to the child.

The local authority party is likely to agree to provide those key documents which would be disclosed in the ordinary process of discovery.

However, you do not have the statutory right of access to local authority records, which children's guardians have under Section 42 of the Children Act 1989 meaning local authorities are required to comply with data protection legislation. Where necessary you should discuss a consensual way forward with the local authority party.

Given time and financial constraints this step may be difficult to achieve in some cases and you may exercise your professional judgement in deciding whether to collate these documents.

3.1.2 CONSIDER THE EVIDENCE OF OTHER PARTIES

You should hear the evidence of the local authority and other parties and make submissions on whether they have made their cases on the evidence. You should critically appraise the local authority's actions and evidence in support of those actions, and seek a direction to require the filing of further evidence if appropriate, in order:

- to probe and test their case; and
- to ensure that the court has sufficient evidence on which to base its decisions; and
- to test the evidence of all parties at any contested interim hearing.

You may raise issues for the other parties to consider: you may not recommend a particular course of action.

3.2 Ensuring the child's needs are met

You should be familiar with *Good Practice in Child Care Cases* (The Law Society 2004 with the Association of Lawyers for Children, the Child Care Law Joint Liaison Group, and Resolution (formerly SFLA)), the Public Law Outline and the President's Interim Guidance.

You should also become familiar with any duty guardian scheme/protocol which has been duly approved by the Designated Family Judge in accordance with the President's Interim Guidance, and is in operation in the court.

3.2.1 Your suitability

You should continue to self-assess your suitability after accepting a court appointment of this nature.

You should also be alert and sensitive to whether there is a good reason why this particular child may or may not be better represented by someone of a specific gender or ethnic background or culture, or with knowledge, skills or experience relevant to the case.

Practitioners should not continue with cases which are outside their expertise.

3.2.2 Your contact with the child

You should attempt to see the child as soon as possible, if appropriate. You should exercise professional judgement as to whether a visit is appropriate, particularly if the subject is a baby or very young child. It is generally appropriate to meet the child if you are competent to do so, the child would benefit from the visit or the visit would assist the court, unless there is a good reason not to.

Ideally the meeting should take place after you have read the papers and before the first hearing. Meetings should be conducted in an appropriate setting and tone, in order for you to:

- identify family members and other persons who the child regards as significant

- understand the wishes and feelings of the child where it is possible to do so
- ascertain whether the child is able to give her/his own instructions.

You should report to the court any wishes and feelings articulated by the child, and consider seeking directions for discovery and disclosure as necessary, including in relation to previous Children Act proceedings and concurrent criminal proceedings

As appropriate to the child's age and understanding, you should help them to understand the court process, prepare them for court proceedings and explain the outcome of interim court decisions and any appeal.

3.2.3 Conditions for interim care

You should consider whether it is appropriate to request a transfer to the care centre, based on the information available, and make any application to do so if necessary.

You should consider and provide advice based on evidence, not personal feelings as to whether the interim care plan and arrangements are both:

- safe, and
- suitable for the age and circumstances of the child.

You must not recommend that an Interim Care Order be made but can advise the court as to whether the evidence presented satisfies the test for making an Interim Care Order.

3.2.4 Family contact

You should be aware of any contact issues for children separated from their families. Check whether contact with parents, siblings and other family members is being properly explored and whether the arrangements are appropriate and safe. In doing so you should establish factors such as:

- frequency
- venue
- travel arrangements
- opportunities for care giving
- level of supervision

You should ensure that contact with the father and extended paternal family is being properly explored, even where the father has apparently not played a key role to date.

3.2.5 Tracing family members or other carers

You should ascertain from the local authority any enquiries made in relation to the identity and whereabouts of the father or putative father and paternal grandparents, and the early identification of other family members or people of importance to the child who might offer care and/or with whom the child might want, or benefit from, contact.

You should ensure that all appropriate steps have been taken to trace any such parties and check with parents' representatives that parents have been asked and given information about relevant members of the extended family.

3.3   Appointment of a children's guardian

You should continue to seek the appointment of a children's guardian by Children and Family Court Advisory and Support Service (CAFCASS). You may make a repeat request if the case becomes more urgent or adequate time has passed.

You should keep the issue of the non-appointment of a children's guardian under constant review. This includes advising the court at the outset. You may do this by informing the clerk of your view on the level of priority for appointment. In formulating this advice you should consider, together with the other parties, whether there are urgent decisions to be made on any of the following issues:

- separation and placement;
- the removal or return of the child including initial risk assessment;
- the separation of siblings;
- contact including sibling contact;
- the need for immediate expert evidence on causation;
- the type of placement.

The matter should be brought back before the court as quickly as possible after the first hearing and continue to be an issue for every hearing until resolved.

3.3.1   Welfare issues

CAFCASS should be kept informed of any changes or issues arising that affect your advice on the level of urgency in relation to allocation of a guardian.

If urgent and specific welfare issues arise which cannot await the allocation of a guardian, and advice from any duty guardian is insufficient to deal with the problem, you should consider applying to the court for leave to consult an expert social worker or other appropriate expert to advise the court on those specific welfare issues.

You should invite the court to record on the face of the order the reasons for the urgency and consider obtaining prior authority from the Legal Services Commission before proceeding with any resulting instruction.

3.4   Case management and court procedures

You should consider Articles 6 (the right to fair trial) and 8 (the right to respect for family life) of the European Convention on Human Rights (enshrined in domestic law in the Human Rights Act 1998) and ensure that proceedings are conducted with due regard to such rights.

With regards to court procedure you should:

- consider whether a split hearing is necessary;
- consider whether or not to appeal any court adjudication;
- check and become familiar with any duty guardian scheme or protocol which has been duly approved by the Designated Family Judge in accordance with the President's Interim Guidance and is in operation at the court.

You should also be generally aware of, and play a leading role in, case management and time tabling issues to enable smooth running of the proceedings as a whole.

3.4.1   Statements

You may:

- seek directions for the filing of parents' statements, together with those of any other relevant party
- consider the issue of joinder of additional parties
- identify and suggest to other parties, where appropriate, that they interview any witnesses.

3.4.2   Medical or psychiatric assessments

You should consider the need for medical/psychiatric or other expert assessments and evidence, having regard in particular to the competence of the child to give instructions and the joinder of additional parties.

It can be difficult to take an initiative on this point without instructions from a guardian, but you may identify issues where it might be more appropriate for the local authority or parents to consider instructing an expert.

You may also respond to suggestions by others and play a role in clarifying instructions and approving draft letters of instruction and time tabling.

4   More information

4.1   Professional conduct

The following section of the Solicitors' Code of Conduct 2007 is relevant to this issue:

- Rule 2.01: Taking on clients

4.2 Legal and other requirements

- Children Act 1989
- Rule 4.12 of the Family Proceedings Rules 1991
- European Convention on Human Rights articles 6 and 8
- Human Rights Act 1998

4.3 Further products and support

4.3.1 Law Society publications

- "Appointing a solicitor for the child in specified proceedings: guidelines for courts" April 2007

4.3.2 Law Society Children Panel

Law Society online resources for children law practitioners include publications, policy documents and event announcements.

4.3.4 Practice Advice Line

The Law Society provides support for solicitors on a wide range of areas of practice. Practice Advice can be contacted on 0870 606 2522 from 09:00 to 17:00 on weekdays.

4.3.5 Resolution

Resolution is the national organisation of family lawyers. This advice has been endorsed by Resolution.

4.4 Status of this practice note

Practice notes are issued by the Law Society for the use and benefit of its members. They represent the Law Society's view of good practice in a particular area. They are not intended to be the only standard of good practice that solicitors can follow. You are not required to follow them, but doing so will make it easier to account to oversight bodies for your actions.

Practice notes are not legal advice, nor do they necessarily provide a defence to complaints of misconduct or of inadequate professional service. While care has been taken to ensure that they are accurate, up to date and useful, the Law Society will not accept any legal liability in relation to them.

For queries or comments on this practice note contact the Law Society's Practice Advice Service.

4.5 Terminology in this practice note

"Must" – a specific requirement in the Solicitor's Code of Conduct or legislation. You must comply, unless there are specific exemptions or defences provided for in the code of conduct or relevant legislation.

"Should" – good practice for most situations in the Law Society's view. If you do not follow this, you must be able to justify to oversight bodies why this is appropriate, either for your practice, or in the particular retainer.

"May" – a non-exhaustive list of options for meeting your obligations. Which option you choose is determined by the risk profile of the individual practice, client or retainer. You must be able to justify why this was an appropriate option to oversight bodies.

A3.8   APPENDIX 8:
PREPARING FOR CARE AND SUPERVISION PROCEEDINGS

Best Practice Guide
August 2009

Preparing for Care and Supervision Proceedings

A best practice guide for use by all professionals involved with children and families pre-proceedings and in preparation for applications made under section 31 of the Children Act 1989.

Produced by the Care Proceedings Programme, Ministry of Justice, August 2009.

Foreword

This comprehensive best practice guide is based on the findings of inter agency workshops and has been extensively peer reviewed. It sets out examples and puts forward suggestions as to how we can all work together, valuing and understanding the work and roles of colleagues, and puts the needs of the child firmly back at the heart of care proceedings.

The guide will complement the Statutory Guidance and Public Law Outline but it is not intended to be prescriptive. However, it describes the processes involved; the respective roles of those involved; tackles some of the most difficult and frequently raised areas of uncertainty; and provides examples of good practice. It also acts as a sign post towards the regulations and Statutory Guidance on specific issues and is one of a range of measures aimed at developing a consistent and practical approach to care proceedings.

The publication of this guide is particularly timely in view of the recommendations in Lord Laming's report "The Protection of Children in England: A progress report", published in March 2009. The UK Government has accepted all 58 of Lord Laming's recommendations, and published an action plan on 6 May 2009, setting out the detailed response to the recommendations. The action plan is available at: *www. everychildmatters.gov.uk/laming.*

The Welsh Assembly Government has put in place a programme of measures to strengthen arrangements to safeguard children. These include new arrangements to establish teams to provide intensive support to families whose children may be subject of a care order.

The guide has the full support of the National Family Justice Board. We would like to express our thanks to all those practitioners who have co-operated and contributed to this publication and in particular to the Family Law Bar Association and the Law Society for their endorsement.

Contents

*sw	Social work professionals
lfc	lawyers for children
lfp	lawyers for parents or those with PR
lfLA	lawyers for the Local Authority
hmcs	court staff and magistrates' legal advisers

cg   Children's Guardians

j   Judiciary

Abbreviations

ACA 2002	Adoption and Children Act 2002
ALDT/CLDT	Adults with Learning Difficulties Team/Community Learning Disability Team or LA equivalent
CA 1989	Children Act 1989
CA 2004	Children Act 2004
Cafcass	Child and Family Court Advisory Service
CAFCASS CYMRU	The Welsh Assembly Government Service in Wales
CMC	Case Management Conference
Experts PD	Practice Direction: Experts in Family Proceedings Relating to Children (President of the Family Division, April 2008)
FA	First Appointment
FGC	Family Group Conference
FH	Final Hearing
Framework	Framework for the Assessment of Children in Need and their Families, 2000, Department of Health. Framework for the Assessment of Children in Need and their Families, 2001, Welsh Assembly Government
HMCS	Her Majesty's Court Service
IRH	Issues Resolution Hearing
IRO	Independent Reviewing Officer
LA	Local Authority
LbP	Letter before Proceedings
LSCB	Local Safeguarding Children's Board
LSC	Legal Services Commission
Parent	The term "parent" is used throughout but should be read to include "parent(s) or other person(s) with PR"
PD	Practice Direction: Guide to Case Management in Public Law Cases (Judiciary of England & Wales and Ministry of Justice, April 2008)
PLO	Public Law Outline (this is contained in the PD and replaces the previous 2003 protocol)
PPM	Pre-Proceedings Meeting
PR	Parental responsibility, defined in section 3 of the Children Act 1989
SG	Statutory Guidance The Children Act 1989 Guidance and Regulations, Volume 1: Court Orders (Department for Children, Schools and Families, April 2008) and the Welsh equivalent, The Children Act 1989 Guidance and Regulations, Volume 1: Court Orders (Wales)
Working Together	Working Together under the Children Act 2004 to Safeguard Children: Every Child matters. A guide to inter-agency working to safeguard and promote the welfare of children, 2006, HM Government Wales – Safeguarding Children – Working Together under the Children Act 2004

Chapter 1 – Introduction

1.1 Background to the reforms

Following the *Review of the Child Care Proceedings System in England and Wales*[1], reforms to s 31 CA 1989 proceedings were brought into effect in April 2008 by two key documents:

1 The Practice Direction: Guide to Case Management in Public Law Cases[2]; and

2 The Children Act 1989 Guidance and Regulations, Volume 1: Court Orders[3] in England, and The Children Act 1989 Guidance and Regulations, Volume 1: Court Orders (Wales)[4] in Wales.

The aim of the reforms can be broadly stated as an intention to make the system for s 31 CA 1989 proceedings more efficient by reducing delay and to improve the outcomes for children and families who may become the subject of court proceedings. The Statutory Guidance focuses on social work undertaken pre-proceedings for two principal reasons. In many cases there will still be an opportunity for the social worker to work with the child and family with a view to avoiding the need for court proceedings. Secondly, work done at these stages can impact on the proceedings (if proceedings are later initiated) and the ability for the proceedings to be conducted as smoothly and expeditiously as possible providing the best possible outcome for the child and his/her family.

1 Review of the Child Care Proceedings System in England and Wales, Department of Constitutional Affairs, Department for Education and Skills and Welsh Assembly Government (May 2006). Accessible at: http://www.dca.gov.uk/publications/reports_reviews/childcare_ps.pdf

2 The Practice Direction: Guide to Case Management in Public Law Cases, Judiciary of England & Wales and Ministry of Justice (April 2008). Accessible at: http://www.judiciary.gov.uk/docs/public_law_outline.pdf

3 The Children Act 1989 Guidance and Regulations, Volume 1: Court Orders, Department for Children, Schools and Families (April 2008). Accessible at: http://www.dcsf.gov.uk/localauthorities/_documents/content/childrensactguidance.pdf

4 The Children Act 1989 Guidance and Regulations, Volume 1: Court Orders, Welsh Assembly Government and NHS Wales (March 2008). Accessible at: http://new.wales.gov.uk/dhss/publications/children/guidance/actguidance/courtorderse.pdf?lang=en

1.2 The status of this best practice guide

Ten initiative areas[1] tested elements of the PLO prior to it being finalised. Professionals from those areas were well placed to share information about how their areas were dealing with the reforms "on the ground". The Ministry of Justice's Care Proceedings Programme Office[2] held two workshops in July 2008 (Reading and Liverpool). The "Moving Forward Workshops" brought together professionals from all fields of expertise (HMCS, legal, social work and Cafcass/CAFCASS CYMRU) from the initiative areas. A wealth of information came out of the workshops. We learned about the many examples of good practice, which some areas had already implemented and were working to; many of those ideas have been incorporated into this guide. We also learned of challenges, which some professionals were experiencing. We have sought to bring all that information into this one comprehensive guide to both share the ideas of good practice already operating but also to address and assist with some of the perceived problems.

The guide is not Statutory Guidance: it has no legal status. We have taken careful steps to ensure that various experts in their respective fields reviewed this guide before it was finalised. We hope practitioners may find it a useful additional source of information and explanation but it is no substitute for acting within the statutory framework set out in the Children Act 1989 and the regulations made under Part 3 of the Act and the Statutory Guidance on it.

1   Birmingham, London, Liverpool, Warrington/Chester, Newcastle/Sunderland, Exeter/Plymouth, Leicester, Milton Keynes/Oxford, Swansea, Portsmouth.

2   An inter-agency group set up to deliver the recommendations arising from the 2006 Care Review at: *http://www.justice.gov.uk/guidance/careproceedings.htm*

1.3   Who should read this guide

This guide is written for all professionals who work with or for children and families where s 31 CA 1989 care proceedings are being considered or applied for. In the main those who we hope will find the guide of most use to their work are: LA social workers, LA managers, lawyers for the LA and for parents, Children's Guardians, lawyers for children, HMCS court staff and legal advisers, the judiciary and expert assessors who may be instructed pre-proceedings and within proceedings.

1.4   How to use this guide

This guide is separated into two parts. Chapter 2 covers the pre-proceedings stages up to the point that a s 31 CA 1989 application is issued at court. Chapter 3 looks at the stages from the point that the LA issues a s 31 CA 1989 application through to disposal of the application and conclusion of the proceedings.

Some of the aspects discussed in this guide will be connected or relate to other aspects. We have used cross-referencing where this is the case. The intention of the guide is that it should act as a quick-reference tool to good practice. As the guide has been written to cater for all parties involved in care proceedings readers should gain a better understanding of the roles and responsibilities of other professionals involved. To make the guide as user-friendly as possible the contents identify the paragraphs which are recommended reading for the various professionals involved in s 31 CA 1989 proceedings.

Chapter 2 – Pre-proceedings stages

2.1   Introduction

In this document the term pre-proceedings is used to indicate the several stages of interaction between the child, family and the LA which occur prior to a court application being issued for a s 31 CA 1989 order. It is straightforward to ascertain the "end" of pre-proceedings because this will be the date that the application to court is issued. Where the pre-proceedings stages "begin" however, is less well defined. On the one hand all stages of involvement prior to an application being made could be termed "pre-proceedings" but for the purposes of the recent reforms the use of the term pre-proceedings is rather precise. It denotes the stages from the point that the LA is considering making an application to court to protect the child but the risk of harm to the child is manageable if an application is not made immediately. Effectively, the LA's approach will be to further attempt to engage with the parent in order to put an agreement in place which reduces the risk of significant harm to the child to a manageable level at that stage.

The point at which pre-proceedings stages nominally commence in view of the recent reforms is where the legal gateway/planning meeting (section 2.3) has been held and the LA makes the decision to send a Letter before Proceedings (LbP) (section 2.4).

2.2   Social work

Volume 1 of the Children Act Guidance and Regulations is issued under section 7 of the Local Authority Social Services Act 1970. Local Authorities must, in exercising their social services functions, act under this guidance.

The Children Act 1989, the Adoption and Children Act 2002, and the Children Act 2004 combined with Regulations made under those statutes and the Statutory Guidance set out the statutory framework within which social workers should perform functions on behalf of the LA. The Statutory Guidance seeks to provide advice to the LA on relevant matters. In relation to care proceedings the Guidance stipulates the "matters to be considered by the LA before making an application for a care or supervision order"[1]. The LA has many duties and obligations with which it must comply. The most relevant (at this stage) is the general duty to safeguard and promote the welfare of children in need and "so far as is consistent with that duty, to promote the upbringing of such children by their families by providing a range and level of services appropriate to those children's needs" (s 17(1) CA 1989).

The original version of Volume 1 was published in 1991. The revised Guidance gives updated advice to LAs on how they should meet their duties. Some key points from the Guidance are:

- That voluntary arrangements for the provision of services should be fully explored together with consideration of potential alternative carers
- That prior to proceedings, work should be undertaken to explore alternative care solutions for the child, assess the suitability of those arrangements and consider the legal status of those arrangements.

1   Statutory Guidance, paras 3.22–3.33.

2.3   The legal gateway/planning meeting

The purpose of a legal gateway or planning meeting is for the LA to seek legal advice about a particular case. These meetings should be attended by the child's social worker and managers together with the lawyer advising the LA. The social work team will usually set out the facts of the case, their concerns and explain what has been done to work with the child and family. The ultimate question will be "is the threshold criteria met and are court proceedings necessary at this stage?"

In those cases where it is agreed that it will be necessary to initiate Care Proceedings the LA will consider if it is appropriate to write to the parent to inform him or her that an application to court will be made shortly and to explain that he or she should seek legal advice. A template letter can be found at Annex A. There are two important points to note about sending such a letter to the parent:

- This letter is not intended to be a "LbP" and therefore may not act as the trigger letter for Family Help Lower (level 2) publicly funded advice and assistance (section 2.6.3). However, the parent may still be eligible for means-tested advice under Legal Help (level 1) from a solicitor. Parents should be advised to seek further guidance from a solicitor on this point; and
- It will not be appropriate to send this letter in all cases where immediate issue of proceedings is decided. Whether or not to send the letter requires very careful assessment by the LA. For example, there may be concerns that if a parent knows that the LA is going to apply to court for an order allowing it to remove the child from his or her care, the parent and their children may leave the area.

2.4   The Letter before Proceedings (LbP)

If following a legal gateway/planning meeting it is decided that there is time to work with the family to avoid proceedings, and the short term safety and welfare of the child permits, a LbP should be issued. The LbP allows social workers to structure their work with the child and family and to consider alternative options and services which could be provided to the family. Once the LbP inviting a parent to a Pre Proceedings Meeting (PPM) is sent out, the LA has an opportunity to work with the family and to explore all options prior to making an application to court. Some LAs have indicated that the use of the LbP has helped to stop the drift in more long-standing cases. We found that many LAs have given lots of time and effort to adjusting the template LbP contained in the Statutory Guidance to their particular areas and we have been informed that generally parents have found the LbP useful as it sets out in one place the LA's concerns.

2.4.1   OWNERSHIP

As the LbP is a new stage in the process introduced by the revised Statutory Guidance (SG) we are aware that LAs have varying experiences of its use. The template LbP which is annexed to the SG envisages that the signature carried on the LbP will be that of the social worker's team manager.

The LA should request that their legal department check the contents of this letter to ensure that it includes all information relevant to the grounds for proceedings.

2.4.2 TIMING

In deciding the timing about when best to send the LbP, the LA will have first considered and sought legal advice about whether it should make an application to the court (section 2.3). If it makes an "in principle" decision that it would be appropriate to apply for an order but also concludes that the risk can be managed without an immediate application, the LA is effectively concluding that it can see a window of opportunity to try to continue to work with the family to maintain their children safely with their parents. The LbP should be sent at this point.

Once the LbP is sent the LA should utilise this opportunity to secure a plan or agreement to protect the child safely at home and work towards reducing the risk of significant harm to the child.

Where a local authority judges that there is not a window of opportunity to work with the family to continue to maintain the child at home, given its assessment of the safeguarding concerns in the case, the LA will need to apply immediately to court even on short notice for a s 31 CA 1989 order. Where this is the case LAs should consider using the immediate issue template letter at Annex A.

2.4.3 CONTENTS

The Letter before Proceedings (LbP) is an important letter and should be carefully drafted. It is the trigger for non-means, non-merits tested publicly funded legal advice and assistance under "Family Help Lower" (also referred to as Level 2 advice) (sections 2.6.2 & 2.6.3). It will be filed with the court, and it needs to be concise, clear and focused. For this reason the template LbP in the Statutory Guidance should be used as the basis for the letter.

It is important that the LbP is understood by the recipient. The template LbP in the Statutory Guidance uses very simple English and is jargon free so that it can be understood by recipients. If applicable it should be translated into the language used by the parent or carer. It is important that there should be no surprises in the LbP. Although the parent should already have had notice or knowledge of the LA's concerns, the purpose of the LbP is to be clear (in one place) about the concerns and what the LA needs to change or improve in order to reduce those concerns. Finally, it acts as formal notification that the parent should seek legal advice, together with a final warning that court proceedings may follow if the situation fails to improve.

The LbP also invites the parent to a Pre Proceedings Meeting (PPM) to discuss matters and hopefully finalise a plan or agreement. There needs to be sufficient time balanced against risk to the child to allow the recipient of the LbP to actually receive the letter, consider it and to seek advice from a lawyer in advance. Social workers will need to consider these factors when proposing the date and time of the PPM in the LbP.

2.4.4 PLANS AND AGREEMENTS

The Letter before Proceedings will state what concerns need to be addressed by the parent and what support will be provided by the LA to help. These issues will be reflected in the existing child in need/child protection or care plan. The plan may be one of the following formats:

(*a*) a care plan because the child is looked-after by the LA pursuant to a s 20 CA 1989 agreement; a looked after child's plan can only be amended at a Statutory review at which the parents will (hopefully) be present;

(*b*) a child protection plan if the child is already the subject of child protection measures;

(*c*) a Child in Need plan if the child is not looked-after but is deemed to be "in need" of services pursuant to s 17 CA 1989.

It follows that the LA should update the plan and send it to the parent as a draft plan (ideally with the LbP) which he or she will be asked to agree at the PPM.

The Pre Proceedings Meeting (PPM) will work best where both the LA and the parent have had a good opportunity to prepare. For the parent this will mean considering the LbP and understanding the plan which he or she is being asked to agree to. The LbP must actively encourage the parent to see a solicitor for advice; ideally he or she will have given instructions and at least sought some brief advice before coming to the PPM with the solicitor. Parents should understand the details of the concerns about the child's developmental needs, including the need for safeguarding and the plan to meet them in order to know what is required of them and how they can fulfil the requirements or discuss the issues if they feel unable to make a meaningful change. Alternatively, they will be in a position to suggest factual corrections or amendments to the proposed plan through the negotiation that will take place during the PPM.

2.4.5 COMMUNICATING MESSAGES

It is important to be sensitive and careful in communicating messages from the LbP. Nothing in the proposed plan should be new or a surprise to the parent. The concerns will have continuously been referred to during meetings, case conferences, documents or correspondence between the LA and the parent.

- The LA should consider hand delivering the LbP (taking into account if it is safe to do so) so that the social worker can be sure that the LbP was actually delivered.
- The social worker may wish to ask the parent to sign a "receipt" to evidence delivery of the LbP. Feedback informs us that parents are more likely to attend the PPM where the LA has met the parent to deliver the LbP to reinforce its meaning and purpose.
- If communication is difficult it will be even more important to record on the LA file the methods attempted by the social worker to deliver the letter.
- Where the LbP is being posted then use recorded delivery.

The expectation is that the parents will seek legal advice and take the LbP to their solicitor.

The Ministry of Justice's Care Proceedings Programme Office will be issuing in 2009 a written pack for parents to encourage better engagement during the pre-proceedings stages. The material's target audience will be parents who are involved with the LA at the pre-proceedings stages. It is hoped that social workers and lawyers for parents will be able to refer parents to the material to aid their understanding of the pre-proceedings stages. It is intended that the material will be made more widely available within voluntary sector agencies/organisations whose service-user groups include parents involved with the LA in relation to their children.

2.5   The Pre Proceedings Meeting (PPM)

2.5.1   TIMING

The Letter before Proceedings will have stated a date, time and venue for the PPM. Consideration should be given to re-scheduling when requested by the parents so long as this not does affect the child's safety and welfare.

2.5.2   ORGANISATION AND CO-ORDINATION

Ethos: The aim of the PPM is to reach an agreement on the proposed plan between the family and the LA. Although agreement may not be able to be reached in all cases or about all areas of the plan, a conciliatory approach is encouraged of the participants and their lawyers. It should be noted that the PPM is not intended to be adversarial in nature and therefore it would be unhelpful for any participant to take such an approach. It must be borne in mind that the PPM is a social work led meeting and not a court or tribunal where a judge or arbiter listens to evidence, argument and makes decisions. Neither is the PPM a forum for disputed facts to be determined, such as in a fact finding hearing. If there are disputed facts or issues, the participants can through negotiation agree facts or narrow issues down voluntarily. The PPM will not however, decide on anything which fundamentally remains contested or disputed. No participant should feel pressured to agree to anything that he or she does not want to. Legal advice during the meeting will assist the parent with this. It is vital for the parent to understand that the proposed plan being put forward by the LA warrants careful thought so that the parent is aware of what is likely to happen in the event that an agreement to the plan or amended plan cannot be secured.

Venue of the PPM: We know that in certain familial situations the issue of where the PPM takes place can be "make or break" in terms of whether the parent will attend and engage in the PPM. The decision regarding venue will be taken by the social worker in conjunction with his or her manager and the person who will chair the PPM. The social worker will be key in influencing this decision – having the most detailed knowledge of the circumstances of the family.

Agenda for the PPM: Many LAs have formulated an outline agenda for use at the PPM. They have found that this is helpful as it formalises the meeting, ensures that everything is covered and demonstrates to the participants that the PPM is of a more serious nature than perhaps other routine meetings between a parent and the LA. Annex C is a list of points/agenda items which may be considered for inclusion in any agenda for such meetings. It remains, of course, for each LA to decide how it wishes to conduct the meetings and whether it chooses to create its own agenda using some or all of the suggestions contained in Annex C.

Engaging the parent: There may be times when a parent will either refuse to attend the PPM or disagree with the proposed plan. This can be a difficult process but there may still be an opportunity to narrow some of the issues. A brief case example is given at the bottom of Annex C.

Minutes of the PPM: It is good practice for minutes to be taken of the PPM and then for those to be approved by the LA and circulated to the parent as quickly as possible. The parent will then have the opportunity to suggest corrections or additions which the LA can then consider. We suggest that the LA adopt a similar practice regarding minutes of the PPM as they will have in place for child protection case/review conferences. Minutes are important for any formal meeting and it is preferable that they are provided in relation to all PPMs.

Communicating plans: The plan and any agreement which has been reached during the meeting will be a material document and it is important that it is accurate, and comprehensive.

2.5.3 PARTICIPANTS

Legal: If parents attend with their lawyer the LA lawyer should also attend.

Wider family members: Should a parent wish to bring a person in a supportive role it is in the discretion of the LA to allow this.

One possible tool that the LA might re-consider at this point is the use of a Family Group Conference/Family meeting which might assist identification of wider family support. However, it must be remembered that the child's welfare is paramount and also that the parents should be central to this process and their agreement obtained at the outset and throughout the process.

Other agencies/organisations: The PPM is not a multi-disciplinary meeting or forum and it is not appropriate for other agencies to attend.

Chairing the PPM: Some LAs have stated that they have not found it helpful for the child's social worker or manager to chair the PPM. Some suggestions on people who might be better suited to chair the PPM are:

- A senior manager from the LA; or
- A contracted person who is suitably qualified akin to an Independent Reviewing Officer.

In either case, it is preferable that the person who does chair should be someone with no prior direct involvement with the child and family and where practicable that this person should chair all the PPMs in that LA. LAs who are operating a system of one nominated person as chair for all meetings are finding this is beneficial to the outcome.

If this person has no prior involvement the chances of a productive meeting increase as the parent will hopefully look to the chair as someone who is fresh to the case, less likely to have preconceived ideas about the child or family, perhaps be more impartial than the child's social worker, and is sufficiently distanced to have a wider perspective on the issues. If the chair is able to gain the trust of the participants in the meeting, the meeting will proceed more effectively.

2.5.4 ATTENDEES WITH PARTICULAR NEEDS

Given the nature, sensitivity and seriousness of the issues which fall to be discussed at the PPM it is crucial that the participants understand and are able to follow the discussions.

Some of the issues which come within the remit of the pre-proceedings stages are just as important as some of those that arise within proceedings. Where a person lacks the capacity to follow the litigation within proceedings, it is likely that he or she would also find it difficult to understand everything that is being said and asked of him or her pre-proceedings. Where an informal assessment suggests a parent may struggle to follow the pre-proceedings discussions or otherwise may have a learning disability or mental health problems which affect the parent's ability to follow the issues, then an immediate and urgent referral must be made to the Adults with Learning Disability Team/Community Learning Disability Team (ALDT/CLDT) or LA equivalent. Lord Justice Wall's comments in a recent case have clarified the Court's expectations in this instance:

> "It is, I think, inevitable that in its pre-proceedings work with a child's family, the local authority will gain information about the capacity of the child's parents. The critical question is what it does

with that information, particularly in a case where the social workers form the view that the parent in question may have learning difficulties." (para 175).

"At this point, in many cases, the local authority will be working with the child's parents in an attempt to keep the family together. In my judgment, the practical answer in these circumstances is likely to be that the parent in question should be referred to the local authority's adult learning disability team (or its equivalent) for help and advice. If that team thinks that further investigations are required, it can undertake them: it should, moreover, have the necessary contacts and resources to commission a report so that as soon as the pre-proceedings letter is written, and proceedings are issued, the legal advisers for the parent can be in a position, with public funding, to address the question of a litigation friend. It is, I think, important that judgments on capacity are not made by the social workers from the child protection team." (para 176).

"In the pre-proceedings phase local authorities should feel free to do whatever is necessary in social work terms to assist parents who may become protected parties. My view, however, is that this is best achieved by members of the adult learning disabilities team who do not have responsibility for the children concerned." (para 181).

P v. Nottingham City Council and the Official Solicitor [2008] EWCA Civ 462.

On a practical level ALDT/CLDT must be asked to assess the parent and to make recommendations as to capacity to understand the information being discussed and shared at the pre-proceedings meetings. It may be that the parent can properly engage during pre-proceedings if supported by a social worker from the ALDT/CLDT. Alternatively, a voluntary sector organisation may be able to provide an advocate who is experienced in working with those with learning disability. If those options fail then the LA may wish to consider inviting a close family member or friend to support the parent during the PPM. That however is not ideal. Ultimately, if the social worker or the lawyer for the parent believes that the parent is unable to understand and follow the subject matter properly in order to then give considered instructions to the solicitor, it may be the case that the LA will have to issue an application to court so that the Official Solicitor can be invited to act for the parent within the proceedings.

Language barriers must also be considered where a parent's capacity to understand is clearly limited and the LA should make arrangements for a suitable independent interpreter and not rely on a family member or friend.

2.5.5 REVIEWING PLANS

The objective of the PPM is to:

- Agree a plan; and

- Track and monitor progress to implementing the plan.

The plan for the child might be that the child will be accommodated by the local authority. This is a key option for the child even if only as a temporary measure (section 2.8). If it is agreed that the child should be looked-after under s 20 1989 the LA must comply with all statutory duties in relation to looked after children.

Where the child is not a looked-after child because he or she will remain in the care of the family or be subject to a private fostering arrangement between the parent and a third person (such as a family friend or more distant relative) it is likely that the child will remain a child in need for the requisite period. The LA will however be responsible for checking and supervising any private fostering arrangements. If the arrangements are brokered by the LA then the child becomes a looked-after child under a s 23 placement.

2.5.6 CHILDREN'S PARTICIPATION AND THE PARTICIPATION OF THE CHILD

So far as it is reasonably practicable and consistent with the child's welfare, every child should be notified in age appropriate language by the LA that a PPM is to be held, with an explanation that the purpose is to help parents to keep them safe. The child should then be given the chance to make written representations to the PPM. The social worker has an ongoing duty to ascertain the wishes and feelings of the child[1]. The social worker should be in a position to feed those wishes and feelings into the PPM. Acting in the best interests of the child will be the responsibility which pervades everything the social worker does in a particular case. The social worker is therefore in a position to make clear the child's views at the PPM.

Additionally, the LA must decide in each individual case whether to invite the child to the PPM. In considering the matter, there will be a variety of factors which will be taken into account including:

- The child's age;
- The child's level of understanding as to what is involved;
- The child's coping skills; and
- Whether it is appropriate for the child to be present for all or for part of the PPM.

If the child is invited and attends the meeting, the LA should review agenda items, as there may be information that could be difficult for a child to manage within this forum. The social worker should also inform the chair of the PPM that the child will be attending.

If it is felt inappropriate to invite the child to attend the PPM or the child rejects the invitation, the social worker must consider how the child's wishes and feelings could be heard at the PPM.

The LA should ascertain the parent's views towards the child's attendance at the meeting. If the parents oppose the child's attendance at the meeting it must be remembered that the LA does not have parental responsibility at this stage.

If parents do not wish the child to attend, the child should be informed about the LAs complaints procedure. In these circumstances the LA should consider other methods of ensuring that the child's voice is heard, such as:

- the child making written representations for the meeting;
- the social worker having a meeting with the child;
- the child being referred to a local advocacy service able to support the child.

A template letter to the child can be found at Annex B. This should be tailored and adapted where the LA decide to notify a child about the PPM in writing. If the child does not attend the meeting the social worker will explain the plan to the child and take account of their wishes and feelings. As in all issues pre, during and after proceedings there must be a child focused timetable.

1   Amendments were made by s 53 CA 2004 to the following sections of CA 1989: s 17(4A), s 47(5A) and s 20(6) (all of which relate to ascertaining wishes and feelings of the child).

2.5.7   THE ROLE OF LAWYERS

The role of lawyers in PPMs is to provide impartial legal advice in private to a client if appropriate.

If the lawyer is able to familiarise himself or herself with the relevant papers at the outset this will aid his or her ability to properly advise the client when needed. Lawyers for LAs are likely to first hear about a particular case during the legal gateway/planning meeting. It may however, be some time later when the LA come back to the lawyer for further advice or to ask that the lawyer be present at the PPM. Reading updated social work documents is useful at this point. In relation to lawyers for parents, in some circumstances the lawyer will have been instructed even prior to the LbP being sent (section 2.6.1). Where this is the case, the lawyer may have already seen documents or will have sought disclosure from the LA. Otherwise the first involvement for the lawyer for the parent will be where the parent brings in the LbP to the first attendance with the solicitor. There may be very little time between instruction of lawyers and the PPM taking place.

2.5.8   LAWYER FOR THE PARENT

If the PPM is to have the best possible chance of resolving issues or identifying an alternative care solution it is vital that both the LA and the parent have appropriate advice from their qualified legal advisors.

2.6   Public funding (Legal Help and Legal Aid)

2.6.1   LEGAL HELP – PUBLIC LAW

Some parents may have had a lawyer during other stages of their involvement with the LA. In those cases the lawyer will have assessed the client's eligibility for Legal Help (referred to as "Level 1 Advice"). Unlike Family Help Lower this level of service is means-tested and therefore not all parents will be financially eligible. There is also a merits-test which has a low threshold ("the sufficient benefit test"). This is payable by way of a fixed fee.

2.6.2   IMPORTANCE OF THE LbP

Each local authority will have sent the parent a Letter before Proceedings (LbP) inviting the recipient of the letter to a meeting to discuss concerns and plans for the child and family. From the moment that the letter is received, the person to whom it is addressed automatically becomes eligible for advice and assistance. It is vital that the LA ensure that the parent receives the LbP (section 2.4). Only then will he or she be able to secure non-means, non-merits tested advice and assistance from a solicitor on this basis; the LbP acting as the trigger for eligibility. The LA are encouraged to enclose with the LbP a list of firms/organisations who do such work and in particular those that have staff who are members of the Solicitors Regulation Authority's (formerly the Law Society) Children Panel.

2.6.3   FAMILY HELP LOWER

Advice and assistance is provided by the legal advisor under a scheme called Family Help Lower (also referred to as "Level 2 Advice"). This is a form of Controlled Work and therefore it is for the lawyer to assess whether the person seeking assistance is eligible for this level of service. Any parent or person with Parental Responsibility (PR) who receives a LbP is entitled to this level of service; it is non-means and non-merits tested. The parent is free to instruct any firm or organisation which does public funded family work.

The level of service (Family Help Lower) is remunerated as a standard fee. The LSC has calculated this fee based upon Controlled Legal Representation rates, which are higher than Legal Help and are similarly used in mental health and immigration cases involving priority clients. The LSC has increased the fee so that it currently represents over 7 hours of work.

2.6.4   EXCEPTIONAL CASES

There may be cases where the issues are very complex or great in numbers. For example there may be several persons with PR or the LA has had long-standing involvement and so there are many historic but relevant issues and documents or the assisted person (client) has significant learning difficulties or mental health problems. Those circumstances may make taking instructions, advising the client or negotiation on behalf of the client difficult and complicated. Work done under either Legal Help, Family Help Lower (or both levels of service) when compared to hourly rates may exceed the fixed fee. Where the work was justified and the time spent (based on applicable hourly rates) amounts to three times or over the fixed fee the firm/organisation will be able to claim their costs on a full hourly rates basis rather than being restricted to the fixed fee.

2.6.5   FURTHER INFORMATION

Further information about publicly funded family services can be found on the Legal Service Commission's website: *www.legalservices.gov.uk*[1]. A list of LSC family regional contacts can be found at: *http//www. legalservices.gov.uk/civil/civil_justice_system_initiatives.asp*.

   1   A Q&A document is also helpful reading and is accessible at: *http://www.legalservices. gov.uk/docs/cls_main/QandAPublicLawCareProceedings050308.pdf*

2.7   Assessments

2.7.1   ADAPTING TO CHANGE

The assessment of children and their families is a key task for social work professionals. What the reforms do is to focus on purposeful, analytical and evidence based assessments and their importance. The child's allocated social worker is responsible for coordinating the work on that child's case with support from team/service managers and possibly other agencies. The assessment process is discussed in the Statutory Guidance[1] and in Working Together[2]. Assessments, both Initial and Core should be undertaken in accordance with these documents and the detailed guidance set out in the Framework for the Assessment of Children in Need and their Families (DH et al (2000)). The LA must not work in isolation and it is imperative that the appropriate sharing of information between the professional network continues to take place to ensure that the child's safety and welfare is kept central to the process.

Where cases rely on specialist assessments to inform the assessment which may not be completed within the target time frame, the core assessment should still be completed and should note any timescales agreed with partners who may be undertaking specialist assessments documented[3]. Planning, intervention and urgent work to safeguard the child's welfare will need to continue not withstanding an incomplete or outstanding core assessment.

The core assessment is the means by which LAs gather and analyse information about the child and family as it undertakes its s 47 CA 1989 enquires[4]. It is the process by which evidence is gathered which is important to the LA's case when it applies to court[5]; the LA will file the core assessment record with the court as its primary piece of evidence to support its application. As it is a live document it will continue to be updated during the LA's involvement with the child and it may well evolve as circumstances change and new information about the family is obtained. Assessment is a continuing process and not a single event.

1   Statutory Guidance, paras 3.12–3.18.
2   *Working Together*, paras 5.60–5.67.
3   Statutory Guidance, para 3.16.
4   Statutory Guidance, para 3.15.
5   Statutory Guidance, para 3.16.

2.7.2   CHANGE OF CIRCUMSTANCES

It is essential that the extent to which a child is suffering, or is likely to suffer, harm is kept under constant review and that if necessary the matter proceeds immediately to court irrespective of whether or not the LA has completed its preparation or documentation.

Where the LA decides (usually having taken legal advice) that it needs to take steps to protect a child who it considers to be suffering or likely to suffer significant harm, the LA may take immediate protective measures which could include requesting police protection or an application at court for an order. This may be for an emergency protection order (EPO)[1] because the LA believes the child is in imminent danger, or for an interim care or supervision order[2] in order to safeguard the child. It is recognised that in some cases a core assessment will not have been completed or even started at the point that an application is made to the court. Where however, the LA has been involved with a family for some time and/or has already commenced enquiries pursuant to s 47 CA 1989 it should be conducting the enquiries via a core assessment and documenting findings from the assessment process in a core assessment record. Where the core assessment is not available or completed at the time of issue, the LA will inform the court of the reason why it has not been filed and of the expected date of filing. That information should be given at column (*d*) of Part 1 ("Pre-proceedings checklist") of the Supplementary PLO1 form. See the Practice Direction 10.2 and 10.3 for guidance on compliance with the pre-proceedings checklist.

1   Statutory Guidance, paras 4.25–4.63.
2   Statutory Guidance, paras 3.44–3.47.

2.7.3   SPECIALIST ASSESSMENTS (PRE-PROCEEDINGS)

The key question for the LA to ask itself is "is there an element or aspect of the core assessment process which cannot be completed because specialist expertise is required".

Specialist assessments are those assessments which the LA believe are required when for example there is a particular aspect of the child's or family's circumstances which require a specialist assessment from a professional other than a social worker such as an adult mental health assessment. The specialist assessment will only address that specific aspect and it will feed into the core assessment.

Where a specialist assessment is thought to be required, the decision to commission such an assessment must be made as soon as possible to avoid introducing unnecessary delay into resolution of the proceedings. Consideration should also be given to the joint instruction of experts. The PPM can be used for this purpose.

Any specialist assessments commissioned pre proceedings should be presented by the LA in any proceedings, and for that reason it is suggested that the LA consider the requirements of the Experts PD[1], particularly those that relate to pre-proceedings assessments.

1   *http://www.hmcourts-service.gov.uk/cms/files/Experts-PD-flagB-final-version-14-01-08.pdf*

2.8   *Alternative care for children*

SECTION 20 CHILDREN ACT 1989 AND THE FUNCTION OF THE INDEPENDENT REVIEWING OFFICER (IRO)

There will be some circumstances where it will be appropriate for children to be looked after by the local authority following agreement with those who have parental responsibility that this arrangement would be the best way to meet the child's needs. Where the authority provides accommodation for a child under a voluntary agreement, then the LA does not share parental responsibility for the child and the parents may remove the child from the arrangement at any time. The parents' wishes regarding the care of their child must be respected, unless they are putting the child at risk of significant harm, and the parents and the child must be consulted before any decisions are taking that affect their child. Providing services to children in this way will not be appropriate where there are continuing concerns about significant harm to the child.

Children accommodated under s 20. like every other looked after child, must have a care plan based on a comprehensive assessment of their needs, setting out how the authority intends to meet those needs in partnership with the child's parents. This will include detail about how the authority intends to establish legally secure care arrangements for the child (e.g. permanency options might include making arrangements to reunite the child with their birth family or planning for the child to be placed in a permanent substitute family or long term foster care). The care plan must be regularly reviewed. Review meetings must be held at minimum statutory intervals – within 28 days of placement, then within 3 months and six monthly thereafter. Reviews must involve the child, their carers and representatives of the local authority responsible for their care, most reviews will also involve other appropriate professionals. The LA must appoint an Independent Reviewing Officer (IRO) to chair reviews.

The IRO's functions are to

(*a*)   Participate in the review of the case of each looked after child
(*b*)   Monitor the authority's functions in respect of the review

(c)   Refer a case to Cafcass/CAFCASS CYMRU if the failure to implement the care plan might be considered to breach the child's human rights

Regulations require IROs to fulfil the following responsibilities

(a)   To ensure that the views of children and young people are understood and taken into account (in care planning);

(b)   that the person's responsible for implementing any decision taken in consequence of the review are identified; and

(c)   that any failure to review the case or to take proper steps (to implement review recommendations) is brought to the attention of person's at an appropriate level of seniority within the responsible authority.

The review meeting is one of the key components within the core processes of working with children and families. The purpose of the review meeting is to consider the plan for the welfare of the child and then to monitor the progress of the plan and make decisions to amend the plan as necessary in light of changed knowledge and circumstances. The appropriate legal status for the child's care must be considered at every review meeting and the review should make recommendations to senior managers in children's services if the child's legal status no longer seems appropriate to the child's needs. For example, where the circumstances of a child accommodated under s 20 have changed such that it may be necessary for the authority to consider making application for a care order to make legally secure plans to meet the child's future needs.

DCSF are currently re-writing all the Children Act 1989 regulations and guidance and the NMS for fostering and adoption services. In addition DCSF will be issuing Strategic Guidance for consultation in October 2009 on a new framework for family and friends care which will contain a model for assessing relative carers.

2.9   Safeguarding and child protection

2.9.1   THRESHOLD

S 31 (2) Children Act 1989 sets out the threshold criteria. A court has no power to make a care or supervision order in favour of a local authority unless, as a matter of fact, it is satisfied that:

(a)   the child concerned is suffering, or is likely to suffer, significant harm, and

(b)   that the harm or likelihood of harm is attributable to either (i) the care given to a child or likely to be given to him if the order were not made not being what it would be reasonable to expect a parent to give him or (ii) the child is beyond parental control.

Harm includes impairment from seeing or hearing the ill treatment of another.

The court will only act on evidence and will make findings of fact about whether the child is suffering significant harm. If the LA have reasonable cause to suspect that a child is suffering significant harm they will make, or cause to be made, such enquiries as they consider necessary to enable them to decide whether they should take any action to safeguard or promote a child's welfare. The court has to establish that it is more probable that the fact(s) in question occurred than they did not. Mere suspicions are not sufficient. It has to be shown that the child is or is likely to suffer significant harm, with significant being the key word. The harm has to be due to unreasonable parenting i.e. parents not giving the care it would be reasonable for a parent to give that child.

The threshold is established as a matter of fact on the evidence at the point when protective measures are implemented.

Only once the court is satisfied that this threshold has been established does the court have the power to make a care or supervision order.

Finding that threshold is proven does not mean that the court must automatically make a care order. Once threshold is established, the court will then go on to hear argument and evidence to determine what order is in the best interests of the child having regard to the welfare checklist set out in section 1 of the Children Act 1989. This might be a care or supervision order or, for example where a suitable kinship carer has been identified, it might be a residence order. The final outcome may also be an order of "No Order" where the court believes that the interests of the child would be best served by no order being made.

The Public Law Outline usually needs to be considered in the context of whether or not there is a need for an order at that stage and the focus should be upon whether the risk is manageable without an order.

2.9.2 MANAGING SIGNIFICANT HARM

Managing possible harm to the child whilst working with families is a delicate task which demands careful social work judgement in discussion with line managers. The Statutory Guidance emphasises the importance of taking pre-proceedings steps such as the Pre Proceedings Meeting which follows the Letter before Proceedings (LbP) and investigating alternative care solutions, it also recognises that there will be some cases where an immediate application to court will be required. The LA may consider that a case may fit into this category and that certain pre-proceedings steps e.g. dispatch of the LbP cannot be complied with because it might place the child at increased risk of harm or fail to stop the child suffering harm. A typical example might be where the social worker considers there is a real risk of a parent absconding with the child if he or she were to become aware that that the LA is considering applying to court. This is entirely a decision for the LA, making a judgement based on its professional experience of child protection and its knowledge of the child and the family.

When the court application is prepared there may be some information or documentation which cannot be submitted with the application such as the LbP or kinship assessments which may not yet be completed. It is again essential to emphasise that if the child is suffering or likely to suffer significant harm and s 31 threshold has been established following legal advice, the matter must proceed to court. The supplementary form PLO1 lists the documentation, which should accompany the application form itself. Column (*d*) on that form allows the Applicant Authority to state any reason why it has not filed any document. In an emergency LAs are not required to provide pre-proceedings documentation on issue but will be required to file it later.

2.10   Working with partner organisations and agencies

2.10.1   SHARING INFORMATION

Sharing information arising from the PPM is subject to the usual guidance and practice which governs the LA sharing of information. The general position is that "the consent of children, young people and their parents or caregivers should be obtained when sharing information, unless to do so would place the child at risk of significant harm. Decisions should also be made with their agreement, whenever possible, unless to do so would place the child at risk of significant harm"[1].

Where consent to sharing information cannot be secured it will generally be safe to share information where this is justified in the public interest. For example, where there is a clear risk of significant harm to a child or adult it will usually be justified to share information so long as sharing that information is in the best interest of the child's safety and welfare. Detailed guidance can be found in "Information sharing: Practitioners' guide"[2].

1   *Working Together* p 101.
2   "Information sharing: Practitioners' guide", HM Government 920020. Accessible at: *http://www.everychildmatters.gov.uk/_files/ ACB1BA35C20D4C42A1FE6F9133A7C614.pdf*

Chapter 3 – Making a section 31 CA 1989 application[28]

3.1   Preparing an application for court

3.1.1   THE FORMS

Set out below is a list of some of the forms available at the present time with advice on their completion:

- **PLO1 – Application for a care order or supervision order: Supplementary form:** To be filed by the LA with its application. Part 1 is a checklist of the necessary documents. Part 2 is the Record of Case Management Documents filed and to record which case management documents are filed as the case progresses.

---

28   This material must now be read subject ot the revised PLO.

- **PLO2 – Local Authority Case Summary**: This standard form should be filed by the LA setting out its position, before the First Appointment (FA), Case Management Conference (CMC) and Issues Resolution Hearing (IRH) and will include details of: proceedings relating to the child, living arrangements, summary of incidents/concerns, key issues in the case and directions for the court to consider.
- **PLO3 – Case Management Order:** This contains standard provisions designed to help the parties, their legal representatives and the court, and has three sections: 1) Preliminary, 2) Order and 3) Recitals. The LA should prepare an initial draft in advance of each advocates' discussion/meeting and share this with all advocates involved in the case, as this document forms the basis of discussions at the advocates' meeting. Following each advocates' discussion/meeting, it is the responsibility of the local authority advocate to file the draft order with the court at least one working day before either the CMC or IRH.
- **PLO4 – Allocation Record and Timetable for the Child**: To be filed by the LA with its application. It sets out an allocation proposal regarding the appropriate tier of court. It will also be used to record the court's allocation decision and reasons. The LA also uses it to provide important dates in the child's life to assist the court set a suitable Timetable for the Child.
- **PLO5 – Standard Directions and allocation on issue of proceedings**
- **PLO6 – Standard Directions and allocation at First Appointment**: Forms PLO 5 and 6 are completed by a judge or legal adviser once an application is lodged at court and at the First Appointment. The court will consider giving standard directions appropriate to each case at Issue and First Appointment stages using these forms.

3.1.2   THE DOCUMENTATION

All pre-proceedings checklist documents should be filed with the application where available.

The documents which the LA are called upon to create specifically for filing with the application are:

1   The Schedule of Proposed Findings;
2   Initial Social Work Statement;
3   Care Plan for each child;
4   The Allocation Record; and
5   Timetable for the Child.

The Public Law Outline is explicit about the required documents that should be filed and issued by the court.

LAs should file and serve under the category of the "Other relevant reports and records" (see item 7 on form PLO1, Part 1) the child's full birth certificate or relevant ID as this is likely to be required by the court at some stage and therefore would be useful to be filed at the outset.

3.2 Parties with particular needs

In s 31 CA 1989 proceedings where the social worker or any party believes that a parent may not have capacity to conduct the litigation the court can be asked to make a direction inviting the Official Solicitor to act on that person's behalf. It must be considered that appropriate social work expertise within the local authority disability team can be used pre or post proceedings to inform a decision on their client's capacity. The Official Solicitor is a "litigation friend of last resort" and will only accept that invitation if there is no one else who is willing and suitable to conduct the litigation on the parent's behalf. Invariably in family proceedings it will be difficult to say with any certainty that another family member is suitable because he or she may have a view which is in conflict with the parent or otherwise because he or she is very close to the subject of the litigation so will not be able to present the parent's views properly. It is important that the Official Solicitor is approached as soon as possible if required to assist:

> "if all the professionals involved with the proceedings and with the parents, including the judges, solicitors, barristers, advocates, and court staff, are aware of the need from the start of the proceedings to take time to consider the parent and whether the proceedings are proving too much for the parent to fully understand. If at any time there is a genuine concern about the parent's capacity to understand the proceedings and to instruct their solicitor, the parent should be able to ask for, and to receive assistance without being made to feel stigmatised by their disability."

> *http://www.officialsolicitor.gov.uk/docs/parentsnetworkarticle.doc*

3.3 Advocates' meetings

3.3.1 ATTENDEES

A Children's Guardian (CG) is a social work professional appointed by a court to independently represent a child subject a care or adoption procedures. They are officers of Cafcass/CAFCASS CYMRU. Children's Guardians and social workers must not attend Advocates' Meetings but they should be notified of the time and date of the meeting and they should be contactable throughout so that counsel may take instructions as necessary.

The Advocates' Meeting should not take place on the morning of the hearing but in accordance with the requirements of the PLO. It is advisable to book the meeting promptly following any previous meeting. When advocates are considering timetabling a meeting, due consideration should be given to utilising telephone or video conferencing where attendance in person is impractical.

It is recognised that it is sometimes unhelpful to a party to have a different advocates representing him or her at various hearings. At times, this can have a bearing on the smooth running of the proceedings. Any client should be free of constraints to choose who he or she wishes to instruct as his or her representative and therefore the Practice Direction (PD) cannot be prescriptive on the issue. Nevertheless the PD does acknowledge the concern and provides a reminder to advocates (for all parties) that the advocate who represents at the final hearing should be the same advocate representing the client at the CMC and IRH. Where this is not possible the PD suggests that an advocate who is familiar with the issues in the case should attend[1].

1   PD, para 16.

3.3.2 PREPARATION

The aim of the Advocates' Meeting is to facilitate agreement between the parties and narrow the issues in dispute[1]. In order to save valuable court time the Advocates' Meeting also acts as a forum where the draft Case Management Order is discussed and prepared[2]. Meetings will only be productive if all the advocates have prepared what is the background to and the issues in the case, what their respective client seeks to achieve from the proceedings, and up to date instructions from their clients in advance but as close to the Advocates' Meeting as possible.

To aid the smooth running of the Advocates' Meeting the draft Case Management Order should be prepared as an initial draft by the LA in advance of the Advocates' Meeting itself. If this is circulated to the other parties even a day before the Advocates' Meeting is scheduled to take place, it will act as a working document which all can come to the meeting armed with comments on. It will also act as the agenda for the meeting which would be helpful.

If proceedings are to run smoothly and with as little delay as possible, it will be important that all parties comply with the filing of evidence and in time. Where compliance with a particular direction is not looking possible, the relevant party's representative must seek agreement from all the parties for an extension of time or draw the non compliance to the attention of the court.

1   PD, para 3.11.
2   PD, paras 13.1–13.7.

3.3.3 DRAFTING THE CASE MANAGEMENT ORDER

During the Advocates' Meeting there will be a discussion about the Case Management Order and the Applicant's advocate (usually the LA) will take the lead in preparing or drafting that document together with the other advocates. Ideally matters can be agreed and the Case Management Order can be filed as a single agreed case management tool to assist the judge at the hearing. Where that is not possible the advocates will specify on the Case Management Order (or on a separate document if necessary) the provisions which they agree and disagree1. There must be a clear narrative detailing what the LA is asking the court to do, with the CMO fully completed. Detailed standard variable directions are available from the HMCS website to provide assistance on the full and appropriate wording to be used when considering the required directions for the draft case management order.

1 PD, para 13.5.

3.4 Care planning

The plan for the care of the child should be based on findings from the initial and core assessments. It should set out the aims of the plan and intended outcomes for the child, informed by the findings from the assessments ie. The identified developmental needs of the child and the capacity of the parents to respond to the child's needs in the context of their wide family and environmental factors. It will set out clearly what the plan for the child if the Court makes a care order.

In those relatively few cases where the identified permanence option, at the point of the commencement of proceedings, is for the adoption of the child, and where the decision that the child should be placed for adoption has been taken in accordance with the Adoption Agencies Regulations 2005 (SI 2005/389), the local authority must apply for a placement order issued simultaneously with, or as soon as possible after, the issue of the care proceedings.

3.5 Role of the Children's Guardian and the Independent Reviewing Officer

Where possible the Children's Guardian (CG) should meet with the child, where age appropriate, and with other parties in advance of the First Appointment (FA). The Guardian must have read the court papers and provided the required analysis.

The Practice Direction defines Case Analysis & Recommendation (A&R) as being a "written or oral outline of the case from the child's perspective prepared by the Children's Guardian or other officer..."[1]. A list follows that paragraph of the PD setting out the particular points that the Case A&R should address. It is anticipated that the CG may not always be in a position to file a written Case A&R and this is why the definition allows for an oral outline to be provided by the CG at the FA. Where an oral report is given it is suggested that the child's solicitor takes a note of the oral report and then files it as an agreed note. However, in Wales practice guidance requires that the CG provides an initial analysis in written form at the earliest stage and if feasible by the FA.

In subsequent hearings, the CG should be up to speed and in a position to provide written Case A&R that will be filed by the child's solicitor as per the court's directions.

The child's care plan must be maintained by the local authority and kept under review at the statutory intervals and whenever significant changes are proposed to the plan throughout proceedings. It will be good practice for the Children's Guardian and the IRO to maintain a constructive working relationship throughout proceedings. Both the Children's Guardian and the IRO should be properly informed about the local authority's plans for the child so they are able to scrutinise these plans to make sure that they are based on good quality assessment so that the plan demonstrates how the child's needs will be met, with the child being provided with the opportunity to be meaningfully involved in planning for their care. The local authority will need to take the views of the IRO on the quality of planning into account in formulating the final care plan to be put to the Court[2].

Where a child is accommodated by the LA upon issue of proceedings e.g. under s 20 of the CA 1989, it is good practice for the LA to serve a copy of the LA Case Summary (form PLO2) together with a copy of the Initial Social Work Statement, Schedule of Proposed Findings, Care Plan and Allocation Record and timetable for the child on the IRO. Additionally the LA should provide the parties and the Children's Guardian with the name and contact details of the IRO together with the dates of any statutory reviews which have been arranged.

At the conclusion of proceedings IROs may well have an important role in ensuring that the implications of the agreed care plan are understood by all professionals, cares and family members, as there will no longer be any oversight by the Court of the care planning process. In particular, the IRO will have a role in enabling the child to understand their plan and to participate in future care planning.

1　PD, para 25(8).
2　The Children and Young Person Act includes provision which significantly strengthens the IRO function. In future each looked after child must have their own personal named IRO; the IRO will be responsible for monitoring the quality of the local authority's care planning function; and ensure that in every care plan due consideration has been given to the child's wishes and feelings.

3.6　Issues Resolution Hearings and Final Hearings

The purpose of the Issues Resolution Hearing (IRH) is to narrow the issues in so far as to conclude proceedings if possible.

There is some concern amongst professionals that a final hearing is only listed by the court at the IRH. This seems to have given rise to some anxiety about the List Office's ability to secure a date in the court diary for a final hearing soon after the IRH. Where the court is able to do this, some are worried that there will not be an opportunity to give adequate notice to experts and that this may also cause difficulty for the consistency of advocates.

The Practice Direction itself does not require final hearings to only be listed at the IRH. The PD states that at the Case Management Conference (CMC) the court will set a date for the IRH and "if necessary, specify a period within which the Final Hearing of the application is to take place unless a date has already been set"[1]. Rather than taking a prescriptive approach the PD is flexible about the listing of final hearings leaving it for the court to decide when it lists the final hearing and in accordance with its case management functions. The Timetable for the Child will greatly influence how the court manages its case especially in regard to the listing of hearings.

1   PD, para 14.5(2).

3.7   Collective participation and co-operation

All professionals involved in public law proceedings will work together with the court to assist achievement of the overriding objective. The parties have a duty to do this, which is enshrined in the PD[1].

It is also emphasised[2] that the parties and their representatives should co-operate with the court in case management. Furthermore, the parties and representatives should monitor compliance (generally) with the Court's directions and inform the court or court officer about any failure to comply with a direction of the court or any other delay within the proceedings[3]. A number of courts have a case progression officer (CPO) who should be the first point of contact with regard to Public Law cases.

1   PD, para 2.3.
2   PD, para 5.4.
3   PD, para 5.5.

3.8   The nature of the Public Law Outline

The purpose of the PLO is to reduce delay in these important proceedings concerning the short and long-term placement future of children. It has had to be robust in order to achieve its objectives and to secure outcomes for children and families involved within the target timeframe set by the Timetable for the Child (which is one of the case management tools)[1]. It should be borne in mind that the PD does acknowledge that the court has flexible powers. At any stage in the proceedings the court may exercise those powers[2].

The expectations[3] are that the proceedings should be conducted using the Case Management Tools and Documentation and determined in accordance with the stages in the Timetable for the Child (together with the timeframes indicated for the various stages within the PLO). It is however, acknowledged that the child's welfare in some cases may require a more tailored approach; possibly one that does not fall firmly within the stages and expectations of the PLO. In those cases it will be for the court to determine the appropriate case management directions and timetable[4] but the court must record on the face of any order its reasons for departing from the PLO's general approach. This aids the parties' understanding of why the court is managing its case in the way it is and it also protects the court itself from any potential criticism for departing from the PLO's expectations.

1   PD, paras 3.2–3.4.
2   PD, paras 17.1–17.3.
3   PD, para 4.1.

4 PD, para 4.2.

Annex A: Immediate Issue Letter (template)

SENT BY [RECORDED DELIVERY/BY HAND]

Office Address

Contact

Direct line

My ref

Fax

E-mail

Date

Dear [parent and/or full name(s) of all people with parental responsibility]

Re: [insert name of Local Authority] CONCERNS ABOUT [insert name(s) of child]

I am writing as you were told I would, when you spoke to [name of social worker] on [insert date of last interaction]. As you are aware [name of Local Authority] is extremely worried about your care of [name(s) of child/ren]. We told you about these main concerns in [reference to the Letter before Proceedings/PPM/child protection case conference/any social work meetings].

We have tried to work with you to help you improve your care of [name(s) of child/ren] but unfortunately things have not changed. We are writing to tell you again that we will be going to court to try and make sure [name of child] is safe. You will soon receive a copy of our application to the court and other important documents, which set out the key issues.

We would urge you, if you have not done so already, to get advice from a solicitor. We have sent with this letter a list of local solicitors who specialise in work with children and families. They are not part of Children's Services (Social Services).

Yours sincerely

[name]
Team Manager
Local office/service

cc. Social Worker [name]
Local Authority in house Legal Team

Enc. List of Law Society Children Panel Solicitors

Annex B: Letter notifying a child about a Pre-Proceedings Meeting (template)

Delivered by Hand

Office Address

Contact

Direct line

My ref

Fax

E-mail

Dear [name]

As you know, there have been some concerns about how your parents/carers [delete as appropriate and/or name] have been looking after you.

Although we have been trying hard to sort out these problems, unfortunately, at the moment, we are still worried that you may be at risk of harm.

Our next step therefore is to hold a "pre-proceedings meeting". At that meeting we will try to agree a plan with your parents/carers about what needs to be done to deal with our worries about you.

If we cannot sort things with your parents/carers at this meeting, it may mean that our only option is to go to court. Hopefully this will not happen but if it does, you will be given plenty of information about what happens and your role in it all.

I am now writing to invite you to attend the pre-proceedings meeting which is being held on [date] at [time] at [venue]. This will give you the chance to tell the meeting about your thoughts, wishes and feelings. If you would rather not attend the meeting, that is fine. You can always put your thoughts in writing if that is easier.

I shall be present at the meeting, with my manager, [name] and our legal advisor. Your parents have of course been invited and may have their lawyer with them.

I shall call you soon to check if you would like to attend all or part of the meeting. It may be that you would like an adult (who should be unconnected to the family) to support you during the meeting.

Alternatively, I may be able to arrange for an advocate to attend the meeting with you. An advocate's job is to make sure that a young person's views are heard, either through speaking for a young person or helping a young person speak for him or herself. Please let me know if you would like any more information on this and you can telephone me on [...........].

If you have any questions or worries please contact me on the above number.

Yours sincerely

Social Worker [name]
Local office/service

Annex C: List of potential agenda items for a Pre-Proceedings Meeting

- Introductions
- Setting out any special requirements (interpreter, sign language interpreter, presence of an advocate)
- Outline the purpose of the meeting and establish ground rules and specify roles
- Outline duty of the LA to protect children, duty (where possible) to promote the child living with the family, balance of that against need to protect and promote welfare of the child. Explaining why it may be that a court application is necessary but that the LA hopes that the meeting may avoid the need for that
- Explain the concerns of the LA and referencing the LbP
- Initial views and opinions of the parent and specifying or clarifying any areas of agreement and disagreement
- Discuss what can be done to help improve the child's situation on the part of the parent including any assessment outcomes and gaps identified
- Discuss what services have been be provided to the family by the LA and can be provided to help i.e. promoting the idea of collaborative working between family and the LA in the best interests of the child
- Discuss the outcome of the Family Group Conference/Family meeting
- Identification of alternative carers (this will be a revisit to the concept as it will have been discussed previously within the assessment process)
- Lead into a discussion of the proposed plan for the child including the need for any further assessments (the auspices of that plan i.e. Child in Need plan or Child Protection Plan)
- Break away for both parent and the LA to take advice from their respective lawyers
- Initial views from parent as to their thoughts on the plan/agreement
- Reconvene for focused discussion on the plan. Can an agreement be reached on the plan/agreement as it stands in draft or can revisions/amendments be agreed now to avoid proceedings

- If no agreement can be reached such that the LA believes it will have to issue an application with the court consider scope for discussion as to any issues which may be resolved now.

Brief case example: mother abuses alcohol and her partner is abusive to her. Both elements raise safeguarding concerns. At the PPM the plan is that mother should (1) agree to cease excessive drinking and agree to attend a community drugs and alcohol programme; and (2) agree to her partner moving out of the family home and to seek assistance from domestic abuse support group/project to support mother with skills/knowledge to leave a violent relationship and to avoid entering into similar relationships in the future. Mother agrees to do (1) but not to do (2). Mother provides details for the first time of alternative carers but refuses to agree to information being disclosed to those persons. The LA decides that it will need to seek an interim care order to safeguard the child. Although proceedings have not been avoided, one crucial issue has (potentially) been resolved and the LA will now be able to press ahead with consideration of alternative carers whilst not disclosing information which the mother has not consented to.

A3.9   APPENDIX 9:
GUIDELINES FOR JUDGES MEETING CHILDREN WHO ARE SUBJECT TO FAMILY PROCEEDINGS

Practice Note
April 2010

Produced by the Family Justice Council and approved by the President of the Family Division. April 2010

In these Guidelines –

- All references to 'child or 'children' are intended to include a young person or young people the subject of proceedings under the Children Act 1989.
- 'Family proceedings' includes both public and private law cases.
- 'Judge' includes magistrates.
- Cafcass includes CAFCASS CYMRU.

Purpose

The purpose of these Guidelines is to encourage Judges to enable children to feel more involved and connected with proceedings in which important decisions are made in their lives and to give them an opportunity to satisfy themselves that the Judge has understood their wishes and feelings and to understand the nature of the Judge's task.

Preamble

– In England and Wales in most cases a child's needs, wishes and feelings are brought to the court in written form by a Cafcass officer. Nothing in this guidance document is intended to replace or undermine that responsibility.

– It is Cafcass practice to discuss with a child in a manner appropriate to their developmental understanding whether their participation in the process includes a wish to meet the Judge. If the child does not wish to meet the Judge discussions can centre on other ways of enabling the child to feel a part of the process. If the child wishes to meet the Judge, that wish should be conveyed to the Judge where appropriate.

– The primary purpose of the meeting is to benefit the child. However, it may also benefit the Judge and other family members.

Guidelines

1 The Judge is entitled to expect the lawyer for the child and/or the Cafcass officer:

(i)   to advise whether the child wishes to meet the Judge;

(ii)   if so, to explain from the child's perspective, the purpose of the meeting;

(iii)   to advise whether it accords with the welfare interests of the child for such a meeting take place; and

(iv)   to identify the purpose of the proposed meeting as perceived by the child's professional representative/s.

2 The other parties shall be entitled to make representations as to any proposed meeting with the Judge before the Judge decides whether or not it shall take place.

3 In deciding whether or not a meeting shall take place and, if so, in what circumstances, the child's chronological age is relevant but not determinative. Some children of 7 or even younger have a clear understanding of their circumstances and very clear views which they may wish to express.

4 If the child wishes to meet the Judge but the Judge decides that a meeting would be inappropriate, the Judge should consider providing a brief explanation in writing for the child.

5 If a Judge decides to meet a child, it is a matter for the discretion of the Judge, having considered representations from the parties –

(i)   the purpose and proposed content of the meeting;

(ii)   at what stage during the proceedings, or after they have concluded, the meeting should take place;

(iii)   where the meeting will take place;

(iv)   who will bring the child to the meeting;

(v)   who will prepare the child for the meeting (this should usually be the Cafcass officer);

(vi)   who shall attend during the meeting – although a Judge should never see a child alone;

(vii)   by whom a minute of the meeting shall be taken, how that minute is to be approved by the Judge, and how it is to be communicated to the other parties.

It cannot be stressed too often that the child's meeting with the judge is not for the purpose of gathering evidence. That is the responsibility of the Cafcass officer. The purpose is to enable the child to gain some understanding of what is going on, and to be reassured that the judge has understood him/her.

6   If the meeting takes place prior to the conclusion of the proceedings –

(i)   The Judge should explain to the child at an early stage that a Judge cannot hold secrets. What is said by the child will, other than in exceptional circumstances, be communicated to his/her parents and other parties.

(ii)   The Judge should also explain that decisions in the case are the responsibility of the Judge, who will have to weigh a number of factors, and that the outcome is never the responsibility of the child.

(iii)   The Judge should discuss with the child how his or her decisions will be communicated to the child.

(iv)   The parties or their representatives shall have the opportunity to respond to the content of the meeting, whether by way of oral evidence or submissions.

Sir Nicholas Wall

President of the Family Division and Head of Family Justice

A3.10   APPENDIX 10:
BASIC GUIDANCE TO GOOD PRACTICE IN CARE PROCEEDINGS ACROSS LONDON

Introduction

1.   The Public Law Outline Monitoring Group set up by the Designated Family Judge for London comprises members across the disciplines in care proceedings and makes recommendations to seek to achieve and maintain consistency of good practice in the carriage of care proceedings across London.

2.   The guide produced by the Ministry of Justice in August 2009 entitled 'Preparing for Care and Supervision Proceedings' is a comprehensive best practice guide for use by all professionals involved with care proceedings. The guidance issued by the Justices'

Clerks' Society with the support of the Magistrates' Association in November 2009 entitled 'Dealing with the Public Law Outline in Family Proceedings Courts' is a detailed best practice document issued to legal advisers in family proceedings courts in order to provide a guide in public law cases.

3.   The purpose of this Basic Guidance setting out the recommendations of the Public Law Outline Monitoring Group for London is to simply highlight basic requirements of good practice during the currency of care proceedings.

4.   It is to be read in the context of the Initial Local Plan for London of the 10th April 2008 of the Designated Family Judge for London and the *Practice Direction: Public Law Proceedings Guide to Case Management* of April 2010 of Sir Mark Potter reported at [2010] 2 FLR 472 whose detailed provisions should be actively considered by all those concerned in the carriage of care proceedings. The overriding objective is set out at 2.1 of the Practice Direction.

5.   It is understood that each care case has its own differing requirements to be to be considered by the court on its individual facts. It is understood that there are varying and well-known significant challenges, in relation to resources and otherwise, to the childcare system.

6.   The recommendations of the Group in this Guidance are intended to assist the parties, who are required to help the court further the overriding objective, to achieve and maintain consistency of good practice in the carriage of care proceedings

7.   It is intended that this Basic Guidance to Good Practice in care proceedings should be made available to all of those involved in the carriage of care proceedings across London.

The timetable for the child

8.   As stated at 3.5 of the Practice Direction, due regard should be paid to the timetable for the child to ensure that the parties and the court remain child-focused throughout the progress of public law proceedings.

9.   The parties and the court should always be considering how in practice to achieve the least delay in care proceedings and the earliest possible finalisation consistent with fairness and the best interests of the child.

10.   The court and the parties should actively consider in this regard that part of the Practice Direction of April 2010 which gives guidance as

to stages 1 to 4 of care Proceedings and in particular the time periods within which stages of the proceeding should be heard: see [2010] 2 FLR pages 482 to 484.

11. It is also understood and accepted that care proceedings should, as a guide, be finalised within 40 weeks of their issue, earlier if circumstances permit.

12. It is recommended to be good practice for the parties and the court to have available to them in writing from the outset of proceedings a short schedule indicating for the particular case the time periods within which the 4 stages of the proceedings should be heard. This is to be described as the 'Case Timetable'.

13. Any procedural steps proposed under the Public Law Outline are to be considered in the context of significant events in the life of the child who is the subject of the proceedings.

14. When setting the timetable for the child accordingly, the court must take into account the significant steps in the life of the child who is the subject of the proceedings.

15. These include not only legal steps but also social, care, health and education steps.

16. Paragraph 3.4 of the Practice Direction gives examples of the dates the court will take into account when setting the timetable for the child.

17. It is for the parties, led by the local authority, to outline to the court, on the individual facts of a case, the significant events in the child's life relevant to the timetable to be set by the court for that child

Active case management

18. Active case management includes essentially identifying the timetable for the child and avoiding unnecessary delay in the proceedings.

Draft case management orders

19. It is essential for a local authority as applicant in care proceedings to provide to the court at each and every court hearing within such proceedings (as well as a case summary) a fully drafted case management order. The lead, as indicated, will be taken by the local authority but it is the obligation too of the other advocates in the case to assist in both drafting and ensuring such orders are before the court. Whilst a draft case management order is no longer

required in PLO3 format, it is still a basic requirement and necessity for the court to be provided with draft orders. Attention is drawn to paragraph 26 (12) of the April 2010 Practice Direction: this sets out the checklist factors to be taken into account in drafting case management orders.

Position statements

20. Position statements from the parties are of material help to the court and are expected to be provided at each and every court hearing.

The advocates meeting and the CMC hearing

21. The parties should actively consider the full provisions set out in the Practice Direction of April 2010 relevant to the Advocates Meeting and the CMC hearing.

22. The Advocates Meeting and the CMC hearing remain pivotal in enabling the court to best set the timetable for the child and avoid unnecessary delay.

23. It is not acceptable to adjourn the CMC hearing and all necessary preparation should be done in advance. Adjournment of the CMC hearing may only be considered in exceptional circumstances.

24. The parties are expected to have available at the CMC hearing details of the nature and timing of proposed experts and/or assessors with the dates the latter are available to give evidence at any hearing to be fixed by the court.

25. The parties must be ready at the CMC hearing for all steps to be timetabled up to IRH or final hearing, as the court so determines.

Compliance with active case management directions

26. It is the responsibility of the parties to adhere to the timetable the court has set for the child. This enables the court to ensure the case is dealt with justly under the overriding objective. A failure by the parties to enable the active case management of the case may jeopardise the timetable for the child and cause unnecessary delay in the proceedings.

27. It is the responsibility of the parties to bring to the attention of the court any material departure from case management directions jeopardizing the timetable for the child set by the court.

28. Active case management includes encouraging the parties to cooperate with each other in the conduct of the proceedings.

29.   It is the responsibility of the parties to speedily address and seek to remedy by agreement between themselves any difficulties that arise in compliance with case management directions, in such a way that the timetable for the child set by the court can be maintained and not jeopardised.

Transfers

30.   If a care case is to be transferred from one court to another, such a transfer, if merited, should occur in practice at the earliest stage after the issue of proceedings. The court to which the case is transferred can then actively case manage it in such a way as to avoid jeopardising the timetable for the child and causing undue delay in the finalisation of proceedings.

31.   Attention is drawn generally to the Family Law Allocation and Transfer of Proceedings Order 2008 and the Practice Direction "Allocation and Transfer of Proceedings" issued the 3rd November 2008, but also in particular to paragraph 3.20 (2) of the April 2010 Practice Direction which states:

> 'Active case management includes identifying the appropriate court to conduct the proceedings and transferring the proceedings as early as possible to that court.'

32.   Late transfers may jeopardise the timetable for the child and cause undue delay in the finalisation of proceedings.

Split hearings/fact-finding

33.   The court and the parties should give active consideration to the Guidance of the President of the Family Division of May 2010 in relation to the subject of split hearings.

Expedited final hearings for certain types of care cases

34.   The court and the parties should be alert to those cases which may be suitable for an expedited hearing. It is not necessarily easy to be prescriptive as to the categories of cases which may be so suitable. In cases involving very young children the court will wish to consider whether the case may be so suitable for expedition.

35.   There may be clear cases of full parental engagement after the issue of proceedings leading to the likelihood of a speedy reunification. There may be cases of clear parental disengagement or abandonment in relation to a child leading to the likelihood of the child not being so reunified.

36. In such circumstances, the local authority should present the court a clear timetable setting out the date by which its final recommendation will be made.

37. In cases meriting expedition, a speedy conclusion of the care proceedings is likely to be possible well within the guide period of 40 weeks referred to previously.

38. Where more than one child is the subject of care proceedings, the individual circumstances of the case may cause the court and the parties to consider whether a separate timetable for the finalisation of the proceedings may be set for one or other of those children. It may be apparent that an expedited hearing is suitable for one or more but not all of the children who are subjects of the proceedings.

Experts and Assessors

39. Attention is drawn generally to the detailed terms of the Practice Direction: Experts in Family Proceedings Relating to Children dated April 2008.

40. In relation to expert evidence and differing types of assessments in care proceedings, it is to be expected of practitioners that such experts and assessors should be asked to take into account specifically the timetable for the child as set by the court, when setting a timetable for their own reports.

41. A failure to do this may jeopardise the timetable for the child as set by the court and cause unnecessary delay in the finalisation of the proceedings.

The Children's Guardian

42. The purpose of this basic guidance to good practice is not to consider the challenges currently faced by Cafcass and their effect on care proceedings. Attention is drawn to the joint message and agreement between the President of the Family Division and the Chief Executive of Cafcass dated the 1st October 2010 entitled "Arrangements to assist Cafcass pending implementation of the Family Justice Review."

43. In relation to good practice from the point of view of the child, there is much importance to be attached to the intervention of a children's guardian from the outset of proceedings, so that he or she may see the children early on and have full input into the recommendations being made to the court in relation to parental assessments, expert evidence and otherwise.

44. A failure in the appointment of a guardian to act throughout the proceedings may jeopardise the timetable for the child and cause unnecessary delay to the proceedings.

Parallel Planning

45. Applicant local authorities in care proceedings will be giving primary consideration to whether a child may be parentally re-unified. They should in practice also place sufficient emphasis on the importance of active parallel planning during the currency of such proceedings.

46. This should apply from the outset of proceedings through to their determination.

47. The court will be giving primary consideration to whether a child may be parentally reunified and will accordingly give case management directions in relation to parental assessment.

48. The court in its case management order should also consider reflecting in its directions the importance to the case of active parallel planning by way of a general clause in its case management order to the effect that 'the local authority is to carry out active parallel planning through the proceedings, whether as to kinship assessments within the extended family or seeking potential alternate carers for the child outside of the family.'

49. A failure to carry out active parallel planning throughout proceedings may jeopardise the timetable for the child and cause undue delay to the proceedings.

Kinship assessments

50. It is important to ascertain at the outset of care proceedings which member or members of the family should be subject to assessment. An applicant local authority in issuing care proceedings should itself be considering the identification of any family member or members who may be suitable as kinship carers and who accordingly should be urgently assessed by it. In cases with a complex family structure, the provision by the local authority of a genogram at the outset of proceedings is to be viewed as good practice.

51. The court should always consider at the early stage of proceedings giving specific directions as to kinship assessments. The local authority may have a kinship assessment underway or already completed. The court order may direct the parents to notify the local authority expeditiously of the name or names of any member or members of the family they wish to be assessed. The court at the

early stage of proceedings similarly may direct the local authority to carry out, within a specified time, an assessment of any such member or members of the family the parents reasonably seek to be assessed.

52. The prospect of an unforeseen approach by a member of the extended family late in the proceedings can be diminished by active case management early on in the proceedings. The failure of any such active case management early on may jeopardise the timetable for the child set by the court and cause unnecessary delay in the proceedings.

Parallel planning outside of the extended family

53. The court should consider at the early stage of case management a general clause to the effect that 'the local authority is to ensure, by way of parallel planning only, the subject child is placed before such permanency panel as may be appropriate in advance of the substantive determination of the case.'

The disclosure of material by the Metropolitan Police

54. An appropriate order for consideration in case management is:

'Any party requiring disclosure of material in the possession of the Metropolitan Police shall within 7 days of the First Appointment (or by such later date as may be specified by the court) file and serve written confirmation that a request has been sent in accordance with Annex B to the Protocol for Disclosure by the Police of Information in Family Proceedings. If obtained, the requiring party shall within 7 days of disclosure serve copies of such documents on the other parties. Where police object to disclosure and/or no agreement can be reached, the requesting party shall apply on notice for an order for disclosure and request a hearing date. Provision of the requested information in advance of the hearing should be deemed compliance with the proposed order for disclosure.'

Communicating with the Home Office

55. Attention is drawn to the recently re-issued Practice Direction of October 2010 of the President of the Family Division (replacing and amalgamating previous guidance issued in 2002,2004 and 2006) entitled 'Communicating with the Home Office in Family Proceedings.'

56. This is usually referable to cases which require clarification as to the immigration status of a party or parties in proceedings.
57. It is the responsibility of the parties led by an applicant local authority in such cases to obtain and complete the form EX660 in advance of seeking such a direction in court. A sample completed

EX660 form is attached to the recent guidance. The parties are also to ensure a suitable court order is drawn requesting the Home Office to provide to the court within a specified period its response to the information sought. A sample court order is attached to the recent guidance.

District Judge Richard Harper
The Chair, on behalf of the PLO Monitoring Group for London

Approved by the Designated Family Judge for London
His Honour Judge John Altman

October 2010

A3.11   APPENDIX 11:
ARRANGEMENTS TO ASSIST CAFCASS PENDING IMPLEMENTATION OF THE FAMILY JUSTICE REVIEW

President's Joint Direction
1 October 2010

Note—The Agreement between the President of the Family Division and the Chief Executive of Cafcass dated 1 October 2010 expired on 30 September 2011. It was felt that the good practice generated by it was now so well established that it would continue without the need for any formal agreement (see President's Joint Message at **A3.12** below).

Agreement between the President of the Family Division and the Chief Executive of Cafcass

This Agreement is supported by the Ministry of Justice and the Department for Education and shall remain in force for a period of 12 months from 1st October 2010 (unless renewed within that period). The effect of the Agreement shall be monitored by the Ministry of Justice, HMCS and the Department for Education with a view to further discussions between government, Cafcass and the judiciary three months in advance of the end of that period: (that is by 30th June 2011).

The agreement has a four-fold purpose:

1   To build on the valuable inter-agency working which the Interim Guidance has produced.
2   To continue the reduction of backlogs in the allocation of public law guardians and prevent their recurrence where they have been eliminated.
3   To assist guardians to make the best use of their time and
4   To minimise the use of Cafcass nominated 'duty advisers' except where the DFJ has agreed and published circumstances in which they may be used, and then to regulate such use.

Where local arrangements have been agreed and implemented by DFJs with Cafcass under the President's Interim Guidance which have been successful and resulted in eliminating backlogs in the appointment of guardians in public law cases, such arrangements may continue to apply with the concurrence of both the DFJ and the Cafcass Head of Service in so far as those arrangements are not inconsistent with the provisions of the Public Law Outline.

Preamble

1 This Agreement must be read alongside the Public Law Outline (The PLO). It is of the utmost importance that the PLO is fully and effectively implemented by all judges, magistrates, legal advisers and guardians.

Note—See now FPR PD12A.

2 In particular:

Paragraph 3.1(2) of the PLO emphasises the need for judicial continuity. It makes clear that each case must be allocated to one and not more than two case management judges (in the case of magistrates' courts, case managers) who will be responsible for every case management stage of the proceedings through to the final hearing. It is of the greatest importance that this provision is obeyed. Delay most often occurs when there in no case manager taking responsibility for the case. The President is content that arrangements for this have been made in the Principal Registry of the Family Division and he is setting up a similar scheme to govern cases listed in the Royal Courts of Justice. Family Division Liaison Judges, through their Designated Family Judges, and Justices' Clerks will be expected to make similar arrangements on their Circuits.

Paragraph 3.19 of the PLO requires the court to further the overriding objective by actively managing cases.

Paragraph 3.20 makes clear that active case management includes identifying all facts and matters that are in issue at the earliest stage in the proceedings and at each hearing, and that the court must decide promptly which issues need full investigation and which do not. For the avoidance of any doubt, active case management includes (1) discussion with all parties and the guardian and/or the child's legal representative about the issues in the case; and (2) directions to the guardian setting out the issues which the case management judge or case manager requires the guardian to investigate and report upon to the court.

3 While this Agreement reminds courts of their proactive role, it is not intended to diminish the role of the guardian. On the contrary, although the court will at an early stage, and throughout the proceedings indicate to the guardian and the parties the issues which the court perceives as likely to determine the outcome of the case:–

    (*a*)   nothing in this Agreement is designed to prevent or inhibit the guardian identifying and investigating other issues which the guardian perceives to be necessary for the fulfilment of the guardian's duty to safeguard and promote the welfare of the child;

(*b*) at all stages of the proceedings the court will revisit the issues in the case and may at any time indicate to the guardian further or other issues on which the assistance of the guardian is required; and

(*c*) nothing in this Agreement encourages or permits the court's interference with the guardian's duties as set out in statute and court rules.

Agreement

4 Local arrangements have been designed to reduce backlogs in the allocation of guardians and to promote inter-agency working. Arrangements set up by the Designated Family Judge (DFJ) under paragraphs 1–4 of the President's Interim Guidance shall remain in place for

(*a*) Coordination of matters such as hearing dates, filing and service of documents and transmission of information including resolution of urgent problems

(*b*) Provision of information to assist the DFJ to make decisions about management of family business in their courts

(*c*) Arranging meetings of appropriate representatives with the DFJ to assist in and be advised of the formulation of local agreements

(*d*) Publication of details of the arrangements made under this paragraph, and of the local agreements reached

5 In accordance with the PLO, Cafcass will allocate a guardian in every case within three days of being notified by the local authority or the court that proceedings under Part IV of the Act have been instituted.

6 Only, in circumstances agreed and published by the DFJ in accordance with Paragraph 4 above may Cafcass nominate a 'duty adviser.' Any such 'duty adviser' will be fully qualified and in a position to assist the court and the parties up to and at the first appointment and at any urgent interim hearing in which a substantive decision is sought in relation to the child prior to a guardian being allocated (for example whether to make an interim care order or a residential assessment).

7 Where a 'duty adviser' is in place, Cafcass will nonetheless allocate a guardian for the purposes of the proceedings no later than 7 days before the Advocates' Meeting in preparation for the CMC.

8 To the extent that the court makes case management directions and orders in advance of the CMC, and the Cafcass representative is a 'duty adviser', the 'duty adviser' shall record these matters and convey them to the guardian within 24 hours of the guardian's allocation.

9 At every hearing, the court should consider with the parties whether the guardian may be excused attendance at the next hearing in the proceedings in accordance with rule 4.11A(4) FPR 1991 or rule 11A(4) FPC(CA)R 1991

10 If the guardian is of the opinion, taking into account the directions of the court, and paragraph 3 above, that there are no identified tasks to be undertaken by the guardian for a specified period, the guardian must advise the court and the parties of this. The court will then aim to clarify the particular tasks and relevant time frames for any work which remains to be done by all parties and the guardian and make appropriate directions or recordings on the face of any order.

11 During any period when directions or recordings made under paragraph 10 above apply, indicating that there are no tasks to be undertaken by the guardian during a specified period, the guardian must have regard to the statutory duties of a guardian and monitor the progress of the case. The other parties, and in particular the children's solicitor, must bring any relevant change in circumstances or other matter which may require the investigation of the guardian to the attention of the guardian immediately. The case management judge(s) or case manager(s) must be advised by the parties and the guardian of any such change which is likely to affect the issues which need investigation or the timetable fixed by the court in accordance with the Timetable for the Child.

Sir Nicholas Wall
President of the Family Division

Anthony Douglas CBE
Chief Executive, Cafcass & Head of Family Justice

Annex A
Joint message from Sir Nicholas Wall, President of the Family Division and Anthony Douglas, the Chief Executive of Cafcass

With this note, you will receive the Agreement which has been reached between us and the relevant government Departments and which replaces the Interim Guidance, which expires on 30 September 2010.

We think the document speaks for itself, and we express a joint determination to make the family justice system work for the benefit of the disadvantaged children who are caught up in it.

You will see that the thrust of the Agreement is that all involved in the system should work cooperatively to operate the Public Law Outline[1] locally within an environment of increasing and complex workloads to make the most of our available resources.

In deciding what directions should be made in relation to the work of the guardian, the court will usually hear from all parties and especially the representative of the child and will above all take into account that nothing in the Agreement fetters the responsibility of the children's guardian independently to represent the interests of the child in accordance with the statute and court rules.

We expect that the judges and magistrates who have to manage cases and make the decisions in relation to them will understand and respect the changing operational processes of Cafcass. In turn Cafcass recognises that it is the essence of judicial case management that judges and magistrates identify particular pieces of work which they wish the guardian to undertake and that if they regard it necessary from time to time to specify the manner in which such work is undertaken, they have the power to do so.

Sir Nicholas Wall
The President of the Family Division & Head of Family Justice

Anthony Douglas CBE
Chief Executive, Cafcass

> 1   Practice Direction: Public Law Proceedings Guide to Case Management: April 2010

A3.12   APPENDIX 12:
PRESIDENT'S JOINT MESSAGE OF 29 JULY 2011

Joint Message from Sir Nicholas Wall, President of the Family Division and Anthony Douglas CBE, the Chief Executive of Cafcass

Note—The Agreement between the President of the Family Division and the Chief Executive of Cafcass dated 1 October 2010 expired on 30 September 2011. It was felt that the good practice generated by it was now so well established that it would continue without the need for any formal agreement. The expired Agreement is set out above at **A3.11**. It was to be read alongside the Public Law Outline (FPR PD12A) and set out guidelines that aimed to improve interagency working, reduce the backlog in the allocation of public law guardians, assist guardians to make the best use of their time and minimise the use of Cafcass "duty advisers".

On 1 October 2009 and again on 1 April 2010 Sir Mark Potter P and the Chief Executives of HMCS (as it then was) and Cafcass entered into agreements for what were described as "short-term measures" and which became known as his "Interim Guidance" (PIG1 and PIG2). Each was designed initially to last six months.

On the Expiry of PIG2 on 1 October 2010, we came to an Agreement to assist Cafcass to manage constantly increasing demand for its services pending implementation of the Family Justice Review.

The Agreement was to last until 30 September 2011 and contained provision for the Ministry of Justice, HMC(T)S, and the Department for Education to monitor its effect. The Ministry of Justice and the Department for Education have sent the Local Performance Improvement

Groups the results of their 'Review of local arrangements between Cafcass and Designated Family Judges.' This review document concludes that the Agreement, "has been successful in achieving its aims, which is demonstrably clear from the statistical evidence, supported by concurring opinion from frontline practitioners collected through an online survey."

The success of the Agreement has been as a result of two main factors –

1   Cooperative working between the courts, Cafcass and other agencies with strong information-sharing across the system being used to identify ways of improving the system locally.

2   Improved good practice in observing the detailed case management provisions of the Public Law Outline Practice Direction.

While we accept the recommendation in the review document that, "with the continued high levels of s 31 applications being forecast and the consequent continuation of high demand for Cafcass services, there is strong evidence that the successful working practices adopted by local areas to manage current workloads should be maintained", we are confident that the arrangements for good communication and working relations which were already in existence in some areas, but which were formalised by the Designated Family Judges and Cafcass Heads of Service under the PIGs and restated at paragraph 4 of the Agreement will be maintained.

In these circumstances, we have come to the conclusion, after consulting the Designated Family Judges and local Cafcass managers, that it would not be right formally to renew the Agreement and that in any event it is unnecessary to do so.

We are both of the view that the good practice generated by the PIGs and by the Agreement is now well established and should continue without the need for any formal agreement between us. Thus the spirit of the Agreement will continue to operate: local discussions and initiatives will continue and local agreements or protocols will remain in place or new ones be drawn up as the need arises. We are confident that Judges and magistrates hearing cases under the Children Act will continue to manage according to the Public Law Outline and the Private Law Programme and will continue to assist guardians in the manner envisaged in paragraphs 9 to 11 of the Agreement and set out in the final paragraph of the joint message which we sent with the Agreement on 1 October 2010.

Sir Nicholas Wall
President of the Family Division

Anthony Douglas, CBE
Chief Executive, Cafcass

A3.13   APPENDIX 13:
        COMMUNICATING WITH THE HOME OFFICE IN
        FAMILY PROCEEDINGS

President's Guidance
March 2012

1 The 'Communicating with the Home Office in Family Proceedings' protocol enables the family courts to communicate with the Home Office (UK Borders Agency and Identity and Passport Service) to obtain immigration, visa and passport information for family court proceedings.

2 This guidance has been reissued to replace & amalgamate previous guidance issued in 2002, 2004, 2006 & 2010 (including the Communicating with the Passport Service 2004) to reflect the new contact details for the Home Office Liaison Officer who has responsibility for administering requests made under the Protocol. It does not alter the nature or purpose of the Protocol.

3 Where an order is made against the Home Office in Family Proceedings, the court shall draw up the relevant order. The HMCTS form EX660 should be fully completed (including specifying the details of the relevant family members and their relationship to the child). Parties should provide details of *both* mother and father if known, whether or not they are involved in the proceedings.

4 The sealed order and the completed EX660 should be sent immediately to:

Home Office Liaison Officer
Her Majesty's Courts and Tribunal Service
Arnheim House
PO Box 6987
Leicester
LE1 6ZX
Email: homeofficeliaison@hmcts.gsi.gov.uk
Telephone: 0116 249 4309
Fax: 0116 249 4400

5 Please note that all information provided in the EX660 will be forwarded to the Home Office. Parties should ensure that any additional information, such as a case synopsis, which it wishes the Home Office to view, has the required leave of the court, set out in the order, to be disclosed to the Home Office. (Note that it is a contempt of court to disclose this information otherwise).

6 Where the query relates to the proposed adoption of a foreign national minor, the Home Office Liaison Officer can advise as to the additional information which will be required.

7 The order and EX660 should clearly state the time by which the information is required. In order to comply with the agreed four (4) week period in for the Home Office to provide a response to the court, parties and court staff should ensure that the Home Office Liaison Officer receives the court order on the day the order is made.

8 Where it will not be possible for court to send the sealed order to the Home Office Liaison Officer on the day it is made, the court when stating the required date of receipt by the court of the information should allow any additional time necessary for the preparation and sending of the order. This is in order to ensure that Home Office has 4 weeks to provide a response from the time it receives the order from the Home Office Liaison Officer. Any reduction in this period may result in a request by the Home Office for further time in which to reply.

9 The request or order should identify the questions it wishes to be answered by the Home Office.

10 Parties should provide the name and contact details of someone who has agreed and is able to provide further information should it be needed.

11 The order and EX660 should be forwarded to the Home Office Liaison Officer together with such information as is sufficient to enable the Home Office to understand the nature of the case, to identify whether the case involves an adoption, and to identify whether the immigration issues raised might relate to an asylum or non-asylum application.

12 The Home Office Liaison Officer will then send to an appropriate officer in the Home Office the enquiry, together with a copy of any order made. The Home Office official will be personally responsible for either:

(*a*) answering the query themselves, by retrieving the file and preparing a statement for the court; or

(*b*) forwarding the request to a caseworker or relevant official with carriage of that particular file.

13 The Home Office Liaison Officer will follow up as required in order to ensure that the information is received by the court in time, and will receive the information before forwarding it on as instructed by the judge or court making the request.

14 Attached is a sample court order and completed EX660 which should provide further useful guidance. **Please note the change in contact details in the form EX660.**

****

Originally issued December 2002

Re-issued March 2012

Sir Nicholas Wall
President of the Family Division

Note—The contact details in Form EX660 are the same as in para 4.

A3.14   APPENDIX 14:
PRESIDENT'S GUIDANCE IN RELATION TO OUT OF HOURS HEARINGS

President's Guidance
18 November 2010

Out of Hours Hearings

1 It is perhaps not sufficiently appreciated by the general public that there is always a High Court judge of the Family Division on duty "out of hours" – that is to say every day of the year including all holiday periods either: (1) between 16.15 on day one and 10.30 am on day two of a normal court sitting; or (2) between 16.15 on any given Friday and 10.30 the following Monday. In vacations, when the court is not sitting, a similar service is provided at any time of the day or night.

2 It is of the utmost importance that this service is used for its intended purposes and is not abused. It is designed for urgent cases. In this context "urgent" has a specific meaning. It means cases in which an order of the court is required to regulate the position between the moment the order is made and the next available sitting of the court in conventional court hours – that is, usually, 10.30 on the following morning.

3 Judges of the Family Division have no complaint, for example, if, in the middle of the night, they are asked to sanction life saving medical treatment, or if they have to visit a hospital at such a time in order to decide whether a given individual should undergo urgent and specific treatment.

4 Any application that is "urgent" within the definition set out in paragraph 2 above must be capable of being reduced to a faxed sheet of A4 (or its email equivalent), or a short telephone conversation. Whether or not a case is "urgent" will always be a matter for the judge.

5 What is unacceptable is an application which can plainly wait until the normal sitting of the court and/or which involves a substantial amount of documentation. A judge cannot and should not be expected either to receive or to assimilate a substantial volume of documentation in an urgent, out of hours application unless both are absolutely essential to a proper understanding of the order which the judge is being asked to make. Equally, judges who are on duty out of hours should not be expected to make arrangements to sit in court unless such a sitting is strictly necessary to enable an order to be made. The profession should also remember that the judge on duty, whilst always available on the telephone, will be at home, and that "home" may not be in London.

6 Lawyers who abuse the system, particularly those who seek to take advantage of an order not made on notice and out of hours with a speedy return date in hours may not only be the subject of orders for wasted costs, but may find themselves reported to their professional bodies for serious professional misconduct. The profession is thus reminded of the definition of "urgent" set out in paragraph 2 of this note.

7 Nothing in this note supersedes any previous Guidance or Practice Note relating to out of hours applications.

Sir Nicholas Wall
President of the Family Division

A3.15   APPENDIX 15:
CASE MANAGEMENT DECISIONS AND APPEALS THEREFROM (BULLETIN NUMBER 2)

President's Guidance
December 2010

Introduction

If my first "Guidance" (regarding split-hearings, issued in May 2010 and published in the July issue of *Family Law* at [2010] Fam Law 752) began with a note of a health warning, such a health warning applies even more strongly to what follows. I hope, however, that it will, nonetheless, be of assistance.

As I have gone around the country, a number of judges and magistrates have told me that they feel unsupported by appellate jurisdictions. They thus feel, for example, that they must order an expert's report or an additional assessment by an independent social worker for fear that if they do not they will be appealed and criticised on appeal for not having done so.

I cannot, of course, speak for the Court of Appeal, which will deal with any given appeal, or application for permission to appeal, on its merits. Equally, in my view, no court should ever deal with a case on the basis that one discretionary outcome rather than another may find greater favour with an appellate tribunal. I can, however, offer the following by way of guidance.

It seems to me that there are two particular types of case management decisions in which this dilemma principally arises. The first relates to additional reports or assessments of children and their parents in care proceedings. The second is applications under section 38(6) of the Children Act 1989. I propose to deal with each in turn. Before doing so, however, it will, I think, do no harm to repeat a few obvious messages: –

1 As a general proposition, and as a matter of policy, appellate courts recognise that decisions at first instance are often taken quickly and under pressure both of time and other work. It follows that the instinct of the appellate court is to support the decision made below, unless that decision is – as both Asquith LJ and Lord Fraser emphasise "plainly wrong"- see paragraph 3 below.

2 Judicial decisions under the Act are mostly discretionary. A judicial discretion must, of course, be exercised judicially. That said, the discretion is, usually, a wide one, particularly in relation to case management decisions.

3 It is worth remembering always what Atkin LJ said in *Bellenden (formerly Satterthwaite) v Satterthwaite* [1948] 1 All ER 343 at 345 (and cited by Lord Fraser in the Family case of *G v G* [1985] 1 WLR 647 at 651-2, [1985] FLR 894 at 898 namely: –

> "It is, of course, not enough ... to establish that this court might, or would, have made a different order. We are here concerned with a judicial discretion, and it is of the essence of such a discretion that on the same evidence two minds may reach different conclusions in relation to the same subject matter without either being wrong: or, to put it another way, an appellate court cannot reverse a court of first instance unless the decision at first instance is plainly wrong."

4 When exercising a first instance discretion, it is essential for the tribunal to take all relevant matters into account and to exclude all irrelevant matters. The pros and cons should then be weighed and a decision reached. The decision itself must be reasoned and clearly articulated. Provided it follows these rules, the decision should be fireproof.

5 Decisions can, of course, be plainly wrong if judges or magistrates make an error or errors of law. However, such errors in this category of case are unusual. The argument is more likely to centre on the manner in which the discretion has been exercised, and this in turn will depend upon the performance of the balancing exercise.

6 So when you are performing such an exercise, even if you are entirely clear about what you intend to do, I suggest that you take a few moments in your room to jot down or underline the relevant points to ensure that you have taken everything relevant into account and discarded the irrelevant. Itemise the considerations for and against the application and explain why you have decided as you have. Don't labour the fact that you are exercising your discretion, but say so, and remind yourself that it has to be – and is being – exercised judicially.

7 Quite what the factual matrix will be in a given case will, self-evidently, depend upon the facts of that case. However, always bear in mind that assessments or additional reports take time. It is thus always important to take delay and the timing of the application in question into account. There will be cases in which an assessment will not cause additional delay: there will be other cases in which the delay caused by an additional

assessment may be a critical factor which tips the balance against it. Either way, ensure that you have dealt with the point in your judgment.

8 Any hearing you conduct must, of course, be ECHR Article 6 and 8 compliant.

9 Any appeal against a case management decision must be mounted swiftly – see the decisions of the Court of Appeal in *Re A (Residence Order)* [2007] EWCA Civ 899 [2007] Fam Law 1061, *Re S (Child Proceedings: Urgent Appeals)* [2007] EWCA Civ 958, [2007] 2 FLR 1044 and *Re P and P (Care Proceedings: Appointment of Experts)* [2009] EWCA Civ 610, [2009] 2 FLR 1370 (also discussed below).

Guidance

Applications for additional assessments or for expert reports

10 Re-read the experts' practice direction at [2009] 2 FLR 1383. Remember always that it is your case and your decision. An "expert" can only be instructed if you agree, and the function of the expert is "to provide an opinion about a question that is not within the skill and experience of the court" (PD paragraph 1.3). So always ask yourself: do I need this additional report to enable me to make a fair and proper decision? What can this expert add or contribute to the case? If the answer to the first question is "no" and to the second "nothing," you are unlikely to order a report.

11 Process is important in family law, and every hearing you conduct must be ECHR Articles 6 and 8 compliant. This does not, of course, mean that you must accede to every parent's application for a second opinion: each decision is a matter of judgment. What is important is that your conduct of the proceedings is transparent and your conclusion is fair. This will inevitably involve balancing different factors in the manner I have already described before reaching a reasoned conclusion.

12 Always bear in mind the effect which any order you are being asked to make has on the time-table for the child and the case overall.

13 Always remember that issues of fact and credibility (who is believed and who is not) are matters for you, and not for the expert.

14 In public law care proceedings, judges and magistrates cannot make care orders under the Act unless they are satisfied both that the threshold criteria under section 31 of the Act are satisfied and that it is in the best interests of the child for a care order to be made. If the material available to you does not enable you to fulfil your statutory obligations to the child, say so, specifying the gap that needs filling, and – if you make an order for an expert opinion – list that as a principal reason for doing so.

15 Note that by virtue of paragraph 4.3(8) of the Practice Direction the party seeking permission to instruct an expert must explain why the

expert evidence proposed cannot be given by social services undertaking a core assessment or by the children's guardian in accordance with their respective statutory duties.

Applications under section 38(6) of the Act

16 There are additional factors which should be taken into account when dealing with applications under sections 38(6) and (7).

17 It is, I think, worthwhile remembering that section 38 of the Act deals with interim care orders and interim supervision orders. So the court cannot make an order under section 38(6) unless such an order is or will be in place. Section 38(6) is thus an exception to the general rule that where a care order is made, the local authority is in the driving seat and can effectively dictate how parental responsibility is to be exercised under section 33.

18 The two leading cases are the decisions in the House of Lords in *Re C (A Minor) (Interim Care Order: Residential Assessment)* [1997] AC 489, [1997] 1 FLR 1 (*Re C*) and *Re G (A Minor) (Interim Care Order: Residential Assessment)* [2005] UKHL 68. [2006] 1 AC 576, [2006] 1 FLR 601 (*Re G*). They should be re-read.

19 Two points of law were decided by *Re C*. They are: (1) that sections 38(6) and (7) of the Act are to be broadly construed and "confer jurisdiction on the court to order or prohibit any assessment which involves the participation of the child and is directed to providing the court with the material which, in the view of the court, is required to enable it to reach a proper decision at the final hearing of the application for a full care order" (per Lord Browne-Wilkinson); and (2) that the phrase "the medical or psychiatric examination or other assessment of the child" in section 38(6) is not to be interpreted so as to restrict assessments to the medical or psychiatric.

20 In addition, *Re C* makes it clear that it is impossible to assess a young child divorced from his or her environment and thus the assessment includes the relationship between the parents and the child or children concerned.

21 *Re G*, whilst adopting the broad approach set out in *Re C* decides that an assessment under section 38(6) does not include therapy or treatment, particularly for a parent. Inpatient treatment was thus beyond section 38(6) and the court had no power to order it under the sub-section.

22 Lord Scott, who conducts a helpful review of the authorities, specifically agreed with a statement by Holman J in *Re M (Residential Assessment Directions)* [1998] 2 FLR 371 at 381 which I think it useful to follow. Holman J said: –

> "... The court's powers ... are limited to a process that can properly be described as 'assessment' rather than 'treatment' although no doubt all

treatment is accompanied by a continuing process of assessment. And they are limited to a process which bona fide involves the participation of the child as an integral part of what is being assessed."

23 Section 38(6) should thus be seen as part of the essential evidence gathering process. Plainly, if the proposed assessment is in fact a therapeutic intervention for the benefit of the parents, you will refuse the application. If, on the other hand, the assessment falls within Holman J's statement in *Re M*, that will be a factor which opens the door to the exercise of your discretion.

I propose to illustrate this guidance by reference to examples of decisions of the Court of Appeal in which I gave the leading judgment.

In the first, we supported the decision of the judge not to allow a further assessment.

The second is a reversal of the judge's decision, but is largely concerned with an error in law.

The third is an example of further expert evidence being required to assist the court.

The fourth concerns the question of a second opinion, but was wholly exceptional on its facts.

Example 1

24 *Re S* [2008] EWCA Civ 1078, [2008] Fam Law 1267 (not otherwise reported). In this case, the Court of Appeal (Mummery LJ and myself) refused an application for permission to appeal the decision not to allow a section 38(6) assessment. We did so because: –

> (*a*) the judge was exercising a discretion, and had done so judicially;
>
> (*b*) the judge had conducted a careful balancing exercise: he had identified all the factors in favour of an assessment and had balanced them against the factors which militated against it;
>
> (*c*) he cited from and followed the relevant authorities;
>
> (*d*) he expressly weighed the question of delay;
>
> (*e*) he also considered carefully the likely disruption to the child caused by the assessment;
>
> (*f*) the judge was concerned about the information the mother had made available to those proposing the assessment , and took into account what he found to be the mother's lack of frankness in this respect;
>
> (*g*) the judge asked himself the question: would the report give him any important additional information? In this case, although it might not be necessary in all cases, there had been a previous, unsuccessful attempt at a residential assessment;
>
> (*h*) the judge found that, as an exercise of discretion, the "antis" outweighed the "pros" by a significant margin and he refused the application.

25 Such a decision is plainly incapable of being appealed, even if the appellate court would be inclined to disagree with it.

Example 2

26 *Re L and H (Residential Assessment)* [2007] EWCA Civ 213. [2007] 1 FLR 1370, a decision of Thorpe LJ and myself.

27 What is important to note about this decision is that it is a rare example of where we took the view that the judge had made an error of law. The two factors which predominated in the case were: (1) that the judge had refused the assessment on the grounds that it involved a therapeutic element and was thus outside section 38(6); and (2) he gave no weight to the fact that a previous psychological assessment had strongly recommended a residential parenting assessment both to give the professionals involved in the case important information about the mother's practical parenting, and also to provide important, even vital information about how the parents' relationship bore up under stress.

28 In our view, the judge had been plainly wrong to characterise the recommended assessment as outside section 38(6). The psychologist had suggested a concurrent therapeutic intervention by others, not a therapeutic intervention as part of the residential assessment.

29 The judge had also been wrong in saying, as he did, that the assessment would "of necessity give rise to considerable and in my judgement unacceptable delay...". Had he ordered an assessment it would have been completed well in advance of the fixed date for the final hearing.

30 Our decision in *Re L and H*, therefore, was not primarily concerned with the reversal of the judge's discretionary judgment.

31 It is, of course, the case, that I go on to discuss the principles underlying the 1989 Act and describe fairness and a full and proper investigation as points which go to the "root of family justice". I do not, however, think that I am saying more than the following: -

   (1)   that care proceedings are important;
   (2)   that the court has a duty to act in conformity with ECHR Articles 6 and 8;
   (3)   that before making a care order the court has to be satisfied about the threshold criteria and that a care order is in the best interests of the child concerned; and
   (4)   that given the importance of the issues to the child concerned and his or her family every case needs to be fully and properly investigated.

32 In my view, there is nothing in *Re L and H* to lead anyone to the view that they cannot take difficult decisions about disadvantaged children with impunity. This is, after all, what judges and magistrates are doing day in and day out.

Example 3

33 A rare example of a case management decision being reversed is *Re P and P (Care Proceedings: Appointment of Experts)* [2009] EWCA Civ 610, [2009] 2 FLR 1370 in which Smith LJ and I felt compelled to reverse a decision by Coleridge J who had refused permission to a local authority to instruct an paediatric pathologist to investigate an earlier child death which had manifested symptoms similar to those shown by one of the children who were the subject of the care proceedings before the judge.

Coleridge J refused the application on the ground that it would lead to an extensive investigation and that the resulting delay could not be justified. We took the view that his decision was premature: the judge should have ordered the report and then decided upon the direction of the case. He had deprived himself of information which would have enabled him to make an informed decision. The appeal was supported by the guardian, and the enquiries were plainly material.

Example 4

34 *W v Oldham MBC* [2005] EWCA Civ 1247; [2006] 1 FLR 543. A decision of Thorp LJ, Black J (as she then was) and myself.

35 This case, although required reading, was wholly exceptional on its facts. It is an example of circumstances when it is necessary in the interests of fairness and justice to allow a parent a second opinion. The judge thought she was dealing with a medical consensus. In reality, it turned out to be nothing of the sort. All the doctors in the case at first instance simply deferred to the one doctor who had the specialism lacked by the others. When a second specialist was instructed, he took a different view (which proved to be that adopted by the judge). The parents were initially deprived of the opportunity to challenge the medical evidence.

Summary

36 As we stated in *Re P and P* (see 33 above):

> [17] Case management decisions are not to be challenged on a whim, or because one party simply happens to disagree with them. They are discretionary decisions in which the allocated judge enjoys a very wide discretion to deal with the case within the confines of the overriding objective and taking into account the best interests of the child. There must be a point of substance which requires an urgent challenge and speedy resolution. In the overwhelming majority of cases, no such point will arise. Where it does, however, speed is of the essence. Delay, as the 1989 Act makes clear, is usually contrary to the interests of children, as well as being the enemy of justice in most child cases.

Conclusion

37 Having sat in the county court, and having listened to everything which is said to me, I know how difficult and stressful these cases are. But

the message of this guidance, I hope, is that provided it is followed, your work will be respected and supported, even if it may look to you as though the case being heard in the Court of Appeal bears little or no resemblance to the case you heard.

Nicholas Wall

A3.16   APPENDIX 16:
GUIDANCE IN CASES INVOLVING PROTECTED PARTIES IN WHICH THE OFFICIAL SOLICITOR IS BEING INVITED TO ACT AS GUARDIAN AD LITEM OR LITIGATION FRIEND

President's Joint Guidance
December 2010

Public and private law children's cases

1 Many practitioners and judges will know of the Official Solicitor's recent difficulties in accepting requests to act as guardian ad litem/litigation friend for protected parties in proceedings relating to children. Although, currently, there are unallocated cases, the backlog has reduced significantly in recent months.

2 The Official Solicitor is subject to severe budgetary constraints – a situation which is unlikely to ameliorate in the medium term.

3 In all cases, the Official Solicitor will need to be satisfied of the following criteria before accepting a case, and parties may need reminding of the need to provide confirmation of these matters immediately on approaching the Official Solicitor's office:

- satisfactory evidence or a finding by the court that the party lacks capacity to conduct the proceedings and is therefore a protected party;
- confirmation that there is security for the costs of legal representation;
- there is no other person who is suitable and willing to act as guardian ad litem/litigation friend.

4 In order to assist the Official Solicitor in the decisions he makes about allocating case workers, in certain cases, judges should consider whether it may be appropriate to indicate with as much particularity as possible the relative urgency of the proceedings and the likely effect upon the child (and family) of delay. The Official Solicitor will very carefully consider giving priority to such cases.

5 It is and remains the judge's duty in children's cases, so far as he is able, to eradicate delay.

Court of Protection welfare cases (including medical cases)

6 The number of welfare cases brought under the provisions of the Mental Capacity Act 2005 is rising exponentially with concomitant resource implications for the Official Solicitor.

7 Judges should be alert to the problems the Official Solicitor may have in attending at each and every preliminary hearing. Consideration should be given, in appropriate cases, to dispensing with the requirement that he should be present at a time when he is unable to contribute meaningfully to the process. In circumstances where his position has been/will be communicated in writing it may be particularly appropriate for the judge to indicate that the Official Solicitor's attendance at the next directions' hearing is unnecessary.

8 The Court of Protection Rules make clear that the judge is under a duty to restrict expert evidence to that which is reasonably required to resolve the proceedings. The explanatory note to r 121 states that the court will consider what 'added value' expert evidence will give to the case. Unnecessary expert assessments must be avoided. It will be rare indeed for the court to sanction the instruction of more than one expert to advise in relation to the same issue.

9 The Practice Direction – Experts (PD15A) specifies that the expert should assist by "providing objective, unbiased opinion on matters within his expertise, and should not assume the role of advocate". The form and content of the expert's report are prescribed, in detail, by paragraph 9 of the Practice Direction. It is no part of the expert's function to analyse or summarise the evidence. Focused brevity in report writing is to be preferred over discussion.

Mrs Justice Pauffley

A3.17 APPENDIX 17:
PROTOCOL FOR HANDLING SECURE ACCOMMODATION APPLICATIONS UNDER S 25

Introduction:

(1) The purpose of this Protocol is to provide a practice-orientated approach to the case-management of these often very sensitive applications.

(2) Any assertions of fact triggered by the questions set out below will have to be supported by evidence: because it is essential that there should be a clear record of facts as found by the court and for which sworn evidence is necessary.

(3) This Protocol does not cover:

a. A child who has reached the age of 16 and is being provided with accommodation, although an order may be made prior to the age of 16 to extend beyond the child's sixteenth birthday;

b. Children remanded to local authority accommodation, pursuant to Children and Young Person's Act 1969, s. 23.

c. A child under the age of 13, unless there is prior approval from the Secretary of State;

d. A child who is a ward of court, unless there is a direction for secure accommodation from the judge exercising wardship jurisdiction.

Practice management:

1. **Who is the applicant?**

   a. Where a local authority is looking after the child, only the local authority;

   b. Where a health authority, NHS trust or local education authority is providing accommodation for child, only the health authority etc, unless local authority looking after child;

   c. Where child is provided with accommodation in a residential care home, nursing home or mental nursing home, the person carrying on that establishment may apply.

2. **In relation to the child:**

   a. *Full name;*

   b. *Date of birth;*

   c. *Place of birth;*

   d. *Is the child looked after by a local authority?* [see s 22 CA 1989 – also covers child who is bailed with a condition of residence to the local authority].

   e. *Address of current residence* [if this is not secure accommodation, why has LA not invoked the 72 hour margin];

   f. *Health/details of any disease and/or other medical issues;*

   g. *Time-table for the child:*

      i. By when the question relating to the child[ren] should be answered; and

      ii. Why the question has to be answered within this time-frame.

   h. *Parents:*

      i. Full names and dates of birth;

      ii. Current residence[s];

3. **Legal representation for the child:**

   a.   **If no:**

   i.   Has child been informed of his/her right to legal representation?
   ii. If yes, with what response?
   iii. If no, why not?
   iv. Has child been informed of the hearing?

   b.   **If yes:**

   i.   Who represents the child?
   ii. When did that representation commence?

4.   **Service:** Who has been served with the application for a s 25 order?

Sworn evidence is required as to the following:

5.   **History of absconding:**

   a.   *Absconsion[s]:*

   i.   When?
   ii. From where – give address?
   iii. Who was looking after/had control of the child at the time of absconsion?
   iv. Circumstances of absconsion[s];

   b.   *What is the evidence to support each of the matters set out under (a) immediately above giving details of:*

   i.   Witness[s] – full names, and role [e.g. foster parent, social worker etc] giving also dates of any relevant witness statements and/or reports;
   ii. HV records?
   iii. School records?
   iv. Police records [also CRB etc];
   v.   Any letter and/or notes etc. written by the child.

6.   **Has the child at any time in his or her adolescence come to significant harm in any circumstances? If yes –**

   a.   *Set out each occasion / instance;*

   i.   Date;
   ii. Circumstances;
   iii. Medical evidence setting out [if available] harm / injury / impairment sustained.
   iv. Anyone else involved? If yes, full particulars.

   b.   Have the social services and / or the police been involved as a result of any instance? If yes, give details [police records?]

7. **Is there psychiatric evidence available in relation to the child?**

    a. **If no:**

        i. Why not?
        ii. Is it yet to be obtained, and if yes: when, from whom [expert's name, address and qualifications], to what issue, is there a draft letter of instruction?

    b. **If yes:**

        i. Date?
        ii. Name of expert, address, qualifications;
        iii. To what issue.

NB(1) : On an application for a secure accommodation order, an effort should be made to obtain psychiatric evidence to put before the court: *Oxfordshire County Council v R* [1992] 1 FLR 648.
NB(2): Schedule report to the application.

8. **Has the availability of secure accommodation been established?**

    a. **If no:**

        i. Why not?
        ii. When is it anticipated to be available [and where is it]?
        iii. What is to happen to the child in the meantime?

    b. **If yes:**

        i. Where – giving address?
        ii. On what grounds is it contended that the accommodation is secure? [see *A Metropolitan Borough Council v DB* [1997] 1 FLR 767; and *Detention: Medical Treatment* [1997] 2 FLR 180].
        iii. What facilities are available at this secure accommodation including education, psychiatric and psychological therapies etc [if possible, download material from website, if any, and produce to parties and the court].
        iv. What particular therapies [if any] are recommended for the child, by whom, why and with what anticipated result [with particular reference to rehabilitation and improving the prospects of the child in the passage to adulthood]?
        v. Does the guarantee of continuity of care provided by the proposed secure accommodation [resulting in a guarantee of non-interruption of therapies / education etc] assist the overall prognosis and rehabilitation?

9. **Alternative accommodation:**

a.   Is there available a non-secure environment which can provide necessary treatments therapies? If yes –

b.   *If the child were resident there, would he/she be at risk of:*

   i.   Injury to himself/herself? If yes – on what grounds is it so contended?

   ii.   Injury to others? If yes, on what grounds is it so contended?

10. Information particularly required from the child's guardian: given that (i) the s. 1(2) welfare check list does not apply, but s 22(3) continues to apply subject to s 22(6) and (ii) the role of the court is to control the exercise of the LA's power: C(SA)R 1991, reg 7.

a.   S. 22(3) welfare of child [how the child's welfare will or will not be advanced by a s. 25 order];

b.   The criteria justifying the order;

c.   The merits of an order being made [the guardian has to adapt his general duties to the specific requirements of the application before the court and recommend what he/she believes to be in the best interests of the child].

Relevant dicta and equivalent provisions:

•   The Children Act Guidance and Regulations issued under s 7 of the Local Authority Social Services Act 1970 (LASSA 1970) are relevant. The relevant part is para 5 of Vol 1 under the heading 'Court orders'. That provides:

> 'That restricting the liberty of children is a serious step which must be taken only when there is no genuine alternative which would be appropriate. It must be a last resort in the sense that all else must have been comprehensively considered and rejected. Never because no other placement was available at the relevant time, because of inadequacies in staffing, because the child is simply being a nuisance or runs away from his accommodation and is not likely to suffer significant harm in doing so, and never as a form of punishment ... Secure placements, once made, should be for only so long as is necessary and unavoidable.'

•   Per Hoffman LJ in *Re M (A Minor) (Secure Accommodation Order)* [1995] 1 FLR 418 at page 427:

> "Thus I think that the duty of the court is to put itself in the position of a reasonable local authority and to ask, first, whether the conditions in subs (1) are satisfied and secondly, whether it would be in accordance with the authority's duty to safeguard and promote the welfare of the child (but subject to the qualification in s 22(6)) for the child to be kept in secure accommodation and if so, for how long.'

NB: Charles J set that passage in the following context, at para [45] of his judgment in *S v Knowsley BC* [see below]:

> "I pause to note that one of the effects of this passage is that at the stage of an application for a secure accommodation order the court can refuse to make one if it is not satisfied that to do so would be in accordance with the duties of the local authority to safeguard and promote the welfare of the child. As I have mentioned, this passage, in my view, indicates that the court, when making a secure accommodation order, must itself decide whether the s 25(1) criteria are met, but, in my view, it does not indicate that the court should decide the welfare issues relating to the duty to safeguard and promote the welfare of the child. Rather, the passage indicates that the court should assess such welfare issues on the basis that the local authority is the decision-maker and thus on the basis whether a placement of the child in secure accommodation is within the permissible range of options open to a local authority exercising its duties and functions to promote and safeguard the welfare of the child who is being looked after by it. Such a child may be one who is being provided with accommodation by the local authority or, as in this case, a child in respect of whom a care order has been made."

- Per Charles J in *S v Knowsley Borough Council* [2004] EWHC 491 (Fam) at para [37]

> "... the word 'likely' should be construed in the same way as in the threshold criteria in s. 31; namely, in the sense of a real possibility or a possibility that cannot sensibly be ignored.."

- *Re K (Secure Accommodation Order: Right to Liberty)* [2001] 1 FLR 526:

   a.   Per Dame Elizabeth Butler-Sloss at para [29]

   > 'It is a benign jurisdiction to protect the child as well as others: see *Re W (Secure Accommodation Order: Attendance at Court)* [1994] 2 FLR 1092, 1096 per Ewbank J, but it is nonetheless restrictive.'

   b.   Per Judge LJ a para [95] and [101]:

   > '[95] It is worth re-emphasising that it is a pre-requisite to the order that the child is being 'looked after' by the local authority. There is therefore a continuing duty to safeguard and promote the welfare of the child ....

   > [97] In summary, s 25 therefore forms part of the overall framework of the support and welfare of children who present particular difficulties and who, for their own protection and that of others and to ensure their continuing education, require that the accommodation in which they are being looked after should be secure. The necessary authorisation in domestic law enabling

the local authority to restrict the liberty of such children is provided by the court order. Although the maximum length of any order must be specified, the question whether this authorisation should be used and, if so, for how long and in what degree remains with the local authority. If and when the statutory conditions cease to apply, the order may no longer be enforced. (*LM v Essex County Council [1999] 1 FLR 988*)'

'[101] By definition the making of the order means that if accommodation less than adequate for the purpose of restricting liberty is provided, a child is likely to suffer significant harm because there is a history and continuing risk of absconding, with a likelihood of significant harm or injury to himself or others.'

- *Oxfordshire County Council v R* [1992] 1 FLR 648 per Douglas Brown J at page 656:

"That leads me to the last question, ground 7. In the report of the guardian ad litem, reference was made to psychiatric assessments of the appellant. In the absence of such evidence, the magistrates were unable to assess whether the last resort of making a secure accommodation order was justified on the totality of information relating to the appellant's background.

It may not be possible in every case where there is considerable pressure on those preparing the cases, when time is short, for there to be psychiatric evidence called, but I think in these cases where, almost invariably, disturbed young people are being discussed, an effort should be made to obtain psychiatric evidence. The very minimum I think these magistrates should have had was a psychiatric report from one of the psychiatrists who were attached to the secure unit. Of those, Dr Martin Gay is a well-known expert in the field of child and adolescent psychiatry, and the report from him or his registrar would have been extremely valuable. This boy is clearly highly disturbed, and there are dangers for him in either of the options which were open to the magistrates to make the order or to refuse it.'

A3.18   APPENDIX 18: PRACTICE MANAGEMENT: DOMESTIC VIOLENCE

A suggested Protocol to accompany the Practice Direction (PD) of 14 January 2009 (Residence and Contact Orders: Domestic Violence and Harm [2009] 2 FLR 1400 and on the free Family Law website: www.familylaw.co.uk/newswatch

Relevance of this Protocol:

1.   **Introduction:**

    a.   This Protocol is not a substitute for a reading of the PD. What it seeks to achieve is to provide a case-management tool for the vast majority of the cases which are caught by the PD.

    b.   The purpose of this Protocol is to guide the case-management of proceedings to a finding-of-fact hearing.

2.   Time is of the essence in these cases, in two respects:

    a.   Firstly: the time-table for any child, which is a first and paramount consideration; and

    b.   Secondly: the PD itself demands urgent addressing of the factual and welfare issues involved.

Note (1) Implicit throughout this Protocol is s 1(2) of the Children Act 1989: 'In any proceedings in which any question with respect to the upbringing of a child arises, the court shall have regard to the general principle that any delay in determining the question is likely to prejudice the welfare of the child.'

Note (2) If there has been any delay in applying for a fact-finding hearing, there must be filed with the court at least two working days before the relevant hearing, a particularised chronology explaining how the delay arose.

3.   Domestic Violence (DV):

    a.   Is DV in these proceedings raised by either party as an issue? If yes, which party?

    b.   Even if DV is not raised by a party, does it otherwise arise? If yes, how?

4.   If the answer to '3(a) or 3(b)' above is 'yes.'

    a.   Precisely what are the allegations [explain in short-hand succinctness, setting out who makes them/how they arise], and

    b.   Then please go to point '5' below.

Introductory issues assuming (1) an application for residence and/or contact and (2) domestic violence within the parameters set by paras 1 and 2 of the PD:

5.   List the child(ren) setting out:

    a.   Name;

    b.   Date of birth;

    c.   Age now;

    d.   Where living and with whom (explaining relationship of the carer(s) to the child(ren));

e.   If school, identify the same with address.

6.   In relation to the child(ren):

a.   What is the time-table for that child, explaining why in sufficient detail so that this is immediately clear? Note: Any order must make the following particularly clear on its face as a recital:

   i.   By when the question relating to the child(ren) should be answered; and
   ii.   A clear and succinct explanation as to why this is the time-table; ie why the question has to be answered within this time-frame.

b.   In relation to that child, what are the residence and/or contact options taking into account:

   iii.   Parents;
   iv.   Kinship carers;

Case Management Questionnaire – to be addressed by the court as soon as possible:

7.   Have there been initial Cafcass safeguarding checks?

a.   If yes, when, giving date and with what result?
b.   If no, why not?

Check list: Criminal record? Social services involvement? Any need/risk/ child protection issues to be investigated/assessed?

Note: Settled cases must not be approved without confirmation recorded on the file of the completion of safety checks.

8.   As to the allegations of DV: Is it contended that such allegations, if true, affect the welfare of the child(ren) the subject of the application? If yes:

a.   Who so contends?
b.   Explain clearly in what way?
c.   Are such allegations relevant in deciding whether or not to make an order? If yes – in what way?

9.   If such allegations, if true, would be relevant:

a.   To what extent are they disputed, and by whom?
b.   Is it necessary to have a finding-of-fact hearing and if yes, what are the grounds for so contending (taking into account the

Court of Appeal authority *Re L, V, M, H (Contact: Domestic Violence)* [2000] 2 FLR 334)? As to 'necessary':

    i.   Consider the nature of any allegation or admission of DV and the extent to which any DV which is admitted, or which may be proved, would be relevant in deciding whether to make an order about residence or contact and if so, in what terms?

    ii.   If the issue is in reality, the alleged anger of the father as a risk to mother and/or child(ren), would the risk be capable of adequate acknowledgment and management [if necessary with supervised contact] without a finding-of-fact hearing on the basis of the father undergoing anger-management therapy/DV programme and it being recorded in the order as a recital that he accepts a problem with anger and volunteers for such therapy? (*Re L*: In assessing the relevance of past domestic violence, it is likely to be highly material whether the perpetrator has shown an ability to recognise the wrong he (or less commonly, she) has done, and the steps taken to correct the deficiency in the perpetrator's character).

    iii.   Is there a psychological problem with either party which would be susceptible to a course of therapy? If yes, what therapy precisely, and would the undertaking of such therapy avoid the necessity of such a finding-of-fact hearing, with an express recording as a recital to the order?

  c.   Time-table for hearings:

    i.   **Part 1**: How quickly can a finding-of-fact hearing be prepared and listed?

    ii.   **Part 2**: A further hearing (ie welfare; which has to be before the same judge) must be listed after any finding-of-fact hearing.

10. **If there is to be a *finding-of-fact* hearing, what overriding directions are necessary?** Consider:

  a.   The need for speed: (The factual and welfare issues must be identified at the earliest opportunity);

  b.   Health visitor records;

  c.   Medical records;

  d.   School reports;

  e.   Police disclosure as to incidents of alleged DV and any previous convictions.

  f.   Any other third party (liver function, carbohydrate deficient transferring (CDT), hair strand testing? etc) g.　Other potentially relevant records (eg previous court orders/ judgments; assessments; ss 7 and/or 37 reports; inter-agency materials; Home Office documents; records of discussions with the family; key local authority (LA) and records for the child(ren) including strategy discussion record);

h.　Is it contended that the guardian attend the fact-finding hearing? If yes, who so contends, and on what grounds?

i.　Also consider carefully whether the circumstances are such as to justify the following (and if yes, on what grounds, taking into account specifically the *Practice Guidance: Interim Guidance to Assist Cafcass* of 30 July 2009, [2009] 2 FLR 1407 see also www.familylaw.co.uk/newswatch):

　　i.　Section 7 Cafcass report (if yes, what is the issue, and what is the extent of the enquiries necessarily to be made at this stage? Is it in fact appropriate to secure information on the wishes and feelings of the child before findings of fact have been made?);

　　ii.　Child(ren) to be separately represented? (Rule 9.5; need for compliance with the President's Direction of 5 April 2004, in addition to the President's Interim Guidance of 30 July 2009. Note that application of this Rule is only in very circumscribed cases given the requirement for exceptional circumstances, as explained in Interim Guidance).

11.　**In addition to '10' above, directions must provide for the following to be undertaken *as soon as possible*:**

a.　The facts which the court is to be invited to find as to the nature and degree of the DV must be set out clearly in schedule form in such a way as to identify the precise issues for determination and the evidence in relation to them.

b.　The schedule should have columns to accommodate the following:

　　i.　The allegation number (to be inserted sequentially in the first column);

　　ii.　Each allegation;

　　iii.　The date on which such violence is alleged to have taken place (or if a pattern of behaviour, the range of dates between which it is alleged such pattern of behaviour occurred);

　　iv.　The cross-reference of the particular allegation to the page numbers in the Trial Bundle (TB), of all relevant witnesses setting out in the Schedule also the name of such witnesses and the paragraph in the statement.

> v. The alleged effect of such DV on the child(ren) with all cross-referencing by reference to TB pagination and paragraph numbering.
> vi. The effect of such DV on the parent, with all cross-referencing by reference to TB pagination and paragraph numbering.
> vii. The effect of such DV on another relevant person, identifying the same, with all cross-referencing by reference to TB pagination and paragraph numbering.
> viii. Columns for a full reply by each respondent/relevant witness – each such response also to be cross-referenced by pagination in the TB and paragraph number (leaving the final column for the judge).

Note: It is essential that the schedule fulfil its function as a practice case-management tool to achieve the following: That it makes readily clear to the court the nature and degree of any domestic violence alleged and its effect on the child(ren) and/or child(ren)'s parents and/or any other relevant person.

12. Given an adjournment for a *finding-of-fact* hearing and the need to secure an interim position:

 a. Is an interim order for residence and /or contact in the interest of the child(ren)? If yes –

   i. Why in the interests of the child(ren)?
   ii. Residence, with whom?
   iii. Contact, with whom (including the option of interim contact)?
   iv. What steps are being taken in the interim to manage any potential risk?
   v. Is there a need for a s 7 report on the question of contact, or any other matter relating to the welfare of the child, taking into account the circumscription set out in the *President's Interim Guidance* of 30 July 2009?
   vi. Consider whether contact should be supervised or supported, and if so, where and by whom (taking into account the availability of any appropriate facilities).
   vii. Consider seeking information as to the wishes and feelings of the child(ren) before findings of fact have been made.
 b. Can the safety of the child(ren) and the residential parent be secured before and after contact? (refer to the welfare check-list)
 c. When addressing (a) and (b) above, particular consideration must be given to the likely effect on the child of any contact and any risk of harm, whether physical, emotional or

psychological, which the child is likely to suffer as a consequence of making or declining to make an order.

A3.19 APPENDIX 19: STANDARD VARIABLE DIRECTIONS DOVETAILING WITH THE CASE MANAGEMENT ORDER

Children

- **Join children as parties:** The children are made parties to the proceedings as (the)(**) respondent(s).

- **Appoint children's solicitor:**

  (a) (**) is appointed as the solicitor for the child(ren);
  (b) A solicitor is appointd for the child(ren).

- **Notification of the name of the solicitor appointed:** Adopt the text from C46.

- **Children's attendance at hearings:** The child(ren) is/are not required to attend any further hearings in these proceedings without further direction of the court.

Guardian

- **Appoint children's guardian:**

  (a) (**) is appointed as the children's guardian for the child(ren);
  (b) A children's guardian is appointed for the child(ren).

- **Cafcass to allocate children's guardian:** CAFCASS shall allocate a guardian to represent the child(ren) by 4pm on the (**) or in the event that a guardian is not immediately available shall by the same time on the same day notify the court of the likely date upon which an allocation will be made.

- **Notification of the name of the guardian:** Adopt the text from C46.

Party status

- **Persons to be joined:** The (identify person(s)) is/are joined as (the) (**) respondent(s) to these proceedings.

- **Joinder as party to meet allegations:** The (identify person(s)) is/are joined as the (**) respondent(s) to these proceedings, in order to meet the allegation(s) that the injuries to/sexual abuse of/other the child may have been caused by either one of them (and/or failed to protect the child).

- **Adjourn party status application pending outcome of assessment:** The (identify person) application for party status is adjourned pending the outcome of the local authority (relative carer) assessment/ viability assessment and shall be reconsidered at the (directions) hearing listed on the (date).

- **Refusal of application for party status:** The application of (identify applicant) to be joined as a party to the proceedings is refused.

- **Cease to be a party:** The (party) shall cease to be a party to these proceedings (forthwith) (upon – *specify event*).

Applications for residence/contact/parental responsibility orders

- **Adjourn applications for leave to apply for residence/contact orders:** The application(s) of (identify person) for leave/permission to make applications for residence (and contact) order(s) in respect of the child(ren) are adjourned generally with permission to restore on not less than seven days' notice.

- **Permission to apply for residence/contact orders:** The (identify party) is granted leave/permission to apply for a residence/contact order(s) in respect of the child(ren) in accordance with the application filed with the court.

- **Parental responsibility:** (Identify person) shall have parental responsibility for the child/ren (identify and dates of birth)/The application for parental responsibility is adjourned to final hearing.

Attendance at court

- **Children's attendance at hearings:** The child(ren) is/are not required to attend any further hearings in these proceedings without further direction of the court.

- **Excuse party/children's guardian attendance at hearing:** The (party/children's guardian) shall not be required to attend the hearing (time/date) (provided he/she/they are legally represented).

- **CG's attendance:** The children's guardian shall be required to attend the Finding of Fact Hearing

- **Party's attendance:** The respondent is to attend the next hearing and if the party fails to attend they should understand that the court may proceed to make orders which affect their rights in their absence.

Transfer

- **Note criteria for transfer** – which can be recordings in the recital to an order.

    (a) Complexity;
    (b) Consolidation;
    (c) Length/number of parties;
    (d) Question of law/public interest;
    (e) Urgency;
    (f) Other.

- **Transfer:** The applications(s) of the (description) shall be transferred to (court description) sitting at… for the following purposes:

    (a) For allocation directions to be given.
    (b) For case management directions to be given.
    (c) For specific hearing—

        (i)   For a (**) hearing.
        (ii) For hearing as to …
    (d) Whether (an) interim care (supervision) order(s) should be made.

- **Consent to transfer:** The receiving court, by its justices' clerk, consents to the transfer.

- **Transfer to District Registry of High Court:** The case is/proceedings are transferred to the (**) Registry of the High Court.

- **Transfer to High Court – Reserved Case Management to other judge:** This case is transferred to the (**) Registry of the High Court save that all future case management directions and hearings shall be heard by (identity of judge etc) unless otherwise directed by the allocated High Court judge.

Allocation

- **Allocation for case management:** This case is allocated for case management to the following identified case management judge (identity of judge etc);

- **Allocation to Family Division judge by Clerk to Rules:** The case is to be allocated to a judge of the High Court by the Clerk to the Rules.

- **Allocation to a Family Division judge:** This case is allocated to (Mr(s) Justice (name). All future hearings in this case will be conducted by the allocated judge and NOT by the urgent applications judge or any other judge unless on application to the allocated judge, if necessary in case of urgency by telephone, Fax or e-mail, the allocated judge releases the case to another judge.

- **Allocation to Family Division judge and Identity of Case Management judge:** This case is allocated to (Mr(s) Justice (name)) who will conduct the (Case Management Conference) (the) CMC, the IRH and {if necessary, the Final Hearing on the key issue(s)}. All case management directions (including the Case Management Conference) will be given by (identity of judge) unless otherwise directed by the allocated judge.

- **List Case Management Conference**

Meetings

- **Advocates' meetings:**

  (a) The parties legal advisers (and any un-represented party) shall attend an Advocates' Meeting at (venue) on (date/time (date no later than 1 day before the Case Management or Issues Resolution Hearing) to discuss those matters set out in the 2010 PLO Practice Direction. And shall prepare an updated draft Case Management Order which shall be filed by the local authority solicitor with the court not later than (date/time one day prior to relevant hearing).

  (b) In default of the Advocates' Meeting taking place and in any event, the legal representatives of all parties and any un-represented party shall attend at court on the day of the Case Management Conference not later than 1 hour before the time fixed for the hearing so that they can all meet together to discuss the issues and draft the Case Management Order.

  (c) The parties' legal representatives shall bring to the Advocates' Meeting and to all hearings—

      (i) Their professional diaries for the next 12 months; and

      (ii) Details (so far as can be known) of the names and availability of anybody who it is proposed should conduct any assessment or provide any expert evidence so that a witness availability form can be prepared and filed at the CMC;

      (iii) Details (so far as can be known) of the names and contact details (professional addresses and telephone/fax/DX/e-mail numbers for) for the purposes of the recitals of further orders.

Split trial

- **Model order:** There shall be a finding of fact hearing on ... the ... day of ... (e.l.h. x hours) to include court reading time of y hours) before HHJ ... who will then be responsible for the final hearing. The purpose of the hearing shall be for the finding of facts in relation to the matters relied upon by the local authority as constituting the threshold criteria under s 31(2). In particular (by way of example)—

  (a) The extent to which the parents have been taking illicit drugs/alcohol;

  (b) The extent to which there has been domestic violence including threats of violence between the mother and the father or between any other persons with care of the child; and the extent to which the child may have been involved in or witnessed such violence;

  (c) In relation to the issue of non-accidental injury alleged to have been sustained by the child ... (naming him/her) and in relation to each injury alleged—

    (i)   The nature of the injuries sustained by the child (naming her/her);

    (ii) When and in what circumstances the injuries were sustained;

    (iii) The likely cause of such injuries;

    (iv) Whether injuries were non-accidental in the sense that they had been inflicted intentionally or recklessly;

    (v)   The likely perpetrator or perpetrators of such injuries and in particular whether it is likely that such injuries had been inflicted by ... and/or ... and/or ...

    (vi) When and by whom any medical treatment was sought in respect of the injuries;

    (vii) Whether either parent has failed to protect the child; and

    (viii) Whether the 'threshold criteria' under s 31(2) of the Children Act 1989 are met;

    (ix) In the case of ... or ... or ..., if not the perpetrator, whether there has been a failure to protect, and if so, the nature of such failure.

  (d) By ... on the ... day of ... The LA shall lodge with the court trial bundles and documentation for the finding of fact hearing in accordance with the current PD and serve at the same time a trial bundle index on each respondent;

  (e) There shall be a CMC in relation to the finding of fact hearing before HHJ on ...

  (f) By ... on the ... day of ... 20... the LA to file and serve a Schedule setting out those facts that it intends to ask the court to find and which are relied on to establish the criteria;

(g) The respondents to file and serve their response to the LA Schedule by ...;

(h) Provided applications in proper form are filed and served by ... on ... (x days hence) John Doe and/or Richard Roe shall be joined as respondents to these proceedings in order to meet any allegations that the injuries to the child may have been caused by either one of them and thereupon the direction at para 6 will apply. If no such applications are made, the case will proceed and findings may be made against one or both in their absence;

(i) The LA is directed to serve John Doe and Richard Roe forthwith with notice of the contents of paras 6 and 7 of this order;

(j) The parties may jointly instruct and disclose an agreed bundle of documents including the child's medical records to ... for the purpose of obtaining an expert paediatric radiologist's report on the injuries sustained by the child, such report to be filed and served by ... (x months hence);

(k) The child's solicitor shall be the lead solicitor for the purposes of the instruction of ... and s/he shall provide a draft letter of instruction to all other parties by 4 pm on ... Any comments thereon are to be provided to the child's solicitor by 4 pm on ... and the letter of instruction shall be delivered to ... by no later than ...;

(l) The reasonable cost of the report shall be apportioned equally between the parties and shall be a proper charge on the certificates of those parties who have a public funding certificate;

(m) The parents shall each file and serve a report from ... dealing with their current drug/alcohol abuse, to include details of treatment and medication prescribed, by ... and thereafter shall on a monthly basis serve the results of drug hair testing to be arranged by their respective solicitors. The letters of instruction shall be agreed by the parties' legal representatives and the reasonable cost of the tests and reports shall be a proper charge on the relevant party's public funding certificate;

(n) (Experts' meeting, if necessary).

Evidence and care plans

• In relation to the issues identified in para [ ] above:

(a) The local authority to file and serve its statements of evidence by ... and concurrently file and serve its interim/final care plan. (An interim care plan should be filed very early in the proceedings and then updated).

(b) Each of the respondents in relation to such issues do file and serve their statements in reply by ... Such statements shall be limited to dealing with (the findings of fact contended for by the local authority/the factual basis for the conclusions of the reports with which he/she/they do not agree).

• **Direction to address ethnicity, language, religion and culture:** The (local authority/children's guardian) shall prepare, file and serve by (time/date) a (statement/report) dealing with the ethnicity, language, religion and culture of the child and other significant persons (in the form of a family profile). For the purpose of such report the (local authority/children's guardian) is expressly permitted to instruct further suitably qualified persons for the purpose of obtaining specific information on the religious/cultural beliefs and practices of relevant communities—

(a) The children's guardian shall file and serve by (time/date) an interim/final report;

(b) The oral evidence called by each party shall be limited to those witnesses whose statements have been filed with the court and served upon the other parties.

• **Disclosure of court documents and by other agencies:**

(a) *Criminal proceedings concluded against a party:* The solicitors for the (identify party) shall file and serve by (time/date) copies of the (identify documents eg indictments/witness statements/ any written basis of plea placed before the court/pre-sentence report(s) prepared by the National Probation Service/and other reports before the court/transcript of the judge's sentencing remarks) in relation to the proceedings in the Crown Court (including Calendar Number) in respect of which he/she was sentenced on the (insert date) (together with any record of previous convictions).

(b) *Criminal proceedings against a non-party:* The Chief Constable of (identify police force) is requested to disclose forthwith (or state time limit) to (identify local authority)—

(i) Copies of witness statements/records of interview/charge sheet/other relating to the prosecution of (identify relevant person) pursuant to the complaint made by the (identify relevant person/party) arising out of the incident (specify incident and date(s)); and

(ii) Copies of records of all/any-recorded complaints and officers case recording of incidents of domestic violence between (identify persons or parties concerned).

(c) *Ongoing criminal investigation:* The Chief Constable of (identify police force) is requested to disclose to the local authority by (time/date) all statements/entries in pocket notebooks/transcripts of interviews/photographs/and other material (specify) in the possession of the police relating to the investigation concerning the issue of domestic violence between the parties/ injuries sustained by (identity of child).

(d) *Liberty to apply:* Liberty to apply on not less than 48 hours notice is given to the Chief Constable in the event of any objection being raised to disclosure of the information required by paragraph (insert paragraph number).

(e) *Disclosure of court documents to the police:* Permission is given to the local authority to disclose forthwith copies of the statements/reports of the (identify parties/persons) to (identify police force).

(f) *Service of order on police:* The local authority/children's solicitor/other shall serve a copy of this order on the Chief Constable of (identify police force) forthwith.

(g) *Service of disclosed police documents – domestic violence:* The local authority shall file and serve by (time/date) copies of documents and records relating to complaints to the police of incidents of domestic violence (identify persons/parties) upon receipt of the same from the Chief Constable.

Experts and assessments

- **Local authority schedule of past and current assessments:** The local authority shall file and serve by (time/date) a ... schedule setting out details of its previous and current assessments of the child and family together with a timetable and timescales for completing those that are current.

- **Local authority schedule of proposed assessments:** The local authority shall file and serve by (time/date) a schedule setting out details of its proposed assessments identifying by whom and in respect of whom they are to be undertaken together with a timetable and timescales for completing the same.

- **Local authority obtaining medical records:** The local authority shall by (time/date) obtain the relevant medical records and shall disclose to the court the medical/GP/Hospital/Health Visitor/Mid-Wife/(or specify other) records of (identity of child or other relevant person) and such records shall be disclosed forthwith to the medical experts upon receipt (and copies served on the parties' solicitors).

- **Children's solicitor obtaining medical records:** The children's solicitor shall obtain, file and serve by (time/date) all medical (and hospital) records relating to the child(ren).

- **Instruction of medical expert by children's solicitor:** Permission is granted to the child(ren)'s solicitor to disclose the case papers/an agreed bundle of documents to (identity of expert and nature of expertise) including the medical records, for the purpose of obtaining an expert paediatric/radiological/neurological/ophthalmologic (or specify other field of expertise) report on the following issues (specify) which report shall be filed and served by (time/date). The letter of instruction shall be prepared by the children's solicitor and agreed by the parties' legal representatives and delivered to the expert by no later than (time/date) and filed with the court. The reasonable cost of the report shall be a proper charge on the child(ren)'s Public Funding Certificates (or other relevant cost provision).

- **Joint instruction of medical expert – paediatric etc:** Permission is granted for the (identify party) *child's* solicitor, as the nominated lead solicitor, to disclose the case papers/an agreed bundle of documents to (identity of expert and nature of expertise) including the medical records (or other), for the purpose of obtaining a joint expert paediatric/radiological/neurological/(or specify other) report on the following issues (specify) sustained by the child(ren) which report shall be filed and served by (time/date). The letter of instruction shall be prepared by the lead solicitor and agreed by the parties' legal representatives and delivered to the expert by not later than (time/date) and filed with the court. (** Insert relevant cost provision as appropriate).

- **Instruction of medical expert – specific considerations:** Permission is granted to the (identify party) solicitors to disclose the case papers and medical records/an agreed bundle of documents to (identity of expert and nature of expertise) for the purpose of obtaining a report to address whether circumstances (specify relevant considerations advanced) could have caused or contributed to the child's presentation on (specify date(s)). The expert's report shall be filed and served by (time/date). The letter of instruction shall be prepared by the (identify party) solicitor and agreed by the other parties' legal representatives and delivered to the expert by not later than (time/date) and filed with the court. The reasonable cost of the report shall be a proper charge on the (identify party)'s Public Funding Certificate (** or other relevant cost provision).

- Parties are reminded that the duty of disclosure is ongoing and that all relevant medical records or other assessment information such as for example medical assessments upon reception into care or psychological assessments for the purpose of special educational needs are to be disclosed within the proceedings while they remain current.

Assessments

These are part of the expected documentation for the pre-proceedings checklist; within proceedings other assessments may also be required:

- **Local authority Core/Framework Assessment Reports:** The local authority shall file and serve by (time/date) its report(s) in respect of its current or proposed Core/Framework Assessments (consider purpose and scope) of (identify parties/persons to be subject of assessment).

- **Adult Psychologist Assessment:** Permission is granted to the (identify party)'s solicitor to disclose the case papers/an agreed bundle of documents to (identify expert) Consultant Forensic Psychologist/ Chartered Psychologist/Consultant Clinical Psychologist/other for the purpose of undertaking a psychological assessment of the (identify parties to be subject of assessment) and to prepare a report as to the following specific issues (specify) which shall be filed and served by (time/date) by the solicitor. The letter of instruction shall be prepared by the (identify party)'s solicitor and agreed by the other parties' legal representatives and delivered to the expert by not later than (time/date) and filed with the court. (** Insert relevant cost provision as appropriate).

- **Parent or other party instruction of (treating) psychiatrist:** Permission is granted to the (identify party)'s solicitor to disclose the case papers/an agreed bundle of documents to (identify) Consultant Psychiatrist for the purpose of obtaining a report to be filed and served by (date/time) addressing the issue of (identify party)'s mental health difficulties including details of any diagnosis, prognosis, treatment and medication prescribed. The letter of instruction prepared by the (identify party) solicitor shall be filed and served on the other parties and delivered to (identify psychiatrist) by (time/date) and filed with the court. (** Insert relevant cost provision as appropriate).

- **Independent Social Work Assessment – risk, parenting capacity etc:** Permission is granted to the (identify party) solicitors to disclose the case papers/an agreed bundle of documents to (identity of expert) Independent Social Work Consultant for the purpose of undertaking a risk assessment/assessment of parenting capacity/assessment of their parenting capacity as long term carers (whether under a care order or residence order) for the child(ren) (specify name(s) (or other) (to include consideration of their historical involvement with Social Services, capacity to change and timescale). Permission is granted to (identity of expert) to (arrange in consultation with the local authority to) see the child(ren) (and to observe contact) as he/she may consider necessary (or specify number of times permitted. The report of (identity of expert) is to be filed and served by (time/date). The letter of instruction shall be prepared by the (identify party) solicitor and agreed by the other parties' legal representatives and delivered to the expert by not later than (time/date) and filed with the court. (** Insert relevant cost provision as appropriate).

- **Local authority instructing Independent Social Worker Assessment – shared costs:** Permission is granted to the local authority solicitor to disclose the case papers/an agreed bundle of documents to (identify expert) Independent Social Work Consultant for the purpose of undertaking Core/Framework/Risk/Other Assessments of the (identify parties/persons subject of assessment). To address the following specific issues (specify) and to prepare a report which shall be filed and served by (time/date). (identity of expert) has permission to (arrange in consultation with the local authority to) see the children/observe the children in contact with the (identify relevant persons) should this be necessary as part of his/her assessment. The letter of instruction shall be prepared by the (identify party) solicitor as the nominated lead solicitor and agreed by the other parties' legal representatives and delivered to the expert by not later than (time/date) and filed with the court. (** Insert relevant cost provision as appropriate).

- **Independent Social Work Assessment – joint instruction:** Permission is granted to the (identify party) solicitors as nominated lead solicitor to disclose the case papers/an agreed bundle of documents to (identify expert) Independent Social Work Consultant for the purpose of obtaining a joint expert risk assessment/assessments of parenting capacity/an assessment of parenting capacity as long term carers (whether under a care order or residence order) for the child(ren) (specify name(s)/(or other) (to include consideration of their historical involvement with Social Services or capacity to change). Permission is granted to (identify expert) to (arrange in consultation with the local authority to) see the child (and to observe contact) as he/she may consider necessary. The report of (identify expert) is to be filed and served by (time/date). The letter of instruction shall be prepared by the nominated lead solicitor and agreed by the other parties' legal representatives and delivered to the expert by not later than (time/date) and filed with the court (**Insert relevant cost provision as appropriate.

Expert evidence

- **Drug hair strand tests – specifying drugs to be tested:** The (identify party) solicitors shall arrange for Drugs Strand Hair Tests to be done by (identify testing agency/or other tester) at the following intervals in respect of the father/mother/other for heroin/cocaine/ecstasy/amphetamine/other use and shall file and serve by (time/date) the report/test results or any such earlier date on which such results may be available. The letter of instruction shall be prepared by the (identify party) solicitor and agreed by the other parties' legal representatives and delivered to the (testing agency/or other tester) by not later than (time/date) and filed with the court. The reasonable cost of the tests and report shall be a proper charge on the (identify party)'s Public Funding Certificate. (** or other relevant cost provision).

- **Party's report GP or psychiatrist on mental health** The (identity of party) solicitors shall file and serve by (time/date) a report from his/her General Practitioner/psychiatrist/other (identify) addressing the issue of his/her depression/mental health/drug (abuse) dependency/alcohol (abuse) dependency/other, to include details of any diagnosis, prognosis, treatment and medication prescribed. The letter of instruction shall be sent to the GP/other and served on the other parties' legal representatives by (time/date) and filed with the court. The reasonable cost of the report shall be a proper charge on the (identify party)'s Public Funding Certificate. (**or other relevant cost provision).

- **Blood tests to determine paternity:**

  (a) It is directed pursuant to section 20(1) of the Family Law Reform Act 1969;
  (b) That blood tests (including DNA tests) be used to ascertain whether such tests show that Mr. X is or is not excluded from being the father of the child ... born on the ...;
  (c) That for that purpose, blood samples be taken on or before the ... day of ... from the following persons, namely: Mr. X, Ms Y and the child ...;
  (d) That the person appearing to the court appearing to have care and control of the child ... who is under the age of 16 is Ms. Y;
  (e) That such tests be carried out by ... of ... who shall provide a report on or before ...

- **Meeting of experts:** The solicitor for the (identify party usually the solicitor for the child) shall (if necessary) arrange a meeting of the medical experts between (date) and (date)/(or during the week commencing the (date). All parties agree that the relevant issues/questions to be determined are—

  (a) The experts shall—

     (i) identify and narrow the issues in the case;
     (ii) reach agreement on the expert issues (where feasible);
     (iii) identify the reasons for disagreement on any expert question and to identify what if any action needs to be taken to resolve any outstanding disagreement/question;

    (b)   limit wherever possible the need for experts to attend court to give oral evidence.

An agenda (identifying the relevant issues/questions set out above) shall be prepared by the solicitor and circulated for agreement by the parties' legal advisers and the experts not less than five days in advance of the Meeting. The Meeting shall be chaired by (identify nominee) and minutes of the meeting shall be recorded and a joint Statement of Concurrence/Schedule of Agreement prepared by the (identify party)'s solicitor setting out areas of agreement and/or disagreement and filed and served by (time/date).

- **Permission to disclose case papers to expert:** Permission is granted to the (identify party) solicitor to disclose the case papers/an agreed bundle of documents to (identity of expert and nature of expertise) to obtain a report (identify purpose).

- **Permission to expert to see/examine children:** Permission is grated to (identity of expert) to obtain a report (identify purpose).

- **File and service expert report:** The report of (identity of expert) is to be filed and served by (time/date).

- **Time for preparation, approval and delivery of letter of instruction to expert:** The letter of instruction shall be prepared by the (identify party) solicitor and agreed by the other parties' legal representatives and delivered to the expert by not later than (time/date) and filed with the court.

Care planning, and placement

- **Family Meetings Review Meetings:** It is proposed that the progress of the care plan and/or service delivery for the child will be discussed (on date). The meeting will involve (local authority and other parties).

- **Disclosure of documents, to adoption/permanency panels:** Permission is granted to the local authority to disclose forthwith the report(s) of (specify names & professional status of report writers) to its adoption/permanency panel (or the panel of any adoption agency involved in placement of the child(ren)).

- **Agreement on support and assistance to be provided under interim care plan or supervision order):** The local authority shall file and serve by (time/date) a written agreement setting out the specific support and assistance to be provided to (identify child(ren)) and proposed carer(s) under the proposed current interim care plan or supervision order and details of agreed review procedures (and dates).

Contact arrangements

- **Requirement to make children available:** The child(ren) shall be made available for contact with (the party) by (the local authority, the respondent with whom the child is residing) (on) (details dates, times etc).

- **Permission to refuse contact:** The local authority with whom the child is residing shall have permission to refuse contact between the child(ren) (names) and (party).

- **Specified minimum contact-discretion to supervise:** The local authority shall permit the mother/father (name) to have contact with the (child(ren)'s names) on not less than the following number of occasions each year (frequency/ duration/ venue (** specify number)) and which, in its discretion, shall be supervised.

- **Section 34(4) – matching:**

  (a) *Conditional upon 'matching' for adoption:* The local authority is granted permission to terminate contact between the parents, (names) and the children, (names) pursuant to s 34(4) of the Children Act 1989, subject to the condition in respect of each child that the order will not be implemented until the Adoption Panel has formally approved linking with a prospective adoptive family or further order.

  (b) *Upon 'matching' for adoption – alternative form:* Permission is granted to the local authority to terminate direct contact between the mother/father and the child(ren) (names) upon the child(ren) being formally 'matched' to prospective adopters by the Adoption Panel.

- **Sibling contact** The local authority shall permit the children, (names) to have direct contact with each other on not less than (** specify number) occasions each year (which contact shall be arranged, facilitated and supervised by the local authority).

Ethnicity, language, religion and culture

- **Language interpreters:** The solicitors for the (identify party) are required to arrange for (**) interpreters who are able to communicate with and interpret the proceedings for the (identify party requiring service) using (identify language eg Punjabi, Urdu, French etc) to be available for the hearing on the (insert date) and any subsequent days as may be necessary (** insert any relevant cost provision).

- **Interpreters for the deaf:** The Courts Administration is requested to arrange for (** specify number) interpreters who are able to communicate with and translate the proceedings for the (identify party requiring service eg mother/father/other) using (identify language eg British Sign Language) to be available for the hearing on the (date) and any such other days as may be necessary (being 2 for each parent on each day).

- **Security/vulnerable witnesses:** Arrangements shall be made by the Court Administration to list the hearing in a secure court/a court with video link facilities/or describe other specific steps required (eg provision of screens) to safeguard the position of the vulnerable or intimidated witnesses (identify).

A3.20   APPENDIX 20:
THE CHILDREN ACT 1989 GUIDANCE AND REGULATIONS, VOL 1, COURT ORDERS, A FRAMEWORK FOR THE CARE AND UPBRINGING OF CHILDREN, CHAPTER 3

Care and supervision orders

Summary

3.1 This Chapter focuses on the processes that are to take place before and during public law proceedings under section 31 of the Act. The Chapter opens by describing the referral and assessment processes undertaken by local authorities with responsibilities for children's social care functions, in particular initial and core assessments. If, following or as a result of these local authorities are concerned that children may be suffering or are likely to suffer, significant harm, the guidance then sets out the processes that are to be followed in moving towards making an application to the court for a care or supervision Order. Guidance on the emergency steps that may be taken is set out in Chapter 4.

3.2 Where such concerns arise, they may be so serious that the local authority will reach the view that it is no longer possible, without a care or supervision order (or emergency action), for it any longer to safeguard and promote the welfare of a particular child by promoting their upbringing by their family. In arriving at such a view, the local authority will have considered, through the core assessment process, not only the child's needs but also the needs and capacities both of the child's parents and those to be found in the wider family and community.

3.3 Before making an application for a care or supervision order a local authority is expected to seek legal advice and to communicate with the parents (and child, if of sufficient age and understanding) the nature and extent of their concerns. Prior to submitting an application to the court, and where the short term safety and welfare of the child permits, the local authority should send a 'Letter Before Proceedings' to the parents, the contents of which should also be explained carefully and directly to the parents, taking into account in the way in which information is presented the parents' cognitive and linguistic abilities. The purpose of such a letter is to enable the parents to obtain legal assistance and advice, prior to a meeting with the local authority the intention of which is either to deflect proceedings or, at least, to narrow and focus the issues of concern. It is recognised, of course, that there will be some emergency and other situations where the welfare of the affected child will not permit even a brief period for such correspondence and direct discussions to take place. To assist local authorities and others, a standard template letter is provided as an annex to the guidance.

3.4 Where, regardless of whether the 'Letter Before Proceedings' (see Annex A) process has been followed, the local authority then issues an application, a pre-proceedings checklist sets out clearly the documentation that the local authority needs to provide to the court, comprising material already available to the local authority as well as that which has been recently created specifically for the purposes of the application. Both a flowchart and the relevant Practice Direction, containing a 'pre-proceedings checklist' are annexed to this guidance

3.5 The conditions under which a court may make a care or supervision order are set out as well as the processes that are followed in initial hearings and underpinning the making of any interim orders. The effect of care orders is then described as are the processes that are to be followed where care orders, once made, are discharged and where supervision orders are either discharged or varied. Extensive guidance is provided on arrangements for children in care (who are the subject of care orders) to have contact with their parents and other significant people such as siblings, in the context of the local authority's duty to promote contact. The effects of supervision orders are also described in detail. Guidance is also provided on wardship and the exercise of the inherent jurisdiction of the High Court.

Care and Supervision Proceedings

3.6 The scheme for care and supervision proceedings is founded on a number of principles. The first is that the local authority can only intervene in the care and upbringing of a child without the parents' agreement if the authority obtains a court order following proceedings in which the child, his parents and others who are connected with the child are able fully to participate. The proceedings should establish what action, if any, is in the child's interests, and the procedure must be fair to all concerned. The term 'care' is used in the Act in relation to a child who is the subject of a care order and does not include a child accommodated by a local authority under voluntary arrangements (section 105(1) of the Act).

3.7 Secondly, the local authority has a general duty, under section 17 of the Act, to promote the upbringing of children in need by their families so far as this is consistent with its duty to safeguard and promote the welfare of children, in particular through the provision of family support services to children in need and their families. This means that voluntary arrangements for the provision of services to the child and his family including the consideration of potential alternative carers should always be fully explored ahead of the making of any application under section 31, provided that this does not jeopardise the child's safety and welfare. The local authority should ensure, when assessing the wider family and environmental factors within the core assessment (undertaken in accordance with the *Framework for the Assessment of Children in Need and Their Families*), that it considers the capacity and willingness of the wider family to provide care for the child on a short or a longer-term basis. The local authority should also bear in mind that the court has a duty to make no order unless it considers that doing so would be better for the child than making no order at all (section 1(5) of the Act). It is possible that care proceedings may be avoided altogether or that a different application, such as for a special guardianship order or a residence order, made by a relative or carer, may be more appropriate, rather than a care order application by the local authority.

3.8 A family group conference (FGC) can be an important opportunity to engage wider friend and members of the wider family at an early stage of concerns about a child, either to support the parents or to provide care for the child, whether in the short or longer term. In either case, they can reduce or eliminate the need for the child to become looked after. In presenting a care plan to the court in any application for a care order, the local authority will be required to demonstrate that it has considered family members and friends as potential carers at each stage of its decision making.

3.9 Thirdly, there are common grounds for making care or supervision orders: the local authority must identify the actual or likely significant harm to the child and how this is occurring or may occur. Factors such as the child's parents having learning disabilities or misusing substances are not grounds in themselves for making a care or supervision order, unless they contribute to the harm suffered or likely to be suffered by the child and provide evidence of inadequate, or lack of proper, parenting.

3.10 Fourthly, ascertaining the wishes and feelings of the child in such proceedings is essential (and forms part of the welfare checklist to which the Court must have regard under section 1(3) of the Act). Children and Family Court Advisory and Support Service (Cafcass) Children's Guardians must be appointed in most kinds of public law proceedings unless the court is satisfied that this is not necessary in order to safeguard the child's interests. A Children's Guardian should normally be appointed as soon as practicable after the commencement of proceedings. A Children's Guardian appointed in respect of emergency proceedings (emergency protection order or child assessment order) should, wherever practicable, continue to represent the child in subsequent proceedings for a care or supervision order. The role of the Children's Guardian is to safeguard the interests of the child and, for that purpose, is subject to the duties set out in rules of court.

3.11 Fifthly, when a care order is in force the local authority and parents share parental responsibility for the child, subject to the authority's power to limit the exercise of such responsibility by the parents where it is necessary to do so in order to safeguard or promote the child's welfare (and to some specific limitations on the authority (section 33(6) and (7)). Where a child is in the care of the authority (including where an interim care order has been made), the authority must allow the child reasonable contact with his parents and specified others, subject to court orders and limited local authority powers of action to refuse to allow contact in emergencies (section 34 of the Act and paragraph 15 of Schedule 2 to the Act).

Assessment Processes

3.12 Where a child is referred to the local authority as a child who may be in need, the local authority should decide, within one working day of the referral whether to undertake an initial assessment. This decision would normally follow discussion with the person who has made the referral and consideration of other information which the authority may hold or obtain. Any assessment should be undertaken in accordance with the *Framework for the Assessment of Children in Need and Their Families* (the 'Assessment Framework') (Department of Health et al, 2000). The initial assessment should be completed within seven working days of the date of the referral. Information should be gathered and analysed using the dimensions and domains set out in the Assessment Framework, namely:

- the child's developmental needs;
- the parents' or caregivers' capacity to respond appropriately to those needs; and
- the wider family and environmental factors.

By undertaking an initial assessment, which may be very brief in urgent safeguarding situations, the local authority may then ascertain whether:

- the child is a child in need (a 'child in need' is defined in section 17(10) of the Act); and
- there is reasonable cause to suspect that the child is suffering, or is likely to suffer, significant harm (section 47 of the Act).

3.13 Where concerns about significant harm do not emerge or are not substantiated, but the child is assessed as being a 'child in need', the local authority may have sufficient information to determine what services, if any, should be provided, on the basis of the initial assessment and to agree a 'child in need' plan with the child and family. In determining what

The Framework for Assessment of Children in Need and their Families (extracted from Appendix A)

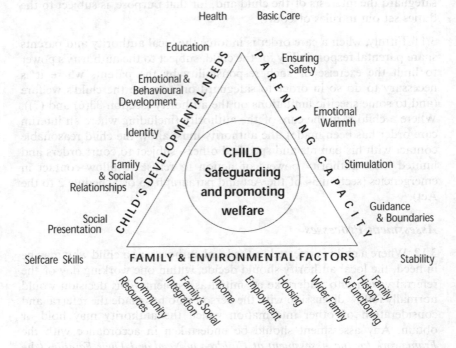

services to provide, the local authority is required to ascertain and take into account the wishes and feelings of the child.[29]

3.14 If the child is assessed as being in need and the local authority is concerned that the child is suffering, or is at risk of suffering, significant harm, the authority is under a duty to make, as soon as practicable and, in any event, within 48 hours of the authority receiving the information, such enquiries as it considers necessary to enable it to decide whether it should take action to safeguard or promote the welfare of the child (section 47(1) of the Act) and what action may be appropriate in the circumstances (also see C4.66 to 4.75). Emergency action may be required, to secure the immediate protection of the child (see Chapter 4 of this guidance and *Working Together to Safeguard Children* (2006) for further guidance on Emergency Protection Orders (section 44 of the Act) and the exercise of police protection powers (section 46 of the Act)). Where emergency action has been taken, such section 47 enquiries as may be necessary should follow quickly.

3.15 The core assessment is the means by which section 47 enquiries are carried out. In all cases where an initial assessment concludes that there is cause to suspect that a child is suffering or is likely to suffer significant harm, a **core assessment should be completed**, informed by the information obtained through the initial assessment. The need to complete a core

---

[29] See s 17(4A) of the Act.

assessment should not deter necessary safeguarding action from being taken. Compliance with the requirement to complete the core assessment will be scrutinised by the responsible court as part of the court's first consideration of any application under section 31 of the Act that it receives.

3.16 A core assessment is 'an in-depth assessment which addresses the central or most important aspects of the needs of a child and the capacity of his or her parents or caregivers to respond appropriately to these needs within the wider family and community context' (Assessment Framework 3.11). The core assessment should build on the initial assessment, utilise any prior specialist assessments that may have been carried out and should be completed within 35 working days of its commencement. It is recognised that newly-commissioned specialist assessments from other agencies or independent professionals will not necessarily be completed within this period, but clear timescales for their completion should have been agreed with those bodies from which they have been commissioned, which should be specified in the core assessment. Once these specialist assessments are available, these will need to be taken into account and, depending on their relevance, may influence the local authority's planning for the child.

3.17 The core assessment forms the central part of the evidence supporting any application that the local authority may make for a care or supervision order under section 31 of the Act. Local authorities must ensure that an up to date core assessment is available in relation to any child who is the subject of a section 31 application under the Act.

3.18 The plan for the care of the child should be based on findings from the initial and core assessments. It should set out the aims of the plan and the intended outcomes for the child, informed by the findings from the assessments i.e. the identified developmental needs of the child and the capacity of the parents to respond to the child's needs in the context of their wider family and environmental context. The structure of the plan should follow the Assessment Framework domains and dimensions in accordance with the Integrated Children's System (ICS) care plan exemplar and be explicit about the services which will be provided by which agency and at what frequency in relation to the dimension headings. The plan should also set out the outcomes which are being sought in relation to the needs and services identified. LAC (99) 29 provides further guidance on the preparation of care plans in applications under section 31 of the Act. Additionally, section 31A of the Act provides that where an application is made, from which a care order might be made with respect to a child, the local authority must within the timetable directed by the court prepare a care plan, and no care order may be made until the Court has considered that plan (section 31(3A)).

Applications for care and supervision orders (sections 31 and 32) – the order-making powers of the court

3.19 A child is in the care of a local authority where the court has made a care order (including an interim order) under section 31. Aside from voluntary accommodation under section 20 or where the court has made a supervision order (including an interim order) under section 31, the only other circumstances in which a child may be placed in local authority accommodation are set out in section 21. These include children who are in police protection, children who are on remand and children who are subject to a supervision order made in criminal proceedings that imposes a local authority residence requirement or a foster parent residence requirement (which are different to a supervision order made under section 31).

3.20 Care and supervision proceedings, and indeed all proceedings under Part 4 of the Act, are 'family proceedings' (see section 8(3) of the Act), and may be heard at any level of the family courts, with most of cases starting in the family proceedings court. The court hearing an application for a care or supervision order may on its own initiative make an order under section 8 or a special guardianship order as an alternative to a care or supervision order. A local authority may apply for a care or supervision order if it considers that the threshold criteria at section 31 of the Act are established and those proceedings may be joined with other proceedings under:[30]

  (a) the inherent jurisdiction of the High Court in relation to children;
  (b) Matrimonial Causes Act 1973;
  (c) Parts 1, 2 and 4 of the Act;
  (d) Schedule 5 to the Civil Partnership Act 2004;
  (e) the Adoption and Children Act 2002;
  (f) the Domestic Proceedings and Magistrates' Courts Act 1978;
  (g) Schedule 6 to the Civil Partnership Act 2004;
  (h) Part 3 of the Matrimonial and Family Proceedings Act 1984;
  (i) the Family Law Act 1996; or
  (j) sections 11 and 12 of the Crime and Disorder Act 1998.

3.21 Although a local authority may not apply for a residence order or special guardianship order, such orders may be made as a result of local authority section 31 applications, though such orders may not be made in favour of a local authority. Specific issue orders and prohibited steps orders cannot be used to achieve what may be achieved by the other section 8 orders, but a local authority may apply for such an order in respect of a child *not* in its care. If the child is the subject of a care order, contact arrangements will be dealt with under section 34 and not by a contact order under section 8.

---

[30] See s 31(4) and s 8(3)–(4).

Matters to be considered by local authorities before making an application for a care or supervision order

3.22 Only a local authority or authorised person (as defined in section 31(9)) may apply for a care or supervision order. At present, only the NSPCC is an authorised person. Its potential role in care proceedings is not addressed in this guidance because it has not exercised these powers for some years.

3.23 The local authority, in applying for an order under section 31, is likely to rely on a range of contributions from others, such as those already involved in the care of the child (including parents and relatives) as well as those providing specific information or findings from specialist assessments. Full inter-agency co-operation, including the sharing of information for the purpose of safeguarding children is essential whenever a potential care or supervision order case is identified, both because of the need to obtain as complete as possible a picture of actual or likely harm to the child but also to plan appropriate provision to meet the child's needs, if the order is made. Information from health professionals is likely to be of particular importance.

3.24 Within the local authority, the legal advisers have a key role to play in providing advice about the requirements of the courts and in relation to the making of the application. Parents, the child (if they are of sufficient age and understanding) and others with a legitimate interest in the child's future should, as far as possible, be involved, in the pre-application assessment processes and should, to the extent that it is possible to do so, be consulted on the local authority's plans for the child. Thus, even before the local authority reaches a decision that it should apply for a care or supervision order, parents will already have been made aware of the local authority's concerns about the child. Before reaching such a decision, the local authority should have taken such steps as are possible, perhaps through a family group conference or other family meeting, to explore whether care for the child can be safely provided by a relative or friend, have assessed the suitability of possible arrangements and have considered the most appropriate legal status of such arrangements.

3.25 Where the local authority decides, having sought and considered legal advice, that it intends to apply for a care or supervision order, the local authority must immediately notify that decision to the parents and others with parental responsibility for the child, using language and methods of communication, both in writing and orally, that will be understood by them. In particular the local authority should consider whether the parent (or other person with parental responsibilities) appears to have the capacity to instruct their legal representative, as the Official Solicitor may act as guardian ad litem/Next Friend/Litigation Friend for parties who lack litigation capacity (within the meaning of the Mental Capacity Act 2005) to represent themselves in proceedings, where there is no other person willing or suitable to do so. Further advice may be obtained from the official Solicitor (http://www.officialsolicitor. gov.uk).

3.26 The parents (and any others with parental responsibility for the child), on receipt of the local authority's written notification of its intention to apply for a care or supervision order, (known as the 'Letter Before Proceedings') are entitled to non-means tested publicly funded legal advice at 'Level 2', which covers liaison and negotiations with the local authority.

3.27 With the exception of those cases where urgent court action, including emergency protection proceedings, is needed to safeguard the child, the local authority should liaise with the parents (and those with parental responsibility) with a view to considering what steps, if any, can be taken to avoid proceedings, including by improving parental engagement with the local authority (where this is in the interests of the child), by further explaining the local authority's position and concerns and, where proceedings cannot be avoided, by narrowing the issues. Once the application for a care or supervision order has been made, parents will be entitled to 'Level 3' legal representation, which is also available on a non-means tested basis.

3.28 Where any affected child is of a sufficient age and level of understanding, the intention to initiate care or supervision proceedings must also be explained to him, unless to do so would exacerbate any significant harm that they might already be suffering, have suffered or be likely to suffer. However, it is recognised that, in a number of cases, there may be parental sensitivity about the local authority's involvement with the child, leading to parental consent for such involvement being withheld, which will mean that such information can only be provided after the commencement of proceedings, at which point the Cafcass Children's Guardian will also have a role to play. In this connection, it will be helpful for Cafcass planning purposes for the local authority to notify it of the prospect of the commencement of proceedings at the point at which parents are notified, though identifying details of the child should only be disclosed to Cafcass with the parents' consent.

3.29 The notification to the parents should, in its written version, take the form of a 'Letter Before Proceedings'. A standard template letter is included as an annex to this guidance (Annex A), but the letter, in cases where it is used, will need to be adjusted to fit the particular circumstances of the case. It should include:

- a summary of the local authority's concerns about the actual or likely harm to the child and the evidence on which these concerns are based;
- information about what the local authority has done to safeguard and promote the child's welfare, what needs to be addressed, what support will be provided and what the outcome will be if the problems are not addressed; and

- information about how to obtain legal help (on a non-means tested basis) and advice (including, in particular, details of local solicitors who provide a legal aid service in public law Children Act 1989 cases) together with encouragement to seek such advice as soon as possible.

3.30 It is recognised there will be some cases where, while inappropriate to be the subject of applications for Emergency Protection Orders, will nevertheless need to be the subject of an immediate section 31 application by the local authority. This is likely to occur where the scale, nature and urgency of the local authority's safeguarding concerns are such that the local authority considers that it is not in the interests of the child for a 'Letter Before Proceedings' to be sent. It may also be the case, in situations of this type, that not all of the other pre- proceedings steps will have been completed. In such circumstances, the local authority's application to the court will need to make explicit the reasons for any missing documentation or absent steps.

3.31 At or immediately after the meeting, the parents (and their legal representative) the local authority should provide in writing any revised plan for the child, setting out what the parents and the local authority are to do to safeguard the child and the steps that the local authority will take if this action is not effective in safeguarding the child. The outcome of the meeting should also be explained orally to the parents by the local authority.

3.32 The follow up letter and, as relevant, the plan for the child should make explicit what consideration has been given to the possibility, in the light of the needs of the child identified by the core assessment, of the child living with a relative or a friend. This plan will be based on findings from the up to date core assessment and any other current assessments or previous plans and the outcome of any previous family group conference or other family meeting, as well as reflecting the outcome of the meeting triggered by the 'Letter Before Proceedings'. It will identify how the child's short term needs will be met (and also set out any longer terms plans if information to support these is available).

3.33 If, despite the meeting following the 'Letter Before Proceedings', the local authority continues to be concerned (or again becomes concerned) that the child is suffering, or is likely to suffer, significant harm, it remains responsible for making an application to the court for a care or supervision order. See Annex C for a flow chart which sets out the pre-proceedings steps that are to be taken by local authorities.

The making of the application

3.34 Once the local authority has obtained information from the relevant range of agencies and disciplines, but before proceeding with an application, the local authority should always obtain and consider legal advice on:

(a) whether, in the circumstances of the case and in the light of the available evidence, the court is likely to be satisfied:
   (i) that the section 31(2) criteria are met; and
   (ii) that an order is in the best interests of the child and that the section 1(5) 'no order' test is likely to be met;[31]

(b) its care plan for the child, which will identify how the child's short term needs will be met (and also set out any longer terms plans if information to support these is available). In those relatively few cases where the identified permanence option, at the point of the commencement of proceedings, is for the adoption of the child, and where the decision that the child should be placed for adoption has been taken in accordance with the Adoption Agencies Regulations 2005 (SI 2005/389),[32] the local authority must apply for a placement order within the care proceedings (in accordance with the Adoption and Children Act 2002, its regulations and guidance[33]). Where the child is subject to a care order and each parent or guardian of the child has consented to the child being placed for adoption under section 19 of the 2002 Act[34] , it is not required that a placement order application be made;

(c) the court to which the application should be made; and

(d) whether to ask the court to make an interim care or supervision order and what directions should be sought (e.g. in relation to further assessments).

Annex B of this guidance is the *Practice Direction – Guide to Case Management in Public Law proceedings*. The table following paragraph 9.2 of this judicial guidance specifies, in the form of a 'pre-proceedings checklist', the documents that are to be disclosed to the court from the local authority's files, in support of the local authority's section 31 application. It also lists those additional documents that are to be prepared for the proceedings.

Conditions for a care or supervision order

3.35 The child must be under seventeen years old (or under 16 if married) at the time the order is made. The court is likely to look particularly carefully at a case for making an order if the young person is approaching his 17th birthday. A care or supervision order ceases to have effect at age eighteen unless brought to an end earlier (section 91 of the Act).

---

[31] The court has made clear that any intervention under Pt IV or V of the Act must be proportionate to the legitimate aims of protecting the welfare and interests of the child. Interference with family life may only be justified by the overriding necessity of the interests of the child. See in particular *Re O (Supervision Order)* [2001] 1 FLR 923; *Re B (Care: Interference with Family Life)* [2003] 2 FLR 813, and summary of Munby J in *XVB (Emergency Protection Orders)* (2004) EWHC 2015 (Fam).
[32] See *Re P-B* [2007] 1 FLR 1106.
[33] See Chapter 2 of and Annex A to the Adoption and Children Act 2002 Guidance.
[34] See s 22 of the Adoption and Children Act 2002.

3.36 The court may not make an order unless satisfied that the threshold conditions are met (section 31(2)):

(a) the child concerned is suffering significant harm, or is likely to suffer significant harm; and

(b) the harm or likelihood of harm is attributable to

(i) the care given to the child, or likely to be given to him if the order were not made, not being what it would be reasonable to expect a parent to give him; or

(ii) the child is beyond parental control.

If the threshold criteria are met the court must go on to apply the welfare checklist at section 1(3) and the 'no order' principle (section 1(5)). The court must consider the wide range of powers to make orders and to give directions. Having done so, the court must make whichever order is most consistent with the welfare interests of the child. In doing this, the court will have as its paramount consideration the welfare of the child. The court will want to be satisfied that a care or supervision order is a necessary and proportionate response to the legitimate aim of protecting the welfare and interests of the child.

3.37 The court must be satisfied that both elements of the threshold criteria have been met. The first focuses on actual or likely significant harm. The second is that the harm is attributable to the parenting of the child or to the child's being beyond parental control.

3.38 The first limb of the definition of 'harm' concerns ill-treatment or the impairment of health or development. This includes impairment suffered from seeing or hearing the ill-treatment of another person.[35] Ill-treatment is defined as including sexual abuse and forms of ill-treatment that are not physical (section 31(9)). Whether the harm suffered by the child is 'significant' is matter for the court to determine on the particular facts of the case.

3.39 In most cases impairment of health or development is likely to provide the evidence of 'harm'. Health is defined as physical or mental health; development as physical, intellectual, emotional, social or behavioural development (section 31(9)). Where the question of whether harm suffered by a child is significant turns on the child's health or development, this will be compared with that which could reasonably be expected of a similar child.

3.40 The second limb requires the court to be satisfied either that the harm, or likelihood of harm, is 'attributable to the care given or likely to be given, to the child not being what it would be reasonable for a parent to give to the child' or that the child is 'beyond parental control'. If the issue is the adequacy of parenting, there must be a direct connection between the harm suffered (or likely to be suffered) by the child and the care given by the parent. Harm caused solely by a third party is not therefore

---

[35] See amendment made to the definition of harm by s 120 of the Adoption and Children Act 2002.

relevant, unless the parent could have been expected to intervene to prevent it and, unreasonably, did not do so. The quality of care given to the child will be compared with what it would be reasonable to expect a parent, having regard to the child's needs, to give the child. 'Care' is not defined but in the context is interpreted as including responsibility for making proper provision for the child's health and welfare (including promoting his physical, intellectual, emotional, social and behavioural development) and not just meeting basic survival needs.

3.41 If the child is determined by the court as being beyond parental control, this means that, whatever the standard of care provided by the parents, the child is suffering or is likely to suffer significant harm because of lack of parental control. This requires the court to determine whether as a matter of fact, the child is beyond control: it is immaterial who, if anyone, is to blame. In such cases, the local authority will need to demonstrate how the child's situation will improve if the court makes an order – how his behaviour can be brought under control, and why an order is necessary to achieve this.

3.42 Case law makes it clear that 'when deciding whether to make a care order, the court should normally have before it a care plan which was sufficiently firm and particularised for all concerned to have a reasonably clear picture of the likely way ahead for the foreseeable future. The court must always maintain a proper balance between the need to satisfy itself about the appropriateness of the care plan and the avoidance of over zealous investigation into matters which were properly within the administrative discretion of the local authority.' (see *Re S and W* (2002) 1 FCR 577). Section 31A provides that on an application for a care order local authorities must prepare a care plan for the future care of the child. While the child remains looked after, both during the course of court proceedings and subsequently, the local authority keep that care plan under review in accordance with the Review of Children's Cases Regulations 1991 (SI 1991/895).

Initial hearings: court requirements and party status

3.43 The local authority's legal adviser will advise on and have conduct of the legal proceedings, on instructions from the relevant local authority member of staff (usually a social worker or social work manager). Proceedings under the Act are governed by a number of statutory instruments including the Family Proceedings Rules 1991 (SI 1991/1247), the Family Proceedings Courts (Children Act 1989) Rules 1991 (SI 1991/1395) as amended and, for placement orders, the Family Procedure (Adoption) Rules 2005 (SI 2005/2795). Further requirements relating to the conduct of proceedings are set out in Practice Directions and in the *Public Law Outline (PLO)* (issued by the President of the Family Division, which is effective from April 2008). This guidance is to be read alongside the *PLO*, which have been prepared alongside one another to ensure consistency.

Interim orders

3.44 Interim care and supervision orders are similar in effect to full care and supervision orders except in two particulars: the court determines the duration of the interim order; and it may give directions to the local authority as to the medical or psychiatric examination of the child or other assessment. Interim orders represent a substantial, if time-limited, intervention in the care and upbringing of the child, and should not be regarded as an automatic stage in the process of an application for a full care or supervision order. Interim care or supervision orders enable the local authority compulsorily to intervene in the family to protect the child, for example after an emergency protection order or at the expiry of a period of police protection where the circumstances necessitate intervention. In addition, courts will wish to be clear about the local authority's immediate plans for the placement of the child under the terms of any interim care order.

3.45 The court may make an interim care order or interim supervision order when it adjourns proceedings relating to an application for a care or supervision order or directs the local authority to investigate a child's circumstances under section 37(1) of the Act in private family law proceedings. Before making an interim order, the court must be satisfied (it will not rubber-stamp an application, even if unopposed) that there are *reasonable grounds for believing* that the child's circumstances fulfil the criteria for a care or supervision order (i.e. that the child is suffering or is likely to suffer significant harm due to inadequate parenting or the child being beyond parental control).

3.46 If the test for making an interim care order is satisfied the court must then address the welfare checklist (s 1(3)) and the no order (s 1(5)) principle. It must determine whether the welfare of the child justifies the making of an interim care or supervision order.[36] In order to make such a determination it will need to consider the local authority's care plan alongside any alternative course which may be proposed by the parents or by the Cafcass children's guardian.

3.47 The court can instead make a section 8 order as an interim measure (section 11(3)), pending final disposal of the proceedings. If it makes a residence order in these circumstances it must also make an interim supervision order unless satisfied that the child's welfare will be satisfactorily safeguarded without one (section 38(3)). A residence order gives the person in whose favour the order is made parental responsibility for the child while it is in force. The order may contain directions about how it is to be carried into effect, impose conditions and deal with other matters such as contact arrangements and educational provision. It is likely to be for a specified period, until the care or supervision application is decided (section 11(7)). This may be particularly relevant in circumstances where the local authority's care plan has identified placement with a relative as a preferred option for permanence.

---

[36] See judgment of Thorpe LJ in *Re M (A child) (Interim Care Order)* (2002) 1 FCR 350.

Duration of interim orders

3.48 The first interim order can last for up to 8 weeks. Subsequent orders can normally only last for up to 4 weeks. The court will consider the appropriate duration for the first and each subsequent interim order having regard to the likely prejudicial effect on the child's welfare of any delay in finally disposing of the proceedings (section 1(2)), the timetable for the case determined by the court, in accordance with the *Public Law Outline* and the limits on the maximum duration of the order set out in section 38(4).

Directions on examination and assessment when an interim order is made

3.49 The Act gives the court the power when making an interim care order or interim supervision order to give any directions it considers appropriate about medical or psychiatric examination or other necessary assessment of the child. However, if the child is of sufficient understanding he may refuse to submit to the examination or assessment (section 38(6)). The court's powers under this provision are limited to a process that can properly be characterised as 'assessment' rather than 'treatment'. Any proposed assessment must be necessary to enable the court to discharge properly its function of deciding whether or not to make a care or supervision order. The court may also direct that no examination or assessment shall take place or make any it subject to its specific approval (section 38(7)). Directions can be given when the order is made or at any other time while it is in force and can be varied on an application made by any party to the proceedings in which the directions were given. In *Re G (A child) (Interim Care Order: Residential Assessment)* [2005] UKHL 68) the House of Lords held that the court hearing care proceedings had no powers to order the local authority to provide specific services for anyone – that was a matter for the authority. The purpose of section 38(6) and (7) was to enable the court to obtain the information it needed.

3.50 The court has similar directions powers when making a child assessment order (section 43(6)(b)) and emergency protection order (section 44(6)(b)) (see Chapter 4). The court's powers are more limited when a final supervision order is made and it does not have power to give any directions when making a final care order as thereafter decisions on examinations and assessment fall within the scope of local authority's parental responsibility. However, the court will have considered the local authority's care plan, prior to making a care order, and will expect that its key elements will be implemented, unless the child's circumstances change markedly.

3.51 A medical, psychiatric or other type of specialist assessment, with or without an examination of the child, will often be an important part of the core assessment, prior to the application for a care or supervision order. Such assessments will have been important in identifying whether there is any evidence that the child is suffering, or is likely to suffer, significant harm. In other cases, as an alternative to section 31 proceedings, the local authority should consider whether satisfactory arrangements for specialist assessments of the child can be made, whether with the agreement of the parents or by making an application for a child assessment order under section 43 of the Act.

3.52 Court directions on examination or assessment do not override the right of the child who is of sufficient understanding to make an informed decision to refuse to submit to an examination or assessment (sections 38(6), 43(8) and 44(7)). Examination or assessment without the child's consent may be an assault. For consent to be valid the person giving consent must be competent, ie understand the nature of what he or she is consenting to (and the risks) and consent must be freely given. A child of 16 is presumed in law to be capable of giving, or withholding, consent unless there is good evidence of incapacity. Children under 16 are not automatically presumed to be legally competent but may be so in relation to a particular issue. There is no specific age at which a child becomes competent to consent to treatment: it depends both on the child and on the seriousness and complexity of the intervention being proposed. Detailed guidance on consent is provided in *'Seeking consent: working with children'* DH 2001 (www.dh.gov.uk/en/ Publicationsandstatistics/Publications/PublicationsPolicyandGuidance/ DH_4007005).

Including an exclusion requirement

3.53 If the court is satisfied that there are reasonable grounds for believing that the child is suffering or is likely to suffer significant harm, and the harm is attributable to the care given to the child not being what it would be reasonable to expect a parent to give him, it has power to include in an interim care order an exclusion requirement (section 38A(1), inserted by the Family Law Act 1996) that:

(a) requires a particular person to leave the child's home;
(b) prohibits a particular person from entering the child's home;
(c) excludes a particular person from a defined area in which the child's home is situated (section 38A(3)).

3.54 This power may be exercised only if the following conditions are satisfied:

(a) that there is reasonable cause to believe that if the relevant person is excluded from the child's home, the child will cease to suffer, or cease to be likely to suffer, significant harm; and
(b) that another person living in the child's home is able and willing to care for the child and consents to the exclusion requirement (section 38A(2)).

3.55 The requirement may last as long as the interim order or may be for a shorter period (sub-section (4)), and the period may be extended on an application to vary or discharge the interim care order. A power of arrest may be attached to the order (sub-section (5)). The exclusion requirement will cease to have effect if the local authority removes the child from his home to other accommodation for more than 24 hours (sub-section (10)).

3.56 In any case where it could impose an exclusion requirement, the court has power to accept an undertaking from the relevant person which is enforceable as if it were an order of the court although a power of arrest cannot be attached (section 38B). An undertaking given under this section ceases to have effect in the same circumstances as an exclusion requirement; that is, when the interim order lapses, when the interim order is varied to that effect or is discharged or when the child is removed to other accommodation for more than 24 hours. LAC(97)15 provides further guidance about this issue (www.dh.gov.uk/en/Publicationsandstatistics/Lettersandcirculars/LocalAuthorityCirculars/AllLocalAuthority/DH_4004746).

Effects of, and responsibilities arising from, interim orders

3.57 Interim care and supervision orders have the same effect and give the same responsibilities to local authorities as full orders, save for the fact that the court specifies the length of any interim order and may also give directions. An interim care order confers on the local authority parental responsibility for the child for as long as the interim care order is in force and, like a care order, its effect is that the local authority is under a duty to allow the child reasonable contact with his parents and others, such as siblings (see section 34). Interim supervision orders do not confer parental responsibility on the local authority and therefore the parents' contact with the child may only be defined by a section 8 contact order. During the currency of an interim care order, the local authority is responsible for ensuring or enabling the provision of services identified in the care plan, which may well inform the development of the local authority's proposals for the future care of the child, which may involve rehabilitation to the child's parents, placement with a relative or friend or permanence outside the child's family of origin. The emergence of such proposals should be notified both to the local authority's legal advisers and to the Cafcass children's guardian.

Effect of care orders

3.58 Section 33 of the Act sets out the effect of a care order and establishes the legal basis for the local authority's welfare responsibilities towards children in care. The effect of a care order on other orders is set out in section 91. At the conclusion of care proceedings the Cafcass Children's guardian will, in all relevant cases, ensure that the care plan, as agreed by the court, is made available to the Independent Reviewing Officer (also see paragraph 3.66).

3.59 The local authority designated by the care order is responsible for looking after the child (section 33(1)). It must provide accommodation for him and maintain him (section 23); safeguard and promote his welfare (section 22(3)(a)); and give effect to or act in accordance with the other welfare responsibilities set out in sections 22 to 26 and in Part 2 of Schedule 2 and in regulations made under the Act.

3.60 The local authority designated in the care order has parental responsibility for the child for as long as the order is in force. The local authority has power to determine the extent to which the child's parents and others with parental responsibility (who do not lose their parental responsibility on the making of the order) may meet their responsibility (section 33(3)(b)). The local authority may only use its powers to limit the parents' and others' exercise of parental responsibility if it is necessary to do so in order to safeguard and promote the child's welfare (section 33(4)); it should be discussed with the parent and child; and recorded in the care plan, ensuring also that any restriction is kept under regular review.

3.61 In exercising its parental responsibility the local authority must also ascertain the wishes and feelings of the child and his parents, and any other person with parental responsibility for the child or whom the authority considers relevant before taking key decisions about the child (section 22(4)). Further specific limitations on the local authority's parental responsibility are set out in section 33(6): the local authority must not cause the child to be brought up in any religious persuasion other than in which he would have been brought up had the order not be made; they do not have the right to agree (or refuse to agree) to the making of an adoption order with respect to the child, or to appoint a guardian for the child. The exercise of parental responsibility by the authority and others is further restricted by sub-section (7): no one can cause the child to be known by a new surname without a court order or the written consent of every other person who has parental responsibility and similarly no one can remove the child from the UK without an order or everyone's consent, except that (sub-section (8)) the local authority has power to take the child abroad for a period of up to one month. This limit does not affect any arrangements that may be made for the child to live outside England and Wales, which are governed by Schedule 2 paragraph 19.

3.62 The child's parents retain all rights, duties, powers, responsibilities or authority in relation to the child and his property which they have under other legislation and also continue to have financial responsibility for the child.

3.63 Subject to the specific restrictions mentioned above, the local authority has all the rights, duties, powers, responsibilities and authority to act as parent of a child for whom it is the authority designated in the care order. It may not transfer any part of the parental responsibility to another, but can arrange for some or all of it to be met by someone else acting on its behalf e.g. a local authority foster parent or a voluntary organisation (section 2(9)).

3.64 A care order automatically discharges the following orders made with respect to the child: a residence order and any other order made under section 8; a supervision order; and a school attendance order. It also brings wardship to an end (section 91). An education supervision order ceases to have effect on the making of a care order with respect to the child (paragraph 15(6)(b) of Schedule 3).

Discharge of care orders and discharge and variation of supervision orders

3.65 The child, local authority and any person having parental responsibility for the child may apply for discharge or variation of a care or supervision order under section 39 of the Act. Other persons with whom the child is living may apply for variation of a supervision order in so far as it affects them (section 39(3)). The welfare principle and the checklist in section 1 apply to the court's decision on an application under section 39 as they do to the court's determination of any other question concerning the upbringing of a child that falls to be determined under section 8 or Part 4 of the Act. The court may on an application for discharge of a care order substitute a supervision order without having to re-establish that the grounds (section 31(2)) for making a supervision order still exist. However, a care order can only be made where the child was subject to a supervision order if the local authority satisfies the court that the criteria in section 31(2) are met. The supervision order is automatically discharged on the making of a care order (section 91(3)).

3.66 A care order is automatically discharged by the making of a residence order (section 91(1)) or by the making of a special guardianship order (section 91(5A). A care order is suspended but not discharged by the making of a placement order (section 29(1) of the Adoption and Children Act 2002) and will revive if the placement order is later discharged. A person in whose favour a residence order is made will have parental responsibility for the child (if he does not already have it) and may apply for discharge or variation of a supervision order under section 39(2)(a).

3.67 Local authorities are required by the Review of Children's Cases Regulations 1991 to consider, at least at every statutory review (of a case of a child in care) whether to apply for discharge of the care order. The reviews must be chaired by an Independent Reviewing Officer (IRO). Part of the IRO's role is to ensure that the child's wishes and feelings are understood and taken into account in the authority's plans for the child's future care. At each review, as appropriate, the child should be informed of steps he can take for himself in relation to the order, or which an eligible adult might take on his behalf. These include applying for:

- discharge of the order;
- an order with respect to contact or for variation of an existing order (section 34);
- leave to apply for a residence order (section 10(8)); or

- leave to apply for a special guardianship order (section 14A).

3.68 A supervision order will last only one year (or less if the court so specifies) unless discharged earlier or the local authority applies for an extension. It can be extended for up to 3 years from the date of the original order. The local authority should consider whether or not to apply for the order to be varied or discharged where it has not been complied with (e.g. where a child of sufficient understanding refuses consent to a medical examination required by the order) or where circumstances have changed so that it may no longer be necessary.

3.69 Where an application for discharge of a care order or supervision order or to substitute a supervision order for a care order has been disposed of, no further application of this kind may be made within six months without leave of the court. This does not apply to interim orders or applications to vary a supervision order (section 91(15) and (16)).

Appeals against care and supervision orders

3.70 Rules of court provide that any one who had party status in the original proceedings may appeal against the making of a care or supervision order, including an interim order, or of an order varying or discharging such an order, or against the court's refusal to make such an order. In certain cases, the permission of the original court may be needed before an appeal may be pursued. The time limits for appeals are set out in Part 8 of the Family Proceedings Rules 1991 (SI 1991/1247), rule 29 of the Family Proceedings Courts (Children Act 1989) Rules 1991 (SI 1991/1395) as amended and, for placement orders, Part 19 of the Family Procedure (Adoption) Rules 2005 (SI 2005/2795).

Contact with children in care

3.71 The local authority, in pursuit of its duty to promote contact, must allow a child who is the subject of a care order to have reasonable contact with his parents and certain other people, unless directed otherwise by a court order, or unless the local authority temporarily decides to refuse contact in urgent circumstances (section 34). The court must consider contact arrangements before making a care order (see section 34(11) and has wide powers to make orders appropriate to the particular circumstances. The underlying principle is that the local authority, the child and other persons concerned should as far as possible agree reasonable arrangements for contact before the care order is made, but should be able to seek the court's assistance if agreement cannot be reached or the authority considers that contact between the child and a person who would otherwise be entitled to it would not be in the child's best interests.

3.72 Section 34 creates the presumption that local authorities should enable contact to take place between children in care and their parents (and other people who are significant to them, such as siblings). The pro-active role given to the court in managing the arrangements during the course of proceedings reflects the importance of contact for the child. Regular contact with parents, grandparents, other relatives and friends will usually be an important part of the child's upbringing in his new environment and will be essential for successful rehabilitation. Lack of contact can, over a period, have serious consequences for the rights of parents and children; it can be a major factor in deciding whether to discharge a care order or to dispense with parental agreement to adoption. Contact arrangements for children in care are handled entirely separately from applications for contact orders under section 8. A section 8 contact order cannot be made when a child is the subject of a care order (section 9(9)), and an existing section 8 order is automatically discharged by the making of a care order (section 91(2)).

3.73 In addition to allowing the child reasonable contact with his parents, the local authority must under section 34 also allow reasonable contact with any guardian or special guardian, any person in whose favour a residence order was in force with respect to the child immediately before the care order was made and any person who had care of the child under wardship immediately before the care order was made.

3.74 There are a number of ways in which the local authority's proposals for contact may be scrutinised or challenged:

(a) the court, before making a care order, must consider the arrangements made or proposed by the authority and ask parties to the proceedings to comment on them (section 34(11)).

(b) any person to whom the Act's presumption of reasonable contact applies, or any other person who has obtained the leave of the court, can apply for an order with respect to contact at any time if he is dissatisfied with the arrangements made or proposed for contact by the local authority;

(c) the child can apply for his contact with another person to be terminated or for any order with respect to contact to be varied or discharged (section 34(4) and (9));

(d) the court, if it is satisfied that it should do so under section 1(5), may make any order about contact that it considers appropriate either in response to an application or on its own initiative, and can impose any conditions it considers appropriate. The conditions can be as specific as the court considers necessary, for example, that contact is supervised or takes place at a particular time or place, or is reviewed at prescribed intervals.

3.75 The local authority has the same powers as the child to apply for an order with respect to contact, and can also refuse contact that would otherwise be required under section 34(1) or a court order made under section 34 for up to 7 days without reference to the court (section 34(6)). The local authority must be satisfied that it is necessary to refuse contact to safeguard and promote the child's welfare, and the refusal must need to be decided on as a matter of urgency. If the authority considers it necessary to refuse contact for a longer period it must apply for an order under section 34(4). The authority, child or other person named in the order may apply at any time for an order to be varied or discharged; and any party to the proceedings (including the local authority) can appeal against the making of, or refusal to make, an order.

3.76 A decision to refuse contact under section 34(6) is a serious step which should not be undertaken lightly. The Contact with Children Regulations 1991 (SI 1991/891) set out the steps that the local authority must take when refusing contact under section 34(6). If the conditions set out in section 34(6) and the 1991 Regulations are not met, the local authority can exercise its parental responsibility in relation to a child subject to a care order to permit or refuse contact between the child and any person with whom it is not required to allow contact by virtue of section 34(1). It should always consult the child and their parents before making such a decision and inform any person denied contact of their right to apply for an order in respect of contact under section 34(3), and of the local authority's procedure for handling representations and complaints made under section 26(3).

3.77 Repeat applications for orders under section 34 are controlled by section 91(17). If an application for an order has been refused, the person concerned may not re-apply for the same order in respect of the same child within six months without the permission of the court. The court has a further power to control applications under Section 91(14) but will consider carefully whether it should use this power, in accordance with the expectation that restrictions on contact and on access to the courts will only be imposed where they are necessary to protect the rights of others.

3.78 Certain other provisions in the Act bear on the question of contact more generally, in relation to all looked after children not just those who are the subject of care orders (paragraph 15 of Schedule 2). In addition to the local authority's general duty to promote contact between the child and his parents (and others – see 3.57 above), it must take reasonable steps to keep parents informed of the child's whereabouts, such as when another authority takes over the provision of accommodation, unless the child is the subject of a care order and there is reasonable cause for believing that giving that information would be prejudicial to the child's welfare. In no other circumstances may the local authority withhold information on the child's whereabouts. Where the authority provides accommodation for a child whether under a care order or otherwise it must ensure that the accommodation is as near his home as is reasonably practicable and consistent with his welfare (section 23(7), so that contact is facilitated.

3.79 The local authority has the power to make payments to assist contact (Schedule 2 paragraph 16) for example towards the costs incurred by parents and others visiting the child or by the child in visiting or maintaining contact by means of letters, telephone or electronic communication.

Supervision orders

3.80 Supervision orders and interim supervision orders have for the most part been dealt with in the preceding sections of this guidance – those on the court's order-making powers, applications, criteria for orders, court directions and variation and discharge of orders, for example – where the provisions are common to both supervision orders and care orders or raise common points. The following paragraphs deal more specifically with supervision orders.

3.81 A supervision order puts the child under the supervision of a designated local authority. The local authority has three specific duties:

(a) to advise, assist and befriend the child;

(b) to take all reasonable steps to see that the order is given effect; and

(c) to consider whether to apply for variation or discharge of the order where it is not being wholly complied with or the authority considers that the order may no longer be necessary (section 35(1).

Where a person is receiving medical treatment pursuant to a condition in the order, the local authority must also refer back to the court specific issues relating to that treatment in accordance with paragraph 5(7) of Schedule 3 should the need arise.

3.82 A supervision order may also require the child to comply with any directions given by the local authority which require him to do all or any of the following:

(a) live at a place specified in directions given by the supervisor;

(b) take part in education or training activities; and

(c) report to particular places at particular times.

The local authority cannot give directions in respect of any medical or psychiatric examination or treatment (Schedule 3 paragraph 2(3)). These are matters for the court to require by order but it should be noted that the court cannot make a direction requiring the child to submit to psychiatric or medical examination or treatment unless the child, if of sufficient understanding to do so, consents to its inclusion in the order (Schedule 3 paragraph 4). The local authority should always consider very carefully when contemplating an application under section 31 whether these powers, coupled with the power of the court and supervisor to impose requirements on a responsible person (Schedule 3 paragraph 3), with the consent of that person, are sufficient to promote and safeguard the welfare of the child. A responsible person is any person with parental responsibility for the child and any other person with whom the child is living (Schedule 3 paragraph1).

3.83 There is no prescribed remedy for breach of a requirement set out in the order itself or of a local authority's direction. In case of breach, the local authority would have to consider whether to apply to the court to vary or discharge the order (section 35(3)). If the supervisor is prevented from visiting the child or having reasonable contact with him under paragraphs 8(1)(b) and (2)(b) of Schedule 3, he may apply to the court for a warrant under section 102. The warrant is intended to enable the person concerned to exercise his powers. If the supervisor considered that urgent action should be taken to protect the child, he should consider whether to apply for an emergency protection order (section 44) or ask a constable to take the child into police protection under section 46.

3.84 Unless otherwise discharged, a supervision order will last for one year (Schedule 3 paragraph 6(1)). Before its expiry, the supervisor can apply for an extension, or further extensions, for any period not exceeding 3 years in total from the date of the first order. A supervision order is otherwise discharged by order of the court; the making of a care order with respect to the child; the making of a placement order under the Adoption and Children Act 2002; the child reaching the age of 18; or if a court takes certain action under the Child Abduction and Custody Act 1985 for example by making an order for the return of the child. An interim supervision order may accompany a residence order in the circumstances described in section 38(3). A local authority, when exercising responsibility for a supervision order, will need to consider whether also to operate a child protection plan or a child in need plan.

Wardship and the inherent jurisdiction of the High Court

3.85 The impact of the Act on the inherent jurisdiction of the High Court was considerable. Section 100 prohibits the use of the court's inherent jurisdiction in general, and wardship in particular, as an alternative to public law orders. If a care order is made in respect of a child who is a ward of court then the wardship comes to an end (section 91(4)). While a child is in care he cannot be made a ward of court (section 100(2) and section 41 of the Supreme Court Act 1981 as amended by paragraph 45 of Schedule 13).

3.86 The inherent jurisdiction remains available as a remedy of last resort where a local authority seeks the resolution of a specific issue concerning the future of a child in its care. But there are restrictions: the local authority must have the High Court's leave to apply for the exercise of its inherent jurisdiction (section 100(3)). Leave may only be granted where the court is satisfied that the local authority could not achieve the desired result through the making of any order other than one under the inherent jurisdiction (section 100(4)). Where there are other statutory remedies, the local authority will be expected to use them instead. Even if there is no other statutory remedy within the Act, the court must be satisfied that there is reasonable cause to believe that the child is likely to suffer significant harm if the inherent jurisdiction is not exercised.

3.87 Since the local authority has parental responsibility for children in its care, it should make decisions that affect the child's welfare in consultation with the parents as appropriate and after taking the child's

wishes and feelings into account. Occasions where recourse to the High
Court is appropriate should be very rare and will relate to matters that are
unusual or highly contentious, or that have the potential to affect
permanently the child's exercise of his human rights. An example might
be the sterilisation of a child in care. Other less extreme situations may
also merit High Court intervention, for example, to restrain harmful
publicity about a child or to provide injunctive protection against third
parties. In such cases when the inherent jurisdiction is the only means of
obtaining the remedy, it should not be too difficult to satisfy the leave
criteria.

3.88 The Act further prevents the High Court from exercising its inherent
jurisdiction 'for the purposes of conferring on any local authority power
to determine any question which has arisen, or which may arise in
connection with any aspect of parental responsibility'. Thus, in making
an order under its inherent jurisdiction, the court cannot confer on the
local authority any degree of parental responsibility it does not already
have (section 100(2)).

A3.21 APPENDIX 21: PRESIDENT'S DIRECTION OF 24 JULY 2000: HUMAN RIGHTS ACT 1998

1 It is directed that the following practice shall apply as from 2 October
2000 in all family proceedings:

Citation of authorities

2 When an authority referred to in s 2 of the Human Rights Act 1998
('the Act') is to be cited at a hearing:

- (a) the authority to be cited shall be an authoritative and complete
  report;
- (b) the court must be provided with a list of authorities it is intended
  to cite and copies of the reports:
  - (i) in cases to which *Practice Direction (Family Proceedings:
    Court Bundles)* (10 March 2000) [2000] 1 FLR 536 applies,
    as part of the bundle;
  - (ii) otherwise, not less than 2 clear days before the hearing; and
- (c) copies of the complete original texts issued by the European
  Court and Commission, either paper based or from the Court's
  judgment database (HUDOC) which is available on the internet,
  may be used.

Note—The *Practice Direction Family Proceedings: Court Bundles* of 10 March 2000, [2000]
1 FLR 536, has been replaced by the *Practice Direction Family Proceedings: Court Bundles
(Universal Practice to be Applied in all Courts other than the Family Proceedings Court)* of
27 July 2006, [2006] 2 FLR 199, and any reference in any other practice direction to *Practice
Direction Family Proceedings: Court Bundles* shall be read as if substituted by a reference to

the *Practice Direction Family Proceedings: Court Bundles (Universal Practice to be Applied in all Courts other than the Family Proceedings Court)* (see *Practice Direction Family Proceedings: Court Bundles (Universal Practice to be Applied in all Courts other than the Family Proceedings Court)* paras 13, 14).

Allocation to judges

3(1) The hearing and determination of the following will be confined to a High Court judge:

(*a*) a claim for a declaration of incompatibility under s 4 of the Act; or

(*b*) an issue which may lead to the court considering making such a declaration.

(2) The hearing and determination of a claim made under the Act in respect of a judicial act shall be confined in the High Court to a High Court judge and in county courts to a circuit judge.

Issued with the concurrence and approval of the Lord Chancellor.

Dame Elizabeth Butler-Sloss
President

A3.22   APPENDIX 22:
PRACTICE DIRECTION 27A
FAMILY PROCEEDINGS: COURT BUNDLES
(UNIVERSAL PRACTICE TO BE APPLIED IN ALL
COURTS OTHER THAN THE FAMILY
PROCEEDINGS COURT)

This Practice Direction supplements FPR Part 27

1.1 The President of the Family Division has issued this practice direction to achieve consistency across the country in all family courts (other than the Family Proceedings Court) in the preparation of court bundles and in respect of other related matters.

Application of the practice direction

2.1 Except as specified in para 2.4, and subject to specific directions given in any particular case, the following practice applies to:

(*a*) all hearings of whatever nature (including but not limited to hearings in family proceedings, Civil Procedure Rules 1998 Part 7 and Part 8 claims and appeals) before a judge of the Family Division of the High Court wherever the court may be sitting;

(*b*) all hearings in family proceedings in the Royal Courts of Justice (RCJ);

(*c*) all hearings in the Principal Registry of the Family Division (PRFD) at First Avenue House; and (*d*)   all hearings in family proceedings in all other courts except for Family Proceedings Courts.

2.2 'Hearings' includes all appearances before a judge or district judge, whether with or without notice to other parties and whether for directions or for substantive relief.

2.3 This practice direction applies whether a bundle is being lodged for the first time or is being re-lodged for a further hearing (see para 9.2).

2.4 This practice direction does not apply to:

(*a*)   cases listed for one hour or less at a court referred to in para 2.1(*c*) or 2.1(*d*); or

(*b*)   the hearing of any urgent application if and to the extent that it is impossible to comply with it.

2.5 The designated family judge responsible for any court referred to in para 2.1(*c*) or 2.1(*d*) may, after such consultation as is appropriate (but in the case of hearings in the PRFD at First Avenue House only with the agreement of the Senior District Judge), direct that in that court this practice direction shall apply to all family proceedings irrespective of the length of hearing.

Responsibility for the preparation of the bundle

3.1 A bundle for the use of the court at the hearing shall be provided by the party in the position of applicant at the hearing (or, if there are cross-applications, by the party whose application was first in time) or, if that person is a litigant in person, by the first listed respondent who is not a litigant in person.

3.2 The party preparing the bundle shall paginate it. If possible the contents of the bundle shall be agreed by all parties.

Contents of the bundle

4.1 The bundle shall contain copies of all documents relevant to the hearing, in chronological order from the front of the bundle, paginated and indexed, and divided into separate sections (each section being separately paginated) as follows:

(*a*)   preliminary documents (see para 4.2) and any other case management documents required by any other practice direction;

(*b*)   applications and orders;

(*c*)   statements and affidavits (which must be dated in the top right corner of the front page);

(*d*)   care plans (where appropriate);

(*e*)   experts' reports and other reports (including those of a guardian, children's guardian or litigation friend); and

(*f*)   other documents, divided into further sections as may be appropriate.

Copies of notes of contact visits should normally not be included in the bundle unless directed by a judge.

4.2 At the commencement of the bundle there shall be inserted the following documents (the preliminary documents):

    (i)   an up to date summary of the background to the hearing confined to those matters which are relevant to the hearing and the management of the case and limited, if practicable, to one A4 page;

    (ii)   a statement of the issue or issues to be determined (1) at that hearing and (2) at the final hearing;

    (iii) a position statement by each party including a summary of the order or directions sought by that party (1) at that hearing and (2) at the final hearing;

    (iv) an up to date chronology, if it is a final hearing or if the summary under (i) is insufficient;

    (v)   skeleton arguments, if appropriate, with copies of all authorities relied on; and

    (vi) a list of essential reading for that hearing.

4.3 Each of the preliminary documents shall state on the front page immediately below the heading the date when it was prepared and the date of the hearing for which it was prepared.

4.4 The summary of the background, statement of issues, chronology, position statement and any skeleton arguments shall be cross-referenced to the relevant pages of the bundle.

4.5 The summary of the background, statement of issues, chronology and reading list shall in the case of a final hearing, and shall so far as practicable in the case of any other hearing, each consist of a single document in a form agreed by all parties. Where the parties disagree as to the content the fact of their disagreement and their differing contentions shall be set out at the appropriate places in the document.

4.6 Where the nature of the hearing is such that a complete bundle of all documents is unnecessary, the bundle (which need not be repaginated) may comprise only those documents necessary for the hearing, but

    (i)   the summary (para 4.2(i)) must commence with a statement that the bundle is limited or incomplete; and

    (ii)   the bundle shall if reasonably practicable be in a form agreed by all parties.

4.7 Where the bundle is re-lodged in accordance with para 9.2, before it is re-lodged:

    (*a*)   the bundle shall be updated as appropriate; and

    (*b*)   all superseded documents (and in particular all outdated summaries, statements of issues, chronologies, skeleton arguments and similar documents) shall be removed from the bundle.

Format of the bundle

5.1 The bundle shall be contained in one or more A4 size ring binders or lever arch files (each lever arch file being limited to 350 pages).

5.2 All ring binders and lever arch files shall have clearly marked on the front and the spine:

- (*a*) the title and number of the case;
- (*b*) the court where the case has been listed;
- (*c*) the hearing date and time;
- (*d*) if known, the name of the judge hearing the case; and
- (*e*) where there is more than one ring binder or lever arch file, a distinguishing letter (A, B, C etc).

Timetable for preparing and lodging the bundle

6.1 The party preparing the bundle shall, whether or not the bundle has been agreed, provide a paginated index to all other parties not less than 4 working days before the hearing (in relation to a case management conference to which the provisions of the *Protocol for Judicial Case Management in Public Law Children Act Cases* [2003] 2 FLR 719 apply, not less than 5 working days before the case management conference).

6.2 Where counsel is to be instructed at any hearing, a paginated bundle shall (if not already in counsel's possession) be delivered to counsel by the person instructing that counsel not less than 3 working days before the hearing.

6.3 The bundle (with the exception of the preliminary documents if and insofar as they are not then available) shall be lodged with the court not less than 2 working days before the hearing, or at such other time as may be specified by the judge.

6.4 The preliminary documents shall be lodged with the court no later than 11 am on the day before the hearing and, where the hearing is before a judge of the High Court and the name of the judge is known, shall at the same time be sent by email to the judge's clerk.

Lodging the bundle

7.1 The bundle shall be lodged at the appropriate office. If the bundle is lodged in the wrong place the judge may:

- (*a*) treat the bundle as having not been lodged; and
- (*b*) take the steps referred to in para 12.

7.2 Unless the judge has given some other direction as to where the bundle in any particular case is to be lodged (for example a direction that the bundle is to be lodged with the judge's clerk) the bundle shall be lodged:

(*a*) for hearings in the RCJ, in the office of the Clerk of the Rules, 1st Mezzanine (Rm 1M), Queen's Building, Royal Courts of Justice, Strand, London WC2A 2LL (DX 44450 Strand);

(*b*) for hearings in the PRFD at First Avenue House, at the List Office counter, 3rd floor, First Avenue House, 42/49 High Holborn, London, WC1V 6NP (DX 396 Chancery Lane); and

(*c*) for hearings at any other court, at such place as may be designated by the designated family judge or other judge at that court and in default of any such designation at the court office of the court where the hearing is to take place.

7.3 Any bundle sent to the court by post, DX or courier shall be clearly addressed to the appropriate office and shall show the date and place of the hearing on the outside of any packaging as well as on the bundle itself.

Lodging the bundle – additional requirements for cases being heard at First Avenue House or at the RCJ

8.1 In the case of hearings at the RCJ or First Avenue House, parties shall:

(*a*) if the bundle or preliminary documents are delivered personally, ensure that they obtain a receipt from the clerk accepting it or them; and

(*b*) if the bundle or preliminary documents are sent by post or DX, ensure that they obtain proof of posting or despatch.

The receipt (or proof of posting or despatch, as the case may be) shall be brought to court on the day of the hearing and must be produced to the court if requested. If the receipt (or proof of posting or despatch) cannot be produced to the court the judge may: (i) treat the bundle as having not been lodged; and (ii) take the steps referred to in para 12.

8.2 For hearings at the RCJ:

(*a*) bundles or preliminary documents delivered after 11 am on the day before the hearing will not be accepted by the Clerk of the Rules and shall be delivered:

(i) in a case where the hearing is before a judge of the High Court, directly to the clerk of the judge hearing the case;

(ii) in a case where the hearing is before a Circuit Judge, Deputy High Court Judge or Recorder, directly to the messenger at the Judge's entrance to the Queen's Building (with telephone notification to the personal assistant to the Designated Family Judge, 020 7947 7155, that this has been done).

(*b*) upon learning before which judge a hearing is to take place, the clerk to counsel, or other advocate, representing the party in the position of applicant shall no later than 3 pm the day before the hearing:

(i)   in a case where the hearing is before a judge of the High
      Court, telephone the clerk of the judge hearing the case;

(ii) in a case where the hearing is before a circuit judge, deputy
      high court judge or recorder, telephone the personal
      assistant to the designated family judge;

to ascertain whether the judge has received the bundle (including the
preliminary documents) and, if not, shall organise prompt delivery by the
applicant's solicitor.

Removing and re-lodging the bundle

9.1 Following completion of the hearing the party responsible for the
bundle shall retrieve it from the court immediately or, if that is not
practicable, shall collect it from the court within 5 working days. Bundles
which are not collected in due time may be destroyed.

9.2 The bundle shall be re-lodged for the next and any further hearings in
accordance with the provisions of this practice direction and in a form
which complies with para 4.7.

Time estimates

10.1 In every case a time estimate (which shall be inserted at the front of
the bundle) shall be prepared which shall so far as practicable be agreed
by all parties and shall:

(*a*) specify separately: (i) the time estimated to be required for
       judicial pre-reading; and (ii) the time required for hearing all
       evidence and submissions; and (iii) the time estimated to be
       required for preparing and delivering judgment; and

(*b*) be prepared on the basis that before they give evidence all
       witnesses will have read all relevant filed statements and reports.

10.2 Once a case has been listed, any change in time estimates shall be
notified immediately by telephone (and then immediately confirmed in
writing):

(*a*) in the case of hearings in the RCJ, to the Clerk of the Rules;

(*b*) in the case of hearings in the PRFD at First Avenue House, to
       the List Officer at First Avenue House; and

(*c*) in the case of hearings elsewhere, to the relevant listing officer.

Taking cases out of the list

11.1 As soon as it becomes known that a hearing will no longer be
effective, whether as a result of the parties reaching agreement or for any
other reason, the parties and their representatives shall immediately notify
the court by telephone and by letter. The letter, which shall wherever
possible be a joint letter sent on behalf of all parties with their signatures
applied or appended, shall include:

(*a*) a short background summary of the case;
(*b*) the written consent of each party who consents and, where a party does not consent, details of the steps which have been taken to obtain that party's consent and, where known, an explanation of why that consent has not been given;
(*c*) a draft of the order being sought; and
(*d*) enough information to enable the court to decide (i) whether to take the case out of the list and (ii) whether to make the proposed order.

Penalties for failure to comply with the practice direction

12.1 Failure to comply with any part of this practice direction may result in the judge removing the case from the list or putting the case further back in the list and may also result in a "wasted costs" order in accordance with CPR, Part 48.7 or some other adverse costs order.

Commencement of the practice direction and application of other practice directions

13.1 This practice direction replaces *Practice Direction (Family Proceedings: Court Bundles) (10 March 2000)* [2000] 1 FLR 536 and shall have effect from 2 October 2006.

14.1 Any reference in any other practice direction to *Practice Direction (Family Proceedings: Court Bundles) (10 March 2000)* [2000] 1 FLR 536 shall be read as if substituted by a reference to this practice direction.

15.1 This practice direction should where appropriate be read in conjunction with *Practice Direction (Family Proceedings: Human Rights)* [2000] 2 FLR 429 and with *Practice Direction (Care Cases: Judicial Continuity and Judicial Case Management)* appended to the *Protocol for Judicial Case Management in Public Law Children Act Cases*. In particular, nothing in this practice direction is to be read as removing or altering any obligation to comply with the requirements of the *Public Law Protocol*.

This Practice Direction is issued:

(i) in relation to family proceedings, by the President of the Family Division, as the nominee of the Lord Chief Justice, with the agreement of the Lord Chancellor; and
(ii) to the extent that it applies to proceedings to which s 5 of the Civil Procedure Act 1997 applies, by the Master of the Rolls as the nominee of the Lord Chief Justice, with the agreement of the Lord Chancellor.

A3.23   APPENDIX 23:
MODEL JUDGMENT TEMPLATE

A Template for a Model Judgment: How Advocates can Assist the Judge

Is there a set form to a judgment? No, as stated by Thorpe LJ in *Re B (Appeal: Lack of Reasons)* [2003] EWCA Civ 881, [2003] 2 FLR 1035:

> 'Certainly it is not incumbent upon the judge to adopt some formula for judgment or simply to parrot statutory provisions. For my part, I would say that the essential test is: does the judgment sufficiently explain what the judge has found and what he has concluded as well as the process of reasoning by which he has arrived at his findings, and then his conclusion.'

There must, however, be sufficient reasoning, as stated in *Re F (Contact: Lack of Reasons)* [2006] EWCA Civ 792, [2007] 1 FLR 65. The judge was under an obligation to determine three issues of fact and to provide a reasoned explanation as to why he had concluded as he had. The headnote, amongst other matters, reads as follows:

> 'The judgment in this case is so lacking in reasoning and substance that it presented at least the appearance of not having engaged fully with the important issues in the case. The judgment was wholly deficient in explanations as to how or why the judge arrived at the conclusion that he had. The judge had not explained why he disbelieved two of the children, nor had he dealt with the question of whether there were inconsistencies in their evidence. The judge had referred to the father's credibility as 'dented' without explaining what he meant or what were the implications of that conclusion. Having made adverse findings about the father in relation to inappropriate communications with two of the children, the judge had failed to consider the implications of those findings. In particular he had failed to acknowledge that if a person had behaved with sexual intent towards some children, less weighty evidence was required to overcome the inherent improbability of his having interfered with another child. The judge had not made clear whether he accepted, in relation to the third allegation, whether that child had made the allegation, whether the allegation was consistent with any other evidence, and why he considered that the evidence was incapable of sustaining the allegation.' (para [19])

For guidance as to how to introduce a judgment, see Wilson LJ in *D McG v Neath Port Talbot County Borough Council* [2010] EWCA Civ 821, [2010] 2 FLR 1827, at para [19]:

> 'On 26 March, apparently almost immediately following his receipt of final submissions, the judge delivered his oral judgment. He would be the first to accept that, under constraints of time, he was not able to compile a very well-organised judgment. We consider that we should be hesitant before criticising judgments in care cases made by Circuit judges and High Court judges under great pressure. It would however be very helpful to this court if, at the outset of a judgment in a care case, the judge were to introduce all the

parties and to explain their different proposals for the future of the children; and then, before turning to the history (and later of course to analysis of the issues), if he were briefly to summarise the current circumstances of the children and of each of the adult protagonists. It is also obviously far preferable if the evidence in relation to particular areas of the case can be collected together rather than that, as this judge was constrained to do, he should, apparently from his notebook, work through – without much comment as to what he accepted and what he did not accept – the evidence given by each witness in the order in which he had received it. It is enough for us to say that, in the light of the facts that the girls had been in short-term foster care for ten months and that there were reports from a number of professional sources indicative of an absence on the part of the mother of any wish to receive external help, the judge concluded that the chance of rehabilitation without repetition of the physical and emotional harm (including neglect) which the girls had suffered in the mother's home was too small to warrant adjournment for the specialist assessment.'

Purpose of this Guidance

The approach to a judgment predicates the approach of the advocate during final submissions. Therefore, the approach of the advocate to final submissions and their reduction, where possible, to **issue** driven, clearly expressed, focussed, written form is immediately relevant to the court's judgment.

Suggested Topics to be Considered before Drafting Final Submissions

The Strategic Framework to Final Submissions

Accepting that there is no 'form', the following are likely to be the core steps (as appropriate) to a judgment in s 31 of the Children Act 1989 cases:

(a)   identify for the judge what documents he/she has seen, what witnesses have been heard, and what undertakings have been/are to be/can be given;

(b)   threshold (*Re H (Minors) (Sexual Abuse: Standard of Proof)* [1996] AC 565, FLR, otherwise known as *Re H and R*);

(c)   if threshold, options and welfare check-list (including 'delay' and Art 8 issues of reasonableness, necessity and proportionality);

(d)   if care, scrutinise care plan;

(e)   if plan for adoption, consent/dispensing; 2002 Act welfare check-list (including 'throughout life' and 'delay').

What can be Agreed Prior to the Drafting of Final Submissions?

To the extent that it is possible, the following should be agreed:

(a)   core facts (including as appropriate, places of birth, addresses, any occupation of the parties and what it involves/time involved; if the names of any party do not obviously suggest gender – stating the gender);

(b)   child(ren): date(s) of birth, parentage, where living, relevant court orders;

(c)   chronology (particularly flagging up the time-table for the child: key dates for the child, including when to be 18);

(d)   statement of relevant law;

(e)   extent of agreement of expert evidence.

Consider what Judgment is to be Sought?

This will involve a clear analysis of the following:

(a)   What are the **issues** in the case which require resolution? (There can only be four categories of **issue**: law, fact, expert/opinion evidence and the exercise of judicial discretion). Note that the primary factual **issues** in care proceedings almost invariably fall within one or more of the categories set out in **Annex 1** below.

(b)   Assuming a statutory framework to the advocate's submissions, provide the judge with that framework.

(c)   If an **issue(s)** of law is the subject matter of contention:

(i)   What are the competing interpretations?
(ii)   On what grounds does the advocate contend for his/her interpretation(s)?

(d)   Is there is an **issue(s)** of fact? If yes:

(i)   What facts is the court to be invited to find and on what grounds (explaining the competing arguments, and substantiating the findings contended for);
(ii)   Is the court to be invited to draw any inferences from those primary facts and if so, what inferences and on what grounds (see *Jones v GWR* (1930) 47 TLR 39)?

(e)   If there is no **issue** as to fact then the advocates should agree, and record in writing for the judge, the factual basis of the case. Key facts which the judge should have available prior to judgment, and which should be agreed if possible by the advocates, are set out in **Annex 2**. (All agreements should be given clear written expression by all parties in final submissions).

(f)   If there is an **issue** of expert/opinion evidence:

(i)   What expert/opinion evidence is the court to be invited to find?

(ii) Why is it in dispute and by whom is it disputed? Is it the factual basis of the opinion (in which case, see above as to 'findings of fact') or is it the approach of the expert/professional: in which case identify the issue involved, the area of dispute between the experts/professionals and set out clearly the grounds why the approach contended for is correct.

(g)   If the **issue** is one of discretion, set out:

(i)   The range of options open to the court; and

(ii) In relation to the option contended for, why that should prevail over the competing options, setting out the grounds for that contention clearly.

Welfare issues will feature in this context, see **Annex 3** below for the check-list, and in this context also keep in mind when preparing final submissions:

(i)   Evidence of attachment.

(ii) Dynamics within the family: if the placement proposed is (for example) with a grandmother or aunt, what is the relationship between that person and other family members (this is relevant also to 'findings').

(iii) If the contention is that the child be brought up within the extended family, keep in mind the theme struck in **Annex 4**.

Summary Thus Far

The above preparatory steps provide the building bricks for the 'template' below. The cardinal rule is that an advocate should, as it were, seek to write the judge's judgment. The template, set out below, focuses primarily on the drafting of final submissions, setting out as it does the material the Judge will need for a judgment.

Template

(1)　Theme of the case: (see Annex 1 below for examples) and set out in just a few sentences the core factual background and issues;

(2)　Applications: for what and by whom;

(3)　Brief introduction of all relevant persons:

(a)　The children concerned and their current circumstances are:

  (i)　...
  (ii)　...
  (iii)　etc

(b)　The other parties concerned are:

  (i)　...
  (ii)　...
  (iii)　etc

(4)　Positions of all parties:

(a)　The local authority's case: (covering care plan if relevant);

(b)　The guardian supports/does not support (explaining clearly any issues between the guardian and the local authority, if any, covering care plan if relevant);

(c)　The mother/father's case is;

(d)　The extended family's case is (see **Annex 4** below).

(5)　Background: context of the applications to cover:

(a)　Any parental family history and childhood experiences which may have impacted on personality or parenting capacity;

(b)　The relationship between the parents, its history and development.

(6)　Law/Disputed Law: in the event of any dispute, set out clearly the competing arguments, and why the interpretation sought is the correct one.

(7)　Disputed facts: set out what they are, together with the relevance of the disputed facts to the **issue[s]**.

(8)　Witness of fact:.

(a)   Set out the relevant parts of evidence vis a vis what is in **issue**;

(b)   Explain reliable and unreliable aspects, including inconsistencies.

(c)   Give an assessment (reliability, accuracy, credibility, demeanour).

(9)   Findings of fact the judge is to be invited to make: Set out the facts the judge is to be invited to find, together with the grounds for the judge being invited to make such findings; also set out here any inferences the judge is invited to draw from the primary facts, and the grounds therefor.

(10)   Expert evidence:

(a)   Facts upon which based (if expert opinion turns also on an **issue** of fact, resolve that issue of fact first);

(b)   As to opinion:

    (i)   Reliability?
    (ii)   Consistency with facts?
    (ii)   Assessment (see *Loveday v Renton* (1990) 1 MLR 117 and *The Ikarian Reefer* (1993) 2 Lloyds Rep 68).

(11)   Findings on expert witnesses the judge is to be invited to make: set out these findings sought. If appropriate, explain why one expert is to be preferred to another (giving clear reasons);

(12)   Guardian:

(a)   Short summary of evidence given/his-her position;

(b)   Issues;

(c)   Assessment of evidence;

(d)   Acceptance or rejection of recommendations.

(13)   Given findings: threshold?

(14)   Disposal:

(a)   Need for a Children Act order? And if yes, what order. Considerations include:

    (i)   Child's history;
    (ii)   Child's identified needs;
    (iii)   Child's timetable for decisions;
    (iv)   Family history;

(v) Carers' profile;

(vi) Assessment of personality and capabilities;

(vii) Impact of difficulties/ factors on parenting capacity and timescale for change.

(b) Welfare check-list/Art 8 ('reasonable', 'proportionate', 'necessary');

(c) Options: care/supervision/no order;

(d) Nature of placement (e g long term fostering/adoption);

(e) Contact (parent, extended family member or inter-sibling);

(f) In relation to each party seeking residence, the benefit/detriment to the child(ren) if such an order made.

(15) Care plan:

(a) Scrutiny;

(b) Approve or not? If not, why not?

(16) If placement application:

(a) Do parents consent?

(b) If no – dispensing/welfare check-list (including 'throughout life' and 'delay') – Art 8 ('reasonable', 'proportionate', 'necessary').

(c) Contact after adoption (ss 26 and 27)?

(17) Conclusion:

(18) Subsidiary matters:

(a) Any undertaking to which any order will be subject?

(b) Any directions (see Annex 6 for examples);

(c) Leave to serve order?

(d) Transcript; at whose expense?

(e) Section 91(14) application;

(f) Exclusion orders?

(g) If appeal pending, stay of operation of order pending appeal?

(h)   Costs.

Annex 1: Issues

- Domestic violence (risk of physical and emotional impact on children);

- Drugs;

- Drink (including of a partner);

- Financial difficulties;

- Chaotic lifestyle;

- Neglect;

- Ill-treatment of children including NAI;

- Lack of control of children;

- School attendances;

- Lack of hygiene;

- Emotional abuse;

- A parent's lack of candour (co-operation with authorities);

- A parent's ability to separate from partner;

- Safety of parenting having regard to above issues.

Annex 2: Key Facts (to complement the Case Management Order and the Local Authority Summary)

Evidence:

- The documents before the court by reference to trial bundle index.

- Documents which have been read out, or taken as read by the agreement of the parties;

- What documents (if any) have been handed up during trial?

- What witnesses were called orally to give evidence, by whom and in relation to which **issues**?

Core facts:

- Names and dates of birth of birth parents and any other significant adult;

- Names and dates of birth of children, the subject matter of the proceedings;

- Names and dates of birth of other siblings (setting out their parentage, if relevant), their residence and with whom;

- Who has parental responsibility in relation to the relevant child(ren).

As to relevant child(ren):

(a) Living with whom?

(b) At what address?

(c) Since when?

Adoption – prospective adopters:

(a) Found? Approved by panel? Suitable matching?

(b) Has guardian been informed of the substance of the adopters' profile and agreed that they would be a suitable match;

(c) Timescale for placement, if a placement order.

Contact after placement:

(a) Local authority's position? Guardian's?

(b) If any recommendation for contact consider:

   (i) Attachment;
   (ii) Age in the context of being able to carry forward memories;
   (iii) Whether those exercising contact would accept an adoptive placement and conduct themselves in a manner which would be supportive of the placement;
   (iv) Consider 'letter box' contact.

Annex 3: Children Act Welfare Checklist Factors

(1) The ascertainable wishes and feelings of the child concerned (considered in the light of his age and understanding);

(2) His/her physical, emotional and educational needs;

(3) The likely effect on him of any change in his circumstances;

(4) His age, sex, background and any characteristics of his which the court considers relevant;

(5) Any harm which he has suffered or is at risk of suffering;

(6) How capable each of his parents, and any other person in relation to whom the court considers the question to be relevant, is of meeting his needs;

(7) The range of powers available to the court under the 1989 Act in the proceedings in question.

Annex 4: Care with Extended Family

If a child is to be brought up within the extended family where there may be an expectation of contact with family members (not only his parents, but also aunts, uncles and cousins etc):

(a) Consider as appropriate: Is she/he/they prepared to give undertakings that he/she/they will not permit any unauthorised contact to either of the parents, and if the local authority had a care order and child x were placed with her/him/them would there be accepted local authority decisions as to the nature and extent of parental contact subject to any contrary rulings of the court.

(b) Consider age of an extended family member, not as an issue in itself, but in the overall context of health, etc.

Annex 5: Examples of Orders the Subject Matter of the Care Jurisdiction

(1) Care order or supervision order;

(2) Discharge of a care order;

(3) Variation or discharge of a supervision order;

(4) Substitution of a supervision order for a care order;

(5) Contact, or refusal of contact, with a child in care;

(6) Consideration of a residence order for a child in care;

(7)   Under para 19(1) Sch 2 to the Children Act 1989: arrangements to assist children to live abroad;

(8)   Under para 6(3) Sch 3 to the Children Act 1989 (imposition of obligations on responsible person);

(9)   Under Part V Children Act 1989 (child assessment orders, emergency protection, exclusion requirement in emergency protection, undertakings and emergency protection, duration of emergency protection, removal and accommodation of children by police in case of emergency, local authority powers to investigate, powers to assist in discovery of children who may be in need of emergency protection, abduction of children in care, recovery of abducted children, refuges for children at risk);

(10)   Where a direction under s 37 Children Act 1989 has been made and the court (has made) (is considering) whether to make an (interim care order) (supervision order);

(11)   Under s 33(7) Children Act 1989 (prohibition of causing child to be known by a new surname or to removed from UK subject to conditions);

(12)   Under s 25 Children Act 1989 (secure accommodation).

Annex 6: Sample Model Orders

(1)   And it is directed:

(a)   That the said child(ren) be not removed from England and Wales without leave of the court until he/she/they shall attain the age of 18 years; provided that if either parent do give a general written undertaking to the court to return the said child(ren) to England and Wales when called upon to do so, and, unless otherwise directed, with the written consent of the other parent, that parent may remove the said child(ren) from England and Wales for any period specified in such written consent; and

(b)   That no step (other than the institution of proceedings in any court) be taken by [set out particulars of person(s)] which would result in any of the said child(ren) being known by a new surname before he or she attains the age of 18 years or, being a female, marries below that age, except with the leave of a judge or the consent in writing of the other parent.

(2)   Prompts:

(a)   Disclosure of judgment to professionals.

(b)   Reporting in anonymous form of any High Court judgment.

A3.24   APPENDIX 24:
WORKING PARTY OF THE FAMILY JUSTICE
COUNCIL GUIDELINES
DECEMBER 2011

These guidelines on the issue of children giving evidence in family proceedings, have been produced by the Family Justice Council Working Party on Children Giving Evidence, chaired by the Rt Hon Lord Justice Thorpe. They have been approved by the Council and I wish to add my endorsement.

The working party was set up following a referral from the Court of Appeal in *Re W* [2010] EWCA Civ 57. The Supreme Court in *Re W* [2010] UKSC 12 subsequently held that there was no longer a presumption or even a starting point against children giving evidence in such cases.

I am sure that these guidelines will be of benefit to members of the judiciary, lawyers and professionals, who have to deal with applications for children to give evidence in family proceedings.

May I take this opportunity to express my gratitude to all the members of the working party, and in particular to Alex Verdan QC, for the final version of these guidelines.

Sir Nicholas Wall

President of the Family Division

Children Giving Evidence in Family Proceedings

1 These Guidelines have been produced by Lord Justice Thorpe's Working Party.

2 This Working Party was set up following a request to the President of the Family Division by the Court of Appeal in *Re W* [2010] EWCA Civ 57, a case which considered the issue of children giving evidence in family proceedings.

3 That same case then went to the Supreme Court and is reported as *Re W* [2010] UKSC 12. It is now the leading authority on this issue. The Supreme Court held that there was no longer a presumption or even a starting point against children giving evidence in such cases.

4 Enquiries by this Working Party suggests that the number of applications for children giving evidence since this decision may be increasing.

5 The aim of these Guidelines is to provide those involved in family proceedings with advice as to what matters should be taken into account in such situations.

6 Hearsay evidence is of course admissible in family proceedings: Children (Admissibility of Hearsay Evidence) Order 1993, SI 1993/621.

7 The issue of whether a child should be further questioned or give evidence in family proceedings should be considered at the earliest possible opportunity by the court and all the parties and not left to the party intending to so apply.

Legal considerations

8 In light of *Re W*, in deciding whether a child should give evidence, the court's principal objective should be achieving a fair trial.

9 With that objective the court should carry out a balancing exercise between the following primary considerations:

(i)   the possible advantages that the child being called will bring to the determination of truth balanced against;

(ii) the possible damage to the child's welfare from giving evidence i.e. the risk of harm to the child from giving evidence;

having regard to:

(*a*)   the child's wishes and feelings, in particular their willingness to give evidence, as an unwilling child should rarely if ever be obliged to give evidence;

(*b*)   the child's particular needs and abilities;

(*c*)   the issues that need to be determined;

(*d*)   the nature and gravity of the allegations;

(*e*)   the source of the allegations;

(*f*)   whether the case depends on the child's allegations alone;

(*g*)   corroborative evidence;

(*h*)   the quality and reliability of the existing evidence;

(*i*)   the quality and reliability of any ABE interview;

(*j*)   whether the child has retracted allegations;

(*k*)   the nature of any challenge a party wishes to make;

(*l*)   the age of the child; generally the older the child the better;

(*m*)   the maturity, vulnerability and understanding, capacity and competence of the child; this may be apparent from the ABE or from professionals' discussions with the child;

(*n*)   the length of time since the events in question;

(*o*)   the support or lack of support the child has;

(*p*)   the quality and importance of the child's evidence;

(*q*)   the right to challenge evidence;

(*r*)   whether justice can be done without further questioning;

(*s*)   the risk of further delay;

(*t*)   the views of the guardian who is expected to have discussed the issue with the child concerned if appropriate and those with parental responsibility;

(*u*)   specific risks arising from the possibility of the child giving evidence twice in criminal or other and family proceedings taking into account that normally the family proceedings will be heard before the criminal; and

(*v*)   the serious consequences of the allegations i.e. whether the findings impact upon care and contact decisions.

10 The Court must always take into account the risk of harm which giving evidence may do to children and how to minimise that harm, although that may vary from case to case but the Court does not necessarily need expert evidence in order to assess the risk.

11 Where there are concurrent or linked criminal proceedings there should be close liaison between the respective parties and the allocated judges and ideally linked directions hearings. The Police/CPS should be informed of any proposal that a child give evidence in family proceedings and their views obtained before any such decision is made.

Alternatives to child giving live evidence at a hearing

12 The Court needs to consider seriously the possibility of further questions being put to the child on an occasion distinct from the substantive hearing so as to avoid oral examination. This option would have significant advantages to the child and should be considered at the earliest opportunity and in any event before that substantive hearing. Such further questioning should be carried out as soon as possible after the incident in question.

The Court will need to take into account practical and procedural issues including:

(*a*)   giving the child the opportunity to refresh his memory;

(*b*)   the appropriate identity of the questioner;

(*c*)   matching the skills of the questioner to the communication needs of the child;

(*d*)   where the questioning should take place;

(*e*)   the type and nature of the questions;

(*f*)   advance judicial approval of any questions proposed to be put to the child;

(*g*)   the need for ground rules to be discussed ahead of time by the judge, lawyers (and intermediary, if applicable) about the examination; and

(*h*)   how the interview should be recorded.

Practical considerations pre-hearing

13 Once a decision has been made that a child should give evidence at a hearing and be questioned at court, the Court must factor in steps to improve the quality of the child's evidence and minimise the risk of harm to the child.

14 At the earliest opportunity and in any event before the hearing at which the child's evidence is taken, the following matters need to be considered:

(a)   if "live" cross examination is appropriate, the need for and use of a registered intermediary (subject to their availability) or other communication specialist to facilitate the communication of others with the child or relay questions directly, if indicated by the needs of the child;

(b)   the use of other "special measures" in particular live video link and screens;

(c)   the full range of special measures in light of the child's wishes and needs;

(d)   advance judicial approval of any questions proposed to be put to the child;

(e)   the need for ground rules to be discussed ahead of time by the judge, lawyers (and intermediary, if applicable) about the examination;

(f)   information about the child's communication skills, length of concentration span and level of understanding e.g. from an expert or an intermediary or other communication specialist;

(g)   the need for breaks;

(h)   the involvement and identity of a supporter for the child;

(i)   the timetable for children's evidence to minimise time at court and give them a fresh clear start in the morning;

(j)   the child's dates to avoid attending court;

(k)   the length of any ABE recording, the best time for the child and the Court to view it (the best time for the child may not be when the recording is viewed by the court);

(l)   admissions of as much of the child's evidence as possible in advance; including locations, times, and lay-outs;

(m)   save in exceptional circumstances, agreement as to (i) the proper form and limit of questioning and (ii) the identity of the questioner.

15 If a child is to give oral evidence at the hearing the following should occur:

(a)   a familiarisation visit by the child to the court before the hearing with a demonstration of special measures, so that the child can make an informed view about their use;

(b)   the child should be accompanied and have a known neutral supporter, not directly involved in the case, present during their evidence;

(c)   the child should see their ABE interview and/or their existing evidence before giving evidence for the purpose of memory refreshing;

(d)   consideration of the child's secure access to the building and suitability of waiting/eating areas so as to ensure there is no possibility of any confrontation with anyone which might cause distress to the child (where facilities are inadequate, use of a remote link from another court or non-court location);

(*e*) identification of where the child will be located at court and the need for privacy.

16 Where possible the children's solicitor/Cafcass should be deputed to organise these matters.

17 A child should never be questioned directly by a litigant in person who is an alleged perpetrator.

Practical considerations at hearing

18 If the decision has been made that the child should give oral evidence at the hearing the following should occur:

(*a*) advocates should introduce themselves to the child;

(*b*) judges and magistrates should ask if the child would like to meet them, to help to establish rapport and reinforce advice;

(*c*) children should be encouraged to let the court know if they have a problem or want a break but cannot be relied upon to do so;

(*d*) professionals should be vigilant to identify potential miscommunication;

(*e*) the child should be told how the live video link works and who can see who;

(*f*) a check should be made (before the child is seated in the TV link room) to ensure that the equipment is working, recordings can be played and that camera angles will not permit the witness to see the Respondents;

(*g*) the parties should agree which documents the child will be referred to and ensure they are in the room where the child is situated for ease of access.

Examination of children

19 If the Court decides a child should give oral evidence, the Court and all parties should take into account the Good Practice Guidance in managing young witness cases and questioning children (part of the NSPCC/Nuffield Foundation research "Measuring Up" July 2009 by Joyce Plotnikoff and Richard Woolfson) and the subsequent Progress Report which Guidance has been endorsed by the Judicial Studies Board, the Director of Public Prosecutions, the Criminal Bar Association and the Law Society: http://www.nspcc.org.uk/Inform/research/findings/measuring_up_guidance_wdf66581.pdf.

20 Examination of the child should take into account the Court of Appeal judgment in *R v Barker* [2010] EWCA Crim 4, para [42], which called for the advocacy to be adapted "to enable the child to give the best evidence of which he or she is capable" and which questioning should:

(*a*) be at the child's pace and consistent with their understanding;

(b)   use simple common words and phrases;
(c)   repeat names and places frequently;
(d)   ask one short question (one idea) at a time;
(e)   let the child know the subject of the question;
(f)   follow a structured approach, signposting the subject;
(g)   avoid negatives;
(h)   avoid repetition;
(i)   avoid suggestion or leading, including "tag" questions;
(j)   avoid a criminal or "Old Bailey" style cross examination;
(k)   avoid "do you remember" questions;
(l)   avoid restricted choice questions;
(m)   be slow and allow enough time to answer;
(n)   check child's understanding;
(o)   test the evidence not trick the witness;
(p)   take into account and check the child's level of understanding;
(q)   not assume the child understands;
(r)   be alert to literal interpretation;
(s)   take care with times, numbers and frequency;
(t)   avoid asking the child to demonstrate intimate touching on his or her own body (if such a question is essential, an alternative method, such as pointing to a body outline, should be agreed beforehand).

Court's overriding duty

21 All advocates have a responsibility to manage the questioning of a child witness fairly. However, the ultimate responsibility for ensuring that the child gives the best possible evidence in order to inform the court's decision rests with the tribunal. It should set out its expectations of the advocates and make it clear to the child witness that they can indicate to the court if they feel they are not saying what they want to say or do not understand what is being said to them.

The court must be scrupulous in the attention it gives to the case management and control of the questioning process and should be prepared to intervene if the questioning is inappropriate or unnecessary.

22 These Guidelines will be reviewed periodically. Those involved in family proceedings are invited to contact the Family Justice Council with any relevant comments.

Working Party of the Family Justice Council

A3.25   APPENDIX 25:
THE NEW CARE MONITORING SYSTEM

Guidance for practitioners

The new care monitoring system (CMS) is a judicially led management information programme intended to provide accurate ongoing information about case volumes, case progress and allocation. The system will provide the case management information necessary to enable leadership judges and the administration to oversee and manage public law caseloads and the allocation of individual cases in their Care Centres. The programme will also assist judges, legal advisers and magistrates to focus on avoiding delay for children and will help identify the real causes of delay. CMS has been jointly developed by the judiciary and HMCTS and has been written to a judicial specification which looks at both the real progress of a case through the court and the DFJ's and JC's responsibilities for all cases within their courts.

The system is being piloted nationwide from the 2nd April 2012 from when **all new care and supervision cases will be entered on to the system**.

The CMS case summary will provide judges/legal advisers/benches with ongoing information updated for every hearing about the ages of the child or children they are dealing with, the length of time a case has been running (measured in weeks), the number of hearings which there have been, any adjournments of hearings and applications for experts.

Tracking the age of the case by reference to the timetable for the child

In preparation for the reforms which are contemplated in the family modernisation programme, and for the purpose of this trial, all cases will be given a standard 26 week timetable on issue. The system will keep track of where the case is in the process and whether it is on time to be completed within the 26 week period.

If, at any point, the court decides that the **timetable for the child** is such that the proceedings will not be completed within 26 weeks of issue then it will make a decision about this. The determination of the timetable for the child must be done at the CMC. This must be done in court in the presence of the parties based on the evidence and information available and what it is necessary to do to conclude the proceedings. The timetable should then be expressed as the expected number of weeks which are necessary to conclude the proceedings. **This must then be recorded on the face of the order (usually in the form of a recital). Staff will use that order to input the data onto the CMS.**

The timetable for two or more children involved in the same proceedings may be different. Once the expected conclusion date has been set as being outside 26 weeks, it cannot be reset; however this does not preclude the case being completed earlier than the expected conclusion date.

The expected conclusion date will be set taking into account **only** the timetable for the child in each case and will not be linked to any other measures.

For the court's assistance and to ensure consistency of data collection, a form of order is included with this guidance which should be incorporated into the directions given at any relevant hearing in order for staff to have the information to populate the CMS.

Adjourning or relisting cases

Each time a case is adjourned or relisted, the system will record the reason for that adjournment. If there is a hearing, then the reason will be given in front of the parties in court and the reason(s) for the adjournment should be recorded on the face of the order (usually in the form of a recital).

Each hearing must be properly described in accordance with the PLO (e.g. if a CMC is being adjourned because the case management is incomplete and the case is not ready for an IRH, it is adjourned to another CMC; or if an IRH is being adjourned but the case is not ready for final hearing without another intervening hearing then the case is being adjourned to another IRH and so on). The system is able to record more than one reason for an adjournment (and it may be that a number will apply).

Shown below are the reasons that currently appear on the system.

Evidence	No/poor pre proceedings preparation by Local Authority
	No poor kinship assessments
	No expert instructed by LA
	No/poor parental evidence
	No/poor core assessment (this includes assessment of parents)
	No Genogram (no friends or family identified before hearing)
	No/poor placement evidence

	No/poor CAFCASS analysis
	Disclosure of medical records or materials from other agencies/ proceedings required
Case Management	No timetable for the child
	No threshold
	Official Solicitor not instructed/ready (re adult capacity)
	Lack of judicial continuity
	No key issue analysis
	CAFCASS not allocated/present
	Insufficient time/No courtroom available
	Non compliance with directions
	New party joined
	Lawyers not present or ready
	Interpreter not available
Planned	Consolidation with other proceedings
	New/alternative care plan (including kinship placement)
	Parallel proceedings (including joint directions with crime)
	New baby/pregnancy

If providing the court with a draft order, please make reference to one or more of the reasons on the system as above to enable the court staff accurately to input information onto the new CMS.

Experts

The number and types of experts' reports requested and allowed and the timescales for compliance with the instruction will also be monitored by the system. Each time a report is requested, the system will be updated with the following details:

- Type of expert

Paediatric	
Paediatric Radiologist	
Other Medical Reports	
Family Centre Assessments (Parenting Skills)	Residential
	Non-Residential
Psychiatric Report	On Child And Parent(s) / Carers
	On Child Only
Adult Psychiatric Report On Parent(s)	
Psychological Report On Child Only	Clinical
	Educational
Psychological Report On Parent(s) Only	
Psychological Report On Parent(s) and Child	
Multi Disciplinary Assessment	
Independent Social Worker	
Other Experts Reports Filed	

- The date the report was requested

- Whether the report was allowed

- The date the report is due and

- when it is received

If preparing draft orders, it would assist the court if they could be in the form of order included with this guidance to enable the court staff accurately to input information onto the new CMS.

Placement of a child

The system records the placement of the child. Please ensure that there is a recital in an order which accurately describes the placement to enable the court staff accurately to input information onto the new CMS. The following examples can be used:

Placement of a child	
Not removed – At home	
Not removed – In RPaCA placement a residential assessment with parent	
Not removed – In another form of placement	
Removed – To kinship placement	
Removed – To foster care	
Removed – To potential adoptive placement (parallel planning)	
Reunification – Assessment placement with parent	
Reunification – Assessment placement with kinship	
Complex needs- In a specialist placement (that is not foster care or residential assessment with parent.)	

Suggested forms of order

TRACKING THE AGE OF THE CASE

ORDER

This is a case in which the best interests of the child will be met by a timetable which involves the completion of the case within 26 weeks/ within [___] weeks.

OR

The timetable for the child is [ ] and the proceedings are to be completed within 26 weeks/ the proceedings cannot be completed within 26 weeks but are to be completed within [ ] weeks.

ADJOURNING OR RELISTING CASES

ORDER

The First Appointment/CMC/IRH/FOF/Final hearing is adjourned to.. [ ]

The brief reasons for the adjournment are [please make reference to the list above]

EXPERTS

ORDER

Application(s) to authorise the instruction of an expert/a number of experts have been made. The expert(s) authorised is/are (please make reference to the list above). The reason for the appointment of the expert is (here please give details e.g. absence of expert evidence from local authority/ Cafcass or an identified necessity on a relevant issue outside the skill and expertise otherwise available to the court.

[The cost of the expert(s) is to be paid by]

CHAPTER 4

EXPERT EVIDENCE IN THE CONTEXT OF THE PLO

4.1   CASE MANAGEMENT

4.1.1   President's Practice Direction on Expert Evidence

The matters set out below must be read subject to the President's Practice Direction on Expert Evidence; see **A4.1** below.

4.1.2   Experts practice points

(a)   **From whom?** Has consideration been given (including by the children's guardian (CG)) as to whether such a professional is genuinely necessary, reasonable and proportionate in the sense that without such opinion there is missing a piece of information essential to the exercise of the court's discretion? Can such evidence be provided by a Social Work Assessor (eg attachment issues) and/or could such evidence be provided by the CG? An expert will not be necessary unless the relevant expertise is outwith the skills and expertise of the court.

(b)   **To what issue?** Just by way of example:[1]

    (i)   unexplained, disputed serious injuries or other harm to a child;
    (ii)   unexplained developmental delay;
    (iii)   serious mental health issues;
    (iv)   severe learning difficulties;
    (v)   major disabilities;
    (vi)   potential to benefit from therapy and timescales.

(c)   **Timetabling?**

(d)   **Joint/cost-apportionment?**

(e)   **Consequential directions:**

---

[1]   See *Re S (Expert Evidence)* [2008] EWCA Civ 365, [2008] Fam Law 729: Experts should be confined to material relevant to the issue and no more.

    (i)   Leave to disclose?

    (ii)   Permission to interview/examine?

(f) **Meetings?** After respective meetings:

    (i)   notes/minutes of meetings;

    (ii)   filing of statements of agreement/disagreement – matters in *issue* that are likely to affect outcome.

4.1.3 Issues and more than one expert

Disruption to the progression of cases can be avoided if there is clear compliance with the following:

(a) In relation to any *issue* on which a professional of a particular discipline is to advise, that *issue* must be the same for each professional instructed from that discipline.

(b) In relation to any *issue*, if there is to be more than one professional advising, then each such professional should be of the same discipline.

(c) It is essential that each such professional is privy to the identical material as the corresponding professional.

4.1.4 Analysis of an expert's report

If an expert's report is an amalgam of fact, inference, speculation and opinion, the inevitable corollary is that at the experts' meeting such amalgam has the potential to solidify into a settled view, the validity of which becomes increasingly difficult to challenge/disentangle. The opinion of an expert should be readily capable of refraction through the following prism (and it will be more transparent if the format of the report dovetails with the six parameters set out below in the order in which they are given):

(1) What is the *issue(s)* upon which advice was sought?

(2) What are the facts which the expert invites the court to find to establish her/his opinion; identifying the evidential source for any such fact (eg by cross-referencing with a core medical bundle)?

(3) Does the expert invite the court to draw any inferences from the primary facts (reasoned deductions as contrasted with speculation?) If yes, what are those inferences and on what grounds does he invite the court to infer them?

(4) What is the expert's clear focused opinion on the *issue*(s) the subject matter of the report?

(5) In relation to any opinion on any *issue* expressed, what precisely are the grounds for that opinion setting them out clearly and succinctly? Are there any other reasonable opinions/options capable of being explained? Why is one opinion/option preferable over another (see the decision of Charles J in *A County Council v K, D & L* [2005] 1 FLR 851 at **4.4.4** below).

(6) A glossary of any learned texts relied upon setting out the core material where necessary, including that core material as a separate indexed and paginated bundle, highlighting the relevant passages in fluorescent ink which will register on a black and white photocopier.

4.1.5 Taking issue with a professional/expert given the above expert report template

If issue is taken by any party as to any opinion advanced by a professional (to include social workers, doctors, psychologists, health visitors etc) then the basis of any dispute is to be made clear.

(a) Is it by reference to the facts upon which an opinion of a professional is based? If yes, precisely what are the facts challenged and what are the grounds for contending that even if such facts are successfully challenged, that such challenge should affect the conclusion to which the professional comes?

(b) Similarly, is it by reference to any inference from those facts?

(c) If the facts (and any inferences) are substantially accepted, is the ground of challenge by reference to the opinion of the professional? If yes:

  (i) Precisely what part of the opinion of the professional is challenged?
  (ii) On what basis is it to be contended that such opinion is wrong; what is challenged precisely in the context of the other expert's reasoning process and why?
  (iii) What instead is the view contended for, and on what grounds is that to be advanced?

4.1.6 Experts' meetings

Practice points pursuant to the PLO, to be read subject to paragraph 6 of the *President's Practice Direction (Experts in Family Proceedings relating to Children)*:

(a) Under the Public Law Outline there is a clear distinction between Advocates' Meetings and Experts' Meetings.

(b) It should not be assumed that agreement among witnesses is indicative of reliability.[2] There is a danger that factors such as the respective standing of experts, as opposed to the methodological rigour of any hypothesis advanced, might result in a common position arrived at through professional deference rather than scientific consensus; see *W v Oldham MBC* [2005] EWCA Civ 1247, [2006] 1 FLR 543.

(c) The agenda for an experts' meeting should include:

    (i) the precise *issues* to be considered, and in relation to each specialty – by whom;

    (ii) source material for the facts relied on to be identified by all those at the meeting and recorded in writing;

    (iii) have all the hospital notes been compiled?

    (iv) tape-recording of meeting to avoid dispute over the notes;

    (v) if any inferences are to be drawn from accepted facts, then such inferences must be expressly identified (it should be stated who invites them to be drawn, and there should also be recorded the facts from which they are drawn together with the grounds for drawing them);

    (vi) check for gaps in evidence;

    (vii) all experts to attend (check that CVs available together with any of their relevant publications);

    (viii) medical aids (Glossary; Illustrations; Anatomical material).

(d) The court will be looking for clear and succinct language, addressing the relevant *issues*. Prolixity may be expected to invite from the court explanation as to why such extensive reportage was deemed by the expert to be necessary.

4.1.7 Checklist for end of experts' meeting

At the end of such a meeting, the experts should address the following checklist:

(a) What specialisms were represented at the meeting? Identify the experts present.

(b) What precisely were the issues identified in each specialism?

(c) Identify clearly the source material for the facts relied on.

---

2   See generally G. Edmond '*After Objectivity: Expert Evidence and Procedural Reform*' [2003] Sydney Law Review 8.

(d)   Were any inferences drawn from primary facts? If yes:

    (i)   What primary facts?
    (ii)   What inferences?
    (iii)   What was the reasoning for drawing inferences?

(e)   Were any gaps in the evidence identified? If yes, identify them precisely. For example, were the medical records complete?

(f)   In relation to each issue identified, was there agreement or disagreement? If disagreement, setting out in relation to each expert:

    (i)   What is the issue?
    (ii)   Which experts disagreed?
    (iii)   What succinctly are the grounds for the view taken by each such expert?
    (iv)   And why do they contend that they are correct and the other wrong?

(g)   Was the meeting recorded? Who has the tape?

(h)   What (if any) of the following were used at the meeting:

    (i)   Glossary?
    (ii)   Illustrations?
    (iii)   Anatomical material?

4.1.8   Challenging an expert

Parties are reminded that:

(a)   If there is no evidence to gainsay the opinion of a professional, then if the court comes to a conclusion different from that advised by the professional, it must give good reasons. Thus if any party is to challenge the opinion of a professional without corresponding expertise, then the grounds for challenging the professional opinion must be clear and firm.

(b)   To seek to challenge the opinion of a professional without clear and firm grounds can result in a delay in the result of a hearing, a wasting of court time together with the unnecessary and unreasonable arousing of false expectations. A fair trial under Article 6 of the European Convention on Human Rights mandates compliance by all parties with the legal principles and procedures and this is of particular importance in the context of children cases where their welfare and the *Timetable for the Child* are paramount.

4.2 EXPERT EVIDENCE AND THE PLO IN THE CONTEXT OF *ISSUE* DRIVEN LITIGATION

4.2.1 Contrasting the role of medical expert and judge

(a) **Taking a history:** When analysing a medical history in a report, it is suggested that the following approach may be helpful:

  (i)   The role of a doctor when taking a history is therapeutic; the history may be the best source of data she/he has, even if it is flawed.

  (ii) In contrast, the court is looking at the primary facts, and the inferences that can logically be derived from those facts,[3] when assessing the foundation for any expert opinion built on such facts and inferences.

  (iii) Thus, whereas a relatively uncritical approach to a history is central to the medical therapeutic function, it is completely antithetical to the scrupulous care with which the court must approach the assessment of such history.

(b) **The legal/medical interface – room for misapprehension:** Does a doctor with his/her training understand the forensic process which is central to the lawyer with his/her training? There is room for misunderstanding between the provider and receiver of a letter of instruction.

(c) **Expert interviewing and assessing:**[4] If experts' reports are based also on assessments and interviews (which by definition are subjective interpretation as contrasted with objectively distilled fact), what is the weight to be attached to the material elicited and how does that affect the weight/structure of the medical opinion?[5]

(d) **Judge decides:**[6] '*The expert advises, but the judge decides.*' The court is entitled to depart from the opinion of an expert although, if it does so, it must provide a reasoned explanation.[7]

4.2.2 Law relating to expert evidence

See **4.4** below.

---

3   See *Jones v GWR* (1930) 47 TLR 39.

4   See *Re CS (Expert Witnesses)* [1996] 2 FLR 115 at 120.

5   See *Re CB and JB* [1998] 2 FLR 211 at para 224(b)–225(f).

6   See *Re B (Care: Expert Witnesses)* [1996] 1 FLR 667, CA.

7   See *Oxfordshire County Council v DP, RS and BS* [2005] EWHC 2156 (Fam), [2008] Fam Law 839.

4.3 ISSUES ARISING OUT OF THE JOINT INSTRUCTION OF EXPERTS

4.3.1 Joint instruction?

Joint instruction is encouraged.[8]

4.3.2 As to bringing in a second/additional expert (*Daniels v Walker* [2000] 1 WLR 1382)

Lord Woolf MR proposed the following steps in the instruction of an expert (or experts) where the court has ordered a joint approach:

> '(a) Parties endeavour to instruct on the basis of an agreed letter;
> (b) Failing that, parties write separately;
> (c) If one party, for reasonable reasons, is discontented with the report, he can put questions to the expert;
> (d) If that does not resolve the position, then one or both parties may seek a direction as to the calling of further evidence. Such a direction will be considered on the basis of proportionality to the issues and money involved.'

4.3.3 Cases following on from *Daniels v Walker*[9]

Cosgrove v Pattison (*2001*) *The Times, 13 February*

This case identifies relevant factors as to the nature and number of issues between the parties, the reasons for wishing to call one's own expert, the amount at stake and any delay in making the application or caused to the hearing (see further, CPR 1998, r 35.8).

GW & PW v Oldham MBC [2005] EWCA Civ 1247, [2006] 1 FLR 543[10]

Where the medical evidence of NAI or unascertained infant death became pivotal, the court would be slow to decline an application for a second expert, since such evidence was not easily challenged in the absence of another expert opinion. Such a second opinion should normally be permitted where the question to be addressed went to an *issue* of critical importance. The principle is '*Dominant Issue*'. The ruling is underpinned by a logical symmetry. The LA will almost invariably be supported by the CG. Thus there are two professional reports outside the medical arena on

---

8 See *Best Practice Guide and Instructing a Single Joint Expert* [2003] 1 FLR 573.
9 As to a "shadow expert", see *Re J (Application for a Shadow Expert)* [2008] 1 FLR 1501.
10 Also see *Re SK (Local Authority: Expert Evidence)* [2007] EWHC 3289 (Fam).

the dominant issue. If the joint report is challenged and no further report is ordered, there will only be one medical report on the dominant issue.

Re S, WSP v Hull City Council [2006] EWCA Civ 981, [2007] 1 FLR 90

The judge had been correct – or at the very least entitled – to favour the joint instruction of single experts. The *Oldham* case was no authority for the submission that the parents were entitled unilaterally to instruct four experts to prepare reports at the outset of proceedings for use at the fact-finding stage of the hearing. The *Oldham* case had not intended to suggest that the court should routinely favour the instruction of two or more experts in the same discipline additional to such experts already destined to give evidence because of their clinical involvement in the child's case: it also stressed that justification for a second opinion lay only in circumstances in which the first opinion was 'pivotal' and until the first set of reports was to hand, it could not be discerned where any of them, and if so, which one, was the pivot around which the others turned.

Re B (Care Proceedings: Expert Witness) [2007] EWCA Civ 556, [2007] 2 FLR 979

Where in a seemingly hopeless case the mother sought her own independent expert evidence to test the opinion of the local authority's experts and to follow the national protocol.

Held:

The parents ought to be permitted to instruct an expert of their own. It was very important that parents who were at risk of losing a child forever should have confidence in the fairness of proceedings, and that inevitably meant the even-handed nature of the proceedings. Furthermore, if the parents' expert shared the opinion of the local authority experts, there would be a measurable chance that the anticipated two-day hearing would either be unnecessary or could be abbreviated.

Re C [2011] EWCA Civ 1451

In 2008 father accepted two cautions for having had sexual intercourse with under-aged girls. The father's application for a second psychiatric assessment was rejected. The President inter alia said:

'33. Family proceedings relating to children are unique in the control which the judge has over expert evidence. No expert can be instructed without judicial permission. It follows that a judge now decides each application for a second opinion on its merits by reference to the criteria set out in the Overriding Objective, the Practice Direction and the Family Procedure Rules 2010 (the FPR). In each case it is a matter of judgment, and the critical questions remain: Do I need this report in order to enable me to deal justly with the case? What will the additional expert add to the case?'

4.3.4 The concept of a fair trial in the context of the jointly instructed expert

Re L (Care: Assessment: Fair Trial) [2002] 2 FLR 730, per Munby J

'[113] ... where a jointly instructed or other sole expert's report, though not binding on the court is 'likely to have a preponderant influence on the assessment of the facts by [the] court' there may be a breach of Article 6 if a litigant is denied the opportunity – before the expert produces his report—
(a)   to examine and comment on the documents being considered by the expert, and
(b)   to cross-examine witnesses interviewed by the expert and on whose evidence the report is based – in short to participate effectively in the process by which the report is produced.'

Peet v Mid Kent Healthcare Trust Practice Note [2002] 1 WLR 210

'When, if at all, should one party, without the consent of the other party, be permitted to have sole access to a single joint expert, ie an expert instructed and retained by both parties? *Never.*'

4.3.5 Additional references

(a)   Disagreement, however eminent the witnesses involved, did not absolve the family judge from the responsibility of making a decision, applying the civil standard of proof. In *A Local Authority v SW and T*[11] it was recognised that some medical issues, such as the force required to produce fatal brain injuries, were genuinely controversial, that understanding in this area was continuing to develop, and that some of the old certainties had now been strongly questioned. It follows that disagreement should come as no surprise, even amongst doctors of the highest repute.

(b)   It was incorrect to treat the distinction between criminal and civil standards as 'largely illusory'.[12] The standard of proof to be applied in Children Act cases was the balance of probabilities and the approach to these difficult cases was laid down by Lord Nicholls of Birkenhead in *Re H (Minors) (Sexual Abuse: Standard of Proof)* [1996] 1 FLR 80, HL.

---

[11]   [2004] 2 FLR 129, per Hedley J.
[12]   *Re U, Re B* [2004] 2 FLR 263.

(c)   When photographs were taken, suitable local protocols should be devised as soon as possible to enable all photographs to be released to all the relevant experts when they received instructions to report in care proceedings. This required consideration at a national level of discussion between the judiciary and all the relevant disciplines.[13] It was held that one of the medical experts had been placed in a most difficult and unsatisfactory position, in that he had not had the opportunity to see and examine the child and was dependent entirely upon information provided by others. It was clear that, at the new trial, the medical evidence had to be re-evaluated in circumstances in which the medical experts had access to all the relevant documents and photographs and could give fully informed evidence to the judge. Photographs had become an increasingly important part of medical evidence.

(d)   Hypotheses – Wall J inter alia held in *Re AB (Child Abuse: Expert witnesses)* [1995] 1 FLR 181:
'(a)   Where an expert advances a hypothesis to explain a given set of facts, he owes a very heavy duty to explain to the court that what he is advancing is a hypothesis, that is controversial (if it is), and to place before the court all the material which contradicts the hypothesis.
(b)   The expert must also make all his material available to the other experts in the case.
(c)   Where the medical evidence points overwhelmingly to non-accidental injury, any expert who advises the parents and the court that the injury has an innocent explanation has a heavy duty to ensure that he has considered carefully the available material and is expressing an opinion that can be objectively justified.'

4.4   PRINCIPLES UNDERPINNING EXPERT EVIDENCE IN FAMILY PROCEEDINGS

4.4.1   Medical evidence in the context of the *issue* of credibility

In the context of expert evidence of a specific character (particularly as to physical injuries) apart from the rare cases where it was demonstrated that professional opinion was not capable of withstanding logical analysis, the judge was not entitled to reject un-contradicted medical findings and opinion and to conclude that that opinion was either unreasonable or irresponsible:

- *Re B (Split Hearing: Jurisdiction)* [2000] 1 FLR 334, per Butler-Sloss P (cited in *Re B (Non-accidental Injury: Compelling Medical Evidence)* [2002] EWCA Civ 902):

---

[13]   *Re T (Abuse: Standard of Proof)* [2004] 2 FLR 838.

'The credibility or otherwise of the lay witness on the facts of this case
... cannot stand so high as to make the evidence of the two consultant
radiologists of no effect.'

- *Re M (Residence)* [2002] EWCA Civ 1052, [2002] 2 FLR 1059, held
  inter alia:

    (i)   The assessment of the father's credibility was primarily the
           judge's task, but the assessment of his core personality and the
           extent to which damage resulting from his early life experience
           was disabling and permanent was primarily for the experts,
           whose professional training, qualification and clinical expertise
           equipped them for the task. Given that the experts were
           unanimous on this vital aspect, it was not open to the judge to
           reject their conclusions, either on the basis of his own
           impressions of the father or upon the basis of the prejudice to
           the father's case caused by management decisions of the local
           authority and prison authority during the interlocutory stages.
    (ii)   Insofar as the judge was fully entitled to depart from the
           experts in relation to issues of management, placement and
           welfare, it was incumbent upon him to give full reasons for such
           departure.
    (iii) There was no reasoned rejection of the guardian's evidence,
           which was largely based on the expert evidence given by others.
           The report was also based on the guardian's considerable
           experience. It was necessary therefore for the judge to explain
           why he was rejecting the guardian's views.

- *Re B (Care: Expert Witness)* [1996] 1 FLR 667 at 674 by way of
  contrast in the context of management, placement and welfare per
  Butler-Sloss LJ:

    'It is important to remember that the decision is that of the judge and
    not of the professional expert.'

Against that backdrop the ruling was: The judge did not err in law in
departing from the opinion of the experts and the guardian ad litem.
The judicial task was to make a decision in the light of all the
available evidence. In this case the judge's finding was not against the
weight of the evidence taken as a whole, including that of the
mother, health visitors and the contact supervisor. The judge had
given proper reasons for departing from the recommendations of the
experts and the guardian ad litem.

4.4.2 Credibility in the context of psychometric testing

This is primarily for the judge (as contrasted with psychometric testing pursuant to the *Eysenck Personality Questionnaire – Revised*) – *Re S (Care: Parenting Skills: Personality Tests)* [2005] 2 FLR 658, CA:

> 'The judge had given undue prominence to the personality testing evidence, and had failed to accept the subsequent qualifications made by the relevant expert, and his oral evidence that the child should remain with the mother. Very little reliance could be placed upon psychometric testing of this sort, which should not ordinarily have any place in cases of this kind. Questions of credibility were for the judge to decide; judges did not need personality tests to assist them in deciding such questions of credibility and were probably far better off without them. Personality testing of the sort used in this case could not be used to resolve issues such as parenting skills unless validated by other evidence. If a judge were, exceptionally, minded to rely upon the results of personality tests, he had first to assess their validity, both generally and for the purposes of the case (see paras [57], [58], [63], [67], [71]).'

The court had to be cautious of declining to follow uncontradicted expert evidence but it was not bound by it. The assessment of adult credibility as to the responsibility for harming a child remained the function of the court.[14]

4.4.3 Fairness and scrutiny of source material

Where an expert's report was likely to have a preponderant influence on the court's assessment of the facts, a breach of Art 6 could occur if the litigant had no opportunity, before the production of the report, to examine and comment on documents being considered and to cross-examine witnesses interviewed and relied upon in the report (see *Re L (Care: Assessment: Fair Trial)* [2002] EWHC 1379 (Fam) [2002] 2 FLR 730).

Per curiam:

The court laid down guidelines in relation to the conduct and recording of meetings and the provision of documents, which in summary cover:

(a)   The duty of social workers to notify parents of material criticism and advise how to remedy (now part of the pre-action protocols).

(b)   The need to keep full, balanced and comprehensive notes.

(c)   The duty on a LA to make early and full and frank disclosure.

---

[14]   See also in this context *A County Council v K, D & L* [2005] 1 FLR 851; *Birmingham CC v H, H & S* [2005] EWHC 2885 (Fam).

(d) Social workers and guardians should routinely exhibit to their reports and statements notes of relevant meetings, conversations and incidents.

(e) For a professionals' meeting: an agenda, clear written notice, the opportunity for a parent to make representations/right to attend, clear full and balanced minutes with agreement as soon as possible after the meeting.

(Reference should be made to the report for the full context.)

4.4.4 As to how experts should approach the issue and likelihood of the cause(s) of death, harm or injuries

A County Council v. K, D & L [2005] 1 FLR 851 per Charles J covering the questions experts should be asked and how they should approach the *issue* and likelihood of the cause(s) of death, harm or injuries:

Per curiam:

In civil cases concerning children it might be more helpful if the medical experts were not asked to express a view as to the cause of the relevant death, injuries or harm on the balance of probabilities but were rather asked to: identify possible causes of the relevant death, injuries or harm setting out in respect of each the reasons why it might be a cause and thus why it should be considered; state their views as to the likelihood of each possibility being the cause of the relevant death, injuries or harm and the reasons why they include or reject it as a reasonable (as opposed to a fanciful or merely theoretical) possible cause; compare the likelihood of the cause (or causes) identified as reasonable possibilities being the actual cause of the relevant death, injuries or harm; state whether they consider that a cause (or causes) was (were) the most likely cause (or causes) of the relevant death, injuries or harm and their reasons for that view; and to state whether they consider that a cause (or causes) was (were) more likely than not to be the cause (or causes) of the relevant death, injuries or harm and their reasons for that view (see para [89]).

4.4.5 Costs sharing

As a general rule, the proportionate approach of sharing the costs of joint expert reports between all of the parties was to be preferred to the 'moiety' approach contended for by the Legal Services Commission (LSC) (LSC suggested a moiety of 50% and the local authority to carry the balance of 50%).[15] The court identified some non-exhaustive considerations when considering who should bear the costs of reports produced by joint experts in public law cases, per Bodey J:

---

[15] *Calderdale MBC v S & LSC* [2005] 1 FLR 751.

'The court should apportion the relevant costs fairly and reasonably, bearing in mind all the circumstances of the particular case; the court would have regard to the reasonableness of how the local authority had conducted the information-gathering process and with what degree of competence and thoroughness; competence and thoroughness were relevant because there might be cases where a local authority had done little preparation or had prepared poorly; the court would have regard to the extent to which the report went merely to satisfying the 'threshold' for state intervention, as distinct from helping the court to decide more generally what overall 'disposal' would best serve the interests of the child's welfare; 'treating experts' and others who had had a 'hands on' role with the family were more likely to be paid for by the local authority, whereas the fees of a purely forensic expert were more likely to be ordered to be shared in principle between the parties; the sharing of the costs of a forensic expert gave each party confidence in the integrity of the forensic process, but if a party had genuinely opposed the commissioning of the joint report, then this would be a relevant factor; the fact that a party was publicly funded was not a reason for making a different decision about costs from that which would otherwise have been made (see para [35]).'

Also see in this context *Lambeth LBC v S.*[16] The costs of a residential assessment under s 38(6) can be apportioned between the parties (even where they are publicly funded) rather than being borne just by the local authority.[17]

4.4.6   Quality control testing of the expert's report

If a court rigorously considers the broader context of expert evidence, that is the social, educational and healthcare history, there must surely be less likelihood of inappropriate reliance on what may transpire to be insufficiently cogent and sometimes frankly incorrect expert evidence even where it is un-contradicted.[18]

4.4.7   Sundry cases as to the court's approach to expert evidence and the role of the judge

*   **Addressing a conflict:** *Re J (Expert Evidence: Hearing)* [1999] 2 FLR 661
    Where there is a conflict between experts, the court must address and resolve the conflict in so far as it is relevant to the issues before the court and it is entitled to give greater weight to the opinion of one expert against that of another, provided that proper reasons are given.

---

[16]   [2005] 2 FLR 1171.
[17]   And see *Sheffield City Council v V (Legal Services Commission Intervening)* [2007] 1 FLR 279 per Bodey J as to guidelines.
[18]   *A County Council v A Mother, A Father and X, Y & Z* [2005] 2 FLR 129.

- **Understanding the limitations of the diagnostic function of a medical expert:** *Re B (Non-accidental injury)* [2002] EWCA Civ 752, [2002] 2 FLR 1133

  'It seems that on very carefully stated and carefully balanced appraisal the judge would have been failing in his primary protective function if he were to have acceded to some submission that because the doctor had not been prepared to say in medical language that there was a confident diagnosis therefore there was no evidence of risk of harm. The elevation of a medical opinion to the status of a confident medical diagnosis is very much a matter of art and bounded by medical conventions that are fully recognised and, indeed, negotiated at a professional level. What this doctor was saying was that the child's condition was entirely consistent with non-accidental injury and that there was no other more probable explanation. The case, in my view, is as straightforward as that.

  [16] The expert of ultimate referral was there to guide the judge as to the relevant medical and scientific knowledge, inevitably expressing himself in medical language. The judge's function was a very different one. He had to consider the question posed by s 31 of the Children Act 1989 as to whether he was a child suffering or likely to suffer significant harm and whether that harm or likelihood of harm was attributable to the care given to the child, or likely to be given to him if the order were not made.'

And in this context see also *Re M (Care Proceedings: Best Evidence)* [2007] EWCA Civ 589, [2007] 2 FLR 1006.

4.4.8 Suggested protocol for format of experts' reports

The report should have as page 1 a precise and succinct précis of what the report says:

(a) the conclusions;

(b) the grounds for those conclusions;

(c) the foundation facts underpinning those conclusions; it is suggested that this should be recorded on no more than one side of A4 at the beginning of the report.

4.5 CASE DIGEST

R v Bowman [2006] EWCA Crim 1077

The report of an expert should include: (i) details of the witness's qualifications, experience and accreditation relevant to the opinions expressed in the report and the range and extent of the expertise and any limitations thereon; (ii) a statement setting out the substance of the instructions received, however received, the questions upon which an opinion was sought, the materials provided, and the materials which were relevant to the opinions expressed or upon which they were based; (iii) information as to who had carried out any tests etc, and their methodology, and whether such work was carried out under the supervision of the witness; (iv) where there was a range of opinion in the matters dealt with in the report, a summary of the range of opinion and the reasons for the opinion given; any material facts or matters which detracted from the witness's opinion and any points which should be made against it; (v) relevant extracts from the literature or other material which might assist the court; (vi) a statement that the witness had complied with the duty to the court to provide independent assistance by way of objective unbiased opinion in relation to matters within his or her expertise and an acknowledgment that the witness would inform all parties and, where appropriate, the court in the event of any change of opinion on the material issues; and these guidelines applied equally to supplementary reports.[19]

Meadow v GMC [2006] EWCA Civ 1390, [2007] 1 FLR 1398

Immunity should not extend to the situation where a judge before whom the expert had given evidence (or the Court of Appeal where appropriate) had referred the expert's conduct to the relevant disciplinary body when satisfied that his conduct had fallen so far below that which was to be expected as to merit some disciplinary action; for this purpose, the witness's shortcomings had to be sufficiently serious for the judge to believe that the witness might need to be removed from practice or at least to be subjected to conditions regulating his practice; normally, evidence given honestly and in good faith would not merit such a referral; but the precise boundaries of the immunity would have to be established on a case-by-case basis.

R v Harris, R v Rock, R v Cherry and R v Faulder [2006] 1 Cr App R 55(5)

As to such evidence in general, it should be and be seen to be the independent product of the expert uninfluenced as to form or content by the exigencies of litigation; an expert should provide independent assistance to the court by way of objective unbiased opinion in relation to matters within his expertise and should never assume the role of advocate; the facts or assumptions on which his opinion is based should be stated and he should not omit to consider material facts which detract from his concluded opinion; an expert should make it clear when a particular question or issue falls outside his expertise, and if his opinion has not been properly researched because he considers that insufficient data is

---

[19]   *R v Bowman* (2006) *The Times*, 24 March, CA approving the statement of an expert witness's duties at trial contained in *R v Harris, R v Rock, R v Cherry, R v Faulder* [2006] 1 Cr App R 55(5), CA.

available then he should say so with an indication that his opinion is no more than a provisional one; and, if after exchange of reports, an expert changes his view on material matters, such change of view should be communicated to the other side without delay and, when appropriate, to the court; in cases where there is a genuine disagreement on a scientific or medical issue, or where it is necessary for a party to advance a particular hypothesis to explain a given set of facts, the tribunal of fact will have to resolve the issue which is raised, but the expert who advances such a hypothesis owes a heavy duty to explain to the court that what he is advancing is a hypothesis, that it is controversial (if it is) and to place before the court any material which contradicts the hypothesis; and he must make his material available to the other experts in the case.

The Ikarian Reefer [1993] 2 Lloyd's Rep 68, Cresswell J

'[1] Expert evidence presented to the court should be, and should be seen to be, the independent product of the expert uninfluenced as to form or content by the exigencies of litigation ...

[2] Independent assistance should be provided to the court by way of objective unbiased opinion regarding matters within the expertise of the expert witness ... An expert witness in the High Court should never assume the role of advocate.

[3] Facts or assumptions upon which the opinion was based should be stated together with material facts which could detract from the concluded opinion.

[4] An expert should make it clear when a question or issue fell outside his experience.

[5] If the opinion was not properly researched because it was considered insufficient data was available then that had to be stated with an indication that the opinion was provisional ... If the witness could not assert that the report contained the truth, the whole truth and nothing but the truth then that qualification should be stated in the report.

[6] If after exchange of reports, an expert witness changed his mind on a material matter then the change of view should be communicated to the other side through legal representatives without delay and, when appropriate, to the court ...'

This case was cited in *R v Harris* [2006] 1 Cr App R 55(5) and the Court of Appeal then went on to say in this context:

'[272] Wall J, as he then was, sitting in the Family Division also gave helpful guidance for experts giving evidence involving children (see *Re AB (Child Abuse: Expert Witnesses)* 1995 1 FLR 181). Wall J pointed out that there will be cases in which there is a genuine disagreement on a scientific or medical issue, or where it is necessary for a party to advance a particular hypothesis to explain a given set of facts. He added (see p 192):

> "Where that occurs, the *jury* will have to resolve the issue which is raised. Two points must be made. In my view, the expert who advances such a hypothesis owes a very heavy duty to explain to the court that what he is advancing is a hypothesis, that it is controversial (if it is) and placed before the court all material which contradicts the hypothesis. Secondly, he must make all his material available to the other experts in the case. It is the common experience of the courts that the better the experts the more limited their areas of disagreement, and in the forensic context of a contested case relating to children, the objective of the lawyers and the experts should always be to limit the ambit of disagreement on medical issues to the minimum."

(The word *jury* has been substituted for *judge* in the above passage.)

[273] In our judgment the guidance given by both Cresswell J and Wall J are very relevant to criminal proceedings and should be kept well in mind by both prosecution and defence. The new Criminal Procedure Rules provide wide powers of case management to the Court. Rule 24 and Paragraph 15 of the Plea and Case Management form make provision for experts to consult together and, if possible, agree points of agreement or disagreement with a summary of reasons. In cases involving allegations of child abuse the judge should be prepared to give directions in respect of expert evidence taking into account the guidance to which we have just referred. If this guidance is borne in mind and the directions made are clear and adhered to, it ought to be possible to narrow the areas of dispute before trial and limit the volume of expert evidence which the jury will have to consider.

[274] We see nothing new in the above observations.'

Loveday v Renton [1990] 1 Med LR 117, per Stuart-Smith LJ

'In reaching my decision a number of processes have to be undertaken. The mere expression of opinion or belief by a witness, however eminent, that the vaccine can or cannot cause brain damage, does not suffice. The court has to evaluate the witness and the soundness of his opinion. Most importantly this involves an examination of the reasons given for his opinions and the extent to which they are supported by the evidence. The judge also has to decide what weight to attach to a witness's opinion by examining the internal consistency and logic of his evidence; the care with which he has considered the subject and presented his evidence; his precision and accuracy of thought as demonstrated by his answers; how he responds to searching and informed cross-examination and in particular the extent to which a witness faces up to and accepts the logic of a proposition put in cross-examination or is prepared to concede points that are seen to be correct; the extent to which a witness has conceived an opinion and is reluctant to re-examine it in the light of later evidence, or demonstrates a flexibility of mind which may involve changing or modifying opinions previously held; whether or not a witness is biased or lacks independence.

Criticisms have been made by Counsel of some of the witnesses called on either side and I shall have to consider these in due course ...

'There is one further aspect of a witness's evidence that is often important; that is his demeanour in the witness box. As in most cases where the court is evaluating expert evidence, I have placed less weight on this factor in reaching my assessment. But it is not wholly unimportant; and in particular in those instances where criticism has been made of a witness, on the grounds of bias or lack of independence, which in my view are not justified, the witness's demeanour has been a factor that I have taken into account.'

A4.1 APPENDIX: PRACTICE DIRECTION 25A – EXPERTS AND ASSESSORS IN FAMILY PROCEEDINGS

FPR Pt 25

This Practice Direction supplements FPR Part 25

Introduction

1.1 Sections 1 to 9 of this Practice Direction deal with the use of expert evidence and the instruction of experts, and section 10 deals with the appointment of assessors, in all types of family proceedings. The guidance incorporates and supersedes the *Practice Direction on Experts in Family Proceedings relating to Children* (1 April 2008) and other relevant guidance with effect on and from 6 April 2011.

Where the guidance refers to "an expert" or "the expert", this includes a reference to an expert team.

1.2 For the purposes of this guidance, the phrase "proceedings relating to children" is a convenient description. It is not a legal term of art and has no statutory force. In this guidance it means –

(*a*) placement and adoption proceedings; or
(*b*) family proceedings which –
    (i) relate to the exercise of the inherent jurisdiction of the High Court with respect to children;
    (ii) are brought under the Children Act 1989 in any family court; or
    (iii) are brought in the High Court and county courts and "otherwise relate wholly or mainly to the maintenance or upbringing of a minor".

AIMS OF THE GUIDANCE ON EXPERTS AND EXPERT EVIDENCE

1.3 The aim of the guidance in sections 1 to 9 is to:

(*a*) provide the court with early information to determine whether expert evidence or assistance will help the court;
(*b*) help the court and the parties to identify and narrow the issues in the case and encourage agreement where possible;
(*c*) enable the court and the parties to obtain an expert opinion about a question that is not within the skill and experience of the court;
(*d*) encourage the early identification of questions that need to be answered by an expert; and
(*e*) encourage disclosure of full and frank information between the parties, the court and any expert instructed.

1.4 The guidance does not aim to cover all possible eventualities. Thus it should be complied with so far as consistent in all the circumstances with the just disposal of the matter in accordance with the rules and guidance applying to the procedure in question.

PERMISSION TO INSTRUCT AN EXPERT OR TO USE EXPERT EVIDENCE

1.5 The general rule in family proceedings is that the court's permission is required to call an expert or to put in evidence an expert's report: see rule 25.4(1). In addition, in proceedings relating to children, the court's permission is required to instruct an expert: see rule 12.74(1).

1.6 The court and the parties must have regard in particular to the following considerations:

- (*a*) Proceedings relating to children are confidential and, in the absence of the court's permission, disclosure of information and documents relating to such proceedings may amount to a contempt of court or contravene statutory provisions protecting this confidentiality.
- (*b*) For the purposes of the law of contempt of court, information relating to such proceedings (whether or not contained in a document filed with the court or recorded in any form) may be communicated only to an expert whose instruction by a party has been permitted by the court (see rules 12.73 and 14.14).
- (*c*) In proceedings to which Part 12 of the FPR applies, the court's permission is required to cause the child to be medically or psychiatrically examined or otherwise assessed for the purpose of the preparation of expert evidence for use in the proceedings; where the court's permission has not been given, no evidence arising out of such an examination or assessment may be adduced without the court's permission (see rule 12.20).

1.7 In practice, the need to have the court's permission to disclose information or documents to an expert, or (under rule 12.20) to have the child examined or assessed, means that in proceedings relating to children the court strictly controls the number, fields of expertise and identity of the experts who may be first instructed and then called.

1.8 Before permission is obtained from the court to instruct an expert in proceedings relating to children, it will be necessary for the party seeking permission to make enquiries of the expert in order to provide the court with information to enable it to decide whether to give permission. In practice, enquiries may need to be made of more than one expert for this purpose. This will in turn require each expert to be given sufficient information about the case to decide whether or not he or she is in a position to accept instructions. Such preliminary enquiries, and the disclosure of information about the case which is a necessary part of such enquiries, will not require the court's permission and will not amount to a contempt of court: see sections 4.1 and 4.2 (Preliminary Enquiries of the Expert and Expert's Response to Preliminary Enquiries).

1.9 Section 4 (Proceedings relating to children) gives guidance on applying for the court's permission to instruct an expert, and on instructing the expert, in proceedings relating to children. The court, when granting permission to instruct an expert, will also give directions about the preparation and filing of the expert's report and the attendance of the expert give evidence: see section 4.4 (Draft Order for the relevant hearing).

1.10 In proceedings other than those relating to children, the court's permission is not required to instruct an expert. Section 5 (Proceedings other than those relating to children) gives guidance on instructing an expert, and on seeking the court's permission to use expert evidence, prior to and in such proceedings. Section 5 emphasises that the use of a single joint expert should be considered in all cases where expert evidence is required.

WHEN SHOULD THE COURT BE ASKED FOR PERMISSION?

1.11 Any application (or proposed application) for permission to instruct an expert or to use expert evidence should be raised with the court – and, where appropriate, with the other parties – as soon as possible. This will normally mean –

  (*a*)   in public law proceedings under the Children Act 1989, by or at the Case Management Conference: see rule 12.25;

  (*b*)   in private law proceedings under the Children Act 1989, by or at the First Hearing Dispute Resolution Appointment: see rule 12.31;

  (*c*)   in placement and adoption proceedings, by or at the First Directions Hearing: see rule 14.8;

  (*d*)   in financial proceedings, by or at the First Appointment: see rule 9.15;

  (*e*)   in defended matrimonial and civil partnership proceedings, by or at the Case Management Hearing: see rules 7.20 and 7.22.

In this practice direction the "relevant hearing" means any hearing at which the court's permission is sought to instruct an expert or to use expert evidence.

General matters

SCOPE OF THE GUIDANCE

2.1 Sections 1 to 9 of this guidance apply to all experts who are or may be instructed to give or prepare evidence for the purpose of family proceedings in a court in England and Wales. The guidance also applies to those who instruct, or propose to instruct, an expert for such a purpose. Section 10 applies to the appointment of assessors in family proceedings in England and Wales.

2.2 This guidance does not apply to proceedings issued before 6 April 2011 but in any such proceedings the court may direct that this guidance will apply either wholly or partly. This is subject to the overriding objective for the type of proceedings, and to the proviso that such a direction will neither cause further delay nor involve repetition of steps already taken or of decisions already made in the case.

PRE-APPLICATION INSTRUCTION OF EXPERTS

2.3 When experts' reports are commissioned before the commencement of proceedings, it should be made clear to the expert that he or she may in due course be reporting to the court and should therefore consider himself or herself bound by this guidance. A prospective party to family proceedings relating to children (for example, a local authority) should always write a letter of instruction when asking a potential witness for a report or an opinion, whether that request is within proceedings or pre-proceedings (for example, when commissioning specialist assessment materials, reports from a treating expert or other evidential materials); and the letter of instruction should conform to the principles set out in this guidance.

EMERGENCY AND URGENT CASES

2.4 In emergency or urgent cases – for example, where, before formal issue of proceedings, a without-notice application is made to the court during or out of business hours; or where, after proceedings have been issued, a previously unforeseen need for (further) expert evidence arises at short notice – a party may wish to call expert evidence without having complied with all or any part of this guidance. In such circumstances, the party wishing to call the expert evidence must apply forthwith to the court – where possible or appropriate, on notice to the other parties – for directions as to the future steps to be taken in respect of the expert evidence in question.

ORDERS

2.5 Where an order or direction requires an act to be done by an expert, or otherwise affects an expert, the party instructing that expert – or, in the case of a jointly instructed expert, the lead solicitor – must serve a copy of the order or direction on the expert forthwith upon receiving it.

ADULTS WHO MAY BE PROTECTED PARTIES

2.6 The court will investigate as soon as possible any issue as to whether an adult party or intended party to family proceedings lacks capacity (within the meaning of the Mental Capacity Act 2005) to conduct the proceedings. An adult who lacks capacity to act as a party to the proceedings is a protected party and must have a litigation friend to conduct the proceedings on their behalf. The expectation of the Official Solicitor is that the Official Solicitor will only be invited to act for the protected party as litigation friend if there is no other person suitable or willing to act.

2.7 Any issue as to the capacity of an adult to conduct the proceedings must be determined before the court gives any directions relevant to that adult's role in the proceedings.

2.8 Where the adult is a protected party, that party's representative should be involved in any instruction of an expert, including the instruction of an expert to assess whether the adult, although a protected party, is competent to give evidence. The instruction of an expert is a significant step in the proceedings. The representative will wish to consider (and ask the expert to consider), if the protected party is competent to give evidence, their best interests in this regard. The representative may wish to seek advice about "special measures". The representative may put forward an argument on behalf of the protected party that the protected party should not give evidence.

2.9 If at any time during the proceedings there is reason to believe that a party may lack capacity to conduct the proceedings, then the court must be notified and directions sought to ensure that this issue is investigated without delay.

CHILD LIKELY TO LACK CAPACITY TO CONDUCT THE PROCEEDINGS ON WHEN HE OR SHE REACHES 18

2.10 Where it appears that a child is –

    (*a*)   a party to the proceedings and not the subject of them;

    (*b*)   nearing age 18; and

    (*c*)   considered likely to lack capacity to conduct the proceedings when 18,

the court will consider giving directions for the child's capacity in this respect to be investigated.

The Duties of Experts

OVERRIDING DUTY

3.1 An expert in family proceedings has an overriding duty to the court that takes precedence over any obligation to the person from whom the expert has received instructions or by whom the expert is paid.

PARTICULAR DUTIES

3.2 An expert shall have regard to the following, among other, duties:

(*a*) to assist the court in accordance with the overriding duty;

(*b*) to provide advice to the court that conforms to the best practice of the expert's profession;

(*c*) to provide an opinion that is independent of the party or parties instructing the expert;

(*d*) to confine the opinion to matters material to the issues between the parties and in relation only to questions that are within the expert's expertise (skill and experience);

(*e*) where a question has been put which falls outside the expert's expertise, to state this at the earliest opportunity and to volunteer an opinion as to whether another expert is required to bring expertise not possessed by those already involved or, in the rare case, as to whether a second opinion is required on a key issue and, if possible, what questions should be asked of the second expert;

(*f*) in expressing an opinion, to take into consideration all of the material facts including any relevant factors arising from ethnic, cultural, religious or linguistic contexts at the time the opinion is expressed;

(*g*) to inform those instructing the expert without delay of any change in the opinion and of the reason for the change.

CONTENT OF THE EXPERT'S REPORT

3.3 The expert's report shall be addressed to the court and prepared and filed in accordance with the court's timetable and shall –

(*a*) give details of the expert's qualifications and experience;

(*b*) include a statement identifying the document(s) containing the material instructions and the substance of any oral instructions and, as far as necessary to explain any opinions or conclusions expressed in the report, summarising the facts and instructions which are material to the conclusions and opinions expressed;

(*c*) state who carried out any test, examination or interview which the expert has used for the report and whether or not the test, examination or interview has been carried out under the expert's supervision;

(*d*)   give details of the qualifications of any person who carried out the test, examination or interview;

(*e*)   in expressing an opinion to the court –

   (i)   take into consideration all of the material facts including any relevant factors arising from ethnic, cultural, religious or linguistic contexts at the time the opinion is expressed, identifying the facts, literature and any other material including research material that the expert has relied upon in forming an opinion;

   (ii)   describe their own professional risk assessment process and process of differential diagnosis, highlighting factual assumptions, deductions from the factual assumptions, and any unusual, contradictory or inconsistent features of the case;

   (iii)   indicate whether any proposition in the report is an hypothesis (in particular a controversial hypothesis), or an opinion deduced in accordance with peer-reviewed and tested technique, research and experience accepted as a consensus in the scientific community;

   (iv)   indicate whether the opinion is provisional (or qualified, as the case may be), stating the qualification and the reason for it, and identifying what further information is required to give an opinion without qualification;

(*f*)   where there is a range of opinion on any question to be answered by the expert –

   (i)   summarise the range of opinion;

   (ii)   identify and explain, within the range of opinions, any "unknown cause", whether arising from the facts of the case (for example, because there is too little information to form a scientific opinion) or from limited experience or lack of research, peer review or support in the relevant field of expertise;

   (iii)   give reasons for any opinion expressed: the use of a balance sheet approach to the factors that support or undermine an opinion can be of great assistance to the court;

(*g*)   contain a summary of the expert's conclusions and opinions;

(*h*)   contain a statement that the expert –

   (i)   has no conflict of interest of any kind, other than any conflict disclosed in his or her report;

   (ii)   does not consider that any interest disclosed affects his or her suitability as an expert witness on any issue on which he or she has given evidence;

   (iii)   will advise the instructing party if, between the date of the expert's report and the final hearing, there is any change in circumstances which affects the expert's answers to (i) or (ii) above;

    (iv) understands their duty to the court and has complied with that duty; and

    (v) is aware of the requirements of Part 25 and this practice direction;

  (*i*) be verified by a statement of truth in the following form –

"I confirm that I have made clear which facts and matters referred to in this report are within my own knowledge and which are not. Those that are within my own knowledge I confirm to be true. The opinions I have expressed represent my true and complete professional opinions on the matters to which they refer."

(Part 17 deals with statements of truth. Rule 17.6 sets out the consequences of verifying a document containing a false statement without an honest belief in its truth.)

Proceedings relating to children

Preparation for the relevant hearing

PRELIMINARY ENQUIRIES OF THE EXPERT

4.1 In good time for the information requested to be available for the relevant hearing or for the advocates' meeting or discussion where one takes place before the relevant hearing, the solicitor for the party proposing to instruct the expert (or lead solicitor or solicitor for the child if the instruction proposed is joint) shall approach the expert with the following information –

  (*a*) the nature of the proceedings and the issues likely to require determination by the court;

  (*b*) the questions about which the expert is to be asked to give an opinion (including any ethnic, cultural, religious or linguistic contexts);

  (*c*) the date when the court is to be asked to give permission for the instruction (or if – unusually – permission has already been given, the date and details of that permission);

  (*d*) whether permission is to be asked of the court for the instruction of another expert in the same or any related field (that is, to give an opinion on the same or related questions);

  (*e*) the volume of reading which the expert will need to undertake;

  (*f*) whether or not permission has been applied for or given for the expert to examine the child;

  (*g*) whether or not it will be necessary for the expert to conduct interviews – and, if so, with whom;

  (*h*) the likely timetable of legal and social work steps;

  (*i*) in care and supervision proceedings, any dates in the Timetable for the Child which would be relevant to the proposed timetable for the assessment;

  (*j*) when the expert's report is likely to be required;

(*k*)   whether and, if so, what date has been fixed by the court for any hearing at which the expert may be required to give evidence (in particular the Final Hearing); and whether it may be possible for the expert to give evidence by telephone conference or video link: see section 8 (Arrangements for experts to give evidence) below;

(*l*)   the possibility of making, through their instructing solicitors, representations to the court about being named or otherwise identified in any public judgment given by the court.

It is essential that there should be proper co-ordination between the court and the expert when drawing up the case management timetable: the needs of the court should be balanced with the needs of the expert whose forensic work is undertaken as an adjunct to his or her main professional duties.

EXPERT'S RESPONSE TO PRELIMINARY ENQUIRIES

4.2 In good time for the relevant hearing or for the advocates' meeting or discussion where one takes place before the relevant hearing, the solicitors intending to instruct the expert shall obtain confirmation from the expert –

(*a*)   that acceptance of the proposed instructions will not involve the expert in any conflict of interest;

(*b*)   that the work required is within the expert's expertise;

(*c*)   that the expert is available to do the relevant work within the suggested time scale;

(*d*)   when the expert is available to give evidence, of the dates and times to avoid and, where a hearing date has not been fixed, of the amount of notice the expert will require to make arrangements to come to court (or to give evidence by telephone conference or video link) without undue disruption to his or her normal professional routines;

(*e*)   of the cost, including hourly or other charging rates, and likely hours to be spent, attending experts' meetings, attending court and writing the report (to include any examinations and interviews);

(*f*)   of any representations which the expert wishes to make to the court about being named or otherwise identified in any public judgment given by the court.

Where parties have not agreed on the appointment of a single joint expert before the relevant hearing, they should obtain the above confirmations in respect of all experts whom they intend to put to the court for the purposes of rule 25.7(2)(*a*) as candidates for the appointment.

THE PROPOSAL TO INSTRUCT AN EXPERT

4.3 Any party who proposes to ask the court for permission to instruct an expert shall, by 11 a.m. on the business day before the relevant hearing, file and serve a written proposal to instruct the expert, in the following detail –

- (*a*) the name, discipline, qualifications and expertise of the expert (by way of C.V. where possible);
- (*b*) the expert's availability to undertake the work;
- (*c*) the relevance of the expert evidence sought to be adduced to the issues in the proceedings and the specific questions upon which it is proposed that the expert should give an opinion (including the relevance of any ethnic, cultural, religious or linguistic contexts);
- (*d*) the timetable for the report;
- (*e*) the responsibility for instruction;
- (*f*) whether or not the expert evidence can properly be obtained by the joint instruction of the expert by two or more of the parties;
- (*g*) whether the expert evidence can properly be obtained by only one party (for example, on behalf of the child);
- (*h*) why the expert evidence proposed cannot be given by social services undertaking a core assessment or by the Children's Guardian in accordance with their respective statutory duties;
- (*i*) the likely cost of the report on an hourly or other charging basis: where possible, the expert's terms of instruction should be made available to the court;
- (*j*) the proposed apportionment (at least in the first instance) of any jointly instructed expert's fee; when it is to be paid; and, if applicable, whether public funding has been approved.

DRAFT ORDER FOR THE RELEVANT HEARING

4.4 Any party proposing to instruct an expert shall, **by 11 a.m. on the business day before the relevant hearing**, submit to the court a draft order for directions dealing in particular with –

- (*a*) the party who is to be responsible for drafting the letter of instruction and providing the documents to the expert;
- (*b*) the issues identified by the court and the questions about which the expert is to give an opinion;
- (*c*) the timetable within which the report is to be prepared, filed and served;
- (*d*) the disclosure of the report to the parties and to any other expert;
- (*e*) the organisation of, preparation for and conduct of an experts' discussion;
- (*f*) the preparation of a statement of agreement and disagreement by the experts following an experts' discussion;
- (*g*) making available to the court at an early opportunity the expert reports in electronic form;

(*h*)   the attendance of the expert at court to give oral evidence
        (alternatively, the expert giving his or her evidence in writing or
        remotely by video link), whether at or for the Final Hearing or
        another hearing; unless agreement about the opinions given by
        the expert is reached at or before the Issues Resolution Hearing
        ("IRH") or, if no IRH is to be held, by a specified date prior to
        the hearing at which the expert is to give oral evidence ("the
        specified date").

Letter of Instruction

4.5 The solicitor or party instructing the expert shall, **within 5 business
days after the relevant hearing**, prepare (in agreement with the other
parties where appropriate), file and serve a letter of instruction to the
expert which shall –

(*a*)   set out the context in which the expert's opinion is sought
        (including any ethnic, cultural, religious or linguistic contexts);
(*b*)   set out the specific questions which the expert is required to
        answer, ensuring that they –
        (i)   are within the ambit of the expert's area of expertise;
        (ii)   do not contain unnecessary or irrelevant detail;
        (iii) are kept to a manageable number and are clear, focused and
               direct; and
        (iv)   reflect what the expert has been requested to do by the
               court.

        (The Annex to this guidance sets out suggested questions in letters
        of instruction to (1) child mental health professionals or
        paediatricians, and (2) adult psychiatrists and applied psychologists,
        in Children Act 1989 proceedings.)

(*c*)   list the documentation provided, or provide for the expert an
        indexed and paginated bundle which shall include –
        (i)   a copy of the order (or those parts of the order) which gives
               permission for the instruction of the expert, immediately
               the order becomes available;
        (ii)   an agreed list of essential reading; and
        (iii) a copy of this guidance;
(*d*)   identify any materials provided to the expert which have not been
        produced either as original medical (or other professional)
        records or in response to an instruction from a party, and state
        the source of that material (such materials may contain an
        assumption as to the standard of proof, the admissibility or
        otherwise of hearsay evidence, and other important procedural
        and substantive questions relating to the different purposes of
        other enquiries, for example, criminal or disciplinary proceed-
        ings);

(e) identify all requests to third parties for disclosure and their responses, to avoid partial disclosure, which tends only to prove a case rather than give full and frank information;

(f) identify the relevant people concerned with the proceedings (for example, the treating clinicians) and inform the expert of his or her right to talk to them provided that an accurate record is made of the discussions;

(g) identify any other expert instructed in the proceedings and advise the expert of their right to talk to the other experts provided that an accurate record is made of the discussions;

(h) subject to any public funding requirement for prior authority, define the contractual basis upon which the expert is retained and in particular the funding mechanism including how much the expert will be paid (an hourly rate and overall estimate should already have been obtained), when the expert will be paid, and what limitation there might be on the amount the expert can charge for the work which they will have to do. In cases where the parties are publicly funded, there should also be a brief explanation of the costs and expenses excluded from public funding by Funding Code criterion 1.3 and the detailed assessment process.

ASKING THE COURT TO SETTLE THE LETTER OF INSTRUCTION TO A SINGLE JOINT EXPERT

4.6 Where possible, the written request for the court to consider the letter of instruction referred to in rule 25.8(2) should be set out in an e-mail to the court (or, by prior arrangement, directly to the judge dealing with the proceedings) and copied by e-mail to the other instructing parties. In the Family Proceedings Court, the request should be sent to the legal adviser who will refer it to the appropriate judge or justices, if necessary). The court will settle the letter of instruction, usually without a hearing to avoid delay; and will send (where practicable, by e-mail) the settled letter to the lead solicitor for transmission forthwith to the expert, and copy it to the other instructing parties for information.

KEEPING THE EXPERT UP TO DATE WITH NEW DOCUMENTS

4.7 As often as may be necessary, the expert should be provided promptly with a copy of any new document filed at court, together with an updated document list or bundle index.

Proceedings other than those relating to children

5.1 Wherever possible, expert evidence should be obtained from a single joint expert instructed by both or all the parties ("SJE"). To that end, a party wishing to instruct an expert should first give the other party or parties a list of the names of one or more experts in the relevant speciality whom they consider suitable to be instructed.

5.2 Within 10 days after receipt of the list of proposed experts, the other party or parties should indicate any objection to one or more of the named experts and, if so, supply the name(s) of one or more experts whom they consider suitable.

5.3 Each party should disclose whether they have already consulted any of the proposed experts about the issue(s) in question.

5.4 Where the parties cannot agree on the identity of the expert, each party should think carefully before instructing their own expert because of the costs implications. Disagreements about the use and identity of an expert may be better managed by the court in the context of an application for directions (see paragraphs 5.8 and 5.9 below).

AGREEMENT TO INSTRUCT SEPARATE EXPERTS

5.5 If the parties agree to instruct separate experts –

(a) they should agree in advance that the reports will be disclosed; and

(b) the instructions to each expert should comply, so far as appropriate, with paragraphs 4.5 to 4.7 above (Letter of instruction).

AGREEMENT TO INSTRUCT AN SJE

5.6 If there is agreement to instruct an SJE, **before instructions are given** the parties should –

(a) so far as appropriate, comply with the guidance in paragraphs 4.1 (Preliminary inquiries of the expert) and 4.2 (Expert's confirmation in response to preliminary enquiries) above;

(b) have agreed in what proportion the SJE's fee is to be shared between them (at least in the first instance) and when it is to be paid; and

(c) if applicable, have obtained agreement for public funding.

4.7 The instructions to the SJE should comply, so far as appropriate, with paragraphs 4.5 to 4.7 above (Letter of instruction).

SEEKING THE COURT'S DIRECTIONS FOR THE USE OF AN SJE

5.8 Where the parties seek the court's directions for the use of an SJE, they should comply, so far as appropriate, with paragraphs 4.1 to 4.4 (Preparation for the relevant hearing) above.

5.9 The instructions to the SJE should comply, so far as appropriate, with paragraphs 4.5 to 4.7 above (Letter of instruction).

The Court's control of expert evidence: consequential issues

WRITTEN QUESTIONS

6.1 Where –

(a) written questions are put to an expert in accordance with rule 25.6, the court will specify the timetable according to which the expert is to answer the written questions;

(b) a party sends a written question or questions under rule 25.6 direct to an expert, a copy of the questions must, at the same time, be sent to the other party or parties.

EXPERTS' DISCUSSION OR MEETING: PURPOSE

6.2 In accordance with rule 25.12, the court may, at any stage, direct a discussion between experts for the purpose outlined in paragraph (1) of that rule. Rule 25.12(2) provides that the court may specify the issues which the experts must discuss. The expectation is that those issues will include-

(a) the reasons for disagreement on any expert question and what, if any, action needs to be taken to resolve any outstanding disagreement or question;

(b) explanation of existing evidence or additional evidence in order to assist the court to determine the issues.

One of the aims of the specification of those issues for discussion is to limit, wherever possible, the need for the experts to attend court to give oral evidence.

EXPERTS' DISCUSSION OR MEETING: ARRANGEMENTS

6.3 Subject to the directions given by the court under rule 25.12, the solicitor or other professional who is given the responsibility by the court ("the nominated professional") shall – **within 15 business days after the experts' reports have been filed and copied to the other parties** – make arrangements for the experts to meet or communicate. Subject to any specification by the court of the issues which experts must discuss under rule 25.12(2), the following matters should be considered as appropriate –

(a) where permission has been given for the instruction of experts from different disciplines, a global discussion may be held relating to those questions that concern all or most of them;

(b) separate discussions may have to be held among experts from the same or related disciplines, but care should be taken to ensure that the discussions complement each other so that related questions are discussed by all relevant experts;

(c) **5 business days prior to a discussion or meeting**, the nominated professional should formulate an agenda including a list of questions for consideration. The agenda should, subject always to the provisions of rule 25.12(1), focus on those questions which are intended to clarify areas of agreement or disagreement.

Questions which repeat questions asked in the letter of instruction or which seek to rehearse cross-examination in advance of the hearing should be rejected as likely to defeat the purpose of the meeting.

The agenda may usefully take the form of a list of questions to be circulated among the other parties in advance and should comprise all questions that each party wishes the experts to consider.

The agenda and list of questions should be sent to each of the experts **not later than 2 business days before the discussion;**

(d)   the nominated professional may exercise his or her discretion to accept further questions after the agenda with list of questions has been circulated to the parties. **Only in exceptional circumstances should questions be added to the agenda within the 2-day period before the meeting. Under no circumstances should any question received on the day of or during the meeting be accepted**. This does not preclude questions arising during the meeting for the purposes of clarification. Strictness in this regard is vital, for adequate notice of the questions enables the parties to identify and isolate the expert issues in the case before the meeting so that the experts' discussion at the meeting can concentrate on those issues;

(e)   the discussion should be chaired by the nominated professional. A minute must be taken of the questions answered by the experts. Where the court has given a direction under rule 25.12(3) and subject to that direction, a Statement of Agreement and Disagreement must be prepared which should be agreed and signed by each of the experts who participated in the discussion. In accordance with rule 25.12(3) the statement must contain a summary of the experts' reasons for disagreeing. The statement should be served and filed **not later than 5 business days after the discussion has taken place;**

(f)   in each case, whether some or all of the experts participate by telephone conference or video link to ensure that minimum disruption is caused to professional schedules and that costs are minimised.

MEETINGS OR CONFERENCES ATTENDED BY A JOINTLY INSTRUCTED EXPERT

6.4 Jointly instructed experts should not attend any meeting or conference which is not a joint one, unless all the parties have agreed in writing or the court has directed that such a meeting may be held, and it is agreed or directed who is to pay the expert's fees for the meeting or conference. Any meeting or conference attended by a jointly instructed expert should be proportionate to the case.

COURT-DIRECTED MEETINGS INVOLVING EXPERTS IN PUBLIC LAW
CHILDREN ACT CASES

6.5 In public law Children Act proceedings, where the court gives a
direction that a meeting shall take place between the local authority and
any relevant named experts for the purpose of providing assistance to the
local authority in the formulation of plans and proposals for the child, the
meeting shall be arranged, chaired and minuted in accordance with the
directions given by the court.

Positions of the Parties

7.1 Where a party refuses to be bound by an agreement that has been
reached at an experts' discussion or meeting, that party must inform the
court and the other parties in writing, **within 10 business days after the
discussion or meeting or, where an IRH is to be held, not less than 5 business
days before the IRH**, of his or her reasons for refusing to accept the
agreement.

Arrangements for Experts to give evidence

PREPARATION

8.1 Where the court has directed the attendance of an expert witness, the
party who is responsible for the instruction of the expert shall, **by the
specified date or, where an IRH is to be held, by the IRH**, ensure that –

- (*a*)   a date and time (if possible, convenient to the expert) are fixed for
  the court to hear the expert's evidence, substantially in advance of
  the hearing at which the expert is to give oral evidence and no
  later than a specified date prior to that hearing or, where an IRH
  is to be held, than the IRH;
- (*b*)   if the expert's oral evidence is not required, the expert is notified
  as soon as possible;
- (*c*)   the witness template accurately indicates how long the expert is
  likely to be giving evidence, in order to avoid the inconvenience of
  the expert being delayed at court;
- (*d*)   consideration is given in each case to whether some or all of the
  experts participate by telephone conference or video link, or
  submit their evidence in writing, to ensure that minimum
  disruption is caused to professional schedules and that costs are
  minimised.

EXPERTS ATTENDING COURT

8.2 Where expert witnesses are to be called, all parties shall, **by the
specified date or, where an IRH is to be held, by the IRH**, ensure that –

(a) the parties' advocates have identified (whether at an advocates' meeting or by other means) the issues which the experts are to address;

(b) wherever possible, a logical sequence to the evidence is arranged, with experts of the same discipline giving evidence on the same day;

(c) the court is informed of any circumstance where all experts agree but a party nevertheless does not accept the agreed opinion, so that directions can be given for the proper consideration of the experts' evidence and opinion and of the party's reasons for not accepting the agreed opinion;

(d) in the exceptional case the court is informed of the need for a witness summons.

Action after the Final Hearing

9.1 **Within 10 business days after the Final Hearing**, the solicitor instructing the expert shall inform the expert in writing of the outcome of the case, and of the use made by the court of the expert's opinion.

9.2 Where the court directs preparation of a transcript, it may also direct that the solicitor instructing the expert shall send a copy to the **expert within 10 business days after receiving the transcript**.

9.3 After a Final Hearing in the Family Proceedings Court, the (lead) solicitor instructing the expert shall send the expert a copy of the court's written reasons for its decision **within 10 business days after receiving the written reasons**.

Appointment of assessors in family proceedings

10.1 The power to appoint one or more assessors to assist the court is conferred on the High Court by section 70(1) of the Senior Courts Act 1981, and on a county court by section 63(1) of the County Courts Act 1984. In practice, these powers have been used in appeals from a district judge or costs judge in costs assessment proceedings – although, in principle, the statutory powers permit one or more assessors to be appointed in any family proceedings where the High Court or a county court sees fit.

10.2 **Not less than 21 days before making any such appointment**, the court will notify each party in writing of the name of the proposed assessor, of the matter in respect of which the assistance of the assessor will be sought and of the qualifications of the assessor to give that assistance.

10.3 Any party may object to the proposed appointment, either personally or in respect of the proposed assessor's qualifications.

10.4 Any such objection must be made in writing and filed and served **within 7 business days of receipt of the notification from the court of the**

proposed appointment, and will be taken into account by the court in deciding whether or not to make the appointment.

Annex

(drafted by the Family Justice Council)

Suggested questions in letters of instruction to child mental health professional or paediatrician in Children Act 1989 proceedings

A. The Child(ren)

1 Please describe the child(ren)'s current health, development and functioning (according to your area of expertise), and identify the nature of any significant changes which have occurred

- Behavioural
- Emotional
- Attachment organisation
- Social/peer/sibling relationships
- Cognitive/educational
- Physical
    - Growth, eating, sleep
    - Non-organic physical problems (including wetting and soiling)
    - Injuries
    - Paediatric conditions

2 Please comment on the likely explanation for/aetiology of the child(ren)'s problems/difficulties/injuries

- History/experiences (including intrauterine influences, and abuse and neglect)
- Genetic/innate/developmental difficulties
- Paediatric/psychiatric disorders

3 Please provide a prognosis and risk if difficulties not addressed above.

4 Please describe the child(ren)'s needs in the light of the above

- Nature of care-giving
- Education
- Treatment

in the short and long term (subject, where appropriate, to further assessment later).

B. The parents/primary carers

5 Please describe the factors and mechanisms which would explain the parents' (or primary carers) harmful or neglectful interactions with the child(ren) (if relevant).

6 What interventions have been tried and what has been the result?

7 Please assess the ability of the parents or primary carers to fulfil the child(ren)'s identified needs now.

8 What other assessments of the parents or primary carers are indicated?

- Adult mental health assessment
- Forensic risk assessment
- Physical assessment
- Cognitive assessment

9 What, if anything, is needed to assist the parents or primary carers now, within the child(ren)'s time scales and what is the prognosis for change?

- Parenting work
- Support
- Treatment/therapy

C. Alternatives

10 Please consider the alternative possibilities for the fulfilment of the child(ren)'s needs

- What sort of placement
- Contact arrangements

Please consider the advantages, disadvantages and implications of each for the child(ren).

Suggested questions in letters of instruction to adult psychiatrists and applied psychologists in Children Act 1989 proceedings

1 Does the parent/adult have – whether in his/her history or presentation – a mental illness/disorder (including substance abuse) or other psychological/emotional difficulty and, if so, what is the diagnosis?

2 How do any/all of the above (and their current treatment if applicable) affect his/her functioning, including interpersonal relationships?

3 If the answer to Q1 is yes, are there any features of either the mental illness or psychological/emotional difficulty or personality disorder which could be associated with risk to others, based on the available evidence base (whether published studies or evidence from clinical experience)?

4 What are the experiences/antecedents/aetiology which would explain his/her difficulties, if any, (taking into account any available evidence base or other clinical experience)?

5 What treatment is indicated, what is its nature and the likely duration?

6 What is his/her capacity to engage in/partake of the treatment/therapy?

7 Are you able to indicate the prognosis for, time scales for achieving, and likely durability of, change?

8 What other factors might indicate positive change?

(It is assumed that this opinion will be based on collateral information as well as interviewing the adult).

CHAPTER 5

PROTECTED PARTIES/PARTIES UNDER A DISABILITY

5.1 ADULTS

The legal presumption that adults are competent to conduct proceedings until otherwise proved, may be displaced in any case by evidence to the contrary on the balance of probabilities.

The Mental Capacity Act 2005 has substituted a new test of capacity in the civil courts to that hitherto used by the courts which was derived from the Mental Health Act 1983.

The new Act clearly separates the issues of mental health and capacity. A person suffering from mental health problems may also be found to be incapable of conducting proceedings under the MCA 2005, but from October 2007 the Civil Procedure Rules and Family Procedure Rules have abandoned the old language of 'patient' and 'person under a disability', as well as references to the test in the Mental Health Act.

The principles of CPR 1998, Pt 21 and Practice Direction now appear in FPR 2010, Pt 15 and confirm:

- 'lacks capacity' means lacks capacity within the meaning of the 2005 Act;

- 'protected party' means a party, or an intended party, who lacks capacity to conduct proceedings;

- a protected party must have a litigation friend to conduct proceedings on his behalf.

The Family Procedure Rules 2010 carry through these changes formally into the language of family proceedings. However the person who conducts the proceedings on the patient's behalf, referred to as the litigation friend in civil proceedings, is still in family proceedings to be referred to as the next friend if they apply for an order; or the guardian ad litem if they act as respondent. In specified proceedings, therefore, there will be a children's guardian for the children who are the subject of proceedings, and a next friend or guardian ad litem for any protected party.

5.2   A TEST FOR CAPACITY – MENTAL CAPACITY ACT 2005

By s 2 of the MCA 2005:

'2. People who lack capacity

(1) ... a person lacks capacity in relation to a matter if at the material time he is unable to make a decision for himself in relation to the matter because of an impairment of, or a disturbance in the functioning of, the mind or brain.

(2) It does not matter whether the impairment or disturbance is permanent or temporary.

(3) A lack of capacity cannot be established merely by reference to–
(a)   a person's age or appearance, or
(b)   a condition of his, or an aspect of his behaviour, which might lead others to make unjustified assumptions about his capacity.

(4) In proceedings under this Act or any other enactment, any question whether a person lacks capacity within the meaning of this Act must be decided on the balance of probabilities ...

3. Inability to make decisions

(1) For the purposes of section 2, a person is unable to make a decision for himself if he is unable–
(a)   to understand the information relevant to the decision,
(b)   to retain that information,
(c)   to use or weigh that information as part of the process of making the decision, or
(d)   to communicate his decision (whether by talking, using sign language or any other means).

(2) A person is not to be regarded as unable to understand the information relevant to a decision if he is able to understand an explanation of it given to him in a way that is appropriate to his circumstances (using simple language, visual aids or any other means).

(3) The fact that a person is able to retain the information relevant to a decision for a short period only does not prevent him from being regarded as able to make the decision.

(4) The information relevant to a decision includes information about the reasonably foreseeable consequences of–
(a) deciding one way or another, or

(b) failing to make the decision.'

The Act and its supporting Code of Practice can be accessed at www.publicguardian.gsi.gov.uk.

Learning difficulties, mental health problems, brain injury, communication difficulties, and physical disabilities may all lead to a similar difficulty in negotiating legal proceedings to the inexpert eye.

Capability should not be confused with capacity, although it may equally require special measures to ensure equal treatment. Many parties to proceedings may have learning difficulties that would bring them within the definition of disability for the purposes of the Disability Discrimination Act 1995 and the legislation related to the provision of services for disabled persons, but they will have capacity for the purposes of the Mental Capacity Act 2005.

5.3 CHILDREN

In the amended Rules children – ie aged under 18 – are no longer universally described with relevant adults as being 'under a disability', but simply as children.

Children may be involved in specified proceedings where they are not the subject of the application for care or supervision and also where they themselves are applicants; eg for orders for contact. Such children will also need to act through a litigation friend in the CPR terminology.

A court may make an order permitting a child who is a party to carry on proceedings without a next friend or guardian ad litem (FPR 2010, r 16.6 and PD).

5.4 CHILDREN WHO ARE PARENTS

Children who are parents of children who are the subject of proceedings are 'parents' for the purposes of interpretation, and references to children within the procedural rules refer, unless the context otherwise requires, to the subject children.

The human rights of the child applicant are themselves of great significance, and may be expected to be given the enhanced weight of the child as against the adult party. The court will consider the welfare checklist as relevant in determining the balance in relation to that applicant, but will conduct the analysis systematically for each application under consideration.

The power of the court to direct that the child may carry on proceedings without a litigation friend may be appropriate where a child is of sufficient age and understanding, but it is a decision which must be addressed on a case-by-case basis, and cannot be assumed from the fact of the child's own parentage of the child who is the subject of proceedings.

5.5   OTHER PARTIES WHO ARE PROTECTED PARTIES

Non-parents may be protected parties themselves (separately represented applicants), for an alternative disposal such as a residence order, or persons joined for a limited purpose such as persons implicated as perpetrators for a finding of fact hearing. They will be subject to the same procedural and other considerations as parents who are protected persons for the currency of their involvement in proceedings.

5.6   PARENTS OR OTHER PARTIES WITH MENTAL HEALTH PROBLEMS

A history of mental health problems in a parent or other party is a factor which will need careful consideration in children proceedings. Where it is argued that the nature of the problem may affect the particular issue that the court has to decide, or where there is an associated issue of capacity for litigation purposes or capability to carry through plans for the child it is likely that there will be a need for psychiatric expert evidence. Psychiatric evidence should be obtained from the relevant specialty within psychiatry depending on the type of illness/injury.

It is rarely appropriate to rely solely on the evidence of current treating physicians if the mental health of a party is likely to be a factor in the issues before the court. There will always be the problem of professional objectivity and importantly the loss of confidentiality and trust in this relationship might have an adverse impact upon the health of the party involved possibly in the long term.

Decision-making and expert evidence should address the separate factors that the mental health problem presents in the case. Instructions, invariably joint, should be compiled with great care and histories (which may be difficult to trace accurately) checked and included:

(1)   Is there associated lack of capacity, and is this permanent, long-term, transitory or episodic?

(2)   Is there a lack of capability to meet needs or recognise problems?

(3)   Risk assessment: is there increased risk, is this long-term, short-term or episodic, what is the level of risk and what counter-measures are appropriate?

(4)   What is the diagnosis, prognosis and relevant history?

(5)   Is treatment effective?

5.7   SERVICES TO ASSIST PARENTS WITH A LEARNING DISABILITY

Those acting for parents with moderate or mild learning difficulties will wish to ensure that their clients are receiving the support services that will maximise the chances of successfully parenting their children, by reference to *Fair Access to Care Services: Guidance on eligibility criteria for adult social care* (DoH, 2002).

The Department of Health and DFES have also jointly issued *Good Practice Guidance on Working with Parents with a Learning Disability* (2007) which identifies five key features of good practice in working with parents with learning disabilities:

(1)   accessible information and communication;

(2)   clear and coordinated referral and assessment procedures and processes, eligibility criteria and care pathways;

(3)   support designed to meet the needs of parents and children based on assessment of their needs and strengths;

(4)   long-term support, where necessary;

(5)   access to independent advocacy.

Local authorities should set local protocols that clearly specify responsibilities for assessment and care planning.

Services should be targeted at families who have additional need, which may require a different interpretation of the criteria relating to the threshold for service provision than that currently operated by specialist teams for adult services generally.

The combination of impairment and parenting responsibilities within the overall context of the individual family's circumstances may generate a higher degree of need for support than a personal assessment of the disabled/ill adult alone.

> 'Disabled parents or children of disabled parents should automatically be entitled to an assessment' (Norfolk County Council, 2006 policy statement).

Adults with a learning disability may have an extensive history of dependence on services, reliance on professional advice and decision-making, and be especially disempowered in any debate with those services in the absence of advocacy.

5.7.1   Issues

- Has there been a full cognitive functioning assessment?

- Has there been a proper assessment of eligibility for adult support services and has this been reviewed against the party's needs as a parent?

- Have wider family resources been engaged and utilised?

- Are appropriate specialist support services being provided? (Eg specialist health visitor/structured programmes.)

- Have child protection social workers taken advice from adult services workers in conducting assessments and devising interventions?

- Has 'Person Centred Planning' been carried out?

- Has a communication strategy been devised which takes into account the special vulnerability of the parent?

- Has advocacy been offered and what steps have been taken to demonstrate that the family understand the issues?

- Have appropriate expert help/services been sought to respond to special needs?

5.8   PROCEDURE WHERE A PARENT OR OTHER PARTY IS A PROTECTED PARTY

Without the permission of the court, a protected party may not take any step in proceedings, save for issuing and service of proceedings, without the appointment of a litigation friend/guardian ad litem.

Proceedings may not be continued without such an appointment where lack of capacity becomes apparent only as matters progress. This is not uncommon, as applying the tests outlined above, those instructed by people with learning disabilities may wish this issue to be reviewed. This may particularly be the case where the quality of decisions becomes more complex.

The Official Solicitor will be invited by the procedural judge to act where lack of capacity becomes apparent whereas previously this issue required transfer to the county court, now under the Family Procedure Rules 2010 Part 15 (and associated Practice Directions). Magistrates and family proceedings courts may also invite the Official Solicitor to become involved.

The Family Justice Council recommend that Standard Directions, if a professional litigation friend or the Official Solicitor is to be invited to act, should be as follows:

> 'That X (named party) forward to Y/Official Solicitor forthwith:
> (a) a copy of the order appointing the litigation friend/inviting the Official Solicitor to act;
> (b) a detailed letter of background information, including the stage of proceedings reached and the date of any pending hearing;
> (c) a paginated bundle with summary, statement of issues, and chronology.'

Before consenting to act, the Official Solicitor will require a report from some suitably qualified person (usually a psychiatrist or psychologist) confirming lack of capacity.

The Official Solicitor has issued Practice Notes for appointment in family proceedings and urgent appointments. In the absence of any other willing and suitable person (who may be someone in the family circle provided no insuperable conflict of interest arises) the Official Solicitor will act as next friend or guardian ad litem for a person under a disability, or for a child party whose own welfare is not the subject of family proceedings. Under the Public Law Outline, initial telephone contact may be advisable to ensure that decisions are made as to representation, in time for case management hearings.

Where, as may be more commonly the case in private law proceedings, the court is asked to approve the appointment of some person other than the Official Solicitor (who will always require to be paid) it is of the utmost importance to bear in mind the Practice Direction to FPR 2010, Part 15 which requires that the person has no interest adverse to that of the protected party and can fairly and competently conduct proceedings on their behalf. Experience shows that this condition may not always be or remain satisfied, and removal is therefore occasionally necessary.

Previously, service rules were criticised because, illogically, a court could decide that it was not satisfied that a person had capacity to conduct proceedings, yet serve that order upon the person. FPR 2010 completely revise these procedures in relation to service of documents on persons under a disability – dealing with service not only where a litigation friend has already been appointed but also prospectively where it is anticipated one should be appointed, under the procedure set out in FPR 2010, r 15.8.

The court may still also direct service upon the person themselves and it should be remembered that this new and complete procedural code builds on many principles previously confined to the civil courts to allow the court to deal flexibly and imaginatively with many routine procedural difficulties of this nature.

Where a parent lacks litigation capacity the court equally will have to consider carefully how it deals with matters expressed to be 'by consent'. In such cases, it must be appreciated that it is very improbable that s/he has the capacity to consent to other decisions intended to have legal effect outside the court process, for example to their child being accommodated under s 20 of CA 1989. This doubt will become certainty after a court has adjudicated upon a permanent lack of capacity, and parties equally should consider with care where other capacity-related processes have taken place which raise the inference that the person concerned lacks capacity on a permanent basis. In *Re W (Care Proceedings)*[1] the court did not accept that a guilty plea for the purposes of criminal proceedings over an injury to the child was conclusive in view of the alleged perpetrator's borderline and fluctuating capacity and conducted a fact-finding hearing.

Those under a duty to make decisions on behalf of those who lack capacity are obliged to consider the 'best interests' of that person and the revised Public Law Outline of April 2010 specifically reminds representatives of their duty to consider how best interests may be served in the way they contribute to proceedings.

Where vitiated capacity or poor mental health makes it more difficult to cope with proceedings the court is likely to consider this a relevant factor in considering the presence of media in or reporting of proceedings in order to protect the human rights of the party to be fully involved in those proceedings. In cases of substantial public interest, limited reporting may be permitted 'on the basis that it was for the media to demonstrate what should be allowed, rather than the vulnerable adult having to show what should be restricted'.

It can be helpful to address vitiated capacity imaginatively in the conduct of proceedings. Familiar advocates may assist the legal representative and the party. Decision-making may be broken down into discrete parts, or a hearing may address issues in step-wise fashion. Simple summaries of outcomes can be written and a menu for future hearings. It is essential that the court properly adjust its processes to balance the needs of all parties, including those with capacity issues.

Local authorities anticipating the need to issue specified proceedings should demonstrate they have considered these aspects pre-proceedings.

---

[1]   [2008] EWHC 1188.

Notwithstanding the rule revision permitting magistrates to invite the Official Solicitor to act, in care cases the FJC advise that if there is evidence as to lack of parental capacity to conduct the proceedings, the FPC should transfer the case immediately for first appointment in the Care Centre.

5.9   THE OVERRIDING OBJECTIVE

There is one provision of the FPR 2010 that will be of particular interest to those involved in cases with protected parties, or people with any degree of vitiated capacity or disability, and that is the terminology of the new Overriding Objective.

This, the cornerstone of the FPR, is contained in r 1.1(1) and is designed to give a new ethos to all family litigation.

> 'These rules are a **new** procedural code with the overriding objective of enabling the court to deal with cases justly, **having regard to any welfare issues involved.**'

Practitioners should note that 'any welfare issues' may arise not only in cases involving children, but also in those involving adults, to include adults who lack mental capacity, or are in some other way vulnerable. The extent of lack of capacity will comprise those who are protected parties but is not limited to this group.

All that has been said above, about the need to adopt procedures inside and outside the court which are adapted to the needs of those with capacity issues, is reinforced by the terminology with which this rule continues:

> '(2) Dealing with a case justly includes, so far as is practicable–
>   ...
> (c)   ensuring that the parties are on an equal footing;
>   ...'

5.10   GOOD PRACTICE IN PROCEEDINGS WHERE A PARENT HAS LEARNING DIFFICULTIES

The case of *Enfield London Borough Council v SA, FA and KA*[2] involved an adult who had alleged abuse and who gave an Achieving Best Evidence interview without the involvement of the Official Solicitor.

It was held that such evidence is admissible under the Court of Protection Rules 2007, r 95(d), its weight to be a matter for specific evaluation in each case. In the absence of absolutely pressing emergency this may be

---

[2]   [2010] EWHC 196 (Admin).

raised with the court, but in every case (even where it is not appropriate to give notice to another party against whom allegations are made) notice should be given to the litigation friend. Even where rules about obtaining evidence from protected parties are broken, the court may decide that evidence may still be used, but the litigation friend will have to be involved in that decision.

A *Protocol on Advice and Advocacy for Parents (Child Protection)*[3] considers the impact of specialist advocacy in supporting parents with learning disabilities.

The court may order that the involvement of a specialist learning disability advocate is an appropriate disbursement on a legal aid certificate, even where the party has sufficient capacity to instruct a solicitor on their own behalf.

During hearings, the principles of communication should be adhered to, in order to supply parents' access needs, and ensure Art 6 compliance: These may include:

- putting written material into an accessible format;

- avoiding the use of jargon;

- taking more time to explain things;

- telling parents things more than once.

Care is needed in selection of the appropriate expert to report on the party in question. While an initial assessment of capacity may be sought from a general practice psychiatrist, it will generally be necessary for any more detailed expert assessment to be obtained from a practitioner specialising in learning disabilities, brain injury, dual diagnosis, or whatever description of disability or difficulty the individual presents. The voluntary sector may be able to advise on selection of the appropriate expert.

5.11 PRINCIPLES OF DECISION-MAKING WHERE A PARENT HAS LEARNING DIFFICULTIES

- The best person to bring up a child is the natural parent. It matters not whether the parent is wise or foolish, rich or poor, educated or illiterate, provided the child's moral and physical health are not endangered.[4]

---

3   dh4018900 (Department of Health).
4   *Re KD (A Minor) (Ward: Termination of Access)* [1988] AC 806.

- Care proceedings are not social engineering.[5]

- Changes are to be expected when a child is in foster care.[6]

- Caution in extrapolating future risk.[7]

- Diagnostic psychometric assessments can provide information about whether a parent has a learning disability and about their skills and abilities. However:[8]

  > 'Although such information is useful, it must be stressed that there is no direct correlation between the results of these tests and parental adequacy.'

5.12 MORE THAN ONE DIAGNOSIS

It can be especially difficult to assess capacity, autonomy, responsibility, and capacity to change where a party has overlaying conditions affecting their functioning.

The phrase 'dual diagnosis' can be used to cover people with substance abuse and mental health issues, or with mental health and learning disability conditions, so it is best avoided.

In each such case, the court requires appropriate evidence to determine the following:

- What is the condition/conditions? (Consider any overlap and complication)

- What specific difficulties does this present in parenting?

- What are the appropriate services and have they been offered?

- What issues are generated by the condition for working successfully with services?

- What are the range of outcomes and what plans are appropriate?

---

5   *Re L (Children) (Care Proceedings: Significant Harm)* [2006] EWCA Civ 1282.
6   *Re L* [2007] 1 FLR 2050 – ibid first instance.
7   *Re W (A Child) (Care Proceedings)* [2007] EWCA Civ 102.
8   McGaw and Newman *What Works for Parents with Learning Disabilities?* (Jessica Kingsley Publishers, 2005), p 27; and see *Re L (Children) (Care Proceedings: Significant Harm)* [2006] EWCA Civ 1282 (over-reliance on psychometric testing criticised).

PART II

PRIVATE LAW

CHAPTER 6

DECLARATION OF PARENTAGE AND PARENTAL RESPONSIBILITY

6.1 DECLARATION OF PARENTAGE

6.1.1 Overview

This section sets out the law and procedure for securing a legally binding pronouncement by a court concerning parentage, whether by confirming the applicant's position as:

(i)   the parent of a particular child;

(ii)   as the child of an identified adult; or

(iii) by identifying the other parent of a child who is the recognised child of the applicant.

6.1.2 The law

6.1.2.1 The legal basis

The Family Law Act 1986

The statutory basis is to be found in s 55A of the Family Law Act 1986 which was inserted by the Child Support, Pensions and Social Security Act 2000, s 83(1), (2). It provides for a single common procedure for obtaining a declaration as to parentage replacing the procedures set out in s 56 of the Family law Act 1986 and s 27 of the Child Support Act 1991. It was effective for all proceedings commencing from 1 April 2001.

6.1.2.2 Requirements

There are certain requirements which must be satisfied in order to bring an application for a declaration. They are as follows:

(a) Jurisdiction

Before the court will hear the application either the applicant or the person named in the application must be, either:

(i) domiciled in England and Wales on the date of the application;[1] or

(ii) have been habitually resident in England and Wales for one year by the date of the application being made.[2]

If the relevant person has died then the same criteria must have been applicable at the date of death.[3]

(b) Sufficient personal interest

A court shall not hear an application for a declaration unless the applicant has a sufficient personal interest in the determination of the application[4]. No definition of sufficient personal interest is provided; therefore reliance should be placed upon the ordinary meaning of the words. Examples of such an interest would include where issues of succession or inheritance are involved or issues arising out of health or genetic facts.

A sufficient personal interest is automatically considered to be present in the following cases:

(i) where a person is seeking to establish that they are the parent of a child;

(ii) where a person is seeking to establish whether they are a child of a particular person;

(iii) where a person is seeking to establish whether another person is the other parent of a child of the applicant.[5]

When an application is made because of a denial of paternity in connection with statutory child maintenance payments, if the applicant is the person with care of the child s/he is deemed to have sufficient personal interest.[6] If the application is made by the Secretary of State the sufficient personal interest test does not apply.[7]

---

[1] Family Law Act, s 55A(2)(a).
[2] Family Law Act, s 55A(2)(a).
[3] Family Law Act 1986, s 55A(2)(c)(i), (ii).
[4] Family Law Act, s 55A(3).
[5] Family Law Act 1986, s 55A(4).
[6] Child Support Act 1991, s 27(2)(a).
[7] Child Support Act 1991, s 27(2)(b).

(c) The best interests of the child

The hearing of an application may be refused where a child is named in the application and the determination of the application would not be in the best interests of that child.[8]

Information as to true identity and genetic inheritance, acknowledgement of official recognition and accuracy as to official registration documentation would all be considered as positive reasons for a declaration to be made.[9] Similarly the likely impact upon a child's existing relationships and the likely impact upon the child of granting the declaration sought should be considered.[10]

Where a court determines that an application should not be determined it may require an applicant to obtain permission from the court before making any future similar application.[11]

In addition to the above requirements before making the declaration sought a court must consider the following matters.

(d) The standard of proof

The burden is on the applicant who is required to satisfy the court. The standard to be applied, even when seeking to rebut a presumption of paternity, is not proof beyond reasonable doubt. However, parentage is an issue of significance which requires evidence commensurate with the seriousness of the issue. Accordingly a court will require a high degree of probability in order to be satisfied that a declaration should be made.[12] Note, however, the decision of the House of Lords in *Re B (Care Proceedings: Standard of Proof)*[13] that in family proceedings there is only the single (civil) standard of proof.

(e) Public policy considerations

A court, even if satisfied that the applicant has established the truth of the proposition to be proved to the requisite standard, shall not make the declaration sought if to do so would be manifestly contrary to public policy.[14]

Having considered those matters if the court is satisfied that the declaration sought should be made then the following matters are important:

---

8   Family Law Act 1986, s 55A(5).
9   *M v W (Declaration of Parentage)* [2007] 2 FLR 270.
10   *Re T (Paternity: Ordering Blood Tests)* [2001] 2 FLR 1190.
11   Family Law Act 1986, s 55A(6).
12   *Serio v Serio* (1983) 4 FLR 756.
13   [2008] UKHL 35.
14   Family Law Act 1986, s 58(1).

- the scope of the declaration;

- the court has no power, if dismissing an application, to make a declaration that was not the subject of the application;[15]

- the declaration is binding when made and requires no further process to make it absolute, unlike a decree of divorce;

- the declaration is conclusive as to status and binding upon all persons, including the Crown. However it will not affect any final judgment or decree already pronounced or made by any court of competent jurisdiction.[16]

A court when dealing with an application for a declaration under s 55A is exercising an express statutory jurisdiction and the only available relief is a declaration on the issue of parenthood.[17]

6.1.3 Procedural requirements

It had been stated that the route to a declaration is beset by procedural formalities.[18] However, the position has been simplified by the adoption of the unitary code that is the Family Procedure Rules 2010.[19]

6.1.3.1 The rules

Whether in the High Court, county court or family proceedings court the procedure is governed by the Family Procedure Rules 2010 (FPR 2010), rr 8.18–8.22.

6.1.3.2 Applications

(a) The court

The proper court in which to commence the process can be the High Court, the county court or the family proceedings court. The provision stating that, if proceeding in the county court, a Divorce County Court is not an appropriate venue, has not been replicated in the new Rules.

(b) The parties

The position is governed by FPR 2010, r 8.20(1) and the table set out there.

---

[15] *Re L (Family Proceedings Court)(Appeal: Jurisdiction)* [2005] 1 FLR 210.
[16] Family Law Act 1986, s 60(3).
[17] *Law v Inostroza Ahumuda* [2011] 1 FLR 708.
[18] *Re AB (Care Proceedings: Service on Husband Ignorant of Child's Existence)* [2004] 1 FLR 527, per Thorpe LJ at [11].
[19] SI 2010/2955.

The applicant is:

- the person whose parentage is in question;

- the person seeking to establish whether they are a parent of a particular child; or

- some other person with a sufficient personal interest.

The respondents are:

- the person whose parentage is in issue;

- any person who is, or who is alleged to be, the parent of the person whose parentage is in issue.

Any other party may be joined following a request for directions made to the court and served upon the respondents as to other persons who should be made parties or notified of the proceedings.[20]

Any person notified of the proceedings as a result of the direction hearings shall have 21 days after service of the notice to apply to be made a party.[21]

(c) The role of the Attorney-General

There is no requirement to serve the Attorney-General with a copy of the petition[22] but the court should consider at the directions stage referred to above whether an invitation should be extended to the Attorney-General to argue any point in the proceedings.[23]

The reason for this particular point is to be found in the binding nature of declarations and therefore the importance attached to them. A declaration will bind third parties, including the State, in its conferral of benefit or status and therefore the possibility of fraud or collusion in the obtaining of the same cannot be discounted and is to be guarded against. Further a declaration should be made upon satisfaction of the necessary proof, save where public policy issues require otherwise. The Attorney-General is the appropriate advocate of such arguments.

The court can at any stage of the proceedings for a declaration send the papers to the Attorney-General who may intervene in the proceedings in

---

[20]   FPR 2010, r 8.20(4).
[21]   FPR 2010, r 8.20(5).
[22]   FPR 2010, r 8.21(1).
[23]   FPR 2010, r 8.21(4).

such manner as is thought necessary or expedient[24] and argue before the court any point which the court thinks necessary to have fully argued.[25]

(d) Starting the process and documentation

The process is begun by the filing of Form C63[26] which has incorporated the details previously required to be included within the initiating petition.

The Guidance Notes at the end of the form incorporate the following information:

- the application form must be accompanied by:

  (i)   any written evidence to be relied upon;
  (ii) a copy of the birth certificate of the person whose parentage is in question.

- written evidence must be verified by a statement of truth;

- a copy of the form shall be served on each respondent personally or by post;

- a respondent shall respond by way of acknowledgement of service;[27]

- a respondent should serve as many copies of the acknowledgement of service as there are parties to the proceedings.

(e) Directions for trial

A judge shall give directions for trial on the written request of the applicant or any party who is defending a cause upon being satisfied that:

- a copy of the application form has been duly served upon every person required to be served;

- the time provided for the filing of a notice of intention to defend by any party has expired without such notice having been given;

- the time for the filing an acknowledgement of service has expired.[28]

Further interlocutory proceedings are dealt with in accordance with FPR 2010, Pt 19.

---

24   Family Law Act 1986, s 59(1).
25   Family Law Act 1986, s 59(2).
26   FPR 2010, PD 5A.
27   FPR 2010, r 8.20(3), PD 5A, Form FP5.
28   FPR 2010, r 19.9.

(f) Hearings in camera

The court may direct that an application for a declaration may be heard in whole or in part in camera and any application to the court for such a direction shall itself be heard in camera unless otherwise directed by the court.[29]

(g) Upon making of the declaration

The proper officer of the court (being the Court Manager or other officer of the court acting on their behalf) should send a copy of the declaration to the Registrar General of Births, Deaths & Marriages within 21 days[30] who has a discretion to amend the Register in accordance with the declaration.[31]

In the family proceedings court, where a transfer of the application to the county court is being considered, the criteria for transfer are set out in art 15 of the Allocation and Transfer of Proceedings Order 2008[32] as follows:

- the transfer will significantly accelerate the determination of the proceedings;

- there is a real possibility of difficulty in resolving conflicts in the evidence of witnesses;

- there is a real possibility of a conflict in the evidence of two or more experts;

- there is a novel or difficult point of law;

- there are proceedings concerning the child in another jurisdiction or there are international law issues;

- there is a real possibility that enforcement proceedings may be necessary and the method of enforcement or the likely penalty is beyond the powers of a magistrates' court;

- there is another good reason for the proceedings to be transferred.

---

[29]   Family Law Act 1986, s 59(4).
[30]   FPR 2010, r 8.22(2).
[31]   Registration of Births, Deaths and Marriages Act 1953, s 14A.
[32]   SI 2008/2836.

(h) Appeal

A right of appeal lies to the county court:

- from any decision to grant a declaration;

- to refusal to make a declaration; or

- to make an order prohibiting future application without leave of the court pursuant to s 55A(6).[33]

If an issue of parentage arises in the course of proceedings under the Child Support Act 1991, s 20, it is transferred for hearing from the first-tier tribunal to the family proceedings court. However the family proceedings court hearing an appeal under the Child Support Act 1991, s 20 cannot make a declaration under s 55A in the absence of any application for such a declaration and where the child in question has not been made a party.[34]

The order is made on Form C63A.

6.1.4 Case Digest (Declaration of parentage)

6.1.4.1 *When to make an application for a Declaration*

Re R (IVF: Paternity of Child) [2003] 1 FLR 1183

It is usually more convenient to seek findings of parentage in the course of proceedings for a substantive order about the child. However, if the case raises a difficult issue of law or public policy, or if re-registration of the child would be desirable even without a substantive order, or if the child is grown up, then the procedure under s 55A should be used.

Re AB (Care Proceedings: Service on Husband Ignorant of Child's Existence) [2004] 1 FLR 527

A mother who made an application in care proceedings to exclude her husband from the proceedings on the basis that the child concerned was not his should have sought a declaration under s 55A as to the status of the child. She could then have made an application to the court for some relaxation of the rule that her husband should be a respondent in those proceedings.

---

[33]   Family Law Act 1986, s 60(5).
[34]   *Re L (Family Proceedings Court) (Appeal: Jurisdiction)* [2005] 1 FLR 210.

6.1.4.2   Parties

Re R (IVF: Paternity of Child) [2003] 1 FLR 1183

A parent includes a person who is to be treated as a parent by virtue of the Human Fertilisation and Embryology Act 1990, s 27 or 28.

6.1.4.3   The standard of proof

Serio v Serio (1983) 4 FLR 756

In cases involving an application for a declaration the standard of proof to be applied was not a mere balance of probabilities but a standard commensurate with the seriousness of the issue involved; where the issue was the paternity of a child it was an issue of great gravity.

6.1.4.4   Public policy

M v W (Declaration of Parentage) [2007] 2 FLR 270

An adopted person's application for a declaration that a particular man and woman were his natural parents was granted, there being no objections from interested parties nor reason of public policy for not doing so.

6.1.4.5   Procedure

Re AB (Care Proceedings: Service on Husband Ignorant of Child's Existence) [2004] 1 FLR 527

The court would be reluctant to grant any relaxation as to the rules requiring service of an application upon a prospective respondent in the absence of the most extreme circumstances.

Law v Inostroza Ahumuda [2011] 1 FLR 708

A court when dealing with an application for a declaration under s 55A is exercising an express statutory jurisdiction and the only available relief is a declaration on the issue of parenthood.

6.1.4.6   Appeals

Re L (Family Proceedings Court) (Appeal: Jurisdiction) [2005] 1 FLR 210

A family proceedings court hearing an appeal under the Child Support Act 1991, s 20 cannot make a declaration under s 55A where no application has been made for such a declaration and the child in question has not been made a party.

6.2 PARENTAL RESPONSIBILITY

6.2.1 What is parental responsibility?

- Parental responsibility is defined as all the rights, duties, powers, responsibilities and authority which by law a parent of a child has in relation to the child and his property.[35]

- There is no precise definition of its extent, powers or limitations to be found in the Children Act 1989. This was a deliberate recommendation of the Law Commission.[36] Neither is there significant statutory assistance to be found elsewhere in English law.

- In the Guidance which accompanies the Children Act 1989 it has been described as the limited powers to carry out parental duties.[37]

- In substituting the term parental responsibility for notions of parental rights of custody, care and control the emphasis is now upon obligations and requirements arising from 'the duty to care for the child and to raise him to moral, physical and emotional health'.[38]

- Parental responsibility should not be confused with parenthood; whilst the two overlap they are not identical. A parent derives from a genetic fact or a legal status, a social or psychological relationship between an adult and child does not confer the status of parent upon that adult.[39]

- A person can be a parent by reason of his being a biological co-creator of the child and yet not hold parental responsibility for that child. Conversely a person may have parental responsibility for a child with whom there is no genetic link.

- Obligations which exist by virtue of parenthood (eg a statutory duty to provide financial maintenance for a child pursuant to the Child Support Act 1991) are not avoided by reason of the absence of parental responsibility. Conversely the holding of parental responsibility does not automatically create a statutory responsibility to provide financial support.[40]

---

[35] CA 1989, s 3(1).
[36] Law Commission No 172, para 2.6.
[37] The Children Act 1989, Guidance and Regulations, Volume 2.
[38] Department of Health Introduction, Pt 1.4.
[39] *Re A (Joint Residence: Parental Responsibility)* [2008] 2 FLR 1593.
[40] *T v B (Parental Responsibility: Financial Provision)* [2010] 2 FLR 1966.

6.2.2 Scope

Parental responsibility is wide in scope and can encompass any aspect of a child's life. Examples include:

- the provision of accommodation;

- the names to be given to a child;

- emigration and foreign travel;

- the provision of medical treatment;

- religious upbringing and instruction;

- schooling and education issues;

- legal representation;

- the administration of discipline;

- the administration of financial and property interests;

- publicity and the media.

6.2.3 The limits of parental responsibility

A person in whom parental responsibility is vested does not have an absolute right to determine any issue in relation to the upbringing of a child. There are a variety of constraints and restrictions which may impinge upon the exercise of parental responsibility.

6.2.3.1 *The welfare principle*

Notwithstanding the generous margin of appreciation in personal morals, beliefs and ideas which are accorded to a person in relation to how they consider their child should be brought up, personal choice over the parenting of children has its limits. The premise underpinning the concept of parental responsibility is that decisions are taken which are in the child's best interest.

Accordingly a parent's ability to decide upon a course of action is limited by consideration of the welfare principle and those who are deemed to be acting contrary to a child's interests can find their right to do so curtailed.[41]

---

41 *Gillick v West Norfolk and Wisbech Area Health Authority and Another* [1986] 1 FLR 224.

6.2.3.2   The development of the child's wishes and feelings

A more common frustration to the untrammelled exercise of parental authority over the child is the development of the child's own views as they move from dependent child to fiercely independent adolescent. Parental responsibility (in its earlier guise of parental right) has been aptly described as having a 'dwindling' nature which 'starts with the right of control and ends with little more than advice.'[42] Parental responsibility ends in any event upon the child reaching the age of 18 but the courts give weight and respect to the views of children well within their minority.[43]

6.2.3.3   The duration for which parental responsibility is held

The extent of the parental responsibility may be limited by the period for which it is held. Parental responsibility can be held for a variety of reasons (see below) and the holder may not be in a position to make long-term decisions if their authority is for a short period only. Parental responsibility is conferred by the making of an emergency protection order which has a maximum duration of 15 days[44] but the scope of the parental responsibility which can be applied in the light of that time limit will necessarily be limited.[45] Similarly the holder of a residence order who thereby holds parental responsibility,[46] the duration of which is expressly limited, will lack the authority to implement changes in a child's life extending significantly beyond their limited period of responsibility.

6.2.3.4   Statutory exceptions

There are statutory restrictions imposed upon those with parental responsibility. Where a residence order is in force no person may cause the child to be known by a new surname or remove him from the United Kingdom for a period in excess of one month without the written consent of every person who has parental responsibility for the child or the leave of the court.[47] Where there are two or more holders of parental responsibility the consent of all of them is required before a child can be placed for adoption.[48]

Parental responsibility cannot be applied in a way that would conflict with any order made by a court under the Children Act 1989.[49]

---

[42]   *Hewer v Bryant* [1970] 1 QB 357, at 369.
[43]   *Re P (A Minor)(Education)* [1992] 1 FLR 316, *Re Roddy (A Child) (Identification: Restriction on Publication)* [2004] 2 FLR 949 but note the different view when issues of refusal to consent to medical treatment are involved *Re W (A Minor)(Medical Treatment: Court's Jurisdiction)* [1993] 1 FLR 1.
[44]   See Children Act 1989, s 45(1) and (5).
[45]   Children Act 1989, s 44(5)(b).
[46]   See Children Act 1989, s 12(2) and below.
[47]   Children Act 1989, s 13(1).
[48]   Adoption and Children Act 2002, s 47.
[49]   Children Act 1989, s 2(8).

Accordingly a parent holding parental responsibility in respect of a child who is the subject of an order determining issues such as residence and contact or in respect of whom a prohibited steps, specific issue, special guardianship, care or supervision order has been made is required to abide by the terms of that order notwithstanding the ability to do otherwise provided by parental responsibility.

6.2.3.5 *Any requirement for unanimity of agreement*

Parental responsibility can be held by more than one person at the same time[50] but securing the agreement of all other holders of parental responsibility is not necessary before decisions are taken.[51] However this is subject to the judicially expressed view that, notwithstanding the clear words of the statute, prior to any important step in the life of a child there should be consultation with any other holders of parental responsibility. Examples include: a change of school[52] and irreversible medical treatment (eg sterilisation, circumcision).[53]

6.2.4 Who has parental responsibility?

Parental responsibility is not merely confined to parents although they are the most likely holders of it in the majority of cases.

Parental responsibility is or can be held by the following:

WHO	HOW	WHEN	UNTIL
Mother	By her status as mother[54]	Birth	(i) Child reaching 18 (ii)subsequent adoption of child
Father	Married to the child's mother at birth[55]	Birth	As (i) and (ii) above

---

[50] Children Act 1989, s 2(5).
[51] Children Act 1989, s 2(7).
[52] *Re G (Parental Responsibility: Education)* [1994] 2 FLR 964.
[53] *Re J (Specific Issue Orders: Child's Religious Upbringing and Circumcision)* [2000] 1 FLR 571.
[54] Children Act 1989, s 2(1) and (2)(a).
[55] Children Act 1989, s 2(1).

WHO	HOW	WHEN	UNTIL
	Unmarried at the time of birth but subsequent legitimation of child (eg by the parents' subsequent marriage)[56]	Date of legitimation	As (i) and (ii) above
	Since 1 December 2003 registered (or re-registered) as the father on the Register of Births[57]	Date of registration	As (i) and (ii) above or (iii) upon order discharging his parental responsibility
	Makes a parental responsibility agreement with the mother[58]	Upon filing of agreement with Principal Registry	As (i) and (ii) above or (iv) upon order discharging parental responsibility agreement
	Court makes parental responsibility order	Date of order	As (i) and (ii) above or (v) upon order discharging parental responsibility order
	Court makes a residence order (and a parental responsibility order)[59]	Date of order	As (i) and (ii) and (v) above
Step-parent	By entering into a parental responsibility agreement with all other holders of parental responsibility[60]	Upon filing of agreement with Principal Registry	As (i) and (ii) and (v) above

---

[56] Children Act 1989, s 2(3).
[57] Children Act 1989, s 4(1)(a).
[58] Children Act 1989, s 4(1)(b).
[59] Children Act 1989, s 12(1).
[60] Children Act 1989, s 4A(1)(a).

WHO	HOW	WHEN	UNTIL
	Court makes a parental responsibility order[61]	Date of order	As (i) and (ii) and (v) above
Second female parent	By registration as a parent on the Register of Births[62]	Date of registration	As (i) and (ii) above
	By entering into a parental responsibility agreement with the mother of the child[63]	Upon filing of agreement with Principal Registry	As (i) and (ii) and (iii) above
	Court makes a parental responsibility order[64]	Date of order	As (i) and (ii) and (v) above
Guardian	Appointed by a parent with parental responsibility[65]	Either: if residence order in force in favour of parent making the appoint- ment on the death of that parent; or on the death of the last surviving parent with parental responsibil- ity	As (i) and (ii) and (v) above
	Appointed by the court as guardian[66]	Making of the order	As (i) and (ii) and (v) above

---

[61] Children Act 1989, s 4A(1)(b).
[62] Children Act 1989, s 4ZA(1)(a).
[63] Children Act 1989, s 4ZA(1)(b).
[64] Children Act 1989, s 4ZA(1)(c).
[65] Children Act 1989, s 5(3).
[66] Children Act 1989, s 5(1).

WHO	HOW	WHEN	UNTIL
	Appointed by the child's then guardian[67]	Date of death of the then guardian	As (i) and (ii) and (v) above
Special guardian	Court makes a special guardianship order[68]	Date of making of the order	As (i), (ii) and (vi) court discharges special guardian-ship order
Local authority	On making of an emergency protection order[69]	Date of making of the order	Discharge or expiration of the order
	Making of an interim care order[70]	Date of making of the order	Discharge or expiration of the order
	Making of a care order[71]	Date of making of the order	Discharge or expiration of the order
	If acting as the adoption agency and authorised to place a child by parental consent or court order	Date of achieving consent or making of order	Upon the making of an adoption order
Adoption Agency	As above	As above	As above
Commis-sioning parent (surro-gacy)	Upon making of a parental order[72]		As (i) and (ii) above

---

[67] Children Act 1989, s 5(4).
[68] Children Act 1989, s 14A.
[69] Children Act 1989, s 44(4)(c).
[70] Children Act 1989, s 33(3)(a).
[71] As above.
[72] Human Fertilization and Embryology Act 1990, s 30.

WHO	HOW	WHEN	UNTIL
Adoptive parent	On the making of the adoption order	From the making of the order	As (i) above or (vii) revocation of the adoption order
	On placement of the child by Adoption Agency[73]	From placement	Removal of the child
Any person	Upon the making of a residence order[74]	From making of the order	Cessation of the order

6.2.5 The acquisition of parental responsibility

As can be seen above there are four principal methods for the acquisition of parental responsibility by those individuals not automatically entitled to it:

(i) by marrying (or entering into a civil partnership) with the mother of the child;

(ii) by registration (including re-registration) as a parent on the Register of Births;

(iii) by making a parental responsibility agreement; or

(iv) by court order.

6.2.5.1 By registration

The unmarried father of a child or the second female parent who is not a civil partner of the mother of the child can acquire parental responsibility by their being registered as a parent of the child.[75] The Joint Birth Registration Regulations (when enacted) will require both parents to register as parents rather than it being the sole responsibility of the mother under the previous regime.

---

[73] Adoption and Children Act 2002, s 25(3).
[74] Children Act 1989, s 12(2).
[75] Registration of Births, Deaths and Marriages Act 1953, s 10(1B) and s 10A(1B) respectively.

6.2.5.2   *Parental responsibility agreements*

The ability to acquire parental responsibility by use of a parental responsibility agreement is limited to:

(a)   the father of the child;

(b)   the second female parent of the child who is not the civil partner of the mother; or

(c)   a step-parent (including civil partner) of the parent holding parental responsibility for that child.

A parental responsibility agreement is made only with the consent of those parents already holding parental responsibility for the child. The decision to enter into a parental responsibility agreement is a decision which is not subject to the consent of a local authority even when it also has parental responsibility by virtue of the existence of a care order.[76] It is not an exercise of parental responsibility which can be reviewed and countermanded by a court.

To be effective the agreement must be completed, lodged and registered in accordance with detailed regulations – the Parental Responsibility Agreement Regulations 1991,[77] as amended by the Parental Responsibility Agreement (Amendment) Regulations 2005.[78]

Further guidance is given in the Notes annexed to the form of agreement to be used, copies of which are set out in Appendix 1.

In summary the procedure in respect of a father or second female parent is as follows:

- obtain the correct form: (C(PRA1) for unmarried father, C(PRA2) for second female parent or C(PRA3) for step-parent;

- in sufficient quantities to ensure that a separate form is used for each child in respect of whom parental responsibility is to be conferred;

- the completed unsigned forms should be taken to a court (can be family proceedings court, county court or the Principal Registry of the Family Division);

- the mother of the child must produce the child's birth certificate and evidence of her own identity (eg a passport, photopass or official card);

---

[76]   *Re X (Parental Responsibility Agreement)* [2000] 1 FLR 517.
[77]   SI 1991/1478.
[78]   SI 2005/2808

- the father/second female parent should produce evidence of their identity (as above);

- the appropriate court official will witness the signatures of the adult parties;

- the signed forms and the copies should then be sent to the Principal Registry of the Family Division;

- the original will be retained at the Principal Registry and the copies sealed and returned to each parent.

In relation to a step-parent/civil partner the procedure is as above save:

- each parent with parental responsibility must produce evidence of their parental responsibility;

- each parent must also produce evidence of their identity;

- the step-parent must produce evidence of the marriage or civil partnership as well as evidence of their own identity.

6.2.5.3   Parental responsibility orders

Like agreements a parental responsibility order can only be made in favour of a father, a second female parent or a step-parent. Any other person in whose favour a residence order is made is deemed to have parental responsibility for the duration of that order but no specific parental responsibility order is made unless that person is also the father of the child.[79]

An order confers upon the recipient the status of parent which nature (and now in the light of s 4ZA and s 4A, scientific ingenuity), custom or expediency has delivered. The making of an order is not dependent upon the immediate or regular exercise of that responsibility and can be made at the same time as any opportunity for the use of that responsibility is curtailed or controlled by ancillary orders.[80]

In the absence of statutory criteria for the making of an order for parental responsibility other than that set out in s 1(1) and (5) of the Children Act 1989 the following principles have emerged from the case-law:

(1)   The applicant must demonstrate commitment, attachment and good reason for making the application.[81]

---

[79]   Children Act 1989, s 12(1). This section has not been amended to include a step-parent.
[80]   *Re S (Parental Responsibility)* [1995] 2 FLR 648.
[81]   *Re H (Illegitimate Children: Father: Parental Rights) (No 2)* [1991] 1 FLR 214.

(2)   These criteria are not exhaustive but if evident the court should make the order absent any countervailing reasons.[82]

(3)   However, all the circumstances have to be considered and the issue turns on welfare.[83]

(4)   Even where the criteria are fulfilled the presence of adverse matters may cause the application to be refused.[84]

(5)   The application should be considered separately from any application for a section 8 order.[85]

(6)   It is not necessary for an applicant to be exercising contact or otherwise in direct communication with a child for a parental responsibility order to be made.[86]

(7)   A parental responsibility order should be refused where its use would be to undermine the role of the primary carer in a manner which could not be controlled by the use of section 8 orders.[87]

(8)   A parental responsibility order cannot be suspended.[88]

6.5.2.4   *Applying for a parental responsibility order*

(a) By application only

A parental responsibility order must be sought by application. There is no power of a court to make such an order of its own motion.[89]

(b) The court and the relevant procedural rules

Applications for a parental responsibility order can be made to a family proceedings court, county court or the High Court and the procedure is governed by FPR 2010, rr 12.3 ff and PD 12B.

(c) The applicants

There are only three categories of applicants:

- a father to a child;[90]

---

[82]   *Re G (A Minor)(Parental Responsibility Order)* [1994] 1 FLR 504.
[83]   *Re H (Illegitimate Children: Father: Parental Rights) (No 2)* [1991] 1 FLR 214.
[84]   *Re H (Parental Responsibility)* [1998] 1 FLR 855.
[85]   *Re J (Parental Responsibility)* [1999] 1 FLR 784.
[86]   *Re H (Minors) (Parental Responsibility)* [1993] 1 FLR 484.
[87]   *Re M (Contact: Parental Responsibility)* [2001] 2 FLR 342.
[88]   *Re G (Parental Responsibility Order)* [2006] 2 FLR 1092.
[89]   Children Act 1989, ss 4(1), 4ZA(1) and 4A(1).
[90]   Children Act 1989, s 4(1)(c).

- a second female parent of the child;[91] and

- a step-parent married (including civil partner) to a parent with parental responsibility.[92]

(d) The application

An application for a parental responsibility order is governed by the Revised Private Law Programme set out in FPR 2010, PD 12B which provides a step-by-step guide to the making of the application.

The application (and the order cannot be made by the court of its own motion) is made within 'family proceedings'.[93]

The correct application to be made is dependent upon whether the application is made:[94]

- as a freestanding application, in which case Form C1 should be used; or

- within existing proceedings requiring the use of Form C2.

If necessary, Form C1A (Supplemental Information) should be filed if allegations of harm are raised in the initiating document[95] (see 'Documents' below).

The applicant should attempt to include as much relevant material as possible when completing the appropriate Forms. The application may be made in respect of more than one child but sufficient copies of the original documents filed must be provided to the court to allow service upon each respondent.

Once received by the court the proper officer of the court will:

- fix a date for the hearing or directions appointment;

- endorse the date upon the date on Form C6 and if appropriate C6A;

- return the documents to the applicant for service as set out below together with Form C7 and Form C1A.[96]

In either case an applicant is required:

---

91   Children Act 1989, s 4ZA(1).
92   Children Act 1989, s 4A(1)(b).
93   Children Act 1989, s 8(3)(4).
94   FPR 2010, Pt 12.
95   FPR 2010, r 12.5
96   FPR 2010, r 12.7.

- to serve copies of the application on each respondent together with Form C6 and Form C7 and, if applicable, Form C1A as provided by the court;

- to serve Form 6A upon those entitled to notice of the proceedings.

(e) Service

The applicant must serve each respondent with the application and documents specified in PD 12C no later than 14 days prior to the date of the hearing endorsed upon the documentation.[97]

Persons to whom notice must be given of the proceedings should be served at the same time and in any event so as to comply with the 14-day period.

A statement of service should be filed (Form C9) by or before the date of the first directions appointment.

(f) The respondents

The respondents are:

- every person whom the applicant believes has parental responsibility for the child; and

- if a care order is in force in relation to that child, every person who the applicant believes had parental responsibility prior to the making of that order.

In addition the following persons are entitled to be served with notice of the proceedings:

- a local authority proving accommodation for the child;

- any person caring for the child at the time when proceedings are commenced;

- if the child is staying in a refuge believed to be certified under s 51(1) or (2) the person who is providing the refuge.

Further a person may file a request (Form C2) that he be joined as a party.

Each respondent should within 14 days of service file and serve on the other parties his acknowledgement (Form C7) and, if appropriate, Form C1A.

---

[97] FPR 2010, r 12.8.

(g) The directions hearing

The date endorsed by the proper officer on the documents served by the applicant will be the date of the first directions hearing of the application at which time the court will consider the following issues:[98]

- the timetable for the proceedings;

- the attendance of the parties;

- the submission of evidence (see Documents below);

- the preparation of any welfare (section 7) report;

- the transfer of proceedings to another court (including at the same jurisdictional level or to an upper or lower tier);

- the consolidation of the proceedings with any other relevant proceedings.

(h) Documents

The documents which are required for an application for parental responsibility are:

(1) The applicant's initiating documents:

    (a) Form C1 or C2;
    (b) Form C1A.

(2) The documents to be served by the applicant on each respondent:

    (a) those Forms submitted to the proper officer of the court;
    (b) Form C6;
    (c) a blank version of Form C1A.

(3) The documents to be served by the applicant upon those persons to whom notice of proceedings must be given:

    (a) Form C6A.

(4) Further documents to be filed and served:

    (a) any written statement of evidence to be relied upon at the hearing of the application;

---

[98] FPR 2010, r 12.12.

(b)   copies of any experts' reports to be relied upon.[99]

Written statements of evidence should:

- contain the substance of the oral evidence intended to be adduced;

- refer to all relevant matters;

- avoid reference to matters which are unrelated to the issues with which the court is concerned;

- avoid excessive hearsay;

- make clear any source of information other than the maker of the statement where that information is included within the statement;

- comply with the following procedural requirements:

    (a)   contain a statement of truth;
    (b)   be dated;
    (c)   be signed by the person making the statement;
    (d)   contain a declaration that the maker of the statement believes it to be true and understands that it will be placed before the court;
    (e)   set out in the top right-hand corner of the first page:

        (i)   the initials and surname of the maker of the statement;
        (ii)   the number of that statement;
        (iii)   the date on which it was made;
        (iv)   on whose behalf it is filed (the party).

Note that statements of evidence are intended to stand as evidence-in-chief at the final hearing.[100]

(i) The final hearing

Order of procedure:

- For the submission of evidence:

    (a)   the applicant;
    (b)   any party with parental responsibility;
    (c)   any other respondents.

- For the order of speeches during argument:

---

[99]   In which case note the provisions of *PD25A Experts and Assessors in Family Proceedings*.
[100]   *Practice Direction (Case Management)* [1995] 1 FLR 456.

(a)   any other respondents;

(b)   any party with parental responsibility;

(c)   the applicant.

(j) The order

It is a common error to include a parental responsibility order within other orders which a court might make at the same time (whether private law or public law orders). A parental responsibility order is a separate order of the court and is made on Form C45.

6.2.6   Loss of parental responsibility

Parental responsibility cannot be surrendered or transferred permanently to another but can be delegated to a greater or lesser extent to one or more individuals who act on the behalf of and with the authority of any holders of parental responsibility.[101]

Parental responsibility can be brought to an end in the following ways:

• the death of the child;

• the child attaining the age of 18;

• the discharge of a parental responsibility agreement or a parental responsibility order by court order;

• the adoption of the child or the making of a parental order;

• the discharge or expiration of the residence, care or emergency protection order under by which it was conferred;

• the relinquishment of the position as guardian.

An application for the discharge of a parental responsibility agreement or parental responsibility order follows the same procedure as that set out above.

The issues for the court in considering whether to discharge parental responsibility are:

• the welfare of the child;

• whether making the order is better than making no order at all;

---

[101]   Children Act 1989, s 2(9).

- whether on the facts the court would make a parental responsibility order if none existed;[102]

- whether there are continuing benefits to the child by the exercise of parental responsibility by the person from whom it is sought to be discharged;[103]

- how the continuation of parental responsibility impacts upon any other holders of parental responsibility.[104]

6.2.7 The absence of parental responsibility

Even in the absence of parental responsibility a person who has the care of the child is still able to do what is reasonable in all the circumstances of the case for the purpose of safeguarding or promoting the child's welfare.[105]

What is reasonable in all the circumstances will depend upon:

- the nature and gravity of the problem facing the child;

- the ability to effectively communicate with any person who does hold parental responsibility;

- the immediacy of necessary response;

- the impact which any necessary action may have on the child in the longer term.

---

[102] *Re P (Terminating Parental Responsibility)* [1995] 1 FLR 1048.
[103] Ibid.
[104] Ibid.
[105] Children Act 1989, s 3(5).

6.2.8 Form C(PRA1)

Parental Responsibility Agreement
Section 4(1)(b) Children Act 1989

Keep this form in a safe place
*Date recorded at the Principal Registry
of the Family Division:*

**Read the notes on the other side
before you make this agreement.**

This is a Parental Responsibility Agreement regarding

the Child	*Full Name* _____

Boy or Girl   *Date of birth*   *Date of 18th birthday*

Between
    the Mother   *Name*

                Address

and   **the Father**   *Name*

                Address

We declare that   we are the mother and father of the above child and we agree that the child's father shall have parental responsibility for the child (in addition to the mother having parental responsibility).

Signed **(Mother)**   Signed **(Father)**

Date   Date

**Certificate
of witness**

The following evidence of identity was produced by the person signing above:	The following evidence of identity was produced by the person signing above:
Signed in the presence of: *Name of Witness*	Signed in the presence of: *Name of Witness*
Address	*Address*
Signature of Witness	*Signature of Witness*
[A Justice of the Peace] [Justices' Clerk] [An assistant to a justices' clerk] [An officer of the court authorised by the judge to administer oaths]	[A Justice of the Peace] [Justices' Clerk] [An assistant to a justices' clerk] [An Officer of the Court authorised by the judge to administer oaths]

Notes about the Parental Responsibility Agreement

Read these notes before you make the agreement.

About the Parental Responsibility Agreement

The making of this agreement will affect the legal position of the mother and the father. You should both seek legal advice before you make the Agreement. You can obtain the name and address of a solicitor from the Children Panel (020 7242 1222)

or from   • your local family proceedings court, or county court

              • a Citizens Advice Bureau

              • a Law Centre

              • a local library.

You may be eligible for public funding.

When you fill in the Agreement

Please use black ink (the Agreement will be copied). Put the name of one child only. If the father is to have parental responsibility for more than one child, fill in a separate form for each child. **Do not sign the Agreement.**

When you have filled in the Agreement

Take it to a local family proceedings court, or county court, or the Principal Registry of the Family Division (the address is below).

A justice of the peace, a justices' clerk, an assistant to a justices' clerk, or a court official who is authorised by the judge to administer oaths, will witness your signature and he or she will sign the certificate of the witness. **A solicitor cannot witness your signature.**

To the mother: When you make the declaration you will have to prove that you are the child's mother so take to the court the child's full birth certificate.

               You will also need evidence of your identity showing a photograph and signature (for example, a photocard, official pass or passport). **Please note that the child's birth certificate cannot be accepted as sufficient proof of your identity.**

To the father: You will need evidence of your identity showing a photograph and signature (for example, a photocard, official pass or passport).

When the Certificate has been signed and witnessed

Make 2 copies of the Agreement form. You do not need to copy these notes.

Take, or send, this form and the copies to **The Principal Registry of the Family Division, First Avenue House, 42-49 High Holborn, London, WC1V 6NP.**

The Registry will record the Agreement and keep this form. The copies will be stamped and sent back to each parent at the address on the Agreement. The Agreement will not take effect until it has been received and recorded at the Principal Registry of the Family Division.

Ending the Agreement

Once a parental responsibility agreement has been made it can only end

              • by an order of the court made on the application of any person who has parental responsibility for the child

              • by an order of the court made on the application of the child with permission of the court

              • When the child reaches the age of 18.

6.2.9   Form C(PRA2)

**Step-Parent Parental
Responsibility Agreement**
Section 4A(1)(a) Children Act 1989

Keep this form in a safe place
*Date recorded at the Principal Registry
of the Family Division:*

Read the notes on the other side before you make this agreement.

This is a Step-Parent Parental Responsibility Agreement regarding

the Child	*Full Name* _____

	Boy or Girl *Date of birth*	*Date of 18th birthday*

Between
   Parent A   *Name*

                  Address

and
   *the other parent   *Name*
   (with parental
   responsibility)   *Address*

and
   the step-parent   *Name*

                  Address

**We declare
that**   we are the parents and step-parent of the above child and we agree that the above mentioned step-parent shall have parental responsibility for the child (in addition to those already having parental responsibility).

Signed (Parent A)	*Signed (Other Parent)	Signed (Step-Parent)
Date	Date	Date

Certificate of witness	The following evidence of identity was produced by the person signing above:	The following evidence of identity was produced by the person signing above:	The following evidence of identity was produced by the person signing above:
	Signed in the presence of: *Name of Witness*	Signed in the presence of: *Name of Witness*	Signed in the presence of: *Name of Witness*
	Address	*Address*	*Address*

*If there is only one parent with parental responsibility, please delete this section.

Signature of Witness	*Signature of Witness*	*Signature of Witness*
[A Justice of the Peace] [Justices' Clerk] [An assistant to a justices' clerk] [An Officer of the Court authorised by the judge to administer oaths]	[A Justice of the Peace] [Justices' Clerk] [An assistant to a justices' clerk] [An Officer of the Court authorised by the judge to administer oaths]	[A Justice of the Peace] [Justices' Clerk] [An assistant to a justices' clerk] [An Officer of the Court authorised by the judge to administer oaths]

C(PRA2) (12.05)   HMCS

Notes about the Step-Parent Parental Responsibility Form
Read these notes before you make the Agreement

About the Step-Parent Parental Responsibility Agreement

The making of this agreement will affect the legal position of the parent(s) and the step-parent. You should seek legal advice before you make the Agreement. You can obtain the name and address of a solicitor from the Children Panel (020 7242 1222) or from:

- your local family proceedings court, or county court,
- a Citizens Advice Bureau,
- a Law Centre,
- a local library.

You may be eligible for public funding.

When you fill in the Agreement

Please use black ink (the Agreement will be copied). Put the name of one child only. If the step-parent is to have parental responsibility for more than one child, fill in a separate form for each child. **Do not sign the Agreement.**

When you have filled in the Agreement

Take it to a local family proceedings court, or county court, or the Principal Registry of the Family Division (the address is below).

A justice of the peace, a justices' clerk, an assistant to a justices' clerk, or a court official who is authorised by the judge to administer oaths, will witness your signature and he or she will sign the certificate of the witness. **A solicitor cannot witness your signature.**

To Parent A and the Other Parent with parental responsibility:

When you make the declaration you will have to prove that you have parental responsibility for the child. You should therefore take with you to the court one of the following documents:

- the child's full birth certificate and a marriage certificate to show that the parents were married to each other at the time of birth or subsequently,
- a court order granting parental responsibility,
- a registered Parental Responsibility Agreement Form between the child's mother and father,
- if the birth was registered after the 1 December 2003, the child's full birth certificate showing that the parents jointly registered the child's birth.

C(PRA2) (Notes) (12.05)

You will also require evidence of your (both parents') identity showing a photograph and signature (for example, a photocard, official pass or passport) **(Please note that the child's birth certificate cannot be accepted as sufficient proof of your identity.)**

To the step-parent: When you make the declaration you will have to prove that you are married to, or the civil partner of, a parent of the child so take to the court your marriage certificate or certificate of civil partnership.

You will also need evidence of your identity showing a photograph and signature (for example, a photocard, official pass or passport).

When the Certificate has been signed and witnessed

Make sufficient copies of the Agreement Form for each person who has signed the form. You do not need to copy these notes.

Take, or send, the original form and the copies to: **The Principal Registry of the Family Division, First Avenue House, 42-49 High Holborn, London, WC1V 6NP.**

The Registry will record the Agreement and retain the original form. The copies will be stamped with the seal of the court and sent back to every person with parental responsibility who has signed the Agreement Form and to the step-parent. The Agreement will not take effect until it has been received and recorded at the Principal Registry of the Family Division.

Ending the Agreement

Once a step-parent parental responsibility agreement has been made it can only end:

- by an order of the court made on the application of any person who has parental responsibility for the child,
- by an order of the court made on the application of the child with permission of the court,
- when the child reaches the age of 18.

6.2.10 CASE DIGEST (PARENTAL RESPONSIBILITY)

Case	Citation	Judge	Principle
Re H (A Minor) (Parental Responsibility)	[1993] 1 FLR 484	Nolan LJ Hollis J	Parental responsibility orders are separate from other Children Act 1989 orders and may be made in circumstances where those other applications are dismissed.
Re CB (A Minor) (Parental Responsibility Order)	[1993] 1 FLR 920	Waite J	An application for a parental responsibility order requires specific assessment by the court. The absence of an ability to exercise parental responsibility does not preclude the making of an order.
Re G (A Minor) (Parental Responsibility Order)	[1994] 1 FLR 504	Balcombe LJ Beldam LJ	Where an applicant father fulfils the criteria of commitment, attachment and of good reason for making the application prima facie an order for parental responsibility should be made. The criteria are indicative only, not exhaustive.
Re P (A Minor) (Parental Responsibility Order)	[1994] 1 FLR 578	Wilson J	An order for parental responsibility did not give the holder a right to interfere with the day-to-day arrangements of the primary carer.
Re G (Parental Responsibility: Education)	[1994] 2 FLR 964	Glidewell LJ Hirst LJ	Holders of parental responsibility should be consulted prior to the taking of any important step in the life of the child.
Re E (Parental Responsibility: Blood Tests)	[1995] 1 FLR 392	Balcombe LJ Mann LJ Saville LJ	A parental responsibility order should be made where the applicant had demonstrated evidence of commitment and attachment and there was no countervailing evidence of detriment by the making of the order.

Case	Citation	Judge	Principle
Re P (Terminating Parental Responsibility)	[1995] 1 FLR 1048	Singer J	An application to discharge parental responsibility was not a weapon to be used by a dissatisfied parent. The welfare of the child was paramount. The court should consider whether a parental responsibility order would be made on the facts or whether the evidence demonstrated forfeiture of parental responsibility to be appropriate.
Re S (Parental Responsibility)	[1995] 2 FLR 648	Butler-Sloss LJ Simon Brown LJ Ward LJ	Parental responsibility conferred upon a father the status of parenthood and it was wrong to concentrate upon notions of rights and duties.
Re P (Parental Responsibility)	[1997] 2 FLR 722	Lord Woolf Millett LJ Ward LJ	An inability to exercise parental responsibility by virtue of incarceration was a factor to take into account in determining whether parental responsibility should be granted.
Re C and V (Contact and Parental Responsibility)	[1998] 1 FLR 392	Nourse LJ Evans LJ Ward LJ	Applications for contact and parental responsibility were separate applications to be independently considered from different perspectives. An application for parental responsibility posed a general question: had this applicant shown genuine concern for the child and demonstrated a genuine wish to take on the responsibilities in law already given by nature?
Re H (Parental Responsibility)	[1998] 1 FLR 855	Butler-Sloss P Henry LJ Potter LJ	The test for parental responsibility was not exhaustive and the court was required to consider all the circumstances in the case with the welfare of the child being paramount. A finding that commitment, attachment and good reasons was not sufficient for an order to be made.

Case	Citation	Judge	Principle
Re P (Parental Responsibility)	[1998] 2 FLR 96	Hirst LJ Wall J	A parental responsibility order should not be refused where a father might use parental responsibility inappropriately but should be where a finding was made that inappropriate use would be made of it.
Re S (Parental Responsibility: Jurisdiction)	[1998] 2 FLR 921	Butler-Sloss P Mantell LJ Sir John Vinelott	There was no requirement that a child should be within or even habitually resident in the jurisdiction for a parental responsibility order to be made.
M v M (Parental Responsibility)	[1999] 2 FLR 737	Wilson J	An application for parental responsibility presupposes capability by the applicant of exercising rights, performing duties and wielding powers on behalf of a child. Where an applicant could not demonstrate such capacity parental responsibility should not be granted.
Re X (Parental Responsibility Agreement: Children in Care)	[2000] 1 FLR 517	Wilson J	The making of a parental responsibility agreement is not in itself an exercise of parental responsibility and a local authority itself with parental responsibility was not entitled to prevent the same.
Re D (Parental Responsibility: IVF Baby)	[2001] 1 FLR 972	Butler-Sloss P Hale LJ Arden LJ	Where a father demonstrated commitment and a good reason for the making of a parental responsibility application but had not had the opportunity to know the child it was appropriate to adjourn the application to see if commitment was maintained.
Re M (Contact: Parental Responsibility)	[2001] 2 FLR 342	Black J	The test for parental responsibility was not exhaustive and where the grant of application might lead to the undermining of the position of the primary carer of the child it should not be made.

Case	Citation	Judge	Principle
Re L (Contact: Genuine Fear)	[2002] 1 FLR 621	Bruce Blair QC	Parental responsibility should not be conferred where there was little benefit for the child, distress would be caused to the mother and the father was not in a position to participate in decisions concerning the child.
Re G (Parental Responsibility Order)	[2006] 2 FLR 1092	Thorpe LJ Moses LJ Hedley J	A parental responsibility order could not be suspended. Where the tests for the making of an order were met but the welfare of the child predicated against the making of an order the application should be adjourned.
Re B (Role of Biological Father)	[2008] 1 FLR 1015	Hedley J	The 'hallowed ground' of commitment, attachment and good reason for making the order did not trump the overarching need to give paramount consideration to the child's welfare.
Re E & F (Female Parents: Known Father)	[2010] 2 FLR 383	Bennett J	A parental responsibility order was subject to the issue of welfare and a relationship with an absent parent could be promoted by contact without the need for the disruption which a parental responsibility order might generate.
Re R	[2011] 2 FLR 1132	Peter Jackson J	It was implicit in the statutory provision that for a step-parent to be awarded parental responsibility s/he should be in-coming rather than out-going.

CHAPTER 7

ORDERS UNDER SECTIONS 8 AND 13 OF THE CHILDREN ACT 1989

7.1 PROCEDURE FOR SECTION 8 APPLICATIONS

7.1.1 Which court?

Applications for section 8 orders can be commenced in any of the following:

- the family proceedings court;

- the county court;

- the High Court.

Where the proceedings arise from related matrimonial proceedings the application should be made to the court in which those related proceedings are already listed.

Following the issuing of an application, proceedings can be transferred upwards to a superior court, downwards to a lower court or to a different court in the same jurisdictional tier.[1]

The following are matters which should *not* be dealt with in the family proceedings courts:

- an application for contact with a child who has been adopted;[2]

- a case involving a conflict with the law of another jurisdiction;[3]

- where there is a conflict of evidence between expert witnesses;

- a case involving complicated issues of psychological harm;[4]

---

[1]   Allocation and Transfer of Proceedings Order 2008, SI 2008/2836.
[2]   *Re T (Adopted Children: Conflict)* [1995] 2 FLR 792.
[3]   Allocation and Transfer of Proceedings Order 2008, SI 2008/2836, art 15(1)(e).
[4]   *Berkshire County Council v B* [1997] 1 FLR 171.

- an application for leave to remove from the jurisdiction.[5]

The following are matters which should be transferred to the High Court:

- an application involving the removal of a child to a state which is not a signatory to the Hague Convention;

- an application involving the removal of a child to a state where 'mirror orders' will be required;[6]

- an application in respect of which communication with a foreign court or consideration of a foreign order will be required;

- an application by a child for leave to make an application;[7]

- where in the course of proceedings applications will be made to limit the information or documentation to be provided to a party to the proceedings;

- an application concerning a significant medical issue e g sterilisation, potentially life-threatening surgery, issues arising from blood transfers.

7.1.2 Which judge?

Within the same jurisdictional level not all judges will have equal judicial powers.

The Family Proceedings (Allocation to Judiciary) Directions 1999 specify the limits of jurisdiction and before whom applications may be considered.

- a High Court Judge may deal with any application, whether contested or unopposed;

- a circuit judge or recorder nominated to hear private family law applications may deal with any application, whether contested or unopposed, save where it involves an issue which should be heard in the High Court;

- a District Judge of the Principal Registry may deal with any application, whether contested or unopposed;

---

5   *MH v GP (Child: Emigration)* [1995] 2 FLR 106.
6   *Re K (Removal from the Jurisdiction: Practice)* [1999] 2 FLR 1084.
7   Allocation and Transfer of Proceedings Order 2008, SI 2008/2836.

- a district judge nominated to hear private family law applications may deal with any application, whether contested or unopposed, save where it involves an issue which should be heard in the High Court;

- a district judge without a private law family 'ticket' has jurisdiction limited to:

  - Interlocutory matters;
  - unopposed hearings; or
  - opposed hearings where:

    (a) the application is for a contact order and the principle of contact with the applicant is unopposed; or

    (b) the order:

      (i) is (or is one of a series of orders which is) to be limited in time until the next hearing or order; and

      (ii) the substantive application is returnable before a judge who has full jurisdiction in all circumstances;

- a deputy district judge has jurisdiction to deal with interlocutory matters or unopposed hearings.

7.1.3 The importance of mediation

Under Family Procedure Rules 2010, r 3.2 the court must consider 'at every stage in the proceedings, whether alternative dispute resolution is appropriate'.

This is emphasised by Practice Direction 3A which requires parties to comply with the pre-application protocol for mediation information and assessment (included as Annex A to the Direction). It sets out an expectation that a potential applicant for an order will undertake mediation first unless the conditions set out in Annex C to the Direction apply. Form M1 should be completed to demonstrate either that mediation has been attempted or that it was considered unsuitable prior to commencing litigation.

Attendance at mediation is not compulsory and the court cannot decline jurisdiction by reason of any party's unwillingness to have attempted mediation prior to litigation.

7.1.4   The parties

7.1.4.1   The applicant

A person seeking to apply for a s 8 order will initially fall into one of two categories:

- entitled to make the application;

- required to obtain permission to make the application.

Applications by right

Those entitled to make an application as of right for any s 8 order are the following:[8]

- any parent, guardian or special guardian of the child;

- any step-parent (including civil partner to a parent) of the child;

- any person in whose favour a residence order has been made in respect of that child.

There is a separate category of those entitled to make an application as of right only for a residence or contact order which comprises:[9]

- any party to a current or former marriage or civil partnership in relation to whom the child is a child of the family;

- any person with whom the child has lived for at least 3 years;

- a person who has the consent of the following:
  - those who hold parental responsibility for the child;
  - any residence order holder(s) in relation to the child;
  - the local authority where the child is in their care.

A parent is a person with the necessary genetic relationship with the child and not someone who might have a close social or psychological relationship.[10]

Where a child has lived with a local authority foster parent for at least one year that foster parent may apply for a residence order.[11]

---

[8]   Children Act 1989, s 10(4).
[9]   Children Act 1989, s 10(5).
[10]   *T v B (Parental Responsibility: Financial Provision)* [2010] 2 FLR 1966.
[11]   Children Act 1989, s 10(5A).

A person shall have the right to apply for the variation or discharge of any order if it was either:[12]

- made on his application; or

- the order in question is a contact order and he is a person named in the order.

The 3-year period of residence referred to above must have commenced within the 5 years immediately preceding the date of the application and not have concluded more than 3 months prior to that date.[13]

Note that any of the above classes of person will be required to obtain leave when the application concerns an application for a residence order in relation to a child who is the subject of a special guardianship order.[14]

Applicants seeking leave

Leave is required in the following cases:

- for any person who cannot on the facts qualify in one of the above categories;

- where a child is seeking to make an application whether concerning himself or a different child (see below);

- where a person has been made subject to a direction pursuant to s 91(14) of the Children Act 1989.

In the absence of entitlement to make an order a filtering process has been set up. The basis upon which permission is granted is set out in s 10(9)(a)–(d)(ii) of the Children Act 1989:

> 'Where the person applying for leave to make an application for a section 8 order is not the child concerned, the court shall, in deciding whether or not to grant leave, have particular regard to—
> (a)   the nature of the proposed application for the section 8 order;
> (b)   the applicant's connection with the child;
> (c)   any risk there might be of that proposed application disrupting the child's life to such an extent that he would be harmed by it; and
> (d)   where the child is being looked after by a local authority—
>   (i)   the authority's plans for the child's future; and
>   (ii)   the wishes and feelings of the child's parents.'

It should be noted that:

---

[12]   Children Act 1989, s 10(6).
[13]   Children Act 1989, s 10(10).
[14]   Children Act 1989, s 10(7A).

- the section is not exhaustive of the criteria to be considered;

- the welfare of the child is not the paramount consideration.[15]

The following points have emerged from the case law in relation to applications for leave:

- the application should be heard on notice;[16]

- the court should hear evidence from the parties where there are substantial issues of fact;[17]

- the grant of leave is a substantial judicial decision to be made in the presence of the parties;[18]

- when considering the issue of whether to grant permission the court should refuse the application if:[19]

  - it is frivolous, vexatious or an abuse of process;
  - it demonstrates no real or only a remote prospect of success;
  - it does not disclose a serious issue to try;
  - it does not demonstrate a good, arguable case;

- the statutory criteria should not be supplanted by any convenient formula and should be the prism by which the application is judged.[20]

The child as applicant

An applicant who is himself a child will fall into one of two categories:

(1) he will be the child who is the subject of the proceedings (the child concerned); or

(2) a child seeking an order in relation to a different child (eg an application for contact by a sibling).

When the applicant for a s 8 order is the child concerned the basis upon which leave is given is set out in s 10(8) and s 10(9) does not apply.

---

[15]   *Re A and W (Minors) (Residence Orders: Leave to Apply)* [1992] 2 FLR 154.
[16]   *Re M (Prohibited Steps Order: Application for Leave)* [1993] 1 FLR 275.
[17]   *Re F and R (Contact Order: Grandparent's Application)* [1995] 1 FLR 524.
[18]   *Re W (Contact Application: Procedure)* [2000] 1 FLR 263.
[19]   *Re M (Care: Contact: Grandmother's Application for Leave)* [1995] 2 FLR 86.
[20]   *Re J (Leave to Issue Application for a Residence Order)* [2003] 1 FLR 114.

The court 'may only grant leave if it is satisfied that he has sufficient understanding to make the proposed section 8 order.' In practice this means:

- the child's ability to give instructions to a legal representative; and

- to participate as a party in the proceedings; and

- to appreciate the consequences of involvement in litigation.

In addition the court will consider:

- the nature of the proposed application;

- the length of time in which the proceedings have been ongoing;

- the likely conduct of the proceedings in the future, whether the child would have to be cross-examined;

- the likelihood of the proposed application succeeding.

Where the applicant is not the child concerned the court will apply the criteria set out in s 10(9) above.[21]

Applicants seeking leave following a s 91(14) direction

An applicant seeking leave to make an application following the making, in earlier proceedings, of a direction under s 91(14) that no application for an order under the Children Act 1989 should be made without leave of the court.

When later leave of the court is sought to make the application a different, more simple test is required than s 10(9).

The question to be asked is: does this application demonstrate that there is any need for renewed judicial investigation? If so the options open to the court are wide and do not automatically commit the parties to preparing for trial. The outcome of the grant of leave may be limited to a review of the current position with or without the input of any professional assistance.[22]

The initiating process

The procedure for applications for s 8 orders has now been simplified by the coming into effect of the Family Procedure Rules 2010 which apply to all tiers of the court structure which deal with applications for s 8 orders.

---

[21] *Re S (Contact: Application by Sibling)* [1998] 2 FLR 897.
[22] *Re A (Application for Leave)* [1998] 1 FLR 1.

The Rules specific to Children Act applications (both Private Law applications and Public Law applications) are contained in Part 12 and in the Practice Directions set out thereafter with Part 4 being of particular relevance to Private Law applications.

The relevant Practice Directions are:

12B	The Private Law Programme
12C	Service of Proceedings
12E	Urgent Business
12G	Communication of Information
12I	Reporting Restriction Orders
12J	Residence and Contact Orders: Domestic Violence and Harm
12L	Risk Assessments
12M	Family Assistance Orders
12N	Enforcement of Contact Order: Disclosure

7.1.4.2   The application

The application is one made within 'family proceedings'.[23]

The correct application to be made is dependent upon whether the application is made:[24]

- as a freestanding application, in which case Form C100 should be used; or

- within existing proceedings requiring the use of Form C2; or

- when leave is sought, in which case both C100 and C2 are required.

All of the forms relevant to Children Act proceedings are now to be found listed in Practice Direction 5A.

If necessary, Form C1A (Supplemental Information) should be filed if allegations of harm are raised in the initiating document.[25]

---

23   Children Act 1989, s 8(3), (4).
24   FPR 2010, PD 5A.
25   Form C100 para 9.

The applicant should attempt to include as much relevant material as possible when completing the appropriate Forms. The application may be made in respect of more than one child but sufficient copies of the original documents filed must be available to allow service upon each respondent. Service will be effected by the applicant unless the court directs otherwise or a rule or practice requires service by the court.[26]

7.1.4.3   *Without notice orders*

There is provision for without notice orders to be made, where being made in the family proceedings court with the leave of the Clerk to the Justices.[27]

When such application is made the following points should be noted:

- there is a duty for full and frank disclosure to the court of all relevant material;

- if the order is made the respondent should be provided with full details of all of the evidence and any other supporting material relied upon to obtain the order;

- the applicant (or his legal solicitor/counsel) is under an obligation to keep a note of the without notice hearing and to provide a copy to the respondent on request;

- the application should be filed within 24 hours if made by telephone, or at the time if made in person and served on the respondents in any event within 48 hours;

- the court would generally require an applicant seeking an order without notice to give the following undertakings:

  - to issue and serve proceedings on the respondent, either as soon as practicable or within a specified period where not already done so;
  - to swear and serve:

    (i)   an affidavit if not already filed setting out in detail the basis upon which the order was obtained;
    (ii) a sealed copy of the order, the material relied upon and notification of the return date.

In practice without notice orders are the exception rather than the rule, particularly in the case of applications for residence orders which, absent

---

[26]   FPR 2010, r 6.24.
[27]   FPR 2010, r 12.16.

the circumstances of a snatch situation, should normally be adjourned to allow for hearing before all parties albeit that the time for service may be abridged.[28]

Once received by the court the proper officer of the court will:

- fix a date for the hearing or directions appointment;

- endorse the date upon the date on Form C6 and if appropriate C6A;

- return the documents to the applicant for service as set out below together with Form C7 and Form C1A.[29]

In either case an applicant is required:

- to serve copies of the application on each Respondent together with Form C6 and Form C7 and, if applicable, Form C1A as provided by the court;

- to serve Form 6A upon those entitled to notice of the proceedings.

7.1.4.4   *Applications for leave*

Where leave is required as a preliminary consideration prior to making the application, in the absence of consent to leave being granted a hearing should be held. This is particularly appropriate where adjudication is required in respect of factual issues. However, even where such matters are not obvious from the papers those who may well be affected by the grant of leave should be notified of it and have an opportunity of considering their position.[30]

7.1.4.5   *Service*

Provisions for service of documentation are now set out in FPR 2010, Practice Direction 12C to which reference should be made.

The applicant must serve each respondent with the application and Forms received from the court no later than 14 days prior to the date of the hearing endorsed upon the documentation.[31]

Persons to whom notice must be given of the proceedings should be served at the same time and in any event so as to comply with the 14-day period.

28	*Re G (Minors)(Ex Parte Interim Residence Order)* [1993] 1 FLR 910.
29	FPR 2010, r 12.5.
30	*Re W (Contact Application: Procedure)* [2000] 1 FLR 263.
31	FPR 2010, PD 12C.

Service is effected:

- Where the person is acting by a solicitor:

    - by delivery or sending by first class post to the solicitor's office;
    - by DX'ing it to the solicitor's office;
    - by fax.[32]

- Where it is believed that no solicitor has been instructed:

    - by personal delivery to the person;
    - by delivery or sending by first class post to his residence or last known residence.[33]

Note that a statement of service should be filed (Form C9) by or before the date of the first directions appointment. Good Practice regarding service in the context of family law proceedings is set out by Resolution (formerly the SFLA) at [1995] Fam Law 206.

7.1.4.6   The respondents

The respondents are:

- every person whom the applicant believes has parental responsibility for the child; and

- if a care order is in force in relation to that child, every person who the applicant believes had parental responsibility prior to the making of that order.[34]

In addition the following persons are entitled to be served with notice of the proceedings:[35]

- a local authority proving accommodation for the child;

- any person caring for the child at the time when proceedings are commenced;

- if the child is staying in a refuge believed to be certified under s 51(1) or (2), the person who is providing the refuge.

Full details of the parties to applications under the Children Act 1989 can be found in the table accompanying FPR 2010, r 12.3.

---

[32]   FPR 2010, r 6.23.
[33]   FPR 2010, r 6.25.
[34]   See FPR 2010, r 12.3.
[35]   See FPR 2010, PD 12C.

Further a person may file a request (Form C2) that he be joined as a party.[36]

Each respondent should within 14 days of service file and serve on the other parties his Acknowledgement (Form C7) and, if appropriate, Form C1A.

The court will be slow to disapply the requirements of service upon any person who should ordinarily be notified of the proceedings.[37]

7.2   THE PRIVATE LAW PROGRAMME

Announced in November 2004 and, since January 2006, in practice in the High Court, county court and family proceedings courts the Private Law Programme establishes a common procedure for all applications under Part II of the Children Act 1989, including therefore all s 8 orders.

The programme was revised and re-issued in April 2010 to take into account legislative changes (eg contact activity directions), the increasing fluidity of the family court in allowing cases to be transferred both up and down the judicial hierarchy, the need for risk assessments to be undertaken prior to arrangements concerning children to be approved by the courts, the impact of domestic violence and the need, where possible, to properly involve children within the process by which their futures were determined.

In addition the Revised Private Law Programme is intended to work in conjunction with the emphasis upon mediation and alternative dispute resolution set out within the Family Procedure Rules 2010 and thereby to further the Overriding Objective which is the principled basis for the new procedural code set out in the Family Procedure Rules 2010.

The Revised Private Law Programme is now incorporated into the Family Procedure Rules 2010 as Practice Direction 12B and is set out in Chapter 3 of this work at **A3.5**.

7.2.1   The principles

The Revised Private Law Programme is a scheme of national effect but which allows for local adaptation to ensure that good local practice responsive to regional issues is allowed to prosper where it serves a local need.

---

[36]   FPR 2010, r 12.3.
[37]   *Re AB (Care Proceedings: Service on Husband Ignorant of Child's Existence)* [2004] 1 FLR 527.

The aim is for early intervention to remove from the court arena those cases for which alternative forms of dispute resolution, including conciliation and the provision of mediation services, are identified as being suitable.

The court seeks to implement the overriding objective of the family justice system in the following respects:

- using the First Hearing as a dispute resolution hearing and achieving the following:

  - identifying immediate safety issues;
  - establishing the aim of the court process;
  - allowing Cafcass intervention at dispute resolution level;
  - in the absence of exceptional circumstances re-directing cases to local sources of ADR, medication, conciliation etc;

- ensuring effective court control by continuous and active case management to allow for:

  - judicial availability;
  - judicial continuity;
  - continuous case management;
  - the avoidance of unnecessary delay;
  - the enabling of transfer between levels of family court;
  - monitoring of outcomes;
  - enforcing orders;
  - controlling costs;

- matching resources to families by the use of referrals and effective facilitation:

  - to make best use of Cafcass practitioners;
  - to encourage Parenting Plans;
  - to apply varying powers to achieve rehabilitation, training, therapy, enforcement and treatment.

As the application to which the Revised Private Law Programme applies is a section 8 application the court will apply the welfare principle as its paramount consideration in the determination of the substantive issues. In the process employed to arrive at that determination the court will apply the Overriding Objective as set out in FPR 2010, r 1.1 of enabling the court to deal with cases justly, having regard to any welfare issues involved.

'(2) Dealing with a case justly includes, so far as is practicable—
(a) ensuring that it is dealt with expeditiously and fairly;

(b)   dealing with the case in ways which are proportionate to the nature, importance and complexity of the issues;

(c)   ensuring that the parties are on an equal footing;

(d)   saving expense; and

(e)   allotting to it an appropriate share of the court's resources, while taking into account the need to allot resources to other cases.'

7.2.2   The process

There are four stages to the Private Law Programme:

(1)   before the First Hearing Dispute Resolution Appointment (FHDRA);

(2)   at court;

(3)   before the judge;

(4)   after the FHDRA.

7.2.2.1   Before the FHDRA

- Applications are issued on the day of receipt.

- Cafcass are sent a copy on issue.

- Information Sheets are sent to the parties with the Notice of Hearing.

- The application is listed for a FHDRA no later than 6 weeks after issue (and usually no earlier than 4 weeks post issue).

- Cafcass receives a copy of the Acknowledgement Form when received by the court.

- Cafcass:

    –   undertake a paper risk assessment[38] without discussing any substantive issues with any party;
    –   advise the judge on the forum for discussions dependent upon the existence of risk or safety issues; and
    –   identify those complex, urgent or risk-laden cases which require an alternative framework.

---

[38]   Note that since 1 October 2007 Cafcass are required to undertake a risk assessment and provide it to the court when given 'cause to suspect the child concerned is at risk of harm': Children Act 1989, s 16A.

7.2.2.2 *At court*

- The application is listed before a judge/magistrate/legal advisor to allow for early dispute resolution.

- Parents are expected to attend and also legal advisors.

- A mediator may attend subject to local practice arrangements, in which case the parties will be invited to work with the mediator in enabling papers to be read and legal professional privilege to be waived if it will assist the mediator in resolving the disputed issues between the parties.

- The attendance of children is dependent upon local practice and suitable facilities.

- Further risk assessment may be undertaken by Cafcass prior to any joint meeting.

- The aim is to reach agreement.

7.2.2.3 *Before the judge*

- If agreement is reached consider the terms and whether an order is necessary.

- Where issues remain directions to be given dealing with those issues.

- Timetable further hearings.

- Identify whether a Cafcass report is necessary, if so as to what issues?

- Record the terms of any agreement, the issues identified, the nature of any monitoring or of referrals (using Annex F as the template for draft orders).

7.2.2.4 *After the FHDRA*

- Ensure follow-up in respect of orders or agreements:

    - for compliance;
    - that directions were carried out;
    - that CAFCASS are properly informed in respect of problems which arise.

- Ensure mechanisms for informing the court are agreed and set out.

- Ensure immediate/swift re-listing can be achieved where compliance issues require judicial intervention.

- Ensure judicial continuity where possible.

7.2.3 Further hearings

Where the application of the Revised Private Law Programme does not enable a working agreement or order to be arrived at the application will be made ready for trial and relevant issues thereafter attended to. Such issues may include:

- the timetable for the proceedings including the identification of the issues which require adjudication and the order in which they shall be determined (note the *President's Guidance: Split Hearings* issued in May 2010, available at [2010] Fam Law 752);

- the attendance of the parties;

- the submission of evidence;

- the preparation of any welfare (s 7) report;

- the transfer of proceedings to another court (including at the same jurisdictional level or to an upper or lower tier);

- the consolidation of the proceedings with any other relevant proceedings.

7.2.4 Preparation for final hearing

Good practice in relation to case preparation for any s 8 hearing requires consideration of the following.

7.2.4.1 Case management

- Identification of issues:

  - what is the outcome which is sought?
  - what is the evidence necessary to achieve that?

- Agreement as to the relevant issues:

  - can a schedule be drawn up identifying the issues with which the court will be concerned?

- Agreeing a realistic time estimate:

- based upon a sensible witness template;
- identifying the necessary oral evidence;
- ensuring the availability of witnesses coincides with the witness template;
- allowing sufficient time for pre-reading and the preparation of judgment.[39]

7.2.4.2 *Bundles*

- In the proper structure.

- Incorporating skeleton arguments, opening position statements, schedules of issues and witness templates.

- Clearly identifying agreed documentation and that which is not agreed.

- Marking clearly where parties are relying upon material which is not agreed.

- See Practice Direction 27A, FPR 2010.

7.2.4.3 *Documentation*

- Should be legible.

- Paginated.

- Available to the witness.

- Provided in good time.

- Updated in the Bundle as required.

- Written statements of evidence:

  - should contain the substance of the oral evidence intended to be adduced;
  - should refer to all relevant matters;
  - should avoid reference to matters which are unrelated to the issues with which the court is concerned;
  - should avoid excessive hearsay;
  - should make clear any source of information other than the maker of the statement where that information is included within the statement;
  - should comply with the following procedural requirements:

---

[39]   See *Re D (Minors: Time Estimates)* [1994] 2 FLR 336.

(i) be dated;

(ii) be signed by the person making the statement;

(iii) contain a declaration that the maker of the statement believes it to be true and understands that it will be placed before the court;

(iv) set out in the top right-hand corner of the first page:

    (a) the initials and surname of the maker of the statement;

    (b) the number of that statement;

    (c) the date on which it was made;

    (d) on whose behalf it is filed (the party).

– be re-intended to stand as evidence-in-chief at the final hearing.[40]

7.2.4.4 *Experts*

The issue of the use of expert evidence in family proceedings has become a much discussed topic in recent years, not least because of the increasing costs of such expertise and the declining numbers of suitably qualified experts willing to involve themselves in the family justice system.

As a consequence, considerable judicial energy has been given to the proper use of expert evidence, the frequency of expert reports, the instruction given to the authors of such reports, the preparation of those reports and the necessity for the expert to attend court as opposed to engage in less expensive and more focused discussions with fellow experts aimed at minimising the areas of disagreement and settling the forensic disputes.

Much benefit will be gained by a detailed reading of FPR 2010, Practice Direction 25A into which the collected guidance on the appropriate use of expert evidence has been distilled.

The headline points are:

- experts should be instructed only where there is clear identification of the issue which their evidence will address, that such issue is relevant to the determination of the application before the court and that issue is not within the knowledge of the court;

- the appropriate specialism should be carefully identified;

- the agreed letter of instruction should set out with clarity the instructions of each expert and the parameters of their professional responsibilities;

---

[40] *Practice Direction (Case Management)* [1995] 1 FLR 456.

- there shall be a clear timetable for the instruction of the expert, the filing of the report and of any consequential questions and answers flowing from that report which will assist in the clarification of the relevant issues;

- experts so instructed in court proceedings have a duty to the court rather than to any particular party and their reports should explicitly acknowledge such duty when filed;

- the contents of the expert's report should follow a logical structure and should ensure compliance with para 3.3 of PD25A;

- there are clear rules governing the holding of any experts' meetings, the preparation for them, the minuting of them and the structure of them;

- reference should be made to:

  - the Code of Guidance for Expert Witnesses in Family Proceedings;
  - the Good Practice Guidance for letters of instruction to be found at www.family-justice-council.org.uk;
  - Annex B of the Report of the Chief Medical Officer, 'Bearing Good Witness: Proposals for Reforming the delivery of medical expert evidence in family law cases';
  - the guidance given by Charles J in *A County Council v K, D and L*;[41]
  - the guidance given by Ryder J in *Oldham County Council v W*.[42]

7.3 GENERAL PRINCIPLES TO BE APPLIED WHEN CONSIDERING APPLICATIONS FOR S 8 ORDERS

When considering an application for any s 8 order a court will apply certain uniform principles:

- the child's welfare shall be the paramount consideration;[43]

- that welfare will be prejudiced by delay in determining the application;[44]

- the application shall be decided with reference to a checklist of factors;[45]

---

[41]   [2005] 1 FLR 851.
[42]   [2007] 2 FLR 597.
[43]   Children Act 1989, s 1(1).
[44]   Children Act 1989, s 1(2).
[45]   Children Act 1989, s 1(3).

- an order will only be made if doing so is better than not making an order.[46]

7.3.1 Welfare

The classic definition of welfare was given by Lord McDermott in *J v C*:[47]

> '... when all the relevant facts, relationships, claims and wishes of parents, risks, choices and other circumstances are taken into account and weighed, the course to be followed will be that which is most in the interests of the child's welfare as that term is now understood. That is ... the paramount consideration because it rules on and determines the course to be followed.'

7.3.2 The application of the principle

The court is required to make welfare the paramount consideration whenever the court is concerned with a question with respect to the upbringing of a child[48]. The statutory guidance accompanying the children states that the welfare principle applies whenever the court is considering whether to make *any* s 8 order.[49]

The welfare principle does not apply unless the issue before the court is concerned with the 'upbringing' of a child, defined as including 'the care of the child'[50] and therefore is not applicable where the issue does not directly concern his care or upbringing. Hence the following issues would not require welfare to be the paramount consideration:

- a decision whether to make a person a party to proceedings;

- whether to give leave to a person to make an application for a s 8 order;

- an application under s 15 and Sch 1 for financial provision.

The court is concerned with the child whose upbringing is in issue before the court.

However, an application may concern more than one child or an application may be brought by a child and concern a different child (eg an application by one sibling for contact with another). In which case the following principles apply:

---

[46]   Children Act 1989, s 1(5).
[47]   (1969) FLR Rep 360.
[48]   Children Act 1989, s 1(1)(a).
[49]   *The Children Act 1989 Guidance and Regulations*, Vol 1, para 2.57.
[50]   Children Act 1989, s 105(1).

- the welfare with which the court is concerned is that of the child who is the subject of the application;[51]

- where an application concerns more than one child it is the welfare of each child with which the court is concerned which must be considered by the court and the respective benefits and detriments to each child which must be weighed in determining the appropriate outcome.[52]

The central importance of welfare as the primary determinant of an application concerning a child has been demonstrated clearly by the decisions in *Re G (Children)*[53] and *Re B (A Child)*.[54] By those decisions the notion of parental right or presumptions in determining the issue of residence of a child was consigned to history.

7.3.3   Delay

The Children Act has placed a premium upon the avoidance of systemic delay overtaking the irreplaceable time of childhood. There is a constant tension between the conflicting aims of delivering an effective and just system of law which meets the needs of children and doing so as quickly as possible.

There will always be some degree of delay between the issuing of an application and its final determination. In many cases instant decisions would run counter to the need to make the most informed and considered judgement which will meet the child's needs, both immediate and in the longer term. The avoidance of delay is in fact a precept to avoid loss of valuable time in a child's life through drift, when the child's time is allowed to elapse without good reason and for no benefit.

The general principle is that delay is prejudicial to welfare[55] and therefore, given that, the court must give paramount consideration to the child's welfare and it should not countenance delay.

This principle is general and not absolute and therefore may be capable of being rebutted depending upon the facts of the case. Delay may be accepted where:

- it is for the purpose of gathering information necessary to enable a court to make a fully informed decision;

---

[51]   *Birmingham City Council v H (No 3)* [1994] 1 FLR 224.
[52]   *Re T and E (Proceedings: Conflicting Interests)* [1995] 1 FLR 581.
[53]   *Re G (Children)* [2006] UKHL 43.
[54]   *Re B (A Child)* [2009] UKSC 5.
[55]   Children Act 1989, s 1(2).

- further developments are expected which may have a significant impact upon the outcome;

- time is required to allow an arrangement to settle down following a period of change.

The acceptance of delay is because it is perceived to offer some benefit to a child, delaying the determination of an outcome for the benefit of an adult is not acceptable.[56]

In order to give practical effect to the general principle of avoiding delay upon the issuing of an application for a s 8 order the court shall require a timetable to be drawn up with the aim of avoiding delay.[57] The accent of avoiding delay has been strengthened with the coming into effect of the Family Procedure Rules 2010. The FPR 2010 has as the first part of its Overriding Objective the requirement to deal with the case expeditiously and fairly. In addition Practice Directions 12A and 12B respectively incorporate the Revised Public Law Outline and the Private Law Programme which separately and specifically require cases to be expeditiously conducted and timetabled at each stage (see Procedure).

7.3.4 The welfare checklist

Section 1(3) of the Children Act 1989 sets out the following:

'... a court shall have regard in particular to –
(a) the ascertainable wishes and feelings of the child concerned (considered in the light of his age and understanding);
(b) his physical, emotional and educational needs;
(c) the likely effect on him of any change in his circumstances;
(d) his age, sex, background and any characteristics of his which the court considers relevant;
(e) any harm which he has suffered or is at risk of suffering;
(f) how capable each of his parents, and any other person in relation to whom the court considers the question to be relevant, is of meeting his needs;
(g) the range of powers available to the court under this Act in the proceedings in question.'

This is known as the welfare checklist. It exists for the following reasons:

- the court's paramount consideration is the welfare of the child;

- welfare is a multi-faceted concept which evolves and adapts depending upon the factual circumstances which exist at the point of consideration;

---

[56] *B v B (Minors)(Interviews and Listing Arrangements)* [1994] 2 FLR 489.
[57] Children Act 1989, s 11(1).

- by setting out a frame of reference for consideration of the child's welfare the court is required to look at the child's situation from a number of different perspectives and in so doing arrive at a more informed and child-centred decision.

The checklist has the following additional benefits:

- it provides a structure around which a case can be based;

- issues can be more readily identified;

- more focused and targeted evidence can be presented;

- decisions and judgments of the court will be better structured by dealing with the relevant aspects of the checklist so as to lead to greater clarity as to the reasons for the decision which has been made.

In addition the following points should be noted:

- The checklist is to be applied for any contested s 8 order.[58]

- The checklist should also be used whenever an application is made for permission to remove from the jurisdiction.[59]

- The checklist is not intended to be exhaustive of all the relevant factors which a court might consider in determining any particular application.

- The matters set out in the checklist should not be ignored, the section states that the court 'shall have regard' to them.

- It is open to the court to include within its deliberations any other matter which is considered to be relevant to the application.

- It is not obligatory for judges to refer to each factor when delivering judgment upon an application[60] but it is certainly useful to approach the decision-making process on that basis.[61]

- In difficult or finely balanced cases it is a great help for judges to consider each of the factors in the checklist individually so as to ensure that each factor is given the weight which it should properly have.[62]

---

[58]   Children Act 1989, s 1(4).
[59]   *Payne v Payne* [2001] 1 FLR 1052.
[60]   *H v H (Residence Order: Leave to Remove from Jurisdiction)* [1995] 1 FLR 529.
[61]   *B v B (Residence Order: Reasons for Decision)* [1997] 2 FLR 602.
[62]   *Re G (Children)* [2006] UKHL 43.

- Justices sitting in the family proceedings court are expected to make express reference to the various factors in the welfare checklist when announcing the reasons for their decision.[63]

7.3.5 The No Order principle

Section 1(5) requires the court to consider whether it would be better for the child if an order were made:

> 'Where a court is considering whether or not to make one or more orders under this Act with respect to a child, it shall not make the order or any of the orders unless it considers that doing so would be better for the child than making no order at all.'

This short but important provision raises a number of important points:

- it is applicable whenever the court is considering whether to make any order under the Children Act 1989;

- there is no presumption against making an order;

- the court is specifically required to consider whether, from the point of view of the child, the making of an order confers a positive benefit;

- where an issue is the subject of contested proceedings the need for an order may be obvious;

- even where agreement has been reached there may be a basis for making an order to:
  - confer parental responsibility where it might not otherwise exist;
  - confirm arrangements for the child;
  - clarify the position to avoid future confusion;
  - give impetus to the development of proper contact arrangements;
  - assist in the state allocation of public resources or financial benefits;
  - evidence the contact arrangements for the purpose of the Child Support Agency.

An important but secondary aspect of the no order principle is the adoption of a policy of a least interventionist approach.[64] Recognised in

---

63 *R v Oxfordshire County Council (Secure Accommodation Order)* [1992] Fam 150.
64 *Re O (Care or Supervision Order)* [1996] 2 FLR 755.

the sphere of public law, it is consistent with the principle of deferring to those to whom responsibility was primarily given save where good reason justifies intervention.

7.4 DIRECTIONS, CONDITIONS AND PROVISIONS

Unlike the previous orders involving 'custody, care and control' section 8 orders were intended to be flexible and capable of targeting a particular aspect of a child's life. In so doing the orders are consistent with the least interventionist approach implied within the 'no order' principle of s 1(5) of the Children Act 1989.

An important but under-used provision in support of those twin aims is the power of the court to attach to any order conditions, directions or provisions.

By reason of s 11(7) of the Children Act 1989 any section 8 order may:

'(a) contain directions about how it is to be carried into effect;
(b) impose conditions which must be complied with by any person—
    (i)   in whose favour the order is made;
    (ii)   who is a parent of the child concerned;
    (iii) who is not a parent of his but who has parental responsibility for him; or
    (iv)   with whom the child is living,
    and to whom the conditions are expressed to apply;
(c) be made to have effect for a specified period, or contain provisions which are to have effect for a specified period;
(d) make such incidental, supplemental or consequential provision as the court thinks fit.'

There are three aspects of this section:

(1) the power to give directions as to *how* an order shall be implemented;

(2) the power to impose *conditions* upon those *who* fall within the classes of persons set out in (b)(i)–(iv) above;

(3) the power to make *provision* in relation to the order.

The intention of this important subsection is to enable a standard statutory scheme to have the maximum flexibility to provide tailor-made solutions to individual cases.

Directions as to the implementation of an order can allow for careful planning of the attainment or development of the purpose intended by the order, for example:

- phasing the change of residence of a child from one carer to another by setting out planned stages;

- structuring arrangements for contact to provide for the timing and location of handovers;

- making an 'interim' order by including a direction as to when the order will expire.[65]

Conditions can be imposed which qualify the authority or requirement otherwise conferred by the order. Conditions can be specific to a particular person or be general in their application. A condition is not necessarily concerned merely with the implementation of the order but its long-term operation.

Examples of conditions which have been made in respect of section 8 orders are:

- allowing the child to be permanently removed from the jurisdiction only upon completion of specified steps;

- requiring the parent with whom the child resides to read to the child any indirect contact material sent by the absent parent;[66]

- requiring a resident parent to provide to a non-resident parent photographs, information on the child's progress and medical reports;

- restricting the discretion of parental responsibility by setting prohibitions upon certain behaviour.

However despite the aim of achieving individual flexibility there are limitations upon the nature of the conditions which may be imposed:

- in the absence of exceptional circumstances arising from the individual facts of a case no condition of location should be imposed upon the making of a residence order;[67]

- no condition should be made which has as its purpose or result the suspension or removal of rights of occupation;[68]

---

65 Also achieved by the operation of s 11(3) of the Children Act 1989.
66 *Re O (Contact: Imposition of Conditions)* [1995] 2 FLR 124.
67 *Re E (Residence: Imposition of Conditions)* [1997] 2 FLR 638.
68 *D v N (Contact Order: Conditions)* [1997] 2 FLR 797.

- no condition or direction can be made which restricts or otherwise interferes with the statutory powers or obligations of other statutory bodies;[69]

- conditions should not be imposed upon a residence order where, as a result, the child will be residing beyond the jurisdiction;[70]

- those against whom conditions can be made are limited to those specifically set out in subsection (b) and it is not open to the court to impose conditions on others;[71]

- a condition must be within the scope and purpose of the section 8 order to which it is attached and should not seek to import by some circuitous route results which do not fall within that context.[72]

Provisions are broader in scope as they are not limited to implementation or as to the class of persons in respect of whom they may be made. An example of a provision of a section 8 order was to give permission to a non-party to apply to vary an order in which he is named.[73]

7.5   RESIDENCE ORDERS

7.5.1   The nature of a residence order

A residence order 'means an order settling the arrangements to be made as to the person with whom a child is to live'.[74]

- The order does not determine where a child should live only with whom.

- It does not extinguish the parental responsibility which is held by any other person but does limit the ability to use it.[75]

- A residence order is intended to confirm the practical arrangements then existing as to with whom a child lives at any particular time.

Although there will only be one residence order in place at any one time, the arrangements made may involve more than one person and more than one location.[76]

---

[69]   *D v D (County Court Jurisdiction: Injunctions)* [1993] 2 FLR 802.
[70]   *Re H (Residence Order: Placement out of Jurisdiction)* [2006] 1 FLR 1140.
[71]   *Leeds County Council v C* [1993] 1 FLR 269.
[72]   *Re D (Prohibited Steps Order)* [1996] 2 FLR 273.
[73]   *Re H (Prohibited Steps Order)* [1995] 1 FLR 638.
[74]   Children Act 1989, s 8(1).
[75]   Children Act 1989, s 2(8).
[76]   Children Act 1989, s 11(4).

There are various types of residence order:

- *a sole residence order* – confirming that a child lives with an identified individual who is the holder of the residence order;

- *a joint residence order* – an order identifying two or more individuals who live in the same household but each will be able to exercise parental responsibility for the child who is the subject of the order;

- *a shared residence order* – an order identifying two or more individuals who live in separate households but with whom a child spends an appreciable period of time (although not necessarily equal periods).

Although a shared residence order will not be the outcome in every case where a child spends time with different carers the idea that such an order was only to be made in exceptional circumstances or where there was an obvious benefit to a child is no longer the case, good reasons would have to be shown why such an order should *not* be made in a situation where a child's time was (roughly) equally divided between the respective households.[77] Where such an order is made the time spent by the child with any person identified in the order is not 'contact' and should not be considered as such.[78]

7.5.2　The effect of a residence order

The *effect* is that a residence order:

- confers parental responsibility upon a person who would not otherwise have it[79] for the period during which the order operates (note the different position of a father in whose favour a residence order is made[80]);

- enables the holder to apply to the court for financial assistance for the child;[81]

- discharges any pre-existing care order;[82]

- prevents a change of surname of the child;[83]

---

[77]　*Re P (Shared Residence Order)* [2006] 2 FLR 347.
[78]　*Re W (Shared Residence Order)* [2009] EWCA Civ 370, [2009] 2 FLR 436.
[79]　Children Act 1989, s 12(2).
[80]　Children Act 1989, s 12(4).
[81]　Children Act 1989. s 15 and Sch 1.
[82]　Children Act 1989, s 91(1).
[83]　Children Act 1989, s 13(1)(a).

- prevents the removal of the child from the United Kingdom (not just England and Wales[84]) for periods greater than one month.[85]

It is no longer the case that a residence order can only continue after a child has reached the age of 16 where exceptional circumstances are found.[86]

7.5.3   The limitations of a residence order

The *limitations* of a residence order are:

- it cannot be made in favour of a local authority;[87]

- it will cease to have effect 6 months after the residence order holder (where a parent of the child) has lived with the child's other parent where both parents have parental responsibility for that child;

- it cannot be made in relation to a child who has achieved their 16th birthday in the absence of exceptional circumstances.

The *enhanced* residence order which could previously be made under s 12(5) and (6) of the Act is no longer available. The special guardianship order would now be considered the appropriate order in the circumstances where an enhanced residence order might have been made.

A residence order (like all s 8 orders) is intended to act to promote the welfare of the child and therefore can be applied with both flexibility as to its application and elasticity in its operation. In addition to the conditions, provisions and directions that can be added to it (see relevant section) its operation, including dates of implementation and terms of application, can be separately considered. The aim is to provide bespoke justice to the particular case before the court.[88]

Such flexibility does not, however, extend to the provision of accommodation for the child. A shared residence order should not be made unless it is reasonably likely that each person shall have accommodation in which the child can in fact reside. A shared residence order is not a means by which a provider of accommodation (whether a local authority or other) can be made subject to pressure to allocate scarce housing stock.[89]

---

[84]   See *Re H (Children) (Residence Order: Condition)* [2001] 2 FLR 1277.
[85]   Children Act 1989, s 13(1)(b).
[86]   Children Act 1989 1989, s 9(6).
[87]   Children Act 1989, s 9(2).
[88]   *Re A (Suspended Residence Order)* [2010] 1 FLR 1679.
[89]   *Holmes-Moorhouse v Richmond-upon-Thames London Borough Council* [2009] UKHL 7.

In seeking to promote a child's welfare a residence order should not be made in favour of a natural parent over any other person (eg a grandparent, former partner or civil partner) unless that person is also considered to be the person most able to care for that child. The concept of a 'natural parent presumption' which was thought to apply in favour of a parent over anyone else should not cause a court to ignore evidence which would otherwise result in another person being granted the order. The fact of biological parentage is a factor which will be taken into consideration but is not determinative.[90] Considerations of parenthood must be examined in the light of what was in the child's best interests.[91] The same position is applicable where surrogate parents are involved.[92]

7.6   CONTACT ORDERS

7.6.1   The legal framework

7.6.1.1   Definition

A contact order is defined as:

'an order requiring the person with whom a child lives, or is to live, to allow the child to visit or stay with the person named in the order, or for that person and the child otherwise to have contact with each other'.[93]

The practical effects of a contact order are as follows:

- it is a court order capable of being enforced in the event of non-compliance;

- to be effective it requires a settled set of arrangements to be in place in respect of the child's primary residence as it is an order directed against the person or persons with whom the child lives (but does not require the making of a residence order as a prerequisite);

- it is not an order directing a person to have contact with a child, no such legal compulsion exists, there is no duty to have contact, there is no right (in English law) to have contact with a child;[94]

- it is not limited to direct contact (ie a face-to-face meeting between the child and the person named in the order) but can take the form of letters, cards, presents, telephone calls, texts, emails, social network communications, videos/DVDs or webcams;

---

90   *Re G* [2006] UKHL 43, [2006] 2 FLR 629.
91   *Re B* [2009] UKSC 5, [2010] 1 FLR 551.
92   *Re P (A child) (Residence Order)* [2007] EWCA Civ 1053, [2008] 1 FLR 198.
93   Children Act 1989, s 8(1).
94   *Re S (Contact: Promoting Relationship with Absent Parent)* [2004] 1 FLR 1279.

- arrangements can be general, undefined and vague (often defined as 'reasonable contact') or specific as to date, time, location and include stipulations as to mode of travel, state of health, activities included or excluded from contact.

Applications for contact orders are governed by s 10 as to entitlement to apply and the requirement of leave (see Applications for s 8 orders).

The court may make a contact order of its own motion whilst considering any s 8 application[95] An order may be made on a without notice basis, as a final order at the conclusion of the proceedings or 'at any time during the course of the proceedings in question'.[96] Care should be taken when considering 'interim' contact in cases where either the principle of contact is in dispute or substantial factual issues exist.[97]

Contact is not limited to a parent but the presumption that contact is in the best interests of a child does not automatically fall to be applied where the applicant is not a parent or a sibling. The extent to which a court will consider that contact should take place with any particular person (including grandparents, same sex partners and former spouses or partners) will depend upon an assessment of a number of factors including the relationship with the child, its significance, strength and history, the view of the parent with care and the likelihood of contact taking place to any related persons without contact to the applicant taking place.

Cases of significant inter-parental contact dispute can distort the view as to where the child's welfare lies and in such cases it is appropriate for the child to be separately represented with the assistance of a guardian.[98] Reference in such cases should be made to FPR 2010, Practice Direction 16A Representation of Children.

No order directing contact between a child and a parent may continue for longer than 6 months after the resumption of cohabitation between the child's parents.[99] An order requiring that the person with whom the child lives shall *not* allow contact with a named person (an order for no contact) is a contact order.[100]

---

[95] Children Act 1989, s 10(1)(b).
[96] Children Act 1989, s 11(3).
[97] *Re D (Contact: Interim Order)* [1995] 1 FLR 495.
[98] *Re A (A Child)(Contact: Separate Representation in Contact Proceedings)* [2001] 1 FLR 715.
[99] Children Act 1989, s 11(6).
[100] *Nottinghamshire County Council v P* [1993] 1 FLR 514.

7.6.1.2   The legal principles upon which an application for contact is determined

A succinct submission of the essential principles in relation to the court's approach to the grant of contact is found in the judgment of Wall J in *Re P (Contact: Supervision)*:[101]

(1)   Overriding all else, as provided by s 1(1) of the 1989 Act, the welfare of the child is the paramount consideration, and the court is concerned with the interests of the mother and the father only insofar as they bear on the welfare of the child.

(2)   It is almost always in the interests of a child whose parents are separated that he or she should have contact with the parent with whom the child is not living.

(3)   The court has power to enforce orders for contact, which it should not hesitate to exercise where it judges that it will overall promote the welfare of the child to do so.

(4)   Cases do, unhappily and infrequently but occasionally, arise in which a court is compelled to conclude that in existing circumstances an order for immediate direct contact should not be ordered, because so to order would injure the welfare of the child: see *Re D (A Minor) (Contact: Mother's Hostility)*.[102]

(5)   In cases in which, for whatever reason, direct contact cannot for the time being be ordered, it is ordinarily highly desirable that there should be indirect contact so that the child grows up knowing of the love and interest of the absent parent with whom, in due course, direct contact should be established.

The advent of the Human Rights Act 1998 and the consequent introduction of the jurisprudence of the European Court of Human Rights have allowed for further scrutiny of the approach adopted in relation to contact applications:[103]

- the right under Article 8 of an individual to have a family life is not absolute and will give way to the needs of a child;

- the effect of the application of the European jurisprudence has served to clarify the interrelationship between the rights of the different individuals affected by the application;

---

[101]   [1996] 2 FLR 314.
[102]   [1993] 2 FLR 1, 7G, per Waite LJ.
[103]   *Re D (Intractable Contact Dispute: Publicity)* [2004] 1 FLR 1226.

- whilst there is no absolute right to have contact with a child a parent has a right to expect a state to put in place effective means by which a parent separated from a child will be reunited;

- that right must be considered in the light of the rights of others in relation to their privacy and family life;

- the effectiveness of the methods for the resumption of contact are measured primarily in the time taken for implementation as the elapse of time may disproportionately affect the relationship between adult and child;

- coercion of an unwilling parent to allow contact is one of several measures to be applied;

- skilled, professional assistance must be available for the most difficult of cases.

It has been suggested that the relevant principles can be cast in terms of the checklist set out at s 1(3) of the Children Act 1989 and the question asked whether the fundamental need of every child to have an enduring relationship with both parents is outweighed by the depth of harm which may be caused.[104]

The principles are applicable when the aim is to maintain a current relationship or to restore a former one although different considerations may apply where the aim is to create a new relationship.[105]

7.6.1.3 *Parental opposition to contact*

Parental Alienation Syndrome or, more properly, 'implacable hostility' is a particular problem affecting opposition to applications for contact. The court should start from the position that, despite the objections being expressed, the presumption in favour of contact meets the child's welfare for reasons of identity and a continuing relationship.[106]

The court will consider any application for contact in the light of the welfare checklist and in particular will give careful scrutiny where the parent with whom the child lives is hostile to the principle of contact. The proper approach for the court to adopt is:

- **Are there any rational grounds for the parent's hostility?**

---

[104] *Re M (Contact: Welfare Test)* [1995] 1 FLR 274.
[105] *Re L (Contact: Domestic Violence); Re H (Contact: Domestic Violence); Re M (Contact: Domestic Violence); Re H (Contact: Domestic Violence)* [2000] 2 FLR 334.
[106] *Re H (A child) (Mother's Opposition)* [2001] 1 FCR 59.

If not then in the absence of evidence (usually a psychiatric report) of a serious risk of emotional harm to the child contact should be ordered.

- **If there are grounds for the hostility:**
  Are they sufficient to displace the presumption that contact would be in this child's best interests?
  If no, then why should an order for contact not be made?
  If yes, the fact of parental hostility is largely irrelevant to the existence of grounds for refusing the application.
  But:

- **Is there any countervailing argument in favour of contact notwithstanding the grounds for not making an order?**
  If yes, is the hostility a factor which when measured as to its effect upon the child important, or even determinative, of the application?[107]

Where a court has made a contact order, despite a finding of implacable hostility, and the operation of that order is being thwarted by the resident parent the removal of the child to the care of the contact parent should not be viewed as a punishment of one parent but a review of previously considered welfare arrangements for a child in the light of developments such as a failure of adherence to them.[108] It remains the judicial weapon of last resort.

7.6.1.4 *Domestic violence and contact*

The previous infliction of domestic violence by a person seeking contact upon a child or the person with care of that child is not in itself an automatic prohibition to contact.[109] It is, however, a factor which will be of significance when considering any application.

The principles for dealing with cases where there are allegations of domestic violence are set out in the case of *Re L (Contact: Domestic Violence)*:[110]

(1) the effect of children being exposed to domestic violence of one parent as against the other should not be ignored nor underestimated;

(2) any allegations of domestic violence which if proved might have an effect upon the outcome of the application should be properly investigated at a Finding of Fact hearing;

---

[107] *Re P (Contact: Discretion)* [1998] 2 FLR 696.
[108] *Re G* [2006] 2 FLR 629.
[109] *Re H (Minors)(Contact: Domestic Violence)* [1998] 2 FLR 42.
[110] [2000] 2 FLR 334.

(3)   any allegations of domestic violence which are found to be proved
      do not create a presumption of no contact which must thereafter be
      surmounted by the applicant;

(4)   where established the effect of domestic violence on children exposed
      to it, and the risk to the residential carer are highly relevant factors
      in considering orders for contact and their form;

(5)   in assessing the relevance of past domestic violence, it is likely to be
      highly material whether the perpetrator has shown an ability to
      recognise the wrong he (or less commonly she) has done, and the
      steps taken to correct the deficiency in the perpetrator's character;

(6)   domestic violence is not to be elevated to some special category; it is
      one highly material factor amongst many which may offset the
      assumption in favour of contact when the difficult balancing exercise
      is carried out by the judge applying the welfare principle and the
      welfare checklist, s 1(1) and (3) of the Children Act 1989.

Whether a Finding of Fact hearing was required should be identified at
an early stage in the proceedings and, once listed, should not be vacated
without good reason[111] and should not be concluded after hearing only
the evidence of one party[112] or accede to a submission of no case to
answer.[113]

Where allegations of violence have been made which may, if proved, be
relevant to the question of whether contact is ordered or how contact is
operated then it is not normally appropriate prior to that finding of fact
hearing to make an order for interim contact.[114]

Particular assistance is gained from considering the Guidelines for Good
Practice on Parental Contact in cases where there is Domestic Violence
(reprinted here as Appendix 1). When considering the issues arising in
these cases it is necessary to have regard to Family Procedure Rules 2010
Practice Direction 12J – Residence and Contact Orders: Domestic
Violence and Harm (Appendix 2).

Further assistance is gained from considering the report of Dr Glaser and
Dr Sturge, Consultant Child Psychiatrists, commissioned for the purpose
of the conjoined hearings reported as *Re L*.[115]

---

[111]   *Re FH (Dispensing with Finding of Fact Hearing)* [2009] 1 FLR 349.
[112]   *Re Z (Unsupervised Contact: Allegations of Domestic Violence)* [2009] 2 FLR 877.
[113]   *Re R (Family Proceedings: No Case to Answer)* [2009] 2 FLR 83.
[114]   *S v S (Interim Contact)* [2009] 2 FLR 1586.
[115]   See [2000] Fam Law 615.

7.6.1.5   *Facilitation of contact*

Upon making an order for contact a variety of options are available to the court including:

- an order for reasonable contact which allows the parties to set up the arrangements for contact, determining timing, frequency, venues and duration, such order may include provision for staying contact, extended staying contact, visiting contact and additional forms of indirect contact;

- a prescriptive order specifying to whatever degree of particularity is required the precise details of the contact.

Where some degree of supervision of contact is required the use of a Child Contact Centre may be necessary. A Protocol for the referral of Judges and Magistrates to Child Contact Centres has been issued, supported by the President of the Family Division which should be adhered to. (The Protocol is reproduced as Appendix 3).

Recent amendments made to the Children Act 1989[116] have been made to enhance the powers of the court with respect to the better operation of contact orders. Section 11A–11P sets out the provisions whereby a court can:

- direct the attendance of a person at a contact activity (defined in Cafcass Guidance as information meetings about mediation, parenting information programmes and domestic violence prevention programmes);

- provide financial assistance to enable individuals to participate in such activities;

- impose a monitoring requirement upon Cafcass (s 11J) to report as to the extent to which any party has complied with their obligations under the contact order made;

- issue a warning notice as to the consequences if a breach of the order is proved, such consequences can include an enforcement order requiring the party in breach to undertake unpaid work or to pay financial compensation for losses arising from the failure to comply with the order.

Where a contact order has been made but is not operating smoothly there is a duty upon the court to strive to make it work and it is not ordinarily

---

[116] Sections 11A–11P, inserted by the Children and Adoption Act 2006.

appropriate to dismiss applications for enforcement of the order or make prohibitions against further applications.[117]

7.7 APPLICATIONS FOR CHANGE OF NAME

7.7.1 The Law

7.7.1.1 *Naming the child*

There is a social convention that a child takes the surname of the father; however, there is no legal requirement that this be so.[118] There is a legal requirement that the name of a child must be registered no later than 42 days after birth.[119] Where the parents are married, registration may be effected by either parent, otherwise registration is the responsibility of the mother, even where the father has parental responsibility for the child.[120] The father in such a situation has no authority within the process of registration.

7.7.1.2 *Registration of the name*

The register cannot be altered following completion of the registration process save by the addition of a name within 12 months of the date of registration.[121] The registration of a particular name for a child is a factor of significance when consideration is given to any change but it is not determinative of the question of whether a change could in the future be made.[122]

7.7.1.3 *The right to change a name*

Parents (together with any other persons also holding parental responsibility) acting jointly may make any change to the names of their child. Where a child is the subject of a residence order the child's name can only be changed where the consent of all those holding parental responsibility is given *in writing*.[123] Any application for such a change is made by application under s 13(1).

---

[117] *Re C (Contact Order: Variation)* [2009] 1 FLR 869.
[118] *Dawson v Wearmouth* [1999] 1 FLR 1167.
[119] Births and Deaths Registration Act 1953, s 2.
[120] Births and Deaths Registration Act 1953, s 10.
[121] *Re H (Child's Name: First Name)* [2002] 1 FLR 973.
[122] *Dawson v Wearmouth* [1999] 1 FLR 1167.
[123] Children Act 1989, s 13(1) and s 14C(3).

Where there is no residence order in place the consent of all those with
parental responsibility must be first obtained, notwithstanding s 2(7) of
the Children Act 1989.[124] In the absence of consent an application for a
specific issue order must be made.

Where only one parent has parental responsibility the position is as
follows:

- that person alone has the authority to change the child's name;[125]
  but

- following *Dawson v Wearmouth* the better course is to give advance
  notice to those interested parties who might otherwise object.[126]

7.7.1.4   *The principles involved*

The principles with which the court will be concerned on an application
are neatly set out in *Re W, Re A, Re B (Change of Name)*.[127]

(a)   If parents are married, they both have the power and the duty to
register their child's names.

(b)   If they are not married the mother has the sole duty and power to do
so.

(c)   After registration of the child's names, the grant of a residence order
obliges any person wishing to change the surname to obtain the leave
of the court or the written consent of all those who have parental
responsibility.

(d)   In the absence of a residence order, the person wishing to change the
surname from the registered name ought to obtain the relevant
written consent or the leave of the court by making an application
for a specific issue order.

(e)   On any application, the welfare of the child is paramount and the
judge must have regard to the s 1(3) criteria.

(f)   Among the factors to which the court should have regard is the
registered surname of the child and the reasons for the registration,
for instance recognition of the biological link with the child's father.
Registration is always a relevant and an important consideration but
it is not in itself decisive. The weight to be given to it by the court

---

[124]   *Re T(A Minor)(Change of Surname)* [1998] 2 FLR 620.
[125]   *Re PC (Change of Surname)* [1997] 2 FLR 730.
[126]   *Dawson v Wearmouth* [1999] 1 FLR 1167.
[127]   [1999] 2 FLR 930.

will depend upon the other relevant factors or valid countervailing reasons which may tip the balance the other way.

(g)   The relevant considerations should include factors which may arise in the future as well as the present situation.

(h)   Reasons given for changing or seeking to change a child's name based on the fact that the child's name is or is not the same as the parent making the application do not generally carry much weight.

(i)   The reasons for an earlier unilateral decision to change a child's name may be relevant.

(j)   Any changes of circumstances of the child since the original registration may be relevant.

(k)   In the case of a child whose parents were married to each other, the fact of the marriage is important and would suggest that there would have to be strong reasons to change the name from the father's surname if the child was so registered.

(l)   Where the child's parents were not married to each other, the mother has control over registration. Consequently, on an application to change the surname of the child, the degree of commitment of the father to the child, the quality of contact, if it occurs, between father and child, the existence or absence of parental responsibility are all relevant factors to take into account.

7.7.1.5   *The application*

The application is either:

•   a freestanding one under s 13(1), where a residence order is in force in relation to a child; or

•   an application for a specific issue order where no residence order has been made.

7.7.1.6   *The procedure*

When the application is made as an application for a specific issue order the procedure to be followed is as set out for a section 8 application (see Procedure).

When the application is a freestanding application under s 13(1) the procedure to be followed is above. Note that there is no requirement when the application is brought under s 13(1) to have regard to the welfare checklist set out at s 1(3) of the Children Act 1989 but its consideration as a valuable 'aide-memoire' has been endorsed.[128]

Reference should be made to *Practice Direction (20th December 1994)* [1995] 1 FLR 458.

7.7.1.7 Factors to consider

When dealing with an application for change of name the following matters should be considered:

- The welfare of the child is the paramount consideration.

- What is the motivation for the change?

  - convenience for the parent with care is not a strong factor;[129]
  - the siblings all having the same surname is a not a factor.

- What is the registered name? Is the change from the registered name or a return to it?

- In the case of a child of a marriage is the registered name also the marital name?

- If objection to a change is being raised by a parent with whom the children do not live:

  - is the change from the name of the absent parent (the link with a father may be considered to be a strong factor against change)?
  - what is the degree of attachment and commitment to the children by the absent parent?
  - is there contact with that absent parent? With what degree of frequency and/or regularity? If not, why not?

- If there has already been a change which is now being challenged, when did the change take place? Has the child adjusted to that change?

- Where does the positive benefit to the child lie – with a change of name or a retention of a name?

---

[128] *Re B (Change of Surname)* [1996] 1 FLR 791.
[129] *Re T (Change of Surname)* [1998] 2 FLR 620.

7.7.1.8   The order

An order will made on Form C43 (Specific Issue order) or C44 (application under Children Act 1989, s 13).

7.8   PROHIBITED STEPS ORDERS

A prohibited steps order is an order preventing any person from taking an action which could be taken by a parent in meeting his parental responsibility for a child, and which is of a kind specified in the order, without the consent of the court.[130]

The prohibited steps order is an attempt to preserve the utility of the wardship jurisdiction within a limited, more focused context. Whereas within wardship proceedings no important step in the child's life could be taken without the consent of the court, a prohibited steps order seeks to regulate or restrict the particular exercise of identified aspects of parental responsibility whilst leaving all other aspects of the child's life free from court involvement.

The order is broad in its application as it is not limited to the regulation of a parent but to any person who seeks to act in respect of the child. However, it is also narrow in that it deals only with the particular issue of concern and does not affect the exercise of any other aspect of parental responsibility.

The order is prohibitive as against the person acting in respect of the child, it does not act as an injunction upon the child who is the subject of the application. Accordingly a prohibited steps order cannot forbid a child from taking any action, even of the type specified in the order.

Examples of prohibited steps orders and the exercise of parental responsibility are:

- preventing the child from being removed from the jurisdiction;

- preventing the child's name being changed;

- preventing the authorisation of specific surgery (eg circumcision);

- preventing a person (not the person with whom the child lives) from coming into contact with the child.

The following would not be considered an exercise of parental responsibility and therefore a prohibited steps order would not be available:

---

[130] Children Act 1989, s 8(1).

- preventing parents from meeting;

- making a parental responsibility agreement;[131]

- prohibiting the media from publishing information about a child;

- excluding a parent from the family home.[132]

7.8.1   Restrictions

A prohibited steps order cannot be used in the following situations:

- where the result could be achieved by the making of a residence or contact order;[133]

- in any way which is denied to the High Court by s 100 of the Children Act 1989 in the exercise of the inherent jurisdiction;[134]

- where the child has reached the age of 16 in the absence of exceptional circumstances;[135]

- where the child is subject to a care order, but note that this restriction does not apply to a child who is a 'Looked After Child' or the subject of a supervision order.[136]

It should be noted that whilst open to a local authority to apply for a prohibited steps order it is essentially a private law remedy and should not be preferred where a local authority is acting by reason of its child protection duties.[137] A prohibited steps order cannot be used to prevent a local authority from exercising its statutory powers (for example with regard to child protection) but could be imposed against a parent to prevent them from involving statutory agencies.[138]

As with the other s 8 orders the eligibility to apply for a prohibited steps order and the requirement to seek leave for those not so eligible are governed by s 10 of the Children Act 1989 (see Procedure).

---

[131] *Re X (Parental Responsibility Agreement: Children in Care)* [2000] 1 FLR 517.
[132] *Pearson v Franklin* [1994] 1 FLR 246.
[133] Children Act 1989, s 9(5)(a).
[134] Children Act 1989, s 9(5)(b).
[135] Children Act 1989, s 9(6).
[136] Children Act 1989, s 9(1).
[137] *Langley v Liverpool City Council* [2006] 1 FLR 342.
[138] *D v D (County Court Jurisdiction: Injunctions)* [1993] 2 FLR 802.

7.9   SPECIFIC ISSUE ORDERS

A specific issue order is an order giving directions for the purpose of determining a specific question which has arisen, or which may arise, in connection with any aspect of parental responsibility for a child.

The purpose of a specific issue order is to provide both a forum and a mechanism for resolution of 'any aspect of the manner in which parental responsibility falls to be exercised'[139] which is in dispute between those who are otherwise entitled to exercise that responsibility. It is a necessary consequence of the evolution from custody orders, which would entitle the holder of such an order to wield sole authority, to the concept of multi-party parental responsibility.

Specific issue orders can be used to determine a wide range of issues including:

- education;

- religion;

- medical treatment;

- the return of a child to the jurisdiction;

- the removal of a child from the jurisdiction;

- the provision of information to a child of paternity;

- the determination of a child's surname (in the absence of the existence of a residence order).[140]

The order is not limited to those who actually have parental responsibility for a child. A local authority may, with leave (see restrictions below) apply for a specific issue order where the court's guidance is sought but the issue involved would not justify the local authority seeking a care or supervision order.

The order may be made alone or in conjunction with any other combination of s 8 orders.

---

[139]   *Re J (Specific Issue Order: Leave to Apply)* [1995] 1 FLR 669.
[140]   Otherwise Children Act 1989, s 13, should be relied upon.

7.9.1 Restrictions

- A specific issue order cannot be made where the result could be achieved by the making of a residence or contact order.[141]

- The substance of a specific issue order must be related to an issue of parental responsibility, otherwise the wardship jurisdiction is more appropriate.

- The order cannot be made so as to achieve a result denied to the High Court in the exercise of its inherent jurisdiction with respect to children.[142]

- The order cannot be made in relation to a child in the care of the local authority.[143]

- A local authority may itself apply for a specific issue order but subject to the provisos set out above (and the requirement to seek permission to make the application).

- In the absence of exceptional circumstances no order can be made which will have effect upon a child:

  – who has already attained their 16th birthday;
  – beyond the attainment of their 16th birthday.

- An order should not be made which achieves an objective for which specific statutory criteria are otherwise available and required.[144]

In common with other s 8 orders the eligibility to apply for a prohibited steps order and the requirement to seek leave for those not so eligible are governed by s 10 of the Children Act 1989 (see Procedure). Further the court may give ancillary directions as to how its decision on the substantial point shall be carried into operation.

A specific issue application may be made by a child but when considering the issue of whether to give leave to the child to make such an application (as required under s 10) the issue with which the application is concerned should be one of importance.[145] In determining a specific issue application the court should decide the matter and not abdicate its

---

[141] Children Act 1989, s 9(5).
[142] Children Act 1989, s 100(2).
[143] Children Act 1989, s 9(1).
[144] *Pearson v Franklin (Parental Home: Ouster)* [1994] 1 FLR 246.
[145] *Re C (A Minor) (Leave to seek a Section 8 Order)* [1994] 1 FLR 26.

primary obligation to resolve the issue by determining that one parent as opposed to the other should decide the issue.[146]

7.10 APPLICATION FOR LEAVE TO REMOVE FROM THE JURISDICTION

7.10.1 When is leave required?

Leave is required to remove a child from the United Kingdom in every case *except* the following:

- where all those with parental responsibility consent to the child's removal; or

- where there is a residence order in place and the removal:

  - is for a period less than one month; and
  - is by a person in whose favour the residence order has been made;[147] and
  - that person is travelling with the child for the duration of that holiday;[148] or

- where there is a special guardianship order in place and the removal is for:

  - a period less than 3 months; and
  - is by a person in whose favour the special guardianship order has been made;[149] or

- where those with parental responsibility have delegated such responsibility to the person removing the child and the period of removal is less than one month.

Note the reference is to the United Kingdom. Leave is not required to move a child internally within the United Kingdom even where such a move involves moving to a different jurisdiction.[150]

Upon application leave can be given generally or for specified purposes.[151]

---

[146] *Re P (Parental Dispute: Judicial Determination)* [2002] EWCA Civ 1627, [2003] 1 FLR 286.

[147] Children Act 1989, s 13(2).

[148] *Re N (Leave to Remove: Holiday)* [2006] 2 FLR 1124.

[149] Children Act 1989, s 14C(4); in the absence of authority to the contrary the *Re N (Leave to Remove: Holiday)* [2006] 2 FLR 1124 point would also apply in this scenario.

[150] *Re H (Children)(Residence Order: Condition)* [2001] 2 FLR 1277.

[151] Children Act 1989, s 13(3).

7.10.2 What application should be made?

The application will be either:

- a freestanding application under s 13 of the Children Act 1989; or

- an application for a specific issue order under s 8 of the Children Act 1989.

7.10.3 Considerations for an application for permission to remove

In each case the general principles which will apply will be:

- the welfare of the child is paramount;[152]

- delay is being prejudicial to the welfare of the child;[153]

- the factors set out in the welfare checklist[154] (this is the case whether the application is made under s 8 or s 13).

Leave to remove cases are generally fact-specific and therefore little reliance can be placed upon decided cases as examples of fact as opposed to indicators of the principles to be applied.[155]

7.10.3.1 The 'traditional case' v the 'modern approach'

An important distinction must be drawn between those cases which reflect the common position of permission being sought by the parent who is also the settled, long-standing primary carer for the children and those where shared residence orders are in existence or where a pattern of shared residence is in fact the reality for the children. In recent years a different approach has been adopted for the latter type of case.

The traditional case

Where permission is sought by the parent with care the leading authority in relation to applications for leave to remove from the jurisdiction is *Payne v Payne*.[156] Although not immune from criticism as to whether its reasoning properly reflects the current dynamics in family life it remains the receptacle of distilled judicial wisdom and from which the following principles are derived:

(1) The welfare of the child is always paramount.

---

[152] Children Act 1989, s 1(1).
[153] Children Act 1989, s 1(2).
[154] Children Act 1989, s 1(3).
[155] *Re B (Children)* [2008] EWCA Civ 1034.
[156] *Payne v Payne* [2001] 1 FLR 1052.

(2)   There is no presumption in favour of the applicant parent, even where that parent is established as the primary carer.

(3)   The *reasonable* proposals of the parent with a residence order wishing to live abroad carry great weight.

(4)   The proposals have to be scrutinised with care and the court needs to be satisfied that there is a *genuine* motivation for the move and not the intention to bring contact between the child and the other parent to an end.

(5)   The effect of a refusal of leave upon the applicant parent and the new family of the child is very important.

(6)   The effect upon the child of the denial of contact with the other parent and in some cases his family is very important.

(7)   The opportunity for continuing contact between the child and the parent left behind may be very significant.

THE JUDICIAL CHECKLIST FOR *PAYNE* CASES

The questions to be considered by the judge when considering whether to grant leave to remove are the following:

(a)   Is the application genuine in the sense that it is not motivated by some selfish desire to exclude the other parent from the child's life?

(b)   Is the application realistic, is it founded on practical proposals both well researched and investigated?

If the application fails either of these tests refusal will inevitably follow. If, however, the application passes these tests then there must be a careful appraisal of any opposition to the application:

(a)   Is it motivated by genuine concern for the future of the child's welfare or is it driven by some ulterior motive?

(b)   What would be the extent of the detriment to the remaining parent and the future relationship with the child were the application granted?

(c)   To what extent would that be offset by any extension of the child's relationships with the removing parent and the new home?

(d)   What would be the impact on the applicant, either personally or in the context of any new family relationships, of a refusal of a realistic proposal? (NB. 'In any evaluation of the welfare of the child as the paramount consideration great weight must be given to this factor.'[157])

(e)   Consider the answers to those questions within an overriding review of the child's welfare as the paramount consideration, directed by the statutory checklist insofar as appropriate.

Although *Payne v Payne* has been regularly held up by the Court of Appeal as articulating the questions to be asked by judges in dealing with these applications it is to be viewed as guidance and not an embodiment of principle from which no deviation may be allowed.[158]

The modern approach

Where family life has not settled into the more common role of primary carer and contact parent but is reflective of a dual-centred approach more akin to a shared residence arrangement the *Payne* guidance is of limited effect and a different approach is to be followed. The position in these types of cases is set out by Hedley J in the case of *Re Y*:

> 'What it seems to me I must do is to remind myself of the opening provisions of the Children Act 1989, section 1(1) says that when a court determines any question with respect to the upbringing of a child, the child's welfare shall be the court's paramount consideration, and in considering these issues I have to take a number of matters into account as required by s 1(3).'

The judge went on to state:

> 'It seems to me that of those matters, the ones that are important in this case are the educational and emotional needs of *Y*, the likely effect on him of any change in his circumstances, and his age and background so far as his life is presently concerned. It seems to me that I need to remind myself that the welfare of this child is the lodestar by which the court at the end of the day is guided.'[159]

In effect when operating outside of the traditional/*Payne* situation the proper approach is to look at the case from the general perspective of welfare, identify those factors which, on the facts of the case as admitted or found, are likely to impact upon welfare (whether the application is granted or refused) and balance those factors against each other in order to determine how the welfare of the relevant child is best met.

---

[157]   Per Thorpe LJ, *Payne v Payne* at [41].
[158]   *K v K (Relocation: Shared Care Arrangement)* [2011] EWCA Civ 793.
[159]   *Re Y (Leave to Remove from the Jurisdiction)* [2004] 2 FLR 330.

7.10.3.2   General points

The following points should be noted:

- There is one test to be applied when considering relocation cases, irrespective of whether the intention of the remover is to return home or to make a 'lifestyle choice' and seek to improve the family situation.[160]

- The impact of refusal upon the family, including any prospective step-parent, applied with greater force where the intention was to emigrate to the jurisdiction where the step-parent was based.[161]

- In the case of a cross-border family there will be less scrutiny of the proposals of a parent who is returning to a familiar jurisdiction.[162]

- Where the child's home is shared equally between two parents the principles set out in *Payne* are not applicable.[163]

- Where the court is in fact concerned with cross applications for residence then the principles in *Payne* are not applicable.[164]

- Where a parent presents a genuine application for a removal from the jurisdiction but the plans post removal are incomplete, leave may be granted subject to meeting conditions concerning the finalisation of those plans.[165]

- In granting leave a court should have assessed all risks and have developed reasonable safeguards against their occurrence rather than simply accepting undertakings from a parent soon to depart from the jurisdiction.[166]

7.10.4   Documentation

Applications for leave should be made on Form C100 irrespective of whether the application is made pursuant to s 13 or s 8.

---

[160] *Re B (Leave to Refuse: Impact of Refusal)* [2005] 2 FLR 239.
[161] *Re B (Children: Removal from the Jurisdiction); Re S (A Child) (Removal from the Jurisdiction)* [2003] 2 FLR 1043.
[162] *Re F and H (Children)* [2007] EWCA Civ 692.
[163] *Re Y (Leave to Remove from the Jurisdiction)* [2004] 2 FLR 330.
[164] *Re J (Leave to Remove: Urgent Case)* [2007] 1 FLR 2033.
[165] *Re M (Leave to Remove Child from Jurisdiction)* [1999] 2 FLR 334.
[166] *Re K (Removal from the Jurisdiction: Practice)* [1999] 2 FLR 1084.

7.10.5   Procedure

The procedure follows the application for a section 8 order (see Procedure).

7.10.6   Essential requirements

There are a number of matters which should be covered when making this application:

- Why is the application being made?

- What is the connection with the proposed jurisdiction?

- What are the current arrangements which would be lost by a move and can they be compensated by alternative arrangements post removal?

- What arrangements will be in place for:

  - accommodation?
  - employment?
  - education of the children?
  - contact with the absent parent/those family members remaining in this jurisdiction?

- How practical are those arrangements?

- Can those arrangements be presented in such a way as to enable a court to fully appreciate them, eg:

  - photographs or (more effective) a video/DVD of the accommodation, location, schools and amenities;
  - the curriculum of the proposed school, confirmation of a place there;
  - evidence from individuals in that jurisdiction with whom the children would be living or meeting (eg members of the family of a step-parent)?

- Will contact take place in both jurisdictions or only one?

- What is the cost of contact trips (transport, accommodation and subsistence)?

- What will be the impact of a refusal in terms of:

  - family dynamics?
  - future employment opportunities?

   –   maintenance of any current family unit?

- Is evidence of the foreign legal system required and its methods of enforcement in the event of a non-return? It should be noted that where the country in question is not a signatory to the Hague Convention the starting point is that such evidence *is* required – even where the leave sought is for a temporary duration.[167]

7.10.7 The Order

An order will be made on Form C43 (specific issue order) or C44 (application under s 13 of the Children Act 1989).

7.11 CASE DIGEST

7.11.1 Residence orders

CASE NAME	CITATION	PRINCIPLE
Re W (A Minor) (Residence Order)	[1992] 2 FLR 332	Rebuttable presumption that a baby is best placed with the mother.
B v B (A Minor) (Residence Order)	[1992] 2 FLR 327	A residence order could be made for the purpose of conferring parental responsibility.
Re H (Shared Residence: Parental Responsibility)	[1995] 2 FLR 883	The making of a joint residence order was appropriate where the benefit to the child was the conferring of parental responsibility upon a step-father with whom the child also lived.
B v B (Residence Order: Restricting Applications)	[1997] 1 FLR 139	Although siblings should ordinarily be brought up together there were circumstances where separation was justified.
D v D (Shared Residence Orders)	[2001] 1 FLR 495	Exceptional circumstances were not required before the court would consider making a shared residence order.

---

[167] *Re M (Removal from Jurisdiction: Adjournment)* [2011] 1 FLR 1943, applying *Re K (Removal from Jurisdiction: Practice)* [1999] 2 FLR 1084.

CASE NAME	CITATION	PRINCIPLE
A v A (Shared Residence)	[2004] 1 FLR 1195	A shared residence order did not require the co-holders to be capable of working harmoniously together.
B v B (Residence: Condition Limited Geographic Area)	[2004] 2 FLR 979	Only in exceptional circumstances could a court impose a condition upon a capable parent which had the effect of restricting where they could reside.
Re P (Shared Residence Order)	[2006] 2 FLR 347	Good reasons would have to be shown why such an order should not be made in a situation where a child's time was (roughly) equally divided between the respective households.
Re H (Children) (Residence Order: Condition)	[2001] 2 FLR 1277	Where a residence order is in force no permission was required to remove a child from one part of the United Kingdom to another.
Re G (Residence: No Order Principle)	[2006] 1 FLR 771	No presumption against an order where this has been agreed between the parents.
Re G (Children)	[2006] 2 FLR 629	In determining residence welfare was the paramount consideration and not any presumption in favour of a parent, although the fact of parentage was not irrelevant.
Re M (Children) (Residence Order)	[2005] 1 FLR 656	Clear judicial reasoning must be provided for the rejection of a CAFCASS recommendation.
Re J (Children: Ex Parte orders)	[1997] 1 FLR 606	Ex parte residence orders should only be made in exceptional circumstances.

CASE NAME	CITATION	PRINCIPLE
Re W (Shared Residence Order)	[2009] 2 FLR 436	Where time spent with each parent is more akin to residence than contact the same should not be reflected in a contact order but a shared residence order.
Re A (Suspended Residence Order)	[2010] 1 FLR 1679	The court has power through its use of directions and conditions to provide a bespoke answer to meet the welfare needs of the child.
Holmes-Moorhouse v Richmond-upon-Thames LBC	[2009] UKHL 7	A shared residence order is not a means by which a provider of accommodation (whether a local authority or other) can be made subject to pressure to allocate scarce housing stock.
Re B (A Child)	[2010] 1 FLR 551	All consideration of the importance of parenthood in private law disputes about residence must be firmly rooted in an examination of what was in the child's best interests, which was the paramount consideration. It was only as a contributor to the child's welfare that parenthood assumed any significance; in common with all the other factors bearing on what was in the best interests of the child, it must be examined for its potential to fulfil that aim.

7.11.2   Contact orders

CASE NAME	CITATION	PRINCIPLE
Re R (A Minor) (Contact)	[1993] 2 FLR 762	A child has a right to be informed as to its natural parentage, even when immediate contact could not be ordered.
Re H (A Minor) (Parental Responsibility)	[1993] 1 FLR 484	Contact may be refused, despite the bona fides of the applicant, where to do so would significantly disrupt the child's stability and security.

CASE NAME	CITATION	PRINCIPLE
Re H (A Minor) (Contact)	[1994] 2 FLR 776	There is no presumption of contact in favour of a step-parent although the social and psychological links with the child may be of significance in the assessment of whether contact was in the child's best interest.
Re O (A Minor: Imposition of Conditions)	[1995] 1 FLR 124	The court has power to impose conditions when making a contact order with which a residential parent must comply.
Re K (Contact: Mother's Anxiety)	[1999] 2 FLR 703	The genuine anxiety of the parent with care may be of such significance as to preclude contact with the absence parent.
Re L, Re V, Re M, Re H (Contact: Domestic Violence)	[2000] 2 FLR 334	Important guidance given as to the proper assessment of applications in which violence was alleged. The positive benefits to the child would have to be set against any risks found to be posed.
Re M (Intractable Contact Dispute: Interim Care Order)	[2003] 2 FLR 636	Where implacable hostility prevented contact from taking place there was scope for the making of public law orders to enable the child to have contact.
Re T (Contact: Alienation: Permission to Appeal)	[2003] 1 FLR 531	The court should investigate the reasons for an alleged alienation of a child from a parent and its findings should be the basis for assessments thereafter.
Re D (Intractable Contact Dispute: Publicity)	[2004] 1 FLR 1226	Allegations should be investigated when made and not allowed to fester. Allegations made late in proceedings should be viewed with scepticism. Contact disputes required effective case management.

CASE NAME	CITATION	PRINCIPLE
V v V (Contact: Implacable Hostility)	[2004] 2 FLR 851	Where a parent continually sabotaged court ordered contact plans and sought to alienate children from their parent the court should balance the risks of a transfer of residence against the risk of emotional harm by continued exposure to the present circumstances.
Re S (Contact: promoting Relationship with the Absent Parent)	[2004] 1 FLR 1279	There is no duty on a parent to have contact with an absent child and no right of that parent to have contact.
Re D (Contact: Interim Order)	[1995] 1 FLR 495	Care should be taken when considering 'interim' contact in cases where either the principle of contact is in dispute or substantial factual issues exist.
Re A (A Child) (Contact: Separate Representation in Contact Proceedings)	[2001] 1 FLR 715	Cases of significant inter-parental contact can distort the view as to where the child's welfare lies and in such cases it is appropriate for the child to be separately represented with the assistance of a guardian.
Nottinghamshire County Council v P	[1993] 1 FLR 514	An order requiring that the person with whom the child lives shall not allow contact with a named person (an order for no contact) is a contact order.
Re M (Contact: Welfare Test)	[1995] 1 FLR 274	In determining an application in which harm is alleged the question to be asked is whether the fundamental need of every child to have an enduring relationship with both parents is outweighed by the depth of harm which may be caused.

CASE NAME	CITATION	PRINCIPLE
Re H (A Child)(Mother's Opposition)	[2001] 1 FCR 59	In cases where a parent is opposed to contact the court should start from the position that, despite the objections being expressed, the presumption in favour of contact meets the child's welfare for reasons of identity and a continuing relationship.
Re P (Contact: Discretion)	[1998] 1 FLR 696	Guidance given as to how the court should weigh and assess the objections of a parent when determining the principle of contact.
Re B (A Child) (Child Support: Reduction of Contact)	[2007] 1 FLR 1949	There was no correlation between contact and financial support and the court should not seek to assess the benefits of competing financial arrangements dependent upon division of a child's time between parents.
Re F-K (A Child)(Contact: Departure from Evidence)	[2005] 1 FCR 388	No principle of 'issue estoppel' in contact cases, so that a later court may, in appropriate circumstances, rehear allegations and make new findings of fact.
Re B (Minors)(Contact)	[1994] 2 FLR 1	Provided the hearing is fair a judge has a broad discretion as to how a contact application should be determined.
Re W (A Minor)(Staying Contact)	[1998] 2 FCR 453	Staying contact should not be ordered where serious allegations are made and which require findings to be made.
Re FH (Dispensing with Finding of Fact Hearing)	[2009] 1 FLR 349	Whether a Finding of Fact hearing was required should be identified at an early stage in the proceedings and, once listed, should not be vacated without good reason.

CASE NAME	CITATION	PRINCIPLE
Re Z (Unsupervised Contact: Allegations of Domestic Violence)	[2009] 2 FLR 877	A finding of fact hearing should not be concluded following the hearing of only one party to the proceedings.
Re R (Family Proceedings: No Case to Answer)	[2009] 2 FLR 83	There is no place in the determination of allegations of violence for the submission of 'no case to answer'.
S v S (Interim Contact)	[2009] 2 FLR 1586	Where allegations of violence have been made which may, if proved, be relevant to the question of whether contact is ordered or how contact is operated then it is not normally appropriate prior to that finding of fact hearing to make an order for interim contact.
Re C (Contact Order: Variation)	[2009] 1 FLR 869	Where a contact order has been made but is not operating smoothly there is a duty upon the court to strive to make it work and it is not ordinarily appropriate to dismiss applications for enforcement of the order or make prohibitions against further applications.

7.11.3 Prohibited steps orders

CASE NAME	CITATION	PRINCIPLE
Re D (Prohibited Steps Order)	[1996] 2 FLR 273	It was not a proper use of a prohibited steps order to exclude a parent from a family home.
Re X (Parental Responsibility Agreement: Children in Care)	[2000] 1 FLR 517	An agreement to make a parental responsibility agreement with the other parent was not an exercise of parental responsibility and therefore not subject to the jurisdiction of a prohibited steps order.

CASE NAME	CITATION	PRINCIPLE
Re H (Minors)	[1995] 1 FLR 638	It was a proper use of a prohibited steps order to make an order prohibiting a person from seeking to have contact with a child.
Re H (Children) (Residence Order: Condition)	[2001] 2 FLR 1277	Where the intention was to seek to prevent a child from being removed to a different part of the United Kingdom the proper order was a residence order with a condition and not a prohibited steps order.
Re S and D (Children) (Powers of the Court)	[1995] 2 FLR 456	There is no power to prevent a parent from removing a child from local authority accommodation under s 20(8) of the Children Act 1989.
Langley v Liverpool City Council	[2006] 1 FLR 342	Whilst open to a local authority to apply for a prohibited steps order it is essentially a private law remedy and should not be preferred where a local authority is acting by reason of its child protection duties.

7.11.4　Specific issue orders

CASE NAME	CITATION	PRINCIPLE
Re HG (Specific Issue Order: Sterilisation)	[1993] 1 FLR 587	For the purpose of bringing a specific issue application there must be a question to be answered; it was not necessary that there were competing protagonists.
Re R (A Minor) (Blood Transfusion)	[1993] 2 FLR 757	A local authority could obtain leave to make an application for a specific issue order where the child was not in its care.

CASE NAME	CITATION	PRINCIPLE
Re C (A Minor) (Leave to Seek Section 8 Orders)	[1994] 1 FLR 26	The granting of applications by children for specific issue orders should be reserved for matters of importance and the jurisdiction exercised cautiously. The issue of whether a child was allowed to go on holiday was not such a matter.
Re J (Specific Issue Order: Leave to Apply)	[1995] 1 FLR 669	A specific issue order would be inappropriate to determine the question of whether J was a child in need. The question whether a child was in need was not one which arose in connection with any aspect of parental responsibility, since a specific issue order could only be made where a specific aspect of the practical application of the exercise of parental responsibility arose.
Re F (Specific Issue: Child Interview)	[1995] 1 FLR 819	It was an appropriate use of a specific issue order to determine whether a child should be interviewed in relation to criminal proceedings concerning one of his parents.
Re K (Specific Issue Order)	[1999] 2 FLR 280	A specific issue application was appropriate when the issue between the parents was whether the child should be informed about his paternity.
Re J (Specific Issue Orders: Muslim Upbringing and Circumcision)	[1999] 2 FLR 678 [2000] 1 FLR 571	Only in unusual circumstances would a court require a child to be brought up in a religion not that of the parent with whom the child resided. Where parents agreed a child could be circumcised but in the absence of agreement the matter was one for the court.

CASE NAME	CITATION	PRINCIPLE
Re C (HIV Test)	[1999] 2 FLR 1004	The local authority could use a specific issue order to enable a child to undergo an HIV test in the face of united parental opposition.
Re A (Specific Issue Order: Parental Dispute)	[2001] 1 FLR 121	A specific issue order was the appropriate order in a dispute concerning the type and nature of schools to be attended in the future.
Re P (Parental Dispute: Judicial Determination)	[2003] 1 FLR 286	On an application for a specific issue order the court should not abdicate its decision-making responsibility in favour of one parent.
Re C (Welfare of Child: Immunisation)	[2003] 1 FLR 1054, [2003] 1 FLR 1095	Where parents were in dispute about the immunisation of a child against infectious disease, neither parent had the right to make the decision alone and immunisation should be carried out only where a court decided that this was in the best interests of the child, s 2(7) of the Children Act 1989 notwithstanding. There was no general proposition of law that a court would not order non-essential invasive medical treatment in the face of strong opposition from the child's primary carer.

CASE NAME	CITATION	PRINCIPLE
Chief Constable of Greater Manchester v KI and KW (by their Children's Guardian, CAFCASS Legal) and NP	[2008] 1 FLR 504	The grant or refusal of consent to the interview of a child was an aspect of parental responsibility that could be controlled by the court, in its modern jurisdiction, by the use of a specific issue order. The test to be applied by the court was a balance of rights of interests within which the child's welfare was not the paramount consideration, because a reasonable parent would weigh their child's interests against the public interest, and could not rely exclusively on the child's interests where to do so would interfere with the rights of others.

7.11.5   Change of name

CASE NAME	CITATION	PRINCIPLE
Dawson v Wearmouth	[1999] 1 FLR 1167	The fact of registration of a name was significant but not determinative. A change of name required a positive welfare consideration for the application to succeed.
Re W , Re A, Re B (Change of name)	[1999] 2 FLR 930	Registration in a particular name was relevant but not decisive. An application based solely on a wish for the child to share a surname with the applicant would be unlikely to succeed. Where the application was made by a father, his connection with the child and commitment to contact and the existence or absence of parental responsibility would all be relevant.

CASE NAME	CITATION	PRINCIPLE
Re H (Child's Name: First Name)	[2002] 1 FLR 973	Surnames were of particular significance, insofar as they denoted the family to which the child belonged, but given names had a much less concrete character, and a number of different names might be used over the course of a child's life. When issues relating to given names arose, judges must look in a worldly, common-sense way at what was best for the child, and must not place too much emphasis upon the statutory process of registration.
Re D, L and LA (Care: Change of Forename)	[2003] 1 FLR 339	Changes of names were important matters and had to be treated with appropriate seriousness. No foster parent or carer should unilaterally change the forename of a child. If for any reason foster parents or other such carers thought that a child's name should be changed, they should go straight to the social worker in charge of the case, or the adoption placement officer, and ask for the change and explain why. In foster placements the parents should be consulted and allowed to express their views. If the change could not be achieved by consent, it might be necessary to invoke the inherent jurisdiction of the court.
Re T (A Minor)(Change of Surname)	[1998] 2 FLR 620	Where there is no residence order in place the consent of all those with parental responsibility must be first obtained, notwithstanding s 2(7) of the Children Act 1989.

CASE NAME	CITATION	PRINCIPLE
Re PC (Change of Surname)	[1997] 2 FLR 730	Where only one parent has parental responsibility that person alone has the authority to change the child's name but the better course of action is to consult and secure consent.
Re B (Change of Surname)	[1996] 1 FLR 791	When an application for a change is made pursuant to s 13(1) the welfare checklist should be used as a valuable aide-memoire.
Re T (Change of Surname)	[1998] 2 FLR 620	An application for a change founded upon the convenience of ensuring uniformity of names for the parent with care is unlikely to succeed.

7.11.6   Leave to remove from the jurisdiction

CASE NAME	CITATION	PRINCIPLE
Payne v Payne	[2001] 1 FLR 1052	Guidance given on the proper approach to adopt in considering applications for leave to remove.
Re C (Permission to Remove from Jurisdiction)	[2003] 1 FLR 1066	To be reasonable an application must be (a) genuine and (b) practical. There was no presumption that a reasonable application would be automatically granted. The harm generated by a refusal is likely to be greater than the harm suffered by the reduction in contact.
L v L (Leave to Remove Children from Jurisdiction: Effect on Children)	[2003] 1 FLR 900	Account should be taken of the disadvantage to the whole family from a refusal of an application.

CASE NAME	CITATION	PRINCIPLE
Re Y (Leave to Remove from Jurisdiction)	[2004] 2 FLR 330	Application refused where a child enjoyed shared care. Principles of *Payne* inapplicable in shared care arrangement.
R v R (Leave to Remove)	[2005] 1 FLR 687	An application to return to France by a mother with French family was refused where the intention was more in the belief that life would be better there but contact would be significantly disrupted.
Re G (Removal from Jurisdiction)	[2005] 2 FLR 166	An applicant did not have to establish that psychiatric damage would follow from a refusal of an application. The impact on the applicant was to be looked at in terms of well-being.
Re B (Leave to Remove: Impact of Refusal)	[2005] 2 FLR 239	No distinction is to be drawn between 'lifestyle' cases and returning home cases. The reason for relocation and the reasonableness of the primary carer's proposals lay at the core of the case. It was important to give great weight to the emotional and psychological well-being of the primary carer, not merely to take note of the impact on the primary carer of a refusal.
Re B (Children: Removal from the Jurisdiction) Re S (A Child) (Removal from the Jurisdiction)	[2003] 2 FLR 1043	The impact of refusal upon the family, including any prospective step-parent, applied with greater force where the intention was to emigrate to the jurisdiction where the step-parent was based.
Re Y (Leave to Remove from the Jurisdiction)	[2004] 2 FLR 330	Where the child's home is shared equally between two parents the principles set out in *Payne* are not applicable.

CASE NAME	CITATION	PRINCIPLE
Re J (Leave to Remove: Urgent Case)	[2007] 1 FLR 2033	Where the court is in fact concerned with cross applications for residence then the principles in *Payne* are not applicable.
Re M (Leave to Remove Child from Jurisdiction)	[1999] 2 FLR 334	Where a parent presents a genuine application for a removal from the jurisdiction but the plans post removal are incomplete leave may be granted subject to meeting conditions concerning the finalisation of those plans.
Re K (Removal from the Jurisdiction: Practice)	[1999] 2 FLR 1084	In granting leave a court should have assessed all risks and have developed reasonable safeguards against their occurrence rather than simply accepting undertakings from a parent soon to depart from the jurisdiction.
K v K (Relocation: Shared Care Arrangement)	[2011] EWCA Civ 793	*Payne* guidance not appropriate when starting point is a shared care arrangement.
Re N (Leave to Remove: Holiday)	[2006] 2 FLR 1124	Permission not required where child removed from the United Kingdom for one month and accompanied by residence order holder.
Re B (Children)	[2008] EWCA Civ 1034	Leave to remove cases are generally fact-specific and therefore little reliance can be placed upon decided cases as examples of fact as opposed to indicators of the principles to be applied.
Re M (Removal from Jurisdiction: Adjournment)	[2011] 1 FLR 1943	Starting point when considering removal to non-Hague signatory state is that evidence of foreign legal system is required.

7.11.7 Principles to be applied when making section 8 order

CASE NAME	CITATION	PRINCIPLE
Birmingham City Council v H	[1993] 1 FLR 224	The welfare with which the court is concerned is that of the child who is the subject of the application.
Re T and E (Proceedings: Conflicting Interests)	[1995] 1 FLR 581	Where an application concerns more than one child it is the welfare of each child with which the court is concerned which must be considered by the court and the respective benefits and detriments to each child which must be weighed in determining the appropriate outcome.
B v B (Minors) (Interviews and Listing Arrangements)	[1994] 2 FLR 489	The acceptance of any delay must be because it is considered to have some benefit for a relevant child. Delay which only assists an adult is not acceptable.
H v H (Residence Order: Leave to Remove from the Jurisdiction)	[1995] 1 FLR 529	It is not obligatory for judges to refer to each factor when delivering judgment upon an application.
B v B (Residence Order: Reasons for Decision)	[1997] 2 FLR 602	It is certainly useful to approach the decision-making process on the basis that reference to the individual components of the welfare checklist will provide clarity to the judicial reasoning process.
R v Oxfordshire County Council (Secure Accommodation Order)	[1992] Fam 150	Justices sitting in the family proceedings court are expected to make express reference to the various factors in the welfare checklist when announcing the reasons for their decision.

CASE NAME	CITATION	PRINCIPLE
Re O (Care or Supervision Order)	[1996] 1 FLR 70	The court should begin with a preference for the less interventionist rather than the more interventionist approach. This should be considered to be in the better interests of the children, again unless there are cogent reasons to the contrary.
Re G (Children)	[2006] 1 FLR 771	Section 1(5) does not create a presumption one way or another; the court is required to answer the question: in the light of all the circumstances of the case, is it better for the child to make the order than to make no order at all?
Re A (Leave to Remove: Religious and Cultural Considerations)	[2006] 2 FLR 572	The primary focus for the court is upon the welfare of the child and not the views or considerations of the adults involved.
Birmingham City Council v H (No. 2)	[1993] 1 FLR 883	The focus for the court when considering the welfare of a child is on the child who is the subject of the application and not any other children involved in the proceedings.
Re T and E (Proceedings: Conflicting Interests)	[1995] 1 FLR 581	Where more than one child is the subject of an application the court must consider the benefits and detriments of each course of action as they might well impact upon each child.
C v Solihull MBC	[1993] 1 FLR 290	In exceptional cases delay may benefit the child and is a positive factor which will be allowed by the court.

CASE NAME	CITATION	PRINCIPLE
Re P (Minors) (Interim Order)	[1993] 2 FLR 742	Having regard to the principles of the Children Act 1989, the court has a duty to determine current questions relating to the upbringing of a child as they arise and to do so with finality and as much speed as is consistent with justice and the welfare of the child. Once a question has been determined, it can seldom, if ever, be right for the court to continue adjourning a case.
Re P (A Minor)(Education)	[1992] 1 FLR 742	Whilst not necessarily being determinative of the question the views of older children are important and carry great weight.
Re C (HIV Test)	[1999] 2 FLR 1004	There is a rebuttable presumption that the united appraisal of both parents will be correct in identifying where the welfare of their child lies.
C v C (Minors) (Custody)	[1988] 2 FLR 291	There is a general proposition that all things being equal siblings should be brought up together.
Re G (Children)	[2006] 2 FLR 629	Whilst there is no natural parental presumption the fact of parenthood (particularly genetic and gestational) is a factor which must be weighed when undertaking the welfare assessment.
Re B (A Child)	[2009] UKSC 5	The notion of parental presumption cannot trump an assessment of the welfare of the child.

7.11.8   Procedure upon making section 8 orders

CASE NAME	CITATION	PRINCIPLE
Re T (Adopted Children: Conflict)	[1995] 2 FLR 792	Applications after adoption should be designed to ensure that adopters are not necessarily disturbed but the judge should have as much relevant information as possible. The adoption agency should in the first instance normally be given notice of the application for leave, but this should not be treated as if it were the substantive application. It may be necessary to transfer the application to the High Court and to involve the Official Solicitor but this should not be a general rule.
Berkshire County Council v P	[1997] 1 FLR 171	The likelihood of conflicting expert opinion upon which adjudication is required is a reason for the allocation of a case to a higher jurisdiction than the Family Proceedings Courts.
MH v GP (Child: Emigration)	[1995] 2 FLR 106	Applications for the removal of children permanently from the jurisdiction of the court do not necessarily have to be heard in the High Court but should be transferred for determination either in the county court or the High Court, depending on the complexity and difficulty of the decision.
Re K (Removal from the Jurisdiction: Practice)	[1999] 2 FLR 1084	Applications involving consideration of the legal system in foreign states and which may require the putting in place of mirror orders, should ordinarily be dealt with by a judge of the Family Division.

CASE NAME	CITATION	PRINCIPLE
Re A and W (Minors) (Residence Orders: Leave to Apply)	[1992] 2 FLR 154	On an application under ss 8 and 10(9) of the Children Act 1989 for leave to apply for a residence order, the child's welfare was not the paramount consideration. Particular regard must be had to a local authority's plans for the child's future, the mother's wishes and feelings and any risk of disruption to the child's life to such an extent that he would be harmed by it. In granting or refusing such an application for leave, the upbringing of the child was irrelevant. That question only arose for determination on the substantive application.
Re M (Prohibited Steps Order: Application for Leave)	[1993] 1 FLR 275	Justices making a decision under the Family Proceedings Courts (Children Act 1989) Rules 1991, r 3.2, as to whether or not to give notice to other parties of an application for leave under s 10, had a discretion to grant the request forthwith or give directions for notices of that request to be served upon the other parties. This discretion must be exercised judicially. When hearing the application for leave, the justices had to have regard, inter alia, to the matters set out in s 10(9), including the risk that the making of the proposed application might disrupt the child's life and the local authority's plans for the child's future. Except in cases of emergency, the interests of justice required that notice be given to parties likely to be affected. The requirement of leave was an important step and the court ought not ordinarily to grant leave ex parte.

CASE NAME	CITATION	PRINCIPLE
Re F and R (Contact Order: Grandparent's Application	[1995] 1 FLR 524	Where facts are disputed an oral hearing should take place, not necessarily covering every aspect of the evidence, but allowing sufficient view to be taken of the disputed issues.
Re W (Contact Application: Procedure)	[2000] 1 FLR 263	The grant of leave was a significant exercise of judicial discretion, to be undertaken in the presence of the parties, recorded in writing and allowing opportunities for the presentation of evidence and its testing.
Re J (Leave to issue an application for a Residence Order)	[2003] 1 FLR 114	The statutory checklist set out at s 10(9) needed to be given its proper weight and recognition and should not be substituted by any judicial formula. The minimum essential protection of the rights enjoyed pursuant to Articles 6 and 8 was a proper judicial inquiry.
Re A (Application for Leave)	[1998] 1 FLR 1	Applications under s 91(14) are distinct applications which are not subject to the s 10(9) criteria; and when considering applications for leave under s 91(14), the simple question for the court was: did this application demonstrate that there was any need for renewed judicial investigation? If the answer was in the affirmative, leave should be granted.

CASE NAME	CITATION	PRINCIPLE
Re G (Minors) (Ex parte Interim Residence Order)	[1993] 1 FLR 910	A without notice residence order was reserved for issues of child protection or where a snatch situation had occurred. The normal position will be the preservation of the status quo existing prior to the interruption of the routine. In exceptional cases where compelling reasons exist such an order could properly be made.
Re AB (Care Proceedings: Service on Husband Ignorant of Child's Existence)	[2004] 1 FLR 527	The responsibilities of a public authority, the rights of the child, the rights of the husband and the rights of the mother's other children could not be minimised or suppressed. It was manifest that the court would be exceptionally slow to grant a relaxation of the rules of service in any circumstances, other than the most extreme.
Re X (Care: Notice of Proceedings)	[1996] 1 FLR 186	When considering whether to disapply service requirements, including notifying as to proceedings, the welfare of the child is not necessarily the court's paramount consideration.
Re S (Ex Parte orders)	[2001] 1 FLR 308	Detailed guidance given as to the proper approach to adopt when making a without notice application.
T v B (Parental Responsibility: Financial Provision)	[2010] 2 FLR 1966	A parent is a person with the necessary genetic relationship with the child and not someone who might have a close social or psychological relationship.

7.11.9 Directions, conditions and provisions

CASE NAME	CITATION	PRINCIPLE
Re O (Contact: Imposition of Conditions)	[1995] 2 FLR 124	Section 11(7) of the Children Act 1989 conferred wide and comprehensive powers on the court to ensure contact between the child and the non-custodial parent, where it promoted the welfare of the child, including obligations upon each parent where appropriate.
Re E (Residence Order: Imposition of Conditions)	[1997] 2 FLR 638	Although s 11(7) was wide enough to cover a requirement as to location such a condition should not be imposed upon an otherwise suitable carer absent exceptional circumstances.
D v N (Contact Order: Conditions)	[1997] 2 FLR 797	Section 11(7) should not be used to impose conditions which were in fact aimed at the protection of one parent from another.
D v D (County Court Jurisdiction: Injunctions)	[1993] 2 FLR 802	The breadth of s 11(7) was not so wide as to prevent a local authority from undertaking its statutory duties.
Re H (Residence Order: Placement out of Jurisdiction)	[2006] 1 FLR 1140	It is not appropriate to use s 11(7) where the court would not be in a position to exercise control over the conditions imposed or which ran counter to the plans for the children.
Leeds County Council v C	[1993] 1 FLR 269	The categories of persons against whom conditions may be imposed are limited to those set out in s 11(7)(b)(i)–(iv) and conditions could not be applied to those not identified therein.

CASE NAME	CITATION	PRINCIPLE
Re D (Prohibited Steps Order)	[1996] 2 FLR 273	Section 11(7) is ancillary to the making of a s 8 order and cannot be used as the conduit for the importation of different statutory provisions.
Re H (Prohibited Steps Order)	[1995] 1 FLR 638	A person named in a section 8 order need not be present before the court nor notified of the intention to make the order. It is sufficient if permission is given to enable an application for its variation or discharge to be made for which there is jurisdiction by way of the ancillary to make provision.

A7.1 APPENDIX 1:
GUIDELINES FOR GOOD PRACTICE ON PARENTAL CONTACT IN CASES WHERE THERE IS DOMESTIC VIOLENCE

Court to give early consideration to allegations of domestic violence

In every case in which domestic violence is put forward as a reason for refusing or limiting contact the court should at the earliest opportunity consider the allegations made (and any answer to them) and decide whether the nature and effect of the violence alleged by the complainant (or admitted by the respondent) is such as to make it likely that the order of the court for contact will be affected if the allegations are proved.

Steps to be taken where the court forms the view that its order is likely to be affected if allegations of domestic violence are proved

Where the allegations are disputed and the court forms the view that the nature and effect of the violence alleged is such as to make it likely that the order of the court will be affected if the allegations are proved the court should:

(a) consider what evidence will be required to enable the court to make findings of fact in relation to the allegations;

(b) ensure that appropriate directions under section 11(1) of the Children Act 1989 are given at an early stage in the application to enable the matters in issue to be heard as speedily as possible; including consideration of whether or not it would be appropriate for there to be an initial hearing for the purpose of enabling findings of fact to be made;

(c) consider whether an order for interim contact pending the final hearing is in the interests of the child; and in particular that the safety of the child and the residential parent can be secured before during and after any such contact;

(d) direct a report from a children and family reporter on the question of contact unless satisfied that it is not necessary to do so in order to safeguard the child's interests;

(e) subject to the seriousness of the allegations made and the difficulty of the case consider whether or not the children in question need to be separately represented in the proceedings; and, if the case is proceeding in the Family Proceedings Court whether or not it should be transferred to the County Court; if in the County Court whether or not it should be transferred to the High Court for hearing.

Directions to the Children and Family Reporter in cases involving domestic violence

(a) Where the court orders a welfare report under section 7 of the Children Act 1989 in a disputed application for contact in which it considers domestic violence to be a relevant issue, the order of the court should contain specific directions to the children and family reporter to address the issue of domestic violence; to make an assessment of the harm which the children have suffered or which they are at risk of suffering if contact is ordered; to assess whether the safety of the child and the residential parent can be secured before, during and after contact; and to make particular efforts to ascertain the wishes and feelings of the children concerned in the light of the allegations of violence made.

(b) Where the court has made findings of fact prior to the children and family reporter conducting his or her investigation, the court should ensure that either a note of the court's judgment or of the findings of fact made by the court is made available to the children and family reporter as soon after the findings have been made as is practicable.

(c) Where in a case involving allegations of domestic violence the whereabouts of the child and the residential parent are known to the court but not known to the parent seeking contact; and where the court takes the view that it is in the best interests of the child or children concerned for that position to be maintained for the time being, the court should give directions designed to ensure that any welfare report on the circumstances of the residential parent and the child does not reveal their whereabouts, whether directly or indirectly.

Interim Contact pending a full hearing

In deciding any question of interim contact pending a full hearing the court should:

(a) specifically take into account the matters set out in section 1(3) of the Children Act 1989 ('the welfare check-list');

(b) give particular consideration to the likely risk of harm to the child, whether physical and/or emotional, if contact is either granted or refused;

(c) consider, if it decides such contact is in the interests of the child, what directions are required about how it is to be carried into effect; and, in particular, whether it should be supervised, and if so, by whom; and generally, in so far as it can, ensure that any risk of harm to the child is minimised and the safety of the child and residential parent before during and after any such contact is secured;

(d)   consider whether it should exercise its powers under section 42(2)(b) of the Family Law Act 1996 to make a non-molestation order;

(e)   consider whether the parent seeking contact should seek advice and/or treatment as a precondition to contact being ordered or as a means of assisting the court in ascertaining the likely risk of harm to the child from that person at the final hearing.

Matters to be considered at the final hearing

At the final hearing of a contact application in which there are disputed allegations of domestic violence:

(a)   the court should, wherever practicable, make findings of fact as to the nature and degree of the violence which is established on the balance of probabilities and its effect on the child and the parent with whom the child is living;

(b)   in deciding the issue of contact the court should, in the light of the findings of fact which it has made, apply the individual items in the welfare checklist with reference to those findings; in particular, where relevant findings of domestic violence have been made, the court should in every case consider the harm which the child has suffered as a consequence of that violence and the harm which the child is at risk of suffering if an order for contact is made and only make an order for contact it can be satisfied that the safety of the residential parent and the child can be secured before during and after contact.

Matters to be considered where findings of domestic violence are made

In each case where a finding of domestic violence is made, the court should consider the conduct of both parents towards each other and towards the children; in particular, the court should consider:

(a)   the effect of the domestic violence which has been established on the child and on the parent with whom the child is living;

(b)   whether or not the motivation of the parent seeking contact is a desire to promote the best interests of the child or as a means of continuing a process of violence against or intimidation or harassment of the other parent;

(c) the likely behaviour of the parent seeking contact during contact and its effect on the child or children concerned;

(d) the capacity of the parent seeking contact to appreciate the effect of past and future violence on the other parent and the children concerned;

(e) the attitude of the parent seeking contact to past violent conduct by that parent; and in particular whether that parent has the capacity to change and/or to behave appropriately.

Matters to be considered where contact is ordered in a case where findings of domestic violence have been made

Where the court has made findings of domestic violence but, having applied the welfare checklist, nonetheless considers that direct contact is in the best interests of the child or children concerned, the court should consider (in addition to the matters set out in paragraphs 5 and 6 above) what directions are required to enable the order to be carried into effect under section 11(7) of the Children Act 1989 and in particular should consider:

(a) whether or not contact should be supervised, and if so, by whom;

(b) what conditions (for example by way of seeking advice or treatment) should be complied with by the party in whose favour the order for contact has been made;

(c) whether the court should exercise its powers under section 42(2)(b) of the Family Law Act 1996 to make a non-molestation order;

(d) whether such contact should be for a specified period or should contain provisions which are to have effect for a specified period;

(e) setting a date for the order to be reviewed and giving directions to ensure that the court at the review has full information about the operation of the order.

Information about local facilities

The court should also take steps to inform itself (alternatively direct the children and family reporter or the parties to inform it) of the facilities available locally to the court to assist parents who have been violent to their partners and/or their children, and, where appropriate, should impose as a condition of future contact that violent parents avail themselves of those facilities.

Reasons

In its judgment or reasons the court should always explain how its findings on the issue of domestic violence have influenced its decision on the issue of contact; and in particular where the court has found domestic violence proved but nonetheless makes an order for contact, the court should always explain, whether by way of reference to the welfare check-list or otherwise why it takes the view that contact is in the best interests of the child.

NOTE

Although not part of our formal guidelines, we think that all courts hearing applications where domestic violence is alleged should review their facilities at court and should do their best to ensure that there are separate waiting areas for the parties in such cases and that information about the services of Victim Support and other supporting agencies is readily available.

Background Information

* The Report and Guidelines were published over Easter 2000.

* The Guidelines were referred to by the Court of Appeal in the Judgment in Re L (a child) and Others, handed down on the 19th June 2000.

* On the 6th March 2001 Jane Kennedy, Parliamentary Secretary in the Lord Chancellor's Department, announced in the House of Commons that the Government endorsed the report of the Children Act Sub-Committee entitled 'Parental Contact in Cases where there is Domestic Violence', and the Guidelines for Good Practice. Ms Kennedy also outlined that the Government will work in partnership with the President of the Family Division to ensure the widest promulgation of the Guidelines, will work in partnership with the Sub-Committee to monitor the effectiveness of the Guidelines, and that at the end of the monitoring period will consider the need for amending legislation in the light of that monitoring.

* The Report uses the term court welfare officer. This term has since been amended by the Family Proceedings (Amendment) Rules 2001 and the Family Proceedings Courts (Children Act 1989) (Amendment) Rules 2001 to children and family reporter. The terms court welfare officer's report and welfare officer's report have now been replaced by welfare report. This document reflects those changes.

Family Policy Division
Lord Chancellor's Department
April 2001

A7.2   APPENDIX 2:
PRACTICE DIRECTION 12J – RESIDENCE AND
CONTACT ORDERS: DOMESTIC VIOLENCE AND
HARM

This Practice Direction supplements FPR Part 12

1 This Practice Direction applies to any family proceedings in the High Court, a county court or a magistrates' court in which an application is made for a residence order or a contact order in respect of a child under the Children Act 1989 ("the 1989 Act") or the Adoption and Children Act 2002 ("the 2002 Act") or in which any question arises about residence or about contact between a child and a parent or other family member.

2 The practice set out in this Direction is to be followed in any case in which it is alleged, or there is otherwise reason to suppose, that the subject child or a party has experienced domestic violence perpetrated by another party or that there is a risk of such violence. For the purpose of this Direction, the term 'domestic violence' includes physical violence, threatening or intimidating behaviour and any other form of abuse which, directly or indirectly, may have caused harm to the other party or to the child or which may give rise to the risk of harm.

> ('Harm' in relation to a child means ill-treatment or the impairment of health or development, including, for example, impairment suffered from seeing or hearing the ill-treatment of another: Children Act 1989, ss 31(9), 105(1))

General principles

3 The court must, at all stages of the proceedings, consider whether domestic violence is raised as an issue, either by the parties or otherwise, and if so must:

- identify at the earliest opportunity the factual and welfare issues involved;
- consider the nature of any allegation or admission of domestic violence and the extent to which any domestic violence which is admitted, or which may be proved, would be relevant in deciding whether to make an order about residence or contact and, if so, in what terms;
- give directions to enable the relevant factual and welfare issues to be determined expeditiously and fairly.

4 In all cases it is for the court to decide whether an order for residence or contact accords with Section 1(1) of the 1989 Act or section 1(2) of the

2002 Act, as appropriate; any proposed residence or contact order, whether to be made by agreement between the parties or otherwise must be scrutinised by the court accordingly. The court shall not make a consent order for residence or contact or give permission for an application for a residence or contact order to be withdrawn, unless the parties are present in court, except where it is satisfied that there is no risk of harm to the child in so doing.

5 In considering, on an application for a consent order for residence or contact, whether there is any risk of harm to the child, the court shall consider all the evidence and information available. The court may direct a report under Section 7 of the 1989 Act either orally or in writing before it makes its determination; in such a case, the court may ask for information about any advice given by the officer preparing the report to the parties and whether they or the child have been referred to any other agency, including local authority children's services. If the report is not in writing, the court shall make a note of its substance on the court file.

Issue

6 Immediately on receipt of an application for a residence order or a contact order, or of the acknowledgement of the application, the court shall send a copy of it, together with any accompanying documents, to Cafcass or Cafcass Cymru, as appropriate, to enable Cafcass or Cafcass Cymru to undertake initial screening in accordance with their safeguarding policies.

Liaison

7 The Designated Family Judge, or in the magistrates' court the Justices' Clerk, shall take steps to ensure that arrangements are in place for:

- the prompt delivery of documents to Cafcass or Cafcass Cymru in accordance with paragraph 6
- any information obtained by Cafcass or Cafcass Cymru as a result of initial screening or otherwise and any risk assessments prepared by Cafcass or Cafcass Cymru under section 16A of the 1989 Act to be placed before the appropriate court for consideration and directions
- a copy of any record of admissions or findings of fact made pursuant to paragraphs 12 & 21 below to be made available as soon as possible to any Officer of Cafcass or Welsh family proceedings officer or local authority officer preparing a report under section 7 of the 1989 Act.

Response of the court on receipt of information

8 Where any information provided to the court before the first hearing, whether as a result of initial screening by Cafcass or Cafcass Cymru or

otherwise, indicates that there are issues of domestic violence which may be relevant to the court's determination, the court may give directions about the conduct of the hearing and for written evidence to be filed by the parties before the hearing.

9 If at any stage the court is advised by Cafcass or Cafcass Cymru or otherwise that there is a need for special arrangements to secure the safety of any party or child attending any hearing, the court shall ensure that appropriate arrangements are made for the hearing and for all subsequent hearings in the case, unless it considers that these are no longer necessary.

First hearing

10 At the first hearing, the court shall inform the parties of the content of any screening report or other information which has been provided by Cafcass or Cafcass Cymru, unless it considers that to do so would create a risk of harm to a party or the child.

> (Specific provision about service of a risk assessment under section 16A of the 1989 Act is made by rule 12.34 of the Family Procedure Rules 2010.)

11 The court must ascertain at the earliest opportunity whether domestic violence is raised as an issue and must consider the likely impact of that issue on the conduct and outcome of the proceedings. In particular, the court should consider whether the nature and effect of the domestic violence alleged is such that, if proved, the decision of the court is likely to be affected.

Admissions

12 Where at any hearing an admission of domestic violence to another person or the child is made by a party, the admission should be recorded in writing and retained on the court file.

Directions for a fact-finding hearing

13 The court should determine as soon as possible whether it is necessary to conduct a fact-finding hearing in relation to any disputed allegation of domestic violence before it can proceed to consider any final order(s) for residence or contact. Where the court determines that a finding of fact hearing is not necessary, the order shall record the reasons for that decision.

14 Where the court considers that a fact-finding hearing is necessary, it must give directions to ensure that the matters in issue are determined expeditiously and fairly and in particular it should consider:

- directing the parties to file written statements giving particulars of the allegations made and of any response in such a way as to identify clearly the issues for determination;
- whether material is required from third parties such as the police or health services and may give directions accordingly;
- whether any other evidence is required to enable the court to make findings of fact in relation to the allegations and may give directions accordingly.

15 Where the court fixes a fact-finding hearing, it must at the same time fix a further hearing for determination of the application. The hearings should be arranged in such a way that they are conducted by the same judge or, in the magistrates' court, by at least the same chairperson of the justices.

Reports under Section 7

16 In any case where domestic violence is raised as an issue, the court should consider directing that a report on the question of contact, or any other matters relating to the welfare of the child, be prepared under section 7 of the 1989 Act by an Officer of Cafcass or a Welsh family proceedings officer (or local authority officer if appropriate), unless the court is satisfied that it is not necessary to do so in order to safeguard the child's interests. If the court so directs, it should consider the extent of any enquiries which can properly be made at this stage and whether it is appropriate to seek information on the wishes and feelings of the child before findings of fact have been made.

Representation of the child

17 Subject to the seriousness of the allegations made and the difficulty of the case, the court shall consider whether it is appropriate for the child who is the subject of the application to be made a party to the proceedings and be separately represented. If the case is proceeding in the magistrates' court and the court considers that it may be appropriate for the child to be made a party to the proceedings, it may transfer the case to the relevant county court for determination of that issue and following such transfer the county court shall give such directions for the further conduct of the case as it considers appropriate.

Interim orders before determination of relevant facts

18 Where the court gives directions for a fact-finding hearing, the court should consider whether an interim order for residence or contact is in the interests of the child; and in particular whether the safety of the child and the residential parent can be secured before, during and after any contact.

19 In deciding any question of interim residence or contact pending a full hearing the court should: –

(a) take into account the matters set out in section 1(3) of the 1989
     Act or section 1(4) of the 2002 Act ('the welfare check-list'), as
     appropriate;
(b) give particular consideration to the likely effect on the child of
     any contact and any risk of harm, whether physical, emotional or
     psychological, which the child is likely to suffer as a consequence
     of making or declining to make an order;

20 Where the court is considering whether to make an order for interim
contact, it should in addition consider

(a) the arrangements required to ensure, as far as possible, that any
     risk of harm to the child is minimised and that the safety of the
     child and the parties is secured; and in particular:
     (i)   whether the contact should be supervised or supported, and
           if so, where and by whom; and
     (ii) the availability of appropriate facilities for that purpose

(b) if direct contact is not appropriate, whether it is in the best
     interests of the child to make an order for indirect contact.

The fact-finding hearing

21 At the fact-finding hearing, the court should, wherever practicable,
make findings of fact as to the nature and degree of any domestic
violence which is established and its effect on the child, the child's parents
and any other relevant person. The court shall record its findings in
writing, and shall serve a copy on the parties. A copy of any record of
findings of fact or of admissions must be sent to any officer preparing a
report under Section 7 of the 1989 Act.

22 At the conclusion of any fact-finding hearing, the court shall consider,
notwithstanding any earlier direction for a section 7 report, whether it is
in the best interests of the child for the court to give further directions
about the preparation or scope of any report under section 7; where
necessary, it may adjourn the proceedings for a brief period to enable the
officer to make representations about the preparation or scope of any
further enquiries. The court should also consider whether it would be
assisted by any social work, psychiatric, psychological or other assessment
of any party or the child and if so (subject to any necessary consent) make
directions for such assessment to be undertaken and for the filing of any
consequent report.

23 Where the court has made findings of fact on disputed allegations, any
subsequent hearing in the proceedings should be conducted by the same
judge or, in the magistrates' court, by at least the same chairperson of the
justices. Exceptions may be made only where observing this requirement
would result in delay to the planned timetable and the judge or
chairperson is satisfied, for reasons recorded in writing, that the detriment
to the welfare of the child would outweigh the detriment to the fair trial
of the proceedings.

In all cases where domestic violence has occurred

24 The court should take steps to obtain (or direct the parties or an Officer of Cafcass or a Welsh family proceedings officer to obtain) information about the facilities available locally to assist any party or the child in cases where domestic violence has occurred.

25 Following any determination of the nature and extent of domestic violence, whether or not following a fact-finding hearing, the court should consider whether any party should seek advice or treatment as a precondition to an order for residence or contact being made or as a means of assisting the court in ascertaining the likely risk of harm to the child from that person, and may (with the consent of that party) give directions for such attendance and the filing of any consequent report.

Factors to be taken into account when determining whether to make residence or contact orders in all cases where domestic violence has occurred

26 When deciding the issue of residence or contact the court should, in the light of any findings of fact, apply the individual matters in the welfare checklist with reference to those findings; in particular, where relevant findings of domestic violence have been made, the court should in every case consider any harm which the child has suffered as a consequence of that violence and any harm which the child is at risk of suffering if an order for residence or contact is made and should only make an order for contact if it can be satisfied that the physical and emotional safety of the child and the parent with whom the child is living can, as far as possible, be secured before during and after contact.

27 In every case where a finding of domestic violence is made, the court should consider the conduct of both parents towards each other and towards the child; in particular, the court should consider;

(*a*) the effect of the domestic violence which has been established on the child and on the parent with whom the child is living;

(*b*) the extent to which the parent seeking residence or contact is motivated by a desire to promote the best interests of the child or may be doing so as a means of continuing a process of violence, intimidation or harassment against the other parent;

(*c*) the likely behaviour during contact of the parent seeking contact and its effect on the child;

(*d*) the capacity of the parent seeking residence or contact to appreciate the effect of past violence and the potential for future violence on the other parent and the child;

(*e*) the attitude of the parent seeking residence or contact to past violent conduct by that parent; and in particular whether that parent has the capacity to change and to behave appropriately.

Directions as to how contact is to proceed

28 Where the court has made findings of domestic violence but, having applied the welfare checklist, nonetheless considers that direct contact is in the best interests of the child, the court should consider what if any directions or conditions are required to enable the order to be carried into effect and in particular should consider:

(a)   whether or not contact should be supervised, and if so, where and by whom;

(b)   whether to impose any conditions to be complied with by the party in whose favour the order for contact has been made and if so, the nature of those conditions, for example by way of seeking advice or treatment (subject to any necessary consent);

(c)   whether such contact should be for a specified period or should contain provisions which are to have effect for a specified period;

(d)   whether or not the operation of the order needs to be reviewed; if so the court should set a date for the review and give directions to ensure that at the review the court has full information about the operation of the order.

29 Where the court does not consider direct contact to be appropriate, it shall consider whether it is in the best interests of the child to make an order for indirect contact.

The reasons of the court

30 In its judgment or reasons the court should always make clear how its findings on the issue of domestic violence have influenced its decision on the issue of residence or contact. In particular, where the court has found domestic violence proved but nonetheless makes an order, the court should always explain, whether by way of reference to the welfare check-list or otherwise, why it takes the view that the order which it has made is in the best interests of the child.

31 This Practice Direction is issued by the President of the Family Division, as the nominee of the Lord Chief Justice, with the agreement of the Lord Chancellor.

****

A7.3   APPENDIX 3:
PROTOCOL FOR REFERRALS OF FAMILIES BY JUDGES AND MAGISTRATES TO CHILD CONTACT CENTRES

The National Association of Child Contact Centres (NACC) has issued a Protocol, endorsed by the President of the Family Division, for the referral of families to Child Contact Centres. It provides guidance as to which categories of cases are suitable for this service, the practical steps to be taken in order to get in touch with an appropriate centre and suggested wording for court orders requiring the attendance of parties and children at the centre. The Protocol reads as follows:

'Before making an Order for Contact (whether interim or final) which involves the use of a Child Contact Centre, please check that the matters listed below have been addressed.'

Please note in particular that most Child Contact Centres do *not* offer Supervised Contact. The provision which most offer is SUPPORTED CONTACT which is described in the Manual of Guidance produced by the National Association of Child Contact Centres (NACCC) as:

– low vigilance;

– several families at a time in one or a number of rooms;

– volunteers and staff keeping a watchful eye;

– conversations not being monitored.

If you are considering making an Order for contact in a case where domestic violence is an issue, please ensure that you have addressed that issue, and in particular:

(1) that you have considered the effect on the resident parent and the children concerned of any domestic violence you have found or which is alleged and that;

(2) notwithstanding these matters you are satisfied that supported contact is appropriate. If this is *not appropriate*, is supervised contact appropriate and is it available?

Things to check

(1) That the Child Contact Centre Co-ordinator has been contacted and has confirmed:

(a) The referral appears to be suitable for that particular Centre. Child Contact Centres can refuse to accept families if the circumstances appear inappropriate for the Centre.

(b) The intended day and times are available at the particular Centre concerned.

(c) A vacancy is available or a place on a waiting list has been allocated.

(2) That you have directed that a copy of the order is provided to the Centre by one or other of the parties within a specified time together with any other injunctive or relevant Orders on the court file.

(3) That it has been agreed who will have responsibility for completing and returning the Centre's referral form. Solicitors for both parties should agree the contents and it should be forwarded to the Child Contact Centre within 24 hours of the court hearing.

(4) If contact is to be observed at the Child Contact Centre by a family court welfare officer (CAFCASS officer) or other third party, that this is a facility offered by that Centre and that the Centre has agreed to this course of action. (many do not permit such attendance).

(5) That the parties understand whether the Centre offers supported or supervised contact and appreciate the difference.

(6) That it is agreed who is going to tell the children where and when they will see their non-resident parent.

(7) That the Order clearly defines whether or not any other family members are to be a part of the contact visit.

(8) That it has been agreed who will be responsible for informing the Centre when the place is no longer required.

(9) That a date has been set for a review of the contact and any other steps parties have been ordered or undertaken to take which are relevant to the contact issue and for further directions if necessary. Only in exceptional circumstances should use of a Centre be open-ended.

Please also note

(1) The order should be worded: 'Subject to the parties attendance at a pre-contact meeting (if applicable), the availability of a place and the parties abiding by the rules of the centre '
Note: it is a requirement of some Centres that the parents and children attend a pre-contact meeting (parents are seen separately) so that the Centres can follow their own risk assessment procedure. Others will either welcome or insist on a pre-contact visit by the resident parent to acclimatise the child(ren). Non-resident parents are also welcome.

(2) *Ben's Story*, a children's book about visiting a Child Contact Centre is available from NACCC or can be ordered from most good bookshops (ISBN: 0-9536548-0-X). Cost £1.99 plus 35p post and packaging. It is also printed in Welsh – *Stori Ben*.

(3) The Centre or Centres at which you direct contact to take place will very much welcome a visit from you or from your colleagues. It will be greatly appreciated by the volunteer staff if the local judiciary takes a positive interest in its local Centres, and such visits will also help you understand the facilities on offer and thus the type of case which is most suited to contact in the local Child Contact Centre.

CHAPTER 8

SPECIAL GUARDIANSHIP ORDERS

8.1 THE LEGISLATION

The relevant provisions are sections 14A–14G of the Children Act 1989, as inserted by s 115 of the Adoption and Children Act 2002.

A special guardianship order provides a halfway house between an adoption or residence order in that it:

- allows natural parents to retain their parental responsibility (unlike adoption) (s 14C(2) and (3));

- is more secure than a residence order, to the extent that the special guardian secures 'exclusive' parental responsibility over and above the natural parents (s 14C(1)); and

- natural parents have to obtain the leave of the court to discharge a special guardianship order and have to show a change of circumstances (s 14D(5)).

8.2 MAKING AN APPLICATION

An application can be made in care proceedings (and may be part of a local authority's care plan) or as an application by way of private proceedings. The court also has the power to make a special guardianship order of its own motion where it seems to be the best order to meet a child's welfare needs (s 14A(6)(b)).

An application for a special guardianship order is made on Form C100, or on Form C13A if there are no other proceedings before the court.

If the application is made within other proceedings, eg within care proceedings, Form C2 is needed.

8.3 THOSE WITH THE AUTOMATIC RIGHT TO MAKE AN APPLICATION (S 14A(5))

- Person with residence order.

- Formal guardian.

- Someone the child has lived with for 3 of the last 5 years.

- A local authority foster carer where the child has lived with them for a year.

- Someone supported by the local authority if the child is in care eg under a care plan.

- Someone supported by all those with parental responsibility, or by someone who holds a residence order.

All other applicants need the leave of the court to make an application.

8.4 WHO NEEDS TO KNOW YOU ARE MAKING AN APPLICATION?

Notice of the application must be given to everyone who has parental responsibility for the child eg parents, local authority with a care order, anyone with a residence order and the child themself (via their children's guardian) if they are subject to care proceedings, or via the local authority if subject to a care order. In the latter case, a children's guardian will be appointed as one of the first directions (see FPR 2010).

8.5 RULES

The provisions of the Family Procedure Rules 2010 should be borne in mind in the context particularly of stand-alone special guardianship applications, or in relation to those cases where these follow the making of a residence order some time previously in favour of a carer from the child's extended family.

In addition to bearing in mind the overriding objective in FPR 2010, Pt 1, the court and parties may frequently find that in this category of cases (where parties may also be unrepresented) contact with the child's own relatives has been lost or is not easy to re-establish. The court will want to consider the service provisions in FPR 2010, Pt 6 carefully in these circumstances.

Delay, whether from problematic service or from late filing of reports, is also a very frequent problem in an area of work which struggles to retain any priority in the allocation of social services resources, and parties may wish from time to time to ask the court to make orders without attendance, using its powers under FPR 2010, rr 1 and 4.

8.6 NOTICE TO THE LOCAL AUTHORITY TO PREPARE A REPORT (S 14A(7))

Before making the application, notice must be given to the local authority of the intention to apply. This will be either the local authority where the applicant lives or any local authority with a care order in respect of the child. The local authority so notified must prepare a special guardianship report. The report considers information about the potential carers and their suitability to care for the child in question, the needs of the child and the appropriateness of special guardianship as an order for that child. The report must also consider the financial and support needs of the carers in looking after the child.

In the case of automatically entitled applicants, notice given to the local authority triggers their duty to prepare a special guardianship report forthwith. In the case of applicants who need leave, the local authority's duty only begins at the point when such an applicant obtains the court's leave to pursue their application.[1]

If the court decides to make a special guardianship order of its own motion, it still requires a special guardianship report.[2] If such a decision is likely, the provision of the SGO report must be considered and borne in mind when timetabling proceedings.

8.7 WHICH COURT?

If there is an existing order in force e g care order or residence order, the application should be made to the court which made that order. The same applies if there are existing proceedings concerning the child.

In all other cases there is a choice whether to issue proceedings at the family proceedings court, county court or High Court. Which court is chosen will depend on complexity and convenience, in accordance with the usual principles for issue of any proceedings.

---

[1]   *Re R (A Child) sub nom Birmingham City Council v LR (by the OS), PNG, AK, KW & MRR (by her Guardian)* [2006] EWCA Civ 1748, (2006) *The Times*, 29 December.

[2]   *Re S (A Child) (No 2)* [2007] EWCA Civ 90, [2007] 1 FLR 855.

8.8 WHEN WILL THE COURT MAKE A SPECIAL GUARDIANSHIP ORDER?

There is guidance from the Department for Children, Families and Schools (DCSF) and the British Association for Adoption and Fostering (BAAF) setting out particular circumstances in which it has been envisaged that special guardianship may be more appropriate than adoption. These include:

- where carers are relatives, e g grandparents, aunts and uncles, so that family relationships are not skewed by adoptive parenthood;

- where an older child has a relationship with their natural family and does not wish to be adopted or lose that family link but wishes for permanency with a foster carer or other alternative carer;

- cases where there are religious or cultural objections to adoption;

- in the case of unaccompanied asylum seeking children whose family may not have been traced, but who retain the hope that their parents are alive and want to maintain a potential family link.

8.9 THE CASE LAW

It is clear from the case law that the decision as to whether an SGO should be made depends entirely on the *welfare of the child* as assessed in the particular circumstances of the case. The court should address carefully all aspects of the welfare checklist (Children Act 1989, s 1) and if the alternative order is adoption then the assessment should consider the effect of that order throughout the child's life (Adoption and Children Act 2002, s 1). The DCFS/BAAF guidelines may still have some merit but are not binding, as is made clear by the cases.

Consider the cases of:

- *Re S* [2007] EWCA Civ 54, [2007] 1 FLR 819;

- *Re AJ* [2007] EWCA Civ 55, [2007] 1 FLR 507;

- *Re MJ* [2007] EWCA Civ 561, [2007] 1 FLR 691, further discussed in Chapter 15 under adoption.

8.10 THE EFFECT OF A SPECIAL GUARDIANSHIP ORDER

A special guardianship order gives the special guardian:

- exclusive parental responsibility for the child until they are aged 18 (unlike a residence order which generally only lasts to 16) (s 14C(1));

- the right to make decisions about their care, save for a change of name or removal from the country for over 3 months (s 14C(3));

- the right to appoint a testamentary guardian for the child in the case of the special guardian's death;

- entitlement to be assessed by the local authority for support, financial and otherwise, to support the carer in caring for the child (Special Guardianship Regulations 2005, reg 14F).

Parents retain:

- parental responsibility and the right to be consulted on major decisions e g name change, religion (s 14C(2));

- the right to apply for contact or specific issue orders concerning the child, without leave of the court.

8.11 SUPPORT FOR SPECIAL GUARDIANS (S 14F CHILDREN ACT 1989 AND SPECIAL GUARDIANSHIP REGULATIONS 2005)

The local authority has a duty to provide support for people caring for a child under a special guardianship order. They also have a duty to assess applicants for a special guardianship order to ascertain what support they need in caring for the child. Support may be by way of financial assistance and other practical support e g counselling, mediation with the parents, support for contact with parents and support groups.

The support regulations are particularly relevant for applicants who have previously cared for the child under a care order, whether as a foster carer or as a relative carer. Responsibility for the assessment and provision of support lies with the local authority placing the child for the first 3 years, even if placement is with carers outside that local authority area (see Special Guardianship Regulations 2005).

A statement detailing the assessment undertaken and any support and services to be provided must be filed by the local authority along with the Special Guardianship Report. Parties representing applicants will wish to ensure that the special guardianship order details or refers to both the basis upon which allowances are to be paid and the services which the local authority undertakes to provide to support the child and the family.

See *Re L (A Child) (Special Guardianship: Surname)*[3] where contact orders to the mother were made at the same time as a special guardianship order. The judge ruled that the child was to continue to remain registered as a child in need and receive a support package from the local authority to include contact supervision and life story. The special guardians' objections to this interference with their parental responsibility were rejected on appeal.

In the judicial review case of *B v X MBC*[4] the local authority set the special guardian's allowance at two-thirds of the core fostering allowance. It was held (ordering payment of arrears and re-assessment) 'Payment at this rate by policy represented a substantial departure from para 65 of the Guidance and was not justified on rational grounds'. A substantial departure required substantial justification which was absent here.

8.12   HOW CAN YOU DISCHARGE A SPECIAL GUARDIANSHIP ORDER? (S 14D)

The birth parent needs to show a change of circumstances to obtain leave (s 14D(5)). 'Change of circumstances' is not yet defined but it is likely to include recovery from what led to inability to parent in the first place.

The child can obtain leave to challenge the order, provided they have sufficient understanding (s 14D(4)). They do not have to show change of circumstances.

The court also has the power to vary or discharge a special guardianship order of its own motion, within existing proceedings, if it seems to be in the interests of the child to do so (s 14D(2)).

Application is made by Form C1 and C13A in the same way as an application to obtain the original order.

---

3   [2007] EWCA Civ 196.
4   [2010] EWHC 467 (Admin).

8.13   SPECIAL GUARDIANSHIP ORDER FLOWCHART

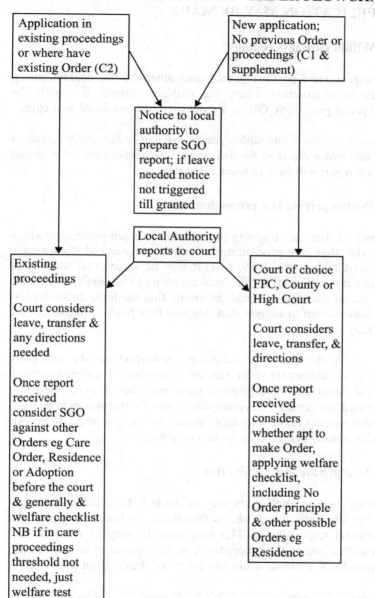

Application in existing proceedings or where have existing Order (C2)

New application; No previous Order or proceedings (C1 & supplement)

Notice to local authority to prepare SGO report; if leave needed notice not triggered till granted

Local Authority reports to court

Existing proceedings

Court considers leave, transfer & any directions needed

Once report received consider SGO against other Orders eg Care Order, Residence or Adoption before the court & generally & welfare checklist NB if in care proceedings threshold not needed, just welfare test

Court of choice FPC, County or High Court

Court considers leave, transfer, & directions

Once report received considers whether apt to make Order, applying welfare checklist, including No Order principle & other possible Orders eg Residence

8.14 SITUATIONS WHEN A SPECIAL GUARDIANSHIP APPLICATION MAY BE MADE

8.14.1 Within care proceedings

Either in response to a positive viability assessment by the local authority, particularly in a situation where the children already live with the potential special guardians, OR as a request to be considered as a carer.

In this scenario the main timetabling framework will be the care proceedings timetable into which the time for assessment and preparation of a special guardianship report will have to be incorporated.

8.14.2 Within private law proceedings

For example, if there are ongoing proceedings between parents in which there is a risk that care proceedings might be commenced (following a report under Children Act 1989, s 37) it may be agreed that the way to forestall care proceedings is for the local authority to assess the alternative carers as special guardians instead, assuming that the local authority has sufficient information to suggest that this may be a positive placement for the child(ren).

In this scenario the special guardianship application can be separately timetabled as a continuation of the existing proceedings. It will be necessary to review all earlier directions given to make sure that they are consistent with the revised timetable eg extending timescales for statements to be filed, altering final hearing dates – to take account of the fact that the special guardianship assessment can take up to 3 months.

8.14.3 As a private law application

For example, such an application may be made if the child(ren) already live with the alternative carer who wishes to secure his/her position and obtain parental responsibility. This may arise by way of the potential special guardian issuing the proceedings, or in response to an application by the parent for a residence order and return of the children to their care.

In this scenario the timetable will be set as the main set of directions for the proceedings.

8.14.4 As an application to discharge an existing care order

For example, is the applicant a local authority foster carer or relative carer acting under a care order.

In this scenario the proceedings will be public law proceedings, requiring notice to local authority and children's guardian to be joined as parties to the proceedings. The timetable will therefore be more akin to the timetable for care proceedings.

8.15 SPECIAL GUARDIANSHIP: CHECKLIST OF STEPS AND TIMETABLE TO FINAL HEARING

8.15.1 Within care proceedings

8.15.1.1 Application – documents

If care proceedings have been issued, that will have been done by the local authority. The application for a special guardianship order within care proceedings must therefore be on a C2, as follows:

Form C2

• Cover: Name of court and full name of the child.

(1) Name, address and details of applicant and solicitor's details.

(2) Order(s) applied for – this will be:

    (a) leave to be joined in the proceedings;
    (b) leave to issue the application (if needed);
    (c) substantive application for special guardianship order;
    (d) any ancillary applications e g for change of name, religion etc.

(3) People to be served, names, addresses and relationship to child.

(4) Domestic abuse, violence or harm – this is where the fact that the children are already subject to care proceedings should be indicated – a Form C1A will also be needed.

(5) Reasons for applying – set out basis of application ie involvement with child; ability to meet child's needs; relationship with child's parents; proposals for contact between the child, parents and others important to the child; social services contact and their view of application, e g viability assessments.

(6) Any need for support at court e g interpreters.

Form C1A

• Cover: Name of court and full name of the child

Section 1

(1)	Name, address and details of applicant.

(2)	Applicant's solicitor's details.

Section 2

(1)	Can be ignored as this is the respondent's comments on any allegations of harm or domestic violence.

Section 3

(1)	Details of involvement with outside agencies – provide as much information as is known by the applicant of social services/police concerns.

(2)	Incidents of violence or harm.

(3)	Involvement of the children in those incidents.

(4)	Details of any witnesses.

(5)	Details of any medical treatment or assessment of the children.

(6)	Any incidents of abduction.

(7)	Steps or orders needed to protect applicant or children – consider whether an injunction might be needed if there is any threat or possibility of harassment from the parents or any others.

(8)	Any need for support at court eg interpreters.

NB – If the applicant has little detail concerning the grounds for the child protection proceedings, it may be appropriate simply to refer to the fact that it is known that there are concerns that have led to proceedings, rather than completing the C1A.

Form C13A

This is the specific supplement required to apply for a special guardianship order. If the applicant knows from the outset that this is the order sought, the Form C13A should also be completed as follows:

•	Cover: Court, names of the children

(1)	Relationship of applicant to the child(ren) and whether permission is needed to make the application.

(2) Details of the local authority to which notice of the need to prepare a special guardianship report has been given, or is to be given, and whether an adoption application has been made.

(3) Reasons for making the application.

(4) Details of plans for the child(ren), including any need to vary or discharge an existing order e g residence or care; contact arrangements and any orders needed as to conditions to be attached to the order.

However, if at the time of issuing the Form C2 the applicant is not sure whether a care or special guardianship order might be more appropriate, it is possible for the court to make a special guardianship order of its own motion without a Form C13A having been issued.

8.15.1.2   *Directions needed*

(1) Local authority to prepare the special guardianship report in line with the Schedule to the Special Guardianship Regulations 2005: this includes:

    (a) information about the child's background and needs, including any assessment undertaken in the existing proceedings;

    (b) information about the child's parents, including reports from assessment in the proceedings;

    (c) information about the potential special guardian(s) and their capacity to meet the child's needs, including managing contact with parents etc;

    (d) special guardianship support plan – detailing what support is available for the special guardian(s) in raising the child, including financial support, help with legal costs and the costs of any future proceedings e g over contact.

Report to be filed by [xxx] date – no later than 3 months from date of notice.

(2) Parties to file statements in response to the local authority's evidence, which will include the special guardianship report, final care plan and final statement; this may already have been timetabled earlier in the proceedings.

(3) Directions for children's guardian's report.

8.15.1.3   *Issues for Final Hearing*

(1) **Findings** – If there is a decision to be made as between a care or supervision order and a special guardianship order, there will need to be agreement or findings made about the threshold criteria.

(2) **Appropriate placement for the child** – Should the child be placed with
     the applicant(s) for special guardianship? Or should the child be
     placed back with parent(s)? Or outside the family e g for adoption or
     long term fostering?

(3) **Appropriate order for the placement** – If the placement is to be with
     the applicant for special guardianship it will have to be considered
     whether special guardianship is the best order to meet the child's
     welfare – following the welfare checklist – or whether some other
     order is more appropriate.

(4) **Care or special guardianship order?** – The court will need to consider
     whether—

     (a) the special guardian can exercise parental responsibility to meet
          the child's needs on his/her own or whether the local authority
          needs to share parental responsibility;
     (b) the local authority does not need to share parental
          responsibility if the carer simply needs some support; the key
          will be whether the carer has an appropriate understanding of
          the child's needs and can meet them and exercise parental
          responsibility without too much guidance from the local
          authority;
     (c) the impact of social services' intervention on the child and
          whether support can be provided other than by a care order;
     (d) if all that is needed is practical support (e g resources, assistance
          with supervising contact), then this can be provided under the
          special guardianship support package and may not need a care
          order.

(5) **Special guardianship or adoption?** – Adoption may be more
     appropriate than special guardianship in situations where—

     (a) there might be a threat of disruption to the placement from the
          parents;
     (b) where an ongoing relationship with the natural parents may not
          be possible;
     (c) where the child needs the stability of a placement without state
          intervention.

(6) **Special guardianship or residence order?**
     If there is—

     (i) a prospect of parents recovering sufficiently to share or even
          resume the care of the children; and
     (ii) they can share parental responsibility with the carers without
          undermining or disrupting placement with the alternative
          carers in the meantime, then a residence order may be more

appropriate than a special guardianship order as the hurdles to changing the order are less for the former than for the latter.

(7) The basis for a decision as to which is the best order is the welfare checklist. It is for this reason that a Threshold Document identifying 'significant harm' is not needed (as a matter of strict legal process) if proceedings are to be concluded with a special guardianship order. However, to identify why care proceedings were issued and why the children cannot be returned to their parents, a set of threshold facts is still useful. It is likely that this will have been dealt with as a matter of course within the care proceedings in any event, either by way of a fact finding hearing or by agreement.

(8) Other points to note:

(a) as a matter of law and regulation applications for special guardianship do not have to be considered by adoption or fostering panels although some local authorities may include this step within their own internal approval processes;

(b) as a matter of law and regulation the Schedule for a special guardianship report does not require CRB checks. However, as a matter of good practice CRB and SIDs checks are appropriate to ensure that the placement is safe or, that if there are any risks, they are known and can be managed. In addition, some courts ask for such information as a prelude to private as well as public proceedings in any event;

(c) in these two respects special guardianship orders are treated more like residence orders than equivalent to adoption or care orders;

(d) in any situation where the court considers making a special guardianship order of its own motion the court must direct that the local authority prepare a special guardianship report prior to the final hearing. This direction should be given at the earliest opportunity once it is realised that a special guardianship order might be an appropriate disposal of the case.

8.15.2 In private law proceedings

8.15.2.1 *Application – documents*

If there are already private law proceedings ongoing and the special guardianship application intervenes in those proceedings, much of the process will be similar to the checklist outlined above (save for references to the local authority, guardian or threshold criteria). The application for a special guardianship order within existing private law proceedings is also made on Form C2, as follows.

–   Cover: Name of court and full name of the child

(1)   Name, address and details of applicant and solicitor's details.

(2)   Order(s) applied for – this will be:

    (a)   leave to be joined in the proceedings;

    (b)   leave to issue the application (if needed);

    (c)   substantive application for special guardianship order;

    (d)   any ancillary applications e g for change of name, religion etc.

(3)   People to be served, names, addresses and relationship to child.

(4)   Domestic abuse, violence or harm – this is where to indicate that the children are already subject to care proceedings – a Form C1A will also be needed.

(5)   Reasons for applying – set out basis of application: ie involvement with child; ability to meet child's needs; relationship with child's parents; proposals for contact between the child, parents and others important to the child; social services contact and their view of application e g viability assessments.

(6)   Any need for support at court e g interpreters.

Form C1A

–   Cover: Name of court and full name of the child

Section 1

(1)   Name, address and details of applicant.

(2)   Applicant's solicitor's details.

Section 2

(1)   Can be ignored as this is the respondent's comments on any allegations of harm or domestic violence.

Section 3

(1)   Details of involvement with outside agencies – provide as much information as is known by the applicant of social services/police concerns or involvement e g by way of a s 37 report.

(2)   Dates and details of incidents of violence or harm.

(3)   Involvement of the children in those incidents.

(4)   Details of any witnesses.

(5)   Details of any medical treatment or assessment of the children.

(6)   Any incidents of abduction.

(7)   Steps or orders needed to protect applicant or children – consider whether an injunction might be needed if there is any threat or possibility of harassment from the parents or any others.

(8)   Any need for support at court eg interpreters.

In the event that the applicant for special guardianship institutes proceedings the following forms will need to be completed:

Form C1

–   Cover: Name of court and full name of the child.

(1)   Name, address and details of applicant and solicitor's details.

(2)   Children's details and orders applied for.

(3)   Details of any other cases involving the children, now or in the past – details of social services and/or children's guardian involved.

(4)   The automatic respondents: ie everyone with parental responsibility, including parents, local authority if the child is subject to a care order.

(5)   Others to whom notice is to be given; eg a father or step-parent without parental responsibility, former carer for the child under a residence order.

(6)   Care of the children: where they live now and who cares for them.

(7)   Domestic violence, abuse or harm.

(8)   Social services involvement.

(9)   Education and health of the child(ren).

(10) Details of the child(ren's) parents, including names, addresses.

(11) Any other siblings or half siblings of the child(ren) in respect of whom the application is made along with their details.

(12) Any other adults who live with the child(ren).

(13) Reasons for the application and plans for the children, including contact.

(14) Attending court – any support needed.

(15) Parenting information checklist.

Form C1A

This will be required if information is given about domestic violence or abuse; details required to be given include:

– Cover: Name of court and full name of the child.

Section 1

(1) Name, address and details of applicant.

(2) Applicant's solicitor's details.

Section 2

(1) Can be ignored as this is the respondent's comments on any allegations of harm or domestic violence.

Section 3

(1) Details of involvement with outside agencies: provide as much information as is known by the applicant of social services/police concerns or involvement eg by way of a s 37 report.

(2) Dates and details of incidents of violence or harm.

(3) Involvement of the children in those incidents.

(4) Details of any witnesses.

(5) Details of any medical treatment or assessment of the children.

(6) Any incidents of abduction.

(7) Steps or orders needed to protect applicant or children – consider whether an injunction might be needed if there is any threat or possibility of harassment from the parents or any others.

(8) Any need for support at court eg interpreters.

Form 13A

– Cover: Court, names of the children.

(1) Relationship of applicant to the child(ren) and whether permission is needed to make the application.

(2) Details of the local authority to which notice of the need to prepare a special guardianship report has been given or is to be given and whether an adoption application has been made.

(3) Reasons for making the application.

(4) Details of plans for the child(ren), including any need to vary or discharge an existing order eg residence or care; contact arrangements and any directions needed as to conditions to be attached to the order.

8.15.2.2 *Directions needed*

(1) Direction addressed to the local authority to prepare the special guardianship report. Although the local authority is not a party to proceedings this direction operates in the same way as does a direction for a report under Children Act 1989, s 37. The report must cover the issues set out in the Schedule to the Special Guardianship Regulations 2005 including:

   (a) information about the child's background and needs;
   (b) information about the child's parents;
   (c) information about the potential special guardian(s) and their capacity to meet the child's needs, including managing contact with parents etc;
   (d) special guardianship support plan – detailing what support is available for the special guardian(s) in raising the child, including financial support, help with legal costs and the costs of any future proceedings eg over contact.
   Report to be filed by [xxx] date – no later than 3 months from date of notice.

(2) Parties to file statements in response to the application for special guardianship and in response to the report when filed. Statements may also need to respond to any earlier statements and reports eg s 7 or s 37, that have been filed by other agencies. Directions already timetabled earlier in the proceedings will need to be reviewed to ensure consistency of timetabling to the final hearing.

(3) Directions for children's guardian's report – this may still be needed if a children's guardian has been appointed under r 9.5;

(4)   NB – In proceedings initiated by the potential special guardian it
      may be necessary to consider whether there are any other
      assessments or reports needed eg psychological assessments of the
      parents or of the child(ren). If so these will need to be timetabled
      whereby they can be considered by the local authority in the
      preparation of the special guardianship report. This is most likely to
      arise if there is a contest between parents and applicant for special
      guardianship and eg if there is background history of mental illness,
      domestic violence or substance misuse and/or any significant
      concerns about the child's physical or emotional health.

8.15.2.3   *Issues for final hearing*

(1)   **Appropriate placement for the child** – Should the child be placed with
      the applicant(s) for special guardianship? Or should the child be
      placed back with either or both parent(s) – depending upon who has
      applied?

(2)   **Appropriate order for the placement** – If the placement is to be with
      the applicant for special guardianship, it will have to be considered
      whether special guardianship is the best order to meet the child's
      welfare or whether some other order is more appropriate. The most
      obvious choice is between special guardianship and residence orders.
      The court will consider:

      (a)   the extent of involvement of any other holders of parental
            responsibility in care of and decision-making for the child, and
            whether this would be disrupted by the special guardianship
            order;
      (b)   likely developments during the period of the child's minority;
      (c)   the need for formal support from the local authority in the
            form of a special guardianship order support package.

(3)   **Care or special guardianship order?** – A care order would only be
      possible in the context of private proceedings if the court was not
      satisfied that the potential special guardian could meet the child's
      needs, and that concerns are so serious that the threshold test of s 31
      is satisfied; any such order would be an interim order under s 38. The
      court will need to consider whether –

      (a)   the special guardian can exercise parental responsibility to meet
            the child's needs or whether the local authority needs to share
            parental responsibility;
      (b)   the local authority does not need to share parental
            responsibility if the carer simply needs some support. The key
            will be whether the carer has an appropriate understanding of

the child's needs and can meet them and exercise parental responsibility without too much guidance from the local authority;

(c) the impact of social services intervention on the child and whether support can be provided other than by a care order;

(d) if all that is needed is practical support (eg resources, assistance with supervising contact) then this can be provided under the special guardianship support package and may not need a care order.

If the court considers that a local authority does need to share parental responsibility, then it will have to order a s 37 report from the local authority. This could be problematic as it is likely to be the same local authority that has prepared the special guardianship report. However, it is possible that the outcome of a special guardianship assessment is negative which may prompt the local authority itself to issue care proceedings.

(4) **Special guardianship or adoption?** – This may arise in a situation where eg a long term foster carer seeks to care for the child by way of application for adoption instead of long term fostering. It is also open to the court to consider in a special guardianship application of its own motion whether adoption may be suggested to the applicants to be more appropriate than special guardianship. Factors to be taken into account will include whether:

(a) there might be a threat of disruption to the placement from the parents;

(b) whether an ongoing relationship with the natural parents is possible;

(c) whether an open adoption is more appropriate and secure than a special guardianship order which can be challenged;

(d) whether it might be appropriate to secure the special guardianship order by means of s 91(14) orders to restrict future disruptive applications over contact or specific issue orders;

(e) the child's wishes and feelings about adoption or maintaining the link with their birth family via special guardianship; and

(f) all other factors in the welfare checklist.

(5) **Special guardianship or residence order?** – If there is: (i) a prospect of parents circumstances changing sufficiently to share or even resume the care of the children; and (ii) they can share parental responsibility with the carer without undermining or disrupting placement with the alternative carers in the meantime, then a residence order may be more appropriate than a special guardianship order. This is because the hurdles to changing the order are less for a residence than for a special guardianship order.

(6) In all situations, the underlying basis for decisions as to which is the best order is the welfare checklist. The test of 'significant harm' is not relevant but the court will need to make clear (partly in case there are future applications for leave to overturn the special guardianship order) why the child is not living with his/her natural parents.

(7) Other points to note – As for care proceedings – see **8.15.1.3** above.

8.15.3 Other public proceedings – application for discharge of care order and substitution by special guardianship or adoption

(1) This will be commenced in the same way as outlined above ie the applicant for special guardianship will complete Forms C1, C1A and C13A if they commence the proceedings or by Form C2 and C13A if within existing proceedings eg by parents to discharge the care order or a foster carer to adopt. It might be that when a foster carer seeks to adopt a child, other family members seek to care for the child.

(2) Notice will need to be given to the guardian and local authority as parties.

(3) The timetabling issues will be similar to those for the public law proceedings. It may also be that further, up to date assessments of parenting capacity, changes in psychological profile or medical issues are needed; these will need to be timetabled alongside the preparation of the special guardianship assessment and report and their conclusions considered within it.

8.16 CASE DIGEST

8.16.1 Adoption order or special guardianship order

Re S [2007] EWCA Civ 54, [2007] 1 FLR 819

Application by foster carer to adopt a 6-year-old child fostered for half her life. The Court of Appeal upheld a special guardianship order made by HHJ Kushner QC as best reflecting the child's welfare and direct contact with her biological family. The Court of Appeal emphasised the need to respect judicial discretion as to the best order for the child's needs, assessed by careful reference to the welfare checklist. The guardian's support for adoption was so finely balanced that it did not amount to a recommendation; it did not therefore matter that the judgment overlooked his evidence. The making of s 91(14) orders was approved to ensure that challenges to the special guardian's parental responsibility, not just applications to revoke, required leave. Also confirmed that special guardianship can be imposed on a carer applying for a different order, in contrast to *Re K* [1995] 1 FLR 675, which held that a residence order could not be forced on a carer who wanted a care order.

Re AJ [2007] EWCA Civ 55, [2007] 1 FLR 507; Re MJ [2007] EWCA Civ 56, [2007] 1 FLR 691

Decisions to grant adoption and not special guardianship to relative carers, as adoption was needed for security of the placements. Although special guardianship was envisaged as appropriate for relative carers, to avoid distortion of family relationships, it was still open to courts to make adoption orders to relatives.

8.16.2 Special guardianship or adoption outside the family

Re EN (A Child) [2007] Civ 264

Adoption outside the family preferable to special guardianship with grandmother, despite grandmother's move of house, to cut ties with family who could undermine her protection of the child. What she gained in distance from the family she lost in support. The child would not have a normal family life as there was much of the family he could not have contact with. Grandmother could not meet the child's needs, even with a special guardianship order; the child needed a new family and identity.

Haringey LBC v C & Mrs E, Mr E, Mrs F and Kenya [2006] EWHC 1620

Kenyan baby purportedly born to E, who claimed maternity by miracle. The court found the baby was trafficked. The applications were by: (a) E, who believed herself to be the mother and whose false belief would place the child at risk of emotional harm; (b) a white foster carer who sought special guardianship; and (c) the local authority which sought adoption by more culturally appropriate carers than the foster carer. Held that even though special guardianship preserves links with birth family it does not overcome the need, where possible, to ensure appropriate cultural matching.

8.16.3 Parental responsibility under SGO

L (A Child) [2007] EWCA Civ 196

Court of Appeal upheld the first instance decision that the applicant grandmother should have a special guardianship order and not adoption order as she did not promote the child's Afro-Caribbean heritage or life story work. Whilst a special guardianship order granted exclusive parental rights over biological parents, it was not free of judicial oversight. The court made a contact order to the parents who had been 'sidelined but not totally displaced' by the special guardianship order. The change of name sought by grandmother was also refused because of her difficulties in promoting the child's identity.

8.16.4   Special guardianship reports

Re R (A Child) sub nom Birmingham City Council v LR (by the OS) [2006] EWCA Civ 1748, [2007] 1 FLR 564

Section 14A(8) of the Children Act 1989 required local authorities to prepare suitability reports for SGO *only* when a person with automatic entitlement to seek a special guardianship order gave notice *or* when someone who required leave obtained the court's leave to apply. It was not possible to give notice to the local authority prior to leave being granted.

Re S (A Child) (No 2) [2007] EWCA Civ 90, [2007] 1 FLR 855

Arising from *Re S* [2007] EWCA Civ 54. Where a judge, under s 14A(6)(b) of the Children Act 1989, makes a special guardianship order as an alternative to another order, the special guardianship order cannot be made until a special guardianship suitability report is prepared (s 14A(8) and s 14A(11) of the Children Act 1989). Where a report was already before the court with most of the information required, the local authority could provide the missing information, cross referenced to the existing report.

8.16.5   Assessment of relatives

Re B & G [2007] EWCA Civ 358

Judge entitled to refuse late application by foster sister as potential carer; she was too tardy in coming forward and evidence suggested would be unsuitable.

A8.1   APPENDIX:
TABLE REPRODUCED FROM RE AJ [2007] 1 FLR 507

SCHEDULE OF MAIN DIFFERENCES BETWEEN SPECIAL GUARDIANSHIP ORDERS & ADOPTION

	SPECIAL GUARDIANSHIP	ADOPTION
1 <u>STATUS OF CARER</u>	**Special Guardian:** *If related to child retains existing relative status.*	**Parent for all purposes:** *If related to child existing relative status changes.*
2 <u>STATUS OF CHILD</u>	**A child living with relatives/carers who remains the child of birth parent.**	**The child of the adoptive parent as if born as a child of the marriage and not the child of any other person** *therefore adoption includes a vesting of 'parenthood'* *Section 39(1), (2) of the Adoption Act 1976 (the 1976 Act)/s 67 of the Adoption and Children Act 2002 (the 2002 Act).*
3 <u>DURATION OF ORDER</u>	**Ceases automatically on reaching 18 if not revoked by court earlier** **whether also ceases on death?** *The legal relationship created is therefore time limited and not lifelong.* *Section 91(13) of the Children Act 1989 (the 1989 Act).*	**Permanent** *The legal relationship is lifelong.* *Section 39(1) of the 1976 Act/s 67 of the 2002 Act.*
4 <u>EFFECT ON BIRTH PARENT PR</u>	**PR retained by birth parent** *SG can impose limitations in use (see 6 below)* *Section 14C(1), (2) of the 1989 Act.*	**Birth Parent PR extinguished** *Section 39(2) of the 1976 Act/s 46 of the 2002 Act.*
5 <u>CARER'S PR</u>	**PR vests in special guardian/s** *Section 14C(1), (2) of the 1989 Act* *Subject to limitations (see 6 below).*	**PR vested in adopter/s** *Section 39(1) of the 1976 Act/s 49of the 2002 Act/s 2 of the 1989 Act* *No limitations (but see joint operation* below).*

	SPECIAL GUARDIANSHIP	ADOPTION
6 LIMITATION/RESTRICTION OF PR		
(a) removal from jurisdiction	(a) up to 3 months without leave, thereafter only with written consent of all PR holders or leave of court unless court gave general leave on making SG order. *Section 14C(3)(b) and 14C(4)/14B(2)(b)of the 1989 Act.*	(a) No restriction
(b) change of name	(b) can not change surname without written consent of all PR holders or order of the court. *Section 14C(3)(a)/14B(2)(a) of the 1989 Act.*	(b) No restriction *name change may take place at time of making adoption order or thereafter*
(c) consent to adoption	(c) consent required from birth parents _and_ special guardians or court must dispense with consent of birth parents _and_ special guardians. *Sections 19,20,52 and 144 of the 2002 Act/s 14C(2)(b) of the 1989 Act.*	(c) consent required from adopters only or court must dispense with consent of adopters only.
(d) medical treatment	(d) may be difficulties where each special guardian agrees but birth parents do not in the following circumstances: **Sterilisation of a child** *This is the example given in the government guidance to SGO in 'Every Child Matters; in Relation to effect of s 14C(2)(a) – no authority is cited.* **Ritual Circumcision** See *Re J (Specific Issue Orders: Child's Religious Upbringing and Circumcision)* [2000] 1 FLR 571 *Suggests that like sterilisation the consent of all PR holders would be required for this procedure.*	(d) no restrictions where each adoptive parent agrees (subject to age/Gillick competence of child) on giving consent for medical treatment. *However where adoptive parents themselves disagree in these scenarios a court order may be required (see below).*

	SPECIAL GUARDIANSHIP	ADOPTION
(d) medical treatment contd.	**Immunisation** See *Re C (Welfare of Child: Immunisation)* [2003] EWCA Civ 1148, [2003] 2 FLR 1095 *This added contested immunisations to the small group of important decisions where the consent of both parents was required.* **Life prolonging/Life shortening** *If the above scenarios require consent of all with PR surely it must then extend to issues of whether treatment should be given or withheld in terminal cases.* **Section 14C(1)(b) with (2)(a)** *Section 14(C)(1)(b) does not effect the operation of any enactment or rule of law which requires the consent of more than one person with PR in a matter effecting the child.* *If consent of all PR holders is required for these type of decisions does this then impose a duty upon SG to consult with birth parents in advance and to bring the matter back to court for determination if birth parents indicate an objection?*	***Section 2(7) of the 1989 Act*** *Where more than one person has PR for a child each may act alone and without the other but nothing in this part shall be taken to affect the operation of any enactment which requires the consent of more than one person in a matter affecting the child.*
(e) voluntary accommodation	(e) If SG objects LA cannot accommodate child unless court order. If all SGs consent but birth parents object would appear that LA cannot accommodate child unless court order if birth parent willing and able to provide accommodation or arrange for accommodation to be provided.	(e) where adoptive parents agree they can accommodate voluntarily.

	SPECIAL GUARDIANSHIP	**ADOPTION**
(e) voluntary accommodation contd.	*This is not the case if there is in force a residence order and the residence order holder consents nor if there is a care and control order pursuant to wardship or inherent jurisdiction and the person in whose favour the order is made consents.*	
(f) removal from voluntary accommodation	(f) Any person may remove from voluntary accommodation at any time. *This is not the case if residence order holder of carer under wardship/inherent jurisdiction agrees to the voluntary accommodation.* *How is the 'exclusive' nature of the SG's PR intended to operate in these circumstances? It appears that the statute requires the consent of all PR holders therefore if SGs consent to accommodation but parents do not the parents can simply remove the child.* ***Section 20 (7),(8) and (9) of the 1989 Act***	(f) adoptive parents can remove from voluntary accommodation.
(g) consent to marriage under 18	(g) if all SG agree no restriction *the Marriage Act 1949 has been amended to enable SGs to give valid consent where SGO in force (unless also care order in force)* **s 3(1), (1A)(a) and (b)**	(g) if all agree no restriction

	SPECIAL GUARDIANSHIP	ADOPTION
7 DEATH OF CHILD	Special guardian must notify parents with PR *Section 14C(5) of the 1989 Act.*	No requirements for notification.
	Special guardians may not be able to arrange for burial/cremation in circumstances where parents wish to undertake such a task if the SGO ends on death. See by way of analogy R v Gwynedd County Council ex parte B [1991] 2 FLR 365	*The rights and duties of legal parents do not end on death therefore would be no such conflict.*
8 REVOCATION OF ORDER	Specific statutory provision for birth parents to apply for discharge of SGO with leave of the court, leave not to be granted unless there has been a significant change of circumstances.	No statutory provision for revocation.
	Specific statutory provision four court to discharge of its own motion even where no application in any 'family proceedings'. *Section 14D of the 1989 Act.*	*In wholly exceptional circumstances court may set aside adoption order, normally limited to where has been a fundamental breach of natural justice. See for example Re K (Adoption and Wardship)* [1997] 2 FLR 221.
9 FUTURE APPLICATIONS BY PARENTS	(a) Leave required	(a) Leave required
(a) Residence	(b) no automatic restriction	(b) Leave required
(b) Contact	(c) no automatic restriction	(c) Leave required
(c) Prohibited Steps	(d) no automatic restriction *Section 10(4)(7A) and (9) of the 1989 Act A parent is entitled to apply for any section 8 order except residence where is SGO.*	(d) Leave required *Section 10(2)(b), (4) and (9) of the 1989 Act.*
(d) Specific Issue		

	SPECIAL GUARDIANSHIP	ADOPTION
10 **RESPONDENTS TO FUTURE LEGAL PRODEEDINGS RE CHILD**	Birth parents would be respondents in addition to the SGs to any applications in relation to the child for s 8 orders, EPOs, Care/Supervision Orders, Secure accommodation etc.	Only adopters would be automatic respondents.
11 **MAINTENANCE**	Does not operate to extinguish any duty on birth parents to maintain the child.	Operates to extinguish any duty on birth parents to maintain the child *Section 12(3)(b) of the 1976 Act/s 46(2)(d) of the 2002 Act.*
12 **INTESTACY**	Child placed under SGO will not benefit from the rules relating to intestacy if the SGs die intestate.	Adopted Child will have rights of intestate succession.

Lorna Meyer QC
David Crowley
Graham Jones

CHAPTER 9

SCIENTIFIC TESTS

9.1 A DIRECTION FOR SCIENTIFIC TESTING

The power of the court to direct testing to establish proof of parentage
has evolved with the scientific advances that have been made in the
development of identification through examination of individual DNA
profiles. As originally enacted the provisions of the Family Law Reform
Act 1969 (FLRA 1969) were concerned with the use of blood samples to
assist in the determination of paternity by excluding those who were less
likely to be the father of a child. As currently enacted ss 20–25 now enable
the court to direct the taking and testing of bodily samples for the
purposes of positively identifying whether a person is in fact the parent of
a child.

9.2 THE LAW

9.2.1 The scope of the court's power

Under FLRA 1969, s 20 when the court is hearing civil proceedings
requiring the determination of the parentage of a person it can give a
direction for:

- the use of scientific tests to ascertain whether a party to proceedings
  is or is not the father or mother of that person; and

- the taking of bodily samples[1] from the person whose parentage is to
  be determined, a party alleged to be the father or mother and any
  other party to the proceedings.

The following are therefore requirements:

- That there are civil proceedings already in existence; an application
  for a direction is not a freestanding application.[2] These proceedings
  may include applications under the Children Act 1989 (eg contact

---

[1] Defined as bodily fluid or bodily tissue by s 25 of the Act.
[2] *Re E (Parental Responsibility: Blood Tests)* [1995] 1 FLR 392.

orders), the Child Support Act 1991, the Inheritance (Provision for Family and Dependents) Act 1975 or for an application for a declaration pursuant to s 55A of the Family Law Act 1986.

- That those proceedings require the determination of an issue relating to parentage and which is not in fact secondary to the issue before the court (eg an attempt to prove that a wife has committed adultery).

- The court of its own motion may direct the use of the tests without application by any individual.

- The section does not confer a compulsory power but a permissive direction. The direction permits the use of tests and the taking of bodily samples for those purposes. Save in one respect in relation to children the consent of the person from whom a sample is sought must be obtained (see Consent below). It is a discretionary remedy and should only be used if considered to be in the interests of the child concerned (see Principles below).

- The reference to any party includes an intervener to the substantive proceedings or a person named in a petition for a declaration of parentage. Any person not already a party to the application in which the issue of a direction arises will be made a party for the purposes of the determination of this issue. Note however that there is no power in the family proceedings courts for a party to be joined for this purpose (see Procedure below).

- Tests may only be administered by a body accredited by the Ministry of Justice.[3]

9.2.2   Consent

There are three issues in relation to the capacity to give consent:

(1) **Adults** – Even following the making of the direction the court cannot compel the taking of a bodily sample from an adult identified in the direction[4] save where that person is incapable of giving consent by reason of mental disorder and both consent is given by the person with care and control of him and the treating doctor certifies that such testing will not be prejudicial to his care and treatment.[5]

(2) **Children over the age of 16** – A minor who has attained the age of 16 years can give his own consent to the taking of a bodily sample

---

3   FLRA 1969, s 20(1A).
4   FLRA 1969, s 21(1).
5   FLRA 1969, s 21(4).

irrespective of a refusal to do so by a parent.[6] The statute does not state whether a refusal by such a person can be overridden by the court although a similar provision in s 8 of the same Act has been interpreted so as to allow the court or a person with parental responsibility to override such a refusal in the case of medical treatment.[7] However, there is authority for the proposition that older children capable of understanding the situation and forming a view should not be subject to such a procedure against their will.[8]

(3) **Children under the age of 16** – A different position is taken in respect of children who have yet to attain the age of 16. Bodily samples may be taken for the purposes of testing where either the person with care and control of the child gives their consent to the procedure, or where such consent is not given where the court considers that it would be in the best interest of the child for the sample to be taken.[9] The consent of the child, even the *Gillick* competent child, can be overridden by the clear words of the statute although the court will be mindful of the wishes and feelings of the child in determining the issue of whether the direction should be given.

9.2.3 The principles to be applied

The direction is discretionary and the statute does not set out the basis upon which the court's discretion should be exercised. The principles to be applied have been determined by the courts in the light of the improvements made to the science of genetic testing and the advent of legal developments such as the enactment of the Human Rights Act 1998. The following principles have emerged from the jurisprudence:

- the welfare of the child concerned is a relevant but not the paramount factor as the court is not considering an issue as to the upbringing of the child;[10]

- the court should refuse the direction where it would be against the child's interests to order it;[11]

- a refusal by a party to consent to the testing does not preclude the court from giving the direction;[12]

---

6   FLRA 1969, s 21(2).
7   FLRA 1969, s 8, and see *Re W (A Minor) (Consent to Medical Treatment)* [1993] 1 FLR 1.
8   *S v S, W v Official Solicitor* [1972] AC 24.
9   FLRA 1969, s 21(3).
10   *S v S, W v Official Solicitor* [1972] AC 24.
11   Ibid.
12   *Re H (Paternity: Blood Test)* [1996] 2 FLR 65.

- the likely outcome of the application within which the issue of parentage has arisen is not a factor in the determination of the issue of whether testing should be directed;[13]

- the welfare of a child will more often be best served by the ascertainment of truth as to the child's parentage;[14]

- the interests of justice require that issues before the court should be determined upon best evidence which, given the advances in scientific testing, is achieved through DNA testing rather than the application of a presumption;[15]

- since the enactment of the Human Rights Act the interests of other individuals must be considered as well as those of the child;[16]

- Article 8 does not provide an absolute right to the establishment of identity but where individuals' rights conflict the balance should be weighed in favour of a child having certainty of parentage.[17]

9.2.4   The effect of a failure to comply with the direction

The giving of the direction is not dependent upon achieving the consent of all parties. However, there is no power to enforce a direction once made.[18] Where a party refuses to comply with the direction to provide a bodily sample the court may draw such inference from the non-compliance as appears proper in the circumstances.[19] The court's power to draw the forensic inference results from the view that a failure to comply derives from an attempt to hide the truth. Accordingly the inference of paternity will be virtually inescapable for the man who fails to comply with a direction to provide a sample for a paternity test.[20] Very clear reasons would be required to justify a refusal and those reasons must be held to be just, fair and reasonable to put forward.[21] The inference can be drawn even where a presumption would otherwise apply in the absence of any rebutting evidence.[22] An applicant for relief who fails to comply with a direction may have their application dismissed.

Upon the making of a direction the substantive application should be adjourned pending the receipt of the tester's report.

---

[13]   Ibid.
[14]   *Re H and A (Paternity: Blood Tests)* [2002] 1 FLR 1145.
[15]   Ibid.
[16]   *Re T (Paternity: Ordering Blood Tests)* [2001] 2 FLR 1190.
[17]   *Lambeth London Borough Council v S, C, V and J* [2007] 1 FLR 152.
[18]   *Re O and J (Paternity: Blood Tests)* [2000] 418 declining to follow *Re R (Blood Test: Child: Inherent Jurisdiction)* [1998 1 FLR 745.
[19]   FLRA 1969, s 23(1).
[20]   *Re A (A Minor) (Paternity: Refusal of Blood Test)* 1994 2 FLR 463.
[21]   Ibid.
[22]   FLRA 1969, s 23(2).

9.3 PROCEDURE

9.3.1 Procedure for making the application

9.3.1.1 The relevant procedural code

The relevant procedural code is dependent upon whether:

- the direction is sought within an application for a declaration of parentage, in which case the procedure is set out in the Family Procedure Rules 2010[23] (FPR 2010), Pt 8; or

- as an application in existing family proceedings, in which case it is made pursuant to FPR 2010, Pt 18.

Note however that CPR 1998 Practice Direction 23B remains applicable and is applied to the Family Procedure Rules 2010 by Practice Direction: *Practice Directions relating to Family Proceedings in force before 6 April 2011*, which support the FPR 2010. For applications to which the Civil Procedure Rules 1998 apply see Part 23 and Practice Direction 23B (see also *Practice Direction (Blood Tests)* [1972] 1 WLR 353).

The procedure to be followed is set out in FPR 2010, Pt 18 and attention should be paid to PD 18A.

- An application for a direction may be made by any party to proceedings already before the court.

- The application shall be made on Form FP2 to all parties to the proceedings in which the application is made and to any other person from whom a sample is to be sought.

- An application in respect of a person who is either under 16 or suffering from a disorder within the meaning of the Mental Heath Act 1983 and incapable of understanding the nature and purpose of scientific tests shall be served on the person who is stated in the summons as being the person with care and control of that person.

- Any person named in the direction from whom a bodily sample is to be sought who is not already a party to the proceedings must be served personally.

- The time for service of the application is 2 clear days prior to the hearing of the application.

---

[23] SI 2010/2955.

- Any person who is served but is not already a party to the proceedings may be made so at any time by direction of the court.

- A draft of the order sought should be submitted with the application.

- The court may deal with the application without a hearing if deemed appropriate or if all parties agree on the proposed order sought.

In the Magistrates Court the procedure is governed by the Magistrates Courts (Blood Tests) Rules 1971[24] and lays down the following procedure:

- Any party to existing proceedings may write to the court seeking a direction and the designated officer may write to the other party to the proceedings to inform them of the making of the application and informing them that they may consent to the making of the direction prior to the hearing of the same.[25]

- Where consent has been given a court may give the direction in the absence of either or both parties.[26]

- The direction shall be in Form 2 (see below) and a copy shall be provided to every person referred to including any person with care and control of any subject under a disability.[27]

- Within 14 days of the giving of the direction (or such period as is stipulated in the direction) the person seeking the direction must pay to the court the fees of the sampler and tester.[28]

- Within 14 days of the service of the direction each subject or person having care and control of any subject who has attained the age of 12 months by the date of the direction must provide a photograph of themselves/the subject to the proper officer of the court.[29]

- A failure to comply with these conditions may cause either the direction to be revoked or the court to resume the application and make such findings as it considers appropriate.[30]

- Where the condition has been complied with the court may make the arrangements for the testing or require the solicitors so to do.[31]

---

[24] SI 1971/1991.
[25] Magistrates Courts (Blood Tests) Rules 1971, r 4.
[26] Magistrates Courts (Blood Tests) Rules 1971, r 5.
[27] Magistrates Courts (Blood Tests) Rules 1971, r 6–7.
[28] Magistrates Courts (Blood Tests) Rules 1971, r 8.
[29] Magistrates Courts (Blood Tests) Rules 1971, r 9.
[30] Magistrates Courts (Blood Tests) Rules 1971, r 10.
[31] Magistrates Courts (Blood Tests) Rules 1971, r 11.

- When the arrangements have been made the proper officer of the court will give notice of those arrangements (see Form 3 below) to each subject from whom samples are to be taken for testing and will send to the sampler who will obtain the samples in respect of each subject Parts I and II of a direction form.[32]

- When the direction form is returned, if it is not accompanied by a tester's report, then a copy of the direction form shall be made available to all parties to the proceedings and the court shall make such order in relation to the direction or the original proceedings as appears appropriate.[33]

- A copy of any report filed shall be served upon every party to the proceedings, which shall be effected by either first class post to the subject's address or the office of his solicitor.[34]

It should be noted that there is no power under these rules, unlike the power in the High Court and county court, to join as a party for the purposes of the direction any person not a party to the original proceedings. Under the language of the rules the persons to be tested who are not parties to the proceedings are referred to as subjects.

9.3.1.2 *Whether the child should be joined as a party?*

The court has power to order the separate representation of a child upon an application for a direction. Any guardian appointed to represent the child's interests does not have the power to consent or refuse to the provision of samples for a test, that being the prerogative of the person with care and control.

Where an application for a direction for the use of scientific testing is made it would not be the normal practice for a child to be made a party and separately represented as to the issue as to whether the direction should be made because:

- in the absence of compliance with the terms of the direction there is no power to enforce it and the court may be required to rely upon a presumption as to paternity;

- a child should not be bound as a party by such finding;

- in any event a child has the right even after a finding by a court to apply for a declaration of parentage.[35]

---

[32] Magistrates Courts (Blood Tests) Rules 1971, r 12.
[33] Magistrates Courts (Blood Tests) Rules 1971, r 13.
[34] Magistrates Courts (Blood Tests) Rules 1971, rr 14, 16.
[35] *Re O and J (Paternity: Blood Tests)* [2000] 1 FLR 418, at 433.

Upon receipt of the report:

- questions may be asked of the tester pursuant to s 20(4) of the FLRA 1969;

- any party requiring the tester to attend at court to give evidence must comply with s 20(5) of the FLRA 1969 by giving notice to the court and the other parties within 14 days of receipt of the report.

The costs of the report shall be deemed to be costs in the proceedings but shall be borne by the party on whose application the direction was given.[36]

9.3.2   Procedure for proper conduct of the test

The relevant regulations are the Blood Test (Evidence of Paternity) Regulations 1971.[37]

The onus to make the arrangements lies with the solicitor for the party seeking the direction.[38]

In summary the procedure is:

- Obtain the list of organisations accredited to test samples for the purpose of a direction pursuant to s 20 of the FLRA 1969 available at http://www.justice.gov.uk/docs/list-bodies-parentage-test.pdf.

- Obtain Parts I and II of the direction form from the court.

- Attempt to agree the identity of the proposed tester failing which the matter must be returned to court for further directions.

- Contact the proposed tester to make arrangements for the sending of the samples and identify with the tester the most suitable samplers to take the samples from each person identified in the direction.

- Make the arrangements for samples to be taken from each subject. A registered medical practitioner should be the sampler.

- Upon the making of the arrangements provide the completed Parts I and II to the district judge for signing. The district judge will sign the forms and provide to the solicitor a copy of the notes for the guidance of samplers.

---

[36]   FLRA 1969, s 20(6).
[37]   SI 1971/1861. See also Home Office Circular 248/1971 and Home Office Circular 41/1989.
[38]   See Practice Direction [1972] 1 WLR 353.

- In every case where the subject has attained the age of 12 months a photo of that subject must be attached to Part III of the direction form before sending to the sampler.[39]

- Arrangements for the taking of samples may be altered by the sampler if necessary.

- A sampler should be informed if there is a possibility of any subject not complying with the direction and arrangements made to ensure that any sample to be taken from a child should be taken last to avoid it not being tested due to non-compliance by another subject.

- Where a sample is not taken according to the arrangements made and no other arrangements are subsequently made the sampler shall return the form to the court setting out his reason for not taking the sample and any reason provided by the subject for not complying.[40]

- Samples shall be sent to the tester by the sampler.

- The same tester should test all samples as far as practicable.

- On completion of the tests the tester should send to the court a report (see Form 2 below) together with the appropriate direction forms.

- A sampler may charge a fixed fee of £27.50 in each case whether or not a sample is taken.[41]

9.3.3 Good Practice Guidance with regard to DNA testing

Since the first edition of this publication an important decision in this area has been given. *Re F (Children) (DNA Evidence)*,[42] a decision of Mr Anthony Hayden QC sitting as a Deputy High Court Judge, has laid down the following guidance:

- Any order for DNA testing made by the family courts should be made pursuant to FLRA 1969 (and not CA 1989, s 38(6) or the inherent jurisdiction).

- The order should specify that it is being made pursuant to FLRA 1969 and should either name the company to be instructed to undertake the testing or provide that only a company on the MOJ accredited list is to be used.

---

[39] Blood Tests (Evidence of Paternity) Regulations 1971, r 6(2).
[40] Blood Tests (Evidence of Paternity) Regulations 1971, r 5(5).
[41] Blood Tests (Evidence of Paternity) Regulations 1971, r 12.
[42] [2008] 1 FLR 348.

- The taking of samples from children should only occur pursuant to an express order of the court. Any subsequent further samples must also be authorised by a subsequent court order. These requirements are to be expressly communicated to the instructed DNA company.

- The company should be instructed via formal letter of instruction, save where the issue is solely confined to paternity testing.

- The letter of instruction should stress that the DNA expert's responsibilities are identical to those of any other expert reporting in a family case.

- The letter of instruction should set out in clear terms precisely what relationships are to be analysed and, if available, the belief of the parties as to the extent of their relatedness.

- The DNA expert should take care to describe the test results in clear language and refer to the likely ratios to be derived from the results. The author should explain the parameters within which the test results are to be considered.

9.4   THE SPECIMEN FORM OF WORDS FOR A DIRECTION FOR SCIENTIFIC TESTING

'It is directed pursuant to s 20(1) of the Family Law Reform Act 1969 (as amended):

(a)   that scientific tests (including DNA tests) be used to ascertain whether such tests show that [Mr A] is or is not excluded from being the father of [child B] born on [. . ..]; and

(b)   that for that purpose bodily samples be taken on or before [. . ..] from the following persons: [Mr A], [Mrs X (mother of child B)] and [child B]; and

(c)   that the person appearing to the court to have care and control of [child B], who is under the age of 16, is [Mrs X];

(d)   that such tests be carried out by [Mr CD of].'

9.5   CASE DIGEST

9.5.1   Scope of the court's power

Re A (A Minor) (Paternity: Refusal of Blood Test) [1994] 2 FLR 463, CA

No definitive answer as to whether a mother could make successive claims, leading to further applications under s 20, against two or more putative fathers where a first or subsequent claim had failed, although it would be illogical to deny her the ability to do so.

Re E (A Minor) (Child Support: Blood Test) [1994] 2 FLR 548

A refusal by justices to direct blood testing does not necessarily prevent a further application and direction for blood tests.

Re E (A minor) (Parental Responsibility) [1995] 1 FLR 392, CA

The court has no jurisdiction to make a free-standing order for blood tests.

In Re D (Paternity) [2007] 2 FLR 26

Distinguishing between the principle and the question of when the direction should take effect Hedley J made an order for scientific testing but stayed the order without limit of time (with liberty to restore) where it was in the child's best interests to know the truth but on the facts it was not to pursue the point at that time.

LG v DK [2011] EWHC 2453 (COP)

Wall P concluded that the court had the power under s 21(4) of the 1969 Act to consent to the taking of a bodily sample from a person lacking capacity notwithstanding the absence of a specific application within COP proceedings putting the parentage of an individual in issue. He noted that ultimately it would require unusual facts for the man's best interests to depart from the ascertainment of the truth or the interests of justice.

9.5.2   Principles

Re CB (A Minor) (Blood Test) [1994] 2 FLR 762

Wall J refused to order a blood test mainly because of a real risk that, if the man were found to be the father, the child would, because of the intense hostility between him and the mother, 'be projected into an emotional maelstrom in which the court, even in the exercise of its coercive powers, would be hard pushed to protect her'.

O v L (Blood Tests) [1995] 2 FLR 930

The mother was seeking a test to prevent contact between the child and her husband but no precise definition of the nature of the relationship between the husband and the child was needed in order for contact between them to develop.

Re H (A Minor) (Blood Tests: Parental Rights) [1996] 2 FLR 65

This case has formulated the following principles:

(1) the parentage issue must be judged as a free-standing application entitled to consideration on its own;

(2) the outcome of the substantive proceedings must be taken into account in so far as it bears on the welfare of the child;

(3) any gain to the child from preventing any disturbance to his security must be balanced against the loss to him of the certainty of knowing who he is;

(4) the parentage issue is not to be judged by the criteria set out in the Children Act 1989, s 10(9);

(5) while the outcome of the substantive proceedings and the risk of disruption to the child's life, both by the continuance of the parentage issue and pursuit of the substantive proceedings, are factors which impinge on the child's welfare, they are not determinative of the scientific testing question.

(6) If a child has a right to know the truth then the sooner he was told the truth the better.

Re H (Paternity: Blood Test) [1996] 2 FLR 65, CA

The court is required to make a direction, and not an order, since the court cannot order the taking of samples against a person's consent. A summary of the matters to be considered when the court exercises its discretion are:

(1) a parent's refusal to comply with a direction was not determinative of the issue of whether or not a direction should be made;

(2) the welfare of the child is a relevant but not paramount factor in deciding whether or not to make a direction; the interests of other persons may also be involved (and see *S v S, W v Official Solicitor* (above));

(3) the outcome of the proceedings in which the direction is sought is not a factor in deciding whether to make a direction: the paternity question was a free-standing application entitled to its own considerations; and

(4) a child's welfare generally demands that it know the truth about his or her parentage.

Re T (Paternity: Ordering Blood Tests) [2001] 2 FLR 1190

Bodey J considered the correct approach under the ECHR, Art 8 in a contested s 21(3) application. The Art 8 rights of each relevant party will be in play, but the rights and best interests of the child fall particularly to be considered and a child's right to know his true identity is likely to emerge as the weightiest consideration.

Re H and A (Paternity: Blood Tests)

'The points of principle to be drawn from [recent cases are]: first, that the interests of justice are best served by the ascertainment of the truth and, secondly, that the court should be furnished with the best available science and not confined to such unsatisfactory alternatives as presumptions and inferences.'[43]

Lambeth London Borough Council v S, C, V and J (By His Guardian) [2007] 1 FLR 152

Ryder J held:

(1)   there is no absolute right under Art 8 to establish one's identity in the sense that there is no absolute right of access to genetic information. Access to genetic information may be controlled by the State, but such control must be in accordance with Art 8(2);

(2)   in cases where parentage is in issue or unknown, having regard to the more modern practice of balancing parallel rights the court would expect that balance to be weighed in favour of a child having certainty of parentage as against the inevitable interference with the Art 8 rights of a parent.

9.5.3   The application of the presumption

Re A (A Minor) (Paternity: Refusal of Blood Test) [1994] 2 FLR 463

If a mother makes a paternity allegation (and monetary claim) against one of three possible men and that man chooses to exercise his right not to submit to be tested, the inference that he is the father should be virtually inescapable. He would have to advance very clear reasons for his refusal – reasons which it would be just and fair and reasonable for him to be allowed to maintain.

---

[43]   [2002] 1 FLR 1145, CA, at [29].

Re CB (A Minor) (Blood Tests) [1994] 2 FLR 762

The power to draw such an inference applies whether it is the mother or putative father who refuses to agree to testify.

Re H (Paternity: Blood Test) [1996] 2 FLR 65, CA

If an inference is to be drawn from the refusal of a test, such inference can be drawn, even though a direction has not been made, if a parent clearly indicates an intention not to comply with any direction made by the court.

Re G (Parentage: Blood Sample), [1997] 1 FLR 360 (and followed in Secretary of State for Work and Pensions v Jones [2003] EWHC 2163; [2004] 1 FLR 282)

The Court of Appeal held that where a putative father refused to submit to blood tests then a forensic inference should be drawn and, since the forensic process was advanced by the truth being told in court, those who obstruct that process will have an adverse inference drawn against them.

Znamenskaya v Russia (Application No 77785/01) [2005] 2 FCR 406, ECtHR

The European Court of Human Rights has ruled that it is a violation of Art 8 of the European Convention if a legal presumption is allowed to prevail over biological and social reality, without regard to both established facts and the wishes of those concerned and without actually benefiting anyone. The application of the presumption in those circumstances is not compatible, even having regard to the margin of appreciation left to the state, with the obligation to secure effective respect for private and family life.

9.5.4   Procedure

Re J (A Minor) (Wardship) [1988] 1 FLR 65

A court can grant an injunction to restrain the mother of a ward of court from leaving the jurisdiction where she has been directed to undergo DNA fingerprinting to establish paternity. The court will as a general rule order surrender of her passport.

Re F (Children: DNA Evidence) [2008] EWHC 3235 (Fam) [2008] 1 FLR 348

Any order for DNA testing made by the family courts should be made, and specify that it was being made, pursuant to the Family Law Reform

Act 1969. The order should either identify the company undertaking the testing, or direct that the company be selected in accordance with the Act; only accredited companies could be instructed. Taking samples from children should only be undertaken pursuant to the express order of the court; further samples might be taken only with court approval, following a written application to the judge. These requirements should be communicated to the identified DNA company in the letter of instruction. Save in cases where the issue was solely confined to paternity testing, all requests for DNA testing should be by letter of instruction, which should: emphasise that the DNA expert's responsibilities were identical to those of any expert reporting in a family case and that their overriding obligation was to the court; set out in clear terms precisely what relationships were to be analysed and, where available, the belief of the parties as to the extent of their relatedness; and make it clear that if the DNA experts considered there was any lack of clarity, or any ambiguity in their written instructions, or required further guidance, they should revert to the solicitor instructing them, who should keep a note or memo of any such request. If any test carried out cast any doubt on or appeared relevant to the hypothesis set by their instructions, the DNA experts had to regard themselves as being under a duty to draw that to the attention of the court and the parties. Reports prepared by the DNA experts should bear in mind that they were addressing lay people; such reports should strive to interpret their analysis in clear language. Care should be taken to explain results within the context of identified conclusions, and particular care should be taken in the use of phrases such as this result provides good evidence; such expressions should always be set within the parameters of current DNA knowledge and identify in plain terms the limitations as to the reliability of any test carried out. Where any particular test and subsequent ratio of likelihood was regarded as in any way controversial within the mainstream of DNA expertise, the use of the test and the reasons for its use should be signalled to the court within the report.

PART III

PUBLIC LAW

CHAPTER 10

LOCAL AUTHORITY PROCEDURES PRIOR TO ISSUING CARE PROCEEDINGS

10.1 OVERVIEW

All applications for care or supervision orders under s 31 of the Children Act 1989 are made by local authorities.[1] The powers and duties of local authorities in this respect are contained in Parts III and IV of the Children Act 1989. Such orders will only be made where the threshold criteria are met and if it would be better for the child for an order to be made, than not.

Prior to issue, the role of local authorities is to determine whether the threshold criteria (Children Act 1989, s 31) are met. Where they suspect that this is the case, they must investigate and assess the needs of the child(ren) in question and also plan how the child(ren) can best be provided for in the long-term. The details and conclusions of these processes are recorded in standardised documents[2] that must be filed with the court at the same time as the application is made.

The procedures themselves are varied and frequently overlapping. Throughout the process of preparing s 31 applications, the authority must have continual regard for the welfare of the child and must take any emergency or interim action required to promote or protect this.

The local authority has a duty to promote the upbringing of children in need by their families so long as this is compatible with its duty to safeguard the welfare of the child.[3] Voluntary co-operation rather than compulsory orders are preferred: the authority must have regard for this principle throughout proceedings and must consider all alternatives to issuing s 31 proceedings including alternative applications (guardianship, residence) and possible kinship care options.

---

[1] Although the NSPCC also has statutory authorisation to do so, it does not exercise this power at present.

[2] http://webarchive.nationalarchives.gov.uk/20090813152455/dcsf.gov.uk/everychildmatters/safeguardingandsocialcare/integratedchildrenssystem/icspracticeresources/icsexemplarsdocuments/docs/

[3] See *The Children Act 1989 Guidance and Regulations*, Vol 1: Court Orders, para 3.7 (DFES, revised 2008).

All such proceedings must be fair to the child and its family who should be able to participate fully.

10.2 STATUTORY FRAMEWORK AND GUIDANCE DOCUMENTS

In May 2006 the *Review of the Child Care Proceedings System in England and Wales ('The Care Review')* was published.[4] *The Care Review* examined the procedures employed in s 31 cases (care and supervision) from pre-proceeding investigations through to final order and found numerous areas of serious concern, including unnecessary delay caused by poorly prepared applications and ineffective case management.[5]

In order to address these problems a new protocol: 'The Public Law Outline' ('PLO') was devised and came into force on 1 April 2008. A new revision of this protocol came into force on 6 April 2010 and replaces the 2008 Protocol. The original and revised PLO are intended to ensure better and timelier case management by reducing the burden of documentary requirements at issue, clarifying the 'Timetable for the Child' principle and improving the PLO forms. The overall framework of the original PLO has not been affected by the revised protocol. The PLO 2010 places particular emphasis on pre-proceedings preparation and is designed to ensure that applications are only made in appropriate circumstances and where all the alternatives have been fully explored. Under the Protocol, local authorities are provided with a checklist of documents that should be prepared prior to issuing proceedings and guidance as to how these should be created is provided in the latest revision of 'The Children Act 1989 Guidance and Regulations Volume 1 Court Orders' ('Guidance and Regulations') — set out in this work at **A3.20**.

The revised 'Guidance and Regulations' pulls together the existing statutory guidance from two primary sources: The *Framework for the Assessment of Children in Need and their Families ('the Framework')*[6] provides guidance as to the proper assessment of children in need; and *Working Together to Safeguard Children*[7] ('Working Together') sets out procedures for the proper investigation and protection of children at risk of, or known to be suffering, significant harm.[8] These documents form part of the Integrated Children's System.[9]

---

[4]   *Review of the Child Care Proceedings System in England and Wales* (DCA, DFES, Welsh Assembly Government, 2006).

[5]   Ibid, para 1.4.

[6]   *Framework for the Assessment of Children in Need and their Families* (DoH, DFEE, HO, 2000).

[7]   *Working Together to Safeguard Children: A Guide to Interagency Working to Safeguard and Promote the Welfare of Children* (DfES, 2006).

[8]   The Framework and Part One of *Working Together* are both issued under s 7 of the Local Authority Social Services Act 1970. This legislation requires local authorities in their social services functions to act under the general guidance of the Secretary of

It should be noted that the new revised Protocol applies to all applications commenced after 6 April 2010 but does not apply retrospectively. All applications made before this date will be managed under the previous protocol.[10]

10.3 PRE-PROCEEDINGS CHECKLIST

The 2010 Protocol and statutory guidance both place a strong emphasis on efficient and thorough pre-proceeding preparation by local authorities. It is hoped that thorough preparation will lead to fewer unnecessary applications thereby fulfilling the 'no compulsory action except where required' principle. It is expected that all necessary steps will have been taken to avoid delay once proceedings have been issued. Once a child has been referred, local authorities are required not only to complete the relevant assessment and planning processes prior to issuing an application for a s 31 order, but also to demonstrate that they have shared information with the parents and wider families of the child(ren) and have fully investigated alternatives to proceedings.

Each of these processes should be carefully recorded and reports made of the conclusions. A chronology should also be prepared. In order that the court may be sure that these procedures have been properly followed, the following documents should be attached and filed with the application form C1:

- previous orders and judgments/reasons;

- any relevant assessment materials;

- section 7 & 37 reports;

- relatives and friends materials (eg a genogram);

- other relevant reports and records;

- single, joint or inter-agency materials (eg health & education/Home Office & immigration documents);

- records of discussions with the family;

- key local authority minutes & records for the child (including Strategy Discussion Record);

State. As such the guidance in these documents, whilst not statute, should be complied with unless exceptional local circumstances justify a variation.

9   http://webarchive.nationalarchives.gov.uk/20090813152455/dcsf.gov.uk/ everychildmatters/safeguardingandsocialcare/integratedchildrenssystem

10   The Public Law Outline replaced the Protocol: http://www.judiciary.gov.uk/publications-and-reports/guidance/index/guide-case-management

- pre-existing care plans (eg child in need plan, looked after child plan & child protection plan).

Form C110 is the new application form for care and supervision orders introduced under the revised PLO. Form C110 contains an 'Annex' with a list of the six documents that need to be filed with the application at the time of issue:

- Social Work Chronology;

- Initial Social Work Statement;

- Initial and Core Assessments;

- Letters before Proceedings;

- Schedule of Proposed Findings;

- Care Plan.

By introducing Form C110, there will no longer be a requirement to use the existing prescribed application forms C1 and C13 to apply for a care or supervision order. Also, a series of forms were introduced for use under the 2008 PLO Practice Direction, which will NOT be applicable to applications issued on or after 6 April 2010:

- PLO1 Pre-proceedings Checklist – this is because the information has been incorporated into the new C110 application form.

- PLO2 Local Authority Case Summary – A local authority Case Summary is still required, although no longer on a particular form. The information to be included is specified in the 2010 PLO.

- PLO4 Allocation Record and Timetable for the Child(ren) – this is because the information has been incorporated into the new C110 application form.

- PLO5 Standard Directions Form on Issue – A new PLO 8 will be issued that is 'suggested' for use under the requirements of the 2010 PLO.

- PLO6 Standard Directions Forms at First Appointment – A new Form PLO9 is 'suggested' for use under the requirements of the revised PLO.

10.4 REFERRAL

Many cases will begin with a referral to social services or initial contact with a child. A referral is defined as a request for services to be provided by the social services department.[11]

Where a referral or initial contact is made, whether the information comes from the child, a family member, a third party or from elsewhere within the authority, the nature of the concerns, how and why they have arisen and the apparent needs of the child and family should be determined.[12] The details of any referral should be accurately recorded.[13] The factors that should be considered as relevant are set out in the *Framework for Assessment of Children in Need and their Families*.[14]

In some cases it may be apparent at this stage that the criteria for initiating s 47 enquiries is already met in which case a strategy discussion should be held (see **10.6** below). Whether or not this is the case, the local authority must decide within one day of receiving the referral, whether an initial assessment should be undertaken.[15] The decision to undertake an initial assessment is likely to be made following a discussion with the person who has made the referral and after considering any other information that the local authority may already hold or can quickly obtain.[16]

Even if it is decided that no further action should be taken following a referral, this decision should be recorded and the referrer should be informed both of the decision and its rationale, as should the parents or care givers and the child(ren), if appropriate.[17]

The referral may also come via the court as a result of concerns raised in the course of private law proceedings. Where parents in such proceedings have made allegations against each other, or the CAFCASS officer has grounds for concern, CA 1989, s 37 confers on the court the power to order that the relevant local authority investigates the matter. The court may only make such an order where it appears that it may be appropriate for the local authority to apply for a care or supervision order. The procedure should not be used unless there are good grounds for believing

---

[11] *Framework for the Assessment of Children in Need and their Families* (DoH, DfEE, HO, 2000), para 3.8.

[12] *Working Together*, para 5.31.

[13] *Framework for the Assessment of Children in Need and their Families* (DoH, DfEE, HO, 2000), para 3.3.

[14] Ibid, App C.

[15] *The Children Act 1989 Guidance and Regulations*, Vol 1: Court Orders (DfES, revised 2008), para 3.1.

[16] Ibid.

[17] *Framework for the Assessment of Children in Need and their Families* (DoH, DfEE, HO, 2000), para 3.8.

that the threshold criteria will be met.[18] The s 37 report is not a general welfare report and should focus on the question of whether or not there is a need to apply for a care or supervision order. Where the application has come from this route the s 37 report should be filed with the application form.[19]

10.5   ASSESSMENT

If it is decided, following referral, that further action should be taken, the local authority must then assess the child(ren). This process can be broadly divided into two phases: initial and core assessment. The revised statutory guidance sets out timeframes for each of these but it should be recognised that where a child is at risk of immediate harm, and emergency protective measures are required, pre-application processes are likely to be concluded quicker.

Assessment of any child(ren) believed to be in need must be carried out in accordance with the *Framework for the Assessment of Children in Need and their Families* (*'the Framework'*). The Framework is a conceptual map for gathering and analysing information about all children and their families. It features three inter-related 'domains':

- Child's Developmental Needs;

- Parenting Capacity;

- Family and Environmental Factors.

Each of these has within it a number of 'critical dimensions'. Assessment of a child is intended to examine the interaction of these domains with the aim of understanding how they affect the child. This analysis in turn informs the planning and action to secure the best outcomes for the child (see Appendix 1 below).[20]

The assessment process has several overlapping phases:[21]

- clarification of source of referral and reason;

- acquisition of information;

- exploring facts and feelings;

---

[18]   If the court is concerned that the child is potentially in need but such orders will be inappropriate then it should request a s 7 report instead.

[19]   PLO – Pre-proceedings Checklist.

[20]   *Framework for the Assessment of Children in Need and their Families* (DoH, DfEE, HO, 2000), para 2.2.

[21]   Ibid, para 3.1.

- giving meaning to the situation which distinguishes the child and the family's understanding and feelings from those of the professionals;

- reaching an understanding of what is happening, problems, strengths and difficulties, and impact on the child (with the family wherever possible);

- drawing up an analysis of the needs of the child and parenting capacity within their family and community context as a basis for formulating a plan.

10.5.1 Initial assessment

The decision to gather more information constitutes an initial assessment. An initial assessment is defined as a 'brief assessment of each child referred to social services with a request for services to be provided'.[22]

Initial assessments are carried out predominantly by members of social services. The purpose of the initial assessment is to determine not only whether the child is 'in need'[23] but also the nature of any services required, how and within what timescale they will be provided and, lastly, whether a further more detailed core assessment should be undertaken. Such assessments must be completed within seven working days of the date of referral.[24] Where the criteria for initiating s 47 enquiries has already been met at the point of referral, the initial assessment is likely to be very brief[25] as a core assessment will almost certainly be required.

As part of any initial assessment, the child should be seen (observation and discussion will vary depending on age).[26] An initial assessment may also include some or all of the following:[27]

- interviews with family members as appropriate;

- involvement of other agencies in gathering and providing information as appropriate;

- consultation with supervisor/manager;

- record of initial analysis;

---

[22] Ibid, para 3.9.
[23] Children Act 1989, s 17(1).
[24] *The Children Act 1989 Guidance and Regulations*, Vol 1: Court Orders (DfES, revised 2008), para 3.12; *Framework for the Assessment of Children in Need and their Families* (DoH, DfEE, HO, 2000), para 3.9.
[25] *Working Together*, para 5.37.
[26] *Framework for the Assessment of Children in Need and their Families* (DoH, DfEE, HO, 2000), para 3.10.
[27] Ibid.

- decisions on further action/no action;

- record of decisions/rationale with family/agencies;

- informing other agencies of the decision;

- statement to the family of decisions made and, if the child is in need, the plan for providing support.

The processes undertaken in the course of the assessment must be noted, together with any conclusions reached, in the Initial Assessment Record.[28] The Initial Assessment Record must be filed at the point of application for an order under s 31.[29]

The parent(s) and child(ren), if appropriate, should be informed in writing, and/or in another more appropriate medium, of the decisions made and should be offered the opportunity to record their views. Agencies involved in the assessment should be similarly informed with reasons for the decisions.[30]

At the conclusion of the initial assessment, the local authority should be able to determine whether the child concerned is a child 'in need' (CA 1989, s 17(10)) and whether there is reasonable cause to suspect that the child is suffering or is likely to suffer significant harm.

If the child is found to be 'in need' then the local authority has a duty to provide for the child and so must decide the extent and nature of the child's needs and how best they can be met.[31] For this purpose a more in depth core assessment may be required.

In all cases where the conclusion of the initial assessment is that the child(ren) is not only in need but also suspected to be suffering or likely to suffer significant harm, then the provisions of Children Act 1989, s 47 come into play (if they have not already done so) and a core assessment should be completed.[32]

10.5.2   Core assessment

A core assessment is defined as:[33]

---

28   Initial Assessment Record (DoH, 2002).

29   Protocol Pre-procedure Checklist.

30   *Framework for the Assessment of Children in Need and their Families* (DoH, DfEE, HO, 2000), para 3.13.

31   Children Act 1989, s 17.

32   *The Children Act 1989 Guidance and Regulations*, Vol 1: Court Orders (DfES, revised 2008), para 3.15.

33   Ibid, para 3.16; *Framework for the Assessment of Children in Need and their Families* (DoH, DfEE, HO, 2000), para 3.11.

'an in-depth assessment which addresses the central or most important aspects of the needs of a child and the capacity of his or her parents or caregivers to respond appropriately to these needs within the wider family and community context'.

A core assessment will be carried out in any case where an initial assessment identifies a child as being in need, but more information is required as to the extent of those needs. Where significant harm is a possibility, a core assessment must be carried out with the purpose of establishing whether there is reasonable cause to suspect that this child is suffering or is likely to suffer significant harm and whether any emergency action is required to secure the safety of the child.[34]

Because of its integrated role in s 47 investigations (see **10.6**), the core assessment forms the central part of the evidence submitted in support of any application under s 31. The new Protocol requires that local authorities file the completed core assessment at the point of application.[35] It is crucial therefore, that local authorities ensure that an up-to-date core assessment document is available in relation to any child who is subject to proceedings.[36] Compliance with the requirement to complete the core assessment will be scrutinised by the judge or magistrate as part of the court's initial consideration of any application under s 31 of the Children Act 1989.[37]

The core assessment should be led by a qualified and experienced social worker with additional specialist assessments commissioned from external agencies where required.[38] The assessment itself should be informed by the results of the initial assessment[39] and the information gathered therein should be given primary importance when considering whether the child is suffering, or is likely to suffer, significant harm.[40] Any prior specialist assessments that may have been carried out should also be utilised. All relevant dimensions of the Framework should be covered before the assessment is completed[41] (see **A10.1**).

Such assessments are conducted by way of interviews with the child(ren) and adults who are personally or professionally associated with the child(ren) together with specific examinations or assessments of the child(ren) by independent professionals. Guidance as to appropriate content and methods of such assessments are set out in the *Framework*

---

[34]   *Framework for the Assessment of Children in Need and their Families* (DoH, DfEE, HO, 2000), para 3.15.
[35]   Protocol Pre-procedure Checklist.
[36]   *The Children Act 1989 Guidance and Regulations*, Vol 1: Court Orders (DfES, revised 2008), para 3.17.
[37]   Ibid, para 3.15.
[38]   *Working Together*, para 5.60.
[39]   *The Children Act 1989 Guidance and Regulations*, Vol 1: Court Orders (DfES, revised 2008), para 3.16.
[40]   *Working Together*, para 5.60.
[41]   Ibid.

and *Working Together*. If the child's parents frustrate any attempts at assessment the authority may apply for an assessment order.

Where there is evidence that a crime has been committed and the assessment team and the police interview children jointly, these interviews should be conducted in accordance with the *Achieving Best Evidence (ABE) Guidelines*.[42]

In the course of the core assessment the possibility that members of the wider family could care for the child should be examined and assessed. Both the capacity and willingness of these individuals should be examined, as should the timeframe within which they may be able to assist, whether that be in the short or long term.[43]

A completed core assessment should include an analysis of the child's developmental needs and the parent's capacity to respond to those needs. The core assessment should be completed within 35 working days of its commencement and is deemed to have commenced at the point the initial assessment ended.[44] Where newly commissioned specialist assessments from external agencies or independent professionals will not be available within the 35-day timeframe, it is expected that clear timescales for their completion will be agreed and it will be specified in the core assessment when those additional reports will be expected to be completed.[45] When such reports later become available their contents will need to be taken into account and may influence the local authority's care plan.

Where emergency action is required to safeguard the welfare of the child the core assessment should still be completed. The deadlines specified in the statutory guidance still apply, although where the child is subject to an emergency protection order the local authority should endeavour to determine as quickly as possible whether a long-term order is going to be necessary.

10.6   SECTION 47: ENQUIRIES AND EMERGENCY PROTECTIVE ACTION

Where a local authority is informed that a child in its area is in police protection or is subject to an emergency protection order, or the authority itself has reasonable cause to suspect that the child has suffered or is likely to suffer significant harm, Children Act 1989, s 47 imposes a duty on the

---

[42]   *Achieving Best Evidence in Criminal Proceedings: Guidance for Vulnerable or Intimidated Witnesses including Children* (HO, DoH, CPS, 2002).

[43]   *The Children Act 1989 Guidance and Regulations*, Vol 1: Court Orders (DfES, revised 2008), para 3.18.

[44]   *Framework for the Assessment of Children in Need and their Families* (DoH, DfEE, HO, 2000), para 3.11.

[45]   *The Children Act 1989 Guidance and Regulations*, Vol 1: Court Orders (DfES, revised 2008), para 3.16.

authority to investigate. In such circumstances the authority must undertake any such enquiries that they consider necessary to enable a decision as to whether any action needs to be taken in order to safeguard or promote the welfare of the child(ren) concerned and if so, what action is appropriate in the circumstances.[46]

Before undertaking any enquiries the authority is required to convene a strategy discussion. This should take place as soon as is practicable. The purpose of such meetings is to establish both the requirements of any subsequent enquiries and also any need for immediate protective action. Throughout the investigative process the strategy should be reviewed and if necessary amended. The investigations will take the form of an initial and core assessment (see above).

Section 47 enquiries may run concurrent to any police investigations and will in some circumstances be linked to the criminal proceedings.[47]

Where in the course of any enquiries the local authority or its representatives are denied access to the child or knowledge of his/her whereabouts, s 47(6) confers upon the authority duty to apply for an emergency protection,[48] child assessment,[49] care[50] or supervision[51] order, unless they are satisfied that the child(ren)'s welfare can be satisfactorily safeguarded without doing so.

Where there is a risk to the life of a child or a likelihood of serious immediate harm, the local authority or the police should act to secure the immediate safety of the child. Such action may be required as soon as the referral is received or at any point in involvement with the child and their family.[52] Whenever such action is planned the authority should consider also whether there are any other children in the household who require the same protection.[53] The decision as to whether emergency action should be taken will normally be made at a strategy discussion meeting.

Emergency action may take the form of an emergency protection order,[54] an exclusion requirement within an interim care order or emergency protection order,[55] or police action to either remove or prevent removal (eg from hospital) of the child under CA 1989, s 46.

---

[46]   Children Act 1989, s 47(1).
[47]   *Working Together*, para 5.69.
[48]   See **11.1**.
[49]   See **11.3**.
[50]   See **13.3**.
[51]   See **13.4**.
[52]   *Working Together*, para 5.49.
[53]   Ibid, para 5.50.
[54]   See **11.1**.
[55]   See **11.1.7.1**.

Emergency action only addresses the immediate circumstances of the child and so does not usurp the requirement for a full investigation of the child's needs. Section 47 enquiries should still take place and should be completed as quickly as is possible.[56] Where an emergency protection order applies, the local authority must decide quickly whether to initiate proceedings for a care order.[57]

At the conclusion of s 47 enquiries the outcome should be recorded in the Outcome of s 47 Enquiries Record (Department of Health 2002)[58] and copies of this document should be provided to the child (where of sufficient age and appropriate level of understanding), their parents and any agencies or professionals substantially involved in the investigation.[59]

If at the conclusion of the s 47 investigation, concerns are not substantiated, there may still be a need for help and support or future monitoring. If concerns are substantiated but the child is not judged to be at continuing risk of significant harm, for example where the risk has been removed and/or the parent/carer is willing to co-operate, the local authority should draw up a plan for proposed future involvement (after obtaining the child's views and taking account of their wishes and feelings according to their age and understanding). In such cases, a Child Protection Conference may not be necessary. Where concerns are substantiated and the child is judged to be at continuing risk of significant harm a Child Protection Conference should be convened.

10.7 STRATEGY DISCUSSIONS

Wherever there is reasonable cause to suspect that a child is suffering or is likely to suffer, significant harm, a strategy discussion should be held in order to determine how to proceed. This may occur following referral or at any other time when concerns emerge.[60]

Such discussions should be attended by representatives of the local authority's social care department, the police and any other bodies such as the referring agency or the child's school as is deemed appropriate. If the child is in hospital or has been subjected to a medical examination, a senior doctor with knowledge of the case should also be present.[61]

The purpose of a strategy discussion is to:

---

56   *Working Together*, para 5.53.
57   Ibid.
58   http://webarchive.nationalarchives.gov.uk/20090813152455/dcsf.gov.uk/everychildmatters/safeguardingandsocialcare/integratedchildrenssystem/icspracticeresources/icsexemplarsdocuments/docs/
59   *Working Together*, para 5.72.
60   Ibid, para 5.54.
61   Ibid.

- share the available information;

- agree the conduct and timing of any criminal investigation;

- decide whether a core assessment (s 47 enquiries) should be initiated or continued if it has already begun;

- plan how the core assessment (s 47 enquiries) should be undertaken (if one is to be initiated), by whom, when and for what purpose;

- agree what action is required immediately to safeguard and promote the welfare of the child, and/or provide interim services and support;

- determine what information if any will be shared with the family;

- determine if legal action is required.

The strategy discussion should be used to agree what further information is required about the child(ren) and their family and how it should be obtained and recorded in the course of the s 47 enquiries. A list and timetable for interviewees should be agreed as should plans for ascertaining the wishes and feelings of the child(ren).[62]

In complex cases several strategy discussions are likely to be required. The authority's social care representatives should accurately note any decisions reached at such meetings in the Record of Strategy Discussion.[63] This document is part of the Integrated Children's System. The records of all strategy discussions should be filed at point of issue in accordance with the pre-proceedings checklist.[64]

10.8 CHILD PROTECTION PLANS AND CONFERENCES

A child protection conference is a multi-disciplinary, multi-agency meeting at which the groundwork for any future application for a s 31 order will be carried out. The aim of a child protection conference is to enable those professionals most involved with the child of the family and the family themselves to assess all relevant information and plan how best to safeguard and promote the welfare of the child.[65] If as a result of the conference it is decided that the child(ren) is at continuing risk of significant harm, a plan for their future protection is then drafted (Child

---

[62] *Working Together*, para 5.56.
[63] *Record of Strategy Discussion* (DoH, 2002): http://webarchive.nationalarchives.gov.uk/
20090813152455/dcsf.gov.uk/everychildmatters/safeguardingandsocialcare/
integratedchildrenssystem/icspracticeresources/icsexemplarsdocuments/docs/
[64] PLO Pre-proceedings Checklist.
[65] *Working Together*, para 5.79.

Protection Plan, Department of Health 2002)[66] and their at risk status is recorded on the local authority's child protection register.

The timing of the initial Child Protection Conference depends on the urgency of the case but in any event should take place within 15 working days of the strategy discussion or the last strategy discussion if more than one has been held. It is likely therefore, that the core assessment will be ongoing when the conference is held.

Those attending conferences should be there because they have a significant contribution to make arising from professional expertise, knowledge of the child or family or both. As a minimum at every conference there should be in attendance the local authority's children's social worker and at least two other professional groups or agencies who have had direct contact with the child who is the subject of the conference.[67] The chair of the conference should be a professional who is independent of operational or line management responsibilities for the case.[68]

Before the conference takes place its purpose should be explained to the parents and where appropriate to the child. If the child(ren) is old enough they will normally be invited to attend and to bring with them an advocate, friend or supporter. If they are not old enough to attend or if for some other reason it is not appropriate for them to do so, then their views and wishes should be ascertained and relayed to the conference by a member of social services.[69]

The child(ren)'s parents will normally be invited to attend and should be helped to participate fully. However, it is not a breach of natural justice for parents not to be invited to attend such a conference[70] and the authority may exclude parents or other family members if there is deemed to be a risk of violence or intimidation[71] by the individual. When parents do attend such conferences, their solicitors are permitted to accompany them but in the capacity of observers only.

Parental and legal involvement in the child protection conference and review system is mainly regulated by the governmental guidance currently contained in *Working Together to Safeguard Children; a guide to inter-agency working to safeguard and promote the welfare of children*

---

[66] http://webarchive.nationalarchives.gov.uk/20090813152455/dcsf.gov.uk/
       everychildmatters/safeguardingandsocialcare/integratedchildrenssystem/
       icspracticeresources/icsexemplarsdocuments/docs/
[67] *Working Together*, para 5.83.
[68] Ibid, para 5.87.
[69] Ibid, para 5.84.
[70] *R v Harrow London Borough Council ex parte D* [1990] Fam 133; *R v East Sussex County Council ex parte R* [1991] 2 FLR 358; *R v Devon County Council ex parte L* [1991] 2 FLR 541.
[71] *Working Together*, para 5.84.

(Department of Health, 2000) (*'Working Together 1999'*). A fundamental change in the new guidance is the removal of any reference to the family's solicitor at the child protection conference. As a result, the Law Society's advice is that solicitors should clarify their role at the conference with the chair, prior to its commencement, 'which may vary according to local practices and circumstances'.[72] Subsequently the court has held that a blanket ban on solicitors attending the Child Protection Conference was contrary to the Statutory Guidance and was therefore unlawful. However, restrictions can be placed upon their role.[73]

Attendance by solicitors at child protection conferences is provided for under the legal aid allowance in respect of pre-proceeding advice and assistance. However, since this is a fixed fee allowance it is likely that parents will generally need to pay privately if they want their solicitor to attend.[74]

The local authority's social worker should provide the conference with a written report. This should summarise and analyse the information obtained in the course of the initial assessment and the core assessment undertaken under Children Act 1989, s 47 (insofar as this has been completed within the available time period) and also information in existing records relating to the child and family.[75]

The child will be deemed to be at such risk if either of two tests is met. Firstly, if it can be shown that s(he) has previously suffered ill treatment or impairment of health or development as a result of physical, emotional or sexual abuse or neglect and the professional judgment is that further ill treatment or impairment are likely. Alternatively, if professional judgments substantiated by the findings of enquiries in the case, or by research evidence, is that the child is likely to suffer ill treatment or the impairment of health or development as a result of physical, emotional or sexual abuse or neglect.[76]

If a child is made the subject of a protection plan this must be recorded on the local authority's child protection register. The child must be recorded as having been abused or neglected in one or more of four specified categories: physical, emotional, sexual abuse or neglect. The decision as to which categories are appropriate is made at the conference and should reflect the outcome of all investigations into the child's welfare undertaken by that point in time. The category(ies) used will then indicate

---

[72] Attendance of Solicitors at Child Protection Conferences, guidance issued by Law Society's Family Law Committee (July 1997).
[73] *R v Cornwall County Council ex parte LH* [2000] 1 FLR 236.
[74] See Chapter 1.
[75] *Working Together*, para 5.89.
[76] Ibid, para 5.94.

to those consulting the child's social care record, the primary presenting concerns at the time the child became the subject of a Child Protection Plan.[77]

A child may not be the subject of a Child Protection Plan but he or she may nonetheless require services to promote his or health or development. In such circumstances what support could be offered to the family should be considered and this may involve the need to continue and complete a core assessment of the child's needs.[78]

Where a child is to be the subject of a Child Protection Plan it is the responsibility of the conference to consider and make recommendations on how agencies, professionals and the family should work together to ensure the child will be safeguarded from harm in the future.[79]

The outline child protection plan should:[80]

- identify the factors associated with the likelihood of the child suffering significant harm and ways in which the child can be protected;

- establish short and long term aims and objectives linked to reducing likelihood of future harm;

- set out who has responsibility for what actions and in what timescales;

- outline plans for monitoring and evaluating progress against planned outcomes.

Once a child protection plan has been made following a conference, a key worker and core group should be appointed. The key worker will be an experienced member of social work staff who will coordinate future work between the family, agencies and local authority.[81] The core group will include the key worker, child where appropriate, family and professionals or foster carers who have direct contact with the family. The role of the core group is to ensure that the child protection plan is implemented, refined and monitored. The first meeting of the core group should take place within 10 days of the initial child protection conference.[82]

Once the plan has been implemented, it should be reviewed regularly at further conferences. The first child protection review conference should be

---

[77] Ibid, para 5.141.
[78] Ibid, para 5.98.
[79] Ibid, para 5.99.
[80] Ibid, para 5.100.
[81] Ibid, para 5.108.
[82] Ibid, para 5.111.

held no later than 3 months after the initial conference and thereafter conferences should be held at intervals of no more than 6 months.[83]

The child protection plan will come to an end when the child is no longer judged to be at risk of harm, has reached 18 years of age, or has left the area or UK permanently.[84]

Where a core assessment under s 47 gives rise to concerns that an unborn child may be at risk of significant harm upon being born, the local authority may decide to convene an initial child protection conference prior to the child's birth. Such conferences will proceed in the same way as ordinary child protection conferences and are subject to the same rules regarding reviews.[85]

10.9   THE CARE PLAN

The results of the initial and core assessments together with the findings of any other reports should be used by the local authority to draft a care plan for the child.[86] No final care order may be made with respect to a child until the court has considered a care plan (also known as a 'section 31A plan')[87] which must be filed with the initial application for an order under s 31.[88]

The purpose of the plan is to enable the court to make an informed decision as to whether it should make an order and if so, what kind of order it should make. The structure of the plan should follow the Assessment Framework domains and dimensions in accordance with the Integrated Children's System (ICS) care plan exemplar.[89]

The care plan should set out the authorities stated aims and planned outcomes for the child and these must of course relate to the findings of the assessments. The outcomes sought should also relate directly to the aims and services specified.[90] The care plan should state explicitly what services will be provided and by whom. The frequency with which services should be provided in relation to the framework dimension headings should also be set out.[91]

---

[83]   Ibid, para 5.128.

[84]   Ibid, para 5.133.

[85]   Ibid, para 5.140.

[86]   *The Children Act 1989 Guidance and Regulations*, Vol 1: Court Orders (DfES, revised 2008), para 3.18.

[87]   Children Act 1989, s 31(3A).

[88]   PLO 2010 Pre-proceedings Checklist.

[89]   *The Children Act 1989 Guidance and Regulations*, Vol 1: Court Orders (DfES, revised 2008), para 3.18; http://media.education.gov.uk/assets/files/pdf/c/children%20act%20 1989%20guidance%20and%20regulations.pdf

[90]   *The Children Act 1989 Guidance and Regulations*, Vol 1: Court Orders (DfES, revised 2008), para 3.18.

[91]   Ibid.

Where appropriate, the care plan should state explicitly what consideration has been given to the possibility that the child could live with family or friends.[92]

While the application is pending, the authority must keep any care plan prepared by them under review and, if they are of the opinion some change is required, revise the plan, or make a new plan, accordingly.[93]

10.10 FAMILY GROUP CONFERENCES

10.10.1 Overview

The new Protocol and revised guidance both encourage the use of Family Group Conferences (FGCs) in the pre-proceedings process.[94] FGCs are an effective way of identifying and enabling family members to come forward as potential carers.

A Family Group Conference (also sometimes called a Family Group Meeting) is a decision-making and planning process involving the wider family group and intended to explore the care options for a child who has been identified as being in need. In this context the 'family' includes both blood relatives and non-related significant family friends or neighbours. One of the strengths of this process is that the child will often participate in the conference.[95]

Even where emergency action is taken in respect of the child(ren), the duty of the authority to explore the possible care options available for the future persists and so the core assessment should still incorporate the use of FGC unless this is inappropriate for some other reason.

The FGC comprises five distinct stages:

10.10.2 Referral

The local authority begins the process by making a referral to an FGC service. Provided that someone with parental responsibility for the child agrees to the conference and the necessary sharing of information the conference can proceed. Where the local authority has parental

---

[92] *The Children Act 1989 Guidance and Regulations*, Vol 1: Court Orders (DfES, revised 2008), para 3.32.

[93] Children Act 1989, s 31A(2).

[94] *Using Family Group Conferences for children who are, or may become, subject to court proceedings: A Guide for Courts, Lawyers, CAFCASS officers and Child Care Practitioners* (Family Rights Group in consultation with the Family Group Conference Network, September 2007), p 1.

[95] Ibid.

responsibility and the wider family wishes to go ahead with the FGC but the parents do not, the authority can consent to the FGC in spite of the parent's opposition.[96]

At the referral stage an independent coordinator is appointed. This individual should reflect the ethnicity and culture of the child's family and share the same first language.[97] The coordinator will also be completely neutral in that they have no previous involvement with the child and no case-holding or decision-making responsibilities in relation to the child.[98]

10.10.3 Preparation

The coordinator then identifies appropriate participants from the child's family and where appropriate discusses with the child how they can participate and whether they would like a nominated supporter or advocate at the meeting.[99]

It is unusual for a solicitor to attend the FGC because the emphasis is on problem solving away from the court arena. If one person brings a solicitor it can result in an inequality or alternatively a situation where all the family members want to bring somebody, resulting in an escalation of the atmosphere of the meeting. Nevertheless, if a solicitor has relevant information, they may be invited to attend the information-giving part of the meeting provided that all the family members present agree to their attendance.

CAFCASS officers may attend if they have information to contribute. They may only attend the information-giving and final stages of the meeting so that they may clarify the support available to the family if their plan is agreed.

Once the participants are agreed, the coordinator liaises with the family and referrer. Any relevant agencies or professionals are invited to provide information to the family about the child welfare issues that need to be considered at the conference and the services that might assist both the child and their family.[100]

The preparation stage normally takes 4 to 6 weeks.[101] Once this has been completed the conference can take place.

---

[96]   Ibid.
[97]   Family rights group website: What is a Family Group Conference? www.frg.org.uk/fgc_ model.html.
[98]   *Using Family Group Conferences for children who are, or may become, subject to court proceedings: A Guide for Courts, Lawyers, CAFCASS officers and Child Care Practitioners* (Family Rights Group in consultation with the Family Group Conference Network, September 2007), p 1.
[99]   Ibid, p 2.
[100] Ibid.
[101] Ibid.

10.10.4   Conference

During the conference information is first given to the family members about the child's welfare, the resources and support they could supply as well as the action that will be taken if the plan cannot be agreed.

Once the family have the information they need, they are left to talk among themselves and come up with a plan based on what they have been told. The fundamental principle of the conference is that the family is the key decision making group and that they are enabled to make decisions through informed private discussion.[102]

When the family are ready to propose a plan the referring authority, the information givers and the referrer return to the conference to discuss and if possible agree the plan. At this point the resources that will be needed are discussed.

It is presumed that the plan proposed by the family will be approved by the referring agency unless it would put the child at risk of harm and further that the support asked for will be provided unless it is either unreasonable or unnecessary.[103] If the plan is not agreed, the reasons must be explained to the family.[104]

If a plan has been agreed, it is then implemented within agreed timescales. There should be a clear process of reviewing the implementation. A review FGC can be arranged subject to the same criteria as the first.[105]

10.11   NOTIFICATION

As soon as a local authority decides that it intends to apply for a care or supervision order, it must immediately notify that decision to the parents and any other adult with parental responsibility for the child concerned.[106] The notification should take the form of a Letter before Proceedings, a template of which can be used and should include:[107]

* a summary of the local authority's concerns about the welfare of the child;

---

[102] Ibid.
[103] *Using Family Group Conferences for children who are, or may become, subject to court proceedings: A Guide for Courts, Lawyers, CAFCASS officers and Child Care Practitioners* (Family Rights Group in consultation with the Family Group Conference Network, September 2007), p 3.
[104] Ibid.
[105] Ibid.
[106] *The Children Act 1989 Guidance and Regulations*, Vol 1: Court Orders (DfES, revised 2008), para 3.25.
[107] Ibid, para 3.29.

- a summary of the evidence on which the concerns are based;

- information about the timing of the planned application;

- information about how to obtain legal help and advice;

- details of local solicitors firms;

- encouragement to seek such advice;

- the care plan.

Such individuals should be notified using methods of communication that they can understand. This can be written or oral. If possible or appropriate, the local authority should liaise with the parents or other individuals with parental responsibility, with a view to seeing what steps can be taken to avoid proceedings. This is likely to involve further explaining the position of the local authority and its concerns.[108]

Where parental engagement might avert proceedings this should be discussed, and if proceedings simply cannot be averted then the issues should be narrowed at this stage.[109]

Where the child is old enough to understand the situation, the intention of the local authority should also be explained to the child. It should be recognised, however, that this may exacerbate the situation, in which case this should not be done until after proceedings have commenced and a guardian is instructed. Parental sensitivity will also be a factor in deciding whether this is appropriate.[110]

Upon receiving the written notification from the local authority of an intention to commence proceedings, such individuals are entitled to non-means tested publicly funded legal advice through 'Family Help Public' at Level 2.[111] This covers liaison and negotiation with the local authority aimed at avoiding or in any event limiting proceedings.[112]

---

[108] Ibid, para 3.25.
[109] Ibid.
[110] *The Children Act 1989 Guidance and Regulations*, Vol 1: Court Orders (DfES, revised 2008), para 3.28.
[111] Ibid, para 3.26.
[112] Ibid.

10.12   FLOWCHARTS

Flowchart 1: Referral[113]

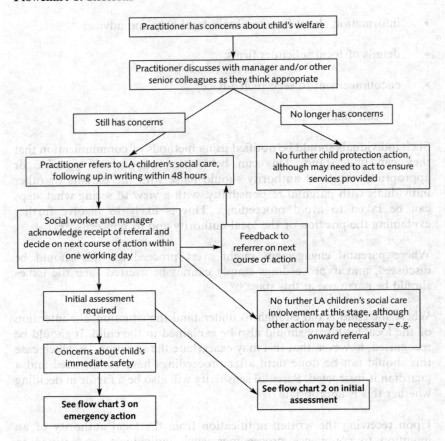

Practitioner has concerns about child's welfare

↓

Practitioner discusses with manager and/or other senior colleagues as they think appropriate

Still has concerns

No longer has concerns

Practitioner refers to LA children's social care, following up in writing within 48 hours

No further child protection action, although may need to act to ensure services provided

Social worker and manager acknowledge receipt of referral and decide on next course of action within one working day

Feedback to referrer on next course of action

Initial assessment required

No further LA children's social care involvement at this stage, although other action may be necessary – e.g. onward referral

Concerns about child's immediate safety

See flow chart 2 on initial assessment

See flow chart 3 on emergency action

---

[113] Taken from *Working Together*, p 142.

Flowchart 2: What happens following initial assessment?[114]

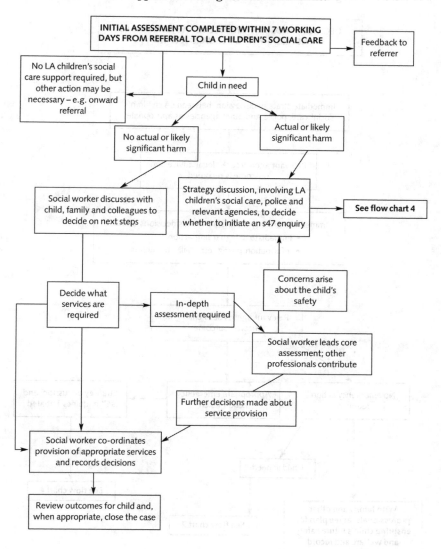

Flowchart 3: Urgent action to safeguard children[115]

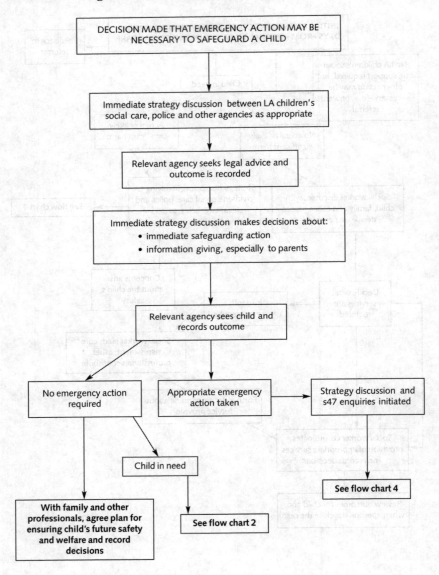

DECISION MADE THAT EMERGENCY ACTION MAY BE NECESSARY TO SAFEGUARD A CHILD

Immediate strategy discussion between LA children's social care, police and other agencies as appropriate

Relevant agency seeks legal advice and outcome is recorded

Immediate strategy discussion makes decisions about:
- immediate safeguarding action
- information giving, especially to parents

Relevant agency sees child and records outcome

No emergency action required

Appropriate emergency action taken

Strategy discussion and s47 enquiries initiated

Child in need

See flow chart 4

With family and other professionals, agree plan for ensuring child's future safety and welfare and record decisions

See flow chart 2

---

[115] Taken from *Working Together*, p 144.

Flowchart 4: What happens after the strategy discussion?[116]

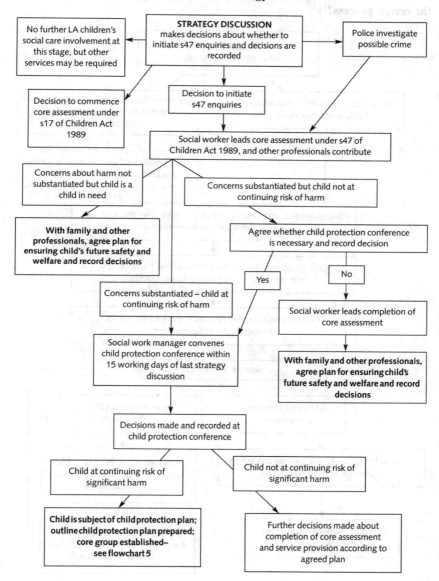

Flowchart 5: What happens after the child protection conference, including the review process?[117]

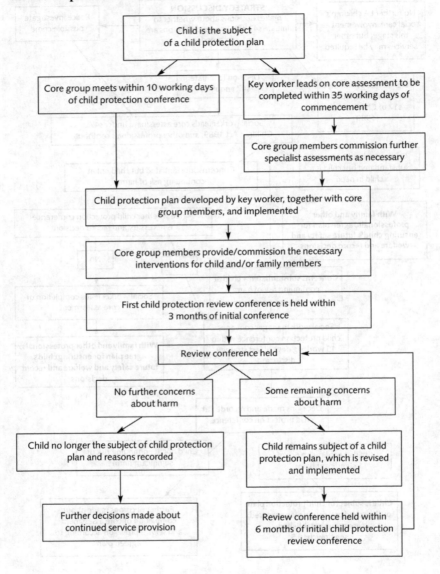

Flowchart 6: *Working Together to Safeguard Children* – **Individual cases flowchart**

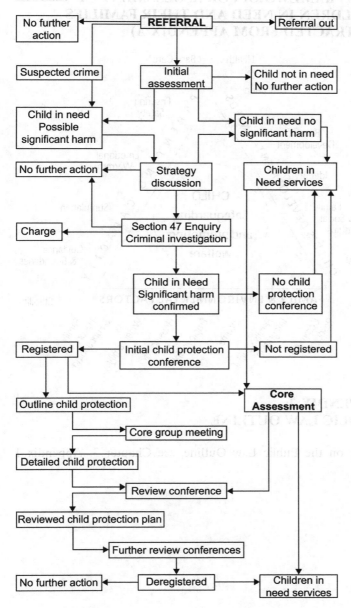

A10.1   APPENDIX 1: THE FRAMEWORK FOR ASSESSMENT OF CHILDREN IN NEED AND THEIR FAMILIES (EXTRACTED FROM APPENDIX A)

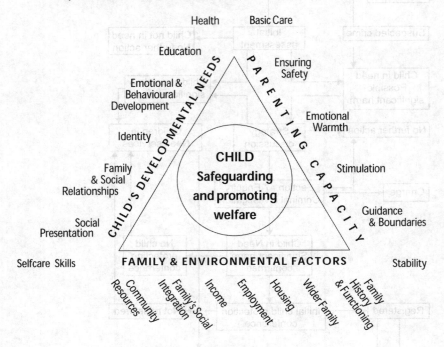

A10.2   APPENDIX 2: PUBLIC LAW OUTLINE

For Guidance on the Public Law Outline, see Chapter 3, Appendix 1 (**A3.1**).

CHAPTER 11

EMERGENCY PROTECTION PROCEDURES

11.1 EMERGENCY PROTECTION ORDERS

An emergency protection order (EPO) can be made by any person but will usually be made by a local authority.

Emergency protection orders are specifically provided for in the Children Act 1989.[1]

11.1.1 Effect

A successful applicant acquires parental responsibility for the child once an EPO has been granted and during the continuance of the order.[2]

The applicant also acquires a number of specific rights and duties but parental responsibility can only be used reasonably and in pursuit of safeguarding or promoting the welfare of the child (during the duration of the order). Accordingly, any use of parental responsibility must be proportionate.

While an order is in force it:

- Operates as a direction to any person who is in a position to do so to comply with any request to produce the child to the applicant;

- Authorises—

    (i) The removal of the child at any time to accommodation provided by or on behalf of the applicant and his being kept there; or
    (ii) The prevention of the child's removal from any hospital or other place in which he was being accommodated immediately before the making of the order.[3]

---

1   Children Act 1989, s 44.
2   Children Act 1989, s 44(4)(c).
3   Children Act 1989, s 44(4)(a), (b).

11.1.2   Grounds for granting an EPO

The grounds which must be satisfied in order to obtain an emergency protection order vary depending on who makes the application. However, there is one common ground which applies to every applicant:

11.1.2.1   *Common ground*

Whoever is the applicant must satisfy the court that:

- There is reasonable cause to believe that the child is likely to suffer significant harm if:

    (i)   He is not removed to accommodation provided or on behalf of the applicant; or

    (ii) He does not remain in the place in which he is then being accommodated.[4]

Where the applicant is the local authority

Section 44(4)(b)

- Enquiries are being made in respect of the child under s 47(1)(b); and

- Those enquiries are being frustrated by access to the child being unreasonably refused to a person authorised to seek access and the applicant has reasonable cause to believe that access to the child is required as a matter of urgency.

Where the applicant is an 'authorised person'[5]

Section 44(4)(c)

- The applicant has reasonable cause to suspect that a child is suffering, or is likely to suffer, significant harm;

- The applicant is making enquiries with respect to the child's welfare; and

- Those enquiries are being frustrated by access to the child being unreasonably refused to a person authorised to seek access and the applicant has reasonable cause to believe that access to the child is required as a matter of urgency.

---

4   Children Act 1989, s 44(1)(a)(i), (ii).
5   'Authorised person' – NSPCC and any person authorised by order of the Secretary of State to bring proceedings under s 31: Children Act 1989, s 31(9).

When determining an application:

- the child's welfare is the paramount consideration when deciding whether an order should be made;[6]

- the court must not make the order unless doing so would be better for the child than making no order at all.[7]

However, it should be noted:

- the statutory checklist need not be applied;[8] and

- an EPO does *not* fall within the definition of 'family proceedings'. Accordingly the court cannot make any other order.[9]

11.1.3 Duration

An EPO may be made for a maximum of 8 days.

- If granting the order for a maximum period where the eighth day falls on a bank holiday or Sunday, the court may specify a period which ends at noon on the first later day which is not such a holiday.[10]

- Where the child was taken into care pursuant to police protection powers and subsequently the 'designated officer'[11] has applied on behalf of the local authority for an EPO, the maximum 8-day period runs from the date of the child being received into police protection rather than the date of the making of the order.[12]

- The order can be extended once only, for a period not exceeding 7 days.[13]

11.1.4 Procedure

Where there is a risk to the life of the child or a likelihood of serious immediate harm, an agency with child protection powers should act

---

[6]   Children Act 1989, s 1(1).
[7]   Children Act 1989, s 1(5).
[8]   Children Act 1989, s 1(4)(a), (b).
[9]   Children Act 1989, s 8(4).
[10]   Children Act 1989, s 45(1), (2)(a), (b).
[11]   An officer designated for the purposes of the Act by the Chief Officer of the police area concerned: Children Act 1989, s 46(3)(e).
[12]   Children Act 1989, s 45(3).
[13]   Children Act 1989, s 45(5), (6).

quickly to secure the immediate safety of the child. Emergency action may be necessary as soon as a referral is received or at any point when involved with children and families.

When considering whether emergency action is required, an agency should always consider whether action is also needed to safeguard and promote the welfare of other children in the same household, the household of an alleged perpetrator or elsewhere.

Planned emergency action normally takes place following an immediate strategy discussion between police, local authority children's social care and other agencies, as appropriate. Where a single agency has to act immediately to protect a child, a strategy discussion should take place as soon as possible after such action to plan the next steps. The decisions taken at any strategy discussion must be recorded.[14] Decisions about immediate action should be kept under review.

Legal advice should normally be obtained before initiating legal action, in particular when an EPO is sought. This was reinforced by McFarlane J:[15]

> 'The importance of the local authority lawyer on an EPO application was not to be underestimated. That person was under a duty to present the case for the applicant and ensure that it was presented fairly and the bench made fully aware of the legal context within which the application was made.'

The local authority in whose area a child is found, in circumstances that require emergency action, is responsible for taking that action. If the child is looked after by or is the subject of a child protection plan in another authority, the first authority should consult the authority responsible for the child. Only when the second authority accepts responsibility is the first authority relieved of the responsibility to take emergency action. Such acceptance should subsequently be confirmed in writing.

An application for an EPO must be made in the family proceedings court[16] unless the application is made as a result of a court-directed investigation (in which case the application must be made to the court which directed the investigation), or the application is made while there are other proceedings pending (in which case the application must be made to the court which made the original order).

The Application should be made on a Form C1 with Supplement C11[17] and, unless it is ex parte, must be served on the appropriate respondents.

---

14 Department of Health, 2002.
15 *Re X (Emergency Protection Orders)* [2006] EWHC 510 (Fam), [2006] 2 FLR 701.
16 Allocation and Transfer of Proceedings Order 2008, SI 2008/2836, art 5(2).
17 Family Procedure Rules 2010, SI 2010/2955; Practice Direction 12C.

11.1.4.1 *Ex parte applications*

An application for an EPO may be made without notice.[18] In the family proceedings court, leave of the justices' clerk is required.[19] A without notice application should only be made in wholly exceptional circumstances justified by a genuine emergency, or the need for extreme urgency, or where there are compelling reasons for believing that the child's welfare would be compromised by giving notice.[20]

Where the application is made without notice, the applicant must, if the application is made by telephone, file the application within 24 hours of the application (or if in the family proceedings court, as directed by the justices' clerk), or at the time of making the application; and serve a copy of the application on each respondent within 48 hours after the making of an order.[21] Copies of the supporting evidence, a note of any oral evidence and the court's reasons for making the order should be prepared and served on the parents as soon as possible.[22]

Any without notice hearing must be recorded verbatim and a copy provided for the parents unless there is a very good reason not to.[23]

11.1.4.2 *Applications on notice*

In relation to EPO proceedings, the application may be made by any person. The application must be served on all the respondents to the application.[24] Automatic respondents will be:

• every person whom the applicant believes to have parental responsibility for the child;

• where the child is the subject of a care order, every person whom the applicant believes to have had parental responsibility immediately prior to the making of the care order;

• in the case of an application to extend, vary or discharge an order, the parties to the proceedings leading to the order which it is sought to have extended, varied or discharged;

---

[18] FPR 2010, r 12.16(1).
[19] FPR 2010, r 12.16(3).
[20] *X Council v B (Emergency Protection Orders)* [2004] EWCH 201 (Fam), [2005] 1 FLR 341; *Haringey London Borough Council v C and E* [2004] EWCH 2580 (Fam), [2005] 2 FLR 47.
[21] FPR 2010, r 12.16(3).
[22] *X Council v B (Emergency Protection Orders)* [2004] EWCH 201 (Fam), [2005] 1 FLR 341; *Haringey London Borough Council v C and E* [2004] EWCH 2580 (Fam), [2005] 2 FLR 47.
[23] *Re X (Emergency Protection Orders)* [2006] EWHC 510 (Fam), [2006] 2 FLR 701.
[24] Practice Direction 12C (para 1.1)

- in the case of specified proceedings, the child.[25]

The applicant must serve:

- the application Form C1(including any supplementary forms; C11 for an EPO) with the hearing or directions date endorsed and a notice of proceedings on Form C6, with the date and place of the hearing, within one day of the hearing or directions appointment.[26]

Notice of any hearing or directions must be given to non-parties on Form C6A. The following are to be considered as non-parties to the application:

- local authority providing accommodation for the child;

- persons who are caring for the child at the time when the proceedings are commenced;

- in the case of proceedings brought in respect of a child who is alleged to be staying in a refuge which is certified under s 51(1) or (2) of the 1989 Act, the person who is providing the refuge, at the same time as serving the application; and

- every person whom the applicant believes to be a parent of the child.

If a person with parental responsibility requests to be a party to proceedings, the court will direct that the person with parental responsibility be made a party to proceedings.[27]

Further, the court may at any time direct that any person or body be made a party to proceedings, or a party be removed.[28]

Once a 'with notice' application has been filed and served, the matter will be listed for hearing. The procedure is the same as for a care order.

---

[25] FPR 2010, r 12.3(1).
[26] FPR 2010, r 12.8 and Practice Direction 12C.
[27] FPR 2010, r 12.3(2).
[28] FPR 2010, r 12.3(3).

11.1.4.3   *Common ground*

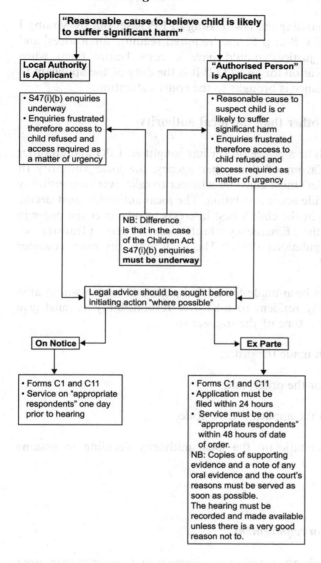

"Reasonable cause to believe child is likely to suffer significant harm"

Local Authority is Applicant

"Authorised Person" is Applicant

- S47(i)(b) enquiries underway
- Enquiries frustrated therefore access to child refused and access required as a matter of urgency

- Reasonable cause to suspect child is or likely to suffer significant harm
- Enquiries frustrated therefore access to child refused and access required as matter of urgency

NB: Difference is that in the case of the Children Act S47(i)(b) enquiries **must be underway**

Legal advice should be sought before initiating action "where possible"

On Notice

Ex Parte

- Forms C1 and C11
- Service on "appropriate respondents" one day prior to hearing

- Forms C1 and C11
- Application must be filed within 24 hours
- Service must be on "appropriate respondents" within 48 hours of date of order.
NB: Copies of supporting evidence and a note of any oral evidence and the court's reasons must be served as soon as possible.
The hearing must be recorded and made available unless there is a very good reason not to.

11.1.5   Good practice guidance

The 14 points summarising the law relating to EPOs set out by Munby J in *X County Council v B* at p 57 are 'required reading' for justices' and legal advisors and justices should have a copy before them when considering an application for an EPO.[29] It is the duty of the applicant to ensure that this guidance is brought to the court's attention.

11.1.6   Applicant other than the local authority

Where a person such as a police officer has sought an EPO and an order has been made in favour of that other agency, the local authority (if informed of this order) must consider whether to take over responsibility for the child or provide accommodation. The local authority must decide whether it would be in the child's best interests to take over the order in accordance with the Emergency Protection Orders (Transfer of Responsibilities) Regulations 1991.[30] The local authority must consider the welfare checklist.

When a decision has been made for a local authority within whose area the child is ordinarily resident to take over responsibility, it must give notice of the date and time of the transfer to:

- the court which made the order;

- the applicant for the order; and

- those to whom the applicant gave notice.

The transfer is automatic on the local authority deciding to assume responsibility.

11.1.7   Law

11.1.7.1   Exclusion requirement

The court may include an exclusion requirement in an interim care order (ICO) or EPO.[31] This allows a perpetrator to be removed from the home instead of removing the child. The court must be satisfied that:

- there is reasonable cause to believe that if the person is excluded from the home in which the child lives, the child will cease to suffer, or cease to be likely to suffer, significant harm, or that enquiries will cease to be frustrated; and

---

[29]   *X County Council v B* [2006] EWCH 510 (Fam).
[30]   SI 1991/1414.
[31]   Children Act 1989, ss 38A and 44A.

- another person living in the home is able and willing to give the child the care that it would be reasonable to expect a parent to give, and consents to the exclusion requirement.

A person to whom an exclusion requirement applies may apply for a variation or discharge of the requirement. Such application must be made on notice.

11.1.7.2   *Variation and discharge*

An EPO can be challenged either by attendance at the hearing or by an application to discharge it. Those entitled to challenge the making of the order or to apply for discharge are:

- the child;

- a parent of the child;

- any other person with parental responsibility;

- any person with whom the child was living before the order was made.

An application to discharge the order can be made immediately after its making, but cannot be heard before the expiry of 72 hours.[32] The application must be made on Form C1 and must be made on notice and the application must be filed in sufficient time to allow service on each respondent.

11.1.7.3   *Contact*

While an EPO is in force, the applicant must allow reasonable contact with:

- the child's parents;

- any other person with PR;

- any person with whom the child was living when the order was made;

- any person who has a contact order;

- any person who is allowed contact pursuant to s 34 (contact with a child in care);

---

[32]   Children Act 1989, s 45(9).

- any person acting on behalf of those persons;
- any person who has access to a child pursuant to an existing order for access.[33]

The basic position may be altered by a court direction e g that a particular person is not to have contact.

11.1.7.4   *Appeal*

There can be no appeal from the making of an order, a refusal to make an order or any of the directions made in connection with the order.[34]

11.2   POLICE PROTECTION ORDERS

11.2.1   Procedure

The officer that takes the child into police protection must ensure that the case is inquired into by an officer designated for the purpose by the chief officer of the police area concerned. Both officers have defined responsibilities but neither acquire parental responsibility. The designated officer may apply for an EPO on behalf of the local authority.

11.2.1.1   *Responsibilities of the constable taking the child into police protection*

- Inform the local authority within whose area the child was found of his action and intended action, and the reasons why.

- Give details to the local authority in whose area the child is usually resident of where the child is.

- If the child is capable of understanding, tell them the steps that have been taken and what further steps may be taken.

- Take reasonable steps to ascertain the child's wishes and feelings.

- Ensure the case is inquired into by the 'designated officer'.

- If the child is removed to accommodation that is not local authority or refuge accommodation, ensure that they are moved to local authority accommodation.

---

33 Children Act 1989, s 44(13).
34 Children Act 1989, s 45(10).

- Take reasonable steps to inform the following parties: – parents, anyone with PR, anyone with whom the child was living immediately before the removal – of what he has done and why and what further steps may be taken.

11.2.1.2 *Responsibilities of the designated officer*[35]

The designated officer must do what is reasonable in the circumstances to safeguard or promote the child's welfare.

The designated officer must:

- release the child from police protection if after conducting his inquiry he does not consider that there is reasonable cause to believe that the child is likely to suffer significant harm if released;

- allow such contact as he considers reasonable and in the child's best interests to:

  (i) the parents;
  (ii) anyone with PR;
  (iii) any person with whom the child was living immediately before being taken into police protection;
  (iv) any person with a contact order;
  (v) anyone who has access to the child pursuant to an existing access order;
  (vi) anyone acting on behalf of those persons above.

Only the designated officer may apply for an EPO when the child is in police protection.

11.2.2 Law

Under s 46 of the Children Act 1989, where a police officer has reasonable cause to believe that a child would otherwise be likely to suffer significant harm s/he may:

- remove the child to suitable accommodation and keep him or her there; or

- take reasonable steps to ensure that the child's removal from any hospital, or other place in which the child is then being accommodated is prevented.

---

[35] An officer designated for the purposes of the Act by the Chief Officer of the police area concerned: Children Act 1989, s 46(3)(e).

No child may be kept in police protection for longer than 72 hours.[36] If it is felt necessary to keep the child in accommodation longer, an application must be made to the court for an EPO before the expiration of 72 hours.

If it is necessary to remove a child, a local authority should, wherever possible and unless a child's safety is otherwise at immediate risk, apply for an EPO. Police protection powers should only be used in exceptional circumstances, where there is insufficient time to seek an EPO or for reasons relating to the immediate safety of the child.

A police officer does not have the power to enter premises and search for a child without a warrant, unless one of the grounds under PACE 1984, s 17 are satisfied (to arrest a person for an arrestable offence, arrest a person for a breach of the peace, recapture a person unlawfully at large, save life and limb or prevent serious damage to property).

The police power to remove a child may be exercised notwithstanding that there is already an EPO in place.[37] However, a police officer who knows that an EPO is in force should not exercise the s 46 power unless there are compelling reasons to do so.

11.2.3   Conclusion

Emergency action addresses only the immediate circumstances of the child. It should be followed quickly by s 47 enquiries, as necessary. The agencies primarily involved with the child and family should then assess their needs and circumstances and agree action to safeguard and promote the welfare of the child in the longer term. Where an EPO applies, LA children's social care must consider quickly whether to initiate care or other proceedings, or to let the order lapse and the child return home.

---

[36]   Children Act 1989, s 46(6).
[37]   *Langley v Liverpool City Council* [2005] EWCA Civ 1173, [2006] 1 FLR 342.

11.2.4 Police protection flowchart – procedure

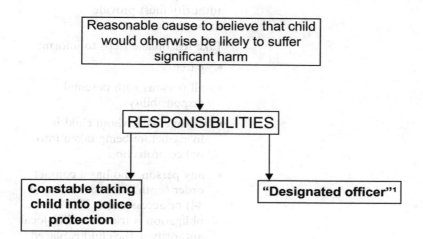

GROUND

Reasonable cause to believe that child
would otherwise be likely to suffer
significant harm

RESPONSIBILITIES

Constable taking child into police protection

Ensure designated officer takes 'certain action'[38]

Inform local authority in whose area child was found of his action, proposed action and why[39]

Give details to local authority in whose area child is ordinarily resident[40]

"Designated officer"[1]

Must release child if after conducting enquiry he does not consider there is still reasonable cause to believe the child is likely to suffer significant harm if released

Allow such contact as he considers reasonable and in the child's best interest to:

- the parents
- anyone with parental responsibility
- anyone with whom the child was living before being taken into police protection

If child has sufficient understanding provide explanation of proposed action[41]

---

[38] The chief officer or chief constable must designate officers for the purposes of the Act: Children Act 1989, s 46(3)(e).
[39] Children Act 1989, s 46(3)(a).
[40] Children Act 1989, s 46(3)(b).
[41] Children Act 1989, s 46(3)(c).

Take reasonably practicable steps to discover child's wishes and feelings[42]

Ensure child is moved to local authority accommodation[43] (local authority must provide accommodation)[44]

Take reasonable steps to inform:

- parents

- all persons with parental responsibility

- anyone with whom child is living before being taken into police protection

- any person who has a contact order (both CA 1989, ss 8 and 34) or access order. This obligation is transferred to local authority if the child is placed in local authority accommodation

- anyone acting on behalf of any of the above persons

What he has done and what further steps need to be taken[45]

11.3   CHILD ASSESSMENT ORDER

11.3.1   Introduction

In any family proceedings the court will have a wide range of powers to make whatever order it deems appropriate. An example of this is if the court considers that a mother needs to be protected from domestic violence, when it may grant a non-molestation order. The parties must always be given notice of the type of order that a court is considering.

There are three types of orders that a court may consider in cases where a child needs urgent protection:

- a child assessment order (CAO);

---

42   Children Act 1989, s 46(3)(d).
43   Children Act 1989, s 46(3)(e).
44   Children Act 1989, s 46(3)(f).
45   Children Act 1989, s 21(2)(a).

- an emergency protection order (EPO);

- a recovery order (RO).

11.3.2 What is a child assessment order

A CAO is defined under the Children Act 1989, s 43(1). On the application of a local authority or authorised person for an order to be made under this section with respect to a child, the court may make the order if, but only if, it is satisfied that:

- the applicant has reasonable cause to suspect that the child is suffering or likely to suffer significant harm;

- an assessment of the state of the child's health or development, or of the way in which he has been treated, is required to enable the applicant to determine whether or not the child is suffering, or is likely to suffer, significant harm; and

- it is unlikely that such an assessment will be made, or be satisfactory, in the absence of an order under this section.

The statutory guidance[46] states that:[47]

> 'Its purpose is to allow the local authority or authorised person to ascertain enough about the state of the child's health or development, or the way in which he has been treated, to decide what further action, if any, is required. It is less interventionist than the emergency protection order, interim care order and interim supervision order, and should not be used where the circumstances of the case suggest that one of these orders would be more appropriate.'

Child assessment orders should be used sparingly and only be contemplated where there is serious concern for the child. The matter should be pursued on a multi-disciplinary basis with a pooling of information on the handling of the case and considered at a case conference.[48]

11.3.3 Persons who may apply

The local authority, the NSPCC or any other authorised person is able to apply. The applicant must do what is reasonably practicable to make sure that notice of the application is given to the child, its parents, carers, anyone else with parental responsibility, or a contact order. A children's

---

[46] *The Children Act 1989 Guidance and Regulations*, Vol 1 Court Orders, para 4.6.

[47] Hershman & McFarlane *Children Law and Practice*, para [201].

[48] *Department of Health Guidelines*, Vol.1, para 4.23.

guardian should be appointed unless it is deemed not necessary to do so to safeguard the interests of the child.

11.3.4   The procedure for an application to court

An application for a CAO should be made on the application Form C1 (including any supplementary forms; C16 for CAO) and Form C6 (Notice of proceedings) together with copies for each respondent.[49] The fee to make an application in the High Court or a county court is £150.[50] There is also a fee of £150 to make an application in the magistrates' court.[51]

11.3.5   Which court

This will usually take place in a family proceedings court unless there are already pending proceedings or an application results from a s 37 investigation by a local authority. If this is the case then the application must be to the court where proceedings are pending or to the court which has requested the investigation.

Application is to the court where there are proceedings pending, or the court which made the original order. Proceedings may be transferable sideways, upwards or downwards; this will depend on the circumstances. Proceedings which have started in the county court or High Court can be transferred between county courts, and also between High Court and county court. They cannot be transferred down to a family proceedings court.

11.3.6   Persons who have power to make an order

A High Court judge, nominated circuit judge or any District Judge of the Principal Registry will be permitted to make such an order.[52]

A nominated district judge outside the Principal Registry (in regards to variation applications under CA 1989, s 39(3), all stages of application; in relation to other s 39 applications, interlocutory matters and unopposed trials only).[53]

A magistrates' court, justices' clerk or single justice cannot make an order.[54]

---

49   FPR 2010, r 12.8 and Practice Direction 12C.
50   Family Proceedings Fees Order 2008, SI 2008/1054, Schedule, fee 2.1(n).
51   Magistrates' Courts Fees Order 2008, SI 2008/1052, Schedule, fee 10.1(k).
52   Family Proceedings (Allocation to Judiciary) Directions 1999, Sch, paras (h), (j) (as substituted by Family Proceedings (Allocation to Judiciary) (Appeals) Directions 2002).
53   Ibid.
54   Ibid.

11.3.7 Respondents

Respondents are cited under FPR 2010, r 12.3, App 3 as being every person whom the applicant believes has parental responsibility, every person whom the applicant believes had parental responsibility prior to the care order, the child and the parties to the original proceedings.

In brief, the respondent will be anyone whom the applicant (such as the local authority) views as having parental responsibility prior to the care order being made.

11.3.8 Service

The local authority or person making the application must serve notice on any person caring for the child at the start of proceedings, any person who is providing accommodation for the child (again this could be the local authority) and persons providing a 'refuge' for the child under CA 1989, s 51. Persons can also include those named in s 43(11).

This must be given at least 7 days before the application, although the court does have the power to abridge service and allow the applicant to give short notice for the application. A statement must be prepared by the applicant and should give details of the application. The relevant forms are C1 and C13.[55]

A copy of the application Form C1, together with Form C6, should be served on the respondent by day 3, pursuant to FPR 2010 r 12.8 and Practice Direction 12C (1.1) and (2.1).

Form C6A should be served on additional persons at the same time as the application etc is served on the respondents (FPR 2010 r 12.8 and Practice Direction 12C (3.1)).

11.3.9 Who are additional persons?

A copy of the application, alongside Form C6, must be served on the respondents at least 1 day before the date of hearing or directions appointment.[56] Form C6A must be served on additional persons as with applications served on respondents.[57] The applicant should file a statement in Form C9 either at or before the first directions appointment or hearing. Form C9 is to prove that the requirements for service have been adhered to.[58]

---

[55] *Children and Families Procedure Manual*: Section D: Family Proceedings and Protection of Children, p 5.
[56] FPR 2010, r 12.8 and Practice Direction 12C (para 2.1).
[57] Ibid.
[58] FPR 2010, Practice Direction 5A.

11.3.10 What factors will the court consider when deciding whether to make the order

The child's welfare must be the court's paramount consideration although the court does not have to apply the welfare checklist.[59]

There are a number of factors which are relevant and may be useful to the court. With regard to any physical or oral examination, the court will need to know what the purpose of the examination is, who will be carrying out the examination and whether that person should be named in the order. Other factors will involve when and where the examination will be taking place and who may be present. The court will also need to consider how many examinations may be permitted and the duration. Other important factors are what aids (if any) will be used in the examination and the method used for recording the examination. The court will also look at whether the child should be allowed to go home either before or during the examination.

Another factor is contact. Again the court will need to consider what sort of contact the child should have with those who are or have been caring for him, for example his parents and persons with parental responsibility.

A factor which has been mentioned previously is the child's sufficient understanding in making informed decisions, namely about whether to refuse to submit to an examination or assessment of any kind. Does the child have sufficient understanding or will the decision be left to the court?[60]

Section 43(8) of the CA 1989 states (regardless of subsection 7), if the child is of sufficient understanding to make an informed decision it is possible for that child to refuse to submit to the assessment.[61]

Section 43(4) of the CA 1989 states:

> '(4) No court shall make a child assessment order if it is satisfied—
> (a)   that there are grounds for making an emergency protection order with respect to the child; and
> (b)   that it ought to make such an order rather than a child assessment order.'

This makes it clear as to when a CAO may *not* be sought.

---

[59] Summarised from the Family Court Bench Book (section 6 Public Law Orders) Judicial Studies Board (December 2006), 6-1, p 41.
[60] *Children and Families Procedure Manual*: Section D: Family Proceedings and Protection of Children, pp 5 and 6.
[61] Summarised from the Family Court Bench Book (Section 6 Public Law Orders) Judicial Studies Board (December 2006) 6-1, p 42.

Section 43(10) deals with the issue of contact in relation to the child whilst he or she is away from home. The order will contain directions that the court thinks suitable.

> '(10) Where the child is to be kept away from home, the Order shall contain such directions as the court thinks fit with regard to the contact that he must be allowed to have with other persons while away from home.'

The factors discussed above will be considered in detail by the court and will form the 'backbone' of the CAO. It is therefore imperative to be as thorough as is possible and to have any appointments for assessments and or examinations already in place so that if an order is made these can take effect immediately.[62]

Section 43(3) states:

> '(3) A court may treat an application under this section as an application for an emergency protection order.'

In effect this allows the courts to regard an application made under this section as an application for an EPO.

11.3.11 Effect of orders

The court has the power to specify the terms of the order.[63] It is important to note that the local authority does not obtain parental responsibility under a CAO.

Section 43(6) states that, where a CAO is in force, any person who is in a position to produce the child, must produce that child to the person named in the order, and must also carry out such directions relating to the assessment of the child as the court deems necessary. Any failure to produce the child when asked to do so may give grounds whereby the local authority can seek to obtain an EPO from the court.[64]

Section 43(7) reads:

> '(7) A child assessment order authorises any person carrying out the assessment, or any part of the assessment, to do so in accordance with the terms of the order.'

For example, the court can specify the type or method of assessment to be carried out and what contact the child should have with its parents, or others, during the duration of the order.[65]

---

[62] Ibid.
[63] Children Act 1989, s 43(7).
[64] Ibid.
[65] Children Act 1989, s 43(10).

Section 43(9) gives three situations whereby the child may be kept away from home:

- if it is in accordance with directions specified in the order;

- if it is deemed necessary for the assessment; and

- for any given period of time as dictated by the order.

11.3.12 Duration of the child assessment order

Section 43(5) states:

> '(5) A child assessment order shall –
> (a) specify the date by which the assessment is to begin; and
> (b) shall have effect for such period, not exceeding 7 days beginning with that date, as may be specified in the order.'

This section deals with the duration of the order. It clarifies the start date of the order and states that it may only last for a maximum of 7 days from the date specified.[66]

A CAO cannot be further applied for until 6 months have elapsed since the disposal of the previous application for an order.[67]

11.3.13 Applications to vary or discharge a child assessment order

An application to either vary or discharge a CAO can be made in any circumstances by:

- the local authority;

- persons referred to under s 43(11)—

  (i)   the child's parents;
  (ii)   any person who is not a parent but still has parental responsibility;
  (iii) any other person who has care of that child;
  (iv)   any person in whose favour a contact order is in force regarding that child;
  (v)   any person who is permitted to have contact with that child under an order made under s 34; and
  (vi)   the child.[68]

---

66   Full details in Hershman & McFarlane *Children Act Handbook* 2012/2013.
67   Summarised from D8.2.1 (iv). The Children and Families Procedure Manual June 1999: Section D: Family Proceedings and Protection of Children.
68   Ibid.

11.3.14 Concluding the assessments

When concluding an assessment it is normally good practice for the review conference to share its conclusions and recommendations for future action. They include:

- family services;

- care proceedings;

- further voluntary assessment;

- no further action.

11.3.15 Public Funding (Legal Aid)

The Legal Services Commission will provide public funding for children; this is defined below.[69]

- Children even if they are under 16 will receive legal help.

- Legal representation will be available for minors (those under 18 years of age).

Legal aid for children is provided in the following ways:[70]

- If the child is seeking advice or assistance in relation to private law proceedings (where the child is competent) then that child has an absolute right to seek advice, as if he or she were an adult. Otherwise the acting solicitor must have the authority of the Area Director to advise the child and the merits of that advice must be established.[71]

- Representation in 'Special Children Act proceedings' is non-means, non-merits tested public funding for certain public law proceedings (care/supervision orders, child assessment orders, applications for secure accommodation – and for the child alone, applications for EPO's etc). In other public law proceedings the normal rules for the grant of public finding will apply.[72]

- A child's application for public funding will be assessed as for any adult. The merits of his/her case will be considered and means (the child's only) are relevant to the financial assessment. The child's solicitor will sign the application and the means form for a child

---

[69] Funding Code Criteria, s 2.2 and FPR 2010, Part 16, Practice Direction 16.
[70] Funding Code, Ch 20 and Funding Code Criteria, s 4.
[71] *Children Law and Practice*: Public Funding (Legal Aid).
[72] Ibid.

under 16 years of age. If the child is over the age of 16 then the child will sign the appropriate financial form applicable to the adult client.[73]

---

73   Ibid.

CHAPTER 12

APPOINTMENT AND REMOVAL OF A CHILDREN'S GUARDIAN

12.1 INTRODUCTION

The involvement of social services in the life of a family attempts to tread the uneasy territory between two extremes. At one extreme is the possibility of the serious injury or even death of a child whose parents do not provide the care which is needed. At the other extreme is the unnecessary, intrusive and damaging intervention of the state in a private sphere. Hence, the role of the children's guardian has evolved to try to protect those caught in the uncomfortable middle ground. This independent officer, appointed by the court, makes his/her own assessment of the issues in the case and scrutinises the actions of the local authority, reporting directly to the court.

12.2 RELEVANT LEGISLATION

Section 41 of the Children Act 1989 (as amended) provides for the appointment of a children's guardian and solicitor for the child. Section 42 provides for access by the children's guardian to local authority records.

Rule 16.3 of the Family Procedure Rules 2010 provides for the appointment of a children's guardian: r 16.20 (including r 16.21 and PD 16A) sets out their powers and duties. Rule 16.29 sets out the role of the solicitor for the child who will often, but not always, be working alongside the children's guardian.

12.3 APPOINTMENT OF A CHILDREN'S GUARDIAN

There is a mandatory obligation upon the court to appoint an officer of Cafcass for the child concerned in specified proceedings unless satisfied that appointment is not necessary in order to safeguard the child's interests (CA 1989, s 41(1)).

It is rare for the court to conclude that appointment is not necessary.

In initial proceedings a guardian will be appointed as an automatic process. It is more likely that a guardian may be dispensed with in non-contentious cases under categories (c), (e) and (f) below.

In *Re J (A Minor) (Change of Name)* [1993] 1 FLR 699 the court dealt with an ex parte application by a local authority for leave to change the name of a child in its care without appointing a guardian ad litem (now children's guardian) on the basis that they could not have added to what was said on behalf of the applicant local authority, and there was no conflict of interest. In proceedings where a s 37 direction is made, appointment should not be automatic but will depend upon the purpose for which a s 37 report is required and whether an interim care order is actually being made or merely being considered. If the latter, the factors requiring appointment should be considered, as should the time available to the guardian to play a useful role and any other safeguards which may already be in place protecting the child's interests (see *Re CE (Section 37 Direction)* [1995] 1 FLR 26).

These older authorities must be regarded with some caution in a time of financial stringency for public services. Over 2008–2010 delays in the appointment of children's guardians became commonplace in many areas of the country. The Law Society issued the following Practice Note to children's solicitors: *Acting in the absence of a Children's Guardian*:[1]

> 'Representation should be given in furtherance of the best interests of the child but not to the extent of advising the court what those best interests are. This will include conduct in accordance with instructions given by the sufficiently competent child.
>
> Within proceedings the court will expect representations as to whether any arrangements or plans are safe and appropriate.
>
> Representation does extend to critical appraisal of the other parties' cases but not recommendation of any particular course of action; this includes representation as to whether the grounds for an order are made out but not advocacy for or against an order being made.'

As a general rule courts may accept cases proceeding to First Appointment or CMC without a guardian where there is a genuine agency issue. After that point, and in any case where an interim care order, removal or other significant step is contested, the court should require the involvement of a guardian formally appointed to the case.

12.4　SPECIFIED PROCEEDINGS (CA 1989, S 41(6))

(a)　An application for a care order or supervision order;

---

[1]　https://www.lawsociety.org.uk/productsandservices/practicenotes/
childrensguardian/3387.article.

(b)   Proceedings in which the court has given a direction under section 37(1) and has made, or is considering whether to make, an interim care order.

(c)   An application for the discharge of a care order or the variation or discharge of a supervision order.

(d)   An application under section 39(4) (where the court is considering substituting a supervision order for a care order on an application for discharge).

(e)   Where the court is considering making a residence order or special guardianship order with respect to a child the subject of a care order.

(f)   Proceedings concerning contact between a child in care and any other person.

(g)   Proceedings under Part V (essentially emergency steps such as child assessment orders, emergency protection orders, police protection orders and proceedings concerning abduction of children in care).

(h)   Appeals concerning care and supervision orders, orders for contact with children in care and applications to vary these, or applications and orders under Part V.

(hh) Applications for the making or revocation of a placement order.

(i)   Proceedings specified by rules of court.

12.5   PROCEDURE

Once specified proceedings have been commenced or transferred to a court, the court or legal advisor must appoint a children's guardian. This should take place as soon as practicable, unless an appointment has already been made and is subsisting, or the court considers appointment is not necessary to safeguard the interests of the child.[2] A party may apply at any stage of specified proceedings for an appointment, or the court may appoint of its own motion.

The Public Law Outline requires the court to appoint a children's guardian on the first day of the process. Cafcass is expected to allocate a children's guardian by day 3. The court officer is to notify the parties and any welfare officer or child and family reporter of the appointment as soon as practicable and serve copies of the application and any documents filed upon the children's guardian.

---

[2]   FPR 2010, r 16.3.

When making its appointment, the court must consider any children's guardian who has previously been involved. An application for a change of guardian, because of a view expressed in earlier proceedings, is likely to fail.[3] Note also that by FPR 2010, r 16.3 where no appointment has yet been made in specified proceedings any party may apply for a children's guardian's appointment at any time and, on refusal, reasons must be given. The court may make an appointment at any time of its own initiative

12.6   PRIVATE LAW

FPR 2010, Part 16 deals comprehensively across the family courts with the representation of children and reports in proceedings involving children, and in FPR 2010, r 16.2 now provides:

> '16.2(1) The court may make a child a party to proceedings if it considers it is in the best interests of the child to do so.'

Under the previous formulation in the FPR 1991, the appointment of children's guardians in private law was an area which frequently became a zone of tension for Cafcass in their efforts to control the appropriate allocation of their resources. Practice Directions at national and local level attempted to address the potential for such appointments to cause problems for the service and so for the courts. In most areas there is a requirement policed locally for all such appointments, where contemplated, to be canvassed prior to the order being made with local Cafcass managers. It will be expected that any Cafcass officer currently involved with the case under CA 1989, s 7 will take the children's guardian appointment if they have sufficient skills and experience for the enhanced role.

On criteria that will be influential before making the child a party under FPR 2010, r 16.4 the practice direction provides:

> 'Before taking the decision to make the child a party, consideration should be given to whether an alternative route might be preferable, such as asking an officer of the Service or a Welsh family proceedings officer to carry out further work or by making a referral to social services or, possibly, by obtaining expert evidence.'

The decision to make the child a party will always be exclusively that of the court, made in the light of the facts and circumstances of the particular case. The following are offered, solely by way of guidance, as circumstances which may justify the making of such an order:

(a)   where a Cafcass officer is of the opinion that the child should be made a party;

---

[3]   *Re J (Adoption: Appointment of Guardian ad Litem)* [1999] 2 FLR 86.

(b)   where the child has a standpoint inconsistent with or incapable of being represented by any of the adult parties;

(c)   where there is an intractable dispute over residence or contact, irrational but implacable hostility to contact or where the child may be suffering harm;

(d)   where the views and wishes of the child cannot be met by a report to the court;

(e)   where an older child is opposing a proposed course of action;

(f)   where there are complex medical or mental health issues;

(g)   where there are international complications;

(h)   where there are serious allegations of physical, sexual or other abuse in relation to the child or there are allegations of domestic violence not capable of being resolved;

(i)   where the proceedings concern more than one child and the welfare of the children is in conflict;

(j)   where there is a contested issue about scientific testing.

But note also:

> 'separate representation of the child may result in a delay in the resolution of the proceedings. When deciding whether to direct that a child be made a party, the court will take into account the risk of delay or other facts adverse to the welfare of the child.'[4]

Rules concerning requirements for child applicants, and connected children's guardian appointments for litigation friends etc, and the inter-relationship with the child's party status are further dealt with in FPR 2010, Part 16.

12.7   POWERS AND DUTIES OF THE CHILDREN'S GUARDIAN

Once appointed, the guardian is under a duty to safeguard the interests of the child in accordance with the rules (s 41(2)(b)). The rules require the guardian to have regard to the general principle against delay at s 1(2) of the Act and to the welfare checklist at s 1(3).

---

[4]   FPR 2010, PD 16.

Where the appointment is in relation to proceedings involving protected parties the guardian must carry out those duties as if the duties imposed by s 1 of CA 1989 were worded with reference to the children's guardian.

The guardian is to contact or seek to interview such persons as he or she thinks appropriate or the court directs, and to obtain such professional assistance as is available or the court directs. The guardian not infrequently takes the role of coordinating the instruction of expert professional witnesses in fulfilment of this duty.

FPR 2010 Practice Direction 16A governs the exercise of the children's guardian's duties. Firstly under specified proceedings:

'6.1 The children's guardian must make such investigations as are necessary to carry out the children's guardian's duties and must, in particular –

(a) contact or seek to interview such persons as the children's guardian thinks appropriate or as the court directs; and

(b) obtain such professional assistance as is available which the children's guardian thinks appropriate or which the court directs be obtained.

6.2 The children's guardian must –

(a) appoint a solicitor for the child unless a solicitor has already been appointed;

(b) give such advice to the child as is appropriate having regard to that child's understanding; and

(c) where appropriate instruct the solicitor representing the child on all matters relevant to the interests of the child arising in the course of proceedings, including possibilities for appeal.

...

6.5 The children's guardian or the solicitor appointed under section 41(3) of the 1989 Act or in accordance with paragraph 6.2(a) must attend all directions hearings unless the court directs otherwise.

6.6 The children's guardian must advise the court on the following matters –

(a) whether the child is of sufficient understanding for any purpose including the child's refusal to submit to a medical or psychiatric examination or other assessment that the court has the power to require, direct or order;

(b) the wishes of the child in respect of any matter relevant to the proceedings including that child's attendance at court;

(c) the appropriate forum for the proceedings;

(d) the appropriate timing of the proceedings or any part of them;

(e) the options available to it in respect of the child and the suitability of each such option including what order should be made in determining the application; and

(f) any other matter on which the court seeks advice or on which the children's guardian considers that the court should be informed.

6.7 The advice given under paragraph 6.6 may, subject to any direction of the court, be given orally or in writing. If the advice is given orally, a note of it must be taken by the court or the court officer.'

The court will invariably set a date for the filing of the guardian's report, which will take into account the timetable set for the proceedings.

The guardian's power under s 42 to inspect local authority documentation goes beyond documentation prepared in connection with the proceedings themselves. It extends to all information relevant to the child, including information compiled by the local authority in its role as adoption agency, as long as it refers to the child who is the subject of proceedings.[5] The guardian is entitled to take copies of the local authority documents and those copies may be admitted in evidence. Note also the PD imposed duty:

'Where the children's guardian inspects records of the kinds referred to in:
(a)   section 42 of the 1989 Act (right to have access to local authority records); or
(b)   section 103 of the 2002 Act (right to have access to adoption agency records)

the children's guardian must bring all records and documents which may, in the opinion of the children's guardian, assist in the proper determination of the proceedings to the attention of –
(i)   the court; and
(ii)   unless the court directs otherwise, the other parties to the proceedings.'

Note also that the FPR 2010 now make provision in relation to informing the child of outcome, by the Practice Direction:

'The children's guardian must ensure that, in relation to a decision made by the court in the proceedings –
(a)   if the children's guardian considers it appropriate to the age and understanding of the child, the child is notified of that decision; and
(b)   if the child is notified of the decision, it is explained to the child in a manner appropriate to that child's age and understanding.'

For those private law situations where the child has been made a party the duties are:

'... fairly and competently to conduct proceedings on behalf of the child. The children's guardian must have no interest in the proceedings adverse to that of the child and all steps and decisions the children's guardian takes in the proceedings must be taken for the benefit of the child.'

---

[5]   *Re T (A Minor) (Guardian ad Litem: Case Record)* [1994] 1 FLR 632.

12.8   SOLICITOR FOR THE CHILD

A child may be represented by a solicitor in public law (and other specified) proceedings.

The appointment of a solicitor for a child in specified proceedings is governed by the provisions of s 41(3)–(5) of the Children Act 1989. The role of the solicitor for the child is regulated by FPR 2010, r 16.29.

Section 41(3)–(5) of the CA 1989 read as follows:

'(3) Where –
(a)   the child concerned is not represented by a solicitor; and
(b)   any of the conditions mentioned in subsection (4) is satisfied

the court may appoint a solicitor to represent him.

(4) The conditions are that –
(a)   no officer of the Service or Welsh family proceedings officer has yet been appointed for the child;
(b)   the child has sufficient understanding to instruct a solicitor and wishes to do so
(c)   it appears to the court that it would be in the child's best interests for him to be represented by a solicitor

(5) Any solicitor appointed under or by virtue of this section shall be appointed, and shall represent the child, in accordance with the rules of the court.'

- NB – the court *may* appoint a solicitor for the child – it does not have to if it is not considered necessary.

- If there is a waiting list for the appointment of a children's guardian, it is likely that a solicitor will be appointed and act on her/his own initially.

- A child who is of sufficient age and understanding may instruct a solicitor of his/her choice (see FPR 2010, Part 16).

12.9   DUTIES OF CHILD'S SOLICITOR

A solicitor who has been appointed either by the children's guardian or by the court (pursuant to s 41(3) of the CA 1989) has specific duties:

- to represent the child in accordance with the instructions of the children's guardian unless the solicitor considers that the child wishes to give instructions which conflict with those instructions, and the child is able to give such instructions, having regard to the child's understanding;

- where no children's guardian has been appointed, to represent the child on the child's instructions (so long as the child has sufficient understanding and wishes to instruct a solicitor);

- where a children's guardian has not been appointed and the child does not have sufficient understanding to give instructions, the solicitor must act in the furtherance of the child's best interests.

(See FPR 2010, r 16.29.)

12.10 TERMINATION OF APPOINTMENT OF CHILD'S SOLICITOR

The children's guardian (r 16.29) may apply to the court for the termination of the appointment of the solicitor for the child. The solicitor and the child/children's guardian must be given the opportunity to make representations on any such application. There is no prescribed form; an application within proceedings on Form C2 is suggested.

- A child's level of understanding may be affected not only by age and level of cognitive functioning, but also by any emotional disturbance to which the child may be subject.

- If a conflict arises between the recommendations of the children's guardian, and the wishes and feelings of a child who is old enough and with sufficient understanding to give instructions, the matter should be referred to the court for the matter to be resolved. The solicitor will, in general, continue to represent the child and the children's guardian may seek other representation.

12.11 TERMINATING THE APPOINTMENT OF THE CHILDREN'S GUARDIAN

- The termination of the appointment of the children's guardian is regulated by FPR 2010, r 16.19. The appointment, once made, is for the currency of the proceedings and comes to an end either when the proceedings end, or if the appointment is terminated by the court (r 16.19).

- The court may only terminate the appointment of a children's guardian if there has been an application for it to do so. Written reasons must be given for terminating the appointment.

- There are no prescribed criteria to which the court should have regard when considering such an application set out in the rules; however acting 'manifestly contrary to the interests of the child' has been considered sufficient, even where the children's guardian has acted in good faith (see *Re A (Conjoined Twins: Medical Treatment) (No 2)*).[6]

---

6 [2001] 1 FLR 267.

CHAPTER 13

CARE ORDERS AND SUPERVISION ORDERS

13.1 INTRODUCTION

A care order is one of the most significant orders which a court can make in English law. It gives the designated local authority parental responsibility (shared with any other person with parental responsibility) but with controlling status. A supervision order, whilst less draconian in its scope, nonetheless gives a local authority certain powers to require families to comply with its lawful directions.

Before either order can be made the applicant authority must satisfy the court on the balance of probabilities that certain criteria have been established. These are known as 'the threshold criteria'. Only if the threshold has been crossed can the court determine the appropriate order to make having regard to the 'welfare checklist' contained in s 1(3) of the Children Act 1989 ('CA 1989'). Every application for a care order or a supervision order must be coupled with a plan, 'the care plan'.[1] This sets out proposals for the future care of the child which the judge must scrutinise to ensure that it meets the welfare needs of the child.

The proposals set out in the care plan may be the precursor to a rehabilitation of the child with his parent or parents, wherever that may be achieved, or placement with a carer within the family. There will, however, be those cases where the plan is the permanent removal of the child from the parents and the natural family. Where a care order is made, a 'placement order'[2] may also be made either simultaneously, or shortly thereafter, leading to the adoption of the child and the termination of parental rights. Such an order clearly impacts upon the human rights of both parent and child.

It is self-evident that faced with decisions of such importance the court needs to ensure that it has the best evidence available before coming to a determination. The nature of care proceedings is largely inquisitorial and judicial case management is fundamental to the process. This is an area where the court is often faced with a changing picture as a case develops.

---

[1]   CA 1989, s 31A.
[2]   Adoption and Children Act 2002, s 21.

Procedures have therefore been developed to allow for both flexibility and to set out a clear path for the courts, and also for parties to follow. It is a statutory principle that delay in the determination of questions concerning the upbringing of a child is likely to prejudice the welfare of the child.[3]

13.2 THE PUBLIC LAW OUTLINE (PLO)

The Protocol for Judicial Case Management in Public Law Children Act Cases came into operation in 2003 with the aim of providing a framework for good practice and case management. The PLO which replaced the Protocol in all cases commenced after 1 April 2008 arose out of a review of the Protocol by the Judicial Review Team in December 2005 and the Government Child Care Proceedings Review 2006. It sought to refine those areas where practice required improvement. Now this has been further refined by the introduction of the 'Public Law Proceedings Guide to Case Management: April 2010' set out in Practice Direction 12A of the 'Practice Directions Supplementing The Family Procedure Rules 2010' (PD) which applies to care and supervision proceedings and insofar as practicable to all other Public Law Proceedings commenced after 6 April 2010. If practicable, however, it will be applied to proceedings not disposed of before that date. Otherwise the 'Practice Guide to Case Management in Public Law Proceedings' dated April 2008 will apply.

One of the more significant aspects of the PLO is that local authorities will now have to follow the pre-action protocol which, as will be seen, is designed to ensure that any assessments perceived to be necessary should have been undertaken by the local authority before the commencement of proceedings, except in emergency situations. In some cases the preliminary work may identify issues which can properly be addressed without the need for proceedings.

Practice Point: Advocates will need to satisfy themselves as to the local authority's compliance with pre-action steps.

This chapter is designed to give a brief overview of the substantive law and a ready reference guide to a range of issues arising where applications for care and supervision orders are made. It should be considered in conjunction with the chapter covering the Public Law Outline (Chapter 3). This gives a clear guide to the procedures and to the overall objectives of the PLO and the practice, which must be followed in the presentation of applications for public law orders, set out therein.

---

[3] CA 1989, s 1(2).

13.3 CARE ORDERS

13.3.1 Part IV of the Children Act 1989

Part IV of the Children Act 1989 sets out the principles, powers and duties in relation to public law applications.

Section 31(1) of the Children Act 1989 provides that:

On the application of any local authority or authorised person, the court may make an order –

(a) placing the child with respect to whom the application is made in the care of a designated local authority; or

(b) putting him under the supervision of a designated local authority.

A 'care order' means an order under subsection (1)(a) above and a 'supervision order' means an order under subsection (1)(b).

13.3.2 The effect of a care order

A care order gives the local authority 'parental responsibility' for the child and the power to determine the extent to which any other person with parental responsibility may meet his parental responsibility for him.[4]

Parental responsibility means: All the rights, duties, powers, responsibilities and authority which by law a parent has in relation to the child and his property.[5]

The local authority may not exercise such parental responsibility unless it is satisfied that it is necessary to do so in order to safeguard or promote the child's welfare.[6]

The local authority has a duty to remove a child from the care of its parent/s where placed at home under a care order in circumstances where the placement is or becomes contrary to the local authority's duty to promote the welfare of the child or would prejudice the safety of the child.[7] It may do so without recourse to the court.[8]

---

[4]   CA 1989, s 33(3)(b)(ii).
[5]   CA 1989, s 3(1).
[6]   CA 1989, s 33(4).
[7]   CA 1989, s 22(3).
[8]   Placement of Children with Parents Regulations 1991, SI 1991/893, reg 11.

13.3.3　Restrictions upon local authorities and other parties under a care order

The order places certain restrictions upon a local authority while a care order is in force. The local authority shall not:

- Cause the child to be brought up in any religious persuasion other than that in which he would have been brought up if the order had not been made.[9]

- Agree or refuse to agree to the making of an adoption order or an order giving parental responsibility to a person who intends to seek an adoption order in another jurisdiction.[10]

- Appoint a guardian for the child.[11]

No person may:

- Cause the child to be known by a new surname.[12]

- Remove him from the United Kingdom.[13]

The above prohibition does not prevent the local authority removing the child for a period of less than one month.

Where there is an absence of agreement between all those with parental responsibility, applications may be made to cause a child to be known by a new surname under s 33(7)(a). The welfare of the child is paramount in determining any such application.

13.3.4　Duration of order

Care orders other than interim care orders continue in force until the child reaches 18 unless brought to an end earlier.[14]

13.3.5　Discharge of care orders

The Children Act s 39(1) provides:

'A care order may be discharged on the application of:
(a)　any person who has parental responsibility for the child;
(b)　the child himself;

9　　CA 1989, s 33(6)(a).
10　CA 1989, s 33(6)(b)(ii).
11　CA 1989, s 33(6)(b)(iii).
12　CA 1989, s 33(7)(a).
13　CA 1989, s 33(7)(b).
14　CA 1989, s 91(12).

(c)   the local authority designated by the order.'

In the case of an application under CA 1989, s 39(1)(a) and/or (b) the application is a free standing order which should be made to the court in which the original order was made.

The provisions of the PLO now govern applications made by the local authority which must have fulfilled the necessary pre-action requirements before filing an application. The court can, if it thinks fit, substitute a supervision order.[15] The threshold criteria need not be re-established in these circumstances.

13.4   SUPERVISION ORDERS

A supervision order is an order under CA 1989, s 31(1)(b).

The principles underlying CA 1989 require that the courts should adopt the least interventionist approach consistent with the welfare of the child. When deciding whether to make a supervision order in a particular case an order should not be made if the court is satisfied that there will be voluntary compliance with a local authority direction.

13.4.1   The duties of the supervisor

While a supervision order is in force it shall be the duty of the supervisor:

(a)   to advise, assist and befriend the supervised child;[16]

(b)   to take such steps as are reasonably necessary to give effect to the order; and[17]

(c)   where:

(i)   the order is not wholly complied with; or
(ii)   the supervisor considers that the order may no longer be necessary, to consider whether or not to apply to the court for its variation or discharge.[18]

---

[15]   CA 1989, s 39(4).
[16]   CA 1989, s 35(1)(a).
[17]   CA 1989, s 35(1)(b).
[18]   CA 1989, s 35(1)(c).

The effect of an order

Under a supervision order the child may be required by the supervisor to:

- comply with directions given from time to time which may include directions as to where the child shall live;[19]

- present himself to a person specified in the directions at a place or places as required and to participate in specified activities at the discretion of the supervisor.[20]

The supervisor cannot compel medical or psychiatric examination or treatment although this may be a requirement of the supervision order.[21]

Further, a supervision order may require the supervised child:

- to keep the supervisor informed of any change of address;[22]

- to allow the supervisor to visit him at the place where he is living.[23]

Or, the responsible person in relation to the child (that is the person/s with parental responsibility and any other person with whom the child is living):

- if asked, to inform the supervisor of the child's address;[24]

- if living with the child, to allow the supervisor reasonable contact.[25]

13.4.3 Limitations on the powers of the court

The court cannot:

- specify the directions to be given by a supervisor and the court cannot attach directions to a supervision order;[26]

- require the supervisor to impose a direction on a responsible person.[27]

It is clear that the statute intends to confer on the supervisor the discretion to determine the requirements under the order. However, the

---

[19] CA 1989, Sch 3, para 2(1)(a).
[20] CA 1989, Sch 3, para 2(1)(b).
[21] CA 1989, Sch 3, para 4.
[22] CA 1989, Sch 3, para 8(1)(a).
[23] CA 1989, Sch 3, para 8(1)(b).
[24] CA 1989, Sch 3, para 8(2)(a).
[25] CA 1989, Sch 3, para 8(2)(b).
[26] *Re V (Care or Supervision Order)* [1996] 1 FLR 776.
[27] *Re H (Supervision Order)* [1994] 2 FLR 979.

case of *Re B (Supervision Order: Parental Undertaking)*[28] suggests that a parent's undertaking to behave in a particular way can be recorded in a preamble to the order. Any failure to honour the agreement could be subsequently brought to the attention of the court.

Note: The supervisor cannot impose any sanction for failure to comply with his requirements other than to return to court for a discharge of the order and the possible imposition of a more draconian order.

13.4.4   Duration of order

Supervision orders last for 12 months from the date of the order unless the order specifies a lesser period.[29]

The order may be extended or further extended if the supervisor applies to the court.[30]

A supervision order may not be extended so as to run beyond a period of 3 years from the making of the original order.[31] The applicant must satisfy the court that the welfare of the child requires that the order be extended.[32]

There is no need to satisfy the court again that the threshold criteria have been met.[33]

Should further statutory orders be required, the threshold test would need to be satisfied again.

13.5   PRINCIPLE SIMILARITIES AND DIFFERENCES BETWEEN CARE AND SUPERVISION ORDERS

13.5.1   Similarities

- They can both only be made on the application of a local authority or authorised person.[34]

- The threshold conditions are the same in each case.[35]

- The child must be under 17 or 16 if married.[36]

---

[28] [1996] 1 FLR 676.
[29] CA 1989, Sch 3, para 6(1).
[30] CA 1989, Sch 3, para 6(3).
[31] CA 1989, s 6, Sch 3.
[32] CA 1989, Sch 3, para 6(4).
[33] *Re A (Supervision Order: Extension)* [1995] 1 FLR 335.
[34] CA 1989, s 31(1).
[35] CA 1989, s 31(2).
[36] CA 1989, s 31(3).

- The welfare test under s 31(1) must be satisfied having regard to the welfare checklist.

13.5.2   Differences

- A care order gives parental responsibility to the local authority; a supervision order does not.

- A care order operates to discharge any existing s 8 orders, eg a residence order.[37]
  A supervision order does not have such an effect and operates in conjunction with existing s 8 orders eg, a residence order to the natural parent.

- A subsequent residence order will automatically discharge the care order;[38] it will not discharge a supervision order.

- A local authority may exercise its parental responsibility under a care order to remove a child from a carer with whom he has been placed, without application to the court.
  In contrast, a local authority may not remove a child under a supervision order from the care of the person or persons with parental responsibility without returning to court to seek an order (save in an emergency where emergency provisions will apply).

- The care order lasts until the child attains the age of 18 or until superseded by a further order.
  In contrast, the supervision order lasts for only 1 year unless renewed and in any event for no longer than 3 years.

13.5.3   Which order should the court make?

The principle behind the Children Act is that the court should opt for the less interventionist order wherever possible. The question in every case where the issue arises will be determined by the level of risk to the child and whether in the circumstances of the particular case he can be sufficiently protected if the lesser order is made. Any order must be proportionate to the risk presented.[39]

---

37   CA 1989, s 91(2).
38   CA 1989, s 91(1).
39   *Re C (Care Order or Supervision Order)* [2001] 2 FLR 466.

13.6 THE DESIGNATED LOCAL AUTHORITY

The care order places a duty on the local authority designated by the order to receive the child named in the order into its care and to keep him in its care while the order remains in force.[40]

A supervision order places the child under the supervision of the designated local authority.

13.6.1 Which local authority is the court to designate?

The courts are sometimes faced with difficult issues as to which local authority is the appropriate authority to designate in a particular case.

Section 31(8) of the CA 1989 provides as follows.

The local authority designated in a care order must be:

(a) the local authority within whose area the child is ordinarily resident; or

(b) where the child does not reside in the area of a local authority, the authority within whose area any circumstances arose a consequence of which the order is being made.

The CA 1989, s 105(6) provides that in determining 'ordinary residence' of a child for any purpose of this Act there shall be disregarded any period in which he lives in any place:

(a) which is a school or other institution;

(b) in accordance with the requirements of a supervision order under this Act or an order under s 63(1) of the Powers of the Criminal Courts (Sentencing) Act 2000; or

(c) while he is being provided with accommodation by or on behalf of a local authority.[41]

Not infrequently the issue arises as to which local authority should be designated. In some instances it may be that the designated local authority will be different from the one bringing proceedings. There are of course resource implications from the respective local authority's point of view.

The exercise for the court is first to determine where the child is ordinarily resident, disregarding any period to which s 105(6) above applies. If the

---

[40] CA 1989, s 33(1).
[41] CA 1989, s 105(6).

child cannot be said to be ordinarily resident anywhere, the court will apply s 31(8) ie the authority to be designated will be the one in which the circumstances arose which triggered proceedings. Even in chronic cases it would be possible to evaluate where the principal issues arose.

This is a question of fact for the court to determine by carrying out a rapid and not overly sophisticated review of the history of the case.

The ordinary residence of a new born baby may be deemed to be that of the mother.[42]

The time to consider designation is the time at which the matter is being considered by the court. The court may reconsider the position of an authority previously designated at an interim stage.[43]

In some cases it will be clear that if a care order is to be made, it will be made to a different authority than the applicant authority (eg where a child moves to live in a different area from that in which the circumstances giving rise to proceedings occurred). It is clearly important that there should be full communication between the applicant and the second authority. The court will need to ensure that a representative of the designated authority attends before a care order is made in order to satisfy the court and the parties that they are willing and able to carry out the care plan.[44]

13.7 WHICH COURT HAS JURISDICTION?

Care proceedings must be commenced in the family proceedings court. The case will then be allocated having regard to the allocation principles set out in the PLO. 'For the Purposes of this Act (Children Act) 'the Court' means the High Court, a county court or a magistrates' court (family proceedings court).'[45] A care order or a supervision order can be made at any level of court.

The court has jurisdiction in respect of a child who is either:

- habitually resident in the England and Wales; or

- present in England and Wales when the application is made.[46]

---

[42]   *C (a child) v Plymouth County Council* [2000] 1 FLR 875.
[43]   *London Borough of Redbridge Newport City Council* [2004] Fam Law 562.
[44]   *L v London Borough of Bexley* [1996] 2 FLR 595.
[45]   CA 1989, s 92(7).
[46]   *Re M (Care Orders: Jurisdiction)* [1997] 1 FLR 456.

13.8   WHEN CAN THE COURT MAKE INTERIM ORDERS?

The court may make an interim care or supervision order:

- when adjourning a care or supervision application;[47]

- when ordering a s 37 report (the court may consider a report under the provisions of Children Act 1989, s 37 where there is the possible need for public intervention. It is to be noted that there will not be a public law application before the court at that stage).

A court shall not make an interim order unless it is satisfied:

- that there are reasonable grounds for believing that the circumstances with respect to the child are as set out in s 31(2) of the CA 1989, ie the threshold criteria set out below;[48] and

- it is satisfied that an order is needed having regard to the welfare of the child.[49]

13.8.1   Duration of interim orders

Interim orders last until the happening of the first of the following events:

- such period as is specified in the order;

- 8 weeks from the date on which the order is first made.

And thereafter:

- on second and subsequent occasions, 4 weeks from the expiry of the previous order;

- the disposal of the application;

- in the case of proceedings linked to a s 37 direction where no application has been made by the local authority, the expiry of the period fixed in the direction or 8 weeks.[50]

---

[47] CA 1989, s 38(1).
[48] CA 1989, s 38(2)(c).
[49] CA 1989, s 1.
[50] CA 1989, s 38(4).

13.9 THE PARTIES TO PROCEEDINGS

13.9.1   Who may apply for a care order or supervision order?

A local authority or an authorised person may apply.

An authorised person means:

(a) the National Society for the Prevention of Cruelty to Children and any of its officers; and

(b) any person authorised by the secretary of state to bring proceedings.[51]

No persons or bodies have thus far been authorised under the section and for all practical purposes the local authority will be the applicant.

13.9.2   Who may become a party to proceedings? – Joinder

The Family Procedure Rules 2010 now provide that the following persons will become respondents:

'•   Every person whom the applicant believes to have parental responsibility for the child;
•   where the child is the subject of a care order every person whom the applicant believes to have had parental responsibility immediately prior to the making of the care order;
•   in the case of an application to extend vary or discharge an order, the parties to the proceedings leading to the order which it is sought to have extended varied or discharged;
•   in the case of specified proceedings, the child.'

Care and supervision proceedings are specified proceedings under the CA 1989 and the child will therefore be a party.[52]

Any person may file a request to become a party in Form C2. In deciding whether to grant party status there is no guidance in the rules. The decision to grant party status will be a matter for the judge's discretion.

The PLO now requires that questions as to party status be considered at the first appointment.

However some of the following considerations are relevant to the exercise of such discretion.

---

51   CA 1989, s 31(9).
52   Family Procedure Rules 2010, SI 2010/2955 (FPR 2010), r 12.3(1).

13.9.3 Factors indicating joinder

- A parent without parental responsibility will usually be made a party unless there are substantial reasons as to why s/he should not.

- A person with a good arguable case.[53]

- A person who seeks to become a party to existing proceedings in order to apply for a s 8 order.

The court may give leave to persons to intervene for a specific purpose or the determination of a particular fact without the need for them to be granted party status.[54]

The fact that an allegation has been made against an individual does not automatically give rise to the presumption that they should be permitted to intervene. The court will have regard to all the circumstances of the case including whether the application is proportionate.

13.9.4 Factors indicating refusal

- Where the applicant's position is the same as that of an existing party.

- It is not necessary to make a person a party in order to make a prohibited steps order against them[55] (although the court would usually give liberty to apply in relation thereto).

- Where an application is made very late in the proceedings without good reason.

- Foster carers will not usually be made parties for policy reasons.

13.9.5 Termination of party status

The court may direct that a party to proceedings cease to be a party either:

- Of its own motion.[56]

- At the request of himself or another.[57]

(Any request should be made on Form C2.)

---

[53] *Re M (Care: Contact: Grandmother's Application for Leave)* [1995] 2 FLR 86, CA.
[54] *Re S (Care: Residence: Intervener)* [1997] 1 FLR 497, CA.
[55] *Re H (Prohibited Steps Order)* [1995] 1 FLR 638, CA.
[56] FPR 2010, r 12.3(3).
[57] FPR 2010, rr 4.3, 12.3(3).

13.9.6   Representation of the child

The court is required to appoint a children's guardian to safeguard the interests of the child within **'specified proceedings'** ie those proceedings specified in CA 1989, s 41(6) unless the court is satisfied that it is unnecessary to do so, as follows:

- applications for care and supervision orders and applications to discharge these;

- cases in which the court is considering making a residence order in respect of a child in care;

- applications for contact with a child in care;

- cases where the court is considering making an interim care order or where a direction has been given under CA 1989, s 37;[58]

- appeals against the above.

13.9.7   Who is the children's guardian?

The children's guardian will be an officer of Cafcass or a Welsh family proceedings officer.[59]

Where a guardian has acted for the child in previous proceedings or has acted for siblings in related proceedings the same guardian should act on behalf of the child in the current proceedings. The advantage of continuity will usually outweigh concerns which may be expressed by the parties as to the fact that the guardian may have reached conclusions adverse to them previously.[60]

13.9.8   The role of the children's guardian

The rules require the guardian to have regard to the principles set out in CA 1989, s 1(2) and s 1(3)(a)–(f) in carrying out his duty ie to have regard to the paramountcy principle and the welfare checklist.[61]

The guardian must unless otherwise directed file a written report advising on the interests of the child in accordance with the timetable set by the court.[62]

The Practice Direction provides as follows:

---

[58]   FPR 2010, r 16.3(1).
[59]   CA 1989, s 41(1).
[60]   *Re J (Adoption: Appointment of Guardian ad Litem)* [1999] 2 FLR 86.
[61]   FPR 2010, r 16.20(3).
[62]   PD16A 6.8(a).

'16-6.6 The children's guardian must advise the court on the following matters –

(a) whether the child is of sufficient understanding for any purpose including the child's refusal to submit to a medical or psychiatric examination or other assessment that the court has the power to require, direct or order;

(b) the wishes of the child in respect of any matter relevant to the proceedings including that child's attendance at court;

(c) the appropriate forum for the proceedings;

(d) the appropriate timing of any proceedings or any part of them;

(e) the options available to it in respect of the child and the suitability of each such option including what order should be made in determining the application;

(f) any other matter on which the court seeks advice or on which the children's guardian considers that the court should be informed.'

The parties are entitled to question the guardian in respect of his advice.

Since the introduction of the PLO the guardian is now required to provide the court with an analysis of the current situation at the first appointment and will thereafter be required to provide updates at the subsequent CMC and Issue Resolution Hearing (IRH) (see Chapter 3).

The guardian is required to attend all directions hearings unless the court directs otherwise.[63]

13.9.9 Records

In the preparation of his report the guardian is entitled to have access tolocal authority records relating to the child; in connection with social services functions; and in connection with the making or proposed making of an application under the Act.[64]

The guardian shall bring to the court's and the parties attention, unless the court otherwise directs, all records and documents which may, in the opinion of the children's guardian, assist the court in the proper determination of the issues.[65]

It is good practice for the guardian to seek the court's direction where the documentation is sensitive and may give rise to issues of public interest immunity (PII), before disclosing the same to the parties.

13.9.10 The guardian's enquiries

The guardian shall make such investigations as are necessary to advise the court and he shall:

---

[63] PD16A 6.6.
[64] CA 1989, s 42.
[65] PD16A 6.10.

(a)   contact or seek to interview such persons as he thinks appropriate or as the court directs;[66]

(b)   obtain such professional assistance as is available to him which he thinks appropriate or which the court directs him to obtain.[67]

In addition to the above the guardian may seek the assistance of such experts as are required, based on his professional opinion as to the child's welfare needs and he will often be the conduit for the joint instruction of experts.

13.9.11   Older children

The guardian must notify the child of such of the contents of his report as he considers appropriate having regard to the age and understanding of the child or explain to the child the contents in an appropriate manner. It is not uncommon for an older child to have views and opinions which differ from those of the guardian. Where it appears to the guardian that the child is capable of instructing a solicitor direct or intends to conduct the proceedings on the child's own behalf he must notify the court of that fact and the court may give directions accordingly.[68] This does not obviate the requirement for the guardian to present his report based on his professional opinion. The guardian may, if the court considers it to be necessary, appoint another solicitor to represent his position.

In some cases a parent may also be a minor and indeed may have a guardian of his/her own. It will be the child's welfare which is paramount wherever a conflict arises.

13.10   THE TWO-STAGE PROCESS

The making of a care or supervision order involves the court in a two-stage process. The first part of that process requires the applicant to establish on the balance of probabilities that the 'threshold criteria' set out in s 31 of the CA 1989 are made out. The threshold findings provide the factual basis for the determination of the appropriate orders to make, having regard to the welfare needs of the child. This is the **'Welfare Stage'**. Although there will be some cases where both stages can be dealt with within the same hearing, it will often be necessary for there to be a split hearing (see **13.14**), particularly in cases where the threshold criteria are disputed.

NB – The threshold criteria must be established before the court can make an order.

---

[66]   PD16A 6.1(a).
[67]   PD16A 6.1(b).
[68]   FPR 2010, r 16.21(1)(a) and (b).

13.11 THE THRESHOLD CRITERIA

Section 31 of the CA 1989 sets out the criteria which must first be established before either a care order or a supervision order can be made.

Section 31(2) provides:

'(2) A court may only make a care order or a supervision order if it is satisfied –
(a) that the child concerned is suffering or is likely to suffer significant harm;
(b) that the harm, or likelihood of harm, is attributable to –
(i) the care given to the child, or likely to be given to him if the order were not made, not being what it would be reasonable to expect a parent to give to him; or
(ii) the child's being beyond parental control.'

13.11.1 The meaning of 'significant harm'

The Act does not define 'significant', which therefore has its ordinary dictionary definition. Where however the issue of whether the harm suffered is 'significant' turns on questions of the child's health or development the Act says that 'his health or development shall be compared with that which could reasonably be expected of a similar child'.[69] In *Re L (Care Threshold Criteria)*,[70] Hedley J said of significant harm: 'It must be something unusual; at least something more than commonplace failure or inadequacy ...'.

Harm is defined in s 31(9):

'"harm" means ill-treatment or the impairment of health or development including, for example, impairment suffered from seeing or hearing the ill treatment of another;

"development" means physical, intellectual, emotional, social or behavioural development;

"health" means physical or mental health; and

"ill-treatment" includes sexual abuse and forms of ill-treatment which are not physical.'

Impairment suffered from seeing or hearing the ill treatment of another was imported into the section by s 120 of the Adoption and Children Act 2002. This recognises the harm caused, for example, by exposure to domestic abuse and domestic violence.

---

[69] CA 1989, s 31(10).
[70] [2007] 1 FLR 2050.

13.11.2   'is suffering'

'Is suffering' is determined as at either:

- the date of the hearing;

- the date of application for a care order or the date on which the local authority initiated child protection proceedings e g an application for an EPO.[71]

13.11.3   'likely to suffer'

'Likely' means a real possibility.[72]

The relevant time is the same as for 'is suffering'.[73]

In her judgment in *Re S-B*[74] Lady Hale states the law as follows:

'If the case is based on actual harm, the court must be satisfied on the balance of probabilities that the child was actually harmed. Second, if the case is based on the likelihood of future harm, the court must be satisfied on the balance of probabilities that the facts upon which that prediction was based did actually happen. It is not enough that they may have done so or that there was a real possibility that they did. Third, however, if the case is based on the likelihood of future harm, the court does not have to be satisfied that such harm is more likely than not to happen. It is enough that there is "a real possibility, a possibility that cannot sensibly be ignored having regard to the nature and gravity of the feared harm in the particular case" (per Lord Nicholls of Birkenhead).'

13.12   SCHEDULE OF FINDINGS OF FACT – SCHEDULE OF ISSUES

It is the duty of the court to satisfy itself that the threshold criteria are satisfied. To assist this process, the applicant authority must provide a draft **schedule of findings of fact** setting out the factual basis upon which it seeks to establish the threshold criteria so that the respondents know the case that they have to meet. The court will require a reply from the respondents. A **schedule of issues** can then be prepared. The schedule of findings of fact should be prepared at the earliest opportunity as revisions can always be made in the light of emerging evidence.

---

[71]   *Re M (A Minor) (Care Order: Threshold Conditions)* [1994] 2 AC 424.
[72]   *Re H and R (Child Sexual Abuse)* [1996] 1 FLR 80.
[73]   *Southwark LBC v B* [1998] 2 FLR 1095.
[74]   [2009] UKSC 17.

13.12.1   Agreed schedules and orders sought

The court will scrutinise the schedule of findings sought in order to determine the issues which need to be tried. Where there is agreement or where there is partial acceptance of the findings sought, the court will need to ensure that:

- those facts which are agreed are sufficient to meet the threshold criteria;

- they provide a sufficient factual basis to identify any assessments which need to be carried out and to determine the issues which need to be assessed having regard to the care plan; and

- where there are different categories of harm, the findings of facts provide a sufficient basis for the management of future risk.

Similarly the fact that the parties may agree to the making of an order, or agree that the threshold criteria are made out, does not obviate the need for the court to satisfy itself as to whether the factual substratum for the findings or orders proposed is sufficient. This is so, even where it is proposed that there should be no statutory orders and that proceedings should be withdrawn.

Leave of the court is required to withdraw proceedings and will only be given 'if the court thinks fit'.

In *A County Council v DP; RS; BS by his Children's Guardian*[75] McFarlane J sets out a list of the factors which are 'likely to be relevant' to the court's determination:

(a)   the interests of the child (which are relevant but not paramount);

(b)   the time that the investigation will take;

(c)   the likely cost to public funds;

(d)   the evidential result;

(e)   the necessity or otherwise of the investigation;

(f)   the relevance of the potential result of the investigation to the future care plans of the child;

(g)   the impact of any fact-finding process upon the other parties;

(h)   the prospect of a fair trial on the issue;

---

[75]   [2005] 2 FLR 1031.

(i)   the justice of the case.

The above factors are equally applicable to the court's acceptance of agreed findings. If there is substantial agreement on the main points then it may not be necessary to determine the remaining issues having regard to the above criteria.

Note – An example of a situation where the court might endorse a partial acceptance of the findings may be where a party does accept some findings of the same type and gravity as those which s/he does not accept.

The position, however, will be different if the significant harm to a child falls under a number of heads. For example, a parent may have both sexually abused a child and also neglected him. If the parent accepts the neglect but not the allegation of sexual abuse, it would usually be necessary to have a finding of fact hearing so that the different categories of risk can be appropriately assessed. In this example a parent may be able to address the concerns relating to neglect to a good enough standard, but the child may remain exposed to actual or potential significant harm.

13.12.2   Practice point: the threshold document

It is of critical importance that the factual basis for an order can be clearly understood. Where there is a judgment, then this will contain the necessary findings.

A transcript will provide the basis for future work in relation to the child. Where the court has accepted agreed threshold criteria, a clear record of the matters agreed should be set out and a threshold document should be prepared. In some cases the schedule of findings will be sufficient. This should be signed by the parties and the document should be appended to the order of the court. Should the order need to be revisited, or should an issue arise in future proceedings, the factual basis for the order will be clear.

13.13   THE BURDEN AND STANDARD OF PROOF

*   The burden of proving the threshold criteria is upon the applicant; and

*   the standard of proof is the civil standard of 'on the balance of probabilities.' See **13.11.3**.

Note however:

- Where the court is satisfied that a child has suffered significant harm but cannot determine which of two or more joint carers inflicted that harm, the threshold criteria will still be established and each of the possible perpetrators will be treated as such at the welfare stage.[76]

> 'It may be difficult for the judge to decide, even on the balance of probabilities, who has caused the harm to the child. There is no obligation to do so ... It is not a necessary ingredient of the threshold criteria.'[77]

It is also important to note that CA 1989, s 31(2)(b) provides: 'that the harm, or likelihood of harm is attributable to (i) the care given to the child, or likely to be given to him if the order were not made, not being what it would be reasonable to expect a parent to give to him.' Thus a parent may bear a burden of responsibility giving rise to intervention without being the perpetrator of the harm actually suffered as in cases of failure to protect.

13.14 SPLIT HEARINGS

Once the threshold criteria are established, the court goes on to determine the appropriate order having regard to the child's welfare. In many cases the court may determine that there should be more than one hearing. Cases where a split trial is likely to be necessary are those where the factual basis is in issue and must be resolved before welfare issues can be considered. Typical examples might be:

- Where there is an issue as to whether an injury is non-accidental.

- Where there is no dispute as to the injury being non-accidental but there is an issue as to the identity of the perpetrator.

- Where there is a disputed allegation of sexual abuse.

- Where there is a dispute that the type of harm alleged has occurred or is significant.

The purpose of the split trial is to enable the court at a finding of fact hearing to make such findings as are necessary to establish the factual basis upon which future welfare planning can be based and the nature and extent of further evidence required. At a later final hearing the court will determine where the child should be placed, with whom and the orders necessary to safeguard the child's welfare. The factual enquiry may be confined to a narrow issue or issues or it may involve a more extensive enquiry.

---

[76] *Re O & N, Re B* [2003] 1 FLR 1169.
[77] Per Lady Hale: *Re S-B* [2009] UKSC 17.

The need for a finding of fact hearing under the PLO should have been identified by the court at the first appointment and by the date of the Case Management Conference ('CMC') the court will have:

(1)   identified the discrete issue or issues of fact to be determined by whom and when;

(2)   identified the evidence required to determine the issue or issues;

(3)   specified any expert evidence to be obtained;

(4)   considered any questions as to disclosure and the provision of documentary evidence.

At every stage the court will have in mind the overriding objective and the timetable for the child.

The court should consider listing the matter for an IRH before listing the finding of fact hearing, in order to ascertain those issues remaining (see Chapter 3).

Once the threshold has been crossed the court will give further directions for the determination of the welfare stage. Where this is so, however, the same judge should determine both aspects of the case and the matter will be treated as part heard where the welfare or disposal hearing takes place on a separate occasion.

13.15   PRACTICE POINTS RELEVANT TO ALL PUBLIC LAW PROCEEDINGS

There are many ways in which a child may sustain or be at risk of sustaining significant harm. The majority of cases coming before the courts tend to fall into three main categories. The type of case may impact upon the procedural course to be taken, particularly having regard to the Public Law Outline. The principle categories are:

- *Acute or emergency cases*
  These are the cases involving non-accidental injury, where an allegation of sexual abuse has been made or in circumstances of acute domestic violence. There is usually a precipitating incident triggering child protection procedures. In many instances further investigation reveals that the precipitating incident is the latest example in a pattern of abuse.
  These cases often give rise to a finding of fact hearing, either as to the fact that the harm complained of has occurred in the manner alleged, or where there is a question mark as to the identity of the perpetrator. Included in this category will be those cases where a

child has sustained fractures, head injuries, burns or bruises and where there is no explanation, or where there are incongruous or inconsistent histories.

- *Chronic or 'slow burn' cases*
  These include cases of neglect, both physical and emotional; cases of failure to thrive; cases where concerns are held by professionals over long periods of time; there may be poor school attendance and/or evidence of the children being disturbed or disruptive within the school setting. There may have been referrals to social services on a number of occasions and interventions may have failed to bring about change.
  This category would also include those cases where the parents capacity to care is affected by one of the following –

  (a) domestic violence;
  (b) dependence upon street drugs of alcohol.
  The long term effects of domestic violence within the home are well known and exposure to violence is likely to be found to be emotionally abusive. Similarly the effects of addiction may render a carer emotionally as well as physically unavailable.
  Factitious illness may fall into this category. This includes a spectrum of harm ranging from the deliberate inducing of symptoms in a child by his carer to the repeated presentation of a child for medical attention/treatment to a degree that is abusive. Clearly the presenting signs may be such as to present an emergency.

- *Lack of parenting capacity*
  These are cases which may exhibit many of the above features where the parents sadly lack the capacity possibly by reason of mental health issues and/or disability to parent and who, despite support and assistance, simply cannot cope with the demands of parenting without significantly harming the child or putting him at risk.

NB – The Public Law Outline now set out at PD12A 10.2 provides a Pre-Proceedings Checklist of documents to be disclosed from the Local Authority's files. One of the principal aims of the PLO is to ensure that the local authority has carried out necessary groundwork before embarking upon proceedings. This will include relevant assessments and a thorough review of the history and chronology of social services involvement. Much of the work previously carried out once proceedings had commenced will now be done in preparation for proceedings. In some cases the need for proceedings will be obviated. An important component of the local authority's pre-action responsibilities is the letter to parents setting out its expectations of the parent and the consequences of non-compliance.

In an acute or emergency situation the local authority must take action to start emergency procedures without delay and then comply with the PLO as soon as reasonably practicable thereafter.

13.16   THE WELFARE STAGE

Prior to this stage the threshold criteria will have been established and the parties and the court will have a factual foundation on which to build. This will flow either from a court approved agreement between the parties or a finding of the court having conducted a finding of fact hearing. The court goes on to determine the appropriate orders to safeguard and promote the minor's present and future welfare having regard to the welfare checklist set out in s 1(3) of the CA 1989; the 'welfare' stage.

Whilst the role of the court comes to an end once a care or supervision order is made, the court must be satisfied as to the applicant authority's proposals for the child in the event that an order is made. These proposals are set out in 'the care plan'.

13.17   THE CARE PLAN

The applicant local authority must produce a care plan upon issuing proceedings, which will need to be reviewed as the case progresses. A 'care plan' means a 'section 31A plan' referred to in s 31A of the 1989 Act.

The local authority must provide a final care plan once the evidence is gathered in and it is in a position to provide the court with the detail of its intentions if and when a final care order is made.

The care plan must be kept under review and amended and revised or replaced as necessary.[78] This is a mandatory requirement.

The care plan should provide:

- overall aims;

- the child's needs;

- placement details and proposed timetable;

- the views of others;

- details of the management of the placement and of any support to be provided.

---

[78]   CA 1989, s 31A(2).

LAC Circular of 17/8/99 (LAC (99)29).

The circular stresses a theme to which the court should also have regard in the management of cases: that is 'achievable time scales leading up to specific outcomes for overall implementation'.

It is the court's duty to scrutinise the care plan in order to satisfy itself that it meets the welfare needs of the child. Whilst the court cannot compel a local authority to change its plan, it can give guidance. A responsible local authority should work co-operatively with the court. The court can refuse to make a care order unless and until it is satisfied that the child's welfare needs are met. The local authority must produce a separate care plan for each child in respect of whom it seeks an order even though the plan for a number of siblings may be identical.[79]

13.18   TWIN TRACK PLANNING

There are some cases in which a local authority recognises that there is some potential for rehabilitation of the child within the natural family but that potential is uncertain. For example there are many cases in which early positive responses to local authority involvement are not sustained. In order to avoid delay and to give the court the necessary information regarding prospects for permanence away from the natural family, the court should be presented at a final hearing with fully researched options.[80]

13.19   THE EVIDENCE

Part 22 of FPR 2010 contains the rules relating to evidence in public law proceedings.

'**22.1.**—(1) The court may control the evidence by giving directions as to—
(a)   the issues on which it requires evidence;
(b)   the nature of the evidence which it requires to decide those issues; and
(c)   the way in which evidence is to be placed before the court.

(2) The court may use its power under this rule to exclude evidence that would otherwise be admissible.

(3) The court may permit a party to adduce evidence, or to seek to rely on a document, in respect of which that party has failed to comply with the requirements of this part.

(4) The court may limit cross-examination.'

---

[79]   CA 1989, s 31A.
[80]   *Re D and K (Care Plan: Twin Track Planning)* [1999] 2 FLR 872.

It is clear that the rules give considerable discretion to the court in order to regulate the evidence required to determine the issues which, in its consideration, require to be determined. Thought will need to be given by practitioners as to the necessity of proving a particular issue and the evidence which is going to be required.

The general rule is that 'any fact which needs to be proved by the evidence of witnesses is to be proved:

(a)   at the final hearing, by their oral evidence; and

(b)   at any other hearing, by their evidence in writing'.[81]

The general rule in proceedings under the CA 1989 is that hearings are held in private and applications for care and supervision orders and related applications fall within the scope of the rule. The rules set out those who may attend. They now include a duly accredited representative of news gathering and reporting organisations.[82] FPR 2010, r 22.3 provides that the court may allow evidence to be given by video link or by other means eg by telephone. This will usually be provided for in those cases of witness vulnerability or where attendance at the hearing is logistically difficult. In *Clibbery v Allen*[83] the Court of Appeal explained the different circumstances in which the court might hold family proceedings in open court, in private and where they are to be regarded as confidential. 'The court may give directions as to service on the other parties of any witness statement of the oral evidence on which a party intends to rely in relation to any issues of fact to be decided at the final hearing.'[84] The court may also give directions as to the order in which witnesses are to be served and as to the need or otherwise for filing of statements with the court.[85] Whilst it may be that the parties need to see a wide range of documents many of these may prove non contentious or irrelevant to the issues before the court. Witness statements must comply with the requirements set out in the PD22A. (Part 17 requires a witness statement to be verified by a statement of truth.)

At both the threshold and welfare stages of the process professional evidence is likely to be needed. The PLO provides for the evidence which must be filed at the commencement of proceedings.

It may be that it is only after the threshold criteria have been established that the court and the parties will be in a position to determine the evidence necessary for the court's determination of the welfare stage, in particular the professional and expert evidence which may be needed.

---

81   RSC 1965, Ord 38, r 2.
82   FPR 2010, r 27.11(1)(a) and (2).
83   [2002] 1 FLR 565.
84   FPR 2010, r 22.5.
85   FPR 2010, r 22.5(3).

13.19.1   Hearsay

'Evidence given in connection with the upbringing, maintenance or welfare of a child shall be admissible notwithstanding any rule of law relating to hearsay.'[86]

13.19.2   Children

A child can give sworn evidence if the court is satisfied that he understands the nature of the oath or he understands that it is his duty to speak the truth and has sufficient understanding to justify his evidence being heard (CA 1989, s 96(1), (2)).

A child is theoretically compellable although leave of the court will be needed. However the court in the case of *R v B County Council ex parte P* [1991] 1 FLR 470 said that the use of a summons under Children Act 1989, s 97 (or by analogy a witness summons or sub poena) for this purpose is inappropriate in care proceedings in view of the admission of hearsay into such cases. The court should be slow to issue a summons if to do so would be inimical to the welfare of the child or its effect would outweigh the interest of the person seeking the summons or where the request is designed to intimidate or to seek attendance solely for the purpose of cross-examination. The correct approach to an application for a child to give evidence has now been determined by the Supreme Court in the case of *Re W (Children) (Family Proceedings: Evidence)*:[87] in such circumstances the court must weigh the competing rights of the applicant's Art 6 rights under the European Convention for the Protection of Human Rights (ECHR) to a fair trial against the Art 8 right of all parties, including the child, to respect for private and family life. No one right has precedence and any assumed presumption against calling the child would be contrary to the ECHR. Calling a child may create a real risk to the welfare of the child which the court must weigh in the balance. The level of risk will vary depending on the individual child and the circumstances of the case. This will have to be weighed in each case but there is neither a presumption that the child will not be called nor is this a starting point either. The essential test is 'can justice be done without further questioning of the child?'

In Practice: in Children Act cases indirect evidence of what a child has said is often introduced in relation to allegations of child abuse. Further the child's guardian or the court welfare officer may convey to the court the child's wishes and feelings. The court will always look to other sources of evidence to determine the necessity of calling the child. Where the evidence has not been tested by cross-examination the court must consider carefully the extent to which it can be relied on (*R v B* above).

---

[86]   Children (Admissibility of Hearsay Evidence) Order 1993, SI 1993/621.
[87]   [2010] UKSC 12.

13.19.3   The parent

The parent is both a competent and a compellable witness.

13.19.4   Other parties

The parties should have identified the evidence upon which they seek to rely at the first appointment or the CMC at the latest.

13.20   ASSESSMENTS

CA 1989, s 38(6) provides that when the court makes an interim care order or an interim supervision order in respect of a child, it may order one or more of the following:

- the medical or psychiatric examination or other assessment of the child as it considers appropriate;[88]

- if the child is of sufficient age and understanding he may refuse to submit to examination or assessment;

- the court may direct that there should be no such examination or assessment save with leave of the court.[89]

The section is directed to providing the court with the material required to reach a proper decision at the final hearing.[90]

The section does not empower the court to order treatment or therapy. Its purpose is confined to gathering information and identification of issues.

However, the assessment of a child may include where appropriate:

- his relationship with his parents;

- the risk that his parents may present to him;

- ways in which any risk may be avoided or managed;

- the services to be provided to the child and his parents must be ancillary to the above end.[91]

The funding of such assessments is an important factor to be taken into consideration and the court must consider the cost of any particular

---

[88]   CA 1989, s 38(6).
[89]   CA 1989, s 38(7).
[90]   *Re B (Interim Care Orders: Directions)* [2002] 1 FLR 545.
[91]   *Re G (Interim Care Order: Residential Assessment)* [2006] 1 FLR 601, HL.

assessment in light of the social services budget as a whole. Where there is an issue as to the provision of an assessment the court may need to hear evidence on the point. The issue may be particularly acute where a residential assessment is proposed.[92]

The court may also need to consider other resources available to the local authority.

A medical or psychological assessment of a parent, or a course of psychotherapy for a parent to enable him/her to parent the child safely, would be outside the ambit of s 38(6).

13.21 THE ROLE OF THE EXPERT

Cases concerning the welfare of children commonly require the input of experts to assist the court in coming to a determination on matters outside the court's expertise. Part 25 of the FPR 2010 sets out the rules relating to the appointment and instruction of experts in family proceedings. The general rule is that 'expert evidence will be restricted to that which is reasonably required to resolve the proceedings'. The rules are supplemented by PD25A which gives comprehensive guidance as to the role of experts and expert evidence. The Practice Direction incorporates and supersedes the Practice Direction on Experts in Family Proceedings Relating to Children (1 April 2008) and other relevant guidance after 6 April 2011. The following is a brief summary of the rules and guidance.

13.22 THE DUTIES OF EXPERTS

13.22.1 Overriding duty

An expert in family proceedings has an overriding duty to help the court on matters within their expertise that takes precedence over any obligation to the person from whom he has received instruction or by whom he is paid.

> 'An expert shall have regard to the following, among other duties:
> (a) to assist the court in accordance with the overriding duty;
> (b) to provide advice to the court that conforms to the best practice of the experts' profession;
> (c) to provide an opinion that is independent of the party or parties instructing the expert:
> (d) to confine the opinion to matters material to the issues between the parties and in relation to questions that are within the experts' expertise (skill and experience);

---

[92] *Re C (Children) (Residential Assessment)* [2001] 3 FCR 164.

(e) where a question had been put which falls outside the expert's expertise, to state at the earliest opportunity and to volunteer an opinion as to whether another expert is required to bring expertise not possessed by those already involved or, in the rare case, as to whether a second opinion is required on a key issue and if possible what questions should be asked of the second expert;

(f) in expressing an opinion to take into consideration all of the material facts including any relevant factors arising from ethnic, cultural, religious, or linguistic contexts at the time the opinion is expressed;

(g) to inform those instructing the expert without delay of any changes in the opinion and of the reason for the change.'[93]

13.22.2   The single joint expert

Where two or more parties wish to submit expert evidence on a particular issue the court may direct that a single joint expert be appointed. This will require parties to endeavour to reach agreement as to the identity of the expert to be instructed. If they cannot agree then the court can decide based on lists provided by the parties. Whilst the opinion of an expert may be significant it is for the judge to determine the weight to be attached to it in every case.

13.22.3   Further provisions relating to expert evidence

It is important to note that no party may call an expert or put in evidence an expert's report without the court's permission.[94]

PD25A 4.1 now provides specific guidance on preliminary enquiries to be made of the expert. The expert shall be provided with the following:

(a) the nature of the proceedings

(b) the questions about which the expert is to be asked to give an opinion;

(c) the date on which the court is to be asked permission for the instruction;

(d) whether permission is to be asked of the court for the instruction of another expert in the same or a related field;

(e) the volume of reading required;

(f) whether permission has been applied for or given for the expert to examine the child;

---

[93]   PD 25A, para 3.2.
[94]   FPR 2010, r 25.4(1).

(g)   the timetable for any legal and social work steps;

(h)   whether or not it will be necessary for the expert to conduct interviews and if so with whom;

(i)   the time table for the child and the proposed timescale for any assessment;

(j)   when the expert's report is likely to be required;

(k)   whether and if so what date has been fixed by the court for any hearing at which the expert may be required to attend;

(l)   the possibility of being named or otherwise identified in any judgment.

The court will not direct an expert to attend a hearing unless it is necessary to do so in the interests of justice.[95]

The court may further direct a party to provide information to the expert.[96]

In those cases where there is more than one expert the court will usually require experts to hold a discussion in order to identify and discuss expert issues and where possible to reach agreement. A joint statement containing heads of agreement and disagreement will usually be ordered.[97]

Rule 25.6 does provide that the parties may put questions to the expert.

The court may give directions as to the timetable for questions and replies.[98]

Expert evidence is to be given in a written report unless the court otherwise directs otherwise.

The court will not direct an expert to attend a hearing unless it is necessary to do so in the interests of justice.[99]

The court may further direct a party to provide information to the expert.[100]

---

[95]   FPR 2010, r 25.5.
[96]   FPR 2010, r 25.9.
[97]   FPR 2010, r 25.12.
[98]   PD25A, para 6.1.
[99]   FPR 2010, r 25.5.
[100] FPR 2010, r 25.9.

In those cases where there is more than one expert the court will usually require experts to hold a discussion in order to identify and discuss expert issues and where possible to reach agreement. A joint statement containing heads of agreement and disagreement will usually be ordered.[101]

Practice points:

Beware: proceedings relating to children are confidential and, in the absence of the court's permission, disclosure of information and documents may amount to a contempt of court or contravene statutory provisions protecting this confidentiality.[102]

Expert witnesses are a rare and possibly expensive resource and the time which they may require to produce a report can be considerable. It is therefore essential to identify the relevant expertise required at the earliest point possible.

It is good practice for parties to attend the CMC armed with data which should include:

• A brief outline of the issue upon which it is submitted expert evidence is required;

• The curriculum vitae of the proposed expert setting out relevant experience;

• Information as to the likely timescale for the preparation of a report;

• Availability (the trial date may not be fixed until the IRH so updates as to availability may be required).

It may not be possible to determine the full range of expert evidence required at the outset. Expert evidence may be required to determine the factual basis upon which welfare issues will be determined. This may be because the threshold criteria are disputed or there may be an acceptance that the threshold is crossed but there may remain disputed allegations which are pertinent to the child's welfare. Once the threshold has been established further assistance may be required to determine welfare issues. At this stage expert opinion is likely to be directed to the issue of risk. In many cases where the carers have drug or drink related issues evidence of their engagement with services and a psychiatric evaluation of their responses and the prognosis may be necessary. A psychological report will also often be necessary to identify those cases where therapeutic input may sufficiently address risk. A child psychologist may also be required to address issues of attachment and bonding both with parents and siblings.

---

[101] FPR 2010, r 25.12.
[102] PD 25A, para 1.6(a).

The table below gives a broad overview of the expertise which may be required in the typical cases outlined above at **13.4**.

13.23 THE ROLE OF THE PAEDIATRICIAN

The paediatrician is likely to play a major role, particularly in cases where the threshold criteria are in dispute. The paediatrician's clinical expertise is as a physician with specialist knowledge in the field of child medicine, including the diagnosis and treatment of the diseases and other conditions of childhood. The paediatrician's remit includes the identification of the signs and symptoms of abuse. He will also monitor child development and be able to identify factors such as failure to thrive or to reach developmental milestones which may be indicative of neglect and/or emotional abuse. He will usually be called in to give an opinion when a child presents at Accident and Emergency with suspicious injuries and he may be responsible for invoking child protection procedures. Alternatively he will often be invited to give an opinion by a concerned local authority. He too may seek further input from experts in other fields. The table is a general guide to the kind of expertise which may be necessary depending on the type of harm with which the court is concerned. (See overleaf.)

13.24 DOCUMENTARY EVIDENCE

In many cases a court will be asked by a party to consider documentary evidence. This may be information under the direct control of another party or it may be in the control of third parties. The usual categories of information are likely to be as follows:

- **Police records**

  - Criminal records relating to a party.
  - Domestic violence logs.
  - Interviews and statements of the parties in connection with either an investigation or a prosecution.

- **Medical records**

  - Medical and hospital records of a party.
  - Medical and or hospital records relating to the child.

- **Social Services records**

  - Memoranda and contemporaneous notes of incidents, reports and conversations relevant to the decision making process of the local authority.

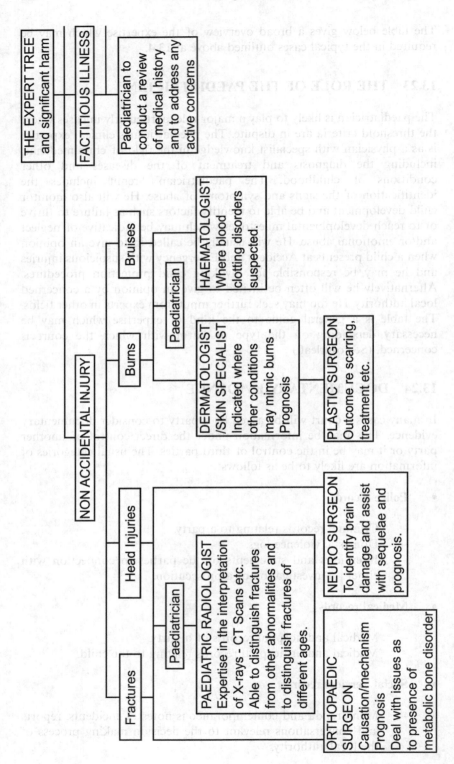

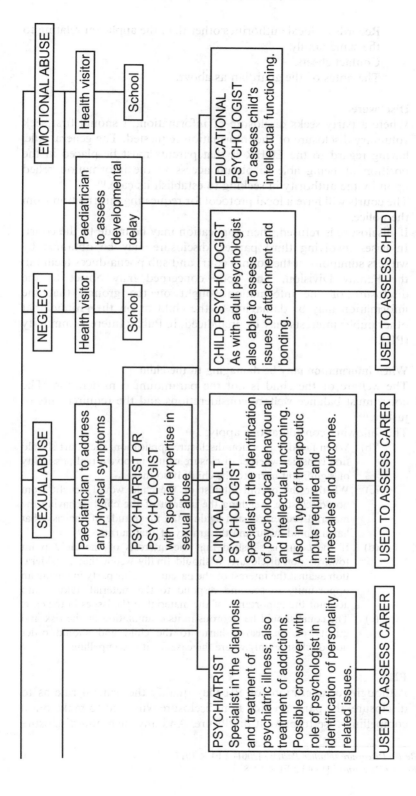

- Records of local authorities other than the applicant relating to the same family.
- Contact sheets.
- The notes of the guardian as above.

- **Disclosure**

  Where a party seeks disclosure of information, it should first seek voluntary disclosure of the information requested. The general rule, having regard to the ECHR is that parents must be placed in the position of being able to obtain access to the information relied upon by the authority in seeking to establish its case.[103]

  The courts will have a local protocol for requesting information from the police.

  If disclosure is refused, then application may be made to the court. In cases involving third parties, disclosure may be obtained by witness summons in the county court and sub poena duces tecum in the Family Division. The body concerned may object to the disclosure of the information sought on the ground that the information may be damaging to the child or on the ground that other public interests may be prejudiced, ie Public Interest Immunity (PII).

- **When information may be damaging to the child**

  The welfare of the child is not the paramount consideration. The court must balance welfare considerations and the requirements of justice.[104]

  The following considerations apply:

  '(b) When faced with a non-disclosure application, the court should first consider whether disclosure would involve a real possibility of significant harm to the child. If so then:

  (c)   Whether the overall interest of the child would benefit from non-disclosure, weighing the interest of the child in having the material properly tested against the magnitude of the risk that harm would occur and the gravity of that harm.

  (d)   If the court is satisfied that the interests of the child point towards non-disclosure, it should finally weigh that consideration against the interest of the parent or other party in having an opportunity to see and respond to the material, taking into account the importance of the material to the issues in the case.

  (e)   The court should be rigorous in its examination of the risk and gravity of the feared harm to the child and should order non-disclosure only where the case for it is compelling.'

- **PII**

  Although considerations of PII may qualify the general rule as to disclosure, the party seeking non-disclosure will need to make out a compelling case to prevent disclosure. And any such non-disclosure

---

[103] *Re B (Disclosure to other Parties)* [2001] 2 FLR 1017.
[104] *Re M (Disclosure)* [1998] 2 FLR 1028.

must be confined to that which is strictly necessary having regard to the public interest in keeping the information secret and the parallel public interest in ensuring the fair administration of justice.

The categories of PII are not closed.

A common example of such an objection might be that if the material concerned was to be revealed it would undermine a police investigation, or reveal a police informer.

Local authorities and children's guardians should be more willing to disclose original notes of meetings and incidents used in the decision making process. Per Charles J in *Re R (Care: Disclosure: Nature of Proceedings)*.[105]

13.25 CARE ORDERS AND THE EUROPEAN CONVENTION FOR THE PROTECTION OF HUMAN RIGHTS

A care order will impact upon the natural parent's right to respect for his family life under Art 8 of the Convention. If complaint is made the court must consider whether, if there has been such an interference with the right, that interference was justified under Art 8(2) as being necessary in a democratic society for the protection of the health and morals and of the rights and freedoms of others. If such interference is justified the court must also consider whether it is proportionate to the aim of protecting the rights of the child concerned.[106]

In judicial decisions where the Art 8 rights of the parents and the child are at stake, the child's interests are the paramount consideration.

13.26 CONTACT

13.26.1 Regulating contact with children in care

- Contact with children in care (including interim care), its variation and discharge are governed by s 34 of the CA 1989 and *not* by s 8 of that Act (any s 8 contact order which exists prior to the making of a care or interim care order will be discharged on the making of such an order). The section also deals with applications for permission to refuse contact with a child in care, and the power of the local authority to refuse contact for a short period of time without the need to make an application to the court.

  Applications for contact with a child who is the subject of a placement order are made pursuant to s 26 of the Adoption and Children Act 2002.

---

[105] [2002] 1 FLR 755.
[106] *Re B (Care: Interference with Family Life)* [2003] 2 FLR 813.

The term 'contact' may apply not only to direct or 'face to face' contact with the child, but may also include telephone calls, sending and receiving letters etc.

• There is a duty upon the local authority to allow *reasonable* contact between a child in its care and a range of people.[107] NB What is 'reasonable' will depend upon the circumstances of the individual case.

• The local authority also has a general duty to *promote* contact between any child being looked after by it and a range of people, namely:

    – parents;
    – any person who is not a parent but who has parental responsibility for the child;
    – any relative, friend or other person connected with the child.

• The local authority, the child, those set out in s 34(1) or any other person who has obtained the leave of the court, may apply for an order providing for contact between the child and any named person (s 34(2) and (3)).

• The local authority or the child can apply to the court for an order *refusing* contact between the child and any person set out at s 34(1)(a)–(d).[108]

If the court makes an order refusing contact, it is a 'permissive' order. If the local authority, for some reason, does not wish to refuse contact having obtained the order, then it does not have to. If the contact re-commences after a cessation which has arisen as the result of the court giving permission to refuse contact, the person (generally the local authority, although the child may also apply for such an order) who has been given permission to refuse contact, should apply to have the order discharged.

• When making a care order with respect to a child, or in any family proceedings in connection with a child who is in the care of a local authority, the *court* may make an order under s 34, even though no application for such an order has been made, if it considers that the order should be made (s 34(5)).

• A local authority may refuse to allow contact which would either be required by s 34(1) or by an order under s 34 if—

---

[107] CA 1989, s 34(1)(a)–(d) (see table at **13.26.2**).
[108] CA 1989, s 34(4).

(a) they are satisfied that it is necessary to do so in order to safeguard or promote the child's welfare; and

(b) the refusal—

    (i)   is decided upon as a matter of urgency; and

    (ii) does not last for more than 7 days.

- An order pursuant to s 34 may be made at the same time as the care order or at a later date (s 34(10)). Before making a care order in respect of a child, the court shall consider the arrangements or the proposed arrangements between the child and any other person and shall invite the parties to comment on those arrangements (s 34(11)) (NB – these arrangements should be set out in the care plan). The court may make an interim order for contact at the time of the making of a final care order, and set a later date for final determination of the contact issues.

- The court may impose such conditions as it deems appropriate when making an order under s 34 (s 34(7)).

- The court may vary or discharge any order made under this section on the application of the local authority, the child or the person named in the order (s 34(9)).

NB – The local authority must address the question of contact arrangements as part of its care plan or interim care plan for a child.

13.26.2 Procedural table

TYPE OF ORDER	WHO CAN APPLY?	WHO ARE RESPONDENTS?	NOTES
Contact order pursuant to s 34(2)	* local authority (s 34(2)) * the child (s 34(2))	* every person believed by the applicant to have parental responsibility for the child	

TYPE OF ORDER	WHO CAN APPLY?	WHO ARE RESPONDENTS?	NOTES
Contact order pursuant to s 34(3)	* the parents (s 34(3)(a)) * any guardian or special guardian (s 34(3)(a)) * any person who, by virtue of CA 1989, s 4A has parental responsibility for the child (s 34(3)(a)) * where there was a residence order with respect to the child in force immediately before the care order was made, the person in whose favour the residence order was made (s 34(3)(a)) * where, immediately before the care order was made, a person had care of the child by virtue of an order made in the exercise of the High Court's inherent jurisdiction, that person (s 34(3)(a)) * any person who has obtained the leave of the court to make the application (s 34(3)(b))	* every person believed by the applicant to have parental responsibility immediately *before* the making of a care order * the child * in the case of an application to extend (also to vary or discharge) an order, the parties to the proceedings leading to the order which the application seeks to extend/vary/discharge * the person whose contact with the child is the subject of the application **NB**: an application for contact with a child in care containing notice of the date, time and place of the hearing must also be served on the following: – any local authority providing accommodation for the child – any person with whom the child is living at the time the proceedings are commenced – if the child is alleged to be staying in a refuge which is certified under s 51(1) or (2), the person who is providing the refuge	Those persons permitted to apply by virtue of s 34(3)(a) are the same as those persons with whom the local authority shall allow reasonable contact with the child pursuant to s 34(1)(a)–(d) **APPLICATION FORMS** Applications for orders pursuant to s 34(2) and (3) are made using Form C1 (if free standing) or C2 (if made within existing proceedings) with supplement C15. **SERVICE** For applications pursuant to ss 34(2), (3), (4) and (9) respondents must be served with a copy of the application endorsed with the date fixed for the hearing at least three days before the hearing

TYPE OF ORDER	WHO CAN APPLY?	WHO ARE RESPONDENTS?	NOTES
Order giving permission to refuse contact with a child in care (s 34(4))	* the local authority * the child	as above	Applications pursuant to s 34(4) are made using Form C1 (if the child is the subject of a final care order) or C2 (if within existing proceedings) supported by supplement C14
Order varying/discharging an order for contact (s 34(9))	* the local authority * the child * the person named in the order to be varied/discharged	as above	Form C1 or C2 as above. No supplement is required

13.26.3 Applications for leave

An individual not falling within one of the categories of person being entitled to apply for contact may apply to the court for permission, or leave, to make a contact application.

The test to be applied by the court on an application for leave is that set out in s 10(9) of the CA 1989, namely:

(a) the nature of the proposed application;

(b) the applicant's connection with the child;

(c) any risk there might be of that proposed application disrupting the child's life to such an extent that it would be harmed by it; and

(d) where the child is looked after by the local authority:

(i) the authority's plans for the child;
(ii) the wishes and feelings of the child's parents.

The court should approach the application by considering the following:

• Is the application frivolous, vexatious or otherwise an abuse of the process of the court? If so, it will fail.

- Does the application fail to disclose that there is any eventual real prospect of success, or are those prospects of success so remote that they are obviously unsustainable? If so, the application will be dismissed.

- Can the applicant satisfy the court that there is a serious issue to try and present a good arguable case? Has the applicant a case which is better than merely arguable, yet not necessarily one which has a better than even chance of success?

13.26.4 Procedure

13.26.4.1 Which court?

Generally, applications for parental contact pursuant to CA 1989, s 34 must be issued in the Family Proceedings Court (Allocation and Transfer of Proceedings Order 2008, art 5(2)), although there are exceptions to this general rule (see further Chapter 2).

13.26.4.2 Which application form?

See the procedural table above.

- Will the application require a C1, and/or C2?

- Is a supplement required?

- Is leave required?

NB – Complete the form as accurately as possible. Give a comprehensive but succinct account of the reasons for the application in the appropriate section. This will help the court at any initial hearing.

13.26.4.3 What else is required when issuing the application?

- Copies of the application form/s for each respondent (see procedural table for who must be served and who must be given notice).

- The appropriate court fee.

13.26.4.4 Service of applications

In respect of an application for a contact order, permission to refuse contact, variation or discharge of a contact order and leave to apply for contact, the applicant must serve relevant documents on the respondent/s and any other person required to be served at least 3 days before the date of the hearing or directions hearing.

A *respondent* must be served with:

- a copy of the application (including any supplement) and the date of the hearing must be endorsed on the application;

- a notice of the proceedings containing the date and place of the hearing.

Each person to whom *notice* must be given must be served with:

- notice of the proceedings;

- the date, time and place of the hearing.

13.26.4.5 The court's approach

- Applications pursuant to CA 1989, s 34 are subject to the welfare principle, and the court must apply the welfare test in s 1(3) to such applications. (NB continuing contact may not be in the interests of the *long-term* welfare of a child in care.) Much will depend upon the plans for the placement of a child and the nature of her/his existing family relationships.

(For a discussion of the approach of the court to the question of welfare, see *Berkshire County Council v B*.[109])

13.26.4.6 Restrictions on applications

- The court may *restrict* a person from applying for contact with a child in care by the imposition of an order pursuant to CA 1989, s 91(14). An order under this section provides that no application for an order under CA 1989 of a specified kind may be made without the leave of the court. Such an order may be made either at the time of making of a final care order, or at a later date if the court is 'disposing of any application for an order' (for example a contact application which has not been finalised at the time of making of a final care order).

- Extensive guidance in relation to s 91(14) orders was set out in *Re P (s 91(14) Guidelines) (Residence and Religious Heritage)*.[110] The power to impose such orders should be used sparingly and be the exception rather than the rule.

- If an application for contact pursuant to s 34 is made and is unsuccessful, a further application may not be made by the person

---

[109] [1997] 1 FLR 171.
[110] [1999] 2 FLR 573.

who made that application for a period of 6 months unless the leave of the court has been obtained (s 91(17)).

13.26.5   Case Digest: Regulating contact with children in care

Re B (Minors) (Care: Contact: Local Authority's Plans) [1993] 1 FLR 543

Two girls born to the mother were the subject of final care orders and to be placed for adoption. The mother had a third child and made strides in her parenting ability sufficient to be able to retain care of him. She began to have frequent unsupervised contact with the girls. The local authority applied for an order under s 34(4) to authorise refusal of contact between the mother and two girls so as to place them with prospective adopters who were not supportive of ongoing contact. Mother opposed and the guardian supported her.

The order was granted at first instance but overturned on appeal. The Court of Appeal emphasised the presumption of continuing reasonable contact unless or until a s 34(4) order was made. Whilst the court had no power to review the local authority's discretionary decisions, it was the court and not the local authority which had the duty to decide on contact between the child and those identified in s 34(1) of the Act. In the exceptional circumstances of this case the court could intervene having the child's welfare as its paramount consideration.

Berkshire County Council v B [1997] 1 FLR 171

Local authority granted a care order with a plan for adoption about which both the guardian and psychiatrist in the case expressed doubts on the basis that the child would be difficult to place. The justices making the care order also ordered contact twice a week under s 34. The local authority appealed.

The Divisional Court refused to interfere with the contact order. The court could order contact in exercising its duty to consider the child's welfare, even if the local authority's plan envisaged a future need for that contact to be terminated.

Re W (Section 34(2) Orders) [2000] 1 FLR 502

The guardian sought a specific order preventing the local authority from permitting staying contact after the conclusion of care proceedings. Refused on appeal. Section 34 may not be used to inhibit the local authority's exercise of its statutory duty in planning contact for a child in its care after the conclusion of proceedings.

Re S (Care: Parental Contact) [2004] EWCA Civ 1397, [2005] 1 FLR 469

Section 34(4) order made although contact was envisaged, to allow for the possibility of the mother not keeping the contact arrangements. Overturned on appeal.

An order refusing contact should not be made against the mere possibility that circumstances may change in the future.

Re H (Termination of Contact) [2005] EWCA Civ 318, [2005] 2 FLR 408

Local authority applied for an order under s 34(4) on the basis that it would need to suspend contact for a settling-in period when the children moved to adoptive carers in accordance with the care plan, although some post adoption contact was subsequently to take place. The adoptive placement had not been identified when the order was sought.

Application refused and refusal upheld on appeal. General principle restated, that contact would be terminated only where there was no likelihood of rehabilitation and post adoption contact was not considered in the child's best interests.

Kirklees Metropolitan District Council v S (Contact to Newborn Babies) [2006] 1 FLR 333

Family proceedings court made an interim order requiring the local authority to allow daily contact between a newborn baby in its care and its mother. On appeal the order was upheld, although described as unusual.

CHAPTER 14

SECURE ACCOMMODATION

14.1 DEFINITION

'Accommodation provided for the purposes of restricting liberty.'[1]

'Restricting the liberty of children is a serious step which must be taken only when there is no genuine alternative which would be appropriate. It must be a 'last resort' in the sense that all else must first have been comprehensively considered and rejected – never because no other placement was available at the relevant time, because of inadequacies in staffing, because the child is simply being a nuisance or runs away from his accommodation and is not likely to suffer significant harm in doing so, and never as a form of punishment. It is important, in considering the possibility of a secure placement and that those providing the accommodation can fully meet those aims and objectives. Secure placements, once made, should be for only so long as is necessary and unavoidable.'[2]

Secure accommodation orders may be made in criminal proceedings and by the family proceedings court. The county court and the High Court may also make a secure accommodation order in the course of other proceedings.

On an application under CA 1989, s 25 by a local authority for a secure accommodation order, the welfare of the child is relevant but is not the paramount consideration and the criteria in s 1 of the CA 1989 do not apply.[3]

Therefore, the role of the children's guardian is not just to advise the court as to the child's welfare but also as to the criteria and merits of an order. The role of the court is to control the exercise of the local authority's power.[4]

The local authority may not place a child in secure accommodation unless it appears:

---

[1]   Children Act 1989, s 25(1).
[2]   *The Children Act 1989 Guidance and Regulations*, Vol 1: Court Orders, para 5.1.
[3]   *Re M (Secure Accommodation Order)* [1995] 1 FLR 418.
[4]   Children (Secure Accommodation) Regulations 1991, SI 1991/1505 (C(SA)R 1991), reg 7.

(a)   that:

    (i)   the child has a history of absconding and is likely to abscond from any other description of accommodation; and

    (ii) if he absconds he is likely to suffer significant harm, or

(b)   if he is kept in any other description of accommodation he is likely to injure himself or other persons.

The criteria are modified for children remanded to local authority accommodation, pursuant to Children and Young Persons Act 1969, s 23. They include children:

(1)   charged with, or convicted of, an offence imprisonable, in the case of a person aged 21 or over, for 14 years or more; or

(2)   charged with or convicted of an offence of violence, or who have been previously convicted of an offence of violence; and

(3)   children detained under PACE 1984, s 38(6).[5]

The criteria in these cases are that children may not be placed or kept in secure accommodation unless it appears that any accommodation other than that provided for the purpose of restricting liberty is inappropriate because:

(i)   the child is likely to abscond from such accommodation; or

(ii) the child is likely to injure himself or other people if he is kept in any such accommodation.[6]

Once the statutory criteria of s 25(1) or reg 6 have been satisfied, the court *must* make an order.[7]

14.2   CHILDREN WHOSE LIBERTY MAY NOT BE RESTRICTED

•   A child under the age of 13 may not be placed in secure accommodation without the prior approval of the Secretary of State.

---

[5]   C(SA)R 1991 reg 6(1).

[6]   C(SA)R 1991 reg 6(2).

[7]   *Re M (Secure Accommodation Order)* [1995] 1 FLR 418; see also *Re W and D (Secure Accommodation)* [1995] 2 FLR 807.

- A child who has reached the age of 16 and is being provided with accommodation, although an order may be made prior to the age of 16 to extend beyond the child's sixteenth birthday.[8]

- A child who is a ward of court may not be placed in secure accommodation unless there is a direction to that effect from a judge exercising the wardship jurisdiction.

14.3 CHILDREN WHOSE LIBERTY IS OTHERWISE RESTRICTED

- The child is detained under the Mental Health Act 1983;

- the child is detained pursuant to CYPA 1933, s 53 (punishment for grave crimes);

- the child is being accommodated under CA 1989, s 20(5);

- the child is being kept away from home under a child assessment order or emergency protection order; or

- the child is being kept in police protection.

Any person who has parental responsibility for a child (who is not in care) may remove them from secure accommodation at any time,[9] subject to restrictions imposed by CA 1989, s 20(9).

The right of persons with parental responsibility to object to a child being provided with accommodation is not an absolute right. The exceptions are:

- where there is a residence order or a special guardianship order in force with respect to the child and the person with the residence order or special guardian agrees to the child being provided with accommodation by the local authority, or if there is a residence order or special guardianship order granted to more than one person and all in whose favour the order was made agree;

- where a person who has care of a child by virtue of an order of the High Court exercising its inherent jurisdiction agrees to the child being provided with accommodation, or if there is more than one person with such an order, all such persons agree;

---

8   *Re G (Secure Accommodation)* [2000] 2 FLR 259.
9   CA 1989, ss 20(8), 25(9).

- if the child is at least 16 and agrees to being looked after by the local authority, and remains in the accommodation provided.[10]

14.4 DURATION

A child who meets the criteria may be placed in secure accommodation for a maximum of 72 hours, in any 28-day period, without court authority.[11] A local authority or other body wanting to keep a child in secure accommodation beyond that period must make an application to the court for authority to do so.

On application to the court, secure accommodation may be authorised:

(i)   for remand cases – the period of remand, except that no such order may extend beyond 28 days;[12]

(ii)   for non-remand cases – for up to 3 months on the first application[13] and for up to 6 months on any further application.[14]

14.5 THE APPLICATION

An application to place a child in secure accommodation may be made by the following who are providing accommodation for a child:[15]

- local authority;

- health authority;

- NHS trust;

- local education authority;

- person carrying on a residential care home, nursing home or mental nursing home.

When a child is looked after by a local authority, it is only that local authority which may apply.

---

[10]   CA 1989, s 20.
[11]   C(SA)R 1991, reg 11(1).
[12]   C(SA)R 1991, reg 13.
[13]   C(SA)R 1991, reg 11; *Re K (Secure Accommodation Order: Right to Liberty)* [2001] Fam 377; *S v Knowsley Borough Council* [2004] 2 FLR 716.
[14]   C(SA)R 1991, reg 12.
[15]   C(SA)R 1991, reg 2.

The court considering the application must not make an order unless the child is legally represented, except where the child has been informed of the right to apply for legal aid and having had an opportunity to do so, has failed or refused to apply.[16]

An application must be made on Form C1 with Supplement C20 and must be served on the appropriate respondents. The application must be made on notice.[17]

Automatic respondents[18] are:

- every person whom the applicant believes to have PR for the child; and

- where the child is the subject of a care order, every person whom the applicant believes to have had PR immediately prior to the making of a care order; and

- the child.

Automatic respondents may be removed by the court and others may be joined. Each respondent should be served the application with the hearing date endorsed and a notice of the proceedings with the date and place of hearing, one day before the date set for hearing.[19]

Notice of the proceedings and of the date, time and place of the hearing or directions appointment (but not the application) must also be served, one day before the date set for hearing, on the following:

- any local authority providing accommodation for the child;

- any person with whom the child is living at the time the proceedings are commenced; and

- where the child is alleged to be staying in a refuge which is certified under s 51(1) or (2), the person providing refuge.[20]

14.6 PROCEDURE

Once an application has been filed and served, the matter will be listed for hearing or directions. Since only one day's notice is required, directions hearings are unlikely. The court may make an interim secure

---

[16] CA 1989, s 25(6).
[17] Family Procedure Rules 2010, SI 2010/2955 (FPR 2010), r 12.8 and Practice Direction 12C (paras 1.1.1 and 3.1.1); Practice Direction 5A.
[18] FPR 2010, r 12.3 and Practice Direction 12C (para 1.1).
[19] FPR 2010, r 12.8 and Practice Direction 12C (para 1.1).
[20] FPR 2010, r 12.8 and Practice Direction 12C, (paras 2.2.6 and (3.1.1).

accommodation order and adjourn the application with directions.[21] Respondents may file an answer. The procedure thereafter is the same as for an application for a care or supervision order.

On an application for a secure accommodation order, an effort should be made to obtain psychiatric evidence to put before the court.[22]

The court can allow the child to be present but under its inherent jurisdiction, can refuse to allow the child into court if s/he is likely to be unruly. The court should only allow attendance if satisfied that it is in the interests of the child to do so.[23]

Before making a secure accommodation order, the court should allow the child to be present or solicitor or counsel representing him to have the opportunity to take instructions. In all but the most exceptional circumstances, a children's guardian should be appointed.[24]

14.7 LOCAL AUTHORITY'S DUTIES

C(SA)R 1991, reg 15 places a duty on the local authority in respect of a child being kept in secure accommodation to appoint three people, one of whom must be independent of the local authority, to review placement within 1 month of the inception of the placement and at regular intervals thereafter, not exceeding 3 months. Those persons must satisfy themselves that the criteria for secure accommodation continue to apply and that the placement continues to be necessary.

The local authority must ensure that, in respect of every child kept in secure accommodation, a case record is kept of:

- the name, date of birth and sex of the child;

- the care order or other statutory provision by virtue of which the child is in the community home and particulars of any other local authority involved;

- the date and time of placement and the name of the officer authorising placement;

- all of the persons informed of the placement;

- any court orders and directions with regard to the placement;

- all reviews in respect of the placement;

---

21 CA 1989, s 25(5).
22 *Oxfordshire County Council v R* [1992] 1 FLR 648.
23 *Re W (Secure Accommodation Order: Attendance at Court)* [1994] 2 FLR 1092.
24 *Re AS (Secure Accommodation Order)* [1999] 1 FLR 103.

- the date and time of any occasion on which the child is locked on his own in any room, other than his bedroom during usual bedtime hours, the name of the person authorising the action, the reason for it and the date on which and time at which the child ceased to be locked in that room;

- the date and time of discharge and the child's address following discharge.[25]

14.8 APPEAL

An appeal from the family proceedings court lies to the High Court against the grant or refusal to authorise a child being kept in secure accommodation.[26] An appeal from a county court or High Court lies to the Court of Appeal.

---

[25] C(SA)R 1991, reg 17, as amended by Children (Homes and Secure Accommodation) (Miscellaneous Amendments) Regulations 1996, reg 3.

[26] CA 1989, s 94(1).

CHAPTER 15

PLACEMENT AND ADOPTION

15.1 INTRODUCTION

- The law of adoption is governed by the Adoption and Children Act 2002, which was brought into effect substantially on 30 December 2005.

- Prior to this the governing statute was the Adoption Act 1976, which has some residual relevance for transitional purposes.

- The Adoption and Children Act 2002 not only governs adoption proceedings but regulates the duties of local authorities connected with adoption.

- The machinery of the Act promotes greater use of adoption and is intended also to improve the efficacy of the adoption service.

15.2 NOTABLE FEATURES AND NEW CONCEPTS OF THE ADOPTION AND CHILDREN ACT 2002

- **Terminology**
  The terminology of the Act echoes the Children Act 1989.

- **Welfare**
  The child's welfare, throughout his/her life, is the paramount consideration not only for the court but also for the Adoption Agency.

- **Checklist**
  The Act introduces a welfare checklist resonant with the checklist applicable under the Children Act 1989, but focused specifically upon issues relevant to adoption.

- **Emphasis**
  The act emphasises the importance of:

  – avoiding delay;

    –   considering the range of powers available; and

    –   only making an order if this is better for the child than no order.

- **What is governed by the Act?**

  The following are all governed by the Act. Its principles apply to any decisions relating to the adoption of a child, whether during proceedings or not.

      –   The Adoption Service.

      –   Adoption Agency placements and placement for adoption.

      –   Restrictions on removal of children.

      –   Those who may apply for adoption orders.

      –   Consent and dispensing with consent.

      –   Contact after placement and after adoption.

      –   Keeping and sharing of information.

      –   The Adoption and Children Act Register.

      –   Inter-country adoption.

- **Consent**

  As far as possible consent is dealt with before the child has been placed with the prospective new family (to reduce the uncertainty of the potential adopters and to *ensure* a fait accompli at the final hearing). One of the aims of the new provisions is to avoid delay in the making of decisions in the adoption process.[1]

- **Parental responsibility**

  In general terms the parent/guardian shares parental responsibility (PR) with the prospective adopters; the role of the local authority is to determine the extent of the PR of the parent/guardian as appropriate. Unlike under the former provisions, a parent does not lose PR on placement.

- **Special guardianship**

  The Act introduces the concept of special guardianship, a less drastic step than adoption.

- **Range of powers**

  The principles of the Act apply to any decision relating to the adoption of a child, whether during proceedings or not.

- **Advance consent**

  This enables a parent (who consents to placement by an adoption agency) concurrently or subsequently giving consent to the making of a future adoption order. Such advance consent:

---

[1]   See s 1(3).

- may be to adoption by the prospective adopters identified in the consent (but if the adoption breaks down, the validity of such consent lapses);
- may be to adoption by any prospective adopters who may be chosen by the agency.

• **Placement orders**
An order authorising placement for adoption will be required in every case where there is no parental consent, before placement may be made.

15.3 CONCEPTS CHANGED BY THE ADOPTION AND CHILDREN ACT 2002

• **Reasonableness no longer the criterion**
If parental consent is not, or has not been, given to the making of an adoption order, it may be dispensed with by the court. The basis for doing so is:

- that the parent or guardian cannot be found; or
- the child's welfare requires the consent to be dispensed with.

The reasonableness or otherwise of the withholding of consent is no longer an issue for the court. The child-centred approach under the new law is underpinned by the welfare checklist governing as it does the dispensing with consent as it applies to the making of an adoption order.

• **The role of the 'placement order' (as contrasted with the previous 'freeing order')**
Where a child has been freed pursuant to a care plan for adoption before the coming into force of the 2002 Act that order will remain valid. However, post the 2002 Act a care plan for adoption must express itself through application for a placement order under the 2002 Act.

• **Who can apply**

- Single people (as before);
- Same sex couples (need not have registered their partnership);
- Heterosexual couples (need not be married).

• **Restrictions on removal**
Under the 2002 Act there are detailed restrictions upon the removal of a child placed for adoption.

• **Adoptions with a foreign element**

The Act sets up a process for the approval of those wishing to adopt from overseas. By way of regulation, it creates criminal offences associated with the trafficking in children for adoption. It also creates a mechanism for the acquisition of parental responsibility by those wishing to remove a child from the jurisdiction for adoption abroad.[2]

15.4   RULES AND FORMS

The Act is supported by the Family Procedure Rules 2010 which incorporate all relevant practice directions and forms.

The wording of the overriding objective in the new FPR 2010, r 1.1 differs from that in the CPR. The wording is however, the same as that used in the Family Procedure (Adoption) Rules 2005 and that in the Public Law Outline (PLO), which has applied by Practice Direction from 2008.

In adoption procedure where there is already provision for the court to give Directions on receipt of applications and reports it will be important to utilise the flexibility imported under the new FPR 2010, r 1.4:

> '1.4 (1) The court **must** further the overriding objective by actively managing cases.
>
> (2) Active case management includes –
> (a)   encouraging the parties to co-operate with each other in the conduct of the proceedings;
> (b)   identifying at an early stage –
>   (i)   the issues; and
>   (ii)   who should be a party to the proceedings; ...'
> (emphasis added)

> '4.1 (3) Except where these rules provide otherwise, the court may –
>   ...
> (e)   hold a hearing and receive evidence by telephone or by using any other method of direct oral communication;
>   ...
> (o)   Take any other step or make any other order for the purpose of managing the case and furthering the overriding objective

The court may exercise its case management powers on an application or on its own initiative (r 4.3(1)).

Where the court proposes to make an order of its own initiative it may:

---

[2]   See ss 85, 86.

- give any person likely to be affected by the order, an opportunity to make representations by a specified time and in a specified manner (r 4.3(2)); or

- hold a hearing to decide whether to make the proposed order, having given at least 5 days' notice of the hearing to each party likely to be affected by the order (r 4.3(3)); or

- make such an order without hearing the parties or having given them an opportunity to make representations (r 4.3(4)).

Where an order has been made under FPR 2010, r 4.3(4):

- a party affected by the order may apply to have it set aside, varied, or stayed; and

- the order must contain a statement of the right to make such an application and within any period specified by the court. (If not specified, the period is within 7 days of the date of service of the order on the party making the application).

15.5 ADOPTION/PLACEMENT ORDER: PROCEDURAL TABLE

Type of order applied for
Adoption order (s 46)
Note: Effect of such an order is—
• extinguishes PR of birth parents;
• gives PR to adopters;
• any existing Children Act orders extinguished;
• any agreement or order for maintenance ceases to have effect;
• order in favour of parent's partner does not affect the parent's PR;
• adopted person is treated in law as if born to the adopters;
• an adopted person is the legitimate child of the adopters (thus becoming legally related to the adopters' family save by reference to some of the prohibited degrees); ➡

- as to peerages and inheritance, see s 71;

- once adopted, the person is recorded on the Adopted Children Register (enabling such person if he/she wishes to trace back to the birth family);

- adoption gives the child the same nationality as the adopters.

Note as to Adoption Contact Register—

- a potential route for birth family members to make links with an adopted person;

- enables an adopted person to establish if there is an expression of interest in contact from the birth family.

Note as to age of child to be adopted—

- must be under age of 18 year at the time the application is made (s 49(4));

- an order may be made up to the 19th birthday (s 47(9)).

Who is the applicant?

The prospective adopters

- a couple (s 50); or

- one person (s 51).
  (NB age and domicile/habitual residence qualifications ss 49–51.)

Notes as to applicant's age—

- an application may be made by a couple when both are 21 years or over (s 50);

- one is the mother or father of child to be adopted and is 18 years or over and the other is 21 years or over;

- an application may be made by one person who is 21 years or over and is not married (s 51); or

- by a person who is 21 years or over if they are the partner of the parent of the child to be adopted;   ➡

There are various saving provisions for those separated from spouses etc.

Note as to domicile and habitual residence—

- At least one adopter must be domiciled in the British Isles; or

- have been habitually resident in part of the British Isles for at least a year ending with date of application.

What is a couple?

- A couple means a married couple, two people who are civil partners of each others, or two people whether of different or the same sex living as parents in an enduring family relationship (s 144(4));

Who is/are the respondents?

- Each parent with PR or guardian of the child unless they have given notice that they do not wish to be informed of any application for an adoption order.

- Any person in whose favour there is provision for contact.

- Any adoption agency with PR for the child (see ss 19, 25, 46).

- Any adoption agency which has, at any stage, taken part in the arrangements for the adoption of the child.

- Any local authority to whom notice of intention to adopt (s 44) has been given.

- Any local authority or voluntary organisation which has PR for, is looking after, or is caring for the child (eg a local authority with a care order in respect of the child).

- The child where permission (leave) has been granted to a parent or guardian to oppose the making of an adoption order (s 47(3) and (5)):

  - s/he opposes the making of an adoption order;
  - a children and family reporter recommends that it is in the best interests of the child for the child to be a party to the proceedings and the court accepts the recommendation;
  - the child is already an adopted child;

- any party to the proceedings or the child is opposed to the arrangements for allowing any person contact with the child, or a person not being allowed contact with the child after the making of the adoption order;
- the prospective adopters are relatives of the child.

Type of order applied for

Placement order (s 21)

Note effect of a placement order—

- A child may only be placed with prospective adopters or left with care who have become prospective adopters if either a parent has given consent under s 19 or the local authority has obtained a placement order.

- Children who are subject to a placement order remain LAC ('looked after children').

Who is the applicant?

A local authority (s 22)

Note as to duty to apply for a placement order—once the LA reaches the view that a child ought to be placed for adoption, a duty arises to apply for a placement order if either: (i) the child is the subject of ongoing care proceedings; or (ii) the child is the subject to a final care order and there is no consent to placement for adoption under section 19.

Discretion to apply—if a final care order has been made and consent to placement for adoption has been given under s 19, the local authority has discretion to apply for a placement order.

Who is/are the respondents?

- Each parent who has parental responsibility or guardian of the child;

- Any person in whose favour an order under the Children Act 1989 is in force;

- Any adoption agency or voluntary organisation who has parental responsibility for, is looking after, or is caring for, the child; ➡

- The parties or any persons who have been parties to proceedings for a care order in respect of the child where those proceedings have led to the application for the placement order.

Type of order applied for

Order varying a placement order (s 23)

Who is the applicant?

Joint application by the local authority authorised by the placement order to place the child for adoption and the local authority which is to be substituted for it (s 23).

Who is/are the respondents?

The parties to the proceedings which led to the placement order which is the subject of the variation application (**except the child**).

Type of order applied for

Order revoking a placement order (s 24)

Who is the applicant?

- The child.

- The local authority authorised to place the child for adoption.

- Where the child is not placed for adoption by the local authority, any other person with the permission of the court to apply (s 23).

Who is/are the respondents?

- The parties to the proceedings which led to the placement order which is the subject of the revocation application.

- Any person in whose favour there is a provision for contact.

(See separate sections for contact (s 26) and adoptions with a foreign element.)

15.6   APPLICATION FOR CONTACT: PROCEDURAL TABLE

Type of order applied for

Contact (ACA 2002, s 26)

When no contact application can be made under CA 1989, s 8 or 34?

During the time when an adoption agency is authorised to place a child for adoption or a child is so placed.

When does a contact order under CA 1989 cease to have effect?

- On adoption agency being authorised to place a child for adoption; or

- placing a child under 6 weeks old for adoption.

After that, application for contact only under ACA 2002, s 26.

What orders can court make under ACA 2002, s 26 (s 26(2)(b))?

- Requiring the person with whom the child lives, or is to live, to allow the child to visit or stay with the person named in the order; or

- for the person named in the order and the child otherwise to have contact with each other.

(Such orders may provide for contact on any conditions appropriate: s 27(5).)

Can parent still apply for contact?

Yes, under CA 1989, s 8 – if appropriate, at the final adoption hearing (s 26(5)).

Who is/are the applicants?

- The *child* or the agency.

- Any *parent/guardian/relative* (for definition of 'relative' see ACA 2002, s 144).

- Any person in whose favour there was provision for *contact under CA 1989* which ceased to have effect on the adoption➡

agency being authorised to place the child for adoption (or placing the child if the child is under 6 weeks old).

- If a *residence order* was in force immediately before the adoption agency was authorised to place the child for adoption (or placed a child under 6 weeks of age), the person in whose favour the residence order was made.

- Any person who, immediately before the adoption agency was authorised to place the child (or placed the child if under 6 weeks old), had *care of the child* by virtue of an order made under the inherent jurisdiction of the High court.

- Any person who has obtained the *leave of the court* to make a contact application.

NB – when making a placement order the court may on its own initiative make a contact order (s 26(4)).

Who is/are the respondents?

- The *adoption agency* authorised to place, or who has placed the child, for adoption.

- The person with whom the child lives.

- Each parent with parental responsibility.

- A guardian of the child.

- A child as defined in FPR 2010, Pt 14, ie—

    (a) the agency authorised to place the child or who has placed the child or a parent with PR *opposes* the making of the order under s 26;
    (b) the child *opposes* the making of a contact order;
    (c) existing provision for contact is to be *revoked;*
    (d) *relatives* of the child *do not agree* to the arrangements for allowing/not allowing any person to have contact with the child;
    (e) the child is suffering/at *risk* of suffering *harm* within the meaning of CA 1989.

Type of order applied for

Application to revoke a contact order (s 27(1)(b)) ➡

- The adoption agency *may refuse to allow contact* which would otherwise be required by virtue of an order under s 26 if it is satisfied that it is necessary to do so in order to safeguard or promote the child's welfare *and* the refusal is decided as a matter of urgency and does not last for more than 7 days.

Who is/are the applicants?

- The child.

- The agency.

- Any person named in the order.

Note—

(i)   A birth parent does not have any status to apply to revoke/vary an order unless they are named in the order.

(ii)   Before making a placement order the court must consider the arrangements which the adoption agency has made or proposes to make for allowing any person contact with the child and invite the parties to the proceedings to comment on those arrangements (s 27(4)(a)).

Who is/are the respondents?

- The parties to the proceedings leading to the contact order which it is sought to have varied/revoked.

- Any person named in the contact order.

15.7   THE PROCESS OF ADOPTION

This table shows the steps to be taken in an adoption application from beginning to end, including steps necessary before the issue of proceedings.

**The Process of
Adoption**

For proceedings with
no foreign element

Day 1   Child arrives in
                                   placement

Either placed by an
adoption agency or as a
result of a private
agreement

Waiting period

Residence requirement
applies unless the court
gives leave. Duration
varies depending upon
type of placement.

Child placed by local authority with a placement order or adoption agency with parental consent.	Agency placement High Court order Applicant (or one applicant) is parent	10 weeks
	Applicant is partner of parent	6 months
	Local authority foster parent(s)	one year
	Other applicants	3 out of last 5 years

Notice

Must be given unless
child was placed by an
adoption agency

When

Must be given not more than 2 years and at least 3 months before the application for the adoption order is made. This could be in the last 3 months of the waiting period.

How

May be given by post and must be in writing. There is no prescribed form.

To whom

Notice must be given to the appropriate local authority. This will usually be the authority for the area in which the applicants have their home. The precise recipient is not specified: it is suggested that notice is sent to the Assistant Director of Social Services with a copy served upon the local authority's legal department. If the applicants do not have a home in England or Wales the relevant local authority is prescribed by the Local Authority (Adoption) (Miscellaneous Provisions) Regulations 2005, SI 2005/3390 ie the last local authority in which they lived.

Notice is not required in the case of an agency placement because the local authority will already be aware of the placement.

The Family Procedure Rules 2010and FPR Practice Directions contain the procedure for dealing with applications in adoption placement and related proceedings, the most significant of which other proceedings will of course be in relation to contact in this context.

Confidentiality by way of serial number is imposed, and it will be important for lawyers to establish internal procedures to ensure that their use of serial numbers is established in office procedures also.

Part 14 of the FPR deals with procedure for applications, and FPR Practice Directions 14A to 14F deal with the following:

14A   Who receives a copy of the application form.

14B   First directions for foreign element adoptions.

14C   This PD is very detailed and requires careful consideration to ensure that reports filed deal adequately with all required matters. There is no doubt that in drafting these practice directions an attempt has been made to ensure that specific answers are given particular to the child and not formulaic responses. There is more emphasis on gauging the parties' positions on important issues and also in establishing an account of dealings of the agencies and parties with each other up to this point.

14D   Health reports.

14E   Communication of information relating to proceedings.

14F   Disclosing information to an adopted adult.

ROUTES TO ADOPTION

Care proceedings
Before taking care proceedings a local authority is likely to have worked with a family to try to improve the home situation.

- There may have been a child protection plan [*or children's names may have been entered on the child protection register*] with regular reviews to assess progress towards identified goals of improvement.

- Alternatively, the local authority may have become involved with a family on an emergency basis and have applied originally for an emergency protection order or

- Had the case referred by the police following the making of a police protection order.

CARE PROCEEDINGS

Local authority forms plan for adoption

Placement order application

Threshold criteria satisfied

Welfare checklist (s 1(3), CA 1989) applied

- **Non-care proceedings**
A parent may give their child to the adoption agency for the purposes of adoption.

- Once the child is at least 6 weeks old, a parent with parental responsibility may consent to the placement of the child for adoption (s 19) and to the child's future adoption (s 20).

- The giving of consent limits the parent's subsequent ability to oppose the making of an adoption order.

RELINQUISHED CHILD

Parent/s with PR consent to adoption

↓

Adoption application

↓

ADOPTION ORDER

↓

| care plan for adoption approved | care plan for adoption not approved/plan is not for adoption | | |

↓   ↓

| Care order Placement order | court is not satisfied that adoption will promote child's welfare throughout his/her life, but local authority requires parental responsibility | long term carers require parental responsibility 'with teeth' | long term carers need parental responsibility, can work with parents |

if either: ↓   ↓   ↓

(a) parent has given consent s 19, or

| | CARE ORDER (long term foster care) | SPECIAL GUARDI- ANSHIP ORDER | RESIDENCE ORDER |

(b) there is no parent or guardian, or

(c) consent should be dispensed with (welfare)

↓

Child placed with prospective adopters who observe the minimum waiting period

(suitability assessment can be before or after application)

↓

ADOPTION APPLICATION

↓

ADOPTION ORDER

15.8 CHECKLISTS

15.8.1   Consent – general, to be completed in any case

(1) **Has consent been given?**
    If yes, give full details (note that the consent will be by a 'parent' or 'guardian' which includes a 'statutory guardian'). Such a 'parent' includes:

    (a)   birth mother;
    (b)   birth father, where he is married to the child's mother at the time of the child's birth or if he subsequently marries the mother;
    (c)   an unmarried father if:

        (i)   he becomes registered as the child's father under the Births and Deaths Registration Act 1953 (*and the child is born after December 2003* – ACA 2002, s 111); or
        (ii) he makes a parental responsibility agreement with the child's mother; or
        (iii) he is granted a parental responsibility order by the court;
    (d)   the child's adoptive parent, where the child has been the subject of a previous adoption.

(2) **If yes, was it given with full understanding of what is involved?**

(3) **As to consent given or withdrawn by a parent or guardian:**

    (a)   Did the parent have PR? (PR is a precondition to a parent giving a valid consent; see s 52(6).)
    (b)   Was consent given when the child was less than six weeks old?
    (c)   Was any consent to the placement of a child for adoption given after an application for an adoption order was made?
    (d)   Was any consent for '*Placing child with parental consent*' (s 19) or for '*Advance consent to adoption*' (s 20) given in the form prescribed by the rules?
    (e)   Was any consent to 'placing child with parental consent' or 'Advance consent to adoption' withdrawn? If yes:

        (i)   was it in the form prescribed by the rules; or
        (ii) by notice given to an agency?

Note (1): There is no need for the person giving consent to know the identity of the persons in whose favour the order will be made (s 52(5)).

Note (2): The following procedure—

(a) Consent to child being placed for adoption (s 19): Form A100.

(b)   Consent to the making of a future adoption order: Form A103.

Note (3): The residence requirement for agency placement is 10 weeks.[3] After that time, it is open to make an adoption application, which once made precludes parental opposition to the making of an adoption order without the court's leave (ss 47(3) and (5)).

15.8.2   Advance consent to adoption

(1)   **Has parent or guardian of the child given the following consent?**

(a)   Consented to the child being placed for adoption by an adoption agency under s 19?

(b)   Consented (at the same or any subsequent time) to the making of a future adoption order?

If the answer to 'a' or 'b' is 'yes' give full particulars of precisely who gave the consent, how it was given (it must be by the prescribed Form to comply with the rules), where and upon whom it was served?

(2)   **In relation to any consent, have any prospective adopters been identified?**

If yes, who are they giving full particulars?

(3)   **Has any consent been withdrawn?**

If yes –

(a)   By whom?

(b)   Notified to whom?

(c)   When?

(d)   How (identifying any document)?

(4)   **Has any parent or guardian by notice to the adoption agency:**

(a)   stated that he/she does not wish to be informed of any application for an adoption order; or

(b)   withdrawn such a statement?

If yes, when was such statement made or withdrawn, by whom, on what date, upon whom was it served and when?

Note: A parent or guardian who has given consent to adoption cannot oppose the making of an adoption order (once applied for) without the court's leave: ss 47(3) and (5). A pre-condition to leave is a change in circumstances: s 47(7).[4]

---

3   See flowchart at **15.7** and s 42(2).

4   *Re P (Adoption Leave Provisions)* [2007] 2 FLR 1069.

15.8.3 Dispensing with consent to a child being placed for adoption or to the making of an adoption order – no foreign element (s 52(1))

(1) *Pre-conditions:*

In order to dispense with consent for placement for adoption there are two alternative grounds:

    (a)   the parent or guardian cannot be found or is incapable of giving consent;[5] or

    (b)   the welfare of the child requires consent to be dispensed with.[6]

(2) *Statement of facts checklist:*

    (a)   What is the procedural history of the case?

    (b)   If it is contended that a parent or guardian cannot be found, what efforts have been made to find them eg via Inland Revenue, DWP, electoral roll? The court must be given sufficient facts to be satisfied.

    (c)   If it is contended that the parent or guardian is incapable of giving consent, what is the evidence eg medical psychological or psychiatric report? The court must be given sufficient facts to be satisfied.

    (d)   If it is contended that the welfare of the child *requires* the consent to be dispensed with, explain in detail why by reference to the welfare check-list; note that s 1(1)(c) and 1(1)(f) must be carefully covered (so court can balance child's rights against birth family under Art 8). Note the word 'requires.' The issue here is not whether it meets the child's 'welfare' to adopt, but whether welfare is so central and immediate as to 'require' consent to be dispensed with.

    (e)   Do not disclose the name of the applicant if a serial number has been assigned.

(3) *Procedure checklist* (r 27, Pt 5):

    (a)   Give notice of the request to dispense with consent, either in the application form or at any later stage, by filing a written request setting out the reasons for the request.

    (b)   File a statement of facts containing the information covered in the checklist above.

    (c)   On receipt of the notice of the request a court officer will:

---

[5]   *Re R (Adoption)* [1967] 1 WLR 34 per Buckley J; and *Re A (Adoption of a Russian Child)* [2000] 1 FLR 539.

[6]   As to the meaning of the word "requires" see *Re P (Placement Orders: Parental Consent)* [2008] EWCA Civ 535 and also *SB v A County Council; Re P* [2008] EWCA Civ 535; Case Digest at **18.3**.

(i)   inform the parent or guardian of the request;

(ii) send a copy of the statement of facts to the parent or guardian, to any children's guardian, to any reporting officer or children and family reporter, to any local authority to whom a notice of intention to adopt has been given or a notice as to parental responsibility prior to adoption abroad.

(d) If the applicant considers that the parent or guardian is incapable of giving consent, the court will consider whether to:

(i)   appoint a litigation friend for the parent or guardian (r 55(1)); or

(ii) give directions for an application to be made under r 55(3), unless a litigation friend is already appointed for that parent or guardian.

(e) Giving of consent:

(i)   *must* be in the form required by the relevant Practice Direction or a form to the like effect, if s 19 (placing) or s 20 (future adoption);

(ii) *may* be given in such form if it is to the making of an adoption order or to the giving of parental responsibility prior to adoption abroad (ACA 2002, s 84).

15.8.4 Placement orders

(1) Is the child subject to a care order?

(2) Is the court satisfied that the threshold criteria (CA 1989, s 31(2)) are met?

(3) Is it the position that the child does not have a parent or guardian?

(4) In the case of each parent or guardian:

(a) Is there the relevant consent which has not been withdrawn?

(b) If no relevant consent – should consent be dispensed with?

Note (1): The court has no jurisdiction to make a placement order unless the answer to *any* of the above question is 'yes'.

Note (2): The inter-action of ss 19 and 21 – a child can only be placed for adoption if there is:

(a) parental consent; or

(b) a placement order.

Note (3): Only local authorities have the jurisdiction to apply for a placement order.

Note (4): 'Placing a child for adoption by an adoption agency' is defined in s 18(5) as including placing a child with prospective adopters.

Note (5): If the adoption agency is a local authority and the child is subject to a care order, the local authority may apply for a placement order.

Note (6): An adoption agency may place a child who is less than 6 weeks' old for adoption ('baby placement') with the voluntary agreement of the parents. The baby is not placed under s 19 or under a placement order during the first 6 weeks: the placement regime does not apply. When the child attains the age of 6 weeks, if adoption continues to be the plan, the agency must obtain the consent of the parents or, if a local authority, a placement order.

Note (7): A care order is suspended when a placement order is in force (s 29(1)).

Note (8): On the making of a placement order, any s 8 (CA 1989) order and any supervision order ceases to have effect.

Note (9): The court has no jurisdiction to make any of the following orders when a placement order is in force: CA 1989, s 8 (residence, contact, specific issue, prohibited steps), s 34(4) contact, supervision or child assessment order; s 29(3).

Note (10): No jurisdiction to make a special guardianship order if a placement order is in force. As to an application for special guardianship at the final adoption hearing, see s 29(5).

Note (11): Section 24 provides—

(a)   A placement order remains in force until revoked or the child reaches the age of 18 or marries.

(b)   An application to revoke can be made without leave:

      (i)   by the child;
      (ii)   by the relevant local authority;

(c)   An application to revoke can be made by a relative or any other person only with leave[7] and where the child is not placed by the authority for adoption.

---

[7]   See *Re F (Placement Order)* [2008] EWCA Civ 439 and also *S-H v Kingston-Upon-Hull City Council* [2008] EWCA Civ 493, [2008] Fam Law 716; Case Digest at **18.3**.

(d)   Where an application for the revocation for a placement order has been made and has not been disposed of, and the child is not placed for adoption by the authority, the child may not without the court's leave be placed for adoption under the placement order: s 24(5) (*Re F (A Child) sub nom C v East Sussex CC* [2008] EWCA Civ 439 CA (Civ Div)).

Note (12): Section 25 governs parental responsibility. In the following circumstances it is shared by the local authority, the birth parents and (where placed with them) the prospective adopters:

(i)   placement by consent;

(ii)   authorising for placement by consent;

(iii) a placement order is in force.

The local authority can control the extent of the PR of birth parents and prospective adopters; s 25(4) and in so doing, it must take into account the welfare checklist, Art 8 and proportionality.

Note (13): Where a placement order is in force no SGO can be made unless:

(a)   an application has been made for an adoption order; and

(b)   the person applying for the SGO has obtained the court's leave under this subsection or, if he is a guardian of the child, has obtained the court's leave under s 47(5).

15.8.5   Placing children with parental consent

(1)   Has a parent or guardian:

    (a)   Consented to the child:

        (i)   being placed for adoption with prospective adopters identified in the consent; or
        (ii)   being placed for adoption with any prospective adopters who may be chosen by the agency?

    (b)   If yes, has such consent been withdrawn (NB such consent can only be withdrawn in the form prescribed by the rules or by notice given to the agency).
        If the answer to (a) or (b) above is 'yes' give full particulars including:

-   any form of consent (give details);
-   date of consent?

- upon whom consent has been served?
- the names of prospective adopters?
- the identity of the agency, with full address and contact details;
- in the event of any consent being withdrawn, full details of when, how, by whom and upon whom served.

(2) Has an application been made on which a care order might be made and the application has not been disposed of?

(3) Has a care order or a placement order been made after the consent was given?

Note (1): Section 19(2) permits a consent which both identifies the foster parents and also provides consent to a subsequent placement with any prospective adopters chosen by the agency.

Note (2): As to withdrawing consent – see ss 19(1) and (4), 52(1), 31, 47(5) and (7).

Note (3): An adoption agency is authorised to place the child for adoption if there is a valid continuing consent. But if the answer to either question 2 or question 3 above is 'yes' the route which the local authority must take is via s 22(2).

Note (4): Where under s 19 a child is placed for adoption or an adoption agency is authorised to place a child for adoption:

(a) a parent or guardian cannot apply for a residence order unless an application for an adoption order has been made or the parent or guardian has obtained the court's leave under s 47(3) or (5);

(b) if an application has been made for an adoption order, a guardian of the child may not apply for a special guardianship order unless he has obtained the court's leave under s 47(3) or (5) (see s 28(1)).

See also s 28.

15.8.6 Local authority application for placement orders

(1) *Mandatory application* – Are the following conditions satisfied:

(a) Is the child voluntarily placed for adoption by a local authority or is it being provided with accommodation by a local authority?

(b) There is no adoption agency with authority to place the child for adoption?

(c) The child has no parent or guardian or the local authority considers that the conditions in s 31(2) of the CA 1989 are not met?

(d) The local authority are satisfied that the child ought to be placed for adoption? (to be Convention compliant, the local authority must have properly considered the alternative options).

(e) No-one has given notice of intention to adopt (or any such notice has expired after 4 months or such application has been withdrawn or refused)?

(f) No application for an adoption order has been made which has yet to be disposed of?

If these conditions are satisfied, the local authority *must* apply to the court for a placement order.

(2) *Mandatory application* – Are the following conditions satisfied:

(a) an application has been made (and has not been disposed of) on which a care order might be made in respect of a child; or

(b) a child is subject to a care order and the local authority are not authorised to place the child for adoption; and

(c) no-one has given notice of intention to adopt (or any such notice has expired after 4 months or such application has been withdrawn or refused); and

(d) no application for an adoption order has been made which has yet to be disposed of; and

(e) the relevant local authority is satisfied that the child ought to be placed for adoption?

If these conditions are satisfied, the local authority *must* apply for a placement order.

(3) *Discretionary application* – A local authority *may* apply for a placement order if the following conditions are satisfied:

(a) the child is subject to a care order; and

(b) the local authority are authorised to place the child for adoption (s 19); and

(c) no-one has given notice of intention to adopt (or any such notice has expired after 4 months or such application has been withdrawn or refused)?

(d) no application for an adoption order has been made which has yet to be disposed of.

15.8.7 Directions on local authority application for placement orders

(1) Has an application for a placement order been made? If yes:

(a) Has it been disposed of?

(b) If no, is there an interim care order in force?

(c) If no, the court may give any directions it considers appropriate for the medical or psychiatric examination or other assessment of the child; but a child who is of sufficient understanding to make an informed decision may refuse to submit to the examination or other assessment (CA 1989, s 38(6) and s 43(8)).

(2) Consent is no longer valid if a care or placement order or an application for one has been made since consent was given (s 19(3)).

15.9 APPLICATION FORMS: REQUIRED INFORMATION

The solicitor will be required to supply the detailed information referred to in the Family Procedure Rules about the legal background to the application, the applicant, local authority, the child, relatives, contact, proposed orders, together with matters that the court requires to know about orders sought, confidentiality issues, or special measures for hearing, and other relevant factors for the proceedings and process.

15.10 ADOPTION: FINAL HEARING

15.10.1 Introduction

• At the final hearing for the adoption order, the court has a range of options (see 'Court's options' at **15.10.2**).

• When considering such options, the court must weigh up and balance each of the options: the duty of the court is to provide a level of security proportionate to the assessed need. Thus an 'adoption order' can only be made if the other options are not sufficient to provide the security which (under the welfare checklist) the child requires.

• When weighing up each of such options, the court has to the forefront of its mind the range of powers (see 'Court's range of powers' at **15.10.3**).

• To achieve the relevant balancing process, the statements of the parties must address these issues clearly and succinctly.

• By way of example, the approach of a local authority may be:

(a) We have considered rehabilitation with birth parents, but discount that for the following reasons on the basis of the following evidence: (*then cite the evidence in the particular case in respect of the parents*).

(b)   And we have considered placement with family members but discount that for the following reasons: (*and cite evidence*) until coming to adoption (*which then must be supported with evidence and positive reasons as to why that is the only course of action which can be taken to secure the relevant level of security and welfare*).

Note: Twin track and concurrent planning continue under the new regime.

- The court can only undertake this comprehensive exercise if the material relevant to the exercise of its discretion is before it, in focused succinct statements. Those statements must be informed by a focus upon the statutory criteria relevant to the child's 'welfare,' (see 'Welfare' at **15.10.4**).

- The court's options, the range of its powers and the 'welfare' issues are the corner stone of any final adoption hearing. All the rules, practice directions and procedures are nothing more than the means to achieve an orderly process to the final hearing without unreasonable delay (see 'Delay' at **15.10.5**).

- Adoption is conditional upon consent; see s 47(2) of the ACA 2002. There are three aspects:

  – consent;
  – advance consent;
  – dispensing with consent.

- Consent – when?

  – in an agency case, the issue of consent arises prior to placement;
  – in a non-agency case, the prospective adopters will apply (if necessary) within the adoption application to dispense with parental consent.

15.10.2   Court's options

- Rehabilitation with birth parent(s).

- Residence with step-parent/extended family/friends/local authority; foster-parent (residence requirement reduced to one year).

- Fostering.

- Special guardianship.

- Adoption. And if no adoption, as to the placement order:

(a)   revoke it; or

(b)   order placement to continue if it decides that the child should still be placed for a future adoption.

15.10.3 Court's range of powers

- Residence order.

- Supervision order.

- Care order.

- Special guardianship order.

- Adoption.

Note: Section 1(6) – The court or adoption agency must always consider the whole range of powers available to it in a child's case. The court must not make any order under ACA 2002 unless it considers that making the order would be better for the child than not doing so.

15.10.4 Welfare

- Child's wishes and feelings (subject to age and understanding, particularly in the context of older children)?

- Child's needs:

  (a) Emotional?
  (b) Educational (special needs?)?
  (c) Religious persuasion?*
  (d) Racial origin?*
  (e) Cultural background?*
  (f) Linguistic background?*
  (g) Social?
  (h) Moral?
  (i) Psychological?
  (j) Health (physical disability)?

- Effect throughout life of the following:

  (a) Ceasing to be a member of original family – consider:

      (i)   Loss of PR?
      (ii) Loss of inheritance?
      (iii) Beneficiary under insurance policy?
      (iv) Nationality?
      (v) Any right of abode?

      (vi) Loss/sense of loss/sense of abandonment of family identity (with birth/extended family)?

  (b) Becoming an adopted person – the check list as above.

- Child's characteristics – consider:

  (a) Age.
  (b) Sex.
  (c) Background (including cultural, racial origin, linguistic etc).
  (d) Any particular characteristics.

- Harm:

  (a) What harm has the child suffered (eg witness to domestic violence)?
  (b) What harm is the child at risk of suffering?

- Relationship with relatives and other persons?

  (a) Who (including siblings), giving name, address, and hard evidence-based fact as to the nature of the relationship.
  (b) Likelihood of such relationship continuing and the value to the child of it doing so, giving hard evidence-based fact including the wishes and feelings of such persons.
  (c) Ability/willingness of such persons to provide child with a secure environment in which the child can develop and otherwise meet the child's needs, giving evidence-based fact.

Note:

(1) The criteria under the welfare checklist and conditions for dispensing with consent compensate for the right reasonably to withhold consent.

(2) Also note the 'least interventionist' approach, s 1(6).

(3) The Asterisk (*) indicates those matters to which the adoption agency must give due consideration, s 1(6).

15.10.5 Delay

- Has the court drawn up a time-table?[8]

- National Adoption Standard:

---

[8]   ACA 2002, s 109(1).

    (a) Has a plan for permanence been made at the local authority's 4-monthly review?

    (b) Has a decision been made on prospective adopters within 6 months of the application?

•   Has the Adoption and Children Act Register been consulted?

Note: ACA 2002, s 1(3) – 'The court or adoption agency must at all times bear in mind that, in general, *any* delay in coming to the decision is likely to prejudice the child's welfare.'

15.11   CASE DIGEST: ADOPTION, PLACEMENT ORDERS AND SPECIAL GUARDIANS

15.11.1   Dispensing with consent and contact orders

Birmingham City Council v P and Seven Others [2007] EWHC 3031 (Fam)

The applicant local authority made two applications for final care orders and placement orders in respect of the third to seventh respondent children. The children concerned were aged from only a few days to 7 years old. The parents of all five children were the first respondent mother (M) and the second respondent father (F). M had married F in Pakistan when she was 13 years old and had the eldest child when she was 15 years old. The local authority had become involved with the family after one of the children was admitted to hospital with extensive non-accidental injuries. The four older children were then placed in foster care, although some of them subsequently went to live with the eighth respondent paternal grandmother (G). A fact finding hearing then took place, and the court found that the children had been physically abused by M on a regular basis, and that F and the family were aware of that. The court concluded that none of the children could be brought up by M and F or their families. F asked for the return of the children, or alternatively that they be placed with family members, or finally, as adoption was an alien concept, that they should be fostered with Sunni Muslims. G sought special guardianship or residence orders in her favour. Together with M and F, she wanted ongoing contact with the children were they to be fostered or adopted.

Held:

Under the Adoption and Children Act 2002, local authorities were under a duty to apply for a placement order where a child was subject to a care order and it was satisfied that the child ought to be placed for adoption, pursuant to s 22(2) of the Act. The court could not make a placement order unless the parent had consented or the parent's consent should be dispensed with under s 21 of the Act. Pursuant to s 52(1)(b) of the Act, the only ground for dispensing with parental consent was that the welfare of the child required it. In the instant case, the children were at risk of significant harm, both physical and emotional, if they were returned to M and F, and no family members could provide sufficient care for them. The welfare of the children would properly be met by adoption and required that consent to their adoption by M and F should be dispensed with. It would not be appropriate to make an order under s 26 of the Act allowing for contact with M and F. Although between the children themselves the need for a s 26 order was stronger, it was in their best interests that such an order should not be made. The children would be made subject to final care orders and placement orders without delay.

15.11.2 Placement order

Re G [2007] EWCA Civ 395

Placement order overturned as the judge failed to evaluate the degree, seriousness and immediacy of risk of emotional or physical harm. It was agreed that the risks would only occur if the parents separated and mother reacted badly. Case remitted for re-hearing.

15.11.3 Assessment of relatives

Re B & G [2007] EWCA Civ 358

Judge entitled to refuse late application by foster sister as potential carer; she was too late in coming forward and evidence suggested would be unsuitable.

15.11.4 Child's welfare: telling relatives and father would cause unwarranted delay

Re C (A Child) v (1) XYZ County Council (2) EC [2007] EWCA Civ 1206, (2007) The Times, 5 December

The appellant mother (M) appealed against the decision of a judge directing the first respondent local authority to disclose the existence and identity of her baby (E) to the extended maternal family and, if he could be identified, the putative father and any extended paternal family, against M's wishes. M gave birth to E when she was 19 years old and unmarried. E was conceived following a one-night stand with the father with whom M had no other relationship. M had kept her pregnancy a secret from her family and immediately after E was born, M made it clear that she wanted E placed for adoption. She declined to identify E's father. At the time of the hearing E was 4 months old and had begun to form bonds with her foster carers who had collected her from hospital after her birth. The local authority applied for a care order under the Children Act 1989. The local authority then applied to the court for guidance on whether extended family members should be approached with a view to finding a home for E within her family against M's consent. The judge directed the local authority to disclose the existence and identity of E to the extended maternal family and, if he could be identified, the putative father and any extended paternal family, on the basis that E should know about her parentage.

Held:

(1) The local authority's application should have been made under the Adoption and Children Act 2002. The 2002 Act did not impose a duty on the local authority to make such enquiries. When a decision was required to be made about the long-term care of a child, whom a mother wished to be adopted, there was no duty to make enquiries which it was not in the interests of the child to make.

(2) Such an interpretation did not violate the father's right to family life under the European Convention on Human Rights 1950, Art 8 because he had no family life with E. It was not a violation of a Convention right to deprive him of the possibility of obtaining a right to respect for family life with E. He therefore had no Convention right under Art 8.

15.11.5 Child's welfare: duty to tell paternal relatives so they could be assessed as carers

Birmingham City Council v (1) S (2) R (3) A (A Child by her Guardian) [2006] EWHC 3065 (Fam), [2007] 1 FLR 1223, [2007] UKHRR 588

Order sought in care proceedings that the parties to the proceedings should not inform the paternal grandparents of a child (X) that X existed. X's mother (S) and her father (R) were together for 2 years but had never cohabited or married. After X was born their relationship ended, but R had regular contact with X. Because of S's previous parenting difficulties and non-accidental injuries suffered by her children from a former marriage, the local authority had issued care proceedings in respect of X soon after her birth. The assessment of S's parenting skills was ongoing but there was a possibility that X would be freed for adoption, which R did not oppose. R lived with his parents, who were devout Muslims. He had not told them about his relationship with S or X's birth. R had previously told X's guardian that if S was unable to care for X, then his own mother might wish to come forward to do so but by time of the instant hearing R stated that if his family learned about X, they would not accept her because of S's background as a prostitute and they would throw him out of their house. The disclosure would cause difficulties for him and his family within the Muslim community.

Held:

The duration of the relationship between R and S, together with their continued friendship and R's good and developing contact with X, indicated that there was family life for the purposes of the Human Rights Act 1998, Sch 1, Pt I, Art 8. R's Art 8 rights were opposed to those of X. Based on principles established in cases concerning mothers who sought to have their child adopted without notifying the father of the child's existence, the court had jurisdiction to grant or to refuse R's application, *Re R (A Child) (Adoption: Duty to Investigate)* [2001] 1 FLR 365 and *Re H (A Child) (Adoption: Consultation of Unmarried Fathers)* [2001] 1 FLR 646 considered. But the matter had to be determined on the facts and there was no evidentially sound basis to conclude that R's parents would reject X. R's change of approach about his parents' likely reaction to the news of X's existence was not convincing and was driven substantially by the upset he feared he would create rather than a genuine appraisal of whether his mother might wish to care for X. Adoption was a last resort for any child and to deprive a significant member of the wider family of the information that a child existed who might otherwise be adopted was a fundamental step that could only be justified on cogent and compelling grounds. There were no such grounds in the instant case. Balancing the Art 8 rights of R and X required that the order sought by R should not be made.

15.11.6 Welfare: assessment of family members

Re A (A Child) (Care Order) [2006] Lawtel, 19 October

The father (F) appealed against a care order in respect of his son (B) in the terms sought by the first respondent local authority. The local authority had brought public law proceedings in respect of three children, including B, for whom a care order with a view to adoption was sought. The application was supported by the guardian. Reports suggested that F, a Turkish national, lacked the potential to care for B himself. F contended that B could be cared for by his sister and his extended family in their village near Istanbul. The guardian consequently visited the family home in Turkey. Following a 6-hour visit the guardian compiled a report raising concerns over, inter alia, the poverty of the village. The judge rejected F's proposal and made the care order. F contended that where the guardian's impression had been formed over such a brief visit the judge ought not to have made the order he had.

Held:

In the circumstances the judge's decision was beyond the bounds of the wide ambit of his discretion in closing down the possibility of care for B within his Turkish family on the basis of a 6-hour visit. The order would, accordingly, be set aside and replaced by an interim care order, and the matter would be remitted so that a fresh case might be prepared and investigated, which would require the involvement of international social services to deliver a report on the family in Turkey in the context of F's proposal to be primary carer.

15.11.7   Fair hearing: a different view of delay

Re B (A Child) [2007] EWCA Civ 556, [2007] 2 FLR 979

The mother and father (M and F) appealed against a decision refusing them permission to instruct independent experts in care proceedings concerning their baby (J). The local authority brought care proceedings to determine the future of J, who had been separated from M and F at birth because of F's history of dangerousness and the failure of F and M as a couple to provide good enough parenting for an earlier child who had been released for adoption. At a directions hearing, M and F sought to persuade the judge to allow their instruction of independent experts in addition to those who had reported for the local authority. The judge, having found that there was nothing relevant that could be added to existing reports, refused that request. It was contended that the judge's decision restricting the ability of M and F to test the experts relied on by the local authority could be perceived as biased. M further submitted that she would separate herself immediately from F, and so sought assessment by a particular expert (B) concerning her ability as a single parent removed from the danger F represented.

Held:

It was important that parents at risk of losing a child forever should have confidence in the fairness and even handed nature of proceedings. In the instant case, whilst the judge had not shown any bias against M and F, it would probably be sensible to allow B to be instructed, particularly where, if B shared the opinion of the other experts, there was a measurable chance that the anticipated final hearing would be unnecessary or could be abbreviated.

15.11.8   Factors in assessing welfare: children's wishes and feelings

Re S & C (Children) [2006] EWCA Civ 1822

The husband (H) and wife (W) appealed against a decision of a judge to reject their application for an adoption order in respect of five children. The biological mother (M) had had four of the children with H, her then husband, and the youngest of the children with another man. H and M subsequently divorced and H married W. Pursuant to the application of H and W for an adoption order, the local authority produced a report that showed that the children were all in support of the plan for adoption. However, the children's guardian also filed a report that, contrary to the local authority's findings, showed that what the children in fact wanted was a continuation of the compromise of living with H and W but maintaining attachment to M. H and W believed that the shift in the children's position resulted from the guardian giving the impression to the children that, in the event of an adoption order, they would lose contact with M. Social workers then wrote a formal letter of complaint to CAFCASS in respect of the guardian's behaviour, a complaint that was subsequently withdrawn. The judge, unaware of the letter of complaint, gave a very short judgment dismissing the application of H and W and made a joint residence order in lieu. During the preparation of the instant appeal, H, W and M agreed that, in respect of the youngest child, it was in his best interests for an adoption order to be made. H and W submitted that the judge had failed to have regard to the oral evidence presented at the hearing and had not sufficiently considered the contradictory nature of the two separate reports.

Held:

Given the age of the children, especially the eldest, and evidence that there was a conflict in accounts between the local authority and the guardian, the judge's treatment of the important factor of the children's wishes had been inadequate. The judge's summary of the evidence omitted the local authority report; even without the knowledge of the complaint made by the social workers it was incumbent upon the judge to focus upon the fundamental difference between the contrary impressions given by each report. Such a deficiency was fatal in that it went to the paramount factor of the children's needs and desires. The only possible outcome therefore was to set aside the joint residence order and direct a retrial of applications in respect of the older children. With regard to the youngest child, the court's first consideration was to his welfare, and the permanent security and stability achieved by an adoption order would plainly promote his welfare; accordingly, an order to that end was made.

15.11.9   Adoption: proportionality

Re F (Children) [2007] EWCA Civ 516, [2007] 2 FLR 891

The local authority appealed against the judge's refusal to make care orders in respect of two children aged 4 and 3. The children's mother had admitted that she had subjected the children to unreasonable chastisement and had caused bruising on their bodies. The children's father was found to have struck a third child (their brother) with a belt. The local authority brought care proceedings and an adoption order was made in respect of the children's brother. The judge was not satisfied that the mother was incapable of providing adequate care for the children and therefore made an interim order placing them in her care until an assessment could be carried out. The judge held that, although the mother's over-chastisement of the children could not be condoned, making care orders in such circumstances would lead to a situation where a disproportionate number of children would be at risk of adoption. The local authority submitted that the judge had arrived at the wrong conclusion in refusing to make immediate care orders in respect of the children.

Held:

The judge had been right in his assessment of the case. The case was one of physical chastisement and was not of sufficient severity to justify removing the children for adoption. In the circumstances, such a measure would have constituted a disproportionate remedy.

15.11.10   Leave to apply for adoption order

Re A sub nom TL (Appellant) v (1) Coventry City Council (2) CC (Respondents) & A (By Her Children's Guardian) (Intervener) [2007] EWCA Civ 1383

The appellant foster mother (M) appealed against refusal of leave to apply for an adoption order for a 9-month old baby (X), who had been in M's care since she was 6 days old. A placement order was made in the family proceedings court authorising the local authority to place X for adoption. M made it known before then to the respondent local authority that she wished to adopt X; the local authority did not believe that M was an optimum long-term placement because she was a single mother, a smoker and because her household (four other children besides X) was too 'busy'. They were also concerned that the birth mother knew M and visited her home and they thought that X's origins would be quickly found out if she remained in the area. Both X's guardian and X's birth mother supported adoption by M. The magistrates declined to allow an adjournment to assess M as a potential adopter. The local authority approved a match with other proposed adopters. M made an application for leave to apply for an adoption order pursuant to the Adoption and Children Act 2002, s 42(4) and (6). The order refusing leave to apply had been made in the county court 3 days before X was due to go and live with the prospective adopters. The judge, heavily influenced by the outcome in the family proceedings court, had read a note describing the stance of X's guardian, had studied the reasons why the local authority was adverse to M's candidacy and had found that the delay that the grant of leave would cause to the finalisation of X's adoption weighed against M. M submitted that the judge had erred in the exercise of his discretion.

Held:

(1)   In the absence of reported decisions concerning the grant of leave to apply for an adoption order under s 42(6) of the Act, the legal principles relevant to the exercise of the discretion in each of the sub-sections of s 42 were identical; *Warwickshire CC v M* (2007) EWCA Civ 1084, (2007) 3 FCR 681 applied. The welfare of the child was relevant but not the paramount consideration. Another relevant consideration was whether the proposed application had a real prospect of success.

(2)   The judge paid attention to the guardian's views at a level below the requisite minimum.

(3)   The judge had undoubtedly been right to consider that delay caused by granting leave was relevant to the issue of discretion, but it would rarely be a proper exercise of discretion for questions of delay to precipitate a refusal of leave to make an application of the instant type.

(4)   While it would be absurd to consider that suitability to foster equated to suitability to adopt, it was equally absurd to conclude that suitability to foster equated to unsuitability to adopt. The judge's approach had been insufficiently independent of the local authority's approach. Although the court had a duty to scrutinise local authority care plans very closely, such scrutiny did not, in principle, extend to an address of any issue as to the identity of the optimum adopter, *Re S (Children)* (2007) EWCA Civ 232, [2007] 2 FLR 275 considered. The judge's repeated references to the alleged facility for M and the guardian to have appealed against the placement order were misplaced.

15.11.11   Leave to defend adoption: child's welfare paramount

Re P (A Child) [2007] EWCA Civ 616, [2007] 2 FLR 1069

The appellant father (F) appealed against a decision refusing him and his wife (M) leave to oppose the making of an adoption order in respect of their child (S). S had been removed from her parents' care by means of an emergency protection order when she was 2 days old. F and M had been in a volatile and violent relationship at that time, exacerbated by mutual abuse of alcohol and illicit drugs. Care proceedings followed and S had been placed with prospective adopters when she was 10 months old. The parents had had another child a month later and having undergone a successful residential assessment were caring for that child together. M was pregnant with their third child. The parents had applied under the Adoption and Children Act 2002, s 47(5) for leave to defend the adoption proceedings on the basis that they had addressed all the deficiencies in their lives and in their parenting of S as identified by the judge in the care and placement order proceedings. The judge had refused leave on the basis that the change in circumstances was not sufficient for the purposes of s 47(7) of the Act, and if that was wrong, that the welfare of S required her to be adopted. F argued that the judge was wrong to find that there had been an insufficient change in circumstances to cross the leave threshold. He also argued that the welfare of S should not have been the court's paramount consideration on an application for leave to defend adoption proceedings.

Held:

(1) A judicial decision whether to give leave for a parent to defend adoption proceedings under s 47 of the Act was 'a decision relating to the adoption of a child' pursuant to s 1(1) as defined in s 1(7). Accordingly such an application was governed by s 1, which provided that the child's welfare was paramount. An application under s 47 involved a two-stage process. Firstly, the court had to be satisfied, on the facts of the case, that there had been a change of circumstances within s 47(7). The change in circumstances had to relate to the grant of leave and had to be of a nature or degree sufficient, on the facts of the case, to warrant the exercise of judicial discretion. Whether there had been a relevant change in circumstances under s 47(7) had to be a matter of fact to be decided by the good sense and sound judgment of the court hearing the application. Secondly, if there had been a change of circumstances, then judicial discretion to permit the parents to defend the proceedings became exercisable and the decision whether to grant leave was governed by s 1. In exercising the discretion the court had to have regard to the matters set out in s 1(3) and (4) of the Act.

(2) The application of s 1 to the facts of the case could not be faulted. He had been bound to give considerable weight to the fact that the plan for adoption had been in place for nearly a year, that the placement with S's prospective adopters had been successful and that she had formed firm attachments with them.

15.11.12 Leave to revoke placement order: change of circumstance; prospect of success

Warwickshire County Council (Appellant) v M (Respondent) & (1) M (2) L (By Their Children's Guardian) (Interveners) [2007] EWCA Civ 1084, (2007) The Times, 21 December

The local authority appealed against an order made under the Adoption and Children Act 2002, s 24(2)(a) granting the respondent mother (M) leave to apply for revocation of placement orders in respect of her two children. Care orders had been made in respect of both children on the basis of concerns about M's care of them and a psychologist had assessed her as unlikely to sustain the changes necessary for the provision of safe parenting in a time-frame acceptable for them. The placement orders had been made shortly after the making of the care orders. A little over 18 months later, M sought leave to apply for revocation of the placement orders on the basis that her circumstances had changed. The judge interpreted s 24(3) of the 2002 Act as meaning that if the court was satisfied that there had been a change in circumstances since the placement order was made then leave must be granted. He found that there had been a change in M's circumstances and concluded that he was required to grant leave. The local authority submitted that the judge's construction of s 24(3) of the 2002 Act was wrong; whilst the establishment of a change in circumstances was the only necessary precursor to the exercise of the court's discretion as to whether or not to grant leave, in exercising that discretion the court had to take into account the welfare of the children.

Held:

(1) In *Re P (A Child) (Adoption Order: Leave to Oppose Making of Adoption Order)* [2007] EWCA Civ 616, [2007] 1 WLR 2556 the court held that in exercising its discretion to grant parents leave to oppose an adoption order under s 47(5) of the 2002 Act, the decision about granting leave was an action to be taken within s 1(7)(b) of the Act. Thus, the welfare of the child under ACA 2002, s 1 was the court's paramount consideration, in a decision under s 47(5), *P (A Child)* explained. However, welfare was not paramount in an application under s 24(3) of the 2002 Act for leave to apply to revoke a placement order, because determining such an application was a decision about granting leave for the initiation of proceedings by an individual under the Act and did not fall within s 1(7). Nevertheless, it did not follow that the welfare of the child was not relevant at all. It was well established that a determination whether to grant leave to apply for an order relating to a child could require the court to exercise a discretion in which the child's welfare, although relevant, was not paramount. It was not clear why Parliament should have provided that the child's welfare should be paramount in the discretionary exercise under s 45(7) but not in that under s 24(3). There was no situation other than s 45(7) in which the facility to participate in proceedings relating to a child was governed by the paramountcy of a child's welfare. Therefore, in relation to a child's application for leave under the Children Act 1989, s 10(8), the approach taken in *Re SC (A Minor) (Leave to Seek Residence Order)* [1994] 1 FLR 96 was preferred to that taken in *Re C (A Minor) (Leave to Seek Section 8 Orders)* [1994] 1 FLR 26, *Re SC (A Minor)* approved, *C (A Minor)* disapproved.

(2) In conducting the discretionary exercise under s 24(3), the court might usefully borrow the language of the test set out in CPR 1998, r 52.3(6) and ask whether the applicant would have a real prospect of success. On establishment of a change of circumstances, a discretion arose in which the welfare of the child and the prospect of success had both to be weighed. Analysis of the prospects of success would not always, but would almost always, include analysis of the welfare of the child. The judge's approach to s 24(3) was wrong. In the circumstances, M's applications had no real prospect of success and it would not serve the welfare of the children for her to be granted leave to apply to revoke the placement orders.

15.11.13   Leave to revoke placement order: change of circumstances

Cumbria County Council v (1) W (2) C (3) J & K & L (By Their Children's Guardian F) (4) B [2007] EWHC 2932 (Fam)

The mother, W, applied for permission to revoke a placement order concerning her daughter (L). W had a history of alcohol misuse and drug dependency. The local authority obtained emergency protection orders in respect of L and her two siblings. They were placed with their maternal grandmother (B). The children later became the subject of interim care orders. However, the local authority then had to remove L from her grandma's care, with the court's approval. At the final hearing W sought for L to be rehabilitated to her by means of a year-long residential programme. However, a care order and placement order were made. Prospective adopters were approved and subsequently matched with L. A statement made by B was filed and indicated that W was engaged in a programme of rehabilitation and was making significant progress. A letter from a care manager of a drugs and alcohol service indicated that W had been accepted for a place at a therapeutic resource.

Held:

It was unnecessary to look further for an exposition of the test in Adoption and Children Act 2002, s 24(2) and (3) than the judgment in the related proceedings, *Re W (A Child)* [2007] EWCA Civ 1079. The statutory provision was declaratory in its wording in s 24(3). The test was not construed to include a requirement that the change be 'significant'. In oral evidence, W was relatively unconvincing as to the nature and extent of the change she asserted. W accepted that she had to change but also asserted that she had changed by freeing herself of her drug dependency, something that was not cogently established. On all the evidence, W had not established a change of circumstances.

Re S-H (a child) sub nom NS-H v (1) Kingston upon Hull City Council (2) MC [2008] EWCA Civ 493, CA

The appellant mother (M) appealed against a refusal to grant her leave to apply for revocation of a placement order for adoption under ACA 2002, s 24(2)(a) made in respect of her son (T). T, born in 2004, had failed to thrive in the home of his parents. At the age of 2 he had been taken into foster care by the respondent local authority and had so remained. T had continued to fail to thrive, demonstrated by the absence of any significant weight gain. The local authority was granted a placement order authorising it to place T for adoption. However, in the intervening 5 months before M's application for leave to apply for revocation of the placement order was heard, the local authority had formed the view that the adoption plans for T should not be pursued until T could thrive, and its initial plan that T would remain with his current foster carers until a foster placement with a view to adoption could be found had been replaced with one that T be moved to a different foster home on the basis that, if his failure to thrive could there be remedied, he would then be moved to an adoptive home. Medical examinations of T had taken place but had resulted in professional conflict as to the right course of action to be taken for T and whilst the local authority was agreeable to a fresh medical appraisal of T, M sought a much wider enquiry than that proposed by the local authority. In exercising his discretion not to grant M leave to apply for revocation of the placement order, the judge considered that he had to consider whether the local authority was failing to act as a reasonable parent. The local authority submitted that as M's proposed application for revocation was not based on any real prospect of T's return to live in her home, it was a contrivance and that M's real aim was to obstruct the removal of T from his present foster carers and to secure the instruction of experts favoured by herself rather than the expert favoured by the local authority.

Held:

The judge had clearly been correct to find under s 24(3) that there had been a change in circumstances since the placement order had been made. However, in his consideration of whether to grant leave he had asked himself the wrong question. The question was not whether the local authority was acting as a reasonable parent but whether in all the circumstances, including M's prospects of success in securing revocation of the placement order and T's interests, leave should be given. It was an insufficient foundation for a placement order that the long-term aim of the court was that the child should be adopted. The necessary foundation, broadly speaking, was that the child was presently in a condition to be adopted and was ready to be adopted. It was also in T's interests that leave should be given and the apparent change in his current suitability for adoption be examined by the court. Such an examination would precipitate enquiry into all the options available for him.

15.11.14　Local authority duties when application for leave to revoke pending

Re F (A Child) sub nom C v East Sussex County Council [2008] EWCA Civ 439

The appellant father (F) appealed against a decision of the judge that the court had no jurisdiction to grant him leave to make an application to revoke a placement order made in respect of his daughter (J). F had had a casual relationship with J's mother, the second respondent, and had not initially been aware that he was J's father. DNA tests later established F's paternity after J had been placed in the care of the first respondent local authority. F subsequently learned that plans for J's adoption were well advanced. In fact, J had already been matched for placement. F sought information as to J's progress towards adoption and the authority informed him that she had not been placed but had been to a matching panel the previous day. F filed an application under ACA 2002, s 24 for leave to revoke the placement order. Due to staff shortages, the county court did not process F's application for nearly 2 weeks, when notices of a hearing were sent to the parties. In the meantime, however, and despite F's emerging challenge, the local authority's decision maker ratified the matching panel's decision. At the hearing, the local authority submitted that the terms of s 24(2)(b) of the Act removed the court's jurisdiction to grant F leave to make the application as J had already been placed for adoption. The judge upheld that submission. F contended that it was open to the court, in reliance on Human Rights Act 1998, s 3 in giving effect to his rights both to a fair hearing and to family life under the ECHR 1950, to interpret s 24(5) of the Act so that the words 'an application for the revocation of a placement order has been made' could include the application for leave to make the application.

Held:

(1)　The words of s 24 of the 2002 Act were clear, unambiguous and capable of only one meaning. The words 'an application for the revocation of a placement order' in s 24(5)(a) meant just that: they did not mean and could not be read as also meaning 'an application for leave to apply for the revocation of a placement order'. Further, s 24 of the 2002 Act, properly applied and implemented, was compliant with the 1998 Act and the Convention. The fact that the 2002 Act had permitted the travesty of good practice which had occurred in the instant case was not a reason for declaring it incompatible with F's human rights or for construing s 24(5) as F had contended.

(2)　There was a need for good practice to supplement the 2002 Act. The conduct of the local authority in the instant case had been disgraceful and was an example of the worst kind of sharp practice.

Local authorities and adoption agencies had to understand that it was the court which was in control and which had been given the responsibility for making those decisions by Parliament. Appeal dismissed.

15.11.15 Agency must approve adoption before placement order application

Re PB (A Child) [2006] EWCA Civ 1016, [2007] 1 FLR 1106

The appellant mother (P) appealed against a care order and placement order made in respect of her son (R). P's ability to care for R, who was being treated for leukaemia, had been adversely affected by her Asperger's syndrome and post natal depression; the local authority had applied for a care order. During the proceedings the local authority submitted seven care plans, all providing for ultimate rehabilitation; but its eighth substituted adoption. It thus applied, after its adoption panel had approved the proposal, for the placement order. The judge dealt with the application at the same time as the care order application, and granted both. P contended that it had been procedurally unfair to permit an application to be made for a placement order at a very late stage of the care proceedings.

Held:

The local authority acted as an adoption agency under the Adoption and Children Act 2002 in deciding that it was satisfied that a child ought to be placed for adoption. Under the terms of s 22 of the 2002 Act the local authority could only be so satisfied, and an application for a placement order made, after its appointed officer had taken the positive decision to endorse the recommendation of the adoption panel. It was not open to the local authority to issue the placement order application any earlier than it did. The judge's decision to permit the consolidation and contemporaneous conclusion of the care order and placement order applications was within the wide ambit of his discretion since it was hard to discern what prejudice that had caused P.

MJ & another v X local authority [2008] EWCA Civ 835

Where the decision of a panel making a 'should be placed for adoption' decision is flawed, eg for lack of information, the agency decision maker cannot ratify that flawed decision and the court cannot make a placement order.

15.11.16   Guidance on when to advertise for adoption

Re K (A Child) (Adoption: Permission to Advertise) [2007]
EWHC 544 (Fam), [2007] 2 FLR 326

Local authorities cannot advertise a child for adoption eg in 'Be my
parent' until such time as the child is 'available for adoption'. This will
generally be once they have a placement order from the court to that
effect. However, the court's leave might be given in exceptional cases
eg where parents agree with advertising earlier or where there is clear
agency approval for adoption and/or there is a final care order with plan
for adoption but as yet no placement order. The court has to weigh up the
child's welfare, which is paramount, against the parents' and family's
Art 6 rights.

15.11.17   Adopters' confidentiality

(1) B (2) B v A County Council [2006] EWCA Civ 1388, [2007]
1 FLR 1189

Appeal by an adopting family (B) against a decision that although the
respondent local authority had broken their duty of care to keep B's
identity confidential during the adoption process, their negligence claim
should be dismissed because the damage on which the action depended,
namely loss by a campaign of harassment by the birth family, had not
been proved. The local authority cross-appealed against the decision that
it owed a duty of care to B. The judge found that the local authority owed
B a duty of care to keep their identity confidential and that the duty had
been breached by release of information to the birth family, but
nonetheless dismissed the action because he did not find it proved that the
birth family carried out the campaign of harassment alleged.

Held:

(1)   The chain of events leading up to the adoption was certainly of
      importance, but it did not suffice to destroy the proximity between
      the parties in the sense in which that concept was used in *Caparo*
      Industries Plc v Dickman (1990) BCC 164, Caparo applied. The
      parties were plainly in close proximity to each other, irrespective of
      whatever was asked for and given in relation to confidentiality and
      remained in that relationship throughout the adoption process.

(2)   The starting point of any adoption, even an open one, would always
      be confidentiality of the adopters. In the instant case to hold the
      local authority liable when an express undertaking was asked for and
      given would not undermine the general system of adoption. The
      judge was very experienced in family work and adoption matters and

his perception of the birth family was based on evidence given to him by trained social workers. The instant court could not disturb the judge's conclusion that the birth family had not been proved to be responsible for the incidents complained of.

15.11.18 Declaration of original parentage: no disruption to adoption

M v W (Declaration of Parentage) [2006] EWHC 2341 (Fam), [2007] 2 FLR 270

M had been placed for adoption shortly after his birth; he sought a declaration of parentage in respect of his natural father (F). M's birth certificate carried the name of his natural mother only; F had returned to Australia after a brief relationship with the birth mother. At the material time, an unmarried father's consent to adoption was not required. M's adoption file contained the name of F, who had married in Australia and had children from that marriage. F had died before meeting M, but M was in friendly contact with F's children in Australia. The natural mother had signed a declaration of acknowledgement of parentage in which she named F as M's father and M had been granted Australian citizenship. M submitted that it was important to him that the state recognised the truth of his origins and that he wished to pass on to his own children and grandchildren as accurate an account as possible of their ancestry.

Held:

There was no public policy issue to preclude the making of a declaration of parentage in an uncontested application if the court was satisfied as to the truth of the claim of parentage, since it would assist the petitioner and would not affect the validity of an adoption order. Recognition of F as M's natural father would satisfy his personal wishes and it could be of value to M and his family to know the identity of his biological father in relation to genetic make-up and pre-disposition to certain medical conditions.

15.11.19 Adoption order or special guardianship order

Re S [2007] EWCA Civ 54, [2007] 1 FLR 819

Application by foster carer to adopt a 6-year-old child fostered for half her life. The Court of Appeal upheld an SGO made by HHJ Kushner QC as best reflecting the child's welfare and direct contact with her biological family. The Court of Appeal emphasised the need to respect judicial discretion as to the best order for the child's needs, assessed by careful reference to the welfare checklist. The guardian's support for adoption was so finely balanced that it did not amount to a recommendation; it did not therefore matter that the judgment overlooked his evidence. The making of s 91(14) orders, was approved to ensure that challenges to the special guardian's exercise of PR, not just applications to revoke, required leave. Also confirmed that special guardianship can be imposed on a carer applying for a different order, in contrast to Re K [1995] 1 FLR 675, which held that a residence order could not be forced on a carer who wanted a care order.

Re AJ [2007] 1 FLR 507; Re MJ [2007] EWCA Civ 56, [2007] 1 FLR 691

Decisions to grant adoption and not special guardianship to relative carers, as adoption was needed for security of the placements. Although special guardianship was envisaged as appropriate for relative carers, to avoid distortion of family relationships, it was still open to courts to make adoption orders to relatives.

S v B and Newport [2007] 1 FLR 1116

The decision was that a special guardianship order supported by an indefinite s 91(14) order and prohibited steps order forbidding direct contact was sufficient for kinship carers of a 6-year-old.

15.11.20 Special guardianship or adoption outside the family

Re EN (A Child) [2007] EWCA Civ 264

Adoption outside the family was preferable to special guardianship with grandmother, despite grandmother's move of house, to cut ties with family who could undermine her protection of the child. What she gained in distance from the family she lost in support. The child would not have a normal family life as there was much of the family he could not have contact with. Grandmother could not meet the child's needs, even with an SGO; the child needed a new family and identity.

Haringey LBC v C & Mrs E, Mr E, Mrs F and Kenya [2006] EWHC 1620

Kenyan baby purportedly born to E, who claimed maternity by miracle. The Court found the baby was trafficked. The applications were by: (a) E, who believed herself to be the mother whose false belief would place the child at risk of emotional harm; (b) a white foster carer who sought special guardianship; and (c) the local authority plan for adoption by more culturally appropriate carers than the foster carer. Even though special guardianship preserves links with birth family, it does not overcome the need where possible to ensure appropriate cultural matching.

15.11.21 Parental responsibility under SGO

Re L (A Child) [2007] EWCA Civ 196

Court of Appeal upheld the first instance decision that the applicant grandmother should have an SGO not adoption order as she did not promote the child's Afro-Caribbean heritage or life story work. Whilst an SGO granted exclusive PR over biological parents, it was not free of judicial oversight. The court made a contact order to the parents who had been 'sidelined but not totally displaced' by the SGO. The change of name sought by grandmother was also refused because of her difficulties promoting the child's identity.

15.12.22 Special guardianship reports

Re R (A Child) sub nom Birmingham City Council v LR (by the OS) & Others [2006] EWCA Civ 1748, [2007] 1 FLR 564

Section 14A(8) of the Children Act 1989 requires local authorities to prepare suitability reports for SGO *only* when a person with automatic entitlement to seek an SGO gave notice OR when someone who required leave obtained the court's leave to apply. It was not possible to give notice to the local authority prior to leave being granted.

Re S (A Child) (No 2) [2007] EWCA Civ 90, [2007] 1 FLR 855

Arising from *Re S* [2007] EWCA Civ 54. Where a judge, under Children Act 1989, s 14A(6)(b), makes an SGO as an alternative to another order, the SGO cannot be made until a special guardianship suitability report is prepared (CA 1989, s 14A(8) and (11)). Where a report was already before the court with most of the information required, the local authority could provide the missing information cross-referenced to the existing report.

15.11.23 Placement for adoption abroad

Re G (A Child: Adoption: Placement outside the Jurisdiction) [2008] EWCA Civ 105

Regulation 10(b)(iv) of the Adoption with a Foreign Element Regulations 2005 (SI 2005/392) requires that the foreign authority has authorised the child's entry into their jurisdiction with the potential adopters before the English court has power to make an order granting those adopters PR under Adoption and Children Act 2002, s 84.

Child Case Management Practice

Haringey London Borough Council v MA and others [2008] EWHC 1722 (Fam)

If potential adopters of a child take the child abroad for a holiday to test the placement with them in the country of their residence, this is not at that stage a placement for adoption. Therefore it is not caught by ACA 2002, s 85 and an order under s 84 is not required at that point. If the child is taken on holiday with the potential adoptive parents, as part of the assessment process, the period of time spent in their home country can be included in the 10 weeks period of residence required for the making of an order granting PR to the prospective under s 84. This should make the assessment of prospective foreign adopters, particularly relatives, a great deal more straightforward.

A15.1 APPENDIX 1:
PRESIDENT'S GUIDANCE OF 3 OCTOBER 2008
LISTING FINAL HEARINGS IN ADOPTION CASES

1 This Guidance is issued with the purpose of clarifying the legal requirements and practical arrangements for final hearings in adoption applications.

2 This Guidance does not apply to any case where the child has been freed for adoption under the provisions of the Adoption Act 1976 or where the parent or guardian of the child cannot be found.

3 In this Guidance:

(a) "the 2002 Act" means the Adoption and Children Act 2002;
(b) any reference to a rule by number is a reference to the rule so numbered in the Family Procedure (Adoption) Rules 2005.

4 Section 141(3) of the 2002 Act and rule 31 place an obligation on the court officer to give to the persons listed in rule 31, including birth parent(s) with parental responsibility, notice of the date and place of the final hearing of an adoption application.

5 The requirement to give notice is mandatory. Notice of the final hearing must be given to any person listed in rule 31 who can be found and there is no discretion to dispense with such notice. The provisions of rule 39 (power of court to dispense with service) do not apply to notice of the final hearing. By rule 32(1) any person who has been given notice under rule 31 has the right to attend the final hearing and, except where rule 32(2) applies[9] , to be heard on the question of whether an adoption order should be made.

6 In some cases the welfare of the child will require arrangements to be made to ensure that the birth parent(s) and the applicant(s) or the child do not meet at or in the vicinity of the court. This will apply particularly to proceedings in which a serial number has been assigned to the applicant under rule 20(2); rule 20(4)(b) provides that, in such a case, the proceedings will be conducted with a view to securing that the applicant is not seen by or made known to any party who is not already aware of his identity except with his consent.

7 Rule 32(6) provides that the court cannot make an adoption order unless the applicant and the child personally attend the final hearing. However, rule 32(6) is subject to rule 32(7), which gives the court a discretion to direct that the applicant or the child need not attend the final hearing; this provision permits the court, where appropriate, to direct that the attendance of the applicant or the child or both of them at the final hearing is not required.

---

[9]   A person whose application for the permission of the court to oppose the making of an adoption order under section 47(3) or (5) of the 2002 Act has been refused is not entitled to be heard on the question of whether an order should be made.

8 When giving directions for the conduct of the final hearing of an adoption application, the court should consider in particular:

- whether to give a direction under rule 32(7) that the applicant or the child need not attend the hearing;
- whether to give a direction under rule 32(4) that any person must attend the hearing;
- whether arrangements need to be made to ensure that the birth parent(s) and the applicant or the child do not meet at or in the vicinity of the court;
- the arrangements for ensuring that the ascertainable wishes and feelings of the child regarding the adoption decision are placed before the court;
- the facilities at the place where the final hearing is to take place, including
  - the availability of suitable accommodation
  - the use of any electronic information exchange and video or telephone conferencing links.

9 In proceedings in which a serial number has been assigned to the applicant under rule 20(2), it will generally be appropriate to excuse the attendance of the child at the final hearing. It may also be appropriate to excuse the attendance of the applicant, if necessary to ensure that confidentiality is preserved. Where in such a case the attendance of the applicant is required, arrangements must be made to ensure that the applicant is not seen by or made known to any party who is not already aware of his identity.

10 In any case in which a direction is given that the applicant or the child need not attend the final hearing, the order and any notice of hearing issued by the court must state clearly that the applicant or the child, as the case may be, should not attend.

11 Each Adoption Centre and each magistrates' court which hears family proceedings must have arrangements in place to provide information to the relevant parties about any special arrangements made for their attendance at and the conduct of the final hearing.

12 The application for an adoption order should be determined at the hearing of which notice has been given under rule 31. If the application is not determined at that hearing, notice of the adjourned final hearing should be given under rule 31 and this Guidance shall apply equally to the adjourned hearing.

13 Where an adoption order is made in the absence of the applicant or the child, the court should consider making facilities available for a celebratory event. The event should not normally be held before the expiry of the appeal period (generally 14 days). Except in exceptional circumstances, the judge or, in the magistrates' court at least one of the

magistrates, who made the adoption order should host the celebratory event. Arrangements for the celebratory event should be made with the applicant(s) by the court.

Sir Mark Potter
President

A15.2   APPENDIX 2:
PLACEMENT/ADOPTION FORMS

Reproduced with the kind permission of Liverpool County Court.

Placement Form

IN THE **COUNTY COURT** **CASE NO.** **CHILD:** **These directions are given pursuant to the Family Procedure (Adoption) Rules 2005 (hereinafter called 'The Rules')**		
☐ Before [District Judge /HH Judge] ☐ At a hearing attended by ☐ Without any of the parties or their legal representatives having been directed to attend Court		
ORDER:–		
Respondents[1]	☐	The Respondents in these proceedings shall be:- ☐ the child [2]. ☐ (hereinafter called "the Respondent Mother")[3]. ☐ (hereinafter called "the Respondent Father") ☐ (specify any other Respondents)[4].
Guardian's Appointment[5]	☐	A Children's Guardian shall be appointed to represent the child (preferably the person who has previously acted in that capacity for h).
Service on Respondents by court	☐	The proper officer of this Court shall serve on all parties [other than the Respondent(s)] all such documents (including this order) as are required by the rules to be served on those parties. **Note for Office:**[6]. ☐ The notice of hearing shall not include a rule 24(iv) notice ☐ The notice of hearing shall include a rule 24(iv) notice and shall refer to an attached statement of facts ☐ The notice of hearing shall include a rule 24(iv) notice and that directions will be given concerning filing and service of a statement of facts.

Personal. Service by Local Authority[7]	☐	The Local Authority shall by 4pm on _____ personally serve on the Respondent(s) :- ☐ a copy of the Applicant's application ☐ a copy of this order ☐ a copy of the notice of hearing provided by the court ☐ a copy of the Applicant's statement of facts ☐ a copy of the response form provided by the court
Tracing missing parents[8]	☐	The Applicant shall make all reasonable efforts to trace the whereabouts of _____ . In the event that the Applicant fail to discover the missing parent's whereabouts despite making all reasonable efforts they may apply to the Court for an order for substituted or deemed service or for an order dispensing with service of the application on that parent. Any such application shall be supported by Affidavit setting out full particulars of the attempts made to trace the missing parent and shall be filed at Court by 4pm on _____ .
Annex B report	☐	The Applicant shall file a report ("the Annex B Report") by 4.00pm on _____ covering those matters referred to in rule 29(3) of the rules.
	☐	The Applicant shall serve suitably anonymised copies of the Annex B Report on the other parties.
Statement of facts	☐	The Applicant(s) shall by 4pm on _____ file at Court a statement of facts setting out a summary of the history of the case and any other facts to satisfy the Court that [the parent(s) of the child cannot be found or is incapable of giving consent/the welfare of the child requires the consent of the child's parent(s) to be dispensed with].

Response to statement of facts	☐	The shall by 4.00pm on send to the Court: (a) a signed and dated statement setting out: (i) h response to the Statement of Facts in support of the application to dispense with h consent to the making of a Placement Order; (ii) h reason for opposing or not consenting to the making of a Placement Order in respect of the child; (iii) particulars of any alternative proposals which h has for the long term care and welfare of the child. (b) details of the means by which he may be contacted by the Children's Guardian to arrange an appointment including the provision of a telephone number.
	☐	If fails to comply with the preceding paragraph of this order within the time prescribed or fails to keep any appointments with the Children's Guardian, the Children's Guardian may complete h investigations and report to the Court without the need to make any further enquiry of the
Guardian's report	☐	The Children's Guardian shall by 4pm on file at Court a Guardian's report [which shall include comment on].
	☐	The Children's Guardian shall disclose suitably anonymised copies of the Report to the other parties.
	☐	If wishes to consent to the making of a Placement Order, the Children's Guardian's appointment shall automatically be converted by this Order to that of Reporting Officer for the purpose of obtaining that consent.
Reporting Officer	☐	It appearing that the parent(s) of the child may be willing to consent to a Placement Order an Officer of the Service (as defined in rule 6 of the Rules) is appointed to be a reporting officer to perform the functions referred to in rules 71 and 72 of the Rules.
	☐	The Reporting Officer shall file at Court a report by 4pm on
Directions hearing	☐	The Application is listed for further consideration at 10.30am on at the Civil and Family Courts, [ELH].
Directions without attendance[9]	☐	The Court file will be referred to a Judge during week commencing with a view to the Court giving further case management directions [which may include the giving of a final hearing date if appropriate].

Final hearing	☐	The Placement Application is listed for final hearing at 10.30am on at the Civil and Family Courts, [ELH]
Attendance	☐	The child is excused from attending all future hearings unless the Court makes a different direction later.
Evidence	☐	The evidence and the judgment in the Care Proceedings relating to the child shall be admitted as evidence in these proceedings.
Permission to apply	☐	Any party may apply to the Court for further or different directions.
Further Information	☐	The shall by 4pm on file at court the following further information:-
Other directions	☐	

Footnotes

1. The form provides for the Judge to specify who the Respondents will be. This is to avoid the necessity of the Court office having to determine who automatic Respondents might be.
2. Rule 23 provides that the child is automatically a Respondent in placement proceedings.
3. Any birth parent with PR is automatically a Respondent, under Rule 23.
4. "Other" automatic Respondents are
    (i)   Any person with a contact order under the 1989 Act;
    (ii) Any adoption agency or voluntary organisation which has PR for the child or who is looking after or caring for the child (but do not confuse with the Local Authority who will be the Applicant in the proceedings);
    (iii) Any persons who are parties in any care proceedings which have led to the application for the placement order.
5. As the child is automatically a Respondent it will also invariably be the case that the appointment of a Guardian is appropriate.
6. In placement proceedings the consent of any birth parent with PR has to be obtained or, alternatively, that consent has to be dispensed with.If the latter, then a Rule 24 for notice, and an appropriate statement of facts will need to be served. It is important that this notice is completed to give guidance to the Court office as to whether such a notice and statement of facts need to be served. In placement proceedings the birth parents are also (unlike in adoption proceedings) entitled to receive a copy of the application form.
7. If the whereabouts of the Respondent Parents are unknown or uncertain it may be appropriate to order that the Local Authority shall serve the necessary papers on the parents. This direction is intended to make clear to the Local Authority precisely what documents need to be served and the documents referred to are documents which the Local Authority will receive itself from the Court at the outset of the proceedings.
8. For what constitutes "cannot be found" refer to re R (Adoption) [1967] 1 WLR 34; re S (Adoption) [1999] 2 FLR 374; re F (An Infant) [1970] 1 QB 385 at 389b; re A (Adoption of Russian Child) [2000] 1 FLR 539.
9. This direction for further directions to be given on paper is intended to be an alternative to a Directions Hearing being fixed at the outset. It might be appropriate where, for example, further information from an Annex A report or the like will clarify whether a Directions Hearing is necessary and, if so, whether the Application for an Adoption Order is likely to be opposed or not.

Adoption Form (1)[1]

<table>
<tr>
<td colspan="2">IN THE CHILD: COUNTY COURT   CASE NO.
These directions are given pursuant to the Family Procedure (Adoption) Rules 2005 (hereinafter called 'The Rules')</td>
</tr>
<tr>
<td colspan="2">☐   Before [District Judge   /HH Judge   ]
☐   At a hearing attended by
☐   Without any of the parties or their legal representatives having been directed to attend Court</td>
</tr>
<tr>
<td colspan="2">ORDER:-</td>
</tr>
<tr>
<td>Applicant's Identity</td>
<td>☐   The Applicant's identity shall be kept confidential and from now on he shall be referred to as: A.</td>
</tr>
<tr>
<td>Respondents[2].</td>
<td>☐   The Respondents in these proceedings shall be:-
    ☐   the[3]child
        ☐   (hereinafter called "the Local Authority")[4].
        ☐   (hereinafter called "the Respondent Mother")[5].
        ☐   (hereinafter called "the Respondent Father")
        ☐   (specify any other Respondents)[6].</td>
</tr>
<tr>
<td>Guardian's Appointment[7]</td>
<td>☐   A Children's Guardian shall be appointed to represent the child (preferably the person who has previously acted in that capacity for h   ).</td>
</tr>
<tr>
<td>Service on Respondents by court</td>
<td>☐   The proper officer of this Court shall serve on all parties [other than the Respondent(s)   ] all such documents (including this order) as are required by the rules to be served on those parties.
Note for Office: [8].
☐   The notice of hearing shall not include a rule 24 (iv) notice
☐   The notice of hearing shall include a rule 24(iv) notice and shall refer to an attached statement of facts.
☐   The notice of hearing shall include a rule 24(iv) notice and that directions will be given concerning filing and service of a statement of facts.</td>
</tr>
<tr>
<td>Personal Service by Local Authority[9]</td>
<td>☐   The Local Authority shall by 4pm on   personally serve on the Respondent(s) :-
☐   a copy of this order
☐   a copy of the notice of hearing provided by the court
☐   a copy of the response form provided by the court
☐   a copy of the Applicant's statement of facts</td>
</tr>
</table>

Tracing missing parents[10]	☐	The Local Authority/Applicant shall make all reasonable efforts to trace the whereabouts of . In the event that the Local Authority/Applicant fail to discover the missing parent's whereabouts despite making all reasonable efforts they may apply to the Court for an order for substituted or deemed service or for an order dispensing with service of the application on that parent. Any such application shall be supported by Affidavit setting out full particulars of the attempts made to trace the missing parent and shall be filed at Court by 4pm on .
Annex A report	☐	The Local Authority shall file a report ("the Annex A Report") by 4.00pm on covering those matters referred to in rule 29(3) of the rules
	☐	The Local Authority shall serve suitably anonymised copies of the Annex A Report on the other parties.
Guardian's report	☐	The Children's Guardian shall by 4pm on file at Court a Guardian's report [which shall include comment on].
	☐	The Children's Guardian shall disclose suitably anonymised copies of the Report to the other parties.

Leave to oppose	☐	The application for leave to oppose the making of an Adoption Order shall be determined as a preliminary issue at a hearing at 10.30am on day of 200 at the Civil and Family Courts, (ELH) and the following directions are given for the purpose of enabling the Court to determine that preliminary issue:- i) By 4pm on 200 the shall file and serve a signed and dated statement setting out:- a) full particulars of the alleged change of circumstances relied upon such as the believes would merit the court granting h leave to pose the making of an Adoption Order; b) particulars of any alternative proposals which h has for the long-term care and welfare of the child; c) details of the means by which h may be contacted by the Children's Guardian to arrange an appointment including the provision of a telephone number. ii) By 4pm on 2000 the Children's Guardian shall file a report covering: • Any alleged change of circumstances; • Those matters setting out in Section 1(4) of the Act; • The overall welfare of the child. iii) The prospective adopters and the child are excused from attending the hearing unless a different order is made later. iv) The is directed to attend the hearing but should note that the Court may proceed in h absence upon proof that h has been served with a copy of this order; IMPORTANT NOTE If the fails to attend the hearing or the application for leave to oppose the making of an adoption order is refused, the Court may go on to hear the adoption application immediately afterwards and <u>make a final order</u>.
Directions hearing	☐	The Application is listed for further consideration at 10.30am on at the Civil and Family Courts, [ELH].
Directions without attendance[11]	☐	The Court file will be referred to a Judge during week commencing with a view to the Court giving further case management directions [which may include the giving of a final hearing date if appropriate].
Final hearing	☐	The Adoption Application is listed for final hearing at 10.30am On at the Civil and Family Courts, [ELH]

Attendance	☐	The Applicants and the child are excused from attending all future hearings unless the Court makes a different direction later.
Evidence	☐	The evidence and the judgment in the [Care and Placement] Proceedings relating to the child shall be admitted as evidence in these proceedings.
Permission to apply	☐	Any party may apply to the Court for further or different directions.
Further Information	☐	The _____ shall by 4pm on _____ file at court the following further information:-
Other directions	☐	

Footnotes

1. This tick box form is intended to be suitable for Adoption cases where Section 47(2) or Section 47(4) of the Adoption and Children's Action 2002 apply. Loosely, those Sections will apply if a Parent has given advanced consent (in the prescribed form) to the making of an Adoption Order or the child was placed for Adoption by an Adoption Agency with the consent of the Parents or the child was placed for Adoption under a Placement Order. A separate tick box form is provided for cases where Section 47 does not apply.

2. The form provides for the Judge to specify who the Respondents will be. This is to avoid the necessity of the Court office having to determine who automatic Respondents might be.

3. Pursuant to Rule 23 a child will only automatically be a Respondent if (i) Section 47 permission has been given to a Parent to oppose the application (ii) the child proposes the application (iii) CAFCASS recommends that the child should be made a Party (and the Court agrees) (iv) there is a foreign element (v) the prospective Adopters are relatives of the child (vi) if the child is already an Adopted child (vii) if any Party to the proceedings is opposed to contact arrangements for the child.

4. Rule 23 provides that if a Local Authority is entitled to receive a Section 44 notice then they are automatic Respondents.

5. a) If a Freeing Order has already been made any Parent or Guardian is divested of P.R. and is therefore not an automatic Respondent under Rule 23

   b) A parent who has given an advance Section 20(4)(a) notice of wish not to be informed of any Adoption application will not automatically be a Respondent.

   c) If a child was born after the 1st December 2003 a Father obtains P.R. by having his name on the Birth Certificate.

6. Pursuant to Rule 23 other automatic Respondents are (i) any person in whose favour there is provision for contact (ii) any Adoption Agency having P.R. for the child (iii) any Adoption Agency which has taken part in the arrangements for Adoption (iv) any Local Authority which has looked after or is caring for the child.

7. Appointment of the child's Guardian is only appropriate if the child has been made a Party.

8. The Rules require that the Court Officer give notice to a Respondent Parent of any request for that Parent's consent to be dispensed with and, also, that the Court Officer serve the Parent with the Applicant's (anonymised if necessary) Statement of Facts. Completion of this note will ensure that the Court Officer is told whether the appropriate notice should be given and whether the Statement of

Facts is to be sent out. In cases where Section 47 applies it will invariably be the case that the consent of the birth parents is not required and, therefore, no rule 24(iv) notice or statement of facts will need to be served on the Respondent parents.

9. If the whereabouts of Respondent Parents are unknown or uncertain it may be appropriate to order that the Local Authority (rather than, for example, a Step Parent Applicant) shall serve the necessary papers on the Parents. The Local Authority will often have to carryout such enquiries in any event in connection with its Annex A Report. This direction is intended to make clear to the Local Authority precisely what documents need to be served and the documents referred to are documents which the Local Authority will receive itself from the Court at the outset of the proceedings. A Respondent Parent is not automatically entitled to a copy of the Adoption Application form.

10. For what constitutes "cannot be found" refer to re R (Adoption) [1967] 1 W LR 34; re S (Adoption) [1999] 2 FLR 374; re F (An Infant) [1970] 1 QB 385 at 389b; re A (Adoption of Russian Child) [2000] 1 FLR 539.

11. This direction for further directions to be given on paper is intended to be an alternative to a Directions Hearing being fixed at the outset. It might be appropriate where, for example, further information from an Annex A report or the like will clarify whether a Directions Hearing is necessary and, if so, whether the Application for an Adoption Order is likely to be opposed or not.

Adoption Form (2)[1]

IN THE	**COUNTY COURT**	**CASE NO.**
CHILD:		
These directions are given pursuant to the Family Procedure (Adoption) Rules 2005 (hereinafter called 'The Rules')		

☐ Before [District Judge /HH Judge] ☐ At a hearing attended by ☐ Without any of the parties or their legal representatives having been directed to attend Court	

ORDER:-

Applicant's Identity	☐	The Applicant's identity shall be kept confidential and from now on he shall be referred to as: A.
Respondents[2]	☐	The Respondents in these proceedings shall be:- ☐ the child [3]. ☐ (hereinafter called "the Local Authority")[4]. ☐ (hereinafter called "the Respondent Mother")[5]. ☐ (hereinafter called "the Respondent Father") ☐ (specify any other Respondents)[6].
Guardian's Appointment[7]	☐	A Children's Guardian shall be appointed to represent the child (preferably the person who has previously acted in that capacity for h).

Service on Respondents by court	☐	The proper officer of this Court shall serve on all parties [other than the Respondent(s)] all such documents (including this order) as are required by the rules to be served on those parties. **Note for Office:**[8] ☐ The notice of hearing shall not include a rule 24 (iv) notice ☐ The notice of hearing shall include a rule 24(iv) notice and shall refer to an attached statement of facts ☐ The notice of hearing shall include a rule 24(iv) notice and that directions will be given concerning filing and service of a statement of facts.
Personal Service by Local Authority[9]	☐	The Local Authority shall by 4pm on personally serve on the Respondent(s) :- ☐ a copy of this order ☐ a copy of the notice of hearing provided by the court ☐ a copy of the response form provided by the court ☐ a copy of the Applicant's statement of facts
Tracing missing parents[10]	☐	The Local Authority/Applicant shall make all reasonable efforts to trace the whereabouts of . In the event that the Local Authority/Applicant fail to discover the missing parent's whereabouts despite making all reasonable efforts they may apply to the Court for an order for substituted or deemed service or for an order dispensing with service of the application on that parent. Any such application shall be supported by Affidavit setting out full particulars of the attempts made to trace the missing parent and shall be filed at Court by 4pm on .
Annex A report	☐	The Local Authority shall file a report ("the Annex A Report") by 4.00pm on covering those matters referred to in rule 29(3) of the rules
	☐	The Local Authority shall serve suitably anonymised copies of the Annex A Report on the other parties.
Statement of facts	☐	The Applicant(s) shall by 4pm on file at Court a statement of facts setting out a summary of the history of the case and any other facts to satisfy the Court that [the parent(s) of the child cannot be found or is incapable of giving consent/the welfare of the child requires the consent of the child's parent(s) to be dispensed with].

Response to statement of facts	☐	The shall by 4.00pm on send to the Court: (a a signed and dated statement setting out: (i) h response to the Statement of Facts in support of the application to dispense with h consent to the making of an Adoption Order; (ii) h reason for opposing or not consenting to the making of an adoption order in respect of the child; (iii) particulars of any alternative proposals which h has for the long term care and welfare of the child. (b) details of the means by which he may be contacted by the Children's Guardian to arrange an appointment including the provision of a telephone number.
	☐	If fails to comply with paragraph ( )(a) and/or (b) of this order within the time prescribed or fails to keep any appointments with the Children's Guardian, the Children's Guardian may complete h investigations and report to the Court without the need to make any further enquiry of the
Guardian's report	☐	The Children's Guardian shall by 4pm on file at Court a Guardian's report [which shall include comment on].
	☐	The Children's Guardian shall disclose suitably anonymised copies of the report to the other parties.
	☐	If wishes to consent to the making of an Adoption Order, the Children's Guardian's appointment shall automatically be converted by this Order to that of Reporting Officer for the purpose of obtaining that consent
Reporting Officer	☐	It appearing that the parent(s) of the child may be willing to consent to an adoption order an Officer of the Service (as defined in rule 6 of the Rules) is appointed to be a reporting officer to perform the functions referred to in rules 71 and 72 of the Rules.
	☐	The Reporting Officer shall file at Court a report by 4pm on
Directions hearing	☐	The Application is listed for further consideration at 10.30am on at the Civil and Family Courts, [ELH].
Directions without attendance[11]	☐	The Court file will be referred to a Judge during week commencing with a view to the Court giving further case management directions [which may include the giving of a final hearing date if appropriate].

Final hearing	☐	The Adoption Application is listed for final hearing at 10.30am on at the Civil and Family Courts, [ELH].
Attendance	☐	The Applicants and the child are excused from attending all future hearings unless the Court makes a different direction later.
Evidence	☐	The evidence and the judgment in the [Care and Placement] Proceedings relating to the child shall be admitted as evidence in these proceedings.
Permission to apply	☐	Any party may apply to the Court for further or different directions.
Further Information	☐	The shall by 4pm on file at court the following further information:-
Other directions	☐	

Footnotes

1.   This tick box form is intended to be suitable for Adoption cases where Section 47(2) or Section 47(4) of the Adoption and Children's Action 2002 do not apply. Loosely, those Sections will apply if a Parent has given advanced consent (in the prescribed form) to the making of an Adoption Order or the child was placed for Adoption by an Adoption Agency with the consent of the Parents or the child was placed for Adoption under a Placement Order. A separate tick box form is provided for cases where Section 47 does apply.

2.   The form provides for the Judge to specify who the Respondents will be. This is to avoid the necessity of the Court office having to determine who automatic Respondents might be.

3.   Pursuant to Rule 23 a child will only automatically be a Respondent if (i) Section 47 permission has been given to a Parent to oppose the application (ii) the child proposes the application (iii) CAFCASS recommends that the child should be made a Party (and the Court agrees) (iv) there is a foreign element (v) the prospective Adopters are relatives of the child (vi) if the child is already an Adopted child (vii) if any Party to the proceedings is opposed to contact arrangements for the child.

4.   Rule 23 provides that if a Local Authority is entitled to receive a Section 44 notice then they are automatic Respondents.

5.   a)   If a Freeing Order has already been made any Parent or Guardian is divested of P.R. and is therefore not an automatic Respondent under Rule 23

        b)   A parent who has given an advance Section 20 (4) (a) notice of wish not to be informed of any Adoption application will not automatically be a Respondent.

        c)   If a child was born after the 1st December 2003 a Father obtains P.R. by having his name on the Birth Certificate.

6.   Pursuant to Rule 23 other automatic Respondents are (i) any person in whose favour there is provision for contact (ii) any Adoption Agency having P.R. for the child (iii) any Adoption Agency which has taken part in the arrangements for Adoption (iv) any Local Authority which has looked after or is caring for the child.

7.   Appointment of the child's Guardian is only appropriate if the child has been made a Party.

8.   The Rules require that the Court Officer give notice to a Respondent Parent of any request for that Parent's consent to be dispensed with and, also, that the Court Officer serve the Parent with the Applicant's (anonymised if necessary) Statement of Facts. Completion of this note will ensure that the Court Officer is told whether the appropriate notice should be given and whether the Statement of Facts is to be sent out. In cases where Section 47 does not apply it will usually be the case that the consent of the birth parents does have to be dispensed with and, therefore, a Rule 24 (iv) notice and a statement of facts will need to be served on the Respondent Parents.

9.   If the whereabouts of Respondent Parents are unknown or uncertain it may be appropriate to order that the Local Authority (rather than, for example, a Step Parent Applicant) shall serve the necessary papers on the Parents. The Local Authority will often have to carry out such enquiries in any event in connection with its Annex A Report. This direction is intended to make clear to the Local Authority precisely what documents need to be served and the documents referred to are documents which the Local Authority will receive itself from the Court at the outset of the proceedings. A Respondent Parent is not automatically entitled to a copy of the Adoption Application form.

10.   For what constitutes "cannot be found" refer to re R (Adoption) [1967] 1 WLR 34; re S (Adoption) [1999] 2 FLR 374; re F (An Infant) [1970] 1 QB 385 at 389b; re A (Adoption of Russian Child) [2000] 1 FLR 539.

11.   This direction for further directions to be given on paper is intended to be an alternative to a Directions Hearing being fixed at the outset. It might be appropriate when, for example, further information from an Annex A report or the like will clarify whether a Directions Hearing is necessary and, if so, whether the Application for an Adoption Order is likely to be opposed or not.

PART IV

INTERNATIONAL ISSUES

CHAPTER 16

CHILD ABDUCTION[1]

16.1 INTRODUCTION

One of the most striking changes of the twentieth century was the increasing ability of the greater part of the world's population to travel – whether to wage wars, explore lost worlds, escape oppression, or merely to relocate or holiday. In recent years in particular, the democratisation of States, the relaxation of border controls and the cheapening of the price of travel has allowed the world to shrink.

This change brought a greater understanding of the need to prevent the unlawful movement of children around the world: what has been called by some, 'child abduction'. The latter terminology is unfortunate as it is, of course, entirely pejorative. It is important at the outset to recognise that there may well be very many different reasons for one parent seeking to abduct a child from the environment of the other: some reasons may objectively be said to be indefensible,[2] others may be said to be wholly

---

[1]   This chapter concentrates (almost exclusively) on international parental child abduction. It was written by Mr Edward Devereux, (barrister, Harcourt Chambers), and Miss Anne-Marie Hutchinson OBE, (solicitor, Dawson Cornwell). It does not seek to consider in any detail the unlawful movement of children *within* the United Kingdom. Nor, indeed, does it seek in any way to provide an exhaustive examination of all aspects of the relevant law relating to international parental child abduction. That would take a book. Indeed, some of the most comprehensive commentaries on the law relating to the international movement of children *are* books: see, Lowe, Everall QC and Nicholls *International Movement of Children Law Practice and Procedure* (Jordan Publishing Limited, 2004); and Beaumont and McEleavy, *The Hague Convention on International Child Abduction* (Oxford University Press, 1999). In addition, see *Rayden & Jackson on Divorce and Family Matters* (LexisNexis Butterworths, 2005); Professor Hugh Bevan *Butterworths Family Law Service* (LexisNexis Butterworths); Hershman and McFarlane *Children Law and Practice* (Jordan Publishing Limited); and Lowe and Douglas *Bromley's Family Law* (Oxford University Press, 10th edn, 2007). In preparing this chapter, we are enormously indebted to all of these helpful texts. We are also very grateful to the following: Mr Justice Baker, Mr Ben Gummer MP, Mr Henry Setright QC, who generously read an early draft of this chapter for the first edition of this book, and Mr Matthew Molloy, Mr Joseph Bernard and Miss Lynne Land, Miss Judith Partington, clerks, Harcourt Chambers, and Mr Simon Boutwood, Chambers Director, Harcourt Chambers and the partners of Dawson Cornwell.

[2]   This appears to be the view of the Court of Appeal (Criminal Division). In *R v Talib Hussein Kayani; R v Madhat Solliman* [2011] EWCA Crim 2871, [2012] 1 Cr App R 16, the Court of Appeal said (at para [54]): 'The abduction of children from a loving parent

laudable: all will in different ways affect the child subject to the abduction. This chapter seeks to set out a short overview of the relevant law and procedure, including consideration of both civil remedies and criminal sanctions, as it is currently applied and practised in the courts of England and Wales.

16.2   THE STARTING POINT: THE STATUTORY BACKGROUND

Any practitioner concerned with child abduction should have a close familiarity with the following:[3]

- The Child Abduction and Custody Act 1985 (the CACA 1985), (which, by virtue of Sch 1, incorporates the 1980 Hague Convention on the Civil Aspects of International Child Abduction, ('the Hague Convention'), and which, by virtue of Sch 2, incorporates The 1980 European Convention on the Recognition and Enforcement of Decisions Concerning Custody of Children and on the Restoration of Custody of Children ('the European Custody Convention'));

- The 1980 Hague Convention on the Civil Aspects of International Child Abduction;[4]

- Council Regulation (EC) No 2201/2003 (Brussels II) of 27 November 2003 concerning Jurisdiction and the Recognition and Enforcement of Judgments in Matrimonial Matters and in the

---

is an offence of unspeakable cruelty to the loving parent and to the child or children, whatever they may later think of the parent from whom they have been estranged as a result of the abduction. It is a cruel offence even if the criminal responsible for it is the other parent.' The Court of Appeal indicated that parental abductors should not always be prosecuted under the Child Abduction Act 1984 but should be prosecuted for the common law offence of kidnapping. In addition, the Court of Appeal suggested that the maximum sentence for child abduction under the Child Abduction Act 1984 should be increased.

3   There is no separate treatment in this chapter of the 1950 European Convention for the Protection of Human Rights and Fundamental Freedoms though of course the jurisprudence of the ECtHR has had a significant impact on child abduction cases in recent years, especially following the Grand Chamber decision of *Neulinger and Shuruk v Switzerland* (Application no. 41615/07) [2011] 1 FLR 122. For discussion of recent decisions of the ECtHR see the Supreme Court's decision of and the Court of Appeal's decision of *Re E (Children) (Abduction: Custody Appeal)* [2011] EWCA Civ 361, [2011] 2 FLR 724, and in particular the judgments of Thorpe LJ and Aikens LJ (which considers the role of the ECtHR).

4   Beaumont & McEleavy *The Hague Convention on International Child Abduction* (Oxford University Press, 1999) although now dated, provides one of the best detailed discussions of the Hague Convention.

Matters of Parental Responsibility, 'Brussels II Revised' (or 'Brussels IIbis' or 'Brussels IIA'), but for the purposes of this chapter, 'Brussels IIR';[5]

- The 1996 Hague Convention on Jurisdiction, Applicable Law, Recognition, Enforcement and Cooperation in respect of Parental Responsibility and Measures for the Protection of Children;[6] and

- The Pakistan Protocol of 17 January 2003.

A list of States to which the Hague Convention is currently in force with England and Wales can be found at Appendix 1 below.

16.2.1 The interaction between Brussels IIR, the Hague Convention and the European Custody Convention

Brussels IIR is the current European statutory framework which determines matters of jurisdiction and recognition in respect of the dissolution of marriage, legal separation and annulment of marriage, and, most importantly for the purposes of this chapter, 'parental responsibility'.[7] It applies to all Member States of the European Union except for Denmark and has applied to those relevant Member States since 1 March 2005. It has direct effect over domestic law. Its impact in respect of the child abduction cases that it governs is very significant. The principal relevant Articles are: Art 8, 10, 11, 15, 40, 42 and 55. In particular, for child abduction cases, it provides a detailed set of provisions that determine which courts have jurisdiction with the overall aim that in cases where a child has been abducted, the jurisdiction to determine matters relating to the child's welfare shall remain in the requesting State until certain events have taken place; it reinforces various international obligations so as to ensure that the relevant child and his or her parents are able, fairly and properly, to participate in the proceedings; it seeks to ensure that Hague Convention proceedings are completed within 6 weeks (unless there are exceptional circumstances); it creates a novel mechanism by which the courts of a requesting State can consider the question of custody of a child after particular Hague Convention non return orders are made; it provides an ability for one Member State to transfer a case to

---

5   A useful resource is Lowe, Everall QC and Nicholls, *The New Brussels II Regulation A Supplement to International Movement of Children* (Jordan Publishing Limited, 2005).

6   As at the time of writing, this has yet to come into force, but is shortly expected to. It is not discussed in this chapter, though it will be of very considerable importance for those practising in international family law.

7   See, in particular Arts 2, 3, and 8 of Brussels IIR. See also, *Re C* (Case C-435/06) [2008] 1 FLR 490. As determined by the European Court of Justice, Brussels IIR applies to both public law and private law disputes as the Regulation covers all decisions on parental responsibility, including measures for the protection of the child: see *Re C* (Case C-435/06) at 497, para [31] and see also *Re A (Area of Freedom, Security and Justice)* (C-523/07) [2009] 2 FLR 1.

another Member State;[8] and it provides a process by which orders can be recognized and enforced between Member States.

Brussels IIR has largely superseded the provisions of the European Custody Convention so as to render them as almost redundant.[9]

By virtue of Art 60(d) and (e) of Brussels IIR, Brussels IIR takes precedence over the Hague Convention and the European Custody Convention insofar as those Conventions concern matters governed by the Regulation. Brussels IIR is, accordingly, said to *complement* and *reinforce* the Hague Convention.[10]

Applications under Brussels IIR and/or the Hague Convention must be determined before an application under the European Custody Convention.[11]

Practitioners may find some of the darker recesses of Brussels IIR illuminated by *The Practice Guide for the Application of the New Brussels II Regulation* (1 June 2005).

16.3   PREVENTING OR REGULARISING A REMOVAL FROM ENGLAND AND WALES: THE PROCEDURE

16.3.1   The use of preventative or regularising court orders

If an abduction from England and Wales is feared or has taken place, then an urgent application should be made to court. Where the particular facts demand it, the application should ordinarily be made to the Urgent High Court Applications' Judge of the Family Division,[12] sitting at the

---

8   Though note the observations of Thorpe LJ in *Re EC (Child Abduction: Stayed Proceedings)* [2006] EWCA Civ 1115, [2007] 1 FLR 57 at 62, para [18].

9   Save, of course, in respect of Denmark. This chapter does not seek to consider the European Custody Convention in any detail.

10   See, for example, Recitals (17) and (18) of Brussels IIR. Baroness Hale has said that the 'Brussels II Revised Regulation was designed to strengthen the application of the [Hague] Convention throughout Europe...': *In re D (A Child) (Abduction: Rights of Custody)* [2006] UKHL 51, [2007] 1 AC 619 at 644, para [68]. Thorpe LJ has described the particular provisions of Brussels IIR relating to child abduction as providing the 'fortification of what were seen, in the light of nearly 20 years of operation, as weaknesses or loopholes through which abductors were escaping': *Vigreux v Michel* [2006] EWCA Civ 630, [2006] 2 FLR 1180 at 1192, para [37]. In *Re Rinau* (Case C-195/08 PPU) [2008] 2 FLR 1495, the European Court of Justice said at 1507, para [52]: 'The Regulation seeks, in particular, to deter child abductions between Member States and, in cases of abduction, to obtain the child's return without delay.'

11   See Art 60(d) of Brussels IIR and 16(4)(c) of the CACA 1985.

12   Or, indeed, a Deputy High Court Judge. But see, generally, *Re K (Removal from the Jurisdiction: Practice)* [1999] 2 FLR 1084, at 1086H–1087A, where Thorpe LJ expressed the view that where a case involved consideration of the legal system of a foreign state, particularly where there were different traditions or culture, and where it might require notarized agreements or mirror orders, ordinarily it should be heard by a Judge of the

Royal Courts of Justice, Strand, London, WC2A 2LL,[13] usually on a without notice basis for any number of a range of preventative or regulatory orders prior to a proper consideration of the matter on an *inter partes* basis. It is better to apply during normal court hours (10.30am – 4.30pm), although in matters of the greatest emergency, contact can be made with the out of hours Family Division duty judge (who can be contacted through the general enquiries telephone number for the Royal Courts of Justice). The Urgent High Court Applications' Judge will usually expect without notice matters to be heard at 10.30am or 2pm (before the listed 'at risk' matters are called on). Practitioners should be alive to the proper procedure in making an application on a 'without notice basis'.[14]

In other cases, say, where the child has not yet been removed but where there is a fear of retention after what is to be an agreed period of contact abroad, an application may be made for various regulatory orders to a circuit judge, or to a circuit judge sitting as a High Court judge by virtue of s 9 of the Senior Courts Act 1981, in the appropriate court that has jurisdiction to hear the case. Indeed, there may well be no need to place the matter before the Urgent High Court Applications' Judge as all circuit judges will be relatively well experienced in determining applications relating to the removal of children from the jurisdiction.

In all cases, however, it is crucial to move *fast*.

16.3.2 A list of potential directions or orders

Depending on the seriousness of the threat of abduction, the cogency of the evidence, and the particular facts of the case (and, in particular, where the potential abductor and the child is), the following directions or range of orders might be contemplated:

- A parental responsibility order.

- A prohibited steps order preventing the removal of the child from the jurisdiction of the courts of England and Wales.[15]

- A contact order with conditions requiring the return of the child at the end of the period of contact (if that contact is to be abroad).

Family Division. See also, for the case of Pakistan, the *Guidance from the President's Office – Implementation of UK – Pakistan Judicial Protocol on Child Contact and Abduction.*

[13] The telephone number for general enquiries is: 020-7947-6000.

[14] See in particular *KY v DD (Injunctions)* [2011] EWHC 1277 (Fam), [2012] 2 FLR 200 at 204–207, paras [13]–[16]. In addition, the practitioner must consider r 12.47 of the FPR 2010.

[15] Though it must be said that orders under section 8 of the Children Act 1989 will not generally be sufficient to deter or prevent an abduction.

- A residence order with or without ancillary injunctions.[16]

- An order making the child a ward of court.[17]

- An order requiring the surrender of a child's passport (under s 37 of the Family Law Act 1986[18] or, if the passport is held by a foreign national, under the court's inherent jurisdiction).[19]

- An order prohibiting the application for further passports or other travel documents.[20]

- An order requiring a person to give up their own passport and restraining them from leaving the jurisdiction (whether under s 5 of the Child Abduction and Custody Act 1985 or the court's inherent jurisdiction).[21]

- An order under s 33 of the Family Law Act 1986 or under s 24A of the CACA 1985 or under the inherent jurisdiction requiring a person[22] who the court has reason to believe may have relevant information as to where the child is to disclose it to the court. Such persons may or may not be required to attend before the court to provide that information.[23]

---

[16] Though note that one cannot attach a penal notice to a residence order so that a breach of such an order cannot, save in the most exceptional circumstances (see, for example, *Jolly v Hull; Jolly v Jolly* [2000] 2 FLR 69) be punishable as a contempt of court: see *In re P (Minors) (Custody Order: Penal Notice)* [1990] 1 WLR 613. For the use of such ancillary injunctions under the inherent jurisdiction of the Senior Courts Act 1981 or the County Courts Act 1984, including against third parties, see *C v K (Inherent Powers: Exclusion Orders)* [1996] 2 FLR 506.

[17] See below for further discussion.

[18] This is a limited provision which can be relied upon only if the court has already made an order 'prohibiting or otherwise restricting the removal of a child from the United Kingdom or from any specified part of it or from a specified dependent territory' and only in respect of United Kingdom passports.

[19] See FPR 2010, PD 12F, paras 4.9–4.13 which appears to have superseded *Practice Direction* [1983] 2 All ER 253, [1983] 1 WLR 558.

[20] FPR 2010, PD 12F, para 4.10 states that: 'The Identity and Passport Service ("IPS") will take action to prevent a United Kingdom passport or replacement passport being issued only where the IPS has been served with a court order expressly requiring a United Kingdom passport to be surrendered, or expressly prohibiting the issue of any further United Kingdom passport facilities to the child without the consent of the court, or the holder of such an order. Accordingly, in every case in which such an order has been made, the IPS must be served the same day if possible, or at the latest the following day, with a copy of the order. It is the responsibility of the applicant to do this ...'. The prohibition, unless varied, will continue until the child's sixteenth birthday.

[21] See *B v B (Injunction: Jurisdiction)* [1998] 1 WLR 329; *Re A-K (Foreign Passport: Jurisdiction)* [1997] 2 FLR 569; and *Gough v Chief Constable of the Derbyshire Constabulary* [2002] 2 All ER 985.

[22] This may be used against a wide range of persons including third parties such as solicitors, the police, and other professionals.

[23] Though note there is only jurisdiction to make an order pursuant to section 33 of the Family Law Act 1986 in proceedings for, or relating to, a 'Part I' order as defined by that

- An order providing for publicity in respect of the abducted child.[24]

- An order under s 34 of the Family Law Act 1986.

- An order under s 36 of the Family Law Act 1986.

- An order directing a Port Alert.[25]

- Passport,[26] Location or Collection orders under the inherent jurisdiction.

- Agency and other orders (against banks, local authorities, government departments, health authorities, telephone (including mobile telephone) providers[27] and orders against airlines.[28]

- Consideration of mirror orders.[29]

- A consent order by which the person who seeks leave to remove the child enters into a bond which can be forfeited to the other party in the case of a breach.[30]

- Undertakings provided to the English court, or sworn declarations before the foreign court.[31]

Act (see s 1 of the Family Law Act 1986). Proceedings under the Hague Convention or the European Custody Convention are not 'Part I' proceedings. Hence recourse should be had, in respect of those Conventions, to rr 12.43–12.51 of the FPR 2010 and s 24A of the CACA 1985.

[24] For a case in which publicity was used, see *Re D (Minor) (Child Abduction)* [1989] 1 FLR 97. See FPR 2012, PD 12F, paras 4.15–4.16.

[25] See below.

[26] About which see *Young v Young* [2012] EWHC 138 (Fam), [2012] 2 FLR 470.

[27] See the *Practice Direction (Disclosure of Addresses)* [1989] 1 WLR 219, [1989] 1 All ER 765, [1989] 1 FLR 307 as amended by *Practice Direction 20 July 1995 (amending PD of 13 February 1989)*.

[28] See FPR 2010, PD 12O (Arrival *of Child in England by Air*), which replaces *Practice Direction (Arrival of Child in England by Air)* [1980] 1 WLR 73, [1980] 1 All ER 288. This provides that a person may apply for information from the airline carrier 'to enable him to meet the aeroplane' where it is expected that a child will be returning to the jurisdiction having previously been removed or retained abroad.

[29] See, for example, *F v F (Minors) (Custody: Foreign Order)* [1989] Fam 1, sub nom *Re F (Minors) (Custody: Foreign Order)* [1989] 1 FLR 335 at 350C; *Re HB (Abduction: Children's Objections)* [1998] 1 FLR 422 at 427H–428A; *Re S (Removal from Jurisdiction)* [1999] 1 FLR 850 at 861F; and, importantly, *Re W (Jurisdiction: Mirror Order)* [2011] EWCA Civ 703.

[30] See the *Guidance of the Family Division Sub-Committee of the Supreme Court Procedure Committee* [1987] Fam Law 263 (which is also set out in *Rayden & Jackson*, vol 1(2) at 46.53), which emphasises that such protective measures should only be contemplated when there is a 'real danger' that the child may not be returned from a trip abroad; *Re T (Staying Contact in Non Convention Country) (Note)* [1999] 1 FLR 262; and *Re L (Removal from Jurisdiction: Holiday)* [2001] 1 FLR 241.

[31] Practical experience, unfortunately, is that some foreign jurisdictions do not appreciate the nature of undertakings given and may accordingly not respect them: see *In re E*

- Registration of orders.

Where there has been a removal from a primary carer and the child remains, and is expected to remain in the jurisdiction, the proper application should be for an immediate and peremptory order for the return of the child to the primary carer. Such an application should be issued at once to a court, which may be the High Court of Justice, Family Division, which has the facility to offer a 24-hour service, or at least a service on every court sitting day, for the issue of an immediate order on a without notice basis and for accommodating the necessary *inter partes* hearing within days thereafter.[32]

16.3.3 Prospective agencies that might be made subject to orders

Amongst others, the following agencies might be made subject to orders:

- The United Kingdom Border Agency.

- The Department for Work and Pensions.

- HM Revenue and Customs.

- The Ministry of Defence.

- The Office for National Statistics.

- The National Health Service.

- The United Kingdom Identity and Passport Service.

- The Child Support Agency.

- The Driver and Vehicle Licensing Agency.

- British Telecommunications PLC and various mobile telephone providers.

- Different departments of local authorities (such as housing and education departments).

(Children) (Abduction: Custody Appeal) [2011] UKSC 27, [2012] 1 AC 144 at 152, para [7]. See *Re T (Staying Contact in Non Convention Country) (Note)* [1999] 1 FLR 262 for the use of undertakings and a notarised agreement made in a foreign jurisdiction as a protective measure to ensure the return of a child; and *Re A (Security for Return to Jurisdiction) (Note)* [1999] 2 FLR 1 for the use of sworn declarations. See also *Re S (Leave to Remove from Jurisdiction: Securing Return from Holiday)* [2001] 2 FLR 507.
[32] Per Thorpe LJ in *Re R (Children: Peremptory Return)* [2011] EWCA Civ 558, [2011] 2 FLR 863, at [22].

16.3.4 The need for clarity in drafting orders

When drawing up such orders care must be had to draft them in such a way as to make their intention abundantly clear to all who will read them (for example, the alleged abductor and anyone who might have to consider the order in any foreign jurisdiction, whether in translated form or otherwise). Thus a residence order might be expressed in wider terms than is usually the case so as to make it unambiguously clear that a child's settled home is in England with one of its parents. Additionally, it might be useful to have asserted that the primary jurisdiction, in the case of any dispute as to matters relating to parental responsibility, would be the English court and that the child was and remains habitually resident in England and Wales. If time allows, it might also be prudent to obtain a proper, certified translation of the order.

If, however, it is felt that an alleged abductor should not be alerted to the provisions of a particular order, then such an order should be drawn up separately and explicit provision should be given to whomsoever the order is directed not to betray the existence of the order to the abductor.

16.3.5 The use of wardship

Wardship is very often invoked to prevent the removal of a child from the jurisdiction. Wardship proceedings are initiated in the High Court.[33] Once a child is made a ward of court no important step can be taken in his or her life without the permission of the court. Thus wardship has the great advantage that immediately on making a child a ward of court, permission is required to take the child out of the jurisdiction (save that if proceedings for divorce, nullity or judicial separation in respect of the marriage of a child's parents are continuing in a court in another part of the UK[34] or in a specified dependent territory, or proceedings for dissolution or annulment or legal separation in respect of a civil partnership of a child's parents are continuing in another part of the UK or a child is habitually resident in another part of the UK or in a specified dependent territory, the child can travel to the other part of the UK or specified dependent territory without any such leave being required: see s 38 of the Family Law Act 1986). If the child is removed without such leave, it is immediately a contempt of court.[35]

16.3.6 The All Ports Warning System

Where there is a fear that a child might be unlawfully removed from the country, a request may be made by any person at any time, day or night,

---

[33] FPR 2010, r 12.36(1).

[34] Which means in a part of the United Kingdom outside the jurisdiction in which the child is a ward.

[35] In direct contrast to the case where only a residence order is in place. For the procedural rules as to wardship see FPR 2010, rr 12.36–12.42 and PD 12D.

for a Port Alert: see FPR 2010, PD 12F (*International Child Abduction*) and *Practice Direction (Minor: Preventing Removal Abroad)*[36] and *Home Office Circular* 21/1986.[37] Before issuing a Port Alert, however, the police or the court must first be persuaded that the danger of removal is 'real and imminent'.[38]

There are, theoretically, two ways by which a Port Alert can be initiated. The first is by application to the Police, but recent experience appears to show that this method is not often used. The second, and more preferable method, is by application to the High Court. In respect of the latter, the order can applied for as a standalone order, or (more usually) as part of a Passport, Location or Collection order.

Once granted a Port Alert will result in details of the child and the alleged abductor, and the person to whom the child should be returned if the child is found, being communicated to relevant officers at ports and airports throughout the country and the National Ports Office. If the child is between the ages of 16 to 18, a Port Alert cannot be made without there first being an order prohibiting the child's removal from the UK.[39] It may be said that an application to the High Court has its advantages: it has a persuasive power of its own, and it might well be possible to persuade a judge to make further orders (such as any of those set out above).

FPR 2010, PD 12F, sets out the matters which should be given to the police[40]. They are:

(a)   the name, sex, date of birth, physical description, nationality and passport number of the child (if known);

(b)   the name, age, physical description, nationality and passport number, relationship to the child, and whether the child is likely to assist him or her of the person likely to remove the child;

(c)   the name, relationship to the child, nationality telephone number and (if appropriate) solicitor's or other legal representative's name and contact details of the person applying for a port alert;

(d)   the likely destination;

---

36   [1986] 1 WLR 475, [1986] 1 All ER 983, [1986] 2 FLR 89.

37   See also *Port Alerts: Guidance by the Child Abduction Unit, Rayden & Jackson,* vol 1 (2) at 46.55.

38   *Practice Direction (Minor: Preventing Removal Abroad)*; *Port Alerts: Guidance by the Child Abduction Unit, Rayden & Jackson,* vol 1 (2) at 46.55; *Home Office Circular* 21/1986; and FPR 2010, PD 12F, paras 4.5–4.8.

39   *Practice Direction (Minor: Preventing Removal Abroad); and Port Alerts: Guidance by the Child Abduction Unit.*

40   Similar details are given to the court in the form completed for the Tipstaff when applying for a Passport Order, Location Order or Collection Order.

(e) the likely time of travel and port of embarkation and, if known, details of travel arrangements;

(f) the grounds for the port alert (whether (i) because there is a suspected offence under s 1 or s 2 of the Child Abduction Act 1984; or (ii) the child is subject to a court order);

(g) the details of the person to whom the child should be returned if intercepted.

Once a non court issued Port Alert has been issued the child's name will remain on what is known as the 'stop list' for four weeks before being automatically removed, unless a further application is made.[41]

16.4 REACTING TO A CHILD ABDUCTION TO, OR FROM, ENGLAND AND WALES

Once there has been a child abduction to or from England and Wales, how should a practitioner react?[42]

There are three matters which need to be considered:

(a) the general procedure relating to *incoming* child abduction cases;

(b) the law relating to *incoming* child abduction cases;[43] and

(c) the law relating to *outgoing* child abduction cases.

16.4.1 Procedure

16.4.1.1 The initial application: Hague Convention cases

If a child has been abducted and brought to England and Wales, and the Hague Convention is to be invoked, an applicant, an institution or other body claiming that a child has been removed or retained in breach of

---

[41] FPR 2010, PD 12F, para 4.8 and *Practice Direction (Minor: Preventing Removal)*.

[42] In respect of the Hague Convention it has been held that there is an obligation on all practitioners to bring to the court's attention any possibility that the Hague Convention may apply: *Re H (Abduction: Habitual Residence: Consent)* [2000] 2 FLR 294 at 305–306.

[43] Although discussion of the Hague Convention will take place in the analysis of *incoming* child abduction cases, the commentary may be useful, in general terms, for practitioners who are faced with assisting a left behind parent to invoke remedies under that Convention (if the State to which the child has been taken is a party to it) in another jurisdiction (ie *outgoing* child abduction cases). There is, however, something of a necessary health warning that goes with this: whilst an autonomous interpretation of the Hague Convention should be encouraged, interpretation in this jurisdiction of certain Articles of the Convention may not always be a reliable guide as to how they are interpreted in other jurisdictions.

custody rights will usually apply, invoking his or her Hague Convention remedies to the Central Authority of his home State who, in turn, will contact the Central Authority for England and Wales, the International Child Abduction and Contact Unit ('ICACU', or, 'the Child Abduction Unit'). It is, however, also possible to apply directly to the Central Authority of England and Wales or to any other Central Authority. If the Child Abduction and Contact Unit has received the application, it will refer the case to one of the specialist solicitors on its panel.

The application to the Central Authority should, as Art 8 of the Hague Convention sets out, contain:[44]

(a) information concerning the identity of the applicant, the child and of the person alleged to have removed or retained the child;

(b) where available, the date of birth of the child;

(c) the grounds on which the applicant's claim for return of the child is based; and

(d) all available information relating to the whereabouts of the child and the identity of the person with whom the child is presumed to be.

In addition, the application may be accompanied by:

(a) an authenticated copy of any relevant document, decision or agreement;

(b) a certificate or an affidavit from a Central Authority, or other competent authority of the State of the child's habitual residence, or from a qualified person, concerning the relevant law of that State; and

(c) any other relevant document.

16.4.1.2 *Public funding*

The usual rule is that an applicant in an incoming Hague Convention (or European Custody Convention) case is entitled to non-means and non-merit tested public funding (so long as the letter of instruction from the Child Abduction Unit to the plaintiff's solicitor is provided to the Legal Services Commission). A respondent to an incoming Hague Convention case must meet the relevant means and merit based criteria that are required by the Legal Services Commission.[45]

---

[44] See below for the detailed requirements of FPR 2010, PD 12F.

[45] See *The Legal Services Commission Manual*, vol 3, Part C, The Funding Code: Decision Making Guidance, 3C – 217.6 at para 20.58.

In incoming non-Convention cases, both parties must meet the relevant means and merit based criteria.

When a final Hague Convention order is made, the applicant's non-means tested funding will immediately cease.

16.4.1.3 The commencement of proceedings: The Hague Convention and the European Custody Convention

The relevant procedural rules which apply to proceedings under the Hague Convention (and the European Custody Convention) are those set out in Part 12, Chapter 6, Section 1, r 12.43–12.57 of the FPR 2010. All Hague Convention (and European Custody Convention) cases are commenced by the issuing of an application (and in respect of the Hague Convention in Form C67), in the Principal Registry of the Family Division.[46]

By virtue of FPR 2010, PD 12F, the application must contain the following information:

(a)   the name and date of birth of the child in respect of whom the application is made;

(b)   the names of the child's parents or guardians;

(c)   the whereabouts or suspected whereabouts of the child;

(d)   the interest of the applicant in the matter (eg mother, father, or person with whom the child lives and details of any order placing the child with that person);

(e)   the reasons for the application;

(f)   details of any proceedings (including proceedings not in England or Wales, and including any legal proceedings which have finished) relating to the children;

(g)   where the application is for the return of a child, the identity of the person alleged to have removed or retained the child and, if different, the identity of the person with whom the child is thought to be.

---

[46]   FPR 2010, r 12.45(a).

In European Custody Convention proceedings, the application must also include a copy of the decision relating to custody or access which is sought to be registered or enforced or in relation to which a declaration is sought.[47]

Where the application is one to which Brussels IIR applies, there is also an obligation for the application to include any details of measures taken by courts or authorities to ensure the protection of the child after its return to the Member State of habitual residence of which the applicant is aware.[48]

The application should be accompanied by all relevant documents including but not limited to (a) an authenticated copy of any relevant decision or agreement; and (b) a certificate of an affidavit from a Central Authority, or other competent authority of the State of the child's habitual residence, or from a qualified person, concerning the relevant law of the State.[49] Ordinarily, the applicant ought to file a statement in support of the application, verified by a statement of truth.[50] In Hague Convention proceedings, the statement ought to consider the key concepts – such as, for example, rights of custody and habitual residence – but ought not to go into extraneous detail about irrelevant matters.

It is important in Hague Convention proceedings, even if the case seeks in the first instance merely to rely on the Hague Convention, or Brussels IIR and the Hague Convention, to include in the application a claim under the inherent jurisdiction so that there is at least the option of pursuing a return (having regard to welfare considerations), if the primary application pursuant to the Hague Convention is unsuccessful. Unhelpfully, different application forms have been created in relation to Hague Convention cases and cases brought under the inherent jurisdiction. This is a procedural anomaly that should not, it is suggested, stand in the way of pleading cases in the alternative.

By virtue of r 12.3(1) of the FPR 2010, the respondents to an application brought under the CACA 1985 are:

(a) the person who is alleged to have brought the child into the United Kingdom;

(b) the person with whom the child is alleged to be;

---

47 FPR 2010, PD 12F, para 2.20.
48 FPR 2010, PD 12F, para 2.11(h). This would appear to be related to the obligation under Article 11(4) of Brussels IIR. Article 11(4) provides that: 'A court cannot refuse to return a child on the basis of Article 13b of the 1980 Hague Convention if it is established that adequate arrangements have been made to secure the protection of the child after his or her return.'
49 FPR 2010, PD 12F, para 2.12.
50 FPR 2010, PD 12F, para 2.13.

(c)   any parent or guardian of the child who is within the United Kingdom and is not otherwise a party;

(d)   any person in whose favour a decision relating to custody has been made if that person is not otherwise a party;

(e)   any other person who appears to the court to have a sufficient interest in the welfare of the child.[51]

16.4.1.4   *The first without notice hearing*

At the first hearing, an applicant's legal representative will attend before the Urgent High Court Applications' Judge sitting at the Royal Courts of Justice, Strand, London WC2A 2LL (usually on a without notice basis), place before the court the application and a statement in support[52] and any other relevant documents, explain the factual background and seek interim directions and orders leading up to an *inter partes* hearing listed usually within seven days. The Tipstaff, or the Deputy or Assistant Tipstaff, should usually be asked to attend – the Associate in court will make contact with the Tipstaff's office – because in many cases either a Passport, Location or Collection order will be needed. Although the Tipstaff drafts and executes (usually through the police) these orders, it is left to the applicant personally, to serve the court's directions order on the respondent (which should happen after the Tipstaff has executed the Passport, Location or Collection order). Once proceedings have commenced, the court must stay other welfare proceedings relating to the child.[53]

In addition, at the first hearing the applicant may seek recourse to a whole range of other orders such as those contemplated at **16.3.2** above.

It is important to see, as soon as possible, whether the respondent intends to resist the return by way of reliance on any of the exceptions to the obligation to return set out within the Hague Convention. Accordingly, the respondent is usually required, within 7 days beginning on the day on which the application is served, to file and serve an answer and (usually) a statement setting out which, if any, Articles are relied upon and why.[54]

Practitioners must take care to recall that the hearing of the application under the Hague Convention or European Custody Convention cannot be

---

[51]   Who exactly might fall within this category was canvassed in *W v W (Abduction: Joinder as Party)* [2009] EWHC 3288 (Fam), [2010] 1 FLR 1342.

[52]   Though, in fact, there is no obligation to file a statement at the outset, it is common practice and advisable to do so; see FPR 2010, PD 12F, para 2.13. See *Re W (Abduction: Procedure)* [1995] 1 FLR 878 for the content of such statements..

[53]   Art 16 of the Hague Convention; CACA 1985, s 9; and r 12.51 of the FPR 2010.

[54]   FPR 2010, r 12.49.

adjourned for a period exceeding 21 days at any one time.[55] Often in order to meet this obligation the case will be listed merely for mention only with the attendance of parties excused.

There is a requirement, unless the court orders otherwise, to file the application at the time when the application is made (or in the case where the application is made by telephone, on the next business day after the making of the application).[56]

16.4.1.5   The first inter partes hearing

When the parties attend for the *inter partes* hearing a number of directions should be settled with a view to obtaining an early trial date if the matter remains contested. By virtue of r 12.48 of the FPR 2010, as soon as practicable after an application pursuant to the Hague Convention or European Custody Convention is made, the court may give directions as to the following matters, among others:

(a)   whether service of the application may be dispensed with;

(b)   whether the proceedings should be transferred to another court under FPR 2010, r 12.54;

(c)   expedition of the proceedings or any part of the proceedings (and any direction for expedition may specify a date by which the court must issue its final judgment in the proceedings or a specified part of the proceedings);

(d)   the steps to be taken in the proceedings and the time by which each step is to be taken;

(e)   whether the child or any other person should be made a party to the proceedings;

(f)   if the child is not made a party to the proceedings, the manner in which the child's wishes and feelings are to be ascertained, having regard to the child's age and maturity and in particular whether an officer of the Service or a Welsh family proceedings officer should report to the court for that purpose;

(g)   where the child is made a party to the proceedings, the appointment of a children's guardian for that child unless a children's guardian has already been appointed;

(h)   the attendance of the child or any other person before the court;

---

[55]   FPR 2010, r 12.51.
[56]   FPR 2010, r 12.47(2).

(i)   the appointment of a litigation friend for a child or for any protected party, unless a litigation friend has already been appointed;

(j)   the service of documents;

(k)   the filing of evidence including expert evidence; and

(l)   whether the parties and their representatives should meet at any stage of the proceedings and the purpose of such a meeting.

Thus, as a brief checklist, the following matters should be considered:

- The filing and serving of an answer[57] and statement by the applicant (if that has not already happened).

- The filing and serving of a statement in reply by the respondent.

- Expert evidence (as to the law of the requesting State or other matters relating to the child and/or the parties).

- Whether requests should be made to the Home Office.[58]

- Whether there ought to be an Article 15 request to the requesting State.[59]

- The date of the final hearing.

- The attendance of the parties at the final hearing and whether each party should attend in person, or whether they should give evidence or participate in the proceedings by video or telephone link.[60]

- Whether oral evidence should be permitted.

---

57   Practitioners should, however, remember the strictures of Roderic Wood J in *Re H (Abduction)* [2009] EWHC 1735 (Fam), [2009] 2 FLR 1513, at 1521, para [21] about parents 'running an entirely bogus defence only to abandon it at the last minute'.

58   About which see the *President's Guidance: Communicating with the Home Office* (January 2006) [2009] 1 FLR 71 (updated and reissued in October 2010).

59   About which see *Re T (Abduction: Rights of Custody)* [2008] EWHC 809 (Fam), [2008] 2 FLR 1794, where Coleridge J said (at 1797, para [11]) 'In these Hague Convention cases it is peculiarly important that issues like rights of custody should be very clearly settled by the foreign law, either directly by reference to statute or to other written material or, if not, by reference to the foreign court's previous decisions. It would be, I think, highly invidious for the English court to trespass into this area unless it was unavoidable.'

60   Though not concerned with Hague Convention proceedings, the guidance given in relation to 'stranded spouses' is important and should be considered by all practitioners and the court when the court is dealing with a case where it is asserted that there is one party unable to travel to this country: *Re S (Wardship: Guidance in Cases of Stranded Spouses)* [2011] 1 FLR 319. This was issued following the case of *Re S (Wardship: Stranded Spouses)* [2010] EWHC 1669 (Fam), [2011] 1 FLR 305.

- Whether it is appropriate to 'hear the child' and how that should best be effected (including contemplation of whether separate representation of the child should be permitted).

- Whether it is appropriate to join another person 'who appears to the court to have sufficient interest in the welfare of the child' pursuant to FPR 2010, r 12.3.[61]

- Collaboration with other authorities.[62]

- The filing and serving of skeleton arguments.

- Contact with the child.

- What undertakings might be offered, or required.[63]

In all cases, the court must ensure that the case reaches a final hearing as soon as is practicable. In cases which are subject to Brussels IIR, there is a duty, except where circumstances make it impossible, for the proceedings at first instance to be completed within 6 weeks. In other cases, that remains the target, though there is no duty to complete the case within that timescale.

16.4.1.6 Mediation

The court and the parties should consider the option of mediation early in the proceedings.[64] Although public funding is not always available for mediation, mediation is often a very worthwhile course to adopt. It is relatively inexpensive and may be able to solve, without too much rancour, all areas of dispute between the parties if there are multiple proceedings – say, as to divorce jurisdiction, abduction and other children matters – contemplated. In England and Wales, *Reunite* has for a number of years provided an effective mediation scheme (although the emphasis is more on children disputes rather than wider jurisdictional and/or financial arguments): see **16.8** below for *Reunite*'s contact details.

---

[61] For which, see *S v B (Abduction: Human Rights)* [2005] EWHC 773 (Fam), [2005] 2 FLR 878 and *W v W (Abduction: Joinder as Party)* [2009] EWHC 3288 (Fam), [2010] 1 FLR 1342, where Baker J considered and granted an application on behalf of a 17-year-old sibling to a child subject to an application under the Hague Convention.

[62] It may well be that there is a relevant immigration issue that impacts on the proceedings. It is important if such an issue arises that there is early collaboration between the family court and the authority determining the issue: see *Re F (Abduction: Removal Outside Jurisdiction)* [2008] EWCA Civ 842, [2008] 2 FLR 1649.

[63] See *Re M (Abduction: Intolerable Situation)* [2000] 1 FLR 930 at 941.

[64] This (unsurprising) approach has been encouraged in a number of authorities, including *Re G (Abduction: Children's Objections)* [2010] EWCA Civ 1232, [2011] 1 FLR 1645, at 1649, para [16].

16.4.1.7 The burden of proof

Whilst Hague Convention proceedings might properly be called *sui generis*, the evidential burden is generally thought to fall on the applicant to establish matters such as habitual residence and the existence and breach of rights of custody. Once those have been properly established, or conceded, the burden falls on the respondent to prove one of the exceptions to the obligation to return.

16.4.1.8 Hearing the child

At the first *inter partes* hearing, consideration must be had as to how best the court should meet its international obligations 'to hear the child'.[65]

Article 11(2) of Brussels IIR provides that:

> 'when applying Articles 12 and 13 of the Hague Convention, it shall be ensured that the child is given an opportunity to be heard during the proceedings unless this appears inappropriate having regard to his or her age or degree of maturity.'

Recital (19) of Brussels IIR explains that:

> 'The hearing of the child plays an important role in the application of this Regulation, although the instrument is not intended to modify national procedures applicable.'

In *In re D (A Child) (Abduction: Rights of Custody)*[66] Baroness Hale held[67] that the principles set out in Art 11(2) of Brussels IIR should apply to all Hague Convention cases. She identified[68] that there were three possible methods by which a child could be 'heard':

(a) through full scale representation;

(b) through an interview with the judge;[69] or

---

[65] See Recital (19) and Art 11(2) of Brussels IIR; Art 12 of the United Nations Convention on the Rights of the Child (20 November 1989); *In re D (A Child) (Abduction: Rights of Custody)* [2006] UKHL 51, [2007] 1 AC 619 at 641–643, paras [57]–[62]; *Re F (Abduction: Child's Wishes)* [2007] EWCA Civ 468, [2007] 2 FLR 697 at 703, para [24]; and *In re M (Children) (Abduction: Rights of Custody)* [2007] UKHL 55, [2008] 1 AC 1288, *sub nom Re M (Abduction: Zimbabwe)* [2008] 1 FLR 251 at 269, para [57].

[66] [2006] UKHL 51, [2007] 1 AC 619.

[67] [2006] UKHL 51, [2007] 1 AC 619 at 641–642, para [58].

[68] [2006] UKHL 51, [2007] 1 AC 619 at 642, para [60].

[69] As happened in *JPC v SLW and SMW* (Abduction) [2007] EWHC 1349 (Fam), [2007] 2 FLR 900; and *De L v H* [2009] EWHC 3074 (Fam), [2010] 1 FLR 1229, though Sir Mark P was careful in the latter case, expressly, not to use the interview as an evidence gathering exercise: see 1241, para [45]. In *Re G (Abduction: Children's Objections)* [2010] EWCA Civ 1232, [2011] 1 FLR 1645, the Court of Appeal, after observing that it might have been better for the judge at first instance to meet with the

(c)   through an interview with a member of the Cafcass High Court
       team based at Sanctuary Buildings, Westminster, London.

Currently, the latter course is the one most usually adopted.

As a very rough rule of thumb, and without determining a particular age
at which a child's views should or will be canvassed, it might be said that
when the court is concerned with children from the age of about six to
seven onwards the expectation will be that the child's views will be
obtained and considered[70] by one of the methods identified in *In Re D (A
Child) (Abduction: Rights of Custody)*.[71]

16.4.1.9   *The question of separate representation*

How the court should approach the question of separate representation
for children in *Hague Convention* proceedings was considered by Baroness
Hale in *In re D (A Child) (Abduction: Rights of Custody)*[72] and
authoritatively decided by her in *In re M (Children) (Abduction: Rights of
Custody)*.[73] It was thereafter given detailed consideration by Ryder J in
respect of both Hague Convention and non-Convention cases in *Re C
(Abduction: Separate Representation of Children)*.[74] These three cases
read together supersede the older authorities (such as *Re H (Abduction)*[75]
and *Re F (Abduction: Joinder of Child as Party)*).[76]

In *In re D (Abduction: Rights of Custody)*[77], Baroness Hale, speaking
generally about children participating as parties in child abduction
proceedings, said that:

> 'whenever it seems likely that the child's views and interests may not be
> properly presented to the court, and in particular where there are legal
> arguments which the adult parties are not putting forward, then the child
> should be separately represented.'

Baroness Hale returned to the issue in *In re M (Children) (Abduction:
Rights of Custody)*[78], where she held that the proper approach of the

---

elder child, met with that child (who was then aged 13) and thereafter, as a result of
further evidence which included representations made in that meeting, set aside the
order for return.

[70]   Of course, this is far from saying that they will be determinative. For consideration of
       the child's objections exception: see below.
[71]   [2006] UKHL 51, [2007] 1 AC 619.
[72]   [2006] UKHL 51, [2007] 1 AC 619.
[73]   [2007] UKHL 55, [2008] 1 AC 1288, [2008] 1 FLR 251.
[74]   [2008] EWHC 517 (Fam), [2008] 2 FLR 6, at 10–20, paras [18]–[36].
[75]   [2006] EWCA Civ 1247, [2007] 1 FLR 242.
[76]   [2007] EWCA Civ 393, [2007] 2 FLR 313. The comments of Thorpe LJ in *Re F
       (Abduction: Removal Outside Jurisdiction)* [2008] EWCA Civ 842, [2008] 2 FLR 1649, at
       1653, para [12] are *obiter*.
[77]   [2006] UKHL 51, [2007] 1 AC 619 at 642, para [60].
[78]   [2007] UKHL 55, [2008] 1 AC 1288, [2008] 1 FLR 251.

court to the consideration of joinder in *Hague Convention* cases, (where settlement under Art 12 of the Hague Convention was not relied upon), was not to apply any general 'exceptionality' test (as was the historic approach) but instead to ask:[79]

> 'whether separate representation of the child will add enough to the court's understanding of the issues that arise under the Hague Convention to justify the intrusion, the expense and delay that may result.'

Where settlement under Art 12 of the Hague Convention was relied upon, the threshold for separate representation will be lower, these cases being regarded as particularly child-centric in their nature.[80] Thus it seems that the normal rule, in these cases, will be that (older) children should be granted separate representation.

In cases where an application is pursued under the inherent jurisdiction, the proper approach is to have regard to r 16 of the FPR 2010 (and PD 16A) and to *Mabon v Mabon*.[81]

Whether a child should be required to act through a Guardian was considered in detail in *WF v FJ, BF and RF (Abduction: Child's Objections)*.[82] In that case, Baker J commented that 'it seems to me clearly preferable, where the time and resources permit, for the child to be seen by the Cafcass High Court Team before any decision is taken as to party status'.[83]

16.4.1.10 *Oral evidence and conflict in affidavit evidence*

Oral evidence is discretionary in proceedings commenced by Originating Summons. Because of the limited ambit, and summary nature of Hague Convention proceedings, in England and Wales it has been held that there is no presumption for any party to call oral evidence. Indeed, oral evidence of the parties will only be allowed in exceptional circumstances, and then normally only relating to very limited areas.[84] Generally

---

[79] Per Baroness Hale in *In re M (Children) (Abduction: Rights of Custody)* [2007] UKHL 55, [2008] 1 AC 1288, sub nom *Re M (Abduction: Zimbabwe)*, [2008] 1 FLR 251 at 270, para [57]. See also *EM (Lebanon) v Secretary of State for the Home Department* [2008] UKHL 64, [2008] 2 FLR 2067, at 2088, para [49].

[80] See *In re M (Children) (Abduction: Rights of Custody)* [2007] UKHL 55, [2008] 1 AC 1288, sub nom *Re M (Abduction: Zimbabwe)* [2008] 1 FLR 251 at 269–270, para [57].

[81] [2005] EWCA Civ 634, [2005] 2 FLR 1011. See also *Re C (Abduction: Separate Representation of Children)* [2008] EWHC 517 (Fam), [2008] 2 FLR 6, at 10–12, paras [18]–[24].

[82] [2010] EWHC 2909 (Fam), [2011] 1 FLR 1153, at 1162–1164, paras [19]–[25].

[83] At 1164, para [25].

[84] *Re F (A Minor) (Child Abduction)* [1992] 1 FLR 548 at 553A–B, where Butler-Sloss LJ held that there was no 'right to give oral evidence' merely a discretion to admit it; and *Re W (Abduction: Domestic Violence)* [2004] EWCA Civ 1366, [2005] 1 FLR 727 at 733, para [23]. The sort of detailed finding of fact hearing conducted by Peter Jackson J in *DT v LBT (Abduction: Domestic Abuse)* [2010] EWHC 3177 (Fam), [2011] 1 FLR 1215

speaking, oral evidence is more often heard in cases where consent or acquiescence[85] is raised. In respect of Art 13(b), it has previously been said that 'to warrant oral exploration of written evidence, the judge must be satisfied that there is a realistic possibility that oral evidence will establish an Art 13(b) case that is only embryonic on the written material'; but the current thinking is that oral evidence in cases where Art 13(b) is raised would only be permitted in the rarest of cases.[86] If oral evidence is allowed, it should usually be time limited.

In *Re K (Abduction: Case Management)*[87] Thorpe LJ said: 'Not only should orders for oral evidence be extremely rare but, in my judgment, they should never be made in advance of the filing of written statements on the point in issue.'

Where there is a conflict between affidavit evidence, and no oral evidence is called, a judge may only reject sworn evidence:

(a)   if there is compelling, independent, extraneous evidence in support of one side's affidavit evidence; or

(b)   if the evidence within an affidavit is itself inherently improbable and therefore unreliable.[88]

If there are no grounds for rejecting the affidavit evidence on either side, the person who has the burden to discharge will have failed to establish his or her case.[89]

16.4.1.11   Interim powers and applications

The court has a wide discretion to use its powers during Hague Convention proceedings to secure the welfare of the child or to prevent

---

is very rare indeed and generally to be avoided. See also *Re K (Abduction: Case Management)* [2010] EWCA Civ 1546, [2011] 1 FLR 1268 at 1271–1272, paras [13]–[14]. As Thorpe LJ put it at para [13]: 'There should be no departure from the well recognised proposition that Hague applications are for peremptory orders to be decided on written evidence amplified by oral submissions.'

85   Though even in relation to acquiescence, Munby LJ in *Re K (Abduction; Case Management)* [2010] EWCA Civ 1546, [2011] 1 FLR 1268 said (at 1276, para [41]): 'In particular it would not, as it seems to me, be appropriate to have oral evidence generally in relation to an issue of acquiescence. And I find it difficult to imagine that outside a very small and unusual category of cases it would be appropriate to have oral evidence on any issues other than consent and acquiescence.'

86   *Re W (Abduction: Domestic Violence)* [2004] EWCA Civ 1366, [2005] 1 FLR 727.

87   [2010] EWCA Civ 1546, [2011] 1 FLR 1268 at 1272 at para [15].

88   *In Re D (Article 13B: Non Return)* [2006] EWCA Civ 146, [2006] 2 FLR 305, Thorpe LJ said (at 309, para [16]) that: 'In weighing the evidence of an abductor seeking to justify or explain conduct, the judge needs to subject the evidence to rigorous and perhaps sceptical scrutiny, particularly where, as here, there is a history of previous abduction and outstanding application for permission to relocate.'

89   *Re F (A Minor) (Child Abduction)* [1992] 1 FLR 548 at 553G–554A.

changes in the circumstances relevant to the determination of the application, whether under s 5 of the CACA 1985 or the inherent jurisdiction.[90] It is quite usual to expect arrangements for direct and indirect contact to be put in place in the period leading up to the final hearing. In *Re A (Abduction: Interim Directions: Accommodation by Local Authority)*[91] the Court of Appeal determined that the powers under s 5 of the CACA 1985 were indeed wide and could be used to order a local authority to provide accommodation for an abductor and his or her child. The section had to be construed widely so as to achieve the aims of the Hague Convention and to safeguard the welfare of children whose vulnerability was generally magnified by the effects of abduction.

In the event that such an application were to be made for accommodation that application should be on notice to all parties and to the local authority against whom the order is sought, and should be supported by evidence.[92]

At an interim stage, it is also possible to make an application to strike out the other side's case, though experience shows that it is rare for such an application to be granted.[93]

16.4.1.12 *Undertakings*

A vital weapon of an applicant, and a shield for the respondent, is the ability to offer, or to request, undertakings or other protective measures. On behalf of an applicant it might be hoped that such protective measures might neutralise or ameliorate any potential harm under Art 13(b), or might seek to meet any concerns that might be relevant to the 'discretion' stage, or might be offered so as to reassure the respondent and the court as to the applicant's goodwill, so as to assist in a return.[94] Generally, they will be offered in order to regulate the position only until

---

90 For an overview of the powers exercisable under section 5 of the CACA 1985 and a use of those powers, see *Re A (Abduction: Interim Directions: Accommodation by Local Authority)* [2010] EWCA Civ 586, [2010] 1 FLR 1; and *Re C (Abduction: Interim Directions: Accommodation by Local Authority)* [2003] EWHC 3065 (Fam), [2004] 1 FLR 653, where Singer J acceded to a request that the abductor be subject to electronic tagging for the duration of the Hague Convention proceedings. If this is contemplated, the judge should make contact with the President of the Family Division's office, there being an electronic tagging protocol conceived for this purpose. Electronic tagging can also be used in proceedings brought under the inherent jurisdiction: see *Re A (Family Proceedings: Electronic Tagging)* [2009] 2 FLR 891, where an example draft 'tagging order' is annexed to the judgment of Parker J.

91 [2010] EWCA Civ 586, [2011] 1 FLR 1.

92 [2010] EWCA Civ, 586, [2011] 1 FLR 1 at 10, para [45].

93 See *Re G (Abduction: Striking out Application)* [1995] 2 FLR 410; and *RS v KS (Abduction: Wrongful Retention)* [2009] EWHC 1494 (Fam), [2009] 2 FLR 1231, at 1238, para [24].

94 Such protective measures were encouraged, indeed one might say required, to be offered and considered in Hague Convention cases by the Supreme Court in *Re E (Children) (Abduction: Custody Appeal)* [2011] UKSC 27, [2012] 1 AC 144.

the court in the requesting State is properly seised of the matter and both parties appear before it.[95] It is appropriate, early in the proceedings, for both parties to set out in detail which undertakings are offered and which are required.[96]

In *Re E (Children) (Abduction: Custody Appeal)*[97] the Supreme Court urged the Hague Conference to consider whether machinery could be put in place whereby, when the courts of the requested State identify specific protective measures as necessary if the Art 13(b) exception is to be rejected, then those measures can become enforceable in the requesting State, for a temporary period at least, before the child is returned.

The following undertakings might be considered:

Contemplated applicant's undertakings

- Not to support or to initiate any criminal prosecution or other civil proceedings against the respondent relating to the abduction.

- Not to molest, harass or pester the respondent.

- Not to remove the child from the care and custody of the respondent until further order in the requesting State.

- To meet the reasonable travel costs of the return to the requesting State of the respondent and the child.

- To provide certain maintenance and/or accommodation for the respondent and the child for a specific time period.

- To provide moneys towards a litigation fund for the respondent.

- Not to make, sooner than 28 days after the respondent's return, any 'without notice' applications relating to the respondent and the child.

- Not to attend at the airport on the date of arrival of the respondent and the child.

---

95   *Re O (Child Abduction: Undertakings)* [1994] 2 FLR 349; and *Re M (Abduction: Undertakings)* [1995] 1 FLR 1021. Though compare the approach in *Re C (A Minor) (Abduction)* [1989] 1 FLR 403 at 409A–G to that in *Re W (Abduction: Domestic Violence)* [2004] EWHC 1247 (Fam), [2004] 2 FLR 499, where Baron J imposed extensive conditions and required a number of undertakings as a prerequisite to the return of the child to South Africa.

96   *Re M (Abduction: Intolerable Situation)* [2000] 1 FLR 930.

97   [2011] UKSC 27, [2012] 1 AC 144, at 161–162, para [37].

- To arrange for the lodging of the return order and any undertakings with the relevant court which is, or will be seised, of the matter upon the respondent's return.

Contemplated respondent's undertakings

- To lodge passports upon the respondent's return with his or her solicitors or an independent third party.

- To provide reasonable contact or agreed contact with the applicant until further order of the court in the requesting State.

- To live at particular accommodation for a specific time period.

- Not to leave the jurisdiction of the requesting State until further order of that court.

- To consent to the applicant using undertakings as evidence in any proceedings in the courts of the requesting State.

16.4.1.13   International judicial cooperation

Both in anticipation of, and perhaps after, the final hearing of any Hague Convention proceedings, there may be opportunities to communicate with the authorities in the relevant foreign jurisdiction, whether with the requesting State's Central Authority or directly to a relevant judge in the foreign jurisdiction, as to matters relating to the case.[98] In *Chorley v Chorley*[99] (although not a child abduction case), Thorpe LJ commended, in particular, the use of the European Judicial Network in appropriate cases. If such international judicial cooperation is agreed upon, then contact will be made by the judge hearing the case with the office of the Head of International Family Justice.[100]

16.4.1.14   The final hearing

The final hearing will take a summary form. Skeleton arguments should be filed in advance in accordance with the President's *Practice Direction of 27th July 2006, (Family Proceedings: Court Bundles) (Universal Practice to be Applied in All Courts other than the Family Proceedings Court)*[101] or other directions made in the proceedings.

---

[98] See Art 55 of Brussels IIR; *Re M and J (Abduction: International Judicial Collaboration)* [2000] 1 FLR 803 and *Re S (Care: Jurisdiction)* [2008] EWHC 3013 (Fam), [2009] 2 FLR 550.

[99] [2005] EWCA Civ 68, [2005] 2 FLR 38 at 45, at para [44].

[100] The current Head of International Family Justice (as at 2012), Thorpe LJ, has a legal secretary who assists in these referrals.

[101] [2006] 2 FLR 199.

The applicant's advocate will begin by setting out a history of the matter and referring to the relevant documents. In the absence of oral evidence, the respondent's advocate will then respond. If oral evidence has been permitted, it will usually be time limited.

Once judgment has been given and orders made, advocates should take care to agree the contents of, and thereafter draft and submit very promptly, any final order. Equally there is an obligation on the court to ensure that the order is sealed promptly once the judgment has been distributed.[102]

16.4.1.15   Costs

The issue of costs in *Hague Convention* proceedings was considered in detail in *EC-L v DM (Child Abduction: Costs)*,[103] where it was held that there was jurisdiction in appropriate cases for the court to make a costs order. The 'expectation', however, is that the usual order will be no order as to costs. Only in cases 'where a party's conduct has been unreasonable or there is a disparity of means' would a court have the ability to consider whether to exercise its discretion in accordance with the rules determining normal civil proceedings.[104]

16.4.1.16   *The order of the court*

Where the respondent has failed to resist an order for return, the terms of Art 12 of the Hague Convention require (in all cases where less than one year has elapsed from the date of wrongful removal or retention) the court to order a return to the country of the child's habitual residence, 'forthwith'.[105] Where over a year has elapsed, there is a requirement merely to order a return.[106] Thus as a general rule, and absent agreement, only in (failed) Art 12 Hague Convention settlement cases will it be appropriate to relax the timetable for return.

It has been held that an order for return or non return is usually a final order. It is therefore not appropriate to seek to return to the first instance judge to set it aside: any such application should be made to the Court of Appeal.[107]

---

[102] *Re M (Abduction: Appeals)* [2007] EWCA Civ 1059, [2008] 1 FLR 699, at 702–703, paras [11] and [12].
[103] [2005] EWHC 588 (Fam), [2005] 2 FLR 772.
[104] *EC-L v DM (Child Abduction: Costs)* [2005] EWHC 588 (Fam), [2005] 2 FLR 772 at 788, para [68]; and see the observations of Munby J in *Re C (Costs: Enforcement of Foreign Contact Order)* [2007] EWHC 1993 (Fam), [2008] 1 FLR 619 at 622, paras [14]–[15].
[105] Article 12(1) of the Hague Convention.
[106] Article 12(2) of the Hague Convention.
[107] *Re M (Minor) (Child Abduction)* [1994] 1 FLR 390, affirmed in *Re M (Abduction: Undertakings)* [1995] 1 FLR 1021. As to undertakings, Butler-Sloss LJ said (in *Re M (Abduction: Undertakings)* [1995] 1 FLR 1021 at 1025D) that: 'undertakings have their

It would appear, however, that the court can attach formal conditions to an order for return, such conditions being prerequisites to a return. In this sort of case, the order takes the form of a 'provisional order', so that it can lie 'within the jurisdiction of the trial judge to entertain and determine any application brought by either party which puts in question whether the extent of compliance has been sufficient to convert what was a provisional order into a final order.'[108]

A different and novel approach to a return order was adopted in *F v M and N (Abduction: Acquiescence: Settlement)*.[109] In that case, Black J, having found that the child was settled for the purposes of Art 12 of the Hague Convention, but having particular regard to the fact that the courts in the requesting State were very well advanced in their conduct of hearings as to the child's welfare, made an order for return, but suspended it for a fixed period of time to allow the defendant to issue applications in the 'home' country seeking either temporary or permanent leave to remove.[110]

16.4.1.17 Appeals

It has been held that the obligation to adhere to a strict timetable in all international family law cases, and especially Hague Convention and Brussels IIR proceedings, imposes a duty on the judge (and the advocates) at the conclusion of any final hearing to consider whether any party wishes to seek permission to appeal. If anyone wishes to seek such permission, they ought in usual circumstances, to seek it immediately from the judge, or as soon as possible afterwards, and the judge should either give such permission or refuse it. He or she should thereafter restrict the time for the filing of the Appellant's Notice in normal cases to 7 days, the period of 21 days (in accordance with CPR Part 52), for the lodging of the Notice being regarded as over-generous.[111]

---

place in the arrangements designed to smooth the return of and to protect the child for the limited period before the foreign court takes over, but they must not be used by parties to try to clog or fetter, or, in particular, to delay the enforcement of a paramount decision to return the child.'

[108] *Walley v Walley* [2005] EWCA Civ 910, [2005] 3 FCR 35, paras [14] and [19].

[109] [2008] EWHC 1525 (Fam), [2008] 2 FLR 1270, at 1293–1294, paras [77] and [78] Macur J also accepted that a suspension of a return order was 'within the armoury of the court at the time of exercising its discretion or considering the timing and imposition of "safeguards" necessary to protect the child upon return': see *RS v KS (Abduction: Wrongful Retention)* [2009] EWHC 1494 (Fam), [2009] 2 FLR 1231, at 1244, para [52].

[110] See also *R v K (Abduction: Return Order)* [2009] EWHC 132 (Fam), [2010] 1 FLR 1456. In that case Ryder J, exercised his discretion (within the confines of a 'forthwith' order) to permit a limited amount of time for the mother to settle her affairs in England and Wales before returning to Poland. It appears, unhelpfully, that the leading case of *F v M and N (Abduction: Acquiescence: Settlement)* [2008] EWHC 1525 (Fam), [2008] 2 FLR 1270 was not cited to him.

[111] *Re F (Abduction: Child's Wishes)* [2007] EWCA Civ 468, [2007] 2 FLR 697, at 703, para [28]; and *Klentzeris v Klentzeris* [2007] EWCA Civ 533, [2007] 2 FLR 996, at 1003, paras [27]–[29].

Practitioners should not delay issuing their Appellant's Notice on the basis that they are awaiting for an approved judgment (as the Court of Appeal should know as early as possible if an appeal in an international case is contemplated so that they may, if necessary, put in place arrangements for an expedited hearing).[112]

16.4.1.18 Enforcement

Once an order for return has been made the practical arrangements for effecting that return will have to be considered. It may be agreed that the child should return with the respondent parent or the applicant parent may travel to this jurisdiction to accompany the child back to the Requesting State. If there are difficulties experienced in effecting a return, then assistance may have to be sought from the Tipstaff to put in place arrangements by which the particular child can be returned to the State of their habitual residence.

16.4.1.19 Hague Convention proceedings: a very quick checklist

• Is it a Brussels IIR case?

• What orders are required regularising the position prior to any trial of the issue?

• Was the child 'habitually resident' in the requesting State prior to removal?

• Does the applicant have 'rights of custody' and was he or she exercising them?

• When was the date of removal/retention?

• What exceptions to the obligation to return are to be relied upon?

• What are the matters of procedure that are relevant?

• How is the child going to be 'heard' (including consideration of whether it is appropriate for the child to be separately represented)?

• What protective measures should be put in place prior to any return?[113]

• Expert and oral evidence?

---

[112] *Re EC (Child Abduction: Stayed Proceedings)* [2006] EWCA Civ 1115, [2007] 1 FLR 57, at 59–60, para [6].

[113] About which see, *Re E (Children) (Abduction: Custody Appeal)* [2011] UKSC 27, [2012] 1 AC 144.

- Attendance of the parties at trial?

- Time estimate for trial?

- Listing within the six week time limit?

- International judicial collaboration?

16.4.2 The law

16.4.2.1 *Incoming child abduction cases*

The Hague Convention

The twin objects[114] of the Hague Convention are set out in Art 1:

'(a) to secure the prompt return of children wrongfully removed to or retained in any Contracting State; and

(b) to ensure that rights of custody and access under the law of one Contracting State are effectively respected in the other Contracting States.'

The Hague Convention is a profoundly child-centric,[115] international instrument which grew out of a recognition, as the Preamble records, that 'the interests of children are of paramount importance in matters relating to their custody', and a desire:

'to protect children internationally from the harmful effects of their wrongful removal or retention and to establish procedures to ensure their prompt return to the State of their habitual residence, as well as to secure protection for rights of access.'[116]

---

[114] In *Re E (Children) (Abduction: Custody Appeal)* [2011] UKSC 27, [2012] 1 AC 144, Baroness Hale said at 152, para [8]: 'The first object of the Hague Convention is to deter either parent (or indeed anyone else) from taking the law into their own hands and pre-empting the result of any dispute between them about the future upbringing of their children. If an abduction does take place, the next object is to restore the children as soon as possible to their home country, so that any dispute can be determined there. The left behind parent should not be put to the trouble and expense of coming to the Requested State in order for factual disputes to be resolved. The abducting parent should not gain unfair advantage by having that dispute determined in the place to which she has come.'

[115] See *In re D (Abduction: Rights of Custody)* [2007] 1 AC 619 at 639, para [48]; *In re M (Children) (Abduction: Rights of Custody)* [2007] UKHL 55, [2008] 1 AC 1288, sub nom *Re M (Abduction: Zimbabwe)*, [2008] 1 FLR 251 at 256, para [12], and at 266, para [42]; and *Maumousseau and Washington v France*, (Application no. 39388/05), ECHR, 2 June 2008, para [68].

[116] Although not incorporated by the CACA 1985, it has been held that it is proper to have regard to the Preamble and Art 1: *In re H and others (Minors) (Abduction: Acquiescence)* [1998] AC 72 at 81C.

What has been termed the 'policy' of the Hague Convention may be said to reflect those underlying objects and principles. Thus, whilst the majority of Hague Convention cases will result in the return of the child to his or her country of habitual residence, the Convention provides for some limited and precise circumstances when the court may find that it is not in the child's interests to return.[117] Although it has now been determined by the Supreme Court that the Hague Convention and Brussels IIR have been devised with the best interests of children generally, and of the individual children involved in such proceedings, as a primary consideration,[118] that does not mean that a child's or the children's welfare is the paramount consideration for the court.[119] On such summary applications, there is simply no room for adjudication of any welfare based custodial dispute between the parties, or a full blown examination of the child's future: that is the province of the child's 'home' courts;[120] what the national court does is not to order a return automatically and mechanically, but instead to examine the particular circumstances of the particular child in order to ascertain whether a return would be in accordance with the Hague Convention.[121]

Article 12 sets out the obligation at the heart of the Hague Convention:

> 'Where a child has been wrongfully removed or retained in terms of Article 3 and, at the date of the commencement of the proceedings before the judicial or administrative authority of the Contracting State where the child is, a period of less than one year has elapsed from the date of the wrongful removal or retention, the authority concerned shall order the return of the child forthwith.

---

[117] And see further paras [24]–[25] of the *Explanatory Report of Professor Elisa Perez-Vera* (April, 1981) and the reasoning of Baroness Hale in *In re D (A Child) (Abduction: Rights of Custody)* [2006] UKHL 51, [2007] 1 AC 619 at 639–641, paras [48]–[56].

[118] *In re E (Children) (Abduction: Custody Appeal)* [2011] UKSC 27, [2012] 1 AC 144, at 155–156, para [18].

[119] See *In re E (Children) (Abduction: Custody Appeal)* [2011] UKSC 27, [2012] 1 AC 144, at 153–154, para [12].

[120] See, *inter alia*, Arts 16 and 19 of the Hague Convention. In *In re E (Children) (Abduction: Custody Appeal)* [2011] UKSC 27, [2012] 1 AC 144, the Supreme Court considered the recent jurisprudence of the ECtHR and in particular the reasoning of the Grand Chamber of the ECtHR in *Neulinger and Shuruk v Switzerland* (Application no. 41615/07) [2011] 1 FLR 122. In relation to this issue, the Supreme Court concluded (at 159, para [26]): 'The most that can be said, therefore, is that both *Maumousseau* and *Neulinger* acknowledge that the guarantees in Art 8 have to be interpreted and applied in the light of the Hague Convention and the UNCRC; that all are designed with the best interests of the child as a primary consideration; that in every Hague Convention case where the question is raised, the national court does not order return automatically and mechanically but examines the particular circumstances of this particular child in order to ascertain whether a return be in accordance with the Hague Convention; but that is not the same as a full-blown examination of the child's future; and that it is, to say the least, unlikely that if the Hague Convention is properly applied, with whatever outcome, there will be a violation of the Art 8 rights of the child or either of the parents ...'

[121] *In re E (Children) (Abduction: Custody Appeal)* [2011] UKSC 27, [2012] 1 AC 144, at 159, para [26].

The judicial or administrative authority, even where the proceedings have been commenced after the expiration of the period of one year referred to in the preceding paragraph, shall also order the return of the child, unless it is demonstrated that the child is now settled in its new environment.'

Hague Convention proceedings are summary proceedings where matters should be dealt with speedily. The Hague Convention provides a remedy of 'hot pursuit'.[122]

Brussels IIR[123] and the Hague Convention

Arts 8, 10, 11 and 15 of Brussels IIR are the most relevant Articles of Brussels IIR in respect of child abduction matters.[124] Those Articles regulate jurisdictional matters (in the event of an abduction); determine how relevant Member States' courts considering cases should consider applications for return orders pursuant to the Hague Convention; and provide a process by which a court in the requesting State can examine the question of custody of the child (in certain situations where a non return order has been made).

Article 10 of Brussels IIR provides that:

'In case of wrongful removal or retention of the child, the courts of the Member State where the child was habitually resident immediately before the wrongful removal or retention shall retain their jurisdiction until the child has acquired a habitual residence in another Member State and:
(a) each person, institution or other body having rights of custody has acquiesced in the removal or retention; or
(b) the child has resided in that other Member State for a period of at least one year after the person, institution or other body having rights of custody has had or should have had knowledge of the whereabouts of the child and the child is settled in his or her new environment and at least one of the following conditions is met:
(i) within one year after the holder of rights of custody has had or should have had knowledge of the whereabouts of the child, no

---

[122] *Re C (Abduction: Grave Risk of Physical or Psychological Harm)* [1999] 2 FLR 478 at 488E.

[123] The terminology of Brussels IIR should be interpreted in accordance with the reasoning of the European Court of Justice. For the interpretation, for example, of 'habitual residence' for the purposes of Article 3 of Brussels IIR see *Marinos v Marinos* [2007] EWHC 2047 (Fam), [2007] 2 FLR 1018.

[124] Article 20 of Brussels IIR is not dealt with in this chapter though it is obviously relevant as it provides a court with a jurisdiction to make certain orders in appropriate cases. In *Re A (Area of Freedom, Security and Justice)* [2009] 2 FLR 1, at 13, para [73] the European Court of Justice held that a protective measure under Art 20 may be decided if a number of conditions are satisfied: (a) the measure must be urgent; (b) it must be taken in respect of persons in the Member State concerned; and (c) it must be provisional. See also the comprehensive analysis of Charles J in *Re S (Care: Jurisdiction)* [2008] EWHC 3013 (Fam), [2009] 2 FLR 550, in particular at 570, para [89] and *Deticek v Sgueglia* (Case C-403/09) [2010] 1 FLR 1381.

request for return has been lodged before the competent authorities of the Member State where the child has been removed or is being retained;

(ii) a request for return by the holder of rights of custody has been withdrawn and no new request has been lodged within the time limit set in paragraph (i);

(iii) a case before the court in the Member State where the child was habitually resident immediately before the wrongful removal or retention has been closed pursuant to Article 11(7);

(iv) a judgment on custody that does not entail the return of the child has been issued by the courts of the Member State where the child was habitually resident immediately before the wrongful removal or retention.'

Article 10 therefore ensures that the courts of the requesting State maintain jurisdiction in respect of matters of parental responsibility until certain events have taken place. It is intended to deter and prevent the abductor gaining a jurisdictional advantage by reason of any abduction.

It contemplates jurisdiction passing to the requested State in only *two* situations:

(a) where the child has acquired habitual residence in the requested Member State and all those with rights of custody have acquiesced in the abduction; or

(b) where the child has acquired habitual residence in the requested Member State and has resided in that Member State for a period of at least one year after those with rights of custody learned or should have learned of the whereabouts of the child and the child has settled in his or her new environment and any one of the following further conditions is met:

(i) no request for the return of the child has been lodged within the year after the left behind parent knew or should have known the whereabouts of the child; or

(ii) a request for return was made but has been withdrawn and no new request has been lodged within that year; or

(iii) a decision on non return has been issued in the requested State and the courts of both Member States have taken the steps required under Art 11(6), but the case has been closed in accordance with Art 11(7) because the parties have not made submissions within 3 months of notification; or

(iv) a court of the requesting State has issued a judgment on custody which does not entail the return of the child.

Article 11(1) and (2) of Brussels IIR provides that:

'Where a person institution or other body having rights of custody applies to the competent authorities in a Member State to deliver a judgment on the basis of the Hague Convention of 25 October 1980 on the Civil Aspects of International Child Abduction (hereinafter 'the 1980 Hague Convention'), in order to obtain the return of a child that has been wrongfully removed or retained in a Member State other than the Member State where the child was habitually resident immediately before the wrongful removal or retention, paragraphs 2 to 8 shall apply.

When applying Articles 12 and 13 of the 1980 Hague Convention, it shall be ensured that the child is given the opportunity to be heard during the proceedings unless this appears inappropriate having regard to his or her age or degree of maturity.'

Article 11(2) therefore provides an obligation for the child to be heard during the proceedings unless it is regarded (by the court) to be inappropriate having regard to his or her age or degree of maturity. The most useful method by which this obligation is met (as has been discussed above) is by the ordering of a report from an officer of the Cafcass High Court team based at Sanctuary Buildings, Westminster, London.

Article 11(3) of Brussels IIR provides that:

'A court to which an application for return of a child is made as mentioned in paragraph 1 shall act expeditiously in proceedings on the application, using the most expeditious procedures available in national law.

Without prejudice to the first subparagraph, the court shall, except where exceptional circumstances make this impossible, issue its judgment no later than six weeks after the application is lodged.'

Article 11(3) places a mandatory duty, except where exceptional circumstances make this impossible, to complete the proceedings within 6 weeks. The need for stringent compliance with the time requirements of Brussels IIR has been emphasised on a number of occasions by the Court of Appeal.[125]

Article 11(4) of Brussels IIR provides that:

'A court cannot refuse to return a child on the basis of Article 13b of the 1980 Hague Convention if it is established that adequate arrangements have been made to secure the protection of the child after his or her return.'

Article 11(4) restricts the ability to rely on Art 13(b) of the Hague Convention. As is made clear in the *Practice Guide for the Application of*

---

[125] See, for example, *Vigreux v Michel* [2006] EWCA Civ 630, [2006] 2 FLR 1180 at 1194, para [44] and 1204–1205, paras [88]–[89].

the New Brussels II Regulation, 'the principle is that the child shall always be returned if he/she can be protected in the Member State of origin'.[126]

The Practice Guide goes on to observe, however, that:

'It is not sufficient that procedures exist in the Member State of Origin for the protection of the child, but it must be established that the authorities in the Member State of origin have taken concrete measures to protect the child in question.

It will generally be difficult for the judge to assess the factual circumstances in the Member State of origin. The assistance of the central authorities of the Member State or origin will be vital to assess whether or not protective measures have been taken in that country and whether they will adequately secure the protection of the child upon his or her return.'[127]

Article 11(5) of Brussels IIR provides that:

'A court cannot refuse to return a child unless the person who requested the return of the child has been given the opportunity to be heard.'

Having regard to the strict time limit required Art 11(3) the Practice Guide suggests the contemplation of the use of video and tele-conference facilities.[128]

Article 11(6), (7) and (8) of Brussels IIR provides that:

If a court has issued an order on non-return pursuant to Article 13 of the 1980 Hague Convention, the court must immediately either directly or through its central authority, transmit a copy of the court order on non return and of the relevant documents, in particular a transcript of the hearings before the court, to the court with jurisdiction or central authority in the Member State where the child was habitually resident immediately before the wrongful removal or retention, as determined by national law. The court shall receive all the mentioned documents within one month of the date of the non return order.

Unless the courts in the Member State where the child was habitually resident immediately before the wrongful removal or retention have already been seised by one of the parties, the court or central authority that receives the information mentioned in paragraph 6 must notify it to the parties and invite them to make submissions to the court in accordance with national law, within three months of the date of notification so that the court can examine the question of custody of the child.

---

[126] Practice Guide for the Application of the New Brussels II Regulation, Part VII, para 2.2.

[127] Practice Guide for the Application of the New Brussels II Regulation, Part VII, para 2.2.

[128] Practice Guide for the Application of the New Brussels II Regulation, para 2.3.

Without prejudice to the rules on jurisdiction contained in this Regulation, the court shall close the case if no submissions have been received by the court within the time limit.

Notwithstanding a judgment of non-return pursuant to Article 13 of the 1980 Hague Convention, any subsequent judgment which requires the return of the child issued by a court having jurisdiction under this Regulation shall be enforceable in accordance with Section 4 of Chapter III below in order to secure the return of the child.'

The provisions of Art 11(6), (7) and (8) are some of the more complicated, and perhaps controversial, provisions contained within Brussels IIR. The intention of these provisions is, essentially, to provide a mechanism which (in the case of a Member State making a non return order by virtue of Art 13[129]), a failed applicant can invoke, so as to require the court in the requesting State, notwithstanding the non return order, to 'examine the question of custody of the child'. If, thereafter, once a court has adjudicated upon this question, the court requires that the child should be returned, then the order will be automatically enforceable (under Arts 11(8), 40(1)(b) and 42 of Brussels IIR).

Singer J has considered these provisions in a number of cases, including, *Re A (Custody Decision after Maltese Non Return Order)*[130] and, importantly, *Re A; HA v MB (Brussels II Revised: Article 11(7) Application)*.[131]

In a detailed judgment, Singer J in *Re A; HA v MB (Brussels II Revised: Article 11(7) Application)* held that neither an order for contact, nor a shared residence order, within such proceedings amounted to a 'judgment' requiring the return of the child for the purposes of Art 11(8) of Brussels IIR. In fact 'the return of the child' for the purposes of Art 11(8) had to be construed having regard to both Arts 10 and 11 of Brussels IIR. It related only to 'a decision that the child should reside with the parent who was [in the home State], not ... [to] an order in effect requiring [a parent] to make [a child] available [for contact].'[132] For the purposes of Brussels IIR, it was also held that a 'judgment' was 'the written order issued by the court'.[133]

---

[129] Though not if the refusal was under Art 12(2) or Art 20 or because the applicant had failed to establish that he or she had rights of custody under Art 3. See *Re RD (Child Abduction) (Brussels II Revised: Arts 11(7) and 19)* [2009] 1 FLR 586 and *Re RC and BC (Child Abduction) (Brussels II Revised: Art 11 (7))* [2009] 1 FLR 574.

[130] [2006] EWHC 3397 (Fam), [2007] 1 FLR 1923.

[131] [2007] EWHC 2016 (Fam), [2008] 1 FLR 289.

[132] [2007] EWHC 2016 (Fam), [2008] 1 FLR 289 at 311–313, paras [95] and [101].

[133] [2007] EWHC 2016 (Fam), [2008] 1 FLR 289 at 319, para [127]. See also the judgment of Ryder J in *Re H (Jurisdiction)* [2009] EWHC 2280 (Fam), [2010] 1 FLR 598 where jurisdiction was maintained (for a period of time) by the English court in order to attempt to persuade the mother to engage in the proceedings; in the event, she did not and an order for contact was made in her absence. See further, *Povse v Alpago* (Case C-211/10) [2010] 2 FLR 1343.

The provisions of Art 11(7) and (8) have also been considered by Charles J in *M v T (Abduction: Brussels II Revised, Art 11(7))*[134] and by Theis J in *D v N and D (By her Guardian ad Litem)*.[135]

In *M v T (Abduction: Brussels II Revised, Art 11(7))*, Charles J stated that as soon as possible after an application under Art 11(7) was made there should be a directions hearing before the court at which the court should consider the approach to be taken in the case and in particular: (a) was the case to be determined on a summary basis and/or was there to be a welfare enquiry and, if so, what was to be the extent of the welfare enquiry and what directions would have to be made in that context? and (b) should the child be joined or not? Indeed, it might be well helpful to consider whether to invite Cafcass to make representations to the court as to the appropriate approach.[136]

In *D v N and D (By her Guardian Ad Litem)*,[137] Theis J summarised the proper approach to applications pursuant to Art 11(6)–(8) of Brussels IIR as follows:

(a) the interrelationship of Art 10 and Art 11(7) and (8) of Brussels IIR permit the State of origin (from where the child has been wrongfully removed or retained) to undertake an examination of the question of the custody of the child, once a judgment of non return pursuant to Art 13 has been made by a State where a request has been made under the Hague Convention 1980;

(b) proceedings under Art 11(7) should be carried out as quickly as possible;

(c) in undertaking the examination of the question of the custody of the child, the judge should be in a position that he or she would have been in if the abducting parents had not abducted the child. Thus the whole range of orders that would normally be available to a judge should be available when examining the question of the custody of the child;

(d) in undertaking the examination of the question of the custody of the child, the court exercises a welfare jurisdiction: the child's welfare shall be the court's paramount consideration;

---

134 [2010] EWHC 1479 (Fam), [2010] 2 FLR 1685.
135 [2011] EWHC 471 (Fam), [2011] 2 FLR 464.
136 [2010] EWHC 2010 EWHC 1479 (Fam), [2010] 2 FLR 1685, at 1692–1693, paras [20]–[21].
137 [2011] EWHC 471 (Fam), [2011] 2 FLR 464, at 471–472, para [39]. This summary has been endorsed and followed by Peter Jackson J in *AF v T and another (Brussels II Revised: Art 11(7) Application)* [2011] EWHC 1315 (Fam), [2011] 2 FLR 891, at 896, para [13] and by Baker J in *Re AJ (Brussels II Revised)* [2011] EWHC 3450 (Fam).

(e) it may not be necessary or appropriate to categorise the jurisdictional foundation for such an inquiry as deriving from, or relying upon, the inherent jurisdiction. The foundation for any examination of the question of the custody of the child is simply through the gateway of Art 11(7);

(f) the court has a well-known and historic ability to order the summary return of the child to and from another jurisdiction;

(g) as part of the court's inquiry under Art 11(7) the court does have the ability to order a summary return of the child to this country to facilitate the decision making process leading to a final judgment;

(h) in deciding whether to order a summary return or to carry out a full welfare inquiry, the court exercises a welfare jurisdiction. It is not altogether clear whether the decision to order a return of the child on a summary basis is more appropriately considered as akin to that which might be ordered under the inherent jurisdiction or whether it is effectively a specific issue order under the Children Act 1989: if it is more appropriately considered as akin to the inherent jurisdiction then – at least as to the question of summary return – it may not be necessary for the court mechanistically and slavishly to direct itself to the welfare checklist; that having been said, once the child has returned and the court is considering what order to make the court should direct itself to the welfare checklist;

(i) any summary return order is directly enforceable through the procedures in Brussels IIR.

Article 15 of Brussels IIR provides (so far as is relevant) that:

'Transfer to a court better placed to hear the case

1   By way of exception, the courts of a Member State having jurisdiction as to the substance of the matter may, if they consider that a court of another Member State, with which the child has a particular connection, would be better placed to hear the case, or a specific part thereof, and where this is in the best interests of the child:
    (a) stay the case or the part thereof in question and invite the parties to introduce a request before the court of that other Member State ...; or
    (b) request a court of another Member State to assume jurisdiction ...
2   Paragraph 1 shall apply:
    (a) upon application from a party; or
    (b) of the court's own motion; or
    (c) upon application from a court of another Member State with which the child has a particular connection, in accordance with paragraph 3.

A transfer made of the court's own motion or by application of a court of another Member State must be accepted by at least one of the parties.

3   The child shall be considered to have a particular connection to a Member State as mentioned in paragraph 1, if that Member State:

(a)   has become the habitual residence of the child after the court referred to in paragraph 1 was seised; or

(b)   is the former habitual residence of the child; or

(c)   is the place of the child's nationality; or

(d)   is the habitual residence of a holder of parental responsibility; or

(e)   is the place where property of the child is located and the case concerns measures for the protection of the child relating to the administration, conservation or disposal of this property.'

This article therefore provides a mechanism by which the court substantively exercising the jurisdiction can decide to transfer the case to another Member State's court. It was considered in detail by Mr Jonathan Baker QC sitting as a Deputy High Court Judge in *Re S-R (Jurisdiction: Contact)*[138] and Munby J in *AB v JLB (Brussels II Revised: Article 15)*.[139]

Key Convention concepts

There are a number of key *Convention* concepts which are summarised briefly below. A useful resource as to their interpretation is the *Explanatory Report of Professor Elisa Perez-Vera* (April 1981), ('the *Perez-Vera Report*'), available from www.hcch.net.

Articles 3 and 5: 'Wrongful removal' and 'rights of custody'

For the Convention to be relied upon, the removal or retention[140] must be 'wrongful' within the meaning of Art 3. Article 3 provides that the removal or retention is wrongful where:

'(a)   it is in breach of rights of custody attributed to a person, an institution or any other body, either jointly or alone, under the law of the State in which the child was habitually resident immediately before the removal or retention; and

---

[138]   [2008] 2 FLR 1741.

[139]   [2008] EWHC 2965 (Fam), [2009] 1 FLR 517.

[140]   These terms were examined and explained in detail in *In re H (Minors) (Abduction: Custody Rights)* [1991] 2 AC 476 at, in particular, 499–500. In *Re G (Abduction: Withdrawal of Proceedings)* [2007] EWHC 2807 (Fam), [2008] 2 FLR 351, Sir Mark Potter P said at 364, para [48]: '...retention is an event which occurs on a specific occasion rather than enjoying its usual and wider connotation of a continuous state of affairs. It occurs when a child who has previously been for a limited period of time outside the state of its habitual residence is not returned to that state on the expiry of that limited period.' At 365, para [50] he went on to say: 'Retention by a parent may take a variety of forms, including not only acts of physical restraint or refusal in response to a request, but also court orders obtained on the initiative of the retaining parent which have the effect of frustrating the child's return to the jurisdiction of its habitual residence.'

(b)　at the time of the removal or retention those rights were actually exercised, either jointly or alone, or would have been so exercised but for the removal or retention.'

Article 3 goes on to state that:

'The rights of custody mentioned in sub-paragraph (a) above, may arise in particular by operation of law or by reason of a judicial or administrative decision, or by reason of an agreement having legal effect under the law of that State.'

Article 5 provides that rights of custody 'shall include rights relating to the care of the person of the child and, in particular, the right to determine the child's place of residence' and that rights of access 'shall include the right to take a child for a limited period of time to a place other than the child's habitual residence'.

The judicial or administrative authorities of a requested State may request that the applicant obtains from the authorities of the State of the child's habitual residence a determination of whether the removal or retention was in fact wrongful (see the discussion of Art 15, below).

It is well established that a broad and autonomous interpretation should be attributed to 'rights of custody'.[141] For the purposes of the Hague Convention it is important that 'rights of access' should be properly distinguished from 'rights of custody' (although a person may have both 'rights of access' and 'rights of custody').[142]

It falls to the applicant to prove that he or she had 'rights of custody' under the law of the requesting State and that he or she was exercising those rights at the time of the removal or retention. This may fall into two distinct questions for the court: the 'domestic law question': what rights, if any, did the applicant have under the law of the State in which the child was habitually resident immediately before the retention or removal?; and, thereafter, the 'Convention question': can those rights properly be categorised as rights of custody?[143] (that is say, did those rights identified equate to rights of custody under the autonomous law of the Hague Convention?[144]) Or put another way: 'do the rights possessed under the

---

[141]　See, for example, *In re H (A Minor) (Abduction: Rights of Custody)* [2000] 2 AC 291, [2000] 1 FLR 374; *Re C (Child Abduction) (Unmarried Father: Rights of Custody)* [2002] EWHC 2219 (Fam), [2003] 1 FLR 252; *Re P (Abduction: Consent)* [2004] EWCA Civ 971, 2 FLR 1057; and *In re D (A Child) (Abduction: Rights of Custody)* [2006] UKHL 51, [2007] 1 AC 619 at 632, para [28].

[142]　*In re D (A Child) (Abduction: Rights of Custody)* [2006] UKHL 51, [2007] 1 AC 619 at 631–632, paras [25]–[26].

[143]　See *Hunter v Morrow (Abduction: Rights of Custody)* [2005] EWCA Civ 976, [2005] 2 FLR 1119 at 1131, paras [46]–[47]; and *In re D (A Child) (Abduction: Rights of Custody)* [2006] UKHL 51, [2007] 1 AC 619 at 635, para [39].

[144]　*Kennedy v Kennedy* [2009] EWCA Civ 986, [2010] 1 FLR 782.

law of the home country by the parent who does not have the day to day care of the child amount to rights of custody or do they not?'[145]

An actual, (as opposed to a potential), right to veto a child's removal to another country will, for the purposes of the Hague Convention, constitute a 'right of custody'.[146]

Ordinarily, in order to be able to determine the position the court would require expert evidence to be given on the issue, or for there to be an Art 15 determination. The court is placed in a highly unsatisfactory position if it simply has, without expert evidence, to come to a judgment as to foreign law. As Sir Mark Potter P stated in *Re F (Abduction: Rights of Custody)*:[147]

> 'evidence is particularly desirable, in a situation where, without it, the court is obliged to form its own conclusion upon the basis of a series of orders translated into English without the assistance of expert evidence as to the nuances of the wording, or guidance as to the nature or extent of the rights of the parties under the relevant law.'[148]

Articles 3 and 4: Age and habitual residence[149]

By virtue of Art 4, the Hague Convention applies only to children under the age of 16 and habitually resident in the requesting State prior to the removal or retention. If a child turns 16 during the course of proceedings, he or she falls immediately outside the confines of the Hague Convention and recourse will have to be had to other remedies, such as powers under the inherent jurisdiction, to secure his return.[150]

The term 'habitual residence' in Arts 3 and 4 is not one that is defined within the *Hague Convention*. It has been held that *where* a child is

---

[145] *In re D (A Child) (Abduction: Rights of Custody)* [2006] UKHL 51, [2007] 1 AC 619, at 631, para [26]; and see also *Kennedy v Kennedy* [2009] EWCA Civ 986, [2010] 1 FLR 782, at 785–786, paras [9]–[10].

[146] *In re D (A Child) (Abduction: Rights of Custody)* [2006] UKHL 51, [2007] 1 AC 619, at 635, paras [37]–[38]; *Abbott v Abbott*, Supreme Court of the United States, No. 08-645, decided 17 May 2010.

[147] [2008] EWHC 272 (Fam), [2008] 2 FLR 1239 at 1244, para [14].

[148] See also *Re T (Abduction: Rights of Custody)* [2008] EWHC 809 (Fam), [2008] 2 FLR 1794, at 1797, para [11] and *Re K (Rights of Custody: Spain)* [2009] EWHC 1066 (Fam), [2010] 1 FLR 57, at 61–62, paras [13]–[14].

[149] In England and Wales, as has been noted, there are now currently different approaches adopted in respect of the interpretation of the concept for the purposes of Brussels IIR and for the Hague Convention: see, for example, *Marinos v Marinos* [2007] EWHC 2047 (Fam), [2007] 2 FLR 1018, which for the purposes of Art 3 of Brussels IIR adopts 'a centre of interests' test.

[150] *Re H (Abduction: Child of 16)* [2000] 2 FLR 51; and *Re C (Abduction: Separate Representation of Children)* [2008] EWHC 517 (Fam), [2008] 2 FLR 6.

habitually resident is to be determined according to the law of the requested State.[151] The burden is generally on the applicant to prove 'habitual residence'.

In England and Wales, the meaning of 'habitual residence' and its application has been the subject of exhaustive examination in numerous authorities. Its interpretation however, remains, controversial, principally because of the difficult interrelationship of various international instruments and because of certain rulings of the European Court of Justice.[152]

Habitual Residence: an interpretation[153]

Speaking generally, a number of propositions, in respect of 'habitual residence', might be regarded as a proper summary of the current position (at least in relation to domestic law):

- The term 'habitual residence'

  'is not to be treated as a term of art with some special meaning, but is rather to be understood according to the ordinary and natural meaning of the two words which it contains ... the question whether a person is or is not habitually resident in a specified country is a question of fact to be decided by reference to all the circumstances of any particular case'.[154]

- Habitual residence:

  'refers to a man's abode in a particular place or country which he has adopted voluntarily[155] and for settled purposes as part of the regular order of his life for the time being, whether of short or of long duration'.[156]

---

[151] See *Re P (Abduction: Declaration)* [1995] 1 FLR 831; and *Re D (Abduction: Habitual Residence)* [2005] 2 FLR 403.

[152] See *Re A (Area of Freedom, Security and Justice)* (C-523/07) [2009] 2 FLR 1. In *Re H-K (Habitual Residence)* [2011] EWCA Civ 1100, [2012] 1 FLR 436, at 441, para [17] Ward LJ said: 'I have no doubt, however, that, at least in the fullness of time, the European meaning of habitual residence will by osmosis shape the autonomous meaning to be given to that phrase in the *International* Hague Convention on Child Abduction with the stress of its international application.'

[153] As has been noted above, there are now currently different approaches as to 'habitual residence' in respect of the Hague Convention and Brussels IIR: see, for the purposes of Art 3 of Brussels IIR (*inter alia*) *Marinos v Marinos* [2007] EWHC 2047 (Fam), [2007] 2 FLR 1018; for the purposes of Art 8 of Brussels IIR see *Re A (Area of Freedom, Security and Justice)* (C-523/07) [2009] 2 FLR 1 at 12, at para [73].

[154] *In re J (A Minor) (Abduction: Custody Rights)* [1990] 2 AC 562 at 578G.

[155] 'The residence must be voluntarily adopted. Enforced presence by reason of kidnapping or imprisonment, or a Robinson Crusoe existence on a desert island with no opportunity to escape, may be so overwhelming a factor as to negative the will to be where one is': *R v Barnet London Borough Council Ex p Shah* [1983] 2 AC at 344B. But see also *DT v LBT (Abduction: Domestic Abuse)* [2010] EWHC 3177 (Fam), [2011]

'...[T]here must be a degree of settled purpose. The purpose may be one; or there may be several. It may be specific or general. All that the law requires is that there is a settled purpose. This is not to say that the 'propositus' intends to stay where he is indefinitely; indeed his purpose while settled, may be for a limited period. Education, business or profession, employment, health, family, or merely love of the place spring to mind as common reasons for a choice of regular abode. And there may well be many others. All that is necessary is that the purpose of living where one does has a sufficient degree of continuity to be properly described as settled'.[157]

- Along with a settled purpose and/or intention, there must be the elapse of 'an appreciable period of time'.[158]

- There is a significant difference between losing habitual residence and acquiring it:

  'A person may cease to be habitually resident in a single day if he or she leaves [country A] with a settled intention not to return to it but to take up long-term residence in country B instead. Such a person cannot, however, become habitually resident in country B in a single day. An appreciable period of time and a settled intention will be necessary to enable him or her to come so. During that appreciable period of time the person will have ceased to be habitually resident in country A but not yet have become habitually resident in country B'.[159]

- Habitual residence may be acquired even though the move was only supposed to be on a short term or trial basis.[160]

- (Generally speaking and probably outside the confines of the Hague Convention) there may be occasions when a person may be found to

---

1 FLR 1215 where Peter Jackson J said (at 1226, para [31]): 'In the present context I am of the view that a person is to be taken as acting voluntarily in adopting habitual residence in a country unless their presence is enforced. Bowing to pressure or agreeing with extreme reluctance does not make presence involuntary. Setting the bar too low would create a test that is difficult to apply, and the question of whether pressure is "illegitimate" is too vague to be reliable.' Furthermore, the 'operation of fraud or mistake may prevent the acquisition of habitual residence...': per Macur J in *Re Z (Abduction)* [2008] EWHC 3473 (Fam), [2009] 2 FLR 298 at 302, para [13].

[156] *R v Barnet London Borough Council Ex p Shah* [1983] 2 AC 309 at 343G.

[157] *R v Barnet London Borough Council Ex. p Shah* [1983] 2 AC 309, at 344C–D.

[158] *In re J (A Minor) (Abduction: Custody Rights)* [1990] 2 AC 562, at 579A.

[159] *In re J (A Minor) (Abduction: Custody Rights)* [1990] 2 AC 562, at 578H–579A; and *Al Habtoor v Fotheringham* [2001] EWCA Civ 186, [2001] 1 FLR 951, at 963, para [25].

[160] *Al Habtoor v Fotheringham* [2001] EWCA Civ 186, 1 FLR 951, at 965, para [37]; *Re R (Abduction: Habitual Residence)* [2003] EWHC 1968 (Fam), [2004] 1 FLR 216; and *Re A (Wardship: Habitual Residence)* [2006] EWHC 3338 (Fam), [2007] 1 FLR 1589, at 1595, para [33]. Though note *Re B (Child Abduction: Habitual Residence)* [1994] 2 FLR 915, at 918E, where it was held that a short period of time, some 2 months, when a reconciliation was attempted between the parties, was insufficiently long 'for a settled intention to have been formed by the mother in relation to her residence'; and see also *E v E* [2007] EWHC 276 (Fam), [2007] 1 FLR 1977.

not be habitually resident in either of the jurisdictions for which claims are made.[161] Alternatively, it is arguable (though not in respect of the Hague Convention or Brussels IIR) that a person may have more than one habitual residence at any time.[162]

- The habitual residence of a child remains a question of fact; indeed, '[it] is not always determinable by reference to the combined intention of the parties'.[163]

- As a general rule, however, a young child in the sole lawful custody of his or her mother will have the same habitual residence as her.[164]

- Where both parents shared equal rights of custody under the law of the country of their habitual residence, no unilateral action by one of them can change the child's habitual residence save by agreement or acquiescence over time or a court order determining rights of residence and custody.[165]

- A party's consent to send a child abroad for a short term purpose is unlikely to change that child's habitual residence.[166]

An authoritative summary of the proper approach to 'habitual residence' in Hague Convention cases is to be found in the judgment of Ward LJ in *Re P-J (Abduction: Habitual Residence: Consent)*.[167]

The interpretation of 'habitual residence' in relation to children covered by Art 8 in Brussels IIR was determined by the European Court of Justice in *Re A (Area of Freedom, Security and Justice)* (C-523/07),[168] The court said as follows:

'The concept of "habitual residence" under Art 8(1) of regulation No 2201/2003 must be interpreted as meaning that it corresponds to the place which reflects some degree of integration by the child in a social and family environment. To that end, in particular the duration, regularity,

---

[161] *Al Habtoor v Fotheringham* [2001] EWCA Civ 186, 1 FLR 951, at 964, para [27].
[162] *Ikimi v Ikimi* [2001] EWCA Civ 873, [2001] 2 FLR 1288.
[163] *Re A (Wardship: Habitual Residence)* [2006] EWHC 3338 (Fam), [2007] 1 FLR 1589, at 1599, para [49].
[164] *In re J (A Minor) (Abduction: Custody Rights)* [1990] 2 AC 562 at 579A.
[165] *Re P (G.E.) (An Infant)* [1965] Ch 568 per Lord Denning MR at 586A–C; *Re M (Abduction: Habitual Residence)* [1996] 1 FLR 887; *B v H (Habitual Residence: Wardship)* [2002] 1 FLR 388 at 399, para [85]; *E v E* [2007] EWHC 276 (Fam), [2007] 1 FLR 1977 at 1983, para [32]; and see *Rayden and Jackson on Divorce and Family Matters* at 2.154.
[166] *Re A (Wardship: Jurisdiction)* [1995] 1 FLR 767; *Re M (Abduction: Habitual Residence)* [1996] 1 FLR 887; *P v P* [2006] EWHC 2410 (Fam), [2007] 2 FLR 439; and *B v D* [2008] EWHC 1246 (Fam), [2008] Fam Law 1067.
[167] [2009] EWCA Civ 588, [2009] 2 FLR 1051, at 1062–1064, para [26]. See also *Re H-K (Habitual Residence)* [2011] EWCA Civ 1100, [2012] 1 FLR 436.
[168] [2009] 2 FLR 1.

conditions and reasons for the stay on the territory of a Member State and the family's move to that State, the child's nationality, the place and conditions of attendance at school, linguistic knowledge and the family and social relationships of the child in State must be taken into consideration. It is for the national court to establish the habitual residence of the child, taking account of all the circumstances specific to each individual case.'[169]

Articles 9 and 11: Minimising delay and the obligation to act within a limited timescale

Central to the good working of the Hague Convention is the obligation to avoid delay. Article 9 obliges a Central Authority which has received an application and which has reason to believe the child is in another Contracting State, to:

> 'directly and without delay transmit the application to the Central Authority of that Contracting State and inform the requesting Central Authority, or the applicant, as the case may be.'

Article 11 further provides that the judicial or administrative authorities of Contracting States shall act expeditiously in proceedings for the return of children. If the judicial or administrative authority has not reached a decision within six weeks from the date of the commencement of the proceedings, either the applicant or the Central Authority of the requested State, either by itself or if asked by the Central Authority of the requesting State, shall have a right to request the reasons why there has been a delay.

Brussels IIR and delay

In addition, Brussels IIR, however, positively *requires* Member States to complete the first instance proceedings[170]) within six weeks unless exceptional circumstances make this impossible.[171] This obligation is reinforced by Arts 6 and 8 of the European Convention for the Protection of Human Rights and Fundamental Freedoms.[172]

---

[169] The Court of Appeal sidestepped any consideration of the different tests in relation to the Hague Convention and Brussels IIR in *Re S (Habitual Residence)* [2009] EWCA Civ 1021, [2010] 1 FLR 1146.

[170] See, for example, *Zaffino v Zaffino (Abduction: Children's Views)* [2005] EWCA Civ 1012, [2006] 1 FLR 410, at 413, para [6]; and *Klentzeris v Klentzeris* [2007] EWCA Civ 533, [2007] 2 FLR 996, at 1003, para [27].

[171] Article 11(3) of Brussels IIR; *Vigreux v Michel* [2006] EWCA Civ 630, [2006] 2 FLR 1180 and *Re M (Abduction: Appeals)* [2007] EWCA Civ 1059, [2008] 1 FLR 699, at para [11].

[172] See, for example, *Iosub Caras v Romania (Application No 7198/04)* [2007] 1 FLR 661; *Carlson v Switzerland (Application no. 49492/06)*, ECHR, 10 November 2008; and *Deak v Romania and United Kingdom (Application no. 19055/05)* [2008] 2 FLR 994.

In both *In re D (A Child) (Abduction: Rights of Custody)*[173] and *Re M (Abduction: Zimbabwe)*[174] the House of Lords emphasised that the further away the court was from being able to secure a prompt return the less potent a factor the policy of the Hague Convention was.[175]

Indeed, where an application for a return order was not made promptly and not prosecuted thereafter promptly, very exceptionally, it could be struck out as an abuse of process.[176]

Article 12: Settlement: the 'gateway' stage

As has been noted, Art 12 provides that:

> 'Where a child has been wrongfully removed or retained in terms of Article 3 and, at the date of the commencement of the proceedings before the judicial or administrative authority of the Contracting State where the child is, a period of less than one year has elapsed from the date of the wrongful removal or retention, the authority concerned shall order the return of the child forthwith.

> The judicial or administrative authority, even where the proceedings have been commenced after the expiration of the period of one year referred to in the preceding paragraph, shall also order the return of the child, unless it is demonstrated that the child is now settled in its new environment.'

'Settled': meaning

It has traditionally been held that 'settled' should be given its ordinary and natural meaning. For the purposes of the Convention it has two constituents: first, it involves a physical element of relating to and being established in a community and an environment; and second, it has an emotional and psychological constituent denoting security and stability (it being required to be shown that the present situation imports stability when looking into the future). The new environment includes a child's 'place, home, school, people, friends, activities and opportunities but not, per se, the relationship with ... [the parent] which has always existed in a close, loving attachment. That can only be relevant insofar as it impinges on the new surroundings'.[177] In cases where there has been concealment

---

[173] [2006] UKHL 51, [2007] 1 AC 619.

[174] [2007] UKHL 55, [2008] 1 FLR 251.

[175] *In re D (A Child) (Abduction: Rights of Custody)* [2006] UKHL 51, [2007] 1 AC 619, at 624 and 639, paras [4] and [48]; and *In re M (Children) (Abduction: Rights of Custody)* [2007] UKHL 55, [2008] 1 AC 1288, sub nom *Re M (Abduction: Zimbabwe)* [2008] 1 FLR at 267 and 269, paras [47] and [54].

[176] *Re G (Abduction: Striking out Application)* [1995] 2 FLR 410.

[177] *Re N (Minors) (Abduction)* [1991] 1 FLR 413 at 417H – 418A, approved in *Cannon v Cannon* [2004] EWCA Civ 1330, [2005] 1 FLR 169 and followed in *Re C (Child Abduction: Settlement)* [2006] EWHC 1229 (Fam), [2006] 2 FLR 797. A less formulaic view of the interpretation of 'settlement' was argued for in *F v M and N (Abduction:*

and subterfuge, the Court of Appeal has held that 'the burden of demonstrating the necessary elements of emotional and psychological settlement is much increased'.[178]

It has now been authoritatively decided that even if a child has been in the requested State for more than a year and is settled in its new environment a discretion still exists for the court to order the child's return to the requesting State (see below for detailed discussion of the 'discretion' stage once an exception under the Hague Convention has been made out).[179]

Article 13: Consent, acquiescence, grave risk of physical and psychological harm or other intolerability and child's objections: the 'gateway' stage

INTRODUCTION

Article 13 provides that:

> 'Notwithstanding the provisions of the preceding Article [12], the judicial or administrative authority of the requested State is not bound to order the return of the child if the person, institution or other body which opposes its return establishes that—
>
> (a) the person, institution or other body having the care of the person of the child was not actually exercising the custody rights at the time of removal or retention, or had consented to or subsequently acquiesced in the removal or retention; or
>
> (b) there is a grave risk that his or her return would expose the child to physical or psychological harm or otherwise place the child in an intolerable situation.
>
> The judicial or administrative authority may also refuse to order the return of the child if it finds that the child objects to being returned and has attained an age and degree of maturity at which it is appropriate to take account of its views.
>
> In considering the circumstances referred to in this Article, the judicial and administrative authorities shall take into account the information relating to the social background of the child provided by the Central Authority or other competent authority of the child's habitual residence.'

Acquiescence: Settlement) [2008] EWHC 1525, [2008] 2 FLR 1270. See also, *M v M (Abduction: Settlement)* [2008] EWHC 2049 (Fam), [2008] 2 FLR 1884.

[178] *Cannon v Cannon* [2004] EWCA Civ 1330, [2005] 1 FLR 169 at 188, para [61].

[179] *In re M (Children) (Abduction: Rights of Custody)* [2008] 1 AC 1288, sub nom *Re M (Abduction: Zimbabwe)* [2008] 1 FLR 251 at 262, para [31], thereby supporting the view taken in *Cannon v Cannon* [2004] EWCA Civ 1330, [2005] 1 FLR 169, (which had allowed an appeal from the decision of Singer J in *Re C (Abduction: Settlement)* [2004] EWHC 1245 (Fam), [2005] 1 FLR 127), although for different reasons: see the reasoning of Baroness Hale in *In re M (Children) (Abduction: Rights of Custody)* [2007] UKHL 55, [2008] 1 AC 1288, sub nom *Re M (Abduction: Zimbabwe)* [2008] 1 FLR 251.

ART 13 (A): CONSENT AND ACQUIESCENCE

Consent and acquiescence are separate from each other although they are often raised together. Any consent takes place before the wrongful removal or retention; any acquiescence takes place after it.

Consent

Consent must (usually) be to the child's permanent removal or retention and should be real, informed, positive[180] and unequivocal.[181] It does not necessarily have to be provided in writing.[182] Once given, and acted upon, it cannot thereafter be withdrawn. Consent, however, is not valid if it has been obtained through 'a calculated and deliberate fraud on the part of the absconding parent' or if it is based on a mistake, misunderstanding or non disclosure.[183]

The position where a party has given advance or future consent to a removal or retention at some future (perhaps unspecified) date was considered in *Re L (Abduction: Future Consent)*.[184] In that case, Bodey J stated that he could:

'see no reason in principle why a consent should not be valid if tied to some future event even of uncertain timing, provided that the happening of the event is of reasonable acertainability. It cannot be something too vague, too uncertain or too subjective. The following should for example be capable of forming the basis of the consent defence: "... if my job application succeeds ..." or (as per the example given in Zenel) "... when the child comes out of hospital".

'But commonsense is everything in this sphere. If the consent was given when the facts were wholly and manifestly different from those prevailing at the time of the removal; or if the consent was given so long ago that it must clearly have lapsed; or if the consenting party had withdrawn that consent before it were acted on by a removal of the child, then in those various circumstances the defence would not be made out. It is all a question of degree.'[185]

---

[180] This does not necessarily mean that it needs to be 'express' consent (i e it is not necessary to have an express statement 'I consent'). There is a line of authority which has held that consent may be inferred from a course of conduct: see, for example, *Re C (Abduction: Consent)* [1996] 1 FLR 414 at 419C; and *Re M (Abduction) (Consent: Acquiescence)* [1999] 1 FLR 171 at 187F.

[181] *Re K (Abduction: Consent)* [1997] 2 FLR 212 at 217H.

[182] *Re C (Abduction: Consent)* [1996] 1 FLR 414; *Re K (Abduction: Consent)* [1997] 2 FLR 212; and *Re M (Abduction) (Consent: Acquiescence)* [1999] 1 FLR 171.

[183] *Re B (A Minor) (Abduction)* [1994] 2 FLR 249; *T v T (Abduction: Consent)* [1999] 2 FLR 912 at 917A–C; *M v T (Abduction)* [2008] EWHC 1383 (Fam), [2009] 1 FLR 1309, at 1316–1317, paras [28]–[33]; and *BT v JRT (Abduction: Conditional Acquiescence and Consent)* [2008] EWHC 1169 (Fam), [2008] 2 FLR 972.

[184] *Re L (Abduction: Future Consent)* [2007] EWHC 2181 (Fam), [2008] 1 FLR 914.

[185] *Re L (Abduction: Future Consent)* [2007] EWHC 2181 (Fam), [2008] 1 FLR 914 at 919, paras [29]–[30].

Furthermore, as Bodey J went on to say:

'Where a removing party knows or assumes that the formerly consenting party would not continue that consent at the time of the actual removal and/or if he or she knew the full facts, it is my view that the consent defence fails even though the original consent may never have been expressly withdrawn.'[186]

The issue of consent should be examined as part of a consideration of Art 13(a) and not Art 3.[187]

In the leading case of *Re P-J (Abduction: Habitual Residence: Consent)*[188] Ward LJ summarised the applicable principles in relation to the defence of consent as follows:

(a) Consent to the removal of the child must be clear and unequivocal.

(b) Consent can be given to the removal at some future but unspecified time or upon the happening of some future event.

(c) Such advance consent must, however, still be operative and in force at the time of the actual removal.

(d) The happening of the future event must be reasonably capable of ascertainment. The condition must not have been expressed in terms which are too vague for both parties to know whether the condition will be fulfilled. Fulfilment of the condition must not depend on the subjective determination of one party; the event must be objectively verifiable;

(e) Consent or the lack of it, must be viewed in the context of the realities of family life, or more precisely, in the context of the realities of the disintegration of family life. It is not to be viewed in the context of nor governed by the law of contract.

(f) Consent can be withdrawn at any time before actual removal. If it is, the proper course is for any dispute about removal to be resolved by the courts of the country of habitual residence before the child is removed.

(g) The burden of proving the consent rests on him or her who asserts it.

---

[186] *Re L (Abduction: Future Consent)* [2007] EWHC 2181 (Fam), [2008] 1 FLR 914 at 921, para [41].

[187] *Re P (Abduction: Consent)* [2004] EWCA Civ 971, [2004] 2 FLR 1057; and see *Re P-J (Abduction: Habitual Residence: Consent)* [2009] EWCA Civ 588, [2009] 2 FLR 1051, at 1075, para [53].

[188] [2009] EWCA Civ 588, [2009] 2 FLR 1051, at 1073, para [48]. See the difference of emphasis though in the judgment of Wilson LJ at 1075–1078.

(h)   The inquiry is inevitably fact specific and the facts and circumstances will vary infinitely from case to case.

(i)   The ultimate question is a simple one even if a multitude of facts bear upon the answer. It is simply this: had the other parent clearly and unequivocally consented to the removal?

Acquiescence

The proper approach of the court to the question of acquiescence has been set out in *In re H (Minors) (Abduction: Acquiescence)*[189] as summarised by Lord Browne-Wilkinson:

> '(1) For the purposes of Article 13 of the convention, the question whether the wronged parent has 'acquiesced' in the removal or retention of the child depends upon his actual state of mind. As Neill LJ said in Re S (Minors) (Abduction: Acquiescence) [1994] 1 FLR 819 at 838: "... the court is primarily concerned, not with the question of the other parent's perception of the applicant's conduct, but with the question whether the applicant acquiesced in fact."
>
> (2) The subjective intention of the wronged parent is a question of fact for the trial judge to determine in all the circumstances of the case, the burden of proof being on the abducting parent.
>
> (3) The trial judge, in reaching his decision on that question of fact, will no doubt be inclined to attach more weight to the contemporaneous words and actions of the wronged parent than to the bare assertions in evidence of his intention. But that is a question of the weight to be attached to evidence and is not a question of law.
>
> (4) There is only one exception. Where the words or actions of the wronged parent clearly and unequivocally show and have led the other parent to believe that the wronged parent is not asserting or going to assert his right to the summary return of the child and are inconsistent with such return, justice requires that the wronged parent be held to have acquiesced.'

Sometimes a left behind parent will not know of his or her Convention remedies or will have been provided with wrong legal advice. Each case will depend on its facts but in *Re S (Abduction: Acquiescence)* Butler-Sloss LJ provided the following guidance:[190]

> 'Knowledge of the facts and that the act of removal or retention is wrongful will normally usually be necessary. But to expect the applicant necessarily to have knowledge of the rights which can be enforced under the Convention is

---

[189]   [1998] AC 72 at 90E–G.
[190]   [1998] 2 FLR 115 at 122C–D. See also *Re D (Abduction: Acquiescence)* [1998] 1 FLR 686 and *B-G v B-G (Abduction: Acquiescence)* [2008] EWHC 688 (Fam), [2008] 2 FLR 965.

to set too high a standard. The degree of knowledge as a relevant factor will, of course, depend on the facts of each case.'

Once acquiescence is given, it cannot be withdrawn.[191] Such a withdrawal will, however, be taken into account when the court comes to consider the 'discretion' stage.

ARTICLE 13(B): GRAVE RISK OF HARM

The Art 13 (b) exception, 'grave risk of harm', is one of the more child-centric exceptions to the obligation to return (along with the child's objections, and settlement, exceptions).[192] It is often invoked but difficult to make out.[193] It has now been considered in detail by two decisions of the Supreme Court: *In re E (Children) (Abduction: Custody Appeal)*[194] and *Re S (A Child) (Abduction: Rights of Custody)*.[195] Thus any guidance in the older authorities has been superseded by the reasoning in these important decisions: as the Supreme Court said in *Re S (A Child) (Abduction: Rights of Custody)*, the decision in *In Re E (Children) (Abduction: Custody Appeal)* 'was primarily an exercise in the removal from [Article 13(b)] of disfiguring excrescence'.[196]

In *In re E (Children) (Abduction: Custody Appeal)*, the Supreme Court, after considering the impact of recent jurisprudence from the European Court of Human Rights,[197] set out how a court should direct itself when the Article 13(b) exception was invoked:[198]

'We share the view expressed in the High Court of Australia in *DP v Commonwealth Central Authority* (2001) 206 CLR 401, paras 9, 44, that there is no need for the article to be "narrowly construed". By its very terms, it is of restricted application. The words of article 13 are quite plain and need no further elaboration of "gloss".

First, it is clear that the burden of proof lies with the "person, institution or other body" which opposes the child's return. It is for them to produce evidence to substantiate one of the exceptions. There is nothing to indicate that the standard of proof is other than the ordinary balance of probabilities. But in evaluating the evidence the court will of course be mindful of the limitations involved in the summary nature of the Hague Convention process. It will rarely be appropriate to hear oral evidence of the

---

[191] *Re S (Abduction: Acquiescence)* [1998] 2 FLR 115 at 122H.
[192] See the *Perez-Vera Report*, paras [29] and [116].
[193] A rare occasion when it succeeded was in *Re D (Article 13 (b): non return)* [2006] EWCA Civ 146, [2006] 2 FLR 305.
[194] [2011] UKSC 27, [2012] 1 AC 144.
[195] [2012] UKSC 10, [2012] 2 FLR 442.
[196] [2012] UKSC 10, [2012] 2 FLR at 453, at para [31]. Indeed, as Lord Wilson put it at 445, para [6], the judgment in *In re E (Children) (Abduction: Custody Appeal)* had sought 'to set out in clear terms the proper approach to a defence under Art 13(b).'
[197] In particular, the decision of *Neulinger and Shuruk v Switzerland* [2011] 1 FLR 122.
[198] See 160–161, paras [31]–[36].

allegations made under article 13(b) and so neither those allegations nor their rebuttal are usually tested in cross-examination.

Second, the risk to the child must be "grave". It is not enough, as it is in other contexts such as asylum, that the risk be "real". It must have reached such a level of seriousness as to be characterized as "grave". Although "grave" characterises the risk rather than the harm, there is in ordinary language a link between the two. Thus a relatively low risk of death or really serious injury might properly be qualified as "grave" while a higher level of risk might be required for other less serious forms of harm.

Third, the words "physical or psychological harm" are not qualified. However, they do gain from the alternative "or *otherwise*" placed "in an intolerable situation" (emphasis supplied). As was said in *In re D* [2007] 1 AC 619, para 52, "'Intolerable' is a strong word, but when applied to a child must mean 'a situation which this particular child in these particular circumstances should not be expected to tolerate'". Those words were carefully considered and can be applied just as sensibly to physical or psychological harm as to any other situation. Every child has to put up with a certain amount of rough and teumplem, discomfort and distress. It is part of growing up. But there are some things which it is not reasonable to expect a child to tolerate. Among these also, we now understand, can be exposure to the harmful effects of seeing and hearing the physical or psychological abuse of her own parent. Mr Turner accepts that, if there is such a risk, the source of it is irrelevant: eg, where a mother's subjective perception of events leads to a mental illness which could have intolerable consequences for the child.

Fourth, article 13(b) is looking to the future: the situation as it would be if the child were to be returned forthwith to her home country. As has often been pointed out, this is not necessarily the same as being returned to the person, institution or other body who has requested her return, although of course it may be so if that person has the right so to demand. More importantly, the situation which the child will face on return depends crucially on the protective measures which can be put in place to secure that the child will not be called upon to face an intolerable situation when she gets home. Mr Turner accepts that if the risk is serious enough to fall within article 13(b) the court is not only concerned with the child's immediate future, because the need for effective protection may persist.

There is obviously a tension between the inability of the court to resolve factual disputes between the parties and the risks that the child will face if the allegations are in fact true. Mr Turner submits that there is a sensible and pragmatic solution. Where allegations of domestic abuse are made, the court should first ask whether, if they are true, there would be a grave risk that the child would be exposed to physical or psychological harm or otherwise placed in an intolerable situation. If so, the court must then ask how the child can be protected against the risk. The appropriate protective measures and their efficacy will obviously vary from case to case and from country to country. This is where arrangements for international cooperation between liaison judges are so helpful. Without such protective measures, the court may have no option but to do the best it can to resolve the disputed issues.'

In *Re S (A Child) (Abduction: Rights of Custody)*,[199] the Supreme Court considered the proper approach when a respondent relied upon her subjective perceptions to make out an Art 13(b) approach. In overturning the decision of the Court of Appeal, and in confirming the position, the Supreme Court said:[200]

> 'The critical question is what will happen if, with the mother, the child is returned. If the court concludes that, on return, the mother will suffer such anxieties that their effect on her mental health will create a situation that is intolerable for the child, then the child should not be returned. It matters not whether the mother's anxieties will be reasonable or unreasonable. The extent to which there will, objectively, be good cause for the mother to be anxious on return will nevertheless be relevant to the court's assessment of the mother's mental state if the child is returned.'

Many different factual situations have given rise to attempts to make out an Art 13(b) exception to return. A summary of some of the leading cases is found at the end of this chapter.

ART 13(2): CHILD'S OBJECTIONS

The child's objections exception was considered in *In re M (Children) (Abduction: Rights of Custody)*[201] where Baroness Hale made it clear that for the exception to be made out at the 'gateway' stage only *two* conditions needed to be met:

(a)   that the child himself objects to being returned; and

(b)   that he has attained an age and degree of maturity at which it is appropriate to take account of her views.[202]

A useful starting point as to the accumulated learning on the issue of child's objections is the decision of Baker J in *WF v FJ, BF and RF (Abduction: Child's Objections)*.[203]

As to whether a particular child objects to a summary return, in *Re K (Abduction: Case Management)*[204] Thorpe LJ said:

---

[199]   [2012] UKSC 10, [2012] 2 FLR 442.
[200]   At 453, para [34].
[201]   [2007] UKHL 55, [2008] 1 AC 1288, [2008] 1 FLR 251, at 266–267, para [46].
[202]   Which Wilson LJ described in *Re W (Abduction: Child's Objections)* [2010] EWCA Civ 520, [2010] 2 FLR 1165, at 1170, para [22] as a 'fairly low threshold requirement'.
[203]   [2010] EWHC 2909 (Fam), [2011] 1 FLR 1153, at 1165–1167, paras [26]–[30].
[204]   [2010] EWCA Civ 1546, [2011] 1 FLR 1268, at 1273, para [24].

'The Hague Convention is clear in its terminology. There must be a very clear distinction between the child's objections and the child's wishes and feelings. The child who has suffered an abduction will very often have developed wishes and feelings to remain in the bubble of respite that the abducting parent will have created, however fragile the bubble may be, but the expression of those wishes and feelings cannot be said to amount to an objection unless there is a strength, conviction and a rationality that satisfies the proper interpretation of the Article.'

Once the discretion comes into play, the court may have to consider the nature and strength of the child's objections, the extent to which they are authentically his own or the product of the influence of the abducting parent, the extent to which they coincide or are at odds with other considerations which are relevant to his welfare, as well as general Hague Convention considerations. The older the child, the greater the weight that his objections are likely to carry.[205]

The English courts, in accordance with views expressed in the *Perez-Vera Report*,[206] and for understandable reasons, have declined to determine a particular chronological age at which the second limb of the exception should be regarded as having been made out (if it is found that the particular child objects). Each case must turn on its own facts.

In *Re W (Abduction: Acquiescence: Children's Objections)* Black J held that two children aged 8 and 6 years old were at an age and level of maturity at which it was appropriate to take account of their views. In so concluding, Black J determined that the decision of *In re D (Child) (Abduction: Rights of Custody)*[207] essentially meant that threshold to be crossed (at this stage) was lower than had previously been thought. However, as Black J said: 'In any given case, one can only determine whether a child has the requisite age and degree of maturity by looking at the attributes of the particular child, the circumstances in which he finds himself, and the nature of the objections.'[208]

Indeed, in *Re W (Abduction: Child's Objections)*[209] (which was the appeal from *Re W (Abduction: Acquiescence: Children's Objections)* (see above) Wilson LJ firmly rejected any criticism of Black J's approach and said:[210]

'... over the last thirty years the need to take decisions about much younger children not necessarily in accordance with their wishes but at any rate in the light of their wishes has taken hold: see Art 12 of the United Nations Convention on the Rights of the Child 1989 and note, for EU states, the subtle shift of emphasis given to Art 13 of the Hague Convention by

---

[205] *In re M (Children) (Abduction: Rights of Custody)* [2007] UKHL 55, [2008] 1 AC 1288, sub nom *Re M (Abduction: Zimbabwe)* [2008] 1 FLR 251 at 267, para [46].
[206] At para [30].
[207] [2006] UKHL 51, [2007] 1 AC 619.
[208] [2010] EWHC 332 (Fam), [2010] 2 FLR 1150; see in particular at 1159, para [37].
[209] [2010] EWCA Civ 520, [2010] 2 FLR 1165.
[210] Paras [17]–[18].

Art 11(2) of Council Regulation (EC) No 2201/2003 (Brussels II Revised). Fortunately Art 13 was drawn in terms sufficiently flexible to accommodate this development in international thinking; and, although her comment was obiter, I am clear that, in context, the observation of Baroness Hale of Richmond in *Re D (Abduction: Rights of Custody)* [2006] UKHL 51, [2007] 1 AC 619, [2006] 3 WLR 989, [2007] 1 FLR 961, at [59], that "children should be heard far more frequently in Hague Convention cases than has been the practice hitherto" related to the defence of a child's objections.

'... There is however a concern, which I share, that the lowering of the age at which a child's objections may be taken into account might gradually erode the high level of achievement of the Convention's objective, namely – in the vast majority of cases – to secure a swift restoration of children to the states from which they have been abducted. Such is consideration of policy which should always carry significant weight in exercise of the discretion whether to refuse to order the return of an objecting child, but particularly so if that child is young ... A considerable safeguard against such erosion is to be found in the well-recognised expectation that in the discretionary exercise the objections of an older child will deserve greater weight than those of a younger child ...'

Prior to the decision in *In re M (Children) (Abduction: Rights of Custody)*,[211] there was some debate as to whether it should be at the 'gateway' or 'discretion' stage that various different considerations should be scrutinised – such as the extent to which the child's reasons for objection are rooted in reality and have been shaped or coloured by parental pressure – and how the court's discretion should be exercised once the 'gateway' had been made out. The proper approach appears to have been settled by the reasoning given by the House of Lords in *In re M (Children) (Abduction: Rights of Custody)*[212] and earlier authorities in respect of the child's objections exception[213] should be read in the light of the reasoning therein and only relied upon insofar as they are not inconsistent with the approach of the House of Lords.[214]

Article 15

Article 15 provides that:

---

[211] [2007] UKHL 55, [2008] 1 AC 1288, [2008] 1 FLR 251.

[212] [2007] UKHL 55, [2008] 1 AC 1288, [2008] 1 FLR 251.

[213] In particular *Re T (Abduction: Child's Objections to Return)* [2000] 2 FLR 192; *Zaffino v Zaffino (Abduction: Children's Views)* [2005] EWCA Civ 1012, [2006] 1 FLR 410; *Vigreux v Michel* [2006] EWCA Civ 630, [2006] 2 FLR 1180; and *Re M (Abduction: Child's Objections)* [2007] EWCA Civ 260, [2007] 2 FLR 72.

[214] Thus, in short, it is more than questionable whether the discipline articulated by Ward LJ in *Re T (Abduction: Child's Objections to Return)* [2000] 2 FLR 192 has been replaced by the reasoning in *In re M (Abduction: Rights of Custody)*. Sir Mark Potter P, though, appears to have thought not in *De L v H* [2009] EWHC 3074 (Fam), [2010] 1 FLR 1229 but he may well be wrong. The approach of Baker J, in his detailed consideration of the child's objections' exception in *WF v FJ, BF and RF (Abduction: Child's Objections)* [2010] EWHC 2909 (Fam), [2011] 1 FLR 1153 is, *pace* Sir Mark Potter P, to be preferred.

'The judicial or administrative authorities of a Contracting State may, prior to the making of an order for the return of the child, request that the applicant obtain from the authorities of the State of the habitual residence of the child a decision or other determination that the removal or retention was wrongful within the meaning of Art 3 of the Convention, where such a decision or determination may be obtained in that State. The Central Authorities of the Contracting States shall so far as practicable assist applicants to obtain such a decision or determination.'

This provision allows the State to which the child has been removed or retained in to request that the State of the child's habitual residence determine whether the removal or retention was 'wrongful' within the meaning of Art 3 of the Hague Convention.[215] Resort to this mechanism, however, because of the inevitable delay that will result from its invocation, should be kept to an absolute minimum.[216]

In cases subject to Brussels IIR, it has been remarked that advocates ought to consider the use of liaison through the European Judicial Network to consider what would be the best possible route to follow in a particular case.[217]

Once the court of the requesting State has made the determination and the court of the requested State has received that determination there is no real room for the instruction of further evidence in the latter court as to the same issue. The determination, in almost all cases, will be conclusive. Only in exceptional circumstances, where the determination, for example, 'has been obtained by fraud or in breach of the rules of natural justice'[218] or 'is clearly out of line with the international understanding of the Convention's terms' ... should the court in the requested state decline to follow it'.[219]

Article 18

Article 18 provides that:

'The provisions of this Chapter do not limit the power of a judicial or administrative authority to order the return of the child at any time.'

---

[215] In relation requests being made to England and Wales, see s 8 of the Child Abduction and Custody Act 1985. For recent examples of the determination of such requests see *A v B (Abduction: Declaration)* [2008] EWHC 2524 (Fam), [2009] 1 FLR 1253; and *X County Council v B (Abduction: Rights of Custody in the Court)* [2009] EWHC 2635 (Fam), [2010] 1 FLR 1197.

[216] For a recent example of the English court making such a declaration, see *A v B (Abduction: Declaration)* [2008] EWHC 2524 (Fam), [2009] 1 FLR 1253.

[217] Per Thorpe LJ in *Re F (Abduction: Refusal to Return)* [2009] EWCA Civ 416, [2009] 2 FLR 1023, at 1029–1030, para [12].

[218] *In Re D (A Child) (Abduction: Rights of Custody)* [2006] UKHL 51, [2007] 1 AC 619, at 637–638, paras [43] and [44].

[219] *In re D (A Child) (Abduction: Rights of Custody)* [2006] UKHL 51, [2007] 1 AC 619, at 636–637, 645 and 648–649, paras [41]–[44], [71], [81] and [83].

The meaning of Art 18 has been regarded, at least in respect of its consideration in England and Wales, as being somewhat obscure. In *Cannon v Cannon*[220] Thorpe LJ held that Art 18 specifically conferred a general discretion so that even if a child was found to be 'settled' for the purposes of Art 12 the court could still exercise its discretion to return the child to its country of habitual residence. When that issue was reconsidered in *In re M (Children) (Abduction: Rights of Custody)*[221] the House of Lords took a contrary view, the majority implying such a discretion into Art 12 without reliance on Art 18. Article 18 accordingly merely allows a party to rely on other domestic powers outside the confines of the Hague Convention to seek the return of an abducted child.

Article 20

Article 20 provides that:

> 'The return of the child under the provisions of Article 12 may be refused if this would not be permitted by the fundamental principles of the requested State relating to the protection of human rights and fundamental freedoms.'

In the *Perez-Vera Report*[222] it was explained that this Article was:

> '... not directed at developments which have occurred on the international level, but is concerned only with principles accepted by the law of the requested State, either through general international law and treaty law, or through internal legislation. Consequently, so as to be able to refuse to return a child on the basis of this article, it will be necessary to show that the fundamental principles of the requested State concerning the subject matter of the Convention do not permit it; it will not be sufficient to show merely that its return would be incompatible, even manifestly incompatible, with these principles.'

Article 20 was not incorporated into the CACA 1985 but because of the incorporation of the European Convention for the Protection of Human Rights and Fundamental Freedoms by virtue of the Human Rights Act 1998, it has been held that 'Article 20 has been given domestic effect by a different route'.[223]

Although a respondent may therefore, in theory, rely on Art 20 it is difficult to conceive of particular circumstances where Art 20 would add anything to reliance upon Art 13(b). Indeed, internationally, Art 20 has been very rarely invoked.

---

[220] [2004] EWCA Civ 1330, [2005] 1 FLR 169, at 188, para [62].
[221] [2007] UKHL 55, [2008] 1 AC 1288, [2008] 1 FLR 251.
[222] At para [118].
[223] Per Baroness Hale in *In re D (A Child) (Abduction: Rights of Custody)* [2006] UKHL 51, [2007] 1 AC 619, at 643, para [65]; and *In re J (A Child) (Custody Rights: Jurisdiction)* [2005] UKHL 40, [2006] 1 AC 80, at 96, para [44].

The proper approach of the court to the 'discretion' stage

Until recently, the courts in this jurisdiction have found it difficult to determine how they should approach the 'discretion' stage, once the 'gateway' stage has been passed, and specifically what factors were relevant and what weight should be given to each of them. Over time a considerable difference in approach had grown up.[224]

In *In re M (Children) (Abduction: Rights of Custody)*,[225] however, the House of Lords gave detailed and authoritative guidance on how the court should approach the 'discretion' stage.

Baroness Hale held that:[226]

> '... it is wrong to import any test of exceptionality into the exercise of discretion under the Hague Convention. The circumstances in which the return may be refused are themselves exceptions to the general rule. That in itself is sufficient exceptionality. It is neither necessary nor desirable to import an additional gloss into the Convention ...'

As to what factors would be relevant in relation to each of the different exceptions, Baroness Hale said:[227]

> 'In [Hague] Convention cases ... there are general policy considerations which may be weighed against the interests of the child in the individual case. These policy considerations include, not only the swift return of abducted children, but also comity between the contracting states and respect for one another's judicial processes. Furthermore, the Convention is there, not only to secure the prompt return of abducted children, but also to deter abduction in the first place. The message should go out to potential abductors that there are no safe havens among the contracting states.
>
> My Lords, in cases where a discretion arises from the terms of the Convention itself, it seems to me that the discretion is at large. The court is entitled to take into account the various aspects of the Convention policy, alongside the circumstances which gave the court a discretion in the first place and the wider considerations of the child's rights and welfare. I would, therefore, respectfully agree with Thorpe LJ in the passage quoted in para [32] above, save for the word 'overriding' if it suggests that the Convention objectives should always be given more weight than the other considerations. Sometimes they should and sometimes they should not.
>
> That, it seems to me, is the furthest one should go in seeking to put a gloss on the simple terms of the Convention. As is clear from the earlier

---

[224] See, for example, *W v W (Child Abduction: Acquiescence)* [1993] 2 FLR 211 at 219B–D; *Re C (Abduction: Settlement) (No 2)* [2005] 1 FLR 938 at 946, para [27]; *Zaffino v Zaffino (Abduction: Children's Views)* [2005] EWCA Civ 1012, [2006] 1 FLR 410 at 418, para [19]; and *Vigreux v Michel* [2006] EWCA Civ 630, [2006] 2 FLR 1180.

[225] [2007] UKHL 55, [2008] 1 AC 1288, [2008] 1 FLR 251.

[226] [2007] UKHL 55, [2008] 1 AC 1288, [2008] 1 FLR 251 at 265–267, para [40].

[227] At paras [42]–[48].

discussion, the Convention was the product of prolonged discussions in which some careful balances were struck and fine distinctions drawn. The underlying purpose is to protect the interests of children by securing the swift return of those who have been wrongfully removed or retained. The Convention itself has defined when a child must be returned and when she need not be. Thereafter the weight to be given to Convention considerations and to the interests of the child will vary enormously. The extent to which it will be appropriate to investigate those welfare considerations will also vary. But the further away one gets from the speedy return envisaged by the Convention, the less weighty those general Convention considerations must be.

By way of illustration only, as this House pointed out in Re D (Abduction: Rights of Custody) [2006] UKHL 51; [2007] 1 AC 619, [2007] 1 FLR 961, para [55], "it is inconceivable that a court which reached the conclusion that there was a grave risk that the child's return would expose him to physical or psychological harm or otherwise place him in an intolerable situation would nevertheless return him to face that fate." It was not the policy of the Convention that children should be put at serious risk of harm or placed in intolerable situations. In consent[228] or acquiescence cases, on the other hand, general considerations of comity and confidence, particular considerations relating to the speed of legal proceedings and approach to relocation in the home country, and individual considerations relating to the particular child might point to a speedy return so that her future can be decided in her home country.

In child's objections cases, the range of considerations may be even wider than those in the other exceptions ... Once the discretion comes into play, the court may have to consider the nature and strength of the child's objections, the nature and strength of the child's objections, the extent to which they are 'authentically her own' or the product of the influence of the abducting parent, the extent to which they coincide or are at odds with other considerations which are relevant to her welfare, as well as the general Convention considerations referred to earlier. The older the child, the greater the weight that her objections are likely to carry. But that is far from saying that the child's objections should only prevail in the most exceptional circumstances.

In settlement cases,[229] it must be borne in mind that the major objective of the Convention cannot be achieved. These are no longer 'hot pursuit' cases. By definition, for whatever reason, the pursuit did not begin until long after the trail had gone cold. The object of securing a swift return to the country of origin cannot be met. It cannot any longer be assumed that that country is the better forum for the resolution of the parental dispute. So the policy of

---

[228] In *C v H (Abduction: Consent)* [2009] EWHC 2660 (Fam), [2010] 1 FLR 225 Munby J (at 237, para [46]) said that he 'was inclined to think that the approach that Hale J [in *Re K (Abduction: Consent)* [1997] 2 FLR 212] set out remains good and wise learning notwithstanding the subsequent elaboration of her thinking as Baroness Hale of Richmond in *Re M*. I am inclined to think that it will be an unusual case in which consent having been established, it is nonetheless appropriate to order a return.'

[229] See, for example, *Re O (Abduction: Settlement)* [2011] EWCA Civ 128, [2011] 2 FLR 1307.

the Convention would not necessarily point towards a return in such cases, quite apart from the comparative strength of the countervailing factors which may well, as here, include the child's objections as well as her integration in her new community.

All this is merely to illustrate that the policy of the Convention does not yield identical results in all cases, and has to be weighed together with the circumstances which produced the exception and such pointers as there are towards the welfare of the particular child ...'

16.4.2.2   *Incoming non-Convention child abduction cases*

When a child has been abducted from a non-Convention country, different principles will apply to the court's adjudication of the dispute. Usually, the wardship jurisdiction will be invoked but even if it is not the court will approach the matter, applying the paramountcy of the child's welfare.[230]

The proper approach of the court is now that set out by Baroness Hale in *In Re J (A Child) (Custody Rights: Jurisdiction)*.[231] From this detailed set of reasoning of Baroness Hale a number of propositions may be distilled:

(a)   any court which is determining any question with respect to the upbringing of a child has a statutory duty to regard the welfare of the child as its paramount consideration. In non Convention cases, the court must act in accordance with the welfare needs – the best interests – of the particular child;[232]

(b)   there is no warrant for the principles of the *Hague Convention* being extended to countries which are not parties to that *Convention*;[233]

(c)   a power did, however, remain, in accordance with the welfare principle, to order the immediate return of a child to a foreign jurisdiction without conducting a full investigation of the merits;[234]

---

[230]   FPR 2010, PD 12F, para. 3.5 also requires that non Convention cases are completed within 6 weeks except where exceptional circumstances make this impossible.
[231]   [2005] UKHL 40, [2006] 1 AC 80. Prior to the opinions of the House of Lords in this case, two competing strands of thought had grown up as to how a court should approach such cases: see, for example, *In re JA (Child Abduction: Non Convention Country)* [1998] 1 FLR 231 and contrast it with *Osman v Elasha* [2000] Fam 2, [2000] 2 WLR 2036. An example of the application of the principles in *In Re J (A Child) (Custody Rights: Jurisdiction)* [2005] UKHL 40, [2006] 1 AC 80 is *Re U (Abduction: Nigeria)* [2010] EWHC 1179 (Fam), [2011] 1 FLR 354.
[232]   At 88–91, Paras [18], [22] and [25].
[233]   At 90, para [22].
[234]   At 90, para [26].

(d)   a trial judge had to make a choice, having regard to the welfare
       principle, between a summary return or a more detailed
       consideration of the merits of the parties' dispute;[235]

(e)   in making the choice between a summary return and a more detailed
       consideration of the merits, the focus must be on the individual child
       and the particular circumstances of the case;[236]

(f)   it was wrong to say that there should be a 'strong presumption' that
       it is 'highly likely' to be in the best interests of a child subject to an
       unauthorised removal or a retention to be returned to his country of
       habitual residence so that any issues which remain can be decided
       there. The most one could say was 'that the judge may find it
       convenient to start from the proposition that it is likely to be better
       for a child to return to his home country for any disputes about his
       future to decided there. A case against his doing so has to be made.
       But the weight to be given to that proposition will vary enormously
       from case to case. What may be best for him in the long run may be
       different from what will be best for him in the short run. It should
       not be assumed ... that allowing a child to remain here while his
       future is decided here inevitably means that he will remain here for
       ever';[237]

(g)   a number of factors were relevant, (amongst all the circumstances of
       the case), in deciding whether to order a summary return or not—

       (i)   the degree of connection of the child with each country: what is
               his 'home country'?;[238]
       (ii)   the length of time that the child has spent in each country;[239]
       (iii)   depending on the particular facts of the case, any differences in
               the legal system of this country and the other country,
               including whether the other country had an absence of a
               relocation jurisdiction (which itself may be 'decisive');[240]
       (iv)   the impact of any decision on the child's primary carer;[241]

(h)   any decision about whether to order a summary return or not should
       be taken swiftly.[242]

In the event that, in an incoming non Convention case, the powers of the
court in wardship and the powers of the Secretary of State interface, it

---

[235]   At 92, para [28].
[236]   At 92, para [29].
[237]   At 92, paras [32]–[33].
[238]   At 93, para [33].
[239]   At 93, para [34].
[240]   At 94–95, paras [37]–[38].
[241]   At 95, para [40].
[242]   At 95, para [41].

has been held that it is highly desirable for there to be communication and collaboration between the two bodies.[243]

16.4.2.3 Outgoing child abduction cases

Where the State to which the child has been taken is a contracting State to the Hague Convention, the usual remedy for the left behind parent would ordinarily be to initiate Hague Convention proceedings in the country where the child has been abducted to.[244] In cases where neither the Hague Convention nor other international treaties apply, the left behind parent is left with an uphill struggle.

In these latter cases, the left behind parent may in the first instance, seek a number of different orders in this jurisdiction. The following are examples: (a) an order making the child a ward of court; (b) a Collection order directed to the Tipstaff; (c) an order that the child be placed in the left behind parent's care; (d) an order directed to the Tipstaff requesting a port alert; and (e) orders requesting that the Foreign and Commonwealth Office and/or Interpol render any assistance that they might be able to. In November 2003, the President of the Family Division issued important guidance to practitioners setting out the 'procedures which are to be followed when a court in England and Wales exercising family jurisdiction seeks to invoke diplomatic assistance': *Guidance from the President's Office – Liaison between courts in England and Wales and British Embassies and High Commissions abroad.*[245]

Some of these orders may have a persuasive effect on the relevant authorities in the requested State. For example, in *Re KR (Abduction: Forcible Removal by Parents)*[246] (which provides a very useful precedent as to how such orders might be drafted), a child was returned to the United Kingdom after a number of orders were made seeking the assistance of the judicial and administrative bodies, and the British High Commission, in the foreign state.

If such orders are not successful in achieving the return of the child, it may well be that other options should be considered. If the abducting parent returns at some point to this jurisdiction without the child, then he

---

[243] Per Thorpe LJ in *Re F (Abduction: Removal Outside Jurisdiction)* [2008] EWCA Civ 842, [2008] 2 FLR 1649, at 1658, para [37].

[244] But see *B v D* [2008] EWHC 1246 (Fam), [2009] 1 FLR 1015, where a mother sought the return of her children from Portugal to the United Kingdom. Instead of issuing Hague Convention proceedings in Portugal, the mother issued an Originating Summons in this country, relying instead on the inherent jurisdiction. Baron J rejected arguments that this was an inappropriate use of the inherent jurisdiction, and that the proper mechanism was a Hague Convention application in Portugal, and ordered the children's return. See also *Re S (Wardship: Peremptory Return)* [2010] EWCA Civ 465, [2010] 2 FLR 1960.

[245] 28 November 2003, [2004] Fam Law 68.

[246] [1999] 2 FLR 542.

or she will be caught by the provisions of any orders previously made. Once in this jurisdiction, efforts can then be made to encourage and seek the return of the child.[247]

Otherwise, the left behind parent might wish to consider seeking to initiate proceedings under the domestic law of the particular country to which the child has been abducted, or, if there is a court order in force in this country, to bring contempt proceedings in this country,[248] or, exceptionally, if there is in existence an extradition treaty between the UK and the state to which the child had been abducted to, extradition proceedings, seeking the extradition of the abductor back to the UK.[249]

How the court should adjudicate upon contempt proceedings brought against an alleged abductor, was considered in *Re A (Abduction: Contempt)*,[250] where the following general propositions as to the law were accepted by the Court of Appeal:

(a) the contempt which has to be established lies in the disodedience to the order to return rather than in the original abduction;

(b) a contempt of court must be proved to the criminal standard and the burden of proof lies at all times on the applicant;

(c) a contempt of court involves a contumelious, ie a deliberate, disobedience of an order; there had to be a clear finding not only of breach but that the breach was deliberate.[251]

It is permissible for a court to make a number of successive mandatory injunctions requiring positive action by an individual notwithstanding a past failure to comply with an identical request. Each time the individual fails to comply with any fresh order, it is open for the court to consider fresh contempt proceedings and to consider, if a breach is found, punishment for any contempt.[252]

---

[247] Though note that there is no power *per se* and absent a finding of contempt to remand an alleged abductor in custody pending the return of a child: see *Re B (Child Abduction: Wardship: Power to Detain)* [1994] 2 FLR 479. See the same case for discussion relating to the issuing of bench warrants.

[248] If security has been given, this might be forfeited. Alternatively, a writ of sequestration might be issued against any assets of the abductor (or indeed a third party) in this country, or an order might be made restraining the person in contempt of court from dealing with or disposing with any of his assets pending the issuing of an application for leave for a writ of sequestration.

[249] See the Extradition Act 1989.

[250] [2008] EWCA Civ 1138, [2009] 1 FLR 1, at 4, para [6].

[251] Thus in that case, where a father was ordered to effect the return of a child, it was stated that 'if it be the case that the father cannot cause the return of the child he is not in contempt of court, however disgraceful and/or criminal the original abduction may have been': see para [6].

[252] *In the matter of W (A Child)* [2011] EWCA Civ 1196, at para [37].

The Pakistan Protocol of 17th January 2003

Anglo-Pakistan child abduction cases are determined in accordance with the Pakistan Protocol which was agreed between the then President of the Family Division and the Chief Justice of Pakistan in January 2003. The Protocol provides that:[253]

> '1. In normal circumstances the welfare of the child is best determined by the courts of the country of the child's habitual/ordinary residence.
>
> 2. If a child is removed from the UK to Pakistan, or from Pakistan to the UK, without the consent of the parent with the a custody/residence order or a restraint/interdict order from the court of the child's habitual/ordinary residence, the judge of the court of the country to which the child has been removed shall not ordinarily exercise jurisdiction over the child, save in so far as it is necessary for the court to order the return of the child to the country of the child's habitual/ordinary residence.
>
> 3. If a child is taken from the UK to Pakistan, or from Pakistan to the UK, by a parent with visitation/access/contact rights with the consent of the parent with a custody/residence order or a restraint/interdict order from the court of the child's habitual/ordinary residence or in consequence of an order from that court permitting the visit, and the child is retained in that country after the end of the visit without consent or in breach of the court order, the judge of the court of the country in which the child has been retained shall not ordinarily exercise jurisdiction over the child, save in so far as it is necessary for the court to order the return of the child to the country of the child's habitual/ordinary residence.'

In *Re H (Child Abduction: Mother's Asylum)*,[254] Wilson J held that the principles underpinning the Protocol should be considered, amongst all the circumstances of the case, even in cases which strictly fall outside its confines.

16.5 THE CRIMINAL LAW

The Child Abduction Act 1984 ('the CAA 1984') which amended the criminal law relating to child abduction, creates two offences relating to the abduction of a child under the age of 16. The first is an offence of abduction by a person 'connected with a child'; the second is an offence of abduction by a person who is not connected with a child. Knowledge of the general terms of this Act (if not the detail), and other relevant criminal offences may be useful as they can be relied upon in the first instance as a preventative tool: it is open to the police to arrest anyone

---

[253] At paras [1]–[3].
[254] [2003] EWHC 1820 (Fam), [2003] 2 FLR 1105.

they reasonably suspect of committing an arrestable offence which includes attempting to commit any such offence.[255]

16.5.1 Abduction by a person 'connected with a child': s 1 of the Child Abduction Act 1984

By virtue of s 1(1) of the CAA 1984, 'a person connected with a child under the age of sixteen commits an offence if he takes or sends a child out of the United Kingdom without the appropriate consent'.[256] A person is 'connected with a child' if:

(a)   he is a parent of the child (s 1(2)(a) of the CAA 1984); or

(b)   in the case of a child whose parents were not married to each other at the time of his birth, there are reasonable grounds for believing that he is the father of the child (s 1(2)(b) of the CAA 1984); or

(c)   he is a guardian of the child (s 1(2)(c) of the CAA 1984); or

(d)   he is a special guardian of the child (s 1(2)(ca) of the CAA 1984); or

(e)   he is a person in whose favour a residence order is in force with respect to the child (s 1(2)(d) of the CAA 1984); or

(f)   he has custody of the child (s 1(2)(e) of the CAA 1984).

The Director of Public Prosecutions must agree to initiate, or give his or her consent to any initiation of, a prosecution under s 1 of the CAA 1984 (though not under s 2 of the CAA 1984): s 4(2) of the CAA 1984. Thus, in respect of s 1 of the CAA 1984 prosecutions, if there are family law orders already in place, it would seem to be the preferred course for any matters to be considered by virtue of contempt proceedings within the family proceedings.

16.5.2 What is 'the appropriate consent'?

'The appropriate consent' means the leave of the court granted pursuant to any part of Part II of the Children Act 1989 (s 1(3)(b) of the CAA 1984), or, if any person has custody of the child, the leave of the court which awarded custody to him (s 1(3)(c) of the CAA 1984), or the consent (whether oral or written) of:

(a)   the child's mother (s 1(3)(a)(i) of the CAA 1984); or

---

[255] See s 24 of the Police and Criminal Evidence Act 1984; and *Home Office Circular No 75/1984*. See also *Re J (Minors) (Ex Parte Orders)* [1997] 1 FLR 606.

[256] An unlawful retention does not constitute a criminal offence for the purposes of CAA 1984, s 1: see, *R (Nicolaou) v Redbridge Magistrates Court and the Crown Prosecution Service* [2012] EWCA 1647 (Admin).

(b)   the child's father, if he has parental responsibility for him (s 1(3)(a)(ii) of the CAA 1984); or

(c)   any guardian of the child (s 1(3)(a)(iii) of the CAA 1984); or

(d)   any special guardian of the child (s 1(3)(a)(iiia) of the CAA 1984); or

(e)   any person in whose favour a residence order is in force with respect of the child (s 1(3)(a)(iv) of the CAA 1984); or

(f)   any person who has custody of the child (s 1(3)(a)(v) of the CAA 1984).

16.5.3   Defences to the offence under s 1 of the CAA 1984

A person does not, however, commit such an offence under s 1 of the CAA 1984 if:

(a)   he does it in the belief that the other person has consented or would consent if he was aware of all of the relevant circumstances (s 1(5)(a) of the CAA 1984); or

(b)   he has taken all reasonable steps to communicate with the other person but has been unable to communicate with him (s 1(5)(b) of the CAA 1984); or

(c)   the other person has unreasonably refused to consent (s 1(5)(c) of the CAA 1984).[257]

Where there is in respect of an offence under s 1 of the CAA 1984 'sufficient evidence to raise an issue as the application' of one of the defences set out above, then it falls to the prosecution to prove that the defence does not apply (s 1(6) of the CAA 1984).

In addition, a person does not commit such an offence if he has in his favour a residence order in respect of the child and he takes or sends him out of the UK for less than one month[258] (s 1(4)(a) of the CAA 1984) or if he is a special guardian of the child and he takes or sends the child out of the country for a period of less than three months (s 4(1) of the CAA 1984).

---

[257] Save that the defence under s 1(5)(c) of the CAA 1984 does not apply if: (a) the person who refused to consent is a person (i) in whose favour there is a residence order in force with respect to the child; or (ii) who has custody of the child; or (b) the person taking or sending the child of the UK is, by so acting, in breach of an order made by a court in the UK.

[258] Of course, this is assuming that there is no order under Pt II of the Children Act 1989 in force such as prohibited steps order in place prohibiting him from so doing: s 1(4A) of the CAA 1984.

There was no defence of necessity available to a defendant to a charge of removing a child from the jurisdiction contrary to s 1 of CAA 1984.[259]

For the purposes of s 1 of the CAA 1984, 'special guardian', 'residence order', 'parental responsibility order' have the same meaning as in the Children Act 1989 (s 1(7)(a) of the CAA 1984) and a person who has custody of a child is a person in whose favour 'there is in force an order of a court in the United Kingdom awarding him (whether solely or jointly with another person) custody, legal custody or care and control of the child' (s 1(7)(b) of the CAA 1984).

16.5.4   Abduction of a child by a person 'connected with a child' when that child is in the care of a local authority, detained in a place of safety, remanded to local authority accommodation or the subject of proceedings or an order relating to placement for adoption or adoption: CAA 1984, Sch, paras 1–5

An offence may also be committed by a person 'connected with a child' where the child under 16 is in the care of a local authority in England and Wales (as defined by the Children Act 1989), detained in a place of safety, remanded to local authority accommodation or the subject of proceedings or an order relating to placement for adoption or adoption and that person takes or sends the child out of the United Kingdom without the relevant 'appropriate consent' as set out in the particular provisions of the Schedule to the CAA 1984.[260]

16.5.5   Abduction by a person not connected with a child: s 2 of the CAA 1984

By virtue of s 2(1) of the CAA 1984, 'a person, other than one mentioned in sub-s (2)[261] commits an offence if, without lawful authority or reasonable excuse, he takes or detains a child under the age of sixteen' either: (a) so as to remove him from the lawful control of any person having that control of the child (s 2(1)(a) of the CAA 1984); or (b) so as to keep him out of the lawful control of any person entitled to lawful control of the child (s 2(1)(b) of the CAA 1984). There is afforded a wide definition to the sorts of persons who might be regarded as having or being entitled to 'lawful control of the child'.[262] It is important to note

---

[259] *R v CS* [2012] EWCA Crim 389.
[260] CAA 1984, Sch, paras [1]–[5].
[261] These persons are: (a) where the father and mother of the child in question were married to each other at the time of his birth, the child's father and mother; (b) where the father and mother of the child in question were not married to each other at the time of his birth, the child's mother; (c) the guardian of the child; (d) the special guardian of the child; (e) a person in whose favour a residence order is in force with respect to the child; and (f) a person who has custody of the child: s 2(2) of the CAA 1984.
[262] *R v Mousir* [1987] Crim LR 561.

that this offence, unlike that provided for by s 1 of the CAA 1984, may be committed irrespective of whether the child in fact leaves England and Wales.

16.5.6   Defences to the offence under s 2 of the CAA 1984

It is a defence to the offence under s 2 of the CAA 1984 if it is proved that: (a) the defendant believed that at the time of the alleged offence the child was 16 or over (s 2(3)(b) of the CAA 1984); or (b) where the mother and father were not married each other at the time of the child's birth, that he is the child's father or that at the time of the alleged offence he reasonably believed himself so to be (s 2(3)(a) of the CAA 1984).

In addition, a person who provides a refuge for a child by virtue of s 51 of the Children Act 1989 does not commit an offence under s 2 of the CAA 1984 (or indeed an offence under the Children Act 1989, for which see below): s 51(5) of the Children Act 1989.

16.5.7   The common law offence of kidnapping and false imprisonment and other offences

In *R v D*[263] the House of Lords in holding that a father could indeed kidnap his own child set out the elements that were required for the offence to be satisfied:

(a)   the taking or carrying away of one person by another;

(b)   by force or fraud;

(c)   without the consent of the person so taken or carried away; and

(d)   without lawful excuse.

The traditional position of the prosecuting authorities was that prosecutions for this common law offence were only brought in the rarest of cases, as a prosecution under the CAA 1984 was to be preferred.[264] However, in *R v Talib Hussein Kayani; R v Madhat Solliman*, Lord Judge CJ said that:

> 'Simply because the child has been abducted by a parent, given current conditions, it no longer necessarily follows that for policy reasons a charge

---

[263]   [1984] AC 788.

[264]   *R v C (Kidnapping: Abduction)* [1991] 2 FLR 252 and see also s 5 of the CAA 1984 which requires that the Director of Public Prosecutions must bring or consent to bringing a prosecution for the offence of kidnapping if it was committed against a child under the age of 16 by a person 'connected with' the child within the meaning of s 1 of the CAA 1984.

of kidnapping must always be inappropriate. To that extent the observation of the court in *R v C* has been overtaken by events and has no continuing authority.'[265]

The offence of false imprisonment is closely related, though distinct from that of kidnapping. A false imprisonment consists in 'the unlawful and intentional or reckless restraint of a victim's freedom of movement from a particular place.'[266]

By virtue of s 49 of the Children Act 1989, it is an offence for a person, knowingly and without lawful authority or reasonable excuse to take or to keep a child away from the 'responsible person' or to induce, assist or incite such a child to run away or stay away from the responsible person.[267] The section applies to a child who is (a) in care; or (b) the subject of an emergency protection order; or (c) in police protection. For the purposes of the offence, a 'responsible person' is defined as a person who for the time being has care of the child by virtue of a care order, police protection order, or emergency protection order.

16.6 LEADING ENGLISH CASES

16.6.1 The Hague Convention 1980: general principles

- *In re H (Minors) (Abduction: Acquiescence)* [1998] AC 72
  The principles and policy of the Hague Convention as considered by the House of Lords.

- *In re D (A Child) (Abduction: Rights of Custody)* [2006] UKHL 51, [2007] 1 AC 619
  An important discussion by the House of Lords of the principles and policy of the Hague Convention; 'rights of custody' and 'rights of access'; the nature and use of Art 15 declarations; the exceptions to the obligation to return; how the 'voice of the child' should be heard; and the role of human rights considerations in child abduction proceedings.

- *In re M (Children) (Abduction: Rights of Custody)* [2007] UKHL 55, [2008] AC 1288
  An important appraisal by the House of Lords of the principles and policy of the Hague Convention and the authoritative direction as to how the court should exercise its discretion once any 'gateway' stage has been made out. Also important for determining: (a) that there was a residual discretion for the court to exercise in Art 12 'settlement' cases; (b) that there was no room for importing an

---

[265] [2011] EWCA Crim 2871, [2012] 1 CR App R 16, para [13].
[266] See, for example, *R v Rahman* 81 Cr App Rep 349.
[267] See s 49(1) of the Children Act 1989.

'exceptionality' test into the 'discretion' stage; and (c) the test for separate representation of children in Hague Convention cases.

- *In re E (Children) (Abduction: Custody Appeal)* [2011] UKSC 27, [2012] 1 AC 143
  A recent and very important consideration by the Supreme Court of the policy and the principles of the Hague Convention, particularly in the light of jurisprudence from the European Court of Human Rights, along with the proper approach when Art 13(b) is raised.

16.6.2 The Hague Convention and Brussels IIR

- *Vigreux v Michel* [2006] EWCA Civ 630, [2006] 2 FLR 1180
  Discussion of Brussels IIR and its impact on the Hague Convention by the Court of Appeal. Reinforcement of the mandatory requirement to hear Hague Convention and Brussels IIR cases within 6 weeks.

- *Re A (Custody Decision after Maltese Non-return Order)* [2006] EWHC 3397 (Fam), [2007] 1 FLR 1923
  The first reported decision where Art 11 (7) of Brussels IIR was invoked.

- *Re A; HA v MB (Brussels II Revised: Article 11 (7) Application)* [2007] EWHC 2016 (Fam), [2008] 1 FLR 289
  Extensive and important consideration of the provisions of, in particular, Art 11 (7) and, generally, Arts 10 and 11 of Brussels IIR. Construction of what constitutes a 'judgment' for the purposes of Brussels IIR. Guidance on the appropriate procedure to be followed in such cases.

- *D v N and D (By her Guardian Ad Litem)* [2011] EWHC 471 (Fam), [2011] 2 FLR 464
  Important guidance on the approach of the court in respect of applications pursuant to Art 11(7) of Brussels IIR.

16.6.3 Rights of Custody

- *In re H (A Minor) (Abduction: Rights of Custody)* [2000] 2 AC 291
  Discussion by the House of Lords of 'rights of custody' in the context of a whether a court could be an 'other body' holding 'rights of custody'.

- *Hunter v Morrow (Abduction: Rights of Custody)* [2005] EWCA Civ 976, [2005] 2 FLR 1119
  Reinforcement of the autonomous nature of the Hague Convention and discussion by the Court of Appeal of Art 15 determinations.

- *In re D (A Child) (Abduction: Rights of Custody)* [2006] UKHL 51, [2007] 1 AC 619
  The leading House of Lords case on 'rights of custody' and Art 15 determinations. A 'right of custody' would include any right arising by court order, agreement or operation of law to insist that the other parent did not remove the child from the home country. A potential right of veto was not a right of custody. Art 15 determinations should in normal circumstances be determinative.

- *Kennedy v Kennedy* [2009] EWCA Civ 2009, [2010] 1 FLR 782
  The court's approach to the determination of whether or not a parent exercised 'rights of custody' involved a two stage process: (1) an investigation of the law of the State of habitual residence; (2) whether the particular parent's rights equate to 'rights of custody' under the autonomous law of the Hague Convention.

16.6.4 Habitual residence

- *R v Barnet London Borough Council Ex p Shah* [1983] 2 AC 309
  An important discussion by the House of Lords of the concept of 'ordinary residence'.

- *In re J (A Minor) (Abduction: Custody Rights)* [1990] 2 AC 562
  A consideration by the House of Lords of the required component parts of 'habitual residence'.

- *Al Habtoor v Fotheringham* [2001] EWCA Civ 186, [2001] 1 FLR 951
  An important consideration of the authorities relating to 'habitual residence' by the Court of Appeal.

- *Marinos v Marinos* [2007] EWHC 2047 (Fam), [2007] 2 FLR 1018
  The construction of 'habitual residence' for the purposes of Brussels IIR. 'Habitually resident' meant 'the place where the person had established, on a fixed basis, his permanent or habitual centre of interests, with all the relevant facts being taken into account for the purpose of determining such residence.'

- *Re P-J (Abduction: Habitual Residence: Consent)* [2009] EWCA Civ 588, [2009] 2 FLR 1051
  The most recent leading case on the relevant principles in respect of habitual residence.

16.6.5 Article 12: settlement

- *Re N (Minors) (Abduction)* [1991] 1 FLR 413
  Construction of the meaning of 'settled' for the purposes of the Hague Convention. The word 'settled' had two constituents: a physical element relating to, being established in, a community and

environment, and an emotional element denoting security, as in permanence, and that the present position imported stability when looking forward into the future.

- *Re C (Abduction: Settlement)* [2004] EWHC 1245 (Fam), [2005] 1 FLR 127
  Extensive review of authorities relating to Art 12 and decision that there was no discretion to be exercised once the 'gateway' stage of Art 12 had been made out.

- *Cannon v Cannon* [2004] EWCA Civ 1330, [2005] 1 FLR 169
  Reversal of *Re C (Abduction: Settlement)* (above). Discussion by the Court of Appeal of the impact of subterfuge and the concealment of a child in child abduction proceedings. In those situations, the burden of demonstrating the necessary elements of emotional and psychological settlement was much increased.

- *Re M (Abduction: Zimbabwe)* [2007] UKHL 55, [2008] 1 FLR 251
  Authoritative statement by the House of Lords that there was indeed a discretion to be exercised once the Art 12 'settlement' gateway stage had been made out.

- *F v M and N (Abduction: Acquiescence: Settlement)* [2008] 2 FLR 1270
  An unduly technical approach to the question of settlement should be resisted.

16.6.6 Article 13 (a): consent

- *Re C (Abduction: Consent)* [1996] 1 FLR 414
  Consent does not have to be in writing. Indeed, it was possible in an appropriate case to infer consent from conduct.

- *Re K (Abduction: Consent)* [1997] 2 FLR 212
  A leading case on consent. Consent must be real, positive and unequivocal. It does not have to be in writing. It can be inferred from conduct.

- *T v T (Abduction: Consent)* [1999] 2 FLR 912
  Consent which is based on a misunderstanding or non disclosure would be vitiated.

- *Re P (Abduction: Consent)* [2004] EWCA Civ 971, [2004] 2 FLR 1057
  Consent fell to be considered within the provisions of Art 13(a) not Art 3 of the Hague Convention.

- *Re L (Abduction: Future Consent)* [2007] EWHC 2181 (Fam), [2008] 1 FLR 914

  Consent could be valid if tied to a future event, even of uncertain timing, provided that the happening of the future event was reasonably ascertainable; it should not be too vague, subjective or uncertain. If the consent was provided based on different facts, or had been withdrawn, then it could no longer be relied upon.

- *Re P-J (Abduction: Habitual Residence: Consent)* [2009] EWCA Civ 588, [2009] 2 FLR 1051

  The leading case on the proper approach to consent in Hague Convention cases.

16.6.7 Article 13 (a): acquiescence

- *In re H (Minors) (Abduction: Acquiescence)* [1998] AC 72

  The leading House of Lords case on acquiescence.

- *Re S (Abduction: Acquiescence)* [1998] 2 FLR 115

  It is not necessary in order for acquiescence to be made out for there to be a specific knowledge of the Hague Convention. Knowledge of the facts and that the act of removal or retention is wrongful will normally usually be necessary. To expect knowledge of the rights which can be enforced under the Hague Convention is to set too high a standard. The degree of knowledge as a relevant factor will depend on the facts of each case. Once acquiescence is given, it cannot be withdrawn.

16.6.8 Article 13 (b)

16.6.8.1 General

- *In re D (A Child) (Abduction: Rights of Custody)* [2006] UKHL 51, [2007] 1 AC 619

  There was a particular risk that an expansive application of Art 13 (b), which focuses on the situation of the child, could lead to courts in the requested State carrying out full welfare enquiries. That said, there would be circumstances in which a summary return would be so inimical to the interests of the particular child that it would be contrary to the objection of the Convention to require it. A restrictive application of Art 13 did not mean that it should never be applied at all. For the purposes of Art 13 (b), 'intolerable' meant 'a situation which this particular child in these particular circumstances should not be expected to tolerate.'

- *In re E (Children) (Abduction: Custody Appeal)* [2011] UKSC 27, [2012] 1 AC 144

The most important and definitive guidance as to the proper approach to Article 13(b).

- *Re S (A Child) (Abduction: Rights of Custody)* [2012] UKSC 10, [2012] 2 FLR 442
  An important consideration of subjective perceptions and Article 13(b) by the Supreme Court.

16.6.8.2 Domestic or other violence

- *Re F (Child Abduction: Risk if Returned)* [1995] 2 FLR 31
  A successful reliance before the Court of Appeal on Art 13 (b), relying on a combination of the child being present whilst violence was being perpetrated; the impact that that had on the child's health; and the lack of available and reliable protective measures in the 'home' state.

- *TB v JB (Abduction: Grave Risk of Harm)* [2001] 2 FLR 515
  A failed attempt to rely on Art 13(b) relating principally to the behaviour of the mother's second husband and her own fragile mental health. The Court of Appeal held that protective measures that could be relied upon were sufficient to allow the court to return the children.

- *Re W (Abduction: Domestic Violence)* [2004] EWHC 1247 (Fam), [2004] 2 FLR 499
  A failed attempt to rely on Art 13(b) based to some extent on domestic violence. A large number of conditions were placed on the order for return so as to attempt to protect the child in the 'home' state.

- *Re D (Article 13B: Non Return)* [2006] EWCA Civ 146, [2006] 2 FLR 305
  A successful reliance on Art 13(b). The mother had been shot in Venezuela by an unknown gunman. Having heard expert evidence, the judge concluded that there was a grave risk of harm to the children arising out of the attempted assassination. The Court of Appeal agreed. However, it cautioned that in weighing the evidence of an abductor seeking to justify or explain conduct, a judge needed to subject that evidence to rigorous and perhaps sceptical scrutiny.

16.6.8.3 Potential abuse of child

- *Re F (Child Abduction: Risk if Returned)* [1995] 2 FLR 31
  A successful reliance before the Court of Appeal on Art 13 (b), relying on a combination of the child being present whilst violence

was being perpetrated; the impact that that had on the child's health; and the lack of available and reliable protective measures in the 'home' state.

- *N v N (Abduction: Article 13 Defence)* [1995] 1 FLR 107
  A failed attempt to rely on Art 13(b), relying on the risk of physical harm (potential sexual abuse of the child) and psychological harm.

- *Re S (Abduction: Return into Care)* [1999] 1 FLR 843
  A failed attempt to rely on Art 13(b), relying on the potential sexual abuse of the child. Protective arrangements, those being the return of the child into an investigatory care home in the requesting State, were such as to negate any Art 13 (b) defence.

- *Re D (Article 13B: Non Return)* [2006] EWCA Civ 146, [2006] 2 FLR 305
  A successful reliance on Art 13(b). The mother had been shot in Venezuela by an unknown gunman. Having heard expert evidence, the judge concluded that there was a grave risk of harm to the children arising out of the attempted assassination. The Court of Appeal agreed. However, it cautioned that in weighing the evidence of an abductor seeking to justify or explain conduct, a judge needed to subject that evidence to rigorous and perhaps sceptical scrutiny.

16.6.8.4 Separation from primary carer

- *C v C (Minor: Abduction: Rights of Custody)* [1989] 1 WLR 654 sub nom *Re C (A Minor) (Abduction)* [1989] 1 FLR 403
  The classic consideration of reliance on the non return of a primary carer as raising an Art 13 (b) defence. To allow a primary carer to create the psychological situation, that being that parent's non return, and then rely on it would be to 'drive a coach and four through the Convention'.

- *S v B (Abduction: Human Rights)* [2005], EWHC 733 (Fam), [2005] 2 FLR 878
  The principle that it would be wrong to allow the abducting parent to rely upon adverse conditions brought about by a situation which they have created by their own conduct was born of the proposition that it would drive a coach and horses through the 1985 Act if that were not accepted as the broad and instinctive approach to a defence raised under Art 13 (b) of the Convention. However it was not a principle articulated in the Convention or the Act and should not be applied to the effective exclusion of the very defence itself, which was in terms directed to the question of risk of harm to the child and not the wrongful conduct of the abducting parent.

16.6.8.5 Separation from siblings

- *Re T (Abduction: Child's Objections to Return)* [2000] 2 FLR 192
  Two children aged 11 and 6 were sought to be returned to the
  requesting State. Given that a child objection's defence in respect of
  the elder child was made out, it would create an Art 13 (b) situation
  if the younger child were to be returned to their State of habitual
  residence and therefore such a return would be refused.

- *S v B (Abduction: Human Rights)* [2005] 2 FLR 878
  A mother raised an Art 13 (b) defence based on the unwillingness of
  her elder 13 child to return to the requesting State and its consequent
  impact on her other child, the elder child's step sibling. The position
  as to the elder child's reluctance to return was to some extent the
  result of the mother's conduct. The reality of the situation was that
  when faced with an order for return both the mother and the elder
  child would return to the requesting State with the younger child. A
  return order would accordingly be ordered.

16.6.8.6 Conditions in the requesting State

- *Re S (Abduction: Intolerable Situation: Beth Din)* [2000] 1 FLR 454
  A failed attempt to rely on Art 13 (b), relying on the potential
  injustice that would derive from the judicial system in the requesting
  State. It was not appropriate to consider in detail the law and
  principle applied in the courts of the requesting State, which was, in
  any event, a signatory to the Hague Convention.

- *Re S (Abduction: Custody Rights)* [2002] EWCA Civ 908, [2002]
  2 FLR 815
  A failed attempt to rely on Art 13(b), relying on the conditions in
  Israel, which was suggested to be in a state of war.

- *In re M (Children) (Abduction: Rights of Custody)* [2007] UKHL
  55, [2008] AC 1288
  The moral and political climate in Zimbabwe was not such as to
  place a child at a grave risk of psychological harm or intolerability.

16.6.8.7 Prospective criminal proceedings

- *Re L (Abduction: Pending Criminal Proceedings)* [1999] 1 FLR 433
  Prospective criminal proceedings awaiting in the courts of the
  requesting State was not enough to justify the making out of a
  Art 13 (b) defence.

- *Re C (Abduction: Grave Risk of Psychological Harm)* [1999] 1 FLR
  1145.

A risk of prosecution in the courts of the requesting State was not sufficient to make out an Art 13 (b) defence.

16.6.9   Child's objections

- *In re S (A Minor) (Abduction: Custody Rights)* [1993] Fam 242 sub nom *S v S (Child Abduction) (Child's Views)* [1992] 2 FLR 492
  The classic early consideration of the child's objection's defence.

- *Re T (Abduction: Child's Objections to Return)* [2000] 2 FLR 192
  A comprehensive consideration by the Court of Appeal of the child's objections defence, containing an approach which would appear to be superseded by *Re M (Abduction: Zimbabwe)*.

- *In re M (Children) (Abduction: Rights of Custody)* [2007] UKHL 55, [2008] AC 1288
  The authoritative guide to the child's objections defence. The child's objections exception was brought into play when only two conditions are met: (a) that the child objected to being returned; and (b) that he had attained an age and degree of maturity at which it was appropriate to take account of his views. Once the discretion came into play, the court might have to consider the nature and strength of the child's objections, the extent to which they were authentically their own or the product of the influence of the abducting parent, the extent to which they coincided or were at odds with other considerations which were relevant to his welfare, as well as general Convention considerations. The older the child, the greater the weight that his objections were likely to carry.

- *Re W (Abduction: Child's Objections)* [2010] EWCA Civ 520, [2010] 2 FLR 1165
  Important decision as to the 'gateway' stage in relation to a child's objections. The 'gateway' stage was a fairly low threshold to be passed.

16.6.10   Article 20

- *In re D (A Child) (Abduction: Rights of Custody)* [2006] UKHL 51, [2007] 1 AC 619
  Article 20 had been given domestic effect by virtue of the Human Rights Act 1998. Human Rights considerations may well be relevant in child abduction cases.

- *Re E (Children) (Abduction: Custody Appeal)* [2011] EWCA Civ 361, [2011] 2 FLR 724
  Consideration by the Court of Appeal of the Article 20 defence.

- *In re E (Children) (Abduction: Custody Appeal)* [2011] UKSC 27, [2012] 1 AC 144

  Consideration by the Supreme Court of (*inter alia*) the Article 20 defence.

16.6.11 The exercise of the court's discretion

- *In re M (Children) (Abduction: Rights of Custody)* [2007] UKHL 55, [2008] AC 1288

  The leading case on the exercise of the court's discretion in Hague Convention cases. There was no room for an 'exceptionality' test at the discretion stage. Where a discretion arose, the discretion was at large: the court was entitled to take into account the various aspects of the Hague Convention policy, alongside the circumstances which gave the court a discretion in the first place and the wider considerations of the child's rights and welfare.

- *F v M and N (Abduction: Acquiescence: Settlement)* [2008] EWHC 1525 (Fam), [2008] 2 FLR 1270

  It was within the powers of the Hague Convention for an order for return to be suspended on terms.

16.6.12 Undertakings

- *Re O (Child Abduction: Undertakings)* [1994] 2 FLR 349

  The use of undertakings to alleviate what otherwise would be an intolerable situation was permissible in Hague Convention proceedings.

- *Re M (Abduction: Undertakings)* [1995] 1 FLR 1021

  Undertakings or conditions attached to an order for return were to make the return of the child easier and to provide for necessities, such as a roof over the head, adequate maintenance, etc, until, and only until, the court of habitual residence could become seized of the proceedings brought in that jurisdiction. The court must be careful not in any way to usurp or to be thought to usurp the functions of the court of habitual residence. Equally, the requirements made in this country must not be so elaborate that their implementation might become bogged down in protracted hearings and investigations. Undertakings have their place in the arrangements designed to smooth the return of and to protect the child for the limited period before the foreign court took over, but they must not be used to try to clog or fetter, or, in particular, to delay the enforcement of a paramount decision to return the child.

16.6.13   Contempt

* *Re A (Abduction: Contempt)* [2008] EWCA Civ 1138, [2009] 1 FLR 1

  In a case where contempt to an order was raised, the contempt that had to be established lay in disobedience to the order to return, rather than the original abduction. Contempt of court must be proved to the criminal standard; it involves a contumelious, that is to say, a deliberate disobedience to the order. If it is that the father cannot cause the return of the child, he is not in contempt of court however disgraceful his conduct is.

16.6.14   Practice and procedure

* *Re W (Abduction: Procedure)* [1995] 1 FLR 878

  Skeleton arguments were required in Hague Convention proceedings.

* *Re M (Abduction: Appeals)* [2007] EWCA Civ 1059, [2008] 1 FLR 699

  In applications for a return under Brussels IIR the obligation was to complete proceedings at first instance within 6 weeks. An order following a judgment ought to be drafted and agreed speedily.

* *Re A (Abduction: Interim Directions: Accommodation by Local Authority)* [2010] EWCA CIv 586, [2011] 1 FLR 1

  There was a wide power under s 5 of the Child Abduction and Custody Act 1985 to give directions on an interim basis to safeguard the position of the child. This included a power to direct the provision of accommodation.

16.6.15   Separate representation

* *Mabon v Mabon* [2005] EWCA Civ 634, [2005] 2 FLR 1011

  Useful guidance and discussion by the Court of Appeal as to the test for separate representation in Children Act 1989 proceedings (which can be applied to such applications in Non Convention cases).

* *In re D (A Child) (Abduction: Rights of Custody)* [2006] UKHL 51, [2007] 1 AC 619

  Only in a few cases would separate representation be necessary. But whenever it seemed likely that the child's views and interests may not be properly presented to the court, and in particular where there were legal arguments which the adult parties were not putting forward, then the child should be separately represented.

* *In re M (Children) (Abduction: Rights of Custody)* [2007] UKHL 55, [2008] AC 1288

To order separate representation in all cases, even in all child's objections cases, might be to send the wrong messages. But it would not send the wrong messages in the very small number of cases where settlement was argued under the second paragraph of Art 12. These are the cases in which the separate point of view of the children was particularly important and should not be lost in the competing claims of the adults. If this were to become routine, there would be no additional delay. In all other cases, the question for the directions judge was whether separate representation of the child would add enough to the court's understanding of the issues that arise under the Hague Convention to justify the intrusion, the expense and the delay that may result. One should hesitate to use the word 'exceptional'. The substance is what counts, not the label.

16.6.16 Oral evidence

• *Re F (A Minor) (Child Abduction)* [1992] 1 FLR 548
The classic early statement by the Court of Appeal of the use of oral evidence in Hague Convention proceedings. There was no right to call oral evidence but a discretion to admit it. Such a discretion should be used sparingly. There was a real danger if oral evidence was generally admitted in Hague Convention cases, it would become impossible for them to be dealt with expeditiously and the purpose of the Convention might be frustrated.

• *Re W (Abduction: Domestic Violence)* [2004] EWCA Civ 1366, [2005] 1 FLR 727
Oral evidence should only be admitted in exceptional cases. In Art 13 (b) cases, to warrant oral exploration of written evidence, the judge must be satisfied that there was a realistic possibility that oral evidence would establish an Art 13 (b) case that was only embryonic on the written material.

16.6.17 Costs

• *EC-L v DM (Child Abduction: Costs)* [2005] EWHC 588 (Fam), [2005] 2 FLR 772
There was a power to make costs orders in child abduction proceedings. It should, however, be the expectation in child abduction cases that the usual orders would be no order as to costs, but where a party's conduct had been unreasonable or where there was a disparity of means, then the court could consider whether to exercise its discretion in accordance with the normal civil principles.

16.6.18 Other (non-Convention) cases

• *In re J (A Child) (Custody Rights: Jurisdiction)* [2005] UKHL 40,
  [2006] 1 AC 80
  The leading case on how the court should adjudicate upon a child
  abduction from a Non Convention country. The House of Lords
  held that the welfare of the child was the court's paramount
  consideration; the court did have a power to order an immediate
  return without a full investigation; and the decision whether to order
  an immediate return or whether to conduct a full investigation was a
  matter to be determined by considering the individual child and the
  particular circumstances of the case.

16.7 PRECEDENTS

16.7.1 Port alert and other orders under ss 34 and 36 of the
          Family Law Act 1986

No. [   ]
IN THE HIGH COURT OF JUSTICE
FAMILY DIVISION
PRINCIPAL REGISTRY

BEFORE MR/MRS JUSTICE [   ] SITTING IN CHAMBERS AT
THE ROYAL COURTS OF JUSTICE, STRAND, LONDON WC2A
2LL ON [   ]

IN THE MATTER OF [   ]
AND IN THE MATTER OF THE CHILDREN ACT 1989 AND THE
FAMILY LAW ACT 1986
[AND IN THE MATTER OF THE INHERENT JURISDICTION OF
THE HIGH COURT AND THE SENIOR COURTS ACT 1981]

BETWEEN
Applicant
Respondent

UPON hearing [Leading] Counsel for the applicant father/mother ('the
father')/('the mother') and [Leading] Counsel for the respondent
mother/father ('the mother')/('the father')
AND UPON reading/considering [   ]
AND UPON the court being satisfied that there is a real and imminent
danger of the child [   ] being unlawfully removed from the United
Kingdom

IT IS DIRECTED THAT:

1.   The National Ports Office be requested to institute and maintain a
       Port Alert in respect the child [   ].

AND IT IS FURTHER ORDERED THAT:

2.   There be an injunction granted until further order restraining any person (whether by himself or his servants or agents or otherwise) from removing the child [   ] from England and Wales.

3.   [   ] do return the child [   ] to the jurisdiction of this court and give him/her up to [   ] immediately.

4.   An officer of the court or a constable is hereby authorised to take charge of the child [   ] and deliver him/her to [   ] and in pursuance of this authority to enter and search any premises in which there is reason to believe that the child [   ] may be found and to use such force as may be necessary to give effect to the purpose of this order

5.   [   ] and any other person in possession of a United Kingdom passport which has been issued to or contains the name if the child [   ] shall surrender it to the court forthwith and on officer of the court or a constable is hereby authorised to secure any such passport and remit it to the court.

6.   [   ] do send a copy of this order to the International Child Abduction and Contact Unit at 81 Chancery Lane, London WC2A 1DD forthwith and do immediately notify them if any change in the circumstances of the child [   ].

7.   The matter be further considered at a hearing before a High Court Judge sitting in the Family Division, Royal Courts of Justice, Strand, London WC2A 2LL as well as, if so advised, by counsel and solicitors on [   ] at 10.30am (time estimate 30 minutes, at risk, subject to confirmation with the Clerk of the Rules).

8.   Costs be reserved.

Dated: [   ]

16.7.2   First without notice hearing order

No. [   ]
IN THE HIGH COURT OF JUSTICE
FAMILY DIVISION
PRINCIPAL REGISTRY

BEFORE MR/MRS JUSTICE [   ] SITTING IN CHAMBERS AT THE ROYAL COURTS OF JUSTICE, STRAND, LONDON WC2A 2LL ON [   ]

IN THE MATTER OF [   ]
[AND IN THE MATTER OF THE CHILD ABDUCTION AND CUSTODY ACT 1985 INCORPORATING THE 1980 HAGUE

CONVENTION ON THE CIVIL ASPECTS OF INTERNATIONAL CHILD ABDUCTION]
[AND IN THE MATTER OF COUNCIL REGULATION (EC) NO 2201/2003 OF 27th NOVEMBER 2003 ('BRUSSELS II REVISED')]
[AND IN THE MATTER OF THE INHERENT JURISDICTION OF THE HIGH COURT AND THE SENIOR COURTS ACT 1981]

BETWEEN
Applicant
Respondent

UPON hearing [Leading] Counsel for the applicant father/mother ('the father')/('the mother')
[AND UPON the Proposed applicant's solicitors undertaking to issue the application by no later than 4pm on [   ] in the form of the draft considered by this court and to pay the relevant fee]
AND UPON reading the [draft] statement [of] [   ] on [   ]
AND UPON the court having made other orders directed to the Tipstaff

IT IS ORDERED THAT:

3.   The Proposed respondent shall attend in person before a High Court Judge sitting in the Family Division, Royal Courts of Justice, Strand, London WC2A 2LL as well as, if so advised, by counsel and solicitors on [   ] at 10.30am (time estimate 30 minutes, at risk, subject to confirmation with the Clerk of the Rules).

4.   In the event that the Proposed respondent wishes to contest the application he/she shall file and serve his/her answer (setting out with full particularity the nature of the defence and the Article or Articles relied upon) together with a statement in support (to include a schedule of any undertakings that might be sought) by 4pm on [   ].

5.   Costs be reserved.

TO: [   ]

[AND TO: ANY OTHER PERSON SERVED WITH A COPY OF THIS ORDER]

YOU MUST OBEY THE DIRECTIONS CONTAINED IN PARAGRAPHS [   ] OF THIS ORDER. IF YOU DO NOT, YOU WILL BE GUILTY OF CONTEMPT OF COURT AND YOU MAY BE SENT TO PRISON.

Dated: [   ]

16.7.3 Agencies order

16.7.3.1 *DWP, Inland Revenue and other agencies order*

No. [   ]
IN THE HIGH COURT OF JUSTICE
FAMILY DIVISION
PRINCIPAL REGISTRY

BEFORE MR/MRS JUSTICE [   ] SITTING IN CHAMBERS AT
THE ROYAL COURTS OF JUSTICE, STRAND, LONDON WC2A
2LL ON [   ]

IN THE MATTER OF [   ]
[AND IN THE MATTER OF THE CHILD ABDUCTION AND
CUSTODY ACT 1985 INCORPORATING THE 1980 HAGUE
CONVENTION ON THE CIVIL ASPECTS OF INTERNATIONAL
CHILD ABDUCTION
[AND IN THE MATTER OF COUNCIL REGULATION (EC) NO
2201/2003 OF 27th NOVEMBER 2003 ('BRUSSELS II REVISED')]
[AND IN THE MATTER OF THE INHERENT JURISDICTION OF
THE HIGH COURT AND THE SENIOR COURTS ACT 1981]

BETWEEN
Applicant
Respondent

UPON hearing [Leading] Counsel for the applicant father/mother ('the
father')/('the mother') and [Leading] Counsel for the respondent
mother/father ('the mother')/('the father')

IT IS ORDERED THAT:

1.   [   ], shall, by its officers, servants or agents forthwith disclose
in writing [to the mother's/father's solicitors/the Tipstaff] all
information within their possession, custody or control relating to
the whereabouts of:

    (a)   the child;

    (b)   the [father/mother];

    (c)   [other parties as appropriate].

2.   [   ] is forbidden from disclosing to the [father/mother or to
any other person named in this order] the existence of the terms of
this order without leave of the court.

3.   The [father's/mother's] solicitors are forbidden to disclose to the
[father/mother] any information passed to them pursuant to this
order without the leave of the court.

4.   There be liberty to [   ] to apply to vary or discharge this order
         upon 24 hours notice.

5.   Costs be reserved.

16.7.3.2   *BT and other telecommunications operators order*

Short order

No. [   ]
IN THE HIGH COURT OF JUSTICE
FAMILY DIVISION
PRINCIPAL REGISTRY

BEFORE MR/MRS JUSTICE [   ] SITTING IN CHAMBERS AT
THE ROYAL COURTS OF JUSTICE, STRAND, LONDON WC2A
2LL ON [   ]

IN THE MATTER OF [   ]
[AND IN THE MATTER OF THE CHILD ABDUCTION AND
CUSTODY ACT 1985 INCORPORATING THE 1980 HAGUE
CONVENTION ON THE CIVIL ASPECTS OF INTERNATIONAL
CHILD ABDUCTION 1]
[AND IN THE MATTER OF COUNCIL REGULATION (EC) NO
2201/2003 OF 27th NOVEMBER 2003 ('BRUSSELS II REVISED')]
[AND IN THE MATTER OF THE INHERENT JURISDICTION OF
THE HIGH COURT AND THE SENIOR COURTS ACT 1981]

BETWEEN
Applicant
Respondent

UPON hearing [Leading] Counsel for the applicant father/mother ('the
father')/('the mother') and [Leading] Counsel for the respondent
mother/father ('the mother')/('the father')

IT IS ORDERED THAT:

1.   [   ] do disclose to the [Tipstaff/the mother/father's solicitors]
         any and all information in its possession in respect of any and all
         accounts held in the name of [   ] and in particular in relation
         to the telephone [   ].

16.7.3.3   *BT and other telecommunications operators order*

Long order

No. [   ]
IN THE HIGH COURT OF JUSTICE
FAMILY DIVISION
PRINCIPAL REGISTRY

BEFORE MR/MRS JUSTICE [   ] SITTING IN CHAMBERS AT THE ROYAL COURTS OF JUSTICE, STRAND, LONDON WC2A 2LL ON [   ]

IN THE MATTER OF [   ]
[AND IN THE MATTER OF THE CHILD ABDUCTION AND CUSTODY ACT 1985 INCORPORATING THE 1980 HAGUE CONVENTION ON THE CIVIL ASPECTS OF INTERNATIONAL CHILD ABDUCTION]
[AND IN THE MATTER OF COUNCIL REGULATION (EC) NO 2201/2003 OF 27th NOVEMBER 2003 ('BRUSSELS II REVISED')]
[AND IN THE MATTER OF THE INHERENT JURISDICTION OF THE HIGH COURT AND THE SENIOR COURTS ACT 1981]

BETWEEN
Applicant
Respondent

UPON hearing [Leading] Counsel for the applicant father ('the father')/('the mother') and [Leading] Counsel for the respondent mother ('the mother')/('the father')
AND UPON the Plaintiff's Solicitors undertaking:

(a)   to pay the reasonable costs of [the Licensed telecommunications operator] (hereinafter described in these recitals and in the terms of the order as [   ]) such costs occasioned by the terms of this order to be taxed if not agreed upon the indemnity basis;

(b)   to use any information supplied by [   ] solely in furtherance of inquiries as to the whereabouts of the [the mother/father and/or the child];

(c)   to use his/her best endeavours to cooperate with [ ] in order for [ ] to comply with the terms of this order and to procure the full written consent of [telephone customer] to provide all reasonable assistance to [ ] in order to give effect to this order;

(d)   to comply with any order the court may make if the court finds that this order has caused loss to any person whose telephone service has been affected and the court decides that the person should be compensated for such loss by the Applicant.

IT IS ORDERED THAT:

1.

(a)   [ ], its servants or agents do take all such steps as are reasonably practicable to trace the telephone numbers of all incoming telephone calls originating in the UK to the telephone number [   ] belonging to the Applicant of [   ] from [   ] until the date specified by paragraph 2 of this order.

(b)   [ ], its servants or agents do take reasonable steps to disclose from time to time to the solicitors for the Applicant [   ], the name and installation address (together with billing address if different) of each current customer of [ ] whose telephone number is provided pursuant to paragraph 1 (a) above on receipt of request in writing by the Applicant's solicitors (provided that such names and addresses are readily available).

(c)   [ ] do take such steps as are reasonable practicable to identify the destination of all calls made from the telephone numbers specified in the schedule from [   ] until [   ].

(d)   [ ] do from time to time provide to the Applicant's solicitors such information as may be reasonably identifiable in the course of its business concerning the telephone numbers and names and addresses of the recipients of the telephone calls whose destination are identified in paragraph 1 (c) above.

2.   This order is to remain in force until the date that the child [   ] is returned to the jurisdiction of the court or until further order or until the said [ ] is notified by the Applicant's solicitor in writing that this information is no longer required or until 28 days after the date of service of this order, whichever shall be the soonest.

3.   There be leave to the Applicant not to serve this order upon the Respondent.

4.   This order is not to be served upon the customers [   ] and [   ] for the telephone numbers specified in the schedule, nor should the terms of this order be brought to their attention without leave of the Court.

5.   There be liberty to anyone affected by this order to apply to vary or discharge it on 24 hours notice in writing to the Applicant's solicitors.

       Dated [   ]

16.7.3.4   *First inter partes hearing order*

No. [   ]
IN THE HIGH COURT OF JUSTICE
FAMILY DIVISION
PRINCIPAL REGISTRY

BEFORE MR/MRS JUSTICE [   ] SITTING IN CHAMBERS AT THE ROYAL COURTS OF JUSTICE, STRAND, LONDON WC2A 2LL ON [   ]

IN THE MATTER OF [   ]
[AND IN THE MATTER OF THE CHILD ABDUCTION AND CUSTODY ACT 1985 INCORPORATING THE 1980 HAGUE CONVENTION ON THE CIVIL ASPECTS OF INTERNATIONAL CHILD ABDUCTION]
[AND IN THE MATTER OF COUNCIL REGULATION (EC) NO 2201/2003 OF 27th NOVEMBER 2003 ('BRUSSELS II REVISED')]
[AND IN THE MATTER OF THE INHERENT JURISDICTION OF THE HIGH COURT AND THE SENIOR COURTS ACT 1981]

BETWEEN
Applicant
Respondent

UPON hearing [Leading] Counsel for the applicant father/mother ('the father')/('the mother') and [Leading] Counsel for the respondent mother/father ('the mother')/('the father')
AND UPON the Tipstaff having executed the Location Order/Passport Order dated [   ]

AND UPON the Tipstaff being respectfully requested to continue the Location Order/Passport Order until further order to the contrary

IT IS ORDERED THAT:

[3.   The respondent shall by no later than 4pm on [   ] file and serve an answer (setting out with full particularity the nature of the defence and the Articles relied upon) and a statement in support (to include a schedule of any undertakings that might be sought)].

4.   The applicant shall by no later than 4pm on [   ] file and serve a statement in reply.

5.   A Cafcass officer from the Cafcass High Court Team at Sanctuary Buildings, Westminster, London shall be appointed and shall interview the child and shall file and serve a report by 4pm on [   ] considering the following matters:

    (a)   the age and degree of maturity of the child [   ];

    (b)   his/her wishes and feelings generally;

    (c)   any objections he/she has in relation to order for his/her immediate return to [   ]

6.   The respondent shall make the child [   ] available for the interview with the Cafcass officer.

7.   The Cafcass officer shall attend the final hearing listed below unless notified by both parties in writing that his/her attendance is not required.

8.   [The application shall be adjourned for consecutive periods of 21 days for mention only (on the basis that neither party shall attend on any of those occasions unless they seek further directions when they should give 48 hours notice to the other party and the Clerk of the Rules)] and the matter be listed for final hearing on [   ] before a High Court Judge sitting at the Royal Courts of Justice, Strand, London, WC2A 2LL at 10.30am [listed as a fixture/at risk subject to confirmation with the Clerk of the Rules] with a time estimate of [   ].

9.   Both parties are to attend the hearing listed in paragraph [   ] above.

11.   Costs be reserved.

[PENAL NOTICE IF REQUIRED]

16.7.3.5   *Final order*

No. [   ]
IN THE HIGH COURT OF JUSTICE
FAMILY DIVISION
PRINCIPAL REGISTRY

BEFORE MR/MRS JUSTICE [   ] SITTING IN CHAMBERS AT THE ROYAL COURTS OF JUSTICE, STRAND, LONDON WC2A 2LL ON [   ]

IN THE MATTER OF [   ]
[AND IN THE MATTER OF THE CHILD ABDUCTION AND CUSTODY ACT 1985 INCORPORATING 1980 THE HAGUE CONVENTION ON THE CIVIL ASPECTS OF INTERNATIONAL CHILD ABDUCTION]
[AND IN THE MATTER OF COUNCIL REGULATION (EC) NO 2201/2003 OF 27th NOVEMBER 2003 ('BRUSSELS II REVISED')]
[AND IN THE MATTER OF THE INHERENT JURISDICTION OF THE HIGH COURT AND THE SENIOR COURTS ACT 1981]

BETWEEN
Applicant
Respondent

UPON hearing [Leading] Counsel for the applicant father/mother ('the father')/('the mother') and [Leading] Counsel for the respondent

mother/father ('the mother')/('the father')
AND UPON the application issued on
AND UPON reading the trial bundle herein
AND UPON the father/mother giving the undertakings set out in the First Schedule hereto
AND UPON the father/mother giving the undertakings set out in the Second Schedule hereto
AND in support of the obligation and power conferred on this court under Article 12 of the 1980 *Hague Convention on the Civil Aspects of International Child Abduction* ('the *Hague Convention*') this court accepts the undertakings given to this court by the father/mother and the mother/father set out in the First and Second Schedules hereto and being part of this order, such undertakings constituting binding and enforceable obligations in this jurisdiction

[BY CONSENT]

IT IS ORDERED THAT:

1.   [   ], ('the child'), shall be returned to the jurisdiction of [   ] by 4pm on [   ] pursuant to Articles 3 and 12 of the *Hague Convention* and shall do so with the [father/mother/such other person who is agreed] unless [he/she] refuses to accompany him/her in which case he/she shall return with the [father/mother].

2.   The passports of the [father/mother] and the child shall be released forthwith by the Tipstaff to the [father's/mother's] solicitors [   ], ('the father's/mother's solicitors'), to be held by them to the order of the court and released by the father's/mother's solicitors or agents to the father/mother at the airport of departure immediately prior to his/her embarkation for [   ] in accordance with the terms of this order. In the event of the father/mother refusing to accompany the child on his return the father's/mother's solicitors shall hand the child's passport to the father/mother who will accompany the child back to [   ] and shall thereafter within 48 hours deliver the father's/mother's passport to her solicitors.

3.   Pending the return to [   ] of the child, the orders of Mr/Mrs Justice [   ] dated [   ] shall remain in effect, save that the [ ] and the child shall be permitted to leave the jurisdiction for the purposes of complying with paragraph 1 herein and upon the child's return to [   ] those orders shall stand discharged.

4.   The parties have permission to disclose the papers filed herein to their legal advisers in [   ] and any [   ] court seised of matters in issue between the parties.

5.   Liberty to the parties to apply as to implementation of this order.

6.   There be no order for costs, including costs reserved, [save that there be a detailed assessment of each parties publicly funded costs.]

Dated [   ]

PENAL NOTICE

To the father and to the mother

TAKE NOTICE that if you disobey the terms of your undertakings and/or of this order you will be in contempt of court and may be liable to imprisonment.

FIRST SCHEDULE

UPON THE BASIS THAT:

(a)   The undertakings herein are given without any admission of fact;

(b)   The financial provisions herein are made without prejudice to the contentions the parties may wish to make to the [   ] court as to the appropriate level of financial support (if any) to be made by the [father/mother] to the [father/mother] for himself/herself and/or the benefit of the child;

(c)   The [father/mother] has advised the [father/mother] that all costs incurred as a result of the child's removal and subsequent return to [   ] will be recorded and taken into account in any financial/children proceedings between the parties; and

(d)   They are given for the sole purpose of returning the child to [   ] and to secure his/her welfare until such time as the courts of [   ] shall exercise jurisdiction over him/her.

THE [FATHER/MOTHER] PROVIDES THE FOLLOWING UNDER-TAKINGS WHICH ARE NOT SPECIFICALLY TIME LIMITED:

1.   Not to pursue or support proceedings in [   ] (whether civil or criminal) for the punishment of the [father/mother] (whether by imprisonment, arrest, fine or howsoever arising) in respect of the child's wrongful removal from [   ].

2.   To cause a copy of this order (recording the parties' undertakings) to be filed with the [   ] Central Authority and with the [relevant court in which proceedings have been initiated].

3.   To arrange and pay for the [father's/mother's] and child's flights back to [   ] so as to facilitate the child's return pursuant to paragraph 1 of this order.

THE [FATHER/MOTHER] PROVIDES THE FOLLOWING UNDER-
TAKINGS UNTIL FURTHER WRITTEN AGREEMENT OR THE
FIRST INTER PARTES HEARING IN [   ], WHICHEVER IS
THE SOONER:

4.   To provide the [father/mother] with the sum of [   ] per
        month, to be paid on or around and at the same time each month
        thereafter, to be paid into a bank account in the name of the child.

5.   Not to remove the child from the care of the [father/mother] (save
        for periods of agreed contact or court ordered contact).

6.   Without prejudice to [his/her] contention that he has never done
        so, not to assault, threaten to assault, harass or pester the
        [father/mother].

SECOND SCHEDULE

THE [FATHER/MOTHER] PROVIDES THE FOLLOWING UNDER-
TAKINGS UNTIL FURTHER WRITTEN AGREEMENT OR THE
FIRST INTER PARTES HEARING IN [ ], WHICHEVER IS THE
SOONER:

1.   Following [his/her] return to [   ] not to remove the child from
        the jurisdiction of the [   ] courts.

2.   Not to apply for any passport or other international travel
        document for the child.

3.   To notify the [father/mother] forthwith upon [his/her] arrival and
        child's arrival in [   ] of that fact.

4.   To surrender the child's passport on arrival in [   ] to a lawyer
        instructed by the [father/mother] or to [his/her] own lawyer.

5.   To live at [   ]

SIGNED: [   ]

Dated: [   ]

16.8   LIST OF HELPFUL CONTACTS AND WEBSITES

The International Child Abduction and Contact Unit
81 Chancery Lane
London WC2A 1DD
Tel: 020 7 911 7045/7047
www.justice.gov.uk
enquiries@offsol.gsi.gov.uk

Foreign and Commonwealth Office
Consular Division
Old Admiralty Building
London SW1A 2PA
Tel: 020 7270 1500
www.fco.gov.uk

International child abduction database of case law
www.incadat.com

Hague Conference database
www.hcch.net

Reunite
PO Box 7124
Leicester
LE1 7XX
Tel: 0116 2556 234/0116 2555 345
www.reunite.org

The Royal Courts of Justice
Strand
London WC2A 2LL
Tel: 020 7947 6000 (general enquiries, available 24 hours)

A16.1 APPENDIX:
LIST OF COUNTRIES TO WHICH THE HAGUE CONVENTION IS IN FORCE WITH ENGLAND AND WALES (AS AT AUGUST 2012)

Country	Date of entry into force with England and Wales
Argentina	1 June 1991
Australia	1 January 1987
Austria	1 October 1988
The Bahamas	1 January 1994
Belarus	1 October 2003
Belgium	1 May 1999
Belize	1 October 1989
Bosnia & Herzegovina	1 December 1991
Brazil	1 March 2005
Bulgaria	1 May 2009
Burkino Faso	1 November 1992

Canada	1 August 1986
Chile	1 May 1994
Colombia	1 March 1996
Croatia	1 December 1991
Cyprus	1 February 1995
Czech Republic	1 March 1998
Denmark	1 July 1991
Ecuador	1 June 1992
El Salvador	1 May 2009
Estonia	1 October 2003
Fiji	1 October 2003
Finland	1 August 1994
France	1 August 1986
Georgia	1 October 1997
Germany	1 December 1990
Greece	1 June 1993
Honduras	1 March 1994
Hong Kong	1 September 1997
Hungary	1 September 1986
Iceland	1 November 1996
Ireland	1 October 1991
Israel	1 December 1991
Italy	1 May 1995
Latvia	1 October 2003
Lithuania	1 March 2005
Luxembourg	1 January 1987
Macao	1 March 1999
Macedonia	1 December 1991
Malta	1 March 2002
Mauritius	1 June 1993
Mexico	1 October 1991
Monaco	1 February 1993
Netherlands	1 September 1990
New Zealand	1 October 1991
Norway	1 April 1989
Panama	1 May 1994

Peru	1 October 2003
Poland	1 November 1992
Portugal	1 August 1986
Romania	1 February 1993
Serbia & Montenegro	1 December 1991
Slovakia	1 February 2001
Slovenia	1 June 1994
South Africa	1 October 1997
Spain	1 September 1987
St Kitts and Nevis	1 August 1994
Sweden	1 June 1989
Switzerland	1 August 1986
Turkey	1 August 2000
Turkmenistan	1 May 1998
Ukraine	
Uruguay	1 October 2003
USA	1 July 1988
Uzbekistan	1 October 2003
Venezuela	1 January 1997
Zimbabwe	1 July 1995

CHAPTER 17

FORCED MARRIAGE AND THE FORCED MARRIAGE (CIVIL PROTECTION) ACT 2007

17.1 INTRODUCTION

17.1.1 How big is the problem?

This chapter is devoted to the law in England and Wales concerning forced marriage and the various mechanisms that have been introduced (within the common law and latterly by statute, and outside of the court process by the domestic authorities) to prevent it, to remedy it where the forced marriage has already taken place, and to protect a victim of forced marriage either in the short term prior to any ceremony or, in certain cases, for an extended period of time after the actual event.

At the time of writing all of the cases that have been in the Family Law Reports have emanated from families of non-English heritage[1] and no doubt in the years to come some interesting anthropological research will be conducted on the resurgence within English society of this practice, since the years when the wardship jurisdiction was refined as a tool to deal with orphaned heiresses being married against their will.

The protective court orders made in this developing area of law have typically followed the template of orders in child abduction proceedings, tailored as necessary to the particular circumstances of each case, and so for the international child practitioner much of what is set out below may seem familiar. The reasons for this are twofold: when a child or an adult (in most cases a woman though there are exceptions – between September 2009 and February 2010 86% of the cases referred to the Forced Marriage Unit ('FMU') related to female victims[2]) is removed or retained forcibly abroad or within this jurisdiction and both her location needs to be ascertained and orders obtained to repatriate her, there is simply no need to reinvent the wheel when judges have carefully constructed orders over the years with precisely this aim in mind, albeit from the perspective of

---

[1] Primarily, but not exclusively, of south east Asian origin.

[2] *R (on the application of Quila and another) (FC) (Respondents) v Secretary of State for the Home Department (Appellant)* [2011] UKSC 45, at [11](b).

child protection.[3] Secondly, in cases where parents claim to have exercised their parental responsibility jointly to remove a child abroad permanently or in cases where the alleged victim is a missing adult, the court that regularly deals with child abduction cases (ie the Family Division of The High Court) and is able to exercise the inherent jurisdiction, has proved to be the most effective and efficient venue for such proceedings.

Drawing on the experience gleaned from dealing with matters of abduction, it was the judges of the Family Division who first put their shoulder to the wheel of the then emerging problem of forced marriage, developing case-law to fill the statutory void that was later filled (in part, with the reservation of the court's powers under the inherent jurisdiction) by the passing of the Forced Marriage (Civil Protection) Act 2007 ('the Act' or 'FM(CP)A 2007').

This chapter is intended first to give a brief background to the development of the 'forced marriage' jurisdiction, before moving on to consider the protection currently available to victims and potential victims of forced marriage and how, from a case management perspective, the various options that are available to practitioners faced with such an application may best be deployed.

17.1.2 The nature of forced marriage – an abuse of human rights

The philosophy underpinning the courts' approach to tackling the issue of forced marriage in the cases determined under the inherent jurisdiction,[4] and thereafter the Government's actions in formulating and passing the Act has been that a forced marriage is a significant and abhorrent violation of the victim's fundamental rights as enshrined within a number of international instruments.[5]

The court has been quick to distance the practice of forced marriage from the entirely separate tradition of consensual arranged marriage[6], which has been deemed to be entitled to respect as a 'common and perfectly acceptable practice'[7], and indeed the comparison between the two, and emphasis upon the consensual nature of the arranged marriage, has provided a useful contradistinction to emphasise the evil of a forced marriage, which has been held to be 'an abuse of human rights. It is a

---

3   For example the suggested orders under the UK-Pakistan Judicial Protocol on Children Matters.
4   For which please see **17.1.4** below.
5   Including, but not limited to Art 16(2) of the Universal Declaration of Human Rights 1948, Art 23(3) of the International Covenant on Civil and Political Rights 1966 and Art 12 of the European Convention on Human Rights and Fundamental Freedoms 1950.
6   Which is, of course, still frequently practiced in numerous cultures and has only relatively recently fallen out of favour in the western world.
7   *R (on the application of Quila and another) (FC) (Respondents) v Secretary of State for the Home Department (Appellant)* [2011] UKSC 45, at [65].

form of domestic violence that dehumanises people by denying them their right to choose how to live their lives'.[8]

In summary, in reliance upon the international instruments enshrining an individual's fundamental rights concerning marriage and in accordance with the courts' traditional approach towards the protection of the fundamental rights of children or adults considered to be vulnerable as a result either of their individual circumstances or the situation in which they are placed by those in whom they trust, the courts have acted robustly in seeking to protect such victims from what would undoubtedly be considered a fundamental breach of their rights.

17.1.3   The prevalence of the problem

Any consideration of the problem of forced marriage must begin from the proposition that a forced marriage is something that is intrinsically hard to detect. It is a relative rarity for a forced marriage to be detected by an agency or individual outside of a particular family unit and as such the statistics that seek to demonstrate the prevalence of the problem are often couched with the caveat that they are reliant upon self-reporting or 'whistle blowing'. It is therefore difficult to seek to obtain empirical data and thereby to identify the precise number of threatened or actual forced marriages that have taken place within England and Wales within a particular period of time. This is exponentially so if the forced marriage has taken place abroad, although attempts have been made to infer a significant number of such marriages from, for example, a study focusing on the number of young girls removed permanently from school during their teenage years.

An accurate and comprehensive 'national picture' has hitherto proved impossible to compile as individual cases seem to be reported to a variety of different agencies (for example police forces, local authorities, government agencies and non-governmental organisations). There is therefore always a possibility that one particular case will have been reported to a number of different authorities in any one area, rendering statistical analysis misleading.

It is for that reason that an assessment of the available statistics in this context can prove difficult. Perhaps the most reliable indicator of the scale of the problem (although in comparison with certain other studies their statistics seem to under-report the problem) comes from the FMU.[9]

The FMU was established in 2005 as a dedicated governmental body tasked with coordinating the various efforts undertaken to combat forced marriage both by the government and otherwise. They also provide a

---

8   Press release announcing the establishment of the Forced Marriage Unit, 27 October 2004.

9   For the most recent available statistics please see below.

valuable resource for both victims and practitioners and a point of liaison between the 'front line' in this jurisdiction and the Foreign and Commonwealth Office and the British High Commissions and Embassies overseas. The FMU log each report of an actual or threatened forced marriage that they receive, grouped into defined categories where possible and divided on a yearly basis. The most recent statistics available[10] relate to 2010, and are as follows:

- 1,468 instances where the FMU gave advice or support relating to a possible forced marriage;

- 78% (1,145) involved females and 22% (323) males;

- 66 of the cases involved people with disabilities;

- 10 of the cases involved people who identified themselves as lesbian, gay, bisexual or transgender.

By way of an example of the difficulties in compiling statistics to demonstrate the exact prevalence of forced marriage in England and Wales it may be of assistance to consider the alternative figures available. In the document entitled 'Forced Marriage – Prevalence and Service Response'[11] it was suggested that there were between 5,000 and 8,000 reported cases of actual or threatened forced marriage within the United Kingdom in 2008.

When considering the issue of forced marriage in an immigration context (and specifically the lawfulness or otherwise of Rule 277 of the Immigration Rules) Sedley LJ has accepted that reported cases will represent only a fraction of the total number of cases of forced marriage, within a given timeframe.[12]

It is therefore apparent, at the very least, that the problem of forced marriage is a widespread one that affects a variety of different communities and people of a broad range of ages.

Prior to the implementation of the Act no statistics were kept regarding the number of applications made for inherent jurisdiction orders. It is apparent, though, from the small number of reported decisions available that the problem was brought to the attention of the courts on a relatively regular basis. It seems to an extent unlikely that the scale of the problem would have been lesser prior to the introduction of legislation. The more likely explanation would seem to be that the increased publicity afforded to the issue following the implementation of the Act has increased

---

[10]   As at 10 January 2012 – reproduced with kind permission of the FMU.

[11]   National Centre for Social Research, DCSF B128 (July 2009).

[12]   *Aguilar Quila and Aguilar, Bibi and Mohammed v Secretary of State for the Home Department* [2011] 1 FLR 1187.

awareness of remedies and therefore reporting. This may be reflected by available statistics regarding the Act's use since its implementation: as of February 2011, 293 orders had been issued across the 15 designated forced marriage courts.[13]

17.1.4   The development of protection through the courts

The courts have typically adopted a culturally sensitive yet robust approach to identifiable situations in which a risk may have arisen that a young person was in the process of being, or had been, forced into a marriage. The first such reported decision in which the court was seen (at the invitation of a 'third party'[14] but based upon reliable information of the wishes and feelings of the person to be protected) to intervene in a forced marriage situation was that of *Re KR (Abduction: Forcible Removal by Parents).*[15] Mr Justice Singer commented that: 'In a wider context, this case also illustrates the sort of pressures to which young persons may be subject, driven by the desire of their parents and family that they should marry in the manner culturally expected of them',[16] in circumstances that may now be recognised as akin to a paradigm case of a removal abroad for the purposes of a forced marriage.

Notwithstanding a recognition that 'approaching these issues from the point of view of her parents and of others within their family and community who share their convictions and their outlook, this outcome is an affront to their traditional values, possibly to their religious tenets, and certainly to their concept of family (and perhaps particularly paternal) authority' Mr Justice Singer held that 'Sensitivity to these traditional and/or religious influences is however likely, in English courts, usually to give way to the integrity of the individual child or young person concerned. In the courts of this country the voice of the young person will be heard and, in so personal a context as opposition to an arranged or enforced marriage, will prevail'.[17]

The English courts' willingness to respond to allegations of forced marriage in a manner sensitive to the needs of the victim whilst maintaining a culturally sensitive approach was next demonstrated, again in a decision of Mr Justice Singer, in *Re SK (Proposed Plaintiff) (An Adult by way of her Litigation Friend).*[18] The court was faced with an application made without the knowledge of the person to be protected[19]

---

[13]   Data provided by the Ministry of Justice to the Home Affairs Select Committee and reported in the Eighth Report of Session 2010–12 dated 10 May 2011.

[14]   The elder sister of the person to be protected.

[15]   [1999] 2 FLR 542.

[16]   Ibid, at 543.

[17]   Ibid, at 548.

[18]   [2005] 2 FLR 230.

[19]   Who was, on application, considered eligible for public funding notwithstanding the unusual circumstances of the case. The Legal Services Commission are to be praised for the pragmatic approach taken to allow the progression of such applications, albeit that

based upon information received through the Community Liaison Unit of the Foreign and Commonwealth Office (who preceded the Forced Marriage Unit in fulfilling this function, the FMU having only been recently established[20]).

Mr Justice Singer, having emphasised that: 'there is a spectrum of forced marriage from physical force or fear of injury or death in their most literal form, through to the undue imposition of emotional pressure which is at the other end of the forced marriage range, and that a grey area then separates unacceptable forced marriage from marriages arranged traditionally which are in no way to be condemned, but rather supported as a conventional concept in many societies'[21] made orders on the basis of the information received designed initially to offer interim protection but primarily 'to ascertain whether or not she has been able to exercise her free will in decisions concerning her civil status and her country of residence'.[22]

The jurisdiction exercised by Mr Justice Singer in *Re SK* was examined in great detail by Mr Justice Munby (as he then was) in the later case of *Re SA (Vulnerable Adult with Capacity: Marriage)*,[23] in which he found that the court's power extended to the provision of protection by way of injunctive order to vulnerable adults with the capacity to instruct lawyers but who, by virtue of their circumstances (or, as in *Re SK*, the circumstances that they appeared to face based upon the information available), were rendered vulnerable. Focusing on forced marriage this vulnerability left them unable to provide valid consent (or, viewed another way, to mount effective opposition), to the ceremony of marriage that it was proposed they undergo.

In *Re SA* it was found that the court was able to exercise 'what is, in substance and reality, a jurisdiction in relation to incompetent adults which is for all practical purposes indistinguishable from its well established parens patriae or wardship jurisdiction in relation to children. The court exercises a "protective jurisdiction" in relation to vulnerable adults just as it does in relation to wards of court'.[24]

Having charted the development of the jurisdiction in respect of vulnerable adults following what is termed its 'rediscovery' by the House of Lords in *Re F (Mental Patient: Sterilisation)*,[25] Mr Justice Munby found that, in summary (and resisting any attempt to define precisely those who may find themselves amenable to the jurisdiction) the

---

the funding is necessarily considered on a means and merits basis. For where to find up-to-date guidance on funding applications of this type, please see **17.6.3**.
20   [2005] 2 FLR 230, at 232.
21   Ibid.
22   Ibid, at 233.
23   [2006] 1 FLR 867.
24   Ibid, at [37].
25   [1990] 2 AC 1, [1989] 2 FLR 376.

invocation of the inherent jurisdiction in the context of a vulnerable adult with capacity may be appropriate where:

> 'a vulnerable adult who, even if not incapacitated by mental disorder or mental illness, is, or is reasonably believed to be, either: (i) under constraint; or (ii) subject to coercion or undue influence; or (iii) for some other reason deprived of the capacity to make the relevant decision, or disabled from making a free choice, or incapacitated or disabled from giving or expressing a real and genuine consent.'[26]

Having elaborated upon the points at sub paragraphs (i), (ii) and (iii), the learned judge summarised the position as follows:

> 'There is, however, in my judgment, a common thread to all this. The inherent jurisdiction can be invoked wherever a vulnerable adult is, or is reasonably believed to be, for some reason deprived of the capacity to make the relevant decision, or disabled from making a free choice, or incapacitated or disabled from giving or expressing a real and genuine consent. The cause may be, but is not for this purpose limited to, mental disorder or mental illness. A vulnerable adult who does not suffer from any kind of mental incapacity may nonetheless be entitled to the protection of the inherent jurisdiction if he or she is, or is reasonably believed to be, incapacitated from making the relevant decision by reason of such things as constraint, coercion, undue influence or other vitiating factors.'[27]

It has thereafter been possible to submit to the court that the full range of powers as are undoubtedly available to protect a child from forced marriage within the wardship jurisdiction are equally available where the case involves an adult.

Whilst the court has not had cause to revisit this decision in the context of a forced marriage, the jurisdiction in respect of vulnerable adults has developed in other contexts and the foundation of the jurisdiction utilised in *Re SA* has throughout lain undisturbed, culminating most recently in *Re HM (Vulnerable Adult: Injunction)*,[28] in which Lord Justice Munby, sitting as a judge of the Family Division, held:

> 'In my judgment, and consistently with previous authority, the court has exactly the same power to make orders of the type referred to in paras [32]–[40] above when it is concerned with an adult who lacks capacity as it undoubtedly has when concerned with a child. In particular, the court has exactly the same powers when it is concerned to locate the whereabouts of a missing or abducted adult lacking capacity as it has when concerned to locate the whereabouts of a missing or abducted child.'[29]

---

[26]   Ibid, at [77].
[27]   Ibid, at [79].
[28]   [2010] 2 FLR 1057.
[29]   Ibid, at [45].

The jurisdiction has very recently been revisited in a protective context by Mrs Justice Theis in *A Local Authority v DL*.[30] Mrs Justice Theis upheld the use of the jurisdiction in a protective capacity having been specifically referred to *Re SA*, confirming that the use of this jurisdiction in respect of adults considered vulnerable but with capacity to litigate had survived the passing of the Mental Capacity Act 2005 and the foundation of the Court of Protection.

There will, however, undoubtedly be cases of this type where the individual subject or potentially subject to a forced marriage lacks the capacity to litigate and as such will require the assistance of the Official Solicitor or alternatively consideration within the Court of Protection. For specific comment on the relevant procedures that will be adopted in such a case please see Chapter 5, which relates specifically to the Court of Protection.

17.1.5   The development and implementation of the Forced Marriage (Civil Protection) Act 2007

The Forced Marriage (Civil Protection) Act 2007 received Royal Assent on 26 July 2007, following an extensive consultation process resulting in the publication of *Forced Marriage, A Wrong Not a Right,* a consultation document issued by the Government in December 2005, and the response to that consultation dated June 2006. The Act was initially introduced as a Private Members Bill by Lord Lester of Herne Hill in November 2006, and was enacted following swift passage through Parliament.[31] The stated objective of the Act was to:

> 'make provision for protecting individuals against being forced to enter into marriage without their free and full consent and for protecting individuals who have been forced to enter into a marriage without such consent: and for connected purposes.'[32]

The Act, whilst offering a statutory footing for the exercise of civil powers in an effort to combat the problem of forced marriage, arguably expands upon the powers previously exercised by the courts.[33] The Act could be said to increase the potential pool of applicants for such orders by specifically providing for application by relevant third parties (currently only extended to local authorities) and to other organisations with the

---

[30] [2011] EWHC 1022 (Fam).

[31] Summary from *One year on: the initial impact of the Forced Marriage (Civil Protection) Act 2007 in its first year of operation.*

[32] Introduction to the Forced Marriage (Civil Protection) Act 2007.

[33] Whilst specifically providing for the possibility of the continued use of such inherent jurisdiction powers concurrently with the Act in appropriate circumstances – Family Law Act 1996 (FLA 1996), s 63R(2) (as inserted by FM(CP)A 2007, s 1).

court's leave where a suitable interest in the case can be demonstrated.[34] Perhaps, though, the greatest benefit has been the codification of the remedies available and the associated publicity of the availability of those remedies both to private individuals and to statutory (and other) agencies, which has pushed the issue of forced marriage to the fore, thereby making many more agencies aware of the remedies available.[35]

The impact of the Act is plain from the statistics available regarding its use,[36] which surpassed the government's expectations in the first two years of its operation.

It may be of great significance that the legislation maintains the court's previous approach of dealing with the culturally sensitive issue of forced marriage in an appropriate, victim-centred, manner with a particular focus upon the wishes and feelings of the person to be protected, insofar as they are reasonably ascertainable.[37] The orders are intended to be protective in their nature, though the discretion afforded to the court regarding the form of order made would seem to be wide.[38]

In a recent examination of the powers available to the courts pursuant to the Act (with a particular focus upon issues of disclosure) Sir Nicholas Wall, President of the Family Division, held in the case of *A Chief Constable and AA v YK*[39] that a forced marriage protection order 'will stand in its protective capacity, and in that capacity may require certain information not to be disclosed'[40] in circumstances in which the disclosure of certain information may have led to a risk of honour-based violence directed towards a party to the case.

Examining the approach required under the Act, the President found the crucial issue to be the 'health, safety and well-being' of the person to be protected, which 'in turn, depends on her wishes and feelings'.[41] In order to determine the wishes and feelings of the person to be protected in this particular case, an expert in honour-based violence and forced marriage was instructed and a report prepared for the court.[42]

---

[34]   FLA 1996, s 63C(3) and (4) (as inserted by FM(CP)A 2007, s 1) – though of course such agencies were entitled to apply for relief pursuant to the inherent jurisdiction (subject to Children Act 1989, s 100).

[35]   Though it is clear, particularly in light of *Forced Marriage*, Eighth Report of Session 2010–12, House of Commons Home Affairs Select Committee, that there is a considerable amount of work to be done in this area.

[36]   For which see **17.1.3**.

[37]   FLA 1996, s 63A(3) (as inserted by FM (CP)A 2007, s 1).

[38]   FLA 1996, ss 63A(1) and 63B(1)(a) and (b) (as inserted by FM (CP)A 2007, s 1).

[39]   [2011] 1 FLR 1493.

[40]   Ibid, at [91].

[41]   Ibid, at [97].

[42]   Though not disclosed to the parties, for a discussion of the approach see the postscript to the judgment at p 1520.

The approach adopted by the English courts in cases decided both pre and post the Act would seem to be significant in the focus upon:

- an appropriate recognition of marriages contracted other than by the traditional method as a culturally appropriate institution (but bearing in mind the 'spectrum of forced marriage' identified by Mr Justice Singer[43]), whilst extending the protection afforded pursuant to the Act to those victims subject (or potentially subject) to a forced ceremony that whilst purporting to be a marriage would not be capable of civil recognition;

- an approach tailored toward providing a victim or potential victim of forced marriage with proper protection, whilst taking steps to identify their views regarding their situation so that appropriate orders can be made;

- a willingness to act creatively in order to ensure that appropriate protection can be provided, including within applications made under the Act;

- an extensive, multi-jurisdictional approach where appropriate to ensure that protection is still available even when the person to be protected has been moved away from the furthest reaches of the jurisdiction of the English court.

As more cases come before the court the range of protection offered could be said to have been extended whilst remaining at all times tailored to the specific circumstances of the case and, where appropriate, sensitive to the needs particularly of the victim but also to their family.

The debate about the impact of the Act upon the issue of forced marriage and protection from it has very recently been re-opened following the publication of the Eighth Report of Session 2010–12 of the House of Commons Home Affairs Committee. The report recognises that the powers under the Act have been effective in combating forced marriage in certain cases, but raises concerns regarding the monitoring process following the grant of an order, and the enforcement procedures available in the event of any breach.

The report also considered the possibility of criminalising forced marriage as a discrete offence, in addition to offering civil protection by way of the injunctions available under the Act. The idea of criminalisation was widely discussed during the drafting stage of the Act, but eventually rejected. A consultation process was then initiated regarding the issue of criminalisation during the course of which public and stakeholder opinion appears to have been similarly polarised, perhaps as a result of an

---

[43] Per *Re SK (Proposed Plaintiff) (An Adult by way of her Litigation Friend)* [2005] 2 FLR 230.

apparent absence of any fresh evidence regarding the potential impact upon reporting incidences of forced marriage that might arise from such a step.[44]

On 8 June 2012 the government announced that forcing someone to marry would become a criminal offence in England and Wales.[45] David Cameron stated that he had 'listened to concerns that criminalisation could force this most distressing issue underground. That is why we have a new comprehensive package to identify possible victims, support those who have suffered first hand and, indeed, prevent criminality wherever possible'; however, at that stage details of the additional support measures mentioned were not made available. It is expected that any legislation implementing this decision is unlikely to be put before parliament before 2013 or 2014.

17.2 THE FORCED MARRIAGE (CIVIL PROTECTION) ACT 2007

17.2.1 An overview of the Act

At the time that the Act received Royal Assent the then minister at the Ministry of Justice, Bridget Prentice, said that the Act 'sends out a clear message that forced marriage, a breach of an individual's basic right to choose who and when they marry, is not acceptable in our society' as part of 'a much wider programme of work already underway to raise awareness of the problem of forced marriages and protect women's rights in this area'.[46]

Section 1 of the Act inserted a new Part IVA of the Family Law Act 1996, which was intended to empower the courts to 'make Forced Marriage Protection Orders to stop someone from forcing another person into marriage' by placing on a statutory footing 'a wide discretion in the type of injunctions they will be able to make to enable them to respond effectively to the individual circumstances of the case and prevent or pre-empt forced marriages from occurring'.[47]

In furtherance of those aims, the Act allows the courts to make such orders as appear necessary in accordance with the particular facts of the case on the application of:

- the victim; or

---

[44] Documents concerning the consultation can be found at http://www.homeoffice.gov.uk/publications/about-us/consultations/forced-marriage/.

[45] http://www.homeoffice.gov.uk/media-centre/news/forced-marriage-new-law.

[46] Ministry of Justice press release, 26 July 2007.

[47] Ibid.

- a relevant third party without leave (at the time of writing limited to local authorities); or

- other third parties with the leave of the court; or

- on the court's own motion during the course of existing family proceedings.[48]

The orders made can protect the victim or any other associated person from any conduct associated with the forced marriage in question.

Whilst the Act provides the court with an extremely wide discretion both in respect of the protection that it grants and in respect of the parties protected against particular respondents, there are particular provisions within the scheme of the legislation that merit closer examination.

17.2.1.1   What is a 'forced marriage' for the purposes of the Act, what evidence is required and to whom can the protection apply?

The 'gateway' to protection under the Act can be found at s 63A(4) of the Family Law Act 1996:

> '(4) For the purposes of this Part a person ("A") is forced into a marriage if another person ("B") forces A to enter into a marriage (whether with B or another person) without A's free and full consent.'

This definition is further expanded by subss (5) and (6):

> '(5) For the purposes of subsection (4) it does not matter whether the conduct of B which forces A to enter into a marriage is directed against A, B or another person.
>
> (6) In this Part—
>
> "force" includes coerce by threats or other psychological means (and related expressions are to be read accordingly) ...'

Consent is not further defined for the purposes of the Act; however, the explanatory notes suggest that the definition is clear in its terms. The scheme of the Act suggests that it refers to 'consent' in plain dictionary terms. This may be argued to suggest that the question is one of simple fact, as opposed to something to be determined upon the application of an elevated standard.[49] Subsections (5) and (6) are explained to provide

---

[48]   Which may include any proceedings conforming with that description, but it is thought will particularly encompass proceedings under the Children Act 1989 – for discussion of the specific retention of the powers of the inherent jurisdiction within a forced marriage context, see **17.4.2.4** and **17.5.2**.

[49]   For example, as can be observed in a nullity context: *Hirani v Hirani* (1983) 4 FLR 232.

that the force can be directed towards those other than the victim,[50] and to provide examples of the type of force as may be used in commissioning a forced marriage. This is not, though, suggested to be an exhaustive list and it is submitted that in considering whether or not a marriage at the centre of an application under the Act is or is not forced the court will need to consider all of the circumstances of the case.[51]

Various other definitions are applied to 'force' in this context or the concept of 'forced marriage' as a whole within the relevant guidance associated with the Act. Amongst the most comprehensive, and to a greater or lesser degree analogous to the definition applied within the explanatory notes, is that found within the best practice guidance, *The Right to Choose: Multi-Agency Statutory Guidance for dealing with Forced Marriage*, in which it is stated that:

> 'In forced marriages, one or both spouses do not (or, in the case of some adults with support needs, cannot) consent to the marriage and duress is involved. Duress can include physical, psychological, financial, sexual and emotional pressure.'[52]

The Act does not impose an evidential hurdle to be surmounted in order to engage the court's powers (as, for example, would be required before the court could intervene on the application of a local authority if an interim care order were sought under similar circumstances), instead the court is to 'have regard to all the circumstances including the need to secure the health, safety and well-being of the person to be protected'.[53] It might be reasonable to anticipate a requirement that there be evidence of a forced marriage, as evidence of molestation is required in order to found an application for a non-molestation order,[54] in respect of which the test for intervention is similarly worded.[55] However, there is no such requirement within the wording of the Act and the experience of practitioners has been that the Act has been read narrowly, with no such elevated definition so far applied.

Although the Act is directed towards the protection of a person from 'being forced into a marriage, or from any attempt to be forced into a marriage' or alternatively the protection of 'a person who has been forced into a marriage',[56] and therefore undoubtedly allows the making of protective orders in relation to the alleged victim, the expanded definition of force at s 63A(5)[57] suggests that in seeking to protect a person from

---

50 FLA 1996, s 63A(5).
51 As per FLA 1996, s 63A(2) (below).
52 http://www.fco.gov.uk/resources/en/pdf/travel-living-abroad/when-things-go-wrong/fmu-right-to-choose.pdf, at p 4, para 1.
53 FLA 1996, s 63A(2).
54 *C v C (Non-Molestation Order: Jurisdiction)* [1998] 1 FLR 554.
55 FLA 1996, s 42(5).
56 FLA 1996, s 63A(1)(a) and (b).
57 As set out above.

being forced into marriage, the court may make orders for the protection of other 'third parties' in an effort to alleviate the resultant pressure exerted upon the alleged victim.

This interpretation allows protection to be extended widely to any person potentially affected by other persons' actions towards them either directly or indirectly in the course of forcing or attempting to force another person into a marriage, and may include family members, boyfriends or other friends against whom threats may be made or pressure exerted. In *A Chief Constable and AA v YK*[58] protection was extended to the former boyfriend of the person to be protected as a result of this section.

17.2.1.2   *What orders may the court make and against whom?*

By virtue of the operation of FLA 1996, s 63B, the court may make orders containing 'such prohibitions, restrictions or requirements [and] such other terms as the court considers appropriate for the purposes of the order'. The orders that the court may make may relate to 'conduct outside England and Wales as well as (or instead of) conduct within England and Wales'.[59]

In practice this section has been taken to grant the court an exceptionally wide discretion to make such orders as may be required in order to protect the subjects of the proceedings, dependent entirely upon the circumstances of the proceedings, the evil against which protection is sought and the imagination of the court. To the authors' knowledge (and without intending to present anything purporting to be an exhaustive list) orders made under the Act have thus far extended to the following, granted in addition to more general injunctive provisions and ranging from the relatively standard to the more extreme:

(a)   the prevention of travel/removal of children or adults from the jurisdiction of England and Wales;

(b)   the removal of travel documents (either with the assistance of the Tipstaff if acting in the High Court, or without[60]);

(c)   non-molestation or, if appropriate, occupation order provisions, within the context of forced marriage protection orders;

(d)   prohibitions on contact;

(e)   the provision of accommodation and, if the local authority will provide it, foster care;

---

58   [2011] 1 FLR 1493.
59   FLA 1996, s 63B(2)(a).
60   Although the powers of a county court judge may be limited to British passports, whereas a High Court judge may make orders against any passport or travel document.

(f) the withholding of certain (or in extreme cases, all) of the evidence filed within the proceedings, if its disclosure could be said to result in risk arising to one or more of the parties to the proceedings or the subject of the orders;[61]

(g) prohibitions upon planned wedding venues or other associated venues hosting the event at which it is intended the forced marriage will take place;

(h) prohibition upon the civil registration of a marriage already solemnised that was, in fact, forced;

(i) the imposition of orders of this type upon those who are outside of the jurisdiction of England and Wales, pursuant to FLA 1996, s 63B(2)(a).[62]

Whilst there is no differing evidential standard applicable to the variety of order sought in any given case, it may be that the more draconian the order sought the more compelling the evidence will need to be in order to persuade the court that the order is at that stage justified. However, the courts have typically shown themselves willing to make unusual and creative orders where those orders have been required and are proportionate to the aim of protecting the person to be forced into a marriage, or associated with such an act.

The court is also granted a wide discretion in respect of the respondents to any application. Pursuant to FLA 1996, s 63B(2)(b) and (c), orders under the Act may be directed against:

'(b) respondents who are, or may become, involved in other respects as well as (or instead of) respondents who force or who attempt to force, or may force or attempt to force, a person to enter into a marriage;

(c) other persons who are, or may become, involved in other respects as well as respondents of any kind.'

The familial nature of forced marriage cases, which may involve grandparents, uncles, aunts, brothers and sisters in addition to the parents, can result in orders directed against a number of actual respondents, with other orders made generally against other persons pursuant to subs (c). Section 63B(3) provides examples, but again not an exhaustive list, of 'involvements in other respects', which includes 'aiding, abetting, counselling, procuring, encouraging or assisting another person

---

[61] As to which, see **17.4.1**.

[62] For further discussion of the complications that arise where one or more of the parties to an application are outside of the jurisdiction of England and Wales, see **17.4.2.4**.

to force, or to attempt to force, a person to enter into a marriage' and 'conspiring to force, or to attempt to force, a person to enter into a marriage'.

Whilst it is suggested that those considering making an application pursuant to the Act consider the involvement of wider family members when making the application, and particularly those against whom the applicant (whether that be the person to be protected, another person with *locus* to make an application or another agency with leave) particularly seeks an order, it is similarly suggested that this is a decision that needs to be taken carefully.

The advantages of having protective orders against a wide variety of family members may be outweighed in certain circumstances by the difficulties associated with casting the net too wide, diminishing the force of the overall application. That said, in cases where it is common for members of a family to instruct or encourage others to take steps in the name of family honour, it may be beneficial to take this decision with an abundance of caution. Those against whom in due course it appears the evidence is insufficient can seek discharge at a return date or alternatively give appropriate undertakings at that or a later stage.

As a result of the test that must be met when making an application under the Act, and particularly the focus upon the wishes and feelings of the person to be protected, it is suggested that if the application is to be made by a person or agency other than the person to be protected the alleged victim should be joined as a party at the earliest stage and, if appropriate, assisted in obtaining specialist representation so that they can be helped to obtain additional support if necessary.[63]

17.2.2   Where to apply?

17.2.2.1   Which courts have power to make orders under the Act?

Power to make orders under the Act has been extended to 15 designated county courts around the country, in addition to the High Court sitting either at the Royal Courts of Justice in London or at any of the District Registries around England and Wales. There are currently 15 specified county courts that can deal with applications made under the Act:[64]

- The Principal Registry of the Family Division

- Birmingham Family Courts

- Blackburn County Court

---

[63]   For a discussion as to the type of support that may be required, see **17.4.2.3**.
[64]   The High Court can also hear such applications (see below).

- Bradford County Court

- Bristol County Court

- Cardiff Civil Justice Centre

- Derby County Court

- Leeds Combined Court

- Leicester County Court

- Luton County Court

- Manchester County Court

- Middlesbrough County Court

- Newcastle County Court

- Romford County Court

- Willesden County Court

When making an application pursuant to the Act it will be necessary to consider firstly whether it is a matter appropriate to be heard in the High Court, and secondly if it is not suitable for the High Court to which of the 15 designated family courts the application should be made.

17.2.2.2   High Court or county court?

The Act was intended, as one of its aims, to make the process of applying for relief in circumstances of forced marriage more easily and widely available. As a result of this aim the application process was simplified (by its similarity to an application pursuant to FLA 1996, as opposed to by originating summons as had previously been the procedure) and the number of courts able to entertain the application increased greatly.

Nonetheless it is suggested that there continue to be cases brought under the Act (often in conjunction with the inherent jurisdiction of the High Court, either by way of wardship or otherwise) which will merit at least the initial application being made in the High Court. Hallmarks of such cases may be:

- if either the person to be protected or one or a number of the respondents are based abroad, in circumstances where it is intended that the order made have extra-territorial effect or be otherwise mirrored abroad (for example in the spirit of the UK-Pakistan Judicial Protocol on Children Matters);

- if the case is substantially domestic, but requires (or may require) liaison with foreign authorities by way of the office of Lord Justice Thorpe as the International Liaison Judge;

- where the services of the Tipstaff are required or orders need be made in relation to a foreign passport (such as may not be available in the county court);

- if complex issues of disclosure arise, which may either necessitate that the case commences and thereafter remains in the High Court, or may be dealt with by a High Court Judge as a preliminary issue before transfer to a county court.

This list is not intended to be exhaustive, and cases that do not fit within the limited criteria suggested above may nonetheless be of such complexity that the powers of the High Court are required. However absent international complications or other complex issues it will generally be appropriate to issue the application in one of the 15 designated forced marriage courts.

17.2.2.3   In which court should the application be issued?

Due to the limited number of forced marriage courts available, choice as to the court to which the application is made may be limited depending on the parties' geographical area. Nonetheless in certain cases careful thought should be given regarding which court is chosen, particularly if the person (or people) to be protected are in a refuge or otherwise in hiding, as it may be dangerous to give away even the general geographical location.

In such a case thought should be given to issuing the application in a neighbouring designated court, thus removing any such risk.

17.2.3   Specific provisions

17.2.3.1   Ex parte orders and powers of arrest[65]

Pursuant to FLA 1996, s 63D(1):

'The court may, in any case where it considers that it is just and convenient to do so, make a forced marriage protection order even though the

---

[65] Whilst it is acknowledged that the Family Procedure Rules 2010 (SI 2010/2955) have discarded the Latin terminology previously applied to without notice hearings, the Act refers to ex parte and inter partes hearings, and as such this language is retained for the purposes of this chapter.

respondent has not been given such notice of the proceedings as would otherwise be required by rules of court.'

In considering whether to exercise its powers on an ex parte basis, the court is to consider all of the circumstances of the case, including:

• any risk of significant harm to the person to be protected or another person if the order is not made immediately;

• whether it is likely that an applicant will be deterred or prevented from pursuing an application if an order is not made immediately; and

• whether there is reason to believe that steps are being taken (or would be taken) to evade service, and the delay in service causes (or would be likely to cause) 'serious prejudice to the person to be protected'.

It is submitted, though, that it would be an extremely rare case in which the application for an order were made with notice to the respondents. The reasons for this are clear, and include (but are not limited to) the following:

• The circumstances of forced marriage often (if not always) involve a serious risk of violence towards the person to be protected (or others associated with them); as part of the process, it is therefore likely that there will be a significant risk of reprisal in the event that it becomes apparent that steps have been taken by or on behalf of the person to be protected to prevent the marriage, or any step that is part of or preparatory to it.

• Therefore it is likely to be necessary to have protective non-molestation type orders in place prior to the serving of the orders.[66]

• In any event a forced marriage protection order will more often than not only prevent the subject of the orders from doing something that they are in any event not entitled to do, and as such their rights will not be unduly infringed by the making of orders on an ex parte basis.

There are a number of examples of cases in which very serious violence has been perpetrated upon a person to be protected under orders notwithstanding a regime of protection put in place, in one case by the police.[67] It is therefore suggested that one cannot be overly cautious when

---

[66] Amongst other measures designed to protect the person alongside the protective orders, as to which please see below.

[67] *Re P (Forced Marriage)* [2011] 1 FLR 2060.

considering an application pursuant to the Act, and it is as such likely to be appropriate to seek ex parte relief, allowing authoritative protection to be put in place prior to the service of the orders.

17.2.3.2 *Powers of arrest and the criminalisation of breaches under the Act*

Where an order is made on an ex parte basis, the court 'may attach a power of arrest to one or more provisions of the order if it considers that there is a risk of significant harm to a person, attributable to conduct of the respondent, if the power of arrest is not attached to the provisions immediately' in circumstances where it considers that 'the respondent has used or threatened violence against the person being protected or otherwise in connection with the matters being dealt with by the order'.[68]

It therefore appears that, upon an ex parte application, the court's power to impose a power of arrest is discretionary and dependent upon establishment of the following:

- evidence that the respondent has used or threatened violence;

- that the threat is against the person to be protected, or another person in connection with the evidence justifying the order (presumably in accordance with FLA 1996, s 63A(5)); and

- that if the power of arrest is not attached, there is a risk of significant harm to the person to be protected attributable to the conduct of the respondent.[69]

It must be presumed, in accordance with the wording of FLA 1996, s 63H(3), that the court will consider the person to be protected at risk of significant harm, attributable to the conduct of the respondent even if that conduct is directed against another person as envisaged by ss 63A(5) and 63H(4), allowing a power of arrest to be attached in such circumstances.

In practice the courts have proved willing to attach a power of arrest to most orders made on an ex parte basis due either to existing evidence of violence or an ascertainable risk of violence when it is discovered by the respondents to the application that the person to be protected has taken steps (or, where the person to be protected is not the applicant, has been the subject of steps taken on their behalf) to prevent a forthcoming forced

---

[68]   FLA 1996, s 63H(3) and (4).

[69]   The approach adopted by the Act is similar in its construction to that which is applied to occupation orders pursuant to FLA 1996, s 47, in that the attachment of a power of arrest is mandatory if, on an inter partes basis 'it appears to the court that the respondent has used or threatened violence against the applicant of a relevant child' but discretionary where the order is made on an ex parte application.

marriage or otherwise thwart the will of the respondents in some other regard associated with a forced marriage.

Where the order is to be made on an inter partes basis, the decision-making process is subject to slightly different conditions as, upon satisfaction as the same conditions as apply to the attachment of a power of arrest to an ex parte order, the court:

> 'must attach a power of arrest to one or more provisions of the order unless it considers that, in all the circumstances of the case, there will be adequate protection without such a power.'[70]

It therefore appears likely that, if the court has attached a power of arrest at the ex parte stage, absent compelling argument from or on behalf of the respondents that either: (a) the evidence giving rise to the attachment of the power of arrest (ie the evidence of the use or threat of violence) is in some way questionable or can be undermined; or (b) alternatively (or perhaps additionally) notwithstanding any previous evidence the person to be protected can be adequately so protected without the need for any associated power of arrest, the power of arrest will continue if or when the order is continued following an inter partes hearing.

At the time the Act was drafted, and following a detailed consultation process including non-governmental organisations and legal practitioners, it was not thought necessary to either criminalise forced marriage as an act or to criminalise the breach of a forced marriage protection order.[71] There has, however, recently been a great deal of debate on this subject, particularly in light of the Eighth Report of the Home Affairs Select Committee dated 10 May 2011.

On 10 October 2011, in the aftermath of the Supreme Court finding against the Government in the matter of *R (Quila) v Secretary of State for the Home Department*,[72] the Prime Minister announced the Government's intention to make the breach of a forced marriage protection order a criminal offence, with a concurrent announcement that there would be a further consultation process into whether the practice should be criminalised in the same manner, by way of example, as female genital mutilation has been by the Female Genital Mutilation Act 2003. The consultation has now concluded and on 8 June 2012 the government announced their intention to criminalise the act of forcing someone into a marriage.

In the intervening period, however, the Forced Marriage etc (Protection and Jurisdiction) (Scotland) Act 2011 ('the Scottish Act'), which was first

---

[70]   FLA 1996, s 63H(2).
[71]   As had relatively recently been done in respect of non-molestation orders by way of an amendment to the FLA 1996.
[72]   [2011] UKSC 45.

laid before Parliament on 26 October 2010 was given Royal Assent on 27 April 2011. Pursuant to the Scottish Act:

> 'Any person who, knowingly and without reasonable excuse, breaches a forced marriage protection order commits an offence.'[73]

The offence is punishable on summary conviction to a term of imprisonment of not greater than 12 months, or on indictment a period of not greater than 2 years.

Alongside the announcement that the act of forcing someone into a marriage was to be criminalised, the government also announced that the breach of a forced marriage protection order would be made a criminal offence, moving the approach under the 2007 Act into line with that currently applied in Scotland.

17.2.3.3   *The inter partes return date*

In accordance with FLA 1996, s 63D(3) the court must give the respondents the opportunity to 'make representations' regarding the continuation of the ex parte order at an on notice hearing listed 'as soon as just and convenient' following the making of the order.

Such a hearing is typically in the form of a return date familiar to those who regularly deal with matters initiated by ex parte application. The court's intention at such a hearing will necessarily be to resolve any matters capable of resolution, to narrow and define the issues insofar as possible and thereafter to list any matters for future determination as require it.

It is, however, suggested that the wording of the opportunity afforded to the respondents is significant, as has been held by the President, Sir Nicholas Wall, in the matter of *A Chief Constable and AA v YK*:

> 'Thus the highest the case is put for any respondents are the requirements where there is an ex parte order; (1) for service and; (2) for the respondent to be given the opportunity to make representations. In other words, there is no requirement for there to be a conventional hearing at which the respondents are alerted to the case against them and have the opportunity to rebut it.'[74]

Further, whilst it was acknowledged that there may be some cases in which factual determination of the issues would be required[75], the President was of the view that:

---

[73]   Forced Marriage etc (Protection and Jurisdiction) (Scotland) Act 2011, s 9.
[74]   [2011] 1 FLR 1493, at [19].
[75]   Of which, on the President's analysis, this case (which might have been considered a paradigm case, albeit one with exceptionally complicated disclosure issues) was not one.

'it is arguable that ECHR Article 6 is not engaged in an application for a FMPO. In any event, since the court permits the exercise of jurisdiction ex parte and on the basis of the applicant's belief, it does not seem to me that a respondent's right to apply to set the order aside entitles him or her to access to information which, if abused, will lead to serious breaches of the rights of the person to be protected.'[76]

Rendering a conventional fact finding hearing impossible in such circumstances.

For the President, the issue as to how an application for a forced marriage protection order should progress was crystallised only upon an application being made to set aside the initial ex parte order which, on the analysis advanced, would be likely to engage both Art 6 and Art 8. Nonetheless it was held that the engagement of such fundamental rights would not necessarily entitle the respondent to sight of any undisclosed material,[77] leading ultimately to the same result when considering the possibility of a fact-finding hearing.

It is respectfully submitted that when considering the directions applicable at a first return date, the following factors are of significance and should at all stages be considered:

(a)   The test applicable in considering whether or not a forced marriage protection order should be made is broad, based on an analysis of all of the circumstances of the case, but is particularly based upon the court having 'such regard to the person's wishes and feelings (so far as they are reasonably ascertainable) as the court considers appropriate in the light of the person's age and understanding'.[78]

(b)   In many cases, but subject of course to the facts as they appear before the court in the individual case, fulfilment of the criteria that must be met to justify the making of the order will be dependent upon an assessment of the wishes and feelings of the person to be protected, rather than determination of disputed facts.

(c)   Nonetheless there may be cases in which the wishes and feelings of the person to be protected are informed by or perhaps entirely derived from factual allegations that are disputed as between the parties.

(d)   In such cases there may be a need for limited factual determination.

(e)   It must be borne in mind that there may be evidence known to the applicant and to the court, but not known to the respondents.

---

[76]   [2011] 1 FLR 1493, at [101].
[77]   Ibid, at [102], applying the analysis of Munby J in *Re B (Disclosure to other parties)* [2001] 2 FLR 1017.
[78]   FLA 1996, s 63A(3).

(f)   If that is the case the court should, as a preliminary point, determine the ongoing need for such information to remain undisclosed, and, if the information is to remain undisclosed, how any disputed facts can be resolved maintaining that position whilst always being mindful of the need to protect any individual from the harmful effects of disclosure.[79]

It is submitted that although there is plainly a need to remain mindful of the possibility that factual determination may be required in a forced marriage case (and within that of the difficulties that may arise inherent in such a hearing), it will be a rare case in which such a process is necessary. Careful consideration should be paid to alternative mechanisms by which the proceedings can be determined without the need for a potentially risky and damaging factual enquiry. Such methods may include the commissioning of an experts report from someone experienced in dealing with forced marriage and honour-based violence cases[80] or alternatively a hearing on submissions only (consistent with allowing the respondent to make representations as to the continuation of the order) based upon the matters raised in FLA 1996, s 63A(2) and (3).

17.2.3.4   *Undertakings*

Pursuant to FLA 1996, s 63E the court may accept an undertaking from a respondent to an application instead of making an order 'if it has power to make such an order'. In accordance with usual practice a power of arrest cannot be attached to an undertaking and the court is prohibited from accepting an undertaking where it otherwise would have attached a power of arrest to the order.

Whilst the power of arrest provisions remain (subject to any amendment as may be made in accordance with the current proposals to criminalise the breach of a forced marriage protection order) there may be limited disadvantage to accepting undertakings at the first return date where the power of arrest provisions would not be applicable. The consequence of breach – namely an application for committal as a result of the said breach – would be the same whether under undertaking or order and there are some distinct advantages, particularly the prompt end to proceedings which may, whilst they remain extant, cause risk to the person to be protected.

---

[79]   The points raised at (e) and (f) are derived from the guidance delivered by McFarlane J in in *Re T (Wardship: Impact of Police Intelligence)* [2009] EWHC 2440 (Fam), [2010] 1 FLR 1048 at [112] (i)–(iii).

[80]   As occurred in *A Chief Constable and AA v YK* [2011] 1 FLR 1493 – see the postscript to the judgment.

17.2.3.5 *Applications to vary and/or discharge protective orders made ex parte*

In accordance with the reasoning adopted by the President in *A Chief Constable and AA v YK*[81] there may be a more persuasive argument that respondents' human rights would be infringed were they not granted a full hearing. It is unclear how in practice this difference in approach has manifested itself. It appears as though the provision providing the respondents to an order with an opportunity to make representations contained within FLA 1996, s 63D extend to applications to vary and/or discharge due to the wording of s 63G and particularly subss (3) and (4).

An approach would therefore be to limit the application to vary or discharge to submissions (or 'representations' only) apart from in exceptional cases where there is a defined area of factual dispute requiring of determination in order for an order to be fairly granted. It is suggested, however, that such cases would be rare due to the 'gateway' to protection under the Act and the focus therein upon the wishes and feelings of the person to be protected.

17.3 FAMILY PROCEDURE RULES 2010, PART 11

The procedural rules governing applications pursuant to the 2007 Act are contained within Part 11 of the Family Procedure Rules 2010. Pursuant to r 11.2 the originating application may be made without notice (in Form FL401A) and where notice is not given the application must be supported by a statement explaining why.

In the event that the person making the application requires leave under s 63C(3) that person must supplement the application in Form FL401A with a Part 18 application[82] setting out:

(i)   the reasons for the application, for the making of which permission is sought ('the proposed application');

(ii)   the applicant's connection with the person to be protected;

(iii) the applicant's knowledge of the circumstances of the person to be protected; and

(iv)   the applicant's knowledge of the wishes and feelings of the person to be protected.

---

[81]   As to which see ibid, at [70] and [71].

[82]   The Part 18 application form can be found at http://www.justice.gov.uk/family-procedure-court-forms/FP2%20Nov%2010.pdf.

It is the applicant's responsibility to serve the proceedings, though if the applicant requests that the court effect service the court *must* do so under the terms of r 11.4(3). Where the person to be protected is not the applicant the application must be served upon them together with a notice containing the following information:

(i)   how to apply to become a party to the proceedings; and

(ii) details of that person's right to make representations in writing or orally at any hearing.[83]

This provision applies unless the person to be protected is a child, a person who lacks or may lack capacity within the meaning of that term prescribed by the Mental Capacity Act 2005 or a protected party in which case the court will give directions regarding service pursuant to r 11.4(5).

In the event that it subsequently becomes apparent that any other person should be made a party to the proceedings, or if any other person not a party wishes to become a party, an application can be made to the court by Part 18 notice seeking party status pursuant to r 11.6.

Following any hearing, it is the applicant's duty to serve the order resulting from that hearing upon the parties to the proceedings and, if not a party, the person to be protected. Where the orders contain a power of arrest the process is altered in accordance with r 11.12, by which the applicant must deliver the power of arrest form and a statement of service of the orders upon the respondents to the officer in charge of the police station responsible for the address at which the person to be protected resides, or any other police station at the direction of the court (unless the court has directed otherwise, in which case the order must be served in accordance with that direction – r 11.12(3)(b)).

Where a person subject to an order has been arrested for its breach that person must be brought before the court. The court may then either: (a) determine whether the facts and the circumstances which led to the arrest amounted to disobedience of the order; or (b) adjourn the proceedings. If the proceedings are adjourned the matter must be restored for disposal within 14 days of the person's arrest unless the court directs otherwise. Should the matter not be dealt with within this period a party may issue an application for committal for contempt.[84]

---

[83]   Though note **17.2.1.2** where it is recommended that the person to be protected be made a party to every case and assistance given to them to obtain representation if such assistance is appropriate.

[84]   FPR 2010, r 11.14.

17.4 SPECIFIC AREAS OF COMPLEXITY

17.4.1 Disclosure

In *A Chief Constable and AA v YK* the President was faced with two difficult questions:

(1) Is it appropriate to withhold information from respondents to an application made under the FM(CP)A 2007, and if so on what basis?

(2) If it is appropriate to withhold such information how can the proceedings continue in a manner that protects the rights of all of the people involved?

The issue arose because there was information known to the court and important to disposal of the application that could not, in order to protect a third party to the application, be revealed to the respondents. It had been considered by previous judges that the information was vital to the proceedings and as such the focus of the eventual hearing was upon how that information could be protected.

The President held that it was possible to withhold information from respondents to proceedings under the Act both on a balance of the fundamental rights of the person to be protected, the provider of the information and the respondents and as part of the inherent protective function of the Act itself.

In anticipation of such a conclusion, it was suggested that the fair disposal of the proceedings necessitated the appointment of special advocates, but this argument was rejected by the President in this case as, focusing upon the wishes and feelings of the person to be protected, it was held that the appropriate approach was to appoint an expert in honour-based violence to meet with the person to be protected and thereafter report to the court.

What was at that stage a very complicated question involving a lengthy process of disclosure, consideration of risk, balancing of rights and ultimate determination of the issue has now been greatly simplified however by the advent of the Family Procedure Rules 2010 and particularly r 11.7(2) which provides that:

> 'The court may direct the withholding of any submissions made, or any evidence adduced, for or at any hearing in proceedings to which this Part applies —
> (a) in order to protect the person who is the subject of the proceedings or any other person; or
> (b) for any other good reason.'

It therefore appears that the complicated decision-making process (as outlined by Mcfarlane J in *Re T (Wardship: Impact of Police Intelligence)*[85]) has now been replaced by a relatively simple determination as to whether the withholding of information can be said to be in the best interests of the person to be protected or there is any other good reason to withhold the said information. If either of the two tests is met the information may be withheld and the proceedings must continue on the basis that the information will not be released.

If that is the case then, absent the exceptional case where the appointment of special advocates is appropriate, it would appear as though factual determination is likely to be impossible which adds weight to the suggestion that even on an application to vary and/or discharge the respondents rights are limited to the making of representations rather than any form of factual enquiry.

It is, however respectfully suggested that McFarlane J's analysis of the approach to withheld evidence remains of assistance in guiding the applicant's consideration. It will be necessary to remain vigilant as to the possibility of withholding information from the commencement of the application and only information that can be disclosed should therefore be included on the application form or any statement that is to be disclosed to the parties. If there is information that it is important that the court receives at the initial application that information may be included in either a statement or position statement clearly marked 'Not for disclosure' and for which leave must be obtained not to disclose at that hearing. It may also be necessary to obtain an order against the recording facilities of the court in which the application is heard to prevent transcription of the hearing.

It is always necessary to be extremely vigilant where there is evidence that should not be disclosed as it is self-evident that if it is inadvertently released there will be a considerable risk to the person to be protected (or another provider of information). Measures such as the holding of any documents containing withheld information in a sealed envelope on the court file, keeping the court file in a secure location or nominating a member of the court staff to be responsible for the file and the flow of information from it may be required and should be imposed at the earliest possible opportunity.

---

[85]   [2009] EWHC 2440 (Fam), [2010] 1 FLR 1048 at [112] (i)–(iii).

17.4.2 Other forms of available protection and the interrelation of the Act with them

17.4.2.1 Domestic proceedings

Whilst the Act provides extensive, flexible and tailored protection to victims and potential victims of a forced marriage (or other acts that might accompany such an abuse) there are other remedies available that may be utilised by victims or those associated with them to provide a full protective package. The protection available may be obtained through the courts (on the application of the person to be protected or person associated with them or otherwise) or via other authorities such as the police.

It is important when considering an application for a forced marriage protection order to keep the following mechanisms in mind and to consider from whom the protection may be best obtained in order to provide for the needs of the particular case.

17.4.2.2 Remedies available through the courts

On the application of the person to be protected a forced marriage protection order may be supplemented by orders made under Part IV of the Family Law Act 1996 and in particular non-molestation and, if appropriate, occupation orders. A non-molestation order, if the relevant criteria set down under the Act are met, may have the particular advantage that its breach constitutes an arrestable offence, thereby providing the person to be protected with immediate protection where, for example, a power of arrest could not be granted under the Act.[86]

An occupation order may be a useful remedy in certain cases, although it must be borne in mind that there is very likely to be a risk of honour-based violence and as such it may be more appropriate to seek alternative accommodation for the person to be protected rather than seeking to establish them in their previous property to the exclusion of their family members who may, as a result of the proceedings, seek to do them harm.

It may also be worth considering whether the Protection from Harassment Act 1997 applies to the circumstances arising within the case, particularly if due to the circumstances of those involved relief by way of a non-molestation order is not available. There has typically been little difficulty in adding non-molestation style provisions to a forced marriage protection order however, and as such further applications outside of the scope of the instant proceedings may prove unnecessary.

---

[86]   Though it is readily recognised that such situations will necessarily be rare.

In certain circumstances, and particularly where either: (a) the person to be protected is a child; or (b) where the person to be protected is an elder child or an adult but there are other children at risk within the household, it may be beneficial to notify the local authority of the application to be made. If instructed by the person to be protected directly this will be a matter for their instructions; if acting on information received whilst the person to be protected is outside of the jurisdiction it may be a matter of judgment. However, the following factors may be of relevance:

(a) If there are children of a similar age to the person to be protected within the home and the person to be protected becomes subject to an order, the respondents may seek to force an alternative child into marriage.

(b) If the person to be protected is outside of the jurisdiction of England and Wales then making any other children within the jurisdiction the subject of orders (either within the proceedings or on the application of the local authority) will prevent their removal and therefore may prevent the family from leaving and frustrating the proceedings.

(c) It may be apparent that any other children within the jurisdiction are at similar risk, and if that is so the duty to protect those children may necessitate action by way of referral.

Even outside of the situations referred to above a referral to the local authority may be of assistance in obtaining information about the family through an authoritative source, perhaps by a court direction to file a report pursuant to s 7 of the Children Act 1989, s 37 of the same Act or otherwise.

The involvement of the local authority may bring about concurrent or alternatively joined care proceedings. There is currently no guidance concerning how these two distinct forms of application might inter-relate, and it is obvious that quite different approaches will apply to them in light of the points raised earlier in this chapter. It is suggested that where there are such concurrent proceedings it will be appropriate to consider and conclude the protective, injunctive remedy pursuant to the Act as a preliminary step in line with the principles espoused herein. The care proceedings can then proceed in the normal way with protection available under the Act as necessary.

It must be stressed that whilst the Act provides a flexible and effective remedy to cases where it is alleged that a person may be or has been the subject of a forced marriage it should not be seen as a panacea appropriate and effective in all cases. There are a number of mechanisms by which a person may be protected and each should be considered for their suitability to a particular case. The possibility that other remedies may in due course become more appropriate should be considered at the outset so that the initial application (whether under the Act or otherwise) can be made in an appropriate venue. By way of example, if it appears likely that care proceedings will involve a forced marriage element, but are commenced in a family proceedings court with no link to a designated forced marriage court, it may be appropriate to issue at a court from which the application can be immediately transferred, so that all aspects of a linked application can be dealt with by the same judge.

17.4.2.3 *Protection from other sources*

In addition to the courts it may be necessary to consider other forms of protection to ensure the safety of those involved (either as the subject or a provider of information) with proceedings under the Act.

The obvious first port of call for such protection will be the local police force, who may be able to provide a number of services, from a safe and well check to full witness protection depending on the particular requirements of the case before the court.

Beyond that it may be appropriate to seek advice and assistance from a number of agencies including but not limited to:

- the Forced Marriage Unit of the Foreign and Commonwealth Office;

- non-governmental organisations (for a list of specialised NGOs see **17.6.2**);

- charities who may provide assistance with accommodation;

- shelters and hostels;

- any other agency as may assist.

It will be particularly important to identify alternative sources of support and accommodation where the person to be protected is continuing to live at home but, in the event that an application is to be issued, will need to leave for their own safety as they may be dissuaded from seeking the protection of the courts without the comfort of knowing they will have an alternative place to go.

It may be that it is the police that seek to issue the application, in which case leave will be required pursuant to the FLA 1996, s 63C(3). Whilst there is no difficulty in an application being commenced in this way, some care is required in the manner in which the initial circumstances are investigated and thereafter progressed due to the possibility that the same police force will move from a protective to an investigative function in the event that either the order is breached or a separate offence is committed within the currency of proceedings. This will particularly be the case if there is information withheld from the respondents in the civil proceedings.

To consider a scenario: A and B (the parents) are forcing C (the person to be protected) to enter into a marriage. C is in a relationship with D (the boyfriend). The prospective groom is E (the groom), he knows about the boyfriend and has sought to dissuade him from seeing the person to be protected. The police force commence an application under the Act on the basis of C's complaint to them, but C does not want the parents to know that she has made this complaint and she wants to remain living at home. The parents do not know about D, and C does not want them to know.

This is a fairly common circumstance within an application under the Act. In such a case an application would be made to withhold the following information from the parents, who would become the respondents to the application:

- the fact of C's complaint to the police force; and

- the fact of C's ongoing relationship with D.

The proceedings continue on this basis, but during the course of the proceedings and before a final order is made E commits assault occasioning actual bodily harm on D, who is badly injured. The police pass the file to the CPS and they intend to prosecute E. The case is transferred to the Crown Court and E's representatives call the police officer involved, who is the same officer as is dealing with the application for a forced marriage protection order to give evidence.

That officer is then in difficulty. Within the civil proceedings relevant information providing E with a motive to attack D is withheld from the parents for the safety of C, the person to be protected. Within the criminal proceedings that is information important to the prosecution and within the knowledge of the police officer who will give evidence. That officer will be unable to withhold that information from the courts.

There is no easy way to resolve such an issue. It is therefore respectfully suggested that prior to initiating any application under the Act, a police force would be assisted by:

- consideration of a separation of responsibility amongst their officers, with some designated to deal with the civil side of the proceedings and other officers to deal with any criminal consequence;

- discussion with the CPS and the force solicitors about what approach should be adopted in such circumstances;

- if it is the force practice to make applications under the Act, it may be beneficial to consider a working protocol to adopt in such circumstances that is made known to the local courts dealing with applications under the Act and any criminal consequence of such an application.

17.4.2.4 *International proceedings*

Whilst there have been a greater number of applications relating to people at risk within the jurisdiction of England and Wales the cases of greatest difficulty under the Act will most often be those where the person to be protected (and, perhaps, certain of the respondents) are outside of the jurisdiction of England and Wales.

The provisions of the Act extend to conduct both within and without the jurisdiction of England and Wales and the courts have typically been swift to extend the protection afforded by the Act (and prior to that the inherent jurisdiction) to those who find themselves in difficulty in foreign countries where it can be found to have jurisdiction to do so.[87]

There are, though, unique challenges that arise in such circumstances including but not limited to the following:

- how any order that is obtained can be enforced against the respondents where they are outside of the jurisdiction;

- how the person to be protected can be returned from the foreign country in which they find themselves;

- what assistance can be obtained from other sources in such cases.

Prior to addressing these difficulties, however, it is necessary to consider certain other practical difficulties.

The first matter to consider is who should be made a respondent to the application if one or both of the primary protagonists are outside of the jurisdiction. In such circumstances it would be beneficial to investigate where possible what other family members are in England and Wales and how they may be involved (if at all). If an address at which the family resides when in England is known a Land Registry search may be performed to find out if the property is owned outright. Similarly enquiries may be made of the Department for Work and Pensions and/or Her Majesty's Revenue and Customs to ascertain if the family are in

---

[87] Typically as a result of habitual residence, though there is no such specific requirement under the Act itself.

receipt of any benefits and if so into what bank accounts those benefits are paid. In the future such information may enable the freezing of assets if the respondents are in breach of orders with which they have been served.

It will be necessary to identify a method of service operable in the jurisdiction in which the respondents are present, whether by e-mail or by process server.

It may also be helpful to make enquiries of the FMU to see if contact can be made with the British Consulate or Embassy in that jurisdiction (in the event that the person to be protected is a British Citizen) so that consular assistance may be provided.

Once these enquiries have been made the form of order sought at the initial hearing should be considered. In order to fulfil the terms of the Act a mechanism must be established by which the wishes and feelings of the person to be protected can be ascertained. Whilst it is possible to attempt this process by telephone call or webcam such methods are fraught with difficulty due to the possibility that either it will not be the person to be protected that speaks on the telephone or, if it is, they may not be in a position to express their true wishes and feelings.

For those reasons it is often more effective either to seek an order that the person to be protected be produced at the nearest British consulate (in the event that they have agreed to assist in the process) or that they be returned to the jurisdiction of England and Wales to express their views directly to the solicitor or, preferably, to the court. Arrangements could then be put in place with the assistance of the police, local authority or other non-governmental organisation to ensure their safety upon return, with appropriate alternative accommodation if desired.

Where proceedings are commenced with the person to be protected outside of the jurisdiction, particularly if they are in a country with a common law history, it can be useful from an enforcement perspective to utilise the inherent jurisdiction,[88] which is readily recognised by such jurisdictions and may add weight to the operation of the Act.

17.5 REMEDYING A FORCED MARRIAGE

Following a forced marriage protection order, or alternatively where a victim of forced marriage had not previously been aware that they were entitled, or perhaps had been unable, to access the protection available from the courts and as such had endured a forced marriage, it is likely that they will seek advice about what remedies are available to them.

---

[88]   The possibility of this being specifically envisaged by FLA 1996, s 63R(2).

Whilst the usual course of action would be to suggest that a person wishing to end a marriage obtain a divorce from their spouse, such an approach is often unpalatable to someone who has been subjected to a forced marriage due to:

- the stigma that is often attached to a divorcee within the communities in which forced marriage is common; and

- the implicit legitimisation of the marriage in circumstances in which the victim is likely to view the marriage as illegitimate as a result of their lack of consent.

There are, however, two available remedies that avoid the stigma of divorce and recognise the illegitimacy of the initial ceremony whilst extracting the victim from the marriage. These are the more traditional route of an application for nullity and the more recently discovered route of a declaration within the inherent jurisdiction of the High Court that there was no marriage capable of recognition in the jurisdiction of England and Wales.

17.5.1 Nullity

Under the Matrimonial Causes Act 1973 (MCA 1973) a marriage may be either void ab initio or alternatively voidable by the issue of a decree of nullity. For a marriage to be void ab initio in a usual forced marriage context, pursuant to MCA 1973, s 11 the following subsections are likely to apply:

(a)   that the parties are within the prohibited degrees of relationship;[89] or

(b)   that either party is under the age of 16.[90]

Where a marriage is void ab initio no further action is necessarily required, although the other party to the marriage may seek to challenge this by seeking a declaration that the marriage was valid at its inception under the relevant provisions within s 55(1) of the Family Law Act 1986.

Where a marriage is forced, however, the provision under which nullity is most often sought is MCA 1973, s 12(c), by which a marriage is voidable where 'either party to the marriage did not validly consent to it, whether in consequence of duress, mistake, unsoundness of mind or otherwise' or alternatively, in an appropriate case 'that at the time of the marriage either party, though capable of giving a valid consent, was suffering (whether continuously or intermittently) from mental disorder within the meaning of [the Mental Health Act 1983] of such a kind or to such an extent as to be unfitted for marriage'. The use of a petition of nullity in

---

[89]   MCA 1973, s 11(a)(i).
[90]   MCA 1973, s 11(a)(ii).

such a case was advocated by Coleridge J in *P v R (Forced Marriage: Annulment: Procedure)*,[91] in which the learned judge said that:

> 'In cases where a forced marriage is alleged the proper course is for a petition under s 12(c) to be brought before the court. I am informed by counsel for the petitioner that there is a real stigma attached to a woman in the petitioner's situation if merely a divorce decree is pronounced and it is desirable from all points of view that where a genuine case of forced marriage exists the court should, where appropriate, grant a decree of nullity and as far as possible remove any stigma that would otherwise attach to the fact that a person in the petitioner's situation has been married.' [92]

The burden of proof is to the ordinary civil standard, to which the petitioner must prove the facts in their petition by oral evidence heard in open court, and particularly, in the case of a forced marriage, that 'the threats, pressure, or whatever it is, is such as to destroy the reality of consent and overbears the will of the individual'.[93]

There are, however, bars to relief to a voidable marriage as set out by MCA 1973, s 13:

> '(1) The court shall not, in proceedings instituted after 31st July 1971, grant a decree of nullity on the ground that a marriage is voidable if the respondent satisfies the court —
> (a) that the petitioner, with knowledge that it was open to him to have the marriage avoided, so conducted himself in relation to the respondent as to lead the respondent reasonably to believe that he would not seek to do so; and
> (b) that it would be unjust to the respondent to grant the decree.
>
> (2) Without prejudice to subsection (1) above, the court shall not grant a decree of nullity by virtue of section 12 above on the grounds mentioned in paragraph (c), (d), (e), (f) or (h) of that section unless —
> (a) it is satisfied that proceedings were instituted within the period of three years from the date of the marriage, or
> (b) leave for the institution of proceedings after the expiration of that period has been granted under subsection (4) below.'

The unfortunate reality of forced marriage cases can be that either: (a) the victims are prevented by their circumstances from seeking relief within 3 years; or, alternatively (b) that they do not realise that they can seek relief by way of nullity until after the expiration of the 3-year period. In such a case, unless the victim can fit themselves within subs (4), by which the time estimate can be extended where the judge is satisfied that the petitioner has suffered from a mental disorder within the 3-year period and it is just to extend the period, they cannot seek relief by way of nullity.

---

[91]   [2003] 1 FLR 661.
[92]   Ibid, at [17].
[93]   *Hirani v Hirani* (1983) 4 FLR 232, per Ormrod LJ.

Previously it had been assumed that where nullity was not available to a forced marriage victim they would have to rely on divorce as a remedy, however a recent line of authority has demonstrated that where nullity is not available a victim of forced marriage may seek relief by way of a declaration under the inherent jurisdiction of the High Court.

17.5.2   Declarations under the inherent jurisdiction of the High Court

In the recent case of *Re P (Forced Marriage)*[94] Baron J considered a case where the wife would have sought nullity on the basis that she did not consent to the marriage were she not disbarred from doing so due to the expiration of the 3-year time limit. In forming her conclusions the judge was referred to recent authorities concerning declaratory relief, including *B v I (Forced Marriage)*,[95] *SH v NB (Marriage: Consent)*[96] and *City of Westminster v IC (By His Friend the Official Solicitor) and KC and NN.*[97]

Baron J accepted that, in a genuine case of forced marriage nullity was the appropriate remedy pursuant to MCA 1973, s 12(c). Where such a remedy was unavailable to a victim of forced marriage the court would be prohibited from making a declaration that the marriage was at its inception void under Family Law Act 1986, s 55. It was, however, possible for the court to grant a declaration under the inherent jurisdiction that the marriage was not capable of recognition in the jurisdiction of England and Wales, drawing on the aforementioned authorities but first established in *City of Westminster v IC (By His Friend the Official Solicitor) and KC and NN.*

In accordance with *SH v NB (Marriage: Consent)* the appropriate application is for a declaration as set out above made by Originating Summons in the High Court. The application can be made by ex parte application in appropriate circumstances, for example where it is necessary to withhold the petitioner's address, where the summons is to be issued without the marriage certificate (if there is one) or, and perhaps most importantly, where it is feared that repercussions may flow from the issue of the summons such as to necessitate an application for protection by way of orders made under FM(CP)A 2007.

In *Re P* Baron J applied the test as established by *Hirani v Hirani* to the question of a declaration – finding in that case that the test was met. It is therefore apparent that the same principles as apply to an application for nullity will be applied to a declaration, notwithstanding the different approach within FM(CP)A 2007 itself.

---

[94]   [2011] 1 FLR 2060.
[95]   [2010] 1 FLR 1721.
[96]   [2009] EWHC 3274 (Fam), [2010] 1 FLR 1927.
[97]   [2008] EWCA Civ 198, [2008] 2 FLR 267.

The additional benefit of the use of such a declaration may be that the mechanism can be used (if considered appropriate or beneficial to the victim of a forced marriage) even where the victim has been compelled to undergo a ceremony purporting to be one of marriage that would not be recognised under English civil law, but which may nonetheless be considered by someone of a particular faith to bind them to a marriage.

It is therefore apparent that notwithstanding any delay in the making of an application it will seldom be necessary for a victim of forced marriage to seek a divorce: remedies are available either under nullity or, if that is not available, within the inherent jurisdiction. Due to the flexibility of the remedies available and the purposive and sensitive approach adopted by the courts to victims of such a fundamental breach of their human rights, a victim of forced marriage need not face the stigma of divorce.

17.6 USEFUL MATERIALS

17.6.1 Key cases

- *A Local Authority v DL* [2011] EWHC 1022 (Fam)

- *R (Quila) v Secretary of State for the Home Department* [2011] UKSC 45

- *R (Quila) v Secretary of State for the Home Department* [2010] EWCA Civ 1482, [2011] 1 FLR 1187

- *Re P (Forced Marriage)* [2010] EWHC 3467 (Fam), [2011] 1 FLR 2060

- *A Chief Constable and AA v YK* [2010] EWHC 2438 (Fam), [2011] 1 FLR 1493

- *B v I (Forced Marriage)* [2010] 1 FLR 1721

- *Re HM (Vulnerable Adult: Injunction)* [2010] EWHC 870 (Fam), [2010] 2 FLR 1057

- *SH v NB (Marriage: Consent)* [2009] EWHC 3274 (Fam), [2010] 1 FLR 1927

- *Re T (Wardship: Impact of Police Intelligence)* [2009] EWHC 2440 (Fam), [2010] 1 FLR 1048

- *City of Westminster v IC (By His Friend the Official Solicitor) and KC and NN* [2008] EWCA Civ 198, [2008] 2 FLR 267

- *Re SA (Vulnerable Adult with Capacity: Marriage)* [2005] EWHC 2942 (Fam), [2006] 1 FLR 867

- *Re SK (Proposed Plaintiff) (An Adult by way of her Litigation Friend)* [2004] EWHC 3202 (Fam), [2005] 2 FLR 230

- *P v R (Forced Marriage: Annulment: Procedure)* [2003] 1 FLR 661

- *Re KR (Abduction: Forcible Removal by Parents)* [1999] 2 FLR 542

17.6.2 Useful contact details

The Forced Marriage Unit
Tel: 0207 008 0151
E-mail: fmu@fco.gov.uk
Website: http://www.fco.gov.uk/en/travel-and-living-abroad/when-things-go-wrong/forced-marriage/

Ashiana Network
Telephone – 0208 539 0427/9656
E-mail – info@ashiana.org.uk
Website – http://www.ashiana.org.uk

Equality and Human Rights Commission
Tel: 0845 604 6610
E-mail: englandhelpline@equalityhumanrights.com
Hyperlink – http://www.equalityhumanrights.com

The Henna Foundation
Tel: 02920 496920
E-mail : info@hennafoundation.org
Website: http://www.hennafoundation.org/

Karma Nirvana
Telephone – 0800 999247 (Honour Network Helpline)
Electronic communication through their webpage at
http://www.karmanirvana.org.uk/contact-us.html
Website: http://www.karmanirvana.org.uk

Southall Black Sisters
Tel: 0208 571 9800 (Helpline)/0208 571 9595 (General Enquiries)
E-mail: info@southallblacksisters.co.uk
Website: http://www.southallblacksisters.org.uk

Reunite
Tel: 01162 556234 (Advice line)/01162 555345 (General Enquiries)
E-mail: reunite@dircon.co.uk
Website: http://www.reunite.org

17.6.3 Further resources

In addition to the resources detailed above (which are directed towards information, help and support) the following may be of assistance when preparing applications to court or otherwise considering cases:

Legal Services Commission guidance on funding
http://www.legalservices.gov.uk/docs/cls_main/
forcedmarriagefundinginformation221208.pdf

CPS Guidelines on Honour-Based Violence and Forced Marriage
http://www.cps.gov.uk/legal/h_to_k/honour_based_violence_and_forced_
marriage/

Ministry of Justice Guidance on Forced Marriage
http://www.justice.gov.uk/guidance/freedom-and-rights/forced-
marriage.htm

Application form for a Forced Marriage Protection Order (Form FL401a)
http://www.familylaw.co.uk/system/uploads/attachments/0002/2163/
fl401A_w.pdf

PART V

CASE DIGEST

CHAPTER 18

CASE SUMMARIES

18.1 INTRODUCTION

The purpose of this Case Digest is to record the important cases of the last 3 years, in a way that can convey their effect and relevance without over-burdening the text.

Further, the cases are set out under category order, the intention being that if one reads all the cases as so digested in that category, one can assimilate the legal framework beyond the individual cases.

In this context, each case is also used as a peg, where possible, to refer to other cases with a nexus, so that a legal issue can be researched speedily, given the time constraints for contemporary practice.

18.2 ABDUCTION

M v M [2008] EWHC 2049 (Fam), per Black J

Ordering of father and two children [9 and 6] back to Poland. This was the second time the father had brought the children to England to live, the first ostensibly on holiday and the second, in flagrant breach of a court order and by deception. Children wished to remain in England in the schools where they had previously been enrolled. **Held: *Children to return*. (1) *'Settlement' not established within the meaning of Art 12 of Hague Convention. For*: Links with the local area and doing well enough in school. *Against*: Children's awareness of the insecurity of their situation and influence of father militating against settling into a normal life in UK. (2) *Art 13 not established:* No weight to be attached to children's views because of considerable influence of father's views preventing children from maturing in a normal way in relation to their feelings as to the future. (3) Mother, through father's fault, had not had knowledge of children's whereabouts for at least a year. Thus *jurisdiction remained with Polish courts* within the meaning of Art 10 of the Council Regulation (EC) No 2201/2003 concerning jurisdiction and the recognition and enforcement of judgments in matrimonial matters and in matters of parental responsibility. **Note:** Where a *period of 1 year has elapsed* between the date of wrongful removal and the commencement of Hague Convention proceedings it is necessary to consider whether the children have become settled in their new environment; **Art 12.** See also *Re M (Abduction: Zimbabwe)* [2007] UKHL 55, [2008] 1 FLR 251, and comment at [2008] Fam Law 298. The observations of Thorpe LJ in *Cannon* [2005] EWCA Civ 1330; [2005] 1 FLR 169 were of particular assistance to Black J in relation to their focus on an *'alleged settlement that is built on concealment and deceit'.*

Re RC and BC (Child Abduction) (Brussels II Revised: Article 11(7)) (28 July 2008) [2009] 1 FLR 574, per Singer J

Father returned to Portugal with one child upon separating from mother with whom he had come from Portugal to England to work *with their 2 children*. Holding that the removal from England was not unlawful, the Lisbon court declined to make a return order on the mother's application under the Hague Convention on Civil Aspects of International Child Abduction 1980 for the return of the elder child (which had been forwarded to the Portugal Central Authority which forwarded it to the Lisbon Family Court). The father had joint parental responsibility for the child and had the right to decide the child's place of residence. The mother appealed in Portugal and commenced High Court proceedings inviting the court to conduct an examination of the issues pursuant to Art 11(7) of Council Regulation (EC) No 2201/2003 concerning jurisdiction and the recognition and enforcement of judgments in matrimonial matters and in matters of parental responsibility, repealing Regulation (EC) No 1347/2000 [2003] OJ L338/1 (*Brussels II R*). **Held:** *Mother's application struck out. Only where the child's non-return was pursuant to Art 13 of the Hague Convention would the English court have been competent to 'examine the question of custody of the child' as envisaged by Art 11(7).* Here child's non-return was not pursuant to Art 13 [Art 13 concerns consent or acquiescence, grave risk of harm to the child or the child's objections. Here, the Portuguese court had held the removal to be lawful].

Re RD (Child Abduction) (Brussels II R: Articles 11(7) and 19) (15 August 2008) [2009] 1 FLR 586, per Singer J

The *boy*, now aged **9**, had been *born in England* and spent his first years here with his father and **Portuguese mother**. The parents separated and later the mother *unilaterally* removed the boy to Portugal where he attended an English school, and lived **with his maternal aunt** while the mother underwent psychiatric treatment. Over a year later a Portuguese court found that the boy had been wrongly removed by the mother under the Hague Convention and made a *non-return order under Article 12* and other orders. In October 2007 the father began High Court proceedings in England seeking *relief under Art 11(7)* of Brussels II R for the return of the boy to England and, in January 2008, for residence and/or contact under the Children Act 1989. **Held**: (1) *Art 11(7) did not apply* because the non-return order had been made pursuant to Art 12 and not Art 13. (2) The English court must defer to the determination of the Portuguese court to proceeding with the *mother's parental responsibility application* with which it was first seised. (3) Comment: Arts 11(6), (7) and (8) of Brussels II R grafts on a wholly new jurisdictional opportunity for the unsuccessful party to Hague litigation in the receiving state to re-litigate the question of return to the child's home state *in the courts of the home state. But for this jurisdiction to kick in, the order for the child's return must have been made pursuant to Art 13 and not Art 12*. Art 13 sets up the defences of 'consent or acquiescence', 'grave risk of harm or an intolerable situation' or the objection of a mature child, and is relevant even where the child was taken less than 12 months before. Where that is the case Art 11(7) of Brussels II R enables the court to 'examine the question of custody of the child' thus instituting a welfare-based enquiry. *However, where the abduction has lasted for longer, Art 12 requires the child to be returned* unless the proceedings had begun more than 12 months after the child's wrongful removal and he was settled in his new environment.

B v D (Abduction: Wardship) [2008] EWHC 1246 (Fam)

Portuguese father, British mother and two children born in London. Mother persuaded to permit children *to move to Portugal temporarily,* on basis of efforts to salvage in England, the marriage. **Held:** In exercise of the inherent jurisdiction of the High Court and ordering the return of the children to the UK as soon as was practicable: **(1)** *No child sent abroad merely for the purposes of education can be said to have changed his or her habitual residence.* The only basis upon which the children in England could have changed their habitual residence was if the mother had given true and voluntary consent: on the facts, she only agreed to them going abroad for short-term education while the parties resolved their differences. She thus did not give the necessary consent in law. **(2)** On the authorities, *attempts to save a marriage or attempts to reach a voluntary agreement for the return of children did not amount to acquiescence*. Here, as a matter of law, there was *no acquiescence.* On the facts, the parents and children were all habitually resident in the UK and the present court thus had unchallengeable jurisdiction. **(3)** Where two remedies were available in different courts in different jurisdictions, the Hague Convention on International Child Abduction did not take automatic precedence. The present court was the primary court with the primary jurisdiction, it was considered it appropriate to exercise that jurisdiction and the Portuguese court was bound to cede jurisdiction under the terms of *Brussels II R.*

Re G (Abduction) [2008] EWHC 2558 (Fam), [2009] 1 FLR 760

Mother *did not return 11 year old daughter to Lithuania* after a summer holiday in England. *Father began 'Hague' proceedings.* Mother *conceded* wrongful retention of child but *argued Article 13.* As to how to approach the issue of a child's objections, Black J identified four questions: **(1)** Are the objections to return made out? Is the child objecting to being returned to the *country of habitual residence,* or simply expressing a *preference to stay* with the abducting parent? **(2)** Has the child reached an *age* and *degree of maturity* at which it is appropriate to take account of his or her views? **(3)** Have those views been shaped or coloured by *undue influence* or pressure directly or indirectly exerted by the abducting parents, to an extent which requires them to be disregarded or discounted? **(4)** If it is appropriate to take account of the child's objections, in exercising the court's discretion whether or not to order return, what *weight should be placed* on those objections in the light of any countervailing factors and in particular, the *philosophy of the Convention* (ie *deterrence* of abductors, *comity* and *respect* for the judicial processes of the requesting state, and welfare considerations directed to the child in question)? **Per curiam:** Hague cases have become increasingly technical, frequently giving rise to sophisticated arguments as to how the Convention, which itself is drafted in really quite broad terms, should be interpreted. This process, by lengthening and complicating cases, is anathema to the ability of the courts to deal with Hague returns speedily and summarily as their international obligations and the interests of children require that they should.

A v B (Abduction: Rights of Custody: Declaration of Wrongful Removal) [2008] EWHC 2524 (Fam), [2009] 1 FLR 1253, per Bodey J.

Father had ex parte orders for parental responsibility and to prevent the mother from abducting the child. *Mother abducted child to France before ex parte orders could be served* and French court dismissed father's Hague application under a misapprehension as to English law, taken from an expert opinion on English law. Father applied under s 8 of the Child Abduction And Custody Act 1985 that he and/or the English court had 'rights of custody' for the purposes of the Convention. **Held: (1)** *English court had jurisdiction* to make the declaration, even though not requested by the French court but by the father: *Re P (Abduction: Declaration)* [1995] 1 FLR 831. **(2)** *In the ex parte situation, the court obtains rights of custody once there has been some judicial determination*, even if only by way of judicial case management and this is all the more so where, as here, the court has made a substantive order; following *Re J (Abduction: Declaration of Wrongful Removal)* [1999] 2 FLR 653 per Hale J and *Re C (Child Abduction: Unmarried Father: rights of Custody)* [2003] 1 FLR 252. **(3)** The ruling was made on the basis that the French court would respect the English court's declaration. This is consistent with the HL decision in

Re D (Abduction: Rights of Custody) [2007] 1 FLR 961 which criticised a lower English court for rejecting an Art 15 declaration made by a Roumania Court but rather solicited expert evidence as to Romanian Law.

Re E (Abduction: Intolerable Situation) [2008] EWHC 2112, [2009] 2 FLR 485, per Moylan J

Refusal to order an 11-year-old child's return to Oregon, when mother had taken the child aged 7 ostensibly for a holiday in England, but settled with her English partner with whom she had a child. **Grounds for ruling in relation to the grounds of defence advanced by the mother:**

- *Defence 1*: *acquiescence?* No – acquiescence was a factual matter of a parent's subjective intention; see *Re H (Abduction: Acquiescence)* [1998] AC 72. **The father had not acquiesced.**

- *Defence 2:* child's objections. The approach to consideration of a child's objections was set out by Baroness Hale is *Re M (Abduction: Zimbabwe)* [2008] 1 FLR 251. The child's objections to return were **Art 13 genuine** and based on his own views, he being of ordinary maturity for an 11-year-old.

- *Defence 3*: grave psychological harm. Whilst the threshold for a grave risk of psychological harm and / or an intolerable situation was a high one, on the facts, **there was such a grave risk under Article 13(b)**. See *Re C (Abduction: Grave Risk of Psychological Harm*) [1999] 1 FLR 1145; and *Re D (A Child) (Abduction: Custody Rights)* [2007] 1 AC 619.

- *Defence 4: Child settled in England? Yes* – the court has to consider not only the **physical** nature of the child's settlement but also the *psychological* and *emotional* elements: *Cannon v Cannon* [2005] 1 FLR 169. *Concealment or other subterfuge by the abductor is an important consideration*. On the facts, the child was settled and the uncertainty as to immigration status was not such as to render the position otherwise.

- *Defence 5*: The English court was in a better position to decide on welfare issues.

M v T [2008] EWHC 1383, [2009] 1 FLR 1309, per Pauffley J

Having lived her life with the father and their children in *Spain,* the mother resolved on a *return to England* and she entered into a *notarised* agreement with the father for *shared* responsibility, with the father having care of the eldest child and the mother care of the youngest with detailed provision as to *contact.* The mother left for England precipitately without saying goodbye to the eldest two children and *breached the agreement* by not returning the youngest child for contact and setting up several obstacles to communication with the father. The father pursuant to the agreement, sent the eldest child to England for contact, but at the end of the contact period and thereafter, he was unable to communicate with the mother or with the two children. The father applied for the return of the oldest and youngest child pursuant to the Hague Convention. **Held:** *The children be returned to Spain.* Vis-à-vis the conventional lines of argument:

- *Acquiescence:* Not established – the father had demonstrated his expectation that contact arrangements would be complied with by flying to England on three occasions.

- *Children's views:* Probably influenced by mother – it was incumbent on the mother to return to Spain and to participate in proceedings there.

- *Grave risk of psychological harm and or intolerable situation vis-à-vis child[ren]:* Not established.

- *Where were the children settled, taking into account psychological and emotional elements?* In Spain.

- *Consent [concealment and subterfuge relevant]*: The mother had never had the slightest of intentions of complying with the notarised order; her cruel deception vitiated the father's consent to the removal of the youngest child.

Per curiam: Even if the mother's defences had been made out, the court would in the exercise of its discretion have ordered the children's return. Reasons for so doing were comity, that they had lived all their lives in Spain, and the mother's attempt to exclude the father from their lives.

Re Z (Abduction) [2008] EWHC 3473 (Fam), per Macur J

Against a backdrop of *matrimonial discord,* after 3 years of living in *Israel* [the family having been *originally habitually resident in England*] the mother *removed the children to England.* The father did not commence proceedings for the children's return to Israel under the Hague Convention on the Civil aspects of International Child Abduction 1980 *until almost one year after the children's removal. Held*: **(1)** As a fact, children had been *habitually resident in Israel.* **(2)** No consent or acquiescence by the father. *The delay of one year* by the father did *not amount to acquiesance.* **(3)** *No* clear and compelling evidence of *grave* risk of harm or other *intolerability.* **(4)** In the circumstances of the children's ages *[7 and 5]* and degree of *maturity*, their objections to return to Israel did not prevail. *Per Curiam*: Had the court had a discretion it would have declined to order the return of the children to Israel. *After a long delay the* *children had settled in England and, but for the Hague Convention, the appropriate forum to determine their long-term interests would have been England.* **Note: (1)** The dismissal of the Art 13 defences raised by the mother is a standard illustration of a failure to meet the high evidential threshold to be met. **(2)** *An individual child's interests are not the paramount consideration* in determining the question of return under the Convention; *the general policy is that long-term welfare issues of children as a class are best determined by the courts of habitual residence.*

AAA v ASH, Registrar-General for England and Wales etc [2009] EWHC 636 (Fam)

'Nikah' marriage between British father and Dutch mother in England not valid. Father registered child's birth without mother, producing Islamic marriage certificate. *Mother 7 months later abducts child to Holland.* Father applies for summary return under Hague Convention. **Held:** 'rights of custody' is to be interpreted in accordance with *autonomous jurisprudence* of the Convention. (2) For registration of child to be valid, both parents had to be in attendance. *(Nikah marriage not void or voidable, but a 'non-marriage').* (3) No presumption of marriage following marriage ceremony. (4) Rights of custody could not arise through estoppel or legitimate expectation. (5) No breach of Arts 6, 8, 9, 12 or 14 under Convention.

RS v KS (Abduction: Wrongful Detention) [2009] EWHC 1494 (Fam)

Lithuanian couple; mother abducts child to England. For the purpose of establishing when the 12 months period under Art 2 of the Convention begins to run, an un-communicated decision not to return the child reached before the agreed date of return does not of itself constitute wrongful retention. **Note**: Given the necessity of dating the point at which a wrongful retention occurred, there seems good reason to *require the decision not return the child be communicated or demonstrated* in some form to the other parent. Macur J held that child would face an intolerable situation and be at grave risk of psychological harm if he were to be returned to Lithuania.

Re H (Abduction) [2009] EWHC 1735 (Fam), [2009] 2 FLR 1513, per Wood J

With a history of domestic violence by father against mother, the parties *divorced* and though the family had lived for *many years in Spain*, the mother *abducted* the *14-year-old girl* and *11-year-old boy* to the UK declaring that she would not return, or return the children. The daughter's transition to the UK had been a *disaster* [94% absence from school, sexual relationship with a boy of 17 who had already fathered a child]; very poor relationship with mother; yet **declared** that she would commit **suicide** if returned to Spain. By contrast, the boy was settling well. **Held: Application to return the children refused.** The court made an interim supervision order, and directed the local authority to prepare a full **report** under **s 37** to be considered at a future directions hearing. The Spanish Court was invited to transfer any private law proceedings to England. **Comment: Hague Convention proceedings are family proceedings for the purposes of the Children Act 1989 and consequently the court is able to consider the lives of children under Part II or Part IV of that Act.** An interim supervision order cannot be made unless the court is satisfied that there are reasonable grounds for believing that the threshold conditions exist. As to the case law considered:

(i)   *Re M (Abduction: Brussels II R)* [2006] EWCA Civ 630, [2006] 2 FLR 1180: The Court of Appeal emphasised the fortifications to the Hague Convention by Brussels II R (BIIR) including the protective measures to nullify an Art 13(b) defence. The policy of BIIR together with the Convention constitute *a very weighty factor in favour of return*, but a return should not be ordered where a defence has been established and the circumstances of the particular case outweigh the policy of the Convention.

(ii) *Re D (Article 13B: Non Return)* [2006] EWCA Civ 146, [2006] 2 FLR 305 made clear that when an abductor was seeking to justify his or her conduct, *the evidence needed to be subjected to rigorous or even sceptical scrutiny.*

(iii) As to the 'harm' defence, see: *Re T (Abduction: Grave Risk of Psychological Harm)* [1999] 1 FLR 1145; *C v B (Abduction: Grave Risk)* [2005] EWHC 2988 (Fam), [2006] 1 FLR 1095; *Re C (Abduction: Grave Risk of Psychological Harm)* [1999] 2 FLR 478; *TB v JB (Abduction: Grave Risk of Harm)* [2001] 2 FLR 515 and *Re D (Abduction: Rights of Custody)* [2006] UKHL 51.

Re K (Rights of Custody: Spain) [2009] EWHC 1066 Fam

Abduction of child of **English** parents by mother from **Spain** to England. **Issue:** Had the father rights of custody under Art 3 pursuant to Spanish law? **Problem: the father did not have parental responsibility under English law, and the Spanish law appeared to be that the Spanish court would defer to the English personal law of the father.** But there was yet an exception under which Spanish law applied. The High Court took a pragmatic view. **Held:** that there were rights of custody under Spanish law, and that the mother had wrongly abducted the child by being in breach of the father's rights of custody under Spanish law.

C v H [2009] EWHC 2660 (Fam)

In *Re M (Abduction: Zimbabwe)* [2008] 1 FLR 251 [Munby J], **discretion was stated by the HL to be** at large and unfettered by any purported gloss of exceptionality; but nevertheless in reality it will be difficult successfully to argue for return of a child once a defence of consent is made out.

K v K (Abduction: Consent) [2009] EWHC 2721 (Fam), per Sumner J

[and also see next case]

Conflicting evidence of two **Polish parents** as to how the mother came to remove the children from their family residence in **Ireland,** to **Leeds**. **Issue:** The father's application under the Hague Convention for return of the children to Ireland. **Held**: On the evidence, the father knew that the mother was leaving with the children in March 2009 and that **he fully consented** to the move before she left. His later regret in relation to that decision did not affect the validity of the earlier consent. When she returned in August 2009, that consent was still operative. Cases referred to: *Re K (Abduction: Consent)* [1997] 2 FLR 212, which made clear that once a **full consent had been given to a permanent move, it could not later be withdrawn.** As to discretion: *Re M (Abduction: Zimbabwe)* [2007] UKHL 55; [2008] 1 FLR 251 per Baroness Hale:

> '... in consent or acquiescence cases ... general considerations of comity and confidence, particularly considerations relating to the speed of legal proceedings and approach to relocation in the home country and individual considerations relating to the particular child might point to the speedy return ...'

K v K (No 2) (Hague Convention: Adjournment) [2009] EWHC 891 (Fam)

Before the order in the above case was **perfected**, the **father** made an **application** for **reconsideration** of the application to adjourn and to admit further evidence which the judge had not seen. **Inter alia held**: Where there was an application to reconsider or reverse a judgment in a Hague Convention case after judgment had been given, it had to **satisfy the test of strong reasons**. Some relaxation of the rule in *Ladd v Marshall* was permitted in respect of **fresh evidence** for the reasons and to the extent set out in *Re M (Abduction: Non-Convention Country)* [1995] 1 FLR 89. If the application in respect of fresh evidence was made after the hearing **but before judgment** the difference was that there was no longer a need to find strong reasons. *Re M* alone would govern the approach to be taken.

R v K (Abduction: Return Order) [2009] EWHC 132 (Fam)

Child allegedly *abducted to England*. Father commenced proceedings in UK for summary return to Poland. Mother filed *a defence of consent and acquiescence* but then decided to *issue proceedings in Poland*. The English High Court was not asked to make findings on those defences. The mother *agreed* to the making of a return order but sought the court's ruling on whether such an order could be stayed or suspended until such time as she could obtain an order from the Polish court giving her interim permission to retain the child in this jurisdiction. **Held:** 17 days allowed before return. **Note:** The *father contended* that, since the court's discretion was not engaged, it was **(1)** prevented from entertaining the mother's application to suspend or delay the return order and **(2)** that general welfare considerations could not therefore be considered by the English court as they were firmly within the remit of the Polish court. Against this, the *mother argued* that **(1)** it was well established that the court had power to timetable a return in accordance with welfare and **(2)** that it was appropriate to suspend the return until after the conclusion of the first Polish hearing. Ryder J granted 17 days to the mother; *not* an amount of time which would enable her to remain here with the child until the conclusion of the Polish hearing. Cases referred to: *Re M (Abduction: International Judicial Collaboration)* [2000] 1 FLR 803, at 808 and 809; and the leading authority: *Re M (Abduction: Undertakings)* [1995] 1 FLR 1021.

X County Council v B (Abduction: Rights of Custody in the Court) [2009] EWHC 2635, [2010] 1 FLR 1197

Care proceedings issued on *5 November 2008*. Children abducted to Ireland on *6 November*. **Held:** Upon a court being *'seized'* of an application which involves the court's discretion and jurisdiction to determine the child's place of residence, then it is seized of *rights of custody* in respect of the child to which the application relates: *Re H (Abduction: Rights of Custody)* [2000] 2 AC 291, [2000] 1 FLR 374. In any case, the *quasi-judicial act* of the FPC legal adviser had already *vested the court* with rights of custody, since she had considered the matter and given directions for the future conduct of the proceedings: *Re C (Child Abduction) (Unmarried Father: Rights of Custody)* [2002] EWHC 2219 (Fam), [2003] 1 FLR 252. Macur J also invoked dicta of Hale J in *Re J (Abduction) (Declaration of Wrongful Removal)* [1999] 2 FLR 653:

> '... the court will be invested in rights of custody if, even before the respondent has been served, the matter comes before a judge who exercises a judicial discretion as to the future conduct of the proceedings, even if he makes no substantive order and only gives directions ... A judicially determined adjournment in the course of proceedings which have not yet been served will be sufficient. An administrative step without judicial involvement will not suffice.' [at [58] and [59]).

Re H (Abduction: Jurisdiction) [2009] EWHC 2280 (Fam)

Child *habitually resident* in UK until abducted by mother to Spain. *Article 10* of *Brussels II R* was critical for the purposes of this case, in providing that *jurisdiction did not pass to the Spanish courts* until 'a judgment on custody that does not entail a return of the child has been issued by the courts of the Member State where the child was habitually resident immediately before the wrongful removal or retention'.

Kennedy v Kennedy [2009] EWCA Civ 986

The *unmarried parents* of *two children* were *British* citizens *habitually* resident in *Spain,* where the children had been borne. The father's legal status had been recognised under Spanish domestic law by the process of *filiacion.* The *mother removed* the children to England *without* the father's *consent. Held:* The removal of the children had been in breach of the *father's right of custody* under Spanish domestic law. Under Spanish law, at the date of the children's removal the *father's paternity* had been established and he had been exercising his *rights of parental control and custody.* To apply the children's foreign personal law to attribute custody of the children to the mother alone would be discriminatory on the basis of status and would *be contrary to Spanish public policy.* To identify the autonomous meaning of *'rights of custody'* in this case, the Court of Appeal had recourse to the decision of the New Zealand Court of Appeal in *Fairfax v Johnson* (24 March 2009) which emphasised the *'fundamental change in attitudes in the relationship between the child and father where parents are unmarried'.*

Re S (Habitual Residence) [2009] EWCA Civ 1021

Clear affirmation that, for the purposes of an abduction case [although governed by the provisions of *Brussels II R*], the meaning to be given to *'habitual residence'* under *Arts 10 and 11* of the Regulation is that of the Hague Convention jurisprudence, and *not the EU law* 'centre of interests' test which applies to decisions under Art 3. **Note:** For the purposes of jurisdiction to make orders concerning the exercise of parental responsibility, arising from an abduction, it is the well-established test as to 'habitual residence' set out in the Hague Convention jurisprudence: **(a)** *physical presence/residence* in the new country; **(b)** for a *reasonable period* of time; and **(c)** for *a settled purpose and* with a *settled intention*: see *Re P-J (Abduction: Habitual Residence)* [2009] EWCA Civ 588, [2009] 2 FLR 1051.

De L v H (Abduction: Child's Objections) [2009] EWHC 3074 (Fam)

The judgment of Sir Mark Potter P expressed in highly articulate and full terms, *a detailed examination* of the requirements needed to satisfy the defence under *Art 13(a)* of the Hague Convention and includes a clear application of *'age and maturity'* matters. The *'gateway'* findings required of the court in relation to the 'child's objections' under Art 13 are:

(a) that the child does, in fact, object; and

(b) that he has attained the age and maturity at which it is appropriate to take his views into account. Once those matters are satisfied a wide range of considerations come into play in relation to the exercise of discretion; and see also *Re M (Abduction: Zimbabwe)* [2007] UKHL 55, [2008] 1 FLR 251.

As to (a): the child's objection must be centred on *a return to the state of habitual residence*, rather than to the care of the other parent: see *Re S (A Minor) (Abduction: Custody Rights)* [1992] 2 FLR 492, [1993] Fam 242) but in most cases, *'the two elements are so inextricably linked that they cannot be separated'* See *Re T (Abduction: Child's Objections to Return)* [2000] 2 FLR 192. The role of the court here is to examine the reasons for their objections so that it can consider their strength and validity when weighed *against the overall purpose of the Convention (the prompt return to the country of habitual residence)*. In the present case, the Cafcass officer, the guardian and the President himself all considered that it was 'clear beyond argument' that the boy objected.

As to (b), it was equally clear that the boy was one whose views *should* be taken into account [he was aged 13]. The President had taken the *unusual* step of *interviewing him* in order to make sure that he understood the purpose and nature of the court's task: the boy fully *demonstrated his understanding* and was able to explain his wishes and state of mind to the judge. When considering the soundness and validity of the objections the President was guided by the four heads articulated by Ward LJ in *Re T* [ibid]: these are:

(i) *'the child's own perspective'* on his interests;

(ii) *'the extent to which his objections are rooted in reality'*;

(iii) *'the extent to which the views are coloured or shaped by undue parental pressure'* and

(iv) *'the extent to which the objections would be modified on return and/or the child's removal from the pernicious influence of the abducting parent'*. In relation to this latter point, the President considered that the boy's objections were likely to be confirmed and enhanced if he was returned. *The test is a strong one and the practice of interviewing the child concerned is to be endorsed*; as to a protocol for so interviewing a child, see *JPC v SLW and SMW* [2007] EWHC 1349, [2007] 2 FLR 900.

W v W [2009] EWHC 3288 (Fam), per Baker J

This was an *application by C,* the sibling of L who was the subject of proceedings under the Child Abduction and Custody Act 1985 *to be joined* as a party to those proceedings. C was aged 17 rising 18 and L was aged 11. Allegations by mother of *violence* by father. Mother took children from *Australia to England.* To *father's application for a summary return* of L to Australia, mother raised *13(b)* defence. C contended that because of the alleged volatility and dysfunctionality of her parents' relationship, *she had taken the role of protecting L* and questioned her mother's capacity alone to protect him in the future. *Held: C's application upheld falling well within r. 6.5(e).* In this context, see *S v B (Abduction: Human Rights)* [2005] EWHC 733 (Fam), [2005] 2 FLR 878. **Note:** Cases referred to as to the interpretation of the words *'sufficient interest'* were: *Re D (Abduction: Rights of Custody)* [2006] UKHL 51; [2007] 1 FLR 961, *Re M (Abduction: Zimbabwe)* [2007] UKHL 55, [2008] 1 FLR 251, and *Re C (Abduction: Separate Representation of Children)* [2008] EWHC 517 (Fam), [2008] 2 FLR 6.

W v W (Abduction: Acquiescence: Children's Objections) [2010] EWHC 332

Mother took children from *Ireland to England.* Issue inter alia of *acquiescence.* Wishes of children to remain in UK and fear of father. *Held:*

(1) Acquiescence depended on the *actual state of mind* of the wronged parent and his *subjective intent* was a question of fact. Here the *mother had not discharged the burden* of establishing that, in all the circumstances, including the father's assistance towards settling the children in London, he had acquiesced in the wrongful retention of the children.

(2) The defence under **Art 13(b)** was rejected in relation to the two older children, albeit that did not dictate the outcome of argument in relation to their objections to returning. However, *as regards the youngest child,* who was *too young* to have his views taken into account, an order for his return and thus a split from his siblings would expose him to harm or otherwise place him in an intolerable position. A return without them would have had a significant detrimental impact upon him.

(3) There was no absolute threshold age below which a child could not be sufficiently mature for the purposes of the child's objections defence. One could only determine whether a child had the requisite age and degree of maturity by looking at the *attributes of the particular child*, the circumstances in which he found himself and the *nature* of the objections.

(4) The two older children objected to returning, on the basis of their fear of the father and their family life in Ireland, and had attained an age and degree of maturity at which it was appropriate to take account of those views. *Weighing up* all material matters, including the nature and strength of the children's objections and the extent to which they coincide with other welfare considerations, the court would *not, in the exercise of its discretion*, order their *return* under the Hague Convention. **Note:** See *Re D (Abduction: Rights of Custody)* [2006] UKHL 51, [2007] 1 FLR 961, at para [57]; and also see dicta of Ward LJ in *Re T (Abduction: Child's Objections to Return)* [2000] 2 FLR 192 as to evaluating a child's views, and as to the discretion then to return them, see *Re M (Abduction: Zimbabwe)* [2007] UKHL 55, [2008] 1 FLR 251.

Re W (Abduction: Appeal) [2010] EWCA Civ 520

Children 8, 6 and 3. *Irish father* and *British mother.* Mother brought children to London from their home in *Ireland* where they had been *habitually resident.* After an attempted reconciliation by the father in London, father issued a summons for return of children to Ireland. **Primary issue:** At first instance Black J found that the two older children objected to being returned to Ireland, that each was of an age and maturity at which it was appropriate to take account of their views and she exercised her discretion against ordering a return. **Held on appeal: (1)** The age of the eldest child [8] did not prevent the court taking into account her objection, recognising that this should nonetheless not erode the policy of the Hague Convention of returning children to their home state. **(2)** The judge had been entitled to accept the Cafcass officer's assessment that the older children objected to returning to Ireland, they being even at their age able to distinguish between life in Ireland and life with the father in Ireland. **(3)** The phrase '*to take into account*' in **Art 13** meant what it said, albeit *bounded by considerations of age and maturity*; it represented *a fairly low threshold requirement.* It did not follow that a court could '*take account*' of a child's objections only if they were so solidly based that they were likely to be determinative of the discretionary exercise to return. **(4)** *Delay by the father* was a significant factor: The family had been settled in London for *9 months*; the father had known of their whereabouts and instead of swiftly taking proceedings he had allowed time to pass, including joining them for 2 months. **Per curiam:** The moment when a concerted effort was about to be launched for judgments in family proceedings to become shorter was not the moment to argue that judges faced reversal of their decisions if they failed to repeat reference to specific facts already made. **Comment:** There is a need to take decisions about younger children, in light of their wishes: see Baroness Hale in *Re D (A Child) (Abduction: Rights of Custody)* [2006] UKHL 51, [2007] 1 FLR 961 at [59]. However *Wilson LJ expressed concern* that the gradual lowering of the age at which a child's objections may be taken into account *would erode* the fundamental objective of the Convention – to return children swiftly to the countries from which they had been wrongly removed.

Re H and L [2010] EWHC 652 (Fam)

- Under *Art 12* of the Hague Convention, where an application was made *no more than one year* after the child had been wrongfully removed or retained, an order for return had to be made *unless it was demonstrated* that the child was now settled in his or her new environment.

- Settlement under Art 12 had a *broad meaning and encompasses wider considerations* than physical whereabouts: *Re N (Minors) (Abduction)* [1991] 1 FLR 413, and *Re M (Abduction: Acquiescence)* [1996] 1 FLR 315.

- The *fact-specific* and *child-centred* approach to settlement cases was emphasised by Baroness Hale in *Re M (Abduction: Zimbabwe)* [2007] UKHL 55, [2008] 1 FLR 251, at [47]–[48].

- *'New environment'* meant the total physical, social, emotional and psychological experience of the children.

- As to the argument that *irregularities in the mother's immigration position* counter-indicated settlement, see *Re L (Abduction: Pending Criminal Proceedings)* [1999] 1 FLR 433, and *Re H (Abduction: child of 16)* [2000] 2 FLR 51 [in these cases, the abducting parent had been 'on the run' and had not been allowed to benefit from that].

- As to acquiescence, see: *Re H (Abduction: Acquiescence)* [1997] 1 FLR 872. The question of whether a parent has acquiesced in the removal or retention of a child depends upon the parent's *actual state of mind, which is a question of fact.* There is *only one exception*: where the words or actions of the left-behind parent clearly and unequivocally show or have led the other parent to believe that the left-behind parent is not asserting or going to assert his or her right to summary return of the child, *justice requires that the left-behind parent be held to have acquiesced.*

ES v AJ [2010] EWHC 1113 (Fam), [2010] 2 FLR 1257, per Sir Nicholas Wall

Mother's wardship summons when children taken by consent to the Cameroons pursuant to an open-ended agreement. *Held*:

(1) The question of **habitual residence** was to be approached in accordance with the guidance given by Lord Brandon in *Re J (A Minor) (Abduction: Custody Rights)* [1990] 2 AC 562 at 578. Habitual residence is a question of fact.

(2) The expression 'habitual residence' was to be **understood according to its ordinary and natural meaning,** to be decided by reference to all the circumstances of the particular case.

(3) Where both parents have parental responsibility, **neither parent could unilaterally change a child's habitual residence** without the consent or acquiescence of the other.

(4) The formulation of the test for habitual residence of a child to be conducted in this context **differs very subtly** (at least in formulation) from that undertaken in the context of Arts 8 and 12 **Brussels II R**: see *Re A (Area of Freedom, Security and Justice)* [2009] 2 FLR 1 and *Re S (Habitual Residence)* [2009] EWCA Civ 1021, [2010] 1 FLR 1146.

(5) Further, the test for habitual residence of a child **under Arts 8 and 12 of Brussels II R** (an essentially factual enquiry) differs from the qualitative 'centre of interest' test applied for the determination of the habitual residence of adults for the purposes of the divorce jurisdiction under Art 3 of that Regulation: *Z v Z (Divorce: Jurisdiction)* [2009] EWHC 2626 (Fam), [2010] 1 FLR 694.

Re W (Abduction: Appeal) [2010] EWCA Civ 520

- The kind of decision **required by the Hague Convention** was more appropriately described **as an exercise of judgment** rather than an exercise of discretion. What protected such a decision from all but radical attack was that it was **a judgment made by the judge on the spot** and who was more likely to be right than an appellate court; distant in time and space.

- Although it was **rare to take account of the views of a child as young as 6**, as Black J had done here, that had been done before by the CA in *Re R (Child Abduction: Acquiescence)* [1995] 1 FLR 716.

- However, the notion that a child as young as 6 could fall within the defence based on a child's objections was outside the contemplation of those who signed the Hague Convention in 1980: *the defence had been devised as an escape route for mature adolescents*.

- Over the years, *the need to take decisions about younger children, in light of their wishes, had taken hold*: *Re D (A Child) (Abduction: Rights of Custody)* [2006] UKHL 51, [2007] 1 FLR 961 at [59].

- Wilson LJ expressed concern that the *gradual lowering of the age* at which a child's objections might be taken into account could erode the fundamental objective of the Convention – to return children swiftly to countries from which they had been wrongfully removed.

M v T (Abduction: Brussels II R Art 11(7)) [2010] EWHC 1479 (Fam)

Article 11(7) proceedings in England, pursuant to Mother's *abduction to Lithuania of a young infant habitually resident here*.

- Proceedings under Art 11(7), whereby despite a court ordering the non-return of a child following abduction proceedings, *the court of habitual residence can revisit the issue and override that decision.*

- An *Art 11(7)* case is *not a summary* procedure, but does require the court to treat the child's *welfare as paramount*, and to apply the Court of Appeal *welfare check-list.*

- As *soon as possible* after an Art 11(7) application is issued:

  - There should be *directions* from the court expressly addressing the approach to be taken in the case: is the case to be determined on a summary basis and/or is there to be a welfare enquiry and if so, what is to be the extent of that enquiry?
  - Cafcass Legal and its High Court Team should be notified as soon as such an application is made and at the first directions hearing the court should consider whether or not the child should be joined and/or whether Cafcass Legal or its High Court Team should be invited to make representations to the court concerning the approach the court should take.
  - If the child is joined and Cafcass are to take an active part, *directions must be given to them* as to the role they are expected to perform, including the nature and extent of the welfare enquiry.
  - At an early stage, there is also a need to consider issues relating to *interim contact,* both as to whether and where it should take place.
  - The *timetable for a final determination* of the proceedings must also be closely looked at, and this must be done by reference to and to reflect the urgency enshrined by Art 11 itself,

remembering the inevitable fact that the court is dealing with a child *who was habitually resident here* and who, as a result of *a wrongful removal* or retention, is in another country.

MA v DB (Abduction: Jurisdiction) [2010] EWHC 1697 (Fam)

Both parents wanted residence for the mother in England, and contact with the father in Greece, to be made subject to an English court order. The question arose as to the *jurisdiction of the court pursuant to Hague Convention proceedings* [which were dismissed] to make such orders. **Held:**

- The child did *not have to be made a ward of court* before the inherent jurisdiction was invoked.

- Once that jurisdiction had been invoked, the *court had power to make any s 8 order* and dispense with all formalities.

- Thus the mother was ordered to issue an *originating summons* pursuant to the inherent jurisdiction in order to provide a proper jurisdictional foundation for the s 8 orders.

Re A (Abduction: Interim Directions: Accommodation by Local Authority) [2010] EWCA Civ 586

Issue as to which local authority should be responsible vis-à-vis accommodation of mother and children pending outcome of proceedings for return of children to Ireland under the *Hague Convention:*

- Although a Convention application is a hot pursuit remedy, the *ordinary discipline* of litigation *should be observed* as far as possible. *An applicant for an order under s 5 should be on notice,* particularly to the local authority against whom the order is sought, and should be supported by evidence.

- An accommodation order may be made to

  - prevent further abduction;
  - to promote the welfare of the abducted child, particularly if the child has special needs;
  - and possibly to promote the efficient preparation of the abductor's defence to the return application.

- *Disputes between local authorities as to which should bear the burden of accommodation are much to be discouraged.* As a *generality,* the burden will fall on the authority within whose area the abductor is present at the date of the making of the order. If a dispute arises on the facts of a particular case, the choice of which authority is to accommodate must be made in the exercise of the judicial discretion having regard to the welfare of the abducted child and within the context of the Convention proceedings. ***Domestic statutory provisions designed to deal with transition from one local authority to another are not engaged.***

- Note: While *Re C (Abduction: Interim Directions: Accommodation by Local Authority)* concerned a child being placed in foster care ***because of a concern that the mother would abduct her again*** (after having concealed their whereabouts from the father for 4 years), the present case involved ***the authority being required to provide accommodation for the mother – an illegal immigrant –*** as well as the children.

McB v E (C-400/10) [2011] 1 FLR 518, PPU Court of Justice of the European Union

The referral by the Irish Supreme Court has enabled the CJEU to provide a clear judgment confirming that, as with the jurisprudence relating to the Hague Convention itself and that of the ECHR, ***EU Law as contained in Brussels II R and the Charter also provides Member States with the leeway to impose restrictions upon the obtaining of parental responsibility by an unmarried father in order, in the view of the CJEU, to ensure that the best interests of the child can be protected.*** See case law on 'rights of custody' under Arts 3 and 5 of the Hague Convention. Also see *Re J (A Minor) (Abduction: Custody Rights)* [1990] 2 AC 562.

Re G (Abduction: Children's Objections) [2010] EWCA Civ 1232

Wrongful abduction to UK by mother with 13 and 9 year old daughters, from Canada where family had lived for 2 years. First instance ***order to return.*** On appeal:

- ***Mediation*** had not been mooted.

- ***A meeting between the judge and the elder girl had not been mooted*** albeit she wrote a letter to him [which was not mentioned in the judgment]. The cogency of the girl's reasons for rejecting Canada and everything she had said about her education, wider family and friends led to the conclusion that the judge may well have refused to order return if he had had the advantage of a meeting with her.

- Courts needed to be ***alive*** to the ***difficulty of implementing*** a return order which involved '***an articulate, naturally determined and courageous adolescent***'.

Thorpe LJ made ***three primary points***:

(1) *The inter-relationship between wrongful removal and applications for relocation*: Note: children may be wrongfully removed if the applicant parent is not granted leave to remove.

(2) The move towards hearing from a child personally rather than through Cafcass.

(3) The *emphasis now being placed on mediation* in wrongful removal cases. If the parents here had tried to address the problems that led to the removal, the father may have realised what the likely outcome of an application to legitimise the removal would be.

Raban v Romania [2010] ECHR 1625

Father an *Israeli* and *Dutch* national, with children *aged 2 and 3* married to a *Romanian*.

- The principal interest of the judgment is that it provides a valuable summary of the principles set out by the Grand Chamber in *Neulinger and Shuruk v Switzerland* [2010] ECHR 1053. The significance of this particular line of Strasbourg jurisprudence lies in its *analysis of the relationship between the European Convention* and *Hague Convention.*

- The task of *assessing the child's best interests in each individual case was thus primarily for the domestic authorities,* who had often had the benefit of *direct contact* with the persons concerned. To that end they enjoyed a certain margin of appreciation which nevertheless remained *subject to review by the Court* under the European Convention: *Hokkanen v Finland* [1995] 19 EHRR 139, and *Kunzer v Germany* [2002] 35 EHRR 25.

WF v FJ, BF and RF (Abduction: Child's Objections) [2010] EWHC 2909 (Fam)

Unlawful removal of three children by their father from Germany to England. Baker J declined to order the children's return:

- The *gateway or threshold for taking account of a child's objections under Art 13 is fairly low*. Thus it is left to the discretion stage to consider the following factors:

  - the *child's own perspective* of what is in her interests;
  - the extent to which the reasons for objection *are rooted in reality* or might appear so to the child;
  - the extent to which the child's views might have been shaped or coloured by *undue influence and pressure exerted by the abducting parent*;

- And how far these might be mollified on return or removal from the parent's influence.

- By virtue of Art 11(2) of *Brussels II R, there is a presumption in EU cases that a child should be given an opportunity to be heard unless it appears inappropriate to the court having regard to the child's age or maturity.*

- Note that *the issue of the child's objection to return* is separate from the Art 13(b) defence that a return would present a '*grave risk of physical or psychological harm, or would otherwise place the child in an intolerable position*'.

- Cases referred to:

  - *Re M (Abduction: Zimbabwe)* [2007] UKHL 55, [2008] 1 FLR 251; *Re W (Abduction: Child's Objections)* [2010] EWCA Civ 520, [2010] 2 FLR 1165; emphasising the child's right to be heard.
  - *Neulinger and Shuruk v Switzerland* [2010] ECHR 1053.

DT v LBT (Abduction: Domestic Abuse) [2010] EWHC 3177 (Fam)

Domestic violence precipitated an *English mother* with *three children living in Rome* with the Italian naval officer father [one of whom was autistic] *to abduct the children back to her homeland, England.* At the time of the hearing, the father, from whom there was inadequate financial support, had not had contact for 6 months. *Held: Refusing the father's* application for the return of the children:

- The children would be at *grave risk of psychological harm* if they returned to Italy.

- The mother was *habitually resident in Italy* with the children – *her will had not been broken by domestic violence* [mother had drawn analogy with forced marriage cases]. Bowing to pressure or agreeing with extreme reluctance did not make presence involuntary.

- Objecting to return, on the part of a child, required a strength of opposition that did not apply in this case.

- The *exceptions* provided by the Hague Convention were *by definition exceptional* and should be approached as such when giving effect to their clear terms.

- The *Article 8 rights of the father were qualified* by the *pernicious* effect his behaviour had had on the family and the rights of the mother were thus *correspondingly given more weight: Neulinger and Shuruk v Switzerland* [2010] ECHR 1053 interpreted on the basis that it *should not be read as a warrant for approaching the exceptions provided by the Hague Convention broadly*, liberally or substantially differently from established practice. The true effect of *Neulinger did not require* the court to carry out an in-depth examination of the entire family *situation in each and every case* as to do so would defeat the very purpose of the Convention.

- *Where an abducting abused parent refused to accompany children* there was no absolute rule that there must be a return: see Sir Mark Potter in *S v B (Abduction: Human Rights)* [2005] EWHC 733 (Fam), [2005] 2 FLR 878.

Re K (Abduction: Case Management) [2010] EWCA Civ 1546

Three defences advanced by mother – (1) *acquiescence*, (2) *grave risk of harm* and (3) *child objection*.

- Hague Convention applications were for peremptory orders to be decided on *written* evidence, *amplified [in exceptional cases] by oral evidence*.

- Outside of a narrow and discrete point in an exceptional case, *oral* evidence was *inappropriate* and likely to cause *confusion*, in Hague Convention proceedings for the return of a child.

- Orders for *oral evidence* should be *extremely rare* and *never* made in advance of the filing of written statement on the point in issue.

- In an *exceptional* case, such as an issue as to *consent* or *acquiescance*, oral evidence *should be limited* to the issue and take no more than *35–40 minutes* from each protagonist.

- There had to be a very clear distinction between a child's objections and his/her wishes or feelings.

- The obligation to make a return order in the present case was *heightened* by the fact that it was an *inter-European abduction* and the Articles of the Hague Convention were accordingly fortified by *Brussels II R*, and in particular Art 13.

Re O (Abduction: Settlement) [2011] EWCA Civ 128

Case authority for the following:

- A judge should *not give* 'Hague Convention Policy Considerations' *overriding significance* vis-à-vis summary return [in this case, to the

USA] without adequately considering its application in relation to *the Art 12* situation of the application being brought after one year and his finding the children were settled in Nigeria; see *Re M (Abduction: Zimbabwe)* [2007] UKHL 55, [2008] 1 FLR 251.

- There was *clear evidence* of factors pointing towards the determination of the welfare issues in Nigeria, not the least of which was the father's own *invoking of the Nigerian court's* jurisdiction at an earlier stage [the reason why the proceedings were in England was because mother had brought the children to England for a holiday].

- *There must not be a generalised approach.* There should have been *evidence* as to the *adaptability* of these young children, aged 7 and 5, as to their ability readily to adapt to a return to the USA; see in this context also *RS v KS (Abduction: Wrongful Retention)* [2009] EWHC 1494 [Fam], [2009] 2 FLR 1231 where Macur J did not take the view that the children would readily adapt: she relied upon reports from the *child's guardian* as to *the impact* upon him of return].

Re E (Children) [2011] UKSC 27

(Supreme Court, Lord Hope, Lord Walker, Lady Hale, Lord Kerr and Lord Wilson, 10 June 2011)

Neulinger does not require a departure from the normal summary process in abduction cases, provided that the decision is not arbitrary or mechanical. The Hague Convention was designed with the interests of children as a primary consideration and, if properly applied, it is highly unlikely that there will be a violation of Art 8. Consideration of grave risk and the focus on protective measures under Art 13(b).

A v P [2011] EWHC 1530 (Fam)

(Family Division, Sir Nicholas Wall P, 21 June 2011)

On the facts, the child's habitual residence had not changed from Poland to England and therefore she should be returned to Poland under the Hague Convention. There was no agreement between the parents to move permanently to England and the mother's position was inconsistent with her Polish divorce petition and other documentation.

Re H-K (Children) (Habitual Residence) [2011] EWCA Civ 1100

(Court of Appeal, Ward, Longmore and Sullivan LJJ, 10 October 2011)

Where a family agreed to move to England for a year, the father's intention to return and the mother's agreement to return did not prevent a change in habitual residence from Australia to England. Permanence is not required; there will be habitual residence where residence is adopted for settled purposes as part of the regular order of a person's life for the time being.

FVS v MGS [2011] EWHC 3139 (Fam)

(Family Division, Holman J, 18 November 2011)

Where the family had moved to England for 2 years for the father's work and that period had been extended, the habitual residence of the child had changed from Spain to England. There was a degree of integration in a social and family environment in England – it was for the time being a settled way of life. The summer visit to Spain did not revive the child's Spanish habitual residence as the father had never consented to that, expressly or tacitly.

J v J (Relinquishment of Jurisdiction) [2011] EWHC 3255 (QB)

(Family Division; Mostyn J; 28 November 2011)

The mother took two children, then aged 5 and one, to Austria and the father initiated Hague proceedings. An order had been made 14 months previously in relation to parental responsibility on the basis that the mother would remain the primary care giver, and there was an expectation that it would be implemented in Austria. The father took no steps to bring the order to the Austrian court's attention but reinstituted Hague proceedings. The Austrian court refused the application to order the child's return.

The father abducted the 5-year-old child to England. The siblings remained apart for 3 months with only Skype contact. The only solution was to order a return of the 5-year-old to Austria for a welfare determination to be carried out.

It was in the best interests of the child to be reunited with its mother and sibling as soon as possible and a decision was made on welfare principles regarding residence and contact. Permission to appeal granted.

S v C [2011] EWCA Civ 1385

(Court of Appeal, Thorpe, Longmore and McFarlane LJJ, 2 December 2011)

Re E is a restatement and not an evolution of the law of the Hague Convention. The stress of an anticipated relocation application following return should not have been a factor elevating the Art 13(b) defence. The crucial question was whether the asserted risks and anxieties were reasonably held in the face of the protective package – not the subjective position. The practice of directing a preliminary issue hearing was not intended by the Supreme Court in *Re E* and should be immediately stifled.

Re J (Abduction: Children's Objections) [2011] EWCA Civ 1448

(Court of Appeal, Thorpe and Hallett LJJ and Sir Mark Potter, 2 December 2011)

In Hague proceedings, the judge had failed to make a finding as to whether the children's objections to a return order were made out, which was the basis for an exercise of discretion. Where older children had expressed a wish not to return to their country of habitual residence following a wrongful retention, and the Cafcass report noted that they would be competent to instruct their own solicitor, the judge should have engaged the children in the process of his own motion. He had erred in not at least raising with the parties the need for him to meet the children face to face and in not applying the President's Practice Note (*Guidelines for Judges Meeting Children who are Subject to Family Proceedings*), which should be taken to apply to all proceedings in which the decision of the court will have a significant impact on the future life of the child.

X v Latvia (Application No 27853/09) [2012] 1 FLR 860

(European Court of Human Rights; 13 December 2011)

The mother was a Latvian national who lived in Australia and acquired citizenship. She met her partner in Australia when she was pregnant. The identity of the father was unknown but the partner lived with the mother. The couple separated, and the mother and child returned to Latvia. The partner applied to the Australian family court to establish his parental rights and made a Hague Convention application.

The Court held the partner shared joint parental responsibility. The Latvian court ordered the mother to return the child to Australia. The mother failed to return to Australia and by chance the partner met the mother and child at a shopping centre in Latvia, where he took the child to Estonia to commence the trip to Australia. A disciplinary investigation in Latvia found there were insufficient regulations to avoid the violent and traumatic execution of the court orders in similar cases.

In Australia the partner was granted sole parental responsibility for the child, the mother was restrained from discussing publicly the child or the partner, she was granted supervised contact and until the child reached 11 the mother was prevented from communicating with the child's pre-school or school facility or with a child or parent of a child attending the same facility. She was also prohibited from communicating with the child in Latvian.

The mother alleged a breach of Arts 6 and 8 of the European Convention. The Latvian court's order for the return of the child had been in accordance with law and in pursuit of a legitimate aim but the court's approach lacked an in-depth examination of the whole family situation which rendered the return order a disproportionate interference. The court should have assessed what safeguards were in place to protect the child's interests and a consideration of whether the child's contact with her mother would be maintained if she were returned to Australia. Breach of Art 8.

R v Kayani and Sollimani [2011] EWCA Crim 2871

(Court of Appeal (Criminal Division); Lord Chief Justice, McFarlane LJ, Royce J; 13 December 2011)

Fathers abducted children for a number of years. Appealed against their sentences. There was a discrepancy between sentencing under the Child Abduction Act 1984 (max 7 years) and the offence of kidnapping (life).

One father abducted his two sons for 9 years to Pakistan, the children were now 17 and 16 and back in the UK but were not willing to have contact with their mother. The father was sentenced to 5 years for two counts of child abduction with a 20% reduction for guilty plea.

The other father abducted three children for 7 years. The children had no relationship with mother. He was sentenced for three counts of 3 years. In both cases the children were distressed at the father's imprisonment. The issue was whether the interests of the children should lead to a reduction in sentence despite the fact that a serious offence and sentencing should serve as a deterrent.

The mothers and children suffered greatly as a result of abduction, any further suffering caused by the sentence was a direct result of father's actions. Did not justify a reduction in sentence, both appeals dismissed.

SH v MM [2011] EWHC 3314 (Fam)

(Family Division, Hedley J, 13 December 2011)

A prohibited steps order properly served, although made without permission under Children Act 1989, s 10, made the mother's removal of the child wrongful. The DJ had been entitled to make the PSO to hold the ring. However, the return order would be stayed for DNA testing and pending the permission application being heard.

18.3 ADOPTION

A Local Authority v C, X and C [2008] EWHC 2555 (Fam) per Eleanor King J

Section 20 consent given when baby was less than *6 weeks* old and therefore ineffective; *s 52*. There is no mirror provision in relation to *s 19* consents. The child had been placed several months before and now the parents sought to decline consent. Their consent was dispensed with. See also s 47 and reg 35 of the Adoption Agencies Regulations 2005 (SI 2005/389).

Re S (Placement Order: Revocation) [2008] EWCA Civ 1333

A *'potential'* adoptive parent is not a *'prospective'* adoptive parent; Adoption and Children Act 2002, *s 18(5)*. The words *'potential'* and *'prospective'* have *distinctly different meanings* – and they have to be interpreted strictly. On the facts of this case, the child had been placed under the fostering, and not the placement, regulations. This case emphasises the importance of keeping clearly in mind *the three necessary stages to the placement of a child*: *First:* Adoption must be considered by the LA as in the best interests of the child. Once the decision that the child should be placed for adoption is made, applying the principles under s 1 of the 2002 Act, the authority must apply for a placement order. *Second:* When that order has been granted the local authority then has the responsibility of considering whether specific individuals are in principle approved as adopters of that child. If yes, then *Third:* the child is matched to the specific prospective adopters and therefore to be placed with them.

Re A (Adoption: Removal) [2008] EWCA Civ 41

The local authority wished to assess an *American couple* as prospective adopters for their niece, who was in the care of the local authority. **Held:** Where the child is not being 'placed for adoption' abroad, but what is proposed is that he or she spend time abroad with a view to *assessing* whether adoption might in fact be a suitable option, it will be possible to make use of the *Children Act 1989, Sch 2*. Should the assessment prove positive, it will then be possible for the prospective adopters to obtain *parental responsibility* for the child under *s 84* of the 2002 Act, even though the assessment has been carried out in a foreign country. The word *'home'* in *s 84(4)* is not geographically defined. As a matter of construction, the phrase, *'child's home was with the applicant'* fits far more readily with a home outside the jurisdiction if that is where the prospective adopters' home truly is.

Webster v Norfolk County Council and the Children (By their Children's Guardian) [2009] EWCA Civ 59

Three children *adopted* after a *finding of non-accidental injury (NAI)* in the context of fractures of one of the three. *Subsequent expert* evidence that *fractures caused not by NAI* but by *scurvy*, resulting from a medically prescribed diet of *Soya* milk. Could parents re-open adoption? **Held:** Although, if the true facts had been known the three children would not have been adopted, the public *policy* considerations relating to adoption and the authorities on that point made it *impossible* for the court *to set aside* the adoption orders even if the parents had suffered a serious injustice. Only *exceptional* circumstances such as *procedural irregularity*, *mistake* or *fraud* can challenge the permanency of an adoption order. Per Wilson LJ:

> ' ... a hypothesis in relation to the causation of a child's injuries must not be dismissed only because such causation would be highly unusual and that, where his history contains a demonstrably rare feature, the possible nexus between that feature and his injuries must be the subject of specialist appraisal at an early stage'.

X and Y v A Local Authority (Adoption: Procedure) [2009] EWHC 47 (Fam)

McFarlane J provided clear and cogent guidance for future cases by highlighting all the mistakes into which the court fell or was led. He noted that *if the court had followed the Family Procedure (Adoption) Rules 2005 the prospects of such failings would have been substantially reduced*, as well as considering in greater detail the more major errors highlighted by this case. This case is therefore *essential reading*. Further, adoption orders and their accompanying contact arrangements were intended to be permanent and final, to the extent that *contact should not be reopened* unless there was a *fundamental change* of circumstances: see *Re C (A Minor)(Adopted Child: Contact)* [1993] 2 FLR 431. The issue of *post-adoption direct contact* should be grappled with and determined prior to the making of the adoption order.

ASB and KBS v MQS Secretary of State for the Home Department Intervening) [2009] EWHC 2491 (Fam)

Childless Pakistani couple resident in UK *adopted* nephew from Pakistan with *6-month visa* into UK in 2007, which was not renewed. Application to adopt in 2009, met with resistance from Home Office for application appeared to be a *misuse of adoption proceedings*. *Held by Bennett J:*

Applicants granted leave to apply for an adoption order. This case makes very clear that the court's obligation to be on guard against the misuse of adoption proceedings has survived the Adoption and Children Act 2002. As Bennett J expressed it the *'misuse of adoption proceedings to gain a right of abode (as opposed to exercising parental responsibility) is most unlikely to be in the child's welfare as undermining immigration policies and procedures'.* Cases referred to: *Re B (A Minor) (Adoption Order: Nationality)* [1999] 2 AC 136, [1999] 1 FLR 907 at 910; and *Re A (Care Proceedings: Asylum Seekers)* [2003] EWHC 1086 (Fam), [2003] 2 FLR 921.

Re M (Adoption: Leave to Oppose) [2009] EWHC 3643 (Fam)

After the making of a *placement order*, mother sought to *oppose the making of an adoption order* on the basis of *fresh evidence* from the USA that the *non-accidental injury* as found was in fact attributable to brittle bone disease. *Held:* **(1)** The route was by an appeal [which had failed] and not by recourse to s 47. **(2)** The evidence from the USA did not amount to a change of circumstances. **(3)** Local authorities should actively consider in every case, whether they should *take steps to restrict* the operation of *parental responsibility* of parents in relation to the child's medical records. **(4)** There may be *a special need for caution* when an overseas expert is instructed; there should be strict compliance with *Practice Direction: Experts in Family Proceedings Relating to Children* [2009] 2 FLR 1383. **(5)** There should be early consideration of any proposal to instruct an overseas expert at the case management conference, with the party seeking permission required to explain *in writing* the *rationale* for the instruction and that the proposed overseas expert has *confirmed a familiarity with the Practice Direction* and a willingness *to comply* with its requirements. **Note:** This decision provides valuable guidance on two aspects of public law proceedings concerning children. *The first* relates to the meaning of *'change of circumstances'* required before a parent may seek leave under s 47. The *second* point worthy of note is the *judge's rejection* of the credentials of the American expert instructed by the mother and her guidance concerning the use of overseas experts.

Re N (Recognition of Foreign Adoption Order) [2010] 1 FLR 1102

Teenager in *Armenia* adopted by *British father* who married Armenian mother in Armenia. The family then relocated to England. *Could father under s 67(3)(b) adopt the boy in England without depriving the mother of parental responsibility?* Held: Yes.

Hofstetter and Hofstetter v London Borough of Barnet [2009] EWHC 3282 (Admin), per Charles J

It is crucial for both prospective adopters and the children they seek to adopt that the *decision-making processes carried out by the relevant authority are clear, fair, unbiased and carried out in line with the Adoption Agencies Regulations 2005 and Adoption Guidance (Adoption and Children Act 2002) by qualified and experienced professionals*. The human consequences and the toll that can be taken when this is not the case are immense. In this judgment Charles J has provided *a thorough review of those processes*. He examines the role of the Adoption Agency [here, the defendant borough], the Adoption and Permanency Panel which makes a recommendation to the decision-maker and the IRM Review Panel which also makes a recommendation to the decision-maker.

Oxfordshire County Council v X, Y and J [2010] EWCA Civ 581

After an adoption and placement order already made, natural parents sought an *annual photograph* of the child. *Held*: No – **(1)** It was *'extremely unusual'* to impose on the adoptive parents some obligation which they were unwilling, voluntarily, to assume [see '**Comment**' below]. **(2)** *The relevant welfare check-list to be applied in the contact application, made after the adoption order had been granted, was that in s 1(3) of the 1989 Act and not that in s 1(4) of the 2002 Act.* **(3)** The fear of the adoptive parents that possession of the photograph would create a risk compelled the conclusion that the photographs should not be given to the natural parents. *The child's welfare was paramount* and depended on the *stability* and *security* of her new parents: a failure to heed their *fears* might *undermine* that stability and damage her welfare. **Comment:** See the point made by Wall LJ in *Re R (Adoption: Contact)* [2005] EWCA Civ 1128, [2006] 1 FLR 373, at [49], that *'the imposition on prospective adopters of orders for contact with which they are not in agreement is extremely, and remains extremely, unusual'*. Also see: *Re C (A Minor) (Adoption Order: Conditions)* [1989] AC 1, [1988] 2 FLR 159 and includes *Re T (Adoption: Contact)* [1995] 2 FLR 251, *Re T (Adopted Children: Contact)* [1996] Fam 34, [1995] 2 FLR 792 and *Re P (Placement Orders Parental Consent)* [2008] EWCA Civ 535, [2008] 2 FLR 625. **Warning about separate representation**: Only where it was clear that there was an unavoidable conflict of interest, as a matter of law, between two parties in the same interest, should they have separate legal representation, especially where public money was involved.

Re W (Adoption Order: Set Aside and Leave to Oppose) [2010] EWCA Civ 1535

Procedural unfairness resulted in the making of an adoption order, *which would have been made anyway*, even if the court had properly served the mother with notice of hearing. Judge at first instance set aside the adoption order despite young child being placed for over a year. *Held:*

- A judge must have great regard to the impact of the grant of permission on the child *within the adoptive family*. In the present circumstances, where the mother had not seen the child since he was two and he had been *placed for over a year,* the profoundly upsetting consequences should not be contemplated unless the applicant for permission demonstrated prospects of success that *were not just fanciful or measurable but had substance and solidity*.

- The judge had *underweighed* the current powerful imperatives in favour of adoption and *overvalued* the 'much more speculative' aspects of the child's future: he had adopted an 'altogether too permissive approach'. A *stringent approach was necessary* and the language of McFarlane J in *X and Y v A Local Authority (Adoption: Procedure)* [2009] EWHC 47 (Fam), [2009] 2 FLR 984, preferred.

Re T (A Child) [2010] EWCA Civ 1527

- The *imposition* on prospective adopters of orders for contact [here with a grandmother] with which they are *not in agreement* is extremely and remains *extremely unusual.*

- Even if *Re P (Placement Orders: Parental Consent)* [2008] EWCA Civ 535, [2008] 2 FLR 625 heralds somewhat greater flexibility in judicial attitude to contact following adoption, the statement of Wall LJ in *Re R* was cited with approval by the Court of Appeal in *Oxfordshire County Council v X, Y and J* [2010] EWCA Civ 581, [2011] 1 FLR 272 and still reflects the general approach: The point robustly confirmed in the *Oxfordshire* case is *that the adoptive parents' well-being is inextricably linked with that of the child* and *must therefore trump* any interests, albeit only of humanity, that remain with the natural parents.

- *Re T and M (Adoption)* [2010] EWHC 964 (Fam): *Issue* as to *recognition* in England where two girls adopted individually in *Nicaragua* which jurisdiction *did not recognise same-sex couple adoption*. Issue complicated by *parents living apart* through an attachment *disorder* of one of the children. Issues: *Held:* Adoptions recognised. Matters to be considered:

- Since Nicaragua was not a signatory to the Hague Convention on Protection and Cooperation with respect to Intercountry Adoption, nor a country named in the Schedule to the Adoption (Designation of Overseas Adoptions) Order 1973, *the Adoption Act 1976 did not apply* and the only route to recognition was under the *common law of England and Wales.*

- The UK court *recognised* the *Nicaraguan adoption* because it had been obtained *fully in compliance* with the laws and procedure of Nicaragua and *remained valid* in that jurisdiction. The Nicaraguan concept of adoption broadly accorded with that of England and Wales; and there were *no public policy considerations that should militate against recognition.*

- The two women came within s 144(4)(b) of the Adoption and Children Act 2002 and were thus *a couple within the meaning of s 50.*

- The *welfare of the child without the attachment disorder* required the making of an adoption order in respect of both parents.

- All *procedural requirements* had been *met*.

- The order would make one of the children *a beneficiary* of certain trusts within the family of one of the adoptive parents.

- Cases considered: *Re Valentine's Settlement* [1965] Ch 831; *D v D (Foreign Adoption)* [2008] EWHC 403 (Fam), [2008] 1 FLR 1475.

- This case is also authority for what is meant in s 144(4)(b) by the words: '*Two people (whether of different sexes or the same sex) living as partners in an enduring family relationship.*'

FL v Registrar General [2010] EWHC 3520 (Fam)

The applicant daughter of an adopted man, now in her 60s, sought disclosure of information from the Registrar General in order to find out more about her father's birth family, to explore whether his possible mental health problems had been exacerbated by adoption. **Held:**

(1) The first case to explore the meaning of 'exceptional circumstances' in s 79(4) of the 2002 Act.

(2) The court would not re-write the plain words of s 98 of the 2002 Act as to include people such as FL within the defined categories of those who had been afforded different rights and different routes to obtaining information.

(3) Guidance derived from *Re H (Adoption: Disclosure of Information)* [1995] 1 FLR 236, *D v Registrar General* [1996] 1 FLR 707 and the appeal arising in that case, *D v Registrar General* [1997] 1 FLR 715.

(4) Case authority for the degree of caution with which the court must approach the exercise of a discretion as a matter of public policy.

Coventry City Council v PGO [2011] EWCA Civ 729

(Court of Appeal, Lord Neuberger MR, Lord Wilson and Dame Janet Smith, 22 June 2011)

When foster parents who have been caring for a child wish to adopt him and prevent his removal by the local authority to other potential adopters the court has jurisdiction to make an injunction and must apply public law principles in deciding whether so to order. Here the judge should not have made the injunction. A child is 'placed' with adopters when he begins to live with them, or in the case of foster parents, when the adoption agency formally allows him to continue living with them in their fresh capacity as adopters.

Re H (Children) [2011] EWCA Civ 1218

(Court of Appeal, Ward, Richards and Hughes LJJ 12 July 2011)

The trial judge had not had the necessary material on which to decide whether there should be adoption and to what extent there should be contact. Before approving the local authority's care plan, there should have been some assessment of the prospects of adoption succeeding and the issue of contact was tied up with that.

Re D O'H (Children) [2011] EWCA Civ 1343

(Court of Appeal, Thorpe and Black LJJ, 10 August 2011)

The Court upheld the judge's decision to make final care orders approving a plan for adoption for the younger child whilst the issue of attachment to and contact with an older sibling remained to be determined. The judge had been entitled to find that adoption was required and that the issue of contact was to be determined within that context.

Re PW (Adoption) [2011] EWHC 3793 (Fam)

(Family Division, Parker J, 12 October 2011)

A 69-year-old woman was orphaned when she was 17 and the parents of her closest friend offered her a home and applied for an adoption order. The order was granted and the woman remained with the adoptive family until she was 23 when she left home and was married. She married in her adoptive name and her children have that name on their birth certificates. After her adoptive mother died the woman challenged the adoption order which she claimed should not have been made and had had a devastating effect on her life. She claimed that her wishes and feelings were not ascertained prior to the order and that she felt pressurised and influenced by her adoptive parents who very much wished to adopt her to the extent that she felt unable to gainsay their wishes. The only available remedy was permission to appeal out of time. The adoption had provided considerable benefits and support for the woman and there were strong policy reasons why adoption orders should not be set aside. The court had to assume the order was validly made on a proper and appropriate basis under the law as it was at the time. There was no prospect of success on appeal and so no basis to grant an extension of time for permission to appeal. Application refused.

18.4 AGREED ORDERS

S v P (30 July 2008) [2008] 2 FLR 2040

Agreements flowing from the *collaborative law* process approved by Coleridge J in the *urgent ex parte applications list* [with prior approval of the President]. *Conditions precedent*:

- a *day's notice* [which could be by telephone] to the judge's clerk;

- the *consent* of the urgent applicants judge, where every aspect of the documentation was agreed;

- the documentation was lodged with the judge the night before; and

- the hearing was not expected to take more than 10 minutes.

As to the *collaborative law* process, also see: 'Collaborative Launch' [2007] Fam Law 7; 'Collaborative Law Developments' [2007] Fam Law 850 and 'Resolution News' [2008] Fam Law 267.

18.5 APPEALS

Re M (Placement Order) [2010] EWCA Civ 1257

Even in the case of a *litigant in person,* an *appeal* must be made in compliance with the *requisite rules*. A failure to abide by them may result in the case being *struck out.*

Re P (Children) [2011] EWCA Civ 1016

(Court of Appeal, Patten and Black LJJ, 29 June 2011)

If permission to appeal on certain grounds has been refused at an oral permission hearing, there can be no renewal on the same grounds at the substantive appeal.

Re A and L (Children) [2011] EWCA Civ 1205

(Court of Appeal, Patten, Munby and Tomlinson LJJ, 27 October 2011)

Practice in relation to an appeal when the adequacy of the trial judge's reasoning is in issue. Here it was appropriate to remit the case to the trial judge to clarify his reasoning on certain points and the appeal was adjourned part-heard pending the judge's response.

18.6 ASSESSMENTS

Re S [2008] EWCA Civ 1078

Appeal as to refusing a residential assessment, *dismissed*. The information likely to have been acquired from the assessment would *not add any relevant or vital data to the picture that had already emerged*; and there was a real risk of losing the ongoing foster placement if such assessment were ordered. *R v L and H* distinguished.

Re J (Residential Assessment: Right of Audience) [2009] EWCA Civ 1210

Two issues – whether there should be a further residential assessment, and 'McKenzie Friends.' (1) This case raised the classic dilemma: What to do when a mother wants a further independent assessment of her capacity to care for her child yet, because she had had unsuccessful assessments in the past, the local authority says 'no'. The situation reached in this case [after 10 children] was '*enough is enough*' after *numerous reports* on the mother, a report by a psychologist and a report by a psychiatrist. Relevant authorities on residential assessments are: *A Local Authority v M (Funding of Residential Assessments)* [2008] EWHC 162 (Fam), [2008] 1 FLR 1579; *Re G (A Minor) (Interim Care Order: Residential Assessment)* [2005] UKHL 68, [2006] 1 FLR 601; *Re L and H (Residential Assessment)* [2009] EWHC 865 (Fam), [2009] 2 FLR 443 and *Re M (Assessment: Official Solicitor)* [2009] EWCA Civ 315, [2009] 2 FLR 950. (2) As to the issue of McKenzie friend: It had been illogical to allow the McKenzie friend to advocate the application for assessment yet be denied the ability to represent the mother on the substantive application. See Munby J in *Re N (McKenzie Friend: Rights of Audience)* [2008] EWHC 2042 (Fam), [2008] 2 FLR 1899.

Islington London Borough Council v EV [2010] EWHC 3240 (Fam), per Eleanor King J

Local authority plan was that *4-year-old child* [with a *sectioned mother* in England] should be taken to *Turkey* for an assessment of his living with the father to be carried out. The issue arose as to whether this should be done under *wardship*, or through para 19 of Sch 2 to the Children Act 1989. *Held:* Under the Children Act 1989, given that all parties consented, save for mother who, in any event did not have capacity. As to relevant authority, see *Re P (Minors) (Interim Order)* [1993] 2 FLR 742.

18.7 BURDEN/STANDARD OF PROOF

Re K (Sexual abuse: Evidence) [2008] EWCA Civ 1307, [2009] 1 FLR 921

Guidance from the Court of Appeal as to how to handle a very difficult private law case where *a 5-year-old* made comments at school, *out of the blue*, as to *sexual abuse* with inadequate evidential procedures thereafter; in the context of a *very difficult family breakdown*. The court should *evaluate* each parent, *weigh* concerns flowing from the child's words against the father's statement to the police and consider the issues which went to credibility. *Re B (Sexual Abuse: Standard of Proof)* [2008] 2 FLR 141 considered.

R(D) v Life Sentence Review Commission [2008] UKHL 33

There is a single standard of proof for civil proceedings, and that is the balance of probabilities. A court must weigh the evidence and reach a view on that evidence as to whether something is more likely to have occurred or not; see also *Re B (Sexual Abuse: Standard of Proof)* [2008] 2 FLR 141.

18.8 CAFCASS

Re A (Children: 1959 UN Declaration) [1998] 1 FLR 354

Unless there are strong reasons to do otherwise, judges should follow the guidance of Thorpe LJ in this case and, *if minded to depart from the recommendation of an experienced Cafcass officer should test any misgivings that they may have with the officer in the witness box before reaching a final decision* [contrast *Re C (Section 8 Order: Court Welfare Officer)* [1995] 1 FLR 617, which was distinguished in this case].

Re CB (Access: Attendance of Court Welfare Officer) [1995] 1 FLR 622, Re W (Residence) [1999] 2 FLR 390

The *general position* is that a clear recommendation of the CAFCASS officer *should only be rejected* after *oral* evidence. However where there *is no such clear* recommendation, it is unnecessary to adjourn to hear the welfare officer: *Re C (Section 8 Order: Court Welfare Officer)* [1995] 1 FLR 617. As to where Lords Justices of Appeal disagreed as to whether a recommendation was equivalent or 'cautiously expressed but unequivocal' see *Re R (Residence Order)* [2009] EWCA Civ 445.

A County Council v K [2011] EWHC 1672

(Family Division, Sir Nicholas Wall P, 4 July 2011)

Where there is an irreconcilable difference of view between a guardian and their manager, the decision of the line manager should not invariably prevail. The proper course is for Cafcass to apply to intervene and for the differing views to be placed transparently before the court. The court will then decide. It was not for Cafcass to replace the guardian or substitute its views for those of the guardian.

R (on the application of R and others) v Child and Family Court Advisory and Support Service [2011] EWHC 1774 (Admin)

(Court of Appeal, Munby LJ and Thirlwall J, 12 July 2011)

Cafcass has a duty to appoint a guardian as soon as reasonably practicable, taking into account its general functions, duties and resources. Cafcass does not owe a specific duty to an individual child. A mere delay in allocation and appointment of guardian did not of itself give rise to any actionable breach of either Art 6 or Art 8.

18.9 CARE PROCEEDINGS/PLANS

Re W (Care Proceedings: Litigation Capacity) [2008] EWHC 1188 Fam

There were *two issues*: (1) To what extent was the father's guilty plea in the criminal courts to non-accidental injury sufficiently open to doubt [by reference to his mental/litigation capacity] to warrant a rehearing of the facts; and (2) the law relating to *litigation capacity*. Cases referred to: *Re B* [1997] Fam 117; [1997] 1 FLR 285 as to the issue of estoppel in care proceedings; and as to mental capacity; *Masterman-Lister v Brutton and Co* [2003] 1 WLR 1511 and *RP v Nottingham City Council and the Official Solicitor* [2008] 2 FLR 1516.

Re C (Care Proceedings: Sexual Abuse) [2008] EWCA Civ 1331

Can a judge take into evidential account as corroboration, allegations of sexual abuse which a local authority has not pursued, in order to prove *'propensity'* in relation to an allegation of sexual abuse which it is pursuing? *No. Findings in care proceedings must not go beyond the case ultimately brought by the local authority*. The appellant could not 'unpick' the primary findings on the basis that the judge's approach had been so tainted throughout as to risk injustice; the judge's findings in relation to the girl who had given evidence were extremely clear and strong and his confidence in her had been well above the balance of probabilities.

Re B-M (Care Orders: Risk) [2009] EWCA Civ 205

Muslim *'honour killing'* case where three children taken into care, fostered with a white non-Muslim family with a s 91(14) order. **Principle:** Everything that had happened from arson and domestic violence, to the mother's refusal to identify her brothers in the fire conspiracy for fear of reprisals and potential revenge – so-called 'honour killings' – was contrary to the best interests of the children and, as Wall LJ noted, *had nothing to do with any 'concept of honour' known to English law.* It was, he said, time to re-think the phrase 'honour killings' and impress upon those who thought otherwise that the law of England which regards parents *as equals* and the *welfare* of children as paramount applied in all cases. Whatever the cultural and religious considerations inherent in a set of facts, *applicants seeking permission to appeal in family cases* had to show that the judge had either made an error of law or had exercised judicial discretion in such a way as to render his or her decision plainly wrong. Further *held*: the Court of Appeal was a *court of review* and did not find facts; *Clarke v Newcombe* (1983) 4 FLR 482, cited with approval in *G v G* [1985] 1 WLR 647 [note the gloss on this case in *Re R (Residence Order)* [2009] EWCA Civ 445 where Moore-Bick LJ said at [73] that:

> 'it must be recognised that the court must look at the substance of the matter and that a failure to take into account one or more relevant factors in the exercise of discretion entitles this court to set aside the decision'.

Re H (Care Order: Contact) [2008] EWCA Civ 1245

Judge made a full care order with long term fostering for a 10-year-old whose parents had separated, and whose mother effectively barred contact with relevant family members including maternal grandmother. *Held: Allowing the appeal, residence order with mother coupled with a supervision order for 12 months.* The judge had erred in that he did not sufficiently take on board the *girl's understanding* of her predicament and *the depth of her feeling*. She had consistently retained a *wish to be with her mother* and demonstrated her distress that she was not with her. The *girl's wishes were a weighty factor* and the judge had erred in failing to perpetuate the fundamental importance of a relationship with, and life with, a parent if that were at all possible. Section 35 *befriending service also adumbrated in the judgment*, pursuant to Children Act 1989, s 35. Ward LJ's analysis also focused on the requirement for judicial consideration of a child's wishes in the light of *'understanding'* as well as *'age'* [*s 1(3)*]. *Comment:* See the opinion of Baroness Hale in *Re D (Abduction: Rights of Custody)* [2007] 1 AC 619, at [57] and at [2000] Fam Law 615 at 624 [*'Contact and Domestic Violence – the Expert's Court*

Report'] that the wishes of a child of around 10 or more should carry 'considerable weight. One should *not just hear* what the child has to say, but *listen*. The *need to respect the wishes* of children was emphasised for example in *Mabon v Mabon* [2005] EWCA Civ 634, [2005] 2 FLR 1011.

Re J (Care Proceedings: Injuries) [2009] EWHC 1383 (Fam); [2009] 2 FLR 99

Small child taken to hospital with a number of *severe injuries* including skull fractures and bruising. The father claimed that he had *accidentally dropped* the child but later *amended his story*. **Held: non-accidental injury not proved.** The court was not satisfied that one of the parents had lost control and inflicted an injury to the child. *It was more likely that a non-accidental injury had not happened but that in some dreadful way an accident had occurred:* the mother had remained consistent in her account; if the injuries had been non-accidental, the parents had had a very short time in which to devise an explanation; the parents had taken the child to hospital immediately; the father was cautious in recalling the events and in a state of shock and stress over what had happened; *the medical evidence could not point to non-accidental injury with any clarity and none of the doctors was prepared to give such evidence.* The court was impressed with the parents and there was no reason why the child should not be returned to their care. *'The use of experienced advocates in complex care proceedings was essential'.* **Commentary in Family Law:**

> 'Counsel had remained committed to the agreed timetable, focused on the relevant issues and concluded on time, resulting in only an 18-week lapse between the date of issue of the proceedings and the end of the fact-finding hearing. The early hearing date meant that the child suffered less disruption than might otherwise have occurred and, as a more tangential spin-off, the costs of the litigation borne by the rate payers and tax payers was reduced.'

Re W-P (Fact-Finding Hearing) [2009] EWCA Civ 216

Appeal allowed in relation to findings fact. **Held:** The format of the judgment had been unusual and arguably unwise in that there was a danger in addressing the three injuries separately. *The judge had failed to stand back and ask himself whether it was probable that the baby would have sustained injuries at the hands of the same man in two unrelated incidents of reckless behaviour within 3 hours.* The logical order of analysis would have been to start with the father's revised explanation of the fracture and then to have considered the competing arguments as to its credibility, with particular reference to the expert evidence. *A judge was entitled to accept part but not all of a witness's evidence, but where the rejected evidence included both an admission against interest and an exaggeration, judicial caution was required and should have been expressly recognised.* The judge's findings on causation of the bruising and scratch had been **extraordinary**: *they were based on the judge's own hypothesis rather than evidence and had not been tested at all by the three experts.*

Re R (Fact-Finding Hearing) [2009] EWCA Civ 1619

Judge effectively accepted a submission of 'no case to answer' on behalf of the father, when the mother was proved to have lied on oath in the context of a Part 1 hearing and a 4-year-old daughter. **Held:** As a general test, trial judges in preliminary fact-finding hearings involving serious allegations of domestic violence **should never terminate the case without hearing all the available evidence. The judge had responsibilities to the child.** The judicial function was the **pursuit of child welfare** and not the adjudication of the rights and wrongs between adults. It was **impossible to envisage circumstances** in which a judge, in a hearing in private law proceedings, should entertain an application that there was **no case to answer**.

Re A (Area of Freedom, Security and Justice) (C-523/07)

This case provides important guidance from the ECJ on certain issues of the interpretation of **Brussels II R**. It: **(a)** confirms that the Regulation applies to care (public law) proceedings in respect of children, as well as to private law aspects of parental responsibility; and see also *Re C* (Case C-435/06) [2008] 1 FLR 490. **(b)** This case articulates for the first time an approach to the determination of the (factual) issue of a **child's habitual residence** for the purposes of Art 8 (which gives primary jurisdiction to the courts of the country in which the child is habitually resident). **A child can be habitually resident in only one country at a time for the purposes of Brussels II R:** *Re A; HA v MB* (*Brussels II R: Art 11(7) Application*) [2008] 1 FLR 289; and **(c)** clarifies the conditions precedent for the exercise of the power to take **provisional measures** under **Art 20**. The national court which has taken the provisional measures is not required to transfer the case to the court of another Member State which has jurisdiction, but, insofar as the child's best interests so require, **should inform that court.**

Re A (Residential Assessment) [2009] EWHC 865 (Fam)

Where there is an interim care order the court also has the power to interfere with the exercise of parental responsibility by virtue of s 38(6). **The dividing line between the local authority's decision-making powers under an interim care order and the court's powers under s 38(6) was delineated by Lord Brown-Wilkinson in** *Re C (Interim Care Order: Residential Assessment)* [1997] 1 FLR 1, at 6–7. Other circumstances in which the court can interfere with the local authority's decision making powers are s 34 (contact) and s 39 (application to discharge a care order).

Re M (Assessment: Official Solicitor) [2009] EWCA Civ 315

Extremely damaged young mother acting through Official Solicitor. Failed residential assessment and psychological report on mother saying 'zero chance'. Judge refused application to instruct independent psychiatrist. **Held on appeal:** Official Solicitor given leave to instruct the psychiatrist and refer the papers for a residential assessment. Issue: *The forensic process must be fair. This was particularly so when the young mother was incapacitated, was on the brink of losing her child to care and/or adoption, and the Official Solicitor appointed to represent her considered that further, independent, information needed to be obtained and put before the court.* The Official Solicitor has a duty to explore all the avenues properly open to him and put before the court 'all relevant evidence necessary for the decision' [see *Re L and H (Residential Assessment)*] [2007] EWCA Civ 213, [2007] 1 FLR 1370. As to the role of the Official Solicitor in these cases, see *RP v Nottingham City Council* [2008] EWCA Civ 462, [2008] 2 FLR 1516; and [2008] Fam Law 835.

Re T (Care Order) [2009] EWCA Civ 121

Young child suffered *serious head injury* while in the care of parents found to be *non-accidental injury*. Parents did not accept issues as to domestic violence, alcohol and anger management. *Parents subsequently proved ability to progress and co-operate.* Local authority and guardian sought a supervision order. Judge made a full care order. **Held on appeal:** Supervision order for 12 months. This was the first reported case in which the court had made a care order despite the unanimous agreement of the parties to the making of a supervision order. *Note* **(i)** *Re O (Supervision Order)* [2001] 1 FLR 923: Hale LJ set out the *differences between care and supervision orders* in terms of the power under a care order to remove a child without recourse to the court; the sharing of parental responsibility; and the potential duration of the orders. **(ii)** Per *Oxfordshire CC v L* [1998] 1 FLR 70, Hale J emphasised the need for *strong and cogent reasons* to be advanced where a *more draconian order* was to be imposed on an authority *than they had asked for*.

> '... the court should, so far as is consistent with the paramountcy of the child's welfare, favour the making of a supervision order, as the sufficient and proportionate response to any risk presented to the child, in preference to the protection afforded by a care order.'

Re D (Care Proceedings: Preliminary Hearing) [2009] EWCA Civ 472

The court *was not required to identify* a perpetrator simply because the child had been assaulted by one or other of two people. At para [15] Lord Hoffman said that '*the question for the tribunal was simply whether it was more probable that one rather than the other was the perpetrator.*' If identification of a perpetrator were not possible, and the judge remained genuinely uncertain, then that was the conclusion that the judge should reach. In other words *'judges should not strain to identify a perpetrator of non-accidental injuries to children'*. This case also emphasised the demand for *judicial continuity* in 'split-hearings' [*not split judging*] but note the *exceptions* referred to in *Re G and B (Children)* [2009] EWCA Civ 10, [2009] 1 FLR 1145.

Re Z (Unsupervised Contact: Allegations of Domestic Violence) [2009] EWCA Civ 430

Counsel saw Judge in Chambers; judge curtailed finding-of-fact hearing and ordered unsupervised contact, notwithstanding allegations of domestic violence. **Held: (1)** *The Practice Direction: Residence and Contact Orders: Domestic Violence and Harm* [2008] 2 FLR 103 was an important document and was there *to be obeyed.* It was not designed to tell judges what to decide but to tell them how to go about deciding issues of residence and contact where there were allegations of *domestic violence*. It placed proper and firm emphasis on the *fact-finding exercise and that process should not be short-circuited.* **(2)** The days for private consultations between the judge and counsel *were long over* and could not survive the Human Rights Act 1998. *Comment: A judge needed to be very cautious before reversing a decision of another judge that a fact-finding hearing was necessary;* see *Re FH (Dispensing with Fact-Finding Hearing)* [2008] EWCA Civ 1249, [2009] 1 FLR 349. Assuming a fact-finding hearing is 'necessary' it is only when the judge has heard *all the evidence* and made findings of fact that he can determine where the best interests of the children really lie.

Re L-A (Care: Chronic Neglect) [2009] EWCA Civ 822

Definitive authority as to the *threshold for an interim care order*. The issue is the fundamental paramountcy of 'welfare': was the order sought by the local authority within the principles of s 1 of the Children Act 1989, taking into account the *welfare checklist*, the provision that no order should be made unless the making of an order was *better than no order at all* and the principle that *delay* was prejudicial to welfare? *Re L (Care Proceedings: Removal of Child)* [2008] 1 FLR 575 explained.

Re MA (Care: Threshold) [2009] EWCA Civ 853

Court could *not* extrapolate from the finding of the treatment of a *5-year-old 'mystery' child*, that there was the *likelihood of harm to the parents' own children*. Wilson LJ dissented. This is an *important case* being the first time the Court of Appeal has had to consider *when the dividing line between harm and significant harm was established*. Ward LJ gave a useful analysis of the meaning of *'significant'*, citing the dictionary definition of *'considerable, noteworthy or important'* and reviewing the evolution of the concept within the 1989 Act: see *Humberside CC v B* [1993] 1 FLR 257. The issue is *'the real possibility of significant harm.'* Also see *Re W (Care: Threshold Criteria)* [2007] EWCA Civ 102, [2007] 2 FLR 98 as to the distinction between harm suffered and likelihood; criticism of the failure by the first instance judge adequately to subject expert evidence as to anal abuse, to critical analysis.

Re C (Care: Contact) [2009] EWCA Civ 959

It is essential that local authorities get basic background information right. Per Sedley LJ: the 'disturbing tally of damaging inaccuracies ... indicate a deplorably casual and inappropriately hostile approach to a sensitive and responsible task on which the fate of families can depend.'

Re C (Care: Discharge of Care Order) [2009] EWCA Civ 955

Mother and 16-year-old child opposed discharge of a care order, the application for discharge having originally been made by mother who had throughout obstructed the care order. *Agenda:* To derive benefit from the *'leaving care'* finance. *Held:* The *purpose of the regulations* was to provide children with the sort of support others would normally expect from their own families and it was clear that the *scheme of the regulations* was to take out of the leaving care provisions those children who were in fact living with their own parents. Consequently the *boy did not* fall within the leaving care provisions anyway. See also *R (M) v Hammersmith and Fulham LBC* [2008] UKHL 14, [2008] 1 FLR 1384.

Re L (Care Proceedings: Risk Assessment) [2009] EWCA Civ 1008

The 6-month-old child suffered *extremely severe, non-accidental injuries.* After Part 1 fact-finding, judge *refused mother's application for independent risk assessment* against backdrop of mother making it clear that she was committed to undertaking any work necessary for achieving the return of her child, in the context of the judge ordering the local authority to serve their final care plan and placement order application with a listing for *final hearing before the date of the criminal trial. Held*: (1) The refusal of the mother's application had the effect of conveying the impression of pre-judging the case. This was not the function of a fact-finding hearing. (2) The outcome of the criminal trial was plainly relevant to the outcome of the care proceedings: *the criminal proceedings should be heard first as they were likely to throw up material which could inform the final hearing of the care proceedings.* As to the interface between care and criminal proceedings, see *SW v Portsmouth City Council; Re W (Care Orders: Sexual Abuse)* [2009] EWCA Civ 644, [2009] 2 FLR 1106. **Note: (1)** The need for a *split trial was questioned by the Court of Appeal,* given that the facts were clear, the injuries extreme and the extensive medical evidence unchallenged. **(2)** In relation to the need for independent expert assessment, see: *Re B (Care Proceedings: Expert Witness)* [2007] EWCA Civ 556, [2007] 2 FLR 979, *Re K (Care Order)* [2007] EWCA Civ 697, [2007] 2 FLR 1066 and *Re M-H (Assessment: Father of Half-Brother)* [2006] EWCA Civ 1864, [2007] 1 FLR 1715.

Re R (Care Order: Threshold Criteria) [2009] EWCA Civ 942

Recorder had not found 'threshold' crossed in relation *to second child of a father different from first child*, where he found threshold *was* crossed. *Held on appeal:* The recorder *did not advert* to the most important feature of Lord Nicholls' judgment in *Re H (Minors)(Sexual abuse: Standard of Proof)* [1996] AC 563, [1996] 1 FLR 80 to the effect that the requirement that significant harm be 'likely' did not mean that it had to be 'probable' in the sense of 'more probable than not'; *but that it had only to be a real possibility or one which could not sensibly be ignored*. What was 'likely' within the interpretation of the Act was *not* to be equated with 'probability.' For an example of where the CA upheld the view that there *was not a 'real possibility' of children suffered significant harm*, see *Re MA (Care Threshold)* [2009] EWCA Civ 853.

Lancashire County Council v R [2008] EWHC 2959 (Fam) Ryder J

Three-month-old child admitted to hospital with chronic and *acute subdural haemorrhage and extensive retinal haemorrhages.* Finding father responsible for each of the two major incidents, *Held*: **(1)** Where a court is considering whether a primary fact in issue is proved, it may have direct evidence of the primary fact *andlor evidence of secondary facts which, if found, enable proper judicial inferences as to the existence of the primary fact to be made.* It is in consideration of all the circumstances and the way in which they inform each other that the judicial fact finding function is based. **(2)** Split fact-finding hearings of necessity should be limited to discrete or serious issue cases *where the proceedings can be expedited or delay contained by the separation of the key issues into separate hearings.* To do otherwise undermines the fact-finding process by removing important contextual material from the court's consideration. **(3)** The identification of the perpetrator is to be established, on the evidence, applying a simple balance of probabilities test [*Re B*]. *The court cannot decide that one parent is the perpetrator but that the other parent cannot be excluded as the perpetrator.* **(4)** It may be forensically unwise to attach much, if any weight to the evidence if it is directed only to the question of propensity: *Re CB and JB (Care Proceedings: Guidelines)* [1998] 2 FLR 211.

Re B (Care Proceedings: Interim Care Order) [2009] EWCA Civ 1254

An interim care order was an 'essentially impartial step, which effectively maintains the status quo and does not give a local authority .... A tactical advantage over other parties; the regime [of the order] should operate as a tightly run procedure closely monitored by the court and affording all parties the opportunity of frequent reviews as events unfold'; see *Re G (Minors) (Interim Care Order)* [1993] 2 FLR 839 and *Re M (A Minor) (Appeal: Interim Order) (No 1)* [1994] 1 FLR 54; *Re L-A (Care: Chronic Neglect)* [2009] EWCA Civ 822. It is not the function of a judge on an interim care application to make findings of fact. It is his or her function, however *to review* the evidence and decide *whether or not* it provides reasonable cause to believe that the threshold criteria in s 31(2) of the 1989 Act are satisfied and if so, *whether or not the child's welfare* requires an interim care order.

Re S-B (Children) [2009] UKSC 17

Held:

(1)   It is now well settled law that the test to be applied to the *identification of perpetrators* is the balance of probabilities, as it is in regard to any other factual issue in the case.

(2)   There is no obligation on the judge to decide, even on the balance of probabilities, who has caused harm to the child. *Unlike a finding of harm, the identification of the perpetrator is not a necessary ingredient of the threshold criteria.*

(3)   *If the judge cannot identify a perpetrator, it is still important to identify the pool of possible perpetrators.*

(4)   If the evidence is not such as to establish responsibility on the balance of probabilities it should nevertheless be such as to establish whether there is *a real possibility* that a particular person was involved. When looking at how best to protect the child and provide for his future, the judge will have to consider *the strength of that possibility* as part of the overall circumstances of the case.

(5)   While it is helpful to have a finding as to who caused injuries to a child if such a finding can be made, *it is positively unhelpful to have the sort of indication of percentages that the judge was invited to give in this case*: dicta of Lord Nichols in *Re O and N; Re B* [2003] UKHL 18, [2003] 1 FLR 1169 explained.

(6)   Where the judge does identify a perpetrator on the balance of probabilities, *all the evidence accepted by the judge relating to all the*

risk factors that the judge had identified remains relevant in deciding what will be best for the child. The judge must remain alive to the possibility of a mistaken identification, and *be prepared to think again* if evidence emerges which casts new light on the evidence which led to earlier findings. The judge is entitled *to revisit an earlier identification of the perpetrator* if fresh evidence warrants this. **Note:** The effect of the full judgment of Baroness Hale seems to be this: In a case like this where the court is dealing with the risk of future harm to a different child, and one of the two possible perpetrators of harm to the first child has not left the scene, then in the absence of any other evidence about the inability of the mother to care adequately for the younger child, the threshold cannot in fact, be satisfied if the court cannot identify the mother as perpetrator – and such identification must be a necessary ingredient of the threshold in these circumstances.

Note: *Re T (Care Proceedings: Appeal)* [2009] EWCA Civ 1208 should now be read subject to *Re S-B*.

Re MW (Case Management) [2010] 1 FLR 1093, per Holman J

The *father at age 17* entered into an *unmarried relationship in 1997* and a child L was born prematurely the next year. The *child died at the age of 6 weeks* having been admitted to hospital. The medical evidence was divergent, some experts considering that NAI caused death. *The father subsequently commenced another relationship and a child M was born in 2008.* M was admitted urgently to hospital at the age of *10 weeks with significant brain damage and retinal haemorrhages.* The local authority commenced care proceedings in relation to M and on discharge from hospital he was placed first with foster carers and subsequently with his maternal grandparents. *Medical evidence indicated that M had suffered fractures prior to his admission to hospital.* Medical opinion was that M had suffered non-accidental shaking and impact injuries. Both parents strongly denied that they had abused or mishandled M. *Held:* Until further order and in any event *until after the fact-finding and threshold hearing in relation to M's injuries, it was not necessary or appropriate for the court to determine the cause of death of L.* However, nothing should prevent the court from later directing that there be a trial of the issue of how and why L died if, *after the fact-finding hearing in relation to M, it appeared to the court that such was necessary.*

Re A (Contact Order) [2010] EWCA Civ 208

Orders for separate representation of children should in the present conditions of restricted funding for the family justice system be issued *very sparingly,* per Thorpe LJ, from which Arden LJ distanced herself.

Thorpe LJ recognised that there are cases involving *'children in the post-pubertal adolescent rebellion for whom it is very difficult for a guardian to act ...'*

Birmingham City Council v AG and A (2009) EWHC 3720 (Fam)

See the extraordinary and brutal facts for the full picture. *Inter alia held*: The child's death [one of six] was caused by and was the responsibility of the mother and the man but, in all probability, had there been an adequate initial assessment and proper adherence by the *educational welfare services* to its guidance, she would not have died. At the very least a *proper initial assessment* should have been completed by the authority according to the Framework for Assessment of Children in Need and their Families.

Re W (Children) (Abuse: Oral Evidence) [2010] UKSC 12

Should a 14-year-old daughter be required to give oral evidence as to sex abuse against her father in the absence of any medical evidence flowing from a medical examination but with her father's DNA on her clothing? *Held:*

(1)   *The existing law* which had erected a presumption against a child giving evidence in family proceedings *could not be reconciled* with the rights of all those concerned in those proceedings under Arts 6 and 8 of the European Convention on Human Rights and Fundamental Freedoms 1950 (the European Convention) and would thus no longer be appropriate.

(2)   Striking *a fair balance between competing Convention rights* in care proceedings may well mean that the child should not be called to give evidence but that would be as a result of the *weighing of considerations* and *not a presumption* or even a starting point.

(3)   The problem of whether the current practice could be reconciled with European Convention rights or even with elementary principles of justice was a *question of law* for the Supreme Court [not as the CA believed, for the FJC], albeit the Court would have preferred the up-to-date advice of an expert multi-disciplinary committee.

Note: Cases referred to: *R v B County Council, ex parte P* [1991] 1 FLR 470, *Re P (Witness Summons)* [1997] 2 FLR 447, *LM v Medway Council* [2007] EWCA Civ 9, [2007] 1 FLR 1698 and *Re W (Care Order: Sexual Abuse)* [2009] EWCA Civ 644, [2009] 2 FLR 1106. **Comment:** The central dilemma rested on *the differences between the criminal and family proceedings.* The focus in criminal proceedings was on the defendant and whether he was guilty or not; he clearly had the right to cross-examine his accuser. *In family proceedings the focus was on the child and whether the* *state was required to intervene for the purpose of protection;* jurisprudence, placing the child's welfare as paramount, had tended to avoid any potential harm to the child by refusing to order her to give oral evidence. The central concern was that settled practice as set out in the relevant family jurisprudence had *tended to marginalise* any notion that fairness to someone like the father here had any part to play in the judicial process.

Practice management: *The court will have to weigh the advantages that the evidence and cross-examination would bring to the fact-finding task against the damage that giving evidence may do to the child.* Factors such as the issues that have to be decided, the *age and maturity* of the child, the *quality* of videoed evidence and any *specific risks* to the child all need to be weighed in the balance. Baroness Hale was clear that risk of harm was a feature that must always be given great weight, albeit that weight would vary from case to case, and concluded with a prediction: if the court were to be called upon to carry out the balancing exercise, *the consequence would usually be that the additional benefits to the court's task in calling the child would not outweigh the additional harm that it would do to the child. '... rarity should be a consequence of the exercise rather than a threshold test.'*

Re B (Interim Care Order) [2010] EWCA Civ 324

Order for children to be separated from mother whilst an assessment was made of the mother's capacity to care safely for them and protect them from the violent father from whom the mother had separated. **Held:** *An interim care order was flexible enough to enable a judge to remove children from their mother temporarily when the local authority considered that an assessment of her capacity to care for and protect them could not be carried out safely while they were living with her.* **Note:** The continued removal of a child had to be *proportionate* to the risk of harm to which she would be exposed if she were allowed to return to the parent's care. Here, the mother had contended that a very high standard had to be established to justify interim removal. *The local authority, and the judge, took the view, however, that there was* a real possibility *that the mother would not disengage from her violent partner despite her best wishes and endeavours.* She was a *vulnerable woman* under the control of a *controlling man:* it was the very sort of case in which children needed an environment in which they were *'ring-fenced away from the gunfire'.* **Note:** Relevant authorities: *Re G (Minors) (Interim Care Order)* [1993] 2 FLR 839 and *Re M (A Minor) (Appeal: Interim Order) (No 1)* [1994] 1 FLR 54. Per *Rayden and Jackson on Divorce,* cited by Wall LJ:

> 'The making of an interim care order is an essentially impartial step which
> effectively maintains the status quo and does not give a local authority in
> whose favour it is granted a tactical advantage over the other parties; the

regime of an interim care order should operate as a tightly run procedure closely monitored by the court and affording all parties the opportunity of frequent reviews as events unfold.'

EH v Greenwich and AA and A (Children) [2010] EWCA Civ 344

(1) *Failings of local authority*: They had *pre-judged* the matter, formed a view *far too early* that the care plan should involve *placement away from the family* and were *utterly reluctant to budge* from that position. Where the mother needed *help to break her relationship* with the abusive father, she was denied it, abruptly and without explanation. *It is now well known that women in abusive relationships with controlling men can find it very difficult to break away*; here the mother had left the father, gone to a refuge and asked for help. It was *not forthcoming*.

(2) *As to the judge*: He fell into a series of traps *with regard to identification evidence* as well as in relation to *his conclusions that his findings of fact led inexorably to adoption.* There was a raft of alternative arguments on the basis of his findings (help in breaking the mother's relationship with the father, and continuation of foster care for example) and it could *simply not be said that a permanent separation from a loving mother was in the children's best interests*. Further, s 1(2) of the 2002 Act requires the court to consider the welfare of the child 'throughout his life'. **Authorities:** The range of relevant cases is: *Re G (Children)* [2006] UKHL 43, [2006] 2 FLR 629, *Re B (Care: Interference with Family Life)* [2003] EWCA Civ 786, [2003] 2 FLR 813, *Re P (Placement Order: Parental consent)* [2008] EWCA Civ 535, [2008] 2 FLR 625; *Re M (Fact-Finding Hearing: Burden of Proof)* [2008] EWCA Civ 1261, [2009] 1 FLR 1177, *Re B (Care Proceedings: Standard of Proof)* [2008] UKHL 35, [2008] 2 FLR 141 and *Re F (Placement Order)* [2008] EWCA Civ 439, [2008] 2 FLR 550.

Re I (Care Proceedings: Fresh Evidence) [2010] EWCA Civ 319; [2010] 2 FLR 1462

Non-accidental injury. Perpetrators. Pool of perpetrators, subsequent child. **Per Curiam**: Where there is fresh evidence, that justifies some revision of the detailed conclusion of the fact-finding trial but not a retrial, this should be appended to the record, possibly as an attachment to the judgment refusing an application for a retrial. **Note:** In *Re K (Non-accidental Injuries: Perpetrator: New Evidence)* [2004] EWCA Civ 1181, [2005] 1 FLR 285 held that *where it might be possible to exclude* someone from the pool of perpetrators as a result of their fresh evidence (in that case, the mother having left the husband's home and wider family and alleging that she had been bullied and abused by them), it was important that *a fresh hearing* should take place. In the instant case, the differing view of a later expert would not have exonerated the mother, but rather widened the pool. *It was right to refuse to re-open the fact-finding stage since it would not affect the ultimate outcome.*

Re S (Care Proceedings) [2010] EWCA Civ 42

58-year-old British father entered into a third marriage, this time with a very young Romanian woman whom he brought to the UK. 2 children – 5 years and 9 months. Finding that father a *'shocking, violent, selfish bully and a sexual predator'*. Local authority proposed *immediate foster care for children*, after first representing to the mother that she could retain care of the children *if she did not pursue the father* in respect of her pressing financial needs. Order thereupon made for children to be removed from mother without any proposals made for contact. *Held:*

(1) The immediate removal of the children from their mother was neither formulated nor communicated to her in a proper manner: *Re G (Care: Challenge to Local Authority's Decision)* [2003] EWHC 551, [2003] 2 FLR 42. *The case was not one which demanded urgent removal of children;* rather, there had been time and opportunity for amended care plans to be drawn and put to the court. This would have enabled the mother to be cross-examined and for the *insubstantiality of the grounds* for the plans to be demonstrated.

(2) The grounds for the change of care plan had *not demonstrated* that the safety of the children *demanded immediate separation* (see *Re LA (Care: Chronic Neglect)* [2009] EWCA Civ 822, [2010] 1 FLR 80.

(3) The judge had been *party to a wholesale misrepresentation to the mother*.

(4) The judge had not properly balanced *the pros and cons of removal:* the baby was only a few months old, the authority had *never questioned the mother's care*, the children were *both well and happy* and neither child had ever spent a night away from the mother. Neither had there been any discussion of the obvious way in which the children might have been protected from the father – ie a return to a refuge.

(5) The judge had been wrong to assess the authority's plans without considering the *issue of contact*. The bond between mother and children was *very strong*.

D McG v Neath Port Talbot County Borough Council [2010] EWCA Civ 821

Issue – if there was only a *small chance of rehabilitation*, should the court cause further delay and uncertainty for the children by *adjourning for a*

specialist parenting assessment of their mother or proceed to making placement and adoption orders without every avenue being explored?
Held:

- There *should be the further enquiry* despite the fact that the children would all be a little older and possibly a little more difficult to place if adoption were finally ordered. The *Draconian nature* of the order and an *assurance that Art 8* of the European Convention on Human Rights had been complied with were powerful factors in that determination.

- When the next appeal against a placement order arrived on the basis of a complaint that there was no *express reference to Art 8*, the Court of Appeal would have to consider whether the instruction of the court in *EH v A London Borough Council* [2010] EWCA Civ 344, [2010] 2 FLR 661 that '... *the terms of Art 8 must be explicit in the judgment ...*' was as absolutist as first appeared.

- It would be very helpful to the court *if, at the outset of a judgment in a care case, the judge were to introduce* all the parties and explain their different proposals for the future well-being of the children; then, before turning to the history if he or she were briefly to summarise the current circumstances of the children and each of the adult protagonists and collect particular areas of evidence together.

Re F (Care Proceedings: Interim Care Order) [2010] EWCA Civ 826

In the context of *twins born against a backdrop of previous children being taken into care, and procedural irregularity*, the Court of Appeal **held**:

- The judge had *fallen into error* and been in breach of the first proposition in *Re LA (Care: Chronic neglect)* [2009] EWCA Civ 822, [2010] 1 FLR 80, by focusing on issues that fell to be addressed at the final hearing and particularly by concluding that the history was, in itself, the determination of the interim care order.

- The judge's elevation of emotional harm as justifying the making of interim care orders and separating parents and children did not begin to meet the high threshold set by the authorities, particularly the second proposition in *Re LA*.

- The judge had prematurely refused the parents' application for leave to instruct an expert: *the designated expert had an obvious role to play in assessing what the parents needed, what was available locally and the time-frame within which the service could be expected to deliver benefit*; per Wall P. Had the test in either *Re B (Care Proceedings: Interim Care Order)* [2009] EWCA Civ 1254, [2010] 1 FLR 1211 or

Re L (Care Proceedings: Removal of Child) [2009] EWHC 3526 (Fam), [2008] 1 FLR 575 been applied, the judge would have reached the same result: it would not have been a proportionate exercise of discretion to remove a child in the circumstances of the present case.

Re D (Care Order; Evidence) [2010] EWCA Civ 100

Issue – *safety and parenting*.

- There was in this case an absence of many of the factors that normally characterised cases in which children were permanently removed: there was *no history of drug or alcohol abuse,* the couple had *been together for 10 years*, the father had a *decent employment history*, there was *no significant violence or sexual misbehaviour*, the *house was kept adequately* clean and the children were *'well enough fed'*.

- The *judge was the decision-maker, not the expert*, and had been entitled to prefer the empirical evidence to the psychological prognosis. He had been right to recognise that he *needed to give reasons for his departure from the undisputed expert opinion* and had correctly *weighed* the expert evidence *against the empirical evidence*.

- The nature of the *test under s 31(2)* was an *objective* one and it was abundantly clear that a parent may fail to provide reasonable care even though he or she was doing his or her incompetent best.

- *Re GR (Interim Care Order)* [2010] EWCA Civ 871: issues as to ICOs and when to make them.

- The difficulty with interim care order applications is that the judge has to look at the case at an interim stage and, as described by Black LJ:

  'be on the alert for **glaring contradictions, frank impossibility** in what is described, or anything else which ought to give rise to **real doubts** in relation to the cogency of the material.'

- This case illustrated the proper *two-stage approach to ICOs*: If the court is satisfied as to s 38(2), *then* it must consider as a discrete issue, whether or not to grant the order. The purpose of the second, welfare, stage is to establish a holding position until a full hearing.

- See *Re H (A Child)(Interim Care Order)* [2002] EWCA Civ 1932, where Thorpe LJ stressed that the decision as to an interim order

> *must be limited to the issues that could not await the final hearing* and that *separation* should only be ordered *if the child's safety demanded it.*

- In *Re M (Interim Care Order: Removal)* [2005] EWCA Civ 1594, [2006] 1 FLR 1043, Thorpe LJ stressed *the very high standard to be met* by the authority to justify the continuing removal of the child, and in *Re K and H* [2006] EWCA Civ 1898, [2007] 1 FLR 2043, Thorpe LJ stressed again that removal should not be sanctioned unless the child's safety so required.

- See also *Re B (Care Proceedings: Interim Care Order)* [2009] EWCA 1254, [2010] 1 FLR 1211, where Wall LJ, with whom Thorpe LJ agreed, found that the child's safety, *including her psychological welfare*, required interim protection. The concept of safety includes both the *physical and emotional / psychological welfare.*

- Note *Re GR (Interim Care Order)* [2010] EWCA Civ 871, reviewing the authorities on ICOs; note also the need to demonstrate *that safety of children demands immediate separation.*

Re WXYZ (Withdrawal of Care Proceedings) [2010] EWHC 1914 (Fam)

Issue was *whether to grant permission to withdraw care proceedings, or conduct a fact-finding hearing leading to no order under s 1(5) of the Children Act 1989* [where children had been summarily removed under an ICO on the basis of factitious induced injury, when further medical opinion demonstrated that there were some genuine medical conditions and that the case was not one of imputed illness *but, rather, over-anxious or dramatic exaggeration*]; see also *London Borough of Southwark v Y* [1993] 2 FLR 559.

Re A and D (Local Authority: Religious Upbringing) [2010] EWHC 2503 (Fam)

Primary issue was *religious upbringing under a care plan* where the father was not able to look after the 5-year-old, the mother had originally converted to Islam, a care order provided for the child to be with maternal grandparents [the grandmother was a practising Catholic] who undertook to rear the child as a Muslim, the maternal grandfather then died and the mother reverted to Catholicism, her birth religion. *The legal argument centered around s 33(6)(a), a provision concerned with the exercise of parental responsibility under a care order* which had never been considered before in a reported case. A central ambiguity in the phraseology – '*the authority should not cause the child to be brought up in any religious persuasion other than that in which he would have been brought up if the order had not been made'*. Baker J held that while the authority were bound to ensure that the child was brought up in the religious persuasion of the parents, they were also bound to have regard to any change of religion – even if only one parent's religion, as here, changed. *This case has highlighted an aspect of parental responsibility for a child in care which may well become a more common issue confronting the authorities given the increasingly multi-cultural nature of the UK*. See also: *Haringey London Borough Council v C (E, E, F and High Commissioner of the Republic of Kenya)* [2006] EWHC 1620 (Fam), [2007] 1 FLR 1035 and *Re P (Section 91(14) guidelines) (Residence and Religious Heritage)* [1999] 2 FLR 573.

Westwater v Secretary of State for Justice; Bryan v Secretary of State for Justice [2010] EWHC 2403 (Admin); [2011] 1 FLR 1989

These two cases were tried together. Each involved the question of a *prisoner's contact with his children*. Both prisoners had been imprisoned for *sexual offences* against children. There were flaws in the procedures taken by the prison governor. **Held:** The decisions as to the level of contact were quashed and it was further directed that assessments in accordance with the guidance issued by the Secretary of State be conducted so that new decisions as to contact could be taken. **Note:**

- 	The exposition of the legal framework was common to the two judgments.

- 	In each case, *the required procedures were not followed*. A *failure to comply with the Framework* will render a local authority's action *unlawful*: *AB and SB v Nottingham County Council* [2001] EWHC Admin 235.

- 	The justification for restriction on a prisoner's Art 8 ECHR rights was analysed by Harrison J in *R (Banks) v Governor of Wakefield Prison* [2001] EWHC Admin 917, at [22], [24]–[25]; para [31] of that judgment *emphasised the supervisory nature of the court's role,* on which see further *Secretary of State for the Home Department v Nasseri* [2009] UKHL 23. The concept of proportionality is well-developed in this field: see *R (Daly) v Home Secretary* [2001] 2 WLR 1622 especially at 1634 per Lord Steyn and *Sporring v Sweden* [1982] 5 EHRR 35.

Re L-W (Enforcement and Committal: Contact); CPL v CH-W [2010] EWCA Civ 1253

Intractable hostility case where the judge at first instance in effect treated the word 'allow' as meaning 'ensure'. A contact order *does not impose* a positive obligation to *ensure* that contact takes place (here in the face of vehement opposition by the child). The judgment of Munby LJ contains a useful analysis of the authorities on the appropriateness of *committal orders in difficult contact cases*: see *Churchard v Churchard* [1984] FLR 635, *Re S (Minors: Access)* [1990] 2 FLR 166, *A v N Committal: Refusal of Contact)* [1997] 1 FLR 533, *Re M (Intractable Contact Dispute: Interim Care Orders)* [2003] EWHC 1024 (Fam), [2003] 2 FLR 636, *Re D (Intractable Contact Dispute: Publicity)* [2004] EWHC 727 (Fam), [2004] 1 FLR 1226, *Re S (Contact: Promoting Relationship with Absent Parent)* [2004] EWCA Civ 18, [2004] 1 FLR 1279, *Re S (A Child) (Contact Dispute: Committal)* [2004] EWCA Civ 1790, [2005] 1 FLR 812, *B v S (Contempt: Imprisonment of Mother)* [2009] EWCA Civ 548, [2009] 2 FLR 1005. In *B v S* Wilson LJ said at [16]:

> 'The days are long gone when mothers can assume that their role as carers of children protects them from being sentenced to immediate terms of imprisonment for clear, repeated and deliberate breaches of contact orders.'

Munby LJ observed: Committal should not be *used unless it is a proportionate response* to the problem nor *if some less drastic remedy* will provide an adequate solution. The 2006 amendments to the Children Act 1989 give the court a wide range of options in an intractable hostility dispute.

AP v TD (Relocation: Retention of Jurisdiction) [2010] EWHC 2040 (Fam), per Parker J

- Principle: Parker J determined that *the parties' agreement to submit to the English jurisdiction on matters of contact, at the time the original relocation order was made, extended to all aspects of parental responsibility* – although it is for the judge hearing the substantive application as to whether he or she will exercise that jurisdiction in the best interests of the child.

- In reaching her conclusions, Parker J considered the Supreme Court decision in *Re I (A Child) (Contact Application: Jurisdiction)* [2009] UKSC 10, [2010] 1 FLR 361, which held that *Brussels II R* Art 12 can apply to children resident outside the EU. Also considered was *Re L (Residence: Jurisdiction)* [2006] EWHC 3374 (Fam), [2007] 1 FLR 1686.

- Further held that there was *no bar in principle* to different aspects of parental responsibility being heard in different jurisdictions; see also *L v L* [2006] EWHC 2385 (Fam).

- In *C v C* [2006] EWHC 3247 (Fam), Hedley J held that an *objective assessment of the mother's litigation conduct* was that she had unequivocally accepted the English court's jurisdiction by participating in proceedings both before and after the parties divorced and she had been given permission to relocate with the children.

- In *Bush v Bush* [2008] EWCA Civ 865, [2008] 2 FLR 1437, the Court of Appeal held that filing a statement of arrangements in divorce proceedings *does not amount to acceptance* of the jurisdiction for the purpose of parental responsibility.

- **File management technique**: This case shows the need for care, when advising on *the terms of any agreement* made on relocation decisions, to ensure that both parties can be *as clear as is possible* as to the effect of any terms preserving (or purporting to preserve) the English courts' jurisdiction for the future determination of disputes over the arrangements for their children.

Re A and B (One Parent Killed by the Other) [2011] 1 FLR 783

The *mother* of two children was *killed by the father*. He was convicted of manslaughter and sentenced to 7 years of imprisonment. Immediately after his arrest the paternal grandparents took over the care of the children and the police referred the case to the local authority. **Per curiam** *[this guidance is intended to provide a framework in cases where one parent has been killed by the other, to ensure that the harm caused to children by the killing is not compounded by poor management and delay]*:

- In all cases where one parent had been killed by the other, the *threshold* criteria in s 31 of the Children Act 1989 would be *met*; the authority should give immediate consideration to *issuing care proceedings* and *appoint a social worker* for the affected sibling group [this in the context of Dr. Harris Hendricks emphasising how 'extraordinarily difficult it was for two halves of a family divided by an unlawful killing to cope with the consequences'].

- A *guardian* should be *appointed* at the *earliest opportunity*, the case transferred to the *High Court* and early consideration given to *interim placement* and *contact arrangements*. There should be *liaison* between the authority solicitor and CPS case manager where there were *concurrent criminal proceedings*; where there was a protocol in place that should be utilised but otherwise consideration should be given to a *joint criminal and care case management hearing*.

- *Professionals* involved should *familiarise* themselves with the *appropriate specialist guidance* and *advice* and any *delay* in the provision of *therapy* for the child kept to a *minimum*. School-age children should be kept informed of their situation.

- Where the **killing** took place in the **family home**, the authority should **liaise with the police** with respect of the recovery of the children's **toys** and **clothes** and immediate **financial and practical support** for carers put in place.

- **Expert advice** should be sought with respect to **planning contact** between the children and other **key relatives** and where there was conflict contact decisions should be made by the court. Consideration should be given to family group conferencing to help to facilitate communication.

- Each case should be considered on its own facts and the merits of each placement looked at individually **without presumptions that the perpetrator's family be discounted**.

In the Matter of A and B [2010] EWCA Civ 1000

The test for s 31(2) of the Children Act 1989 is 'objective'.

'For the avoidance of doubt, the test under section 31(2) is and has to be an **objective** one. If it were otherwise, and the 'care which it is reasonable to expect a parent to give' were to be judged by the standards of the parent with the characteristics of the particular parent in question, the protection afforded to children would be very limited indeed, if not entirely illusory. It would in effect then be limited to protection against the parent who was fully able to provide proper care but either chose not to do so or neglected through fault to do so. That is not the meaning of section 31(2). It is abundantly clear that a parent may unhappily fail to provide reasonable care even though he is doing his incompetent best.'

Re C and D (Photographs of Injuries) [2010] EWHC 3714 (Fam)

- Note judge's comments on the requirements to be met if **photographic evidence** is to be **properly utilised** in cases of **suspected abuse**.

- He noted that the Royal College of Paediatrics and Child Health issued guidance in 2006 on such use but that this failed to indicate the **importance** of taking photographs of bruising as **soon as is reasonably possible**.

- He also pointed out that the photographs were not of **adequate quality** – all the injuries should have been identifiable on the photographs, at least to a medical expert witness, and there **should have been a note in the hospital records** to show the **date** and **time** when they were taken, and identifying the medical professional present.

Re D (A Child: Care Order) [2011] EWCA Civ 34, per Wilson LJ

'In my experience one of the *most difficult tasks* which faces the family judge is to *translate* serious, indeed sickening, *paedophile offences* committed by a father or other adult on the internet into an *assessment of the risk* which he therefore poses to his own child. *In that translation the judges need all the expert help that they can get*.'

The interference with family life must be *necessary* in a democratic society, see *Olsson v Sweden* [1988] 11 EHRR 259, *Johansen v Norway* [1997] 23 EHRR 33, *L v Finland* [2001] 2 FLR 118, *Knutzer v Germany* [2003] 1 FCR 249, *K and T v Finland* [2001] 2 FLR 707 and *MAK and RK v UK* [2010] 2 FLR 451.

TW v A City Council [2011] EWCA Civ 17

Child witness – evidence – *acquittal* in criminal proceedings before a jury on direction of Crown Court judge due to manifest deficiencies in the ABE interview [*Achieving Best Evidence in Criminal Proceedings: Guidance on Interviewing Victims and Witnesses, and Using Special Measures 2007*).

Principles:

(1) It is open to a circuit judge in family proceedings to reach a *different conclusion* on the balance of probabilities from a jury applying the criminal standard of proof. *But* if this is to happen, it is *not sufficient* for the judge to rely primarily on the fact that the child is able, when being interviewed in a thoroughly unsatisfactory manner and contrary to the Guidance, to make a number of exculpatory statements. *A clear analysis of all the evidence* is required and the judge must explain *how* and *why* the criminal trial came to the opposite conclusion and *look carefully* at the evidence available in *each* set of proceedings.

(2) The judge *should* have referred to the *substance* of the rulings of the judge in the *criminal trial* and *examined* those to see if they had an application to the facts of the case as they were presented to her.

Per curiam: Practitioners are *reminded* of the requirements set out in *Practice Direction 52 PD 66 Appeals* and *Practice Statements (Supreme Court: Judgments)* [1998] 1 WLR 825, which require that *relevant authorities* must be copied from the *official law reports* where available; with Bailli reports or those from other series only to be used if no other recognised reports are available and the case really needs to be cited. *Relevant passages in the authorities on which counsel seek to rely must be marked.*

B Local Authority v RM, MM and AM [2010] EWHC 3802 (Fam), [2011] 1 FLR 1635

This is the first case where the question of *a transfer from the court hearing care proceedings under the CA 1989 to the Court of Protection (COP)* dealing with the Mental Capacity Act 2005 has been considered. The judge here initiated the transfer of his own motion, not being convinced that the course of action proposed by either the authority or the mother met the girl's welfare needs. *The COP cannot exercise jurisdiction in respect of any person under 16*. In the instant case, the girl was 17 and *lacked capacity*, thus engaging the jurisdiction of the COP. The question of transfer will only arise as a practical issue where the child, with *lifelong disabilities*, is aged at least 16 at the date of the care hearing.

Re M (Children) [2011] EWCA Civ 1035

(Court of Appeal, Thorpe, Longmore and Stanley Burnton LJJ, 1 July 2010)

The Court of Appeal endorsed the judge's decision to make an interim care order solely to give the local authority power to tell the children about their father's history and conviction for abusing his children from his previous marriage. The judge's personal views were an inevitable part of any welfare decision and his judgment had been admirably balanced.

Re G (Interim Care Order) [2011] EWCA Civ 745

(Court of Appeal, Sir Nicholas Wall P, Rix LJ, 28 June 2011)

A judge had made interim care orders under which children were to be removed from their mother but had not referred to the relevant authorities and had treated the hearing as a final hearing. The orders were set aside and interim orders made pending the final hearing.

A County Council v M and F [2011] EWHC 1804 (Fam)

(Family Division; Mostyn J; 13 July 2011)

During a fact-finding hearing to determine the cause of death and origin of injuries of a 7-month-old child the parents described how they had discovered the child looking lifeless one morning. The paramedics attended and worked forcefully on him but the child was pronounced dead on arrival at hospital. A post-mortem revealed the child had 23 separate injuries but none of which either individually or cumulatively would have caused death and there was no medical explanation for the cause of death. Sudden infant death syndrome was said to be unlikely due to the age of child and the existence of injuries.

Social work assessments of the parents were positive with no apparent cause for concern apart from the fact that the father had taken the baby in a bike buggy from a very young age, despite a warning on the buggy that it was unsuitable for children under 12 months. There was a possibility that the injuries caused by buggy use and/or a serious blood disorder.

The local authority proceeded their case on the basis that the parents had abused the baby throughout his life and murdered him. The histological evidence indicated that the injuries had occurred during the lifetime of child, not after death. The judge found it was extremely improbable that the parents had caused the injuries.

NB v Haringey LBC [2011] EWHC 3544 (Fam)

(Family Division, Mostyn J, 7 October 2011)

An interim care order granted in respect of a 3-year-old. Application to stay pending appeal. The appeal was likely to be heard 3 weeks later. The mother was a drug user with a history of not complying with orders and directions to undertake regular drug testing. She maintained a relationship with the father who was in prison for serious domestic violence against the mother. The mother claimed to have stopped using 6 weeks previously. The mother claimed the interim threshold was not passed, but the guardian disagreed but advised a supervision order. The local authority sought an interim care order. The written analysis of the magistrates' decision to make the interim care order was limited and relied on the domestic violence risk posed by the father with no mention of other factors although clearly they were considered.

Application refused. It was impossible on the material available to say that the appeal had a strong likelihood of success or that the justices had been plainly wrong to make an interim care order as opposed to a supervision order.

Re B-A (Children) (Care Proceedings: Joinder of Grandmother) [2011] EWCA Civ 1643

(Court of Appeal; Thorpe, Kitchin LJJ, Mann J; 1 December 2011)

A local authority sought care orders in respect of three Ghanaian children. The viability study assessed the maternal grandmother as a potential carer. At the time of the assessment the maternal grandmother lost her own mother, travelled to Ghana and did not return until shortly before the hearing. The assessment discounted her as a potential carer but she never received the report. The grandmother applied for an independent assessment and reconsideration of herself as a potential carer. The judge refused to grant her party status. The grandmother appealed claiming the case management process had been unfair. The decision had been difficult but the grandmother had been denied the opportunity to test the evidence against her and test the issue of delay.

Appeal allowed.

Re A and L (Fact-finding Hearing: Extempore Judgment) [2011] EWCA Civ 1611

(Court of Appeal; Patten, Munby, Tomlinson LJJ; 21 December 2011)

The mother appealed a fact-finding judgment which found her two children had been sexually abused by three friends of hers and that she had been involved. The parties had been asked by the judge whether there was any particular area they felt he had not covered but they declined. The mother claimed the judge had provided insufficient reasoning. The case was remitted to the trial judge with an invitation to provide further reasoning. The judge was unable to do so for reasons unconnected with the case.

Appeal remitted to Court of Appeal for determination. Appeal dismissed. Judge's reasoning had been sufficiently clear, reasons had been brief but adequate. The judge had been faced with familiar dilemma of either adjourning to prepare a written judgment and causing further delay or giving an ex tempore judgment so that plans for the children could be made with minimal delay. Ex tempore judgments should not be discouraged. Safeguard is the duty of the parties to seek further elaboration if they feel something is missing.

Re A (Children) (Meeting with Child: Contamination of Proceedings) [2012] EWCA Civ 185

(Court of Appeal; Thorpe, Rimer, Lewison LJJ; 13 January 2012)

Serious allegations of sexual abuse made by five children whilst in foster care due to concerns for emotional harm and neglect. In a last minute meeting with the judge the eldest child told the judge that the allegations were true. Judgment in fact-finding hearing found children had been sexually abused. Parents appealed in relation to the judge's meeting with the child in that they had no opportunity to make representations regarding the proposed meeting and that the judge used the opportunity to gather further evidence. The judge had been clear that he had already formed a view prior to the meeting.

The guidelines for judge's meeting with children were only guidelines but there were obvious risks of contaminating the evidence. Growing perception that meeting with children a valuable opportunity for judges. Appeals dismissed.

Re C (A Child) [2012] EWCA Civ 535

(Court of Appeal; Thorpe, Patten LJJ; 16 February 2012)

A fact-finding hearing concluded that the child had suffered non-accidental injuries caused by one of the parents. After the judge retired, at a subsequent hearing a different judge went further and said he thought the mother was the more likely perpetrator but would not rule the father out entirely.

The mother appealed. The findings were not expressed in the resulting order and so were not ordinarily appealable. However, fairness to the mother required the offending paragraphs of the judgment to be struck out. The second judge had gone beyond the initial findings of the judge who had heard the evidence first hand. The mother's fundamental right to a fair trial had been breached and if the paragraphs remained in the judgment the mother's prospects of developing a harmonious relationship with the child and carers could be blighted. Appeal allowed.

Re E (A Child) [2012] EWCA Civ 537

(Court of Appeal; Thorpe, Etherton LJJ, Ryder J; 15 March 2012)

The mother suffered from borderline personality disorder due to childhood abuse and her three older children had been removed from her care. When she became pregnant with a fourth child the local authority was optimistic she would be able to care the baby as she was now in a supportive relationship. Her partner had joint residence of his two children by a previous relationship but they made their primary home with their mother. The father failed to return the children to their mother following a period of contact due to concerns they were living in an abusive household.

At a hearing regarding his two children, residence was transferred to the father based on the undertaking that the mother would find alternative accommodation. The judge decided against rehabilitation of the mother and her baby and approved plans for adoption. The judge could not be criticised for taking the decision she did which had not been plainly wrong. Appeal dismissed.

Re B (Paternal Grandmother: Joinder As Party) [2012] EWCA Civ 737

(Court of Appeal, Laws, Black LJJ, 31 May 2012)

The paternal grandmother wished to care for the 4-year-old child, who was currently in foster care and applied to become a party to the proceedings. Reports on the paternal grandmother noted excessive alcohol use and a history of choosing violent partners. The judge refused the grandmother permission to become a party to the proceedings. The grandmother appealed.

The judge had not erred in regarding the reports on the grandmother as unfavourable and had balanced the negatives with the fact that this was the child's grandmother and considered her Art 8 rights under the European Convention for the Protection of Human Rights and Fundamental Freedoms 1950. Given the likely delay an assessment would cause the judge was entitled to proceed on the basis that there was already enough evidence available to make a decision. Appeal dismissed.

A and S v Lancashire County Council [2012] EWHC 1689 (Fam)

(Family Division, Peter Jackson J, 21 June 2012)

Two boys, now aged 16 and 14, were accommodated as infants and freed for adoption but were never permanently placed. They had been placed with numerous foster carers throughout their childhood, some of whom were abusive, and became increasingly unsettled and disturbed, causing irreparable damage. Links with their birth family were lost despite their not being adopted and the reviewing system did nothing to correct it.

The court made declarations that the local authority and the reviewing officer had acted incompatibly with the boys' Art 8, 6 and 3 rights under the European Convention for the Protection of Human Rights and Fundamental Freedoms 1950.

18.10 CONTACT

Re P (Contact) [2008] EWCA Civ 1431

Against a fraught background of hate and mistrust, judge reduced contact to indirect pending submissions to be made before him as to the use of counselling to the parents. **Held on appeal:** Contact should not be stopped unless that course was a last resort. **Note:** Every avenue to keep contact alive should be pursued. ***Counselling should have been tried before any reduction in contact.***

Re C (Children) [2008] EWCA Civ 1389

Where a *contact order* was *not operating smoothly*, the court that made the order had a *continuing responsibility* to try to make it work, and that responsibility was all the greater where a *litigant in person* was before the court and *plainly frustrated* by the obstruction. The case also demonstrates how it is *misconceived to have recourse to a s 91(14)* order against the father when he needed the service of the court to address the mechanics of a contact order that was not working; the effect of imposing on the father such a restriction was to place an unnecessary hurdle in his path in applying again.

Re P-B (Contact: Committal) [2009] EWCA Civ 143

A judge in the *county court* has the power to attach a *penal notice* addressed to the *local authority* to a contact order under s 34 of the CA 1989 and to *enforce it by way of committal*. The question of contact with children in care was a matter for the court, *not for the discretion of the authority*. That latter had a responsibility to obey orders of the court as well as parental responsibility for the child. For a parallel case, see *Re S (A Child)* [2008] EWCA Civ 1140.

Re B (Contact: Appointment of Guardian) [2009] EWCA Civ 435

Judge had refused application that NYAS replace guardian in an *intractable hostility dispute* spanning a decade. **Held:** The judge had *properly exercised his discretion in refusing to appoint NYAS as a replacement guardian for for the 14-year-old girl*. Good relationship between experienced guardian and girl. Evidence indicated that the girl was 'sick to death of the litigation', and 'would be disheartened if she had to start explaining her position all over again with some new guardian'.

Re I (Contact: Jurisdiction) [2009] EWCA Civ 965

The judge dismissed the mother's *application for variation of a contact* order in respect of her *son living with paternal grandparents in Pakistan*, on the basis that the court had no jurisdiction to entertain it. **Note:** *The novel point raised on this appeal turned on the interpretation of the reference to 'third state' in Art 12(4): Did this include Pakistan?* The Court of Appeal found the answer not in a literal but in a purposive and 'instructive' construction of the Regulation.

Re E (A Child) [2009] EWCA Civ 1238

In a *split hearing*, after Part 1 – the judge indicated that the father's application for contact was almost bound to fail. *Held:* Judge *should not have so expressed himself* prior to the evidence to be deployed in Part 2;

new judge to take part 2. **Note:** For another example of an exceptional case where there could otherwise have been an impression of judicial bias, see *Re G and B (Fact Finding Hearing)* [2009] EWCA Civ 10, [2009] 1 FLR 1145.

Re M (Children) [2009] EWCA Civ 1216

Judge at first instance refused application for an adjournment in contact application relating to children of 9 and 13, notwithstanding that *father certified as unfit* to give evidence due to *bi-polar affective disorder*. *Held:* On the facts, this was *not an entirely hopeless case*. The judge should have seen that to dismiss the case in its totality at that stage was likely to result in a denial of the father's entitlement to a fair trial and that, given the presence of the *corroboration of his medical condition* and the *absence of any prior failure to attend*, the only acceptable conclusion was to grant the *adjournment for the shortest possible time* that could be arranged with the court office, and *giving the father ample warning* that on the next occasion his attendance was absolutely essential and that further adjournment would not be granted without the fullest corroboration and without evidence of exceptional circumstances.

Re A (Contact: Section 91(14)) [2009] EWCA Civ 1548

This case alerts family lawyers to the '*surprising and unfortunate amount of time*' the Court of Appeal spends '*in reversing orders under s 91(14) made on the summary basis here exemplified*'. The judge in the instant case had no evidence on which to base the order and had invited no submissions on the propriety of making it [see *Re C (Litigant in Person: Section 91(14) Order)* [2009] EWCA Civ 674, [2009] 2 FLR 1461]. Neither had she specified which kinds of applicants were barred without leave and which parent was to be subjected to the bar. Wilson LJ stressed two points arising from the leading case of *Re P (Section 91(14) Guidelines) (Residence and Religious Heritage)* [2000] Fam 15, [1999] 2 FLR 573, at 593B. The *first* was that the power to make the order was to be used *with great care* and *sparingly* pursuant to the four guidelines of Butler-Sloss LJ in that case: a s 91(14) order was '... the *exception* and not the rule'. *Secondly*, such an order was 'generally to be seen as a *useful weapon of last resort* in cases of repeated and untenable applications'.

Re G (Restricting Contact) [2010] EWCA Civ 470, [2010] 2 FLR 692

Section 91(14) permits the court to order that no application under the Children Act 1989 of any specified kind may be made by any person without leave of the court. Such an order is draconic and the jurisdiction is to be exercised sparingly: *Re P (Section 91(14) Guidelines) (Residence and Religious Heritage)* [2000] Fam 15, [1999] 2 FLR 573, *Re S*

(Permission to Seek Relief) [2007] 1 FLR 482 and *Re J (A Child) (Restriction on Applications)* [2006] EWCA Civ 1190, [2008] 1 FLR 369. There are however clear cases when a s 91(14) order is called for in the child's best interest: see *Re N (Section 91(14))* [2010] Fam Law 137.

Re S (Contact Order) [2010] EWCA Civ 705

- Under s 8 of the Children Act 1989, the court on contested applications was permitted *only to make orders for residence and for defined contact* when dividing a child's time between parents.

- There was nothing within the statute permitting the court to impose provisions as to a parent either caring for a child or having the care of a child or of dividing a holiday *other than in the form of a contact order.*

- *An order for contact cannot be made without first determining with whom a child shall live,* since it is the person with whom the child lives who in the terms of s 8(1) allows the child to have contact with the person named in the contact order: *Re B (A Child)* [2001] EWCA Civ 1968.

B v B [2010] EWHC 1989 (Fam)

- Issue: Whether an English court should *retain jurisdiction* over contact in the context of parents who both *originated from Pakistan,* where the child was now *living with the mother in Germany,* where the child was now habitually resident, having *left England* where they had been living for about 2 years. Holman J *dismissed all* continuing proceedings in England and discharged any previous contact orders.

- The *general rule* under *Art 8* of *Brussels II R* is that the courts of the Member State in which the child is habitually resident have jurisdiction in matters of parental responsibility.

- However, *Art 8 is subject to inter alia Art 12* [entitled 'Prerogative Jurisdiction'] para 3 of which provides:

  'The courts of a Member State shall also have jurisdiction in relation to parental responsibility ... where
  (a) a child has a *substantial connection* with that Member State, in particular by virtue of the fact that one of the holders of parental responsibility is habitually resident in that Member State or that the child is a national of that Member State; and
  (b) the jurisdiction of the courts *has been accepted* expressly or otherwise in an unequivocal manner by all the parties to the proceedings at the time the court is seised and it is in the best interests of the child.'

- Holman J assumed that the father was habitually resident in Germany and held that continuing involvement of the English Court was not in the child's bests interests; see also *Re S-R (Jurisdiction: Contact)* [2008] 2 FLR 1741.

Re W (Cross-Examination) [2010] EWCA Civ 1499

- A judge should *not* consider evidence of which all parties were *not aware* and able to make representations.

- *A one hour directions hearing should not have been turned into a final hearing without full evidence and the opportunity for cross-examination.*

Re F (Internal Relocation) [2010] EWCA Civ 1428

Four children. Divorced parents, much shared care. Mother wanted to move from England to one of the Scottish islands, her parents living in *Orkney*. *Held:* Dismissing mother's appeal:

- All four children had been born and brought up throughout their lives in one place and *could not have been more firmly rooted* there. The boy's contact with the father was on a *frequent* basis and was patently important for them, and the tortuous nature of the travel arrangements (up to 19 hours) placed an obvious question mark on the sustainability of the proposed contact regime.

- Although it did not arise for decision, *the relief appropriately to be sought* by an objecting parent to a proposed internal relocation is a *prohibited steps order*.

- NB: Perhaps '*exceptionality*' can be satisfied relatively more easily, in the context of the dicta of Dame Butler Sloss P in *Re S (A Child) (Residence Order: Condition) (No 2)* [2002] EWCA Civ 1795:

  'The general principle is clear that a suitable parent entrusted with the primary care of a child by way of a residence order *should be able to choose* where he/she will live and with whom. It will be most unusual for a court to interfere with that general right of the primary carer. There will however be *exceptional circumstances* in which conditions will have, in order to protect the best interests of the child, to be imposed albeit those conditions will interfere with the general right to choose, where to live within the United Kingdom.'

Re W (Family Proceedings: Applications) [2011] EWHC 76 (Fam)

Authority for the endorsement of the principle that the applicable evidential and procedural rules in *committals applications* are properly obeyed, and for '*redoubled vigilance when the respondent to such proceedings is a litigant in person*'. Further this case is an example of grandparents becoming partisan supporters of 'their' child in the divorce, at the risk of damaging their relationship with the child-in-law and, if the child is not the primary carer, with their grandchildren too. Such a situation can have highly negative effects on the otherwise beneficial role that grandparents can play in maintaining '*a haven*' for the grandchildren away from the disputes of their parents.

Re K (Children) [2011] EWCA Civ 1064

(Court of Appeal, Mummery and Lloyd LJJ and McFarlane J, 20 July 2011)

Although the court has a positive duty to promote contact, here the judge was entitled to conclude that the father, who had convictions for sexual offences against children, should not have face-to-face contact with his children. It was also within the discretion of the judge not to adjourn for instruction of a psychiatrist since this would not affect the decision as to whether there should be contact at this stage.

Re K (Children) [2011] EWCA Civ 1075

(Court of Appeal, Ward LJ and McFarlane J, 28 July 2011)

An order in Children Act proceedings that the father vacate his home to enable the mother to have staying contact with the child there was effectively an ouster order. It was outside the judge's jurisdiction under Children Act 1989, s 11(7) and could not stand.

Re P & L (Minors) [2011] EWHC 3431

(Family Division, Hedley J, 20 December 2011)

The children were aged 6 and 10 had been conceived via artificial insemination. Both parents were in same-sex relationships. Judgment given on parenting roles. The older child suffered significant emotional harm as a result of the breakdown in the relationship between the parents. The child was deeply hostile to the relationship between the parents and had been affected to the extent that she was now refusing contact with her father. Contact ordered for one weekend stay per month with the father and his partner, one annual holiday and one special event per year in respect of the younger child, only indirect contact for the older child. The parents urged to cease litigation and encourage the older child to agree to contact. Contact order was only the default position, parents should agree own regime of contact in best interests of children.

Kopf and Liberda v Austria (Application No 1598/06)

(European Court of Human Rights; 17 January 2012)

The 2-year-old child had been removed from his mother after she set fire to their home after drug use and both had to be rescued. The child remained with foster parents for 46 months and they applied to adopt him. The mother recovered, was allowed access and tried to regain custody. The foster parents applied to have contact with the child. The Austrian civil code provided that the court could grant contact to third persons if failure to do so would endanger the child's well-being. It was evident the child was vehemently opposed to contact and had re-established a good bond with his mother. He had not been in contact with the foster parents for 3 years. The regional court and supreme courts dismissed the foster parent's appeals on Art 8 grounds.

The Austrian courts had failed in the procedural requirement implicit in Art 8 to deal diligently with the request for contact. Proceedings had lasted 3 1/2 years during which time the foster parents had no contact with the child and he had re-established the relationship with his mother. That delay had a direct adverse impact on the foster parents: at the start of proceedings the welfare officer was recommending contact but at the conclusion of proceedings the district court found that if the proceedings had been concluded earlier there would have been good reason to order contact.

Re H (Contact With Biological Father) [2012] EWCA Civ 281

(Court of Appeal; McFarlane LJ, Sir Scott Baker; 27 February 2012)

The husband and wife were unable to conceive and agreed for husband's friend to act as sperm donor. The wife and friend ended up having a full sexual relationship and conceived a child. The father applied for parental responsibility and contact. The husband and wife reconciled during pregnancy. The judge dismissed father's application for parental responsibility and contact. Declaration of child's paternity and birth certificate rectified granting the father parental responsibility. District judge allowed father's appeal and ordered direct contact. Mother appealed.

Appeal allowed. There had not been a sufficient evaluation of the issues and where the child's best interests lay. Remitted the case to a fresh judge.

Re F (Contact) [2012] EWCA Civ 828

(Court of Appeal; Black, Ward, Elias LJJ; 3 April 2012)

The mother's supervised contact with her three children aged 14, 13 and 10 was terminated after she assaulted two of the social workers during a contact session. The mother appealed and sought contact with her children.

The judge had been entitled to accept the evidence of the social workers in relation to the assault and the judge's findings were adequately explained in his judgment. That decision could not be interfered with. Appeal dismissed.

Re H (Contact Order: Permissibility of Judge's Actions)

(Court of Appeal; Thorpe, Laws LJJ; 3 May 2012)

The parents sought a variation of the contact order. The judge allowed further time for negotiations after a discussion with all three counsel where it was agreed the matter could be dealt with by way of submissions only. The guardian reported that the child wished for contact to commence on Saturday morning, instead of Friday night, as he wanted to spend time with the mother. The judge approved that arrangement and the father appealed on the basis that the discussion between counsel and the judge had constituted a breach of his rights under Art 6 of the European Convention on Human Rights and the judge had focused on only one aspect of the welfare checklist.

The father's appeal was dismissed. The judge's approach was sensible and consistent with the general approach of trial judges in court when faced with lengthy negotiations that threatened to prevent completion of contested issues in the time permitted. He had heard lengthy submissions from all three counsel and looked at the matter from the proper welfare perspective and had given great weight to the child's wishes.

Re J (Contact) [2012] EWCA Civ 720

(Court of Appeal; Thorpe, Aikens, Black LJJ; 4 May 2012)

The parents were married in Pakistan and had a child. When the parents separated the mother claimed the father had been physically and emotionally abusive towards her.

In contact proceedings the judge accepted the mother's evidence that the father had threatened to abduct the child and had made threats of violence against the mother's extended family and so made no order for contact between the father and child. The father appealed.

Since the hearing the father had made no attempt to engage with therapeutic services offered to him and the judge had been within the exercise of his discretion to make the decision to order no contact given the findings on the father's behaviour. Appeal dismissed.

18.11 CONTEMPT OF COURT

A v Payne and Williams; A-G and N [2009] EWHC 736 (Fam)

Inadvertent breach of rules by a solicitor and guardian, acting on counsel's advice, to release papers to a mediator in an intractable hostility contact case. **Held:** Contempt but no penalty. **Comment:** The list of people to whom papers can be released omits mediators – no reason has been given. **Warning:** Never disclose papers to anyone without asking: 'Can I?'

Slade v Slade [2009] EWCA Civ 748

There are *three* guiding principles governing *committal proceedings* where, as here, *criminal proceedings had already taken place*: (1) **First:** The court was *not* sentencing for the criminal equivalent of what the contemnor had done; rather the court was sentencing to demonstrate *both* its disapproval of the fact that the contemnor had breached its order *and* to ensure future compliance. (2) **Second:** The court should have as much information as possible about the parties and any current criminal proceedings relating to the same or similar facts. (3) **Third:** The sentences for contempt should not be 'manifestly discrepant' with sentences passed in criminal proceedings for comparable offences. **Relevant authorities set out in the judgment**.

B v S (Contempt: Imprisonment of Mother) [2009] EWCA Civ 548

Guidance as to how to handle a committal order, when a mother is breastfeeding a baby. *Strong message to mothers* of young children regarding the potential serious consequences of deliberate disobedience of contact orders.

Re S-C [2010] EWCA Civ 21

(1)   The Court of Appeal emphasised the need for care to be taken in *spelling out precisely and specifically the terms of an order and its penal consequences* particularly in the context of parties who may have trouble in understanding the implications of court orders and *who may be acting in person* with no one to advise them of the consequences of breach.

(2)   As to s 12 of the Administration of Justice Act 1960, *if the judge wants to bar parties from showing the order of the court to their legal advisers, he needed to make this explicit in the order itself.*

CJ v Flintshire Borough Council [2010] EWCA Civ 393

The Court of Appeal set out criteria to assist judges hearing an application for early discharge of a committal order [here in the context of a 21-month period of imprisonment]:

- whether the contemnor had suffered punishment *proportionate* to the contempt;

- whether the contemnor's contrition was *genuine*;

- whether the *interest of the State* would be significantly prejudiced by early discharge;

- whether he had done all he could to *demonstrate a resolve* not to commit a further breach;

- whether he had done all he reasonably could to construct *practical arrangements* in the event of early discharge;

- whether he had made any *specific proposal* to augment the protection of the children against any further breach;

- what the length of time served in prison was *in relation to the full term imposed* and the term otherwise required to be served prior to release pursuant to s 258(2) of the Criminal Justice Act 2003;

- whether there were any *special factors* which impinged on the court's discretion in any way.

Note:

(1) A favourable answer was not required to all the questions but, according to Wilson LJ, and May LJ in *Enfield*, *the first probably needed an affirmative answer before early discharge could be ordered*.

(2) Committal for civil contempt plainly fell within Art 5 of the European Convention for the Protection of Human Rights etc. When a court as considering whether to commit for contempt in the first place, as well as when it was asked to make an order for early release, it needed to consider the extent to which the order was *necessary and proportionate* in the interests of the *prevention of crime* or disorder and to *uphold the rule* of law and the lawful orders of the court.

Re W (A Child) [2011] EWCA 1196

(Court of Appeal, Hughes, Tomlinson and McFarlane LJJ, 17 August 2011)

It is legally permissible to make successive mandatory injunctions requiring positive action, in relation to which a breach would expose the defaulter to fresh contempt proceedings. Whether this is justified turns on the facts. Here a fresh order had been made requiring disclosure of the child's whereabouts and the father had breached it. A further sentence of imprisonment was justified, despite the first sentence being for the maximum period. The coercive element had not run its course.

18.12 COSTS

Re S (Leave to Remove: Costs) [2009] EWHC 3120 (Fam)

Costs vis-à-vis hearing and appeal as to removal from jurisdiction. **Note:** An award of costs against one parent in cases involving children is *exceptional*. This is to avoid one party feeling punished and thus reducing co-operation between the parents with the consequential knock-on effect on the welfare of the child. The *principles in relation to costs in children cases* remain those set out in *Re T (Order for Costs)* [2005] EWCA Civ 311, [2005] 2 FLR 681 with the *major consideration* being whether one party has been *unreasonable in the conduct of the litigation*; that is, *as opposed to unreasonable with regard to the child's welfare*. If conduct is found to be unreasonable the question *then* has to be asked whether it is *a proper exercise of discretion* in the circumstances of the case, bearing in mind the exceptional nature of the award, to make a costs order. *Re T* now has to be read alongside *WEM v SW* [2009] EWCA 311 where Wall LJ *considered* whether *different costs principles* applied on *appeal* as opposed to on an *original hearing*, albeit he lay down no new principle. His Lordship concluded that, *on appeal, the judge had a broad juridical discretion over the question of costs*: this was because uncertainties about what the judge would decide had already been removed and the respondent had had time to take stock and make offers to compromise the appeal where appropriate. *Litigation misconduct was a factor on appeals but it was not essential before a costs order could be made*.

Re J (Costs of Fact Finding Hearing) [2009] EWCA Civ 1350

Held: The costs incurred by the mother in relation to a fact-find hearing were *wholly referable to her allegations against the father* and did not relate to the paradigm situation to which the general proposition of no costs in children cases referred. The district judge should have considered the *nature* of the enquiry, the *seriousness* and *relevance* of the allegations, the *extent of admissions* by the father and the *extent to which they had and had not been proved* where not admitted.

Re T (Order for Costs) [2005] EWCA Civ 311, [2005] 2 FLR 681

The Court of Appeal observed that in children cases costs awarded against one parent or another are *exceptional* since the court is *anxious to avoid* the situation where *a parent may feel 'punished'* by the other parent which will reduce future co-operation between them, *with adverse impact on a child's welfare*. A further *rationale* for not making a costs order in a children case is *not to discourage* a party with a proper interest in the child's welfare from putting forward views in proceedings which were inquisitorial in nature: *London Borough of Sutton v Davis (Costs) (No 2)* [1994] 2 FLR 569; *C v FC (Children Proceedings: Costs)* [2004] 1 FLR 362. The *conduct* of the parties is in reality the *major consideration* whether or not an exceptional order for costs should be made. A costs order should *only* be made if a party has been *unreasonable in his or her conduct.* In *Re T* the mother was ordered to pay the costs of the fact-finding hearings. *Children hearings which address only welfare issues (the vast majority in the private law context) are the 'paradigm situation' of no order for costs.* Also see: *Re N (A Child)* [2009] EWHC 2096 (Fam), [2010] 1 FLR 454 and see the comment by Professor Douglas in [2009] Fam Law 1030.

Re X, Y and Z (Children) (Care Proceedings: Costs) [2011] 1 FLR 1045

HHJ Bellamy sitting as a Judge of the High Court drew up the following list of points to be of particular importance for the future where *fabricated or induced illness* (FII) and *applications to withdraw proceedings* were concerned:

(1) Before making an allegation of FII a local authority had to be *rigorous* in satisfying itself that the evidence was *capable of establishing the fact* of the fabricated or induced illness to the requisite standard.

(2) In reaching the decision to allege FII the authority should normally seek the views of the *health professionals* involved in the children's care rather than relying on the report of one independent expert.

(3) In a case of suspected FII, the letter of instruction to the expert should make clear that he or she should have regard to *'Fabricated or Induced Illness by Carers (FII): A Practical Guide for Paediatricians'* published by the Royal College of Paediatricians and Child Health in October 2009.

(4) All those involved should consider and review the *expert's report* and raise any relevant points with the expert.

(5) In any case where the authority applied under *FPR, r 4.5* to withdraw proceedings they should state *whether the child was a child in need* for the purposes of s 17. If that were so the application should be accompanied by *a schedule outlining the needs identified and detailing the support and services the authority proposed to make available*. In reaching his determination, the judge drew assistance from: *London Borough of Southwark v B* [1993] 2 FLR 559, *Re X (Emergency Protection Orders)* [2006] EWHC 510 (Fam), [2006] 2 FLR 701 {EPOs should only be made in cases of genuine emergency}, *Re N (Leave to Withdraw Care Proceedings)* [2000] 1 FLR 134, *Re M (Local Authority's Costs)* [1995] 1' FLR 533 and *Re R (Care: Disclosure: Nature of Proceedings)* [2002] 1 FLR 755 alongside *Fabricated or Induced Illness by Carers* (2002, the report of a working party of the Royal College of Paediatrics and Child Health).

A Local Authority; A Mother; A Father; An Aunt v C [2012] EWHC 1637 (Fam)

(Family Division; Peter Jackson J; 15 June 2012)

An 8-year-old girl was adopted by her aunt. The aunt claimed costs of £22,734 from the adoption proceedings. It was not the case that an order for costs against a local authority could only be made where there had been unreasonableness.

A departure from the usual outcome was warranted by the need for some degree of equality of arms between the State body and an unrepresented litigant who was of cardinal importance to the welfare of the child and where the local authority had elected to put her to the test over a protracted period. The local authority was ordered to pay half of the aunt's costs.

18.13 DISCLOSURE/PRIVILEGE – FAMILY PROCEEDINGS

A Local Authority v B [2008] EWHC 1017 (Fam), [2009] 1 FLR 289

The presence of a social worker in the capacity of *'appropriate adult'* during an interview between a 15-year-old boy and his solicitor was subject to *legal professional privilege*, notwithstanding that he had made partial admissions of *sexual misconduct* in the context of his 8-year-old half-sister alleging that he had sexually assaulted her.

Re X; Northumberland County Council v Z, YX and the Government of the Republic of Kenya [2009] EWHC 498 (Fam)

X was born in Kenya in 2004, and placed in a children's home. Y and Z, a British couple, brought her to the UK in 2006, using a false Kenyan birth certificate and passport. The local authority were tipped off about the child in 2007 and removed her to foster care and began care proceedings. Munby J approved their care plan for the return of X to Kenya, where she was subsequently adopted. *The authority sought permission to disclose the transcript* of the judgment to the Chief Constable of the Northumbria Police and the UK Border and Immigration Agency in order to consider what lessons may be learned from the circumstances of X's arrival in the UK and to determine whether any proceedings should be commenced against Y and Z. *The Govt. of Kenya sought disclosure of the statements made by Y and Z to the police in the course of the proceedings*, various other statements made by other witnesses, and the court's judgment. **Held:** *Re EC (Disclosure of Material)* provides a *thorough checklist* of *factors* which must be *weighed in the balance*. The balance fell plainly in favour of permitting the disclosure sought by the local authority. The proper role of the family court in this context *was to work together in co-operation with the criminal justice system* to ensure the *proper administration of criminal justice* without unnecessary let or hindrance by the family court and extending all proper assistance to the criminal justice system: *Re X (Children)* [2007] EWHC 1719 (Fam), [2008] 1 FLR 589 and *Re X (Disclosure for Purposes of Criminal Proceedings)* [2008] EWHC 242 (Fam), [2008] 2 FLR 944. As to who in the Government of Kenya, the local authority and the police would be entitled to see the documents: it was *necessary* for the court to *spell out precisely* the limitations and conditions attached to the use by *a corporate litigant* of the documents generated in family proceedings to which it is a party, *especially where the relevant party is a foreign government* which may not be familiar with the minutiae of English family law as a domestic litigant.

Re H (Care Proceedings: Disclosure) [2009] EWCA Civ 704

Issue: *How much could be disclosed to the police* in an non-accidental injury case where the father had made admissions. **Per curiam:** Rule 10.20A of the Family Proceedings Rules 1991 had now been replaced by Rule 11 (affected by the Family Proceedings (Amendment) (No 2) Rules 2009, SI 2009/857). An application brought under Rule 11 should contain a *clear statement* of the *identity* of the *named officer* within *the child protection unit to* whom the Chief Constable sought release. There should be an equally *clear statement of the purpose to which the information would be put* and *also an application for the exercise of a discretion by the named officer to share the documentation with the CPS* in the event that the conclusion was that the material merited referral to the CPS. *The leading judgment in the field remains that of Swinton Thomas LJ in Re EC [1996] 2 FLR 725* with its emphasis on the *public interest* in the *administration of justice, co-operation between agencies* and the *maintenance of confidentiality* in children cases.

A Local Authority v A [2009] EWHC 1574 (Fam)

At the encouragement of her own mother and sister, *Muslim mother had sex with three men whilst on holiday with child*. Sought to prevent this information from being *disclosed to* her Muslim husband. *Held*: The information was relevant to the mother's capacity to parent the child and to provide stability and consistency. *Disclosure ordered*: There was *no particular reason* to suppose that the male members of the mother's family would place her *at risk*. Order stayed for 2 weeks to enable thought to be given as to how it should be implemented. Relevant case law: *Re M* [1998] 2 FLR 1028 and *Re X* [2002] 2 FLR 476.

Re N (Family Proceedings: Disclosure) [2009] EWHC 1663 (Fam)

Father sought an order to disclose to the General Medical Council (GMC), *a critique* of the methodology of the psychiatric assessment of the mother. *Held by Munby J*: Under the new Rule 11.4(1) no need for an order, because the new [far wider] regime permitted disclosure. *But*: GMC would have to be very careful. Guidance given:

(1) There was *no entitlement to communicate the information to the public at large* without the permission of the family court.

(2) That a failure to comply with the provisions of the rule would be a *contempt*.

(3) *That there was an obligation to preserve confidentiality and ensure that there were effective safeguards against abuse*. This third point is to be strongly emphasised now that information can be communicated without prior judicial sanction, without the knowledge of the other parties involved in the proceedings and, as Munby J said, 'in circumstances where the complainant's real agenda may not be immediately obvious'.

Local Authority v M, F and M and M [2009] EWHC 3172 (Fam); [2010] 1 FLR 1355

Hedley J. Father a *violent criminal* from a violent criminal family. Mother [from a *drug dealing* family] at an address with children unbeknown to father. Local authority brought care proceedings because they wanted to assess whether the mother could maintain her separation from the paternal family. *Should father be discharged from the proceedings* [of which he was in ignorance] to prevent any possibility of disclosure to him of the mother's address? *Held*:

(1)   Although incarcerated, the father *represented a real and substantial risk* to the children and the mother and the court was satisfied that he would pursue her without worrying about ensuring the children's safety.

(2)   When the actual *unfairness to the father* of a discharge from the proceedings was *weighed against the risk* of disclosure leading to discovery of the mother and children and the consequences of discovery there was no doubt where the *balance* lay. **Note:** The jurisdiction to make such an order is found in *FPR 1991, r 4.7(5)(b)*; the only occasion it has ever been considered by the Court of Appeal is the case of *Re AB (Care Proceedings: Service on Husband Ignorant of Child's Existence)* [2003] EWCA Civ 1842, [2004] 1 FLR 527. Also note: *Re T (Wardship: Impact of Police Intelligence)* [2009] EWHC 2440 (Fam), [2010] 1 FLR 1048, *where a special advocate was appointed to represent a father who had made threats against the mother and child*.

Re C (Children: Disclosure) [2010] EWCA Civ 239

Father had taken children to his MP as to children's wishes vis-à-vis residence. Judge inter alia ordered the father to *disclose all letters and emails* between himself and the MP to the guardian's solicitor. *Held*:

(1)   No leave to appeal.

(2)   It was *fundamental that allegations made by children against an absent parent be investigated*; the guardian was plainly bound to see whether the communications between the father and the MP and local councillor *shed any light* on that question.

(3)   *Article 8* of the European Convention on Human Rights guaranteed respect for an individual's correspondence; that included email communications with an MP but was, nonetheless, a *qualified right*. The judge had taken Art 8 into account and had met the requirement of *proportionality*, in particular, by providing that the disclosure was to be *to the guardian alone* in the first instance.

London Borough of Lewisham v D (Disclosure of DNA Samples to Police) [2010] EWHC 1238 (Fam)

Per Stephen Cobb QC *Stage 1 Proceedings*. **Facts:** Suspicion that 'mother' of four children engaged in child trafficking. Collaterally police had DNA of mother. Mother had agreed to DNA testing in the family proceedings but after DNA taken from children, mother declined. **Issue:** Could there be disclosure of the children's DNA to the police in the family proceedings? *Held*:

(1) The local authority *should disclose* the children's DNA samples and the results of testing, *to the police.* It was important that barriers should not be erected between one branch of the judicature and another because that may be inimical to justice: *Re EC (Disclosure of Material)* [1997] Fam 76, [1996] 2 FLR 725.

(2) The police *had already co-operated* with the local authority and family court in providing information and evidence valuable to the family court: *it was relevant to the question of disclosure to consider and weigh in the balance a reciprocity of attitude and/or co-operation.*

(3) The *public interest* in the prosecution of those who were guilty of offences against children was engaged in the present case. Child trafficking was a serious offence and the evidence sought here was fundamental to its investigation and the *foundation stone of prosecution:* The importance of the evidence gravitated *strongly in favour of disclosure.*

(4) *Welfare was an important factor, albeit not paramount;* if the children had been brought into the country as a result of trafficking then that was likely to have serious implications for their welfare and for the welfare of others generally.

(5) The preservation of *confidentiality*, while important, did not weigh heavily in the scales given the nature of the disclosure sought. *Although disclosure did interfere with the children's Art 8 rights it was necessary and proportionate that it took place.* Additionally, the opportunity to match DNA would enable the children *to learn more about their parentage* which, although not a heavily weighted factor, was an *interest that would be served* by disclosure. Understanding and determining identity was a fundamental part of private life. *Commentary:* See also: *Re X (Children)* [2007] EWHC 1719 (Fam), [2008] 1 FLR 589 and *Re H (Care Proceedings: Disclosure)* [2009] EWCA Civ 704, [2009] 2 FLR 1531. *These cases endorse the wider recognition of the importance of sharing information between relevant agencies*; they underlined the importance of *collaborative working.* The judge ordered the disclosure not only of the DNA report, but of the samples also: he *endorsed the various proposed safeguards* which would be put in place around the storage and ultimate destruction of that DNA. Vis-à-vis *Re X* Munby J set out the factors to be considered, etc; ruling inter alia:

> 'The factors to be considered when considering whether to order disclosure included *the interests of the children* in care proceedings and of other children, although their welfare was not paramount. There was also the need to maintain *confidentiality and encourage frankness*. These factors were set against the *public interest in the administration of justice* and *prosecution of serious crime,* the *gravity* of the offence and *relevance of the evidence* sought to be disclosed, *the co-operation of*

agencies working with children, fairness concerning *incriminating questions and fair trial of the defendant* and *any disclosure* that had already taken place (see paras [24], [27], [28]).' [emphasis added]

London Borough of Lewisham v D (Disclosure of DNA Samples to Police) [2010] EWHC 1238 (Fam)

Per Stephen Cobb QC *Stage 2 Proceedings*. The facts are as above in *Stage 1*. The *issue*: Could there be disclosure from the police to the local authority of the result of the matching of the children's DNA with that of the mother? *Held*: Refusing the local authority's application, the result of the police exercise was caught by s. *64(1B)(b) of PACE 1984* – it was '*information derived from the sample*' because it arose directly from the samples themselves: See *London Borough of Lambeth v S, C and Others* [2006] EWHC 326 (Fam), [2007] 1 FLR 152 where it was held that police DNA evidence was governed by PACE 1984. **Comment:** The court was sympathetic to the local authority's wish to formulate a care plan based on the most reliable information about the children's identities and parentage. *As it was, the authority would have to wait weeks or months before some step was taken in the criminal process which yielded more information.* The right to know one's parentage had to wait. In other words, the ascertainment of truth about identity and interests of justice thereby served, [see *Re H and A (Paternity: Blood Tests)* [2002] EWCA Civ 383, [2002] 1 FLR 1145 at [29]] were *clearly subordinate to the statutory imperatives of the 1984 Act*.

A Local Authority v A [2009] EWCA Civ 1057

The starting point for issues of non-disclosure of evidence is the speech of Lord Mustill in *Re D (Adoption Reports: Confidentiality)* [1996] AC 593, [1995] 2 FLR 687 where it was noted that **non-disclosure was the exception rather than the rule** and that the court should be rigorous in its examination of the risk and gravity of the feared harm. To carry out the balancing exercise the judge needed to be in a position to assess the risk, weigh it against the steps that might be taken in its mitigation, and consider whether the material could be disclosed '*in a less complete form but in a sufficient way still to provide a fair trial*'.

A County Council v SB, MA and AA [2010] EWHC 2528 (Fam)

Disclosure application in the context of 'honour' based violence where a 17-year-old girl was placed in foster care, an order was made under the Forced Marriage (Civil Protection) Act 2007, and she was later made the subject of an interim care order at the renewal of which, an 'honour' related abuse assessment from an expert was ordered. *This case considered the extent of the duty of an expert to disclose what he had been told*. Per Sir Nicholas Wall P.

- An *expert in Children Act cases* could *not* receive information 'in confidence' from any body. His or her duty was to be *objective* and *wholly free from bias* and the report would invariably be disclosed whatever it said.

- 'Confidentiality' in that context meant that the information contained in the papers filed with the court for the purpose of the proceedings was *confidential to the court* and, with very few exceptions, *could not be disclosed to those who were not parties.*

- Although power existed to withhold disclosure in exceptional cases, *the normal rule of disclosure applied in the instant case* [all cases, these particularly, are fact sensitive and here the court addressed very carefully the risk of harm to the girl from disclosure but held that the parents' rights to a fair hearing under Art 6 of the ECHR outweighed a risk to the girl that disclosure of the information was likely to cause her harm].

- The approach adopted in *Re T (Wardship: Review of Police Protection Decision) (No 2)* [2008] EWHC 196 (Fam), [2010] 1 FLR 1026 *that full disclosure of relevant material should be made to the court with the court then deciding whether the Art 6 rights of the parties required disclosure to them was the approach to be adopted* [as to secure editing of documents, see *Re R (Secure Editing of Documents)* [2007] 2 FLR 759]. Disclosure is the rule and the circumstances have to be *exceptional* for it not to take place; see *Re D (Adoption Reports: Confidentiality)* [1996] AC 593, [1995] 2 FLR 687.

- In cases such as this, the disclosure of information given by a witness to an expert could well put the witness or the source of the information *at risk. In relation to the discretion not to order disclosure in case involving children*, see also: *Official Solicitor v K* [1965] AC 201, *Re M (Disclosure)* [1998] 2 FLR 1028, and see also *R v H, R v C* [2004] UKHL 3 and *Secretary of State for the Home Department v MB and AF* [2007] UKHL 46.

- The instant case is also a useful reminder of the duties of experts in relation to the court. The watchwords should be *openness* and *sound preparation* with expert prepared for everything they do and say to be the subject of challenge.

Re G and B (Disclosure Protocol) [2010] EWHC 2630 (Fam)

Guidance from the President as to the smooth running of the *Practice Direction: Revised Private Law Programme* [2010] 2 FLR 717 in the context of an incomplete Cafcass report.

- First, in carrying out their *safeguarding checks*, Cafcass were provided with information by the police pursuant to the Protocol and were under a duty to comply with the Data Protection Act 1998 whenever they processed sensitive personal information. Cafcass thus received police information but were unable to reproduce it if it was not relevant to the particular child. *According to the Protocol, personal data had to be processed fairly and lawfully, was only to be obtained for a specified and lawful purpose and was not to be further processed in any incompatible manner*.

- Secondly, in their reports, Cafcass were *not permitted* to refer to police information which was not relevant to the child or give a copy of that information to any of the parties or their representatives.

- Thirdly, in the instant case, it had not been open to Cafcass to disclose the first draft *report because it contained information that went beyond what was permitted by the Protocol*.

Re A (Disclosure of Third Party Information) [2012] EWHC 180 (Fam)

(Family Division; Peter Jackson J; 16 February 2012)

Contact order in place for 9-year-old child to have staying contact with her father when he visited the UK. Allegations by a young girl that the father had sexually abused her when she was young. Mother applied to vary contact order and sought disclosure of the allegations. Physical and mental health of the young girl had been affected by sexual abuse. Application for disclosure dismissed.

Compelling her to give evidence would be oppressive and wrong and would have a severe impact on her health. Unresolved allegation left real difficulties for the question of contact. Unsupervised contact would not automatically be ordered.

18.14   EVIDENCE

Re L (Identity of Birth Father) [2008] EWCA Civ 1388

Issue as to contact between a man claiming to be the biological father and a 13-year-old boy suffering considerable mental health problems whose mother had married and *whose husband the boy believed to be his biological father*. The mother did not want adduced in evidence the opinion of a psychiatrist that news of the boy's true paternity would '*have a massive impact on [the boy] and would certainly result in a deterioration in his behaviour and also his performance at school.*' Judge made order in absence of such evidence. **Held**: Evidence *crucial* and matter remitted to trial judge for further consideration.

Re B (Fact-finding Hearing: Evidence) [2008] EWCA Civ 1547

Trial judge could not reject *reputable expert evidence* without very clear and *sound reasons*.

Re G and B (Fact-Finding Hearing) [2009] EWCA Civ 10

(1) Appeal allowed where a fact-finding judge had held father unlawfully to have killed the child which went beyond the expert evidence, and there was *no material* to provide reasons for *rejecting* the expert's evidence.

(2) Further held that where the LA's schedule of proposed findings had been prepared with care and the hearing itself the subject of a directions appointment, *it required very good reasons for the judge to depart from the schedule of proposed findings*. If a judge goes 'off piste' and makes findings of fact not contained within the schedule or sought by the local authority, *the judge must ensure* that those findings are securely founded in evidence.

(3) Given the unexpected allegation of unlawful killing and the father's need to assemble medical evidence, the judge was plainly wrong to refuse him an adjournment.

Per curiam: Distinguishing the dicta of Baroness Hale in *Re B (Care Proceedings)* [2008] 2 FLR 141, there were *exceptions* to the general rule that the same judge should hear both limbs of a split care hearing: where a judge had *died* or was *ill*, for example, it was unlikely to be proportionate or in the interest of the child or in conformity with the overriding objective for the court to start again from scratch. Similar considerations applied where a litigant *had legitimately lost confidence in the judge* or where, as in the present case, there could be an appearance of bias. *As to guidance on dealing with expert evidence, judicial assessment of credibility and the need for full reasons for departure from experts' views, see Re M (Residence) [2002] 2 FLR 1059.*

Re M (Fact-Finding Hearing: Burden of Proof) [2008] EWCA Civ 1261

Mother **admitted leg fractures** to the baby at 4 weeks, but **denied head injuries** suffered at 2 months. Judgment at first instance: '… [g]iven that mother was the main carer, I find that she was the most likely perpetrator, but I cannot exclude [the father] …' **Held:** Where the judge was dealing with a child of only 2 months with an extensive skull fracture, who only a month or so earlier had suffered fractures to her legs, the judge was entitled to look critically at any parental explanation of such serious injuries and **it was not a reversal of the burden of proof for the judge to disbelieve the mother or to find that the mother's explanation did not account for all the injuries that the child had**.

Note: This case reinforces the point emphasised in *Re B (Care Proceedings: Standard of Proof)* [2008] 2 FLR 141 that, **when applying the balance of probabilities standard of proof, once the judge finds that it was more likely than not that a particular person was the perpetrator, then the finding is that that person was the perpetrator, thus ruling out anyone else**. Further, the Court of Appeal emphasised the imperative of practitioners seeking *a clarification of a judgment* from the trial judge rather than resorting to seeking leave to appeal when a judgment appears *unclear* or *unambiguous*; see also in this context: *Re A (Child Abuse)* [2008] 1 FLR 1423.

F and L v A Local Authority and A [2009] EWHC 140 (Fam)

Did fresh evidence cause an earlier finding of non-accidental injury to be upset? *Held:* The test was by reference to the civil standard of proof, and on the evidence, *no*. *Re B (Care Proceedings: Standard of Proof)* [2008] 2 FLR 141, applied.

Re L (A Child) [2009] EWCA Civ 1239

Care proceedings were commenced regarding two children, aged 13 and 9, who came to this country to join their parents from the *Ivory Coast*. An *issue* arose as to the *paternity of the younger child*. The putative father refused to be tested and Coleridge J directed that samples be taken from both children on the basis that the elder sibling's DNA profile could shed light on the younger child's parentage. The children appealed. *Held*:

(1)   There should be a clear distinction between s 20 and s 21 of the Family Law Reform Act 1969. Under s 20, *the test* was not whether taking the sample would be in the sibling's best interests, *but rather, whether it would be adverse to her best interest: S (An Infant) v S* [1972] AC 24. The court did *not need* to be satisfied before ordering the test that the outcome therefore *would be for the benefit* of the sibling.

(2)   The testing of the sibling was premature; *expert evidence was needed to determine the implications of taking the sample from the child, and revealing to (or concealing from) her, the reasons why it was needed*. It was more appropriate to await the welfare stage of the care proceedings when, if necessary, *appropriate expert evidence* could be obtained to decide whether her interests would preclude the taking

of the sample. **Note:** The suggestion that the result should be kept from the girl herself was *hardly compatible*, as Ward LJ pointed out, with the view that *'honesty is the best policy'* in determining issues of *parentage*.

Re M (Allegations of Rape: Fact-Finding Hearing) [2010] EWCA Civ 1385

Per Thorpe LJ: It was:

> 'high time that orders were made reflecting what was found. It was perfectly simple to attach a schedule to the judgment setting out exactly what findings were made.'

Re M (Sexual Abuse: Evidence) [2010] EWCA Civ 1030

Issue of the weight to be attached to *the evidence of a 5- and 3-year-old* in family proceedings in the context of *sexual abuse*; see also *Re W (Children) (Abuse: Oral Evidence)* [2010] UKSC 12, [2010] 1 FLR 1485.

Re X (A Child) [2011] EWHC 3401 (Fam)

(Family Division, Theis J, 9 December 2011)

Applying the balancing exercise in *Re W* a 17-year-old with Asperger's syndrome should not give oral evidence to the court in care proceedings. An important factor was the sort of support that would be required for him to give evidence that would affect the value of the evidence and risked harmful delay. The judge raised concerns regarding the funding of support for giving evidence.

Re R (Children) (Care Proceedings: Appeal) [2011] EWCA Civ 1795

(Court of Appeal; Mummery, Munby LJJ and Hedley J; 9 June 2011)

Two children aged 6 and 3 subject to a series of interim care orders due to allegations of sexual abuse and domestic violence by their father. The father appealed judge's finding that children had been sexually abused. Appeal dismissed.

The procedural deficiencies in the ABE interviews had not been sufficient to justify allowing the appeal, the judge was entitled to attach sufficient weight to the interviews in combination with the other evidence to make the findings he did.

Re M (A Child) [2012] EWCA Civ 165

(Court of Appeal; Thorpe, Rimer LJJ, Dame Janet Smith; 19 January 2012)

A fact-finding hearing found fractures of 10-week-old child had been non-accidental and perpetrated by the mother and father. A placement order was made and contact with the mother was terminated and the child was placed with prospective adopters. The mother sought permission to appeal the placement order and the fact-finding determination. The mother instructed an American paediatrician and sought permission to have his report admitted as fresh evidence.

Application refused. The Court of Appeal emphasised that (i) an applicant seeking permission to appeal, or an appellant who had been granted permission to appeal, in a family case needed the court's permission to instruct a fresh expert. (ii) When seeking to instruct a fresh expert from some other jurisdiction, the matters requiring explanation included why a United Kingdom expert had not been used, what efforts had been made to identify UK experts, and the financial implications of instructing an overseas expert.

Re I-A (Children) [2012] EWCA Civ 582

(Court of Appeal; Thorpe, Etherton, Lewison LJJ; 21 March 2012)

A 12-year-old girl alleged that her stepfather had sexually abused her. Following the allegation and initiation of child protection procedures the stepfather immediately left the home and had only supervised contact with the four children. At a fact-finding hearing the judge failed to consider the evidence of the parents and found in favour of the local authority. Following further submissions from counsel the judge issued an afterword including a summary of the stepfather's evidence but without any analysis.

The stepfather appealed. The only evidence in support of the allegations had been the words of the child who had been known to fantasise and not tell the truth. The evidence of the parents was particularly important and the judge's failure to deal with it was a fundamental flaw and the conclusion was unsustainable. Appeal allowed.

18.15   EXPERT EVIDENCE

O-M GM (and KM) v The Local Authority, LO and EM [2009] EWCA Civ 1405, [2010] 2 FLR 58

Issue: Could non-clinical [ie *non-treating*] expert opinion make a contribution to the case, where in the context of one of two children being diagnosed by Great Ormond Street as having non-accidental injuries, the existing evidence was extensive and [although it had been generated by *clinicians*] it had already embraced an external international consultant based in another part of the UK. **Note:**

(1)   The fact that *no independent expert* has been called is not, in itself, a reason to do so, although there may be cases where a second expert opinion is needed in order that the process is 'not only fair but seen to be fair'.

(2)   There is a distinction between a court appointed expert and a clinician: *'the role of the expert to treat is not to be muddled with the role of the expert to report'*: Re B *(Sexual Abuse: Expert's Report)* [2000] 1 FLR 871 at [46].

(3)   *Some clinical involvement did not affect the doctor's capacity to act as an expert witness*: W v Oldham MBC [2005] EWCA Civ 1247, [2006] 1 FLR 543, per Wall LJ.

(4)   A *'blanket approach which precludes treating clinicians from becoming jointly instructed experts in respect to children they have in fact treated runs the risk of the court being deprived of expertise and excellence'*.

(5)   It is also important to keep the context in mind. A clinical decision about what is required for the child's treatment is different from a *forensic decision* about what is *necessary to determine the issue*: Re M *(Care Proceedings: Best Evidence)* [2007] EWCA Civ 589, [2007] 2 FLR 1006 and it is not up to the expert to advise on a forensic justification for a test.

(6)   *Common sense, fairness and reasonableness*, in the circumstances of a case, are the *key precepts* underlying the authorities.

A Local Authority v S [2009] EWHC 2115 (Fam)

The local authority brought care proceedings in relation to the older child [now 3] alleging that the baby of a few weeks old had died as the result of a shake or shaking/impact injury: the classic *triad* of injuries – *encephalopathy*, *subdural haemorrhage* and *retinal haemorrhage* – were all present but there was *dispute as to the precipitating* factor leading to those injuries. Although the many experts accepted that a non-accidental head injury was one of the possible causes of death, *two of the experts subscribed to the Geddes III hypothesis* and took the controversial view that an *absence of external injuries* meant there was no reliable evidence of shaken baby syndrome; that hypoxia would have been the cause of the subdural bleeding. *Held:* Finding the threshold under s 31 established:

(1) Of the three potential precipitating primary events – namely a *cardiac event, choking* and *trauma – only trauma provided an explanation for the baby's sudden catastrophic collapse and the presence of the triad of injuries*. Trauma not only provided a unified picture of all that was found post-mortem but was also the view of the majority medical opinion. On one view that meant it was unnecessary to examine the mass of medical issues raised but, given the polarisation of the experts' opinion, the court viewed it as important to consider *a number of aspects of the alternative cause for the subdural and retinal haemorrhages*.

(2) The overwhelming preponderance of evidence was to the effect that, as of the present day, medical opinion was that *hypoxia did not lead to subdural and retinal haemorrhages* of the type found in the baby.

(3) *It was crucial that each expert kept within the bounds of their own expertise* and worked in a *collaborative way* with the other experts, deferred to the expertise of others more qualified to comment on certain areas and did so *with acknowledgment* of that greater expertise and knowledge.

(4) Experts must be *accurate* in their use of *source material*, not only drawing the court's attention to research that was contrary to their view but being *rigorous in the use made of research papers*. The particular two experts *had developed a scientific prejudice* and, as a consequence had *allowed convictions to lead analysis*.

Note (1): By way of background, see *R v Harris, Rock, Cherry and Faulder* [2005] EWCA Crim 1980 which concluded that the 'triad' of injuries was central to a diagnosis of non-accidental head injury *when there were no other external signs of trauma such as bruises or fracture*. That case also summarised the alternative hypothesis named Geddes III.

Note (2): In *Re U (Serious Injury: Standard of Proof); Re B* [2004] EWCA Civ 567, [2004] 2 FLR 263 following *R v Cannings* [2004] EWCA Crim 1, the *Court of Appeal provided guidelines in relation to interpreting medical evidence*; in particular Butler-Sloss P noted that the court 'must always be on guard against the over-dogmatic expert, the expert whose reputation or amour propre is at stake, or the expert who has developed scientific prejudice'.

Re M-W (Care Proceedings: Expert Evidence) [2010] EWCA Civ 12

In the context of an inadequate judgment as to threshold, a Court of Appeal had three options: **(i)** Sending the case back with an invitation to the judge to '*reconsider and fill in the gaps*'; *English v Emery Reimbold and Stric Limited* [2002] EWCA Civ 605, [2002] 2 WLR 2409; **(ii)** starting again with a fresh judge albeit leaving in place the judge's findings about the mother in light of the paediatrician's evidence; or **(iii)** directing a complete re-hearing before a judge to be allocated by the designated family judge in consultation with the liaison judge and the President of the Family Division. In the instant case, the Court of Appeal opted for the *third outcome* because there was no alternative, notwithstanding the regrettable delay which would ensue.

Re L (Psychologist: Duty to the Court)

(Family Division; HHJ Bellamy, sitting as a High Court judge; 20 December 2011)

A fact-finding hearing determined that the mother had caused some of the injuries suffered by the baby and that one or both parents had caused a number of other injuries. The maternal grandmother had cared for child following discharge from hospital and with the consent of the parents, but not of the court, moved the child to Ireland. The Irish court ordered the child's return to England.

Following their return the parents had been allowed supervised contact and the father commenced staying contact at the paternal grandparents' home. The paternal grandparents, supported by the father, the local authority and the guardian sought a residence order. The mother supported the maternal grandmother's application for a residence order. The report of an independent consultant forensic psychologist report strayed into areas beyond her expertise including medical evidence regarding the child's injuries. The father claimed she had been biased towards the mother.

It was unsafe to place any reliance on the report and it was in the child's best interests to reside with the father and paternal grandparents for five nights per week and the maternal grandmother for the other two. Supervision order in favour of the local authority granted for 12 months.

18.16 FORCED MARRIAGE

B v I (Forced Marriage) [2010] 1 FLR 1721, per Baron J

Held: Declaration granted under the court's inherent jurisdiction that *the ceremony in Bangladesh had not given rise to a marriage capable of recognition* in the jurisdiction of England and Wales. **Note:** This case followed recent authorities as to the *permissible form of declaration as to non-recognition*, namely: *Westminster City Council v IC* [2008] EWCA Civ 198, [2008] 2 FLR 267 and *SH v NB* [2009] EWHC 3274 (Fam), [2010] 1 FLR 1927. Also see *Hudson v Leigh (Status on Non-Marriage)* [2009] EWHC 1306 (Fam), [2009] 2 FLR 1129. **Quaere:** Whether the form of declaration made in these cases is available where a ceremony has taken place within the jurisdiction of England and Wales rather than overseas. *As to the stigma that can be associated with divorce in cases of forced marriage*, see the dicta of Baron J and also *P v R (Forced Marriage: Annulment Procedure)* [2003] 1 FLR 661.

18.17 HUMAN RIGHTS

G v N County Council [2008] EWHC 975 (Fam), [2009] 1 FLR 774, per McFarlane J

Local authority [with justification] *resolved summarily* to change a care plan *but without consulting mother, peremptorily removed* child from school and placed him in foster care. **Held:**

(1) The actions of the local authority had to be *lawful, proportionate* to the level of concern, *procedurally fair* and must *involve* the parent in the decision-making.

(2) Change of care plan had to take place *after proper consideration* and assessment of all the available evidence and in a way that met the human rights of the child and mother.

(3) The quality of the decision-making process was to be higher *than with an EPO*.

(4) There should have been a *formal comprehensive assessment* giving the parent a chance to *contribute*. But – had the processes been properly exercised, the result would have in substance been the same. McFarlane J spelt out the 10 failings of the LA, which is in the nature of a *file-management quality control check-list*. They include:

  (i) the local authority had *not told* mother they had power to remove the child;

  (ii) they had told her they *may have to go back to court*;

(iii) she had *not been told the time* of the meeting she failed to attend; there had been *no 'letter before action'*;

(iv) they did *not involve the mother* in the decision-making process. See also: *Re W (Removal into Care)* [2005] 2 FLR 1022; *Re G (Care: Challenge to Local Authority's Decision)* [2003] 2 FLR 42, and *X Council v B (Emergency Protection Orders)* [2005] 1 FLR 341. Note: Involvement in the decision-making process must be proportionate to the issues at stake: *Jucius and Juciuviene v Lithuania* (Application No 14414/03) [2008] ECHR 1524.

Adam v Germany (Application No 44036/02) [2008] ECHR 1578

In both private and public law children proceedings, national courts have a positive duty to ensure *an expeditious timetable of hearings*, lest the very issue before the court be effectively determined by lapse of time. In this case, it was a *contact dispute.* Note the *Children and Adoption Act 2006* which is intended to promote and, if necessary, enforce, contact between children and non-resident parents. This Act repeals s 16(3)(a) of the Children Act 1989 removing the requirement for FAOs to be made only in exceptional circumstances [s 6(2)]. It inserts a new s 16(4A) to provide that where an *FAO* is to be in force at the same time as a contact order, the officer may give advice and assistance to establish, improve and maintain contact to the persons named in the contact order. *It increases the maximum duration of an FAO from 6 to 12 months.*

London Borough of Richmond v B, W, B and CB [2010] EWHC 2903 (Fam)

- The **PD** '*Experts in Family Proceedings Relating to Children 2008'* [2009] 2 FLR 1383 applied to *all expert evidence,* including *chemical analysis,* and only rarely would the results not be used and interpreted for the purposes of expert opinion evidence. Expert evidence needed to be given in accordance with the principles underlying the Practice Direction. Ie Chemical analysis should be treated as expert evidence just as much as, for example, medical opinion evidence.

- Experts can also rely on their *own experience* and on *unpublished material,* see *R v Weller* [2010] EWCA Crim 1085.

- Experts must ensure that the *basis of any asserted opinion* is made clear and that their reports are expressed in terms *understandable by lay people.*

- The evidence in the instant case highlighted the need for the exercise of considerable caution when hair tests for alcohol were being interpreted and relied upon both generally and particularly in isolation. *Hair testing should only form part of the evidential picture.*

Plymouth County Council v G [2010] EWCA Civ 1271

Held: The *assessment* of an expert witness was a *sophisticated process* involving many factors which interacted with each other. It was *not always practical* for a judge to identify in writing every consideration that had entered into the assessment. Per Lord Hoffman in *Piglowska v Piglowska* [1999] 2 FLR 763: '... *the reasons for judgment will always be capable of having been better expressed*'.

Re H [2011] EWCA Civ 1009

(Court of Appeal, Thorpe and Black LJJ, 7 July 2011)

In the circumstances of this case there was jurisdiction for the judge to grant an injunction under HRA 1998, s 8 where she considered the local authority's plan to remove the child from her mother under an interim care order was contrary to Art 8.

Sneersone and Kampanella v Italy (App No 14737/09) [2011] 2 FLR 1322

(ECtHR, 12 July 2011)

An order for the return of a child under Art 11(7) BIIR was in breach of the mother and child's Art 8 rights since it had not reasonably taken account of the child's best interests. The principles in *Neulinger* were applied.

R (O) v London Borough of Hammersmith and Fulham [2011] EWCA Civ 925

(Court of Appeal, Rix Lloyd and Black LJJ, 28 July 2011)

The child's needs could be met by the parents' preferred placement or by that proposed by the local authority. Mandamus was therefore not appropriate and there was no interference with Art 8 rights.

DL v London Borough Council of Newham [2011] EWHC 1890 (Admin)

(Administrative Court, Charles J, 7 September 2011)

Where a decision had been declared procedurally unfair and therefore a fresh decision had been made, which was not challenged, a finding and a remedy could still be available if there was a substantive breach of Art 8 (which could be founded by the termination of the child's placement with proposed adopters). Here, however, the child would have been removed even if there had been a fair process, so there was no substantive impact.

YB v BCC [2011] EWHC 3355 (CoP)

(Court of Protection, Mostyn J, 21 December 2010)

The provision of accommodation to a child under s 20(1),(3),(4) or (5) will never give rise to a deprivation of liberty within ECHR, Art 5 since the parents could remove the child at any time. The child was, therefore, accommodated at their behest rather than that of the state and they had consented on behalf of the child in exercise of their parental responsibility.

18.18 INHERENT JURISDICTION

Re D (Unborn Baby) [2009] EWHC 446 (Fam)

Local authority applied for removal of baby at birth, fearful of harm to mother and baby from past experience of mother. **Held:** Anticipatory declaratory relief in the exercise of the inherent jurisdiction of the court.

(1)   Court **had jurisdiction** even though child **not yet born** to adjudicate whether local authority acting in compliance with Art 8.

(2)   Court **had jurisdiction** to declare that local authority would be acting lawfully.

(3)   Circumstances **so exceptional** and **degree of risk so great** as to **justify** the local authority's step of **not engaging fully and frankly** with the parents in the pre-birth planning process. **Cases:** As to the general rule that the parents have a right to be fully involved in the planning of a public authority intervention in their lives and those of their children, whether before, during or after care proceedings; see *W v UK* [1998] 10 EHRR 29; and *Re G (Care: Challenge to Local Authority's Decision)* [2003] EWHC 551 (Fam), [2003] 2 FLR 42. As to jurisdiction to take a drastic step, see Hale LJ in *Re O (Supervision Order)* [2001] EWCA Civ 16, [2001] 1 FLR 923.

18.19   JURISDICTION

Re I (A Child) (Contact Application: Jurisdiction) [2009] UKSC 10

This ruling means that the courts in this jurisdiction can hear proceedings *if the parties are held to have accepted jurisdiction and it is in the child's interests for the case to be heard here*. That second question [child's interests] is a *'forum conveniens'* issue – and not a consideration of what is the child's substantive best interests.

18.20   LITIGANT IN PERSON AND MCKENZIE FRIENDS

Re N (McKenzie Friend: Rights of Audience) [2008] EWHC (Fam), per Munby J

The discretion to appoint a McKenzie Friend under the Courts and Legal Services Act 1990 was unfettered. The courts were faced with a very wide range of relevant circumstances which it was impossible to classify or categorise. Criteria for appointment are 'good reason' in the context of the statutory 'general objective' and 'general principle.' See s 27(2)(c) of the Courts and Legal Services Act 1990. Where a proposed advocate held himself out as providing advocacy services – a 'professional' McKenzie friend – the court would only make an order in exceptional circumstances; where he was a family member the position was likely to be very different. **Note:** In the light of this decision, the *President's Guidance: McKenzie Friends* of 14 April 2008 has been withdrawn and the Guidance reissued on 14 October 2008 in the light of this case, following amendment to the penultimate paragraph.

18.21   LOCAL AUTHORITY

GC v LD and Others [2009] EWHC 1942 (Fam)

The issue here was whether or not the child continued to be provided with accommodation by the local authority following the residence order and therefore remained a 'looked after' child. *The statutory interpretation exercise and analysis of Black J needs to be read in full.*

Re (A) v Croydon LBC etc [2009] UKSC 8

The issues were whether the appellant was *over or under the age of 18* years vis-à-vis the jurisdiction under s 20 of the Children Act 1989 and *how 'age'* was to be assessed. *Held*: The question of a person's age was a question to which there was a right or a wrong answer. *It was a question of fact to be determined on the evidence by a court rather than by other kinds of decision-makers.* That the remedy was, by coincidence, via judicial review did not dictate to the court the way in which it should decide the question. *By way of contrast* where the issue was *what service the local authority should provide*, it was entirely reasonable to assume that Parliament intended such evaluative questions to be determined by the authority, subject to control of the courts on the ordinary principles of judicial review.

O v Orkney Island Council [2009] EWHC 3173 (Fam)

A couple living in England were fostering a vulnerable and sick child from Orkney to whom they were distantly related. Issues of 'looked after' child.

R (SA) v Kent County Council [2011] EWCA Civ 1303

(Court of Appeal, Ward and Rimer LJJ and Sir Stephen Sedley, 10 November 2011)

The Court of Appeal upheld the judge's decision that the child who was living with her grandmother was a looked-after child under a s 23(2) arrangement. The Court also agreed with the judge that if not bound by authority it would not draw the distinction between s 23(2) and s 23(6) regarding the looked-after status of a child, but it was so bound.

Re D (A Child) (Care Order: Designated Local Authority) [2012] EWCA Civ 627

(Court of Appeal; Ward, Stanley Burnton, Elias LJJ; 14 May 2012)

The baby was placed with foster parents by the local authority soon after birth due to concerns of neglect, the vulnerability of the mother and the volatility within the parents' relationship.

The mother had been a child in care herself and had lived with foster carers in the area in which she now lived with her child. However, the mother had been born in a neighbouring local authority and they retained responsibility for her care. The issue arose as to the application of s 105(6) of the Children Act 1989 and which local authority was responsible for providing accommodation for the baby. The mother had not lived within the neighbouring authority for a number of years and the child had never lived there.

The baby's ordinary residence was dependent on that of the mother which was determined to be the one she had lived in since she was removed from her mother, in line with the ordinary meaning of the term 'ordinary residence'. Appeal dismissed.

18.22 MEDIA ACCESS AND PUBLICITY

Re Child X (Residence and Contact: Rights of Media Attendance: FPR Rule 10.28(4)) [2009] EWHC 1724 (Fam)

- *The primary issue*: To decide whether or not to exclude the media from the court-room in the welfare or privacy interests of a party or third party: at [46].

- *'Celebrity' cases*: No different in principle from any other: at **[51]**.

- *The issue is not one of 'discretion'*: The Art 8/10 balancing exercise is *not* a simple issue of *'discretion'* as between two equally legitimate competing rights; it is a test of *'necessity'*: at **[56]**. Thus references to the Court's *'discretion'* in *paragraph 3.1* and in the heading to *paragraph 5* of the **PD** of 20 April 2009 are a misnomer: at **[48]** and **[56]**. *'Necessary'* is the yardstick for any of the statutory grounds of exclusion: at **[53]**. It demands a strong interpretation; *R v Shayler* [2003] 1 AC 247, at 268: at **[54]** and **[89]**.

- *Balancing exercise*: The court must conduct the balancing exercise and process of parallel analysis in respect of the interplay between Arts 8 and 10: see *Campbell v MGN Ltd* [2004] 2 AC 457, *Re S (A child)* [2005] 1 AC 593: at **[46]**; recognising in this context that the issue is one of statutory *'necessity'* to exclude – as contrasted with *'Campbell'* and *'S'* which concerned issues of what could be reported. Note under Rule 10.28(4): To what extent is the *'watchdog'* function of the court engaged: at **[58]** and **[65]**.

- *Burden of proof*: Easier for partial as contrasted with total exclusion: at **[57]**.

Re Stedman [2009] EWHC 935 (Fam), per Eleanor King J

The case of the *15-year-old mother of a child*, of which a *13-year-old boy* professed to be the father. Publicity with press and photos. DNA testing thereafter proved that the boy was not the father. Local authority applied for injunction vis-à-vis publicity and photos. *Held:* Balancing exercise between Arts 8 and 10. Media circus immediately following birth, so *matters already in public domain*. The welfare of the child is *not the paramount* consideration when the court is exercising its protective (ie non-custodial) jurisdiction; see eg *Re Z (A Minor) (Freedom in Publication)* [1997] Fam 1; [1996] 1 FLR 191 etc.

A v Ward [2010] EWHC 16 (Fam) [2010] 1 FLR 1497, per Munby LJ

In an alleged non-accidental injury, the judge found *in favour of the parents.* The parents wished to tell their story through a *BBC documentary* but the professionals involved took legal steps *to preserve their anonymity.* *Held: Openness and transparency* where professionals are involved must, apart from *exceptional* circumstances, be part and parcel of the practice and procedure of all the family courts. **Note:** This case is the delayed sequel to *Re Ward, BBC v Cafcass Legal* [2007] EWHC 616 (Fam), [2007] 2 FLR 765. The case addressed points of pure principle, relevant to practice and procedure in the Family Division. Cases referred to: *Re F (A Minor) (Publication of Information)* [1977] Fam 58, *In Re S (Minors)*

(Wardship: Police Investigation) [1987] Fam 199, *Re W (Disclosure to Police)* [1998] 2 FLR 135, *Re M (Disclosure: Children and Family Reporter)* [2002] EWCA Civ 1199, [2002] 2 FLR 893 and *Re B (A Child) (Disclosure)* [2004] EWHC 411, [2004] 2 FLR 142.

S v Ward [2010] EWHC 538 (Fam), per Munby LJ

This is the sequel to the above case. **Comment:** In his earlier judgment, Munby LJ had held that the question of whether it was in the child's best interests to put information about the child protection proceedings in the public domain was a matter for the parents, not for the court. Paragraph 1 of the order of 8 January 2010 permitted them to do so, disapplying s 12 of the Administration of Justice Act 1960. On the BBC's subsequent application, Munby LJ emphasised the purpose of para 1 of the Order of 8 January 2010, **which gave only the parents the liberty of publication**. Furthermore, the parents were **personally injuncted from identifying the treating clinicians,** which restriction could **not** be circumvented by third parties. **Hence the amendment had to be carefully restricted to permitting third parties to publish only such material as had been supplied to them by the parents.**

News Media Ltd v A (By the Official Solicitor) [2009] EWHC 2858 (Fam)

This case provided the first opportunity to reflect upon the problems of privacy and public interest created by the new jurisdiction of the Court of Protection created by the Mental Capacity Act 2005. There is a tension between the essentially private subject-matter of the proceedings of the court and the legitimate public interest in the practice and exercise of its powers.

Re BBC (Care Proceedings: Costs: Identification of Local Authority) [2011] 1 FLR 977

There was a **legitimate public interest in the local authority being named.** The local population had an interest in knowing of the authority's **failings and the remedial steps** that had been taken. Any restriction on those rights was not proportionate to the potential breach of the children's rights. See also: *Re B; X Council v B* [2007] EWHC 1622 (Fam), [2008] 1 FLR 482; *Re S (Identification: Restriction on Publication)* [2004] UKHL 47, [2005] 1 FLR 591.

Re Jane (Publicity) [2010] EWHC 3221 (Fam)

Section 12(2)(a) of the Human Rights Act 1998 made clear that for a reporting **restriction order** covering **all press and media** to be made, **all practicable steps** to notify had to have been taken or **compelling reasons** for not notifying a respondent provided. This was a case *where the right to freedom of expression* and the Convention provisions protecting that right trumped, in terms, the *child's need for protection from media* intrusion into her life and upbringing. Holman J did what he could to protect the latter but was bound by the clear provisions governing the former.

CDE and FGH v MGN Ltd and LMN [2010] EWHC 3308 (QB)

Minor celebrity, wife and children – naïve and vulnerable single mother conducted a 'quasi relationship' with the celebrity. Comment:

- The judge had to decide what the outcome of the trial is likely to be *on the basis of incomplete, conflicting and untested evidence*. In the present case, for example, the woman's explanation that she changed her mind about selling her story because she had received independent legal advice 'as to her "victim" status' needed a full investigation.

- Eady J was intent upon transparency and the important element of open justice: *he considered that legal practitioners should be able to monitor the court's processes and form a view as to whether judges were applying a consistent, fair and balanced approach*. He examined the various *public interest* arguments, addressed questions of the *defendant's vulnerability* and possible exploitation, and reached conclusions within the context of *human rights* and *proportionality*: see *Mosley v News Group Newspapers Ltd* [2008] EMLR 20.

- Eady J's answer to the argument that the present judgment should not be anonymised was essentially '*that which it is intended should be kept private until the trial, would to all intents and purposes become public – and there would be no point in having a trial*'.

- On the question of anonymity Eady J referred to *Donald v Ntuli* [2010] EWCA Civ 1276 and *Secretary of State for the Home department v AP (No 2)* [2010] UKSC 26.

18.23 MEDICAL EVIDENCE

R v Arshad [2012] EWCA Crim 18

(Court of Appeal (Crim); President of QBD, Griffith Williams J, Sharp J; 24 January 2012)

The mother was found guilty of manslaughter in respect of her 13-week-old son. The mother appealed in light of *R v Henderson* whether the directions given by the judge were correct. The consultant forensic pathologist found evidence of 'the triad' and the only credible explanation of the child's death was a shaking/impact injury. There was extensive medical evidence by the prosecution and defence. After the trial the Royal College of Pathologists held a meeting with the prominent experts in the field, many of which had given evidence at the trial. The discussion left unresolved many of the well-known disagreements including the significance of the triad of injuries. The mother appealed, and argued that the judge should have directed the jury that this is a developing area of medical science and that they had to consider the realistic possibility of the injuries being due to an unknown cause.

Appeal dismissed. The judge's summing up had been entirely fair in a manner the jury could understand, the jury could have been in no doubt that in an area where medical science was uncertain in light of the findings made by the doctors, they could only convict if they were sure on the evidence the death had been caused in the manner alleged by the Crown and other possibilities had been excluded.

18.24   MEDICAL TREATMENT

Re B (Medical Treatment) [2008] EWHC 1996 (Fam)

Issue: Declaration sought as to whether or not to permit *withholding of life-saving treatment* in respect of a 22-month-old child suffering from profound mental and physical disabilities with a life expectation of less than 5 years. **Held:**

(1)   *Declaration granted.* If circumstances arose where only invasive resuscitation processes could save the child, it would *not* be in her *best interests* for those processes to be undertaken to ensure a *short* further prolongation of life.

(2)   The local authority were probably right in thinking that they [as opposed to the NHS] *did not have sufficient authority* to consent to the declaration. Even if they did have enough authority they were entirely right in taking the understandable line that they did not wish to consent to, or be seen to consenting to, a declaration of the present kind.

(3)   Because the present declaration was less specific than such declarations usually were, and because the doctors admitted that they could not foresee every situation in which the permission they had obtained would be needed, the court suggested *that a short, joint experts' report be attached to the order so that any doctor coming new to the child and to the critical situation in the future would have further guidance to enable them to make what might be a very difficult, sensitive and finely balanced clinical judgment.*

Re RB [2009] EWHC 3269 (Fam)

It is well established case law that the court has jurisdiction to decide what will be in *a gravely ill child's best interests*, and that will turn in every case on the individual facts and special circumstances. See by way of example also: *Wyatt v Portsmouth NHS Trust* [2005] EWCA Civ 1181, [2006] 1 FLR 554 and *Re Wyatt* [2006] EWHC 319 (Fam), [2006] 2 FLR 111.

A Local Authority v SB, AB and MB [2010] EWHC 1744 (Fam), per Sir Nicholas Wall P

As to medical treatment, the law is as set out by Butler-Sloss LJ in *Re T (Wardship: Medical Treatment)* [1997] 1 FLR 502. In that case the Court of Appeal reversed the decision that the child should undergo a life-saving operation as advised by doctors and opposed by her parents. Her Ladyship considered that the child's future treatment should be '*left in the hands of the devoted parents*'. Sir Nicholas Wall P explained how the case illustrates '*the different areas of responsibility which exist within the family justice system and the proper limits of the court's role within that system*'. He went on to say that '*the court should be acute to recognise the limitations of its role*'. Parliament, in passing the Children Act 1989 had placed a sharp and clear division between the functions of the courts and the local authorities.

18.25 PARENTAL RESPONSIBILITY – AND CAPACITY/CAPABILITY

R v E and F (Female Parents: Known Father) [2010] EWHC 417 (Fam)

7-year-old boy brought up by *two women* in a *lesbian* relationship, one of whom was biological mother. Two lesbian women friendly with male biological father who was in a relationship with another male. *Both women had parental responsibility but not the biological father*. Fall out between two couples, issues as to contact and residence. **Note:** In his legal analysis, Bennet J considered two cases in which one of the lesbian partners had become a mother by means of *donated sperm.* These were *Re D (Contact and Parental Responsibility: Lesbian Mothers and Known Father)* [2006] EWHC 2 (Fam) where parental responsibility was granted to the biological father and *Re B (Role of Biological Father)* [2007] EWHC 1952 (Fam), [2008] 1 FLR 1015 where it was refused. Bennet J noted that the courts had been mindful of those cases which stressed the status aspect of parental responsibility, *that parental responsibility was subject to the overriding provisions of s 1(1)* and, importantly, that dicta from well known decisions in what might be called 'conventional' or 'usual' parental responsibility applications did not readily transfer to cases such as the instant one.

R v R [2011] EWHC 1535 (Fam)

(Family Division, Peter Jackson J, 15 June 2011)

It was not appropriate under Children Act 1989, s 4A(1)(b) for the mother's husband to be granted parental responsibility for the child whom he had initially believed to be his own; it would be likely to lead to conflict with the mother. A declaration of parentage was in the interests of the child to make clear his biological paternity.

Z v B, C and Cafcass [2011] EWHC 3181 (Fam)

(Family Division, Theis J, 2 December 2011)

On the facts, the applicant had satisfied the court that he was domiciled in England and Wales for the purposes of HFEA 2008, s 54 and the court, therefore, had jurisdiction to consider the application for a parental order.

18.26   PATERNITY

Ahrens v Germany (App No 45071/09)

(European Court of Human Rights; 22 March 2012)

The applicant alleged German court's failure to allow him to challenge another man's legal paternity of a child violated his Art 8 rights. The paternity declared by the mother's new partner with her consent. The German court prevented applicant from challenging paternity despite having a sexual relationship with the mother around the time of conception. The applicant's relationship with the child was not within the scope of family life as his relationship with the mother ended a year prior to conception and thereafter was purely sexual. Decision not to allow challenge of paternity fell within private life. Decision taken in the best interests of the family unit: the mother, her partner and the child. Decision whether to allow to challenge paternity fell within the State's margin of appreciation.

Case had taken 3 years, 7 months to be determined in Germany, delay did not predetermine issues, procedural requirements of Art 8 had been complied with.

18.27   PATHWAY/ELIGIBLE CHILD

Re S (A Child) (Eligible Child) [2008] EWCA Civ 1140; [2009] 1 FLR 378

Application to discharge care order vis-à-vis *17 year old girl* with *severe disabilities* dismissed by the county court judge on the basis of and in reliance upon undertakings *by LA as to pathway plan,* statement of *transitional arrangements* and *arrangements* as to child's financial affairs and contact. *LA failed to comply with undertakings.* Court of Appeal *allowed* appeal on the basis of frustration of the grounds for the judge's dismissal.

18.28   PRACTICE/PROCEDURE

Re F-H (Dispensing with fact-finding hearing) [2008] EWCA Civ 1249

Judge held a *fact-finding* hearing on sex abuse to be *unnecessary*; in the context of forthcoming criminal proceedings. **Held:** The fact that certain material need not be considered before a conclusion was reached that the court had *power* to make a care order in no way supported a conclusion that it did not need to be considered before deciding whether the *optimum outcome* for the children was to make such an order. *Facts needed to be found in relation to all four children.* Wilson LJ endorsed the *nine matters* identified by McFarlane J in *A County Council v DP and Others* [2005] 2 FLR 1031 in relation to whether to conduct *a particular fact-finding exercise* but extended the list to matters in the present case – a case where the judge considered at the *outset* of a pre-arranged fact-finding hearing whether, in effect, to *abort* it. Wilson LJ noted that it was:

> 'generally unwise for the family court to await the outcome of criminal proceedings in the hope that either a conviction or ... an implosion of the prosecution case would in effect resolve matters for the purposes of the family proceedings.'

As to the importance of *liaison* between the two jurisdictions in the context of *parallel* criminal proceedings, see *Re W* [2009] EWCA Civ 644, [2009] 2 FLR 1106.

Re C (Litigant in Person: s 91(14) Order) [2009] EWCA Civ 674

In the normal course, the application for a *s 91(14) order* had to be in *writing on notice,* so that the court could hear the relevant submissions and make an order one way or the other. But where an application *arose during or at the end of a trial,* on the application of one party or on the court's own initiative, or when one party was *unrepresented*, other matters needed to be *taken into account*. These stressed that while the court could make the order in those circumstances it was of ***utmost importance*** that the party affected by the order (***particularly if they were in person***) understood that the application was being made, understood its meaning and effect and had ***proper opportunity to answer the application.*** Where a party was ***unrepresented,*** there was the possibility of dealing with it without a formal application; but if there were a substantive objection the court required the application to be made ***formally on notice*** in the normal way ***or an adjournment given to enable a party to respond properly***. In particular there was a ***powerful obligation*** on the court to explain matters where the parties were ***litigants in person***: this meant using ***ordinary language*** to describe the meaning, effect and duration of the order and provide proper opportunities for submissions and objections.

WSCC v M [2010] EWHC 1914 (Fam)

Application to withdraw proceedings; principles to be applied:

> 'I have derived considerable assistance on this point from the judgment of Waite LJ in *London Borough of Southwark -v- Y* [1993] 2 FLR 559 C.A. This question is considered between p. 572D and 573H. The effect of the judgment is that Section 1(1) is engaged but because an application for permission falls outside Section 1(4), then Section 1(3) is strictly not engaged. However, Waite LJ continues at p. 572H –
>
> > "I would not expect [that] to make the slightest difference, in practice, to the way in which applications to withdraw care proceedings under r. 4.5 are approached by the courts ... the only practical results, therefore ... is that a court dealing with an application to withdraw proceedings under r. 4.5. is free, when assessing the considerations affecting the welfare of the child so far as they apply to that application, to make specific use of the S. 1(3) checklist if it so wishes, but cannot be criticized if it omits to do so."
>
> It follows from that that Section 1(1) is engaged and Section 1(3) is available for the assistance of the court but its use is not mandatory. The court makes it clear that the consequences of giving permission (i.e. discharging interim care orders) do not determine of themselves the nature of the application. In other words the focus is on permission not on discharge.'

EH v LB of Greenwich [2010] EWCA Civ 344

Importance, when appropriate, of a *'Turnbull'* and *'Lucas'* lies direction in any judgment.

H v City and County of Swansea and Others [2011] EWCA Civ 195

Failure to give a *Lucas* direction to himself affected the judge's analysis of the facts; see *R v Lucas (Ruth)* [1981] QB 720, and per Ryder J in *Z v Z (Divorce: Jurisdiction)* [2009] EWHC 2626 (Fam), [2010] 1 FLR 694, at [4] where he said:

> 'I have reminded myself that a witness may give truthful evidence as to one matter without necessarily being truthful about all matters and vice versa.'

18.29 PRIVACY

RST v UVW [2009] EWHC B24 (QB), per Tugendhat J

A man who had a *public reputation* had *sex* with a woman *on a commercial basis* at his home. Two years later the woman *threatened* the man with disclosure of this information unless she was paid. The parties reached a *confidentiality agreement for consideration*. Eight years later a third party contacted the man and *threatened* to publish the relevant details which it was claimed the woman had disclosed to him. The man made a 'without notice' application for an interim injunction preventing publication, *based not on defamation but on breach of confidence or privacy. Held*: Granting the interim injunction:

(1) Pursuant to *s 12(2)(b)* of the Human Right Act 1998, the compelling reason to make the order 'without notice' was that the facts were such as to give rise to a real prospect that, *if notice were given*, the defendant *might take steps* to *defeat* the purpose of the injunction.

(2) The *established law* in relation to a claim *in defamation* was that *no* interim injunction would be granted when what the defendant was proposing to publish was material which might be defamatory *but which the defendant alleged to be true* (the rule in *Bonnard v Perryman* [1891] 1 Ch 269; *Greene v Associated Newspapers* [2004] EWCA Civ 1462, [2005] QB 972. *The issue of principle was whether that rule applied to the present case even though it was not pleaded in defamation but in confidence or privacy*.

(3) Where an application raised an issue under both Art 8 and Art 10 of the European Convention for the Protection of Human Rights and Fundamental Freedoms 1950, the court was required to carry out the *ultimate fact-sensitive balancing exercise* in which neither article had precedence: *Re S (A Child) (Identification: Restriction on Publication)* [2004] UKHL 47, [2005] 1 FLR 591.

(4) In this case there were issues:

(a) whether the claim was *properly characterised* as a claim in *protect privacy or reputation*;

(b) if the rule in *Bonnard v Perryman* would otherwise apply, *whether it was overridden by the subsequent agreement which had contractual force*; and

(c) whether the court could give the protection of an injunction to information about *sexual encounters of the kind raised* in this case. These issues would have to be debated and determined at the future substantive hearing.

(5) Subject to these issues, the court was satisfied that the application came within the terms of s 12(3) of the Human Rights Act 1998, ie that *the applicant was likely to publish* and that publication should not be allowed. At the interlocutory stage, the test was the *lower threshold test* as explained in *Cream Holdings v Banerjee* [2003] EWCA Civ 103, [2003] Ch 660.

(6) The injunction was granted.

Note: (1) This judgment highlights an interesting issue of principle which will no doubt be fully canvassed at the substantive hearing. The long-established common law rule in *Bonnard v Perryman* [the 'prior restraint' rule] would appear to have been strengthened by Art 10 of the Convention (protection of freedom of speech). However, there is an obvious tension with Art 8 (protection of the right to privacy). The tension was highlighted by Eady J in *CC v AB* [2006] EWHC 3083 (QB), [2007] 2 FLR 301 where an interim injunction was granted restraining the defendant from communication with the media or the internet concerning the claimant's former relationship with the defendant's wife. The instant case raised the characteristic question – *protection of privacy or protection of reputation*? – and *whether the court is obliged to carry out the characterisation exercise* even where the claimant has elected his cause of action (as to which the case-law is not wholly clear: see eg *Gulf Oil v Page* [1987] Ch 327, *Joyce v Sengupta* [1993] 1 WLR 337 and *McKennit v Ash* [2008] QB 73.The issue of what sexual relations can be protected by injunction was raised in *A v B Plc and C* [2002] 1 FLR 179 (Jack J) and *A v B Plc* [2002] EWCA Civ 337, [2002] 1 FLR 1021 [Court of Appeal]. There, an interim injunction restraining publication of a married professional footballer's sexual relationship with two women *was set aside on appeal*: see the comments in [2002] Fam Law 100 and 415 by Professors Douglas and Bailey-Harris respectively.

Terry v Persons Unknown (Formerly referred to as 'LNS') [2010] EWHC 119 (QB)

The applicant *sought an interim injunction* to prohibit the publication of any information or photographs regarding a personal relationship between him and another person. The applicant also sought a *private hearing, anonymity for the persons involved in the relationship*, sealing of the *entire* court file, an order prohibiting *publication of the existence* of the legal proceedings, and that he not be required to provide any third party served with a copy of the order, a copy of any materials read by the judge and/or a note of the hearing. *Held*: **Refusing** the application

(1) It is for the court to decide whether the principle of free speech prevails or not, and it *does not depend solely upon the choice of the claimant as to his cause of action*.

(2) There *was insufficient* evidence to demonstrate that the applicant was likely to establish there had *been a breach of duty of confidence* owed to him, or a *threat to publish intrusive details* in respect of which he had a *reasonable expectation of privacy*.

(3) The nub of the application was *protection of reputation* rather than any other aspect of private life; the applicant was concerned about the impact of any *adverse publicity upon the business* of earning sponsorship and similar income. On that basis, no injunction should be granted, *Bonnard v Perryman* [1891] 2 Ch 269, applied.

(4) The applicant's advisers had come under the impression that *extensive derogations* from *open justice* should be routine in claims for misuse of private information. But while secrecy might be essential in the case of a respondent who, *if tipped off*, is likely to defeat the purposes of an application by publishing the material before he can be shown to have had notice of the injunction or before it can be granted, *it is less easy to show the need for such secrecy where the person targeted by the applicant is a national newspaper*.

(5) *Notice* of the application *should have been* given to the media organisations who the applicant *knew* were interested in publishing the story. Failure to notify meant the court was unable to form a view of the social utility of the speech which the applicant sought to restrain *as no argument had been heard* from any opponent.

(6) *The test to apply at the interim stage is whether the applicant is more likely than not to succeed at trial.*

(7) If the claim could be treated as for a misuse of private information, and the court were wrong in concluding that a defence of public interest could not be made out, then in the exercise of discretion the court would not grant an injunction – the information had already become *widely available* to many people, meaning that an injunction would be *less necessary or proportionate* than would otherwise be the case.

(8) *Where an applicant seeks an order prohibiting reports of the facts of the injunction sought, there must be a return date and grounds for such an application must be set out in the evidence.*

Note: This case limited the use of the '*super injunction*' under which the existence of the proceedings and the terms of the order itself are to be protected from publication – to situations where secrecy is truly necessary.

18.30 PROCEDURE

Re B (Care Order: Adjournment of Fact Finding Hearing) [2009] EWCA Civ 1243

Legal advisers must be fully conversant with the demands, and the facilities, of the court process to ensure that delay can be minimised whilst safeguarding the due process rights of the client. *Urgent matters, especially relating to children, can be dealt with very swiftly if all the machinery of the Royal Courts of Justice is properly utilised.* In this context, also see: *Re S (Child Proceedings: Urgent Appeals)* [2007] EWCA Civ 958, [2007] 2 FLR 1044, at [10]; and *Re P and P (Care Proceedings: Appointment of Experts)* [2009] EWCA Civ 610, [2009] 2 FLR 1370.

Re R-E (Children) [2011] EWCA Civ 1348

(Court of Appeal, Thorpe and Black LJJ, 9 August 2011)

It was generally accepted that there should be a reappraisal of whether a father was the perpetrator of sexual abuse against his daughter. In the circumstances, the Court of Appeal could take a pragmatic approach to a procedural error and revive the father's notice of appeal in place of his application for an Ord 37 review.

Re B-A (Children) [2011] EWCA Civ 1643

(Court of Appeal, Thorpe and Kitchin LJJ and Mann J, 1 December 2011)

Although it was difficult to maintain the momentum of trial and to accommodate the grandmother's very late application for party status, the judge ought to have devised a method for letting the grandmother back into the trial because she had played a large part in the lives of the children.

Re A & L (Children) [2011] EWCA Civ 1611

(Court of Appeal, Patten, Munby and Tomlinson LJJ, 21 December 2011)

Extempore judgments should not be discouraged. The safeguard is the ability – indeed the duty – of the parties to seek further elaboration from the judge if they feel that something is missing. Experienced judges should not be deterred from giving brief judgments where appropriate.

18.31   PROHIBITED STEPS

Re M (Removal from Jurisdiction: Adjournment) [2010] EWCA Civ 888

- ***Obtaining expert evidence in leave to remove from the jurisdiction cases is the norm.*** The guidance from Thorpe LJ in *Re K (Removal from the Jurisdiction: Practice)* [1999] 2 FLR 1084 was to be followed. All practical safeguards had to be first put in place and that there should be an exploration of those practicalities through expert evidence.

- Dealing with the practicalities of a foreign legal system and information about how a return from a non-Hague Convention country could proceed if the child were not returned, ***required the assistance of someone expert in the jurisdiction.***

- ***An expert could assist with the issue of enforcement,*** how the child would be returned ***if*** the father did not comply with his obligation, whether a ***notarised agreement were possible*** at all and whether a mirror order ***were possible or desirable.***

- Where normal practice – the appointment of an expert – was not complied with, ***there needed to be a clear explanation from the judge as to why not.***

18.32   PROOF OF AGE

R (F) v Lewisham London Borough Council and others [2009] EWHC 3542 (Admin), per Holman J

Directions given in five cases involving ***the assessment of the age*** of people claiming to be children for the purposes of the Children Act 1989:

(1) ***First***: Once the court is required to engage on determination of whether the person was on the relevant date a child, it must and should go on to make ***its own determination*** (binding as between the claimant and the local authority) as ***to actual age*** and ***date of birth***. Hence there must be a direction as to a fact-finding hearing on this issue.

(2) **Second**: Permission for the claim to proceed is an ***important filter*** and must not become a matter of formality [Judge considered the criteria for leave];

(3) **Third:** The standard of proof is the ***balance of probability.***

(4) **Fourth**: The question of where the ***evidential burden*** lies may depend upon the facts and circumstances of individual cases.

(5) **Fifth:** In cases where paediatric evidence has already been obtained, reliance upon it at the fact-finding hearings ***cannot be excluded*** by some direction given at an earlier stage.

(6) **Sixth:** Where medical evidence has not previously been obtained, ***it should not be routinely permitted*** until the court has had some opportunity at a fact-finding hearing fully to consider its potential value.

(7) **Seventh:** If local authorities wish to defend these cases by reliance upon assessments [which include matters of fact as well as opinion] of their social workers, ***then they must produce those social workers for cross-examination if required.***

(8) **Eighth**: The extent to which the claimant participates or gives evidence is a matter for the judge at the hearing itself. Model direction:

> 'Any question whether the claimant shall give oral evidence or be cross-examined and any question whether all or any part of the hearing will take place in Chambers, or whether the judge will see the claimant in his private room, will be a matter for the sole discretion of the judge at the final hearing.'

Further ruling as to video evidence etc.

(9) **Nine:** Identification of the category or ***tier of judge*** who hears this type of case is a matter entirely for the court.

(10) **Ten**: The ***sort*** of ***fact-finding*** hearing and judgment involved in this type of case must be dealt with as a single composite exercise with ***an ex tempore judgment*** at the end.

(11) **Eleven:** Directions for bundles, chronology etc.

(12) **Twelve**: Interpreter?

MC v Liverpool City Council [2010] EWHC 2211 (Admin)

C sought asylum and later sought social benefit. He initially asserted that he had been born on 24 March 1992 but subsequently gave the date of 24 March 1994. **Held:** Assessing C's date of birth as being 24 September 1992, the approach of the court was set out in *R (A) v Croydon LBC; R(M) v Lambeth LBC* [2009] UKSC 8, [2010] 1 FLR 959.

R (FZ) v London Borough of Croydon [2011] EWCA Civ 59

Iranian asylum seeker *claiming to be 17* when LA *assessed him as 19.* Comment:

- See also *R (CJ) v Cardiff City Council* [2011] EWHC 23 (Admin).

- The challenge of a young person, typically an unaccompanied asylum seeker, *to an adverse age assessment* was generally by way of *judicial review* on either *orthodox grounds* or simply that the factual assessment had been wrong.

- In *R (A) v Lambeth London BC* [2009] UKSC 8, [2010] 1 FLR 959, the Supreme Court held that the question of age was subject to the *ultimate determination of the courts*, often by adjudication upon *oral* evidence.

- In the instant case, the President of the QBD said *that such oral evidence was a time-consuming process stretching the court's resources.* He noted that the Administrative Court did *not* habitually decide questions of fact on contested evidence and *nor was oral* evidence normally a feature of such proceedings.

- The President of the QBD drew attention to the Upper Tribunal where judges were *experienced in age assessments* and *transferred the present case to that court.*

- *Guidance* on the *appropriate* process in seeking permission to bring judicial review stemmed from *R (B) v Merton LBC* [2003] EWHC 1689 (Admin), [2003] 2 FLR 888 and has developed into what has been called a '*Merton Compliant*' process or interview.

- The parties to the present case agreed that *the correct test* was that formulated by Holman J in *R (F) v Lewisham LBC* [2009] EWHC 3542 (Admin), [2010] 1 FLR 1463: whether there was a realistic prospect or arguable case that the court would conclude that the claimant *was younger than the authority assessed him to be.*

18.33 PUBLICITY

D v Buckinghamshire CC [2008] EWCA Civ 1372, [2009] 1 FLR 881

After a fact-finding hearing, judge drew up a draft order to the effect that the authority had a reasonable belief that the appellant *posed a risk* to young people and was not an appropriate person to have care of them. The *findings* covered *eight schools* where the appellant had been employed and *concerned deceit* over his qualifications and allegations over attitudes to pupils: they did *not amount to findings of indecent assault or active sexual abuse*. **Held**:

(1)   It was *open to the judge to find facts even where there was no live issue* before the court: subject only to the *question of notice*.

(2)   There was to be disclosure to the Secretary of State at the DCSF. **Note**: Authoritative dicta as to the Independent Safeguarding Authority.

S v Rochdale Metropolitan Borough Council [2008] EWHC 3283 (Fam)

Munby J approved a confidentiality agreement [enshrined in a compromise order against a backdrop of Art 8 of the ECHR and alleged serious infringements by the local authority]. Case material in two primary respects:

(1)   The effect of the confidentiality clause was to deny the claimant the right to share her story with others, a right described by the judge as a critically important aspects of the right to private life as guaranteed by Art 8; see also *Re Roddy (A Child) (Identification: Restriction on Publication)* [2004] 2 FLR 949 where judge observed that it was natural to want to talk about ourselves and fundamental to our human condition that we be able to do so.

(2)   In contrast to *Roddy* the compromise was in fact entirely consistent with the child's welfare.

Re B, C and D (By the Children's Guardian) [2010] EWHC 262 (Fam), per Homan J

The parents of *three children* who had been removed from them and *adopted* applied for the discharge of *injunctions preventing them from discussing* (other than with their legal advisers, etc) or otherwise *communicating, encouraging* or *suggesting* that any other person publish matters relating to their family circumstances or the legal proceedings concerning the children. During the proceedings, Holman J held that *the adoptive parents should be informed and consulted*, and the local authority now applied for the injunctions to *bind the media* directly. **Held, amending the terms of the injunctions**:

(1)   *The legal framework is*: The court will have regard to the importance of the convention right to freedom of expression [Human Rights Act 1998, s 12] but the right under Art 10 ECHR does not outweigh that under Art 8 ECHR: *Re S (Identification: Restrictions on Publication)* [2004] UKHL 47, [2005] 1 FLR 591 and *Clayton v Clayton* [2006] EWCA (Civ) 878, [2007] 1 FLR 11.

(2)   If and to the extent that they could be achieved *without causing or risking damage, disruption or upset to the children and their adoptive families*, the parents' desire to gain publicity for their stories was an entirely legitimate objective.

(3)   The welfare and rights of children, individually as well as collectively, clearly outweighed the rights of the birth parents or media under Art 10. It was *necessary*, *justifiable* and *proportionate*.

(4)   Head-note inter alia reads:

> 'It was necessary, proportionate and justifiable to prevent the pictures or names, including the forenames, of the parents from being published in any context and in any way that might lead anyone, including the children themselves, to make any connection between the publication and any of the children. A picture or image of the birth parents could be used only if obscured or disguised; there was no need to disguise their speech or voice. Dates of birth should not be published, but a reference could be made to age. There must be no reference to the gender of the children, as any such reference would increase the risk that the children might be identified, while adding nothing to the story (see paras [46], [47], [48], [49]).'

Re A (A Minor) (Reporting Restriction Order) [2011] EWHC 1764 (Fam)

(Family Division, Baker J, 8 July 2011)

An order was made restricting the reporting of the identity of a child, but having applied the ultimate balancing exercise, no restrictions would be placed on the reporting of the mother's identity and her arrest on suspicion of murdering her two other children.

18.34 RECUSAL

Re L-B (Care Proceedings: Recusal) [2010] EWCA Civ 1118

Recorder recused herself after realising that she was instructed on outstanding issues in another case by the guardian, but refused to set aside her findings in a finding-of-fact hearing involving that guardian. *Held:* She *should have* set aside her findings. **Note:** Relevant case is *Helow v Secretary of State for the Home Department* [2008] UKHL 62; *the objective bystander test. Issues of recusal are not clear cut and will usually be case-specific.*

18.35 RELOCATION

Re Z (A Child) (Relocation) [2012] EWHC 139 (Fam)

(Family Division; Pauffley J; 2 February 2012)

The Australian mother and Belgian father married in Australia where their 6-year-old daughter was born. They relocated to Belgium. When they separated the mother took the child to England and brought proceedings seeking permission to relocate with the child to Australia. The father wrongfully retained the child during contact in Belgium for 11 months. The father sought a shared residence order. Consequences of wrongful retention had been devastating to mother and child, mother had always been primary carer. Residence with the father would be contrary to child's welfare. The mother was isolated, lacking in support in England and feared child would be abducted again. The mother claimed she would bring the child to England for contact once a year and allow extended Skype contact. There was a real potential for deterioration in the mother's mental well-being if application refused. The father had become focused on own needs rather than those of his daughter. The guardian was unable to make definitive recommendation, child undecided about move to Australia. Mother granted residence and permission to relocate to Australia as there was no doubt that that was in the child's best interests.

18.36 REMOVAL FROM JURISDICTION

Re B (Leave to Remove) [2008] EWCA Civ 1034

Provides an *illustration* of a refusal of a relocation application, and such refusals *remain rare*. Each case requires a *highly fact-specific approach* to the welfare enquiry, and judicial findings are of crucial importance. Advocates must be aware that *evidence not challenged at trial cannot be attacked thereafter* if it has become the subject of judicial findings.

Re S and O (Temporary Removal from Jurisdiction) (8 September 2008), per Baron J

Temporary removal for holiday to *Barbados* with father against backdrop of fear by mother that he would keep the children in Barbados and undertaking by father to return. *Security for the undertaking: father's interest in the matrimonial home*, agreed to in writing pursuant to the Law of Property (Miscellaneous Provisions) Act 1989, s 2(1). Given the shortness of time there was *no prospect of a mirror order* being made and *no bonds* were available. Thus the present judgment was given so that the Barbadian court would be clear that the English court had jurisdiction and regarded itself as the primary court of jurisdiction, and that the children were expected to be returned on the specified day so that their long-term needs and care could be determined if the parties could not agree. *Re K (Removal from Jurisdiction: Practice)* [1999] 2 FLR 1084 followed: *All practical safeguards had first to be put in place in the context of a temporary removal*.

Re D (Leave to Remove: Appeal) [2010] EWCA Civ 50

- Permission to appeal refused.

- There was a perfectly *respectable argument* for the proposition (in *Payne v Payne* [2001] EWCA Civ 166) that it placed *too great an emphasis* on the wishes and feelings of the relocating parent, and ignored or relegated the harm done to children by a permanent breach of the relationship which the children had with *the left behind parent*.

- This case provides a lesson by Wall LJ in the *doctrine of precedent* and the application of the *Payne* principles to the present set of facts.

- Note also: *Re G (Leave to Remove)* [2007] EWCA Civ 1497, [2008] 1 FLR 1587; *Re A (Leave to Remove: Cultural and Religious Considerations)* [2006] EWHC 421 (Fam), [2006] 2 FLR 572, where MacFarlane J regarded *Payne* as the 'key decision' and more recently *M v T (Abduction: Brussels II R Art 11(7))* [2010] EWHC 1479 (Fam), where Charles J found the *Payne v Payne* test a *useful one*.

Re H (Leave to Remove) [2010] EWCA Civ 915

Czech wife of English father wrongly abducted 7-year-old back to her patria of the Czech Republic.

- The decision in *Payne v Payne* stressed that the **welfare** of the child was the **paramount consideration** in applications for permission to relocate.

- However the controversy surrounding the proposition that refusal of the primary carer's reasonable proposals was likely to impact detrimentally on the welfare of the children and the conclusion that *the most crucial assessment was the effect of the refusal on the mother*, were acknowledged.

- The court agreed that there was a **respectable argument** for the proposition that, as stated by Wall LJ in *Re D (children)* [2010] EWCA Civ 50, *Payne v Payne* relegated the harm done to children by the permanent breach of a relationship with the left-behind parent *to a level below that of the harm likely to be sustained though the negative impact upon the applicant of a refusal*.

- **Note**: see recent refusal of leave in *Re AR (A Child: Relocation)* [2010] EWHC 1346 (Fam).

Re J v S (Leave to Remove) [2010] EWHC 2098 (Fam)

Swedish father, *Japanese* mother, boys aged *8* and *10 – who spoke Japanese* – divorce, mother seeking leave to move with the boys to Japan, having developed in England a gastro-intestinal illness. Per Eleanor King J:

- In conducting her balancing exercise, she was bound by *Payne* but not limited by the questions posed by Thorpe LJ at **[40]**. Nonetheless, with the judgment of Butler-Sloss P at **[85]**, the welfare checklist and Art 8, she posed and answered those questions to reach her conclusion: that *the impact of a refusal would be so harmful to the mother that it was inimical to the children's welfare*.

  '... the child cannot draw emotional and psychological security and stability from the dependency unless the primary carer herself is emotionally and psychologically stable and secure. The parent cannot give what she herself lacks.'

- The fundamental point for Eleanor King J, and the difference between this case and *Re AR (A Child: Relocation)* [2010] EWHC 1346 (Fam), [2010] 2 FLR 1577, at **[8]** was that the **mother's emotional well being was utterly compromised by her gastric illness**; the mental and physical were inextricably linked.

Re R (Leave to Remove: Contact) [2010] EWCA Civ 1137

- It is a matter for the *judge's discretion* as to whether there should be a *Cafcass report*.

- *Contact* orders *should not* be made *when granting leave to relocate.* They are contrary to principle and the court must recognise that it is *relinquishing jurisdiction to the courts* of the state to which the parent is moving.

- Vis-à-vis criticism of *Payne v Payne* it is widely understood that the most *controversial* factor in *Payne*, the impact on the residential parent if she is not permitted to relocate, inevitably has to be *assessed from the evidence of the surrounding circumstances* rather than reliance upon the parent's own statement.

MK v CK [2011] EWCA Civ 793

(Court of Appeal, Thorpe, Moore-Bick and Black LJJ, 7 July 2011)

The father's appeal against the mother's relocation to Canada was allowed. The judge had rejected the Cafcass officer's clear recommendations without proper analysis and explanation and given insufficient weight to the father's case. The only principle to be drawn from *Payne* is the paramountcy principle; all the rest is guidance. Consideration of leave to remove and application of *Payne* in shared residence cases.

A v B [2011] EWHC 2752 (Fam)

(Family Division, Wall P, 1 November 2011)

Although the mother had returned to England from Sweden with the child and had been inconsistent about her intentions regarding going back to Sweden, the Swedish court was still seised with the proceedings concerning the child and, therefore, the father's English proceedings would be stayed pursuant to Brussels IIR, Art 19. It was for the Swedish court to interrogate the mother and decide whether to order an Art 15 transfer.

18.37 RESIDENCE ORDER

Re G (Residence: Restriction on Further Applications) [2008] EWCA Civ 1468

Frequent applications for contact by father in the face of breaches of contact orders. At first instance: s 91(14) order and almost as an afterthought, a residence order to the mother. On appeal **held:** s 91(14) order *wrong in principle* and *procedurally wrong* and *unfair* that father did not have an opportunity to deal with the residence order issue. **Note:** A residence order gives the mother no added right over and above the father but *simply regulates a factual state of affairs*. Where each parent has parental responsibility, each is as fully entitled to exercise that responsibility while the child is in his or her care as the other. As to s 91(14): This section has to be read in *conjunction with s 1(1)* and, in cases like the present where there is *no history of unreasonable applications*, the court needs to be satisfied that the facts are *exceptional* – that they go beyond the *commonly encountered* need for a time to settle to a regime ordered by the court and that without the imposition of the restriction, the child or the primary carers will be subject to unacceptable strain: see *Re P (Section 91(14) Guidelines) (Residence and Religious Heritage)* [1999] 2 FLR 573.

AB v JLB [2008] EWHC 2965 (Fam), per Munby J

Mother applying to court in England for the English Court to apply under Article 15 of *Brussels II R* to a Dutch court *for transfer of the proceedings* concerning the child to England. **Held:** Dutch Court had already addressed the Art 15 issue. Munby J *formulated a stringent test for applications of this nature*, to preserve *comity* and the *workability* of such conventions; see also *Re S-R (Jurisdiction: Contact)* [2008] 2 FLR 1741.

Re L (Shared Residence: Relocation) [2009] EWCA Civ 20

Shared residence order for 5-year-old with both parents *living in North London*. Mother then applied to vary the terms of the shared residence order to accommodate a relocation to *Somerset*. Judge at first instance found that the mother sought to undermine the shared residence order. Much argument as to the cases on sole and shared residence. Judge refused to vary the order and mother appealed: **Held:** The issue was *not sole or shared residence but welfare* – to approach the case otherwise generated the risk of making the more narrow legalistic point the determining one, thus possibly distorting the *welfare balancing* exercise. **Policy:** It would be *a powerful disincentive* to parties entering into *shared residence orders* if the consequence of doing so was to place a fetter on any *subsequent application to relocate*. **Reading**: See also '*Shared Residence Orders: For and Against*' [2009] Fam Law 131 and the follow-up update: 'Housing and Shared Residence' [2009] Fam Law 263; by Simon Johnson.

Holmes-Moorhouse v London Borough of Richmond on Thames [2009] UKHL 7

Shared residence order made when the *father was homeless. Issue*: Should the local authority have provided a home for the father to facilitate the exercise of the shared residence order? **Held:** The court had no power to order the local authority to act in the best interests of children and *should not make orders which would be 'unworkable'* unless the local authority so acted. By implication, shared residence orders should only be made *where each parent can themselves provide a home which is suitable as a family home*. The shared residence order should *not have* been made. **Note:** the contrast between the decision-making powers of the family court and those of the local authority in allocating scarce resources.

Re C (Family Placement) [2009] EWCA Civ 72

Placement of *5-year-old* boy with *70-year-old grandmother* with whom he had an important relationship and a substantial track record of commitment through contact. **Held:** Yes – the placement was not plainly wrong. *The grandmother was a member of the wider family and thus the bias of the law in favour of the wider family was engaged*. Adoption would have meant the effective elimination of the family relationships and *the view of the judge* enjoyed professional support, *even though he had departed from the view of the guardian and child psychiatrist*. **Note:** It is *fundamental to the Adoption and Children Act 2002 that a child be kept within the wider family if at all possible*. The judge had had to make a choice and it could have gone either way.

Re F (Shared Residence Order) [2009] EWCA Civ 313

Shared residence order with the *bulk of the time* with the father in the context of a mother who had overcome a drug problem and had been violent in the past. **Held:** ruling upheld. *Ward LJ emphasised how the welfare check list applied* – and that the '*status quo*' argument had no special place in that check list save *a factor to be considered* under s 1(3((b) of the Children Act 1989.The judge had made no error of law, nor exceeded *the generous ambit* within which there is room for disagreement; see *G v G (Minors: Custody Appeal)* [1985] FLR 894.

Re R (Residence) [2009] EWCA Civ 358

Intractable hostility case so acute that *guardian advised placement with paternal grandparents*, who had made *no application for residence* and were *not parties*; a recommendation which the Judge acceded to. **Held: Allowing appeal**: Interim residence order to mother with contact to father.

(1) A residence order to the paternal grandparents was *not an order* which was properly open to the judge to make on the material before him.

(2) The judge had not sufficiently grappled with the fundamental proposition that children had a right to be brought up by their *natural parents unless their welfare positively demanded replacement of that right*. His view that the child needed to be taken out of the arena led him to giving that factor undue weight and caused him *to lose sight* of the fact that he was *removing the child from the mother's care* and depriving him of family life with his *half-brother*. Per

Wall LJ '... *separated parents frequently fail to understand that their children love both of them, and have loyalty to both.*'

Re W (Shared Residence Order) [2009] EWCA Civ 370

The trial judge made a *shared residence order* with *contact times* for the father. The mother appealed contending that shared residence was inappropriate given that the child would only spend around *one quarter of her time* with the father under the order. **Held:**

(1)   There is *no requirement* to establish that, unless the time to be spent by the child in the two households is close to being equal, *unusual circumstances* are required before a shared residence order can be made.

(2)   It is a *contradiction in terms* to grant a *contact order* to a person who has a *shared residence order*. Since the child was to 'live' with each parent, the periods which she was to spend in each of their separate households were to be *specified under s 11(4)* of the Children Act 1989 and not in terms of a s 8 contact order. **Note:** The point of a shared residence order is *to stress* the *equality* of the parents in assuming responsibility for the care of their child; see eg *Re P (Shared Residence Order)* [2005] EWCA Civ 1639, [2006] 2 FLR 347 and *Re K (Shared Residence Order)* [2008] EWCA Civ 526, [2008] 2 FLR 380. Whether the order should be for shared residence, or for residence with one parent and contact to the other, *depended on what was in the best interests of the child*. The *court deprecated* the statistical calculation of the amount of time the child would spend with each parent; see *Re F (Shared Residence Order)* [2003] EWCA Civ 592, [2003] 2 FLR 397. The use of a shared residence order *where the parents are 'at loggerheads' is by no means uncommon* – see also *D v D (Shared Residence)* [2001] 1 FLR 495.

Re R (Residence Order) [2009] EWCA Civ 445

Judge failed to give sufficient weight to the views/wishes of a child *of 9* and *the Cafcass officer from whom he had not heard*.

Re A (Residence Order) [2009] EWCA Civ 1141

Judge transferred residence when not satisfied of mother's volte face expression of good faith for the future. *Held on appeal*: Residence to mother and contact to father *in accordance with guardian's recommendations*; mother's volte-face needed *to be tested*, and mother needed to *be warned* that if she did not embrace the letter and spirit of contact then residence could be transferred. **Note:** A transfer of residence, or the threat thereof, remains *a weapon of last judicial resort* in the face of an obdurate parent determined to exclude the non-resident parent. Cases like the present one, said Coleridge J, *'were the scourge of the whole family justice system'* and may require the putting of a *'gun to a parent's head to force him or her to rethink'*. That was a legitimate approach and remedy. However, the weapon must be deployed with care. The welfare of children should *not be eclipsed by the court's frustration with*, and desire to *punish*, the implacable primary carer.

Re B (A Child) (Residence Order) [2009] UKSC 5

The child [now aged *almost 4*] had lived continuously since birth with his maternal *grandmother*. The father had parental responsibility and had regular contact *until he was imprisoned*; the child visited his father in prison. Contact was resumed upon the father's release from prison. The father married and (supported by the child's mother) applied for a residence order. The justices in the family proceedings court found that the child's needs could be met by both the grandmother and the father. *Justices made an order in favour of grandmother*. Court of Appeal made order in favour of father upholding the decision of the High Court on appeal from the justices. *Held by Supreme Court*: In a *dispute about residence under s 8* of the CA 1989, there was *no presumption in favour of a biological parent*. To talk in terms of a child's rights, as opposed to his or her best interests, diverted from the focus that the *child's best interests* should occupy the minds of those called upon to make decisions as to a child's residence. *When Lord Nicholls had said in Re G* that the interest of a child would 'in the ordinary way' be best served by being reared by his or her biological parent, he had not been propounding any general rule but had been doing *no more than reflecting common experience*; many disputes about residence did not follow the ordinary way. The central point set out by the House of Lords in *Re G* was that consideration of the importance of parenthood in private law disputes about residence had to be firmly rooted in an examination of *the child's best interests, which was the paramount consideration*. It was only as a contributor to a child's welfare that parenthood assumed any significance; in common with all the other factors bearing on what was in a child's best interests, it had to be carefully examined for its potential to fulfill that aim. *The justices' decision had not been plainly wrong*; their misapprehension of the true import of *Re G* did not detract from their careful evaluation of the evidence and their weighing of the competing factors involved in determining this child's residence.

TE v SH and S [2010] EWHC 192 (Fam), [2010] 1 FLR 1785

This was a finely balanced case with little between the parties as far as the law was concerned: *Re B (A Child)* [2009] UKSC 5, [2010] 1 FLR 551 and *Re G (Children)* [2006] UKHL 43, [2006] 2 FLR 629 were key authorities. The real difficulty lay in applying the law, particularly given that the judge was being asked to take a step that is usually a last resort *and transfer residence from one parent to the other*; see *Re R (A Child)* [2009] EWCA Civ 1316 and *Re C (Residence Order)* [2007] EWCA Civ 866, [2008] 1 FLR 211. In relation to the application of the law to the facts the judgment *provides a classic textbook illustration of how to go about it*. The judge began his analysis by reference to each factor in the welfare checklist. Having concluded his consideration of each paragraph under s 1(3) of the Children Act 1989 the judge then arranged the factors according to their relationship and *relevance to the status quo – a list of factors representing the status quo, then a list on the other side of the scales*.

Re R (Residence Order) [2010] EWCA Civ 303

This case is a reminder of the provision of CPR, r 52.3.2:

> 'Where the appellant's case changes after the grant of permission, the appellant's representative should write to the appeal court and to the other party, indicating the proposed nature of the case. The court should be asked to indicate whether it will deal with the matter at the beginning of the hearing of the appeal or whether it will give directions on an earlier date. After being informed of the respondent's attitude, the court can decide whether to shut out the new grounds or allow them to be argued ...'

Re H (Contact Order) [2010] EWCA Civ 448

Parties separated after birth of disabled child.

- While the court has power under s 10(1)(b) of the Children Act 1989 to make an order which it considers appropriate although no party has applied for it, making an *order for which no notice* has been given to the other side is quite a different matter.

- The judge had been wrong to make the contact order amounting to a quarter of the child's time at the father's home. He had failed to take into account the most relevant factors under the welfare check list of s 1(3). *He had assumed without supporting evidence that the father had good parenting skills because he was a GP with paediatric experience.* He had failed to give any weight to the fact that the mother was the primary carer of a very small child who was still being breastfed, *and had not properly considered the child's special health needs*. The judge, not having the opportunity to consider evidence, should have concentrated on making an order that was *as neutral as possible* so as not to prejudice the position of either party when it came to the final hearing.

Re M (Placement Order) [2010] EWCA Civ 1257

In the face of *unremitting refusal* to comply with court orders, the court may order a *transfer of residence*, provided, of course, that this will be for the child's welfare. See also in the same context, *Re A (Residence Order)* [2009] EWCA Civ 1141, [2010] 1 FLR 1083.

M v M (Residence) [2010] EWHC 3579 (Fam)

Indian parents in London. Mother with *unrealistic fantasies* vis-à-vis her future as contrasted with *realism* on the part of the father. *Residence order in favour of father with relocation to India;* providing *for contact with the mother to take place in India*; a Family Assistance order; directing that the father undertake for there to be a *mirror image order obtained by him in India*. In the balance, the court weighed the *undoubted distress* that the child would suffer in the *short term* if she moved back to India against the *long term stability* the father could offer and the opportunity that would provide for her to enjoy a relationship with both parents.

18.38   SPECIAL GUARDIANSHIP

B v Kirklees MBC [2010] EWHC 467 (Admin), per HHJ Langan QC

Note: Where a special guardianship order had been made under the Adoption and Children Act 2002 and financial assistance was *necessary* to enable the special guardian to look after the child *then support was payable by the relevant authority.* The issue in the instant case was the level at which such support should be paid. See also: *B v London Borough of Lewisham* [2008] EWHC 738 (Admin), [2008] 2 FLR 523 citing *R v Islington LBC, ex p Rixon* (1997–1998) 1 CCL Rep 119 at 123.

Re G (A Child) (Special Guardianship Order) [2010] EWCA Civ 300

Mother *seeking to have revoked* an earlier special guardianship order in favour of grandmother, on the basis of her now *being able to cope*, as evidenced by her managing a second child. *Held*:

(1)   Where the courts were required to apply statutory tests expressed in much the same language, they should, if possible, approach them in the same way. Whereas leave to apply for revocation of a placement order under s 24 of the Adoption and Children Act 2002 required '*a change in circumstances*', leave to apply for the discharge of a special guardianship order under s 14D(5) of the Children Act 1989 required '*a significant change in circumstances*'. Section 24 cannot have required only proof of an insignificant change whereas s 115 of the same Act [which inserted s 14D(5)] was requiring something different. For the time being the court would proceed in the present case on the basis *that there was no relevant difference between the two*.

(2) The approach should be that commended in *M v Warwickshire County Council* [2007] EWCA Civ 1084, [2008] 1 FLR 1093; that is, the **approach** in that case **to leave to apply** for the revocation of a placement order **should apply to the discharge** of a special guardianship order.

(3) **Section 10(9)** of the 1989 Act **was not** the right approach to determining whether the mother's application for leave should succeed. That subsection applied to those who needed to apply for leave to apply for a s 8 order: **there appeared to be no ground for considering that the matters specified there should be formally weighed upon an application to discharge a special guardianship order.**

18.39 WARDSHIP

Re T (Wardship: Impact of Police Intelligence) [2009] EWHC 2440 (Fam)

A child who had been **abducted to India by his father** had been **returned to the mother's care** and made the subject of wardship proceedings. The father was remanded in custody. The police informed the judge who was hearing the wardship proceedings, that an **anonymous tip** had alleged that the father had taken out a contract to have the **mother murdered** and that she and the child had been removed into **protective custody**. The police opposed any disclosure of the material to the parties. McFarlane J **suggested the appointment of special advocates for the father and paternal** grandparents to represent their interests. He also provided guidance to other courts faced with a similar set of circumstances.

Re T (Wardship: Review of Police Protection Decision) (No 1) [2007] EWHC 3532 (Fam), per McFarlane J

Direct contact could result in the revealing of the mother's address where she lived with child **previously wrongfully abducted by father**; this being the reason why the police opposed direct contact. **Held**: The court balanced the child's needs [the guardian recognising that direct contact would be of value to the child] alongside the police protection issue and the judicial conclusion that the 'target for contact' should not be set too high even if this entailed some risk. The detailed contact arrangements put forward by highly experienced counsel for the father were integral: **these include the mother and child being taken to an undisclosed location in the vicinity of the contact centre; the father and grandparents arriving after a defined period; the presence of an interpreter during contact; the mother and then the child and then the father leaving within defined periods and above all, the father undertaking to do what was necessary to protect the mother's confidentiality and make contact a happy occasion.** Additionally, and importantly, the idea of having the sessions recorded on either *video or by audio means* was canvassed in order that the police would know exactly what had been said.

Re T (Wardship: Review of Police Protection Decision) (No 2) [2008] EWHC 196 (Fam), per McFarlane J

The judge had made an order *for interim contact pending* a full determination of applications by the father and paternal grandparents [See '*(No 1)*' above]. The police indicated that they would withdraw the protective arrangements if such contact took place. The father and grandparents sought declarations that such action by the police would be in breach of their human rights, and sought an injunction requiring the police to continue the protective arrangements. They also argued that the court should require the police to attend the proceedings in order to give evidence and undergo cross-examination on their decision. *Held*:

(1)   The reality of what the applicants were seeking was an order quashing the police decision or otherwise setting it aside and requiring them to act in a way that was contrary to the decision they had made. *Such a claim was a public law claim which could only be brought under the umbrella of judicial review*: *CF v Secretary of State for the Home Department* [2004] EWHC 111 (Fam), [2004] 2 FLR 517 and *R (Anton) v Secretary of State for the Home Department* [2004] EWHC 2730 (Admin).

(2)   It was immaterial that the claim included human rights issues; it was a *judicial review because of the outcome sought* rather than because of the substance of the rights in play in the claim itself.

(3)   Save for any High Court Judge's residual jurisdiction to hear cases of great urgency which may fall outside his assigned position, *any judicial review proceedings which arose as a result of the police decision must be determined within the Administrative Court or by a judge of the Family Division who was a nominated judge of the Administrative Court*. This court therefore did not have jurisdiction to determine the matter.

(4)   Had the court any discretion in the matter, *it would have declined to embark upon such a judicial review of the police action*. The matter had a much wider significance than merely determining the issues in the case.

Re S (Wardship) [2010] EWCA Civ 465

Mother took *child to Spain* to be with its father, after *local authority had real concern* as to the sanitary condition in which the child was living in England, with the potential for an EPO. At first instance, court made the child a ward with an order for peremptory return. *Held*:

(1) The wardship order *properly fell within the residual jurisdiction,* for the case was not able to be resolved under the Children Act 1989; see *Re T (A Minor) (Wardship: Representation)* [1994] Fam 49, [1993] 2 FLR 278.

(2) Given that the child had not been snatched from one parent but taken by the mother to live with the father and his family in another country, there was *'a powerful case for saying that the case was not within the Hague Convention'*, per Wall LJ. Order for *directions* before the first instance judge the *following day* with a *full welfare* hearing *14 days* after under the interim care order, both parents being in the jurisdiction.

Re S (Wardship) [2010] EWHC 1669 (Fam)

• The mother had made out her case *against the father* and her parents-in-law that she was deliberately separated from her baby and *abandoned in Pakistan*.

• The immigration authorities were to be urged to allow the mother to enter the UK for the purposes and duration of the proceedings.

Re A (Fact-Finding: Disputed Findings) [2011] EWCA Civ 12

Twenty complaints by mother of sexual misconduct against father, the parents being Kurdish cousins, and the child being aged 5 years. Fact-finding hearing. **Ruling and Comment:**

(1) It was possible to appeal against findings of fact, *but it was notoriously difficult* to succeed in doing so; see *Re B (Split Hearing: Jurisdiction)* [2000] 1 FLR 334; *AA v NA (Appeal: Fact-Finding)* [2010] EWHC 1282 (Fam) [2010] 2 FLR 1173. As to a judge *being asked to clarify certain* parts of his judgment, see *Re A (Child Abuse)* [2007] EWCA Civ 1058. Also see *Floyd v John Fairhurst & Co* [2004] EWCA Civ 604, at [47]–[59]; *Re C (A Minor) (Adoption: Parental Agreement: Contact)* [1993] 2 FLR 260, at 273 and 275; *In Re D (An Infant) (Adoption: Parent's Consent)* [1977] AC 602, at 626; and *Piglowska v Piglowska* [1999] 1 WLR 1360, at 1372.

(2) Where findings of fact where *based on the demeanour of a witness*, the appeal court would seldom interfere because the trial judge had a special advantage: *Re S (Abduction: Custody Rights)* [2002] EWCA Civ 908, [2002] 2 FLR 815.

(3) As to cultural context, see *Re K: A Local Authority v N* [2005] EWHC 2956 (Fam), [2007] 1 FLR 399 at [26] and [93].

(4) *Notwithstanding the 'binary' system* of split hearings explained in *Re B*, it may be relevant at the subsequent 'welfare' hearing to know, *and therefore for the judge to record*, whether a matter was not found proved because the judge was satisfied that it did not happen *or whether it was not found proved (and therefore in law deemed not to have happened) because the party making the assertion had failed to establish it to the relevant standard of proof* but in circumstances where there was nonetheless on-going *suspicion*. The cardinal principle that the court at the 'welfare' stage had to act on facts and not on suspicion did not preclude this approach. Per Munby LJ at [29]:

> 'In the first place, a judge conducting a fact-finding hearing is entitled to explain his thought processes and his reasoning in whatever seems to him to be an appropriate and illuminating way. And in a case where there is much suspicion and speculation on some matters as well as satisfactory proof on others, it would be not merely artificial but potentially misleading for the judge, if he thinks this will be helpful, to suppress all reference to the one while giving appropriate prominence to the other.'

(5) As to judicial technique in such fact-finding hearings, see Baroness Hale in *Re B*: she explained that judges:

> '... are guided by many things, including the inherent probabilities, any contemporaneous documentation of records, any circumstantial evidence tending to support one account rather than the other, and their overall impression of the characters and motivations of the witnesses.'

H v H (Jurisdiction to Grant Wardship) [2011] EWCA Civ 796

(Court of Appeal, Thorpe and Black LJJ and Sir Henry Brooke, 8 July 2011)

The court did not have jurisdiction to make a child a ward of court where the child had never been habitually resident or present in the jurisdiction and the father had not accepted the jurisdiction of the court.

INDEX

References are to paragraph numbers.